CAS PROFESSIONAL STANDARDS FOR HIGHER EDUCATION

Ninth Edition
2015

Jennifer B. Wells, Ph.D.
CAS Publications Editor
Kennesaw, Georgia

Council for the Advancement of Standards in Higher Education

Washington, DC

CAS Professional Standards for Higher Education
9th Edition

© Copyright 2015 by the Council for the Advancement of Standards in Higher Education

Library of Congress Cataloging-in-Publication Data
Wells, Jennifer B.
CAS Professional Standards for Higher Education
Includes bibliographic references.

ISBN-13: 978-0-9858819-2-4
1. Student Affairs, 2. Student Services, 3. Professional Standards, 4. Advising,
5. Counseling, 6. Higher Education, 7. Learning Assistance

Interior Design: Jennifer B. Wells, Kennesaw State University, Kennesaw, GA
Cover Design: Ed Bonza, Kennesaw State University, Kennesaw, GA
Cover Photography: "Aspen trees" by Daniel Schwen, used under CC-BY-SA-3.0
Printing and Binding: HBP, Inc., Hagerstown, MD
CAS Staff Assistants: Léna Kavaliauskas Crain, Noah Henry-Darwish,
Dawn M. Simounet, and Lindsey L. Templeton

This book is a revision of CAS Professional Standards previously published in 1986, 1997, 1999, 2001, 2003, 2006, 2009, and 2012.

Council for the Advancement of Standards in Higher Education

CAS Professional Standards for Higher Education (9th ed.)

Table of Contents

New or revised since 2012 edition

Appendices

CAS President's Letter to the Profession

It is my privilege and pleasure, as President of CAS, to present this 9th edition of *CAS Professional Standards for Higher Education*. This edition includes a number of changes from previous editions: the General Standards that are embedded in every set of functional area standards have been updated and 13 of sets of standards have been revised since the 8th edition. All of the contextual statements have been reviewed to reflect changes in each functional area.

CAS has been in existence for over 35 years and finds itself at a crucial crossroads in regard to its vision and mission. Since the beginning under the leadership of Ted Miller with 11 member associations, CAS has operated under a consensus model for decision-making and has emphasized the need for self-assessment. That model still exists with the support of 41 member associations today.

In our most recent strategic planning activities, the CAS Board of Directors approved new values, vision and mission for the organization. The values of *Collaboration & Consensus, Collective Expertise, Integrity, Learning & Improvement, and Responsiveness to Change* confirm how we have and will continue to do business as a Council.

The new vision of *Setting the standard for quality in higher education* sets our path and defines the Council of the future. Our strategic plan identifies three strategies and seven strategic priorities that will guide us there.

Finally, our revised mission reflects our current work and is *CAS, a consortium of professional associations in higher education, promotes the use of its professional standards for the development, assessment, and improvement of quality student learning, programs, and services.* Our work of creating and revising standards will always be our priority, but we are hearing from our users that they need and expect more from us. Because of their needs, we are in the initial stages of creating standards with cross-functional purposes and for those in the international market. We have recreated our Self-Assessment Guides to be more relevant and increasingly user-friendly. More resources are being developed for those struggling to create and assess student learning and development outcomes. Our new partnership with Campus Labs will bring an entirely new dimension to how the formal program review process can work.

All of this work would not be possible if it was not for the many hours of work that is completed by the members of our Board of Directors that voluntarily represent your professional associations. Our collaborative efforts and collective expertise makes our standards stronger and more reflective of the current trends within higher education and the needs of our students.

I must also thank Jen Wells, our editor, and Marybeth Drechsler Sharp, our Executive Director, for their commitment and expertise in making this 9th edition the best ever.

It is my hope that this edition of *CAS Professional Standards for Higher Education* continues to serve practitioners, preparation program faculty, and graduate students across higher education as we work together to create high quality programs and services for the benefit of our institutions and, ultimately, our students.

Deborah A. Garrett
CAS President
Vice Chancellor for Student Services, Arkansas State University-Beebe

Editor's Note

In 2007, I received a phone call from Dr. Laura Dean, our current CAS Past President, asking me if I was interested in accepting a position as the doctoral-level graduate assistant for CAS. At the time, I knew little of what this meant, but knew enough to say "yes," of course. Thus, my relationship with CAS began. Mentored and guided by Laura, then Editor and soon-to-become President, I learned about the value of assessment and the contributions of CAS to assuring quality in our profession. Nearly 8 years later, I am now the CAS Editor and a full-time assessment professional. Most importantly, I am delighted to present to you the newest edition of the CAS Book, a publication our CAS community has prepared over the past several years as an update and revision to our prior editions.

I'm extraordinarily proud of this edition for many reasons. It includes a new set of General Standards embedded into each functional area and 13 revised standards. We took care in trying to provide a new look to this edition, while still honoring the past. Inside, you may notice several new design aspects and a fresh font. On the back cover and on the last page, you will find support for the work of CAS by higher education and student affairs professionals who have eloquently captured the essence of CAS. And, most noticeably, the ninth edition cover design introduces full color for the first time in a CAS publication, and the image of a forest of trees encapsulates the very nature of CAS. Ed Bonza, thank you so much for your work in designing this new cover and seeking to understand CAS so you could honor it here.

Pictured on this "blue book" is a grove of aspen trees, known for their ability to thrive in many different soil types, whether barren, sandy, gravelly, or saturated. In abundant sunshine, aspens thrive and provide habitats for countless wildlife species. The roots of aspens sprout to produce new trees, creating colonies where the root system outlives any individual tree. Akin to the CAS initiative, the aspens ensure the longevity of their stand when conditions shift or environments change, and even when wildfires engulf them.

The hardy, generative root system of aspen trees can be likened to standards produced by the CAS consortium of 41 professional associations. Collectively, the CAS standards serve as the roots of our student programs and services, enabling programs to grow and thrive in challenging situations. Taken as a whole, the CAS standards may appear as an aspen grove—sharing roots, similar in appearance, and providing a big picture image for our profession—yet each functional area also exhibits characteristics and needs as unique as any single tree reaching skyward.

The adage, "it takes a village" certainly captures the experience of editing a CAS Book. Without the assistance of so many individuals, my vision for this edition could not have come to fruition. Marybeth Drechsler Sharp, CAS Executive Director, provided more support and assistance than I could possibly acknowledge here. One contribution she made, which we hope you will notice in your reading, is that Marybeth reconsidered, reshaped, and revised the opening chapters of the book to provide helpful insight about CAS and how it is used. Our CAS interns and staff assistants—Léna Kavaliauskas Crain, Noah Henry-Darwish, Dawn Simounet, and Lindsey Templeton—helped immeasurably by editing and amending content throughout the book.

Thank you very much to the CAS Board of Directors, Executive Committee, and President Deb Garrett for honoring me with the role of Editor, as well as for supporting me in my desire to create a lot of "new" for the ninth edition. Thank you to Ted Miller, Laura Dean, and Dorothy Mitstifer for paving the way as Editors—it is an honor and a privilege to be listed among you.

I'd also like to extend a personal thank you to my family, especially my mom, for their endless support. Many thanks also go to my sweet dog, Max, who continues to be the best writing partner I've ever known.

Jennifer B. Wells, Ph.D
CAS Publications Editor
Director of Planning and Assessment in Student Affairs, Kennesaw State Unversity

The Case for CAS

Educators at post-secondary institutions face daily trials as they endeavor to provide quality programs, services, and learning experiences to their students. Students and families scrutinize the costs and investment returns of higher education, government involvement challenges principles of academic freedom, and employers demand new knowledge and evolving skills from the next generation of the global workforce.

Today's clarion calls echo the last thirty years of pressure for institutions of higher education to adapt. As a result of continued focus on post-secondary reform, faculty and staff members may find it necessary to implement their responsibilities in new and different ways. Approaches and strategies that were previously successful may need to be amended as programs evolve and student populations and characteristics shift. As institutions and their constituents change, so too must the vehicles that guide practice within the shifting culture. New developments, resulting in previously unrecognized or newly identified student needs, require programs and services to evolve as well. In post-secondary education environments, where change is a constant force, these CAS standards also must be viewed as a living document that will shift over time, reflecting evolving contexts and functions. With each edition of the *CAS Professional Standards for Higher Education*, General Standards that form the core of each document are revised, contextual statements are updated, and new and revised standards are included.

The Evolving Relevance of Professional Standards

CAS was founded over thirty-five years ago for purposes of developing and promulgating standards of professional practice to guide higher education practitioners and their institutions, especially in regard to work with college students.

Credibility within the whole of higher education is more effectively gained through collective action than through narrowly defined initiatives of individuals or associations. Although some professional associations or inter-association collectives establish standards of good practice for specific student support services, their products and models are unlikely to become part of the wider educational culture unless they are viewed as an enhancement to the broad educational interests of students and institutions. For standards of professional practice to be truly viable, they must reflect the interests and values of multiple professional organizations and the functional areas they champion. CAS strives to provide this collaborative avenue for establishing thoughtful, balanced, and achievable standards upon which all can rely.

Responding as a Unified Voice

CAS has a long history, rooted in the development of the student affairs profession and in the accountability movement. The Council for the Advancement of Standards in Higher Education, a name adopted in 1992 to reflect the expanded context of the Council's higher education focus, was originally established in 1979 as a nonprofit organization called the Council for the Advancement of Standards for Student Services/Development Programs. CAS was created as a direct response to the emerging student services profession's need to establish standards to guide both preparation and practice.

By the 1960s, the need was apparent for a profession-wide entity to speak as one voice for post-secondary student services. An initial attempt to establish such a group, the Council of Student Personnel Associations in Higher Education (COSPA), was mounted in the late 1960s by 10 student affairs associations. This consortium is best remembered for its promotion of an enlightened approach to student affairs practice reflected in a statement published in 1972 by its Commission of Professional Development entitled "Student Development Services in Post-Secondary Education" (Cooper, 1975). Unfortunately, COSPA was dissolved in 1976, largely as a result of member disillusionment resulting from unresolved political issues.

In 1979, CAS was established as a consortium comparable to COSPA for an equally important, though more concentrated, purpose. Whereas COSPA was intended to function on a full range of professional issues, CAS endeavored to focus on shared values rather than special interests and to avoid politicization. Consequently, the purposes and objectives of CAS are highly focused on professional standards and assessment of practice, which enables members to collaborate around this designated purpose and the processes used to accomplish its mission.

A Legacy of Collaboration

The impetus for CAS's existence was a movement on the part of several national associations to develop accreditation standards for academic programs that prepare counselors and counselor educators. This movement, which culminated in the establishment of the Council for the Accreditation of Counseling and Related Educational Programs (CACREP) in 1980, spurred the American College Personnel Association (ACPA) to devise preparation standards for use in master's level college student affairs administration programs. Rather than promulgating these standards as its own, ACPA sought out other professional associations interested in the development of standards for student affairs preparation and practice. The National Association of Student Personnel Administrators (NASPA) shared an interest in the project, and the two associations jointly issued invitations to a meeting of interested professional associations. Seven additional student affairs-oriented organizations sent representatives to the exploratory meeting held in Alexandria, Virginia, in June 1979. This meeting resulted in the creation of an inter-association consortium for purposes of developing and promulgating professional standards to guide both student affairs practice and academic preparation of those who administer student support programs and services. A subsequent organizational meeting in

September 1979 resulted in the development of CAS as a nonprofit consortium of 11 charter member associations (see Appendix A).

Today, after more than three decades of collaboration and a name change to reflect its expanded interests, CAS is composed of 41 member associations from the U.S. and Canada, representing more than 100,000 higher education professionals and service providers. This edition of *CAS Professional Standards for Higher Education* represents the ninth major iteration of CAS standards, the first having been published under the auspices of the American College Testing Program (CAS, 1986). CAS has generated and promulgated 43 sets of functional area standards and guidelines and one set of master's level academic program standards for college student affairs administration preparation. Also, CAS has devised a statement regarding characteristics of individual excellence for professionals in higher education, a statement of the ethical principles that are held in common across the many areas of professional practice represented at CAS, and a learning and development outcomes model that reflects the most current thought on the intended results of quality practice.

By working collaboratively and speaking collectively on behalf of practitioners and their functional area specialties, CAS has facilitated the development of profession-wide criteria of good practice through standards. In effect, CAS desires to represent every college and university educator and functional area specialist who believes the learning and development of all students to be the essence of higher education.

Core CAS Tenets

A standard to guide practice is an essential characteristic of any established profession. During the evolution of a mature profession, it is vital that a relevant set of standards be developed and promulgated by and for those working in that arena. CAS was founded as a profession-wide entity to establish reasonable and achievable standards to guide practice of those educators supporting students in post-secondary institutions.

During the twentieth century, college and university student support programs evolved from a few faculty members being assigned part-time to attend to students' needs beyond the classroom to institutional divisions designed to complement the educational goals of academic affairs. Contemporary student support programs employ many full-time, well-qualified staff members, most with advanced degrees and highly specialized knowledge and skills. The complexity of student support services has increased as organizational structures have expanded. Largely in response to the increasing complexity of role, function, and purpose of student support programs and services, the CAS standards were developed.

As the field matured and the responsibilities of its practitioners expanded, a complementary need for accountability increased. It is no longer feasible or desirable for practitioners to function on the basis of best guesses or intuition when creating environments conducive to student learning and development. Educators have demanded that standards be developed to guide the quality of practice, and the CAS functional area standards and guidelines have helped meet these important professional needs.

CAS was created as a bellwether for the profession at large. To ensure cross-fertilization of theories, research, and application strategies from the field as a whole, experienced representatives from CAS member associations bring the most current thinking into the standards development process from the functional areas they represent and champion. This commitment to collaboration among functional area specialties ensures that no single perspective will dominate the foundations that underlie the generation, revision, and presentation of each CAS standard. Although the standards reflect a broad range of interests, they are clearly values-driven. Underlying them is a set of fundamental principles upon which CAS was founded and by which it continues to be guided.

Principles that Guide the CAS Standards

The fundamental principles that undergird the work of CAS and guide its initiatives were derived from the theories and conceptual models implicit within human development, group dynamics, student learning, organizational management, and administration that inform the work of higher education professionals who support students. The guiding principles for CAS can be organized into five broad categories, as illustrated in Figure 1.

Students and Their Environments	**Diversity and Multiculturalism**
The whole student is shaped by environments that provide learning opportunities reflective of society and diversity, with students having ultimate responsibility for learning	Institutions embracing diversity and eliminating barriers with justice and respect for differences, binding individuals to community
Organization, Leadership, and Human Resources	**Health Engendering Environments**
Quality of leaders possessing sound preparation is essential, with success directly correlated to clarity of mission	Education prospers in benevolent environments that provide students with appropriate challenge and necessary support
Ethical Considerations Educators exhibit impeccable ethical behavior in professional and personal life	

Figure 1. Categories of CAS Guiding Principles

CAS was developed in the U.S., and while the membership includes Canadian representation, the guiding principles are grounded in a Western, and specifically American, perspective. There is interest in CAS and in professional standards in a number of other countries; however, as the CAS standards are considered for adaptation to different cultures, professionals must identify those underlying assumptions and aspects that need to be adjusted to better reflect the values of that new context.

Students and Their Environments
The initial eight principles guiding CAS work pertain to how students learn and the environmental conditions that institutions need to emphasize for learning and development to occur. Derived from the 1938 and 1949 editions of the *Student Personnel Point of View* (Miller & Prince, 1976, p. 4; see also American Council on Education, 1937; American Council on Education, 1949), the first four principles reflect fundamental "truths" upon which the CAS standards and guidelines are based.
1.   The student must be considered as a whole person.
2.   Each student is a unique person and must be treated as such.
3.   The student's total environment is educational and must be used to achieve full development.
4.   Students seek higher education in responsible ways and will, when encouraged to do so, access appropriate educational resources when they are provided, made known, and relevant to students' felt educational and developmental needs.

Principles five through eight reflect environmental perspectives that complement the student-focused viewpoint from the *Student Personnel Point of View* documents.
5.   Institutions of higher learning are purposeful and function as social and cultural resources to provide opportunities for students to learn and develop in holistic ways.
6.   The primary responsibility for learning and development rests with the student.
7.   Institutions of higher learning reflect the diversity of the societies and cultures in which they exist.
8.   Institutions are responsible for creating learning environments that provide a choice of educational opportunities and challenge students to learn and develop while providing support to nurture their development.
When combined, these eight principles represent the presuppositions upon which student support programs and services are founded.

Each CAS functional area standard was created to inform practitioners about the criteria that represent fundamental levels of programmatic and organizational quality that must be met if higher education environments are to be effective in facilitating student learning and development. When a college or university provides programs and services that meet or exceed the CAS criteria, it will have successfully implemented an intentional educational environment conducive to the learning and development of its students.

The CAS standards do not dictate that students, individually or collectively, must conform to a prescribed standard of involvement or behavior. Rather, they call for institutions and student support programs to meet a standard of programmatic and organizational efficiency and effectiveness sufficient to provide opportunity and encouragement for students to grow, develop, and achieve individual potentials. They further call upon institutions and their programs and services to identify the outcomes that they intend students to achieve and to assess those outcomes to determine the extent to which they have been accomplished. The institutional environment and educational programs are social resources that provide individuals opportunities to expand their horizons and capacities to serve society.

Diversity and Multiculturalism
The CAS standards assert that institutions of higher education must affirm the importance of diversity and consider its influence when creating and implementing educational and developmental initiatives. In an increasingly complex global environment, students must learn to function justly and effectively when exposed to ideas, beliefs, values, physical and mental abilities, religious and spiritual practices, sexual orientations, gender expressions, and cultures that differ from their own. Two principles in this regard are embedded in the CAS standards.
- Recognizing the ubiquitous nature of human diversity, institutions endeavor to eliminate barriers that impede student learning and development, attending especially to establishing and maintaining diverse human relationships essential to survival in a global society.
- Justice and respect for differences bond individuals to community; thus education for multicultural awareness and positive regard for differences is essential to the development and maintenance of a health engendering society.

The CAS standards call for institutions and their student programs and services to recognize the increasingly diverse cultures to be served and the imperative of enhancing students' capacities to competently interact and engage within the context of constantly shifting environments and opinions. CAS recognizes that the spirit of affirmative action is inherent in the delivery of effective student programs and services, and discrimination against any student population or employment category is antithetical to belief in the dignity of the individual. This proposition is fundamental to student development theory and its applications to practice.

The CAS standards reinforce that those responsible for creating educational environments need to be open to and accepting of differences, and they must recognize that such environments are important for enhancing the quality of the education provided and the learning achieved. Further, the standards consistently call for staffing with personnel whose demographic characteristics reflect those of the institution's constituencies. In addition, all students must have access to the educational and co-curricular resources available to the academic community at large; no student, for any reason, should be denied access to them.

Organization, Leadership, and Human Resources
The CAS standards reflect the belief that form follows function; consequently, the structure of an organization should mirror the purposes for which it was established. It is essential that institutions, programs, and services be based on a mutually determined, clearly and publicly stated, and well-understood purpose. Without a clearly defined mission, an institution and its programs are virtually rudderless and will ultimately founder. Unmistakably defined lines of authority must be drawn, detailed duties and job responsibilities described, and policies and procedures established to guide the desired processes. Those who lead and administer student support programs in higher education must remember that because "theory without practice is empty and practice without theory is blind," it is essential that the theory embraced be connected to the purposes sought, in pursuit of quality practice (Cross, 1981).

Three basic principles concerned with these organizational factors also underlie the CAS standards:
- Capable, credible, knowledgeable, and experienced leadership is essential for institutional success; organizational units are most successful when their missions and outcome expectations are effectively documented and understood by all concerned.
- Effective programs and services require well-qualified staff members who understand and support the student learning and development outcomes the programs are intended to promote.
- Student learning and personal development will be enhanced when staff members at all levels of responsibility possess appropriate, relevant, and adequate educational preparation and practical experience.

CAS standards do not prescribe organizational or administrative structures to which institutions and programs are expected to adhere. CAS is guided by the belief that every institution is unique and must establish the frame of administrative reference most appropriate to its particular mission. Consequently, the standards do not prescribe specific requirements, but rather provide fundamental criteria that practitioners can use to judge the effectiveness of their current or projected structures. For example, certain elements clearly are essential to functional success, including employing leaders who possess viable visions of how and what is to be achieved while suitably positioned with access to the highest administrative levels. Leaders and staff members alike must possess effective managerial skills, be properly titled, and be well qualified by both education and experience. Under-educated and under-experienced staff members, good intentions notwithstanding, will virtually always fail to accomplish the program's objectives over the long term.

Health-Engendering Environments
Institutional environments of quality combine educational philosophies and values in conjunction with adequate physical facilities, human resources, and fiscal support to create positive influence on the education and development of students. The establishment of effective, health-generating environments is an important aspect of the CAS standards.
- Student support and developmental programs and services prosper in benevolent environments that provide students with appropriate levels of challenge and support.

The primary purpose of education has always been to promote change, both in individuals and in society. College and university student support programs are primarily educational enterprises. Clearly, the Student Learning Imperative (ACPA, 1996) prevails throughout each CAS functional area standard because an important purpose of the standards is to provide criteria that can be used to judge a program's capacity and effectiveness in creating learning and development opportunities. The establishment of educational environments conducive to student learning and development is essential if an institution of higher learning is to achieve its educational purposes.

Ethical Considerations
A major component in each CAS standard incorporates the fundamental ethical expectations to which all student support practitioners must adhere to ensure fair and equitable practice. Just as a mission statement is essential to provide programs with direction, ethical standards are essential to guide the behavior of staff members in ways that enhance the overall integrity of both the program and the institution.
- Because special mentoring relationships exist between students and those who facilitate their learning and development, support service providers must exemplify impeccable ethical behavior in both their professional relationships and their personal lives.

As an essential task of every profession's emergence, it establishes and codifies ethical standards to guide the behavior of its members. The CAS standards provide the essential ethical foundations upon which to build humane, ethical practice. Without a clearly defined code of ethics, staff members would have little or no guidance for establishing and maintaining a reasonable level of effective moral and ethical behavior. The best of intentions are insufficient if they are not founded on a solid ethical base that can be understood and acknowledged by all concerned. Practitioners can be informed by their own association's ethical codes, the relevant criteria in the CAS standards, and the *CAS Statement of Shared Ethical Principles*.

Characteristics of CAS work
Collaboration and Consensus
By design, CAS brings together professionals from across the broad student services field to write, revise, and vet professional standards. Each member organization appoints up to two representatives to be involved on the council, and these individuals bring an array of experiences and viewpoints. Current council members include professionals from two-year, four-year, public, private, and proprietary institutions; the council includes faculty members and scholar-practitioners, senior student affairs officers, department and program chairs, association leaders, and functional area experts. The diversity of experiences is one of CAS's great strengths.

Since its founding, CAS has adopted a consensus-based decision-making model for reviewing and revising standards of professional practice. Working toward consensus requires dialogue and compromise; the rewards are shared understanding, unanimous agreement, and standards applicable across different contexts. Parker Palmer (2005) encapsulates the benefits of employing consensus within group efforts, explaining "When we make decisions by consensus, we are not allowed to 'resolve' the tension of conflicting viewpoints prematurely" (p. 237). By seeking consensus around each set of CAS standards, collective expertise emerges above individual experiences and perspectives. "Not only are we more likely to be drawn toward a resolution superior to anything anyone had envisioned at the outset, but in the process we have deepened our sense of community instead of breaking into the … fragments that majority rule can breed" (Palmer, 2005, p. 237).

The process for standards development and revision is multi-layered, involving input from various constituents and CAS representatives. Individuals appointed to CAS by member associations serve on working committees for standards development or revision. At different points in the process, internal CAS experts and external functional area experts contribute relevant research, literature, and practical perspectives to the standards. Upon completion of a standards draft, the representatives from the CAS member associations review, provide suggestions, and ultimately approve a final standards document. This conscientious, rigorous process ensures that the CAS standards both systematically organize existing quality practices and represent the broad range of programs and services in post-secondary education (e.g., differing institutional types, control, resources, missions). The collaborative, consensus-based CAS approach results in a profession-wide perspective rather than a narrow or limited viewpoint.

Philosophy of Self-Regulation
Although the standards can be useful for institutional and program accreditation purposes, CAS has not established an accrediting or credentialing process. CAS recognizes individualized institutional and program "self-regulation" as the ideal approach to ensuring program quality and effectiveness. Self-regulation is motivated and directed within an institution; goals of self-regulation are to create, maintain, and enhance high-quality programs and services. Programs and services committed to self-regulation continually assess their work, identify areas for improvement, and address those needs to maintain high quality programs and services. Philosophically, CAS perceives this approach as preferable to externally motivated regulation, because individuals within an institution have clear understanding of its mission, goals, resources, and capabilities.

In its Preamble (Appendix B), CAS identified the following essential elements of self-regulation:
1. Institutional culture that values involvement of all its members in decision making
2. Quality indicators that are determined by the institution
3. Standards and guidelines in quality assurance
4. Collection and analysis of data on institutional performance
5. Commitment to continuing improvement that presupposes freedom to explore and develop alternative directions for the future

Mutual respect between an institution and its members is key to the success of self-regulatory processes. Individuals must be valued, trusted, and cared for within self-regulating environments. Visions, goals, and processes must be collectively shared and cultivated among institutional community members.

In an environment that practices self-regulation, individuals can adopt profession-wide quality indicators like the CAS standards by which to examine their practices. When engaging in self-directed assessment, institutional members must meticulously examine their work, reliably articulate their findings, and intentionally strive to make necessary improvements.

Cross-functional Approaches
Within higher education settings, increasingly issue- and topic-driven activities, programs, and services have emerged, requiring perspectives beyond the scope and responsibility of individual functional areas. As institutions change their organizational approaches to addressing complex, intersecting needs and challenges in educational settings, these efforts must be collaborative and strategic across traditional boundaries or silos. Examples of academic and student life intersections occur around topics of civic engagement, sustainability, and career planning.

CAS provides standards for practice that frequently coalesce around single programs, departments, or functions; however, the standards common across all functional areas – or General Standards – and the embedded CAS learning and development outcomes provide cross-functional direction for leaders and professionals. CAS recognizes the emergent presence of interdisciplinary thinking and practice, as well as encourages users to combine or tailor the resources available to meet the changing needs and overlapping areas of practice on a case-by-case basis. The CAS standards and outcomes emphasize pervasive and well-tested approaches to tackling interdisciplinary, interrelated topics. For example, as professionals partner across divisions and institutions to address critical topics, they can consult the CAS General Standards to help shape their thinking around cross-functional topics aimed at student success, retention, and completion. Although CAS standards do not directly address broad themes common to cross-functional approaches, such as wellness, emergency response, behavior management, and student success initiatives, they do provide guidance for important structures, processes, and stakeholders to be included in development and assessment of emerging areas.

Given the wide variability of student support service organizations and structures, CAS representatives are hesitant to prescribe specific means of reconfiguring units. Historically, CAS has provided guidance about structure and process, as well as focused on codifying existing practice. In most institutions, programs and services continue to be organized in functional area structures. Although cross-functional approaches are gaining attention and being used in some places, they have not coalesced in ways that CAS can yet identify and articulate what standards of practice or cross-functional structures would apply across all settings and that represent recommended ways of configuring programs and services. CAS users are encouraged to consider how they might combine multiple sets of standards to reflect cross-functional initiatives (see descriptions of General/Specialty Standards for further information about integration).

Current Issues

Envisioning the Future for Quality Education

In its vision statement – "Setting the standard for quality in higher education" – CAS encapsulates its commitment to articulating the agreed-upon standard of quality and its aspiration to become even more relevant and recognized as the primary resource for quality practice. Originally founded to implement profession-wide initiatives, with emphasis on the development and promulgation of professional standards, CAS has evolved to accomplish several complementary tasks. In 2015, the mission is:

> CAS, a consortium of professional associations in higher education, promotes the use of its professional standards for the development, assessment, and improvement of quality student learning, programs, and services.

As the mission implies, a primary purpose for CAS is to provide a forum in which representatives from higher education organizations can meet and interact for purposes of articulating the fundamental principles of quality practice that lead to enhanced programs and services for students. The CAS initiative provides a forum where voices from across the profession can be heard in the creation of current, relevant, and useful standards to guide contemporary practice. This approach encourages valuable links among professional associations, most of which focus on highly specialized functions. This professional collaboration results in the creation of standards that represent a profession-wide perspective rather than a narrow and limited viewpoint.

CAS provides a vehicle for the development of functional area and academic preparation standards. In addition, it provides a well-recognized and credible profession-wide entity to publish and promulgate standards and related materials and to encourage and educate practitioners to apply the standards effectively in their work. Further, the CAS consortium speaks with a single voice that bridges numerous specialty areas and represents the profession-at-large on matters concerning professional standards and quality assurance.

Influence of CAS on Practice

The professional role of the Council for the Advancement of Standards in Higher Education has become increasingly important over the past 35 years, and many chapters and articles are available describing the organization and its philosophy, the CAS approach to writing standards, and how professionals can use CAS for quality assurance (Dean, 2011; Dean, 2013; Dean & Jones, 2014; Komives & Arminio, 2011; Miller, 2012; Scott, 2014). Within current research literature, CAS is frequently cited as justification for conducting studies, situating a phenomenon in the higher education context, or establishing the perceived importance of a phenomenon of study; however, research on use of CAS standards in practice remains sparse. In 2003, CAS past-president Don Creamer offered several CAS-related research questions he felt needed to be addressed in order to better understand the influence of CAS and its initiatives, including:

1. What is the level of use of CAS Standards by functional area and geographic area?
2. What is the type and frequency of use of CAS Standards and Guidelines?
3. How do CAS Standards shape professional practice?
4. What is the role of CAS in shaping educational programs and services?
5. Do practitioners perceive that the use of CAS Standards and Guidelines improves their performance?
6. Does CAS benefit professionals' learning and development?
7. Are programs and services that meet CAS Standards and Guidelines more effective in meeting learning goals than those that do not?
8. How does professional practice that is influenced by CAS in turn influence student learning?

In recent years, numerous studies have tackled aspects of this CAS research agenda, although many questions remain.

In a 2004 CAS-sponsored study, Arminio and Gochenaur surveyed over 5,000 individual members from 22 CAS member associations. Among respondents, 62.5% had heard of CAS (i.e., 85 percent of responding vice presidents; 67% of functional area directors, 66% of new professionals, and 31% of faculty members). Of respondents who stated that CAS has positively influenced their programs, 27% believed CAS positively influenced programs through assessing current programs, 22% in expanding current programs, 13% through clarifying mission and goals, 10% by justifying current programs, 8% by emphasizing student and staff training, 5% as a guide for new programs, and 4% to influence budget programs. From the population of vice presidents and associate vice presidents for student affairs included in the study, 82% stated that CAS standards were positively associated with learning outcomes.

Various authors studying aspects of student affairs preparation and higher education administration programs turn to the CAS standards for preparation programs to provide rationale for their assertions about necessary program elements (Wilson & Meyer, 2011; Cuyjet, Longwell-Grice, & Molina, 2009). In recent studies, researchers have found that CAS competencies are being well taught in professional preparation programs (Cuyjet et al.; Young & Janosik, 2007), but there are opportunities to improve the existing CAS standards for master's students to better prepare new professionals (Young & Dean, 2015). Overall, as Cuyjet et al. summarized, "recent graduates agreed that the CAS competencies are important for their current jobs" (p. 108).

Although prior research affirmed that CAS standards articulated important competencies for recent graduates (Cuyjet et al., 2009), outcomes of a 2014 study by Liddell et al. (2014) surprised researchers, who discovered that 18% of their respondents did not know if their graduate programs met CAS standards. Liddell and her colleagues concluded, "this finding suggests two things worthy of further exploration: either CAS standards were not addressed in the curriculum or faculty did not address their programs' CAS compliance with their students" (Liddell et al., p. 80-81).

A number of researchers recently have explored CAS use within functional areas. Young, Dean, Franklin, and Tschepikow (2014) discovered that 40% of collegiate recreation professionals in their study on assessment practices used CAS materials in their efforts. In a study of student conduct professionals, Tschepikow, Cooper, and Dean (2010) found that 72% of respondents indicated that they were assessing student conduct programs. More than half of participants conducting assessment reported using CAS materials in their processes. The researchers also discovered that CAS was significantly related to respondents' creating learning and development outcomes for the first time as well as to launching a comprehensive assessment plan. Using a qualitative approach, Keeling (2010) explored the use of CAS standards in academic advising. Through her comparative case study of five academic advising offices, Keeling determined that advising practices typically aligned with CAS standards, although they are most influential when championed by a campus leader. Keeling also revealed that few advisors with whom she spoke were familiar with CAS, although their practices seemed aligned with the thresholds. Similarly, Barbour (2010) found that barriers, including human and financial resource limitations, influenced how career services directors at two-year public community colleges employed CAS standards; largely, he identified that career services directors of who used CAS were using the standards as references for evaluation and planning.

There can be little doubt that the CAS initiative has been fruitful during its thirty-five year existence. Although there is much work yet to do, the Council for the Advancement of Standards in Higher Education has made a difference in practice and is prepared to continue its important efforts toward professionalizing programs and services in higher education.

CAS Initiatives and Outreach

CAS is a profession-wide collaborative body committed to developing and promulgating standards for post-secondary student programs and services. In the rich discussions within the CAS consortium, ideas supporting the scope and purpose of CAS emerge. While continuing to develop and revise functional area standards, CAS has explored and undertaken projects that support and enhance the consortium's work. These initiatives have focused on promoting student learning and development outcomes, enhancing individual practice, and encouraging self-assessment for the improvement of practice.

A significant and influential CAS initiative was the 2003 revision of the CAS General Standards, which added a major emphasis on student learning and development in the Part 2: Program component of each functional area standard. The standards contained 16 student learning and development outcome domains designed to guide practitioners in their attempts to both emphasize and assess student learning and development. A 2008 revision built upon this work, maintaining the focus on student learning and development, but re-conceptualizing the structure and expression of the outcome domains. Rather than the previous 16 areas, the current version is comprised of six broad learning and development categories, called domains, which are further defined into narrower dimensions to assist practitioners in implementing them. This outcomes revision resulted from the proliferation of many different sets of outcomes in the field (e.g., *Learning Reconsidered 2*, AAC&U's Liberal Education & America's Promise [LEAP]); subsequently, CAS convened a "think tank" of experts to integrate and build on the previous approaches. The resulting CAS Learning and Development Outcomes statement and chart were amended and approved by the CAS Board of Directors. This process and product exemplify CAS's role in higher education—creating collaborative strategies to address challenges to good practice, serving as a clearinghouse and mechanism for consensus, and disseminating the results to help practitioners and bring coherence to the field.

In 2006, CAS published a companion book to the standards, called *The Frameworks for Assessing Learning and Development Outcomes* (FALDOs), to assist practitioners in developing sound and effective strategies for assessing outcomes. Because they were based on the previous 16 student learning and development outcome domains rather than the current structure, the

FALDOs have not been reprinted; however, they are still available as an electronic download, and they continue to provide useful insight into the process of understanding and designing ways to assess intended learning and development outcomes.

CAS also has used its collective voice and inter-association collaboration to develop two statements related to the work of individual professionals in higher education. The first, the *CAS Characteristics of Individual Excellence for Professional Practice in Higher Education*, articulates a list of essential attributes for professionals in higher education that is broader than competencies and includes other markers of professionalism. Although CAS has historically focused on quality assurance with regard to programs and services, the Characteristics were created to suggest the hallmarks of quality on an individual basis. The second statement, the *CAS Statement of Shared Ethical Principles*, articulates values that underlie the ethics statements of CAS member associations. By identifying themes present in those documents, the statement highlights the shared ethical values and beliefs of professionals working across the range of functional areas in higher education. Like the standards themselves, the *Characteristics of Individual Excellence* and the *Statement of Shared Ethical Principles* seek to identify, articulate, and promulgate quality practices in the work that we do.

Finally, because it is part of the CAS mission to promote improvement of programs and services and to encourage self-assessment, CAS seeks to reach practitioners in increasingly direct ways. CAS takes seriously its responsibility to inform and educate the higher education community and the public about the importance of professional standards and their utility for institutional and program self-assessment. Over the years, CAS members have represented the council in numerous conferences, assessment institutes, workshops, and instructional activities. Each of these presentations are designed to inform members of the higher education community in the U.S. and abroad about CAS initiatives and to instruct practitioners in using the standards. Most CAS member associations include CAS-related presentations and workshops in their conference programs. CAS has been represented internationally at the European Association of Institutional Research in Prague, through invited seminars in South Africa, and at conferences in Qatar and China. In 2006 and 2009, CAS held two national symposia to further educate participants on the implementation of the CAS approach and materials, as well as provide opportunities for practitioners to share experiences.

CAS continues to explore other initiatives to further the work of the council. CAS employs technology and social media channels to further provide opportunities for training and supporting CAS users. Additional training resources, including videos and slide decks, are available on the CAS website (http://www.cas.edu). CAS is represented in webinars sponsored by member organizations and others in the assessment field. In 2014, CAS entered into partnership with Campus Labs to work together to promote the use of data, assessment, and self-study for the continued development of quality programs and services. From the earliest conversations over 35 years ago, the intention of enhancing student learning and development across post-secondary institutions is the thread that has been constant throughout the development, discussions, and initiatives of the Council for the Advancement of Standards, and that is the goal that will continue to inform our work into the future.

The CAS standards provide an important tool that expresses to students, faculty, and administrators alike the complex and vital nature of student support programs and services and their relationship to student learning and development. Within higher education, there is sometimes a lack of appreciation for the importance of creating supportive, health-engendering environments for students as an important condition that enhances their experiences. Over the years, those providing students with co-curricular programs and support services have often been viewed as irrelevant or ancillary participants in achieving the academic mission, rather than integral contributors to it. The articulation and application of these standards have empowered professionals to create quality programs and services that support student learning and development and lead ultimately to student success.

References, Readings and Resources

American Council on Education. (1937). *The student personnel point of view: A report of a conference on the philosophy and development of student personnel work in colleges and universities.* Washington, DC: Author. Retrieved from http://www2.bgsu.edu/sahp/pages/1937STUDENTPERSONNELnew.pdf

American Council on Education. (1949). *The student personnel point of view (revised).* Washington, DC: Author. Retrieved from http://www2.bgsu.edu/sahp/pages/1949SPPVrev.pdf

American College Personnel Association (ACPA). (March/April 1996). Special issue: The student learning imperative. *Journal of College Student Development, 37*(2), 118-122.

Association of American Colleges, Universities (AAC&U), & National Leadership Council (NLC) (US). (2007). *College Learning for the New Global Century: A report from the National Leadership Council for Liberal Education & America's Promise.* Association of American Colleges.

Arminio, J. & Gochenaur, P. (2004). After 16 years of publishing standards, do CAS standards make a difference? *College Student Affairs Journal, 23,* 51-65.

Barbour, W. C. (2010). *Use of the Council for the Advancement of Standards (CAS) by career services directors at two-year public community colleges.* Unpublished doctoral dissertation, Morgan State University. (UMI No. 3419531)

Cooper, A. C. (1975). Student Development Services in Post-Secondary Education. *Journal of College Student Personnel, 16*(6), 524-528.

Council for the Advancement of Standards (CAS). (1986). *CAS standards and guidelines for student service/development programs.* Iowa City, IA: American College Testing Program.

Council of Student Personnel Associations in Higher Education. (1994; 1972). Student development services in post-secondary education (pp. 428-447). In A. L. Rentz (Ed.), *Student affairs: A profession's heritage.* Washington, DC: American College Personnel Association.

Creamer, D. G. (2003). Research needed on the use of CAS standards and guidelines. *College Student Affairs Journal, 22*(2), 109-124.

Cross, P. (1981). *Adults as learners.* Washington, DC: Jossey-Bass.

Cuyjet, M. J., Longwell-Grice, R., & Molina, E. (2009). Perceptions of new student affairs professionals and their supervisors regarding the application of competencies learned in preparation programs. *Journal of College Student Development, 50*(1), 104-119. doi: 10.1353/csd.0.0054

Dean, L. A., & Jones, G. M. (2014). The Council for the Advancement of Standards in Higher Education and the role of standards in professional practice. In S. Freeman, Jr., L. S. Hagedorn, L. F. Goodchild, & D. A. Wright (Eds.), *Advancing higher education as a field of study: In quest of doctoral degree guidelines – Commemorating 120 years of excellence* (pp. 93-109). Sterling, VA: Stylus.

Dean, L. A. (2013), Using the CAS Standards in assessment projects. *New Directions for Student Services,* 25–33. doi: 10.1002/ss.20046

Dean, L. A. (2011). *What does "excellence" look like?: Program evaluation and outcomes assessment in college counseling.* Retrieved from http://counselingoutfitters.com/vistas/vistas11/Article_14.pdf

Liddell, D. L., Wilson, M. E., Pasquesi, K., Hirschy , A. S. & Boyle, K. M. (2014). Development of professional identity through socialization in graduate school. *Journal of Student Affairs Research and Practice, 51*:1, 69-84. doi:10.1515/jsarp-2014-0006

Keeling, R. P. (Ed.) (2006). *Learning reconsidered 2: Implementing a campus-wide focus on the student experience.* Washington, DC: American College Personnel Association, Association of College and University Housing Officers-International, Association of College Unions-International, National Academic Advising Association, National Association for Campus Activities, National Association of Student Personnel Administrators, National Intramural-Recreational Sports Association.

Keeling, S. (2010). The influence of the CAS standards on academic advisors and advising programs. *NACADA Journal, 30*(2), 9-18. doi: 10.12930/0271-9517-30.2.9

Komives, S. R., & Arminio, J. (2011). Promoting integrity through standards of practice. *New Directions for Student Services, 135.* 27-34. doi: 10.1002/ss.401

Miller, T. K., & Prince, J. S. (1976). *The Future of Student Affairs: A Guide to Student Development for Tomorrow's Higher Education.* San Francisco, CA: Jossey-Bass.

Miller, M. A. (2012). CAS standards for academic advising programs and transfer student services. In T. J. Grites & Duncan, C. (Eds.), *Advising Student Transfers: Strategies for Today's Realities and Tomorrow's Challenges* (NACADA Monograph Series, No. 24). Manhattan, KS: National Academic Advising Association.

Palmer, P.J. (2005). *The politics of the brokenhearted: On holding the tensions of democracy.* Fetzer Institute.

Scott, R. M. (2014). Using professional standards for higher education to improve student affairs. *New Directions for Community Colleges,* 55–61. doi: 10.1002/cc.20102

Tschepikow, W. K., Cooper, D. L., & Dean, L. A. (2010). Effects of CAS standards on assessment outcomes in student conduct programs. *Journal of Student Conduct Administration, 3*(1), 6-24.

Wilson, J. A., & Meyer, K. A. (2011). A Time and a place: Social justice in a doctoral program. *Journal of College Student Development, 52*(6), 753-759. doi: 10.1353/csd.2011.0080

Young, D. G., & Dean, L. A. (2015). Validation of subject areas of CAS professional studies standards for master's level student affairs professional preparation programs. *Journal of College Student Development, (56)*4, 386-391.

Young, D. G., & Dean, L. A., Franklin, D., & Tschepikow, W. K. (2014). Effects of assessment on collegiate recreation programs. *Recreational Sports Journal, 38,* 82-95. doi: 10.1123/rsj.2013-0023

Young, D. G., & Janosik, S. M. (2007). Using CAS standards to measure learning outcomes of student affairs preparation programs. *NASPA Journal, 44*(2), 341-365.

Chapter Contributors:

Current Edition
Marybeth Drechsler Sharp, CAS Executive Director

Previous Editions
Laura A. Dean, CAS President (2011-2014) and Editor (2004-2011)
Ted K. Miller, CAS President (1979-1989) and Editor (1979-2004)

Putting CAS to Work

Overview of the Ninth Edition

This 2015 edition of *CAS Professional Standards for Higher Education,* often referred to as the *CAS Blue Book* or the *CAS Book of Standards*, is the ninth iteration of professional standards generated and promulgated by the Council for the Advancement of Standards in Higher Education (CAS). This edition contains 43 sets of functional area standards and the standard for Masters-Level Student Affairs Professional Preparation Programs. All of the standards have been refreshed with updated General Standards, and 12 standards have undergone significant revision since the eighth edition. CAS continues to attract interest from professionals across higher education, whether they are seeking to use existing professional standards or to develop new ones.

The standards that have been revised since the 2012 edition include those focused on Academic Advising Programs; Alcohol and Other Drug Programs; Civic Engagement and Service-Learning Programs; College Honor Society Programs; Education Abroad Programs and Services; Financial Aid Programs; Housing and Residential Life Programs; Masters-Level Student Affairs Professional Preparation Programs; Orientation Programs; Sexual Violence-Related Programs and Services; Student Conduct Programs; and Women's and Gender Programs and Services. As has been increasingly true in previous editions, the breadth of CAS standards focuses attention not only on functions that comprise the traditional student affairs areas, but also on other educational functions essential to institutional effectiveness that may be less focused on direct work with students. This expanded CAS vision reflects an increased emphasis on developing standards to guide professional practice throughout the whole of higher education.

In addition to the major revisions of the aforementioned existing standards, each set of standards has been embedded with the updated General Standards, which were revised in 2014. The General Standards appear verbatim within nearly every set of standards and represent areas of practice that are essential regardless of functional area. CAS regularly reviews and updates the General Standards to ensure their currency; typically, the General Standards review and revision process occurs on a three-year cycle.

Also included in this edition are two documents that CAS developed to reflect the consensus of perspectives across differing areas, the *CAS Characteristics of Individual Excellence* and the *CAS Statement of Shared Ethical Principles.* Both the result of extended work within CAS, these materials have expanded the work of CAS to include the consideration of the hallmarks of high quality professional practice and of the ethical values that we hold in common.

Using the CAS Standards and Self-Assessment Guides

CAS standards and guidelines are conceived and crafted with care to be instructive and useful to practitioners and educational leaders. Based upon professional judgment and societal expectations, they include principles that are fundamental to student learning and development in conjunction with guidelines for practice for particular functional areas.

Because CAS believes in the importance of self-assessment, the standards and guidelines, as well as other CAS-related materials, are offered as criteria that can be used in multiple ways toward the goal of assuring and enhancing quality practice. As noted in the 1994 *CAS Preamble* (Appendix B) which outlines the organization's historic aims and justification, CAS standards can be used for design of new programs and services, for determining the efficacy of programs, for staff development, or for programmatic assessment as part of an institutional self-study. CAS does not prescribe or proscribe ways of using the standards; rather, they are intended to be tools for practitioners to improve practice.

Understanding the Standards and Guidelines

The initial CAS "Blue Book," *CAS Standards and Guidelines for Student Service/Development Programs* (CAS, 1986), emerged with the premise that practitioners needed access to a comprehensive and valid set of criteria by which to judge program quality and effectiveness. Further, it was essential that the CAS standards represent quality practices that any college or university program could reasonably achieve. Thus, the standards are intended to represent the threshold of good practice, the minimum acceptable level, rather than an aspirational level of best practice that only some may reach.

CAS functional area standards were created as living, evolving documents. The Council established a periodic review cycle to ensure that each standard undergoes regular review and updating, which is described in the preceding chapter (see The Case for CAS). Protocols to guide the development of new standards and the revision of existing standards are in place and appear in Appendix C. These protocols identify the processes, participants, and procedures used by CAS to create and review its standards. Completion of a typical standard review takes approximately one year from initiation to CAS adoption. It may take slightly longer to complete a new standard because an initial draft must be written before the CAS review process can be initiated. Historically, by the time a functional area standard has undergone the long and arduous development and review, the CAS representatives have nearly always been unanimous in its decision to adopt a new or revised standard, and in fact, the CAS review process is designed to lead to consensus.

What is a Functional Area?
In the CAS Glossary (Appendix D), a functional area is defined as a distinct grouping of activities, programs, and services within higher education that can be differentiated from other groups (e.g., departments) by its focus, mission, purpose, policies, practices, budget, body of literature, professional interests and backgrounds of its practitioners. In many cases, functional areas are what are often referred to as offices or departments, but CAS uses the term functional area to indicate a program or service that may not have the separate organizational structure typically associated with a department. Examples of functional areas include academic advising, internships, housing and residential life, and student leadership programs. Typically, one or more professional associations represent a functional area.

Defining functional areas within post-secondary student support services requires thinking about things as "both/ands," rather than "either/ors." The CAS functional area standards address processes, populations served, and necessary facilities or services. Employing complex "both/and" thinking, one can simultaneously perceive a functional area as both narrow and broad. CAS uses the inclusive term "functional area" in a way that can provide creative tension, enabling programs and services both to be what they are and to envision different ways of organizing themselves. For example, an internship program may exist within career services but also intersect with academic departments and service-learning initiatives.

The current slate of 44 functional area standards identified and addressed by CAS reflects the context and time during which each area was added to the canon of CAS standards. The scope and definition of a functional area is also informed by the timing of its conception. For example, in the 1990s, issues surfacing around alcohol, ADA legislation, HIV, and the Internet influenced the work of post-secondary student support services and, thus, CAS efforts to codify quality practice in the field. In the early 2000s, CAS work reflected the field's shifting focus on learning outcomes, undergraduate research, distance education, and globalization; and in the 2010s, CAS standards have responded to the increasing attention on veteran students, sexual violence, intersectional identities, and cross-functional thinking.

A Common Core: The CAS General Standards
From the CAS perspective, all functional areas of practice, no matter how specialized, have identifiable commonalties with other functions. For example, an institution's admission, academic advising, campus activities, and dining services programs, although established to accomplish clearly different purposes, will each benefit from establishing a written mission statement that is compatible with the mission of the institution. Likewise, the same is true for human, fiscal, physical, and technological resources; legal responsibilities; and ethical considerations, among others. Consequently, CAS developed and has incorporated a number of common criteria that have relevance for each and every functional area, no matter what its primary focus. These common criteria are referred to as "General Standards," and this boilerplate text forms the core of all functional area standards.

The General Standards are composed of 12 subsections, including mission; program; organization and leadership; human resources; ethics; law, policy, and governance; diversity, equity, and access; internal and external relations; financial resources; technology; facilities and equipment; and assessment. The standards statements included in these subsections are broad enough to apply across the different specialized functional areas, yet targeted enough to provide meaningful direction for professionals. The CAS General Standards are reviewed and revised prior to the publication of each new edition of the *CAS Professional Standards for Higher Education*.

These General Standards are designed to overcome the "silo effect" so common throughout higher education in which autonomous administrative units, programs, and services function independently and sometimes inconsistently. In effect, the general standards make the CAS standards highly utilitarian and promote inter-departmental, inter-program, and inter-service cooperation and collaboration. Users are encouraged to view the CAS standards and guidelines as vehicles that interconnect administrative units. Because what these various functional units have in common (e.g., educational purpose, student learning and development) often exceeds their differences, the effective practitioner will find that collaboration between and among units will enhance the educational environment in many important ways.

Another use of the General Standards is in offices or areas for which no CAS standards have been developed. While the General Standards do not offer the specialty standards designed to specifically address the particular functional area, they do offer essential standards of practice that are applicable to all areas and so can be used where no other standards exist. The General Standards are also useful in conducting an assessment of an office that has multiple functional responsibilities (e.g., activities, leadership, and orientation). Since the General Standards are present in each set of standards, practitioners can identify both points of overlap and portions that speak to the various functions, enabling them to merge the General Standards and specialized aspects into one non-repetitive set of standards that reflects the complex nature of the office.

Although the General Standards have evolved over CAS's history, the Council has reaffirmed and reinforced that the commonalities underlying different functional areas are indispensable and must be incorporated in all CAS standards.

Distinguishing the "Musts" from the "Shoulds"
The CAS standards and guidelines are written using similar language to clearly reflect the intent of the statements. All CAS standards use the auxiliary verbs "**must**" and "**shall**" and appear in **bold print** so that users can quickly identify them. As

previously noted, all functional areas have specialty standards in addition to the general standards. Specialty standards are essential to accomplishing a support program's purpose and appear in **bold print,** as do the General Standards.

CAS standards are constructed to represent criteria that every higher education institution and its student support programs should be expected and able to meet with the application of reasonable effort and diligence. Although the standards are carefully worded, it is sometimes helpful to amplify them by providing additional information to facilitate the user's ability to interpret them accurately. Also, when programs are organizationally mature, there is need to provide users with additional criteria that may be used to make good programs even better. Consequently, as a supplement to its standards, CAS has established "guidelines" designed to clarify and amplify the standards. Guidelines may be used to guide enhanced practice when a program has previously achieved high levels of effectiveness. Guidelines use the auxiliary verbs "should" and "may" and are printed in lightface type to distinguish them from the standards.

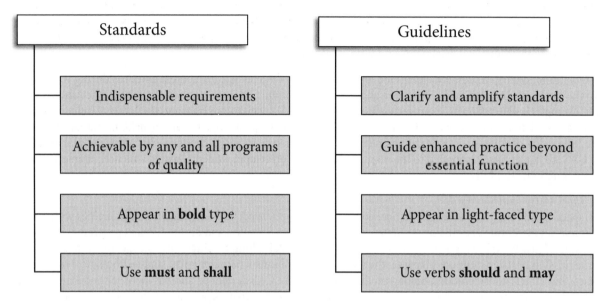

Figure 1. Distinguishing between CAS standards and guidelines

In summary, CAS functional area standards and guidelines are basic statements that should be achievable by any program in any higher education institution when adequate and appropriate effort, energy, and resources are applied. The CAS standards reflect a level of good practice generally agreed upon by the profession-at-large. In addition to the standards, guidelines are incorporated into each functional area to amplify and explain the standards and to guide enhanced practice. This dual presentation is helpful because functional area programs in both early and advanced stages of development, and at both small and large institutions, can use the CAS standards effectively. Most important is the fact that the CAS standards have been conceived and developed via a profession-wide process that can ensure continuity and consistency of practice among all higher education institutions. In addition, each set of standards is reviewed regularly to assess currency and determine need for revision.

Recognizing Context: U.S. Values Inherent in CAS Standards
In considering the CAS standards and guidelines, it is important to note and understand that they are not value-neutral. As discussed in the prior chapter (see The Case for CAS), there is a clear set of values that serves as the underpinning for the standards. They are derived from the theories and models that inform work in post-secondary student programs and services as well as from the historical documents that have guided the development of the field in North America, and particularly in the U.S.; they serve today as important touchstones for the ideas that shape current approaches and that have shaped these standards. While these ideas have been consistently incorporated in the development of the standards to date, CAS acknowledges they are reflective of the democratic culture of U.S. higher education and not sufficiently inclusive for application in all global higher education environments. As users of CAS standards continue to broaden into international settings, new situations and voices may inform future development of the standards, but at this point, they remain grounded in American ideals.

Self-Regulation and Self-Study
Enabling professionals to critically reflect on their practice with an eye toward enhancing quality programs and services has been a CAS goal since its inception. According to Dean and Jones (2014),

> From the beginning, the founders of CAS chose to base their approach on a belief that given the appropriate tools, professionals could do an effective job of self-regulation. Their belief was grounded in part in the recognition that expectations for practice need to be contextualized by the mission and structure of the institution. (p. 97)

Many practitioners today face the task of developing an assessment process, and CAS can be an important tool as part of the larger picture.

Upcraft and Schuh (1996), in describing a comprehensive assessment model, asserted that it should include
- keeping track of who uses student services, programs, and facilities
- assessing of student and other clientele needs
- assessing clientele satisfaction
- assessing campus environments and student cultures
- assessing outcomes
- conducting comparable institutions assessment (i.e., benchmarking)
- using nationally accepted standards to assess

An institution, division, program, or service with an assessment plan that incorporates all of these elements will have abundant documentation with which to complete a CAS self-study. Assessing the separate elements of the program or service supplies the evidence with which to support ratings in the self-study process.

Using CAS standards to assess practice responds directly to Upcraft and Schuh's (1996) recommendation for high quality assessment. The CAS standards define effective practice and are intended to be achievable by well-designed programs of quality. "If practitioners are to call a specific program a 'best practice' (i.e., of high quality and worthy of the adjective 'best'), then they must be able to point to some evidence that demonstrates a significant level of effectiveness based on clearly stated outcomes" (Shutt, Garrett, Lynch, & Dean, 2012, p. 6).

The most thorough and productive use of the standards involves a self-study process for program evaluation. Also referred to as "program review," this process involves others at the institution in examining evidence to determine collectively whether the program is in compliance with the standards. Involvement of others serves several purposes; it ensures a broader and more objective perspective, increases knowledge and awareness of the program across the institution, and develops support for implementation of identified improvements. Self-assessment offers a meaningful opportunity for institutions to be reflective. The results of self-studies can be organized into reports that divisions and institutions can use to enhance the student experience and to guide continuous improvement and strategic planning, and support accreditation efforts.

1. Plan the Process	5. Develop an Action Plan
Map out steps for process, develop timeline, build buy-in with all stakeholders, and explicitly identify desired outcomes of the self-study	Identify discrepancies, corrective action, and recommended steps (e.g., identify strengths, weaknesses, recommendations, benchmarks for achievement, resources, timeframe, and responsible individuals)
2. Assemble and Educate the Self-Assessment Team	6. Prepare a Report
Determine who should be on the team and how to educate the team about the self-study process	Identify audience for report(s); describe the self-study process, evidence gathering, rating process, and evaluations; summarize strengths and weaknesses; describe the action plan; and draft an executive summary
3. Identify, Collect, and Review Evidence	7. Close the Loop
Define what constitutes evidence; then gather, collect, manage, and review evidence	Put action plans into practice; work to navigate politics and secure resources; identify barriers to overcome; and build buy-in to the program review results
4. Conduct and Interpret Ratings Using Evaluative Evidence	
Clarify team's rating criteria; employ a process for rating [small group, individual, staff]; negotiate rating differences; and manage group ratings	

Figure 2. Steps of CAS program review process

Program Review Process
For each set of standards and guidelines, CAS provides a Self-Assessment Guide (SAG) that includes a recommended comprehensive self-study process for program evaluation. Seven basic steps to using a SAG are suggested for implementing a functional area self-study. The following self-study process, presented in Figure 3 and in summary form, is recommended.

1. Plan the Process
Prior to initiating a program review self-study, division and functional area leaders need to determine the area (or areas) to be evaluated and the reasons for the project. This may be dictated by institutional program review cycles or planning for accreditation processes, or it may result from internal divisional goals and needs. Explicitly identifying desired outcomes and key audiences for a self-study will help leaders facilitate a process that makes the most sense for the project.

Critical first phases of a self-study include mapping out the planned steps for the review and developing timelines. Leaders will also want to build buy-in to the review process with stakeholders of the functional area. In the initial planning stage of the self-study process it is desirable to involve the full functional area staff, including support staff members, knowledgeable students, and faculty members when feasible. This approach provides opportunity for shared ownership in the evaluation.

2. Assemble and Educate the Self-Assessment Team

Identifying the appropriate team members for a program review process will emerge as a result of planning. When leaders know their intended outcomes, approach, and audience, they can determine who should be included on the review team. For a self-study of a single functional area, a representative group of three to five members, including one or more knowledgeable individuals from outside the area under review, should be selected to compose the primary self-study team. For a larger department or divisional review, the team may include seven or eight individuals; the team size should reflect the anticipated workload while remaining nimble enough to schedule and work at the desired pace. In either case, the leader of the unit under review may serve as a resource to the committee but CAS recommends that person not chair it; appointing another leader will enhance the credibility of the self-study and facilitate honest responses and review.

Once team members are recruited or appointed, leaders will want to consider how to educate the team about the self-study process. In preparing the team for the self-study, it is imperative to train the team on the CAS standards, as well as self-assessment concepts and principles. The team should familiarize itself with each relevant CAS functional area standard before making individual or group judgments. It is important that all members understand the standard in similar fashion. Team training should be conducted to ensure that members' interpretive differences are resolved before initiating the study. Likewise, review teams will need to establish and agree upon ground rules for the study. Team members should realize that disagreement is natural, healthy, and probably inevitable, but the resulting debates will usually strengthen the team's understanding and ultimate consensus on the matter.

The team also should discuss whether any of the guidelines (included with the standards to indicate areas where practice can be enhanced beyond the minimum expectations) should be treated as a standard for self-study purposes. For example, a functional area guideline might include the statement "facilities should include a private office where individual consultations can be held." The study team may decide that this guideline statement, which is not a CAS standard compliance requirement, is imperative at the institution and should therefore be treated as a standard for purposes of their self-study. If so decided, a criterion measure statement such as "private office space is available for staff members to use for consultation purposes" would be inserted as a criterion measure to be rated along with the other criterion measures included in the SAG and evaluated accordingly.

3. Identify, Collect, and Review Evidence

Gathering and documenting evidence of program effectiveness is an important step in the program review process. No self-assessment is complete without relevant data and related documentation being used. It is good practice for programs to collect and file relevant data routinely, which then can be used to record program effectiveness over time. Although the review team may identify additional information that is needed to complete the review, having basic documents from the functional area available at the outset will assist them in making progress in their work.

It is suggested that program review team members use the CAS Functional Area Self-Assessment Guide (SAG) to direct the self-study. The steps guide members to define what is relevant evidence; identify and collect existing evidence; determine how to collect evidence that does not already exist; manage the evidence; and review available documentation.

Judging the program by rating it against the standard's criterion measures and identifying program strengths and weaknesses does not constitute a completed self-study. Rather, the process requires documentation of the evidence that supports each criterion measure rating. The nature of such documentary evidence may be quantitative, qualitative, or a combination of the two. For example, quantitative measures might include the staff-to-student ratio for a given activity, an analysis of the cost-effectiveness of a given activity, or the results of an assessment of student outcome achievement. Qualitative documentation, on the other hand, might include notes on the process used to develop the program's mission or outcome objectives or structured interviews with students. Essential documentation includes relevant publications (e.g., student and staff handbooks), program descriptions (e.g., career decision-making workshop outlines), program evaluation data (e.g., program assessment results), institutional data (e.g., student profiles), and research initiated for the self-study (e.g., student survey or focus group results). No self-study can be considered complete without relevant data and related documentation to support and validate the team's judgments. These data can be collected over time and stored in a database or data management system for self-study purposes. Such data also have utility for preparing annual reports and supporting accreditation efforts.

The Program section of the CAS standards for every functional area includes learning and development outcome domains for which programs must demonstrate outcomes. It is particularly important that outcomes assessment information be available for review, since assessing the results of our work is a crucial part of determining the effectiveness of the program or service.

4. Conduct and Interpret Ratings Using Evaluative Evidence

When the program review team has gathered and reviewed necessary evidence, they will be able to assign ratings to individual criterion measures. Collectively, the team will want to discuss and clarify their individual approaches to rating items.

Assessment criterion measures are used to judge how well areas under review meet CAS standards. The SAG provides a 4-point scale from *Does Not Meet* to *Exceeds* for rating the criterion measures, which reflect the essence of the standards. This rating scale is designed to estimate broadly the extent to which a given practice has been performed. Under rare circumstances, it may be determined that a criterion measure used to judge the standard is not applicable for the particular program (e.g., a single sex or other unique institution that cannot meet a criterion measure for that reason). In such instances, raters may use a *Does Not Apply* (DNA) rating and, in the self-study report, describe their rationale for excluding the practice in the criterion measure. Also, an *Insufficient Evidence/Unable to Rate* (IE) response can be used when relevant data are unavailable to support a judgment.

The review team will need to ascertain their process for rating, and CAS suggests a two-tiered (individual and group) judgment approach for determining the extent to which the program meets the CAS standard. First, the self-assessment team members should individually rate each criterion measure using the CAS SAG. In addition, they will need to document their reasoning and evidence for the rating assigned to each subsection in the space provided for *Rationale*. This individualized rating procedure is then followed by a collective review and analysis of the individual ratings.

The individual ratings should be reviewed and translated into a collective rating before the team is ready to conduct the interpretation phase of the self-assessment. Interpretation typically incorporates discussion among team members to assure that all aspects of the program were given fair and impartial consideration prior to a final collective judgment. At this point, persistent disagreements over performance ratings may call for additional data collection. The team should discuss and respond to the *Overview Questions* that immediately follow the rating section of each of the 12 components. Answers to the *Overview Questions*, which are designed to stimulate summary thinking about overarching issues, can be used to facilitate interpretation of the ratings and development of the self-study report. After the team review and rating is completed, a meeting with relevant administrators, staff members, and student leaders should be scheduled for a general review of the self-assessment results.

5. Develop an Action Plan
The next step, including discussion of alternative approaches that might be used to strengthen and enhance the program, is to generate phases and activities to be incorporated into an action plan. Review team members should compare their ratings and interpretations of program characteristics, accomplishments, strengths, and shortcomings against the criteria expressed in the standard.

The team members should carefully review each criterion measure and related practice that they rated as *Insufficient Evidence/ Unable to Rate*, *Does Not Meet*, or *Partly Meets* and where significant rater differences were noted. A specific rationale should be prepared for each shortcoming identified. Three core components to include in an action plan are identified discrepancies, corrective actions, and recommended steps.

Discrepancies. When discrepancies are noted between the assessment criteria and actual practice, the team can then identify existing operational problems that need resolution. For example, each standard calls for the existence of a program mission statement consistent with the nature and goals of the institution. If the program has no written mission statement or an outdated one, then the discrepancy between the standard and actual program practice clearly calls for the creation of a current, relevant program mission statement that is consistent with the institution's mission.

Corrective actions. The self-study team should describe in detail the adjustments that need to be implemented for the program to achieve the quality and effectiveness to which it aspires. For example, returning to the case of the program mission, the action required would call for program staff members to draft a statement delineating the elements they believe are agreed upon, circulate them for review and comment, and then prepare and disseminate a final program mission statement to guide the program and its services.

An important point to note in regard to corrective action is the importance of subdividing the overall task into manageable parts. Trying to revise a total functional area in one step is neither a desirable nor an effective approach to program development. It is important that the review team list specific actions identified in the self-study that require implementation. The review team and/ or the functional area staff members should set priorities on the list by order of importance, need, feasibility, and achievability of the desired change. When possible, the review team and functional area staff members should also identify necessary resources, possible timeframe, responsible individuals, and benchmarks for achievement.

Recommended Steps. Even excellent programs can be further refined to provide more desirable and effective outcomes. Unless staff members are satisfied with meeting basic standards only, additional initiatives can be implemented to enhance program quality and effectiveness. This can be accomplished by listing each specific action identified in the self-study that would enhance and strengthen services and by setting priorities among them for follow-up purposes. The guidelines provide possibilities for identifying enhanced practice.

As the program review self-study process comes to closure, it is important for functional area staff members to identify and establish priorities to influence the program's future direction. This process entails comparing past performance with desired outcomes. Staff members should carefully review the self-study process that was conducted to ensure that all relevant program issues are addressed. The post-self-assessment action plan should acknowledge the program's strengths as well as its shortcomings as it moves toward establishing a strategic approach for correcting deficiencies and initiating enhancements. The primary goal of this step is to identify and set priorities for future actions and directions after comparing the results of the self-study with the aspirational outcomes of the program.

6. Prepare a Report

To complete the program review process, a summary document should be produced that (a) explains the mission, purpose, and philosophy of the program; (b) describes the self-study process, evidence gathering, rating process, and evaluations; (c) reviews the outcome of the assessment, including program strengths and weaknesses; and (d) recommends specific plans for action. This final report must include the comprehensive action plan for implementing program changes. The report must identify resources (i.e., human, fiscal, physical) that are essential to program enhancement, dates by which specific actions are to be completed, responsible parties to complete the action steps, and a tentative start-up date for initiating a subsequent self-study.

An extension of the final report may also involve drafting an executive summary, brief presentation, or talking points about the program review. A report that can be easily disseminated and reviewed by stakeholders and divisional leadership can be considerably shorter than the final report, with the primary focus being on prescribed actions.

7. Close the Loop

Finally, to close the loop on a program's self-study process, functional area staff members must implement the recommended changes to enhance the quality of their program. In this final step, the staff endeavors to put action plans into practice. In some cases, there will be institutional politics to be navigated; continued support from functional area leaders remains essential. Staff members will want to work collectively to secure resources, identify barriers to implementation, and build stakeholder buy-in to the results. CAS recommends that closing the loop on a self-study process be integrated into regular staff meetings, individual supervision, trainings, assessment projects, and annual reports. A key to successfully using program review in post-secondary student programs and services is weaving the entire process, from planning through initiating action, into the fabric of the functional area, departmental, and divisional culture.

Other Uses and Applications of the CAS Standards

In addition to the model presented for program evaluation, the CAS standards are a resource that can be used for a number of other purposes. The following examples illustrate how CAS standards may be applied in practice and for purposes of professional development. The uses outlined here are representative; because the CAS standards and guidelines are tools to be used by practitioners, there are not really "wrong" ways to use them as long as the values and spirit underlying them are honored.

Design of New Programs and Services

As student and institutional needs change, opportunities may arise to develop new programs or services, expand existing offerings, and restructure current areas. The functional area standards and guidelines are helpful criteria that outline, guide, and ground planning when needed. The Mission and Program sections are particularly beneficial for specifying important goals and components relevant to the functional area being developed.

The CAS standards can be helpful when advocating for and broadening administrators' understanding of what is required to meet basic essentials of programs and services. Too often, administrators limit their initial thinking about a new program to relatively basic issues, such as access, rather than considering how a new program could help students become better integrated into the campus community or enhance their learning and development. The CAS standards can illuminate for institutional leaders the importance of comprehensive programming.

From a program design perspective, the CAS standards have special utility for emerging student support areas. For example, the National Clearinghouse for Commuter Programs (NCCP) frequently receives requests from institutions desiring to establish on-campus commuter programs. Most practitioners interested in such initiatives initially struggle to comprehend the scope of the functions essential to a comprehensive program. Often, the initiator is interested in establishing a particular type of program (e.g., peer mentoring or orientation for commuters) or service (e.g., off-campus housing referral, commuter newsletter). When such requests are made, the CAS standards are readily available as a professionally sanctioned tool to provide guidance for supporting such populations.

Professional Development

Staff members can study the CAS standards to determine how well they and their colleagues are implementing the criteria in their daily work with students. The relevant functional area standards can be used as an orientation device to assist new professionals in understanding and reviewing their areas, as a point of discussion for supervisors and staff to discuss program strengths and weaknesses, as a resource for educating others at the institution about what is involved in a sound program, or as the format by which annual program reports are prepared. The more the CAS standards are used within a division or institution, the more it will lead to a common language and shared perception of the elements of good practice.

A comprehensive staff development program using CAS functional area standards or the General Standards as a training device could encompass a half- or full-day of meeting time during which staff members share responsibility for leading discussions about the various standard components. This approach is particularly valuable when a program or division self-study is in the offing. In such an instance, staff members learn how CAS standards can be used to influence good practice and how standards can provide a vehicle for self-study. Training staff members before conducting a self-study typically produces a more comprehensive and valuable program evaluation.

Academic and Professional Preparation

The CAS standards have a valuable educational application as a resource in formal academic preparation programs in both student affairs preparation and higher education administration, especially in introductory courses concerned with student-oriented functions common to institutions of higher learning. The CAS functional area standards and their accompanying contextual statements, as well as the statements regarding individual characteristics, shared ethical principles, and learning and development outcomes, provide an excellent primer for those entering the field. The contextual statements summarize the roles and functions of key program and service units, their primary purposes, historical perspectives, and relevant resources available to explore the areas in greater detail. These succinct summary statements provide an introduction for those unfamiliar with the areas under study. The CAS standards provide an in-depth description of the characteristics common to and expected of the various functional areas.

"Quality assurance" can be an ambiguous concept for graduate students, especially at the master's level. The idea of applying standards to practice is more concrete, and students can quickly come to understand the role, function, and utility of professional standards. As a result, many academic preparation programs have integrated the CAS standards into their curricula, as well as using the preparation program standards to guide development of the program overall. From the outset, students can begin to internalize the professional interests of self-regulation and improvement.

CAS standards also are incorporated easily into experiential components of academic preparation programs. For students examining a given functional area in greater detail or participating in a practicum, internship, or other field-based experience, the CAS Self-Assessment Guide provides a unique resource for learning the basics of functional areas and obtaining a comprehensive understanding. Each functional area SAG includes the standards, guidelines, and criterion measures that can be used to judge the level of compliance a program exhibits in regard to the standards. Using a SAG, students can readily identify a program's strengths and shortcomings. Also, the SAG has utility as a vehicle for both students and supervisors to examine together and discuss the various components of the area under study. Students may complete a "mini-self-study" of the functional areas to which they are assigned as part of their supervised practice experiences, ensuring that future professionals are familiar and experienced with putting CAS standards into practice as they move into entry level positions.

Credibility and Accountability

Any profession, along with its practitioners, must exhibit a reasonable level of credibility if it is to survive. Credibility is essential to the existence of post-secondary student programs and services, and, by adhering to professional standards, institutions can help assure potential student users and the general public of their competence. Both higher education consumers and professionals alike attribute credibility to programs and institutions that meet stringent standards; compliance with such standards demonstrates that quality is present.

Institutional and academic program credibility is typically established through accreditation, a voluntary process by which agencies encourage and assist institutions and their sub-units (e.g., colleges, schools, departments, and programs) to evaluate and improve their programs and services (Eaton, 2001). Information about the institutions and programs that voluntarily meet or exceed acceptable standards of quality and effectiveness is made public by the accrediting body. It is not uncommon for institutions lacking accreditation to be denied federal aid or other resources available to accredited institutions. Graduates of non-accredited institutions may be denied admission to graduate schools or certain employment opportunities. Accreditation is intended to assure the public that an institution and its programs do indeed provide quality education.

However, the general public cannot be assured that individuals who have diplomas, certificates, or degrees from accredited institutions and programs are, in fact, effective practitioners. Consequently, various structures have been established by professional and governmental oversight agencies to judge the professional qualifications of service providers in education, health, and social service areas.

Three primary methods have been established to enable individuals to document their professional qualifications: registry, certification, and licensure. CAS, a consortium of higher education professional associations, focuses minimal attention on credentialing options, although some have encouraged CAS to expand its focus into registry or certification, which are often initiated by non-governmental professional bodies. Licensure is largely the province of governments. For instance, licenses based on generally comparable criteria are required of physicians, psychologists, and lawyers in all states; counselors and engineers, on the other hand, may be judged by diverse criteria from state to state.

As demand for accountability in higher education increases, so too does demand for practitioner accountability. CAS endorses self-regulation as the most viable approach to program accountability, calling for each institution to initiate a program of self-assessment for its student programs, services, and related personnel. Whether student programs and services are administratively assigned to student affairs, academic affairs, business affairs, or elsewhere in the organizational hierarchy, CAS encourages program review and evaluation on a continuing basis using the CAS standards. From this perspective, self-regulation becomes a preferred strategy to establish and maintain credibility.

When appropriate and desirable, functional areas may invite representatives from peer institutions or professionals with particular expertise in the areas being studied to review their self-assessment reports as part of a validation process. Self-regulation requires institutions and their leaders to establish their own policies and procedures for institutional assessment and to adhere to them when evaluating quality and effectiveness. Through continuing assessment, institutions can compile and maintain the internal documentation required by regional accrediting bodies and governmental oversight agencies. Self-regulation provides institutions as well as student programs and services with tools to achieve and demonstrate quality. If institutions accept responsibility for initiating meaningful and well-considered assessment processes and procedures, there is less likelihood that external oversight agencies, governmental or otherwise, will seek to do so.

Institutional Program Review

From an institutional perspective, many practitioners view the CAS standards as a staple for conducting comprehensive program reviews. For example, one institution's policy requires that a standard external to the institution be used to implement periodic comprehensive program reviews. CAS standards are readily available, easily understood, and consistent across functional areas; thus, they often are the standard of choice for administrative unit reviews. The fact that operational versions of the standards in the form of CAS Self-Assessment Guides are also available has increased the ease with which the standards can be used for program review purposes. In addition, the existence of the CAS standards informs practitioners that professional practice is not based simply on instinct or history. Rather, it consists of the application of the collective wisdom of the profession and is enhanced by continuous assessment and improvement.

References

Council for the Advancement of Standards (CAS) (1986). *CAS standards and guidelines for student service/development programs.* Iowa City, IA: American College Testing Program.

Dean, L. A., & Jones, G. M. (2014). The Council for the Advancement of Standards in Higher Education and the role of standards in professional practice. In S. Freeman, Jr., L. S. Hagedorn, L. F. Goodchild, & D. A. Wright (Eds.), *Advancing higher education as a field of study: In quest of doctoral degree guidelines – Commemorating 120 years of excellence* (pp. 93-109). Sterling, VA: Stylus.

Eaton, J. S. (March/April 2001). Regional accreditation reform: Who is served? *Change Magazine,* 39-45. doi: 10.1080/00091380109601786

Shutt, M. D., Garrett, J. M., Lynch, J. W., & Dean, L. A. (2012). An assessment model as best practice in student affairs. *Journal of Student Affairs Research and Practice, 49*(1), 1–16. doi:10.2202/1949-6605.6227

Upcraft, M. L., & Schuh, J. H. (1996). *Assessment in student affairs: A guide for practitioners.* San Francisco, CA: Jossey-Bass.

<u>**Chapter Contributors:**</u>
Current Edition
Marybeth Drechsler Sharp, CAS Executive Director

Previous Editions
Laura A. Dean, CAS President (2011-2014) and Editor (2004-2011)
Ted K. Miller, CAS President (1979-1989) and Editor (1979-2004)

CAS Characteristics of Individual Excellence for Professional Practice in Higher Education
CAS Contextual Statement

Defining competencies of student affairs and other professionals in higher education who plan, implement, and offer programs and services is the mark of a maturing profession. A number of authors and organizations have framed competencies in several broad areas. For example, Pope, Reynolds, and Mueller (2004) identified competencies in the areas of a) administration and management, b) multicultural awareness, knowledge, and skills, c) helping and advising, d) assessment and research, e) teaching and training, f) ethics and professional standards, and g) translation and use of theory to guide practice. This document seeks to define a list of necessary attributes for professionals in higher education that is broader than competencies and includes other markers of professionalism. These characteristics of excellence can be used in an evaluative format, both self-evaluation and in the context of "360 degree" (Tornow, London, & Associates, 1998) or supervisory format.

There are numerous purposes for the creation and use of this document. One purpose is to move the student affairs profession and other professionals within the higher education context to more concrete, concise, and agreed upon characteristics that are expected of professionals who provide, implement, and facilitate programs and services in higher education. Another purpose is to assist in the enculturation of new professionals into the profession by defining what it means to be a professional in higher education. This document also seeks to clarify the context within which people are choosing to work. In response to the literature on supervision that indicates that supervision in higher education is often irregular and when it does occur stresses operational tasks rather than professional development (Arminio & Creamer, 2001; Saunders, Cooper, Winston, & Chernow, 2000; Winston & Creamer, 1997), this document was created to provide aspirational expectations for higher education professionals (Carpenter, 2003).

Because it is the intent of this document to honor individual differences that people bring to their practice, when perceived differences from the expected characteristics are identified these differences need to be discussed. It is through these discussions with supervisors and colleagues that such differences can be acknowledged and their implications explored.

This document offers direction for professional development whether prompted by self-evaluation or from supervisory evaluation. In either case, this document is intended to be used in collaboration and discussion with a supervisor, supervisees, students, and/or colleagues. From these discussions an individual professional development plan can be created and accomplishment of that plan can be evaluated.

References

Arminio, J. & Creamer, D. G. (2001). What quality supervisors say about quality supervision. *College Student Affairs Journal, 21*, 35-44.

Carpenter, D. S. (2003). Professionalism. In S. R. Komives & D. Woodard Jr (Eds.). *Student services: A handbook for the profession* (4th edition; pp. 573-592). San Francisco, CA: Jossey-Bass.

Pope, R. L., Reynolds, A. L., & Mueller, J. A. (2004). *Multicultural competence in student affairs.* San Francisco, CA: Jossey-Bass.

Saunders, S. A., Cooper, D. L. Winston, R. B. Jr., & Chernow, E. (2000). Supervising staff in student affairs: Exploration of the synergistic approach. *Journal of College Student Development, 41*, 1281-191.

Tornow, W. W., London, M., & Associates (1998). *Maximizing the value of 360-degree feedback.* San Francisco, CA: Jossey-Bass.

Winston, R. B., Jr., & Creamer, D. G. (1997). *Improving staffing practices in student affairs.* San Francisco, CA: Jossey-Bass.

CAS Characteristics of Individual Excellence for Professional Practice in Higher Education

Evaluating individual professional practice in higher education requires the identification of ideal performance characteristics that describe excellence in professional practice. This document has evolved from multi-faceted professional competencies that are inherent in the purpose, development, and application of the CAS Standards and Guidelines. It assumes a philosophy and practice of life-long learning and professional development shared by individual practitioners and their institutions. Characteristics are grouped into **General Knowledge and Skills**, **Interactive Competencies**, and **Self Mastery.**

General Knowledge and Skills
General Knowledge
1. Understands and supports the broad responsibility of the institution for enhancing the collegiate experience for all students

2. Possesses appropriate knowledge of relevant theories, literature, and philosophies on which to base informed professional practice

3. Knows values, historical context, and current issues of one's profession

4. Has developed, can articulate, and acts consistently with a sound educational philosophy consistent with the institution's mission

5. Understands and respects similarities and differences of people in the institutional environment

6. Understands relevant legal issues

General Skills
7. Manages and influences campus environments that promote student success

8. Works to create campus and related educational environments that are safe and secure

9. Effectively utilizes language through speaking, writing, and other means of communication

10. Engages disparate audiences effectively

11. Teaches effectively directly or through example

12. Thinks critically about complex issues

13. Works collaboratively

14. Is trustworthy and maintains confidentiality

15. Exercises responsible stewardship of resources

16. Engages in evaluation and assessment to determine outcomes and identify areas for improvement

17. Uses technology effectively for educational and institutional purposes

18. Bases decisions on appropriate data

19. Models effective leadership

Interactive Competencies
With students:
20. Counsels, advises, supervises, and leads individuals and groups effectively

21. Knows the developmental effects of college on students

22. Knows characteristics of students attending institutions of higher education

23. Knows students who attend the institution, use services, and participants in programs

24. Interacts effectively with a diverse range of students

25. Provides fair treatment to all students and works to change aspects of the environment that do not promote fair treatment

26. Values differences among groups of students and between individuals; helps students understand the interdependence among people both locally and globally

27. Actively and continually pursues insight into the cultural heritage of students

28. Encourages student learning through successful experiences as well as failures

With Colleagues and the Institution
29. Supervises others effectively

30. Manages fiscal, physical, and human resources responsibly and effectively

31. Judges the performance of self and others fairly

32. Contributes productively in partnerships and team efforts

33. Demonstrates loyalty and support of the institution where employed

34. Behaves in ways that reflect integrity, responsibility, honesty, and with accurate representation of self, others, and program

35. Creates and maintains campus relationships characterized by integrity and responsibility

36. Effectively creates and maintains networks among colleagues locally, regionally, nationally, and internationally

37. Contributes to campus life and supports activities that promote campus community

Self Mastery
38. Commits to excellence in all work

39. Intentionally employs self reflection to improve practice and gain insight

40. Responds to the duties of one's role and also to the spirit of one's responsibilities

41. Views his or her professional life as an important element of personal identity

42. Strives to maintain personal wellness and a healthy lifestyle

43. Maintains position-appropriate appearance

44. Stays professionally current by reading literature, building skills, attending conferences, enhancing technological literacy, and engaging in other professional development activities

45. Manages personal life so that overall professional effectiveness is maintained

46. Belongs to and contributes to activities of relevant professional associations

47. Assumes proper accountability for individual and organizational mistakes

48. Espouses and follows a written code of professional ethical standards

49. Abides by laws and institutional policies and works to change policies that are incongruent with personal and professional principles

50. Re-evaluates continued employment when personal, professional, and institutional goals and values are incompatible and inhibit the pursuit of excellence

CAS Statement of Shared Ethical Principles

The Council for the Advancement of Standards in Higher Education (CAS) has served as a voice for quality assurance and promulgation of standards in higher education for more than thirty-five years. CAS was established to promote inter-association efforts to address quality assurance, student learning, and professional integrity. It was believed that a single voice would have greater impact on the evaluation and improvement of services and programs than would many voices speaking for special interests by individual practitioners or by single-interest organizations.

CAS includes membership of 41 active professional associations and has established standards in 44 functional areas. It has succeeded in providing a platform through which representatives from across higher education can jointly develop and promulgate standards of good practice that are endorsed not just by those working in a particular area, but by representatives of higher education association.

CAS cites George Washington, who said, "Let us raise a standard to which the wise and honest can repair." CAS has raised standards; it is now time to focus on the attributes, such as wisdom and honesty, of those professionals who would use the standards. Professionals working to provide services in higher education share more than a commitment to quality assurance and standards of practice. A review of the ethical statements of member associations demonstrates clearly that there are elements of ethical principles and values that are shared across the professions in higher education.

Most of the member associations represented in CAS are guided by ethical codes of professional practice enforced through the prescribed channels of its association. CAS acknowledges and respects the individual codes and standards of ethical conduct of their organizations. From these codes, CAS has created a statement of shared ethical principles that focuses on seven basic principles that form the foundation for CAS member association codes: autonomy, non-malfeasance, beneficence, justice, fidelity, veracity, and affiliation. This statement is not intended to replace or supplant the code of ethics of any professional association; rather, it is intended to articulate those shared ethical principles. It is our hope that by articulating those shared beliefs, CAS can promulgate a better understanding of the professions of those in service to students and higher education.

Principle I - Autonomy
We take responsibility for our actions and both support and empower an individual's and group's freedom of choice.
- We strive for quality and excellence in the work that we do
- We respect one's freedom of choice
- We believe that individuals, ourselves and others, are responsible for their own behavior and learning
- We promote positive change in individuals and in society through education
- We foster an environment where people feel empowered to make decisions
- We hold ourselves and others accountable
- We study, discuss, investigate, teach, conduct research, and publish freely within the academic community
- We engage in continuing education and professional development

Principle II – Non-Malfeasance
We pledge to do no harm.
- We collaborate with others for the good of those whom we serve
- We interact in ways that promote positive outcomes
- We create environments that are educational and supportive of the growth and development of the whole person
- We exercise role responsibilities in a manner that respects the rights and property of others without exploiting or abusing power

Principle III - Beneficence
We engage in altruistic attitudes and actions that promote goodness and contribute to the health and welfare of others.
- We treat others courteously
- We consider the thoughts and feelings of others
- We work toward positive and beneficial outcomes

Principle IV - Justice
We actively promote human dignity and endorse equality and fairness for everyone.
- We treat others with respect and fairness, preserving their dignity, honoring their differences, promoting their welfare
- We recognize diversity and embrace a cross-cultural approach in support of the worth, dignity, potential, and uniqueness of people within their social and cultural contexts
- We eliminate barriers that impede student learning and development or discriminate against full participation by all students
- We extend fundamental fairness to all persons
- We operate within the framework of laws and policies

- We respect the rights of individuals and groups to express their opinions
- We assess students in a valid, open, and fair manner and one consistent with learning objectives
- We examine the influence of power on the experience of diversity to reduce marginalization and foster community

Principle V - Fidelity

We are faithful to an obligation, trust, or duty.

- We maintain confidentiality of interactions, student records, and information related to legal and private matters
- We avoid conflicts of interest or the appearance thereof
- We honor commitments made within the guidelines of established policies and procedures
- We demonstrate loyalty and commitment to institutions that employ us
- We exercise good stewardship of resources

Principle VI - Veracity

We seek and convey the truth in our words and actions.

- We act with integrity and honesty in all endeavors and interactions
- We relay information accurately
- We communicate all relevant facts and information while respecting privacy and confidentiality

Principle VII – Affiliation

We actively promote connected relationships among all people and foster community.

- We create environments that promote connectivity
- We promote authenticity, mutual empathy, and engagement within human interactions

When professionals act in accordance with ethical principles, program quality and excellence are enhanced and ultimately students are better served. As professionals providing services in higher education, we are committed to upholding these shared ethical principles, for the benefit of our students, our professions, and higher education.

Some concepts for this code were adopted from
Kitchener, K. (1985). Ethical principles and ethical decisions in student affairs. In H. Canon & R. Brown (Eds.), *Applied ethics in student services* (New Directions in Student Services, No. 30, pp. 17-30). San Francisco, CA: Jossey-Bass.

CAS Learning and Development Outcomes
CAS Contextual Statement

Learning outcomes continue to serve as a way to satisfy the increasing demands for accountability in higher education. These statements, meant to identify the aspects of learning experienced by students through engaging with programs, disciplines, or other learning opportunities, are typically paired with assessment techniques in order to effectively measure their magnitude (AAC&U & NLC, 2007; Bowman, 2013; CHEA, 2003). In a brief published by the National Institute for Learning Outcomes Assessment (NILOA), Bresciani (2011) states that assessment is the only way to demonstrate accountability for student learning.

The Council for the Advancement of Standards in Higher Education (CAS) promotes standards to enhance opportunities for student learning and development from higher education programs and services. CAS supports the integration of learning and development outcomes and assessment tools to guide practice and create quality programs for student learning.

The Role of Student Affairs

The initial emergence of formal learning outcomes in higher education was centered on academic affairs and educational disciplines (AAC&U & NLC, 2007; Adelman, 2015). However, the philosophy on learning has since shifted from classroom-specific to a more holistic student learning and development approach, a view championed by the American Association of Colleges and University's (AAC&U) Liberal Education and America's Promise (LEAP) Initiative. This initiative defines holistic learning as "liberal education," or "a comprehensive set of aims and outcomes that are essential for all students because they are important to all fields of endeavor" and encompasses curricular and co-curricular components (AAC&U & NLC, 2007, p. 4). This more holistic view is not new in student affairs; in fact, one of the earliest documents in the field argued that a primary task of higher education was to

> …assist the student in developing to the limits of his [sic] potentialities and in making his contribution to the betterment of society…This philosophy imposes upon educational institutions the obligation to consider the student as a whole…It puts emphasis, in brief, upon the development of the student as a person rather than upon his intellectual training alone. (American Council on Education, 1937/1994, p. 68)

With an increased focus on the whole student experience comes an increased responsibility for student affairs professionals to join faculty in developing outcomes and measuring student learning. While the contribution of student affairs to student learning and development has sometimes been, according to Schuh and Gansemer-Topf (2011), "overlooked and underutilized" (p. 3), the authors present three ways to showcase the contributions of student affairs to student learning:

1. Link the student affairs mission to the institutional mission, purpose, and strategic plan
2. Foster partnerships with faculty
3. Share existing expertise on student learning and development

By incorporating learning outcomes and assessment as a routine part of student affairs work, a more balanced understanding of the elements impacting student learning and development can be achieved.

CAS Standards and Outcome Domains

CAS illustrates support for student affairs professionals' documentation of their contributions to student learning by incorporating the use of learning outcomes as a general standard for all functional areas. To comply with CAS standards, institutional programs and services must identify relevant and desirable learning from specific domains, assess that relevant and desirable learning, and articulate how their programs and services contribute to domains not specifically assessed.

CAS historically had listed desirable outcomes of programmatic efforts, but in the early editions of the book, they were simply examples such as intellectual growth, clarification of values, and achievement of personal goals. Then, in response to the increased focus on student outcomes, CAS in 2003 articulated sixteen domains of learning outcomes, with associated "examples of achievement indicators." Finally, after the publication of Learning Reconsidered (NASPA & ACPA, 2004), and Learning Reconsidered 2 (Keeling, 2006) and other outcomes related literature, CAS reviewed the learning outcomes it had promoted and decided an integration of multiple learning outcomes models would enhance the profession's efforts in promoting student learning and development. Consequently, CAS hosted a "think tank" involving writers of Learning Reconsidered and Learning Reconsidered 2, CAS directors, and prominent practitioners and faculty members in student affairs to make recommendations for a revised learning outcomes document.

The revised student learning and development outcomes model includes six broad categories (called domains): knowledge acquisition, construction, integration and application; cognitive complexity; intrapersonal development; interpersonal competence; humanitarianism and civic engagement; and practical competence.

This learning outcomes model further defines or clarifies each of the six domains by identifying more specific learning outcome dimensions within each domain. Offering dimensions of learning allows for a more focused assessment approach and more opportunities for alignment with institutional mission and priorities. For each of the dimensions, CAS also offers examples illustrating achievement of the student learning outcomes.

The CAS Board of Directors reviewed and approved the six domains, learning outcome dimensions, and examples of learning and development outcomes at its October 2008 meeting. The domains and learning outcome dimensions are embedded in each functional area standard within the 'Program' section, demonstrating that the identification, facilitation, and assessment of student outcomes must be an integral part of the work in every program and service.

Additional Resources

While CAS promotes the incorporation of learning and development outcomes centered on these domains, CAS also recognizes the existence of several other related resources. Among these are AAC&U's LEAP (2011), Learning Reconsidered (NASPA & ACPA, 2004) and Learning Reconsidered 2 (Keeling, 2006), learning outcomes detailed by academic accrediting agencies (Drechsler Sharp, Komives, & Fincher, 2011), and the Degree Qualifications Profile (DQP) (Adelman, Ewell, Gaston, & Schneider, 2011), which focuses on the knowledge and skills students should have upon degree completion. Each of these resources offers learning domains similar to those promoted by CAS, as detailed in the Figure 1 below.

CAS Domains (2008)	Learning Reconsidered (2004)	LEAP [AAC&U] (2007)	Disciplines (2011)	Degree Qualifications Profile [DQP] (2011)
• Knowledge Acquisition, Construction, Integration, and Application	• Knowledge Acquisition, Integration, and Application	• Knowledge of Human Cultures and the Physical and Natural World	• Knowledge Bases	• Specialized Knowledge; Broad and Integrative Knowledge
• Cognitive Complexity	• Cognitive Complexity	• Intellectual and Practical Skills	• Critical Thinking	• Intellectual Skills
• Intrapersonal Development • Interpersonal Competence • Humanitarianism and Civic Engagement	• Interpersonal and Intrapersonal Competence • Humanitarianism • Civic Engagement	• Personal and Social Responsibility	• Intrapersonal Attributes and Competencies • Interpersonal relations with diverse others • Ethics • Management & collaborative leadership	• Civic and Global Learning
• Practical Competence	• Practical Competence • Persistence and Academic Achievement	• Integrative and Applied Learning	• Professional Skills • Life-long Learning	• Applied and Collaborative Learning

Figure 1. Mapping learning and development outcomes

Similarities in themes and values are easily recognized across these resources, with word choice being the primary difference. Adelman (2015) advocates for the adoption of a common language for learning outcomes, but no such agreement currently exists. Regardless of specific terminology, CAS advocates for incorporation of learning outcomes, generally, in efforts to enhance the work of student affairs and create quality programs for student learning and development across higher education.

The following pages provide the CAS learning and development outomce domains and dimensions in a chart format, as approved by the CAS Board of Directors in October 2008.

Contextual Statement Contributors:
Current Edition
Lindsey L. Templeton, CAS Intern
Laura A. Dean, CAS President (2011-2014) and Editor (2004-2011)

Previous Editions
Jan Arminio, CAS President (2005-2008)

CAS Learning and Development Outcomes[1]

Student Outcome Domain[2]	Dimensions of Outcome Domain	Examples of Learning and Development Outcomes
Knowledge acquisition, construction, integration, and application	Understanding knowledge from a range of disciplines	Possesses knowledge of human cultures and the physical world; possesses knowledge of [a specific] one or more subjects
	Connecting knowledge to other knowledge, ideas, and experiences	Uses multiple sources of information and their synthesis to solve problems; knows how to access diverse sources of information such as the internet, text observations, and data bases
	Constructing knowledge	Personalizes learning; makes meaning from text, instruction, and experience; uses experience and other sources of information to create new insights; generates new problem-solving approaches based on new insights; recognizes one's own capacity to create new understandings from learning activities and dialogue with others
	Relating knowledge to daily life	Seeks new information to solve problems; relates knowledge to major and career decisions; articulates career choices based on assessment of interests, values, skills, and abilities; provides evidence of knowledge, skills, and accomplishments resulting from formal education, work experience, community service, and volunteer experiences, for example in resumes and portfolios
Cognitive complexity	Critical thinking	Identifies important problems, questions, and issues; analyzes, interprets, and makes judgments of the relevance and quality of information; assesses assumptions and considers alternative perspectives and solutions[3]
	Reflective thinking	Applies previously understood information, concepts, and experiences to a new situation or setting; rethinks previous assumptions
	Effective reasoning	Uses complex information from a variety of sources including personal experience and observation to form a decision or opinion; is open to new ideas and perspectives
	Creativity	Integrates mental, emotional, and creative processes for increased insight; formulates a new approach to a particular problem
Intrapersonal development	Realistic self-appraisal, self-understanding, and self-respect	Assesses, articulates, and acknowledges personal skills, abilities, and growth areas; uses self-knowledge to make decisions such as those related to career choices; articulates rationale for personal behavior; seeks and considers feedback from others; critiques and subsequently learns from past experiences; employs self-reflection to gain insight; functions without need for constant reassurance from others; balances needs of self with needs of others
	Identity development	Integrates multiple aspects of identity into a coherent whole; recognizes and exhibits interdependence in accordance with environmental, cultural, and personal values; identifies and commits to important aspects of self
	Commitment to ethics and integrity	Incorporates ethical reasoning into action; explores and articulates the values and principles involved in personal decision-making; acts in congruence with personal values and beliefs; exemplifies dependability, honesty, and trustworthiness; accepts personal accountability
	Spiritual awareness	Develops and articulates personal belief system; understands roles of spirituality in personal and group values and behaviors; critiques, compares, and contrasts various belief systems; explores issues of purpose, meaning, and faith

Student Outcome Domain[2]	Dimensions of Outcome Domain	Examples of Learning and Development Outcomes
Interpersonal competence	Meaningful relationships	Establishes healthy, mutually beneficial relationships with others; treats others with respect; manages interpersonal conflicts effectively; demonstrates appropriately assertive behavior
	Interdependence	Seeks help from others when needed and offers assistance to others; shares a group or organizational goal and works with others to achieve it; learns from the contributions and involvement of others; accepts supervision and direction as needed
	Collaboration	Works cooperatively with others, including people different from self and/or with different points of view; seeks and values the involvement of others; listens to and considers others' points of view
	Effective leadership	Demonstrates skill in guiding and assisting a group, organization, or community in meeting its goals; identifies and understands the dynamics of a group; exhibits democratic principles as a leader or group member; communicates a vision, mission, or purpose that encourages commitment and action in others
Humanitarianism and Civic Engagement	Understanding and appreciation of cultural and human differences	Understands one's own identity and culture; seeks involvement with people different from oneself; articulates the advantages and impact of a diverse society; identifies systematic barriers to equality and inclusiveness, then advocates and justifies means for dismantling them; in interactions with others, exhibits respect and preserves the dignity of others
	Global perspective	Understands and analyzes the interconnectedness of societies worldwide; demonstrates effective stewardship of human, economic, and environmental resources
	Social responsibility	Recognizes social systems and their influence on people; appropriately challenges the unfair, unjust, or uncivil behavior of other individuals or groups; participates in service/volunteer activities that are characterized by reciprocity; articulates the values and principles involved in personal decision-making; affirms and values the worth of individuals and communities
	Sense of civic responsibility	Demonstrates consideration of the welfare of others in decision-making; engages in critical reflection and principled dissent; understands and participates in relevant governance systems; educates and facilitates the civic engagement of others
Practical competence	Pursuing goals	Sets and pursues individual goals; articulates rationale for personal and educational goals and objectives; articulates and makes plans to achieve long-term goals and objectives; identifies and works to overcome obstacles that hamper goal achievement
	Communicating effectively	Conveys meaning in a way that others understand by writing and speaking coherently and effectively; writes and speaks after reflection; influences others through writing, speaking or artistic expression; effectively articulates abstract ideas; uses appropriate syntax and grammar; makes and evaluates presentations or performances; listens attentively to others and responds appropriately
	Technological competence	Demonstrates technological literacy and skills; demonstrates the ethical application of intellectual property and privacy; uses technology ethically and effectively to communicate, solve problems, and complete tasks; stays current with technological innovations
	Managing personal affairs	Exhibits self-reliant behaviors; manages time effectively; develops strategies for managing finances
	Managing career development	Takes steps to initiate a job search or seek advanced education; constructs a resume based on clear job objectives and with evidence of knowledge, skills, and abilities; recognizes the importance of transferrable skills
	Demonstrating professionalism	Accepts supervision and direction as needed; shows initiative; assesses, critiques, and then improves the quality of one's work and one's work environment
	Maintaining health and wellness	Engages in behaviors and contributes to environments that promote health and reduce risk; articulates the relationship between health and wellness in accomplishing goals; exhibits behaviors that advance the health of communities
	Living a purposeful and satisfying life	Makes purposeful decisions regarding balance among education, work, and leisure time; acts in congruence with personal identity, ethical, spiritual, and moral values

[1] This document is an adaptation of *Learning Reconsidered* (2004) and the CAS Learning Outcomes (2006)
[2] Categories adapted from *Learning Reconsidered (2004)* and Kuh, Douglas, Lund, & Ramin Gyurmek (1994)
[3] These examples are adopted from the George Mason University *Critical Thinking Assessment Report* (2006)

Approved as revised by CAS Board of Directors, October 19, 2008

References

Adelman, C. (2015). To Imagine a Verb: The Language and Syntax of Learning Outcome Statements. *NILOA Occasional Paper, 24.* 1-27.

Adelman, C., Ewell, P., Gaston, P., & Schneider, C. G. (2011). *The degree qualifications profile.* Indianapolis, IN: Lumina Foundation.

American Council on Education (1937). *The student personnel point of view: A report of a conference on the philosophy and development of student personnel work in colleges and universities.* Washington, DC: Author. Retrieved from http://www2.bgsu.edu/sahp/pages/1937STUDENTPERSONNELnew.pdf

Association of American Colleges & Universities (AAC&U), & National Leadership Council (NLC) (US). (2007). *College learning for the new global century: A report from the National Leadership Council for Liberal Education & America's Promise.* Washington, DC: Association of American Colleges & Universities.

Bowman, N. A. (2013). Understanding and addressing the challenges of assessing college student growth in student affairs. *Research and Practice in Assessment, 8*(2), 5-14.

Bresciani, M. J. (2011). Making assessment meaningful: What new student affairs professionals and those new to assessment need to know. *NILOA Assessment Brief,* 1-5.

Council for the Advancement of Standards in Higher Education (2006). *CAS professional standards for higher education* (6th ed.). Washington, DC: Author.

Council for Higher Education Accreditation (CHEA) (2003). *Statement of mutual responsibilities for student learning outcomes: Accreditation, institutions, and programs.* Washington, DC: Author.

Drechsler Sharp, M., Komives, S. R., & Fincher, J. (2011). Learning outcomes in academic disciplines: Identifying common ground. *Journal of Student Affairs Research and Practice, 48*(4), 481–504. doi:10.2202/1949-6605.6246

George Mason University (2006). Critical Thinking Assessment Report. Retrieved from https:assessment.gmu.edu StudentLearningCompetencies/Critical/AssessProposal.html

Keeling, R. P. (Ed.) (2006). *Learning reconsidered 2: Implementing a campus-wide focus on the student experience.* American College Personnel Association, Association of College and University Housing Officers-International, Association of College Unions-International, National Academic Advising Association, National Association for Campus Activities, National Association of Student Personnel Administrators, National Intramural-Recreational Sports Association.

Kuh, G. D., Douglas, K. B., Lund, J. P., & Ramin Gyurmek, J. (1994). *Student learning outside the classroom: Transcending artificial boundaries.* (ASHE-ERIC Higher Education Report No. 8.). Washington, D.C.: The George Washington University, Graduate School of Education and Human Development.

National Association of Student Personnel Administrators (NASPA) & American College Personnel Association (ACPA). (2004). *Learning reconsidered: A campus-wide focus on the student experience.* Washington, DC: Authors.

Schuh, J. H., & Gansemer-Topf, A. M. (2010). The role of student affairs in student learning assessment. *NILOA Occasional Paper, 7,* 1-14.

CAS General Standards
CAS Contextual Statement

For more than 35 years, higher education professionals, including members of associations representing student and academic affairs programs and services, have utilized the professional standards, values, and principles developed and promulgated by the Council for the Advancement of Standards in Higher Education (CAS). The CAS standards fulfill a three-fold purpose:

- to foster and enhance student learning and development;
- to recognize and promote fundamental and indispensable standards of practice and the assessment of related programmatic and student outcomes; and
- to provide a foundation to develop, guide, assess, and improve programs and services.

The Oxford Dictionaries (2014) define a standard as a "required or agreed level of quality or attainment" (¶1.1). The CAS standards embody the distilled wisdom of higher education professionals with expertise in the specialty of their subject matter and an understanding of the needs of the students they serve and the organizations they represent. The CAS standards describe the practice requirements (known as *standards*) and guidelines for 43 higher education specialties (known as *functional areas*) that touch college students' lives. CAS standards also comprise a measure, norm, or model useful for self-study or comparative evaluations, and they thereby enhance credibility, demonstrate accountability, and underpin program and service improvement for assessment initiatives and action planning.

Professionals in higher education use the vetted and agreed upon CAS Standards as benchmarks to inform practice, management of programs, delivery of services, and assessment processes. The CAS standards have also been used effectively to help advance or leverage existing or new programs and services. More recently, the student learning and development domains of the standards have provided a framework for identifying the student learning and development outcomes that are intended to result from engagement with programs and services.

With the creation and publication of the first 16 functional area standards in 1986, CAS members noted a number of commonalities, which culminated in two fundamental principles:

- The functional areas must include a core, global set of standards that advance common goals (i.e., relevant to various types of higher education institutions as well as to programs and services, regardless of specialty).
- Student learning and development are fundamental to mission and program and must be incorporated into standards.

These principles led to the creation of the CAS General Standards, the set of core standards statements that apply

across functional areas and are embedded in each set of functional area standards.

The CAS General Standards are informed by the expertise and diverse backgrounds of representatives from CAS member associations and by their collective wisdom and experiences across institutional programs and services. The CAS General Standards are reviewed and revised every three years prior to the publication of each new edition of *CAS Professional Standards for Higher Education*.

Although not designed to stand alone, CAS General Standards are presented here to remind and inform educators that despite differences among institutions and within functional areas, significant commonalities exist across the multitude of postsecondary programs and services. The General Standards challenge "'silo' thinking, in which each functional area carries on its own business with limited awareness of the activities, needs, and resources of other divisions and departments" (Fried, 2007, p. 6) and with limited awareness of the ways they contribute to overall student learning and development. Moreover, the General Standards, as embedded within functional area standards, provide the framework for all those in higher education to develop "programs, services and experiences that contribute to student learning experiences that are valued at their institution and, moreover, that are empirically verified as adding value to the student experience at their institutions" (Schuh & Gansemer-Topf, 2010, p. 6).

To ensure that the CAS General Standards apply to and benefit all functional areas (e.g., a one-person student support operation as well as complex programs and services staffed by multiple specialists), the CAS Board of Directors consults with member associations and solicits comments from practitioners. The CAS directors consider differences across functional areas and institutions (e.g., mission and goals, programs, organizational structures, culture and values, student populations served, campus environments, facilities, reporting channels, and resources). The regular revision cycle for the General Standards ensures responsiveness to a changing postsecondary environment and recognition of widely acknowledged and accepted practices. When used for self-assessment and program review, each functional area standard (with the embedded General Standards) provides criteria by which leaders in an institution and functional area can judge the quality and effectiveness of current educational efforts. In functional areas with no standards, stakeholders can employ the General Standards as the starting place to create new programs and services and to design assessment of current ones. In settings where multiple areas are using CAS, the General Standards provide a common language and common expectations, enhancing communication and understanding among areas.

CAS directors recognize the potential impact that institutional programs and services can exert upon student learning and development. Following the publication of *Learning Reconsidered* (NASPA & ACPA, 2004), CAS integrated a revised set of student learning outcomes within the General Standards to enhance efforts for promoting student learning and development. CAS hosted a think tank involving writers of *Learning Reconsidered*, CAS directors, and prominent practitioners and faculty members to recommend revisions to the CAS student learning and development domains. In 2008 the CAS Board of Directors adopted revisions to the student learning and development outcomes, contained in the General Standards and referred to as domains:

- knowledge acquisition, construction, integration, and application;
- cognitive complexity;
- intrapersonal development;
- interpersonal competence;
- humanitarianism and civic engagement; and
- practical competence.

Each domain is further defined or clarified by several learning outcome *dimensions*, which allow for more focused program development and assessment. Examples describing achievement of the student learning outcomes for each of the dimensions appear in the CAS Learning and Development Outcomes chart.

The 2008 revision of the General Standards required programs and services to include student learning and development in mission statements, identify relevant and desirable learning from the six domains, assess relevant and desirable learning, and articulate the ways the programs and services contribute to student learning and development. By recognizing the centrality of student learning and development as well as requiring assessment of learning outcomes, CAS affirms and reinforces expectations of leaders in higher education and accrediting associations. Specifically, CAS provides a vetted framework for self-review of student-oriented programs and services.

In 2011 the CAS Board of Directors adopted significant revisions to the General Standards. In support of *Professional Competency Areas for Student Affairs Practitioners* (ACPA & NASPA, 2010), it revised required competencies for professionals to align appropriately with ACPA/NASPA competencies, most notably in the section on Organization and Leadership. The 2011 revisions also indicated recognition of the pervasiveness of distance learning and the need for those in all functional areas to address the needs of distance education students (Shelton, 2011).

The current General Standards, as revised and approved in 2014, include rewritten or added standards that reflect broadly applicable and high quality practices pertaining to issues of access as well as changes and trends in student populations, technologies, and assessment efforts. With a growing focus on accountability and budget planning, as well as environmental and ethical purchasing practices, new standards were added to the section on Financial Resources. CAS also paid particular attention to the growth in distance education and online learning, new venues for accessing higher education, and

expectations for program and service delivery. Recognizing the importance of clarity in use of terms or phrases, CAS updated the Glossary of CAS Terms (Appendix D).

An understanding of the General Standards and the Glossary of CAS Terms will enhance and facilitate the appropriate use of the standards for self-study and program review and will ensure that the CAS standards constitute a reliable basis for professionals to share values and expectations across institutional programs and services.

References, Readings, and Resources

ACPA-College Student Educators International, & NASPA-Student Personnel Administrators in Higher Education. (2010). *Professional competency areas for student affairs practitioners.* Washington, D.C.: ACPA, NASPA.

Fried, J. (2007, March-April). Higher education's new playbook: Learning reconsidered. In *About Campus,* pp. 2–7.

National Association of Student Personnel Administrators (NASPA) and the American College Personnel Association (ACPA). (2004). *Learning reconsidered: A campus-wide focus on the student experience.* Washington, DC: Author

National Task Force on Civic Learning and Democratic Engagement. (2012). *A crucible moment: College learning and democracy's future.* Washington, DC: Association of American Colleges and Universities.

Schuh, J. H., & Gansemer-Topf, A. M. (2010). *The role of student affairs in student learning assessment.* Urbana, IL: University of Illinois and Indiana University, National Institute for Learning Outcomes Assessment.

Shelton, K. (2011). *A quality scorecard for the administration of online education programs.* Retrieved from http://sloanconsortium.org/quality_scoreboard_online_program

Standard. (2014). In *Oxford Dictionaries.* Retrieved from http://www.oxforddictionaries.com/us/definition/american_english/standards

Contextual Statement Contributors

Current Edition:
Patricia Carretta, George Mason University, NACE
Marsha Miller, Kansas State University, NACADA
Marjorie Savage, University of Minnesota, AHEPPP

Previous Editions:
Jan Arminio, Shippensburg University, NACA
Laura A. Dean, University of Georgia, ACCA
Ted K. Miller, University of Georgia, ACPA/CAS

CAS General Standards
CAS Standards and Guidelines

Part 1. Mission

Programs and services must develop, disseminate, implement, and regularly review their missions, which must be consistent with the mission of the institution and with applicable professional standards. The mission must be appropriate for the institution's students and other constituents. Mission statements must reference student learning and development.

Part 2. Program

To achieve their mission, programs and services must contribute to

- students' formal education, which includes both the curriculum and the co-curriculum
- student progression and timely completion of educational goals
- preparation of students for their careers, citizenship, and lives
- student learning and development

To contribute to student learning and development, programs and services must

- identify relevant and desirable student learning and development outcomes
- articulate how the student learning and development outcomes align with the six CAS student learning and development domains and related dimensions
- assess relevant and desirable student learning and development
- provide evidence of impact on outcomes
- articulate contributions to or support of student learning and development in the domains not specifically assessed
- use evidence gathered to create strategies for improvement of programs and services

STUDENT LEARNING AND DEVELOPMENT DOMAINS AND DIMENSIONS

Domain: knowledge acquisition, integration, construction, and application

- Dimensions: understanding knowledge from a range of disciplines; connecting knowledge to other knowledge, ideas, and experiences; constructing knowledge; and relating knowledge to daily life

Domain: cognitive complexity

- Dimensions: critical thinking, reflective thinking, effective reasoning, and creativity

Domain: intrapersonal development

- Dimensions: realistic self-appraisal, self-understanding, and self-respect; identity development; commitment to ethics and integrity; and spiritual awareness

Domain: interpersonal competence

- Dimensions: meaningful relationships, interdependence, collaboration, and effective leadership

Domain: humanitarianism and civic engagement

- Dimensions: understanding and appreciation of cultural and human differences, social responsibility, global perspective, and sense of civic responsibility

Domain: practical competence

- Dimensions: pursuing goals, communicating effectively, technical competence, managing personal affairs, managing career development, demonstrating professionalism, maintaining health and wellness, and living a purposeful and satisfying life

[LD Outcomes: See *The Council for the Advancement of Standards Learning and Development Outcomes* statement for examples of outcomes related to these domains and dimensions.]

Programs and services must be

- intentionally designed
- guided by theories and knowledge of learning and development
- integrated into the life of the institution
- reflective of developmental and demographic profiles of the student population
- responsive to needs of individuals, populations with distinct needs, and relevant constituencies
- delivered using multiple formats, strategies, and contexts
- designed to provide universal access

Programs and services must collaborate with colleagues and departments across the institution to promote student learning and development, persistence, and success.

Part 3. Organization and Leadership

To achieve program and student learning and development outcomes, programs and services must be purposefully structured for effectiveness. Programs and services must have clearly stated and current

- goals and outcomes
- policies and procedures
- responsibilities and performance expectations for personnel
- organizational charts demonstrating clear channels of authority

Leaders must model ethical behavior and institutional citizenship.

Leaders with organizational authority for the programs and services must provide strategic planning, management and supervision, and program advancement.

Strategic Planning
- articulate a vision and mission that drive short- and long-term planning
- set goals and objectives based on the needs of the populations served, intended student learning and development outcomes, and program outcomes
- facilitate continuous development, implementation, and assessment of program effectiveness and goal attainment congruent with institutional mission and strategic plans
- promote environments that provide opportunities for student learning, development, and engagement
- develop, adapt, and improve programs and services in response to the changing needs of populations served and evolving institutional priorities
- include diverse perspectives to inform decision making

Management and Supervision
- plan, allocate, and monitor the use of fiscal, physical, human, intellectual, and technological resources
- manage human resource processes including recruitment, selection, professional development, supervision, performance planning, succession planning, evaluation, recognition, and reward
- influence others to contribute to the effectiveness and success of the unit
- empower professional, support, and student personnel to become effective leaders
- encourage and support collaboration with colleagues and departments across the institution
- encourage and support scholarly contributions to the profession
- identify and address individual, organizational, and environmental conditions that foster or inhibit mission achievement
- use current and valid evidence to inform decisions
- incorporate sustainability practices in the management and design of programs, services, and facilities
- understand appropriate technologies and integrate them into programs and services
- be knowledgeable about codes and laws relevant to programs and services and ensure that programs and services meet those requirements
- assess and take action to mitigate potential risks

Program Advancement
- advocate for and actively promote the mission and goals of the programs and services
- inform stakeholders about issues affecting practice
- facilitate processes to reach consensus where wide support is needed
- advocate for representation in strategic planning initiatives at divisional and institutional levels

Part 4. Human Resources

Programs and services must be staffed adequately by individuals qualified to accomplish mission and goals.

Programs and services must have access to technical and support personnel adequate to accomplish their mission.

Within institutional guidelines, programs and services must
- establish procedures for personnel recruitment and selection, training, performance planning, and evaluation
- set expectations for supervision and performance
- provide personnel access to continuing and advanced education and appropriate professional development opportunities to improve their competence, skills, and leadership capacity
- consider work/life options available to personnel (e.g., compressed work schedules, flextime, job sharing, remote work, or telework) to promote recruitment and retention of personnel

Administrators of programs and services must
- ensure that all personnel have updated position descriptions
- implement recruitment and selection/hiring strategies that produce a workforce inclusive of under-represented populations
- develop promotion practices that are fair, inclusive, proactive, and non-discriminatory

Personnel responsible for delivery of programs and services must have written performance goals, objectives, and outcomes for each year's performance cycle to be used to plan, review, and evaluate work and performance. The performance plan must be updated regularly to reflect changes during the performance cycle.

Results of individual personnel evaluations must be used to recognize personnel performance, address performance issues, implement individual and/or collective personnel development and training programs, and inform the assessment of programs and services.

Personnel, when hired and throughout their employment, must receive appropriate and thorough training.

Personnel, including student employees and volunteers, must have access to resources or receive specific training on
- institutional policies pertaining to functions or activities they support
- privacy and confidentiality policies
- laws regarding access to student records
- policies and procedures for dealing with sensitive institutional information
- policies and procedures related to technology used to store or access student records and institutional data

- how and when to refer those in need of additional assistance to qualified personnel and have access to a supervisor for assistance in making these judgments
- systems and technologies necessary to perform their assigned responsibilities
- ethical and legal uses of technology

Personnel must engage in continuing professional development activities to keep abreast of the research, theories, legislation, policies, and developments that affect their programs and services.

Administrators of programs and services must ensure that personnel are knowledgeable about and trained in safety, emergency procedures, and crisis prevention and response. Risk management efforts must address identification of threatening conduct or behavior and must incorporate a system for responding to and reporting such behaviors.

Personnel must be knowledgeable of and trained in safety and emergency procedures for securing and vacating facilities.

PROFESSIONAL PERSONNEL

Professional personnel either must hold an earned graduate or professional degree in a field relevant to their position or must possess an appropriate combination of educational credentials and related work experience.

INTERNS OR GRADUATE STUDENTS

Degree- or credential-seeking interns or graduate assistants must be qualified by enrollment in an appropriate field of study and relevant experience. These students must be trained and supervised by professional personnel who possess applicable educational credentials and work experience and have supervisory experience. Supervisors must be cognizant of the dual roles interns and graduate assistants have as both student and employee.

Supervisors must
- adhere to parameters of students' job descriptions
- articulate intended learning outcomes in student job descriptions
- adhere to agreed-upon work hours and schedules
- offer flexible scheduling when circumstances necessitate

Supervisors and students must both agree to suitable compensation if circumstances necessitate additional hours.

STUDENT EMPLOYEES AND VOLUNTEERS

Student employees and volunteers must be carefully selected, trained, supervised, and evaluated. Students must have access to a supervisor. Student employees and volunteers must be provided clear job descriptions, pre-service training based on assessed needs, and continuing development.

Part 5. Ethics

Programs and services must
- review applicable professional ethical standards and must adopt or develop and implement appropriate statements of ethical practice
- publish and adhere to statements of ethical practice and ensure their periodic review
- orient new personnel to relevant ethical standards and statements of ethical practice and related institutional policies

Statements of ethical standards must
- specify that programs and services personnel respect privacy and maintain confidentiality in communications and records as delineated by privacy laws
- specify limits on disclosure of information contained in students' records as well as requirements to disclose to appropriate authorities
- address conflicts of interest, or appearance thereof, by personnel in the performance of their work
- reflect the responsibility of personnel to be fair, objective, and impartial in their interactions with others
- reference management of institutional funds
- reference appropriate behavior regarding research and assessment with human participants, confidentiality of research and assessment data, and students' rights and responsibilities
- include the expectation that personnel confront and hold accountable other personnel who exhibit unethical behavior
- address issues surrounding scholarly integrity

Programs and services personnel must
- employ ethical decision making in the performance of their duties
- inform users of programs and services of ethical obligations and limitations emanating from codes and laws or from licensure requirements
- recognize and avoid conflicts of interest that could adversely influence their judgment or objectivity and, when unavoidable, recuse themselves from the situation
- perform their duties within the scope of their position, training, expertise, and competence
- make referrals when issues presented exceed the scope of the position

Part 6. Law, Policy, and Governance

Programs and services must be in compliance with laws, regulations, and policies that relate to their respective responsibilities and that pose legal obligations, limitations, risks, and liabilities for the institution as a whole. Examples include constitutional, statutory, regulatory, and case law; relevant law and orders emanating from codes and laws; and the institution's policies.

Programs and services must have access to legal advice needed for personnel to carry out their assigned responsibilities.

Programs and services must inform personnel, appropriate officials, and users of programs and services about existing and changing legal obligations, risks and liabilities, and limitations.

Programs and services must inform personnel about professional liability insurance options and refer them to external sources if the institution does not provide coverage.

Programs and services must have written policies and procedures on operations, transactions, or tasks that have legal implications.

Programs and services must regularly review policies. The revision and creation of policies must be informed by best practices, available evidence, and policy issues in higher education.

Programs and services must have procedures and guidelines consistent with institutional policy for responding to threats, emergencies, and crisis situations. Systems and procedures must be in place to disseminate timely and accurate information to students, other members of the institutional community, and appropriate external organizations during emergency situations.

Personnel must neither participate in nor condone any form of harassment or activity that demeans persons or creates an intimidating, hostile, or offensive environment.

Programs and services must purchase or obtain permission to use copyrighted materials and instruments. References to copyrighted materials and instruments must include appropriate citations.

Programs and services must inform personnel about internal and external governance organizations that affect programs and services.

Part 7. Diversity, Equity, and Access

Within the context of each institution's mission and in accordance with institutional policies and applicable codes and laws, programs and services must create and maintain educational and work environments that are welcoming, accessible, inclusive, equitable, and free from harassment.

Programs and services must not discriminate on the basis of disability; age; race; cultural identity; ethnicity; nationality; family educational history (e.g., first generation to attend college); political affiliation; religious affiliation; sex; sexual orientation; gender identity and expression; marital, social, economic, or veteran status; or any other basis included in institutional policies and codes and laws.

Programs and services must
- advocate for sensitivity to multicultural and

social justice concerns by the institution and its personnel
- ensure physical, program, and resource access for all constituents
- modify or remove policies, practices, systems, technologies, facilities, and structures that create barriers or produce inequities
- ensure that when facilities and structures cannot be modified, they do not impede access to programs, services, and resources
- establish goals for diversity, equity, and access
- foster communication and practices that enhance understanding of identity, culture, self-expression, and heritage
- promote respect for commonalities and differences among people within their historical and cultural contexts
- address the characteristics and needs of diverse constituents when establishing and implementing culturally relevant and inclusive programs, services, policies, procedures, and practices
- provide personnel with diversity, equity, and access training and hold personnel accountable for applying the training to their work
- respond to the needs of all constituents served when establishing hours of operation and developing methods of delivering programs, services, and resources
- recognize the needs of distance and online learning students by directly providing or assisting them to gain access to comparable services and resources

Part 8. Internal and External Relations

Programs and services must reach out to individuals, groups, communities, and organizations internal and external to the institution to
- establish, maintain, and promote understanding and effective relations with those that have a significant interest in or potential effect on the students or other constituents served by the programs and services
- garner support and resources for programs and services as defined by the mission
- collaborate in offering or improving programs and services to meet the needs of students and other constituents and to achieve program and student outcomes
- engage diverse individuals, groups, communities, and organizations to enrich the educational environment and experiences of students and other constituents
- disseminate information about the programs and services

Promotional and descriptive information must be accurate and free of deception and misrepresentation.

Programs and services must have procedures and

guidelines consistent with institutional policy for
- communicating with the media
- distributing information through print, broadcast, and online sources
- contracting with external organizations for delivery of programs and services
- cultivating, soliciting, and managing gifts
- applying to and managing funds from grants

Part 9. Financial Resources

Programs and services must have funding to accomplish the mission and goals.

In establishing and prioritizing funding resources, programs and services must conduct comprehensive analyses to determine
- unmet needs of the unit
- relevant expenditures
- external and internal resources
- impact on students and the institution

Programs and services must use the budget as a planning tool to reflect commitment to the mission and goals of the programs and services and of the institution.

Programs and services must administer funds in accordance with established institutional accounting procedures.

Programs and services must demonstrate efficient and effective use and responsible stewardship of fiscal resources consistent with institutional protocols.

Financial reports must provide an accurate financial overview of the organization and provide clear, understandable, and timely data upon which personnel can plan and make informed decisions.

Procurement procedures must
- be consistent with institutional policies
- ensure that purchases comply with laws and codes for usability and access
- ensure that the institution receives value for the funds spent
- consider information available for comparing the ethical and environmental impact of products and services purchased

Part 10. Technology

Programs and services must have technology to support the achievement of their mission and goals. The technology and its use must comply with institutional policies and procedures and with relevant codes and laws.

Programs and services must use technologies to
- provide updated information regarding mission, location, staffing, programs, services, and official contacts to students and other constituents in accessible formats
- provide an avenue for students and other constituents to communicate sensitive information

in a secure format
- enhance the delivery of programs and services for all students

Programs and services must
- back up data on a regular basis
- adhere to institutional policies regarding ethical and legal use of technology
- articulate policies and procedures for protecting the confidentiality and security of information
- implement a replacement plan and cycle for all technology with attention to sustainability
- incorporate accessibility features into technology-based programs and services

When providing student access to technology, programs and services must
- have policies on the use of technology that are clear, easy to understand, and available to all students
- provide information or referral to support services for those needing assistance in accessing or using technology
- provide instruction or training on how to use the technology
- inform students of implications of misuse of technologies

Part 11. Facilities and Equipment

Programs and services' facilities must be intentionally designed and located in suitable, accessible, and safe spaces that demonstrate universal design and support the program's mission and goals.

Facilities must be designed to engage various constituents and promote learning.

Personnel must have workspaces that are suitably located and accessible, well equipped, adequate in size, and designed to support their work and responsibilities.

The design of the facilities must guarantee the security and privacy of records and ensure the confidentiality of sensitive information and conversations. Personnel must be able to secure their work.

Programs and services must incorporate sustainable practices in use of facilities and purchase of equipment. Facilities and equipment must be evaluated on an established cycle and be in compliance with codes, laws, and accepted practices for access, health, safety, and security.

When acquiring capital equipment, programs and services must take into account expenses related to regular maintenance and life cycle costs.

Part 12. Assessment

Programs and services must develop assessment plans and processes.

Assessment plans must articulate an ongoing cycle of

assessment activities.

Programs and services must
- specify programmatic goals and intended outcomes
- identify student learning and development outcomes
- employ multiple measures and methods
- develop manageable processes for gathering, interpreting, and evaluating data
- document progress toward achievement of goals and outcomes
- interpret and use assessment results to demonstrate accountability
- report aggregated results to respondent groups and stakeholders
- use assessment results to inform planning and decision-making
- assess effectiveness of implemented changes
- provide evidence of improvement of programs and services

Programs and services must employ ethical practices in the assessment process.

Programs and services must have access to adequate fiscal, human, professional development, and technological resources to develop and implement assessment plans.

Revision approved April 2014

Academic Advising Programs
CAS Contextual Statement

Academic advising is an essential element in the success and persistence of postsecondary students (Klepfer & Hull, 2012). Although an institution's culture, values, and practices affect the organization and delivery of advising (Habley, 1997), practitioners directly influence personal, institutional, and societal success. Specifically, they help students "become members of their higher education community, think critically about their roles and responsibilities as students, and prepare to be educated citizens of a democratic society and a global community" (National Academic Advising Association [NACADA], 2006, para. 7); that is, regardless of the delivery mechanism, through academic advising, students learn to make the most of their college experience (Miller, 2012, para. 1). As higher education curricula grow increasingly complex and constituents demand accountability, stakeholders feel the pressure to make students' academic experience as meaningful as possible. Academic advising professionals must be ready to meet these challenges.

The growth of academic advising mirrors the growth and changes in higher education (Cook, 2009; Thelin & Hirschy, 2009). In the 1870s, electives introduced in the academic curriculum meant advisors needed "to guide students in the successful pursuit of their chosen paths" (Kuhn, 2008, p. 5). The 1970s ushered in a new era for academic advising with O'Banion's (1972/1994/2009) and Crookston's (1972/1994/2009) articles advocating a developmental academic-advising approach. Today, the advising community recognizes more than a dozen relational styles of academic advising (Drake, Jordan, & Miller, 2013). Each approach encourages professional, faculty, and peer advisors to help students delineate their academic, career, and life goals as they help students craft the educational plans necessary to complete their postsecondary objectives. These approaches are often customized to meet the diverse needs of today's college student (Drake, Jordan, & Miller, 2013).

In 1977, the National Academic Advising Association (NACADA) was formed to provide direction and purpose for practicing academic advisors (Grites & Gordon, 2009). Today, NACADA flourishes with more than 12,000 members in over 30 countries. The NACADA Statement of Core Values (NACADA, 2005) offers the ethical principles that guide advising practice. Along with the NACADA Concept of Academic Advising (NACADA, 2006) and the CAS Standards, the Core Values serve as a framework all academic advisors can use to examine their professional practice. Information on the NACADA resources, programs, and services can be found at www.nacada.ksu.edu.

As those in higher education, including academic advisors, respond to a changing postsecondary environment, they must structure exemplary practices, pay particular attention to key institutional learning outcomes, serve the distinctive needs of a range of student populations, and promote national agendas on degree completion (Drake, Jordan, & Miller, 2013). The

strong emphasis on research in academic advising reflects today's focus on student retention and graduation. Klepfer and Hull (2012) noted "the strength of academic advising as a factor in persistence. College students who reported visiting with advisors frequently had a much greater likelihood of persisting than their peers who never did" (para. 17). As a result, assessment and research increasingly influence the practices and processes of the field.

Today, advisors utilize many theories and strategies from the social sciences, humanities, and education to inform practice. When applying these paradigms, they foster productive relationships with students in support of their higher education goals. In fact, academic advisors provide "perhaps the only opportunity for all students to develop a personal, consistent relationship with someone in the institution who cares about them" (Drake, 2011, p. 10). Their adherence to CAS Standards advances the common goals of academic advising. Lowenstein (2006) observed that "an excellent advisor does for students' entire education what the excellent teacher does for a course: helps them order the pieces, put them together to make a coherent whole, so that the student experiences the curriculum not as a checklist of discrete, isolated pieces but instead as a unity, a composition of interrelated parts with multiple connections and relationships" (para. 5). Academic advisors meet these obligations through applying frameworks for good practice, including building partnerships with pivotal campus offices such as orientation, first-year student programs, and career services.

As the NACADA *Concept of Academic Advising* (NACADA, 2006) delineates, academic advising objectives differ among institutions based upon the particular mission, goals, curriculum, co-curriculum, and assessment methods established for the respective campus (White, 2000). However, a representative sample of learning outcomes for advising indicates that students will

- craft a coherent educational plan based on assessment of abilities, aspirations, interests, and values;
- use complex information from various sources to set goals, reach decisions, and achieve those goals;
- assume responsibility for meeting academic program requirements;
- articulate the meaning of higher education and the intent of the institution's curriculum;
- cultivate the intellectual habits that lead to a lifetime of learning; and
- behave as citizens who engage in the wider world around them (NACADA, 2006, para. 10).

The increasing public attention placed on college completion means increased visibility for academic advising. Reports such as *Guided Pathways to Success* (Complete College America, 2013) point to academic advising as vital to degree completion. As institutions seek to increase and diversify enrollments, academic advisors are vital to ensuring appropriate matriculation and transfer leading to degree completion for all students. The evolving manner by which students complete college degrees, including the blending of courses offered on a variety of campuses and online, places new challenges on academic advisors, who must possess the tools needed to meet the demands of students in virtual space and across multiple institutions (Compete College America, 2013).

A crucial component of the college experience, academic advising encourages students to cultivate meaning in their lives, make significant decisions about their futures, and access institutional resources. When practiced with competence and dedication, academic advising is integral to student success, persistence, retention, and completion. Therefore, academic advisors must develop the tools and skills necessary to address the many issues that influence student success and do so with respect to the increasing diversity on college and university campuses. The standards and guidelines in the Academic Advising Program Standards provide a framework for developing strong academic advising programs.

References, Readings, and Resources

Complete College America. (2013). *Guided pathways to success: Boosting college completion*. Retrieved from http://cl.s4.exct.net /?qs=5070f0ff3e10c3924002ca86e228acbd43cb18c55cf53cadcf2 211cd38d4367f

Cook, S. (2009). Important developments of academic advising in the United States. *NACADA Journal, 29*(2), 18–40.

Crookston, B. B. (2009). A developmental view of academic advising as teaching. *NACADA Journal, 29*(1), 78–82. (Reprinted from *Journal of College Student Personnel, 13*, 1972, pp. 12-17; *NACADA Journal, 14*[2], 1994, pp. 5–9)

Drake, J. K. (2011, July-August). The role of academic advising in student retention and persistence. *About Campus, 16*(3), 8-12. Available from http://onlinelibrary.wiley.com/doi/10.1002/ abc.20062/abstract. doi: 10.1002/abc.20062

Drake, J. K., Jordan, P., & Miller, M. A. (Eds.). (2013). *Academic advising approaches: Strategies that teach students to make the most of college.* San Francisco, CA: Jossey-Bass.

Grites, T. J., & Gordon, V. N. (2009). The history of NACADA: An amazing journey. *NACADA Journal, 29*(2), 41–55.

Habley, W. R. (1997). Organizational models and institutional advising practices. *NACADA Journal, 17*(2), 39–44.

Hagen, P. L., Kuhn, T. L., & Padak, G. M. (Eds.). (2010). *Scholarly inquiry in academic advising* (Monograph No. 20). Manhattan, KS: National Academic Advising Association.

Klepfer, K., & Hull, J. (2012). *High school rigor and good advice: Setting up students to succeed (at a glance.* Retrieved from http://www.centerforpubliceducation.org/Main-Menu/ Staffingstudents/High-school-rigor-and-good-advice-Setting- up-students-to-succeed#sthash.yizFgEcO.dpuf

Kuhn, T. L. (2008). Historical foundations of academic advising. In V. M. Gordon, W. R. Habley, & T. J. Grites (Eds.), *Academic advising: A comprehensive handbook* (2nd ed.) (pp. 3–6). San Francisco, CA: Jossey-Bass.

Lowenstein, M. (2006, September). The curriculum of academic advising: What we teach, how we teach, and what students learn. *Proceedings from the Fifth Annual Professional Development Conference on Academic Advising.* Retrieved from www.psu.edu/dus/mentor/proc01ml.htm

Miller, M. A. (2012). Structuring our conversations: Shifting to four dimensional advising models. In A. Carlstrom (Ed.), *2011 national survey of academic advising.* (Monograph No. 25). Manhattan, KS: National Academic Advising Association. http://www.nacada.ksu.edu/Resources/Clearinghouse/View- Articles/Structuring-Our-Conversations-Shifting-to-Four- Dimensional-Advising-Models.aspx

National Academic Advising Association (NACADA). (2005). *Statement of core values for academic advising.* Retrieved from http://www.nacada.ksu.edu/Resources/Clearinghouse/ View-Articles/Core-values-of-academic-advising.aspx

NACADA. (2006). *Concept of academic advising.* Retrieved from http://www.nacada.ksu.edu/Resources/Clearinghouse/View- Articles/Concept-of-Academic-Advising.aspx

O'Banion, T. (2009). An academic advising model. *NACADA Journal, 29*(1), 83–89. (Reprinted from *Junior College Journal, 42*, 1972, pp. 62, 63, 66–69; *NACADA Journal, 14*[2], 1994, pp. 10–16)

Thelin, J. R., & Hirschy, A. S. (2009). College students and the curriculum: The fantastic voyage of higher education, 1636 to the present. *NACADA Journal, 29*(2), 9–17.

White, E. R. (2000). Developing mission, goals, and objectives for the advising program. In V. N. Gordon & W. R. Habley (Eds.), *Academic advising: A comprehensive handbook* (pp.180-191). San Francisco, CA: Jossey-Bass.

Contextual Statement Contributors:
Current Edition
Marsha A. Miller, Kansas State University, NACADA
Eric R. White, The Pennsylvania State University, NACADA
Charlie Nutt, Kansas State University, NACADA
Jayne K. Drake, Temple University, NACADA
Daniel Bureau, University of Memphis, AFA
Nancy Vesta, NACADA

Previous Editions
Linda C. Higginson, The Pennsylvania State University

Academic Advising Programs
CAS Standards and Guidelines

Part 1. Mission

The mission of Academic Advising Programs (AAP) is to assist students as they define, plan, and achieve their educational goals. The AAP must advocate for student success and persistence.

AAP must develop, disseminate, implement, and regularly review their missions, which must be consistent with the mission of the institution and with applicable professional standards. The mission must be appropriate for the institution's students and other constituents. Mission statements must reference student learning and development.

The specific model used for AAP should be consistent with the mission, structure, and resources of the institution.

Part 2. Program

To achieve their mission, Academic Advising Programs (AAP) must contribute to
- students' formal education, which includes both the curriculum and the co-curriculum
- student progression and timely completion of educational goals
- preparation of students for their careers, citizenship, and lives
- student learning and development

To contribute to student learning and development, AAP must
- identify relevant and desirable student learning and development outcomes
- articulate how the student learning and development outcomes align with the six CAS student learning and development domains and related dimensions
- assess relevant and desirable student learning and development
- provide evidence of impact on outcomes
- articulate contributions to or support of student learning and development in the domains not specifically assessed
- use evidence gathered to create strategies for improvement of programs and services

STUDENT LEARNING AND DEVELOPMENT DOMAINS AND DIMENSIONS

Domain: knowledge acquisition, integration, construction, and application
- Dimensions: understanding knowledge from a range of disciplines; connecting knowledge to other knowledge, ideas, and experiences; constructing knowledge; and relating knowledge to daily life

Domain: cognitive complexity

- Dimensions: critical thinking, reflective thinking, effective reasoning, and creativity

Domain: intrapersonal development
- Dimensions: realistic self-appraisal, self-understanding, and self-respect; identity development; commitment to ethics and integrity; and spiritual awareness

Domain: interpersonal competence
- Dimensions: meaningful relationships, interdependence, collaboration, and effective leadership

Domain: humanitarianism and civic engagement
- Dimensions: understanding and appreciation of cultural and human differences, social responsibility, global perspective, and sense of civic responsibility

Domain: practical competence
- Dimensions: pursuing goals, communicating effectively, technical competence, managing personal affairs, managing career development, demonstrating professionalism, maintaining health and wellness, and living a purposeful and satisfying life

[LD Outcomes: See *The Council for the Advancement of Standards Learning and Development Outcomes* statement for examples of outcomes related to these domains and dimensions.]

AAP should determine which of the CAS learning and development domains and dimensions are most relevant to the advising functions on their campus and develop appropriate outcomes.

AAP must be
- intentionally designed
- guided by theories and knowledge of learning and development
- integrated into the life of the institution
- reflective of developmental and demographic profiles of the student population
- responsive to needs of individuals, populations with distinct needs, and relevant constituencies
- delivered using multiple formats, strategies, and contexts
- designed to provide universal access

AAP must collaborate with colleagues and departments across the institution to promote student learning and development, persistence, and success.

AAP must provide the same quality of academic advising and in the appropriate accessible forums to distance learners as it does to students on campus.

Advisors must engage students in the shared responsibility of academic advising.

Advisors must provide opportunities that help inform student choices and decisions about academic work and about educational, career, and life goals.

Advisors should inform students that the ultimate responsibility for making decisions about educational plans and life goals rests with the individual student.

AAP must be guided by a set of written goals and objectives that are directly related to its stated mission.

Academic advisors should offer advising sessions in a format that is private and safe. Sessions should be convenient and accessible to the student, employing the use of electronic and multimedia formats and traditional in-person or telephone interactions as appropriate. Advising information sessions may be carried out individually or in groups, depending on the needs of the student and always with the student's consent.

Programs and materials associated with the AAP must
- promote student learning, development, and personal growth to encourage self-sufficiency
- support students, on an ongoing basis, as they establish and evaluate their educational, career, and life goals
- assist students in identifying the realistic timeframe to complete their educational goals and support their efforts
- provide current and accurate advising information
- raise awareness of institutional and community resources and services for students
- provide advisors with training and development for making effective referrals to both on- and off-campus services and agencies
- make advising available to students throughout their time at the institution
- proactively identify academically at-risk students and connect those students with appropriate resources to facilitate student success
- employ appropriate and accessible technology to support the delivery of advising information
- clarify institutional policies and procedures for students
- monitor academic progress and direct students to appropriate resources and programs
- advocate for appropriate resources to facilitate student success
- support learning and professional development for those involved in delivery of academic advising
- collect and distribute relevant data regarding student needs, preferences, and performance for use in institutional decisions and policy

AAP must provide adequate resources to ensure that academic advising caseloads are consistent with the institutional mission and stated goals.

When institutional policy or process interferes with students' learning and development, the AAP must advocate for change using appropriate institutional means.

Factors that affect determination of advising caseloads include mode of delivery, advising approach used, additional advisor responsibilities, student needs, and time required for this activity.

The academic status of the student being advised should be taken into consideration when determining caseloads. Specific students groups (e.g., undecided students or students on academic probation) may require more advising time than upper-division students who have declared their majors.

Workloads should reflect that advisors may work with students not officially assigned to them and that advising related responsibilities may extend beyond direct contact with students.

Part 3. Organization and Leadership

To achieve program and student learning and development outcomes, Academic Advising Programs (AAP) must be purposefully structured for effectiveness. AAP must have clearly stated and current
- **goals and outcomes**
- **policies and procedures**
- **responsibilities and performance expectations for personnel**
- **organizational charts demonstrating clear channels of authority**

Leaders must model ethical behavior and institutional citizenship.

Leaders with organizational authority for AAP must provide strategic planning, management and supervision, and program advancement.

Strategic Planning
- articulate a vision and mission that drive short- and long-term planning
- set goals and objectives based on the needs of the populations served, intended student learning and development outcomes, and program outcomes
- facilitate continuous development, implementation, and assessment of program effectiveness and goal attainment congruent with institutional mission and strategic plans
- promote environments that provide opportunities for student learning, development, and engagement
- develop, adapt, and improve programs and services in response to the changing needs of populations served and evolving institutional priorities
- include diverse perspectives to inform decision making

Management and Supervision
- plan, allocate, and monitor the use of fiscal, physical, human, intellectual, and technological resources

- manage human resource processes including recruitment, selection, professional development, supervision, performance planning, succession planning, evaluation, recognition, and reward
- influence others to contribute to the effectiveness and success of the unit
- empower professional, support, and student personnel to become effective leaders
- encourage and support collaboration with colleagues and departments across the institution
- encourage and support scholarly contributions to the profession
- identify and address individual, organizational, and environmental conditions that foster or inhibit mission achievement
- use current and valid evidence to inform decisions
- incorporate sustainability practices in the management and design of programs, services, and facilities
- understand appropriate technologies and integrate them into programs and services
- be knowledgeable about codes and laws relevant to programs and services and ensure that programs and services meet those requirements
- assess and take action to mitigate potential risks

Program Advancement
- advocate for and actively promote the mission and goals of the programs and services
- inform stakeholders about issues affecting practice
- facilitate processes to reach consensus where wide support is needed
- advocate for representation in strategic planning initiatives at divisional and institutional levels

The campus community must be able to identify the individual or group coordinating academic advising.

AAP may be a centralized or decentralized function with a variety of employees throughout the institution assuming responsibilities.

Specific advisor responsibilities must be clearly delineated, published, and disseminated to the campus community.

Advisors must determine and articulate the need for administrative, technological, and executive support of advising.

Part 4. Human Resources

Academic Advising Programs (AAP) must be staffed adequately by individuals qualified to accomplish mission and goals.

AAP must have access to technical and support personnel adequate to accomplish their mission.

Support personnel and technical staff may maintain student records, organize resource materials, receive students, make appointments, handle correspondence, and meet other operational needs, as well as assist with research, data collection, systems development, and special projects.

Within institutional guidelines, AAP must
- establish procedures for personnel recruitment and selection, training, performance planning, and evaluation
- set expectations for supervision and performance
- provide personnel access to continuing and advanced education and appropriate professional development opportunities to improve their competence, skills, and leadership capacity
- consider work/life options available to personnel (e.g., compressed work schedules, flextime, job sharing, remote work, or telework) to promote recruitment and retention of personnel

Administrators of AAP must
- ensure that all personnel have updated position descriptions
- implement recruitment and selection/hiring strategies that produce a workforce inclusive of under-represented populations
- develop promotion practices that are fair, inclusive, proactive, and non-discriminatory

Personnel responsible for delivery of AAP must have written performance goals, objectives, and outcomes for each year's performance cycle to be used to plan, review, and evaluate work and performance. The performance plan must be updated regularly to reflect changes during the performance cycle.

Results of individual personnel evaluations must be used to recognize personnel performance, address performance issues, implement individual and/or collective personnel development and training programs, and inform the assessment of programs and services.

AAP personnel, when hired and throughout their employment, must receive appropriate and thorough training.

AAP personnel, including student employees and volunteers, must have access to resources or receive specific training on
- institutional policies pertaining to functions or activities they support
- privacy and confidentiality policies
- laws regarding access to student records
- policies and procedures for dealing with sensitive institutional information
- policies and procedures related to technology used to store or access student records and institutional data
- how and when to refer those in need of additional assistance to qualified personnel and have access to a supervisor for assistance in making these judgments
- systems and technologies necessary to perform their assigned responsibilities
- ethical and legal uses of technology

AAP personnel must engage in continuing professional development activities to keep abreast of the research, theories, legislation, policies, and developments that affect their programs and services.

Continuing and regular professional development should address

- theories of student development, student learning, career development, and other relevant theories
- academic advising approaches and best practices
- research, assessment, and evaluation processes
- widely adopted purposes of academic advising and its relevance to student success at the institution
- strategies that contribute to achievement of student learning outcomes
- academic policies and procedures, including institutional transfer policies and curricular changes
- ethical and legal issues including U.S. Family Education and Records Privacy Act (FERPA)/ Canadian Freedom Of Information and Protection of Privacy (FOIPP) and other privacy laws and policies
- technology and software training (e.g., to perform degree audits, web registrations)
- comprehensive knowledge of the institution's programs, academic requirements, policies and procedures, majors, minors, and certificate programs
- institutional and community resources and services (e.g., research opportunities, career services, internship opportunities, counseling and health services, tutorial services)
- non-discrimination and accommodations laws and directives (e.g., Americans with Disabilities Act (ADA)/Canadian Human Rights Act)
- strategies for building strong relationships and connections with students from diverse backgrounds through a variety of advising interactions

Administrators of AAP must ensure that personnel are knowledgeable about and trained in safety, emergency procedures, and crisis prevention and response. Risk management efforts must address identification of threatening conduct or behavior and must incorporate a system for responding to and reporting such behaviors.

AAP personnel must be knowledgeable of and trained in safety and emergency procedures for securing and vacating facilities.

PROFESSIONAL PERSONNEL

AAP professional personnel either must hold an earned graduate or professional degree in a field relevant to their position or must possess an appropriate combination of educational credentials and related work experience.

Academic advising personnel may be full-time or part-time professionals for whom advising is a primary or secondary function; they also may be faculty members whose responsibilities include advising. Paraprofessionals (e.g., graduate students, interns, or assistants) and peer advisors

may assist advisors.

INTERNS OR GRADUATE ASSISTANTS

Degree- or credential-seeking interns or graduate assistants must be qualified by enrollment in an appropriate field of study and relevant experience. These students must be trained and supervised by professional personnel who possess applicable educational credentials and work experience and have supervisory experience. Supervisors must be cognizant of the dual roles interns and graduate assistants have as both student and employee.

Supervisors must

- adhere to parameters of students' job descriptions
- articulate intended learning outcomes in student job descriptions
- adhere to agreed-upon work hours and schedules
- offer flexible scheduling when circumstances necessitate

Supervisors and students must both agree to suitable compensation if circumstances necessitate additional hours.

STUDENT EMPLOYEES AND VOLUNTEERS

Student employees and volunteers must be carefully selected, trained, supervised, and evaluated. Students must have access to a supervisor. Student employees and volunteers must be provided clear job descriptions, pre-service training based on assessed needs, and continuing development.

Part 5. Ethics

Academic Advising Programs (AAP) must
- review applicable professional ethical standards and must adopt or develop and implement appropriate statements of ethical practice
- publish and adhere to statements of ethical practice and ensure their periodic review
- orient new personnel to relevant ethical standards and statements of ethical practice and related institutional policies

Advisors must uphold policies, procedures, and priorities of their departments and institutions.

Statements of ethical standards must
- specify that programs and services personnel respect privacy and maintain confidentiality in communications and records as delineated by privacy laws
- specify limits on disclosure of information contained in students' records as well as requirements to disclose to appropriate authorities
- address conflicts of interest, or appearance thereof, by personnel in the performance of their work
- reflect the responsibility of personnel to be fair, objective, and impartial in their interactions with others

- reference management of institutional funds
- reference appropriate behavior regarding research and assessment with human participants, confidentiality of research and assessment data, and students' rights and responsibilities
- include the expectation that personnel confront and hold accountable other personnel who exhibit unethical behavior
- address issues surrounding scholarly integrity

AAP personnel must
- employ ethical decision making in the performance of their duties
- inform users of programs and services of ethical obligations and limitations emanating from codes and laws or from licensure requirements
- recognize and avoid conflicts of interest that could adversely influence their judgment or objectivity and, when unavoidable, recuse themselves from the situation
- perform their duties within the scope of their position, training, expertise, and competence
- make referrals when issues presented exceed the scope of the position

AAP personnel must recognize their responsibility to ensure the privileged, private, or confidential nature of advisors' interactions with students is not sacrificed.

Part 6. Law, Policy, and Governance

Academic Advising Programs (AAP) must be in compliance with laws, regulations, and policies that relate to their respective responsibilities and that pose legal obligations, limitations, risks, and liabilities for the institution as a whole. Examples include constitutional, statutory, regulatory, and case law; relevant law and orders emanating from codes and laws; and the institution's policies.

Advisors must be knowledgeable about and sensitive to laws, regulations, policies, and procedures, particularly those governing harassment, use of technology, personal relationships with students, privacy of student information, non-discrimination, and equal opportunity policies.

AAP must have access to legal advice needed for personnel to carry out their assigned responsibilities.

AAP must inform personnel, appropriate officials, and users of programs and services about existing and changing legal obligations, risks and liabilities, and limitations.

AAP must inform personnel about professional liability insurance options and refer them to external sources if the institution does not provide coverage.

AAP must have written policies and procedures on operations, transactions, or tasks that have legal implications.

AAP must regularly review policies. The revision and creation of policies must be informed by best practices, available evidence, and policy issues in higher education.

AAP must have procedures and guidelines consistent with institutional policy for responding to threats, emergencies, and crisis situations. Systems and procedures must be in place to disseminate timely and accurate information to students, other members of the institutional community, and appropriate external organizations during emergency situations.

Personnel must neither participate in nor condone any form of harassment or activity that demeans persons or creates an intimidating, hostile, or offensive environment.

AAP must purchase or obtain permission to use copyrighted materials and instruments. References to copyrighted materials and instruments must include appropriate citations.

AAP must inform personnel about internal and external governance organizations that affect programs and services.

Part 7. Diversity, Equity, and Access

Within the context of each institution's mission and in accordance with institutional policies and applicable codes and laws, Academic Advising Programs (AAP) must create and maintain educational and work environments that are welcoming, accessible, inclusive, equitable, and free from harassment.

AAP must not discriminate on the basis of disability; age; race; cultural identity; ethnicity; nationality; family educational history (e.g., first generation to attend college); political affiliation; religious affiliation; sex; sexual orientation; gender identity and expression; marital, social, economic, or veteran status; or any other basis included in institutional policies and codes and laws.

AAP must
- advocate for sensitivity to multicultural and social justice concerns by the institution and its personnel
- ensure physical, program, and resource access for all constituents
- modify or remove policies, practices, systems, technologies, facilities, and structures that create barriers or produce inequities
- ensure that when facilities and structures cannot be modified, they do not impede access to programs, services and resources
- establish goals for diversity, equity, and access
- foster communication and practices that enhance understanding of identity, culture, self-expression, and heritage
- promote respect for commonalities and differences among people within their historical and cultural contexts
- address the characteristics and needs of diverse constituents when establishing and implementing culturally relevant and inclusive programs, services, policies, procedures, and practices

- provide personnel with diversity, equity, and access training and hold personnel accountable for applying the training to their work
- respond to the needs of all constituents served when establishing hours of operation and developing methods of delivering programs, services, and resources
- recognize the needs of distance and online learning students by directly providing or assisting them to gain access to comparable services and resources

Part 8. Internal and External Relations

Academic Advising Programs (AAP) must reach out to individuals, groups, communities, and organizations internal and external to the institution to
- establish, maintain, and promote understanding and effective relations with those that have a significant interest in or potential effect on the students or other constituents served by the programs and services
- garner support and resources for programs and services as defined by the mission
- collaborate in offering or improving programs and services to meet the needs of students and other constituents and to achieve program and student outcomes
- engage diverse individuals, groups, communities, and organizations to enrich the educational environment and experiences of students and other constituents
- disseminate information about the programs and services

Promotional and descriptive information must be accurate and free of deception and misrepresentation.

AAP must have procedures and guidelines consistent with institutional policy for
- communicating with the media
- distributing information through print, broadcast, and online sources
- contracting with external organizations for delivery of programs and services
- cultivating, soliciting, and managing gifts
- applying to and managing funds from grants

For referral purposes, AAP should maintain strong working relationships with relevant external agencies and campus offices. AAP should then provide comprehensive referral information to all who advise.

Part 9. Financial Resources

Academic Advising Programs (AAP) must have funding to accomplish the mission and goals.

In establishing and prioritizing funding resources, AAP must conduct comprehensive analyses to determine
- unmet needs of the unit

- relevant expenditures
- external and internal resources
- impact on students and the institution

AAP must use the budget as a planning tool to reflect commitment to the mission and goals of the programs and services and of the institution.

AAP must administer funds in accordance with established institutional accounting procedures.

AAP must demonstrate efficient and effective use and responsible stewardship of fiscal resources consistent with institutional protocols.

Financial resources should be used to raise awareness of the academic advising program and its value to a range of stakeholders.

Sufficient institutional and financial resources must be provided to assist professional development of academic advisors.

Financial reports must provide an accurate financial overview of the organization and provide clear, understandable, and timely data upon which personnel can plan and make informed decisions.

Procurement procedures must
- be consistent with institutional policies
- ensure that purchases comply with laws and codes for usability and access
- ensure that the institution receives value for the funds spent
- consider information available for comparing the ethical and environmental impact of products and services purchased

Part 10. Technology

Academic Advising Programs (AAP) must have technology to support the achievement of their mission and goals. The technology and its use must comply with institutional policies and procedures and with relevant codes and laws.

AAP must use technologies to
- provide updated information regarding mission, location, staffing, programs, services, and official contacts to students and other constituents in accessible formats
- provide an avenue for students and other constituents to communicate sensitive information in a secure format
- enhance the delivery of programs and services for all students

AAP must employ technologies that facilitate interaction with students in the advising process.

AAP must ensure that online and technology-assisted advising includes appropriate processes for obtaining approvals, consultations, and referrals.

AAP must

- back up data on a regular basis
- adhere to institutional policies regarding ethical and legal use of technology
- articulate policies and procedures for protecting the confidentiality and security of information
- implement a replacement plan and cycle for all technology with attention to sustainability
- incorporate accessibility features into technology-based programs and services

When providing student access to technology, AAP must
- have policies on the use of technology that are clear, easy to understand, and available to all students
- provide information or referral to support services for those needing assistance in-accessing or using technology
- provide instruction or training on how to use the technology
- inform students of implications of misuse of technologies

Part 11. Facilities and Equipment

Academic Advising Programs' (AAP) facilities must be intentionally designed and located in suitable, accessible, and safe spaces that demonstrate universal design and support the program's mission and goals.

Facilities must be designed to engage various constituents and promote learning.

Personnel must have workspaces that are suitably located and accessible, well equipped, adequate in size, and designed to support their work and responsibilities.

AAP must provide work space that is private and free from visual and auditory distractions.

The design of the facilities must guarantee the security and privacy of records and ensure the confidentiality of sensitive information and conversations. Personnel must be able to secure their work.

AAP must incorporate sustainable practices in use of facilities and purchase of equipment. Facilities and equipment must be evaluated on an established cycle and be in compliance with codes, laws, and accepted practices for access, health, safety and security.
When acquiring capital equipment, AAP must take into account expenses related to regular maintenance and life cycle costs.

Part 12. Assessment

Academic Advising Programs (AAP) must develop assessment plans and processes.

Assessment plans must articulate an ongoing cycle of assessment activities.

AAP must
- specify programmatic goals and intended outcomes
- identify student learning and development outcomes
- employ multiple measures and methods
- develop manageable processes for gathering, interpreting, and evaluating data
- document progress toward achievement of goals and outcomes
- interpret and use assessment results to demonstrate accountability
- report aggregated results to respondent groups and stakeholders
- use assessment results to inform planning and decision-making
- assess effectiveness of implemented changes
- provide evidence of improvement of programs and services

AAP must employ ethical practices in the assessment process.

AAP must have access to adequate fiscal, human, professional development, and technological resources to develop and implement assessment plans.

General Standards revised in 2014;
AAP content developed/revised in 1986, 1997, 2005, and 2013

Adult Learner Programs and Services
CAS Contextual Statement

The National Student Clearinghouse (2012) reports 38 percent of all college students are adult learners, over the age of 25. According to Aslanian & Clinefelter (2012), 80 percent of students enrolled in online programs are 25 years of age or older. Rather than being evenly enrolled throughout higher education, adults are much more likely to be enrolled in community colleges and in institutions designed specifically for them than in major research universities and state universities. According to the American Association of Community Colleges (2014), 57 percent of community college students are age 22 or older and 14 percent are over 40. Further, in institutions with admissions criteria and practices highly tailored to traditional-age applicants, adult learners may be disproportionately represented in the non-degree seeking and provisionally admitted ranks of students.

Although institutional definitions of an adult learner vary, they often include age 25 and older, veteran's status, a hiatus in learning, and the performance of multiple adult roles regardless of age. Included within the category of adult learners are full- and part-time employees, recently discharged veterans, unemployed workers, single parents, career changers, and retirees. They may live on campus, in local communities, commute some distance, or study at a distance. They turn to higher education for many reasons such as earning degrees, certificates, or other credentials; taking courses for work-enhancement purposes; positioning themselves for new opportunities in order to increase earning power; and seeking enrichment. Despite the diversity of adult learners and their motivations for enrollment, they seek from higher education an understanding of both their needs and their attributes. They also seek an institution that has a desire to be responsive and interested in enrolling them. It is also critical that higher education institutions offer adults the academic programs they want when they are available to take them.

Given higher education's long-standing focus on traditional-age and residential students, adult learners often have been seen as the purview of ancillary units such as continuing and distance education units in land grant universities, evening and weekend colleges in urban universities, and community colleges that are relative newcomers to the higher education landscape. Faculty in student personnel preparation programs have conducted much of their research on and written about the young, residential students who have been easier to access than adult learners. As a consequence, new professionals may think of college student development solely from the perspectives of 17- to 23-year olds. Although the numbers of traditional-age high school graduates enrolling in higher education have fallen periodically, some institutions including private colleges have changed their practices and policies to serve the adult learner more effectively.

In the meantime, the dislocation of the nation's manufacturing economy has called for the re-education of hundreds of furloughed workers. The knowledge economy has called for adults with high school diplomas, some college, or associate degrees to earn bachelor's and advanced degrees. Divorce, separation, and the death of a spouse have triggered the return to learning by many individuals eager to increase their earning power to improve not only their own standard of living but that of their children. Longer life spans have caused people to turn to higher education for second careers and for intellectual stimulation in their retirement. As these social and economic changes have occurred, adults have sought access to and responsiveness from colleges, academic departments, and support services beyond the units that served them previously.

As adults encountered and began to complain about difficulties with gaining admission to "mainstream" academic programs and access to financial aid, with faculty unwilling to consider awarding credit for prior college-level learning, and with a college environment that they sometimes characterized as lonely, if not hostile, the Adult Learner Programs and Services (ALPS) units began to appear. Other ALPS units were created because college and university faculty and staff realized the social and economic trends as well as the attributes that adult learners brought to higher education and wanted to increase their enrollment; or they learned that adult graduation rates were less than the overall institution's graduation rate and wanted to increase adult learner success.

Many factors, including institutional type, structure, and history as well as the rationale for founding Adult Learner Programs and Services units, have influenced the placement of ALPS in the institutional structure, the mission of ALPS, and the activities and expertise of ALPS staff. For example, ALPS units have been placed in student affairs, continuing and distance education, affirmative action, and academic support divisions. In turn, an ALPS mission may focus more on student access, on supporting enrolled student success, and on select populations of adult learners, or the focus may be more comprehensive. The CAS standards and guidelines provide a basis for institutional self-assessment and program development as institutional leaders seek to respond to projected increases in the number and diversity of adult learners and as they wish to provide a standard of program and service excellence to those whom they currently recruit and enroll.

References, Readings, and Resources

Adult learners in higher education: Barriers to success and strategies to improve results. (March 2007). Report prepared for U.S. Department of Labor, Employment and Training Administration, Office of Policy Development and Research by Jobs for the Future. Retrieved from http://www.doleta.gov/reports/searcheta/occ/

American Association of Community Colleges. (2014). *2014 fact sheet* [Fact sheet]. Retrieved from http://www.aacc.nche.edu/AboutCC/Documents/FactSheet_2014_bw_r2.pdf.

Aslanian, C.B., & Clinefelter, D. L. (2012). *Online college students 2012: Comprehensive data on demands and preferences.*

Louisville, KY: the Learning House, Inc.

Aslanian, C. B. (2001). *Adult students today.* New York, NY: The College Board.

Aslanian, C. B., & Brickell, H. M. (1988). *How Americans in transition study for college credit.* New York, NY: The College Board.

Aslanian, C. B., & Brickell, H. M. (1980). *Americans in transition: Life changes as reasons for adult learning.* New York, NY: The College Entrance Examination Board.

Bash, L. (2003). Adult learners: Why they are important to the 21st century college or university. *The Journal of Continuing Higher Education, 51(3),* 18-26.

Harrison, C. H. (2000, May). *The adult learner: Not a student yet.* A thesis in Adult Education, Penn State University.

Kasworm, C. (2003). *What is collegiate involvement for adult undergraduates?* Paper presented at the Annual Meeting of the American Educational Research Association, Chicago, IL. ERIC Document Reproduction Service No. ED 481 228.

Kasworm, C. E., & Blowers, S. S. (1994). *Adult undergraduate students: Patterns of learning involvement.* Final Research Report, University of Tennessee, Knoxville, TN. Washington, DC: Office of Educational Research and Improvement. Retrieved from ERIC database. (ED 376 321)

Kasworm, C. E., Polson, C. J., & Fishback, S. J. (2002). *Responding to adult learners in higher education.* Malabar, FL: Krieger Publishing Company.

Kilgore, D., & Rice, P. J. (2003). *New directions for student services: Meeting the special needs of adult students.* (No. 102) San Francisco, CA: Jossey-Bass.

National Student Clearinghouse Research Center. (2012). Signature report 3. Retrieved from http://nscresearchcenter.org/wp-content/uploads/NSC_Signature_Report_3.pdf

Pusser, B., Breneman, D. W., Gansneder, B. M., Kohl, K. J., Levin, J. S., Milam, J. H., & Turner, S. E. (2007, March). *Returning to learning: Adults' success in college is key to America's future.* Report of the Lumina Foundation for Education, Indianapolis, IN.

Schlossberg, N. K., Lynch, A. Q., & Chickering, A. W. (1989). *Improving higher education environments for adults.* San Francisco, CA: Jossey Bass Publishers.

Sissel, P. A., Hansman, C. A., & Kasworm, C. E. (2001). The politics of neglect: Adult learners in higher education. *New Directions for Adult and Continuing Education*, 91, 17-27.

Contextual Statement Contributors

Current Edition:
Melissa Mahan, Texas A&M University-San Antonio, NCCP

Previous Editions:
Charlene H. Harrison, Penn State University
Melissa Mahan, Texas A&M University-San Antonio, NCCP

Adult Learner Programs and Services
CAS Standards and Guidelines

The mission of Adult Learner Programs and Services (ALPS) is to ensure that adult learners gain equitable access to all relevant curricular and co-curricular opportunities of the institution. ALPS must ensure that programs and services support adult learner success and advocate for adult learners to ensure that they are treated fairly and justly.

Equitable access may be differentiated based upon degree status, course load, fee payment status, or other criteria.

ALPS must develop, disseminate, implement, and regularly review their missions, which must be consistent with the mission of the institution and with applicable professional standards. The mission must be appropriate for the institution's students and other constituents. Mission statements must reference student learning and development.

Adult Learner Programs and Services (ALPS) must provide direct delivery of programs and services and work collaboratively with other essential institutional units to ensure that adult learners gain full access to and support from all curricular and co-curricular opportunities offered by the institution.

Institutions must clarify the availability of programs and services based upon the student's status.

ALPS must help adult learners gain access to the institution and its academic and financial aid programs.

To assist adult learners in gaining access to the institution and its enrollment, academic, and financial aid programs, ALPS staff members should
- be available to meet and/or communicate one-on-one with prospective adult learners
- articulate admissions, transfer enrollment, re-enrollment, non-degree registration, and financial aid procedures and provide information about topics such as academic refresher resources, child and elder care, and application deadlines
- conduct programs for prospective adult learners on applying for admission, re-enrollment, and financial aid, and on relating careers to academic programs
- monitor the progress of adult learner applicants, re-enrollees, and registrants through the application, acceptance, and registration process and through the financial aid application process
- ensure that recruitment literature, websites, list serves, and other outreach efforts are created that target adult learners and contain messages relevant to their needs and concerns

- represent the institution in the community at workplaces and community centers to help bring prospective adults to the institution
- ensure that institutional resources are available at convenient hours for adult learners

ALPS must provide programs and services that assist in increasing the retention of adult learners.

To increase the success of adult learners, the ALPS staff members should
- plan, deliver, and evaluate (either independently or in collaboration with others) orientation and other programs that acquaint adult learners and their families/support networks (a) with the institution's academic and out-of-class resources that enhance their likelihood of success and (b) with others like themselves
- inform adult learners of the availability of emergency funds, short-term loans, and scholarships
- initiate and advise adult learner honor societies and student organizations
- initiate and conduct recognition programs for adult learners that bring together both the learners and those who support them

ALPS staff members must collect data and conduct research on the institution's adult learners and on policies and practices that disproportionately impact them.

ALPS staff members may engage in these efforts either independently or in collaboration with others.

ALPS staff members must educate others about the characteristics, needs, and contributions of adult learners.

For ALPS staff members to educate others in the institution to adult learners' needs and attributes, they should
- be familiar with literature and research about adult learners
- establish relationships with faculty in adult education and other relevant academic disciplines and with staff members in the institutional research office
- meet with academic advisors, admissions, financial aid and student affairs staff members, and other staff and faculty members
- collaborate and network with colleagues to offer training, provide data, and share research in order to inform decision making and practice
- write articles and reports and deliver programs to campus and community audiences

ALPS staff members must advocate for curricular and co-curricular policies, procedures, and programs that are responsive to the needs and concerns of adult learners.

To advocate for adult learners, ALPS staff members should
- assess and monitor adult learners' needs and the

degree to which the institution is meeting them
- understand and be able to articulate the diverse nature of the institution's adult learners
- support individual adult learners and adult student organizations in their self-advocacy
- promote life experiences as criteria for membership in student organizations, including honor societies and for major awards

ALPS staff members must create affirming environments where prospective and enrolled adult learners may interact with one another.

To achieve their mission, ALPS must contribute to
- students' formal education, which includes both the curriculum and the co-curriculum
- student progression and timely completion of educational goals
- preparation of students for their careers, citizenship, and lives
- student learning and development

To contribute to student learning and development, ALPS must
- identify relevant and desirable student learning and development outcomes
- articulate how the student learning and development outcomes align with the six CAS student learning and development domains and related dimensions
- assess relevant and desirable student learning and development
- provide evidence of impact on outcomes
- articulate contributions to or support of student learning and development in the domains not specifically assessed
- use evidence gathered to create strategies for improvement of programs and services

STUDENT LEARNING AND DEVELOPMENT DOMAINS AND DIMENSIONS

Domain: knowledge acquisition, integration, construction, and application
- Dimensions: understanding knowledge from a range of disciplines; connecting knowledge to other knowledge, ideas, and experiences; constructing knowledge; and relating knowledge to daily life

Domain: cognitive complexity
- Dimensions: critical thinking, reflective thinking, effective reasoning, and creativity

Domain: intrapersonal development
- Dimensions: realistic self-appraisal, self-understanding, and self-respect; identity development; commitment to ethics and integrity; and spiritual awareness

Domain: interpersonal competence
- Dimensions: meaningful relationships,

interdependence, collaboration, and effective leadership

Domain: humanitarianism and civic engagement
- Dimensions: understanding and appreciation of cultural and human differences, social responsibility, global perspective, and sense of civic responsibility

Domain: practical competence
- Dimensions: pursuing goals, communicating effectively, technical competence, managing personal affairs, managing career development, demonstrating professionalism, maintaining health and wellness, and living a purposeful and satisfying life

[LD Outcomes: See *The Council for the Advancement of Standards Learning and Development Outcomes* statement for examples of outcomes related to these domains and dimensions.]

ALPS must be
- intentionally designed
- guided by theories and knowledge of learning and development
- integrated into the life of the institution
- reflective of developmental and demographic profiles of the student population
- responsive to needs of individuals, populations with distinct needs, and relevant constituencies
- delivered using multiple formats, strategies, and contexts
- designed to provide universal access

ALPS must collaborate with colleagues and departments across the institution to promote student learning and development, persistence, and success.

ALPS staff members should be familiar with the Commuter and Off-Campus Living Programs Standards and Guidelines.

Part 3. Organization and Leadership

To achieve program and student learning and development outcomes, Adult Learner Programs and Services (ALPS) must be purposefully structured for effectiveness. ALPS must have clearly stated and current
- goals and outcomes
- policies and procedures
- responsibilities and performance expectations for personnel
- organizational charts demonstrating clear channels of authority

Leaders must model ethical behavior and institutional citizenship.

Leaders with organizational authority for ALPS must provide strategic planning, management and supervision, and program advancement.

Strategic Planning
- articulate a vision and mission that drive short-

and long-term planning
- set goals and objectives based on the needs of the populations served, intended student learning and development outcomes, and program outcomes
- facilitate continuous development, implementation, and assessment of program effectiveness and goal attainment congruent with institutional mission and strategic plans
- promote environments that provide opportunities for student learning, development, and engagement
- develop, adapt, and improve programs and services in response to the changing needs of populations served and evolving institutional priorities
- include diverse perspectives to inform decision making

Management and Supervision
- plan, allocate, and monitor the use of fiscal, physical, human, intellectual, and technological resources
- manage human resource processes including recruitment, selection, professional development, supervision, performance planning, succession planning, evaluation, recognition, and reward
- influence others to contribute to the effectiveness and success of the unit
- empower professional, support, and student personnel to become effective leaders
- encourage and support collaboration with colleagues and departments across the institution
- encourage and support scholarly contributions to the profession
- identify and address individual, organizational, and environmental conditions that foster or inhibit mission achievement
- use current and valid evidence to inform decisions
- incorporate sustainability practices in the management and design of programs, services, and facilities
- understand appropriate technologies and integrate them into programs and services
- be knowledgeable about codes and laws relevant to programs and services and ensure that programs and services meet those requirements
- assess and take action to mitigate potential risks

Program Advancement
- advocate for and actively promote the mission and goals of the programs and services
- inform stakeholders about issues affecting practice
- facilitate processes to reach consensus where wide support is needed
- advocate for representation in strategic planning initiatives at divisional and institutional levels

ALPS leaders must inform themselves about program and service approaches that are successful in other higher education or professional settings and establish working relationships with a network of colleagues who are dedicated to serving adult learners optimally.

ALPS must inform institutional leaders of its role in creating, reviewing, and implementing institutional policies and procedures that are responsive to the assessed needs of adult learners.

Part 4. Human Resources

Adult Learner Programs and Services (ALPS) must be staffed adequately by individuals qualified to accomplish mission and goals.

ALPS must have access to technical and support personnel adequate to accomplish their mission.

Within institutional guidelines, ALPS must
- establish procedures for personnel recruitment and selection, training, performance planning, and evaluation
- set expectations for supervision and performance
- provide personnel access to continuing and advanced education and appropriate professional development opportunities to improve their competence, skills, and leadership capacity
- consider work/life options available to personnel (e.g., compressed work schedules, flextime, job sharing, remote work, or telework) to promote recruitment and retention of personnel

Administrators of ALPS must
- ensure that all personnel have updated position descriptions
- implement recruitment and selection/hiring strategies that produce a workforce inclusive of under-represented populations
- develop promotion practices that are fair, inclusive, proactive, and non-discriminatory

Personnel responsible for delivery of ALPS must have written performance goals, objectives, and outcomes for each year's performance cycle to be used to plan, review, and evaluate work and performance. The performance plan must be updated regularly to reflect changes during the performance cycle.

Results of individual personnel evaluations must be used to recognize personnel performance, address performance issues, implement individual and/or collective personnel development and training programs, and inform the assessment of programs and services.

ALPS personnel, when hired and throughout their employment, must receive appropriate and thorough training.

ALPS personnel, including student employees and volunteers, must have access to resources or receive specific training on
- institutional policies pertaining to functions or activities they support
- privacy and confidentiality policies
- laws regarding access to student records

- policies and procedures for dealing with sensitive institutional information
- policies and procedures related to technology used to store or access student records and institutional data
- how and when to refer those in need of additional assistance to qualified personnel and have access to a supervisor for assistance in making these judgments
- systems and technologies necessary to perform their assigned responsibilities
- ethical and legal uses of technology

ALPS personnel must engage in continuing professional development activities to keep abreast of the research, theories, legislation, policies, and developments that affect their programs and services.

Administrators of ALPS must ensure that personnel are knowledgeable about and trained in safety, emergency procedures, and crisis prevention and response. Risk management efforts must address identification of threatening conduct or behavior and must incorporate a system for responding to and reporting such behaviors.

ALPS personnel must be knowledgeable of and trained in safety and emergency procedures for securing and vacating facilities.

PROFESSIONAL PERSONNEL

ALPS professional personnel either must hold an earned graduate or professional degree in a field relevant to their position or must possess an appropriate combination of educational credentials and related work experience.

INTERNS OR GRADUATE ASSISTANTS

Degree- or credential-seeking interns or graduate assistants must be qualified by enrollment in an appropriate field of study and relevant experience. These students must be trained and supervised by professional personnel who possess applicable educational credentials and work experience and have supervisory experience. Supervisors must be cognizant of the dual roles interns and graduate assistants have as both student and employee.

Supervisors must
- adhere to parameters of students' job descriptions
- articulate intended learning outcomes in student job descriptions
- adhere to agreed-upon work hours and schedules
- offer flexible scheduling when circumstances necessitate

Supervisors and students must both agree to suitable compensation if circumstances necessitate additional hours.

STUDENT EMPLOYEES AND VOLUNTEERS

Student employees and volunteers must be carefully selected, trained, supervised, and evaluated. Students must have access to a supervisor. Student employees and volunteers must be provided clear job descriptions, pre-service training based on assessed needs, and continuing development.

Part 5. Ethics

Adult Learner Programs and Services (ALPS) must
- review applicable professional ethical standards and must adopt or develop and implement appropriate statements of ethical practice
- publish and adhere to statements of ethical practice and ensure their periodic review
- orient new personnel to relevant ethical standards and statements of ethical practice and related institutional policies

Statements of ethical standards must
- specify that ALPS personnel respect privacy and maintain confidentiality in communications and records as delineated by privacy laws
- specify limits on disclosure of information contained in students' records as well as requirements to disclose to appropriate authorities
- address conflicts of interest, or appearance thereof, by personnel in the performance of their work
- reflect the responsibility of personnel to be fair, objective, and impartial in their interactions with others
- reference management of institutional funds
- reference appropriate behavior regarding research and assessment with human participants, confidentiality of research and assessment data, and students' rights and responsibilities
- include the expectation that personnel confront and hold accountable other personnel who exhibit unethical behavior
- address issues surrounding scholarly integrity

ALPS personnel must
- employ ethical decision making in the performance of their duties
- inform users of programs and services of ethical obligations and limitations emanating from codes and laws or from licensure requirements
- recognize and avoid conflicts of interest that could adversely influence their judgment or objectivity and, when unavoidable, recuse themselves from the situation
- perform their duties within the scope of their position, training, expertise, and competence
- make referrals when issues presented exceed the scope of the position

Part 6. Law, Policy, and Governance

Adult Learner Programs and Services (ALPS) must be in compliance with laws, regulations, and policies that relate to their respective responsibilities and that pose legal obligations, limitations, risks, and liabilities for the institution as a whole. Examples include constitutional, statutory, regulatory, and case law; relevant law and orders emanating from codes and laws; and the institution's policies.

ALPS must have access to legal advice needed for personnel to carry out their assigned responsibilities.

ALPS must inform personnel, appropriate officials, and users of programs and services about existing and changing legal obligations, risks and liabilities, and limitations.

ALPS must inform personnel about professional liability insurance options and refer them to external sources if the institution does not provide coverage.

ALPS must have written policies and procedures on operations, transactions, or tasks that have legal implications.

ALPS must regularly review policies. The revision and creation of policies must be informed by best practices, available evidence, and policy issues in higher education.

ALPS must have procedures and guidelines consistent with institutional policy for responding to threats, emergencies, and crisis situations. Systems and procedures must be in place to disseminate timely and accurate information to students, other members of the institutional community, and appropriate external organizations during emergency situations.

Personnel must neither participate in nor condone any form of harassment or activity that demeans persons or creates an intimidating, hostile, or offensive environment.

ALPS must purchase or obtain permission to use copyrighted materials and instruments. References to copyrighted materials and instruments must include appropriate citations.

ALPS must inform personnel about internal and external governance organizations that affect programs and services.

Part 7. Diversity, Equity, and Access

Within the context of each institution's mission and in accordance with institutional policies and applicable codes and laws, Adult Learner Programs and Services (ALPS) must create and maintain educational and work environments that are welcoming, accessible, inclusive, equitable, and free from harassment.

ALPS must not discriminate on the basis of disability; age; race; cultural identity; ethnicity; nationality; family educational history (e.g., first generation to attend college); political affiliation; religious affiliation; sex; sexual orientation; gender identity and expression; marital, social, economic, or veteran status; or any other basis included in institutional policies and codes and laws.

ALPS must
- advocate for sensitivity to multicultural and social justice concerns by the institution and its personnel

- ensure physical, program, and resource access for all constituents
- modify or remove policies, practices, systems, technologies, facilities, and structures that create barriers or produce inequities
- ensure that when facilities and structures cannot be modified, they do not impede access to programs, services, and resources
- establish goals for diversity, equity, and access
- foster communication and practices that enhance understanding of identity, culture, self-expression, and heritage
- promote respect for commonalities and differences among people within their historical and cultural contexts
- address the characteristics and needs of diverse constituents when establishing and implementing culturally relevant and inclusive programs, services, policies, procedures, and practices
- provide personnel with diversity, equity, and access training and hold personnel accountable for applying the training to their work
- respond to the needs of all constituents served when establishing hours of operation and developing methods of delivering programs, services, and resources
- recognize the needs of distance and online learning students by directly providing or assisting them to gain access to comparable services and resources

On campuses where adult learners constitute a distinct minority and under-served population, they should be considered an under-represented population. Means for serving this under-represented population could include a task force on adult learner recruitment and retention and/or an adult learner commission with faculty, staff, and student membership.

Part 8. Internal and External Relations

Adult Learner Programs and Services (ALPS) must reach out to individuals, groups, communities, and organizations internal and external to the institution to
- establish, maintain, and promote understanding and effective relations with those that have a significant interest in or potential effect on the students or other constituents served by the programs and services
- garner support and resources for programs and services as defined by the mission
- collaborate in offering or improving programs and services to meet the needs of students and other constituents and to achieve program and student outcomes
- engage diverse individuals, groups, communities, and organizations to enrich the educational environment and experiences of students and other constituents
- disseminate information about the programs and services

ALPS staff members should serve on committees that address policies and procedures that affect adult learners.

If there is more than one campus unit whose clientele are principally adult learners, ALPS should share information and collaborate with those offices. Examples of on-campus units with which ALPS staff members should collaborate include continuing and distance education, commuter and off-campus living programs, campus information and visitor services programs, graduate and professional student services, veterans' programs, child care center(s), and critical access and service-providing units such as admissions, financial aid, the registrar's office, the library, career services, and learning and advising centers. This collaboration also should ensure that students enrolled at off-site locations are provided with equitable access to institutional resources.

The community agencies with which ALPS staff members should have a working relationship include local community education and literacy programs, TRIO and other equal opportunity programs, community libraries, retiree programs, veterans' programs, vocational rehabilitation offices, and social service agencies.

Promotional and descriptive information must be accurate and free of deception and misrepresentation.

ALPS must have procedures and guidelines consistent with institutional policy for
- **communicating with the media**
- **distributing information through print, broadcast, and online sources**
- **contracting with external organizations for delivery of programs and services**
- **cultivating, soliciting, and managing gifts**
- **applying to and managing funds from grants**

Part 9. Financial Resources

Adult Learner Programs and Services (ALPS) must have funding to accomplish the mission and goals.

In establishing and prioritizing funding resources, ALPS must conduct comprehensive analyses to determine
- **unmet needs of the unit**
- **relevant expenditures**
- **external and internal resources**
- **impact on students and the institution**

ALPS must use the budget as a planning tool to reflect commitment to the mission and goals of the programs and services and of the institution.

ALPS must administer funds in accordance with established institutional accounting procedures.

ALPS must demonstrate efficient and effective use and responsible stewardship of fiscal resources consistent with institutional protocols.

Financial reports must provide an accurate financial overview of the organization and provide clear, understandable, and timely data upon which personnel can plan and make informed decisions.

Procurement procedures must
- **be consistent with institutional policies**
- **ensure that purchases comply with laws and codes for usability and access**
- **ensure that the institution receives value for the funds spent**
- **consider information available for comparing the ethical and environmental impact of products and services purchased**

Adult learners should benefit equitably from fee-supported programs and services, including the establishment of programs and services that address their unique needs.

Part 10. Technology

Adult Learner Programs and Services (ALPS) must have technology to support the achievement of their mission and goals. The technology and its use must comply with institutional policies and procedures and with relevant codes and laws.

ALPS must use technologies to
- **provide updated information regarding mission, location, staffing, programs, services, and official contacts to students and other constituents in accessible formats**
- **provide an avenue for students and other constituents to communicate sensitive information in a secure format**
- **enhance the delivery of programs and services for all students**

ALPS must
- **back up data on a regular basis**
- **adhere to institutional policies regarding ethical and legal use of technology**
- **articulate policies and procedures for protecting the confidentiality and security of information**
- **implement a replacement plan and cycle for technology with attention to sustainability**
- **incorporate accessibility features into technology-based programs and services**

When providing student access to technology, ALPS must
- **have policies on the use of technology that are clear, easy to understand, and available to all students**
- **provide information or referral to support services for those needing assistance in accessing or using technology**
- **provide instruction or training on how to use the technology**
- **inform students of implications of misuse of technologies**

ALPS should be responsive to adult learner differences in competencies, knowledge, and comfort levels with technology.

Part 11. Facilities and Equipment

Adult Learner Programs and Services' (ALPS) facilities must be intentionally designed and located in suitable, accessible, and safe spaces that demonstrate universal design and support the program's mission and goals.

Facilities must be designed to engage various constituents and promote learning.

ALPS staff should advocate for access to facilities that are physically close to campus programs to enable adult learners to engage with staff and faculty members and to interact with prospective and enrolled students.

To create an affirming environment in which prospective and enrolled adult learners may interact with one another and the ALPS staff members, ALPS should advocate for access to facilities that include

- lounge and reception areas that are welcoming and comfortable
- kitchenette space to prepare and store meals
- locker facilities
- study area which permits the consumption of food and beverages
- computers and printers
- use of traditional and electronic means of communication, including display racks, bulletin boards, websites, and on-line portals
- traditional and/or electronic library of books, articles, videos, and other resources about adult learners and on topics useful to them such as study skills, financing one's education, and managing multiple roles
- toys, games, and other items for the use of children who accompany their parents/guardians to campus

ALPS staff members should work with other units such as commuter and off-campus living programs, continuing and distance education, and child care programs to assure the availability of facilities that meet adult learners' needs.

Adult learner student organizations should have access to facilities that support successful operations.

Personnel must have workspaces that are suitably located and accessible, well equipped, adequate in size, and designed to support their work and responsibilities.

The design of the facilities must guarantee the security and privacy of records and ensure the confidentiality of sensitive information and conversations. Personnel must be able to secure their work.

ALPS must incorporate sustainable practices in use of facilities and purchase of equipment. Facilities and equipment must be evaluated on an established cycle and be in compliance with codes, laws, and accepted practices for access, health, safety, and security.

When acquiring capital equipment, ALPS must take into account expenses related to regular maintenance and life cycle costs.

Part 12. Assessment and Evaluation

Adult Learner Programs and Services (ALPS) must develop assessment plans and processes.

Assessment plans must articulate an ongoing cycle of assessment activities.

ALPS must
- **specify programmatic goals and intended outcomes**
- **identify student learning and development outcomes**
- **employ multiple measures and methods**
- **develop manageable processes for gathering, interpreting, and evaluating data**
- **document progress toward achievement of goals and outcomes**
- **interpret and use assessment results to demonstrate accountability**
- **report aggregated results to respondent groups and stakeholders**
- **use assessment results to inform planning and decision-making**
- **assess effectiveness of implemented changes**
- **provide evidence of improvement of programs and services**

ALPS assessment activities should include a focus on demographics of adult applicants and enrollees, academic performance variables, retention studies, use of and satisfaction with campus programs and services, the impact on adult learners of institutional policies and practices, access to and receipt of financial aid, and student use of the institution's prior learning assessment options, e.g., College Level Examination Program (CLEP).

ALPS must employ ethical practices in the assessment process.

ALPS must have access to adequate fiscal, human, professional development, and technological resources to develop and implement assessment plans.

General Standards revised in 2014;
ALPS content developed in 2008

Alcohol and Other Drug Programs
CAS Contextual Statement

Historically, abuse of alcohol and other drugs has been a major concern for institutions of higher education. Colleges and universities have employed a variety of approaches over the years to address alcohol and other drug (AOD) abuse and associated problems. Since the mid-twentieth century, significant research has documented the prevalence of alcohol and other drug abuse on America's college campuses, as well as college and university campuses around the world. "Of all health issues facing young adults today, alcohol consumption is the only issue where the college creates greater risk than for age matched peers not enrolled in higher education" (Substance Abuse and Mental Health Services Administration [SAMHSA], 2012). Additionally, new research has identified effective strategies to reduce illegal and high-risk AOD use and abuse on college campuses.

The 2002 landmark report, "A Call to Action: Changing the Culture of Drinking at U.S. Colleges," outlined for the first time recommendations for effective alcohol prevention in the college population. This included the call for an overarching comprehensive program framework and the delineation of four tiers of effectiveness. Utilizing the four tiers of effectiveness, campuses can identify, evaluate, and select prevention strategies most relevant to college student drinking and most strongly supported by empirical evidence. Elements of many of these approaches have been highlighted and deconstructed in "Experiences in Effective Prevention: The U.S. Department of Education's Alcohol and Other Drug Prevention Models on College Campuses Grants" published in 2007 by the U.S. Department of Education's Higher Education Center for Alcohol and Other Drug Abuse and Violence Prevention.

One significant strategy for effective AOD abuse prevention on college campuses is to move beyond the approach where a single staff member or single office is solely charged with addressing AOD issues and implement an approach that includes all relevant stakeholders across campus. Some stakeholders may seem obvious such as AOD prevention services or specialists, health and wellness offices/staff, counseling and health services, student conduct offices, campus police, security and safety, residential living, fraternity and sorority life, athletics, and of course students. Other stakeholders who are equally important but may be less obvious include faculty, staff, alumni, parents/guardians, and families. Offices such as admissions or enrollment management, institutional advancement, institutional research, and administrators at all levels, including the president of the institution, must be included.

Strong leadership, no matter where located in the institution, is also a key element of success. The Presidents Leadership Group, founded in 1997 by the Center for College Health and Safety, urged higher education presidents to make prevention both a personal and institutional priority. Institutions that show such leadership are more likely to have success in reducing illegal and high risk AOD use than institutions that do not have the president out front and center. The comprehensive approach begs for a university wide workgroup, coalition, or task force, and the best way to make this happen is to have the call for change and actions come from the president or chancellor of an institution.

With strong institutional leadership comes a greater likelihood of connecting with community partners, another element of a strong comprehensive approach. Shared responsibility extends to institutional friends and neighbors such as local community or civic associations, AOD service providers, bars and restaurants, elected officials, state liquor control boards, and city, county, and state agencies tasked with prevention. Such agencies may be part of the NASADAD National Prevention Network or the Community Anti-Drug Coalitions of America (CADCA). Also included are stakeholders at the federal level such as the Substance Abuse and Mental Health Services Administration, the National Institute on Alcohol Abuse and Alcoholism, the U.S. Department of Education, and the White House Office of National Drug Control Policy that are demonstrating a greater commitment to addressing AOD issues in, and partnering with, higher education. This is most recently and prominently evidenced in a joint letter from Director Gil Kerlikowske of the White House Office of National Drug Control Policy and Secretary of Education Arne Duncan, dated September 23, 2011, to leaders in higher education inviting them to join with other Federal agency partners to work collaboratively to prevent illegal drug use and high-risk drinking in our Nation's college and university communities (www.whitehouse.gov/blog/2011/09/23/).

One area of the field that continues to receive a great deal of attention is assessment, whether that be in the assessment of student behavior that grew in the 1990s or the assessment of the effectiveness of AOD education, prevention, and intervention programs that have grown in the last decade. Programming now being offered and assessed on many campuses includes motivational interviewing, policies restricting access, individual counseling, support groups, recovery houses, social norms marketing, campus-community task forces, peer education, brief interventions, curriculum infusion, educational sanctions, policy promotion, medical amnesty policies, web-based educational programs, and the list goes on. Not every program is right for each campus, but through intentional programming and thorough assessment, ineffective programs can be discarded, effective ones retained, and new programs added. The CAS standards offer guidance for AOD program development and evaluation, necessary components in the pursuit of effective practice.

There will always be new issues, substances, and strategies to consider when looking at reducing illegal and high risk alcohol and other drug use. Strong leadership, shared responsibility, and program assessment are key elements of the CAS standards for Alcohol and Other Drug Programs. Use of these standards for self-assessment offers a useful approach to addressing current and future AOD issues in higher education.

References, Readings, and Resources

A Call to Action: Changing the Culture of Drinking at U.S. Colleges: www.collegedrinkingprevention.gov/media/TaskForceReport.pdf

AMA Office of Alcohol & Other Drug Abuse: www.ama-assn.org/ama/pub/category/3337.html

American College Health Associations ATOD Coalition: http://www.acha.org/about_acha/ctfs/coalition_atd.cfm

Amethyst Initiative. (2008). *Initiative description.* Retrieved from http://www.amethystinitiative.org

Anderson, D. S., & Milgram, G. G. (1996). *Promising practices: Campus alcohol strategies sourcebook.* Fairfax, VA: George Mason University.

BACCHUS and GAMMA Peer Education Network: www.bacchusgamma.org

Califano, J. A., Jr. (2007). Accompanying statement. In National Center on Addiction and Substance Abuse at Columbia University (CASA), *You've Got Drugs! IV: Prescription Drug Pushers on the Internet.* Retrieved from http://www.casacolumbia.org/addiction-research/reports/youve-got-drugs-perscription-drug-pushers-internet-2007

Coombs, R. H., & Ziedonis, D. (1995). *Handbook on drug abuse prevention: A comprehensive strategy to prevent the abuse of alcohol and other drugs.* Boston, MA: Allyn & Bacon.

Core Institute. (2000). *1999 statistics on alcohol and other drug use on American campuses,* Carbondale, IL: Core Institute.

Johnston, L. D., O'Malley, P. M., Bachman, J. G., & Schulenberg, J. E. (2004). *National survey results on drug use for the monitoring the future study, 1975-2003.* Rockville, MD: National Institute on Drug Abuse.

Journal of Drug Education. Amityville, NY: Baywood Publishing Co.

Lucey, R. (2006). Substance abuse on campus: A brief history. In R. Chapman (Ed.), *When they drink: Practitioner views and lessons learned.* Glassboro, NJ: Rowan University Press.

McCabe, S. E., Knight, J. R., Teter, C. J., & Wechsler, H. (2005). Nonmedical use of prescription stimulants among U.S. college students: Prevalence and correlates from a national survey. *Addiction, 99,* 96–106.

National Clearinghouse for Alcohol and Drug Information (NCADI): www.health.org

National Institute of Drug Abuse (NIDA): www.drugabuse.gov

National Institute on Alcohol Abuse and Alcoholism (NIAAA): www.collegedrinkingprevention.gov

NIAAA Report (2005). *Call to action information.* Retrieved from http://www.campushealthandsafety.org/niaaa/

Strauss, R., & Bacon, S. D. (1953). *Drinking in college.* New Haven, CT: Yale University Press.

Substance Abuse and Mental Health Services Administration (SAMHSA): www.samhsa.gov/

Substance Abuse and Mental Health Administration (SAMHSA). (2012, February 7). *Nearly half of college student treatment admissions were for primary alcohol abuse.* Retrieved from http://www.samhsa.gov/data/spotlight/Spotlight054College2012.pdf.

The Network Addressing Collegiate Alcohol and Other Drug Issues: http://www.thenetwork.ws/

U.S. Department of Education's Higher Education Center publications: www.edc.org/hec

Wechsler, H., Dowdall, G., Davenport, A., & Castillo, S. (1995). Correlates of college student binge drinking. *American Journal of Public Health, 85,* 7.

Wilk A. I., Jensen N. M., Havighurst, T. C. (1977). Meta-analysis of randomized control trials addressing brief interventions in heavy alcohol drinkers. *Journal of General Internal Medicine, 12,* 274–283.

Contextual Statement Contributors

Current Edition:
John Watson, Drexel University

Previous Editions:
Carole Middlebrooks, University of Georgia

Alcohol and Other Drug Programs
CAS Standards and Guidelines

For the purpose of this document, the term "alcohol and other drug use or abuse" includes the illegal and high risk use of alcohol, tobacco, prescription and over-the-counter medications, and other drugs.

Part 1. Mission

The mission of Alcohol and Other Drug Programs (AODP) is to promote a safe, healthy, and learning-conducive environment and healthy choices concerning the use of alcohol and other drugs.

In addition, AODP must
- acknowledge and mitigate the inherent risks to individuals, the institution, and the surrounding community associated with alcohol and other drug use or abuse
- emphasize the elimination of illegal and high-risk use of alcohol and other drugs and related violence
- develop, disseminate, and support the enforcement of campus regulations that are consistent with institutional policies, as well as relevant local, state/provincial, and federal laws
- identify and implement AODP policies and practices for prevention, education, training, intervention, evaluation, referral, and treatment
- develop shared ownership of the issue by involving key entities of the institution and community that may include, but are not limited to, governing boards, administrators, faculty and staff members, students, parents/family members, and community leaders for the purpose of taking action
- protect the legal rights of students

AODP must develop, disseminate, implement, and regularly review their missions, which must be consistent with the mission of the institution and with applicable professional standards. The mission must be appropriate for the institution's students and other constituents. Mission statements must reference student learning and development.

Part 2. Program

To achieve their mission, Alcohol and Other Drug Programs (AODP) must contribute to
- students' formal education, which includes both the curriculum and the co-curriculum
- student progression and timely completion of educational goals
- preparation of students for their careers, citizenship, and lives
- student learning and development

To contribute to student learning and development, AODP must

- identify relevant and desirable student learning and development outcomes
- articulate how the student learning and development outcomes align with the six CAS student learning and development domains and related dimensions
- assess relevant and desirable student learning and development
- provide evidence of impact on outcomes
- articulate contributions to or support of student learning and development in the domains not specifically assessed
- use evidence gathered to create strategies for improvement of programs and services

STUDENT LEARNING AND DEVELOPMENT DOMAINS AND DIMENSIONS

Domain: knowledge acquisition, integration, construction, and application
- Dimensions: understanding knowledge from a range of disciplines; connecting knowledge to other knowledge, ideas, and experiences; constructing knowledge; and relating knowledge to daily life

Domain: cognitive complexity
- Dimensions: critical thinking, reflective thinking, effective reasoning, and creativity

Domain: intrapersonal development
- Dimensions: realistic self-appraisal, self-understanding, and self-respect; identity development; commitment to ethics and integrity; and spiritual awareness

Domain: interpersonal competence
- Dimensions: meaningful relationships, interdependence, collaboration, and effective leadership

Domain: humanitarianism and civic engagement
- Dimensions: understanding and appreciation of cultural and human differences, social responsibility, global perspective, and sense of civic responsibility

Domain: practical competence
- Dimensions: pursuing goals, communicating effectively, technical competence, managing personal affairs, managing career development, demonstrating professionalism, maintaining health and wellness, and living a purposeful and satisfying life

[LD Outcomes: See *The Council for the Advancement of Standards Learning and Development Outcomes* statement for examples of outcomes related to these domains and dimensions.]

AODP must be
- intentionally designed
- guided by theories and knowledge of learning and development
- integrated into the life of the institution
- reflective of developmental and demographic profiles of the student population
- responsive to needs of individuals, populations with distinct needs, and relevant constituencies
- delivered using multiple formats, strategies, and contexts
- designed to provide universal access

AODP must collaborate with colleagues and departments across the institution to promote student learning and development, persistence, and success.

AODP must involve a wide representation of constituent groups from the institution and the community in the development and implementation of programs and services to reduce alcohol and other drug use and abuse.

Constituent groups should include students, faculty members, senior administration, staff members, parents or family members, and community leaders.

In development of programs and services, AODP must take into account
- evidence-based strategies
- assessment, counseling, and referral
- community collaboration
- environmental management strategies
- institutional policies
- student leadership and involvement
- stakeholder training and education
- biennial or other review as required by law

AODP must develop and make available education/ training on policies, laws, prevention, risks, and responsibilities associated with alcohol and other drug use and abuse, healthy living, intervention, and treatment resources.

AODP education and training programs should take into account the specific cultural, economic, psychosocial, and geographical factors of the students as well as the institution's rituals and traditions that often represent times of increased alcohol and other drug use and abuse.

AODP education and training should be focused on local high-risk groups as identified through campus assessments.

AODP should review all education, prevention, treatment, and support programs annually to enhance the effort of the biennial review.

AODP must develop techniques and protocols for identifying and referring students with problems to appropriate campus and off-campus entities. These entities include but are not limited to AODP Centers/Offices, Counseling Centers, Student Health Centers, Wellness Centers/Offices, Health Promotion Offices, Community Treatment Centers, and Outpatient Services.

AODP must develop, provide, and advocate strategies that model practical applications of prevention theories and research results and that are evidence-based or evidence informed such as environmental approaches, risk reduction approaches, brief interventions, and student support programs.

In order to develop a fully comprehensive approach, AODP should consider the following supplemental strategies: curricular infusion projects, substance-free housing options, late-night programming, web-based educational programs, social marketing, social norms approaches, students in recovery programs, on-campus task forces, and campus and community coalitions.

AODP must use public health prevention strategies that are evidence-based and have demonstrated effectiveness in reducing heavy and high-risk drinking and other drug use in college populations.

Programs should consider strategies that have demonstrated effectiveness at the community level and may be appropriate for the college populations.

AODP should advocate for incorporating alcohol and other drug information within relevant courses and expanding campus library holdings.

AODP must provide access to support services for students who use or abuse alcohol and other drugs who self-refer as well as those who are mandated through the campus conduct (judicial) process.

The support services should include confidential individual assessment for students to explore and evaluate their attitudes, perceptions, and behaviors; explore and evaluate the consequences, risk factors, and relationship to alcohol or other drugs; and make decisions based on the student's individual situation.

Support services should include a coordinated system for intervention and referral services for all students. Support services should include campus and community entities that offer effective treatment, education, and support to students, family members, and friends. Such services may include structured education and counseling sessions for individuals and groups, community service work, and disability support services.

Support services should address the needs of students in recovery by offering self-help groups such as Alcoholics Anonymous, Narcotics Anonymous, Al-Anon, and Adult Children of Alcoholics; support groups; recovery living/ housing; and detoxification and in-patient therapy.

Part 3. Organization and Leadership

To achieve program and student learning and development outcomes, Alcohol and Other Drug Programs (AODP) must be purposefully structured for effectiveness. AODP must have clearly stated and current

- goals and outcomes
- policies and procedures
- responsibilities and performance expectations for personnel
- organizational charts demonstrating clear channels of authority

Leaders must model ethical behavior and institutional citizenship.

Leaders with organizational authority for AODP must provide strategic planning, management and supervision, and program advancement.

Strategic Planning
- articulate a vision and mission that drive short- and long-term planning
- set goals and objectives based on the needs of the populations served, intended student learning and development outcomes, and program outcomes
- facilitate continuous development, implementation, and assessment of program effectiveness and goal attainment congruent with institutional mission and strategic plans
- promote environments that provide opportunities for student learning, development, and engagement
- develop, adapt, and improve programs and services in response to the changing needs of populations served and evolving institutional priorities
- include diverse perspectives to inform decision making

Management and Supervision
- plan, allocate, and monitor the use of fiscal, physical, human, intellectual, and technological resources
- manage human resource processes including recruitment, selection, professional development, supervision, performance planning, succession planning, evaluation, recognition, and reward
- influence others to contribute to the effectiveness and success of the unit
- empower professional, support, and student personnel to become effective leaders
- encourage and support collaboration with colleagues and departments across the institution
- encourage and support scholarly contributions to the profession
- identify and address individual, organizational, and environmental conditions that foster or inhibit mission achievement
- use current and valid evidence to inform decisions
- incorporate sustainability practices in the management and design of programs, services, and facilities
- understand appropriate technologies and integrate them into programs and services
- be knowledgeable about codes and laws relevant to programs and services and ensure that programs

and services meet those requirements
- assess and take action to mitigate potential risks

Program Advancement
- advocate for and actively promote the mission and goals of the programs and services
- inform stakeholders about issues affecting practice
- facilitate processes to reach consensus where wide support is needed
- advocate for representation in strategic planning initiatives at divisional and institutional levels

AODP leaders must identify and communicate to senior administrators about the effect of drinking/drug use on institutional priorities such as enrollment, retention, academic performance, and cost management. In addition, AODP leaders must provide institutional and community leaders with information on AODP issues and prevention strategies to ensure coordinated support across the institution and within the larger community.

AODP leaders must encourage senior administrators to communicate a clear, strong message regarding expectations of student behavior related to the use of alcohol and other drugs.

The AODP director, coordinator, or campus designee must be positioned within the institution's organizational structure in order to promote cooperative interaction with appropriate campus and community entities and to develop the support and engagement of high-level administrators.

Engagement with and access to senior leadership is critical to the success of an institution's prevention efforts.

The scope and structure of AODP should be defined by the size, nature, complexity, and stance of the institution.

AODP should maintain an advisory board of knowledgeable members of the campus and surrounding community for advice and support on policies and programs.

AODP must lead in the development of policies to
- promote an educational, social, and living environment which aims to reduce alcohol and other drug use and abuse
- maintain consistency and compliance with laws and regulations
- define geographic jurisdictions to which policies pertain
- define individual and group behaviors and group activities that are prohibited both on campus property and at off-campus events controlled by the institution
- specify consequences for using or possessing, distributing, or manufacturing different amounts and/or classes of alcohol and other drugs
- establish protocols and procedures for the involvement of campus and community law enforcement, campus conduct offices, and other campus entities when a student has been found to be in violation of the institution's alcohol or drug

policies and or laws
- establish protocols and procedures for referring individuals with alcohol or other drug use and abuse problems to appropriate sources for assistance
- define campus procedures on the availability and marketing of alcoholic beverages on campus controlled property or at events
- define appropriate procedures for any permitted use of alcohol or drugs

Part 4. Human Resources

Alcohol and Other Drug Programs (AODP) must be staffed adequately by individuals qualified to accomplish mission and goals.

AODP must have access to technical and support personnel adequate to accomplish their mission.

Within institutional guidelines, AODP must
- establish procedures for personnel recruitment and selection, training, performance planning, and evaluation
- set expectations for supervision and performance
- provide personnel access to continuing and advanced education and appropriate professional development opportunities to improve their competence, skills, and leadership capacity
- consider work/life options available to personnel (e.g., compressed work schedules, flextime, job sharing, remote work, or telework) to promote recruitment and retention of personnel

Administrators of AODP must
- ensure that all personnel have updated position descriptions
- implement recruitment and selection/hiring strategies that produce a workforce inclusive of under-represented populations
- develop promotion practices that are fair, inclusive, proactive, and non-discriminatory

Personnel responsible for delivery of AODP must have written performance goals, objectives, and outcomes for each year's performance cycle to be used to plan, review, and evaluate work and performance. The performance plan must be updated regularly to reflect changes during the performance cycle.

Results of individual personnel evaluations must be used to recognize personnel performance, address performance issues, implement individual and/or collective personnel development and training programs, and inform the assessment of programs and services.

AODP personnel, when hired and throughout their employment, must receive appropriate and thorough training.

AODP personnel, including student employees and volunteers, must have access to resources or receive specific

training on
- institutional policies pertaining to functions or activities they support
- privacy and confidentiality policies
- laws regarding access to student records
- policies and procedures for dealing with sensitive institutional information
- policies and procedures related to technology used to store or access student records and institutional data
- how and when to refer those in need of additional assistance to qualified personnel and have access to a supervisor for assistance in making these judgments
- systems and technologies necessary to perform their assigned responsibilities
- ethical and legal uses of technology

AODP personnel must engage in continuing professional development activities to keep abreast of the research, theories, legislation, policies, and developments that affect their programs and services.

Administrators of AODP must ensure that personnel are knowledgeable about and trained in safety, emergency procedures, and crisis prevention and response. Risk management efforts must address identification of threatening conduct or behavior and must incorporate a system for responding to and reporting such behaviors.

AODP personnel must be knowledgeable of and trained in safety and emergency procedures for securing and vacating facilities.

AODP staff should also have training and experience in prevention, intervention, assessment, treatment issues, and strategies as well as experience with, and an understanding of, the developmental needs of college students.

AOPD should provide training for professional and support staff, pre-professionals, and paraprofessionals in other campus units on alcohol and other drug problem recognition and referral procedures.

PROFESSIONAL PERSONNEL

AODP professional personnel either must hold an earned graduate or professional degree in a field relevant to their position or must possess an appropriate combination of educational credentials and related work experience.

AODP staff should be managed by staff members who have a graduate or professional degree from an accredited institution in fields of study such as health education, student affairs, public health, psychology, social work, counseling, education, and other appropriate health-related areas.

INTERNS OR GRADUATE ASSISTANTS

Degree- or credential-seeking interns or graduate assistants must be qualified by enrollment in an appropriate field of study and relevant experience. These students must be trained and supervised by professional personnel who possess applicable educational credentials and work experience and have supervisory experience. Supervisors must be cognizant of the dual roles interns and graduate assistants have as both student and employee.

Supervisors must
- adhere to parameters of students' job descriptions
- articulate intended learning outcomes in student job descriptions
- adhere to agreed-upon work hours and schedules
- offer flexible scheduling when circumstances necessitate

Supervisors and students must both agree to suitable compensation if circumstances necessitate additional hours.

STUDENT EMPLOYEES AND VOLUNTEERS

Student employees and volunteers must be carefully selected, trained, supervised, and evaluated. Students must have access to a supervisor. Student employees and volunteers must be provided clear job descriptions, pre-service training based on assessed needs, and continuing development.

Part 5. Ethics

Alcohol and Other Drug Programs (AODP) must
- review applicable professional ethical standards and must adopt or develop and implement appropriate statements of ethical practice
- publish and adhere to statements of ethical practice and ensure their periodic review
- orient new personnel to relevant ethical standards and statements of ethical practice and related institutional policies

Statements of ethical standards must
- specify that AODP personnel respect privacy and maintain confidentiality in communications and records as delineated by privacy laws
- specify limits on disclosure of information contained in students' records as well as requirements to disclose to appropriate authorities
- address conflicts of interest, or appearance thereof, by personnel in the performance of their work
- reflect the responsibility of personnel to be fair, objective, and impartial in their interactions with others
- reference management of institutional funds
- reference appropriate behavior regarding research and assessment with human participants, confidentiality of research and assessment data, and students' rights and responsibilities
- include the expectation that personnel confront and hold accountable other personnel who exhibit unethical behavior
- address issues surrounding scholarly integrity

AODP personnel must
- employ ethical decision making in the performance of their duties
- inform users of programs and services of ethical obligations and limitations emanating from codes and laws or from licensure requirements
- recognize and avoid conflicts of interest that could adversely influence their judgment or objectivity and, when unavoidable, recuse themselves from the situation
- perform their duties within the scope of their position, training, expertise, and competence
- make referrals when issues presented exceed the scope of the position

Part 6. Law, Policy, and Governance

Alcohol and Other Drug Programs (AODP) must be in compliance with laws, regulations, and policies that relate to their respective responsibilities and that pose legal obligations, limitations, risks, and liabilities for the institution as a whole. Examples include constitutional, statutory, regulatory, and case law; relevant law and orders emanating from codes and laws; and the institution's policies.

AODP must have access to legal advice needed for personnel to carry out their assigned responsibilities.

AODP must inform personnel, appropriate officials, and users of programs and services about existing and changing legal obligations, risks and liabilities, and limitations.

AODP must inform personnel about professional liability insurance options and refer them to external sources if the institution does not provide coverage.

AODP must have written policies and procedures on operations, transactions, or tasks that have legal implications.

AODP must regularly review policies. The revision and creation of policies must be informed by best practices, available evidence, and policy issues in higher education.

AODP must have procedures and guidelines consistent with institutional policy for responding to threats, emergencies, and crisis situations. Systems and procedures must be in place to disseminate timely and accurate information to students, other members of the institutional community, and appropriate external organizations during emergency situations.

Personnel must neither participate in nor condone any form of harassment or activity that demeans persons or creates an intimidating, hostile, or offensive environment.

AODP must purchase or obtain permission to use copyrighted materials and instruments. References to copyrighted materials and instruments must include appropriate citations.

AODP must inform personnel about internal and external governance organizations that affect programs and services.

If AODP uses parental notification as an element of the

program, it must seek advice from institution's legal counsel on privacy and disclosure of student information.

Part 7. Diversity, Equity, and Access

Within the context of each institution's mission and in accordance with institutional policies and applicable codes and laws, Alcohol and Other Drug Programs (AODP) must create and maintain educational and work environments that are welcoming, accessible, inclusive, equitable, and free from harassment.

AODP must not discriminate on the basis of disability; age; race; cultural identity; ethnicity; nationality; family educational history (e.g., first generation to attend college); political affiliation; religious affiliation; sex; sexual orientation; gender identity and expression; marital, social, economic, or veteran status; or any other basis included in institutional policies and codes and laws.

AODP must
- advocate for sensitivity to multicultural and social justice concerns by the institution and its personnel
- ensure physical, program, and resource access for all constituents
- modify or remove policies, practices, systems, technologies, facilities, and structures that create barriers or produce inequities
- ensure that when facilities and structures cannot be modified, they do not impede access to programs, services, and resources
- establish goals for diversity, equity, and access
- foster communication and practices that enhance understanding of identity, culture, self-expression, and heritage
- promote respect for commonalities and differences among people within their historical and cultural contexts
- address the characteristics and needs of diverse constituents when establishing and implementing culturally relevant and inclusive programs, services, policies, procedures, and practices
- provide personnel with diversity, equity, and access training and hold personnel accountable for applying the training to their work
- respond to the needs of all constituents served when establishing hours of operation and developing methods of delivering programs, services, and resources
- recognize the needs of distance and online learning students by directly providing or assisting them to gain access to comparable services and resources

AODP must consider all populations and diverse needs in educational program messages and in access to prevention, intervention, and treatment services.

Part 8. Internal and External Relations

Alcohol and Other Drug Programs (AODP) must reach out to individuals, groups, communities, and organizations internal and external to the institution to
- establish, maintain, and promote understanding and effective relations with those that have a significant interest in or potential effect on the students or other constituents served by the programs and services
- garner support and resources for programs and services as defined by the mission
- collaborate in offering or improving programs and services to meet the needs of students and other constituents and to achieve program and student outcomes
- engage diverse individuals, groups, communities, and organizations to enrich the educational environment and experiences of students and other constituents
- disseminate information about the programs and services

Promotional and descriptive information must be accurate and free of deception and misrepresentation.

AODP must have procedures and guidelines consistent with institutional policy for
- communicating with the media
- distributing information through print, broadcast, and online sources
- contracting with external organizations for delivery of programs and services
- cultivating, soliciting, and managing gifts
- applying to and managing funds from grants

AODP must gather and disseminate information to the campus community, including students, their parents/guardians, staff, and faculty members on alcohol, tobacco, and other drug problems, risk reduction strategies, resources, and related topics.

AODP must maintain effective working relationships with various institutional offices and community groups and agencies to promote a healthy environment in which the use or abuse of alcohol and other drugs does not interfere with the learning, performance, or social aspects of college life.

Community agencies may include relevant governmental agencies and authorities such as the governmental liquor store control authority, governmental alcohol agency, the office of highway traffic safety, mayor and council, neighborhood associations, faith community, family, parents or guardians, school systems, area health care and treatment providers, support groups, and alumni as well as representatives from the local chamber of commerce and the hospitality industry.

AODP should engage the campus and community in the issues of access and availability of alcohol and other drugs and in the enforcement of the law.

AODP should establish an all-campus task force or campus-community coalition to address on-going concerns and environmental strategies.

Part 9. Finanical Resources

Alcohol and Other Drug Programs (AODP) must have funding to accomplish the mission and goals.

In establishing and prioritizing funding resources, AODP must conduct comprehensive analyses to determine
- unmet needs of the unit
- relevant expenditures
- external and internal resources
- impact on students and the institution

AODP must use the budget as a planning tool to reflect commitment to the mission and goals of the programs and services and of the institution.

AODP must administer funds in accordance with established institutional accounting procedures.

AODP must demonstrate efficient and effective use and responsible stewardship of fiscal resources consistent with institutional protocols.

Financial reports must provide an accurate financial overview of the organization and provide clear, understandable, and timely data upon which personnel can plan and make informed decisions.

Procurement procedures must
- be consistent with institutional policies
- ensure that purchases comply with laws and codes for usability and access
- ensure that the institution receives value for the funds spent
- consider information available for comparing the ethical and environmental impact of products and services purchased

AODP should receive sufficient baseline funding from the institution, including adequate resources for staffing needs, so that staff members may spend the majority of their time on planning, programming, providing, and evaluating services.

The institution should provide support for AODP to explore external funding sources when needed.

Part 10. Technology

Alcohol and Other Drug Programs (AODP) must have technology to support the achievement of their mission and goals. The technology and its use must comply with institutional policies and procedures and with relevant codes and laws.

AODP must use technologies to
- provide updated information regarding mission, location, staffing, programs, services, and official contacts to students and other constituents in accessible formats
- provide an avenue for students and other constituents to communicate sensitive information in a secure format
- enhance the delivery of programs and services for all students

AODP must
- back up data on a regular basis
- adhere to institutional policies regarding ethical and legal use of technology
- articulate policies and procedures for protecting the confidentiality and security of information
- implement a replacement plan and cycle for all technology with attention to sustainability
- incorporate accessibility features into technology-based programs and services

When providing student access to technology, AODP must
- have policies on the use of technology that are clear, easy to understand, and available to all students
- provide information or referral to support services for those needing assistance in accessing or using technology
- provide instruction or training on how to use the technology
- inform students of implications of misuse of technologies

Part 11. Facilities and Equipment

Alcohol and Other Drug Programs' (AODP) facilities must be intentionally designed and located in suitable, accessible, and safe spaces that demonstrate universal design and support the program's mission and goals.

Facilities must be designed to engage various constituents and promote learning.

Facilities should accommodate a range of services, including prevention, education, assessment, intervention, counseling, programming, a resource center, and support for students in recovery.

AODP should be provided facilities that ensure confidentiality and a location in which students, faculty members, and staff might access and read information on alcohol and other drug use/abuse.

AODP office space should be physically separate from human resources, campus security, and student conduct programs.

Personnel must have workspaces that are suitably located and accessible, well equipped, adequate in size, and designed to support their work and responsibilities.

The design of the facilities must guarantee the security and privacy of records and ensure the confidentiality of sensitive information and conversations. Personnel must be able to secure their work.

AODP must incorporate sustainable practices in use of facilities and purchase of equipment. Facilities and equipment must be evaluated on an established cycle and be in compliance with codes, laws, and accepted practices for access, health, safety, and security.

When acquiring capital equipment, AODP must take into account expenses related to regular maintenance and life cycle costs.

Part 12. Assessment

Alcohol and Other Drug Programs (AODP) must develop assessment plans and processes.

Assessment plans must articulate an ongoing cycle of assessment activities.

AODP must
- specify programmatic goals and intended outcomes
- identify student learning and development outcomes
- employ multiple measures and methods
- develop manageable processes for gathering, interpreting, and evaluating data
- document progress toward achievement of goals and outcomes
- interpret and use assessment results to demonstrate accountability
- report aggregated results to respondent groups and stakeholders
- use assessment results to inform planning and decision-making
- assess effectiveness of implemented changes
- provide evidence of improvement of programs and services

AODP must assess systematically the following campus factors:
- attitudes, beliefs, and behaviors regarding alcohol and other drug use, abuse, and dependency
- consequences of alcohol or other drug use or abuse on academic performance; property damage; policy violations; health, counseling, and disciplinary caseloads
- perceptions of campus alcohol and other drug use norms
- features of the environment that abet high-risk alcohol use and other drug use, marketing and promotion that promotes heavy or underage consumption of alcohol, inconsistent enforcement of campus policy and community law, and lack of availability of alcohol-free social and recreational options on campus and in the surrounding community

AODP should assess the norms, behaviors, and behavioral consequences of specific focus populations.

AODP and other campus entities must exchange general and non-confidential assessment results of mutual application and benefit.

AODP must employ ethical practices in the assessment process.

AODP must have access to adequate fiscal, human, professional development, and technological resources to develop and implement assessment plans

General Standards revised in 2014;
AODP (formerly Alcohol, Tobacco, and Other Drug Programs) content developed/revised in 1990, 1997, 2003, & 2013

Assessment Services
CAS Contextual Statement

Assessment was an important element in higher education well before the founding of higher education in the United States; juried reviews were used to demonstrate student learning at the University of Bologna as early as 1063 CE (Bresciani, Moore Gardner, & Hickmott, 2009). Although the need for assessment and program evaluation in American higher education has long been acknowledged, it remains a pressing need today. With fiscal restraints and calls for accountability coming from multiple constituents (ranging from parents to regional accrediting bodies), the ability to document and evaluate the impact of our programs and services is a critical responsibility.

Early proponents of outcomes assessment included William Rainey Harper, President of the University of Chicago. In 1889, he called on colleges and universities to adopt a program of research with the college student as the subject "in order that the student may receive the assistance so essential to his [sic] highest success, another step in the onward evolution will take place. This step will be the scientific study of the student" (as cited in Rentz, 1996, p. 28).

Responding to Harper's vision, the *Student Personnel Point of View* (American Council of Education, 1937) challenged the field of student services to employ "studies designed to improve these functions and services" (p. 42). Later in the document, four specific kinds of studies were identified: student out-of-class life and its connection to the educational mission, faculty and student out-of-class relationships, financial aid to students, and after-college studies to ascertain the effects of college on careers and personal adjustment.

The 1949 revision of the *Student Personnel Point of View* (American Council of Education) stated that the "principal responsibility of personnel workers lies in the area of progressive program development . . . this means that each worker must devote a large part of time to the formulation of new plans and to the continuous evaluation and improvement of current programs (p. 34). This document also stressed the importance of personnel workers being "thoroughly trained in research methods as a part of their professional preparation" (p. 35). Ultimately, the standard for student affairs programs, according to the 1949 document, is in "the difference it makes in the development of individual students" (p. 34).

Historical and foundational documents in the field give clear evidence that the role of assessment and program evaluation in higher education and student affairs is important in the education of the "whole" student. Although most agree about the importance of conducting research on students and programs, still relatively few student affairs divisions have considered it a vital part of their operations.

In the past decade, student affairs documents have continued the call for assessment and accountability of program effectiveness as it relates to student learning and development. *The Student Learning Imperative* (1996) charged student affairs

staff to "participate in efforts to assess student learning . . . and periodically audit institutional environments to reinforce those factors that enhance, and eliminate those that inhibit student involvement in educationally-purposeful activities" (p. 6). The *Principles of Good Practice for Student Affairs* (1996) asserted the need to use systematic inquiry to improve student and institutional performance. Specifically, "student affairs educators who are skilled in using assessment methods acquire high-quality information; effective application of this information to practice results in programs and change strategies . . . [that] improve student achievement" (p. 3). In *Learning Reconsidered* (2004), the language of assessment and student learning was more comprehensive. "Student Affairs must lead broad, collaborative institutional efforts to assess overall student learning and to track, document, and evaluate the role of diverse learning experiences . . . assessment should be a way of life—part of the institutional culture" (p. 26). According to *Assessment Reconsidered*, the companion to *Learning Reconsidered*, assessment is a collaborative exercise influenced by external forces but "more importantly emerges from the desire of faculty members, student affairs professionals, parents, students, and institutional administrators to know, and improve, the quality and effectiveness of higher education (Keeling, Wall, Underhile, & Dungy, 2008, p. 1).

Assessment is a process with dual purposes: accountability and continuous improvement (Suskie, 2009). According to Bresciani (2006),

> . . . in assessment faculty and staff articulate what the program intends to accomplish in regard to its services, research, student learning, and faculty/staff development programs. The faculty and/or professionals then purposefully plan the program so that the intended results (e.g., outcomes) can be achieved; implement methods to systematically–over time–identify whether end results have been achieved; and, finally, use the results to plan improvements or make recommendations for policy considerations, recruitment, retention, resource allocation, or new resource requests. (p. 14)

The terms assessment, research, and evaluation are often used interchangeably, but there are distinctions.

> Briefly, research concerns theory: forming it, confirming it, and disconfirming it. Research assumes broader implications than one institution or program. Assessment, on the other hand, is more focused on the outcomes of participant programs, though this can be very broad to include an entire institution. It does not infer individual student outcomes. The purpose of assessment is to guide practice rather than to relate practice to theory. Evaluation is even more particular to a specific program and is concerned with the satisfaction, organization, and attendance of a program. (Jones, Torres, & Arminio, 2006, p. 30)

Recently, student affairs literature focused on enabling practitioners to implement assessment. These texts provide information about the assessment planning process, writing outcomes, designing instruments, and performing qualitative as well as quantitative assessments (Bresciani, Zelna, & Anderson, 2004). These resources include the self-assessment guides published by CAS, Schuh and Associates' *Assessment Methods for Student Affairs* (2009), Suskie's *Assessing Student Learning: A Common Sense Guide* (2009), and *Demonstrating Student Success* (2009) by Bresciani, Moore Gardner, and Hickmott. Other guides include *Building a Culture of Evidence in Student Affairs, A Guide for Leaders and Practitioners* (Culp & Dungy, 2012), *Accreditation and the Role for the Student Affairs Educator* (Allen, Elkins, Henning, Bayless, & Gordon, 2013), *Assessment in Practice: A Companion Guide to the ASK Standards* (Timm, Davis Barham, McKinney, & Knerr, 2013), *Five Dimensions of Quality: A Common Sense Guide to Accreditation and Accountability* (Suskie, 2014), and *Using Evidence of Student Learning to Improve Higher Education* (Kuh, Ikenberry, Jankowski, Cain, Ewell, Hutchings, & Kinzie, 2015). In addition, professional associations have begun to provide their members with assessment tools, as have numerous for-profit companies. Campuses today should have a comprehensive assessment plan that includes consideration of learning outcomes, student needs and inputs, campus environments, student motivation, student use and satisfaction, and cost effectiveness (Schuh & Upcraft, 2001).

Bresciani, Zelna, & Anderson (2004) offered reasons and uses for conducting assessment in student affairs, based on a compilation of other works, including those by the American Association for Higher Education (1994), Bresciani (2003), Ewell (1997a), Maki (2004), Palomba and Banta (1999), and Upcraft and Schuh (1996). These reasons are applicable 11 years later. These sources noted the multiple reasons for carrying out assessment: reinforcing or emphasizing unit missions; improving a program's quality or performance; comparing a program's quality or value to the program's previously defined principles; informing planning, decision-making, and policy discussions at the local, state, regional, and national levels; evaluating programs and personnel; assisting in the request for additional funds from the college or university and external community; assisting in the reallocation of resources; assisting in meeting accreditation requirements; identifying models of best practices and national benchmarks; celebrating successes while reflecting on the attitudes and approaches taken in improving learning and development; and creating a culture of continuous improvement—a culture of accountability, learning, and improvement.

Assessment efforts may take many forms. Assessment can employ both qualitative and quantitative data collection methods such as interviews, focus groups, observations, rubrics, portfolios, surveys, and questionnaires. The evolution of technology has eased the collection and management of assessment data.

Assessment is a process that can be used to discover an institution's best practices and to bring about continual improvement within the unique context of each institution. Student affairs divisions undertaking assessment efforts should not be discouraged by the seeming enormity of the task. The important consideration is to be purposeful and systematic and to use sound assessment methods that improve operations incrementally. The assessment process can be disaggregated into its component parts for easier implementation. There are many resources available to assist with the task.

Assessment Services (AS) as a functional area is sometimes organized as a single unit, while at other institutions it is a collective of institutional or departmental assessment bodies. In any case, collaboration and consultation is imperative between and within the AS and various individuals and departments as well as with institutional leadership. For a discussion of specific skills necessary to work in the AS in addition to those discussed in the attached CAS standards, the ACPA Assessment Skills and Knowledge (ASK) standards and the ACPA/NASPA Assessment, Evaluation, and Research professional competencies may be informative. The standards articulated here offer principles for assessment that are valuable for those working in or directing an assessment office as well as for those conducting assessments as a part of their position responsibilities in another functional area.

Groups that exist to support assessment practice include ACPA Commission for Assessment and Evaluation, NASPA Assessment, Evaluation, and Research Knowledge Community, Student Affairs Assessment Leaders (SAAL), the Association for the Assessment of Learning in Higher Education (AALHE), and the Association for Higher Education Effectiveness. Each organization provides web resources, hosts listservs, and sponsor annual conferences.

References, Readings, and Resources

Allen, K., Elkins, B.. Henning, G., Bayless, L., & Gordon, T. (2013). *Accreditation and the role of the student affairs educator* (pp. 6-13). Washington, D.C.: American College Personnel Association.

American Association of Higher Education (1994). *Nine principles of good practice for assessing student learning* [On-line]. Retrieved from http://www.iuk.edu/%7Ekoctla/assessment/9principles.shtml

American College Personnel Association (1996). *The student learning imperative: Implications for student affairs* [On-line]. Retrieved from http://www.acpa.nche.edu/sli/sli.htm

American College Personnel Association. (2006). *ASK standards: Assessment skills and knowledge content standards for student affairs practitioners and scholars.* Washington, DC: Author.

American College Personnel Association & National Association of Student Personnel Administrators. (2010). *Professional competency areas for student affairs practitioners.* Washington, D.C.: Authors.

American Council on Education (1937). *The student personnel point of view: A report of a conference on the philosophy and development of student personnel work in colleges and universities.* Washington, DC: Author. Retrieved from http://www2.bgsu.edu/sahp/pages/1937STUDENTPERSONNELnew.pdf

American Council on Education (1949). *The student personnel point of view (revised).* Washington, DC: Author. Retrieved from http://www2.bgsu.edu/sahp/pages/1949SPPVrev.pdf

Angelo, T. A., & Cross, K. P. (1993). *Classroom assessment techniques: A handbook for college teachers (2ⁿᵈ Ed)*. San Francisco, CA: Jossey-Bass.

Banta, T. W., Lund, J. P., Black, K. E., & Oblander, F. W. (Eds.). (1996). *Assessment in practice: Putting principles to work on college campuse*s. San Francisco, CA: Jossey-Bass.

Banta, T. W., & Kuh, G. D. (1998, March/April). A missing link in assessment: Collaboration between academic and student affairs professionals. *Change*, 40-48.

Blimling, G. S., & Whitt, E. J. (1999). *Good practices in student affairs: Principles to foster student learning*. San Francisco, CA: Jossey-Bass.

Bresciani, M. J. (2003). *An updated outline for assessment plans*. NetResults [On-line]. Retrieved from http://www.naspa.org/

Bresciani, M. J., Zelna, C. L., & Anderson, J. A. (2004). *Assessing student learning and development*. Washington, DC: NASPA.

Bresciani, M. J. (2006). *Outcomes-based academic and co-curricular program review: A compilation of institutional good practices*. Sterling, VA: Stylus.

Bresciani, M. J., Moore Gardner, M., & Hickmott, J. (2009). *Demonstrating student success: A practical guide to outcomes-based assessment of learning and development in student affairs*. Sterling, VA: Stylus.

Culp, M. & Dungy, G. (2012). *Building a culture of evidence in student affairs: A guide for leaders and practitioners*. Washington, D.C.: National Association of Student Personnel Administrators.

Driscoll, A., & Wood, S. (2007). *Developing outcomes-based assessment for learner-centered education*. Sterling, VA: Stylus.

Ewell, P. T. (1997a). From the states: Putting it all on the line—South Carolina's performance funding initiative. *Assessment Update*, 9(1), 9-11.

Huba, M. E., & Freed, J. E. (2000). *Learner-centered assessment on college campuses: Shifting the focus from teaching to learning*. Boston: Allyn and Bacon.

Jones, S. R., Torres, V., & Arminio, J. (2006). *Negotiating the complexities of qualitative research*. New York: Routledge.

Keeling, R. P. (Ed.) (2006). *Learning reconsidered 2: Implementing a campus-wide focus on the student experience*. Washington, DC: American College Personnel Association, Association of College and University Housing Officers-International, Association of College Unions-International, National Academic Advising Association, National Association for Campus Activities, National Association of Student Personnel Administrators, National Intramural-Recreational Sports Association.

Keeling, R. P., Wall, A. F., Underhile, R., & Dungy, G. J. (2008). *Assessment reconsidered: Institutional effectiveness for student success*. International Center for Student Success and Institutional Accountability.

Kuh, G., Ikenberry, S., Jankowski, N., Cain, T., Ewell, P., Hutchings, P., & Kinzie, J. (2015). *Using evidence of student learning to improve higher education*. San Francisco, CA: Jossey-Bass.

Maki, P. (2010). *Assessing for learning (2ⁿᵈ Ed)*. Sterling, VA: Stylus.

National Association of Student Personnel Administrators & American College Personnel Association. (2004) *Learning reconsidered: A campus-wide focus on the student experience*. Washington, DC: NASPA & ACPA. Retrieved from http://www.myacpa.org/pub/documents/LearningReconsidered.doc

Palomba, C. A., & Banta, T. W. (1999). *Assessment essentials: Planning, implementing and improving assessment in higher education*. San Francisco, CA: Jossey-Bass.

Rentz, A. L. (1996). *A history of student affairs*. In A. L. Rentz (Ed.), Student affairs practice in higher education (pp. 28-55). Springfield, IL: Thomas.

Schuh, J. & Associates. (2009). *Assessment methods in student affairs*. San Francisco, CA: Jossey-Bass.

Schuh, J., & Upcraft, M. L. (1998, Nov/Dec). Facts and myths about assessment in student affairs. *About Campus*, 2-8.

Schuh, J. H., Upcraft, M. L., & Associates, (2001). *Assessment practice in student affairs: An application manual*. San Francisco: Jossey-Bass.

Suskie, L. (2009). *Assessing student learning: A common sense guide (2ⁿᵈ Ed.)*. Bolton, MA: Anker.

Suskie, L. (2014). *Five dimensions of quality: A common sense guide to accreditation and accountability*. San Francisco, CA: Jossey-Bass.

Strayhorn, T. L. (2006). *Frameworks for assessing learning development outcomes*. Washington, DC: Council for the Advancement of Standards in Higher Education.

Timm, D. M., Davis Barham. J., McKinney, K., & Knerr, A. R. (2013). *Assessment in practice: A companion guide to the ASK standards*. Washington, DC: ACPA-College Student Educators International. Available from http://www.myacpa.org/commae

U.S. Department of Education. (2006). *A test of leadership: Charting the future of U.S. Higher Education*. Jessup, MD: Ed Pubs.

Upcraft, M. L., & Schuh, J. H. (1996). *Assessment in student affairs: A guide for practitioners*. San Francisco, CA: Jossey-Bass.

Walvoord, B. E. (2004). *Assessment clear and simple: A practical guide for institutions, departments, and general education*. San Francisco, CA: Jossey-Bass.

Wehlburg, C. M. (2008). *Promoting integrated and transformative assessment: A deeper focus on student learning*. San Francisco, CA: Jossey-Bass.

Williamson, E. G., & Biggs, D. A. (1975). *Student personnel work: A program of development relationships*. New York, NY: John Wiley & Sons.

Contextual Statement Contributors

Current Edition:
Gavin Henning, New England College, ACPA

Previous Editions:
Gavin Henning, New England College
Jan Arminio, Shippensburg University
Joel H. Scott, University of Georgia
Cara Skeat Ray, Gainesville State College/University of Georgia
Roger B. Winston, Jr., University of Georgia

Assessment Services
CAS Standards and Guidelines

Part 1. Mission

The mission of Assessment Services (AS) is to develop a comprehensive assessment program to increase the institution's knowledge about students, the educational environment, and institutional effectiveness to continuously improve student programs and services and to enhance student learning.

AS must develop, disseminate, implement, and regularly review their missions, which must be consistent with the mission of the institution and with applicable professional standards. The mission must be appropriate for the institution's students and other constituents. Mission statements must reference student learning and development.

Part 2. Program

To achieve their mission, Assessment Services (AS) must contribute to
- students' formal education, which includes both the curriculum and the co-curriculum
- student progression and timely completion of educational goals
- preparation of students for their careers, citizenship, and lives
- student learning and development

To contribute to student learning and development, AS must
- identify relevant and desirable student learning and development outcomes
- articulate how the student learning and development outcomes align with the six CAS student learning and development domains and related dimensions
- assess relevant and desirable student learning and development
- provide evidence of impact on outcomes
- articulate contributions to or support of student learning and development in the domains not specifically assessed
- use evidence gathered to create strategies for improvement of programs and services

STUDENT LEARNING AND DEVELOPMENT DOMAINS AND DIMENSIONS

Domain: knowledge acquisition, integration, construction, and application
- Dimensions: understanding knowledge from a range of disciplines; connecting knowledge to other knowledge, ideas, and experiences; constructing knowledge; and relating knowledge to daily life

Domain: cognitive complexity
- Dimensions: critical thinking, reflective thinking, effective reasoning, and creativity

Domain: intrapersonal development
- Dimensions: realistic self-appraisal, self-understanding, and self-respect; identity development; commitment to ethics and integrity; and spiritual awareness

Domain: interpersonal competence
- Dimensions: meaningful relationships, interdependence, collaboration, and effective leadership

Domain: humanitarianism and civic engagement
- Dimensions: understanding and appreciation of cultural and human differences, social responsibility, global perspective, and sense of civic responsibility

Domain: practical competence
- Dimensions: pursuing goals, communicating effectively, technical competence, managing personal affairs, managing career development, demonstrating professionalism, maintaining health and wellness, and living a purposeful and satisfying life

[LD Outcomes: See *The Council for the Advancement of Standards Learning and Development Outcomes* statement for examples of outcomes related to these domains and dimensions.]

AS must be
- intentionally designed
- guided by theories and knowledge of learning and development
- integrated into the life of the institution
- reflective of developmental and demographic profiles of the student population
- responsive to needs of individuals, populations with distinct needs, and relevant constituencies
- delivered using multiple formats, strategies, and contexts
- designed to provide universal access

AS must collaborate with colleagues and departments across the institution to promote student learning and development, persistence, and success.

Regardless of its structure, AS must collaborate and consult with institutional research or various departments to ensure that assessment efforts address institutional needs.

AS may be organized as a functional area or be a collective body of assessment initiatives across an institution.

Whenever there are both AS and an institutional research

function in an institution, there should be clear delineation of responsibilities.

In institutions that do not have AS, a senior officer must be an advocate for assessment and program evaluation and must collaborate and consult with, and otherwise provide support to, institutional assessment efforts.

AS must include activities that assess student needs and student learning and development outcomes, assess whether goals are being achieved, describe student characteristics, determine whether professional standards are being met, and determine effectiveness of programs and services for students. Results of these studies must be disseminated to appropriate personnel and students in the institution.

AS must

- **describe the demographics, personal characteristics, and behaviors of students**
- **conduct regular assessments of student needs**
- **review and use available literature about the characteristics and developmental changes of post-secondary students**
- **assess whether the work of AS is consistent with and achieves stated objectives**
- **use appropriate professional standards, tools, and instruments for assessment**
- **study the extent to which students, programs, departments, and institutions meet their overall educational goals and determine conditions that enhance or hamper goal achievement**
- **study the impact of the college experience on students and alumni**
- **examine retention and graduation rates**
- **compare institutional practices against professional standards**
- **investigate the impact of campus culture**
- **assist others in the effective use of assessment to inform decisions and guide the development and improvement of services, programs, and policies**

AS should examine cost effectiveness and the level of student satisfaction with programs and services.

AS practices must be conducted in the context of existing and developing strategic initiatives.

AS should provide assessment and evaluation support for other institutional offices and institutional decision makers.

AS should

- collect and analyze student data beginning with pre-enrollment characteristics and continuing through follow-up studies of graduates and other former students
- plan, coordinate, or conduct regular studies of various programs, facilities, services, classes, and student sub-groups
- describe students' intellectual, emotional, social, moral, spiritual, vocational, and physical development and behavior; such data should be

regularly collected, updated, and disseminated
- analyze data to identify trends in student behavior and attitudes to consider the implications for institutional policies and practices
- analyze data to identify retention trends to consider the implications for institutional policies and practices
- collect and analyze data, including cost effectiveness data, to be used for making decisions about the continuation, modification, or termination of programs and services
- compare institutional practices against benchmarks
- coordinate assessment plans across units and act as a resource to faculty and staff regarding assessment and evaluation efforts
- disseminate information about assessment and evaluation findings to members of the campus community
- guide and evaluate research and assessment efforts conducted by students
- track campus studies, for example in theses and dissertations, in which campus students are participants

Part 3. Organization and Leadership

To achieve program and student learning and development outcomes, Assessment Services (AS) must be purposefully structured for effectiveness. AS must have clearly stated and current

- **goals and outcomes**
- **policies and procedures**
- **responsibilities and performance expectations for personnel**
- **organizational charts demonstrating clear channels of authority**

Leaders must model ethical behavior and institutional citizenship.

Leaders with organizational authority for AS must provide strategic planning, management and supervision, and program advancement.

Strategic Planning

- **articulate a vision and mission that drive short- and long-term planning**
- **set goals and objectives based on the needs of the populations served, intended student learning and development outcomes, and program outcomes**
- **facilitate continuous development, implementation, and assessment of program effectiveness and goal attainment congruent with institutional mission and strategic plans**
- **promote environments that provide opportunities for student learning, development, and engagement**
- **develop, adapt, and improve programs and services in response to the changing needs of populations served and evolving institutional priorities**

- include diverse perspectives to inform decision making

Management and Supervision
- plan, allocate, and monitor the use of fiscal, physical, human, intellectual, and technological resources
- manage human resource processes including recruitment, selection, professional development, supervision, performance planning, succession planning, evaluation, recognition, and reward
- influence others to contribute to the effectiveness and success of the unit
- empower professional, support, and student personnel to become effective leaders
- encourage and support collaboration with colleagues and departments across the institution
- encourage and support scholarly contributions to the profession
- identify and address individual, organizational, and environmental conditions that foster or inhibit mission achievement
- use current and valid evidence to inform decisions
- incorporate sustainability practices in the management and design of programs, services, and facilities
- understand appropriate technologies and integrate them into programs and services
- be knowledgeable about codes and laws relevant to programs and services and ensure that programs and services meet those requirements
- assess and take action to mitigate potential risks

Program Advancement
- advocate for and actively promote the mission and goals of the programs and services
- inform stakeholders about issues affecting practice
- facilitate processes to reach consensus where wide support is needed
- advocate for representation in strategic planning initiatives at divisional and institutional levels

AS leaders must
- understand the foundations of higher education
- understand the educational value and objectives of programs and services
- interpret assessment results to guide educational practice
- advocate for institutional response to assessment findings
- serve as an expert in administering effective and efficient assessment programs
- stay current about trends in assessment
- work to ensure that students are not over-assessed
- understand and be able to use various research and assessment methodologies and methods

Because outcomes assessment and program evaluation efforts are conducted on most campuses in cooperation with other institutional research and evaluation efforts,

a staff member must be designated to manage specific assessment activities, priorities, and timelines.

Assessment goals should result from a collaborative effort between leaders of AS, those responsible for the various programs and services being assessed, and others responsible for institutional research efforts.

Part 4. Human Resources

Assessment Services (AS) must be staffed adequately by individuals qualified to accomplish mission and goals.

AS must have access to technical and support personnel adequate to accomplish their mission.

Within institutional guidelines, AS must
- establish procedures for personnel recruitment and selection, training, performance planning, and evaluation
- set expectations for supervision and performance
- provide personnel access to continuing and advanced education and appropriate professional development opportunities to improve their competence, skills, and leadership capacity
- consider work/life options available to personnel (e.g., compressed work schedules, flextime, job sharing, remote work, or telework) to promote recruitment and retention of personnel

Administrators of AS must
- ensure that all personnel have updated position descriptions
- implement recruitment and selection/hiring strategies that produce a workforce inclusive of under-represented populations
- develop promotion practices that are fair, inclusive, proactive, and non-discriminatory

Personnel responsible for delivery of AS must have written performance goals, objectives, and outcomes for each year's performance cycle to be used to plan, review, and evaluate work and performance. The performance plan must be updated regularly to reflect changes during the performance cycle.

Results of individual personnel evaluations must be used to recognize personnel performance, address performance issues, implement individual and/or collective personnel development and training programs, and inform the assessment of programs and services.

AS personnel, when hired and throughout their employment, must receive appropriate and thorough training.

AS personnel, including student employees and volunteers, must have access to resources or receive specific training on
- institutional policies pertaining to functions or activities they support
- privacy and confidentiality policies
- laws regarding access to student records
- policies and procedures for dealing with sensitive

institutional information

- policies and procedures related to technology used to store or access student records and institutional data
- how and when to refer those in need of additional assistance to qualified personnel and have access to a supervisor for assistance in making these judgments
- systems and technologies necessary to perform their assigned responsibilities
- ethical and legal uses of technology

AS personnel must engage in continuing professional development activities to keep abreast of the research, theories, legislation, policies, and developments that affect their programs and services.

Administrators of AS must ensure that personnel are knowledgeable about and trained in safety, emergency procedures, and crisis prevention and response. Risk management efforts must address identification of threatening conduct or behavior and must incorporate a system for responding to and reporting such behaviors.

AS personnel must be knowledgeable of and trained in safety and emergency procedures for securing and vacating facilities.

PROFESSIONAL PERSONNEL

AS professional personnel either must hold an earned graduate or professional degree in a field relevant to their position or must possess an appropriate combination of educational credentials and related work experience.

INTERNS OR GRADUATE ASSISTANTS

Degree- or credential-seeking interns or graduate assistants must be qualified by enrollment in an appropriate field of study and relevant experience. These students must be trained and supervised by professional personnel who possess applicable educational credentials and work experience and have supervisory experience. Supervisors must be cognizant of the dual roles interns and graduate assistants have as both student and employee.

Supervisors must
- adhere to parameters of students' job descriptions
- articulate intended learning outcomes in student job descriptions
- adhere to agreed-upon work hours and schedules
- offer flexible scheduling when circumstances necessitate

Supervisors and students must both agree to suitable compensation if circumstances necessitate additional hours.

STUDENT EMPLOYEES AND VOLUNTEERS

Student employees and volunteers must be carefully selected, trained, supervised, and evaluated. Students must have access to a supervisor. Student employees and volunteers must be provided clear job descriptions, pre-service training based on assessed needs, and continuing development.

Within the institution, a qualified professional AS staff member must be designated to coordinate the assessment efforts and must work closely with or be responsive to leaders of programs and services.

The number of staff members assigned to assessment efforts should be a function of the size, complexity, and purpose of the institution. Institutions unable to assign a full-time professional staff member should devote a portion of their institutional research program's resources to this effort.

Staff assigned responsibility for assessment should possess effective communication and consultation skills and have an appropriate combination of coursework, training, and experience in the following areas: research methodology, design, and analysis; computer literacy; program planning implementation and evaluation; and human development theory, including the study of student sub-group cultures. When staff members lack adequate knowledge in any of these critical areas, they should seek expertise from appropriate resources.

Part 5. Ethics

Assessment Services (AS) must
- review applicable professional ethical standards and must adopt or develop and implement appropriate statements of ethical practice
- publish and adhere to statements of ethical practice and ensure their periodic review
- orient new personnel to relevant ethical standards and statements of ethical practice and related institutional policies

Statements of ethical standards must
- specify that AS personnel respect privacy and maintain confidentiality in communications and records as delineated by privacy laws
- specify limits on disclosure of information contained in students' records as well as requirements to disclose to appropriate authorities
- address conflicts of interest, or appearance thereof, by personnel in the performance of their work
- reflect the responsibility of personnel to be fair, objective, and impartial in their interactions with others
- reference management of institutional funds
- reference appropriate behavior regarding research and assessment with human participants, confidentiality of research and assessment data, and students' rights and responsibilities
- include the expectation that personnel confront and hold accountable other personnel who exhibit unethical behavior
- address issues surrounding scholarly integrity

AS personnel must

- employ ethical decision making in the performance of their duties
- inform users of programs and services of ethical obligations and limitations emanating from codes and laws or from licensure requirements
- recognize and avoid conflicts of interest that could adversely influence their judgment or objectivity and, when unavoidable, recuse themselves from the situation
- perform their duties within the scope of their position, training, expertise, and competence
- make referrals when issues presented exceed the scope of the position

AS must seek from the institutional review board approval to study human subjects for studies whose findings will be published beyond internal review of the institution. AS must know and adhere to the human subjects policies and procedures of the institution.

AS should seek approval to conduct assessment studies through the institution's human subjects review process.

AS must ensure that the privacy or anonymity of study participants and the confidential nature of data are not breached.

AS must regularly purge identifiable information collected about students and other participants to protect their privacy, consistent with institutional policies and federal guidelines.

AS should maintain raw data for a number of years, based on applicable policy, after the study's written report is completed to respond to subsequent questions. Instances involving research on sensitive topics may require protections such as a Certificate of Confidentiality.

AS must acknowledge methodological limitations of assessment studies.

These limitations could include unrepresentative samples, low response rate, or errors in trying to make decisions from ungeneralizable qualitative findings.

Part 6. Law, Policy, and Governance

Assessment Services (AS) must be in compliance with laws, regulations, and policies that relate to their respective responsibilities and that pose legal obligations, limitations, risks, and liabilities for the institution as a whole. Examples include constitutional, statutory, regulatory, and case law; relevant law and orders emanating from codes and laws; and the institution's policies.

AS must have access to legal advice needed for personnel to carry out their assigned responsibilities.

AS must inform personnel, appropriate officials, and users of programs and services about existing and changing legal obligations, risks and liabilities, and limitations.

AS must inform personnel about professional liability insurance options and refer them to external sources if the institution does not provide coverage.

AS must have written policies and procedures on operations, transactions, or tasks that have legal implications.

AS must regularly review policies. The revision and creation of policies must be informed by best practices, available evidence, and policy issues in higher education.

AS must have procedures and guidelines consistent with institutional policy for responding to threats, emergencies, and crisis situations. Systems and procedures must be in place to disseminate timely and accurate information to students, other members of the institutional community, and appropriate external organizations during emergency situations.

Personnel must neither participate in nor condone any form of harassment or activity that demeans persons or creates an intimidating, hostile, or offensive environment.

AS must purchase or obtain permission to use copyrighted materials and instruments. References to copyrighted materials and instruments must include appropriate citations.

AS must inform personnel about internal and external governance organizations that affect programs and services.

Part 7. Diversity, Equity, and Access

Within the context of each institution's mission and in accordance with institutional policies and applicable codes and laws, Assessment Services (AS) must create and maintain educational and work environments that are welcoming, accessible, inclusive, equitable, and free from harassment.

AS must not discriminate on the basis of disability; age; race; cultural identity; ethnicity; nationality; family educational history (e.g., first generation to attend college); political affiliation; religious affiliation; sex; sexual orientation; gender identity and expression; marital, social, economic, or veteran status; or any other basis included in institutional policies and codes and laws.

AS must

- advocate for sensitivity to multicultural and social justice concerns by the institution and its personnel
- ensure physical, program, and resource access for all constituents
- modify or remove policies, practices, systems, technologies, facilities, and structures that create barriers or produce inequities
- ensure that when facilities and structures cannot be modified, they do not impede access to programs, services, and resources
- establish goals for diversity, equity, and access
- foster communication and practices that enhance

- understanding of identity, culture, self-expression, and heritage
- promote respect for commonalities and differences among people within their historical and cultural contexts
- address the characteristics and needs of diverse constituents when establishing and implementing culturally relevant and inclusive programs, services, policies, procedures, and practices
- provide personnel with diversity, equity, and access training and hold personnel accountable for applying the training to their work
- respond to the needs of all constituents served when establishing hours of operation and developing methods of delivering programs, services, and resources
- recognize the needs of distance and online learning students by directly providing or assisting them to gain access to comparable services and resources

AS must ensure inclusion of persons with disabilities in data collection efforts in compliance with local, state/provincial, and federal guidelines.

AS must design studies and collect data so that potential differential outcomes based on diversity among sub-groups can be explored.

Part 8. Internal and External Relations

Assessment Services (AS) must reach out to individuals, groups, communities, and organizations internal and external to the institution to
- establish, maintain, and promote understanding and effective relations with those that have a significant interest in or potential effect on the students or other constituents served by the programs and services
- garner support and resources for programs and services as defined by the mission
- collaborate in offering or improving programs and services to meet the needs of students and other constituents and to achieve program and student outcomes
- engage diverse individuals, groups, communities, and organizations to enrich the educational environment and experiences of students and other constituents
- disseminate information about the programs and services

Promotional and descriptive information must be accurate and free of deception and misrepresentation.

AS must have procedures and guidelines consistent with institutional policy for
- communicating with the media
- distributing information through print, broadcast, and online sources
- contracting with external organizations for

delivery of programs and services
- cultivating, soliciting, and managing gifts
- applying to and managing funds from grants

AS must adhere to all institutional policies with respect to the communication of student data.

Regular and effective communication systems for the dissemination of results must be established and maintained with academic and administrative offices, institutional governance bodies, and other appropriate constituencies.

Part 9. Financial Resources

Assessment Services (AS) must have funding to accomplish the mission and goals.

In establishing and prioritizing funding resources, AS must conduct comprehensive analyses to determine
- unmet needs of the unit
- relevant expenditures
- external and internal resources
- impact on students and the institution

AS must use the budget as a planning tool to reflect commitment to the mission and goals of the programs and services and of the institution.

AS must administer funds in accordance with established institutional accounting procedures.

AS must demonstrate efficient and effective use and responsible stewardship of fiscal resources consistent with institutional protocols.

Financial resources should be sufficient to support study conceptualization, data collection, data entry and analysis, and the dissemination of assessment and research findings, as well as methodological training for staff.

Financial reports must provide an accurate financial overview of the organization and provide clear, understandable, and timely data upon which personnel can plan and make informed decisions.

Procurement procedures must
- be consistent with institutional policies
- ensure that purchases comply with laws and codes for usability and access
- ensure that the institution receives value for the funds spent
- consider information available for comparing the ethical and environmental impact of products and services purchased

Part 10. Technology

Assessment Services (AS) must have technology to support the achievement of their mission and goals. The technology and its use must comply with institutional policies and procedures and with relevant codes and laws.

AS must use technologies to

- provide updated information regarding mission, location, staffing, programs, services, and official contacts to students and other constituents in accessible formats
- provide an avenue for students and other constituents to communicate sensitive information in a secure format
- enhance the delivery of programs and services for all students

AS must

- back up data on a regular basis
- adhere to institutional policies regarding ethical and legal use of technology
- articulate policies and procedures for protecting the confidentiality and security of information
- implement a replacement plan and cycle for all technology with attention to sustainability
- incorporate accessibility features into technology-based programs and services

When providing student access to technology, AS must

- have policies on the use of technology that are clear, easy to understand, and available to all students
- provide information or referral to support services for those needing assistance in accessing or using technology
- provide instruction or training on how to use the technology
- inform students of implications of misuse of technologies

AS must have access to sufficient data analysis software for efficient data collection, storage, retrieval, and analysis.

Both statistical analysis software and qualitative analysis software should be available.

AS must have timely access to appropriate institutional records.

AS should advocate for integration of institutional databases.

Part 11. Facilities and Equipment

Assessment Services' (AS) facilities must be intentionally designed and located in suitable, accessible, and safe spaces that demonstrate universal design and support the program's mission and goals.

Facilities must be designed to engage various constituents and promote learning.

Personnel must have workspaces that are suitably located and accessible, well equipped, adequate in size, and designed to support their work and responsibilities.

The design of the facilities must guarantee the security and privacy of records and ensure the confidentiality of sensitive information and conversations. Personnel must be able to secure their work.

AS must have sufficient secure storage facilities to maintain materials related to studies.

AS must incorporate sustainable practices in use of facilities and purchase of equipment. Facilities and equipment must be evaluated on an established cycle and be in compliance with codes, laws, and accepted practices for access, health, safety, and security.

When acquiring capital equipment, AS must take into account expenses related to regular maintenance and life cycle costs.

Part 12. Assessment

Assessment Services (AS) must develop assessment plans and processes.

Assessment plans must articulate an ongoing cycle of assessment activities.

AS must

- specify programmatic goals and intended outcomes
- identify student learning and development outcomes
- employ multiple measures and methods
- develop manageable processes for gathering, interpreting, and evaluating data
- document progress toward achievement of goals and outcomes
- interpret and use assessment results to demonstrate accountability
- report aggregated results to respondent groups and stakeholders
- use assessment results to inform planning and decision-making
- assess effectiveness of implemented changes
- provide evidence of improvement of programs and services

AS should model good assessment practices related to its own operations as well as when a assisting other entities within the institution.

AS must employ ethical practices in the assessment process.

Programs and services must have access to adequate fiscal, human, professional development, and technological resources to develop and implement assessment plans.

General Standards revised in 2014;
AS (formerly Outcomes Assessment and Program Evaluation) content developed/revised in 1986, 1997, & 2008

Auxiliary Services Functional Areas
CAS Contextual Statement

Student affairs and auxiliary services are names used to describe multi-functional umbrella organizations that, through a variety of means, address the out-of-classroom needs of students, faculty, staff, and visitors on college and university campuses. Auxiliary services typically encompass functional areas that follow business practices and principles in their service design and provision. Student affairs functional areas are more likely to focus upon student life, personal development, student learning, and well-being. This distinction will vary from campus to campus, and each campus determines the heading under which each student service functional area will exist.

Over the past thirty years, several business processes and structures have been introduced to auxiliary services at colleges and universities and to describe the Auxiliary Services Functional Areas (ASFA). The following terms are among those commonly used:

Vendor. A service provider that has permission to deliver a service, using its own resources, consistent with conditions and parameters set forth by the institution. Examples may include ice cream/hot dog trucks, dry cleaning services, and pizza deliverers.

Outsourced Provider. A service provider that is hired by the institution to fill a specific need. Examples may include transportation services, travel offices, and copy services.

Contracted Provider. An entity contractually assigned to provide a continuous service, usually over multiple years, within detailed specifications, on the premises of the institution. Examples may include bookstores and food services.

Licensor. A branded provider of services who contractually sells rights to the institution for use of their name, products, and/or processes, consistent with the institution's and the licensor's guidelines and standards for providing the service. Examples may include fast food outlets and mail packaging/service shops.

Auxiliary (Ancillary) Service. A service wholly owned by the institution, either directly or through a 501(c) 3 subsidiary, which exists solely to serve the institution's students, faculty, staff, and visitors. Examples may include institutionally operated stores and dining programs.

Self-supporting Service. An institutional service that functions net-neutral, under normal circumstances, but may be called upon from time to time to fill an institutional funding need. Examples may be found within any of the aforementioned classifications of service.

Auxiliary services may include but are not limited to housing, student unions, bookstores, dining services, food courts with nationally recognized brands, conference services, health services, campus card programs, parking/transportation, mail services, telecommunications, cable and internet services, student athletics, campus recreation centers, retail outlets, convenience stores, banking services, computer kiosks, other retail outlets, and contracted services. As with all campus services, the ASFA, through its quality, reliability, and ease of use, is expected to positively impact student recruitment and retention and enhance the life experience of students. Organizationally, although many campuses include the ASFA within student life, it may also report through administrative officers or be structured as a separate division of the institution. ASFA may also be structured independently as a 501(c) 3 auxiliary services corporation. When outsourced companies provide services, the auxiliary services role may be as intermediary between private service providers and the institution.

Today's institutions face decreasing state and federal support, pressure to minimize tuition increases, the need to find alternative sources of revenue, an increasingly diverse student population, and calls to improve undergraduate student learning. Within this context are students and parents who want sophisticated and varied campus services. In general, the ASFA faces declining institutional funding and is expected to generate revenue, offer new services, provide excellent customer service, give exceptional value, and use the best technology to deliver services. In addition to following general standards of practice germane to all functional areas in higher education, it is necessary also that the ASFA follows the best business enterprise standards and guidelines to accomplish its mission.

Although ASFA professionals are concerned with providing quality campus services and funding those services, they are equally concerned with supporting the academic mission of their institutions. Among their many roles, ASFA gives students places to live, eat, buy their textbooks and supplies, recreate, meet, study, attend campus events, socialize, and work on campus. As a major source of on-campus student employment, the ASFA plays an important role in promoting individual student success (Indiana University, 1999).

The CAS Standards and Guidelines for ASFA may be used to assess a multi-functional auxiliary service organization, or they may be used to augment the CAS General Standards in development and revision of standards and guidelines for individual functional areas that are structured as auxiliary services.

References, Readings, and Resources

Indiana University Center for Postsecondary Research. (1999). *National Survey of Student Engagement*. Bloomington. IN, Author.

Contextual Statement Contributors
Jeffrey Pittman, Regent University, NACAS
Pat Perfetto, University of Maryland
Bob Hassmiller, Past NACAS CEO

Auxiliary Services Functional Areas

CAS Standards and Guidelines

Part 1. Mission

Auxiliary Services Functional Areas (ASFA) are multi-functional organizations that address many of the out-of-classroom needs of students, faculty, staff, and visitors on college and university campuses. Typical ASFA follow business practices and principles in their service design, and they operate enterprises that provide goods and services on campus.

ASFA must adhere to ethical, effective, efficient, and sustainable business practices in the provision of relevant, quality, on-campus services that support and enhance the campus environment for students, faculty, staff, and visitors, and provide opportunities for student development.

ASFA must develop, disseminate, implement, and regularly review their missions, which must be consistent with the mission of the institution and with applicable professional standards. The mission must be appropriate for the institution's students and other constituents. Mission statements must reference student learning and development.

Part 2. Program

To achieve their mission, Auxiliary Services Functional Areas (ASFA) must contribute to
- students' formal education, which includes both the curriculum and the co-curriculum
- student progression and timely completion of educational goals
- preparation of students for their careers, citizenship, and lives
- student learning and development

To contribute to student learning and development, ASFA must
- identify relevant and desirable student learning and development outcomes
- articulate how the student learning and development outcomes align with the six CAS student learning and development domains and related dimensions
- assess relevant and desirable student learning and development
- provide evidence of impact on outcomes
- articulate contributions to or support of student learning and development in the domains not specifically assessed
- use evidence gathered to create strategies for improvement of programs and services

STUDENT LEARNING AND DEVELOPMENT
DOMAINS AND DIMENSIONS

Domain: knowledge acquisition, integration, construction, and application
- Dimensions: understanding knowledge from a range of disciplines; connecting knowledge to other knowledge, ideas, and experiences; constructing knowledge; and relating knowledge to daily life

Domain: cognitive complexity
- Dimensions: critical thinking, reflective thinking, effective reasoning, and creativity

Domain: intrapersonal development
- Dimensions: realistic self-appraisal, self-understanding, and self-respect; identity development; commitment to ethics and integrity; and spiritual awareness

Domain: interpersonal competence
- Dimensions: meaningful relationships, interdependence, collaboration, and effective leadership

Domain: humanitarianism and civic engagement
- Dimensions: understanding and appreciation of cultural and human differences, social responsibility, global perspective, and sense of civic responsibility

Domain: practical competence
- Dimensions: pursuing goals, communicating effectively, technical competence, managing personal affairs, managing career development, demonstrating professionalism, maintaining health and wellness, and living a purposeful and satisfying life

[LD Outcomes: See *The Council for the Advancement of Standards Learning and Development Outcomes* statement for examples of outcomes related to these domains and dimensions.]

ASFA must be
- intentionally designed
- guided by theories and knowledge of learning and development
- integrated into the life of the institution
- reflective of developmental and demographic profiles of the student population
- responsive to needs of individuals, populations with distinct needs, and relevant constituencies
- delivered using multiple formats, strategies, and contexts
- designed to provide universal access

ASFA must collaborate with colleagues and departments across the institution to promote student learning and development, persistence, and success.

Auxiliary Services Functional Areas (ASFA) are expected to provide programs that target specific needs; facilities; items for sale that the ASFA and institution consider appropriate to the campus community; support services for students, faculty members, staff, and visitors; administration; information; clearly stated schedules and hours of operation; value; efficiency; and a fair cost structure.

ASFA, in conjunction with appropriate partners, must
- **introduce and orient students to facilities, services, staff members, and functions**
- **educate students on relevant safety, security, and emergency concerns**
- **clearly explain policies, procedures, and expectations**
- **develop an atmosphere conducive to educational pursuits, community, and interpersonal growth, in a safe and non-threatening environment**
- **provide a balanced variety of social, cultural, and intellectual options that is reflective of the diversity of the campus**
- **remain transparent and open to dialogue with customers and stakeholders**

ASFA, in conjunction with appropriate partners, may be expected to
- establish formal relationships and agreements with other campus service units
- collaborate with specific academic and campus units in design and provision of ASFA services
- provide opportunities for student employment, management training, and leadership development
- contribute to the socialization of students
- be self-funding (self-supporting) and contribute financially to the institution
- adhere to generally accepted practices of accounting, audit, and business records management
- function as an ancillary enterprise (separate but in concert with the academic enterprise)
- supervise contract-managed functional areas and services

Part 3. Organization and Leadership

To achieve program and student learning and development outcomes, Auxiliary Services Functional Areas (ASFA) must be purposefully structured for effectiveness. ASFA must have clearly stated and current
- goals and outcomes
- policies and procedures
- responsibilities and performance expectations for personnel
- organizational charts demonstrating clear channels of authority

Leaders must model ethical behavior and institutional citizenship.

Leaders with organizational authority for ASFA must provide strategic planning, management and supervision, and program advancement.

Strategic Planning
- **articulate a vision and mission that drive short- and long-term planning**
- **set goals and objectives based on the needs of the populations served, intended student learning and development outcomes, and program outcomes**
- **facilitate continuous development, implementation, and assessment of program effectiveness and goal attainment congruent with institutional mission and strategic plans**
- **promote environments that provide opportunities for student learning, development, and engagement**
- **develop, adapt, and improve programs and services in response to the changing needs of populations served and evolving institutional priorities**
- **include diverse perspectives to inform decision making**

Management and Supervision
- **plan, allocate, and monitor the use of fiscal, physical, human, intellectual, and technological resources**
- **manage human resource processes including recruitment, selection, professional development, supervision, performance planning, succession planning, evaluation, recognition, and reward**
- **influence others to contribute to the effectiveness and success of the unit**
- **empower professional, support, and student personnel to become effective leaders**
- **encourage and support collaboration with colleagues and departments across the institution**
- **encourage and support scholarly contributions to the profession**
- **identify and address individual, organizational, and environmental conditions that foster or inhibit mission achievement**
- **use current and valid evidence to inform decisions**
- **incorporate sustainability practices in the management and design of programs, services, and facilities**
- **understand appropriate technologies and integrate them into programs and services**
- **be knowledgeable about codes and laws relevant to programs and services and ensure that programs and services meet those requirements**
- **assess and take action to mitigate potential risks**

Program Advancement
- **advocate for and actively promote the mission and goals of the programs and services**
- **inform stakeholders about issues affecting practice**
- **facilitate processes to reach consensus where wide support is needed**
- **advocate for representation in strategic planning initiatives at divisional and institutional levels**

ASFA leaders should provide all employees with guidance on

- using effective and appropriate strategies for communicating with customers and stakeholders
- staying current with student needs, issues, perspectives, and desires
- cultivating and perpetuating relations with all campus departments
- working with student, campus, and academic leaders and organizations
- exercising safety and the safe provision of ASFA programs, goods, and services
- facility maintenance and efficient use of campus facilities, equipment, and financial and human resources
- employing standards, best practices, and processes for budgeting, contracting, purchasing, accounting, reporting, auditing, personnel administration, and record keeping
- establishing and maintaining effective relations with community and business agencies and offices
- promoting equal access to services, programs, and facilities for all students, faculty members, staff, and other customers
- implementing effective practices and responses to trends in the respective ASFA functional area community or industry

ASFA must maintain accurate and current documentation on
- **operational policies and procedures**
- **agreements (e.g., contracts, leases) with outsourced service providers and vendors including good faith agreements and amendments**
- **memoranda of understanding with campus service providers**
- **standards of performance and other expectations of service providers**
- **access provisions for clients and employees with disabilities**
- **day-to-day operations such as fiscal controls, maintenance of physical plant and equipment, provision of services, supervision of personnel, and customer relations**

ASFA must consult with members of the campus community regarding its operations, governance, and programming structure, and the formulation of ASFA policies and procedures.

ASFA, in consultation with students, faculty members, staff, administration, and other constituents, must determine and document facility operating polices, budgets, allocations of funds, employment policies, space allocation, products and services to be offered, and hours of operation.

When these areas of consideration are part of a contractual agreement, it may be necessary to address them within pre-determined review or renewal time frames.

ASFA should be organized to
- deliver successful programs, goods, and services

that are supportive of the institution's mission
- operate its business enterprises effectively and efficiently
- conduct satisfaction surveys, learning outcomes evaluations, and other assessment
- meet or exceed fiscal expectations, consistent with its organizational structure
- maintain its physical plant resources
- exercise enterprising and entrepreneurial leadership in a manner that does not detract from the core mission of the institution

Involvement of the campus community may include students, faculty members, staff, visitors, alumni, and other constituents and stakeholders, as appropriate. Typically such involvement is through advisory, governing, and program boards, committees, or through feedback via surveys and focus groups.

Additional areas for consideration in determining structure and management of the ASFA may include:
- availability and characteristics of facilities
- size, nature, and mission of the institution
- size, scope, proximity, and availability of services in the surrounding community
- ratio of residential to commuter/off-campus student populations
- budget and finance expectations
- institutional philosophy, policies, and preferences concerning outsourcing and privatization
- variety of delivery methods being employed or available to the institution
- degree of integration with academic disciplines and academic service units
- goals of ASFA and its partners

Part 4. Human Resources

Auxiliary Services Functional Areas (ASFA) must be staffed adequately by individuals qualified to accomplish mission and goals.

ASFA must have access to technical and support personnel adequate to accomplish their mission.

Within institutional guidelines, ASFA must
- **establish procedures for personnel recruitment and selection, training, performance planning, and evaluation**
- **set expectations for supervision and performance**
- **provide personnel access to continuing and advanced education and appropriate professional development opportunities to improve their competence, skills, and leadership capacity**
- **consider work/life options available to personnel (e.g., compressed work schedules, flextime, job sharing, remote work, or telework) to promote recruitment and retention of personnel**

Administrators of ASFA must
- **ensure that all personnel have updated position**

descriptions
- implement recruitment and selection/hiring strategies that produce a workforce inclusive of under-represented populations
- develop promotion practices that are fair, inclusive, proactive, and non-discriminatory

Personnel responsible for delivery of ASFA must have written performance goals, objectives, and outcomes for each year's performance cycle to be used to plan, review, and evaluate work and performance. The performance plan must be updated regularly to reflect changes during the performance cycle.

Results of individual personnel evaluations must be used to recognize personnel performance, address performance issues, implement individual and/or collective personnel development and training programs, and inform the assessment of programs and services.

ASFA personnel, when hired and throughout their employment, must receive appropriate and thorough training.

ASFA personnel, including student employees and volunteers, must have access to resources or receive specific training on
- institutional policies pertaining to functions or activities they support
- privacy and confidentiality policies
- laws regarding access to student records
- policies and procedures for dealing with sensitive institutional information
- policies and procedures related to technology used to store or access student records and institutional data
- how and when to refer those in need of additional assistance to qualified personnel and have access to a supervisor for assistance in making these judgments
- systems and technologies necessary to perform their assigned responsibilities
- ethical and legal uses of technology

ASFA personnel must engage in continuing professional development activities to keep abreast of the research, theories, legislation, policies, and developments that affect their programs and services.

Administrators of ASFA must ensure that personnel are knowledgeable about and trained in safety, emergency procedures, and crisis prevention and response. Risk management efforts must address identification of threatening conduct or behavior and must incorporate a system for responding to and reporting such behaviors.

ASFA personnel must be knowledgeable of and trained in safety and emergency procedures for securing and vacating facilities.

PROFESSIONAL PERSONNEL

ASFA professional personnel either must hold an earned graduate or professional degree in a field relevant to their position or must possess an appropriate combination of educational credentials and related work experience.

INTERNS OR GRADUATE ASSISTANTS

Degree- or credential-seeking interns or graduate assistants must be qualified by enrollment in an appropriate field of study and relevant experience. These students must be trained and supervised by professional personnel who possess applicable educational credentials and work experience and have supervisory experience. Supervisors must be cognizant of the dual roles interns and graduate assistants have as both student and employee.

Supervisors must
- adhere to parameters of students' job descriptions
- articulate intended learning outcomes in student job descriptions
- adhere to agreed-upon work hours and schedules
- offer flexible scheduling when circumstances necessitate

Supervisors and students must both agree to suitable compensation if circumstances necessitate additional hours.

STUDENT EMPLOYEES AND VOLUNTEERS

Student employees and volunteers must be carefully selected, trained, supervised, and evaluated. Students must have access to a supervisor. Student employees and volunteers must be provided clear job descriptions, pre-service training based on assessed needs, and continuing development.

Staff must include persons reasonably capable of providing temporary oversight for entire units as well as their specialty, should the need require it.

Staff members must have technical skills, training, and experience pertinent to their work.

All ASFA staff members must understand and comply with financial, legal, personnel, and safety laws, regulations, and policies, as they relate to the core function of their unit.

Administrators in charge of ASFA and facilities must have appropriate education, experience, and credentials to adequately and safely provide a level of management consistent with industry standards and institutional expectations.

ASFA staff members must be knowledgeable about programs, goods, and services offered directly.

ASFA staff members should be familiar with related services offered by other campus agencies.

In addition to providing fair wages, ASFA should treat student employment as an important part of a student's education and intentionally incorporate career-related skills, training, and professional responsibilities into the employment experience.

ASFA should provide living wages to all employees.

A thorough job training program should be provided for all employees and volunteers and should include leadership and personal development opportunities.

ASFA staff members should strive to develop and maintain staff relations in a climate of mutual respect, support, trust, and interdependence. Recognizing the strengths and limitations of each professional staff member, professional development opportunities should be regularly made available, consistent with needs and budgets.

Relationships between ASFA and their shareholders will depend heavily on the effectiveness, cooperation, support, and behavior of front line service personnel. Training should be closely supervised and monitored, and current industry practices should be evident in service processes, standards, and evaluation.

Desirable qualities of ASFA staff members should include
- knowledge of and ability to use management and leadership principles
- ability to train, influence, supervise, and evaluate student employees and volunteers, particularly at entry levels
- experience in assessment and planning
- interpersonal skills applicable to a variety of cultures
- ability to explain the ASFA mission and articulate the program's relationship to the mission of the institution
- knowledge of and ability to apply student development and learning theories

Desirable qualities of staff members may include
- technical proficiency certification
- knowledge of environmental and industry trends
- effective professional communication and presentation skills
- attributes necessary to meet job-related physical requirements

Part 5. Ethics

Auxiliary Services Functional Areas (ASFA) must
- **review applicable professional ethical standards and must adopt or develop and implement appropriate statements of ethical practice**
- **publish and adhere to statements of ethical practice and ensure their periodic review**
- **orient new personnel to relevant ethical standards and statements of ethical practice and related institutional policies**

Statements of ethical standards must
- **specify that ASFA personnel respect privacy and maintain confidentiality in communications and records as delineated by privacy laws**
- **specify limits on disclosure of information contained in students' records as well as requirements to disclose to appropriate authorities**
- **address conflicts of interest, or appearance thereof,**

by personnel in the performance of their work
- **reflect the responsibility of personnel to be fair, objective, and impartial in their interactions with others**
- **reference management of institutional funds**
- **reference appropriate behavior regarding research and assessment with human participants, confidentiality of research and assessment data, and students' rights and responsibilities**
- **include the expectation that personnel confront and hold accountable other personnel who exhibit unethical behavior**
- **address issues surrounding scholarly integrity**

ASFA personnel must
- **employ ethical decision making in the performance of their duties**
- **inform users of programs and services of ethical obligations and limitations emanating from codes and laws or from licensure requirements**
- **recognize and avoid conflicts of interest that could adversely influence their judgment or objectivity and, when unavoidable, recuse themselves from the situation**
- **perform their duties within the scope of their position, training, expertise, and competence**
- **make referrals when issues presented exceed the scope of the position**

Marketing and advertising, when conducted, must be informative, accurate, respectful, non-deceptive, and useful to students, faculty members, staff, and visitors.

Private information disclosed by clients, students, faculty members, staff, and visitors in the course of conducting business (e.g., credit card information, medical conditions) must be treated as confidential unless clearly indicated otherwise by the person providing it.

ASFA representatives must not accept gifts from those who seek to do business or who intend to bid on contracts.

They should avoid activities that give the appearance of favoritism or advantage to any entity seeking to do business with ASFA.

Ethical standards of relevant professional associations should be considered.

ASFA should consider the ethical standards and expectations of suppliers and contractors with whom they do business.

Each ASFA staff member should respect students as individuals, each with rights and responsibilities, each with goals and needs, and with this in mind, should seek to create and maintain environments that enhance learning and personal development.

ASFA should exercise professionalism, expertise, and care in the development and handling of requests for proposals, bids, and contracts related to purchases, lease agreements, contractual service agreements, and any agreement that affects students and/or the institution.

Part 6. Law, Policy, and Governance

Auxiliary Services Functional Areas (ASFA) must be in compliance with laws, regulations, and policies that relate to their respective responsibilities and that pose legal obligations, limitations, risks, and liabilities for the institution as a whole. Examples include constitutional, statutory, regulatory, and case law; relevant law and orders emanating from codes and laws; and the institution's policies.

ASFA must have access to legal advice needed for personnel to carry out their assigned responsibilities.

ASFA must inform personnel, appropriate officials, and users of programs and services about existing and changing legal obligations, risks and liabilities, and limitations.

ASFA must inform personnel about professional liability insurance options and refer them to external sources if the institution does not provide coverage.

ASFA must have written policies and procedures on operations, transactions, or tasks that have legal implications.

ASFA must regularly review policies. The revision and creation of policies must be informed by best practices, available evidence, and policy issues in higher education.

ASFA must have procedures and guidelines consistent with institutional policy for responding to threats, emergencies, and crisis situations. Systems and procedures must be in place to disseminate timely and accurate information to students, other members of the institutional community, and appropriate external organizations during emergency situations.

Personnel must neither participate in nor condone any form of harassment or activity that demeans persons or creates an intimidating, hostile, or offensive environment.

ASFA must purchase or obtain permission to use copyrighted materials and instruments. References to copyrighted materials and instruments must include appropriate citations.

ASFA must inform personnel about internal and external governance organizations that affect programs and services.

ASFA leaders must have specific knowledge of legal issues and requirements that apply to functional areas under their control.

ASFA must continually monitor liability for potentially harmful, wrongful, or negligent activities and situations.

ASFA professionals must be aware of and understand due process, employment procedures, equal opportunity, civil rights, and liberties.

ASFA may be required to carry insurance if not sufficiently covered under the institution's policy.

Part 7. Diversity, Equity, and Access

Within the context of each institution's mission and in accordance with institutional policies and applicable codes and laws, Auxiliary Services Functional Areas (ASFA) must create and maintain educational and work environments that are welcoming, accessible, inclusive, equitable, and free from harassment.

ASFA must not discriminate on the basis of disability; age; race; cultural identity; ethnicity; nationality; family educational history (e.g., first generation to attend college); political affiliation; religious affiliation; sex; sexual orientation; gender identity and expression; marital, social, economic, or veteran status; or any other basis included in institutional policies and codes and laws.

ASFA must

- advocate for sensitivity to multicultural and social justice concerns by the institution and its personnel
- ensure physical, program, and resource access for all constituents
- modify or remove policies, practices, systems, technologies, facilities, and structures that create barriers or produce inequities
- ensure that when facilities and structures cannot be modified, they do not impede access to programs, services, and resources
- establish goals for diversity, equity, and access
- foster communication and practices that enhance understanding of identity, culture, self-expression, and heritage
- promote respect for commonalities and differences among people within their historical and cultural contexts
- address the characteristics and needs of diverse constituents when establishing and implementing culturally relevant and inclusive programs, services, policies, procedures, and practices
- provide personnel with diversity, equity, and access training and hold personnel accountable for applying the training to their work
- respond to the needs of all constituents served when establishing hours of operation and developing methods of delivering programs, services, and resources
- recognize the needs of distance and online learning students by directly providing or assisting them to gain access to comparable services and resources

ASFA should provide services and information through a variety of appropriate formats including web sites, e-mail, walk-ins during office hours, telephone, individual appointments, and customer service systems.

ASFA should ensure that services provided through third

parties are offered on a fair and equitable basis and in a manner consistent with the mission of the institution.

ASFA may provide manuals, instructions, policies, signs, and training, in one or more languages in addition to English for predominant groups of employees who speak a language other than English.

All institutional units and contractors that provide services to students must share responsibility for meeting the needs of the wide variety of students on campus. Coordinated efforts to promote multicultural sensitivity and the elimination of prejudicial behaviors in all functional areas on campus must be encouraged.

ASFA should make reasonable effort to address and educate the campus community concerning cultural, religious, racial, socioeconomic, and other aspects of identity that are unique to ASFA services, such as food, holiday recognition, and products offered for sale.

Outsourced programs and services are accountable to the institution. As such, a diversity liaison should exist within each outsourced ASFA to help ensure that a diverse workplace and environment exist, consistent with the goals of the institution.

Part 8. Internal and External Relations

Auxiliary Services Functional Areas (ASFA) must reach out to individuals, groups, communities, and organizations internal and external to the institution to
- **establish, maintain, and promote understanding and effective relations with those that have a significant interest in or potential effect on the students or other constituents served by the programs and services**
- **garner support and resources for programs and services as defined by the mission**
- **collaborate in offering or improving programs and services to meet the needs of students and other constituents and to achieve program and student outcomes**
- **engage diverse individuals, groups, communities, and organizations to enrich the educational environment and experiences of students and other constituents**
- **disseminate information about the programs and services**

Promotional and descriptive information must be accurate and free of deception and misrepresentation.

ASFA must have procedures and guidelines consistent with institutional policy for
- **communicating with the media**
- **distributing information through print, broadcast, and online sources**
- **contracting with external organizations for delivery of programs and services**
- **cultivating, soliciting, and managing gifts**
- **applying to and managing funds from grants**

When services are managed by outside contractors, processes must be in place to ensure that administration of the services remains the responsibility of the institution.

ASFA should share information, initiate and promote program opportunities, encourage staff development, and enhance ASFA program visibility by
- establishing cooperative relationships with procurement, student affairs, and academic departments, and direct service providers such as campus programs, alumni, parking, visitor services, libraries, bookstore, enrollment management, athletics, institutional advancement, campus information, and visitor services
- encouraging staff participation in civic and community organizations such as Rotary, Kiwanis, and Chamber of Commerce as well as involvement in ASFA professional associations
- nurturing cooperative relationships with local, state/provincial, and federal governmental entities

ASFA should adhere to institution-wide processes that systematically involve academic affairs, student affairs, and administrative units such as police, physical plant, and business offices.

ASFA should collaborate with campus agencies, as appropriate, and meet regularly with other service providers to coordinate schedules and facility use and to review services and activities under development.

ASFA should serve as a resource to the campus and community by providing professional advice on market demand, development of new auxiliary services, related business issues, and current industry activities.

ASFA should value marketing as a core function for education about, and promotion of, equal access to ASFA products and services by all constituent groups.

ASFA should provide quality customer service to all constituents and ensure they are fairly represented on ASFA governing and advisory boards.

Students should be the principal beneficiaries of ASFA, although outreach should include all constituents, including faculty members, staff, alumni, visitors, members of the community, and others.

Student government and similar groups should have ongoing involvement with ASFA and their operations.

Student publications and electronic media should be used for communicating information about ASFA.

Relationships among campus administrative staff and employees/representatives of outside contractors should be cultivated and supervised carefully.

Relations with contract service providers should receive close and frequent attention and review. Assessment of these services should be collaborative and continuous.

ASFA should foster partnerships that engage and involve campus and contract service providers in all segments of the campus community.

ASFA should foster initiatives that ensure all service providers become stakeholders in advancing the mission of the institution.

Part 9. Financial Resources

Auxiliary Services Functional Areas (ASFA) must have funding to accomplish the mission and goals.

In establishing and prioritizing funding resources, ASFA must conduct comprehensive analyses to determine
- **unmet needs of the unit**
- **relevant expenditures**
- **external and internal resources**
- **impact on students and the institution**

ASFA must use the budget as a planning tool to reflect commitment to the mission and goals of the programs and services and of the institution.

ASFA must administer funds in accordance with established institutional accounting procedures.

ASFA must demonstrate efficient and effective use and responsible stewardship of fiscal resources consistent with institutional protocols.

Financial reports must provide an accurate financial overview of the organization and provide clear, understandable, and timely data upon which personnel can plan and make informed decisions.

Procurement procedures must
- **be consistent with institutional policies**
- **ensure that purchases comply with laws and codes for usability and access**
- **ensure that the institution receives value for the funds spent**
- **consider information available for comparing the ethical and environmental impact of products and services purchased**

Funds to support the ASFA, insofar as it is possible and desirable, should be generated from pricing set at fair market rates.

For self-support programs
- when net operating income is achieved, ASFA should establish operating reserve funds as a buffer against future shortfalls and capital reserve funds for facilities renewal
- when lower than expected revenue in any one-year results in a deficit, ASFA should access reserve funds to offset the deficit

Financial planning and projections should include budget data for both current and long-term expenditures, including capital expenditures and deferred maintenance costs.

A program of asset management should be in place so that resources are adequate for meeting future repair and replacement requirements for key equipment and facilities.

ASFA should underwrite a fair proportion of overhead costs associated with shared services that support the entire campus.

The institution's budget commitment to ASFA should be sufficient to achieve its mission and to provide appropriate services, facilities, and programs deemed necessary to maintain standards and diversity of programs, goods, and services, commensurate with the organizational structure, aspirations, image, and the reputation of the institution.

ASFA should maintain adequate financial resources to ensure reasonable pricing of services, adequate programming, staffing, proper maintenance, and professional development.

ASFA may be expected to fund specific campus needs and contribute to the general fund.

Part 10. Technology

Auxiliary Services Functional Areas (ASFA) must have technology to support the achievement of their mission and goals. The technology and its use must comply with institutional policies and procedures and with relevant codes and laws.

ASFA should use current and appropriate technology to facilitate, improve, assess, and extend access to its programs, products, services, and facilities.

ASFA must use technologies to
- **provide updated information regarding mission, location, staffing, programs, services, and official contacts to students and other constituents in accessible formats**
- **provide an avenue for students and other constituents to communicate sensitive information in a secure format**
- **enhance the delivery of programs and services for all students**

ASFA must
- **back up data on a regular basis**
- **adhere to institutional policies regarding ethical and legal use of technology**
- **articulate policies and procedures for protecting the confidentiality and security of information**
- **implement a replacement plan and cycle for all technology with attention to sustainability**
- **incorporate accessibility features into technology-based programs and services**

When providing student access to technology, ASFA must
- **have policies on the use of technology that are clear, easy to understand, and available to all students**
- **provide information or referral to support services for those needing assistance in accessing or using technology**
- **provide instruction or training on how to use the**

technology
- inform students of implications of misuse of technologies

Part 11. Facilities and Equipment

Auxiliary Services Functional Areas' (ASFA) facilities must be intentionally designed and located in suitable, accessible, and safe spaces that demonstrate universal design and support the program's mission and goals.

Facilities must be designed to engage various constituents and promote learning.

Personnel must have workspaces that are suitably located and accessible, well equipped, adequate in size, and designed to support their work and responsibilities.

The design of the facilities must guarantee the security and privacy of records and ensure the confidentiality of sensitive information and conversations. Personnel must be able to secure their work.

ASFA must incorporate sustainable practices in use of facilities and purchase of equipment. Facilities and equipment must be evaluated on an established cycle and be in compliance with codes, laws, and accepted practices for access, health, safety, and security.

When acquiring capital equipment, ASFA must take into account expenses related to regular maintenance and life cycle costs.

ASFA must periodically review and evaluate equipment and facilities to assess current and future needs.

Regularly scheduled cleaning of public areas must be provided, and grounds associated with ASFA facilities, which may include streets, paved walks, and parking lots, must be clean and well maintained.

Recycling, energy conservation, and sustainability efforts must be implemented throughout the ASFA and be compliant with institutional guidelines, government regulations, and contractual agreements.

ASFA facilities may include retail outlets; dining centers; vending operations; restaurants; residences; recreation and athletic facilities; event venues; office buildings; parking lots and transportation structures; manufacturing and production operations; maintenance shops; and shipping, receiving, and storage centers.

ASFA facilities should be sufficient to meet the needs of the program, consistent with agreements among institutional and community agencies and with students.

Size of facilities should comply with minimum effective service standards established by appropriate professional organizations for each functional area.

Facilities should be accessible, clean, reasonably priced, appropriately designed, well maintained, and have adequate safety and security features.

Facilities with multi-use capability, such as dining rooms and lounges, should be available for campus events and programs at times when they are not needed to support ASFA functions.

New construction projects should be responsive to the current and future needs of the campus community. Decisions about new construction should be based upon clearly defined needs and consistent with the mission of the institution, which may include adherence to institutional standards for sustainability.

Maintenance and renovation programs should be implemented in all operations and should include:
- preventive maintenance and audit procedures to ensure physical safety
- replacement reserves
- timely repair of equipment, vehicles, facilities, and building systems
- modifications to facilities and systems to keep them attractive, effective, efficient, and safe
- sustainable designs and practices whenever feasible

Systematically planned replacement cycles should exist for furnishings, mechanical and electrical systems, maintenance equipment, floor/wall/window treatments, and serving/point of service equipment.

The institution should be reimbursed for campus services, facilities, technology, and equipment that are used to support ASFA.

ASFA should monitor their impact on the community surrounding the campus and should work to maintain amicable relationships with affected non-university entities.

Part 12. Assessment

Auxiliary Services Functional Areas (ASFA) must develop assessment plans and processes.

Assessment plans must articulate an ongoing cycle of assessment activities.

ASFA must
- specify programmatic goals and intended outcomes
- identify student learning and development outcomes
- employ multiple measures and methods
- develop manageable processes for gathering, interpreting, and evaluating data
- document progress toward achievement of goals and outcomes
- interpret and use assessment results to demonstrate accountability
- report aggregated results to respondent groups and stakeholders
- use assessment results to inform planning and decision-making
- assess effectiveness of implemented changes
- provide evidence of improvement of programs and services

Cost analysis and market research must be conducted at

least annually when setting fees for goods and services to be offered to students, faculty members, and staff.

ASFA must maintain accurate and current documentation on program data such as usage rates, peak times of usage, learning outcomes, sales and revenue, student satisfaction, and value contribution.

Both internal and external evaluations and assessments should be encouraged.

Periodic reports, statistically valid research, outside reviews, and other tools measuring student needs and opinions should be utilized.

ASFA should collaborate with institutional research units to generate data that could be useful, such as in projecting contributions to the local economy, increasing student enrollment, or stimulating research.

A representative cross-section of qualified people from campus communities should be involved in reviewing ASFA.

ASFA should generate and disseminate an annual report identifying overall goals, program data, changes in services provided, financial contributions, regular feedback from participants, and opportunities that contribute to the overall effectiveness and quality of the institution.

ASFA must employ ethical practices in the assessment process.

ASFA must have access to adequate fiscal, human, professional development, and technological resources to develop and implement assessment plans.

General Standards revised in 2014;
ASFA content developed in 2007

Campus Activities Programs
CAS Contextual Statement

One of the first noted formal campus organizations established for the purpose of bringing students together, primarily for debating important issues of the day, was the Oxford Union founded in 1823. The Union's clubs also provided educational opportunities beyond the classroom through such group activities as discussions of literature and poetry and involvement in hobbies and recreational activities. Today, numerous clubs and organizations (hundreds on some campuses) offer students opportunities to learn through their involvement in campus life. There is little debate now that the collegiate experience involves what occurs outside the classroom and that a college education includes more than what goes on in the classroom.

Campus activities describes in part the combined efforts of clubs and organizations established for and/or by students, including, but not limited to, governance, leadership, service, cultural, social, diversity, recreational, artistic, political and religious activities. Many of these efforts focus on programs that serve to educate, develop, or entertain club, organization, or group members, their guests, and the campus community.

Theory of involvement contends that the amount of energy—both physical and psychological—that students expend at their institution positively affects their development during college. Studies indicate that students who are involved in campus life devote considerable energy to their academic programs, spend considerable time on campus, participate actively in student organizations, and interact frequently with other students (Astin, 1996; Kuh, Douglas, Lund, Ramin-Gyurmek, 1994). The campus activities program is one of the vehicles for involving students with the institution.

Although students' efforts are the backbone of campus activities, campus activity advisors serve as the catalysts for these efforts. They plan and implement training for student leaders and group members to assist them in attaining their goals, primarily regarding working with others; provide continuity for student clubs and organizations from year to year; educate students about institution policy, related legal matters, and fiscal responsibility; mediate conflicts between individuals and groups; encourage innovation and responsibility in program implementation; provide opportunities to practice leadership and organizational skills; integrate knowledge gained in the classroom with actual practice; and instruct about ethics, diversity, and other critical values.

The role of campus activity advisors is certainly linked to the quality of a student's involvement experience and thus a student's development. The CAS Standards and Guidelines that follow offer direction for campus activity advisors to create quality campus activity programs that are engaging, developmental, and experiential.

References, Readings, and Resources

ACPA—College Student Educators International (ACPA): http://www.myacpa.org

Association of College Unions International (ACUI): www.acui.org

Astin, A. W. (1996a). Involvement in learning revisited: Lessons we have learned. *Journal of College Student Development, 37,* 123-134.

Boatman, S. (1997). Leadership programs in campus activities. *The management of campus activities.* Columbia, SC: National Association of Campus Activities Education Foundation.

Cuyjet, M. J. (1996). Program development and group advising. In S. R. Komives & D. B. Woodward, Jr. (Eds.), *Student services: A handbook for the profession* (3rd ed., pp. 397-414). San Francisco, CA: Jossey-Bass.

Julian, F. (1997). Law and campus life. *The management of student activities.* Columbia, SC: National Association for Campus Activities.

Kuh, G. D., Douglas, K. B., Lund, J. P., & Ramin-Gyurmek, J. (1994). *Student learning outside the classroom: Transcending artificial boundaries.* ASHE-ERIC Higher Education Report No. 8, Washington, DC: The George Washington University, Graduate School of Education and Human Development.

Meabon, D., Krehbiel, L., & Suddick, D. (1996). Financing campus activities. *The management of student activities.* Columbia, SC: National Association for Campus Activities.

Metz, N. D. (1996). *Student development in college unions and student activities.* Bloomington, IN: Association of College Unions International.

National Association for College Activities (NACA): http://www.naca.org

Nejman, M. R. (1995). *Diversity, student activities, and their roles in community colleges: Developing an effective program to achieve unity through diversity.* Columbia, SC: National Association for Campus Activities.

Roberts, D. C. (2003). Community building and programming. In S. R. Komives & D. B. Woodard (Eds.), *Student Services: A handbook for the profession* (4th ed.) (pp. 539-554). San Francisco, CA: Jossey-Bass.

Skipper, T. L., & Argo, R. (Eds.). (2003). *Involvement in campus activities and the retention of first-year college students.* Columbia, SC: National Resource Center for the First-Year Experience & Students in Transition and National Association of Campus Activities.

Contextual Statement Contributors
Current Edition:
Jan Arminio, George Mason University, NACA

Previous Editions:
Jan Arminio, Shippensburg University, NACA

Campus Activities Programs
CAS Standards and Guidelines

Part 1. Mission

The purpose of Campus Activities Programs (CAP) must be to enhance the overall educational experience of students through development of, exposure to, and participation in programs and activities that improve student cooperation and leadership while preparing students to be responsible advocates and citizens and complementing the institution's academic programs.

These activities could be intellectual, social, recreational, cultural, multicultural, and spiritual in nature. Programs could pertain to leadership, governance, community service, healthy lifestyles, and organizational development.

CAP must develop, disseminate, implement, and regularly review their missions, which must be consistent with the mission of the institution and with applicable professional standards. The mission must be appropriate for the institution's students and other constituents. Mission statements must reference student learning and development.

CAP must provide opportunities for students to
- participate in co-curricular activities
- participate in campus governance
- advocate for their organizations and interests
- develop leadership abilities
- develop healthy interpersonal relationships
- use leisure time purposefully
- develop ethical decision-making skills
- advocate for student organizations and interests

Part 2. Program

To achieve their mission, Campus Activities Programs (CAP) must contribute to
- students' formal education, which includes both the curriculum and the co-curriculum
- student progression and timely completion of educational goals
- preparation of students for their careers, citizenship, and lives
- student learning and development

To contribute to student learning and development, CAP must
- identify relevant and desirable student learning and development outcomes
- articulate how the student learning and development outcomes align with the six CAS student learning and development domains and related dimensions
- assess relevant and desirable student learning and development
- provide evidence of impact on outcomes
- articulate contributions to or support of student

learning and development in the domains not specifically assessed
- use evidence gathered to create strategies for improvement of programs and services

STUDENT LEARNING AND DEVELOPMENT DOMAINS AND DIMENSIONS

Domain: knowledge acquisition, integration, construction, and application
- **Dimensions: understanding knowledge from a range of disciplines; connecting knowledge to other knowledge, ideas, and experiences; constructing knowledge; and relating knowledge to daily life**

Domain: cognitive complexity
- **Dimensions: critical thinking, reflective thinking, effective reasoning, and creativity**

Domain: intrapersonal development
- **Dimensions: realistic self-appraisal, self-understanding, and self-respect; identity development; commitment to ethics and integrity; and spiritual awareness**

Domain: interpersonal competence
- **Dimensions: meaningful relationships, interdependence, collaboration, and effective leadership**

Domain: humanitarianism and civic engagement
- **Dimensions: understanding and appreciation of cultural and human differences, social responsibility, global perspective, and sense of civic responsibility**

Domain: practical competence
- **Dimensions: pursuing goals, communicating effectively, technical competence, managing personal affairs, managing career development, demonstrating professionalism, maintaining health and wellness, and living a purposeful and satisfying life**

[LD Outcomes: See *The Council for the Advancement of Standards Learning and Development Outcomes* statement for examples of outcomes related to these domains and dimensions.]

CAP must be
- intentionally designed
- guided by theories and knowledge of learning and development
- integrated into the life of the institution
- reflective of developmental and demographic profiles of the student population
- responsive to needs of individuals, populations with distinct needs, and relevant constituencies

- delivered using multiple formats, strategies, and contexts
- designed to provide universal access

CAP must collaborate with colleagues and departments across the institution to promote student learning and development, persistence, and success.

CAP must be comprehensive and reflect and promote the diversity of student interests and needs, allowing especially for the achievement of a sense of self-esteem and community pride.

A comprehensive CAP program should include offerings that vary in type, size, scheduling, and cost.

CAP must be of broad scope, inclusive of all educational domains for student learning and development.

Programs should include activities that
- complement classroom instruction and academic learning
- offer instruction and experience in leadership and working in groups
- promote physical and psychosocial wellbeing
- promote understanding of and interaction with people of one's own culture and other cultures
- foster meaningful interactions between students and members of the faculty, staff, and administration
- build specific group communities and identity with the campus community

CAP must offer and encourage student participation in student-led campus activities.

Additional encouragement can come from club advisors, faculty members, staff, parents, peers, administrators, and others.

CAP should create environments in which students can
- explore activities in individual and group settings for self-understanding and growth
- learn about diverse cultures and experiences
- explore ideas and issues through the arts
- design and implement programs to enhance social, cultural, multicultural, social justice, intellectual, recreational, service, and campus governance involvement
- comprehend institutional policies and procedures and their relationship to individual and group interests and activities
- learn of and use campus facilities and other resources
- plan, market, implement, and assess programs

CAP should enhance the retention and graduation of students and strengthen campus and community relations. Programs and events should be planned and implemented collaboratively by students, professional staff, and faculty members.

CAP must ensure that the institution has a policy for the registration and recognition of student organizations.

CAP must include these fundamental functions: implementing campus programs that add vibrancy to the campus, advising student organizations that implement programs or services, advising student governing organizations, ensuring the proper and efficient stewardship of funds including the student activity fee and institutional allocation, and implementing training, development, and educational opportunities.

Programs may evolve from CAP office or from student organizations and student governing bodies and should add richness to the institution and its integral functions. The CAP should strive to build student institutional loyalty and allegiance while promoting citizenship and civility.

Student and student organizations' awards programs should be based on fair and equitable criteria.

These functions may be achieved directly or in collaboration or consultation with other campus entities.

Programs sponsored by CAP must be produced and promoted according to professional and institutional practices and protocols.

Promotion methods CAP may use include the creation and dissemination, either in print or on-line, of activities calendars, organizational directories, student handbooks, and programming and financial management guides.

Entertainment programs should
- reflect the values stated in the institution and CAP mission statements
- maintain admission fees at levels that encourage widespread student attendance
- implement hospitality requirements that prohibit the provision of alcohol to entertainers where appropriate
- include a constituency-based advisory system for activities planning, implementation, and evaluation, to ensure coordination within the larger campus academic calendar

Contracts must be signed by an appropriate authority identified by institutional policies and procedures.

CAP should provide guidance and training that enables students to recruit, negotiate with, and select performers.

Advising

CAP must provide effective administrative support for student organizations. Every student organization must have an advisor. The criteria for who may serve as an advisor and the role and responsibilities of advisors must be defined by the institution.

Responsibilities of advisors can include attending organization meetings, meeting with organization officers as a group or individually, overseeing budget and financial transactions, serving as an advocate for the organization, serving as a liaison between the institution and students, assisting the organization in problem-solving, and overseeing the election and/or appointment of new officers. Advising can take place through face-to-face meetings or via telephone, email, instant messaging, or other communication methods.

Advisors should be institutional faculty members, staff, or graduate student employees.

Advisors must be knowledgeable of legal issues and institutional policies, especially regarding risk management.

CAP must provide information and training opportunities for advisors.

CAP staff should be available to provide oversight and to consult and problem-solve with advisors. Advisors who volunteer their time should be recognized by the institution for their contributions.

Advisors should
- be knowledgeable of student development theory and philosophy to appropriately support students and also to encourage learning and development.
- have adaptive advising styles in order to be able to work with students with a variety of skill and knowledge levels
- have interest in the students involved in the organization
- have expertise in the topic for which the student group is engaged
- understand organizational development processes and team building

Student Governance
Student governance groups must have a written mission, purpose, and process for continuity of leadership that is regularly reviewed. Criteria for student involvement must be clear, widely publicized, easily accessible, and consistently followed. Budgeting and fiscal procedures must be clearly defined and must follow all applicable laws. Clearly defined grievance procedures must exist to settle disagreements regarding continuity of leadership, budgeting procedures, and ethics violations by student leaders.

Student governance groups could include undergraduate and graduate student government associations, residence hall associations, campus center governing boards, sports club councils, fraternity and sorority governance councils, media boards, and college councils.

Student governance groups must be encouraged to operate in accordance with institutional values, mission, and policies, and be informed of possible consequences for failure to do so.

Student governance groups may conduct a wide variety of activities and services, including executive, judicial, legislative, business or service functions, and educational or entertainment programming.

Institutions must have policies and procedures for providing an advisor to student governance organizations.

Training, Education, and Development
CAP must ensure that there are training, education, and development opportunities for students involved in student organizations.

Many CAP are responsible for the training, education, and development of students who are involved in student organizations. As outlined in the CAS Standards for Student Leadership Programs, training involves those activities designed to prepare students to assume leadership positions, improve performance of the individual in the role presently occupied, and enhance participants' knowledge and understanding of specific leadership theories, concepts, models, and institutional policies and procedures needed to work effectively. Successful developmental opportunities often occur in an environment that empowers students to mature and develop toward greater levels of leadership complexity.

CAP training, education, and development activities must be delivered by a diverse range of faculty members, students, and staff, using diverse pedagogies, and take place in a variety of ways.

Training, education, and development activities may take the form of retreats; one-on-one conversations; manuals, handbooks, and other publications; workshops and conferences; seminars; mentoring; and for-credit courses.

CAP training, education, and development opportunities must take into account differing student developmental levels.

Students should be trained in leadership concepts and skills, organizational development, ethical behavior, and other skills particular to distinctive programming requirements, such as contracting for entertainment.

Additional information on leadership programs for students can be found in the CAS Student Leadership Programs standards and guidelines.

Part 3. Organization and Leadership

To achieve program and student learning and development outcomes, Campus Activities Programs (CAP) must be purposefully structured for effectiveness. CAP must have clearly stated and current
- **goals and outcomes**
- **policies and procedures**
- **responsibilities and performance expectations for personnel**
- **organizational charts demonstrating clear channels of authority**

Leaders must model ethical behavior and institutional citizenship.

Leaders with organizational authority for CAP must provide strategic planning, management and supervision, and program advancement.

Strategic Planning
- **articulate a vision and mission that drive short-**

and long-term planning
- set goals and objectives based on the needs of the populations served, intended student learning and development outcomes, and program outcomes
- facilitate continuous development, implementation, and assessment of program effectiveness and goal attainment congruent with institutional mission and strategic plans
- promote environments that provide opportunities for student learning, development, and engagement
- develop, adapt, and improve programs and services in response to the changing needs of populations served and evolving institutional priorities
- include diverse perspectives to inform decision making

Management and Supervision
- plan, allocate, and monitor the use of fiscal, physical, human, intellectual, and technological resources
- manage human resource processes including recruitment, selection, professional development, supervision, performance planning, succession planning, evaluation, recognition, and reward
- influence others to contribute to the effectiveness and success of the unit
- empower professional, support, and student personnel to become effective leaders
- encourage and support collaboration with colleagues and departments across the institution
- encourage and support scholarly contributions to the profession
- identify and address individual, organizational, and environmental conditions that foster or inhibit mission achievement
- use current and valid evidence to inform decisions
- incorporate sustainability practices in the management and design of programs, services, and facilities
- understand appropriate technologies and integrate them into programs and services
- be knowledgeable about codes and laws relevant to programs and services and ensure that programs and services meet those requirements
- assess and take action to mitigate potential risks

Program Advancement
- advocate for and actively promote the mission and goals of the programs and services
- inform stakeholders about issues affecting practice
- facilitate processes to reach consensus where wide support is needed
- advocate for representation in strategic planning initiatives at divisional and institutional levels

Opportunities for student learning and development could include activities boards; student governance bodies; academic, performance, cultural, arts, religious, recreational,

and special interest organizations; program boards; theatrical productions; and media boards.

The CAP should be aware of the institutional strategic plan and be ready to respond to contemporary conditions and emergency preparedness. These conditions could include response to natural disasters, celebrations of notable achievements, and the changing nature of the student population.

CAP may be organized as an autonomous unit or may be organized in the same unit as the campus union or other programming units.

Part 4. Human Resources

Campus Activities Programs (CAP) must be staffed adequately by individuals qualified to accomplish mission and goals.

CAP must have access to technical and support personnel adequate to accomplish their mission.

Within institutional guidelines, CAP must
- establish procedures for personnel recruitment and selection, training, performance planning, and evaluation
- set expectations for supervision and performance
- provide personnel access to continuing and advanced education and appropriate professional development opportunities to improve their competence, skills, and leadership capacity
- consider work/life options available to personnel (e.g., compressed work schedules, flextime, job sharing, remote work, or telework) to promote recruitment and retention of personnel

Administrators of CAP must
- ensure that all personnel have updated position descriptions
- implement recruitment and selection/hiring strategies that produce a workforce inclusive of under-represented populations
- develop promotion practices that are fair, inclusive, proactive, and non-discriminatory

Personnel responsible for delivery of CAP must have written performance goals, objectives, and outcomes for each year's performance cycle to be used to plan, review, and evaluate work and performance. The performance plan must be updated regularly to reflect changes during the performance cycle.

Results of individual personnel evaluations must be used to recognize personnel performance, address performance issues, implement individual and/or collective personnel development and training programs, and inform the assessment of programs and services.

CAP personnel, when hired and throughout their employment, must receive appropriate and thorough training.

CAP personnel, including student employees and volunteers, must have access to resources or receive specific training on

- **institutional policies pertaining to functions or activities they support**
- **privacy and confidentiality policies**
- **laws regarding access to student records**
- **policies and procedures for dealing with sensitive institutional information**
- **policies and procedures related to technology used to store or access student records and institutional data**
- **how and when to refer those in need of additional assistance to qualified personnel and have access to a supervisor for assistance in making these judgments**
- **systems and technologies necessary to perform their assigned responsibilities**
- **ethical and legal uses of technology**

CAP personnel must engage in continuing professional development activities to keep abreast of the research, theories, legislation, policies, and developments that affect their programs and services.

Appropriate continuous training opportunities should be offered for all CAP staff members. This can include training in leadership, organizational planning, diversity, ethical decision making, and communication skills. Staff members should seek to enhance their resourcefulness, empathy, creativity, and openness to serving diverse student populations. Staff members should also seek to increase their knowledge of current issues. Training and development opportunities could be achieved through participation with professional organizations.

Administrators of CAP must ensure that personnel are knowledgeable about and trained in safety, emergency procedures, and crisis prevention and response. Risk management efforts must address identification of threatening conduct or behavior and must incorporate a system for responding to and reporting such behaviors.

CAP personnel must be knowledgeable of and trained in safety and emergency procedures for securing and vacating facilities.

Depending upon the scope of campus activities programs, the staff may include an activities director, a program coordinator, organization and program advisors, orientation and leadership specialists, a technology specialist, and a bookkeeper/financial officer.

PROFESSIONAL PERSONNEL

Professional personnel either must hold an earned graduate or professional degree in a field relevant to their position or must possess an appropriate combination of educational credentials and related work experience.

Relevant fields may include college student affairs, higher education administration, organizational development, or other related programs. Graduate studies should include courses in the behavioral sciences, management, recreation, student affairs, student development, and research techniques. The CAP may require particular training and experience appropriate to serving distinct campus populations and specialized campus or community needs.

The primary functions of full-time professional staff members may include the administration and coordination of campus activities programs; assessment of student interests and needs; planning, implementing, and evaluating programs with students; assisting student organizations in planning and implementing their programs; advising student groups; advising student governance organizations; and providing training, education, and development opportunities for students and advisors involved in student organizations.

Campus activities staff members should include the following additional qualifications:

- ability to collaborate with faculty members, administrators, staff colleagues, students, and all other constituencies
- capacity to interpret or advocate student concerns and interests to the campus community
- expertise in the development of students
- ability to create and deliver programs, activities, and services to students and to student groups
- experience in promoting student leadership
- capability of serving as a role model for ethical behavior
- commitment to professional and personal development
- knowledge of group dynamics and ability to work effectively with groups
- ability to supervise a variety of staff including students, support staff, and professional staff
- knowledge of contracting procedures and contract negotiations
- skills in working with agents and performers
- experience in effectively managing budgets
- appropriate expertise in the use of technology
- ability to supervise student staff members
- ability to balance the role of student advocate and the interest of the institution

At least one professional staff member should be assigned responsibility for campus activities programs.

INTERNS OR GRADUATE ASSISTANTS

Degree- or credential-seeking interns or graduate assistants must be qualified by enrollment in an appropriate field of study and relevant experience. These students must be trained and supervised by professional personnel who possess applicable educational credentials and work experience and have supervisory experience. Supervisors must be cognizant of the dual roles interns and graduate assistants have as both student and employee.

Supervisors must
- **adhere to parameters of students' job descriptions**

- articulate intended learning outcomes in student job descriptions
- adhere to agreed-upon work hours and schedules
- offer flexible scheduling when circumstances necessitate

Supervisors and students must both agree to suitable compensation if circumstances necessitate additional hours.

STUDENT EMPLOYEES AND VOLUNTEERS

Student employees and volunteers must be carefully selected, trained, supervised, and evaluated. Students must have access to a supervisor. Student employees and volunteers must be provided clear job descriptions, pre-service training based on assessed needs, and continuing development.

Thorough training should be provided for student employees and volunteers to enable them to carry out their duties and responsibilities and to enhance their personal experiences with campus activities programs.

Joint staff development efforts should be encouraged with colleagues in allied programs such as recreational sports, residence hall programming, and special programs for international students and students from traditionally underrepresented groups.

Identification of staff with authority to enter into binding contracts must be made by the institution and clearly disseminated and explained to students and advisors.

Part 5. Ethics

Campus Activities Programs (CAP) must
- review applicable professional ethical standards and must adopt or develop and implement appropriate statements of ethical practice
- publish and adhere to statements of ethical practice and ensure their periodic review
- orient new personnel to relevant ethical standards and statements of ethical practice and related institutional policies

Applicable statements may include principles and standards pertaining to
- civil and ethical conduct
- accuracy of information (i.e., accurate presentation of institutional goals, services, and policies to the public and the college or university community, and fair and accurate representation in publicity and promotions)
- conflict of interest
- role conflicts
- fiscal accountability
- fair and equitable administration of institutional policies
- student involvement in relevant institutional decisions
- free and open exchange of ideas through campus

activities programs
- fulfillment of contractual arrangements and agreements
- role modeling of ethical leadership practices

Statements of ethical standards must
- specify that CAP personnel respect privacy and maintain confidentiality in communications and records as delineated by privacy laws
- specify limits on disclosure of information contained in students' records as well as requirements to disclose to appropriate authorities
- address conflicts of interest, or appearance thereof, by personnel in the performance of their work
- reflect the responsibility of personnel to be fair, objective, and impartial in their interactions with others
- reference management of institutional funds
- reference appropriate behavior regarding research and assessment with human participants, confidentiality of research and assessment data, and students' rights and responsibilities
- include the expectation that personnel confront and hold accountable other personnel who exhibit unethical behavior
- address issues surrounding scholarly integrity

CAP personnel must
- employ ethical decision making in the performance of their duties
- inform users of programs and services of ethical obligations and limitations emanating from codes and laws or from licensure requirements
- recognize and avoid conflicts of interest that could adversely influence their judgment or objectivity and, when unavoidable, recuse themselves from the situation
- perform their duties within the scope of their position, training, expertise, and competence
- make referrals when issues presented exceed the scope of the position

Part 6. Law, Policy, and Governance

Campus Activities Programs (CAP) must be in compliance with laws, regulations, and policies that relate to their respective responsibilities and that pose legal obligations, limitations, risks, and liabilities for the institution as a whole. Examples include constitutional, statutory, regulatory, and case law; relevant law and orders emanating from codes and laws; and the institution's policies.

CAP must have access to legal advice needed for personnel to carry out their assigned responsibilities.

CAP must inform personnel, appropriate officials, and users of programs and services about existing and changing legal obligations, risks and liabilities, and limitations.

CAP must inform personnel about professional liability

insurance options and refer them to external sources if the institution does not provide coverage.

CAP must have written policies and procedures on operations, transactions, or tasks that have legal implications.

CAP must regularly review policies. The revision and creation of policies must be informed by best practices, available evidence, and policy issues in higher education.

CAP must have procedures and guidelines consistent with institutional policy for responding to threats, emergencies, and crisis situations. Systems and procedures must be in place to disseminate timely and accurate information to students, other members of the institutional community, and appropriate external organizations during emergency situations.

Personnel must neither participate in nor condone any form of harassment or activity that demeans persons or creates an intimidating, hostile, or offensive environment.

CAP must purchase or obtain permission to use copyrighted materials and instruments. References to copyrighted materials and instruments must include appropriate citations.

CAP must inform personnel about internal and external governance organizations that affect programs and services.

CAP staff members should be well informed about current campus and student legal issues, including risk management, free speech, organization recognition and registration procedures, contractual issues, and student fees.

Part 7. Diversity, Equity, and Access

Within the context of each institution's mission and in accordance with institutional policies and applicable codes and laws, Campus Activities Programs (CAP) must create and maintain educational and work environments that are welcoming, accessible, inclusive, equitable, and free from harassment.

CAP must not discriminate on the basis of disability; age; race; cultural identity; ethnicity; nationality; family educational history (e.g., first generation to attend college); political affiliation; religious affiliation; sex; sexual orientation; gender identity and expression; marital, social, economic, or veteran status; or any other basis included in institutional policies and codes and laws.

CAP must
- advocate for sensitivity to multicultural and social justice concerns by the institution and its personnel
- ensure physical, program, and resource access for all constituents
- modify or remove policies, practices, systems, technologies, facilities, and structures that create barriers or produce inequities
- ensure that when facilities and structures cannot be modified, they do not impede access to programs, services, and resources
- establish goals for diversity, equity, and access
- foster communication and practices that enhance understanding of identity, culture, self-expression, and heritage
- promote respect for commonalities and differences among people within their historical and cultural contexts
- address the characteristics and needs of diverse constituents when establishing and implementing culturally relevant and inclusive programs, services, policies, procedures, and practices
- provide personnel with diversity, equity, and access training and hold personnel accountable for applying the training to their work
- respond to the needs of all constituents served when establishing hours of operation and developing methods of delivering programs, services, and resources
- recognize the needs of distance and online learning students by directly providing or assisting them to gain access to comparable services and resources

Outreach efforts could include electronic voting for student elections and student fee assessments and online communities.

CAP staff must design and implement strategies for involving and engaging diverse student populations.

CAP must provide educational programs that emphasize self assessment and personal responsibility for creating and improving relationships across differences.

CAP must support and participate in creating a welcoming and nurturing educational environment for all students.

Part 8. Internal and External Relations

Campus Activities Programs (CAP) must reach out to individuals, groups, communities, and organizations internal and external to the institution to
- establish, maintain, and promote understanding and effective relations with those that have a significant interest in or potential effect on the students or other constituents served by the programs and services
- garner support and resources for programs and services as defined by the mission
- collaborate in offering or improving programs and services to meet the needs of students and other constituents and to achieve program and student outcomes
- engage diverse individuals, groups, communities, and organizations to enrich the educational environment and experiences of students and other constituents
- disseminate information about the programs and services

Promotional and descriptive information must be accurate

and free of deception and misrepresentation.

CAP must have procedures and guidelines consistent with institutional policy for

- communicating with the media
- distributing information through print, broadcast, and online sources
- contracting with external organizations for delivery of programs and services
- cultivating, soliciting, and managing gifts
- applying to and managing funds from grants

CAP should encourage faculty and staff members throughout the campus community to be involved in campus activities. Faculty members should serve as valuable resources related to their academic disciplines, especially as lecturers, performers, artists, and workshop facilitators. Faculty and staff members who serve as advisors should work directly with organizations in program and leadership development and should be supported by CAP staff. Faculty and staff members, administrators, and students may serve together on advisory boards to provide leadership for important initiatives.

CAP is a highly visible operation both on and off campus and may be influential in forming public opinion about the institution and creating a positive environment for the entire community. In that regard, to build bridges and connections, CAP staff may volunteer for campus-wide or community-based committees, initiatives, and programs beyond the traditional student affairs areas.

Part 9. Financial Resources

Campus Activities Programs (CAP) must have funding to accomplish the mission and goals.

In establishing and prioritizing funding resources, CAP must conduct comprehensive analyses to determine
- **unmet needs of the unit**
- **relevant expenditures**
- **external and internal resources**
- **impact on students and the institution**

CAP must use the budget as a planning tool to reflect commitment to the mission and goals of the programs and services and of the institution.

CAP must administer funds in accordance with established institutional accounting procedures.

CAP must demonstrate efficient and effective use and responsible stewardship of fiscal resources consistent with institutional protocols.

Financial reports must provide an accurate financial overview of the organization and provide clear, understandable, and timely data upon which personnel can plan and make informed decisions.

Procurement procedures must
- **be consistent with institutional policies**
- **ensure that purchases comply with laws and codes for usability and access**

- **ensure that the institution receives value for the funds spent**
- **consider information available for comparing the ethical and environmental impact of products and services purchased**

Methods for establishing, collecting, and allocating student and user fees must be clear and equitable. The authority and processes for decisions relevant to campus activities fees must be clearly established and funds must be spent consistent with established priorities.

Authority for decisions relevant to campus activities fees should rest in large part with students and are typically initiated by a vote of the student body. The fees, once approved through institutional processes, may be managed and allocations distributed by representative student governing bodies or by other allocation boards or committees.

Finance committees of student organizations or student governments should work collaboratively with staff members to establish campus activities fees and priorities. Students and staff members should share responsibility for budget development and implementation according to mutually established program priorities.

Students who have fiscal responsibility must be provided with information and training regarding institutional regulations and policies that govern accounting and the appropriate handling of funds.

CAP should provide educational programs and training to students about the basics of financial management.

Due to the large amounts of money generated by campus activities and the transience of the student population, good business practice dictates that reasonable safeguards be established to ensure responsible management of and accounting for the funds involved. Student organizations may be required to maintain their funds with the institution's business office in which an account for each group is established and where bookkeeping and auditing services are provided. When possible, it is recommended that processes be established to permit individual student organizations to manage their own business transactions. Within this framework, CAP works collaboratively with student organizations on matters of bookkeeping, budgeting, and other matters of fiscal accountability, including contract negotiations, consistent with institutional practices.

Funds for CAP may be provided through state/provincial appropriations, institutional budgets, activities fees, user fees, membership and other specialized fees, revenues from programming or fundraising projects, grants, and foundation resources. Funds may be supplemented by income from ticket sales, sales of promotional items, and individual or group gifts consistent with institutional policies.

In conjunction with students, CAP must establish clear policies and procedures for funding and managing major campus events and entertainment programs necessitating large financial commitments, including concerts, athletic

rivalries, homecoming, alumni days, campus traditions, and family weekend.

Campus Activities Programs (CAP) must have technology to support the achievement of their mission and goals. The technology and its use must comply with institutional policies and procedures and with relevant codes and laws.

Technological capabilities should accommodate all common communication systems including email, on-line calendars, electronic portfolios, pod casts, instant messaging, web browsing, telephone and video conferencing, and other emerging technologies.

CAP must use technologies to
- provide updated information regarding mission, location, staffing, programs, services, and official contacts to students and other constituents in accessible formats
- provide an avenue for students and other constituents to communicate sensitive information in a secure format
- enhance the delivery of programs and services for all students

CAP must
- back up data on a regular basis
- adhere to institutional policies regarding ethical and legal use of technology
- articulate policies and procedures for protecting the confidentiality and security of information
- implement a replacement plan and cycle for all technology wth attention to sustainability
- incorporate accessibility features into technology-based programs and services

When providing student access to technology, CAP must
- have policies on the use of technology that are clear, easy to understand, and available to all students
- provide information or referral to support services for those needing assistance in accessing or using technology
- provide instruction or training on how to use the technology
- inform students of implications of misuse of technologies

Part 11. Facilities and Equipment

Campus Activities Programs' (CAP) facilities must be intentionally designed and located in suitable, accessible, and safe spaces that demonstrate universal design and support the program's mission and goals.

Facilities must be designed to engage various constituents and promote learning.

Facilities should be located conveniently and designed with flexibility to serve the wide variety of functions associated with campus activities. Appropriate facilities, accessible to all members of the college community, should be provided, including student organization offices and adequately sized and equipped public performance spaces.

The CAP may be located in the college union. [See CAS Standards and Guidelines for College Unions.] In addition to their traditional programming, social, and service facilities, unions typically house campus activities programs, student organization offices, and related meeting, work, and storage rooms. Campus activities may also take place in residence halls, recreation centers, fraternity and sorority houses, sports facilities, worship centers, and other locations. CAP space should be designed to encourage maximum interaction among students and between staff members and students.

Personnel must have workspaces that are suitably located and accessible, well equipped, adequate in size, and designed to support their work and responsibilities.

The design of the facilities must guarantee the security and privacy of records and ensure the confidentiality of sensitive information and conversations. Personnel must be able to secure their work.

CAP must incorporate sustainable practices in use of facilities and purchase of equipment. Facilities and equipment must be evaluated on an established cycle and be in compliance with codes, laws, and accepted practices for access, health, safety, and security.

When acquiring capital equipment, CAP must take into account expenses related to regular maintenance and life cycle costs.

Part 12. Assessment

Campus Activities Programs (CAP) must develop assessment plans and processes.

Assessment plans must articulate an ongoing cycle of assessment activities.

CAP must
- specify programmatic goals and intended outcomes
- identify student learning and development outcomes
- employ multiple measures and methods
- develop manageable processes for gathering, interpreting, and evaluating data
- document progress toward achievement of goals and outcomes
- interpret and use assessment results to demonstrate accountability
- report aggregated results to respondent groups and stakeholders
- use assessment results to inform planning and decision-making
- assess effectiveness of implemented changes
- provide evidence of improvement of programs and services

Assessment instrumentation and methods should be scientifically designed and implemented, and when possible, staff should seek advice and guidance and work collaboratively with institutional research offices.

The CAP should be evaluated regularly and the findings should be disseminated to appropriate campus agencies and constituencies including appropriate student organizations. Evaluation procedures should yield evidence relative to the achievement of program goals, student learning outcomes, quality and scope of program offerings, responsiveness to expressed interests, program attendance and effectiveness, cost effectiveness, quality and appearance of facilities, student success and retention, and equipment use and maintenance. Data sources should include students, staff, alumni, faculty members, administrators, community members, and relevant documents and records. Student self-assessment should be encouraged through the use of such techniques as electronic portfolios.

Records of program evaluations should be maintained in the office of the administrative leader of the CAP and should be accessible to planners of subsequent programs.

CAP must employ ethical practices in the assessment process.

CAP must have access to adequate fiscal, human, professional development, and technological resources to develop and implement assessment plans.

General Standards revised in 2014.
Campus Activities content developed/revised in 1986, 1997, & 2006

Campus Information and Visitor Services
CAS Contextual Statement

The development of the campus information and visitor services field was a direct result of the increasing diversity, size, complexity, and specialization of institutions of higher learning during the 20th century. This pattern particularly occurred on campuses in the United States and necessitated the development of information centers to address the many informational needs of large and complex campus communities. Often these centers evolved into, or were combined with, visitor services to become comprehensive campus gateway operations providing entry points to institutions for all visitors, including prospective students, alumni, and others. The common objective of campus information and visitor services (CIVS) is to bring people, programs, and campus services and resources together through increased accessibility to information.

Some of the earliest examples of visitor services and centers include the establishment in 1951 of the Visitor Center at the U.S. Military Academy at West Point and the creation of the Visitor Information Center at the University of California at Berkeley in 1965. Historically, these programs originated as extensions of institutional recruitment activities and efforts. One of the earliest examples of specialized information and referral services can be traced to the 1970 establishment of the Campus Assistance Center at the University of Wisconsin-Madison. Specialized information and referral programs were often established as information and rumor control efforts responding to the rapid expansion of campuses and increasing lack of trust in traditional institutional communication methods. By providing inquirers with the information and services they needed, or referring them to the appropriate resources when necessary, these programs were quickly judged to be highly useful in providing improved communication opportunities and increasing the quality of campus life. These early campus information and visitor service programs quickly became permanent campus operations with philosophies focused on access and individualized service. Additionally, many of the programs established clear guidelines for assisting inquirers in a friendly, sensitive manner and assuring appropriate confidentiality. CIVS programs have had a profound impact on campus communities through commitment to the principle of providing inquirers with clear, concise, thorough, and nonjudgmental information and referrals in the most welcoming environment possible.

By the late 1980s, the increasing institutional pressure for better accountability, outreach, and service to the broader campus community resulted in an increase in the number of campus information and visitor services operations. Easy accessibility to appropriate and timely information is a critical component for institutions in reaching instructional, research, and outreach goals. For many constituents, especially during downtimes—evenings, weekends, and breaks—campus information and visitor services programs become the physical embodiment of an institution. Increasing emphasis on quality improvement and service within the higher education community has been another driving force in the growing number of campus information and visitor services programs. The importance of the Internet, mass communication (e.g., radio and cable television), and new media (e.g., streaming video, podcasts) in the provision of information, and the need for support services that can assure the accuracy and relevance of this information, have also served to increase the importance of campus information and visitor services programs. By having access to an easily available and credible information and visitor services program, inquirers are assisted in making well-informed choices, planning wise courses of action, and taking advantage of the available and/or unique resources of the institution and the surrounding community.

These standards and guidelines provide a framework for excellence in the provision of campus information and visitor services. CIVS is the process of linking people who have campus-related questions to the appropriate resources and services. Also, CIVS provides feedback to service providers and discovers gaps and duplication in campus programs and services that should be addressed. This feedback loop can lead to quality service improvements that make campus operations more efficient. Inquiries can comprise anything related to the campus community, such as directions to a campus building or event; how to contact a department or a faculty or staff member; or whom to contact or where to go for issues of a personal nature, to resolve a problem, or to apply for admission. Inquirers may be current students, faculty or staff members, alumni, prospective students and their families, other visitors, or anyone needing information about the institution. CIVS programs serve as a gateway to the institution, providing one-on-one information to inquirers. When a direct answer is not possible, then the goal is to make a referral, paying careful attention to the needs of the inquirer, assessment of appropriate resources and response modes, identification of programs and services capable of meeting those needs, provision of sufficient information about each program and service to help inquirers make informed choices, location of alternative resources when services are unavailable, and active linking of the inquirer to needed services when necessary. The standards and guidelines that follow are intended to assist in the development of CIVS programs that make such high quality service possible.

References, Readings, and Resources

Hefferlin, J.B. L. (1971). *Information services for academic administration.* San Francisco, CA: Jossey-Bass.

Alliance of Information and Referral Systems. (n.d.). *Out of the shadows: Information and referral bringing people and services together.* Seattle, WA: Author.

Alliance of Information and Referral Systems. (n.d.). T*he ABC's of I & R: A self-study guide for information and referral staff.* Seattle, WA: Author.

Collegiate Information and Visitor Services Association (CIVSA): http://www.civsa.org

Contextual Statement Contributors

Current Edition:

Matthew J. Weismantel, Rutgers University, CIVSA

Previous Editions:

Matthew J. Weismantel, Rutgers University, CIVSA

Campus Information and Visitor Services
CAS Standards and Guidelines

The mission of Campus Information and Visitor Services (CIVS) is to facilitate welcome and access to the institution by providing timely and accurate information and appropriate referrals. CIVS offers a primary point of contact with and access to the institution by providing comprehensive contact information and general descriptions for many programs and services of the institution. CIVS must meet the introductory informational needs of the campus community: students, faculty members, staff, prospective students and their family members, alumni, and general visitors.

To accomplish this mission, CIVS must
- be readily accessible
- provide a welcoming environment
- emphasize personal communication and interaction
- provide accurate information and referrals

CIVS must have a strong commitment to student learning and development, contributing generally to institutional and other agency missions, and acknowledging that students play an integral part in mission delivery. This commitment must be reflected in its mission statement and demonstrated through quality supervision, staff development, and performance appraisals.

CIVS must develop, disseminate, implement, and regularly review their missions, which must be consistent with the mission of the institution and with applicable professional standards. The mission must be appropriate for the institution's students and other constituents. Mission statements must reference student learning and development.

Campus Information and Visitor Services (CIVS) must be responsive to the information and visitor needs and interests of all inquirers.

A broad array of programs and services must be available to ensure that accurate informational resources are provided in a timely manner that accommodates the needs of inquirers.

These services may include telephone or other electronic means of contact, or a walk-in facility, such as a visitor or information center, in which the inquirer has one-to-one, human contact and easy access to information resources such as catalogs, calendars, booklets, schedules, fliers, maps, books, and brochures. Additionally, this may include a variety of tour programs, presentation and conference facilities, and other information distribution methods across campus including video and Internet services.

Multiple media approaches must be used to provide information, services, and programs.

Such approaches may involve Internet-based resources including a website, virtual and downloadable applications, email, social networking, signage, maps, telephone information services, or emergency information devices.

To achieve their mission, CIVS must contribute to
- students' formal education, which includes both the curriculum and the co-curriculum
- student progression and timely completion of educational goals
- preparation of students for their careers, citizenship, and lives
- student learning and development

To contribute to student learning and development, CIVS must
- identify relevant and desirable student learning and development outcomes
- articulate how the student learning and development outcomes align with the six CAS student learning and development domains and related dimensions
- assess relevant and desirable student learning and development
- provide evidence of impact on outcomes
- articulate contributions to or support of student learning and development in the domains not specifically assessed
- use evidence gathered to create strategies for improvement of programs and services

STUDENT LEARNING AND DEVELOPMENT DOMAINS AND DIMENSIONS

Domain: knowledge acquisition, integration, construction, and application
- Dimensions: understanding knowledge from a range of disciplines; connecting knowledge to other knowledge, ideas, and experiences; constructing knowledge; and relating knowledge to daily life

Domain: cognitive complexity
- Dimensions: critical thinking, reflective thinking, effective reasoning, and creativity

Domain: intrapersonal development
- Dimensions: realistic self-appraisal, self-understanding, and self-respect; identity development; commitment to ethics and integrity; and spiritual awareness

Domain: interpersonal competence
- Dimensions: meaningful relationships, interdependence, collaboration, and effective

leadership

Domain: humanitarianism and civic engagement

- **Dimensions: understanding and appreciation of cultural and human differences, social responsibility, global perspective, and sense of civic responsibility**

Domain: practical competence

- **Dimensions: pursuing goals, communicating effectively, technical competence, managing personal affairs, managing career development, demonstrating professionalism, maintaining health and wellness, and living a purposeful and satisfying life**

[LD Outcomes: See *The Council for the Advancement of Standards Learning and Development Outcomes* statement for examples of outcomes related to these domains and dimensions.]

CIVS must be

- **intentionally designed**
- **guided by theories and knowledge of learning and development**
- **integrated into the life of the institution**
- **reflective of developmental and demographic profiles of the student population**
- **responsive to needs of individuals, populations with distinct needs, and relevant constituencies**
- **delivered using multiple formats, strategies, and contexts**
- **designed to provide universal access**

CIVS must collaborate with colleagues and departments across the institution to promote student learning and development, persistence, and success.

CIVS must provide specific information and referral to existing campus programs and services or, when such programs do not exist, actively link inquirers to alternative community and other programs that can meet their specific needs.

CIVS programs must be easily accessible to assist a diverse populations of inquirers in making well-informed choices, planning appropriate courses of action, and taking advantage of available institutional resources.

CIVS must develop and maintain an accurate information retrieval and delivery system of available campus and community resources. This system must be updated regularly to ensure timeliness, accuracy, and comprehensiveness of information.

CIVS must be available at locations and times that meet the needs of the inquirers.

CIVS must provide feedback to appropriate campus officials regarding conditions that may negatively influence an inquirer's interaction with the institution and propose interventions to remedy such conditions.

Feedback topics may include statistics, data analysis, relevant

documentation of service use (e.g., identifying unmet needs, gaps, and services duplication), service quality at other campus locations, and inquirer characteristics.

CIVS must strive to assist inquirers in a friendly, caring, sensitive, and non-judgmental manner and provide clear, concise information. CIVS must protect the privacy of individuals within the campus community from inappropriate inquiry.

CIVS must establish and maintain a planned program of activities to increase campus and community awareness of its services, mission, goals, and objectives.

Campus information and visitor services may include

- campus orientation and tour programs
- display and presentation space
- broadcast and electronic informational resources and support
- visitor reception space including appropriate support services and facilities adequate in size and scope to meet the volume of inquirers to be assisted

CIVS should be a principal provider of structure and content to the institution's on-line information systems.

A range of information should be provided to inquirers, including brief responses, such as names or phone numbers, as well as details about an organization's policies and procedures.

Program activities may include

- participation in training programs of other offices and departments
- provision of printed materials such as brochures, posters, directional information and exhibits
- public service announcements
- hosting informational tours and special events for diverse audiences
- information-based Web site
- role as a resource for other campus and community support services

Part 3. Organization and Leadership

To achieve program and student learning and development outcomes, Campus Information and Visitor Services (CIVS) must be purposefully structured for effectiveness. CIVS must have clearly stated and current

- **goals and outcomes**
- **policies and procedures**
- **responsibilities and performance expectations for personnel**
- **organizational charts demonstrating clear channels of authority**

Leaders must model ethical behavior and institutional citizenship.

Leaders with organizational authority for CIVS must provide strategic planning, management and supervision, and program advancement.

Strategic Planning
- articulate a vision and mission that drive short- and long-term planning
- set goals and objectives based on the needs of the populations served, intended student learning and development outcomes, and program outcomes
- facilitate continuous development, implementation, and assessment of program effectiveness and goal attainment congruent with institutional mission and strategic plans
- promote environments that provide opportunities for student learning, development, and engagement
- develop, adapt, and improve programs and services in response to the changing needs of populations served and evolving institutional priorities
- include diverse perspectives to inform decision making

Management and Supervision
- plan, allocate, and monitor the use of fiscal, physical, human, intellectual, and technological resources
- manage human resource processes including recruitment, selection, professional development, supervision, performance planning, succession planning, evaluation, recognition, and reward
- influence others to contribute to the effectiveness and success of the unit
- empower professional, support, and student personnel to become effective leaders
- encourage and support collaboration with colleagues and departments across the institution
- encourage and support scholarly contributions to the profession
- identify and address individual, organizational, and environmental conditions that foster or inhibit mission achievement
- use current and valid evidence to inform decisions
- incorporate sustainability practices in the management and design of programs, services, and facilities
- understand appropriate technologies and integrate them into programs and services
- be knowledgeable about codes and laws relevant to programs and services and ensure that programs and services meet those requirements
- assess and take action to mitigate potential risks

Program Advancement
- advocate for and actively promote the mission and goals of the programs and services
- inform stakeholders about issues affecting practice
- facilitate processes to reach consensus where wide support is needed
- advocate for representation in strategic planning initiatives at divisional and institutional levels

Campus Information and Visitor Services (CIVS) must be delivered in an atmosphere of staff teamwork, assessment, and continuous improvement.

The information retrieval and delivery system used by CIVS must be organized according to a standardized search system. The information system must have the capacity to accept changes in a very short time frame for information that may change in between regularly scheduled updates.

CIVS must have well developed policies regarding the type, breadth, and currency of information contained in the information retrieval and delivery system.

CIVS must develop and maintain accurate, up-to-date information about available campus resources and procedures for verifying accuracy.

Informational resources should be profiled to include
- official name, common name, and acronym address (i.e., room, building name, street, city, zip code)
- e-mail address
- telephone number, fax number, hours and days of service
- Internet addresses
- type and description of service(s) provided
- population(s) served
- eligibility guidelines
- intake procedures
- required documents
- cost
- waiting period for service
- contact person
- auspices (i.e., city, state/province, private, social service, campus)
- date of last update

CIVS must establish and use a system of collecting and organizing inquirer data for appropriate referral and feedback to the campus community.

CIVS should pursue meaningful research to review and improve programs and services. Members of the campus community should be involved in the review of these findings, as well as in the design and governance of campus information and visitor services. Students, faculty members, staff, and appropriate external agencies should be involved through committees, councils, and boards.

Part 4. Human Resources

Campus Information and Visitor Services (CIVS) must be staffed adequately by individuals qualified to accomplish mission and goals.

CIVS must have access to technical and support personnel adequate to accomplish their mission.

Within institutional guidelines, CIVS must
- establish procedures for personnel recruitment and selection, training, performance planning, and evaluation
- set expectations for supervision and performance
- provide personnel access to continuing and

advanced education and appropriate professional development opportunities to improve their competence, skills, and leadership capacity

- consider work/life options available to personnel (e.g., compressed work schedules, flextime, job sharing, remote work, or telework) to promote recruitment and retention of personnel

Administrators of CIVS must

- **ensure that all personnel have updated position descriptions**
- **implement recruitment and selection/hiring strategies that produce a workforce inclusive of under-represented populations**
- **develop promotion practices that are fair, inclusive, proactive, and non-discriminatory**

Personnel responsible for delivery of CIVS must have written performance goals, objectives, and outcomes for each year's performance cycle to be used to plan, review, and evaluate work and performance. The performance plan must be updated regularly to reflect changes during the performance cycle.

Results of individual personnel evaluations must be used to recognize personnel performance, address performance issues, implement individual and/or collective personnel development and training programs, and inform the assessment of programs and services.

CIVS personnel, when hired and throughout their employment, must receive appropriate and thorough training.

CIVS personnel, including student employees and volunteers, must have access to resources or receive specific training on

- **institutional policies pertaining to functions or activities they support**
- **privacy and confidentiality policies**
- **laws regarding access to student records**
- **policies and procedures for dealing with sensitive institutional information**
- **policies and procedures related to technology used to store or access student records and institutional data**
- **how and when to refer those in need of additional assistance to qualified personnel and have access to a supervisor for assistance in making these judgments**
- **systems and technologies necessary to perform their assigned responsibilities**
- **ethical and legal uses of technology**

CIVS personnel must engage in continuing professional development activities to keep abreast of the research, theories, legislation, policies, and developments that affect their programs and services.

Continuing staff development experiences should include in-service training programs, professional conferences, workshops, and on-site training to enhance employee familiarization with the institution's visitor destinations, programs, services, and employees.

A formal training program must be required for all staff, especially those who will be providing direct service.

Training programs should include experiences for initial employee orientations as well as on-the-job training, in-service group training, supervisory coaching, and individualized training based on employee needs.

Staff-training programs should include

- emergency /crisis management
- strategies for understanding campus and community resources
- information retrieval, delivery and data collection
- overview of mission, vision, strategic goals, role, purpose, function, structure, policies, and procedures of the unit
- student development theory and practice
- customer service and basic communication skills such as interviewing, listening, empathy, clarification and problem-solving
- strategies for supporting persons with disabilities and language differences

Administrators of CIVS must ensure that personnel are knowledgeable about and trained in safety, emergency procedures, and crisis prevention and response. Risk management efforts must address identification of threatening conduct or behavior and must incorporate a system for responding to and reporting such behaviors.

CIVS personnel must be knowledgeable of and trained in safety and emergency procedures for securing and vacating facilities.

PROFESSIONAL PERSONNEL

CIVS professional personnel either must hold an earned graduate or professional degree in a field relevant to their position or must possess an appropriate combination of educational credentials and related work experience.

CIVS staff positions must be filled based on a defined set of qualifications such as level of education, work experience, and personal characteristics (e.g., integrity, communication skills, leadership ability).

INTERNS OR GRADUATE ASSISTANTS

Degree- or credential-seeking interns or graduate assistants must be qualified by enrollment in an appropriate field of study and relevant experience. These students must be trained and supervised by professional personnel who possess applicable educational credentials and work experience and have supervisory experience. Supervisors must be cognizant of the dual roles interns and graduate assistants have as both student and employee.

Supervisors must

- **adhere to parameters of students' job descriptions**

- articulate intended learning outcomes in student job descriptions
- adhere to agreed-upon work hours and schedules
- offer flexible scheduling when circumstances necessitate

Supervisors and students must both agree to suitable compensation if circumstances necessitate additional hours.

STUDENT EMPLOYEES AND VOLUNTEERS

Student employees and volunteers must be carefully selected, trained, supervised, and evaluated. Students must have access to a supervisor. Student employees and volunteers must be provided clear job descriptions, pre-service training based on assessed needs, and continuing development.

Every CIVS staff member must show respect for all inquirers.

Part 5. Ethics

Campus Information and Visitor Services (CIVS) must
- review applicable professional ethical standards and must adopt or develop and implement appropriate statements of ethical practice
- publish and adhere to statements of ethical practice and ensure their periodic review
- orient new personnel to relevant ethical standards and statements of ethical practice and related institutional policies

Statements of ethical standards must
- specify that CIVS personnel respect privacy and maintain confidentiality in communications and records as delineated by privacy laws
- specify limits on disclosure of information contained in students' records as well as requirements to disclose to appropriate authorities
- address conflicts of interest, or appearance thereof, by personnel in the performance of their work
- reflect the responsibility of personnel to be fair, objective, and impartial in their interactions with others
- reference management of institutional funds
- reference appropriate behavior regarding research and assessment with human participants, confidentiality of research and assessment data, and students' rights and responsibilities
- include the expectation that personnel confront and hold accountable other personnel who exhibit unethical behavior
- address issues surrounding scholarly integrity

CIVS personnel must
- employ ethical decision making in the performance of their duties
- inform users of programs and services of ethical obligations and limitations emanating from codes and laws or from licensure requirements
- recognize and avoid conflicts of interest that could

adversely influence their judgment or objectivity and, when unavoidable, recuse themselves from the situation
- perform their duties within the scope of their position, training, expertise, and competence
- make referrals when issues presented exceed the scope of the position

Part 6. Law, Policy, and Governance

Campus Information and Visitor Services (CIVS) must be in compliance with laws, regulations, and policies that relate to their respective responsibilities and that pose legal obligations, limitations, risks, and liabilities for the institution as a whole. Examples include constitutional, statutory, regulatory, and case law; relevant law and orders emanating from codes and laws; and the institution's policies.

CIVS must have access to legal advice needed for personnel to carry out their assigned responsibilities.

CIVS must inform personnel, appropriate officials, and users of programs and services about existing and changing legal obligations, risks and liabilities, and limitations.

CIVS must inform personnel about professional liability insurance options and refer them to external sources if the institution does not provide coverage.

CIVS must have written policies and procedures on operations, transactions, or tasks that have legal implications.

CIVS must regularly review policies. The revision and creation of policies must be informed by best practices, available evidence, and policy issues in higher education.

CIVS must have procedures and guidelines consistent with institutional policy for responding to threats, emergencies, and crisis situations. Systems and procedures must be in place to disseminate timely and accurate information to students, other members of the institutional community, and appropriate external organizations during emergency situations.

Personnel must neither participate in nor condone any form of harassment or activity that demeans persons or creates an intimidating, hostile, or offensive environment.

CIVS must purchase or obtain permission to use copyrighted materials and instruments. References to copyrighted materials and instruments must include appropriate citations.

CIVS must inform personnel about internal and external governance organizations that affect programs and services.

Part 7. Diversity, Equity, and Access

Within the context of each institution's mission and in accordance with institutional policies and applicable codes and laws, Campus Information and Visitor Services

(CIVS) must create and maintain educational and work environments that are welcoming, accessible, inclusive, equitable, and free from harassment.

CIVS must not discriminate on the basis of disability; age; race; cultural identity; ethnicity; nationality; family educational history (e.g., first generation to attend college); political affiliation; religious affiliation; sex; sexual orientation; gender identity and expression; marital, social, economic, or veteran status; or any other basis included in institutional policies and codes and laws.

CIVS must
- advocate for sensitivity to multicultural and social justice concerns by the institution and its personnel
- ensure physical, program, and resource access for all constituents
- modify or remove policies, practices, systems, technologies, facilities, and structures that create barriers or produce inequities
- ensure that when facilities and structures cannot be modified, they do not impede access to programs, services, and resources
- establish goals for diversity, equity, and access
- foster communication and practices that enhance understanding of identity, culture, self-expression, and heritage
- promote respect for commonalities and differences among people within their historical and cultural contexts
- address the characteristics and needs of diverse constituents when establishing and implementing culturally relevant and inclusive programs, services, policies, procedures, and practices
- provide personnel with diversity, equity, and access training and hold personnel accountable for applying the training to their work
- respond to the needs of all constituents served when establishing hours of operation and developing methods of delivering programs, services, and resources
- recognize the needs of distance and online learning students by directly providing or assisting them to gain access to comparable services and resources

Part 8. Internal and External Relations

Campus Information and Visitor Services (CIVS) must reach out to individuals, groups, communities, and organizations internal and external to the institution to
- establish, maintain, and promote understanding and effective relations with those that have a significant interest in or potential effect on the students or other constituents served by the programs and services
- garner support and resources for programs and services as defined by the mission
- collaborate in offering or improving programs and

services to meet the needs of students and other constituents and to achieve program and student outcomes
- engage diverse individuals, groups, communities, and organizations to enrich the educational environment and experiences of students and other constituents
- disseminate information about the programs and services

Promotional and descriptive information must be accurate and free of deception and misrepresentation.

CIVS must have procedures and guidelines consistent with institutional policy for
- communicating with the media
- distributing information through print, broadcast, and online sources
- contracting with external organizations for delivery of programs and services
- cultivating, soliciting, and managing gifts
- applying to and managing funds from grants

CIVS should collaborate closely with other campus offices and external agencies to ensure accuracy, timeliness, and reliability of information being provided to inquirers.

When appropriate, inquirers should be referred to other resources, and staff may actively participate in this linking process. This referral process is often integrated with information dissemination, intervention, and advocacy. Inquirers should be encouraged to re-contact the CIVS if additional information or assistance is needed.

Within institutional guidelines, CIVS should intervene and advocate for inquirers when information is inaccurate or misleading and/or inquirer needs have not been addressed satisfactorily. Follow-up on more complex problem situations should occur to determine the extent to which inquirer needs have been met.

Part 9. Financial Resources

Campus Information and Visitor Services (CIVS) must have funding to accomplish the mission and goals.

Institutional funds for CIVS should be allocated on a permanent basis.

In addition to institutional commitment of general funds, other funding sources may be considered including state/provincial appropriations, federal resources, fees and generated revenue, local community funding, and donations.

In establishing and prioritizing funding resources, CIVS must conduct comprehensive analyses to determine
- unmet needs of the unit
- relevant expenditures
- external and internal resources
- impact on students and the institution

CIVS must use the budget as a planning tool to reflect commitment to the mission and goals of the programs and services and of the institution.

CIVS must administer funds in accordance with established institutional accounting procedures.

CIVS must demonstrate efficient and effective use and responsible stewardship of fiscal resources consistent with institutional protocols.

Financial reports must provide an accurate financial overview of the organization and provide clear, understandable, and timely data upon which personnel can plan and make informed decisions.

Procurement procedures must
- be consistent with institutional policies
- ensure that purchases comply with laws and codes for usability and access
- ensure that the institution receives value for the funds spent
- consider information available for comparing the ethical and environmental impact of products and services purchased

Financial resources should be sufficient to provide inquirers with high quality personal interaction as well as print and electronic information.

Part 10. Technology

Campus Information and Visitor Services (CIVS) must have technology to support the achievement of their mission and goals. The technology and its use must comply with institutional policies and procedures and with relevant codes and laws.

CIVS must use technologies to
- provide updated information regarding mission, location, staffing, programs, services, and official contacts to students and other constituents in accessible formats
- provide an avenue for students and other constituents to communicate sensitive information in a secure format
- enhance the delivery of programs and services for all students

CIVS must
- back up data on a regular basis
- adhere to institutional policies regarding ethical and legal use of technology
- articulate policies and procedures for protecting the confidentiality and security of information
- implement a replacement plan and cycle for all technology with attention to sustainability
- incorporate accessibility features into technology-based programs and services

When providing student access to technology, CIVS must
- have policies on the use of technology that are clear, easy to understand, and available to all students

- provide information or referral to support services for those needing assistance in accessing or using technology
- provide instruction or training on how to use the technology
- inform students of implications of misuse of technologies

Part 11. Facilities and Equipment

Campus Information and Visitor Services' (CIVS) facilities must be intentionally designed and located in suitable, accessible, and safe spaces that demonstrate universal design and support the program's mission and goals.

Facilities must be designed to engage various constituents and promote learning.

Personnel must have workspaces that are suitably located and accessible, well equipped, adequate in size, and designed to support their work and responsibilities.

The design of the facilities must guarantee the security and privacy of records and ensure the confidentiality of sensitive information and conversations. Personnel must be able to secure their work.

CIVS must incorporate sustainable practices in use of facilities and purchase of equipment. Facilities and equipment must be evaluated on an established cycle and be in compliance with codes, laws, and accepted practices for access, health, safety, and security.

When acquiring capital equipment, CIVS must take into account expenses related to regular maintenance and life cycle costs.

CIVS must play an active role in the design and decision-making process for campus signage.

The CIVS facility should include space for confidential interviewing, display of materials, visitor reception, and information and referral operations. State-of-the-art telephone and computer capability should be included.

The CIVS facility should be accessible to and by public transportation and be at a location that can best represent the "front door" of the institution.

Part 12. Assessment

Campus Information and Visitor Services (CIVS) must develop assessment plans and processes.
Assessment plans must articulate an ongoing cycle of assessment activities.

CIVS must
- specify programmatic goals and intended outcomes
- identify student learning and development outcomes
- employ multiple measures and methods
- develop manageable processes for gathering,

interpreting, and evaluating data
- document progress toward achievement of goals and outcomes
- interpret and use assessment results to demonstrate accountability
- report aggregated results to respondent groups and stakeholders
- use assessment results to inform planning and decision-making
- assess effectiveness of implemented changes
- provide evidence of improvement of programs and services

CIVS must maintain an on-going process to collect inquirer use and inquirer satisfaction information.

CIVS must employ ethical practices in the assessment process.

CIVS must have access to adequate fiscal, human, professional development, and technological resources to develop and implement assessment plans.

General Standards revised in 2014;
CIVS content developed/revised in 2000 & 2010

Campus Police and Security Programs
CAS Contextual Statement

The issue of crime on American college and university campuses has been around since at least the early 19th century when a series of student disruptions rocked the campuses of a number of colleges (Gregory, 2001). The image of campus crime in recent years is in stark relief to former impressions due to high-profile incidents on campus, the perception that institutions were hiding campus crime (Gregory, 2002), and suggestions that university officials needed to take more responsibility for the safety of their students (Bickel & Lake, 1999).

Campus Police and Security refers to that agency and those individuals who, either as employees of the institution or through some sort of contracted service, provide for a safer campus environment, protect members of the university community, and may enforce institutional policy and relevant laws and codes. There are a wide variety of arrangements on college and university campuses in the United States and Canada by which these services are provided. These may include "sworn" police agencies at public institutions that are operated as any municipal, state, or province police agency may be and in which officers are trained similarly. On some independent institution campuses, the agency may operate under state or provincial law as "company police" or "special deputies" who have law enforcement authority but whose authority is limited to the campus itself. Some institutions contract with local law enforcement agencies to provide services within the borders of the campus, hire private security companies to protect the institution, or employ their own security officers who do not have arrest authority. Finally, some institutions use a combination of these methods to provide services on and around campus.

In the United States, all campus police and security programs operating on university campuses that receive federal funds must adhere to the *Jeanne Clery Disclosure of Campus Security Policy and Campus Crime Statistics Act* (2000). This federal law, originally passed in 1990, requires the reporting of campus crime statistics in certain categories, includes reporting on campus fire safety, requires the provision of certain information about campus policies, and has a number of other requirements with which university officials must comply. In 2014, the law was amended to add stalking, dating violence and domestic violence to the list of reportable crimes, and clarifies the definitions of several crimes. In addition, all U.S. states and Canadian provinces have laws and regulations that control how and under what types of arrangements campus police and security may operate.

The United States Department of Education has responsibility for enforcement of the Clery Act (http://www2.ed.gov/admins/lead/safety/campus.html), may fine institutions for violation of the Act, and in extreme cases may remove the authority of institutions to receive federal funds. The U.S. Department of Education also provides a great deal of information to assist university authorities to make their campuses safer and to comply with the Act. These include *The Handbook for Campus Safety and Crime Reporting* (Westat, Ward & Mann, 2011)

The family of Jeanne Clery, for whom the Clery Act is named, set up a non-profit advocacy group called Security on Campus, Inc. (2012). This group, for over twenty years, monitored compliance with the act, advocated for strict enforcement of the law, and lobbied Congress for additional laws to improve safety on American institutions of post-secondary education. While still engaged in compliance and lobbying efforts, the organization, which has changed its name to the Clery Center for Security on Campus, now serves primarily as an educational agency that supports institutions in their compliance efforts.

The International Association of Campus Law Enforcement Administrators (IACLEA) advances public safety for educational institutions by providing educational resources, advocacy, and professional development services. IACLEA is the leading voice for the campus public safety community.

IACLEA was created by 11 college and university security directors who met in November of 1958 at Arizona State University to discuss job challenges and mutual problems and to create a clearinghouse for information and issues shared by campus public safety directors across the country. Today, IACLEA membership represents more than 1,200 colleges and universities in 20 countries. In addition to the colleges and universities that are institutional members, IACLEA has 2,000 individual memberships held by campus law enforcement staff, criminal justice faculty members, and municipal chiefs of police" (IACLEA, 2012).

According to Fisher and Sloan (2007), "[t]he past 20 or so years ha[ve] seen key development in the context of campus security: the *professionalization* of the individuals and departments charged with the sometimes daunting task of reducing opportunities for on-campus victimization, responding to calls for assistance, and providing services to crime victims. The professionalization has touched almost all aspects of campus security and has resulted in significant changes in, and upgrades to, security policies" (p. 14). The authors indicated that the movement from service as a "night watchman" to the current role on many campuses of high-tech police departments, which may also have "information security and infrastructure protection" (p. 14) responsibilities, has been a dramatic role change.

Sloan and Lanier (2007) described the evolution of community policing on college and university campuses and noted other current trends that related to campus police and security policies. Bromley (2007) explained the evolution of campus police and security services in some detail and laid out his view of the modern campus police and security agency. CAS standards should guide campus police and security programs to best practices in their new roles.

References, Readings, and Resources

Bickel, R. D., & Lake, P. F. (1999). *The rights and responsibilities of the modern university: Who assumes the risks of college life?* Chapel Hill, N.C.: Carolina Academic Press.

Bromley, M. L. (2007). The evolution of campus policing: Different models for different eras. In Fisher, B. S., & Sloan III, J. J. (Eds.). *Campus crime: Legal, social and policy issues* (2nd ed., pp. 280-304). Springfield, IL: Charles C. Thomas.

Clery Center for Security on Campus (nd). http://www.clerycenter.org

The Clery Center for Security on Campus (2012). Jeanne Clery and the SOC story. Retrieved from http://www. clerycenter.org/

Fisher, B. S., & Sloan III, J. J. (Eds.). (2007). Campus crime policy. Legal, social and security contexts (pp 3-22) in *Campus crime: Legal, social and policy issues* (2nd ed., pp. 3-22). Springfield, IL: Charles C. Thomas.

Fisher, B. S., Hartman, J. L., Cullen, F. T., & Turner, M. G. (2002). Making campuses safer for students: The Clery Act as a symbolic legal reform. *Stetson Law Review, 32*(1), 61-89. Retrieved from http://www.law.stetson.edu/lawrev/abstracts/PDF/32-1Fisher.pdf

Gregory, D. E. (2001). Crime on campus: Compliance, liability and safety. *Campus Law Enforcement Journal, 31*(4), 27-32.

Gregory, D. E. (2002, November-December). Hiding crime on campus: Current reality or paranoia from the past? *Campus Safety and Student Development, 4*(2), 17, 30-32.

Gregory, D. E., & Janosik, S. M. (2002). The Clery Act: How effective is it? Perceptions from the field - The current state of the research and recommendations for improvement. *Stetson Law Review, 32*(1), 7-59. Retrieved from http://www.law.stetson.edu/lawrev/abstracts/PDF/32-1Gregory.pdf

International Association of Campus Law Enforcement Administrators (IACLEA). http://www.iaclea.org/visitors/about/

Janosik, S. M. (2004). Parents' views of the Clery Act and campus safety. *The Journal of College Student Development, 45*(1), 43-56.

Janosik, S. M., & Gehring, D. D. (2003). *The impact of the Jeanne Clery Act Disclosure of Campus Security Policy and the Campus Crime Statistics Act on student decision-making.* EPI Policy Paper No. 10. Blacksburg, VA: Virginia Tech.

Janosik, S. M., & Gregory, D. E. (2003). The Clery Act and its influence on campus law enforcement practices. *NASPA Journal, 44*(1), 182-199. Retrieved from http://publications.naspa.org/cgi/viewcontent.cgi?article=1311&context=naspajournal

Jeanne Clery Disclosure of Campus Security Policy and Campus Crime Statistics Act. (2000). 20 U.S.C. § 1092(f).

Nicoletti, J., Spencer-Thomas, S., & Bollinger, C. (Eds) (2010). *Violence goes to college: The authoritative guide to prevention and intervention* (2nd Ed.). Springfield, IL: Charles C. Thomas.

Seng, M. (1995). The Crime Awareness and Campus Security Act: Some observations, critical comments and suggestions. In B. Fisher & J. Sloan, III (Eds.), *Campus crime: Legal, social and policy perspectives.* (pp. 38-52). Springfield, IL: Charles C. Thomas.

Seng, M., & Koehler, N. (1993). The Crime Awareness and Campus Security Act: A critical analysis. *Journal of Crime and Justice, 16*, 97-110.

Sloan III, J. J., & Lanier, M. M. (2007). Community policing on university campuses: Tradition, practices, and outlook. In Fisher, B. S., & Sloan III, J. J.(Eds.). (2007). *Campus crime: Legal, social and policy issues* (2nd ed.). Springfield, IL: Charles C. Thomas.

Smith, M. C. (1988). *Coping with crime on campus.* New York, NY: American Council on Education: Macmillan

Smith, M. C. (1989). *Crime and campus police: A handbook for police officers and administrators.* Asheville, NC: College Administration Publications.

Smith, M. C., & Fossey, R. (1995). *Crime on campus: Legal issues and campus administration.* Westport, CT: Greenwood Press.

Westat, Ward, D., and Mann, J.L. (2011). *The handbook for campus safety and security reporting.* U.S. Department of Education, Office of Postsecondary Education, Retrieved from https://www2.ed.gov/admins/lead/safety/handbook.pdf

Contextual Statement Contributors
Current Edition:
Dennis E. Gregory, Old Dominion University

Previous Editions:
Dennis E. Gregory, Old Dominion University

Campus Police and Security Programs
CAS Standards and Guidelines

Campus Police and Security Programs (CPSP) serve to provide a safe and orderly campus by enforcing the law, enforcing institutional and community standards, and fostering students' learning and development through the provision of safety education.

CPSP must develop, disseminate, implement, and regularly review their missions, which must be consistent with the mission of the institution and with applicable professional standards. The mission must be appropriate for the institution's students and other constituents. Mission statements must reference student learning and development.

CPSP must develop goals that address the institution's needs to maintain a safe and orderly campus:
- communicate and enforce applicable laws and ordinances
- collaborate with appropriate institutional agencies and programs to develop, disseminate, interpret, and enforce campus policies and procedures
- protect rights of students, employees, pre-college program participants, and campus visitors in the administration of campus police and security programs and enforcement of the law
- respond to student behavioral problems and violations of the law in a fair and consistent manner
- facilitate and encourage respect for the law, campus safety, and institutional governance
- initiate and encourage educational activities that serve to reduce violations of the law and of campus regulations

CPSP should encourage appropriate individual and group behavior as well as serve the campus community by reducing disruption, harm, and violation of institutional policy and the law.

CPSP should be conducted in ways that will serve to foster the ethical development and personal integrity of students and promote an environment that is consistent with the overall educational goals of the institution.

To achieve their mission, Campus Police and Security Programs (CPSP) must contribute to
- students' formal education, which includes both the curriculum and the co-curriculum
- student progression and timely completion of educational goals
- preparation of students for their careers, citizenship, and lives
- student learning and development

To contribute to student learning and development, CPSP must
- identify relevant and desirable student learning and development outcomes
- articulate how the student learning and development outcomes align with the six CAS student learning and development domains and related dimensions
- assess relevant and desirable student learning and development
- provide evidence of impact on outcomes
- articulate contributions to or support of student learning and development in the domains not specifically assessed
- use evidence gathered to create strategies for improvement of programs and services

STUDENT LEARNING AND DEVELOPMENT DOMAINS AND DIMENSIONS

Domain: knowledge acquisition, integration, construction, and application
- Dimensions: understanding knowledge from a range of disciplines; connecting knowledge to other knowledge, ideas, and experiences; constructing knowledge; and relating knowledge to daily life

Domain: cognitive complexity
- Dimensions: critical thinking, reflective thinking, effective reasoning, and creativity

Domain: intrapersonal development
- Dimensions: realistic self-appraisal, self-understanding, and self-respect; identity development; commitment to ethics and integrity; and spiritual awareness

Domain: interpersonal competence
- Dimensions: meaningful relationships, interdependence, collaboration, and effective leadership

Domain: humanitarianism and civic engagement
- Dimensions: understanding and appreciation of cultural and human differences, social responsibility, global perspective, and sense of civic responsibility

Domain: practical competence
- Dimensions: pursuing goals, communicating effectively, technical competence, managing personal affairs, managing career development, demonstrating professionalism, maintaining health and wellness, and living a purposeful and satisfying life

[LD Outcomes: See *The Council for the Advancement of Standards*

Learning and Development Outcomes statement for examples of outcomes related to these domains and dimensions.]

CPSP must be
- **intentionally designed**
- **guided by theories and knowledge of learning and development**
- **integrated into the life of the institution**
- **reflective of developmental and demographic profiles of the student population**
- **responsive to needs of individuals, populations with distinct needs, and relevant constituencies**
- **delivered using multiple formats, strategies, and contexts**
- **designed to provide universal access**

CPSP must collaborate with colleagues and departments across the institution to promote student learning and development, persistence, and success.

CPSP must establish authority and policies within the context of the mission and purpose. A written statement describing the authority, philosophy, jurisdiction, and procedures of the CPSP must be developed and disseminated to all members of the campus community.

This CPSP statement should address
- the jurisdiction
- the authority
- the distinction between security and policing responsibilities
- the relationship between campus police and security programs and external law enforcement agencies with a clear description, including guidelines regarding when external law enforcement authorities will be called in
- the relationship that campus police and security programs have with institutional student conduct programs
- the impact of the "Clery Act" in the USA and other laws governing CPSP operations
- the CPSP intention to respond to and protect the constitutional or contractual rights of members of the community and the community itself

The institutional policy statement should
- describe whether the CPSP is a police agency, a campus security agency, or some combination thereof
- indicate whether the institution contracts with a security agency or a local law enforcement agency to provide services to the campus or whether the CPSP is a branch of the institution
- applicable laws, ordinances, or policies that govern the CPSP operations

If an institution chooses, or is required by law, to provide a CPSP that is maintained and operated by the institution as a separate internal agency, it must
- **clearly identify the authority of this agency**
- **determine the levels of authority within the agency**

(e.g., ranks of officers, supervisory structure, task assignments)
- **determine whether the agency will include sworn police officers, non-sworn security personnel, or some combination of both.**

Roles and functions of CPSP personnel who operate within the institution as a separate agency, an external non-police agency, or a local law enforcement agency may include
- patrolling campus and surrounding property
- enforcing applicable laws
- enforcing institutional policy to include participation in the student conduct system
- investigating violations of law or institutional policy
- enforcing institutional traffic and parking regulations
- examining and ensuring the integrity and safety of institutional facilities
- advising students and others on their rights and responsibilities
- providing institutional safety and crime awareness programs for members of the community and external entities
- maintaining accurate records of all actions

A CPSP officer may be assigned responsibility for training student conduct board members and other student conduct personnel regarding laws and policies related to the institution and for informing faculty, administration, and staff about legal and disciplinary matters.

If an institution chooses to contract with an external non-police agency such as a private security company, it must clearly identify the authority, responsibility, and limits of this agency and its personnel. The institution must make this information available to employees, students, and visitors and identify the institutional employee to whom this agency and its personnel report.

The institution must inform local law enforcement agencies of the authority, responsibility, and limits of any contracted agency and its personnel.

If an institution contracts with a local law enforcement agency to provide police and security services on campus, it must
- **clearly identify any additional or extraordinary responsibilities of these personnel while working on behalf of the institution**
- **provide training to these personnel regarding their responsibility for enforcement of institutional policy**
- **identify an institutional employee to whom this agency and its personnel report while working on behalf of the institution**

Part 3. Organization and Leadership

To achieve program and student learning and development outcomes, Campus Police and Security Programs (CPSP) must be purposefully structured for effectiveness. CPSP must have clearly stated and current
- **goals and outcomes**

- policies and procedures
- responsibilities and performance expectations for personnel
- organizational charts demonstrating clear channels of authority

Leaders must model ethical behavior and institutional citizenship.

Leaders with organizational authority for CPSP must provide strategic planning, management and supervision, and program advancement.

Strategic Planning
- articulate a vision and mission that drive short- and long-term planning
- set goals and objectives based on the needs of the populations served, intended student learning and development outcomes, and program outcomes
- facilitate continuous development, implementation, and assessment of program effectiveness and goal attainment congruent with institutional mission and strategic plans
- promote environments that provide opportunities for student learning, development, and engagement
- develop, adapt, and improve programs and services in response to the changing needs of populations served and evolving institutional priorities
- include diverse perspectives to inform decision making

Management and Supervision
- plan, allocate, and monitor the use of fiscal, physical, human, intellectual, and technological resources
- manage human resource processes including recruitment, selection, professional development, supervision, performance planning, succession planning, evaluation, recognition, and reward
- influence others to contribute to the effectiveness and success of the unit
- empower professional, support, and student personnel to become effective leaders
- encourage and support collaboration with colleagues and departments across the institution
- encourage and support scholarly contributions to the profession
- identify and address individual, organizational, and environmental conditions that foster or inhibit mission achievement
- use current and valid evidence to inform decisions
- incorporate sustainability practices in the management and design of programs, services, and facilities
- understand appropriate technologies and integrate them into programs and services
- be knowledgeable about codes and laws relevant to programs and services and ensure that programs and services meet those requirements
- assess and take action to mitigate potential risks

Program Advancement
- advocate for and actively promote the mission and goals of the programs and services
- inform stakeholders about issues affecting practice
- facilitate processes to reach consensus where wide support is needed
- advocate for representation in strategic planning initiatives at divisional and institutional levels

A member of the campus community who possesses appropriate training and experience must be designated as the person to whom the CPSP reports.

This person should be at a senior administrative level, beyond the internal command structure of the CPSP.

The person responsible for the CPSP should have an educational background in the behavioral sciences (e.g., college student affairs, psychology, sociology, student development including moral and ethical development, higher education administration, counseling, law, criminology, or criminal justice).

The person responsible for the CPSP, the most senior person within the CPSP command structure, and all other professional staff members in CPSP should possess
- a clear understanding of the legal requirements for substantive and procedural due process
- legal knowledge sufficient to confer with attorneys involved in law enforcement as well as student disciplinary proceedings and other aspects of the student conduct services system
- a general interest in and commitment to the welfare and development of students who violate the law or institutional policies
- demonstrated skills in decision-making processes and conflict resolution
- teaching and consulting skills appropriate for educating, advising, and coordinating CPSP personnel
- the ability to communicate and interact with students and other members of the community regardless of race, sex, disability, sexual orientation, and other personal characteristics
- an understanding of the requirements relative to confidentiality and security of law enforcement and student conduct programs files
- the ability to create an atmosphere in which staff feel free to ask questions and obtain assistance

Part 4. Human Resources

Campus Police and Security Programs (CPSP) must be staffed adequately by individuals qualified to accomplish mission and goals.

CPSP must have access to technical and support personnel adequate to accomplish their mission.

Within institutional guidelines, CPSP must
- establish procedures for personnel recruitment and selection, training, performance planning, and

evaluation
- set expectations for supervision and performance
- provide personnel access to continuing and advanced education and appropriate professional development opportunities to improve their competence, skills, and leadership capacity
- consider work/life options available to personnel (e.g., compressed work schedules, flextime, job sharing, remote work, or telework) to promote recruitment and retention of personnel

Administrators of CPSP must
- ensure that all personnel have updated position descriptions
- implement recruitment and selection/hiring strategies that produce a workforce inclusive of under-represented populations
- develop promotion practices that are fair, inclusive, proactive, and non-discriminatory

Personnel responsible for delivery of CPSP must have written performance goals, objectives, and outcomes for each year's performance cycle to be used to plan, review, and evaluate work and performance. The performance plan must be updated regularly to reflect changes during the performance cycle.

Evaluation of the CPSP should include
- performance evaluations of all staff members by their supervisors
- periodic performance evaluations of individual hearing boards
- ongoing evaluation of training programs and publications
- periodic review of applicable laws and current case law to ensure compliance

Results of individual personnel evaluations must be used to recognize personnel performance, address performance issues, implement individual and/or collective personnel development and training programs, and inform the assessment of programs and services.

CPSP personnel, when hired and throughout their employment, must receive appropriate and thorough training.

CPSP personnel, including student employees and volunteers, must have access to resources or receive specific training on
- institutional policies pertaining to functions or activities they support
- privacy and confidentiality policies
- laws regarding access to student records
- policies and procedures for dealing with sensitive institutional information
- policies and procedures related to technology used to store or access student records and institutional data
- how and when to refer those in need of additional assistance to qualified personnel and have access

to a supervisor for assistance in making these judgments
- systems and technologies necessary to perform their assigned responsibilities
- ethical and legal uses of technology

Initial and inservice training of all CPSP personnel must be provided.

In order for CPSP personnel to fulfill their roles and functions, initial training must include
- police-related training that is the same as or equal to the training provided to personnel of other police agencies
- a review of constitutional and other relevant individual and institutional legal rights and responsibilities
- a description of the organization of the CPSP
- information regarding the authority of the CPSP
- policies regarding the use and carry of weapons
- offensive and defensive weapons training if weapons are authorized to be carried
- information regarding informal and formal agreements with local law enforcement agencies off campus
- records documenting that the needs of the agency are addressed and that there is accountability for all training provided

Training for CPSP agencies that provide security services and for CPSP personnel who do not provide policing duties (e.g., security and other non-sworn personnel) must be appropriate to their responsibilities. This training may differ from police training.

Inservice training should include participation in relevant and on-going workshops, seminars, and conferences. A library containing current resources about campus police and security issues should be maintained and be accessible to CPSP personnel.

CPSP personnel must engage in continuing professional development activities to keep abreast of the research, theories, legislation, policies, and developments that affect their programs and services.

Administrators of CPSP must ensure that personnel are knowledgeable about and trained in safety, emergency procedures, and crisis prevention and response. Risk management efforts must address identification of threatening conduct or behavior and must incorporate a system for responding to and reporting such behaviors.

Because CPSP personnel may also be involved in the student conduct process, they must be provided with
- an overview of all student conduct policies and procedures of the institution
- an explanation of the operation of the student conduct process at all levels, including authority and jurisdiction
- an overview of the institution's philosophy on student conduct and the role of CPSP in this

process
- roles and functions of all student conduct bodies and their members
- an explanation of sanctions
- an explanation of institutional policies and privacy laws regarding access to student records and other sensitive institutional information (e.g., in the U.S., the Family Educational Rights and Privacy Act, FERPA) and the differences between "education records" and "law enforcement records" that result from this law
- an explanation of pertinent ethics, including particularly the importance of privacy of student disciplinary records and addressing bias and conflict of interest in the student conduct process
- a description of available personal counseling programs and referral resources
- an outline of conditions and interactions that may involve external enforcement officials, attorneys, witnesses, parents of accused students, and the media
- training in the developmental and interpersonal issues likely to arise among college students

Personnel must be knowledgeable of and trained in safety and emergency procedures for securing and vacating facilities.

PROFESSIONAL PERSONNEL

CPSP professional personnel either must hold an earned graduate or professional degree in a field relevant to their position or must possess an appropriate combination of educational credentials and related work experience.

INTERNS OR GRADUATE ASSISTANTS

Degree- or credential-seeking interns or graduate assistants must be qualified by enrollment in an appropriate field of study and relevant experience. These students must be trained and supervised by professional personnel who possess applicable educational credentials and work experience and have supervisory experience. Supervisors must be cognizant of the dual roles interns and graduate assistants have as both student and employee.

Supervisors must
- adhere to parameters of students' job descriptions
- articulate intended learning outcomes in student job descriptions
- adhere to agreed-upon work hours and schedules
- offer flexible scheduling when circumstances necessitate

Supervisors and students must both agree to suitable compensation if circumstances necessitate additional hours.

STUDENT EMPLOYEES AND VOLUNTEERS

Student employees and volunteers must be carefully selected, trained, supervised, and evaluated. Students must have access to a supervisor. Student employees and volunteers must be provided clear job descriptions, pre-

service training based on assessed needs, and continuing development.

Students in academic programs, particularly in areas such as police science, forensic science, criminalistics, law, or criminology, may assist the campus police and security programs through student employment, practicums, internships, and assistantships.

Students who participate in some services to the CPSPs (with proper supervision) may be awarded academic credit. Clear objectives and assignments should be outlined to ensure that a student's grade for this participation is in no way influenced by his or her decisions on a particular case.

Part 5. Ethics

Campus Police and Security Programs (CPSP) must
- review applicable professional ethical standards and must adopt or develop and implement appropriate statements of ethical practice
- publish and adhere to statements of ethical practice and ensure their periodic review
- orient new personnel to relevant ethical standards and statements of ethical practice and related institutional policies

Statements of ethical standards must
- specify that CPSP personnel respect privacy and maintain confidentiality in communications and records as delineated by privacy laws
- specify limits on disclosure of information contained in students' records as well as requirements to disclose to appropriate authorities
- address conflicts of interest, or appearance thereof, by personnel in the performance of their work
- reflect the responsibility of personnel to be fair, objective, and impartial in their interactions with others
- reference management of institutional funds
- reference appropriate behavior regarding research and assessment with human participants, confidentiality of research and assessment data, and students' rights and responsibilities
- include the expectation that personnel confront and hold accountable other personnel who exhibit unethical behavior
- address issues surrounding scholarly integrity

CPSP personnel must
- employ ethical decision making in the performance of their duties
- inform users of programs and services of ethical obligations and limitations emanating from codes and laws or from licensure requirements
- recognize and avoid conflicts of interest that could adversely influence their judgment or objectivity and, when unavoidable, recuse themselves from the situation
- perform their duties within the scope of their position, training, expertise, and competence

- make referrals when issues presented exceed the scope of the position

Part 6. Law, Policy, and Governance

Campus Police and Security Programs (CPSP) must be in compliance with laws, regulations, and policies that relate to their respective responsibilities and that pose legal obligations, limitations, risks, and liabilities for the institution as a whole. Examples include constitutional, statutory, regulatory, and case law; relevant law and orders emanating from codes and laws; and the institution's policies.

CPSP must have access to legal advice needed for personnel to carry out their assigned responsibilities.

CPSP must inform personnel, appropriate officials, and users of programs and services about existing and changing legal obligations, risks and liabilities, and limitations.

CPSP must inform personnel about professional liability insurance options and refer them to external sources If the institution does not provide coverage.

CPSP must have written policies and procedures on operations, transactions, or tasks that have legal implications.

CPSP must regularly review policies. The revision and creation of policies must be informed by best practices, available evidence, and policy issues in higher education.

CPSP must have procedures and guidelines consistent with institutional policy for responding to threats, emergencies, and crisis situations. Systems and procedures must be in place to disseminate timely and accurate information to students, other members of the institutional community, and appropriate external organizations during emergency situations.

Personnel must neither participate in nor condone any form of harassment or activity that demeans persons or creates an intimidating, hostile, or offensive environment.

CPSP must purchase or obtain permission to use copyrighted materials and instruments. References to copyrighted materials and instruments must include appropriate citations.

CPSP must inform personnel about internal and external governance organizations that affect programs and services.

The institution's policies regarding the administration of applicable laws must be clearly described in writing. Elements to be addressed in this policy must include
- CPSP personnel arrest authority
- circumstances under which, and by whom, weapons will be carried by CPSP personnel
- the roles of various personnel within the CPSP
- a formal or informal agreement with local law enforcement personnel regarding jurisdiction
- policies regarding campus crime reports, crime

logs, and other required documentation
- threat assessment procedures

Procedures and processes must be designed by the CPSP to ensure that all relevant legal requirements are met and, if within a private institution, how private status impacts the institution with regard to law enforcement.

CPSP should provide a statement of relevant state/provincial and local laws regarding status as "special police or deputies" or other designations that allow law enforcement responsibilities.

CPSP should assist all employees and students of the institution to understand the sources and lines of authority of the CPSP.

The institution must be clear about how it defines the jurisdiction of the CPSP to include whether officers have authority beyond the borders of the campus and policy addressing the pursuit of suspects who leave the campus, the areas of patrol for CPSP personnel, and the relationship of the CPSP with local law enforcement agencies beyond the surrounding community.

Agreements should be reached between law enforcement agencies in adjoining jurisdictions or within the agency's jurisdiction to provide assistance to each other in the event of disaster, mass disorder, terrorism, or other emergency situations.

CPSP must maintain records of patrol activities, actions taken by CPSP personnel, information for a campus crime log, evidence to be used by CPSP personnel in law enforcement activities, and student conduct proceedings on campus.

The institution must clearly state the legal issues and conduct regulations that apply to student organizations, the procedures that will be followed in the enforcement of cases related to student organizations, and the guidelines used to determine if actions of individual members or small groups within an organization constitute action by the organization.

The institution must clearly state the legal issues and conduct regulations that apply off campus and which are, as a result, the responsibility of CPSP personnel. These include dealing with individual students and dealing with off-campus enforcement at residential facilities owned and operated by student organizations.

Appropriate policies and practices to ensure compliance with regulations should include notification to all constituencies of their rights and responsibilities under applicable laws as well as the student conduct system; a written description; accurate record keeping of all aspects of the campus police and security operations; and regular reviews of the campus police and security policies and practices.

CPSP must work with the institution to develop clear policy about the protocols for the use of video surveillance.

Part 7. Diversity, Equity, and Access

Within the context of each institution's mission and in accordance with institutional policies and applicable codes and laws, Campus Police and Security Programs (CPSP) must create and maintain educational and work environments that are welcoming, accessible, inclusive, equitable, and free from harassment.

CPSP must not discriminate on the basis of disability; age; race; cultural identity; ethnicity; nationality; family educational history (e.g., first generation to attend college); political affiliation; religious affiliation; sex; sexual orientation; gender identity and expression; marital, social, economic, or veteran status; or any other basis included in institutional policies and codes and laws.

CPSP must
- advocate for sensitivity to multicultural and social justice concerns by the institution and its personnel
- ensure physical, program, and resource access for all constituents
- modify or remove policies, practices, systems, technologies, facilities, and structures that create barriers or produce inequities
- ensure that when facilities and structures cannot be modified, they do not impede access to programs, services, and resources
- establish goals for diversity, equity, and access
- foster communication and practices that enhance understanding of identity, culture, self-expression, and heritage
- promote respect for commonalities and differences among people within their historical and cultural contexts
- address the characteristics and needs of diverse constituents when establishing and implementing culturally relevant and inclusive programs, services, policies, procedures, and practices
- provide personnel with diversity, equity, and access training and hold personnel accountable for applying the training to their work
- respond to the needs of all constituents served when establishing hours of operation and developing methods of delivering programs, services, and resources
- recognize the needs of distance and online learning students by directly providing or assisting them to gain access to comparable services and resources

Part 8. Internal and External Relations

Campus Police and Security Programs (CPSP) must reach out to individuals, groups, communities, and organizations internal and external to the institution to
- establish, maintain, and promote understanding and effective relations with those that have a significant interest in or potential effect on the students or other constituents served by the programs and services
- garner support and resources for programs and services as defined by the mission
- collaborate in offering or improving programs and services to meet the needs of students and other constituents and to achieve program and student outcomes
- engage diverse individuals, groups, communities, and organizations to enrich the educational environment and experiences of students and other constituents
- disseminate information about the programs and services

Promotional and descriptive information must be accurate and free of deception and misrepresentation.

CPSP must have procedures and guidelines consistent with institutional policy for
- communicating with the media
- distributing information through print, broadcast, and online sources
- contracting with external organizations for delivery of programs and services
- cultivating, soliciting, and managing gifts
- applying to and managing funds from grants

Representatives of the CPSP should meet regularly with pertinent campus constituencies (e.g., student government, student development offices, staff, faculty members, academic administrators, legal counsel) to exchange information concerning their respective operations and to identify ways to work together to prevent behavioral problems and to correct existing problems. Such collaborative efforts may include educational programs and joint publications.

CPSP representatives should also meet periodically with relevant external agencies (e.g., local police, district attorneys, and service providers) to ensure their understanding about the campus police and security programs as well as to address student behavior problems in an effective manner.

CPSP must publish information about its specific programs for the campus community.

CPSP publications must contain
- the Clery Act (in the USA) campus crime statistics report
- campus policies, such as those concerning legal representation by campus legal services if available, the maintenance of law enforcement records, and the destruction of records
- campus procedures, such as filing a crime report or request for disciplinary action, gathering information, conducting an investigation
- a general explanation of how and when non-campus law enforcement officials are engaged.

Publications must be distributed to all members of the campus community.

Dissemination methods may include electronic media; the

institutional catalog; orientation programs; the student handbook; specific publications related to requirements of the Clery Act and the Drug Free Schools and Community Act (in the USA) and other legal requirements; and admissions, registration, and billing materials.

Part 9. Financial Resources

Campus Police and Security Programs (CPSP) must have funding to accomplish the mission and goals.

In establishing and prioritizing funding resources, CPSP must conduct comprehensive analyses to determine
- unmet needs of the unit
- relevant expenditures
- external and internal resources
- impact on students and the institution

CPSP must use the budget as a planning tool to reflect commitment to the mission and goals of the programs and services and of the institution.

CPSP must administer funds in accordance with established institutional accounting procedures.

CPSP must demonstrate efficient and effective use and responsible stewardship of fiscal resources consistent with institutional protocols.

Financial reports must provide an accurate financial overview of the organization and provide clear, understandable, and timely data upon which personnel can plan and make informed decisions.

Procurement procedures must
- be consistent with institutional policies
- ensure that purchases comply with laws and codes for usability and access
- ensure that the institution receives value for the funds spent
- consider information available for comparing the ethical and environmental impact of products and services purchased

Part 10. Technology

Campus Police and Security Programs (CPSP) must have technology to support the achievement of their mission and goals. The technology and its use must comply with institutional policies and procedures and with relevant codes and laws.

CPSP must use technologies to
- provide updated information regarding mission, location, staffing, programs, services, and official contacts to students and other constituents in accessible formats
- provide an avenue for students and other constituents to communicate sensitive information in a secure format
- enhance the delivery of programs and services for all students

CPSP must
- back up data on a regular basis
- adhere to institutional policies regarding ethical and legal use of technology
- articulate policies and procedures for protecting the confidentiality and security of information
- implement a replacement plan and cycle for all technology with attention to sustainability
- incorporate accessibility features into technology-based programs and services

When providing student access to technology, CPSP must
- have policies on the use of technology that are clear, easy to understand, and available to all students
- provide information or referral to support services for those needing assistance in accessing or using technology
- provide instruction or training on how to use the technology
- inform students of implications of misuse of technologies

Part 11. Facilities and Equipment

Campus Police and Security Programs' (CPSP) facilities must be intentionally designed and located in suitable, accessible, and safe spaces that demonstrate universal design and support the program's mission and goals.

Facilities must be designed to engage various constituents and promote learning.

CPSP facilities should include private rooms where individual consultations may be held, hearing room facilities, a meeting room for small groups, a library or resource area, and a secure location for records. The facilities should also be designed to promote the personal safety of the individuals involved in the CPSP (e.g., campus alert systems, multiple methods of egress, and panic buttons).

Personnel must have workspaces that are suitably located and accessible, well equipped, adequate in size, and designed to support their work and responsibilities.

The design of the facilities must guarantee the security and privacy of records and ensure the confidentiality of sensitive information and conversations. Personnel must be able to secure their work.

CPSP must incorporate sustainable practices in use of facilities and purchase of equipment. Facilities and equipment must be evaluated on an established cycle and be in compliance with codes, laws, and accepted practices for access, health, safety, and security.

When acquiring capital equipment, CPSP must take into account expenses related to regular maintenance and life cycle costs.

Part 12. Assessment

Campus Police and Security Programs (CPSP) must

develop assessment plans and processes.

Assessment plans must articulate an ongoing cycle of assessment activities.

CPSP must

- specify programmatic goals and intended outcomes
- identify student learning and development outcomes
- employ multiple measures and methods
- develop manageable processes for gathering, interpreting, and evaluating data
- document progress toward achievement of goals and outcomes
- interpret and use assessment results to demonstrate accountability
- report aggregated results to respondent groups and stakeholders
- use assessment results to inform planning and decision-making
- assess effectiveness of implemented changes
- provide evidence of improvement of programs and services

Assessment and evaluation activities may include

- the degree to which CPSP personnel are appropriately following institutional procedures and guidelines to gather feedback from students, faculty, staff, and the community on the performance and effectiveness of the campus police and security system and the learning and development effects on students and other members of the institutional community
- annual trends in crime statistics, case load, rates of recidivism, and types of offenses
- the effects of programming designed to prevent crime, increase safety related behaviors, provide a safe environment, and prevent behavioral problems

CPSP must employ ethical practices in the assessment process.

CPSP must have access to adequate fiscal, human, professional development, and technological resources to develop and implement assessment plans.

General Standards revised in 2014;
CPSP content developed in 2012

Campus Religious and Spiritual Programs
CAS Contextual Statement

The pursuit of religious liberty drove the founding of colonial America, many early colonists being religious dissenters. In order to reinforce and protect the ideal of free religious expression, they founded the early colleges to educate colonial leadership, weaving Protestant Christian values throughout the curriculum and college life. The continuing turmoil in England and Europe—wars, famine, population growth and urbanization, and religious intolerance—combined with expanding trade to encourage the migration of settlers to the New World. With these immigrants came an increasing diversity of religious belief that challenged standing practices of religious liberty. New pragmatic pressures on the colonial colleges forced curricular changes to prepare the growing merchant and governing class. While religion continued to figure centrally in college life, the curriculum gradually diversified to meet the vocational needs of the growing colonies and, upon independence from England, of the new nation (Geiger, 2015; Thelin, 2011; Waggoner, 2011).

The 19th century brought continued geographic and population expansion of the United States, and colleges grew and developed along with the needs of the country. Numerous Protestant and fewer Catholic colleges followed the westward expansion, and their missions continued to differentiate in response to the increasing complexity of the nation's activities. The achievements of Europe's new philosophical ideas and sciences began to traverse the Atlantic, fostering innovations in higher education; chief among these were German-style research and alternative critical study of Biblical texts that challenged traditional unmediated readings. Religion's primacy as the chief interpreter of experience was being challenged by the promise of science and technology (Reuben, 1996). The place of religion in education was debated widely and internationally; in the U.S. the implications of the First Amendment for a society of increasing religious plurality continued to be worked out in the courts.

As state-supported universities developed, particularly with federal land grants through the Morrill Acts of 1862 and 1890, the place of religion was mediated by the requirements of emergent constitutional doctrine. Direct university involvement with religion became more restrained, and new co-curricular outlets developed for facilitating religious expression on public campuses. These would later grow into organizations including the YMCA, InterVarsity Fellowship, Catholic Newman Clubs, Jewish Hillel Centers, the Muslim Student Association, and many more. In the meantime, religiously-affiliated institutions continued to flourish, providing a protected space for free religious expression along the lines of particular beliefs. This differentiated model of religion in higher education became the common practice through the 20th century (Geiger, 2015; Schmalzbauer, 2013; Thelin, 2011).

The 1960s brought a challenge to several cultural authorities, including religion. The Vatican Council of 1962 initiated what many saw as liberalizing reforms in the Roman Catholic Church. Several theologians announced the Death of God. Ruling in *Engel v. Vitale* in 1962, the U.S. Supreme Court decided that a prayer approved by the New York Board of Regents for use in opening exercises violated the Establishment Clause of the First Amendment and was therefore impermissible. One year later in *Abington School District v. Schempp*, the Court disallowed Bible reading for similar reasons. The reaction was immediate and intense. These decisions, however, opened the door to teaching *about* religion (as opposed to educating in a particular religious tradition). Soon after, religious studies departments began to appear in colleges and universities, displacing many more theology-oriented programs. The Immigration Act of 1965 initiated a stream of new citizens who brought with them Asian religious practices. The 1960s counterculture helped popularize Eastern ideas, evolving them into a New Age Spirituality to challenge conventional U.S. religious practices. A period of experimentation ensued, much of which originated on college campuses; however, such innovation was challenged in the larger society by new and vocal conservative religious leaders and their organizations (Waggoner, 2011).

The September 11, 2001, attacks on the U.S. brought Islam to the forefront of American consciousness and galvanized interest in religion throughout the world, especially on college campuses. Religious studies courses filled. Discussions and debates on religion and spirituality flourished across all campuses, in and out of classrooms. Conflict also arose as institutional policies were contested over competing perspectives on what the First Amendment's "free exercise" of religion clause meant. Minority religion adherents and increasingly vocal atheist and other non-religious voices argued for access to institutional resources including facilities, student fee allocations, and official media outlets. Majority religion representatives' previously unchallenged dominance now faced a new multi-faith environment. Interfaith relations, dialogue, and programming became a new dimension of student affairs work on increasingly pluralist college and university campuses (e.g., Interfaith Youth Core).

This is the milieu today—a heightened interest in the role of religion in public life with higher education as a major arena where these ideas are being explored. Faculty of all disciplines, student affairs staff, chaplains and campus ministers, and students themselves are all potential resources in this discussion. A rich literature addressing these topics has emerged, and numerous promising practices are being developed.

Sharon Daloz Parks' seminal work, *Big Questions, Worthy Dreams* (2011), provided the theoretical base for conceptualizing faith and spiritual growth in college by extending the work of James Fowler (1981) into young-adult, college-age development. Parker Palmer (1993; Palmer & Zajonc, 2010) made the case in a series of books over 20 years that spiritual development is inextricably bound up with the educational enterprise. Three important social science databases were developed by the Astin team (Astin, Astin, & Lindholm, 2010) at UCLA through the multi-year *Spirituality in Higher Education* national (U.S.) study, by Christian Smith and associates at the University of Notre Dame (Smith, 2009), and by Robert Putnam and David Douglas also at the University of Notre Dame (2010).

Professional associations began to focus on religion, spirituality, and higher education. Among them was NASPA, which created a Knowledge Community focusing on this area and sponsoring the online *Journal of College and Character*. The *Journal of College Student Development* of ACPA began to feature work in this area. Other journals published progress in this emerging area of interest, including *Religion & Education* for coverage across varying faith and spiritual perspectives, and *Christian Higher Education, Catholic Education: A Journal of Inquiry and Practice,* and the *Journal of Jewish Education* for tradition-specific concerns.

Campus religious and spiritual programs can and do vary widely in focus and intent. Spirituality, while it can be associated with religious traditions, is a perspective that deals with questions of meaning, purpose, and well-being apart from religion (Astin, Astin, & Lindholm, 2010). CAS standards and guidelines for campus religious and spiritual programs should be used as a guide to help assess the needs of students and to structure programs to meet the religious and spiritual needs of students. As students look toward more diverse options to fulfill their religious or spiritual development, and as professional practice in the field continues to evolve quickly, institutions must continue to equip their staff members with knowledge of relevant issues. Robert Nash, with colleagues Michele Murray (2010) and Jennifer Jang (2015), provides useful guidance for both faculty and student affairs administrators to help students with questions of purpose and meaning.

Campus religious and spiritual programs may be structured differently on individual campuses according to the needs and limitations of each institution. There is no preferred organizational or programming structure. Organizational structures may range from coordinating committees to individual staff members working directly with these organizations. Institutional type, size, goals, and mission are just a few of the factors that do and should guide both structure and function of religious and spiritual programs on a campus.

One major and important difference among institutions is between those affiliated with a religious tradition and those that are not. Religiously-affiliated institutions may have particular mission statements, creeds, training, or directives that can influence how programs are organized and implemented on their campuses. For U.S. institutions not so affiliated, organization and programming must be guided in the U.S. by Supreme Court decisions relative to First-Amendment guarantees prohibiting the establishment of religion yet allowing free religious expression. In general, the law provides that the state will be neutral in its relations with persons who profess belief or disbelief in any religion. Legal standards are continually evolving in the area of religion in public life. Consequently, those who administer Campus Religious and Spiritual Programs (CRSP) must maintain familiarity with relevant case law.

References, Readings, and Resources

Association of College and University Religious Affairs: www.acuraonline.org

Astin, A., Astin, H., & Lindholm, J. (2010). *Cultivating the spirit: How college can enhance students' inner lives.* San Francisco, CA: Jossey-Bass.

Christian Higher Education: www.tofconline.com/uche

Fowler, J. W. (1981). *Stages of faith: The psychology of human development and the quest for meaning.* San Francisco, CA: Harper & Row.

Geiger, R. L. (2015). *The history of American higher education.* Princeton, NJ: Princeton University Press.

Interfaith Youth Core: www.ifyc.org

Jewish Campus Life: www.hillel.org

Journal of Catholic Education

Journal of College Student Development: www.jcsdonline.org/

Journal of College and Character: www.journals.naspa.org/jcc/

Muslim Student Association: www.msanational.org

Nash, R. J., & Jang, J. J. (2015). *Preparing students for life beyond college.* New York, NY: Routledge.

Nash, R. J., & Murray, M. C. (2010). *Helping college students find purpose: The campus guide to meaning-making.* San Francisco, CA: Jossey-Bass.

National Association of College and University Chaplains, www.nacuc.net

National Association of Student Personnel Administrators (NASPA) Spirituality and Religion in Higher Education Knowledge Community, www.naspa.org/kc

Palmer, P. J. (1993). *To know as we are known: Education as a spiritual journey.* San Francisco, CA: Harper Collins.

Palmer, P. J., & Zajonc, A. (2010). *The heart of higher education: A call to renewal.* San Francisco, CA: Jossey-Bass.

Parks, S. D. (2011). *Big questions, worthy dreams: Mentoring emerging adults in their search for meaning, purpose, and faith* (2nd ed.). San Francisco, CA: Jossey-Bass.

Putnam, R. D., & Campbell, D. E. (2010*). American grace: How religion divides us and unites us.* New York, NY: Simon & Schuster.

Religion & Education, www.tandfonline.com/urel

Reuben, J. A. (1996). *The making of the modern university: Intellectual transformation and the marginalization of morality.* Chicago, IL: University of Chicago Press.

Schmalzbauer, J. (2013). Campus religious life in America: Revitalization and renewal. *Society, 50*(2), 115-131.

Secular Student Alliance: www.secularstudents.org/

Smith, C. (2009). *Souls in transition: The religious and spiritual lives of emerging adults.* New York, NY: Oxford University Press.

Thelin, J. R. (2011). *A history of American higher education* (2nd ed.). Baltimore, MD: Johns Hopkins University Press.

Waggoner, M. D. (2011). *Sacred and secular tensions in higher education: Connecting parallel universities.* New York, NY: Routledge.

Contextual Statement Contributors
Current Edition:
Michael D. Waggoner, University of Northern Iowa

Previous Editions:
Diane L. Cooper, University of Georgia
Merrily S. Dunn, University of Georgia
S. Bryan Rush, University of Georgia/Erskine College
J. D. White, University of Georgia/Student Voice

Campus Religious and Spiritual Programs
CAS Standards and Guidelines

Part 1. Mission

The purpose of Campus Religious and Spiritual Programs (CRSP) is to provide access to programs that enable interested students to pursue full spiritual growth and development and to foster a campus atmosphere in which interested members of the college community may freely express their religion, spirituality, and faith.

A private or religiously affiliated institution may state its preference for a particular faith or spiritual tradition and may directly use its own resources for this purpose.

CRSP must develop, disseminate, implement, and regularly review their missions, which must be consistent with the mission of the institution and with applicable professional standards. The mission must be appropriate for the institution's students and other constituents. Mission statements must reference student learning and development.

Public institutions without formal religious and/or spiritual programs should make provisions for religious and spiritual programs indirectly, that is, through cooperation with off-campus agencies that provide religious services and programs.

The goals of CRSP should provide opportunities for interested students to
- receive the religious and/or spiritual support they seek
- articulate a personal philosophy
- acquire skills and knowledge to address issues of values, ethics, and morality
- examine the interaction of faith, intellectual inquiry, and social responsibility as bases for finding and affirming meaning and satisfaction in life
- participate in dialogue between and among representatives of the religious and/or spiritual and the secular
- participate with others in the expression of their faith(s)

Part 2. Program

To achieve their mission, Campus Religious and Spiritual Programs (CRSP) must contribute to
- students' formal education, which includes both the curriculum and the co-curriculum
- student progression and timely completion of educational goals
- preparation of students for their careers, citizenship, and lives
- student learning and development

To contribute to student learning and development, CRSP must
- identify relevant and desirable student learning and development outcomes

- articulate how the student learning and development outcomes align with the six CAS student learning and development domains and related dimensions
- assess relevant and desirable student learning and development
- provide evidence of impact on outcomes
- articulate contributions to or support of student learning and development in the domains not specifically assessed
- use evidence gathered to create strategies for improvement of programs and services

STUDENT LEARNING AND DEVELOPMENT DOMAINS AND DIMENSIONS

Domain: knowledge acquisition, integration, construction, and application
- Dimensions: understanding knowledge from a range of disciplines; connecting knowledge to other knowledge, ideas, and experiences; constructing knowledge; and relating knowledge to daily life

Domain: cognitive complexity
- Dimensions: critical thinking, reflective thinking, effective reasoning, and creativity

Domain: intrapersonal development
- Dimensions: realistic self-appraisal, self-understanding, and self-respect; identity development; commitment to ethics and integrity; and spiritual awareness

Domain: interpersonal competence
- Dimensions: meaningful relationships, interdependence, collaboration, and effective leadership

Domain: humanitarianism and civic engagement
- Dimensions: understanding and appreciation of cultural and human differences, social responsibility, global perspective, and sense of civic responsibility

Domain: practical competence
- Dimensions: pursuing goals, communicating effectively, technical competence, managing personal affairs, managing career development, demonstrating professionalism, maintaining health and wellness, and living a purposeful and satisfying life

[LD Outcomes: See *The Council for the Advancement of Standards Learning and Development Outcomes* statement for examples of outcomes related to these domains and dimensions.]

CRSP must be
- intentionally designed

- guided by theories and knowledge of learning and development
- integrated into the life of the institution
- reflective of developmental and demographic profiles of the student population
- responsive to needs of individuals, populations with distinct needs, and relevant constituencies
- delivered using multiple formats, strategies, and contexts
- designed to provide universal access

CRSP must collaborate with colleagues and departments across the institution to promote student learning and development, persistence, and success.

CRSP will vary depending on the requirements and beliefs of specific denominations and faiths, as well as the needs and traditions of the particular institution.

To the extent either required or prohibited by constitutional, statutory, or regulatory provisions, institutions must provide reasonable opportunities for students to

- question, explore, understand, affiliate with or avoid, and express or reject various religious faiths and/or spiritual beliefs and practices
- seek individual counseling or group associations for the examination and application of religious and/or spiritual values and beliefs
- worship communally and individually
- pray and meditate

In public institutions, staff members may coordinate programs, while personnel associated with religious groups provide direct service to campus community.

In religiously affiliated and private secular colleges, religious programs and direct service may be provided by staff members of the institution.

The types of religious programs and activities offered may include

- co-curricular religious studies
- opportunities for religious and/or spiritual nurturance
- service opportunities
- where appropriate by law, regulation, or policy, opportunity to propagate religions or faiths
- where appropriate by law, regulation, or policy, opportunity to practice rituals of religion or faith
- advocacy for particular ethical or moral policies in public life
- opportunities to relate religious and spiritual beliefs to academic and professional programs
- programs that mark significant events or experiences in the life of the community, e.g., death, tragedy, memorials, or celebrations

In addition, institutions may provide guidance services to promote spiritual or religious growth. Co-curricular programs (e.g., lectures, discussions, service projects) that are designed to help students understand their faiths and the faiths of others may also be offered.

Part 3. Organization and Leadership

To achieve program and student learning and development outcomes, Campus Religious and Spiritual Programs (CRSP) must be purposefully structured for effectiveness. CRSP must have clearly stated and current

- goals and outcomes
- policies and procedures
- responsibilities and performance expectations for personnel
- organizational charts demonstrating clear channels of authority

Leaders must model ethical behavior and institutional citizenship.

Leaders with organizational authority for CRSP must provide strategic planning, management and supervision, and program advancement.

Strategic Planning

- articulate a vision and mission that drive short- and long-term planning
- set goals and objectives based on the needs of the populations served, intended student learning and development outcomes, and program outcomes
- facilitate continuous development, implementation, and assessment of program effectiveness and goal attainment congruent with institutional mission and strategic plans
- promote environments that provide opportunities for student learning, development, and engagement
- develop, adapt, and improve programs and services in response to the changing needs of populations served and evolving institutional priorities
- include diverse perspectives to inform decision making

Management and Supervision

- plan, allocate, and monitor the use of fiscal, physical, human, intellectual, and technological resources
- manage human resource processes including recruitment, selection, professional development, supervision, performance planning, succession planning, evaluation, recognition, and reward
- influence others to contribute to the effectiveness and success of the unit
- empower professional, support, and student personnel to become effective leaders
- encourage and support collaboration with colleagues and departments across the institution
- encourage and support scholarly contributions to the profession
- identify and address individual, organizational, and environmental conditions that foster or inhibit mission achievement
- use current and valid evidence to inform decisions
- incorporate sustainability practices in the

management and design of programs, services, and facilities
- understand appropriate technologies and integrate them into programs and services
- be knowledgeable about codes and laws relevant to programs and services and ensure that programs and services meet those requirements
- assess and take action to mitigate potential risks

Program Advancement
- advocate for and actively promote the mission and goals of the programs and services
- inform stakeholders about issues affecting practice
- facilitate processes to reach consensus where wide support is needed
- advocate for representation in strategic planning initiatives at divisional and institutional levels

CRSP activities, policies, and procedures should be scrutinized regularly in light of the growing body of law in the area of religion and higher education.

Part 4. Human Resources

Campus Religious and Spiritual Programs (CRSP) must be staffed adequately by individuals qualified to accomplish mission and goals.

CRSP must have access to technical and support personnel adequate to accomplish their mission.

Within institutional guidelines, CRSP must
- establish procedures for personnel recruitment and selection, training, performance planning, and evaluation
- set expectations for supervision and performance
- provide personnel access to continuing and advanced education and appropriate professional development opportunities to improve their competence, skills, and leadership capacity
- consider work/life options available to personnel (e.g., compressed work schedules, flextime, job sharing, remote work, or telework) to promote recruitment and retention of personnel

At public institutions, religious programs may be coordinated by a professional individual and/or a committee. Professional or volunteer persons named (and paid) by the religious and spiritual groups represented on the campus may carry out their respective activities. The title "director" or "coordinator" of religious programs is more appropriate because of the predominantly educational and liaison functions of the position.

At private institutions, campus religious programs are typically coordinated by a professional in an appropriate field or a committee. Additional staff members may be employed by the institution. Religious groups may also provide additional staff for the institution. Religiously related institutions should permit on-campus programs of religions or spiritual beliefs other than those espoused by the institution. Titles for the director or coordinator at private institutions include chaplain, director of religious life or spiritual development, or other title

specific to a religious or spiritual tradition.

Administrators of CRSP must
- ensure that all personnel have updated position descriptions
- implement recruitment and selection/hiring strategies that produce a workforce inclusive of under-represented populations
- develop promotion practices that are fair, inclusive, proactive, and non-discriminatory

Personnel responsible for delivery of CRSP must have written performance goals, objectives, and outcomes for each year's performance cycle to be used to plan, review, and evaluate work and performance. The performance plan must be updated regularly to reflect changes during the performance cycle.

Results of individual personnel evaluations must be used to recognize personnel performance, address performance issues, implement individual and/or collective personnel development and training programs, and inform the assessment of programs and services.

CRSP personnel, when hired and throughout their employment, must receive appropriate and thorough training.

CRSP personnel, including student employees and volunteers, must have access to resources or receive specific training on
- institutional policies pertaining to functions or activities they support
- privacy and confidentiality policies
- laws regarding access to student records
- policies and procedures for dealing with sensitive institutional information
- policies and procedures related to technology used to store or access student records and institutional data
- how and when to refer those in need of additional assistance to qualified personnel and have access to a supervisor for assistance in making these judgments
- systems and technologies necessary to perform their assigned responsibilities
- ethical and legal uses of technology

CRSP personnel must engage in continuing professional development activities to keep abreast of the research, theories, legislation, policies, and developments that affect their programs and services.

Administrators of CRSP must ensure that personnel are knowledgeable about and trained in safety, emergency procedures, and crisis prevention and response. Risk management efforts must address identification of threatening conduct or behavior and must incorporate a system for responding to and reporting such behaviors.

CRSP personnel must be knowledgeable of and trained in safety and emergency procedures for securing and vacating facilities.

PROFESSIONAL PERSONNEL

CRSP professional personnel either must hold an earned graduate or professional degree in a field relevant to their position or must possess an appropriate combination of educational credentials and related work experience.

When the coordinator of religious and/or spiritual programs represents a particular religious and/or spiritual body, that person should possess qualifications consistent with the particular body represented and appropriate for a higher education setting.

Any director or coordinator should have
- an understanding of and a commitment to spiritual and religious development as a part of a student's human growth
- the ability to treat fairly all varieties of campus religious experience and personal faith
- awareness and understanding of the beliefs of religious and spiritual groups affiliated with that campus

Depending upon the legal constraints of the institution, the responsibilities of the director or coordinator for religious and/or spiritual programs may include:
- the development and communication of policies relating to religious and spiritual programs that are educationally sound and legally acceptable
- the development of procedures whereby students may organize for religious, spiritual, or moral purposes and participate in programs and activities aimed at their spiritual and/or religious growth
- the provision of access to campus facilities for those responsible for religious or spiritual programs
- the provision of opportunities for guidance in relation to students' religious or spiritual needs
- coordination with other campus decision makers on matters related to religious and/or spiritual activities such as scheduling and examinations

INTERNS OR GRADUATE ASSISTANTS

Degree- or credential-seeking interns or graduate assistants must be qualified by enrollment in an appropriate field of study and relevant experience. These students must be trained and supervised by professional personnel who possess applicable educational credentials and work experience and have supervisory experience. Supervisors must be cognizant of the dual roles interns and graduate assistants have as both student and employee.

Supervisors must
- adhere to parameters of students' job descriptions
- articulate intended learning outcomes in student job descriptions
- adhere to agreed-upon work hours and schedules
- offer flexible scheduling when circumstances necessitate

Supervisors and students must both agree to suitable compensation if circumstances necessitate additional hours.

STUDENT EMPLOYEES AND VOLUNTEERS

Student employees and volunteers must be carefully selected, trained, supervised, and evaluated. Students must have access to a supervisor. Student employees and volunteers must be provided clear job descriptions, pre-service training based on assessed needs, and continuing development.

Officials should be fair and equitable in relationships with all agencies participating in the program.

Affiliation with appropriate professional organizations is encouraged.

When a staff member represents a particular religious and/or spiritual body, that person should possess qualifications consistent with the particular body they represent and appropriate for a higher education setting.

Part 5. Ethics

Campus Religious and Spiritual Programs (CRSP) must
- review applicable professional ethical standards and must adopt or develop and implement appropriate statements of ethical practice
- publish and adhere to statements of ethical practice and ensure their periodic review
- orient new personnel to relevant ethical standards and statements of ethical practice and related institutional policies

Statements of ethical standards must
- specify that CRSP personnel respect privacy and maintain confidentiality in communications and records as delineated by privacy laws
- specify limits on disclosure of information contained in students' records as well as requirements to disclose to appropriate authorities
- address conflicts of interest, or appearance thereof, by personnel in the performance of their work
- reflect the responsibility of personnel to be fair, objective, and impartial in their interactions with others
- reference management of institutional funds
- reference appropriate behavior regarding research and assessment with human participants, confidentiality of research and assessment data, and students' rights and responsibilities
- include the expectation that personnel confront and hold accountable other personnel who exhibit unethical behavior
- address issues surrounding scholarly integrity

CRSP personnel must
- employ ethical decision making in the performance of their duties
- inform users of programs and services of ethical obligations and limitations emanating from codes and laws or from licensure requirements
- recognize and avoid conflicts of interest that could adversely influence their judgment or objectivity

and, when unavoidable, recuse themselves from the situation
- perform their duties within the scope of their position, training, expertise, and competence
- make referrals when issues presented exceed the scope of the position

Accommodation must be made so that students, faculty members, and staff from various religions and faiths may carry out the essential practices of their belief systems.

CRSP staff members must avoid any actions that favor one particular faith over another.

As the institution carries out its academic program, fair and reasonable consideration should be given to the need of campus members to participate in the basic activities of their faiths. Institutional policies and practices should be reviewed regularly so as to avoid undue interference with the exercise of religious and/or spiritual traditions.

Private institutions that sponsor or require particular religious activities must clearly state so in their pre-admission literature, thus permitting a potential student to exercise choice in this regard before admission.

CRSP staff members must work to provide reasonable access for all groups and points of view to any public forums sponsored by the institution.

Membership requirements for on-campus religious organizations at public institutions must be consistent with the group's stated purposes. All religious and/or spiritual organizations must be accorded the same rights and privileges and be held accountable in the same manner as any other campus organization.

CRSP staff members must attempt to protect students, through policy and practice, from undue influence or harassment from persons advocating particular religious positions or activities.

Part 6. Law, Policy, and Governance

Campus Religious and Spiritual Programs (CRSP) must be in compliance with laws, regulations, and policies that relate to their respective responsibilities and that pose legal obligations, limitations, risks, and liabilities for the institution as a whole. Examples include constitutional, statutory, regulatory, and case law; relevant law and orders emanating from codes and laws; and the institution's policies.

CRSP must have access to legal advice needed for personnel to carry out their assigned responsibilities.
CRSP must inform personnel, appropriate officials, and users of programs and services about existing and changing legal obligations, risks and liabilities, and limitations.

CRSP must inform personnel about professional liability insurance options and refer them to external sources if the institution does not provide coverage.

CRSP must have written policies and procedures on operations, transactions, or tasks that have legal implications.

CRSP must regularly review policies. The revision and creation of policies must be informed by best practices, available evidence, and policy issues in higher education.

CRSP must have procedures and guidelines consistent with institutional policy for responding to threats, emergencies, and crisis situations. Systems and procedures must be in place to disseminate timely and accurate information to students, other members of the institutional community, and appropriate external organizations during emergency situations.

Personnel must neither participate in nor condone any form of harassment or activity that demeans persons or creates an intimidating, hostile, or offensive environment.

CRSP must purchase or obtain permission to use copyrighted materials and instruments. References to copyrighted materials and instruments must include appropriate citations.

CRSP must inform personnel about internal and external governance organizations that affect programs and services.

Part 7. Diversity, Equity, and Access

Within the context of each institution's mission and in accordance with institutional policies and applicable codes and laws, Campus Religious and Spiritual Programs (CRSP) must create and maintain educational and work environments that are welcoming, accessible, inclusive, equitable, and free from harassment.

CRSP must not discriminate on the basis of disability; age; race; cultural identity; ethnicity; nationality; family educational history (e.g., first generation to attend college); political affiliation; religious affiliation; sex; sexual orientation; gender identity and expression; marital, social, economic, or veteran status; or any other basis included in institutional policies and codes and laws.

CRSP must
- advocate for sensitivity to multicultural and social justice concerns by the institution and its personnel
- ensure physical, program, and resource access for all constituents
- modify or remove policies, practices, systems, technologies, facilities, and structures that create barriers or produce inequities
- ensure that when facilities and structures cannot be modified, they do not impede access to programs, services, and resources
- establish goals for diversity, equity, and access
- foster communication and practices that enhance understanding of identity, culture, self-expression, and heritage
- promote respect for commonalities and differences among people within their historical and cultural contexts
- address the characteristics and needs of diverse

constituents when establishing and implementing culturally relevant and inclusive programs, services, policies, procedures, and practices
- provide personnel with diversity, equity, and access training and hold personnel accountable for applying the training to their work
- respond to the needs of all constituents served when establishing hours of operation and developing methods of delivering programs, services, and resources
- recognize the needs of distance and online learning students by directly providing or assisting them to gain access to comparable services and resources

Part 8. Internal and External Relations

Campus Religious and Spiritual Programs (CRSP) must reach out to individuals, groups, communities, and organizations internal and external to the institution to
- establish, maintain, and promote understanding and effective relations with those that have a significant interest in or potential effect on the students or other constituents served by the programs and services
- garner support and resources for programs and services as defined by the mission
- collaborate in offering or improving programs and services to meet the needs of students and other constituents and to achieve program and student outcomes
- engage diverse individuals, groups, communities, and organizations to enrich the educational environment and experiences of students and other constituents
- disseminate information about the programs and services

Promotional and descriptive information must be accurate and free of deception and misrepresentation.

CRSP must have procedures and guidelines consistent with institutional policy for
- communicating with the media
- distributing information through print, broadcast, and online sources
- contracting with external organizations for delivery of programs and services
- cultivating, soliciting, and managing gifts
- applying to and managing funds from grants

Because religion and/or spirituality may be a concern of many academic disciplines and may have an important impact on student development, staff assigned to religious programs should consult with and coordinate their programs with interested colleagues.

The CRSP director or coordinator may interact with faculty and staff formally through advisory councils or through informal contacts.

Continuing attention should be given to developing and improving relationships with both on-campus and off-campus constituencies. Specific religious and/or spiritual programs and action projects may arise from many sources (e.g., academic departments, on-campus functional areas such as residence halls and campus centers, and off-campus organizations, whether local, regional, national, and/or international).

The coordinator, faculty, staff, and administrators of the institution should meet with personnel from religious and/or spiritual groups on a periodic basis.

Part 9. Financial Resources

Campus Religious and Spiritual Programs (CRSP) must have funding to accomplish the mission and goals.

In establishing and prioritizing funding resources, CRSP must conduct comprehensive analyses to determine
- unmet needs of the unit
- relevant expenditures
- external and internal resources
- impact on students and the institution

All institutions must provide sufficient funding for any institutional staff member(s) and the operational costs related to religious and/or spiritual programs.

If this assignment accounts for only a part of an individual staff member's work load, the budget should clearly indicate the portion that is available for religious and spiritual programs.

CRSP must use the budget as a planning tool to reflect commitment to the mission and goals of the programs and services and of the institution.

CRSP must administer funds in accordance with established institutional accounting procedures.

CRSP must demonstrate efficient and effective use and responsible stewardship of fiscal resources consistent with institutional protocols.

Funding for personnel and programs of adjunct agencies (i.e., not directly provided by the institution) must be assumed by the sponsors of the adjunct agency.

Part 10. Technology

Campus Religious and Spiritual Programs (CRSP) must have technology to support the achievement of their mission and goals. The technology and its use must comply with institutional policies and procedures and with relevant codes and laws.

CRSP must use technologies to
- provide updated information regarding mission, location, staffing, programs, services, and official contacts to students and other constituents in accessible formats
- provide an avenue for students and other constituents to communicate sensitive information in a secure format
- enhance the delivery of programs and services for

all students

CRSP must

- back up data on a regular basis
- adhere to institutional policies regarding ethical and legal use of technology
- articulate policies and procedures for protecting the confidentiality and security of information
- implement a replacement plan and cycle for all technology with attention to sustainability
- incorporate accessibility features into technology-based programs and services

When providing student access to technology, CRSP must

- have policies on the use of technology that are clear, easy to understand, and available to all students
- provide information or referral to support services for those needing assistance in accessing or using technology
- provide instruction or training on how to use the technology
- inform students of implications of misuse of technologies

Part 11. Facilities and Equipment

Campus Religious and Spiritual Programs' (CRSP) facilities must be intentionally designed and located in suitable, accessible, and safe spaces that demonstrate universal design and support the program's mission and goals.

Facilities must be designed to engage various constituents and promote learning.

Personnel must have workspaces that are suitably located and accessible, well equipped, adequate in size, and designed to support their work and responsibilities.

The design of the facilities must guarantee the security and privacy of records and ensure the confidentiality of sensitive information and conversations. Personnel must be able to secure their work.

CRSP must incorporate sustainable practices in use of facilities and purchase of equipment. Facilities and equipment must be evaluated on an established cycle and be in compliance with codes, laws, and accepted practices for access, health, safety, and security.

When acquiring capital equipment, CRSP must take into account expenses related to regular maintenance and life cycle costs.

Opportunity must be provided for all student religious and/or spiritual organizations to utilize campus facilities on the same basis as other student organizations.

In public institutions, whenever space is made permanently or exclusively available for specific staff of affiliated agencies, arrangements should be made whereby the institution is appropriately reimbursed for expenses.

Private institutions may provide facilities designed to suit the purpose(s) of a specific religious group(s).

Institutions should provide fair and equitable arrangements and facilities (including in campus centers, academic buildings, or residential units) for specific religious and/or spiritual groups' programming and practices.

Suitable areas should be provided for individual meditation and small group spiritual interaction.

The institution should provide for or coordinate student religious and/or spiritual dietary differences.

Part 12. Assessment

Campus Religious and Spiritual Programs (CRSP) must develop assessment plans and processes.

Assessment plans must articulate an ongoing cycle of assessment activities.

Each institution should require evaluation of its religious program to determine the achievement of goals, the constituencies reached, and its overall effectiveness.

This evaluation may be made in concert with the periodic examination of the diverse needs and interests of students and other members of the campus community.

CRSP must

- specify programmatic goals and intended outcomes
- identify student learning and development outcomes
- employ multiple measures and methods
- develop manageable processes for gathering, interpreting, and evaluating data
- document progress toward achievement of goals and outcomes
- interpret and use assessment results to demonstrate accountability
- report aggregated results to respondent groups and stakeholders
- use assessment results to inform planning and decision-making
- assess effectiveness of implemented changes
- provide evidence of improvement of programs and services

CRSP must employ ethical practices in the assessment process.

Data should be collected from officers and advisors of campus religious and spiritual organizations to determine the effectiveness of policies affecting religious activity.

CRSP must have access to adequate fiscal, human, professional development, and technological resources to develop and implement assessment plans.

General Standards revised in 2014;
CRSP (formerly Religious Programs) content developed/revised in 1986, 1997, & 2006

Career Services
CAS Contextual Statement

The first evidence of assistance in career services dates back to the 19th century, when commercial employment agencies began to place graduates of the nation's teacher training programs, also known as normal schools, into jobs. More than 200 such agencies existed by the late 1800s. By the turn of the century, an increasing number of institutions had begun to realize their responsibility to help graduates find jobs. When the first institutional appointment and placement services were established, faculty members typically took responsibility for them on a part-time basis. Soon many institutions established programs staffed by full-time "appointment secretaries." By 1920, approximately 75 percent of the nation's normal schools had established placement services; as a direct result of the increasing number of college-sponsored placement services, the number of external agencies decreased.

At the beginning of the twentieth century the concept and practice of choosing an occupation were becoming more prevalent, and much of the theory supporting occupational choice was based on the 1909 work of Frank Parsons in *Choosing a Vocation*. Parsons developed a tripartite model—understanding one's self, understanding the requirements of available jobs, and making choices based on true logic. Often referred to as trait and factor theory, it was grounded in a logical, cognitive, and rational approach to selecting occupations. This model was the forerunner of modern theories of career development and was the foundation for vocational guidance and career development practice until the early 1950s.

Following World War II, the economy exploded and employers sought to hire the nation's college graduates to meet expanding needs. More than 65 percent of the current career services centers were established between 1947 and 1960. Over the years, the function of these offices shifted from solely providing placement activities to providing a broad range of career activities, including a focus on career counseling and personal development which were more independent from the volatility of the job market. Accordingly, this shift is reflected by office name changes from "placement office" to "career planning and placement office" to the most commonly used title, "career services." As we moved into the 1990s the focus moved from counseling to networking and developing networks of students, employers and alumni. With the economy fluctuating and growing competition among higher education institutions, the power of the network became integral to career planning and efforts to identify opportunities for students. We now move into an ever-changing economy that continues to develop and evolve at a rapid rate and therefore career services must also evolve to keep pace with the global and technologically advanced and savvy society. In addition, the shift in higher education to a consumer-based environment has elevated the emphasis on graduate destinations and outcomes data, much of which is gathered by career services.

Professional Associations

Both of the first professional associations focusing on job placement for college graduates, the National Institutional Teacher Placement Association and the National Association of Appointment Secretaries, were established in 1924. In 1934, the National Institutional Teacher Placement Association evolved into the Association for School, College, and University Staffing (ASCUS), which later became the American Association for Employment in Education (AAEE).

From its inception, the mission of AAEE was to connect K-12 school recruiters with career services administrators and education faculty from higher education institutions that prepare educators. AAEE provides information, resources, and networking opportunities to assist schools, colleges, and universities in the employment of educators for staffing excellence in education.

The National Association of Appointment Secretaries became the American College Personnel Association (ACPA) in 1931. ACPA's membership and mission have broadened to include all student affairs professionals for the purpose of "support[ing] and foster[ing] college student learning through the generation and dissemination of knowledge, which informs policies, practices, and programs for student affairs professionals and the higher education community." The ACPA Commission for Career Development offers members opportunities to "examine and address the changing and diverse role of career development in higher education within a student development framework."

In addition, the National Vocational Guidance Association (NVGA) was founded in 1913. In 1985 NVGA was renamed and became the National Career Development Association (NCDA). Thus NCDA is the first, longest running and preeminent career development association in the world. Others concerned with business and industrial placement established the Eastern College Personnel Officers in 1926, and by 1951 six other regional associations had been formed, due largely to Post World War II economic conditions. Those original seven organizations have since merged to form four independent regional associations, which together have memberships covering all fifty states.

The Association of School and College Placement, formed in 1940, published the *School and College Placement* magazine. In 1956, the national association was incorporated as the College Placement Publications Council and its name was shortened in 1957 to the College Placement Council. In 1995, the association became the National Association of Colleges and Employers, now a comprehensive national association for career services. Today, the core purpose of NACE is to facilitate the employment of the college educated; it works to meet this mission in a variety of ways, especially by providing an important connection between college career services centers and HR/staffing offices focused on recruiting and hiring new college graduates.

There have been a number of other associations created over the years to also address other aspects of career services and development on college campuses. The National Society for Experiential Education (NSEE), Cooperative Education and Internship Association (CEIA), NACADA: The Global Community for Advising are a few of the organizations that address topics such as experiential learning, cooperative education and internships, and academic advising respectively. The field has also continued to support state, regional, and international associations that serve a need that cannot always be met by the national associations because of cost, general growth of the field or localized challenges facing career services. State associations serve many states with localized professional development and networking while regional associations such as the Southern Association of Colleges & Employers (SoACE), the Eastern Association of Colleges & Employers, the Midwest Association of Colleges & Employers (MWACE), and the Mountain Pacific Association of Colleges & Employers (MPACE) seek to provide resources to a continuously evolving field.

Theoretical Foundations

Concurrent with the growth in institutional enrollments and creation of career services units, new theories began to emerge emphasizing a developmental approach exploring the stages of career development as a function of personal development, often exemplified in the blending of work identity and personal identity. As the complexity of individuals was further explored, the many factors that influence the career decision-making process became more evident and this coincided with the growth of student and career development theory. As career centers evolved so did career theories from vocational theory roots.

The choices of the individual are at the core of many of these more modern theories, but also required is an understanding of external factors that inevitably shape the multiple career decisions an individual will make over the course of their lifetime. Major career development theory categories and some seminal theorists for each include Trait and Factor Theory (Holland), Developmental Theory (Super, Gottfredson), Learning Theory (Krumboltz), Social Cognitive Theory (Bandura, Lent), Values-Based Theory (Brown), Career Information Processing Theory (Peterson, Sampson, and Reardon), Transition Theory (Schlossburg), Contextualist Theory (Young, Valach, and Collins), Narrative (Savickas) and Planned Happenstance Theory (Mitchell). These representative theories of career choice and development are indicative of the complexity of career decision-making and provide practitioners a broad-based framework to guide intervention with students and other clients. Modern career theory is also inclusive of race, gender, and class implications and the related impacts on career decision-making.

Modern Structures of Career Services

Today, the majority of colleges and universities provide career services that often include career advising or career counseling; career resources; programming such as job-search workshops and networking events; career and job fairs; assistance with co-op, internship, and externship programs; on-campus recruiting; and job posting and resume referral services. Many of these services are available electronically through institutional web sites.

Programs and services offered by career services may vary based on the mission of the institution, its classification, and the constituents being served. Alignment of programs, services and outcomes to the institution's mission and strategic priorities is essential. For example, a community college career services office may place a greater emphasis on workforce preparation and gaining work-related experience; a 4-year liberal arts career services may offer more career counseling, internship opportunities and preparation for graduate or professional school; and a for-profit institution career services may have an explicit expectation to assist students secure their next destination plans. There is now a deep and growing respect for the diverse array of aspirations of students' next destination plans whether it be graduate or professional school, military, service year, a year abroad, stay at home parent, and more.

Beginning in the 1990s, "the dot-com boom reengaged employers on college campuses and created a stronger employer relations focus in career centers. Emerging technologies and social media advanced this 'networking paradigm' in the 2000s to a new level of connectedness for students and employers, as well as alumni, faculty and families" (Cruzvergara & Dey, 2014). The 21st century ushered in a new era of career services and many offices were tasked to meet increasingly complex and sophisticated challenges that include responding to economic shifts and changing work-force needs, increasing diversity, changing demographics, increased cost of higher education and growing student debt, globalization, increasing access and graduation rates, embedding career readiness into the learning experience for every student, and increased student engagement through better use of technology. Career services professionals need to be both culturally sensitive in working with students and knowledgeable about career options both in the United States and internationally.

There is an increasing need to prepare students for multiple career transitions over a life span, and to engage in an entrepreneurial approach to personal and career development. Today's traditional-age students, characterized by their high comfort level with and expectation of technology, and "virtual" students, created through distance learning options, require that career services professionals have an increasingly high level of technical competence. Today's career services professionals must balance high-tech and high-touch service in engaging and delivering serves to students and employers. A "new breed" of career services professionals is being sought after among many forward-thinking institutions to address the increased scrutiny facing colleges and universities from many stakeholders including: government agencies (state and federal), accreditors, parents and families, media and the general public.

According to Contomanolis and Steinfeld (2013), some of the skills that may be most marketable after college are change management, understanding the full context of higher education, strategic communication, project management, employer consultant, business development and community organizer. The field must also be prepared to work with growing diversity among clients. Career changers, including alumni, veterans, and others who are working on career transitions, are turning to career services to provide assistance through traditional and nontraditional means.

An increasing focus in higher education on assessment and accountability necessitates career services professionals to find meaningful measures by which to demonstrate their value to stakeholders that include students, faculty, administrators, parents, employers, government entities, and local communities. Additionally, the growing emphasis on assessment of student learning, using measurable outcomes, and evidence based decision-making processes, requires careful planning, effective implementation, and transparent reporting to stakeholders. It has never been more important to develop productive and collaborative relationships not only with employers and community organizations but also with faculty and other campus constituencies such as advising, student success, service learning, leadership development, and international programs. Increased emphasis from employers on career "readiness," internships/co-ops, electronic recruiting, and diversity recruiting require a corresponding emphasis on the part of career services professionals.

Leadership for career services in the 21st century requires a broader range of skills and competencies beyond those once considered traditional for professionals involved in the career planning and development field. The complexity of work and life impacted by global economic pressures, the accelerating pace of knowledge creation, and ubiquitous technology use means career professionals must help students acquire more broad-based career readiness skills, knowledge, technical skills, and the ability to connect their educational experiences to work and life roles. Successful leadership in career services leading to employment of graduates will positively affect the admission and retention of students, collaboration with academic programs, and partnerships with community organizations. Leaders will need sales, management, technical, financial, marketing, public relations, assessment, and analytical skills in addition to a foundation in education, counseling, or student personnel services. A growing area that many leaders must also take into account when considering the role of career services is advocacy – the ability to support the needs of students and also advocate on behalf of institutions in the public sphere and throughout campus is a necessary leadership skill but also a necessity of the work that is being done on campus. All these attributes point to the need for the career services leader to be adept at convening stakeholders, savvy at partnering with institutional leadership, be connected with the vision and brand efforts of their institution, and the analysis and translation of "big data" to portable, impactful, and relevant metrics of success.

NACE, AAEE, ACPA, NCDA, and other organizations play an increasingly important role in the development of this broader set of skills for career services professionals. They deliver value by conducting research on benchmarks and best practices, reporting on current and emerging issues and trends, providing timely and relevant resources and tools, offering training and professional development, and facilitating networking and affiliation among professional colleagues.

References, Readings, and Resources

American Association for Employment in Education (AAEE): www.aaee.org

American College Personnel Association (ACPA), Commission on Career Development: http://www.acpa.nche.edu.

Contomanolis, E., & Steinfeld, T. (Ed.). (2013). Leadership in career services: Voices from the field. Charleston, SC: CreateSpace.

Cruzvergara, C.Y., & Dey, F. (2014, July 15). *10 future trends in college career services.* Retrieved from https://www.linkedin.com/pulse/20140715120815-31028715-10-future-trends-in-college-career-services?trk=prof-post

Dey, F., & Real, M. (2010). Emerging trends in university career services: Adaptations of Casella's career centers paradigm. *NACE Journal, 71*(1), 31-35.

Gysbers, N., Heppner, M., & Johnston, J. (1998). *Career counseling: Process, issues & techniques.* Boston, MA: Allyn and Bacon

Hughey, K. E., Nelson, D. B., Damminger, J. K., McCalla-Wriggins, B., & Associates (2009). *The handbook of career advising.* San Francisco, CA: Jossey-Bass

Isaacson, L. E., & Brown, D. (2000). *Career information, career counseling, and career development* (7th Ed.), Boston, MA: Allyn and Bacon

Mitchell, K. (n.d.). Planned Happenstance. http://plannedhappenstance.com

NACE Attracting New Professionals Task Force. (2004). *Career services in higher education* [PowerPoint presentation]. Bethlehem, PA: National Association of Colleges and Employers. Retrieved from http://www.naceweb.org/Knowledge/Career_Services/Career_Services_in_Higher_Education_(PPT).aspx

NACE Future Trends Committee. (2009). Looking ahead: highlights from the future trends survey. In *NACE Journal* (September 2009) Bethlehem, PA: National Association of Colleges and Employers. www.naceweb.org

National Association of Colleges and Employers (NACE): www.naceweb.org

National Association of Colleges and Employers. NACE Organizational History. http://www.naceweb.org/About/NACE_Organizational_History.aspx

National Association of Colleges and Employers. *The professional standards evaluation workbook* (2013). http://www.naceweb.org/uploadedFiles/Content/static-assets/downloads/products/professional-standards-evaluation-workbook.pdfnace

National Association of Colleges and Employers. *The professional standards for college and university career services* (2013). www.naceweb.org

National Career Development Association: www.ncda.org

Ratcliffe, R. S. (2004). *Use of the CAS standards by career services directors at four-year public colleges and universities* (Doctoral Dissertation, Virginia Polytechnic Institute and State University, 2004). Available at http://scholar.lib.vt.edu/theses/available/etd-07262004-150008/

Reardon, R. C., Lenz, J. G., Sampson, J. P., & Peterson, G. W. (2009). *Career development and planning: A comprehensive approach* (3rd Ed.). Florence, KY: Cengage Learning

Schnider, N. (Ed.). (2009). *Educator supply and demand research report.* Columbus, OH: American Association for Employment in Education.

Schnider, N. (Ed.). (2010). *The job search handbook for educators.* Columbus, OH: American Association for Employment in

Education.

Steinfeld, T., & Contomanolis, M. (2014, May 6). Thriving in the brave new world of career services: 10 essential strategies. Retrieved from https://www.linkedin.com/pulse/20140506212412-2872947-thriving-in-the-brave-new-world-of-career-services-10-essential-strategiesleaders

Steinfeld, T., & Contomanolis, M. (2014, October 16). *The new breed of career services professional: What's in the secret sauce of success?* Retrieved from https://www.linkedin.com/pulse/20141016204534-3053599-the-new-breed-of-career-services-professional-what-s-in-the-secret-sauce-of-success

2014-15 Career Services Survey (March 2015). Bethlehem, PA: National Association of Colleges and Employers. www.naceweb.org

Contextual Statement Contributors

Current Edition:
Patricia Carretta, George Mason University, NACE
Christine Y. Cruzvergara, George Mason University
Jeremy Podany, Colorado State University
Lisa Severy, University of Colorado
Joseph A. Testani, University of Rochester, NACE

Previous Editions:
Marvin Roth, Lafayette College, NACE
Denise Dwight Smith, UNC-Charlotte, NACE
Alison R. Angell, Lesley College, AAEE
Patricia Caretta, George Mason University, NACE
Mimi Collins, NACE
R. Samuel Ratcliffe, Virginia Military Institute, NACE
Mollie Starbuck Fout, Ball State University, NACE
Joseph A. Testani, University of Richmond, NACE

Career Services
CAS Standards and Guidelines

The primary mission of Career Services (CS) is to assist students and other designated clients in developing, evaluating, and implementing career, education, and employment plans.

Consistent with institutional mission, other designated clients may include alumni, faculty, staff, and community members.

In addition, CS must
- **be a resource to the institution on career and workplace issues and employment and workforce data**
- **develop productive relationships with faculty members, administrators, staff, employers, and other external constituencies**
- **support institutional outcomes assessment and relevant research endeavors**

CS must develop, disseminate, implement, and regularly review their missions, which must be consistent with the mission of the institution and with applicable professional standards. The mission must be appropriate for the institution's students and other constituents. Mission statements must reference student learning and development.

In assisting designated clients, CS must consider the needs of all their constituencies when designing the program and delivering services.

The stated mission should be to help students and designated clients to
- develop or clarify self-knowledge related to career choice and performance in the workplace
- develop understanding of the occupational information required to support career decision-making, including current and future trends and projections
- identify and select personally suitable academic programs and experiential opportunities that optimize future educational and employment options
- take responsibility for making informed career decisions and developing further education and employment plans
- understand how their professional interests and competencies relate to occupational and job requirements
- gain experience on or off campus for the purpose of exploring interests and developing their competencies
- develop effective job search and candidate presentation skills
- link with alumni, employers, professional organizations, and others who can provide opportunities to develop professional interests and competencies, integrate academic learning with work, and explore future career possibilities
- utilize technology throughout the career development and job search processes
- prepare to manage their careers after graduation

CS must promote awareness within the institution of the array of domestic and global occupations and the need for and nature of career development over the lifespan.

Because of expertise and knowledge on career-related subjects, CS should seek involvement in relevant administrative decisions related to student services, institutional development, curriculum planning, and external relations.

Because career-related subjects may also be addressed by other student services and academic programs within the institution, career services should consult with them, promote collaboration, and encourage linkages where appropriate.

Career Services (CS) must design programs and services to assist students and other designated clients to make career decisions and pursue the skill development necessary to compete in a rapidly changing, competency-based, global workplace.

CS must be informed by current career development and experiential learning theories and practices, employment and workforce trends, and appropriate assessments and evaluations.

To achieve their mission, CS must contribute to
- **students' formal education, which includes both the curriculum and the co-curriculum**
- **student progression and timely completion of educational goals**
- **preparation of students for their careers, citizenship, and lives**
- **student learning and development**

To contribute to student learning and development, CS must
- **identify relevant and desirable student learning and development outcomes**
- **articulate how the student learning and development outcomes align with the six CAS student learning and development domains and related dimensions**
- **assess relevant and desirable student learning and development**
- **provide evidence of impact on outcomes**
- **articulate contributions to or support of student learning and development in the domains not specifically assessed**
- **use evidence gathered to create strategies for**

improvement of programs and services

STUDENT LEARNING AND DEVELOPMENT DOMAINS AND DIMENSIONS

Domain: knowledge acquisition, integration, construction, and application

- Dimensions: understanding knowledge from a range of disciplines; connecting knowledge to other knowledge, ideas, and experiences; constructing knowledge; and relating knowledge to daily life

Domain: cognitive complexity

- Dimensions: critical thinking, reflective thinking, effective reasoning, and creativity

Domain: intrapersonal development

- Dimensions: realistic self-appraisal, self-understanding, and self-respect; identity development; commitment to ethics and integrity; and spiritual awareness

Domain: interpersonal competence

- Dimensions: meaningful relationships, interdependence, collaboration, and effective leadership

Domain: humanitarianism and civic engagement

- Dimensions: understanding and appreciation of cultural and human differences, social responsibility, global perspective, and sense of civic responsibility

Domain: practical competence

- Dimensions: pursuing goals, communicating effectively, technical competence, managing personal affairs, managing career development, demonstrating professionalism, maintaining health and wellness, and living a purposeful and satisfying life

[LD Outcomes: See *The Council for the Advancement of Standards Learning and Development Outcomes* statement for examples of outcomes related to these domains and dimensions.]

CS must be
- intentionally designed
- guided by theories and knowledge of learning and development
- integrated into the life of the institution
- reflective of developmental and demographic profiles of the student population
- responsive to needs of individuals, populations with distinct needs, and relevant constituencies
- delivered using multiple formats, strategies, and contexts
- designed to provide universal access

CS must collaborate with colleagues and departments across the institution to promote student learning and development, persistence, and success.

CS must be delivered in a variety of formats in recognition of institutional settings, different learning styles, cultural differences, distance learning, and special needs among clients.

Components of CS must be clearly defined, designed, and implemented in alignment with
- the career development needs and educational and occupational interests of students and other designated clients
- current research, theories, and knowledge of career development and learning
- contemporary career services standards and practices
- economic trends, opportunities, constraints, and/or the needs of external constituents
- institutional priorities
- technological advancements
- operational and personnel resources

Program goals must be reviewed and updated regularly, and communicated as appropriate, to stakeholders including students and other designated clients, administrators, faculty, staff, employers, and other constituencies.

CS should disseminate information on the availability, scope, and use of career services through institutional publications, campus media, presentations, outreach, and orientation programs.

CS must work collaboratively with academic divisions, departments, faculty members, student services, other relevant constituencies of the institution, and employers to enhance students' career development and participation in internships and other experiential education programs.

CS must develop and implement intentional marketing strategies and outreach programming to promote awareness and encourage use of the services.

For CS to effectively accomplish its stated purposes, it must include
- career advising, counseling, and education
- information and resources on careers and further education
- opportunities for career exploration through experiential education
- job search services
- graduate and professional school or further education planning
- employer relations and recruitment services
- consultation services to faculty and administrators

Career Advising, Counseling, and Education

Through CS or other units, the institution must offer career advising, counseling, and education that assist designated clients at any stage of their career development to
- clarify interests, competencies, values, experiences, personal characteristics, and desired lifestyles using appropriate assessment tools
- explore occupational, educational, and employment possibilities

- make reasoned, informed educational and career decisions and plans based on accurate self-knowledge and occupational information
- establish short-term and long-term career goals

The institution's career advising, counseling, and education services should

- encourage students to take advantage of career services as early as possible in their academic programs
- recognize that students' career decision-making is inextricably linked to additional psychosocial, personal, developmental, and cultural issues and beliefs
- assist students with career issues relevant to the individual (e.g., dual careers, sexual orientation, disabilities)
- provide scheduled appointments or drop-ins with individuals, group programs, career planning courses, outreach opportunities, special events, web- or computer-based programs, or any other available resources
- help students gain more self-awareness, apply knowledge and skills from their academic programs, and explore careers through part-time employment, internships, and other experiential programs
- assist students to assess their skills, values, and interests and understand how they relate to academic and co-curricular options and career opportunities
- help students develop and apply job search competencies and decision-making skills

CS must refer students to appropriate counseling and resource agencies if assistance is needed beyond the scope of career advising, counseling, and education.

Career advising, counseling, and education should encourage designated clients to access employers and employment information as a part of their career exploration and decision-making process.

Information and Resources on Careers and Further Study
Career Services must make current and comprehensive career information accessible to designated clients and educate them on the effective use of information and resources in exploring and making educational and career decisions.

CS should provide information and resources

- to help clients assess and relate their interests, competencies, needs and expectations, education, experience, personal background, and desired lifestyle to the employment market
- for constituent groups on career and employment topics and the ethical obligations of students, employers, and others involved in the employment process
- on current employment opportunities and on employers to ensure that candidates have broad choices of employment
- to help students identify and pursue future educational objectives

Information and resources must be
- **current and reflective of economic, occupational, and workplace issues and trends**
- **organized with appropriate systems that are user-friendly, flexible, and adaptable to change**

The scope of information and resources available to clients should include

- individual self-assessment and career planning
- occupational and job market information
- options for further study (e.g., four-year colleges and universities; graduate and professional schools)
- job search information
- experiential learning, internship, and job listings
- employer information

Resources on careers and further study must be provided electronically where available for optimal student access.

Career information, resources, and means of delivery must be compatible with the size and nature of the student population, the career and geographic interests of the students, and scope of academic programs.

Career information and resources should be conveniently available in a variety of media appropriate for different learning styles and special needs.

Career information facilities should be managed and staffed with persons who have the appropriate counseling, advising, and information technology competencies to assist students in accessing and using career information.

Opportunities for Career Exploration through Experiential Education
The institution must provide experiential education programs and services to enable students to integrate their academic studies with work experiences and career exploration.

Experiential education may include apprenticeships, cooperative education, internships, peer leadership experiences, service-learning, shadowing experiences, student teaching, undergraduate research, volunteer experiences, and work-study jobs and other campus employment.

CS should take a leadership role in working with their constituents to develop meaningful and intentional on-campus student employment opportunities.

CS may coordinate on-campus student employment.

Experiential education programs administered through CS must
- **provide students with opportunities to define both learning and career objectives and to reflect upon learning and other developmental aspects of their experience**
- **help students to identify employers for career development and potential employment**
- **teach students appropriate search and application**

techniques
- **support institutional efforts to provide students with additional financial resources for attending college and/or opportunities for obtaining academic credit**
- **ensure adequate site supervision**
- **consider appropriate risk management strategies**

Experiential education programs administered through CS should promote mentor/mentee relationships. When experiential education opportunities are provided by other departments, CS should work closely with those departments.

Job Search Services
Job search services must assist students and other designated clients to
- **develop job-search competencies**
- **articulate their strengths, competencies, and achievements applicable to the positions they are seeking**
- **present themselves effectively as candidates for employment**
- **identify and request appropriate references**
- **obtain information on employment opportunities, trends, and prospective employers**
- **connect with employers through campus recruitment programs, job listings, referrals, direct application, networking, publications, and information technology**
- **identify relevant career management issues (e.g., sex, gender, age, sexual orientation, dual career, disability, cultural, mental health)**
- **access and effectively use the Internet to access career and employer resources**
- **make informed choices among a variety of options**
- **identify and practice ethical job search behaviors**

CS must develop and implement strategies that cultivate employment opportunities for students.

Job search services may include offering site visits, campus recruiting, résumé referrals, information sessions, meetings with faculty members, access to alumni for networking, pre-recruiting activities, student access to employer information, posting job openings, and career and job fairs.

Job search services should help students and other designated clients develop skills to uncover less visible job markets related to their career interests.

If CS offers credential services for students and other clients, CS should
- establish a specific time period and procedures for maintaining information contained in student files and a systematic process for destruction of such records
- articulate clearly those record retention policies and procedures to students and other clients
- obtain signed written consent to disclose credential files prior to release of related information
- establish a process to verify legitimate release of

information
- advise employers that CS does not verify accuracy of information contained in a credential file

CS should advise students and other clients about how to identify and approach individuals to provide a reference, what constitutes an effective reference, and legal and ethical considerations germane to students and other clients.

Job search services may assist clients in the development of portfolios.

Graduate and Professional School or Further Education Planning
Career services must offer programs and services that assist students and other designated clients to
- **identify opportunities for further education that match their career goals**
- **obtain information on further education programs through a variety of sources**
- **connect with schools or programs offering further education**
- **present themselves effectively as candidates for further education**
- **identify and request appropriate references**
- **make appropriate decisions regarding further education**

CS may provide information and resources on research and training opportunities; scholarships, grants and fellowships; and other information on financing further education.

Employer Relations and Recruitment Services
Because employers are both vital partners in the educational process and primary customers of career services, CS must offer a variety of services to employers that reflect the match between the students' and the employers' interests and needs.

Employer relations and recruitment services may include: site visits; campus recruiting; résumé referrals; pre-recruiting information sessions with students; student access to timely employer information; posting and publishing of job and internship openings; on-site or virtual career/job fairs; experiential learning options which may include shadowing experiences, internships, externships, student teaching, cooperative education assignments; remote electronic interviewing options; employer participation in career planning, work-force readiness courses, career conferences, résumé preparation, practice interviews, and job search readiness workshops.

To ensure quality employer relations and services, CS must
- **develop strategic objectives for employer relations/ services and job development that yield maximum opportunities for the institution's students, graduates, and designated clients**
- **inform and promote adherence to laws, policies, procedures, and instructions for using the services in accordance with federal, state/provincial, and institutional privacy and non-discrimination mandates**

- develop, maintain and enhance relationships with employers who provide career development and employment opportunities
- enhance customer service and foster continuous improvement by using feedback from employers
- inform, educate, and consult with employers on the nature of services provided and candidates' availability
- actively involve employers in on-campus programs that meet students' and designated clients' career and employment needs
- facilitate employer involvement and communication with faculty, students, and administrators concerning career and employment issues
- consult with employers on opportunities and strategies for establishing long-term relationships with academic units
- promote adherence to professional and ethical standards that serve as conduct models for students and designated clients
- provide employer feedback to faculty, administrators, and students and designated clients on preparation for jobs, the curricula, and the hiring process

CS should

- provide timely, pertinent information to employers regarding the institution's operations, enrollment, academic calendar, academic programs and curricula, and student/class profile in accordance with institutional policy and guidelines and availability of data to the public
- provide information and services to assist employers to communicate their opportunities to targeted populations and enhance their visibility
- educate employers of student demographics, needs, issues, and perspectives
- encourage employers to provide timely information to career services staff on job offers, salaries, and hires
- provide guidance on working with student leaders and student clubs and organizations
- use employers' experiences and expertise in support of institutional activities
- invite employer membership in career advisory boards
- develop and implement marketing strategies as part of a comprehensive employer relations program
- maximize students' exposure to employers

CS must define the various types of employers it will serve and articulate policies that guide its working relationships with these employers.

CS must uniformly and consistently apply policies and procedures to all employers.

CS staff should understand the variety and diversity of needs and employment practices among businesses, corporations, government agencies, schools, and non-profit organizations.

CS must develop policies for working with third-party recruiting organizations. Policies must include recruiter disclosure of the identities of organizations they represent and agreement to abide by the ethical guidelines.

CS should encourage employers to share information related to their organization's policies and practices on such topics as sustainability, social justice, and family friendly work practices.

<u>Consultation Services to Faculty and Administrators</u>
To support the institution's mission and goals, CS must provide faculty and staff and administrative units with information, guidance, and support on career development, and employment issues and linkages with the broader community.

CS should support faculty and staff and administrative units by

- identifying and disseminating information on employment trends and top employing organizations and on co-op and internship sponsors
- providing employer feedback on the preparation of students for jobs, the curriculum, and the hiring process
- raising awareness of appropriate ethical and legal guidelines for student referrals
- providing guidance on effective strategies for engaging employers in programs offered by faculty and administrative units
- increasing awareness of career development issues and available resources
- providing and interpreting aggregate data on student learning, career-related and first-destination outcomes, and employer engagement for purposes such as accreditation, marketing, institutional development, and curriculum development

CS should develop and disseminate guidelines for serving as a reference and writing effective reference letter, including legal and ethical considerations and other key factors.

Part 3. Organization and Leadership

An institution must appoint, position, and empower a leader or leadership team to provide strategic direction, manage programs and services, and align Career Services (CS) with the mission of the institution and the needs of the constituencies served.

If components of career services are offered by several units, the institution must designate a leader or leadership team that will coordinate the institution's programs and services.

Such leadership is necessary to ensure adherence to institutional and unit missions and to enhance program effectiveness and efficiency.

To achieve program and student learning and development outcomes, CS must be purposefully structured for effectiveness. CS must have clearly stated and current
- **goals and outcomes**

- policies and procedures
- responsibilities and performance expectations for personnel
- organizational charts demonstrating clear channels of authority

Leaders must model ethical behavior and institutional citizenship.

Leaders with organizational authority for CS must provide strategic planning, management and supervision, and program advancement.

Strategic Planning
- articulate a vision and mission that drive short- and long-term planning
- set goals and objectives based on the needs of the populations served, intended student learning and development outcomes, and program outcomes
- facilitate continuous development, implementation, and assessment of program effectiveness and goal attainment congruent with institutional mission and strategic plans
- promote environments that provide opportunities for student learning, development, and engagement
- develop, adapt, and improve programs and services in response to the changing needs of populations served and evolving institutional priorities
- include diverse perspectives to inform decision making

Management and Supervision
- plan, allocate, and monitor the use of fiscal, physical, human, intellectual, and technological resources
- manage human resource processes including recruitment, selection, professional development, supervision, performance planning, succession planning, evaluation, recognition, and reward
- influence others to contribute to the effectiveness and success of the unit
- empower professional, support, and student personnel to become effective leaders
- encourage and support collaboration with colleagues and departments across the institution
- encourage and support scholarly contributions to the profession
- identify and address individual, organizational, and environmental conditions that foster or inhibit mission achievement
- use current and valid evidence to inform decisions
- incorporate sustainability practices in the management and design of programs, services, and facilities
- understand appropriate technologies and integrate them into programs and services
- be knowledgeable about codes and laws relevant to programs and services and ensure that programs and services meet those requirements

- assess and take action to mitigate potential risks

Program Advancement
- advocate for and actively promote the mission and goals of the programs and services
- inform stakeholders about issues affecting practice
- facilitate processes to reach consensus where wide support is needed
- advocate for representation in strategic planning initiatives at divisional and institutional levels

CS leaders must conduct regular program evaluations to improve operations and to adjust to changing client needs, evolving institutional priorities, and changes in the workforce and employment conditions.

CS leaders must annually review, update, and communicate goals and objectives to appropriate constituencies.

CS leaders should identify and find means to address individual, organizational, or environmental conditions that inhibit goal achievement.

CS leaders must participate in institutional decisions about career services objectives and policies. CS leaders must participate in institutional decisions related to the identification and designation of clients served.

Decisions about clients served should include type and scope of services offered and the fees, if any, that are charged.

The external and internal organization of CS, including its place within the institution, must support the CS mission and achievement of programmatic and student outcomes.

The unit to which CS reports should support efficient and effective delivery of career services within the institution.

Areas for consideration in determining structure and management of career services should include
- size, nature, and mission of the institution
- needs of students and designated clients
- number and scope of academic-related programs and services
- scope and intent of recruiting services
- philosophy and delivery system for services
- varied delivery methods (e.g., direct contact, technology)

CS should be coordinated with, and complementary to, employment-related services provided by other institutional units.

Part 4. Human Resources

Career Services (CS) must be staffed adequately by individuals qualified to accomplish mission and goals.

CS must have access to technical and support personnel adequate to accomplish their mission.

A technical support person or support service should be available to maintain computer and information technology systems for career services.

Within institutional guidelines, CS must
- **establish procedures for personnel recruitment and selection, training, performance planning, and evaluation**
- **set expectations for supervision and performance**
- **provide personnel access to continuing and advanced education and appropriate professional development opportunities to improve their competence, skills, and leadership capacity**
- **consider work/life options available to personnel (e.g., compressed work schedules, flextime, job sharing, remote work, or telework) to promote recruitment and retention of personnel**

CS must embrace fair employment practices and must be proactive in attracting and retaining a diverse staff.

CS staff must be staffed by persons who, in combination, provide the core competencies to perform primary functions effectively.

The primary functions should include the following core competencies and knowledge domains.

Management and Administration
Core Competencies

Needs assessment and satisfaction measures; program design, implementation and evaluation; strategic and operational planning; program integration and integrity; staffing; staff development and supervision; budget planning and administration; political sensitivity and negotiation skills; synthesize, interpret and report information.

Knowledge Domains

Systems theory; organizational development; research design; statistics; accounting and budgeting procedures; revenue generation; principles; purchasing; staff selection; supervision; performance appraisals; management of information systems; customer service; marketing.

Program and Event Administration
Core Competencies

Needs assessment; goal setting; program planning; implementation and evaluation; budget allocation; time management; problem solving; attention to detail.

Knowledge Domains

Systems, logistics, and procedures; project management; customer service.

Research and Student Learning/Development Outcomes
Core Competencies

Identification of relevant and desirable student learning and development outcomes; outcome-oriented programming; research-based evidence of program impact on student learning and development outcomes

Knowledge Domains

Student and adult development theory; research/assessment procedures; evidence-based decision-making; statistical procedures.

Career Advising/Counseling and Consultation
Core Competencies

Needs assessment and diagnosis; intervention design and implementation; test administration and interpretation; counseling; feedback; evaluation; advising; empathy and interpersonal sensitivity; work with individuals and groups; use of career, occupational, and employment information.

Knowledge Domains

Career development theories; adult development theory and unique issues for special populations; statistics; counseling processes; evaluation of person-job fit; job analysis; career decision making; behavior management; job search, interviews, and resumès.

Teaching/Training/Educating
Core Competencies

Needs assessment; program/workshop design; researching, evaluating, and integrating information; effective teaching strategies; career coaching; career mentoring; work with individuals and groups; work with diverse populations; use of technology for delivery of content.

Knowledge Domains

Setting learning objectives; designing curricula and learning resources for specific content areas; experiential learning; career development and job search process; learning styles.

Marketing/Promoting/Outreach
Core Competencies

Needs assessment and goal setting; written and interpersonal communication; public speaking; domestic and international job and experiential learning opportunity development; relationship development and management; job development; effective use of print, web, personal presentation methods; sales and closing techniques; development/fundraising strategies; marketing principles/strategies.

Knowledge Domains

Customer service; knowledge of institution and its academic programs; career services; employer, alumni, and faculty needs and expectations; recruiting and staffing methods, trends.

Brokering/Connecting/Linking
Core Competencies

Organize information, logistics, people, and processes toward a desired outcome; consulting; building and managing advisory boards; interpersonal skills.

Knowledge Domains

Systems and procedures; candidate/résumé referral; recruiting and experiential learning operations; human resource selection practices.

Information Management
Core Competencies

Organization and dissemination; storage and retrieval; computing systems and applications; data entry and analysis; acquisition of appropriate career resources; web design and management.

Knowledge Domains
Library/resources center organization; computer systems and applications; specific electronic management information systems.

Administrators of CS must
- ensure that all personnel have updated position descriptions
- implement recruitment and selection/hiring strategies that produce a workforce inclusive of under-represented populations
- develop promotion practices that are fair, inclusive, proactive, and non-discriminatory

CS personnel responsible for delivery of CS must have written performance goals, objectives, and outcomes for each year's performance cycle to be used to plan, review, and evaluate work and performance. The performance plan must be updated regularly to reflect changes during the performance cycle.

Results of individual personnel evaluations must be used to recognize personnel performance, address performance issues, implement individual and/or collective personnel development and training programs, and inform the assessment of programs and services.

CS personnel, when hired and throughout their employment, must receive appropriate and thorough training.

CS personnel, including student employees and volunteers, must have access to resources or receive specific training on
- institutional policies pertaining to functions or activities they support
- privacy and confidentiality policies
- laws regarding access to student records
- policies and procedures for dealing with sensitive institutional information
- policies and procedures related to technology used to store or access student records and institutional data
- how and when to refer those in need of additional assistance to qualified personnel and have access to a supervisor for assistance in making these judgments
- systems and technologies necessary to perform their assigned responsibilities
- ethical and legal uses of technology

CS personnel must engage in continuing professional development activities to keep abreast of the research, theories, legislation, policies, and developments that affect their programs and services.

Training should include customer service, program procedures, and information and resource utilization.

Staff training and development should be ongoing and promote knowledge and skill development across program components.

Administrators of CS must ensure that personnel are knowledgeable about and trained in safety, emergency procedures, and crisis prevention and response. Risk management efforts must address identification of threatening conduct or behavior and must incorporate a system for responding to and reporting such behaviors.

All staff must be trained in legal, confidential, and ethical issues related to career services.

CS personnel must be knowledgeable of and trained in safety and emergency procedures for securing and vacating facilities.

PROFESSIONAL PERSONNEL

CS professional personnel either must hold an earned graduate or professional degree in a field relevant to their position or must possess an appropriate combination of educational credentials and related work experience.

INTERNS OR GRADUATE ASSISTANTS

Degree- or credential-seeking interns or graduate assistants must be qualified by enrollment in an appropriate field of study and relevant experience. These students must be trained and supervised by professional personnel who possess applicable educational credentials and work experience and have supervisory experience. Supervisors must be cognizant of the dual roles interns and graduate assistants have as both student and employee.

Supervisors must
- adhere to parameters of students' job descriptions
- articulate intended learning outcomes in student job descriptions
- adhere to agreed-upon work hours and schedules
- offer flexible scheduling when circumstances necessitate

Supervisors and students must both agree to suitable compensation if circumstances necessitate additional hours.

STUDENT EMPLOYEES AND VOLUNTEERS

Student employees and volunteers must be carefully selected, trained, supervised, and evaluated. Students must have access to a supervisor. Student employees and volunteers must be provided clear job descriptions, pre-service training based on assessed needs, and continuing development.

Career information staff should have the appropriate competencies to assist designated clients to access and effectively use career information and resources.

Part 5. Ethics

Career Services (CS) must
- review applicable professional ethical standards and must adopt or develop and implement appropriate statements of ethical practice
- publish and adhere to statements of ethical practice and ensure their periodic review

- orient new personnel to relevant ethical standards and statements of ethical practice and related institutional policies

Statements of ethical standards must
- specify that CS personnel respect privacy and maintain confidentiality in communications and records as delineated by privacy laws
- specify limits on disclosure of information contained in students' records as well as requirements to disclose to appropriate authorities
- address conflicts of interest, or appearance thereof, by personnel in the performance of their work
- reflect the responsibility of personnel to be fair, objective, and impartial in their interactions with others
- reference management of institutional funds
- reference appropriate behavior regarding research and assessment with human participants, confidentiality of research and assessment data, and students' rights and responsibilities
- include the expectation that personnel confront and hold accountable other personnel who exhibit unethical behavior
- address issues surrounding scholarly integrity

Ethical standards or other statements from relevant professional associations should be considered and if adopted for implementation, should be clearly communicated to relevant constituencies.

CS personnel must
- employ ethical decision making in the performance of their duties
- inform users of programs and services of ethical obligations and limitations emanating from codes and laws or from licensure requirements
- recognize and avoid conflicts of interest that could adversely influence their judgment or objectivity and, when unavoidable, recuse themselves from the situation
- perform their duties within the scope of their position, training, expertise, and competence
- make referrals when issues presented exceed the scope of the position

CS should provide guidance and education on these standards to all persons involved in providing career services, including, but not limited to, entry-level professionals, support staff, student staff, interns, graduate assistants, faculty and staff, employers, service providers, and other administrators. CS staff members should provide guidance regarding prevailing ethical expectations to students and other clients using career services.

Part 6. Law, Policy, and Governance

Career Services (CS) must be in compliance with laws, regulations, and policies that relate to their respective responsibilities and that pose legal obligations, limitations, risks, and liabilities for the institution as a whole. Examples include constitutional, statutory, regulatory, and case law; relevant law and orders emanating from codes and laws; and the institution's policies.

CS must have access to legal advice needed for personnel to carry out their assigned responsibilities.

CS must inform personnel, appropriate officials, and users of programs and services about existing and changing legal obligations, risks and liabilities, and limitations.

CS must inform personnel about professional liability insurance options and refer them to external sources if the institution does not provide coverage.

CS must have written policies and procedures on operations, transactions, or tasks that have legal implications.

CS must regularly review policies. The revision and creation of policies must be informed by best practices, available evidence, and policy issues in higher education.

CS must have procedures and guidelines consistent with institutional policy for responding to threats, emergencies, and crisis situations. Systems and procedures must be in place to disseminate timely and accurate information to students, other members of the institutional community, and appropriate external organizations during emergency situations.

Personnel must neither participate in nor condone any form of harassment or activity that demeans persons or creates an intimidating, hostile, or offensive environment.

CS must purchase or obtain permission to use copyrighted materials and instruments. References to copyrighted materials and instruments must include appropriate citations.

CS must inform personnel about internal and external governance organizations that affect programs and services.

CS staff members must be aware of and seek advice from the institution's legal counsel or other appropriate professional resources on
- privacy and disclosure of student information contained in education records
- defamation law regarding references and recommendations on the behalf of students and other designated clients
- laws regarding employment referral practices of the career services office and others employed by the institution that refer students for employment; affirmative action regulations and laws regarding programs for special populations
- liability issues pertaining to experiential learning programs
- laws regarding eligibility to work and contracts governing service provided by outside vendors
- privacy of data maintained in electronic format by entities engaged by career services
- laws regarding grant administration

Contracts with outside vendors must include adherence to ethics, confidentiality, security, and institutional policies, as well as reflect support of career services programs, goals, and standards.

CS must maintain appropriate records for future work with students and other designated clients.

Part 7. Diversity, Equity, and Access

Within the context of each institution's mission and in accordance with institutional policies and applicable codes and laws, Career Services (CS) must create and maintain educational and work environments that are welcoming, accessible, inclusive, equitable, and free from harassment.

These groups may include traditionally under-represented, evening, part-time, commuter, LGBT, and international students, as well as students with disabilities, athletes, veterans, and distance learners.

To respond to the needs of students and other designated clients, career services should provide services in-person, online, and via telephone, e-mail, or other formats. CS should be responsive to the needs of all its constituencies through the establishment of office hours, customer service systems, and online operations.

CS must not discriminate on the basis of disability; age; race; cultural identity; ethnicity; nationality; family educational history (e.g., first generation to attend college); political affiliation; religious affiliation; sex; sexual orientation; gender identity and expression; marital, social, economic, or veteran status; or any other basis included in institutional policies and codes and laws.

CS must address non-adherence by employers to the word and spirit of equal employment opportunity and affirmative action.

CS staff should make every effort to inform or educate faculty members about issues relevant to discriminatory practices related to their referral of students directly to employers.

CS must
- advocate for sensitivity to multicultural and social justice concerns by the institution and its personnel
- ensure physical, program, and resource access for all constituents
- modify or remove policies, practices, systems, technologies, facilities, and structures that create barriers or produce inequities
- ensure that when facilities and structures cannot be modified, they do not impede access to programs, services, and resources
- establish goals for diversity, equity, and access
- foster communication and practices that enhance understanding of identity, culture, self-expression, and heritage
- promote respect for commonalities and differences among people within their historical and cultural

contexts
- address the characteristics and needs of diverse constituents when establishing and implementing culturally relevant and inclusive programs, services, policies, procedures, and practices
- provide personnel with diversity, equity, and access training and hold personnel accountable for applying the training to their work
- respond to the needs of all constituents served when establishing hours of operation and developing methods of delivering programs, services, and resources
- recognize the needs of distance and online learning students by directly providing or assisting them to gain access to comparable services and resources

CS should collaborate with other departments and student organizations to provide educational programs that help clients from diverse backgrounds and individuals with disabilities to identify and address their needs related to career development and employment. CS should initiate partnerships and collaborative programming with other offices representing specific populations to ensure appropriate service delivery.

Part 8. Internal and External Relations

Career Services (CS) must reach out to individuals, groups, communities, and organizations internal and external to the institution to
- establish, maintain, and promote understanding and effective relations with those that have a significant interest in or potential effect on the students or other constituents served by the programs and services
- garner support and resources for programs and services as defined by the mission
- collaborate in offering or improving programs and services to meet the needs of students and other constituents and to achieve program and student outcomes
- engage diverse individuals, groups, communities, and organizations to enrich the educational environment and experiences of students and other constituents
- disseminate information about the programs and services

In order to achieve this, CS should
- develop institutional support for career development and employment services for students and other designated clients
- involve the academic administration and faculty in career planning and employment programs
- raise issues and concerns with the institution's legal counsel regarding compliance with employment laws as they pertain to recruitment and hiring of students, alumni, and other designated clients
- participate in campus activities such as faculty

organizations, committees, student orientation programs, classroom presentations, academic courses in career planning, leadership training, and student organization programs

- exchange information with the academic administration and faculty concerning employment requirements, labor market trends, specific jobs, and employment that may be related to academic planning and curriculum development
- arrange appropriate programs that use alumni experience and expertise
- establish cooperative relationships with other offices and services in order to support mutual referrals, exchange of information, sharing of resources, and other program functions
- partner with other organizations and institutions to address the unique needs of special populations
- provide information and reports to the academic administration, faculty and key offices of the institution regarding career services for students and other designated clients and for employers
- provide feedback to faculty, administrators, and students on the preparation of graduates for employment, graduate/professional school, or further education to aid curriculum development and individual career planning
- encourage dialogue among employers, faculty members, and administrators concerning career issues and trends for students, graduates, and other designated clients
- provide parents and family members with information and relevant data on career education programs and services and key results related to employment, graduate study, and further education outcomes as appropriate

In addition, CS should encourage staff participation in professional associations and community activities related to career and employment issues (e.g., chambers of commerce, workforce development functions, employer open houses, workshops, federally mandated one stop centers, school-to-work efforts).

Promotional and descriptive information must be accurate and free of deception and misrepresentation.

CS must have procedures and guidelines consistent with institutional policy for
- **communicating with the media**
- **distributing information through print, broadcast, and online sources**
- **contracting with external organizations for delivery of programs and services**
- **cultivating, soliciting, and managing gifts**
- **applying to and managing funds from grants**

Part 9. Financial Resources

Career Services (CS) must have funding to accomplish the mission and goals.

In establishing and prioritizing funding resources, CS must conduct comprehensive analyses to determine
- **unmet needs of the unit**
- **relevant expenditures**
- **external and internal resources**
- **impact on students and the institution**

CS must use the budget as a planning tool to reflect commitment to the mission and goals of the programs and services and of the institution.

CS must administer funds in accordance with established institutional accounting procedures.

CS must demonstrate efficient and effective use and responsible stewardship of fiscal resources consistent with institutional protocols.

Financial reports must provide an accurate financial overview of the organization and provide clear, understandable, and timely data upon which personnel can plan and make informed decisions.

Procurement procedures must
- **be consistent with institutional policies**
- **ensure that purchases comply with laws and codes for usability and access**
- **ensure that the institution receives value for the funds spent**
- **consider information available for comparing the ethical and environmental impact of products and services purchased**

Consistent with institutional policy, CS may
- develop a funding strategy that outlines projects, programs, and related activity that can be further enhanced with additional outside funding sources
- cultivate employer support of the institution, including scholarships and other forms of financial support

Outside revenue may be generated to supplement institutional funding.

Fees charged to employers, vendors, students, and other designated clients should be limited and reasonable to carry out stated CS objectives.

Part 10. Technology

Career Services (CS) must have technology to support the achievement of their mission and goals. The technology and its use must comply with institutional policies and procedures and with relevant codes and laws.

CS must use technologies to
- **provide updated information regarding mission, location, staffing, programs, services, and official contacts to students and other constituents in accessible formats**
- **provide an avenue for students and other constituents to communicate sensitive information in a secure format**

- enhance the delivery of programs and services for all students

CS must

- back up data on a regular basis
- adhere to institutional policies regarding ethical and legal use of technology
- articulate policies and procedures for protecting the confidentiality and security of information
- implement a replacement plan and cycle for all technology with attention to sustainability
- incorporate accessibility features into technology-based programs and services

Technology selection must address distance learners and clients with unique needs and interests.

CS staff must be well informed about the array of career-based technological applications that are in current use.

In light of the rapidity of change associated with technology, CS must develop plans for the replacement/updating of existing hardware and software as well as plan for the integration of new technically-based or supported career programs, including systems developed internally by the institution, systems available through professional associations, or private vendor-based systems.

Technological applications specific to CS must include

- Internet-based resources that provide updated information regarding mission, location, staffing, programs, and services available to students and designated clients, as well as contact information
- computer-based assessment and computer-assisted career guidance systems
- online recruiting and employment systems that include job listings and student résumés

Other applications may include student registration systems; student contact, record, and tracking systems; career portfolios; student surveys; employer satisfaction surveys; career fair management systems; résumé writing software; office intranet sites; e-mail-based career advising/counseling; video-based technology; mentoring; and social/professional networking sites.

When providing student access to technology, CS must

- have policies on the use of technology that are clear, easy to understand, and available to all students
- provide information or referral to support services for those needing assistance in accessing or using technology
- provide instruction or training on how to use the technology
- inform students of implications of misuse of technologies

Part 11. Facilities and Equipment

Career Services' (CS) facilities must be intentionally designed and located in suitable, accessible, and safe spaces that demonstrate universal design and support the program's mission and goals.

CS should be in a convenient location for students and employers and project a welcoming, professional atmosphere for its users. Parking for visitors should be adequate and convenient.

Facilities must be designed to engage various constituents and promote learning.

Personnel must have workspaces that are suitably located and accessible, well equipped, adequate in size, and designed to support their work and responsibilities.

CS should provide

- private offices for professional staff in order to perform advising, counseling, or other confidential work
- support staff work areas
- reception, student registration, and waiting area
- career resource center
- storage space sufficient to accommodate resources, supplies, and equipment
- access to computer labs and to conference and large group meeting rooms equipped with appropriate levels of technology
- private interview facilities for employers and a waiting area for students to accommodate the scope of the recruiting program
- private employer workspace

The design of the facilities must guarantee the security and privacy of records and ensure the confidentiality of sensitive information and conversations. Personnel must be able to secure their work.

CS must incorporate sustainable practices in use of facilities and purchase of equipment. Facilities and equipment must be evaluated on an established cycle and be in compliance with codes, laws, and accepted practices for access, health, safety, and security.

When acquiring capital equipment, CS must take into account expenses related to regular maintenance and life cycle costs.

Part 12. Assessment

Career Services (CS) must develop assessment plans and processes.

Assessment plans must articulate an ongoing cycle of assessment activities.

CS must

- specify programmatic goals and intended outcomes
- identify student learning and development outcomes
- employ multiple measures and methods
- develop manageable processes for gathering, interpreting, and evaluating data

- document progress toward achievement of goals and outcomes
- interpret and use assessment results to demonstrate accountability
- report aggregated results to respondent groups and stakeholders
- use assessment results to inform planning and decision-making
- assess effectiveness of implemented changes
- provide evidence of improvement of programs and services

For comparative studies, CS should identify and consult with peers and professional associations.

CS should collaborate with institutional research units, state agencies, accrediting bodies, and other relevant groups that produce assessment and evaluation data. CS should promote institutional efforts to conduct relevant research on career development, institutional issues such as academic success and retention, student learning outcomes, employment trends, and career interests.

Evaluations should include
- review of the strategic plan, mission, human resources needs, diversity efforts, and other areas covered in this document
- regular feedback from participants on events, programs, and services
- systematic needs assessment to guide program development
- first destination surveys at or following graduation
- employer and student feedback regarding experiential learning programs
- alumni follow-up surveys administered at specific times after graduation
- reports and satisfaction surveys from students and other constituencies interacting with career services such as employers, faculty, and other post-secondary institutions

CS should prepare and disseminate annual and special reports, including career services philosophy, goals and objectives, current programs and services, service delivery information, first destination information, and graduate follow-up information.

CS must employ ethical practices in the assessment process.

CS must have access to adequate fiscal, human, professional development, and technological resources to develop and implement assessment plans.

General Standards revised in 2014;
CS content developed/revised in 1986, 1997, 2000, & 2010

Civic Engagement and Service-Learning Programs
CAS Contexual Statement

From the inception of American colleges and universities, one of the purposes of higher education has been to serve society and promote democracy through the education of leaders (Ehrlich, 2000; Hartley, 2009). The growth and proliferation of civic engagement and service-learning programs over the past thirty years illustrate institutions' commitment to civic education for citizenship and the development of civic leadership skills for students (Saltmarsh & Hartley, 2011). Through service experiences coupled with learning activities and reflection, civic engagement and service-learning programs offer educators many pathways to help students develop dispositions toward responsible public service, citizenship, and civic agency (Schnaubelt, 2012; Gorgol, 2012). Civic engagement outcomes may be achieved through experiences within curricular-based learning, as in a service-learning course, or through a well-organized, one-time service activity, a community-based research project, intentional advocacy, or an alternative spring break trip. Civic engagement can be defined as follows:

> Civic engagement means working to make a difference in the civic life of our communities and developing the combination of knowledge, skills, values and motivations to make that difference. It means promoting the quality of life in a community through both political and non-political processes. (Ehrlich, 2000, p. vi)

Of the pedagogies related to civic engagement, service-learning is the most widely-used, well-researched, and respected high-impact teaching practice (Finley, 2011). Service-learning is "a form of experiential education in which students engage in activities that address human and community needs together with structured opportunities intentionally designed to promote student learning and development" (Jacoby, 1996). Research shows that students who participate in service-learning integrate theory with practice, report academic gains, develop a deeper understanding of course material, demonstrate critical reflection skills, develop a sense of social responsibility, and demonstrate a greater ability to work collaboratively (Astin, Sax, & Avalos, 1999; Eyler & Giles, 1999; Gorgol, 2010; Kahne & Sport, 2008; Keen & Hall, 2009; Steinberg, Hatcher, & Bringle, 2011).

Civic engagement and service-learning programs offer many benefits to students, institutions, and communities making it a popular pedagogy and important institutional strategy (Sponsler & Hartley, 2013). To understand this current movement in higher education, it is valuable to look back fifty years. The partnership between higher education and the community became more pronounced as the civil rights movement and social activism of the 1960s and 1970s influenced the role of colleges and universities in civic life. Higher education institutions intentionally engaged with the social, political, and economic strife of their communities. In this period, many students and faculty emphasized diversity and outreach in their programming; these programs included neighborhood development and outreach programs in local communities, racial/ethnic studies, international education, and study abroad.

The 1980s ushered in a new period of activism led by students and college presidents. In 1984, two students formed COOL – The Campus Outreach and Opportunities League - to promote student involvement in community service and social activism. In 1985, three college presidents, from Brown, Georgetown, and Stanford University, with the president of the Education Commission of the States, formed Campus Compact, creating a coalition of college and university presidents who were committed to returning to and fulfilling the public purposes of higher education. These two organizations laid the groundwork for colleges and universities to institutionalize engagement efforts with resources, infrastructure, and technical support for students, faculty, and administrators.

With the support of external organizations like COOL and Campus Compact, the 1990s experienced a significant growth in the range of service-learning courses and civic engagement efforts. From the three founding campuses, Campus Compact membership grew to nearly 1000 by the year 2000. During this time, service-learning, with its emphasis on combining coursework and community service, emerged as the most popular form of civic engagement in education (Gorgol, 2012). Higher education had renewed its commitment to community and democracy.

In the 2000s, there was a broadening of scope; campuses were continuing to offer service-learning courses and were adding an array of course-based strategies and high-impact pedagogies to educate students for citizenship. This was evident by the growth and development of community-based research, alternative spring breaks, campus-wide service days, community based research, activism, and political engagement efforts. These pedagogies and practices offered more opportunities for students to gain the knowledge, skills, and abilities necessary to serve as leaders in their communities. In addition, due to external accountability and awards such as the Carnegie Elective Classification for Community Engagement and the Presidential Honor Roll for Community Engagement, campuses began better documenting the work being accomplished. National associations and organizations such as The Bonner Program, The American Democracy Project of the American Association of State Colleges and Universities, the Democracy Commitment, and NASPA's Lead Initiative were developed to support the growing work of civic engagement on campuses. To accommodate this growth and meet the demands for assessment, campuses have developed a variety of organizational structures to support civic engagement and service-learning. These responsibilities may be housed in academic affairs, student affairs, or a joint structuring between the two; this structure varies from campus to campus (Sponsler & Hartley, 2013).

The growth, expansion and institutionalization of civic engagement and service-learning programs led to a movement--a social movement towards a more democratic form of education (Hartley, 2013). The report, *A Crucible Moment: College Learning and Democracy's Future,* sponsored by the Department of Education, furthered this idea (2012). This report was a national call to action that provided an agenda for civic engagement and education for the future, highlighting the need for a more democratic education (Osteen, 2012; Campus Compact, 2012).

In practice, civic engagement and service-learning programs are designed with service, learning, and the community in mind to be relational, not transactional; it is the relationship that grounds and supports the learning (Jacoby, 1996; Jacoby, 2014). In order to have a transformative experiential educational experience, civic engagement and service-learning programs must be grounded in reflection, based on reciprocal relationships, and designed to create a diverse community of learners.

At the heart of civic engagement and service-learning programs is reflection. "As a form of experiential education, service-learning is based on the pedagogical principle that learning and development do not necessarily occur as a result of the experience itself. Rather, they occur as a result of reflection intentionally designed to promote learning and development" (CAS, 2012). Reflection can take many forms for both students and community and can occur through formal channels (writing papers, presentations, or disciplinary research) or informal channels (conversation, journaling, debate, or discussion).

Mutually beneficial community partnerships, grounded in reciprocity, are critical components of effective civic engagement and service-learning programs (Jacoby, 2014). Reciprocal relationships guarantee that all parties are both educators and learners; the needs and interests to be addressed in a project should be defined by both campus and community. In developing, maintaining, and improving these relationships, asset-based models are preferred. Both campus and community should consider the strengths that each party brings to the relationship. This is not a "helping" relationship but, rather, a reciprocal relationship in which each is served.

The most successful civic engagement and service-learning programs create a diverse community of learners who together grow and develop as citizens while celebrating difference and diversity. Institutions develop, structure, and support civic engagement and service-learning programs in a variety of ways; some programs are housed in student affairs, academic affairs, or in collaborative centers to serve the unique needs and resources of the institution (Sponsler & Hartley, 2013). This work is not a solitary, individual endeavor but is dependent upon interrelated parties--students, campus, and community partners--who come together to solve problems with innovation and creativity to meet the needs of their defined community (Colby, Beaumont, Ehrlich, &

Corngold, 2007; Hartley, 2009; Saltmarsh & Hartley, 2011). This is the essence of a functioning, diverse democracy. Approaching civic engagement and service-learning in this way with a diverse lens affords the opportunity to reflect upon and activate our democracy and celebrate the contributions of all.

Civic engagement and service-learning programs are a powerful form of experiential education; they integrate practical, real-world service experiences with insightful and thoughtful education. As a result of participation, students develop the skills, knowledge, and capabilities to engage reciprocally with their communities through thoughtful reflection, integrated learning, and becoming empowered to work with others to lead, envision, and create change.

The reader is encouraged to recognize that the CAS Civic Engagement and Service-Learning Programs standards compliment and support other CAS standards. Among others, the CAS standards for Academic Advising Programs, Career Services, College Honor Society Programs, Internship Programs and Education Abroad Programs include components supportive of and relevant to civic engagement and service-learning offerings in higher education.

References, Readings, and Resources

Astin, A. W., Sax, L. J., & Avalos, J. (1999). Long-term effects of volunteerism during the undergraduate years. *The Review of Higher Education 22*(2) 187-202.

Campus Compact. (2012). *Deepening the roots of civic engagement: Campus Compact 2011 annual membership survey executive summary.* Boston, MA: Author.

Colby, A., Beaumont, E., Ehrlich, T., & Corngold, J. (2007). *Educating for democracy: Preparing undergraduates for responsible political engagement.* San Francisco, CA: Jossey-Bass.

Ehrlich, T. (2000). *Civic responsibility and higher education.* Westport, CT: American Council of Education and Oryx Press.

Eyler, J.S., & Giles, D.E. (1999). *Where's the learning in service-learning?* San Francisco, CA: Jossey-Bass.

Finley, A. (2011). *Civic learning and democratic engagements: a review of the literature on civic engagement in postsecondary education.* Washington, D.C.: Association of American Colleges and Universities.

Gorgol (Sponsler), L.E. (2012). *Understanding the influence of the college experience on students' civic development.* (Unpublished doctoral dissertation). University of Pennsylvania.

Gorgol (Sponsler), L.E. (2010). *Moving beyond outcomes: next steps for civic engagement research.* Paper presented at ASHE: Association for the Study of Higher Education, Indianapolis, IN.

Hartley, M. (2009). Reclaiming the democratic purposes of American higher education. *Teaching and Learning 2*(3), 11-30.

Hartley, M., Harkavy, I., & Benson, L. (2005). Putting down roots in the grooves of academe: The challenges of institutionalizing service-learning. In D.W. Butin (Ed.), *Service-learning in higher education: Critical issues and directions.* New York, NY: Palgrave, MacMillan

Jacoby, B. (Ed.). (1996). *Service-learning in higher education: Concepts and practices.* San Francisco, CA: Jossey-Bass.

Jacoby, B. (2014). *Service-learning essentials: questions, answers, and lessons learned.* San Francisco, CA: Jossey-Bass.

Kahne, J. E., & Sporte, S. E. (2008). Developing citizens: The impact of civic learning opportunities on students' commitment to civic participation. *American Educational Research Journal*

45(3) 738-766.

Keen, C. & Hall, K. (2009). Engaging with difference matters: Longitudinal student outcomes of co-curricular service-learning programs. *The Journal of Higher Education 80*(1), 60-79.

National Task Force on Civic Learning and Democratic Engagement. (2012). A crucible moment: College learning and democracy's future. Washington, DC: Association of American Colleges and Universities (AAC&U).

Osteen, L. (2012). *A crucible moment: College learning and democracy's future: A national call to action reading guide.* Washington, DC: NASPA – Student Affairs Administrators in Higher Education.

Saltmarsh, J. & Hartley, M. (Eds.). (2011). *To serve a larger purpose: Engagement for democracy and the transformation of higher education*. Philadelphia, PA; Temple University Press.

Schnaubelt, T. (2012). *Stanford's pathways to public service.* Retrieved from: http://studentaffairs.stanford.edu/haas/about/strategicplan/pathways

Sherrod, L.R., Flanagan, C., & Youniss, J. (2002). Dimensions of citizenship and opportunities for youth development: The what, why, when, where, and who of citizenship development. *Applied Developmental Science, 6*(4), 264-272.

Sponsler, L.E. (2013, Summer). Creating the civic minded campus. *NASPA: Leadership Exchange.*

Sponsler, L.E. & Hartley, M. (2013). *Five things student affairs professionals can do to institutionalize civic engagement.* Washington, DC: NASPA Research and Policy Institute.

Steinberg, K., Hatcher, J. A, & Bringle, R. G. (2011). The civic-minded graduate: A north-star. *Michigan Journal of Community Service Learning, 18*, 19-33.

Contextual Statement Contributors

Current Edition:
Laura Sponsler, NASPA
Stephanie Gordon, NASPA
Caroline Donovan White, NAFSA
Dorothy Mitstifer, ACHS
Gayle Spencer, University of Illinois, NACA
Amy Blackford, IUPUI, CIVSA
Tony Ellis, NACS
Barbara Jacoby, University of Maryland
Becky Frawley, Montreat College
Beth Niehaus, University of Nebraska-Lincoln
Eric Hartman, Kansas State University
Jennifer Johnson Kebea, Drexel University
Julie Hatcher, IUPUI
Maggie Stevens, Indiana Campus Compact
Melody Porter, William & Mary

Previous Editions:
Craig Slack, University of Maryland
Barbara Jacoby, University of Maryland

Civic Engagement and Service-Learning Programs
CAS Standards and Guidelines

Part 1. Mission

The mission of Civic Engagement and Service-Learning Programs (CES-LP) is to involve students in learning experiences that serve community needs through direct service, community-based research, advocacy, and engagement opportunities. These programs require reciprocal relationships between the students, institutions, and the community in a mutually beneficial partnership. At the heart of CES-LPs is reflection that is intentionally designed to promote student learning and development.

CES-LP must develop, disseminate, implement, and regularly review their missions, which must be consistent with the mission of the institution and with applicable professional standards. The mission must be appropriate for the institution's students and other constituents. Mission statements must reference student learning and development.

Part 2. Program

To achieve their mission, Civic Engagement and Service-Learning Programs (CES-LP) must contribute to
- students' formal education, which includes both the curriculum and the co-curriculum
- student progression and timely completion of educational goals
- preparation of students for their careers, citizenship, and lives
- student learning and development

CES-LP must contribute to the well-being of the communities that host service-learners.

To contribute to student learning and development, CES-LP must
- identify relevant and desirable student learning and development outcomes
- articulate how the student learning and development outcomes align with the six CAS student learning and development domains and related dimensions
- assess relevant and desirable student learning and development
- provide evidence of impact on outcomes
- articulate contributions to or support of student learning and development in the domains not specifically assessed
- use evidence gathered to create strategies for improvement of programs and services

STUDENT LEARNING AND DEVELOPMENT DOMAINS AND DIMENSIONS

Domain: knowledge acquisition, integration, construction, and application

- Dimensions: understanding knowledge from a range of disciplines; connecting knowledge to other knowledge, ideas, and experiences; constructing knowledge; and relating knowledge to daily life

Domain: cognitive complexity
- Dimensions: critical thinking, reflective thinking, effective reasoning, and creativity

Domain: intrapersonal development
- Dimensions: realistic self-appraisal, self-understanding, and self-respect; identity development; commitment to ethics and integrity; and spiritual awareness

Domain: interpersonal competence
- Dimensions: meaningful relationships, interdependence, collaboration, and effective leadership

Domain: humanitarianism and civic engagement
- Dimensions: understanding and appreciation of cultural and human differences, social responsibility, global perspective, and sense of civic responsibility

Domain: practical competence
- Dimensions: pursuing goals, communicating effectively, technical competence, managing personal affairs, managing career development, demonstrating professionalism, maintaining health and wellness, and living a purposeful and satisfying life

[LD Outcomes: See *The Council for the Advancement of Standards Learning and Development Outcomes* statement for examples of outcomes related to these domains and dimensions.]

CES-LP must be
- intentionally designed
- guided by theories and knowledge of learning and development
- integrated into the life of the institution
- reflective of developmental and demographic profiles of the student population
- responsive to needs of individuals, populations with distinct needs, and relevant constituencies
- delivered using multiple formats, strategies, and contexts
- designed to provide universal access

CES-LP must collaborate with colleagues and departments across the institution to promote student learning and development, persistence, and success.

CES-LP must be integrated into and enhance both the academic and co-curricular programs and the community.

CES-LP must

- allow participants to define their needs and interests
- engage students in responsible and purposeful actions to meet community-defined needs
- enable students to understand needs in the context of community resources
- articulate clear service and learning goals for everyone involved, including students, faculty and staff members, community agency personnel, and those being served
- ensure intellectual rigor within the design of service-learning experiences
- establish criteria for selecting civic engagement and service-learning sites to ensure productive learning opportunities for everyone involved
- educate students regarding the philosophy of service and learning, the particular community service site, the work they will do, and the people they will be serving in the community
- establish and implement risk management procedures to protect students, the institution, and the community agencies
- offer alternatives to ensure that students are not required to participate in activities that violate a religious, spiritual, or moral belief
- engage students in reflection designed to enable them to deepen their understanding of themselves, the community, and the complexity of social problems and potential solutions
- engage students in the examination of assumptions and biases
- raise student awareness of social systems at the root of community needs
- educate students to differentiate between perpetuating dependence and building capacity within the community
- establish mechanisms to regularly assess and evaluate civic, service, and learning outcomes for students and communities
- provide on-going professional development and support to faculty and staff members
- educate students to analyze community action to differentiate acts of charity from transformative change

CES-LP must initiate and maintain collaborative relations within the institution for the design and implementation of CES-LP experiences. They must develop mutually beneficial partnerships with community-based organizations to meet organizations' service needs and to achieve student learning and development outcomes.

When course credit is offered for service-learning, the credit must be for learning, not service. Whether service-learning is for academic credit or not, the focus must be on learning and educational objectives, not on hours served.

CES-LP must offer a wide range of curricular and co-curricular experiences appropriate for students at varied developmental levels and with a variety of interests and abilities.

Examples may include older students, commuter students, students who are parents, part-time students, fully employed students, international students, and students with disabilities.

Experiences may include

- One-time and short-term experiences. These may be designed to achieve a variety of student learning outcomes, including introducing students to civic engagement and service-learning as a critical aspect of their college education, enabling students to learn what types of service best suit their interests, familiarizing students with the community in which the institution is located, and understanding the approaches different agencies take to address community problems. These experiences may be co-curricular or part of the academic curriculum, including first-year seminars.
- Credit-bearing courses. Such courses may be designed to enable students to deepen their understanding of course content, apply knowledge to practice, and test theory through practical application. These courses may be designed for students at any levels. Learning experiences provide opportunities for students to consider how disciplinary or interdisciplinary knowledge may be applied in a socially responsible manner in professional settings.
- Community-based research. Whether integrated into a course or organized as an independent-study, students engage in community-based research work with faculty and community partners to design, conduct, analyze, and report research results to serve community purposes.
- Intensive service-learning experiences. Service-learning experiences may immerse students intensively in a setting or culture, whether domestically or abroad. These experiences may engage students in dialogue and problem solving with the people most affected by the issues and help them develop a sense of solidarity with people whose lives and perspectives differ from their own. These experiences vary in length from a one-week alternative break to a semester- or year-long experience.

The course syllabus or plan for co-curricular experiences must describe

- community-identified needs that the service will address
- desired outcomes of the service and learning for all participants
- activities or assignments that link service to academic content
- opportunities to reflect on one's personal reactions to service and learning experiences
- logistics (e.g., time required, transportation, materials required, description of the setting)

- nature of the service work
- roles and responsibilities of students and community members
- procedures for risk management
- evaluation of the service and learning experiences
- assessment of the degree to which desired outcomes were achieved

CES-LP should foster student leadership, civic learning, and development and should encourage student-initiated and student-led service and learning.

CES-LP that focus on collective action must gather and evaluate information from multiple perspectives in conducting critical inquiry and analysis.

Part 3. Organization and Leadership

To achieve program and student learning and development outcomes, Civic Engagement and Service-Learning Programs (CES-LP) must be purposefully structured for effectiveness. CES-LP must have clearly stated and current

- goals and outcomes
- policies and procedures
- responsibilities and performance expectations for personnel
- organizational charts demonstrating clear channels of authority

Leaders must model ethical behavior and institutional citizenship.

Leaders with organizational authority for the CES-LP must provide strategic planning, management and supervision, and program advancement.

Strategic Planning
- articulate a vision and mission that drive short- and long-term planning
- set goals and objectives based on the needs of the populations served, intended student learning and development outcomes, and program outcomes
- facilitate continuous development, implementation, and assessment of program effectiveness and goal attainment congruent with institutional mission and strategic plans
- promote environments that provide opportunities for student learning, development, and engagement
- develop, adapt, and improve programs and services in response to the changing needs of populations served and evolving institutional priorities
- include diverse perspectives to inform decision making

Strategic planning should include the insights and perspectives of those off-campus partners that serve as co-educators and/or provide service opportunities.

Management and Supervision
- plan, allocate, and monitor the use of fiscal, physical, human, intellectual, and technological resources
- manage human resource processes including recruitment, selection, professional development, supervision, performance planning, succession planning, evaluation, recognition, and reward
- influence others to contribute to the effectiveness and success of the unit
- empower professional, support, and student personnel to become effective leaders
- encourage and support collaboration with colleagues and departments across the institution
- encourage and support scholarly contributions to the profession
- identify and address individual, organizational, and environmental conditions that foster or inhibit mission achievement
- use current and valid evidence to inform decisions
- incorporate sustainability practices in the management and design of programs, services, and facilities
- understand appropriate technologies and integrate them into programs and services
- be knowledgeable about codes and laws relevant to programs and services and ensure that programs and services meet those requirements
- assess and take action to mitigate potential risks

Program Advancement
- advocate for and actively promote the mission and goals of the programs and services
- inform stakeholders about issues affecting practice
- facilitate processes to reach consensus where wide support is needed
- advocate for representation in strategic planning initiatives at divisional and institutional levels

Leaders should ensure CES-LP participants and stakeholders identify the extent to which the goals were achieved and celebrate those achievements.

Part 4. Human Resources

Civic Engagement and Service-Learning Programs (CES-LP) must be staffed adequately by individuals qualified to accomplish mission and goals.

CES-LP must have access to technical and support personnel adequate to accomplish their mission.

Within institutional guidelines, CES-LP must
- establish procedures for personnel recruitment and selection, training, performance planning, and evaluation
- set expectations for supervision and performance
- provide personnel access to continuing and advanced education and appropriate professional development opportunities to improve their competence, skills, and leadership capacity
- consider work/life options available to personnel (e.g., compressed work schedules, flextime, job sharing, remote work, or telework) to promote

recruitment and retention of personnel

Administrators of CES-LP must
- ensure that all personnel have updated position descriptions
- implement recruitment and selection/hiring strategies that produce a workforce inclusive of under-represented populations
- develop promotion practices that are fair, inclusive, proactive, and non-discriminatory

Personnel responsible for delivery of CES-LP must have written performance goals, objectives, and outcomes for each year's performance cycle to be used to plan, review, and evaluate work and performance. The performance plan must be updated regularly to reflect changes during the performance cycle.

Results of individual personnel evaluations must be used to recognize personnel performance, address performance issues, implement individual and/or collective personnel development and training programs, and inform the assessment of programs and services.

CES-LP personnel, when hired and throughout their employment, must receive appropriate and thorough training.

CES-LP personnel, including student employees and volunteers, must have access to resources or receive specific training on
- institutional policies pertaining to functions or activities they support
- privacy and confidentiality policies
- laws regarding access to student records
- policies and procedures for dealing with sensitive institutional information
- policies and procedures related to technology used to store or access student records and institutional data
- how and when to refer those in need of additional assistance to qualified personnel and have access to a supervisor for assistance in making these judgments
- systems and technologies necessary to perform their assigned responsibilities
- ethical and legal uses of technology

CES-LP personnel must engage in continuing professional development activities to keep abreast of the research, theories, legislation, policies, and developments that affect their programs and services.

Professional development of staff and faculty members engaged in civic engagement and service-learning programs should address how to
- build relationships with community agencies
- establish and maintain collaborative relationships with campus functional areas and units
- engage students in community action for the public good
- prepare, mentor, and monitor students to deliver

services according to legal and risk management policies
- employ learning strategies that are effective in achieving learning outcomes
- engage students in structured opportunities for reflection
- develop, implement, and evaluate service and learning goals
- facilitate the process of identifying student and community needs and interests
- clarify the responsibilities of students, the institution, and agencies
- match the unique needs of agencies and students
- sustain genuine and active commitment of students, the institution, and agencies
- educate, train, and support students to facilitate service-learning experiences for their peers
- ensure that the time commitments for service and learning are balanced and appropriate
- foster participation by and with diverse populations
- develop fiscal and other resources for program support

Administrators of CES-LP must ensure that personnel are knowledgeable about and trained in safety, emergency procedures, and crisis prevention and response. Risk management efforts must address identification of threatening conduct or behavior and must incorporate a system for responding to and reporting such behaviors.

CES-LP personnel must be knowledgeable of and trained in safety and emergency procedures for securing and vacating facilities.

PROFESSIONAL PERSONNEL

CES-LP professional personnel either must hold an earned graduate or professional degree in a field relevant to their position or must possess an appropriate combination of educational credentials and related work experience.

To maintain and encourage reciprocity and mutually beneficial partnerships, the leaders of CES-LP and staff should provide professional development for community partners regarding how to work effectively with students, faculty members, and staff in higher education institutions. CES-LP leaders should also create opportunities for community partners to educate CES-LP staff about their organizations and the community.

Faculty and staff members who integrate service-learning into courses should receive institutional recognition and support (e.g., reduced course load, mini-grants, or teaching assistants).

INTERNS OR GRADUATE ASSISTANTS

Degree- or credential-seeking interns or graduate assistants must be qualified by enrollment in an appropriate field of study and relevant experience. These students must be trained and supervised by professional personnel who possess applicable educational credentials and work experience and have supervisory experience. Supervisors must be cognizant of the dual roles interns and graduate assistants have as both student and employee.

Supervisors must

- adhere to parameters of students' job descriptions
- articulate intended learning outcomes in student job descriptions
- adhere to agreed-upon work hours and schedules
- offer flexible scheduling when circumstances necessitate

Supervisors and students must both agree to suitable compensation if circumstances necessitate additional hours.

STUDENT EMPLOYEES AND VOLUNTEERS

Student employees and volunteers must be carefully selected, trained, supervised, and evaluated. Students must have access to a supervisor. Student employees and volunteers must be provided clear job descriptions, pre-service training based on assessed needs, and continuing development.

Part 5. Ethics

Civic Engagement and Service-Learning Programs (CES-LP) must

- review applicable professional ethical standards and must adopt or develop and implement appropriate statements of ethical practice
- publish and adhere to statements of ethical practice and ensure their periodic review
- orient new personnel to relevant ethical standards and statements of ethical practice and related institutional policies

Statements of ethical standards must

- specify that CES-LP personnel respect privacy and maintain confidentiality in communications and records as delineated by privacy laws
- specify limits on disclosure of information contained in students' records as well as requirements to disclose to appropriate authorities
- address conflicts of interest, or appearance thereof, by personnel in the performance of their work
- reflect the responsibility of personnel to be fair, objective, and impartial in their interactions with others
- reference management of institutional funds
- reference appropriate behavior regarding research and assessment with human participants, confidentiality of research and assessment data, and students' rights and responsibilities
- include the expectation that personnel confront and hold accountable other personnel who exhibit unethical behavior
- address issues surrounding scholarly integrity

CES-LP personnel must

- employ ethical decision making in the performance of their duties
- inform users of programs and services of ethical

obligations and limitations emanating from codes and laws or from licensure requirements

- recognize and avoid conflicts of interest that could adversely influence their judgment or objectivity and, when unavoidable, recuse themselves from the situation
- perform their duties within the scope of their position, training, expertise, and competence
- make referrals when issues presented exceed the scope of the position

CES-LP programs must value and respect the voice of the community in the co-creation of programs and initiatives. They must create sustained partnerships with community leaders to ensure candid feedback and mutuality in decision-making.

The faculty members, staff, and students involved in civic engagement and service-learning must be held to the same ethical standards as the CES-LP staff members.

All faculty and staff members responsible for supervising civic engagement and service-learning activities must monitor student performance based on training expertise and competence and alter placements as needed.

Part 6. Law, Policy, and Governance

Civic Engagement and Service-Learning Programs (CES-LP) must be in compliance with laws, regulations, and policies that relate to their respective responsibilities and that pose legal obligations, limitations, risks, and liabilities for the institution as a whole. Examples include constitutional, statutory, regulatory, and case law; relevant law and orders emanating from codes and laws; and the institution's policies.

CES-LP must have access to legal advice needed for personnel to carry out their assigned responsibilities.

CES-LP must inform personnel, appropriate officials, and users of programs and services about existing and changing legal obligations, risks and liabilities, and limitations.

CES-LP must inform personnel about professional liability insurance options and refer them to external sources if the institution does not provide coverage.

CES-LP must have written policies and procedures on operations, transactions, or tasks that have legal implications.

CES-LP must regularly review policies. The revision and creation of policies must be informed by best practices, available evidence, and policy issues in higher education.

CES-LP must have procedures and guidelines consistent with institutional policy for responding to threats, emergencies, and crisis situations. Systems and procedures must be in place to disseminate timely and accurate information to students, other members of the institutional community, and appropriate external organizations during emergency situations.

Personnel must neither participate in nor condone any form of harassment or activity that demeans persons or creates an intimidating, hostile, or offensive environment.

CES-LP must purchase or obtain permission to use copyrighted materials and instruments. References to copyrighted materials and instruments must include appropriate citations.

CES-LP must inform personnel about internal and external governance organizations that affect programs and services.

Part 7. Diversity, Equity, and Access

Within the context of each institution's mission and in accordance with institutional policies and applicable codes and laws, Civic Engagement and Service-Learning Programs (CES-LP) must create and maintain educational and work environments that are welcoming, accessible, inclusive, equitable, and free from harassment.

CES-LP must not discriminate on the basis of disability; age; race; cultural identity; ethnicity; nationality; family educational history (e.g., first generation to attend college); political affiliation; religious affiliation; sex; sexual orientation; gender identity and expression; marital, social, economic, or veteran status; or any other basis included in institutional policies and codes and laws.

CES-LP must
- advocate for sensitivity to multicultural and social justice concerns by the institution and its personnel
- ensure physical, program, and resource access for all constituents
- modify or remove policies, practices, systems, technologies, facilities, and structures that create barriers or produce inequities
- ensure that when facilities and structures cannot be modified, they do not impede access to programs, services, and resources
- establish goals for diversity, equity, and access
- foster communication and practices that enhance understanding of identity, culture, self-expression, and heritage
- promote respect for commonalities and differences among people within their historical and cultural contexts
- address the characteristics and needs of diverse constituents when establishing and implementing culturally relevant and inclusive programs, services, policies, procedures, and practices
- provide personnel with diversity, equity, and access training and hold personnel accountable for applying the training to their work
- respond to the needs of all constituents served when establishing hours of operation and developing methods of delivering programs, services, and resources
- recognize the needs of distance and online

learning students by directly providing or assisting them to gain access to comparable services and resources

Part 8. Internal and External Relations

Civic Engagement and Service-Learning Programs (CES-LP) must reach out to individuals, groups, communities, and organizations internal and external to the institution to
- establish, maintain, and promote understanding and effective relations with those that have a significant interest in or potential effect on the students or other constituents served by the programs and services
- garner support and resources for programs and services as defined by the mission
- collaborate in offering or improving programs and services to meet the needs of students and other constituents and to achieve program and student outcomes
- engage diverse individuals, groups, communities, and organizations to enrich the educational environment and experiences of students and other constituents
- disseminate information about the programs and services

CES-LP should develop productive working relationships with a wide range of campus agencies, including risk management, transportation, health services, academic departments and colleges, leadership programs, new student orientation, student activities, and institutional relationships and development.

Civic engagement and service-learning works best when the institution as a whole is engaged as a responsible partner with its surrounding communities. CES-LP professionals should advocate for the institution to share its resources with its community and to develop a wide range of mutually beneficial campus-community partnerships.

Promotional and descriptive information must be accurate and free of deception and misrepresentation.

CES-LP must have procedures and guidelines consistent with institutional policy for
- communicating with the media
- distributing information through print, broadcast, and online sources
- contracting with external organizations for delivery of programs and services
- cultivating, soliciting, and managing gifts
- applying to and managing funds from grants

Part 9. Financial Resources

Civic Engagement and Service-Learning Programs (CES-LP) must have funding to accomplish the mission and goals.

In establishing and prioritizing funding resources, CES-LP must conduct comprehensive analyses to determine

- unmet needs of the unit
- relevant expenditures
- external and internal resources
- impact on students and the institution

CES-LP must use the budget as a planning tool to reflect commitment to the mission and goals of the programs and services and of the institution.

CES-LP must administer funds in accordance with established institutional accounting procedures.

CES-LP must demonstrate efficient and effective use and responsible stewardship of fiscal resources consistent with institutional protocols.

Financial reports must provide an accurate financial overview of the organization and provide clear, understandable, and timely data upon which personnel can plan and make informed decisions.

Procurement procedures must
- be consistent with institutional policies
- ensure that purchases comply with laws and codes for usability and access
- ensure that the institution receives value for the funds spent
- consider information available for comparing the ethical and environmental impact of products and services purchased

Part 10. Technology

Civic Engagement and Service-Learning Programs (CES-LP) must have technology to support the achievement of their mission and goals. The technology and its use must comply with institutional policies and procedures and with relevant codes and laws.

CES-LP must use technologies to
- provide updated information regarding mission, location, staffing, programs, services, and official contacts to students and other constituents in accessible formats
- provide an avenue for students and other constituents to communicate sensitive information in a secure format
- enhance the delivery of programs and services for all students

CES-LP must
- back up data on a regular basis
- adhere to institutional policies regarding ethical and legal use of technology
- articulate policies and procedures for protecting the confidentiality and security of information
- implement a replacement plan and cycle for all technology with attention to sustainability
- incorporate accessibility features into technology-based programs and services

When providing student access to technology, CES-LP must
- have policies on the use of technology that are clear, easy to understand, and available to all students
- provide information or referral to support services for those needing assistance in accessing or using technology
- provide instruction or training on how to use the technology
- inform students of implications of misuse of technologies

Part 11. Facilities and Equipment

Civic Engagement and Service-Learning Programs' (CES-LP) facilities must be intentionally designed and located in suitable, accessible, and safe spaces that demonstrate universal design and support the program's mission and goals.

Facilities must be designed to engage various constituents and promote learning.

Personnel must have workspaces that are suitably located and accessible, well equipped, adequate in size, and designed to support their work and responsibilities.

The design of the facilities must guarantee the security and privacy of records and ensure the confidentiality of sensitive information and conversations. Personnel must be able to secure their work.

CES-LP must incorporate sustainable practices in use of facilities and purchase of equipment. Facilities and equipment must be evaluated on an established cycle and be in compliance with codes, laws, and accepted practices for access, health, safety, and security.

When acquiring capital equipment, CES-LP must take into account expenses related to regular maintenance and life cycle costs.

Part 12. Assessment

Civic Engagement and Service-Learning Programs (CES-LP) must develop assessment plans and processes.

Assessment plans must articulate an ongoing cycle of assessment activities.

CES-LP must
- specify programmatic goals and intended outcomes
- identify student learning and development outcomes
- employ multiple measures and methods
- develop manageable processes for gathering, interpreting, and evaluating data
- document progress toward achievement of goals and outcomes
- interpret and use assessment results to demonstrate accountability
- report aggregated results to respondent groups and stakeholders
- use assessment results to inform planning and

       decision-making
- **assess effectiveness of implemented changes**
- **provide evidence of improvement of programs and services**

CES-LP must assess the impact of programs on student learning and development.

CES-LP must assess the impact of programs on the community and partnerships.

CES-LP should provide assessment reports in a format that is easily understood and accessible by all stakeholders and partners.

CES-LP must employ ethical practices in the assessment process.

CES-LP must have access to adequate fiscal, human, professional development, and technological resources to develop and implement assessment plans.

General Standards revised in 2014;
CES-LP (formerly Service-Learning Programs) content developed/
revised in 2005 and 2015

Clinical Health Services
CAS Contextual Statement

Society has become increasingly aware of the need for universal access to basic healthcare services as well as the effects of policy and the built environment on an individual's health. New partnerships are being forged so that clinical (individual) and systemic (population) concerns are addressed in the most effective way. The complexity and comprehensiveness of the Clinical Health Services (CHS) provided by an institution of higher education varies extensively by student demographics, institutional mission, and the availability of community resources. For the purposes of these standards, CHS means a single diagnostic, therapeutic, rehabilitative, preventive or palliative procedure or a series of such procedures. Each procedure may be separately identified for billing and accounting purposes. CHS mainly focuses on disease prevention, intervention, community, and individual medical care along with education.

The programs under Clinical Health Services traditionally include preventive health services such as immunizations, maternal-child health care, and communicable disease control. CHS can also have expanded medical services such as primary care for children and adults, and dental services.

The CHS works with other campus and community departments and programs to address communicable diseases, emergency preparedness, and crisis management. Access to medical, nursing, and allied care as well as management of public health needs are important aspects of maintaining a productive living, learning, and working environment. In many cases, the services may be provided directly by the institution; in other cases, external resources may be used and coordinated with the institution. Trends indicate a continuing concern for issues such as, alcohol and drug use, high risk sexual choices and sexual violence, sleep hygiene and neuropsychological disease (also referred to as mental illness). Administrators of CHS face greater demands for timely access to health care, integration with health insurance plans and increasing demands for accountability. Outside accrediting bodies such as Joint Commission and Accreditation Association for Ambulatory Health Care (AAAHC) assist CHS to meet and exceed accreditation standards (U.S. Department of Education, 2006).

CHS has primarily focused on health care for traditional age college students (18-25yrs) with 59% of new full time undergraduate students completing a four-year degree in six years (IES, 2014). The number of students over the age of 25 increased by 41% between 2000 and 2011 and, as such, the demographics and the needs of college populations are shifting (IES, 2014). In addition to changing demographics the face of health care overall is changing in the U.S. with passage of the affordable care act. Directives from within IHE and federal level for CHS to supply immunization tracking, emergency response, public health surveillance, emergency preparedness protocols and procedures, pharmaceutical and paramedic services are not uncommon (IES, 2014). The

scope of practice for an accredited CHS has expanded with the growing global healthcare services industry. Many of the challenges faced by today's providers were not even thought of at the inception of on campus clinical health services over one hundred and fifty years ago.

One such challenge CHS faced was the passage of the American Recovery and Reinvestment Act of 2009. The passage of this law meant that all health care providers are required to be meaningfully utilizing electronic medical records (EMR) by January 1st, 2014. This mandate required not only that a system be in place but that the providers be prepared to demonstrate compliance ("The American Recovery", 2015). College and university health services were not exempt from implementation of this law.

As behavioral intervention teams (BIT) and threat assessment protocols are becoming commonplace on campuses and we know that CHS providers are included in over 40% of those teams (NaBITA, 2012). A majority of the issues faced by BIT groups on campus are mental health concerns such as suicide, substance abuse, and interpersonal violence (NaBITA, 2012) the voice of CHS is critical in responding appropriately to these community wide issues.

In 1860, Edward Hitchcock Jr., physician and professor of hygiene at Amherst College, was charged by the president of the college to develop methods to advance the health of students (Packwood, 1989). In response to this charge, Dr. Hitchcock focused on physical fitness and hygiene education. During the early part of the twentieth century in response to outbreaks and epidemics of communicable diseases and a lack of community resources, campus infirmaries were created to isolate students with infectious diseases. Given the levels of communicable disease and the lack, in the 1940s, of a single-payer system of universal healthcare access, infirmaries were established on college campuses. In the 1950s as veterans returned and took advantage of the GI Bill, physicals and immunizations were added, as they were the standard practice in the military (Packwood, 1989). Societal and behavioral risk factors moved to the forefront in the 1970s, and in the 1990s the Mental Health Parity Act (MHPA) was signed into United States law and brought new institutional investments in psychiatry and psychology as elements of services.

Between 2000 and 2015, the neuropsychological and psycho-pharmaceutical concerns of students moved into the forefront of CHS (APA, 2013). In response to this increase many IHE took a closer look at how mental health needs are met on campus. In the 2010 American College Health Association-National College Health Assessment (ACHA-NCHA) survey, 76% of campuses surveyed (267 campuses, representing 20% of IHE in the US) maintain discrete clinical health and psychological services (ACHA, 2010). The majority of CHS adjusted to the increasing demand for mental health care through collaboration with psychological services, referral and increased health care provider education.

Today the delivery of healthcare is changing to universal access through private purchase third-party insurance, employment compensation packages, or taxpayer-provided insurance coverage. All three of these financing options can cover primary care and other medical services for students off campus or in the community of their parent/spouse. Students who are underinsured may access care through community resources for the underinsured. Fewer students today are uninsured as IHE have begun to mandate proof of insurance to maintain student status. The CHS is often compared to other primary care ambulatory community health clinics. Traditionally, the CHS was just one of the programs and services financed by institutional appropriations or a "health fee." During these next few years, the integration of existing healthcare delivery and application of insurance will create changes in how and where students access healthcare.

As part of the educational mission of the institution, CHS must do all it can to engage the student in the education process regarding accessing clinical healthcare services. Students need to know their rights and responsibilities. They need to have access to accurate information on cost, price, services, and providers. Orientation to the concepts and language of insurance could diminish significant financial risk. These students will be in need of healthcare all their lives, so they must understand the prevailing system and alternatives. Regardless of the institution's specific policies requiring levels of healthcare insurance coverage beyond current law, students need to know how to make an informed decision based in regard to their own healthcare. Immediate access to accurate information will allow students to take responsibility and affect positive change.

Regardless of the financing and access to healthcare, the health issues that pose a threat to students' academic success are more often psychosocial, behavioral, or environmental. Data collected by the American College Health Association National College Health Assessment (ACHA-NCHA, 2014) indicate that students continue to seek out health care for (in order of significance) allergies, back pain, sinus infection, sore throats and UTI. They identified health-related causes for academic problems (in order of significance) continue to be stress, anxiety, sleep, cold/flu/sore throat and depression (ACHA-NCHA, 2014). All of the health concerns cited as most detrimental to academic progress are neuropsychological in nature and are affected by both environmental and policy decisions. Issues that interfere with academic success, like all health concerns, cannot be addressed solely by accessing medicinally focused healthcare. Effecting change requires that our focus include policy development, procedural refinement, educational outreach and environmental adjustments.

The CHS can be one of a variety of methods used to advance the health of students to the extent that such efforts enhance the learning environment. CHS must adapt and make it a priority to first address health risks and problems contextually appropriate to a student's capacity to learn. The most important aspect of any CHS will be its ability to create and maintain necessary, non-duplicate responsive services on campus as well as collaborative relationships with faculty, staff and the larger surrounding community. The maintenance of a comprehensive ambulatory health care facility may not be as important as other coordinated relevant services that CHS can provide the institution. Campuses must maintain a focus on services that support priorities within this academic context.

Although institutions differ in size, scope, and setting, there are universal concepts that affect the level of healthcare services available to college students. Current sociological trends, high-risk identification, public health issues, healthcare insurance finance reform, and changes in preventive medicine have broad institutional implications. The CHS has a unique opportunity to help meet those new challenges through a variety of services, programs, and approaches. These standards and guidelines are offered to serve this process.

References, Readings, and Resources

American College Health Association (ACHA): http://www.acha.org

American College Health Association. (2014). American College Health Association - National College Health Assessment (ACHA-NCHA) Web Summary. Updated January 2015. Available at http://www.acha.org

American College Health Association. (2010). *An ACHA White Paper: Considerations for integration of counseling and health services on college and university campuses.* Baltimore, MD: Author.

American Psychological Association. (2013, June). College students' mental health is growing concern, survey finds. *APA Monitor, 44*(6), 13.

American Recovery and Reinvestment Act of 2009: retrieved from http://www.recovery.gov/arra/About/Pages/The_Act.aspx

Keeling, R. P. (2000). Beyond the campus clinic: A holistic approach to student health. *AAC&U Peer Review, 2*(3), 13-18. *College student personnel services.* Springfield, IL: Charles C. Thomas.

National Behavioral Intervention Teams Association (2014). Retrieved from https://www.nabita.org/wordpress/wp-content/uploads/2012/04/2014-BIT-survey-summary.pdf

US Department of Education, National Center for Education Statistics (2014). The Condition of Education 2014, Institutional retention and graduation rates for undergraduate students. Retrieved from http://nces.ed.gove/fastfacts/display.asp

Patrick, K. (1988). Student health: Medical care within institutions of higher education. *Journal of the American Medical Association, 260,* 3301-3305.

Silverman, D., Underhile, R., & Keeling, R. (2008). Student health reconsidered: A radical proposal for thinking differently about health-related programs and services for students. *Student Health Spectrum,* 4-11.

Swinford, P. (2002). Advancing the health of students: A viewpoint. *Journal of American College Health, 50*(6), 309-312.

Contextual Statement Contributors
Current Edition:
Paula Swinford, University of Southern California, ACHA

Previous Edition:
Paula Swinford, University of Southern California, ACHA
Richard P. Keeling, MD, Keeling and Associates, CAS Public Director
Mary Hoban, ACHA
Victor Lieno, ACHA
Kristen Buzzbee, ACHA

Clinical Health Services
CAS Standards and Guidelines

The purpose of Clinical Health Services (CHS) is to provide, promote, support, and integrate individual healthcare, clinical preventive services, clinical treatment for illness, patient education, and public health responsibilities. Such services must take into consideration the health status of the student population and the learning environment. These services must be consistent with the educational mission of the institution and must comply with relevant legal requirements, state/provincial regulations, and professional standards. The mission must reflect the fundamental assumption that health and social justice are inextricably interconnected. CHS must serve as a method of advancing the health of the students, thereby enhancing the learning environment at the institution of higher education it serves.

The following characteristics exemplify CHS that are consistent with the environment of healthcare delivery and the environment of higher education:
- access to multiple data sources on the characteristics and health status of the population
- a spectrum of services that supports the learning mission of the campus community and health in its broadest sense
- easy and equal access to services by all students
- advocacy for a healthy campus community by providing leadership on policy issues regarding health risks of the population in the context of the learning environment
- evidence of measures of quality, such as accreditation of services, the use of recognized standards, and data on service delivery and effectiveness
- significant student involvement in advising the program's mission, goals, services, funding, and evaluation
- providing leadership during a health-related crises
- collaboration with other campus health-related programs and services

CHS must develop, disseminate, implement, and regularly review their missions, which must be consistent with the mission of the institution and with applicable professional standards. The mission must be appropriate for the institution's students and other constituents. Mission statements must reference student learning and development.

To achieve their mission, Clinical Health Services (CHS) must contribute to
- students' formal education, which includes both the curriculum and the co-curriculum
- student progression and timely completion of educational goals
- preparation of students for their careers, citizenship, and lives
- student learning and development

To contribute to student learning and development, CHS must
- identify relevant and desirable student learning and development outcomes
- articulate how the student learning and development outcomes align with the six CAS student learning and development domains and related dimensions
- assess relevant and desirable student learning and development
- provide evidence of impact on outcomes
- articulate contributions to or support of student learning and development in the domains not specifically assessed
- use evidence gathered to create strategies for improvement of programs and services

STUDENT LEARNING AND DEVELOPMENT DOMAINS AND DIMENSIONS

Domain: knowledge acquisition, integration, construction, and application
- Dimensions: understanding knowledge from a range of disciplines; connecting knowledge to other knowledge, ideas, and experiences; constructing knowledge; and relating knowledge to daily life

Domain: cognitive complexity
- Dimensions: critical thinking, reflective thinking, effective reasoning, and creativity

Domain: intrapersonal development
- Dimensions: realistic self-appraisal, self-understanding, and self-respect; identity development; commitment to ethics and integrity; and spiritual awareness

Domain: interpersonal competence
- Dimensions: meaningful relationships, interdependence, collaboration, and effective leadership

Domain: humanitarianism and civic engagement
- Dimensions: understanding and appreciation of cultural and human differences, social responsibility, global perspective, and sense of civic responsibility

Domain: practical competence
- Dimensions: pursuing goals, communicating effectively, technical competence, managing personal affairs, managing career development,

demonstrating professionalism, maintaining health and wellness, and living a purposeful and satisfying life

[LD Outcomes: See *The Council for the Advancement of Standards Learning and Development Outcomes* statement for examples of outcomes related to these domains and dimensions.]

CHS must be
- **intentionally designed**
- **guided by theories and knowledge of learning and development**
- **integrated into the life of the institution**
- **reflective of developmental and demographic profiles of the student population**
- **responsive to needs of individuals, populations with distinct needs, and relevant constituencies**
- **delivered using multiple formats, strategies, and contexts**
- **designed to provide universal access**

CHS must collaborate with colleagues and departments across the institution to promote student learning and development, persistence, and success.

CHS must acknowledge that health and social justice are inextricably interconnected.

CHS must establish appropriate policies and procedures for responding to emergency situations, especially where CHS facilities, personnel, and resources are not equipped to handle emergencies and/or when services are closed.

CHS must provide an infrastructure to support its services. The program must also create and maintain a network of services throughout the campus and surrounding communities.

Regardless of the size or scope of the institution, CHS must conform to a general level of acceptable practice that is theory-based and data-driven, and compliant with pertinent statutes, regulations, and professional standards.

In determining the scope of services to be offered, the following guidelines should apply:
- data on the affordability and accessibility of local healthcare resources, the insurance coverage of individual students, and the health status of the population should be collected and used to set priorities and tailor the CHS to the specific campus context
- CHS should contribute to the general education of students in the areas of behaviors and environments that promote physical, psychological, spiritual, and social health
- the scope and objectives of the services should be planned and outlined according to standards of practice utilizing data, goals and objectives, focus populations, assessment strategies and evaluative methodologies
- the educational goals of CHS should be consistent with nationally and internationally developed

healthcare objectives
- documented evidence of organized strategic planning and implementation should be available
- CHS should create opportunities to address documented health issues and medical services needs within the student community it serves
- appropriate interdisciplinary and interagency collaboration should occur regularly

In determining the quality of services provided, the following guidelines should apply:
- access for all students to essential medical, nursing, and counseling services
- provision of services in accordance with standards of professional practice and ethical conduct and concern for the costs versus benefits to the health status of the population
- maintenance of accreditation, staff certification, and licensure where appropriate
- cost-effective and relevant services designed to address unique campus configurations
- coordination of services to ensure coverage with no duplication
- identification of less expensive alternative resources for individual healthcare when appropriate
- provision of appropriate referrals for additional or alternative treatments or assessments

Part 3. Organization and Leadership

To achieve program and student learning and development outcomes, Clinical Health Services (CHS) must be purposefully structured for effectiveness. CHS must have clearly stated and current
- **goals and outcomes**
- **policies and procedures**
- **responsibilities and performance expectations for personnel**
- **organizational charts demonstrating clear channels of authority**

Leaders must model ethical behavior and institutional citizenship.

Leaders with organizational authority for CHS must provide strategic planning, management and supervision, and program advancement.

Strategic Planning
- **articulate a vision and mission that drive short- and long-term planning**
- **set goals and objectives based on the needs of the populations served, intended student learning and development outcomes, and program outcomes**
- **facilitate continuous development, implementation, and assessment of program effectiveness and goal attainment congruent with institutional mission and strategic plans**
- **promote environments that provide opportunities for student learning, development, and engagement**

- develop, adapt, and improve programs and services in response to the changing needs of populations served and evolving institutional priorities
- include diverse perspectives to inform decision making

Management and Supervision
- plan, allocate, and monitor the use of fiscal, physical, human, intellectual, and technological resources
- manage human resource processes including recruitment, selection, professional development, supervision, performance planning, succession planning, evaluation, recognition, and reward
- influence others to contribute to the effectiveness and success of the unit
- empower professional, support, and student personnel to become effective leaders
- encourage and support collaboration with colleagues and departments across the institution
- encourage and support scholarly contributions to the profession
- identify and address individual, organizational, and environmental conditions that foster or inhibit mission achievement
- use current and valid evidence to inform decisions
- incorporate sustainability practices in the management and design of programs, services, and facilities
- understand appropriate technologies and integrate them into programs and services
- be knowledgeable about codes and laws relevant to programs and services and ensure that programs and services meet those requirements
- assess and take action to mitigate potential risks

Program Advancement
- advocate for and actively promote the mission and goals of the programs and services
- inform stakeholders about issues affecting practice
- facilitate processes to reach consensus where wide support is needed
- advocate for representation in strategic planning initiatives at divisional and institutional levels

CHS leaders should continuously strive to eliminate duplicate coverage for care and contribute to a campus culture that supports health.

As the institution is legally constituted, the institution must have a defined governance structure that sets policy and is ultimately responsible for the CHS and its operations.

CHS should be defined by the size, nature, complexity, and mission of the institution and by the documented needs and capabilities of the population it serves, as well as the availability of local community resources.

CHS should establish and maintain an advisory board with broad constituent representation, with specific duties and responsibilities for policy, budget, services, facilities, and resources.

CHS should make initial staff appointments, reappointments, and assignment or curtailment of clinical privileges based upon a professional review of credentials and as directed by institutional policy and state/provincial regulations and statutes.

CHS should establish criteria and institute procedures for assessment and evaluation of medical access insurance policies.

The CHS director or coordinator must be placed within the institution's organizational structure to be able to promote cooperative interactions with appropriate campus and community entities.

Part 4. Human Resources

Clinical Health Services (CHS) must be staffed adequately by individuals qualified to accomplish mission and goals.

CHS must have access to technical and support personnel adequate to accomplish their mission.

Within institutional guidelines, CHS must
- **establish procedures for personnel recruitment and selection, training, performance planning, and evaluation**
- **set expectations for supervision and performance**
- **provide personnel access to continuing and advanced education and appropriate professional development opportunities to improve their competence, skills, and leadership capacity**
- **consider work/life options available to personnel (e.g., compressed work schedules, flextime, job sharing, remote work, or telework) to promote recruitment and retention of personnel**

CHS should
- strive to improve the professional competence and skill, as well as the quality of performance of all personnel it employs
- provide personnel with convenient access to on-line library resources that include materials pertinent to operational, administrative, institutional, and research services
- encourage participation of personnel in seminars, workshops, and other educational activities pertinent to its mission, goals, objectives, and the professional role
- verify participation in relevant external professional development programs, when attendance at such activities is required of professional personnel
- monitor the use of resources available to its personnel to identify that activities are relevant to the mission, goals, and objectives, and to maintain the licensure and/or certification of professional personnel
- identify continuing education activities based on quality improvement findings and the education criteria established by recognized professional authorities

Administrators of CHS must
- ensure that all personnel have updated position descriptions
- implement recruitment and selection/hiring strategies that produce a workforce inclusive of under-represented populations
- develop promotion practices that are fair, inclusive, proactive, and non-discriminatory

Personnel responsible for delivery of CHS must have written performance goals, objectives, and outcomes for each year's performance cycle to be used to plan, review, and evaluate work and performance. The performance plan must be updated regularly to reflect changes during the performance cycle.

Results of individual personnel evaluations must be used to recognize personnel performance, address performance issues, implement individual and/or collective personnel development and training programs, and inform the assessment of programs and services.

CHS personnel, when hired and throughout their employment, must receive appropriate and thorough training.

Staff members must take part in training sessions about gender, sexual orientation, racial, cultural, religious and/or spiritual, and ethnic sensitivity and should be aware of and involved in campus and community matters.

CHS personnel, including student employees and volunteers, must have access to resources or receive specific training on
- institutional policies pertaining to functions or activities they support
- privacy and confidentiality policies
- laws regarding access to student records
- policies and procedures for dealing with sensitive institutional information
- policies and procedures related to technology used to store or access student records and institutional data
- how and when to refer those in need of additional assistance to qualified personnel and have access to a supervisor for assistance in making these judgments
- systems and technologies necessary to perform their assigned responsibilities
- ethical and legal uses of technology

CHS personnel must engage in continuing professional development activities to keep abreast of the research, theories, legislation, policies, and developments that affect their programs and services.

Administrators of CHS must ensure that personnel are knowledgeable about and trained in safety, emergency procedures, and crisis prevention and response. Risk management efforts must address identification of threatening conduct or behavior and must incorporate a system for responding to and reporting such behaviors.

CHS personnel must be knowledgeable of and trained in safety and emergency procedures for securing and vacating facilities.

PROFESSIONAL PERSONNEL

CHS professional personnel either must hold an earned graduate or professional degree in a field relevant to their position or must possess an appropriate combination of educational credentials and related work experience.

CHS must establish criteria and implement a procedure to review and verify credentials of staff.

INTERNS OR GRADUATE ASSISTANTS

Degree- or credential-seeking interns or graduate assistants must be qualified by enrollment in an appropriate field of study and relevant experience. These students must be trained and supervised by professional personnel who possess applicable educational credentials and work experience and have supervisory experience. Supervisors must be cognizant of the dual roles interns and graduate assistants have as both student and employee.

Supervisors must
- adhere to parameters of students' job descriptions
- articulate intended learning outcomes in student job descriptions
- adhere to agreed-upon work hours and schedules
- offer flexible scheduling when circumstances necessitate

Supervisors and students must both agree to suitable compensation if circumstances necessitate additional hours.

STUDENT EMPLOYEES AND VOLUNTEERS

Student employees and volunteers must be carefully selected, trained, supervised, and evaluated. Students must have access to a supervisor. Student employees and volunteers must be provided clear job descriptions, pre-service training based on assessed needs, and continuing development.

Specific aspects of the CHS for which staff should be assigned include business and financial management, community relations, and assessment.

Leaders should involve staff members in designing the organizational structure and in creating and reviewing policies and procedures that reinforce and foster health-engendering behaviors.

When CHS staff is involved in formal teaching or supervision, policies governing those activities must be consistent with the mission, goals, policies, and objectives of the institution.

When CHS staff is involved in research and publishing, policies governing those activities must be consistent with mission, goals, priorities, and objectives of the institution and capabilities of the program.

All CHS staff must be informed of the research policies of the institution and CHS.

Part 5. Ethics

Clinical Health Services (CHS) must

- review applicable professional ethical standards and must adopt or develop and implement appropriate statements of ethical practice
- publish and adhere to statements of ethical practice and ensure their periodic review
- orient new personnel to relevant ethical standards and statements of ethical practice and related institutional policies

Statements of ethical standards must

- specify that CHS personnel respect privacy and maintain confidentiality in communications and records as delineated by privacy laws
- specify limits on disclosure of information contained in students' records as well as requirements to disclose to appropriate authorities
- address conflicts of interest, or appearance thereof, by personnel in the performance of their work
- reflect the responsibility of personnel to be fair, objective, and impartial in their interactions with others
- reference management of institutional funds
- reference appropriate behavior regarding research and assessment with human participants, confidentiality of research and assessment data, and students' rights and responsibilities
- include the expectation that personnel confront and hold accountable other personnel who exhibit unethical behavior
- address issues surrounding scholarly integrity

CHS personnel must

- employ ethical decision making in the performance of their duties
- inform users of programs and services of ethical obligations and limitations emanating from codes and laws or from licensure requirements
- recognize and avoid conflicts of interest that could adversely influence their judgment or objectivity and, when unavoidable, recuse themselves from the situation
- perform their duties within the scope of their position, training, expertise, and competence
- make referrals when issues presented exceed the scope of the position

The task of media relations involving individual health status should be assigned to staff members who are knowledgeable about information that can be released.

Staff members should prevent visitors from entering the facility in any manner that would compromise confidentiality.

Products and services should not be promoted for any other reason than the individual's or the community's benefit.

All marketing and advertising concerning the clinical health services must communicate the scope and range of services provided without deception.

Clinical health services should inform individuals of their basic rights and responsibilities regarding service. Such rights and responsibilities should include

- service that is competent, considerate, and compassionate; recognizes basic human rights; safeguards personal dignity; and respects values and preferences
- provision of appropriate privacy, including protection from access to confidential information by faculty members, staff, student workers, and others
- ability to receive services from the staff member of choice
- accurate information regarding competencies and credentials of the clinical health services staff
- use of identified methods to express grievances and make suggestions
- information concerning individual health status and available services
- individual disclosure of complete and full information on health status that will be treated confidentially and for which the individual gives authority to approve or refuse release in compliance with applicable federal and state/provincial laws
- an explicit process to share necessary personal health information with mental health/counseling/psychotherapy services and other higher education faculty and staff on a need-to-know basis
- an explicit process for consent to share necessary personal health information with off-campus entities

Part 6. Law, Policy, and Governance

Clinical Health Services (CHS) must be in compliance with laws, regulations, and policies that relate to their respective responsibilities and that pose legal obligations, limitations, risks, and liabilities for the institution as a whole. Examples include constitutional, statutory, regulatory, and case law; relevant law and orders emanating from codes and laws; and the institution's policies.

CHS must have access to legal advice needed for personnel to carry out their assigned responsibilities.

CHS must inform personnel, appropriate officials, and users of programs and services about existing and changing legal obligations, risks and liabilities, and limitations.

CHS must inform the institutional community of its policies and procedures addressing

- individual rights and responsibilities
- balancing protection of individual health and safety with individual rights to confidentiality and privacy
- risk management
- medical access insurance coverage
- informed consent
- access, release content, and maintenance of

individual records in accordance with legal obligations and limitations
- research
- medical dismissal of students

CHS must inform personnel about professional liability insurance options and refer them to external sources if the institution does not provide coverage.

CHS must have written policies and procedures on operations, transactions, or tasks that have legal implications.

CHS must regularly review policies. The revision and creation of policies must be informed by best practices, available evidence, and policy issues in higher education.

CHS must have procedures and guidelines consistent with institutional policy for responding to threats, emergencies, and crisis situations. Systems and procedures must be in place to disseminate timely and accurate information to students, other members of the institutional community, and appropriate external organizations during emergency situations.

Personnel must neither participate in nor condone any form of harassment or activity that demeans persons or creates an intimidating, hostile, or offensive environment.

CHS must purchase or obtain permission to use copyrighted materials and instruments. References to copyrighted materials and instruments must include appropriate citations.

CHS must inform personnel about internal and external governance organizations that affect programs and services.

CHS must develop and maintain a systematic risk management program appropriate for the organization.

Risk management programs should focus on
- methods by which individuals may be dismissed from or refused services
- methods of collecting unpaid accounts
- review of litigation related to the institution's CHS
- review of all deaths, trauma, or adverse events where there is health risk
- communication with the liability insurance carrier
- methods of dealing with inquiries from government agencies, attorneys, consumer advocate groups, reporters, and the media
- methods of managing a situation with an impaired staff member
- methods for complying with governmental regulations and contractual agreements
- methods of transporting students with medical emergencies
- maintenance of confidential records

Part 7. Diversity, Equity, and Access

Within the context of each institution's mission and in accordance with institutional policies and applicable codes and laws, Clinical Health Services (CHS) must create and maintain educational and work environments that are welcoming, accessible, inclusive, equitable, and free from harassment.

CHS must not discriminate on the basis of disability; age; race; cultural identity; ethnicity; nationality; family educational history (e.g., first generation to attend college); political affiliation; religious affiliation; sex; sexual orientation; gender identity and expression; marital, social, economic, or veteran status; or any other basis included in institutional policies and codes and laws.

CHS must
- advocate for sensitivity to multicultural and social justice concerns by the institution and its personnel
- ensure physical, program, and resource access for all constituents
- modify or remove policies, practices, systems, technologies, facilities, and structures that create barriers or produce inequities
- ensure that when facilities and structures cannot be modified, they do not impede access to programs, services, and resources
- establish goals for diversity, equity, and access
- foster communication and practices that enhance understanding of identity, culture, self-expression, and heritage
- promote respect for commonalities and differences among people within their historical and cultural contexts
- address the characteristics and needs of diverse constituents when establishing and implementing culturally relevant and inclusive programs, services, policies, procedures, and practices
- provide personnel with diversity, equity, and access training and hold personnel accountable for applying the training to their work
- respond to the needs of all constituents served when establishing hours of operation and developing methods of delivering programs, services, and resources
- recognize the needs of distance and online learning students by directly providing or assisting them to gain access to comparable services and resources

CHS should accommodate the unique needs of individuals with disabilities and should encourage faculty, staff, and other students to develop awareness of and sensitivity to individuals with disabilities. Students with disabilities should be encouraged to self-identify individual needs as soon as possible following admission (pre-matriculation) so that accommodations can be made.

For students with physical disabilities, CHS staff should advocate that the institution meet special needs through clinical health services, housing, food services, and counseling services. Whenever possible, the institution should eliminate architectural barriers that create difficulties for students with physical disabilities.

Students with special health risks may be identified by information provided on health history or behavioral assessment forms, or through screening, surveillance, and education services.

Students with chronic health conditions may be identified and informed of support services.

CHS may provide services directly or identify appropriate resources in the community to meet the special needs of these students.

CHS must ensure that students are informed about the importance of medical and dental access insurance and how to make an informed decision based on their needs.

As a condition of enrollment, students may be required to provide evidence that they have adequate medical access through healthcare insurance coverage.

Medical access through insurance coverage should be available to all eligible students.

Every contact should be viewed as an opportunity to recognize and honor diversity to address specific concerns that might impact health and quality of life for the individual and community.

Students should be provided an environment of caring with an inclusive approach, which is essential for establishing levels of confidentiality, trust, and comfort.

CHS should establish procedures for students to discuss with staff their comfort or discomfort with various approaches in delivery of services.

Individuals should be accepted in a free and open manner and in an atmosphere of mutual respect to encourage candid discussion of sensitive personal issues. Staff members should demonstrate sensitivity and understanding to students from diverse backgrounds and cultures to provide satisfactory services.

Part 8. Internal and External Relations

Clinical Health Services (CHS) must reach out to individuals, groups, communities, and organizations internal and external to the institution to
- **establish, maintain, and promote understanding and effective relations with those that have a significant interest in or potential effect on the students or other constituents served by the programs and services**
- **garner support and resources for programs and services as defined by the mission**
- **collaborate in offering or improving programs and services to meet the needs of students and other constituents and to achieve program and student outcomes**
- **engage diverse individuals, groups, communities, and organizations to enrich the educational**

environment and experiences of students and other constituents
- **disseminate information about the programs and services**

Promotional and descriptive information must be accurate and free of deception and misrepresentation.

CHS must have procedures and guidelines consistent with institutional policy for
- **communicating with the media**
- **distributing information through print, broadcast, and online sources**
- **contracting with external organizations for delivery of programs and services**
- **cultivating, soliciting, and managing gifts**
- **applying to and managing funds from grants**

To ensure success, CHS must maintain good relations with students, faculty members, staff, alumni, the local community, contractors, and support agencies.

CHS must comply with these standards even when contracted for or outsourced by the institution.

CHS staff should participate actively with their institution in designing policies and practices and developing further resources and services that have direct impact on the health status of the campus population.

CHS should review and assess health aspects of relevant institutional policies and practices. These issues may include but are not limited to drug use policies and treatment, blood-borne diseases, sexual harassment/assault, suicide and homicide threats, and discrimination of all types.

Policies on requirements for immunization prior to and during matriculation should be implemented and maintained to assure compliance, protect community health, and meet the needs of students at risk.

CHS should collaborate to minimize duplication of services with campus and community partners.

CHS should address the level and the priorities of campus services as determined by institution-specific population health status surveys, available community resources, user data and institutional context. CHS should review potential health hazards or problems related to academic activities.

CHS should identify and utilize community services, whenever appropriate, to build resource/service networks and create awareness within the community about special needs populations.

Part 9. Financial Resources

Clinical Health Services (CHS) must have funding to accomplish the mission and goals.

In establishing and prioritizing funding resources, CHS must conduct comprehensive analyses to determine
- **unmet needs of the unit**
- **relevant expenditures**

- external and internal resources
- impact on students and the institution

CHS must use the budget as a planning tool to reflect commitment to the mission and goals of the programs and services and of the institution.

CHS must administer funds in accordance with established institutional accounting procedures.

CHS must demonstrate efficient and effective use and responsible stewardship of fiscal resources consistent with institutional protocols.

Financial reports must provide an accurate financial overview of the organization and provide clear, understandable, and timely data upon which personnel can plan and make informed decisions.

Procurement procedures must
- be consistent with institutional policies
- ensure that purchases comply with laws and codes for usability and access
- ensure that the institution receives value for the funds spent
- consider information available for comparing the ethical and environmental impact of products and services purchased

Financial planning and projections should include budget data for both current and long-term expenditures that include capital expenditures and deferred maintenance costs.

Part 10. Technology

Clinical Health Services (CHS) must have technology to support the achievement of their mission and goals. The technology and its use must comply with institutional policies and procedures and with relevant codes and laws.

CHS must use technologies to
- provide updated information regarding mission, location, staffing, programs, services, and official contacts to students and other constituents in accessible formats
- provide an avenue for students and other constituents to communicate sensitive information in a secure format
- enhance the delivery of programs and services for all students

CHS must
- back up data on a regular basis
- adhere to institutional policies regarding ethical and legal use of technology
- articulate policies and procedures for protecting the confidentiality and security of information
- implement a replacement plan and cycle for all technology with attention to sustainability
- incorporate accessibility features into technology-based programs and services

When providing student access to technology, CHS must

- have policies on the use of technology that are clear, easy to understand, and available to all students
- provide information or referral to support services for those needing assistance in accessing or using technology
- provide instruction or training on how to use the technology
- inform students of implications of misuse of technologies

Part 11. Facilities and Equipment

Clinical Health Services' (CHS) facilities must be intentionally designed and located in suitable, accessible, and safe spaces that demonstrate universal design and support the program's mission and goals.

Facilities must be designed to engage various constituents and promote learning.

Personnel must have workspaces that are suitably located and accessible, well equipped, adequate in size, and designed to support their work and responsibilities.

The design of the facilities must guarantee the security and privacy of records and ensure the confidentiality of sensitive information and conversations. Personnel must be able to secure their work.

CHS must incorporate sustainable practices in use of facilities and purchase of equipment. Facilities and equipment must be evaluated on an established cycle and be in compliance with codes, laws, and accepted practices for access, health, safety, and security.

When acquiring capital equipment, CHS must take into account expenses related to regular maintenance and life cycle costs.

CHS facilities should support a range of activities including clinical treatment, intervention and consultation, patient education, and policy development. A safe, functional, and efficient environment is crucial to providing appropriate services and achieving desired outcomes.

Depending upon services offered, environmental conditions should include
- necessary facilities, technology, and equipment to handle individual or campus emergencies
- regulations prohibiting smoking
- elimination of hazards that might lead to slipping, falling, electrical shock, burns, poisoning, or other trauma
- adequate reception areas, toilets, and telephones
- parking for guests, patients, and people with disabilities
- accommodations for persons with physical disabilities
- adequate lighting and ventilation
- clean and properly maintained facilities
- facilities that provide for confidentiality and privacy

- of services and records
- testing and proper maintenance of equipment
- a system for the proper identification, management, handling, transport, treatment, and disposition of hazardous materials and wastes whether solid, liquid, or gas
- appropriate alternative power sources in case of emergency
- technology to support services and facilities

Part 12. Assessment

Clinical Health Services (CHS) must develop assessment plans and processes.

Assessment plans must articulate an ongoing cycle of assessment activities.

CHS must

- **specify programmatic goals and intended outcomes**
- **identify student learning and development outcomes**
- **employ multiple measures and methods**
- **develop manageable processes for gathering, interpreting, and evaluating data**
- **document progress toward achievement of goals and outcomes**
- **interpret and use assessment results to demonstrate accountability**
- **report aggregated results to respondent groups and stakeholders**
- **use assessment results to inform planning and decision-making**
- **assess effectiveness of implemented changes**
- **provide evidence of improvement of programs and services**

CHS should maintain an active, organized, peer-based, quality management and improvement program that links peer review, quality improvement activities, and risk management in an organized, systematic way.

Periodically, the organization should assess user and non-user satisfaction with services and facilities provided by the clinical health services and incorporate findings into quality improvement.

To develop criteria used to evaluate services, staff members should understand, support, and participate in programs of quality management and improvement. Data should be collected in an on-going manner to identify unacceptable or unexpected trends or occurrences.

The quality improvement program should address administrative and cost issues and service outcomes.

CHS must employ ethical practices in the assessment process.

CHS must have access to adequate fiscal, human, professional development, and technological resources to develop and implement assessment plans.

General Standards revised in 2014;
CHS (formerly College Health Programs) developed/revised in 2001 &
2006

College Honor Society Programs
CAS Contextual Statement

The purposes of honor societies in colleges and universities are threefold. First, they exist primarily to recognize the attainment of scholarship of a superior quality. Second, a few societies recognize the development of leadership qualities and commitment to service and excellence in research in addition to a strong scholarship record. To accomplish these objectives, it is clear that an honor society must define and maintain a truly high standard of eligibility for membership and achieve sufficient status by so doing that membership becomes something to be highly valued.

The honor society has followed the expansion and specialization of higher education in America. When Phi Beta Kappa was organized in 1776, there was no thought given to its field because all colleges then in existence were for the training of men for the service of the church and the state. With the expansion of education during the late nineteenth century into new fields, Phi Beta Kappa elected to operate in the fields of liberal arts and sciences. Although this was not finally decided until 1898, the trend was evident earlier; the 1880s saw the establishment of Tau Beta Pi in the field of engineering and Sigma Xi in scientific research (Tau Beta Pi, n.d.).

Early in the 20th century, other honor societies came into being. Phi Kappa Phi was organized to accept membership from all academic fields in the university. A few others of this nature had origins in Black, Catholic, or Jesuit colleges and universities. These honor societies became known as general honor societies. Other variations have developed since that time. Leadership honor societies recognized meritorious attainments in all-around leadership and campus citizenship. Numerous societies drew membership from the various disciplines of study, recognizing good work in the student's special field of study. These societies are generally known as specialized honor societies. Another variation recognizes scholastic achievement during the freshman or sophomore year. Yet other variations recognize achievement in associate degree programs and advanced study. In more recent years, many honor societies have become international in scope. The issue of eligibility of international chapters is managed by each society. For example, Beta Gamma Sigma is able to use the accreditation body (AASCSB International) to identify qualifying institutions for chapters. The eligibility status of members is handled by each society to ensure equivalence with U.S. standards.

The national organization of each honor society sets standards for establishing collegiate chapters and requirements for administering them. Chapters are chartered to institutions and have a dual relationship: maintain national honor society standards and requirements and abide by institutional policies and procedures.

The Association of College Honor Societies (ACHS) was founded in 1925 for the establishment and maintenance of useful functions and desirable standards, including criteria for membership, for governance of each member society, and for chapter operation. In addition to defining honor societies, similar student organizations with more liberal membership requirements were named recognition societies. *Baird's Manual of American College Fraternities,* the authoritative reference work on college Greek-letter societies (first published in 1879) until it was last published in 1991 by Baird's Manual Foundation, adopted the ACHS definitions for classification of honor societies and recognition societies.

The standards and functions originally named in the early history of ACHS still have relevance today as ACHS fulfills a certifying function in assuring candidates for membership as well as institutions that member societies have met the high standards. The standards also serve a role for judging credibility of non-member societies.

The challenge in the 21st century is the same as when ACHS was founded: to use academic and operational standards to allay the confusion prevailing on campuses and among the public regarding the credibility and legitimacy of newly emerging honor societies. A plethora of Internet societies, for-profit societies, and an increasingly narrow focus of specialized societies gives rise to the need for the CAS standards to guide colleges and universities in setting regulations for official recognition of campus honor societies. Students, parents, and the public can use the standards as criteria for judging quality.

References, Readings, and Resources

Association of College Honor Societies. (2014). *ACHS handbook*. East Lansing, MI: Retrieved from http://www.achsnatl.org/member-directory.asp

Association of College Honor Societies. (2014). *Standards alert: How to judge the credibility of an honor society*. Retrieved from http://www.achsnatl.org/standards_alert.asp

Association of College Honor Societies. (2014). *Informational alerts*. Retrieved from http://www.achsnatl.org/informational_alert.asp

Tau Beta Pi. (n.d.). *Tau Beta Pi history*. Retrieved from http://www.tbp.org/about/history.cfm.

Warren, J. W. (2000). *Prelude to the new millennium: Promoting honor for seventy-five years*. East Lansing, MI: Association of College Honor Societies. Retrieved from http://www.achsnatl.org/history.asp

Contextual Statement Contributors
Current Edition:
Dorothy I. Mitstifer, ACHS

Previous Editions:
Dorothy I. Mitstifer, ACHS

College Honor Society Programs
CAS Standards and Guidelines

Part 1. Mission

The mission of College Honor Society Programs (CHSP) is to promote the values of higher education and confer distinction for high achievement in undergraduate, graduate, and professional studies; student leadership; service; and research.

College Honor Society Programs (CHSP) must develop, disseminate, implement, and regularly review their missions, which must be consistent with the mission of the institution and with applicable professional standards. The mission must be appropriate for the institution's students and other constituents. Mission statements must reference student learning and development.

CHSP should
- inspire and encourage intellectual development
- preserve traditions and customs of the honor societies
- provide opportunities for members to associate in mutual understanding
- promote activities focused on civic engagement and contribution to the institutions
- work collaboratively to inform the higher education community of the CHSP mission

Part 2. Program

To achieve their mission, College Honor Society Programs (CHSP) must contribute to
- students' formal education, which includes both the curriculum and the co-curriculum
- student progression and timely completion of educational goals
- preparation of students for their careers, citizenship, and lives
- student learning and development

To contribute to student learning and development, CHSP must
- identify relevant and desirable student learning and development outcomes
- articulate how the student learning and development outcomes align with the six CAS student learning and development domains and related dimensions
- assess relevant and desirable student learning and development
- provide evidence of impact on outcomes
- articulate contributions to or support of student learning and development in the domains not specifically assessed
- use evidence gathered to create strategies for improvement of programs and services

STUDENT LEARNING AND DEVELOPMENT DOMAINS AND DIMENSIONS

Domain: knowledge acquisition, integration, construction, and application
- Dimensions: understanding knowledge from a range of disciplines; connecting knowledge to other knowledge, ideas, and experiences; constructing knowledge; and relating knowledge to daily life

Domain: cognitive complexity
- Dimensions: critical thinking, reflective thinking, effective reasoning, and creativity

Domain: intrapersonal development
- Dimensions: realistic self-appraisal, self-understanding, and self-respect; identity development; commitment to ethics and integrity; and spiritual awareness

Domain: interpersonal competence
- Dimensions: meaningful relationships, interdependence, collaboration, and effective leadership

Domain: humanitarianism and civic engagement
- Dimensions: understanding and appreciation of cultural and human differences, social responsibility, global perspective, and sense of civic responsibility

Domain: practical competence
- Dimensions: pursuing goals, communicating effectively, technical competence, managing personal affairs, managing career development, demonstrating professionalism, maintaining health and wellness, and living a purposeful and satisfying life

[LD Outcomes: See *The Council for the Advancement of Standards Learning and Development Outcomes* statement for examples of outcomes related to these domains and dimensions.]

CHSP must be
- intentionally designed
- guided by theories and knowledge of learning and development
- integrated into the life of the institution
- reflective of developmental and demographic profiles of the student population
- responsive to needs of individuals, populations with distinct needs, and relevant constituencies
- delivered using multiple formats, strategies, and contexts
- designed to provide universal access

CHSP must collaborate with colleagues and departments

across the institution to promote student learning and development, persistence, and success.

CHSP must include the following elements:
- educational programming that complements the academic curriculum
- opportunities for recognition by the institution
- faculty, staff, and administrator involvement and interaction with students

The CHSP process for establishment of college honor society chapters must include
- formal chartering of each chapter by institution and college/department petition
- approval by official action of the governing body of the national/international organization, if applicable
- jointly defined relationship between the institution and the college honor society that must be formalized, documented, and disseminated
- support of the institution for identification of qualified candidates
- candidate selection by the chapter
- membership invitation by the chapter

CHSP must assist college honor society chapters in maintaining good standing with their national/international organization policies.

National/international college honor societies recognized by the institution should be governed by its membership and should include
- officers/board members elected by the national/international membership
- chapter representation in the governing body
- national/international membership participation in approving and revising by-laws
- independent financial review and full financial disclosure

Classifications of college honor societies should include general scholarship, general leadership, specialized scholarship, and freshman, sophomore and two-year honor societies. Minimum scholastic qualifications in each classification of college honor societies should include:
- general scholarship – top 20%, not earlier than junior rank
- general leadership – top 35%, not earlier than junior rank
- specialized scholarship – top 35%, not earlier than second semester sophomore rank

First-year, sophomore, and two-year honor societies should adhere to the same high standards with the exception of rank.

"Recognition Societies" are those organizations with lower scholastic criteria.

CHSP must provide support to chapter officers and leaders to offer programs focusing on scholarship, leadership, service, or research.

Part 3. Organization and Leadership

Advisers (faculty or staff member) must represent College Honor Society Programs (CHSP) and the institution in advising chapters of college honor societies. The adviser must model leadership principles, establish a climate and structure that facilitates leadership development, determine expectations of accountability, and fairly assess student performance.

College honor society chapter governance documents and the names of officers and advisers must be filed annually both with CHSP and the national/international organization.

CHSP should maintain a centralized registry of recognized college honor societies organizations.

CHSP should encourage faculty and staff members to advise college honor societies chapters, recognize their advisers and their co-curricular work with students, and value the contributions that college honor societies make to student development and vibrancy of campus life.

CHSP must ensure student participation in the governance of the collegiate chapter.

CHSP must ensure students are elected by their peers to organize chapter activities.

To achieve program and student learning and development outcomes, CHSP must be purposefully structured for effectiveness. CHSP must have clearly stated and current
- goals and outcomes
- policies and procedures
- responsibilities and performance expectations for personnel
- organizational charts demonstrating clear channels of authority

CHSP policies for chapters must include information about the following:
- national/international and chapter relationship
- chapter adviser role
- chapter executive committee governance process
- fiscal management
- membership rights
- risk management policy
- policies for use of name, logo, and other intellectual property

Leaders must model ethical behavior and institutional citizenship.

Leaders with organizational authority for the CHSP must provide strategic planning, management and supervision, and program advancement.

Strategic Planning
- articulate a vision and mission that drive short- and long-term planning
- set goals and objectives based on the needs of the populations served, intended student learning and

development outcomes, and program outcomes

- facilitate continuous development, implementation, and assessment of program effectiveness and goal attainment congruent with institutional mission and strategic plans
- promote environments that provide opportunities for student learning, development, and engagement
- develop, adapt, and improve programs and services in response to the changing needs of populations served and evolving institutional priorities
- include diverse perspectives to inform decision making

Management and Supervision

- plan, allocate, and monitor the use of fiscal, physical, human, intellectual, and technological resources
- manage human resource processes including recruitment, selection, professional development, supervision, performance planning, succession planning, evaluation, recognition, and reward
- influence others to contribute to the effectiveness and success of the unit
- empower professional, support, and student personnel to become effective leaders
- encourage and support collaboration with colleagues and departments across the institution
- encourage and support scholarly contributions to the profession
- identify and address individual, organizational, and environmental conditions that foster or inhibit mission achievement
- use current and valid evidence to inform decisions
- incorporate sustainability practices in the management and design of programs, services, and facilities
- understand appropriate technologies and integrate them into programs and services
- be knowledgeable about codes and laws relevant to programs and services and ensure that programs and services meet those requirements
- assess and take action to mitigate potential risks

Program Advancement

- advocate for and actively promote the mission and goals of the programs and services
- inform stakeholders about issues affecting practice
- facilitate processes to reach consensus where wide support is needed
- advocate for representation in strategic planning initiatives at divisional and institutional levels

Part 4. Human Resources

College Honor Society Programs (CHSP) must be staffed adequately by individuals qualified to accomplish mission and goals.

With very few exceptions, faculty and staff are not employed to be college honor society advisers; most are volunteers but

should have access to college support.

CHSP must have access to technical and support personnel adequate to accomplish their mission.

Within institutional guidelines, CHSP must

- establish procedures for personnel recruitment and selection, training, performance planning, and evaluation
- set expectations for supervision and performance
- provide personnel access to continuing and advanced education and appropriate professional development opportunities to improve their competence, skills, and leadership capacity
- consider work/life options available to personnel (e.g., compressed work schedules, flextime, job sharing, remote work, or telework) to promote recruitment and retention of personnel

Administrators of CHSP must

- ensure that all personnel have updated position descriptions
- implement recruitment and selection/hiring strategies that produce a workforce inclusive of under-represented populations
- develop promotion practices that are fair, inclusive, proactive, and non-discriminatory

Personnel responsible for delivery of CHSP must have written performance goals, objectives, and outcomes for each year's performance cycle to be used to plan, review, and evaluate work and performance. The performance plan must be updated regularly to reflect changes during the performance cycle.

Results of individual personnel evaluations must be used to recognize personnel performance, address performance issues, implement individual and/or collective personnel development and training programs, and inform the assessment of programs and services.

CHSP personnel, when hired and throughout their employment, must receive appropriate and thorough training.

CHSP personnel, including student employees and volunteers, must have access to resources or receive specific training on

- institutional policies pertaining to functions or activities they support
- privacy and confidentiality policies
- laws regarding access to student records
- policies and procedures for dealing with sensitive institutional information
- policies and procedures related to technology used to store or access student records and institutional data
- how and when to refer those in need of additional assistance to qualified personnel and have access to a supervisor for assistance in making these judgments
- systems and technologies necessary to perform

- their assigned responsibilities
- ethical and legal uses of technology

CHSP personnel must engage in continuing professional development activities to keep abreast of the research, theories, legislation, policies, and developments that affect their programs and services.

Administrators of CHSP must ensure that personnel are knowledgeable about and trained in safety, emergency procedures, and crisis prevention and response. Risk management efforts must address identification of threatening conduct or behavior and must incorporate a system for responding to and reporting such behaviors.

CHSP personnel must be knowledgeable of and trained in safety and emergency procedures for securing and vacating facilities.

PROFESSIONAL PERSONNEL

CHSP professional personnel either must hold an earned graduate or professional degree in a field relevant to their position or must possess an appropriate combination of educational credentials and related work experience.

INTERNS OR GRADUATE ASSISTANTS

Degree- or credential-seeking interns or graduate assistants must be qualified by enrollment in an appropriate field of study and relevant experience. These students must be trained and supervised by professional personnel who possess applicable educational credentials and work experience and have supervisory experience. Supervisors must be cognizant of the dual roles interns and graduate assistants have as both student and employee.

Supervisors must
- adhere to parameters of students' job descriptions
- articulate intended learning outcomes in student job descriptions
- adhere to agreed-upon work hours and schedules
- offer flexible scheduling when circumstances necessitate

Supervisors and students must both agree to suitable compensation if circumstances necessitate additional hours.

STUDENT EMPLOYEES AND VOLUNTEERS

Student employees and volunteers must be carefully selected, trained, supervised, and evaluated. Students must have access to a supervisor. Student employees and volunteers must be provided clear job descriptions, pre-service training based on assessed needs, and continuing development.

Part 5. Ethics

College Honor Society Programs (CHSP) must
- review applicable professional ethical standards and must adopt or develop and implement appropriate statements of ethical practice

- publish and adhere to statements of ethical practice and ensure their periodic review
- orient new personnel to relevant ethical standards and statements of ethical practice and related institutional policies

Statements of ethical standards must
- specify that CHSP personnel respect privacy and maintain confidentiality in communications and records as delineated by privacy laws
- specify limits on disclosure of information contained in students' records as well as requirements to disclose to appropriate authorities
- address conflicts of interest, or appearance thereof, by personnel in the performance of their work
- reflect the responsibility of personnel to be fair, objective, and impartial in their interactions with others
- reference management of institutional funds
- reference appropriate behavior regarding research and assessment with human participants, confidentiality of research and assessment data, and students' rights and responsibilities
- include the expectation that personnel confront and hold accountable other personnel who exhibit unethical behavior
- address issues surrounding scholarly integrity

CHSP personnel must
- employ ethical decision making in the performance of their duties
- inform users of programs and services of ethical obligations and limitations emanating from codes and laws or from licensure requirements
- recognize and avoid conflicts of interest that could adversely influence their judgment or objectivity and, when unavoidable, recuse themselves from the situation
- perform their duties within the scope of their position, training, expertise, and competence
- make referrals when issues presented exceed the scope of the position

Part 6. Law, Policy, and Governance

College Honor Society Programs (CHSP) must be in compliance with laws, regulations, and policies that relate to their respective responsibilities and that pose legal obligations, limitations, risks, and liabilities for the institution as a whole. Examples include constitutional, statutory, regulatory, and case law; relevant law and orders emanating from codes and laws; and the institution's policies.

When questions arise regarding chapter operations and personnel, CHSP chapters must use the institutional system for resolving legal issues regarding laws, regulations, and policies.

When questions arise regarding membership status of

members or the chapter, CHSP must use the national/international governing body to resolve legal issues.

CHSP must have access to legal advice needed for personnel to carry out their assigned responsibilities.

CHSP must inform personnel, appropriate officials, and users of programs and services about existing and changing legal obligations, risks and liabilities, and limitations.

CHSP must inform personnel about professional liability insurance options and refer them to external sources if the institution does not provide coverage.

CHSP must have written policies and procedures on operations, transactions, or tasks that have legal implications.

CHSP must regularly review policies. The revision and creation of policies must be informed by best practices, available evidence, and policy issues in higher education.

CHSP must have procedures and guidelines consistent with institutional policy for responding to threats, emergencies, and crisis situations. Systems and procedures must be in place to disseminate timely and accurate information to students, other members of the institutional community, and appropriate external organizations during emergency situations.

Personnel must neither participate in nor condone any form of harassment or activity that demeans persons or creates an intimidating, hostile, or offensive environment.

CHSP must purchase or obtain permission to use copyrighted materials and instruments. References to copyrighted materials and instruments must include appropriate citations.

CHSP must inform personnel about internal and external governance organizations that affect programs and services.

Part 7. Diversity, Equity, and Access

Within the context of each institution's mission and in accordance with institutional policies and applicable codes and laws, College Honor Society Programs (CHSP) must create and maintain educational and work environments that are welcoming, accessible, inclusive, equitable, and free from harassment.

CHSP must not discriminate on the basis of disability; age; race; cultural identity; ethnicity; nationality; family educational history (e.g., first generation to attend college); political affiliation; religious affiliation; sex; sexual orientation; gender identity and expression; marital, social, economic, or veteran status; or any other basis included in institutional policies and codes and laws.

CHSP must
- advocate for sensitivity to multicultural and social justice concerns by the institution and its personnel
- ensure physical, program, and resource access for

all constituents
- modify or remove policies, practices, systems, technologies, facilities, and structures that create barriers or produce inequities
- ensure that when facilities and structures cannot be modified, they do not impede access to programs, services, and resources
- establish goals for diversity, equity, and access
- foster communication and practices that enhance understanding of identity, culture, self-expression, and heritage
- promote respect for commonalities and differences among people within their historical and cultural contexts
- address the characteristics and needs of diverse constituents when establishing and implementing culturally relevant and inclusive programs, services, policies, procedures, and practices
- provide personnel with diversity, equity, and access training and hold personnel accountable for applying the training to their work
- respond to the needs of all constituents served when establishing hours of operation and developing methods of delivering programs, services, and resources
- recognize the needs of distance and online learning students by directly providing or assisting them to gain access to comparable services and resources

CHSP must encourage college honor society chapters to include outreach to under-represented populations in membership recruitment activities and leadership opportunities.

Part 8. Internal and External Relations

College Honor Society Programs (CHSP) must reach out to individuals, groups, communities, and organizations internal and external to the institution to
- establish, maintain, and promote understanding and effective relations with those that have a significant interest in or potential effect on the students or other constituents served by the programs and services
- garner support and resources for programs and services as defined by the mission
- collaborate in offering or improving programs and services to meet the needs of students and other constituents and to achieve program and student outcomes
- engage diverse individuals, groups, communities, and organizations to enrich the educational environment and experiences of students and other constituents
- disseminate information about the programs and services

Promotional and descriptive information must be accurate and free of deception and misrepresentation.

CHSP must have procedures and guidelines consistent with

institutional policy for
- communicating with the media
- distributing information through print, broadcast, and online sources
- contracting with external organizations for delivery of programs and services
- cultivating, soliciting, and managing gifts
- applying to and managing funds from grants

Part 9. Financial Resources

College Honor Society Programs (CHSP) must have funding to accomplish the mission and goals.

In establishing and prioritizing funding resources, CHSP must conduct comprehensive analyses to determine
- unmet needs of the unit
- relevant expenditures
- external and internal resources
- impact on students and the institution

CHSP must use the budget as a planning tool to reflect commitment to the mission and goals of the programs and services and of the institution.

CHSP must administer funds in accordance with established institutional accounting procedures.

CHSP must demonstrate efficient and effective use and responsible stewardship of fiscal resources consistent with institutional protocols.

Financial reports must provide an accurate financial overview of the organization and provide clear, understandable, and timely data upon which personnel can plan and make informed decisions.

Procurement procedures must
- be consistent with institutional policies
- ensure that purchases comply with laws and codes for usability and access
- ensure that the institution receives value for the funds spent
- consider information available for comparing the ethical and environmental impact of products and services purchased

Part 10. Technology

College Honor Society Programs (CHSP) must have technology to support the achievement of their mission and goals. The technology and its use must comply with institutional policies and procedures and with relevant codes and laws.

CHSP must use technologies to
- provide updated information regarding mission, location, staffing, programs, services, and official contacts to students and other constituents in accessible formats
- provide an avenue for students and other constituents to communicate sensitive information in a secure format

- enhance the delivery of programs and services for all students

CHSP must
- back up data on a regular basis
- adhere to institutional policies regarding ethical and legal use of technology
- articulate policies and procedures for protecting the confidentiality and security of information
- implement a replacement plan and cycle for all technology with attention to sustainability
- incorporate accessibility features into technology-based programs and services

When providing student access to technology, CHSP must
- have policies on the use of technology that are clear, easy to understand, and available to all students
- provide information or referral to support services for those needing assistance in accessing or using technology
- provide instruction or training on how to use the technology
- inform students of implications of misuse of technologies

Part 11. Facilities and Equipment

College Honor Society Programs' (CHSP) facilities must be intentionally designed and located in suitable, accessible, and safe spaces that demonstrate universal design and support the program's mission and goals.

Facilities must be designed to engage various constituents and promote learning.

Personnel must have workspaces that are suitably located and accessible, well equipped, adequate in size, and designed to support their work and responsibilities.

The design of the facilities must guarantee the security and privacy of records and ensure the confidentiality of sensitive information and conversations. Personnel must be able to secure their work.

CHSP must incorporate sustainable practices in use of facilities and purchase of equipment. Facilities and equipment must be evaluated on an established cycle and be in compliance with codes, laws, and accepted practices for access, health, safety, and security.

When acquiring capital equipment, CHSP must take into account expenses related to regular maintenance and life cycle costs.

Meeting space for CHSP chapter activities and storage space for chapter materials (memorabilia, documents, files) should be available. Chapter files should be stored electronically and securely.

Part 12. Assessment

College Honor Society Programs (CHSP) must develop

assessment plans and processes.

Assessment plans must articulate an ongoing cycle of assessment activities.

CHSP must
- specify programmatic goals and intended outcomes
- identify student learning and development outcomes
- employ multiple measures and methods
- develop manageable processes for gathering, interpreting, and evaluating data
- document progress toward achievement of goals and outcomes
- interpret and use assessment results to demonstrate accountability
- report aggregated results to respondent groups and stakeholders
- use assessment results to inform planning and decision-making
- assess effectiveness of implemented changes
- provide evidence of improvement of programs and services

CHSP must employ ethical practices in the assessment process.

CHSP must have access to adequate fiscal, human, professional development, and technological resources to develop and implement assessment plans.

General Standards revised in 2014;
CHSP (formerly College Honor Societies) content developed and revised in 2005 and 2015

College Unions
CAS Contextual Statement

Today's college union is a unifying force that brings together students, faculty, administrators, staff, alumni, and guests. It provides a forum for divergent viewpoints and creates an environment where all feel welcome. Optimally the union is a centrally located building where members of the campus community come together, formally and informally.

The word "union" implies a bringing together of the campus community, including its students, faculty, staff, and alumni. The word "university" derives from the Latin *universitas* meaning the whole; and the word "union" from *unio* meaning oneness—a whole made up of united parts. In the educational world the two concepts support and complement each other.

The college union, primarily referring to an organization or program, evolved from the debating tradition of British universities. The earliest college union, founded at Cambridge University in 1815, was literally a "union" of three debating societies. The first North American college union was organized at Harvard in 1832; like its British predecessors, it existed primarily for debating purposes. By the late 1800s, the Harvard Union had embraced the concept of being a general club. The first building erected explicitly for union purposes was Houston Hall at the University of Pennsylvania. Built in 1896, it housed lounges, dining rooms, reading and writing rooms, an auditorium, game rooms, and student offices; it was given to the university by the Houston family as a "place where all may meet on common ground."

In the 1930s, the success of civic recreational and cultural centers influenced college union leaders to view the union as the campus counterpart of the "community center" with an educational and recreational mission to perform. The first extensive period of union building construction took place following World War II, as enrollments surged and colleges and universities sought to better fulfill the needs of students and faculty. A second building boom occurred in the 1990s and 2000s as the original facilities were renovated or replaced. Numerous institutions built their first unions during this second boom as well.

"Traditionally considered the "hearthstone" or "living room" of the campus, today's union is the gathering place of the campus" (ACUI, 2014, para. 3). In the 21st century, the college union movement has concentrated on building community, emphasizing its educational mission, and promoting student learning and leadership. During this time, the names of facilities that embody the union idea have expanded to include memorial union, student union, university commons, college or university center, student center, and campus center, among others. Funding and institutional preferences have led to the variety of names. Regardless of the facility's name, the fundamental principle of college unions remains to bring together and unify its campus community.

The contemporary college union meets many needs expressed by all members of the campus community. College union facilities often include banks, post offices, child care, dining facilities, study lounges, fitness centers, bookstores, and other services the campus community, especially students, relies on during the course of the day. In providing these services, the college union supports the community focus on academic and personal achievement. College unions vary by institutional size, scope, and purpose. No universal formula identifies the optimum size of a college union. However, the Association of College Unions International (ACUI) offers a benchmarking service that allows for institutional comparison in size and facilities.

In 2005, ACUI announced a set of 11 core competencies for the college union and student activities profession. Developed over six years, the core competencies are a composite set of knowledge and behaviors that provide the basis and foundation for professional practice in college union and student activities work. Subsequently, ACUI developed skill sets associated with each competency. The ACUI website (www.acui.org) has more information about these efforts, which may be used to complement the CAS standards.

The college union provides numerous educationally purposeful activities outside the classroom that are "key to enhancing learning and personal development," according to *The Student Learning Imperative* (ACPA, 1996, p.1). The union contributes to the education of the student body-at-large through its cultural, educational, social, and recreational programs; the union also educates students involved in its governance and program boards and those it employs. The *Role of the College Union* defines the union as "a student centered organization that values participatory decision making. Through volunteerism, its boards, committees, and student employment, the union offers firsthand experience in citizenship and educates students in leadership, social responsibility, and values" (ACUI, 2014, para. 2). These models of college union governance foster student/staff partnerships that form the foundation for student development and leadership training.

The modern college union is a complex entity, offering a wide array of programs and services to the campus community. The standards and guidelines that follow outline the characteristics of a college union that offers high-quality experiences and uses informed practice to educate and serve a diverse range of constituents.

References, Readings, and Resources

American College Personnel Association. (1996). *The student learning imperative*. Washington, DC: Author.

Association of College Unions International (ACUI): www.acui.org.

Association of College Unions International (ACUI). (2014). *The role of the college union*. Retrieved from https://www.acui.org/About_ACUI/About_College_Unions/296/

Association of College Unions International. (2006). *51 facts about college unions*. Bloomington, IN: Author.

Association of College Unions International. (2012). *Core*

competencies and skill sets for the college union and student activities profession. Bloomington, IN: Author.

Butts, P., Beltramini, E., Bourassa, M., Connelly, P., Meyer, R, Mitchell, S., Smith, J., & Willis, T. J. (2012). *The college union idea*. (2ⁿᵈ ed.) Bloomington, IN: Association of College Unions International.

Knell, P., & Latta, S. (2006). *College union dynamic: Flexible solutions for successful facilities*. Bloomington, IN: Association of College Unions International.

Mosher, B. (Producer). (2014). *Building campus community* [Documentary]. United States: Visionaries.

Perozzi, B.P. (Ed.). (2009). *Enhancing student learning through college employment*. Bloomington, IN: Association of College Unions International.

Rullman, L., & van den Kieboom, J (Eds.). *Physical place on campus: A report on the summit on building community*. Bloomington, IN: Association of College Unions International.

The Bulletin, ACUI publication, published bimonthly; available from the ACUI Central Office.

Yakaboski, T., & DeSawal, D. M. (Eds.). (2014). The state of the college union: Contemporary issues and trends. *New Directions for Student Services 145*. Hoboken, NJ: Wiley Periodicals, Inc.

Contextual Statement Contributors
Current Edition:
Bob Rodda, College of Wooster, ACUI
Loren Rullman, University of Michigan, ACUI

Previous Editions:
Bob Rodda, College of Wooster, ACUI
Nancy Davis Metz, ACUI

College Unions
CAS Standards and Guidelines

Part 1. Mission

The primary goals of College Unions (CU) must be to bring campus constituents together, build campus community, support and initiate programs, provide services, and maintain facilities that promote student learning and development.

CU must develop, disseminate, implement, and regularly review their missions, which must be consistent with the mission of the institution and with applicable professional standards. The mission must be appropriate for the institution's students and other constituents. Mission statements must reference student learning and development.

The CU should provide educational, social, cultural, and recreational programs, services, and facilities that enhance the quality of campus life.

Students must be the principal constituents of the CU.

The CU should provide opportunities for students to learn and practice leadership, program planning, organizational management, social and civic responsibility, and interpersonal skills.

The vitality, variety, and spontaneity of the CU's activities should stem primarily from student boards, committees, and student-directed initiatives.

The CU must be an inclusive environment where interaction and understanding among individuals from diverse backgrounds occurs.

Part 2. Program

To achieve their mission, College Unions (CU) must contribute to
- students' formal education, which includes both the curriculum and the co-curriculum
- student progression and timely completion of educational goals
- preparation of students for their careers, citizenship, and lives
- student learning and development

To contribute to student learning and development, CU must
- identify relevant and desirable student learning and development outcomes
- articulate how the student learning and development outcomes align with the six CAS student learning and development domains and related dimensions
- assess relevant and desirable student learning and development
- provide evidence of impact on outcomes

- articulate contributions to or support of student learning and development in the domains not specifically assessed
- use evidence gathered to create strategies for improvement of programs and services

STUDENT LEARNING AND DEVELOPMENT DOMAINS AND DIMENSIONS

Domain: knowledge acquisition, integration, construction, and application
- **Dimensions: understanding knowledge from a range of disciplines; connecting knowledge to other knowledge, ideas, and experiences; constructing knowledge; and relating knowledge to daily life**

Domain: cognitive complexity
- **Dimensions: critical thinking, reflective thinking, effective reasoning, and creativity**

Domain: intrapersonal development
- **Dimensions: realistic self-appraisal, self-understanding, and self-respect; identity development; commitment to ethics and integrity; and spiritual awareness**

Domain: interpersonal competence
- **Dimensions: meaningful relationships, interdependence, collaboration, and effective leadership**

Domain: humanitarianism and civic engagement
- **Dimensions: understanding and appreciation of cultural and human differences, social responsibility, global perspective, and sense of civic responsibility**

Domain: practical competence
- **Dimensions: pursuing goals, communicating effectively, technical competence, managing personal affairs, managing career development, demonstrating professionalism, maintaining health and wellness, and living a purposeful and satisfying life**

[LD Outcomes: See *The Council for the Advancement of Standards Learning and Development Outcomes* statement for examples of outcomes related to these domains and dimensions.]

CU must be
- **intentionally designed**
- **guided by theories and knowledge of learning and development**
- **integrated into the life of the institution**
- **reflective of developmental and demographic profiles of the student population**
- **responsive to needs of individuals, populations**

- with distinct needs, and relevant constituencies
- delivered using multiple formats, strategies, and contexts
- designed to provide universal access

CU must collaborate with colleagues and departments across the institution to promote student learning and development, persistence, and success.

CU must include programs, activities and events, services, and facilities that address campus, community, and student needs.

CU programs, activities, and events could include
- student development programs
- social, cultural, intellectual, and diversity programs
- leisure activities and recreational opportunities
- student leadership development programs and opportunities
- service-learning and community service programs
- performances
- entertainment
- tournaments
- outdoor recreation and travel
- social events
- educational programs
- crafts and hobbies
- leisure activities
- continuing education opportunities

CU services could include
- food services
- retail stores and services
- communication technology
- mailing and duplication services
- information center
- campus and community information

CU facilities could include
- commuter accommodations
- rooms of various sizes and configurations for meetings, banquets, conferences, and programs
- office space for student organization including storage
- office space for relevant administrative functions
- recreational facilities
- rest rooms that meet all constituents needs
- technological capabilities including connectivity to campus intranets, the Internet, and emerging technologies
- exhibit spaces
- art galleries
- quiet rooms, lounges, and study spaces
- conference facilities
- studios

CU must provide opportunities for student, staff, and faculty involvement in program planning, policy development, and facility operation.

CU should also provide appropriate opportunities for involvement, participation, and collaboration with alumni and other institutional stakeholders.

Spaces in CU should be comfortable, inviting, and attractive, and appropriate space should be consistently available for informal and spontaneous interactions.

CU should create and support programs that instill an enduring affinity for the institution, including the history, legacy, traditions, and culture of the institution.

Part 3. Organization and Leadership

To achieve program and student learning and development outcomes, College Unions (CU) must be purposefully structured for effectiveness. CU must have clearly stated and current
- **goals and outcomes**
- **policies and procedures**
- **responsibilities and performance expectations for personnel**
- **organizational charts demonstrating clear channels of authority**

Leaders must model ethical behavior and institutional citizenship.

Leaders with organizational authority for CU must provide strategic planning, management and supervision, and program advancement.

Strategic Planning
- articulate a vision and mission that drive short- and long-term planning
- set goals and objectives based on the needs of the populations served, intended student learning and development outcomes, and program outcomes
- facilitate continuous development, implementation, and assessment of program effectiveness and goal attainment congruent with institutional mission and strategic plans
- promote environments that provide opportunities for student learning, development, and engagement
- develop, adapt, and improve programs and services in response to the changing needs of populations served and evolving institutional priorities
- include diverse perspectives to inform decision making

Management and Supervision
- plan, allocate, and monitor the use of fiscal, physical, human, intellectual, and technological resources
- manage human resource processes including recruitment, selection, professional development, supervision, performance planning, succession planning, evaluation, recognition, and reward
- influence others to contribute to the effectiveness and success of the unit
- empower professional, support, and student personnel to become effective leaders

- encourage and support collaboration with colleagues and departments across the institution
- encourage and support scholarly contributions to the profession
- identify and address individual, organizational, and environmental conditions that foster or inhibit mission achievement
- use current and valid evidence to inform decisions
- incorporate sustainability practices in the management and design of programs, services, and facilities
- understand appropriate technologies and integrate them into programs and services
- be knowledgeable about codes and laws relevant to programs and services and ensure that programs and services meet those requirements
- assess and take action to mitigate potential risks

Program Advancement
- advocate for and actively promote the mission and goals of the programs and services
- inform stakeholders about issues affecting practice
- facilitate processes to reach consensus where wide support is needed
- advocate for representation in strategic planning initiatives at divisional and institutional levels

In addition CU leaders must
- promote efforts to build community
- use principles of good organizational management
- facilitate good planning processes and philosophies
- use leadership skills to effectively manage facilities
- demonstrate intercultural competencies
- conduct outreach and marketing that describes and promotes the programs and services of the CU
- ensure excellent customer services
- utilize developmental and learning theories to design and implement learning initiatives and experiences for students
- engage in professional development activities to stay current with research and best practices

CU must be organized to provide effective social, cultural, intellectual, and recreational programming; offer appropriate business enterprises and services; and maintain its physical plant.

CU must involve members of the campus community in its governance and programming structure and in the formulation of CU policies.

Involvement of the campus community should include students, faculty and staff members, and alumni. Involvement could include parents and local community members. Typically such involvement is through advisory, governing, and program boards. These boards should address issues such as (a) facility operating policies related to the use and/or rental of CU facilities by campus and non-campus groups, (b) programming goals, (c) scheduling of events, (d) budget planning, fee structure, and allocation priorities, (e) employment policies, (f) space allocation priorities, and (g) hours of operation.

CU must assure that outsourced programs and services comply with the goals, policies, and procedures of the CU and the institution.

CU must have an emergency preparedness plan and a business continuity plan. The emergency preparedness plan must be compatible with the institution's emergency preparedness plan. The business continuity plan must be in place to respond after an emergency that compromises essential services and access to the facility.

Procedures must be in place to assess and manage events with large numbers of participants, potential volatile content, or dangerous materials and equipment.

Part 4. Human Resources

College Unions (CU) must be staffed adequately by individuals qualified to accomplish mission and goals.

CU must have access to technical and support personnel adequate to accomplish their mission.

Within institutional guidelines, CU must
- establish procedures for personnel recruitment and selection, training, performance planning, and evaluation
- set expectations for supervision and performance
- provide personnel access to continuing and advanced education and appropriate professional development opportunities to improve their competence, skills, and leadership capacity
- consider work/life options available to personnel (e.g., compressed work schedules, flextime, job sharing, remote work, or telework) to promote recruitment and retention of personnel

Administrators of CU must
- ensure that all personnel have updated position descriptions
- implement recruitment and selection/hiring strategies that produce a workforce inclusive of under-represented populations
- develop promotion practices that are fair, inclusive, proactive, and non-discriminatory

Personnel responsible for delivery of CU must have written performance goals, objectives, and outcomes for each year's performance cycle to be used to plan, review, and evaluate work and performance. The performance plan must be updated regularly to reflect changes during the performance cycle.

Results of individual personnel evaluations must be used to recognize personnel performance, address performance issues, implement individual and/or collective personnel development and training programs, and inform the assessment of programs and services.

CU personnel, when hired and throughout their

employment, must receive appropriate and thorough training.

CU personnel, including student employees and volunteers, must have access to resources or receive specific training on

- institutional policies pertaining to functions or activities they support
- privacy and confidentiality policies
- laws regarding access to student records
- policies and procedures for dealing with sensitive institutional information
- policies and procedures related to technology used to store or access student records and institutional data
- how and when to refer those in need of additional assistance to qualified personnel and have access to a supervisor for assistance in making these judgments
- systems and technologies necessary to perform their assigned responsibilities
- ethical and legal uses of technology

CU personnel must engage in continuing professional development activities to keep abreast of the research, theories, legislation, policies, and developments that affect their programs and services.

Cross training should be made available to enable appropriate staff to assume critical operations and responsibilities during unforeseen situations.

Administrators of CU must ensure that personnel are knowledgeable about and trained in safety, emergency procedures, and crisis prevention and response. Risk management efforts must address identification of threatening conduct or behavior and must incorporate a system for responding to and reporting such behaviors.

CU personnel must be knowledgeable of and trained in safety and emergency procedures for securing and vacating facilities.

PROFESSIONAL PERSONNEL

CU professional personnel either must hold an earned graduate or professional degree in a field relevant to their position or must possess an appropriate combination of educational credentials and related work experience.

Graduate degrees should be earned in fields relevant to the CU including, but not limited to, college student affairs; student development; public, business, or higher education administration; and recreation studies.

CU staff responsible for programs, services, and facilities must have appropriate combinations of education, experience, and credentials to adequately and safely provide a level of management and leadership consistent with relevant industry standards and institutional expectations.

INTERNS OR GRADUATE ASSISTANTS

Degree- or credential-seeking interns or graduate assistants

must be qualified by enrollment in an appropriate field of study and relevant experience. These students must be trained and supervised by professional personnel who possess applicable educational credentials and work experience and have supervisory experience. Supervisors must be cognizant of the dual roles interns and graduate assistants have as both student and employee.

Supervisors must

- adhere to parameters of students' job descriptions
- articulate intended learning outcomes in student job descriptions
- adhere to agreed-upon work hours and schedules
- offer flexible scheduling when circumstances necessitate

Supervisors and students must both agree to suitable compensation if circumstances necessitate additional hours.

The CU should offer internships or practicums to graduate students pursuing advanced degrees in college student affairs; student development; public, business, or higher educational administration; and recreation studies. These students should be utilized in a manner consistent with the missions of the CU and graduate programs.

STUDENT EMPLOYEES AND VOLUNTEERS

Student employees and volunteers must be carefully selected, trained, supervised, and evaluated. Students must have access to a supervisor. Student employees and volunteers must be provided clear job descriptions, pre-service training based on assessed needs, and continuing development.

Student employees and volunteers should be an integral part of the CU's operation. Their work experience should be an important part of their educational experience and contribute to increased engagement in the campus community. A thorough training program should be provided for part-time student employees and volunteers and, depending on their assigned duties, might include leadership training, group facilitation skills, communication skills, CU policies, and emergency procedures.

Staff members should possess (a) knowledge of and ability to use management principles, including the effective management of volunteers; (b) understanding of and the ability to apply student development theory; (c) skills in assessment, planning, training, and evaluation; (d) interpersonal skills; (e) technical skills; (f) understanding of CU philosophy; (g) commitment to institutional mission; and (h) safety and emergency management skills.

Staff members may include food service personnel, audio visual technicians, stage hands, information technology staff, maintenance personnel, support staff, attendants, housekeepers, reservationists, sales clerks, and cashiers.

Part 5. Ethics

College Unions (CU) must
- review applicable professional ethical standards

and must adopt or develop and implement appropriate statements of ethical practice
- publish and adhere to statements of ethical practice and ensure their periodic review
- orient new personnel to relevant ethical standards and statements of ethical practice and related institutional policies

Statements of ethical standards must
- specify that CU personnel respect privacy and maintain confidentiality in communications and records as delineated by privacy laws
- specify limits on disclosure of information contained in students' records as well as requirements to disclose to appropriate authorities
- address conflicts of interest, or appearance thereof, by personnel in the performance of their work
- reflect the responsibility of personnel to be fair, objective, and impartial in their interactions with others
- reference management of institutional funds
- reference appropriate behavior regarding research and assessment with human participants, confidentiality of research and assessment data, and students' rights and responsibilities
- include the expectation that personnel confront and hold accountable other personnel who exhibit unethical behavior
- address issues surrounding scholarly integrity

CU personnel must
- employ ethical decision making in the performance of their duties
- inform users of programs and services of ethical obligations and limitations emanating from codes and laws or from licensure requirements
- recognize and avoid conflicts of interest that could adversely influence their judgment or objectivity and, when unavoidable, recuse themselves from the situation
- perform their duties within the scope of their position, training, expertise, and competence
- make referrals when issues presented exceed the scope of the position

Marketing and advertising must be informative, respectful, socially responsible, and useful to students, faculty, staff, and visitors.

Part 6. Law, Policy, and Governance

College Unions (CU) must be in compliance with laws, regulations, and policies that relate to their respective responsibilities and that pose legal obligations, limitations, risks, and liabilities for the institution as a whole. Examples include constitutional, statutory, regulatory, and case law; relevant law and orders emanating from codes and laws; and the institution's policies.

CU must have access to legal advice needed for personnel to carry out their assigned responsibilities.

CU must inform personnel, appropriate officials, and users of programs and services about existing and changing legal obligations, risks and liabilities, and limitations.

CU must inform personnel about professional liability insurance options and refer them to external sources if the institution does not provide coverage.

CU must have written policies and procedures on operations, transactions, or tasks that have legal implications.

CU must regularly review policies. The revision and creation of policies must be informed by best practices, available evidence, and policy issues in higher education.

CU must have procedures and guidelines consistent with institutional policy for responding to threats, emergencies, and crisis situations. Systems and procedures must be in place to disseminate timely and accurate information to students, other members of the institutional community, and appropriate external organizations during emergency situations.

Personnel must neither participate in nor condone any form of harassment or activity that demeans persons or creates an intimidating, hostile, or offensive environment.

CU must purchase or obtain permission to use copyrighted materials and instruments. References to copyrighted materials and instruments must include appropriate citations.

CU must inform personnel about internal and external governance organizations that affect programs and services.

Part 7. Diversity, Equity, and Access

Within the context of each institution's mission and in accordance with institutional policies and applicable codes and laws, College Unions (CU) must create and maintain educational and work environments that are welcoming, accessible, inclusive, equitable, and free from harassment.

CU must not discriminate on the basis of disability; age; race; cultural identity; ethnicity; nationality; family educational history (e.g., first generation to attend college); political affiliation; religious affiliation; sex; sexual orientation; gender identity and expression; marital, social, economic, or veteran status; or any other basis included in institutional policies and codes and laws.

CU must
- advocate for sensitivity to multicultural and social justice concerns by the institution and its personnel
- ensure physical, program, and resource access for all constituents
- modify or remove policies, practices, systems, technologies, facilities, and structures that create barriers or produce inequities
- ensure that when facilities and structures cannot be modified, they do not impede access to programs,

services, and resources
- **establish goals for diversity, equity, and access**
- **foster communication and practices that enhance understanding of identity, culture, self-expression, and heritage**
- **promote respect for commonalities and differences among people within their historical and cultural contexts**
- **address the characteristics and needs of diverse constituents when establishing and implementing culturally relevant and inclusive programs, services, policies, procedures, and practices**
- **provide personnel with diversity, equity, and access training and hold personnel accountable for applying the training to their work**
- **respond to the needs of all constituents served when establishing hours of operation and developing methods of delivering programs, services, and resources**
- **recognize the needs of distance and online learning students by directly providing or assisting them to gain access to comparable services and resources**

CU governing and programming boards should represent campus diversity and institutional goals for inclusion.

CU should conduct outreach to include and engage all populations in the life of the Union.

Outsourced programs and services are accountable to the institution. Therefore, CU should encourage providers of outsourced programs and services to offer a diverse workforce and inclusive environment.

Part 8. Internal and External Relations

College Unions (CU) must reach out to individuals, groups, communities, and organizations internal and external to the institution to
- **establish, maintain, and promote understanding and effective relations with those that have a significant interest in or potential effect on the students or other constituents served by the programs and services**
- **garner support and resources for programs and services as defined by the mission**
- **collaborate in offering or improving programs and services to meet the needs of students and other constituents and to achieve program and student outcomes**
- **engage diverse individuals, groups, communities, and organizations to enrich the educational environment and experiences of students and other constituents**
- **disseminate information about the programs and services**

Examples of relevant individuals, campus offices, and external agencies include students; student organizations, especially student government and program board(s); faculty members; administrative offices; alumni; local community members;

contracted service providers, including lessees; and campus safety offices.

Promotional and descriptive information must be accurate and free of deception and misrepresentation.

CU should use relevant and appropriate student and campus marketing and outreach resources to inform the campus community about CU programs and services. Staff and volunteers throughout CU should be considered for membership on various institutional committees and governing bodies.

CU must have procedures and guidelines consistent with institutional policy for
- **communicating with the media**
- **distributing information through print, broadcast, and online sources**
- **contracting with external organizations for delivery of programs and services**
- **cultivating, soliciting, and managing gifts**
- **applying to and managing funds from grants**

Part 9. Financial Resources

College Unions (CU) must have funding to accomplish the mission and goals.

CU should have financial resources to ensure reasonable pricing of services and adequate programming, staffing, maintenance, and professional development.

In establishing and prioritizing funding resources, CU must conduct comprehensive analyses to determine
- **unmet needs of the unit**
- **relevant expenditures**
- **external and internal resources**
- **impact on students and the institution**

CU must use the budget as a planning tool to reflect commitment to the mission and goals of the programs and services and of the institution.

CU must administer funds in accordance with established institutional accounting procedures.

CU must demonstrate efficient and effective use and responsible stewardship of fiscal resources consistent with institutional protocols.

Financial reports must provide an accurate financial overview of the organization and provide clear, understandable, and timely data upon which personnel can plan and make informed decisions.

Procurement procedures must
- **be consistent with institutional policies**
- **ensure that purchases comply with laws and codes for usability and access**
- **ensure that the institution receives value for the funds spent**
- **consider information available for comparing the ethical and environmental impact of products and services purchased**

When handling student fee funds, CU must manage fees in accordance with approved accounting methods of the institution.

Student fee funds should be used to benefit students directly.

The institution should consider various methods and sources of financial support including, but not limited to (a) direct institutional support (e.g., salaries, utilities, housekeeping, maintenance, and membership fees); (b) student fees; (c) income from sales, services, rentals, and leases; and (d) fundraising initiatives.

Part 10. Technology

College Unions (CU) must have technology to support the achievement of their mission and goals. The technology and its use must comply with institutional policies and procedures and with relevant codes and laws.

CU must use technologies to
- provide updated information regarding mission, location, staffing, programs, services, and official contacts to students and other constituents in accessible formats
- provide an avenue for students and other constituents to communicate sensitive information in a secure format
- enhance the delivery of programs and services for all students

CU must
- back up data on a regular basis
- adhere to institutional policies regarding ethical and legal use of technology
- articulate policies and procedures for protecting the confidentiality and security of information
- implement a replacement plan and cycle for all technology with attention to sustainability
- incorporate accessibility features into technology-based programs and services

When providing student access to technology, CU must
- have policies on the use of technology that are clear, easy to understand, and available to all students
- provide information or referral to support services for those needing assistance in accessing or using technology
- provide instruction or training on how to use the technology
- inform students of implications of misuse of technologies

The CU should use current and appropriate technology to facilitate, improve, assess, and extend access to its programs, products, services, and facilities.

Part 11. Facilities and Equipment

College Unions' (CU) facilities must be intentionally designed and located in suitable, accessible, and safe spaces that demonstrate universal design and support the program's mission and goals.

Facilities must be designed to engage various constituents and promote learning.

Recycling, energy conservation, and other sustainability efforts must be addressed throughout the CU.

CU facilities should be proportional in size to the needs of the campus community and be centrally located.

CU should provide appropriate spaces that meet the unique needs of diverse groups, while simultaneously promoting interaction and community.

Facilities must be accessible, clean, reasonably priced, well maintained, and have adequate safety and security features.

New construction and renovation projects should be responsive to the current and future needs of the campus community. Decisions about new construction and renovation should be based upon clearly defined needs and consistent with the mission of the institution, which may include adherence to institutional standards for sustainability, accessibility, beautification, debt coverage, and historic preservation.

Members of the campus community and the CU staff should be involved in program development of new and renovated facilities. Such planning efforts should include representation by students, faculty, and staff.

Systematically planned replacement cycles should exist for furnishings, mechanical and electrical systems, maintenance equipment, floor/wall/window treatments, technology, and service equipment.

Personnel must have workspaces that are suitably located and accessible, well equipped, adequate in size, and designed to support their work and responsibilities.

The design of the facilities must guarantee the security and privacy of records and ensure the confidentiality of sensitive information and conversations. Personnel must be able to secure their work.

CU must incorporate sustainable practices in use of facilities and purchase of equipment. Facilities and equipment must be evaluated on an established cycle and be in compliance with codes, laws, and accepted practices for access, health, safety, and security.

When acquiring capital equipment, CU must take into account expenses related to regular maintenance and life cycle costs.

Part 12. Assessment

College Unions (CU) must develop assessment plans and processes.

Assessment plans must articulate an ongoing cycle of assessment activities.

CU must
- specify programmatic goals and intended

outcomes
- identify student learning and development outcomes
- employ multiple measures and methods
- develop manageable processes for gathering, interpreting, and evaluating data
- document progress toward achievement of goals and outcomes
- interpret and use assessment results to demonstrate accountability
- report aggregated results to respondent groups and stakeholders
- use assessment results to inform planning and decision-making
- assess effectiveness of implemented changes
- provide evidence of improvement of programs and services

Evaluation should include goal-related progress on such considerations as student satisfaction, attendance at programs, cash flow, appearance of facilities, and vitality of volunteer groups such as programming and governing boards.

Results and summary data from assessment and evaluation should be broadly shared with all appropriate constituencies including students, faculty and staff members, cabinet members, and board members.

CU must employ ethical practices in the assessment process.

CU must have access to adequate fiscal, human, professional development, and technological resources to develop and implement assessment plans.

General Standards revised in 2014;
CU content developed/revised in 1986, 1997, 1998, & 2009

Commuter and Off-Campus Living Programs
CAS Contexual Statement

Commuter and off-campus students are defined as those who do not live in institutional-owned housing on campus (Jacoby, 2000). Commuter and off-campus students attend virtually every institution of higher education and comprise over 85 percent of college enrollment (Horn & Nevill, 2006). Their numbers include students who live at home with their parents, in rental housing, or with their own families. They may attend college full time, part time, or alternate between the two. They may live near the campus or far away; they may commute by car, public transportation, walking, or bicycle. The majority of commuter and off-campus students work, mostly off-campus, and some are employed the equivalent of full-time and/or at more than one job.

Many professionals treat commuter students as a homogenous group and largely ignore the diversity within the group (Jacoby & Garland, 2004). Regardless of differences in backgrounds, living arrangements, and educational goals, commuter and off-campus students face common needs and concerns, such as finding safe and reliable transportation, managing multiple life roles, integrating their off-campus support systems into their higher education experience, and developing a sense of belonging in their campus community. Whether they attend a predominantly residential or commuter institution, the fact that they reside off-campus profoundly affects the nature of their educational experience.

Commuter and off-campus students are a rapidly growing segment of the postsecondary population. The long-standing residential tradition of American higher education has often impeded effective, comprehensive institutional responses to their wide range of lifestyles. Historically, the relationship of commuter and off-campus students to the institution has been neither well understood nor incorporated into the design of policies, programs, and practices. The CAS Standards and Guidelines take the approach that all students must have equitable access to institutional services, engagement opportunities, and the total educational process regardless of place of residence.

Institutions must critically and comprehensively examine their practices from the point of view of all types of commuter and off-campus students to correct any existing inequities. Because the population is so diverse and each institution's population is unique, it is important that each college and university regularly collect data about its commuter and off-campus students and the nature of their college experiences. These standards and guidelines provide a basis for institutional self-assessment and program development.

References, Readings, and Resources

American College Personnel Association, Commission for Commuter Students and Adult Learners: http://www.acpa.nche.edu

Chickering, A. W. (1974). *Commuting versus resident students*. San Francisco, CA: Jossey-Bass.

Donaldson, J. F., & Townsend, B. K. (2007). Higher education journals' discourse about adult undergraduate students. *The Journal of Higher Education, 78*(1), 27-50.

Horn, L., and Nevill, S. (2006). *Profile of Undergraduates in U.S. Postsecondary Education Institutions: 2003–04: With a Special Analysis of Community College Students* (NCES 2006-184). U.S. Department of Education. Washington, DC: National Center for Education Statistics.

Jacoby, B. (Ed.). (2000). Involving commuter students in learning. *New Directions for Higher Education, 109*. San Francisco, CA: Jossey-Bass.

Jacoby, B. (2004). Engaging first-year commuter students in learning. *Metropolitan Universities, 15*(2).

Jacoby, B. & Garland, J. (2004). Strategies for enhancing commuter student success. *Journal of College Student Retention, 6*(1).

Jacoby, B. (1989). The *student as commuter: Developing a comprehensive institutional response*. ASHE-ERIC Higher Education Report No. 7. Washington, DC: School of Education and Human Development, The George Washington University.

Jacoby, B., & Girrell, K. (1981). A model for improving service and programs for commuter students (The SPAR Model). *NASPA Journal, 18*(3).

Kodama, C. M. (2002). Marginality of transfer commuter students. *NASPA Journal, 39*(3), 233-250.

Mahan, M. (2010). NCCP has a new home. *Commuter Perspectives, 31*(3).

Mahan, M. (2011). *Learning about commuter students: Resources within reach* (10th ed). National Clearinghouse for Commuter Programs. Retrieved from http://nccp.nsuok.edu

National Clearinghouse for Commuter Programs, Northeastern State University, Broken Arrow, OK 74014. (918)449-6200. http://nccp.nsuok.edu

Schlossberg, N. K. Lynch, A. Q., & Chickering, A. W. (1989). *Improving higher education environments for adults*. San Francisco, CA: Jossey-Bass.

Stewart, S. S. (Ed.). (1983). Commuter students: Enhancing their educational experience. *New directions for Student Services, 24*. San Francisco, CA: Jossey-Bass.

Contextual Statement Contributors
Current Edition:
Melissa Mahan, Texas A&M University-San Antonio, NCCP
Kristi Mindrup, Western Illinois University-Quad Cities, NCCP

Previous Editions:
Barbara Jacoby, University of Maryland
Melissa Mahan, Texas A&M University-San Antonio, NCCP

Commuter and Off-Campus Living Programs
CAS Standards and Guidelines

Part 1. Mission

The primary mission of Commuter and Off-Campus Living Programs (COCLP) is to ensure that all students have equitable access to programs, services, and engagement opportunities regardless of place of residence.

In addition, COCLP must
- provide services and facilities to meet the basic needs of commuter and off-campus students as determined by institutional assessment
- ensure that all students benefit equitably from the institution's educational programs
- provide engagement opportunities to assist commuter and off-campus students and promote learning and development
- support the institution's vision for the student learning experience

COCLP must develop, disseminate, implement, and regularly review their missions, which must be consistent with the mission of the institution and with applicable professional standards. The mission must be appropriate for the institution's students and other constituents. Mission statements must reference student learning and development.

The COCLP mission should address not only programs and services but also education and advocacy on behalf of commuter and off-campus students.

Commuter and off-campus students may be defined differently at individual institutions; however, this document focuses on the equitable access of all students to institutional resources.

The number of commuter and off-campus students may range from a small minority to the entire student population. The commuter and off-campus students in any higher educational institution should have equitable benefits of the curricular and co-curricular programs and services offered, regardless of full-time or part-time credit load, family status, age, proximity to campus, day or evening enrollment, or dependent versus independent living status.

Part 2. Program

Commuter and Off-Campus Living Programs (COCLP) must provide direct delivery of essential programs and services meeting a wide variety of needs and interests, whether organized as a single office or distributed throughout the institution. In either case, these services and programs must be evaluated to ensure that all students have equitable access to programs, services, and engagement opportunities regardless of place of residence.

To achieve their mission, COCLP must contribute to

- students' formal education, which includes both the curriculum and the co-curriculum
- student progression and timely completion of educational goals
- preparation of students for their careers, citizenship, and lives
- student learning and development

To contribute to student learning and development, COCLP must

- identify relevant and desirable student learning and development outcomes
- articulate how the student learning and development outcomes align with the six CAS student learning and development domains and related dimensions
- assess relevant and desirable student learning and development
- provide evidence of impact on outcomes
- articulate contributions to or support of student learning and development in the domains not specifically assessed
- use evidence gathered to create strategies for improvement of programs and services

STUDENT LEARNING AND DEVELOPMENT DOMAINS AND DIMENSIONS

Domain: knowledge acquisition, integration, construction, and application
- Dimensions: understanding knowledge from a range of disciplines; connecting knowledge to other knowledge, ideas, and experiences; constructing knowledge; and relating knowledge to daily life

Domain: cognitive complexity
- Dimensions: critical thinking, reflective thinking, effective reasoning, and creativity

Domain: intrapersonal development
- Dimensions: realistic self-appraisal, self-understanding, and self-respect; identity development; commitment to ethics and integrity; and spiritual awareness

Domain: interpersonal competence
- Dimensions: meaningful relationships, interdependence, collaboration, and effective leadership

Domain: humanitarianism and civic engagement
- Dimensions: understanding and appreciation of cultural and human differences, social responsibility, global perspective, and sense of civic responsibility

Domain: practical competence

- **Dimensions: pursuing goals, communicating effectively, technical competence, managing personal affairs, managing career development, demonstrating professionalism, maintaining health and wellness, and living a purposeful and satisfying life**

[LD Outcomes: See *The Council for the Advancement of Standards Learning and Development Outcomes* statement for examples of outcomes related to these domains and dimensions.]

COCLP must be
- **intentionally designed**
- **guided by theories and knowledge of learning and development**
- **integrated into the life of the institution**
- **reflective of developmental and demographic profiles of the student population**
- **responsive to needs of individuals, populations with distinct needs, and relevant constituencies**
- **delivered using multiple formats, strategies, and contexts**
- **designed to provide universal access**

COCLP must collaborate with colleagues and departments across the institution to promote student learning and development, persistence, and success.

COCLP must assist students with access to institutional resources and in meeting basic needs such as housing, transportation, parking, security, information and referral, facilities, food, computer and internet access, and childcare.

COCLP should assist students in making informed choices about housing and should provide information about available housing, tenants' rights and responsibilities, utilities, and legal advice and assistance.

Provisions should be made for parking; carpools; emergency vehicle assistance; and walkway, bike path, and parking lot security. Information about transportation alternatives to campus should be provided.

Information about campus services, programs, and current events should be disseminated in a variety of media and formats. Access to services such as course registration should be available via the internet and telephone as well as in traditional modes.

Students should have adequate study and lounge spaces in convenient locations around the campus. These should include access to computers, printers, copiers, and lockers.

Food service should be available in convenient locations at hours when students are on campus, including evenings and weekends.

Institutions should address commuter and off-campus students' need for high-speed internet access for accomplishing course work, and should ensure equitable access to informational resources.

Institutions should provide adequate childcare services, either through the institution or through referrals to community childcare providers. On-campus facilities for infant feeding and changing should be available.

COCLP should work to ensure that all institutional services are available equitably to commuter and off-campus students, including scheduling of classes, events, campus employment, and office hours to accommodate students' varied schedules.

COCLP must provide programs that meet the specific needs of commuter and off-campus students and ensure that all students have equitable access to all educational, recreational, and social programming.

COCLP should provide educational programs that inform students of tenancy ordinances, tenants and landlord rights and responsibilities, legal advice and assistance, personal financial management, roommate and neighbor relations, and conflict-resolution skills. Additional educational programs can include defensive driving, personal security, proper nutrition, and time management.

COCLP should offer programs, or encourage the institution to offer programs, that enable commuter and off-campus students to achieve learning and development outcomes. These include opportunities for interaction with faculty members and peers, activities scheduled at times convenient for commuter and off-campus students, peer mentoring, learning communities that do not require on-campus residence, experiential education, family-oriented activities, programs offered in off-campus locations with dense student populations, and programming using technology (e.g., virtual communities).

Institutions must include the commuter and off-campus student perspective at all appropriate levels of campus planning, policy making, budgeting, program delivery, and governance.

Commuter and off-campus student advocacy should focus on
- access to comprehensive academic advising, student support services, and information
- recognition of the diverse subgroups of the commuter and off-campus student population, including students who are older, married, fully employed, part-time, evening, veterans, or who live at home with parents or guardian.
- equitable fee structure for campus services
- fair representation of all types of commuter and off-campus students in areas of campus employment, internships, and financial aid awards
- faculty and institutional research programs that enhance understanding of the demographic characteristics and unique needs of commuter and off-campus students
- inclusion of the commuter and off-campus student perspective in community decision-making (e.g., transportation route planning, police coverage, and local ordinances)
- minimum standards for use as criteria for listing off-campus housing options

COCLP must collect data and encourage institutional research to understand the characteristics, needs, and experiences of commuter and off-campus students.

Research efforts may include demographic studies, needs assessments, retention studies, environmental assessments, involvement and satisfaction measures, longitudinal studies, and commuter-resident comparisons.

Part 3. Organization and Leadership

To achieve program and student learning and development outcomes, Commuter and Off-Campus Living Programs (COCLP) must be purposefully structured for effectiveness. COCLP must have clearly stated and current
- goals and outcomes
- policies and procedures
- responsibilities and performance expectations for personnel
- organizational charts demonstrating clear channels of authority

Leaders must model ethical behavior and institutional citizenship.

Leaders with organizational authority for COCLP must provide strategic planning, management and supervision, and program advancement.

Strategic Planning
- articulate a vision and mission that drive short- and long-term planning
- set goals and objectives based on the needs of the populations served, intended student learning and development outcomes, and program outcomes
- facilitate continuous development, implementation, and assessment of program effectiveness and goal attainment congruent with institutional mission and strategic plans
- promote environments that provide opportunities for student learning, development, and engagement
- develop, adapt, and improve programs and services in response to the changing needs of populations served and evolving institutional priorities
- include diverse perspectives to inform decision making

Management and Supervision
- plan, allocate, and monitor the use of fiscal, physical, human, intellectual, and technological resources
- manage human resource processes including recruitment, selection, professional development, supervision, performance planning, succession planning, evaluation, recognition, and reward
- influence others to contribute to the effectiveness and success of the unit
- empower professional, support, and student personnel to become effective leaders
- encourage and support collaboration with colleagues and departments across the institution

- encourage and support scholarly contributions to the profession
- identify and address individual, organizational, and environmental conditions that foster or inhibit mission achievement
- use current and valid evidence to inform decisions
- incorporate sustainability practices in the management and design of programs, services, and facilities
- understand appropriate technologies and integrate them into programs and services
- be knowledgeable about codes and laws relevant to programs and services and ensure that programs and services meet those requirements
- assess and take action to mitigate potential risks

Program Advancement
- advocate for and actively promote the mission and goals of the programs and services
- inform stakeholders about issues affecting practice
- facilitate processes to reach consensus where wide support is needed
- advocate for representation in strategic planning initiatives at divisional and institutional levels

Part 4. Human Resources

Commuter and Off-Campus Living Programs (COCLP) must be staffed adequately by individuals qualified to accomplish mission and goals.

COCLP must have access to technical and support personnel adequate to accomplish their mission.

Within institutional guidelines, COCLP must
- establish procedures for personnel recruitment and selection, training, performance planning, and evaluation
- set expectations for supervision and performance
- provide personnel access to continuing and advanced education and appropriate professional development opportunities to improve their competence, skills, and leadership capacity
- consider work/life options available to personnel (e.g., compressed work schedules, flextime, job sharing, remote work, or telework) to promote recruitment and retention of personnel

Administrators of COCLP must
- ensure that all personnel have updated position descriptions
- implement recruitment and selection/hiring strategies that produce a workforce inclusive of under-represented populations
- develop promotion practices that are fair, inclusive, proactive, and non-discriminatory

Personnel responsible for delivery of COCLP must have written performance goals, objectives, and outcomes for each year's performance cycle to be used to plan, review, and evaluate work and performance. The performance plan must be updated regularly to reflect changes during the performance cycle.

Results of individual personnel evaluations must be used to recognize personnel performance, address performance issues, implement individual and/or collective personnel development and training programs, and inform the assessment of programs and services.

COCLP personnel, when hired and throughout their employment, must receive appropriate and thorough training.

COCLP personnel, including student employees and volunteers, must have access to resources or receive specific training on
- institutional policies pertaining to functions or activities they support
- privacy and confidentiality policies
- laws regarding access to student records
- policies and procedures for dealing with sensitive institutional information
- policies and procedures related to technology used to store or access student records and institutional data
- how and when to refer those in need of additional assistance to qualified personnel and have access to a supervisor for assistance in making these judgments
- systems and technologies necessary to perform their assigned responsibilities
- ethical and legal uses of technology

COCLP personnel must engage in continuing professional development activities to keep abreast of the research, theories, legislation, policies, and developments that affect their programs and services.

Administrators of COCLP must ensure that personnel are knowledgeable about and trained in safety, emergency procedures, and crisis prevention and response. Risk management efforts must address identification of threatening conduct or behavior and must incorporate a system for responding to and reporting such behaviors.

COCLP personnel must be knowledgeable of and trained in safety and emergency procedures for securing and vacating facilities.

PROFESSIONAL PERSONNEL

COCLP professional personnel either must hold an earned graduate or professional degree in a field relevant to their position or must possess an appropriate combination of educational credentials and related work experience.

COCLP professional staff should possess the academic preparation, experience, abilities, professional interests, and competencies essential for the efficient operation of the office as charged, as well as the ability to identify and address needs of the commuter and off-campus student population. They should possess the following knowledge and skills:
- ability to work with diverse students
- knowledge of history and current trends in higher education
- knowledge of organizational development, group dynamics, strategies for changes and principles of community development
- ability to design and evaluate programs to meet desired outcomes
- effective written and oral communication skills
- knowledge of theories of college student learning and development
- knowledge of management and budgeting
- ability to work effectively with internal and external agencies
- ability to serve as an effective advocate

INTERNS OR GRADUATE ASSISTANTS

Degree- or credential-seeking interns or graduate assistants must be qualified by enrollment in an appropriate field of study and relevant experience. These students must be trained and supervised by professional personnel who possess applicable educational credentials and work experience and have supervisory experience. Supervisors must be cognizant of the dual roles interns and graduate assistants have as both student and employee.

Supervisors must
- adhere to parameters of students' job descriptions
- articulate intended learning outcomes in student job descriptions
- adhere to agreed-upon work hours and schedules
- offer flexible scheduling when circumstances necessitate

Supervisors and students must both agree to suitable compensation if circumstances necessitate additional hours.

STUDENT EMPLOYEES AND VOLUNTEERS

Student employees and volunteers must be carefully selected, trained, supervised, and evaluated. Students must have access to a supervisor. Student employees and volunteers must be provided clear job descriptions, pre-service training based on assessed needs, and continuing development.

Part 5. Ethics

Commuter and Off-Campus Living Programs (COCLP) must
- review applicable professional ethical standards and must adopt or develop and implement appropriate statements of ethical practice
- publish and adhere to statements of ethical practice and ensure their periodic review
- orient new personnel to relevant ethical standards and statements of ethical practice and related institutional policies

Statements of ethical standards must
- specify that COCLPpersonnel respect privacy and maintain confidentiality in communications and

records as delineated by privacy laws
- specify limits on disclosure of information contained in students' records as well as requirements to disclose to appropriate authorities
- address conflicts of interest, or appearance thereof, by personnel in the performance of their work
- reflect the responsibility of personnel to be fair, objective, and impartial in their interactions with others
- reference management of institutional funds
- reference appropriate behavior regarding research and assessment with human participants, confidentiality of research and assessment data, and students' rights and responsibilities
- include the expectation that personnel confront and hold accountable other personnel who exhibit unethical behavior
- address issues surrounding scholarly integrity

COCLP personnel must
- employ ethical decision making in the performance of their duties
- inform users of programs and services of ethical obligations and limitations emanating from codes and laws or from licensure requirements
- recognize and avoid conflicts of interest that could adversely influence their judgment or objectivity and, when unavoidable, recuse themselves from the situation
- perform their duties within the scope of their position, training, expertise, and competence
- make referrals when issues presented exceed the scope of the position

Part 6. Law, Policy, and Governance

Commuter and Off-Campus Living Programs (COCLP) must be in compliance with laws, regulations, and policies that relate to their respective responsibilities and that pose legal obligations, limitations, risks, and liabilities for the institution as a whole. Examples include constitutional, statutory, regulatory, and case law; relevant law and orders emanating from codes and laws; and the institution's policies.

COCLP must have access to legal advice needed for personnel to carry out their assigned responsibilities.

COCLP must inform personnel, appropriate officials, and users of programs and services about existing and changing legal obligations, risks and liabilities, and limitations.

COCLP must inform personnel about professional liability insurance options and refer them to external sources if the institution does not provide coverage.

COCLP must have written policies and procedures on operations, transactions, or tasks that have legal implications.

COCLP must regularly review policies. The revision and creation of policies must be informed by best practices, available evidence, and policy issues in higher education.

COCLP must have procedures and guidelines consistent with institutional policy for responding to threats, emergencies, and crisis situations. Systems and procedures must be in place to disseminate timely and accurate information to students, other members of the institutional community, and appropriate external organizations during emergency situations.

Personnel must neither participate in nor condone any form of harassment or activity that demeans persons or creates an intimidating, hostile, or offensive environment.

COCLP must purchase or obtain permission to use copyrighted materials and instruments. References to copyrighted materials and instruments must include appropriate citations.

COCLP must inform personnel about internal and external governance organizations that affect programs and services.

Part 7. Diversity, Equity, and Access

Within the context of each institution's mission and in accordance with institutional policies and applicable codes and laws, Commuter and Off-Campus Living Programs (COCLP) must create and maintain educational and work environments that are welcoming, accessible, inclusive, equitable, and free from harassment.

COCLP must not discriminate on the basis of disability; age; race; cultural identity; ethnicity; nationality; family educational history (e.g., first generation to attend college); political affiliation; religious affiliation; sex; sexual orientation; gender identity and expression; marital, social, economic, or veteran status; or any other basis included in institutional policies and codes and laws.

COCLP must
- advocate for sensitivity to multicultural and social justice concerns by the institution and its personnel
- ensure physical, program, and resource access for all constituents
- modify or remove policies, practices, systems, technologies, facilities, and structures that create barriers or produce inequities
- ensure that when facilities and structures cannot be modified, they do not impede access to programs, services, and resources
- establish goals for diversity, equity, and access
- foster communication and practices that enhance understanding of identity, culture, self-expression, and heritage
- promote respect for commonalities and differences among people within their historical and cultural contexts
- address the characteristics and needs of diverse constituents when establishing and implementing culturally relevant and inclusive programs, services, policies, procedures, and practices

- provide personnel with diversity, equity, and access training and hold personnel accountable for applying the training to their work
- respond to the needs of all constituents served when establishing hours of operation and developing methods of delivering programs, services, and resources
- recognize the needs of distance and online learning students by directly providing or assisting them to gain access to comparable services and resources

Part 8. Internal and External Relations

Commuter and Off-Campus Living Programs (COCLP) must reach out to individuals, groups, communities, and organizations internal and external to the institution to

- establish, maintain, and promote understanding and effective relations with those that have a significant interest in or potential effect on the students or other constituents served by the programs and services
- garner support and resources for programs and services as defined by the mission
- collaborate in offering or improving programs and services to meet the needs of students and other constituents and to achieve program and student outcomes
- engage diverse individuals, groups, communities, and organizations to enrich the educational environment and experiences of students and other constituents
- disseminate information about the programs and services

Promotional and descriptive information must be accurate and free of deception and misrepresentation.

COCLP must have procedures and guidelines consistent with institutional policy for

- communicating with the media
- distributing information through print, broadcast, and online sources
- contracting with external organizations for delivery of programs and services
- cultivating, soliciting, and managing gifts
- applying to and managing funds from grants

COCLP must maintain a high degree of visibility within the campus community through direct promotion and delivery of services, involvement with campus programs, and educational efforts to increase all campus community members' understanding of the needs of commuter and off-campus students.

COCLP should coordinate their activities with all offices and agencies whose efforts directly affect commuter and off-campus students. These include such areas as campus safety and security, transportation and parking, campus information and referral services, and other relevant offices and campus committees.

COCLP should maintain active relationship with various community agencies to ensure the inclusion of the commuter and off-campus student perspective in community decision-making.

Part 9. Financial Resources

Commuter and Off-Campus Living Programs (COCLP) must have funding to accomplish the mission and goals.

In establishing and prioritizing funding resources, COCLP must conduct comprehensive analyses to determine

- unmet needs of the unit
- relevant expenditures
- external and internal resources
- impact on students and the institution

COCLP must use the budget as a planning tool to reflect commitment to the mission and goals of the programs and services and of the institution.

COCLP must administer funds in accordance with established institutional accounting procedures.

COCLP must demonstrate efficient and effective use and responsible stewardship of fiscal resources consistent with institutional protocols.

Financial reports must provide an accurate financial overview of the organization and provide clear, understandable, and timely data upon which personnel can plan and make informed decisions.

Procurement procedures must

- be consistent with institutional policies
- ensure that purchases comply with laws and codes for usability and access
- ensure that the institution receives value for the funds spent
- consider information available for comparing the ethical and environmental impact of products and services purchased

Fee-paying students should benefit equitably from fee-supported services. This is especially important regarding access to electronic services such as computer/internet and campus cable television systems.

Part 10. Technology

Commuter and Off-Campus Living Programs (COCLP) must have technology to support the achievement of their mission and goals. The technology and its use must comply with institutional policies and procedures and with relevant codes and laws.

COCLP must use technologies to

- provide updated information regarding mission, location, staffing, programs, services, and official contacts to students and other constituents in accessible formats
- provide an avenue for students and other constituents to communicate sensitive information

in a secure format
- enhance the delivery of programs and services for all students

COCLP must
- back up data on a regular basis
- adhere to institutional policies regarding ethical and legal use of technology
- articulate policies and procedures for protecting the confidentiality and security of information
- implement a replacement plan and cycle for all technology with attention to sustainability
- incorporate accessibility features into technology-based programs and services

When providing student access to technology, COCLP must
- have policies on the use of technology that are clear, easy to understand, and available to all students
- provide information or referral to support services for those needing assistance in accessing or using technology
- provide instruction or training on how to use the technology
- inform students of implications of misuse of technologies

Institutions that provide high speed internet access or campus based cable television programming to residential students should also consider options to increase accessibility to such services to commuter and off-campus students.

Part 11. Facilities and Equipment

Commuter and Off-Campus Living Programs' (COCLP) facilities must be intentionally designed and located in suitable, accessible, and safe spaces that demonstrate universal design and support the program's mission and goals.

Facilities must be designed to engage various constituents and promote learning.

The campus must provide adequate facilities for the use of commuter and off-campus students, including recreational, study, and lounge space; computer and internet access; and dining facilities.

Because commuter and off-campus students do not have a residence on campus in which to spend time before, between, and after classes, a variety of comfortable spaces should be provided for their use. These spaces should be in classroom buildings, as well as in college union and student center buildings, and should include individual lockers, computer and copier access, food preparation facilities, and family support services (e.g., infant feeding and changing areas).

Personnel must have workspaces that are suitably located and accessible, well equipped, adequate in size, and designed to support their work and responsibilities.

The design of the facilities must guarantee the security and privacy of records and ensure the confidentiality of sensitive information and conversations. Personnel must be able to secure their work.

COCLP must incorporate sustainable practices in use of facilities and purchase of equipment. Facilities and equipment must be evaluated on an established cycle and be in compliance with codes, laws, and accepted practices for access, health, safety, and security.

When acquiring capital equipment, COCLP must take into account expenses related to regular maintenance and life cycle costs.

Part 12. Assessment

Commuter and Off-Campus Living Programs (COCLP) must develop assessment plans and processes.

Assessment plans must articulate an ongoing cycle of assessment activities.

COCLP must
- specify programmatic goals and intended outcomes
- identify student learning and development outcomes
- employ multiple measures and methods
- develop manageable processes for gathering, interpreting, and evaluating data
- document progress toward achievement of goals and outcomes
- interpret and use assessment results to demonstrate accountability
- report aggregated results to respondent groups and stakeholders
- use assessment results to inform planning and decision-making
- assess effectiveness of implemented changes
- provide evidence of improvement of programs and services

COCLP must employ ethical practices in the assessment process.

COCLP must have access to adequate fiscal, human, professional development, and technological resources to develop and implement assessment plans.

General Standards revised 2014;
COCLP (formerly Commuter Student Programs) content developed/revised 1986, 1997, & 2005

Conference and Event Programs
CAS Contextual Statement

A higher education campus is a community where people gather to learn, share, and discuss issues of interest in an open, non-threatening, and enlightened atmosphere. It is a place where topics important to society are addressed freely in a number of formats and settings. Campuses are centers for symposia, lectures, public events, demonstrations, conferences, and other teaching and learning programs attended by people from all walks of life, generations, occupations, and educational levels. These events help to identify the campus as a place where scholarly, cultural, social, artistic, athletic, and other activities can freely occur. As institutions become less constrained by physical borders, they have also become the source and home of conferences and events. A department responsible for developing, coordinating, and promoting on- and off-campus conferences and events is typically found at the core of this important educational responsibility.

Conference and event programs address a broad range of organizing, hosting, and logistical service needs. Services provided to a variety of constituents include program planning; managing conference centers; developing conferences in conjunction with faculty and staff members; providing services and support for summer youth camps; coordinating guest services and special celebrations; scheduling facilities; and organizing donor events, inaugurations, groundbreakings, commencements, homecomings, parents weekends, and other traditional gatherings.

Although the portfolios of program responsibilities will vary from campus to campus, one common element is that of helping institutions expand their activities, presence, and influence beyond the traditional roles of faculty, students, and staff. Conference and events programs make the campus a more effective and user-friendly place for all types of learners. They enhance diverse campus cultures, and conference subject matter adds depth and variety to campus dialogue. Conferences and events programs support institutional efforts to function as a center for celebrations and non-traditional educational activities. They provide a forum for free speech, venues for cultural events, opportunities for students and scholars to be exposed to research findings, and a chance for more people to observe what higher education is all about.

Conference and event programs provide activities during periods when fewer students are present to optimize efficient use of campus resources. They provide institutions with additional sources of revenue and contribute to the availability and continuity of employment for faculty and staff. Many of the support and coordination roles typically associated with student affairs are now tailored to these events through a single conference and event programs office.

The Association of Collegiate Conference and Event Directors–International (ACCED-I) estimates that more than 1,500 U.S. institutions of higher learning have offices providing conference and event planning. Their operations may include overseeing the summer operation of residence halls and classrooms; year-round management of full-service conference centers; coordination of large public events held in campus arenas and stadiums; and procurement of services and facilities at off-campus locations. Today, conference and event staff members provide everything from multi-department coordination of services to year-round academic support services and professional event planning consultation.

Several associations for campus conference and event professionals have come into being and flourished. As these associations matured, the need for professional standards became abundantly clear in dialogue among members. In the mid-1990s, a study of service practices by the Canadian University and College Conference Officers Association (CUCCOA) culminated in a summary report that called for establishing international standards for practitioners. In 1997 ACCED-I, CUCCOA, the Association of College and University Housing Officers-International (ACUHO-I), and the British Universities Accommodation Consortium (BUAC), later merged into VENUEMASTERS, collectively agreed on the need for developing professional standards in collaboration with the CAS standards development initiative. The CAS standards and guidelines that follow provide a professional context for the campus conference and event industry and will serve as a useful tool for all who wish to provide conference and event programs in higher education settings.

References, Readings, and Resources

Association of College and University Housing Officers-International (ACUHO-I): http://www.acuho-i.org
Association of Collegiate Conference and Event Directors–International (ACCED-I): http://www.acced-i.org/
Canadian University and College Conference Officers Association (CUCCOA): http://www.cuccoa.org/
United Kingdom: VENUEMASTERS http://www.venuemasters.co.uk/

Contextual Statement Contributors:
Current Edition:
Thomas Flynn, University of Maryland, ACCED-I
Patrick Perfetto, University of Maryland, ACCED-I

Previous Editions:
Thomas Flynn, University of Maryland ACCED-I
Patrick Perfetto, University of Maryland, ACCED-I

Conference and Event Programs
CAS Standards and Guidelines

The primary mission of Conference and Event Programs (CEP) is to manage institutional resources for educational conferences, workshops, events, and activities that are relevant and complementary to the mission of the institution.

CEP must develop, disseminate, implement, and regularly review their missions, which must be consistent with the mission of the institution and with applicable professional standards. The mission must be appropriate for the institution's students and other constituents. Mission statements must reference student learning and development.

The program mission must recognize and accommodate the needs and relevant goals, of users of conference and event services as well as institutional agencies that are integral providers of service.

Conference and Event Programs (CEP) must provide leadership within and for the institution relative to conference and event planning and management.

CEP must communicate effectively among campus agencies concerning activities that may influence or conflict with planned or potential conferences and events and other campus activities.

CEP must provide clear and timely descriptions of conference and event activities on campus events calendars and related information sources.

CEP must be knowledgeable about institutional resources, including facilities, safety, and visitor services.

CEP should
- collaborate with clients and service providers to assure that programs have a positive and compatible presence in the campus community
- exercise state-of-the-art meeting and event planning concepts and procedures
- encourage understanding and appreciation of the values and mission of the institution

In addition, CEP may
- create opportunities for departments to fulfill their programmatic goals
- create opportunities for departments to extend employment for employees and interns beyond the regular academic calendar
- provide additional revenue derived from income-producing facilities and services
- provide employment and experiential opportunities for students and staff members

- enable educational opportunities for the community that would not otherwise exist

To achieve their mission, CEP must contribute to
- students' formal education, which includes both the curriculum and the co-curriculum
- student progression and timely completion of educational goals
- preparation of students for their careers, citizenship, and lives
- student learning and development

To contribute to student learning and development, CEP must
- identify relevant and desirable student learning and development outcomes
- articulate how the student learning and development outcomes align with the six CAS student learning and development domains and related dimensions
- assess relevant and desirable student learning and development
- provide evidence of impact on outcomes
- articulate contributions to or support of student learning and development in the domains not specifically assessed
- use evidence gathered to create strategies for improvement of programs and services

STUDENT LEARNING AND DEVELOPMENT DOMAINS AND DIMENSIONS

Domain: knowledge acquisition, integration, construction, and application
- Dimensions: understanding knowledge from a range of disciplines; connecting knowledge to other knowledge, ideas, and experiences; constructing knowledge; and relating knowledge to daily life

Domain: cognitive complexity
- Dimensions: critical thinking, reflective thinking, effective reasoning, and creativity

Domain: intrapersonal development
- Dimensions: realistic self-appraisal, self-understanding, and self-respect; identity development; commitment to ethics and integrity; and spiritual awareness

Domain: interpersonal competence
- Dimensions: meaningful relationships, interdependence, collaboration, and effective leadership

Domain: humanitarianism and civic engagement
- Dimensions: understanding and appreciation of cultural and human differences, social

responsibility, global perspective, and sense of civic responsibility

Domain: practical competence
- Dimensions: pursuing goals, communicating effectively, technical competence, managing personal affairs, managing career development, demonstrating professionalism, maintaining health and wellness, and living a purposeful and satisfying life

[LD Outcomes: See *The Council for the Advancement of Standards Learning and Development Outcomes* statement for examples of outcomes related to these domains and dimensions.]

Avenues for learning and development may include
- students engaged in the development and implementation of the program
- program participants learning about the institution
- students benefitting from the program brought to the institution

CEP must be
- intentionally designed
- guided by theories and knowledge of learning and development
- integrated into the life of the institution
- reflective of developmental and demographic profiles of the student population
- responsive to needs of individuals, populations with distinct needs, and relevant constituencies
- delivered using multiple formats, strategies, and contexts
- designed to provide universal access

CEP must collaborate with colleagues and departments across the institution to promote student learning and development, persistence, and success.

Part 3. Organization and Leadership

To achieve program and student learning and development outcomes, Conference and Event Programs (CEP) must be purposefully structured for effectiveness. CEP must have clearly stated and current
- goals and outcomes
- policies and procedures
- responsibilities and performance expectations for personnel
- organizational charts demonstrating clear channels of authority

Leaders must model ethical behavior and institutional citizenship.

Leaders with organizational authority for CEP must provide strategic planning, management and supervision, and program advancement.

Strategic Planning
- articulate a vision and mission that drive short- and long-term planning
- set goals and objectives based on the needs of the

populations served, intended student learning and development outcomes, and program outcomes
- facilitate continuous development, implementation, and assessment of program effectiveness and goal attainment congruent with institutional mission and strategic plans
- promote environments that provide opportunities for student learning, development, and engagement
- develop, adapt, and improve programs and services in response to the changing needs of populations served and evolving institutional priorities
- include diverse perspectives to inform decision making

Management and Supervision
- plan, allocate, and monitor the use of fiscal, physical, human, intellectual, and technological resources
- manage human resource processes including recruitment, selection, professional development, supervision, performance planning, succession planning, evaluation, recognition, and reward
- influence others to contribute to the effectiveness and success of the unit
- empower professional, support, and student personnel to become effective leaders
- encourage and support collaboration with colleagues and departments across the institution
- encourage and support scholarly contributions to the profession
- identify and address individual, organizational, and environmental conditions that foster or inhibit mission achievement
- use current and valid evidence to inform decisions
- incorporate sustainability practices in the management and design of programs, services, and facilities
- understand appropriate technologies and integrate them into programs and services
- be knowledgeable about codes and laws relevant to programs and services and ensure that programs and services meet those requirements
- assess and take action to mitigate potential risks

Program Advancement
- advocate for and actively promote the mission and goals of the programs and services
- inform stakeholders about issues affecting practice
- facilitate processes to reach consensus where wide support is needed
- advocate for representation in strategic planning initiatives at divisional and institutional levels

Because of the likely involvement of multiple campus units in the delivery of conference and event services, CEP leaders may need special authorization to manage resources.

CEP leaders should
- ensure that programs are compatible with the

mission and values of the institution
- be aware of the changing needs of clients to assure expectations are congruent with the capabilities of service providers
- encourage the highest possible service provider capabilities to meet changing client expectations
- ensure that effective and appropriate strategies exist for communicating with prospective and current program participants
- consider student as well as staff and faculty member needs, issues, and perspectives
- cultivate relationships with leaders of academic and administrative departments
- work cooperatively with campus organizations and units in developing effective programs
- ensure efficient and appropriate use of institutional resources
- promote equal access for program participants

CEP should be organized to reflect institutional characteristics, priorities, and organizational structures so that the needs of the intended primary customer may be effectively met. Accordingly, not all functions may exist within the same administrative unit. In such cases, coordination among the units is essential to ensure a cohesive system of services for program and event planners.

The institution may centralize most CEP functions in one administrative unit in order to provide one-stop access to, and coordination of, services to planners of conferences, events, and similar gatherings. To accomplish this, the CEP office should
- serve as a central point of contact for multiple campus services, particularly in a decentralized environment
- have reasonable access to campus resources and facilities
- provide effective coordination of multiple services
- exercise appropriate authority with regard to campus resources necessary to support conferences and events in collaboration with campus service providers, through, for example, service agreements and memoranda of understanding.

Before every conference and event, CEP must clearly communicate with clients and service providers about how the program is going to be managed and onsite issues resolved.

Other areas for consideration in determining structure and management of CEP may include
- availability and characteristics of facilities
- size, nature, and mission of the institution
- scope of related academic services
- philosophy and delivery system for services
- variety of delivery methods being employed or available to the institution
- degree of integration with other institutional units
- unique access or service needs of the relevant community

Conference and Event Programs (CEP) must be staffed adequately by individuals qualified to accomplish mission and goals.

CEP must have access to technical and support personnel adequate to accomplish their mission.

Within institutional guidelines, CEP must
- **establish procedures for personnel recruitment and selection, training, performance planning, and evaluation**
- **set expectations for supervision and performance**
- **provide personnel access to continuing and advanced education and appropriate professional development opportunities to improve their competence, skills, and leadership capacity**
- **consider work/life options available to personnel (e.g., compressed work schedules, flextime, job sharing, remote work, or telework) to promote recruitment and retention of personnel**

Administrators of CEP must
- **ensure that all personnel have updated position descriptions**
- **implement recruitment and selection/hiring strategies that produce a workforce inclusive of under-represented populations**
- **develop promotion practices that are fair, inclusive, proactive, and non-discriminatory**

Personnel responsible for delivery of CEP must have written performance goals, objectives, and outcomes for each year's performance cycle to be used to plan, review, and evaluate work and performance. The performance plan must be updated regularly to reflect changes during the performance cycle.

Results of individual personnel evaluations must be used to recognize personnel performance, address performance issues, implement individual and/or collective personnel development and training programs, and inform the assessment of programs and services.

CEP personnel, when hired and throughout their employment, must receive appropriate and thorough training.

CEP personnel, including student employees and volunteers, must have access to resources or receive specific training on
- **institutional policies pertaining to functions or activities they support**
- **privacy and confidentiality policies**
- **laws regarding access to student records**
- **policies and procedures for dealing with sensitive institutional information**
- **policies and procedures related to technology used to store or access student records and institutional data**
- **how and when to refer those in need of additional**

assistance to qualified personnel and have access to a supervisor for assistance in making these judgments
- systems and technologies necessary to perform their assigned responsibilities
- ethical and legal uses of technology

CEP personnel must engage in continuing professional development activities to keep abreast of the research, theories, legislation, policies, and developments that affect their programs and services.

Administrators of CEP must ensure that personnel are knowledgeable about and trained in safety, emergency procedures, and crisis prevention and response. Risk management efforts must address identification of threatening conduct or behavior and must incorporate a system for responding to and reporting such behaviors.

CEP personnel must be knowledgeable of and trained in safety and emergency procedures for securing and vacating facilities.

PROFESSIONAL PERSONNEL

CEP professional personnel either must hold an earned graduate or professional degree in a field relevant to their position or must possess an appropriate combination of educational credentials and related work experience.

INTERNS OR GRADUATE ASSISTANTS

Degree- or credential-seeking interns or graduate assistants must be qualified by enrollment in an appropriate field of study and relevant experience. These students must be trained and supervised by professional personnel who possess applicable educational credentials and work experience and have supervisory experience. Supervisors must be cognizant of the dual roles interns and graduate assistants have as both student and employee.

Supervisors must
- adhere to parameters of students' job descriptions
- articulate intended learning outcomes in student job descriptions
- adhere to agreed-upon work hours and schedules
- offer flexible scheduling when circumstances necessitate

Supervisors and students must both agree to suitable compensation if circumstances necessitate additional hours.

STUDENT EMPLOYEES AND VOLUNTEERS

Student employees and volunteers must be carefully selected, trained, supervised, and evaluated. Students must have access to a supervisor. Student employees and volunteers must be provided clear job descriptions, pre-service training based on assessed needs, and continuing development.

CEP staff members must be proficient in customer service techniques.

CEP staff members must be knowledgeable about services of institutional agencies and facilities such as housing, dining, recreation, parking, and technology services.

CEP staff members may consider obtaining relevant certifications through meeting planning and higher education associations, such as the Certified Meeting Professional (CMP) or Collegiate Conference and Event Professional (CCEP) designations.

Part 5. Ethics

Conference and Event Programs (CEP) must
- review applicable professional ethical standards and must adopt or develop and implement appropriate statements of ethical practice
- publish and adhere to statements of ethical practice and ensure their periodic review
- orient new personnel to relevant ethical standards and statements of ethical practice and related institutional policies

Statements of ethical standards must
- specify that CEP personnel respect privacy and maintain confidentiality in communications and records as delineated by privacy laws
- specify limits on disclosure of information contained in students' records as well as requirements to disclose to appropriate authorities
- address conflicts of interest, or appearance thereof, by personnel in the performance of their work
- reflect the responsibility of personnel to be fair, objective, and impartial in their interactions with others
- reference management of institutional funds
- reference appropriate behavior regarding research and assessment with human participants, confidentiality of research and assessment data, and students' rights and responsibilities
- include the expectation that personnel confront and hold accountable other personnel who exhibit unethical behavior
- address issues surrounding scholarly integrity

CEP personnel must
- employ ethical decision making in the performance of their duties
- inform users of programs and services of ethical obligations and limitations emanating from codes and laws or from licensure requirements
- recognize and avoid conflicts of interest that could adversely influence their judgment or objectivity and, when unavoidable, recuse themselves from the situation
- perform their duties within the scope of their position, training, expertise, and competence
- make referrals when issues presented exceed the scope of the position

CEP must consider whether prospective clients, programs

or events present ethical conflict for the institution. When potential conflict arises, CEP must consult with appropriate institutional authorities.

Advice and information disclosed by clients, students, and faculty and staff members in the course of conducting business should be considered confidential unless otherwise required by law or institutional policy to be disclosed.

Part 6. Law, Policy, and Governance

Conference and Event Programs (CEP) must be in compliance with laws, regulations, and policies that relate to their respective responsibilities and that pose legal obligations, limitations, risks, and liabilities for the institution as a whole. Examples include constitutional, statutory, regulatory, and case law; relevant law and orders emanating from codes and laws; and the institution's policies.

CEP must ensure crisis management policies and procedures are adapted for periods of time when the institution may be closed or operating at reduced capacity (such as break periods or summer months) or for periods during which operational responsibilities are temporarily transferred (such as for residence halls).

CEP must have the authority to initiate and fulfill contracts and written obligations. Agreements must be in place to fairly protect the interests of both the institution and its clients.

CEP must have access to legal advice needed for personnel to carry out their assigned responsibilities.

CEP must inform personnel, appropriate officials, and users of programs and services about existing and changing legal obligations, risks and liabilities, and limitations.

Relevant institutional policies must be clearly evident in agreements with clients.

CEP should be aware of client activities on campus and ensure compliance with institutional policies.

CEP must inform personnel about professional liability insurance options and refer them to external sources if the institution does not provide coverage.

CEP must have written policies and procedures on operations, transactions, or tasks that have legal implications.

CEP must regularly review policies. The revision and creation of policies must be informed by best practices, available evidence, and policy issues in higher education.

CEP must have procedures and guidelines consistent with institutional policy for responding to threats, emergencies, and crisis situations. Systems and procedures must be in place to disseminate timely and accurate information to students, other members of the institutional community, and appropriate external organizations during emergency situations.

CEP staff members should be timely and forthright in informing conference and event staff, participants, and students of extraordinary or changing conditions.

Personnel must neither participate in nor condone any form of harassment or activity that demeans persons or creates an intimidating, hostile, or offensive environment.

CEP must purchase or obtain permission to use copyrighted materials and instruments. References to copyrighted materials and instruments must include appropriate citations.

CEP must inform personnel about internal and external governance organizations that affect programs and services.

Part 7. Diversity, Equity, and Access

Within the context of each institution's mission and in accordance with institutional policies and applicable codes and laws, Conference and Event Programs (CEP) must create and maintain educational and work environments that are welcoming, accessible, inclusive, equitable, and free from harassment.

CEP must not discriminate on the basis of disability; age; race; cultural identity; ethnicity; nationality; family educational history (e.g., first generation to attend college); political affiliation; religious affiliation; sex; sexual orientation; gender identity and expression; marital, social, economic, or veteran status; or any other basis included in institutional policies and codes and laws.

CEP should make reasonable efforts to inform and educate the community about conference and events that feature unique aspects of diversity.

CEP should provide access to services and information through a variety of formats.

Staff members should ensure that program services provided through non-institutional third parties are offered on a fair and equitable basis.

CEP must
- advocate for sensitivity to multicultural and social justice concerns by the institution and its personnel
- ensure physical, program, and resource access for all constituents
- modify or remove policies, practices, systems, technologies, facilities, and structures that create barriers or produce inequities
- ensure that when facilities and structures cannot be modified, they do not impede access to programs, services, and resources
- establish goals for diversity, equity, and access
- foster communication and practices that enhance understanding of identity, culture, self-expression, and heritage
- promote respect for commonalities and differences among people within their historical and cultural contexts

- address the characteristics and needs of diverse constituents when establishing and implementing culturally relevant and inclusive programs, services, policies, procedures, and practices
- provide personnel with diversity, equity, and access training and hold personnel accountable for applying the training to their work
- respond to the needs of all constituents served when establishing hours of operation and developing methods of delivering programs, services, and resources
- recognize the needs of distance and online learning students by directly providing or assisting them to gain access to comparable services and resources

Part 8. Internal and External Relations

Conference and Event Programs (CEP) must reach out to individuals, groups, communities, and organizations internal and external to the institution to

- establish, maintain, and promote understanding and effective relations with those that have a significant interest in or potential effect on the students or other constituents served by the programs and services
- garner support and resources for programs and services as defined by the mission
- collaborate in offering or improving programs and services to meet the needs of students and other constituents and to achieve program and student outcomes
- engage diverse individuals, groups, communities, and organizations to enrich the educational environment and experiences of students and other constituents
- disseminate information about the programs and services

Promotional and descriptive information must be accurate and free of deception and misrepresentation.

CEP must have procedures and guidelines consistent with institutional policy for

- communicating with the media
- distributing information through print, broadcast, and online sources
- contracting with external organizations for delivery of programs and services
- cultivating, soliciting, and managing gifts
- applying to and managing funds from grants

The program should ensure institutional support by

- establishing cooperative relationships with other offices (in addition to direct service providers) such as alumni, enrollment management, athletics, institutional advancement, communications, public relations, and campus information and visitor services
- sharing information, to stimulate program opportunities, and to enhance institutional visibility

- encouraging staff member participation in civic and community organizations (e.g., Convention and Visitors Bureau, Chamber of Commerce, service organizations) and active involvement in professional associations

CEP must adhere to institution-wide processes that systematically involve academic affairs, student affairs, and administrative units such as police and security, physical plant, and business offices.

CEP must collaborate and meet regularly with service providers to coordinate schedules and facility use and to review conferences and events under development.

CEP should serve as a resource to provide professional advice on conference and event-related issues and activities.

Part 9. Financial Resources

Conference and Event Programs (CEP) must have funding to accomplish the mission and goals.

In establishing and prioritizing funding resources, CEP must conduct comprehensive analyses to determine

- unmet needs of the unit
- relevant expenditures
- external and internal resources
- impact on students and the institution

CEP must use the budget as a planning tool to reflect commitment to the mission and goals of the programs and services and of the institution.

CEP must administer funds in accordance with established institutional accounting procedures.

CEP must demonstrate efficient and effective use and responsible stewardship of fiscal resources consistent with institutional protocols.

Financial reports must provide an accurate financial overview of the organization and provide clear, understandable, and timely data upon which personnel can plan and make informed decisions.

Procurement procedures must

- be consistent with institutional policies
- ensure that purchases comply with laws and codes for usability and access
- ensure that the institution receives value for the funds spent
- consider information available for comparing the ethical and environmental impact of products and services purchased

Funds to support the CEP, insofar as possible and desirable, should be self-generated from fees set at fair market rates.

Self-supported CEP should be authorized to establish reserve funds if higher-than-expected revenue results in a surplus, as a buffer against future shortfalls.

Part 10. Technology

Conference and Event Programs (CEP) must have technology to support the achievement of their mission and goals. The technology and its use must comply with institutional policies and procedures and with relevant codes and laws.

CEP must use technologies to
- provide updated information regarding mission, location, staffing, programs, services, and official contacts to students and other constituents in accessible formats
- provide an avenue for students and other constituents to communicate sensitive information in a secure format
- enhance the delivery of programs and services for all students

CEP must
- back up data on a regular basis
- adhere to institutional policies regarding ethical and legal use of technology
- articulate policies and procedures for protecting the confidentiality and security of information
- implement a replacement plan and cycle for all technology with attention to sustainability
- incorporate accessibility features into technology-based programs and services

When providing student access to technology, CEP must
- have policies on the use of technology that are clear, easy to understand, and available to all students
- provide information or referral to support services for those needing assistance in accessing or using technology
- provide instruction or training on how to use the technology
- inform students of implications of misuse of technologies

When CEP offers external constituents access to institutional computing resources, procedures should be in place to support users who encounter technical difficulties, and CEP policies should protect the integrity of institutional data, technological resources, and student access.

Part 11. Facilities and Equipment

Conference and Event Programs' (CEP) facilities must be intentionally designed and located in suitable, accessible, and safe spaces that demonstrate universal design and support the program's mission and goals.

Facilities must be designed to engage various constituents and promote learning.

Personnel must have workspaces that are suitably located and accessible, well equipped, adequate in size, and designed to support their work and responsibilities.

The design of the facilities must guarantee the security and privacy of records and ensure the confidentiality of sensitive information and conversations. Personnel must be able to secure their work.

CEP must incorporate sustainable practices in use of facilities and purchase of equipment. Facilities and equipment must be evaluated on an established cycle and be in compliance with codes, laws, and accepted practices for access, health, safety, and security.

When acquiring capital equipment, CEP must take into account expenses related to regular maintenance and life cycle costs.

Agreements should exist with departments necessary to fulfill needs of the CEP.

Part 12. Assessment

Conference and Event Programs (CEP) must develop assessment plans and processes.

Assessment plans must articulate an ongoing cycle of assessment activities.

CEP must
- specify programmatic goals and intended outcomes
- identify student learning and development outcomes
- employ multiple measures and methods
- develop manageable processes for gathering, interpreting, and evaluating data
- document progress toward achievement of goals and outcomes
- interpret and use assessment results to demonstrate accountability
- report aggregated results to respondent groups and stakeholders
- use assessment results to inform planning and decision-making
- assess effectiveness of implemented changes
- provide evidence of improvement of programs and services

CEP should collaborate with institutional research units to generate data to project CEP contributions to the local economy, increase student enrollment, or stimulate additional research.

A representative cross-section from appropriate campus communities should be involved in reviewing the CEP program on a regular basis.

CEP should produce and disseminate an annual report identifying overall goals, activities and programs served, financial contributions, representative participate feedback, and opportunities that contribute to the overall visibility and promotion of the institution.

Evaluation of CEP may include goal-related progress on such considerations as stakeholder satisfaction, attendance, cash flow, financial health, and appearance of facilities.

Results and summary data from assessment and evaluation should be broadly shared with all appropriate constituencies including students, faculty and staff members, senior administrators, and clients.

CEP must assess and evaluate regularly its effectiveness in providing students with quality learning and development opportunities.

CEP must employ ethical practices in the assessment process.

CEP must have access to adequate fiscal, human, professional development, and technological resources to develop and implement assessment plans.

General Standards revised in 2014;
CEP content developed/revised in 2002 & 2012

Counseling Services
CAS Contextual Statement

The face of college counseling is changing to meet the needs of today's students. It continues to represent the integration of mental health services within the educational environment (Dean & Meadows, 1995). A diverse student body now includes students who are identified as traditional, high achieving and gifted, nontraditional, under-represented, veterans, online, international and first generation enhances the campus environment but also brings greater demand to existing counseling services on campus (Howard, Schiraldi, Pineda, & Campanella, 2006; Twenge, 2006).

The nature and type of the higher education environment and its effects on students are important tools for college counselors. Steenbarger (1990) noted that college counseling exemplifies the developmental framework that has produced a history of creative outreach and support work on campuses. Twenty-five years later programming efforts, although still part of the work of counseling services, are no longer the primary focus of CS staff efforts. The delivery of clinical services to students in higher education has been and is evolving to respond effectively to client needs in an ever-changing environment.

Historically, the role and function of college counseling has changed in response to both external and internal factors. Social needs, political environment, national economy, and changing demographics all exert shifting influences to which counseling services must respond. Change also occurs in response to internal factors unique to each campus environment (e.g., location of the counseling center on campus, , co-location with other offices on campus versus a standalone counseling center). As a result, the breadth and depth of counseling services reflect the intersection of these influences. Davis and Humphrey's (2000) comprehensive work provided a thorough review of the history of college counseling roles and service delivery models, the changing demographics of higher education, and implications for the future. College counselors have a responsibility to stay informed with a strong knowledge of current student needs (Upcraft, Gardner, & Barefoot, 2005).

The current challenges for college counseling are created by external forces including changing ethnic, racial, national, and experiential backgrounds of students; increasing psychological, health, safety, and financial needs of students; increasing competition for resources in higher education; increased emphasis on accountability; new and changing regulations regarding client privacy; and the implications of health and mental health care reform (American College Health Association, 2007; Gallagher, 2007; Kadison & DiGeronimo, 2004; Magoon, 2002). Moreover, the aftermath of tragedies on college campuses such as mass shootings, cluster suicides, and highly public sexual assault response issues along with other global traumatic events highlight the necessity for college counseling programs to be responsive to unanticipated factors. The level of severity of college

students' presenting concerns is also much greater than the traditional presenting problems of adjustment issues and individuation that were typically identified in counseling center research from the 1950s through the early 1980s (Pledge, et al., 1998). Recent research indicates that the rates of self-injury and serious suicidal ideation/gestures are increasing in students seeking help at counseling services (Locke & Shockey, 2014). The level of severity of presenting problems and the complexity of problems continue to increase (ACHA, 2007; Benton et al., 2003; Kadison, 2006). According to a survey of over 100,000 U.S. college students at 130 universities conducted by the Center for Collegiate Mental Health (CCMH), 1 in 5 students report having experienced sexual assault, 1 in 10 have attempted suicide, 1 in 3 take psychiatric medication, 1 in 4 have self-injured and 1 in 3 have experienced a traumatic event (CCMH, 2014). As the severity and complexity of clients' problems expand, it is increasingly important for college counseling professionals to be prepared to work with physicians, community mental health providers, other campus departments, and health care professionals to create an appropriate systemic response to student's needs. An increased focus on retention and outcomes assessment, generated in part by accreditation agencies, has challenged college counseling programs to be more intentional about demonstrating efficacy (Boyer, 2005; Dean & Meadows, 1995; Lifton, Seay, & Bushko, 2004; Tinto, 2006-07).

Recent challenges to state confidentiality laws have changed the expectations of disclosure of mental health information to offices and departments on and off campus. With increasing media scrutiny has come an increased understanding of the need for mental health services on campus. The APA reports that over $300,000 of funding specifically earmarked for clinical mental health services on campus have been secured through the efforts of the Center for Collegiate Mental Health (CCMH) data collection and media exposure of campus issues (CCMH, 2015).

The Americans with Disabilities Act Title II changes no longer allow a university or college to involuntarily remove a student from the institution for suicidal behavior. This behavior is seen as a symptom of a mental health issue that is protected by the ADA (U.S. Department of Justice, 1990). Title IX compliance and regulations have been strengthened and reinforced in response to sexual misconduct on campus (U.S. Department of Justice, 2000). Both of these legal changes directly affect how counseling services operates on campus and more specifically how providers collaborate with their student affairs colleagues.

Threat assessment expectations of counseling services on campus are part of a relatively new set of responsibility for most CS programs. Participating in behavioral intervention teams goes beyond clinical work and focuses our mental health expertise on the safety needs of the community. Over 92% of threat assessment teams on campus have counseling services staff as a standing committee member (Van Brunt et al., 2015).

With these challenges in mind, the earlier work of Stone and Archer (1990) is still very relevant. They stressed a need for counseling services to (a) clearly define boundaries on the types of problems and degree of severity of those clients for whom the counseling professionals will provide services and (b) develop and identify extensive referral and outreach services to effectively transition more severe clients to appropriate community resources. At the same time, college counselors strive to maintain the therapeutic, developmental, preventive, and consultative services that are integral to their work. As Stone and Archer (1990) noted, the concepts of working within limits and achieving balance between demands and resources are significant for college counseling services. Archer and Cooper (1998) further recognized the importance of demonstrating to institutions the positive outcomes of helping students maintain psychological health and develop personally in ways that support retention.

College counselors offer preventive, crisis, outreach, and consultative services, depending on the nature of the campus and students served. A strong commitment to professional development, whether through conducting research, providing training and supervision, maintaining professional credentials, upholding ethical standards of practice, or actively participating in professional organizations or other scholarly activities, is the catalyst for competent responses to the changing social issues and complex developmental, psychosocial, and mental health concerns of students (Boyd et al., 2003).

College attendance creates a unique set of circumstances and stresses that can stimulate significant student growth and development. As students experience change, they often need to address personal issues, work through challenges, and deal with the implications of growth and change. The rapid changes that characterize today's society, compounded by the impact of global crisis, and catastrophic natural events, can exacerbate students' personal and psychological problems (Davis & Humphrey, 2000; Kadison & DiGeronimo, 2004). However, students' access to and success in higher education are maximized as counseling services embrace and use scientific, technological, and psychological advances such as the use of interactional and Internet-based technologies for additional service-delivery options; this is particularly important as more students enroll through distance education options (Humphrey, Kitchens, and Patrick, 2000). Counseling services must offer assistance and resources to students through innovative means in order to serve the needs of all students.

The CAS Counseling Services Standards and Guidelines that follow provide college counselors with criteria to develop, enhance, evaluate, and judge the quality of campus counseling services.

References, Readings, and Resources

American College Counseling Association (ACCA): http://www.collegecounseling.org

American College Health Association (ACHA): http://www.acha.org

American College Health Association. (2007). *American College Health Association – National College Health Assessment: Reference Group Executive Summary*. Baltimore, MD: American College Health Association.

Archer, J., Jr., & Cooper, S. (1998). *Counseling and mental health services on campus: A handbook of contemporary practices and challenges*. San Francisco, CA: Jossey-Bass.

American College Personnel Association (ACPA): http://myacpa.org

American Counseling Association (ACA): http://www.counseling.org

Association for the Coordination of Counseling Center Clinical Services: http://accccs.appstate.edu/

Association of Counseling Center Training Agents (ACCTA): http://www.accta.net

Association of Counselor Education and Supervision (ACES): http://www.acesonline.net/

American Psychological Association (APA): http://www.apa.org/ and Division 17, Counseling Psychology http://www.apa.org/about/division/div17.html

Association of Psychology Postdoctoral and Internship Centers (APPIC): http://www.appic.org/index.html

Association for University and College Counseling Center Directors (AUCCCD): http://www.aucccd.org

Benton, S., Robertson, J., Tseng, W., Newton, F., & Benton, S. (2003). Changes in counseling center client problems across 13 years. *Professional Psychology: Research and Practice, 34*, 66-72.

Boyd, V., Hattauer, E., Brandel, I. W., Buckles, N., Davidshofer, C., Deakin, S. et al. (2003). Accreditation standards for university and college counseling centers. *Journal of Counseling and Development, 81*, 168-177.

Boyer, P. G. (2005). College student persistence of first-time freshmen at a Midwest university: A longitudinal study. *Research for Educational Reform, 10(1),* 16-27.

Center for Collegiate Mental Health (2015). Annual report offers snapshot of U.S. college students' mental health, need. *PennState News*. Retrieved from http://news.psu.edu/story/343727/2015/02/05/research/annual-report-offers-snapshot-us-college-students'mental-health.

Center for Collegiate Mental Health (2014). *Annual Report 2014*. Retrieved from http://www.ccmh.psu.edu.

Clearinghouse for Structured/Thematic Groups & Innovative Programs, University of Texas at Austin: http://www.utexas.edu/student/cmhc/clearinghouse/index.html

Commission VII: Counseling & Psychological Services: http://myacpa.org

Counseling Center Village: http://ub-counseling.buffalo.edu/ccv.html

Dean, L. A., & Meadows, M. E. (1995). College counseling: Union and intersection. *Journal of Counseling and Development, 74*, 139-142.

Davis, D., & Humphrey, K. (2000). *College counseling: Issues and strategies for a new millennium*. Alexandria, VA: American Counseling Association.

Gallagher, R. P. (2006). *National survey of counseling center directors*. Alexandria, VA: International Association of Counseling Services.

Humphrey, K., Kitchens, H., & Patrick, J. (2000). Trends in college counseling in the 21st century. In D. Davis & K. Humphrey, (Eds.) *College counseling: Issues and strategies for a new millennium* (pp.289-305). Alexandria, VA: American Counseling Association.

International Association of Counseling Services (IACS): An Accreditation Association: http://www.iacsinc.org/

Kadison, R. D. (2006). College psychiatry 2006: Challenges and opportunities. *Journal of American College Health, 54(6),* 338-340.

Kadison, R. D., & DiGeronimo, T. F. (2004). *College of the overwhelmed: The campus mental health crisis and what to do about it*. San Francisco, CA: Jossey-Bass.

Lifton, D. E., Seay, S. & Bushko, A. (2004). Measuring undergraduate hardiness as an indicator of persistence to graduation within four years. In I. M. Duranczyk, J. L. Higbee, & D. B. Lundell (Eds.). *Best Practices for Access and Retention in Higher Education*. Minneapolis, MN: Center for Research on Developmental Education and Urban Literacy, General College, University of Minnesota.

Locke, B., & Shockey, J. (2014). *Center for Collegiate Mental Health; 2014 Survey*. Retrieved from Pennsylvania State University, Counseling and Psychological Services web site: http://ccmh.psu.edu/publications.

Magoon, T. (2002). *College and university counseling center directors' 2001-2002 data bank*. College Park, MD: University of Maryland.

Pledge, D., Lapan, R., Heppner, P., Kivlighan, D., and Roehlke, H. (1998). Stability and severity of presenting problems at a university counseling center: A six year analysis. *Professional Psychology: Research and Practice, 29*, 386-389.

National Association of Behavioral Intervention Teams (NaBITA): https://nabita.org.

Stone, G. L., & Archer, J., Jr. (1990). College and university counseling centers in the 1990s: Challenges and limits. *The Counseling Psychologist, 18*, 539-607.

Tinto, V. (2006-2007). Research and practice of retention: What next? *Journal of College Student Retention, 8(1)*, 1-19.

Twenge, J. M. (2004). *Generation me: Why today's young American's are more confident, assertive, entitled – and more miserable than ever before*. New York, NY: Free Press.

U.S. Department of Justice, (2000). Office of Federal Coordination and Compliance, Title IX of the educational amendments of 1972, regulations and requirements Title IX, 34 C.F.R. 106.1et seq. Retrieved from http://www.justice.gov.

U.S. Department of Justice (1990). *Civil Rights Division*. Retrieved from http://www.ada.gov/2010_regs/htm.

Van Brunt, B., Sokolow, B., Lewis, W., Schuster, S. & Golstan, A. (2014). *NaBITA Team Survey*. Retreived from https://www.nabita.org.

Upcraft, M. L., Gardner, J. N., & Barefood, B. O. (2005). *Challenging and supporting the first-year student: A handbook for improving the first-year of college*. San Francisco, CA: Jossey-Bass.

Contextual Statement Contributors

Current Edition:
MJ Raleigh, UNC – Pembroke, ACCA
Hannah Bayne, University of Maryland, ACCA
Laura Dean, University of Georgia, ACCA

Previous Editions:
Carolyn W. Kern, University of North Texas
Angela Shores, Meredith College
Laura A. Dean, University of Georgia, ACCA
Michelle (Stefanisko) Cooper, Western Carolina University

Counseling Services
CAS Standards and Guidelines

The primary mission of Counseling Services (CS) is to assist students in defining and accomplishing personal, academic, and career goals. To accomplish the mission, the scope of CS must include

- individual and group counseling services to students who may be experiencing psychological, behavioral, or learning difficulties
- programming focused on the developmental needs of students to maximize their potential to benefit from the academic environment and experience
- consultative services to the institution to help foster an environment supportive of the intellectual, emotional, spiritual, and physical development of students
- advocacy for a healthy and diverse learning community
- assessment services to identify and address student needs through appropriate services and referrals
- crisis response, including threat assessment

CS must develop, disseminate, implement, and regularly review their missions, which must be consistent with the mission of the institution and with applicable professional standards. The mission must be appropriate for the institution's students and other constituents. Mission statements must reference student learning and development.

A wide variety of counseling, consultative, evaluative, and training functions may be performed by CS as an expression of its institutional mission.

To effectively respond to the educational needs of the institution and of students, CS should have the following complementary functions:

Developmental. The developmental mission is to help students enhance their personal growth. Developmental interventions help students acclimate to and benefit from the academic environment. To facilitate this, counseling services should promote student growth in the areas of positive and realistic self-appraisal, intellectual development, appropriate personal and occupational choices, the ability to relate meaningfully and mutually with others, and the capacity to engage in a personally satisfying and effective lifestyle.

Clinical. The clinical mission recognizes that some students experience significant problems, ranging from serious adjustment issues to more severe psychological disorders that require immediate professional attention. Elements of the clinical mission include diagnosis, treatment, and crisis response, as well as consideration of the effect on the campus community. Clinical services often allow students to continue enrollment and achieve success.

Preventive. The preventive mission is to anticipate environmental conditions and developmental processes that may negatively influence students' wellbeing and initiate interventions that will promote personal adjustment and growth.

Although there are basic similarities in the overall goals of various types of institutions, differences in student populations and institutional priorities may affect emphases of functions within individual counseling services. For these reasons, counseling services at different institutions may emphasize combinations of personal counseling, academic counseling, career counseling, or student development services.

CS should be organized based on institutional characteristics, priorities, and organizational structures. Accordingly, not all functions may exist within the same administrative unit.

CS must be coordinated to ensure a cohesive system of support for students when counseling functions exist in separate administrative units.

To achieve their mission, Counseling Services (CS) must contribute to

- students' formal education, which includes both the curriculum and the co-curriculum
- student progression and timely completion of educational goals
- preparation of students for their careers, citizenship, and lives
- student learning and development

To contribute to student learning and development, CS must

- identify relevant and desirable student learning and development outcomes
- articulate how the student learning and development outcomes align with the six CAS student learning and development domains and related dimensions
- assess relevant and desirable student learning and development
- provide evidence of impact on outcomes
- articulate contributions to or support of student learning and development in the domains not specifically assessed
- use evidence gathered to create strategies for improvement of programs and services

STUDENT LEARNING AND DEVELOPMENT DOMAINS AND DIMENSIONS

Domain: knowledge acquisition, integration, construction, and application

- Dimensions: understanding knowledge from

a range of disciplines; connecting knowledge to other knowledge, ideas, and experiences; constructing knowledge; and relating knowledge to daily life

Domain: cognitive complexity
- Dimensions: critical thinking, reflective thinking, effective reasoning, and creativity

Domain: intrapersonal development
- Dimensions: realistic self-appraisal, self-understanding, and self-respect; identity development; commitment to ethics and integrity; and spiritual awareness

Domain: interpersonal competence
- Dimensions: meaningful relationships, interdependence, collaboration, and effective leadership

Domain: humanitarianism and civic engagement
- Dimensions: understanding and appreciation of cultural and human differences, social responsibility, global perspective, and sense of civic responsibility

Domain: practical competence
- Dimensions: pursuing goals, communicating effectively, technical competence, managing personal affairs, managing career development, demonstrating professionalism, maintaining health and wellness, and living a purposeful and satisfying life

[LD Outcomes: See *The Council for the Advancement of Standards Learning and Development Outcomes* statement for examples of outcomes related to these domains and dimensions.]

CS must be
- **intentionally designed**
- **guided by theories and knowledge of learning and development**
- **integrated into the life of the institution**
- **reflective of developmental and demographic profiles of the student population**
- **responsive to needs of individuals, populations with distinct needs, and relevant constituencies**
- **delivered using multiple formats, strategies, and contexts**
- **designed to provide universal access**

CS must collaborate with colleagues and departments across the institution to promote student learning and development, persistence, and success.

To fulfill its mission, CS must provide the following services directly, through referral, or in collaboration:
- **individual counseling in areas of personal, educational, career development, interpersonal relationships, family, social, and psychological issues**
- **group interventions (e.g., counseling, psychotherapy, support) to help students establish**

satisfying personal relationships and to become more effective in areas such as interpersonal processes, communication skills, decision-making concerning personal relationships and educational or career matters, and the establishment of personal values
- **psychological testing and other assessment techniques to foster client self-understanding and decision-making**
- **outreach efforts to address developmental needs and concerns of students**
- **outreach and counseling support for students from diverse backgrounds**
- **counseling support for students affected by addictions and substance abuse**
- **counseling support to help students assess and overcome specific deficiencies in educational preparation or skills**
- **psychiatric consultation, evaluation, and support services for students needing maintenance or monitoring of psychotropic medications**
- **crisis and violence assessment, intervention, and response**
- **disaster preparedness and response**
- **staff and faculty professional development programs**

In those cases where other institutional agencies address similar issues, such as career counseling and educational counseling, CS must establish cooperative relationships and maintain appropriate mutual referrals.

In those cases where specialized and needed expertise is not available within counseling services, staff members must refer students to resources within the institution or the local community.

CS must play an active role in interpreting and, when appropriate, advocating for addressing the needs of students to administration, faculty members, and staff of the institution.

CS should provide to institutional leaders a perspective that reflects an appropriate balance between administrative requirements and the needs and interests of students. CS should interpret the institutional environment to students and intervene to either improve the quality of the environment or facilitate the development of better interactions between the student and environment.

CS should help identify and advocate for the removal of barriers to student retention. CS should be sensitive to the needs of traditionally underserved populations and students with distinct needs.

CS may engage in research that contributes to knowledge of student characteristics and needs and evaluation of student outcomes in its programs. CS may assist students, faculty, and staff members who conduct individual research on student characteristics or on the influence of specific student development activities.

CS should provide consultation and inservice professional development for faculty members, administrators, staff and student staff members, and paraprofessionals.

Training and supervision of paraprofessionals, practicum students, and interns is an appropriate and desirable responsibility of CS.

Wherever a fee-for-service model is employed, CS must understand students' health care insurance and work with students to utilize their coverage.

Part 3. Organization and Leadership

To achieve program and student learning and development outcomes, Counseling Services (CS) must be purposefully structured for effectiveness. CS must have clearly stated and current
- goals and outcomes
- policies and procedures
- responsibilities and performance expectations for personnel
- organizational charts demonstrating clear channels of authority

Leaders must model ethical behavior and institutional citizenship.

Leaders with organizational authority for CS must provide strategic planning, management and supervision, and program advancement.

Strategic Planning
- articulate a vision and mission that drive short- and long-term planning
- set goals and objectives based on the needs of the populations served, intended student learning and development outcomes, and program outcomes
- facilitate continuous development, implementation, and assessment of program effectiveness and goal attainment congruent with institutional mission and strategic plans
- promote environments that provide opportunities for student learning, development, and engagement
- develop, adapt, and improve programs and services in response to the changing needs of populations served and evolving institutional priorities
- include diverse perspectives to inform decision making

Management and Supervision
- plan, allocate, and monitor the use of fiscal, physical, human, intellectual, and technological resources
- manage human resource processes including recruitment, selection, professional development, supervision, performance planning, succession planning, evaluation, recognition, and reward
- influence others to contribute to the effectiveness and success of the unit
- empower professional, support, and student

personnel to become effective leaders
- encourage and support collaboration with colleagues and departments across the institution
- encourage and support scholarly contributions to the profession
- identify and address individual, organizational, and environmental conditions that foster or inhibit mission achievement
- use current and valid evidence to inform decisions
- incorporate sustainability practices in the management and design of programs, services, and facilities
- understand appropriate technologies and integrate them into programs and services
- be knowledgeable about codes and laws relevant to programs and services and ensure that programs and services meet those requirements
- assess and take action to mitigate potential risks

Program Advancement
- advocate for and actively promote the mission and goals of the programs and services
- inform stakeholders about issues affecting practice
- facilitate processes to reach consensus where wide support is needed
- advocate for representation in strategic planning initiatives at divisional and institutional levels

The director should have the ability to interact effectively with administrators, faculty and staff members, students, colleagues, and community members and should possess all the general qualifications of a counseling staff member.

The director role also should include the following responsibilities:
- provision of counseling information and services to students, faculty members, and staff and, in accordance with the mission of CS and the institution, to the community
- evaluation of services
- provision of consultation/leadership in campus-wide and internal policy formation and program development
- education of staff members regarding legal issues in mental health, medicine, and higher education, as well as those governing the delivery of counseling services

CS leaders should create a work environment inclusive of various professional credentials and preparation. Because the functions of CS are essential to the overall mission of an institution, their value and impact should be clearly articulated to the institution, and their placement within the organizational structure should be such that it facilitates significant interaction with unit heads in academic and student affairs and other relevant areas.

CS should function independently of units directly responsible for making decisions concerning students' official matriculation status, such as student conduct, academic probation, and admissions or re-admissions actions.

Part 4. Human Resources

Counseling Services (CS) must be staffed adequately by individuals qualified to accomplish mission and goals.

Counseling functions must be performed by professionals from the disciplines of counseling and clinical psychology, counseling and counselor education, psychiatry, and clinical social work, as well as by others with appropriate training, credentials, and supervised experience.

CS must have access to technical and support personnel adequate to accomplish their mission.

Within institutional guidelines, CS must
- establish procedures for personnel recruitment and selection, training, performance planning, and evaluation
- set expectations for supervision and performance
- provide personnel access to continuing and advanced education and appropriate professional development opportunities to improve their competence, skills, and leadership capacity
- consider work/life options available to personnel (e.g., compressed work schedules, flextime, job sharing, remote work, or telework) to promote recruitment and retention of personnel

Administrators of CS must
- ensure that all personnel have updated position descriptions
- implement recruitment and selection/hiring strategies that produce a workforce inclusive of under-represented populations
- develop promotion practices that are fair, inclusive, proactive, and non-discriminatory

Personnel responsible for delivery of CS must have written performance goals, objectives, and outcomes for each year's performance cycle to be used to plan, review, and evaluate work and performance. The performance plan must be updated regularly to reflect changes during the performance cycle.

Results of individual personnel evaluations must be used to recognize personnel performance, address performance issues, implement individual and/or collective personnel development and training programs, and inform the assessment of programs and services.

CS personnel, when hired and throughout their employment, must receive appropriate and thorough training.

CS personnel, including student employees and volunteers, must have access to resources or receive specific training on
- institutional policies pertaining to functions or activities they support
- privacy and confidentiality policies
- laws regarding access to student records
- policies and procedures for dealing with sensitive institutional information
- policies and procedures related to technology used to store or access student records and institutional data
- how and when to refer those in need of additional assistance to qualified personnel and have access to a supervisor for assistance in making these judgments
- systems and technologies necessary to perform their assigned responsibilities
- ethical and legal uses of technology

CS personnel must engage in continuing professional development activities to keep abreast of the research, theories, legislation, policies, and developments that affect their programs and services.

CS should maintain an inservice and staff development program that includes supervision, case presentations, research reports, and discussion of relevant professional issues. Institutional budgetary support should be available to provide for inservice and professional development activities.

Administrators of CS must ensure that personnel are knowledgeable about and trained in safety, emergency procedures, and crisis prevention and response. Risk management efforts must address identification of threatening conduct or behavior and must incorporate a system for responding to and reporting such behaviors.

CS personnel must be knowledgeable of and trained in safety and emergency procedures for securing and vacating facilities.

PROFESSIONAL PERSONNEL

CS professional personnel either must hold an earned graduate or professional degree in a field relevant to their position or must possess an appropriate combination of educational credentials and related work experience.

The minimum qualification for counseling staff members must be a master's degree from a regionally accredited institution in a relevant discipline.

Staff members should have completed a supervised practicum/internship at the graduate level, preferably in the counseling of students within a higher education setting, or should be appropriately supervised until they can transfer their skills to this setting. Counseling staff members should hold, or be eligible for, state/provincial licensure or certification in their chosen discipline (e.g., counseling, psychology, social work) where such exists.

Counseling staff members should have appropriate course work and training in psychological assessment; theories of counseling, cognitive development, personality, abnormal psychology, or psychopathology; treatment planning; group counseling; crisis intervention and management; addictions and alcohol and other drug issues; career development; multicultural counseling; legal and ethical issues in counseling; and learning styles. Counseling staff members should keep abreast of current research, including outcome research. Counseling staff members should also demonstrate knowledge of technology, leadership, organizational development, consultation, and relevant federal, regional, and state/provincial statutes.

Counseling staff members, when responsible for supervision of colleagues or graduate interns, should have doctoral degrees, hold degrees commensurate with those being supervised, or meet professional and state/provincial standards for providing clinical supervision, including licensure or certification as a supervisor.

Counseling staff members should participate in appropriate professional organizations and should have the budgetary support to do so. Counseling staff members should be encouraged to participate in community activities related to their profession.

INTERNS OR GRADUATE ASSISTANTS

Degree- or credential-seeking interns or graduate assistants must be qualified by enrollment in an appropriate field of study and relevant experience. These students must be trained and supervised by professional personnel who possess applicable educational credentials and work experience and have supervisory experience. Supervisors must be cognizant of the dual roles interns and graduate assistants have as both student and employee.

Supervisors must
- **adhere to parameters of students' job descriptions**
- **articulate intended learning outcomes in student job descriptions**
- **adhere to agreed-upon work hours and schedules**
- **offer flexible scheduling when circumstances necessitate**

Supervisors and students must both agree to suitable compensation if circumstances necessitate additional hours.

Practicum students and interns, as well as paraprofessional assistants, may perform, under supervision, such counseling functions as are appropriate to their preparation and experience.

STUDENT EMPLOYEES AND VOLUNTEERS

Student employees and volunteers must be carefully selected, trained, supervised, and evaluated. Students must have access to a supervisor. Student employees and volunteers must be provided clear job descriptions, pre-service training based on assessed needs, and continuing development.

The director of counseling services must have an appropriate combination of graduate course work, formal training, and supervised experience.

The director of CS should have a doctoral degree in counseling psychology, clinical psychology, counselor education, medicine with completed specialty training in psychiatry, or other related discipline from an accredited institution, with a minimum of a master's degree in such areas. The director should hold or be eligible for state licensure or certification where such exists or should pursue such credentials. It is highly desirable that the director has a minimum of three years experience as a staff member or administrator in counseling services within higher education. The director should have received supervision (either pre- or post-doctorate) in counseling within higher education.

The level of CS staffing must be established and reviewed regularly with regard to service demands, enrollment, user surveys, diversity of services offered, institutional resources, and other mental health and student services that may be available on the campus and in the local community.

The level of staffing and workloads must be adequate and appropriate for program and service demands.

The student to counselor ratio should be determined locally in light of institutional size and type, student demographics, roles and responsibilities of professional staff members, scope of services provided, and unique features of CS.

In addition to providing direct services, staff time should be allowed for preparation of interviews and reports, updating institutional information, research, faculty and staff contacts, staff meetings, training and supervision, personal and professional development, consultation, and walk-in and emergency counseling interventions, in accordance with individual staff members' qualifications and task assignments. Similarly, teaching, administration, research, and other such responsibilities should be identified as relevant staff functions.

Support staff members who deal directly with students should be carefully selected, because they play an important role in the students' impressions of the counseling services, often must make some preliminary client-related decisions, and may have access to confidential information.

Part 5. Ethics

Counseling Services (CS) must
- review applicable professional ethical standards and must adopt or develop and implement appropriate statements of ethical practice
- publish and adhere to statements of ethical practice and ensure their periodic review
- orient new personnel to relevant ethical standards and statements of ethical practice and related institutional policies

Statements of ethical standards must
- **specify that CS personnel respect privacy and maintain confidentiality in communications and records as delineated by privacy laws**
- **specify limits on disclosure of information contained in students' records as well as requirements to disclose to appropriate authorities**
- **address conflicts of interest, or appearance thereof, by personnel in the performance of their work**
- **reflect the responsibility of personnel to be fair, objective, and impartial in their interactions with others**
- **reference management of institutional funds**

- reference appropriate behavior regarding research and assessment with human participants, confidentiality of research and assessment data, and students' rights and responsibilities
- include the expectation that personnel confront and hold accountable other personnel who exhibit unethical behavior
- address issues surrounding scholarly integrity

CS personnel must

- employ ethical decision making in the performance of their duties
- inform users of programs and services of ethical obligations and limitations emanating from codes and laws or from licensure requirements
- recognize and avoid conflicts of interest that could adversely influence their judgment or objectivity and, when unavoidable, recuse themselves from the situation
- perform their duties within the scope of their position, training, expertise, and competence
- make referrals when issues presented exceed the scope of the position

When the condition of a client is indicative of serious and foreseeable harm to the client or to others, counseling staff members must take reasonable personal action that may involve informing responsible authorities and, when possible, consulting with other professionals. In such cases, counseling staff members must be cognizant of pertinent ethical principles, state/provincial or federal statutes, and local mental health guidelines that stipulate the limits of confidentiality.

Information should be released only at the written request or concurrence of a client who has full knowledge of the nature of the information that is being released and of the parties to whom it is released.

Instances of limited confidentiality must be clearly articulated, reviewed with the client, and acknowledged by signature.

The decision to release information without consent may occur only after careful consideration and under the conditions described above.

CS staff members must conform to relevant federal, state/provincial, and local statutes that govern the delivery of counseling and psychological services.

Staff members must comply with applicable laws related to privacy and confidentiality.

CS staff members must be familiar with and adhere to relevant ethical standards in the field, including those professional procedures for intake, assessment, case notes, and termination summaries as well as the preparation, use, and distribution of psychological tests.

Client status and information disclosed in individual counseling sessions must remain confidential unless written permission to divulge the information is given by the client.

Clients must be made aware of issues such as the limits to confidentiality during intake or early in the counseling process so they can participate from a position of informed consent.

Consultation regarding individual students, as requested or needed with faculty and other institutional personnel is offered in the context of preserving the student's confidential relationship with the counseling services. Consultation with parents, partners, and public and private agencies that bear some responsibility for particular students may occur within the bounds of a confidential counseling relationship.

CS must maintain records in a confidential and secure manner while specifying procedures to monitor access, use, and maintenance of the records.

Part 6. Law, Policy, and Governance

Counseling Services (CS) must be in compliance with laws, regulations, and policies that relate to their respective responsibilities and that pose legal obligations, limitations, risks, and liabilities for the institution as a whole. Examples include constitutional, statutory, regulatory, and case law; relevant law and orders emanating from codes and laws; and the institution's policies.

CS must have access to legal advice needed for personnel to carry out their assigned responsibilities.

CS must inform personnel, appropriate officials, and users of programs and services about existing and changing legal obligations, risks and liabilities, and limitations.

CS must inform personnel about professional liability insurance options and refer them to external sources if the institution does not provide coverage.

CS must have written policies and procedures on operations, transactions, or tasks that have legal implications.

CS must regularly review policies. The revision and creation of policies must be informed by best practices, available evidence, and policy issues in higher education.

CS must have procedures and guidelines consistent with institutional policy for responding to threats, emergencies, and crisis situations. Systems and procedures must be in place to disseminate timely and accurate information to students, other members of the institutional community, and appropriate external organizations during emergency situations.

Personnel must neither participate in nor condone any form of harassment or activity that demeans persons or creates an intimidating, hostile, or offensive environment.

CS must purchase or obtain permission to use copyrighted materials and instruments. References to copyrighted materials and instruments must include appropriate citations.

CS must inform personnel about internal and external governance organizations that affect programs and services.

Part 7. Diversity, Equity, and Access

Within the context of each institution's mission and in accordance with institutional policies and applicable codes and laws, Counseling Services (CS) must create and maintain educational and work environments that are welcoming, accessible, inclusive, equitable, and free from harassment.

CS must not discriminate on the basis of disability; age; race; cultural identity; ethnicity; nationality; family educational history (e.g., first generation to attend college); political affiliation; religious affiliation; sex; sexual orientation; gender identity and expression; marital, social, economic, or veteran status; or any other basis included in institutional policies and codes and laws.

CS must
- advocate for sensitivity to multicultural and social justice concerns by the institution and its personnel
- ensure physical, program, and resource access for all constituents
- modify or remove policies, practices, systems, technologies, facilities, and structures that create barriers or produce inequities
- ensure that when facilities and structures cannot be modified, they do not impede access to programs, services, and resources
- establish goals for diversity, equity, and access
- foster communication and practices that enhance understanding of identity, culture, self-expression, and heritage
- promote respect for commonalities and differences among people within their historical and cultural contexts
- address the characteristics and needs of diverse constituents when establishing and implementing culturally relevant and inclusive programs, services, policies, procedures, and practices
- provide personnel with diversity, equity, and access training and hold personnel accountable for applying the training to their work
- respond to the needs of all constituents served when establishing hours of operation and developing methods of delivering programs, services, and resources
- recognize the needs of distance and online learning students by directly providing or assisting them to gain access to comparable services and resources

Part 8. Internal and External Relations

Counseling Services (CS) must reach out to individuals, groups, communities, and organizations internal and external to the institution to
- establish, maintain, and promote understanding and effective relations with those that have a

significant interest in or potential effect on the students or other constituents served by the programs and services
- garner support and resources for programs and services as defined by the mission
- collaborate in offering or improving programs and services to meet the needs of students and other constituents and to achieve program and student outcomes
- engage diverse individuals, groups, communities, and organizations to enrich the educational environment and experiences of students and other constituents
- disseminate information about the programs and services

CS should develop close cooperation with institutional referral sources and with potential consumers of counseling services consultations. CS should also work closely with all other segments of the institution whose goal is the promotion of psychological, emotional, and career development.

CS should work closely with the senior student affairs and academic affairs administrators to ensure that institutional goals and objectives are met.

Within the institution, CS should establish close cooperation with career services, academic advising, specialized academic support units (e.g., reading and study skills programs, learning assistance programs), and student services (e.g., services for students with disabilities; international and multicultural students; lesbian, gay, bisexual and transgender students; TRIO programs; women; veterans; returning adult students).

CS should establish relationships with a wide range of student groups (e.g., student government; gay, lesbian, bisexual, transgender groups; fraternities and sororities; spiritual groups; organizations for students from underrepresented groups) to promote visibility and serve as a resource to them.

CS should establish and maintain a close working relationship with student health services as counseling staff members are often called upon to refer clients for medical concerns or hospitalization and to serve as consultants to, or to seek consultation from, health services professionals.

CS should foster relationships with academic units and with professionals in admissions, registrar's office, student activities, athletics, residence halls, and campus security where appropriate.

CS should establish effective relationships with the institutional legal counsel and the legal staff of relevant professional organizations in order to effectively respond to pertinent legal issues and precedents that underlie the delivery components of CS.

Where adequate mental health resources are not available on campus, CS must establish and maintain close working relationships with community mental health resources.

CS must have procedures for the referral of students who require counseling beyond the scope of institutional CS.

Promotional and descriptive information must be accurate and free of deception and misrepresentation.

CS must have procedures and guidelines consistent with institutional policy for

- communicating with the media
- distributing information through print, broadcast, and online sources
- contracting with external organizations for delivery of programs and services
- cultivating, soliciting, and managing gifts
- applying to and managing funds from grants

CS must advocate for membership on critical institutional committees, especially those related to crisis response, students at risk, and threat assessment.

Part 9. Financial Resources

Counseling Services (CS) must have funding to accomplish the mission and goals.

In establishing and prioritizing funding resources, CS must conduct comprehensive analyses to determine

- unmet needs of the unit
- relevant expenditures
- external and internal resources
- impact on students and the institution

CS must use the budget as a planning tool to reflect commitment to the mission and goals of the programs and services and of the institution.

CS must administer funds in accordance with established institutional accounting procedures.

CS must demonstrate efficient and effective use and responsible stewardship of fiscal resources consistent with institutional protocols.

Financial reports must provide an accurate financial overview of the organization and provide clear, understandable, and timely data upon which personnel can plan and make informed decisions.

Procurement procedures must

- be consistent with institutional policies
- ensure that purchases comply with laws and codes for usability and access
- ensure that the institution receives value for the funds spent
- consider information available for comparing the ethical and environmental impact of products and services purchased

Part 10. Technology

Counseling Services (CS) must have technology to support the achievement of their mission and goals. The technology and its use must comply with institutional policies and procedures and with relevant codes and laws.

CS must use technologies to

- provide updated information regarding mission, location, staffing, programs, services, and official contacts to students and other constituents in accessible formats
- provide an avenue for students and other constituents to communicate sensitive information in a secure format
- enhance the delivery of programs and services for all students

CS must

- back up data on a regular basis
- adhere to institutional policies regarding ethical and legal use of technology
- articulate policies and procedures for protecting the confidentiality and security of information
- implement a replacement plan and cycle for all technology with attention to sustainability
- incorporate accessibility features into technology-based programs and services

When providing student access to technology, CS must

- have policies on the use of technology that are clear, easy to understand, and available to all students
- provide information or referral to support services for those needing assistance in accessing or using technology
- provide instruction or training on how to use the technology
- inform students of implications of misuse of technologies

CS must maintain secure and ethical use in the application of technology for the provision of counseling services.

CS must select technology that reflects current best pedagogical practices when it is used to facilitate student learning and development.

Part 11. Facilities and Equipment

Counseling Services' (CS) facilities must be intentionally designed and located in suitable, accessible, and safe spaces that demonstrate universal design and support the program's mission and goals.

Facilities must be designed to engage various constituents and promote learning.

Personnel must have workspaces that are suitably located and accessible, well equipped, adequate in size, and designed to support their work and responsibilities.

The design of the facilities must guarantee the security and privacy of records and ensure the confidentiality of sensitive information and conversations. Personnel must be able to secure their work.

CS must incorporate sustainable practices in use of facilities and purchase of equipment. Facilities and equipment must be evaluated on an established cycle and be in compliance with codes, laws, and accepted practices for access, health, safety, and security.

When acquiring capital equipment, CS must take into account expenses related to regular maintenance and life cycle costs.

CS must maintain a physical and social environment that facilitates optimal functioning and ensures appropriate confidentiality.

CS, when feasible, should be physically separate from administrative offices, campus security, and student conduct units.

Individual offices for counseling staff members should be provided, appropriately equipped, and soundproofed. The offices should be designed to accommodate the functions performed by counseling staff members.

There should be a reception area that provides a comfortable and private waiting area for clients.

CS should maintain or have ready access to professional resource materials.

In those instances where counseling services include a career development unit, there should be a resource center that holds institutional catalogs and occupation and career information.

An area suitable for individual and group testing procedures should be available.

CS should maintain or have ready access to group meeting space that provides a confidential setting.

CS should maintain equipment that is capable of providing modern technical approaches, such as biofeedback and secure video conferencing accessibility, to treatment and record keeping and have access to equipment for research and media presentations.

CS with training components should have adequate facilities for recording and, where possible, for direct observations.

Part 12. Assessment

Counseling Services (CS) must develop assessment plans and processes.

Assessment plans must articulate an ongoing cycle of assessment activities.

CS must
- specify programmatic goals and intended outcomes
- identify student learning and development outcomes
- employ multiple measures and methods
- develop manageable processes for gathering, interpreting, and evaluating data
- document progress toward achievement of goals and outcomes
- interpret and use assessment results to demonstrate accountability
- report aggregated results to respondent groups and stakeholders

- use assessment results to inform planning and decision-making
- assess effectiveness of implemented changes
- provide evidence of improvement of programs and services

CS must employ ethical practices in the assessment process.

CS must have access to adequate fiscal, human, professional development, and technological resources to develop and implement assessment plans.

General Standards revised in 2014;
CS content developed/revised in 1986, 1997, 1999, & 2011

Dining Services Programs
CAS Contextual Statement

Institutions of higher education have provided a dining services program, initially as a component of student housing, since the first residential colleges were founded. Over the years the quality and variety of services provided varied greatly depending upon the specific institution. In 1958, with the creation of the National Association of College and University Food Services (NACUFS), the professionalism of those employed in dining services was enhanced, and the potential for the overall improvement of dining services was increased.

The basic principles that underlie any dining services program are to provide students, faculty, staff, and guests with high quality food service and products in a pleasant environment at a reasonable cost. Those principles are shared by professionals throughout the college and university arena, although the specific focus may vary from campus to campus. Although the original scope of the dining services program encompassed simply the providing of nourishment, currently that is only one of the basic elements of a quality program. Meals are important times and places for students, faculty, and staff to exchange ideas, discuss current issues, and share experiences; the design of facilities and menus needs to accommodate these functions. Although reasonable cost to the consumer is an expectation, providing a source of revenue to the institution is usually a desired outcome. Balancing those two imperatives is critical to the success of any program.

Additionally, modern dining services programs must address the dietary needs and wants of an increasingly diverse population. It is no longer sufficient to provide only good nutrition. Programs must address the rising sophistication of students in higher education and the dining experiences they bring with them to campus. Life-style choices must also be addressed in addition to dietary needs. Vegetarian/vegan and/or religious-based diets are but two of an ever-growing list of eating choices made by today's student that must be accommodated successfully.

As dining services programs have dealt positively with the transition from supplying basic needs to providing for expanded expectations, they are now addressing an increasing list of current issues. Among these is the practice of outsourcing of the dining services program. It is incumbent upon the administration of each institution to make the decision to self-operate or privatize based upon what is in the best interest of that particular institution and its students, faculty, and staff. Sustainability is an issue that has recently emerged on many campuses. These institutions are providing products and services that support local businesses and industries in a manner that encourages the continued existence of those resources while balancing the budget. Increasingly, students with food allergies are being served by dining services programs. Title III of the Americans with Disabilities Act of 1990 requires dining programs to make necessary reasonable modifications in policies, practices, and procedures to permit students with food allergies to fully and

equally enjoy the privileges, advantages, and accommodations of its food service and meal plan system. One of the challenges in this area is to provide a specialized diet without students feeling as if they are being singled out as different. Finally, as mentioned above, students bring an increasingly sophisticated and diverse set of dining experiences to campus. Developing a "retail orientation" to better address these expectations is one of the more prevalent changes being implemented across campuses. There is a continuing need to provide a wide variety of services. At times, students may benefit from all-you-care-to-eat service; at other times, they prefer take-out services. Often, late-night service is a need. In other words, today's students want what they want, where they want it, and when they want it. It is the role of dining services to maintain high quality programs while seeking ways to meet these changing needs and expectations. The standards and guidelines that follow offer guidance for the development and assessment of high quality dining services programs.

References, Readings, and Resources

Administering Food Service Contracts: A Handbook for Contract Administrators in College and University Food Services. (n.d.). Okemos, MI: National Association of College and University Food Services (NACUFS).

Academy of Nutrition and Dietetic: http://www.eatright.org

Educational Foundation of the National Restaurant Association: http://www.nraef.org

Foodservice Systems Management Education Council: http://www.fsmec.org

Journal of The National Association of College & University Food Services. (n.d.). Okemos, MI: National Association of College and University Food Services (NACUFS).

Professional Practices in College and University Food Services (5th ed.). Okemos, MI: National Association of College and University Food Services (NACUFS).

Settlement Agreement between the United States of America and Lesley University DJ 202-36-231. Retrieved from http://www.ada.gov/lesley_university_sa.htm.

The National Association of College and University Food Services (NACUFS): http://www.nacufs.org

Contextual Statement Contributors
Current Edition:
Peter J. Napolitano, Binghamton University
Russ Myer, University of Nevada, Reno, NACUFS
Joe Spina, NACUFS

Previous Editions:
Russ Myer, University of Nevada Reno, NACUFS
Joe Spina, NACUFS

Dining Services Programs
CAS Standards and Guidelines

The mission of Dining Services Programs (DSP) must address
- a dining environment that encourages both individual and community development
- engagement of students in learning about sound nutrition practices
- safe and secure facilities that are clean, attractive, well-maintained, and comfortable
- management services that ensure the orderly and effective administration and operation of all aspects of the program
- reasonably priced, quality, safe, diverse, and nutritious food offerings

DSP must develop, disseminate, implement, and regularly review their missions, which must be consistent with the mission of the institution and with applicable professional standards. The mission must be appropriate for the institution's students and other constituents. Mission statements must reference student learning and development.

DSP should clearly define and communicate its vision and mission to staff members and students, to provide the focus for departmental practices.

The institution, when outsourcing, should clearly define what role the contractor has in developing a mission statement or supporting the institution's mission statement.

In addition to dining services, the DSP mission must include, either directly or through collaboration, a provision for educational programs and services and management services.

To achieve their mission, Dining Services Programs (DSP) must contribute to
- students' formal education, which includes both the curriculum and the co-curriculum
- student progression and timely completion of educational goals
- preparation of students for their careers, citizenship, and lives
- student learning and development

To contribute to student learning and development, DSP must
- identify relevant and desirable student learning and development outcomes
- articulate how the student learning and development outcomes align with the six CAS student learning and development domains and related dimensions

- assess relevant and desirable student learning and development
- provide evidence of impact on outcomes
- articulate contributions to or support of student learning and development in the domains not specifically assessed
- use evidence gathered to create strategies for improvement of programs and services

STUDENT LEARNING AND DEVELOPMENT DOMAINS AND DIMENSIONS

Domain: knowledge acquisition, integration, construction, and application
- Dimensions: understanding knowledge from a range of disciplines; connecting knowledge to other knowledge, ideas, and experiences; constructing knowledge; and relating knowledge to daily life

Domain: cognitive complexity
- Dimensions: critical thinking, reflective thinking, effective reasoning, and creativity

Domain: intrapersonal development
- Dimensions: realistic self-appraisal, self-understanding, and self-respect; identity development; commitment to ethics and integrity; and spiritual awareness

Domain: interpersonal competence
- Dimensions: meaningful relationships, interdependence, collaboration, and effective leadership

Domain: humanitarianism and civic engagement
- Dimensions: understanding and appreciation of cultural and human differences, social responsibility, global perspective, and sense of civic responsibility

Domain: practical competence
- Dimensions: pursuing goals, communicating effectively, technical competence, managing personal affairs, managing career development, demonstrating professionalism, maintaining health and wellness, and living a purposeful and satisfying life

[LD Outcomes: See *The Council for the Advancement of Standards Learning and Development Outcomes* statement for examples of outcomes related to these domains and dimensions.]

DSP must be
- intentionally designed
- guided by theories and knowledge of learning and development
- integrated into the life of the institution

- reflective of developmental and demographic profiles of the student population
- responsive to needs of individuals, populations with distinct needs, and relevant constituencies
- delivered using multiple formats, strategies, and contexts
- designed to provide universal access

DSP must collaborate with colleagues and departments across the institution to promote student learning and development, persistence, and success.

To fulfill its mission and goals effectively, DSP must provide students with access to experiences, services, and programs and facilitate

- interaction with faculty and staff members
- respect for self, others, and property
- appreciation of new ideas
- appreciation of cultural differences and other forms of diversity
- development of a balanced lifestyle embracing wellness
- orientation to community expectations, facilities, services, and staff
- understanding of institutional and dining policies, procedures, and expectations, including the potential consequences of a violation
- involvement in programming and policy development
- responsibility for their community through confrontation of inappropriate or disruptive behavior

DSP should support and respond to student dietary and medical requirements, such as vegan diets and food allergies.

DSP should provide access to a registered dietician to assist students in meeting their dietary and medical needs.

DSP must establish appropriate policies and procedures for responding to emergency situations, especially where DSP facilities, personnel, and resources could assist the institution.

Dining Services should be involved in institution emergency planning.

DSP should provide an organizational avenue such as a food advisory board and should have a relationship with appropriate student governance organizations.

Part 3. Organization and Leadership

To achieve program and student learning and development outcomes, Dining Services Programs (DSP) must be purposefully structured for effectiveness. DSP must have clearly stated and current

- goals and outcomes
- policies and procedures
- responsibilities and performance expectations for personnel
- organizational charts demonstrating clear

channels of authority

Leaders must model ethical behavior and institutional citizenship.

Leaders with organizational authority for DSP must provide strategic planning, management and supervision, and program advancement.

Strategic Planning

- articulate a vision and mission that drive short- and long-term planning
- set goals and objectives based on the needs of the populations served, intended student learning and development outcomes, and program outcomes
- facilitate continuous development, implementation, and assessment of program effectiveness and goal attainment congruent with institutional mission and strategic plans
- promote environments that provide opportunities for student learning, development, and engagement
- develop, adapt, and improve programs and services in response to the changing needs of populations served and evolving institutional priorities
- include diverse perspectives to inform decision making

Management and Supervision

- plan, allocate, and monitor the use of fiscal, physical, human, intellectual, and technological resources
- manage human resource processes including recruitment, selection, professional development, supervision, performance planning, succession planning, evaluation, recognition, and reward
- influence others to contribute to the effectiveness and success of the unit
- empower professional, support, and student personnel to become effective leaders
- encourage and support collaboration with colleagues and departments across the institution
- encourage and support scholarly contributions to the profession
- identify and address individual, organizational, and environmental conditions that foster or inhibit mission achievement
- use current and valid evidence to inform decisions
- incorporate sustainability practices in the management and design of programs, services, and facilities
- understand appropriate technologies and integrate them into programs and services
- be knowledgeable about codes and laws relevant to programs and services and ensure that programs and services meet those requirements
- assess and take action to mitigate potential risks

Program Advancement

- advocate for and actively promote the mission and

goals of the programs and services
- inform stakeholders about issues affecting practice
- facilitate processes to reach consensus where wide support is needed
- advocate for representation in strategic planning initiatives at divisional and institutional levels

DSP must promote professionalism, integrity, and ethical behavior in dealing with colleagues, students, administration, faculty, vendors, and the public.

The institution must clearly articulate whether DSP is to be subsidized, self-sustaining, or revenue generating.

Institutions with significant commuter-based populations or other unique circumstances should recognize that subsidizing the operation may be required, depending upon the level of service desired.

The institution, when outsourcing, must clearly state that the relationship is to be mutually beneficial.

It should recognize that when outsourced, the food service provider has a reasonable expectation of profit and should work with the institution to achieve mutual benefit.

DSP must comply with laws, regulations, and policies, with particular attention to health and safety requirements.

DSP should promote a positive relationship with all internal and external customers, especially students, and openly solicit comments from all customers.

DSP must have internal service control systems in place throughout the department to protect the customer and the department without sacrificing the underlying commitment to customer service.

DSP should have clear lines of authority and responsibility, assignment of span of control, and delineation of individual job responsibilities to achieve the mission of the department while maximizing efficient and effective use of human resources.

DSP must plan and conduct all activities around a fundamental commitment to providing quality service.

Resident dining and retail operations should provide a variety of features, offerings, and themes that deliver a quality food service experience, meet the expectations of customers, and contribute positively to the department and institution.

Nutrition education provided by the department should address the assessed needs of customers and staff and contribute to the overall health of the campus community.

Catering services should provide quality products and customer-centered services.

DSP must have written up-to-date internal policies and procedures covering each aspect of the operation.

Where the management of DSP is divided among different offices within the institution and/or contracted to an outside vendor, institutional leaders, stakeholders, and contractors must establish and maintain productive working relationships.

When DSP is contracted for or outsourced, the institution must identify the individual(s) responsible for administering the contract, supervising the service, and the conditions for the contract's continuance or renewal.

The institution and DSP, whether self-operated, contracted, or a combination of self-operated and contracted, must collaborate in providing a balanced dining services program that meets the nutritional, educational, and social needs of students and the college or university community.

DSP should participate in campus emergency planning efforts to ensure that appropriate contingency plans are in place to feed students.

To fulfill its mission and goals effectively, DSP must maintain well-structured management functions, including planning, personnel, property management, purchasing, contract administration, financial control, and information systems.

DSP should use a planning process that increases the probability that the department will successfully accomplish its mission.

DSP should have a formal, written long-range strategic planning document that provides a vision of the future, reflects the department's long-range decision-making process, and supports its short-term operational planning.

DSP and each of its units should prepare operating or action plans for short-term periods that are consistent with the approved long-term plans.

DSP should develop capital improvement plans, guided by the department's long-term strategic plan, by working in cooperation with the institution to meet the projected needs for dining service facilities and programs that will support the future student enrollment of the institution.

DSP should conduct market research to provide an objective basis for planning how to market and manage the department to maximize customer satisfaction and achieve fiscal goals.

DSP should use a menu-planning process that results in a variety of appealing and wholesome food and beverage choices to meet the dining and nutritional needs of customers within the food cost budget goals.

DSP must use safe and effective procedures for preparing, presenting, and holding foods and maintaining the safety, appearance, and nutritional quality of the products.

DSP should have well-organized food production systems in place.

The organization of work flow within dining services should permit the efficient and safe movement of food and beverage products from receiving through storage, issue, preparation, production, holding, distribution, service, and storage of leftovers.

DSP should organize the purchasing functions to ensure the orderly and timely procurement of food products, supplies, services, and equipment at the defined quantity, cost, and quality levels to support the mission of the department.

DSP must fully comply with all applicable federal, state/provincial, and local food safety codes; compliance focuses on managing the food safety risk at critical control points in a manner consistent with a Hazard Analysis Critical Control Point (HACCP) or similar food safety system.

Part 4. Human Resources

Dining Services Programs (DPS) must be staffed adequately by individuals qualified to accomplish mission and goals.

DSP must have access to technical and support personnel adequate to accomplish their mission.

Within institutional guidelines, DSP must
- establish procedures for personnel recruitment and selection, training, performance planning, and evaluation
- set expectations for supervision and performance
- provide personnel access to continuing and advanced education and appropriate professional development opportunities to improve their competence, skills, and leadership capacity
- consider work/life options available to personnel (e.g., compressed work schedules, flextime, job sharing, remote work, or telework) to promote recruitment and retention of personnel

Administrators of DSP must
- ensure that all personnel have updated position descriptions
- implement recruitment and selection/hiring strategies that produce a workforce inclusive of under-represented populations
- develop promotion practices that are fair, inclusive, proactive, and non-discriminatory

Personnel responsible for delivery of DSP must have written performance goals, objectives, and outcomes for each year's performance cycle to be used to plan, review, and evaluate work and performance. The performance plan must be updated regularly to reflect changes during the performance cycle.

Results of individual personnel evaluations must be used to recognize personnel performance, address performance issues, implement individual and/or collective personnel development and training programs, and inform the assessment of programs and services.

DSP personnel, when hired and throughout their employment, must receive appropriate and thorough training.

DSP personnel, including student employees and volunteers, must have access to resources or receive specific training on

- institutional policies pertaining to functions or activities they support
- privacy and confidentiality policies
- laws regarding access to student records
- policies and procedures for dealing with sensitive institutional information
- policies and procedures related to technology used to store or access student records and institutional data
- how and when to refer those in need of additional assistance to qualified personnel and have access to a supervisor for assistance in making these judgments
- systems and technologies necessary to perform their assigned responsibilities
- ethical and legal uses of technology

DSP personnel must engage in continuing professional development activities to keep abreast of the research, theories, legislation, policies, and developments that affect their programs and services.

Administrators of DSP must ensure that personnel are knowledgeable about and trained in safety, emergency procedures, and crisis prevention and response. Risk management efforts must address identification of threatening conduct or behavior and must incorporate a system for responding to and reporting such behaviors. DSP personnel must be knowledgeable of and trained in safety and emergency procedures for securing and vacating facilities.

PROFESSIONAL PERSONNEL

DSP professional personnel either must hold an earned graduate or professional degree in a field relevant to their position or must possess an appropriate combination of educational credentials and related work experience.

INTERNS OR GRADUATE ASSISTANTS

Degree- or credential-seeking interns or graduate assistants must be qualified by enrollment in an appropriate field of study and relevant experience. These students must be trained and supervised by professional personnel who possess applicable educational credentials and work experience and have supervisory experience. Supervisors must be cognizant of the dual roles interns and graduate assistants have as both student and employee.

Supervisors must
- adhere to parameters of students' job descriptions
- articulate intended learning outcomes in student job descriptions
- adhere to agreed-upon work hours and schedules
- offer flexible scheduling when circumstances necessitate

Supervisors and students must both agree to suitable compensation if circumstances necessitate additional hours.

STUDENT EMPLOYEES AND VOLUNTEERS

Student employees and volunteers must be carefully selected, trained, supervised, and evaluated. Students must have access to a supervisor. Student employees and volunteers must be provided clear job descriptions, pre-service training based on assessed needs, and continuing development.

Student employees should be considered as a part of the DSP staff.

Because student employment is an important component of student development, DSP should have an effective program for the recruitment, training, education, development, evaluation, and promotion of student employees.

DSP must maintain up-to-date, accurate, and complete personnel, payroll, and certification records for each staff member of the department.

DSP must provide emergency response training opportunities for staff to learn to respond to emergencies.

These opportunities could include CPR training, Heimlich maneuver, and basic first aid.

DSP should provide all new staff members, including students, a formal orientation, including policies, procedures, rules, and benefits that apply to them.

DSP should use a formal system for providing standardized and consistent job-specific training for staff members, including students.

Staff members include student staff where applicable.

DSP must follow an orderly system for salary and wage administration that complies with applicable laws and institutional policies and procedures.

DSP should provide personnel benefits beyond wage and salary that provide for the basic needs of all eligible staff members.

DSP should promote long-term career opportunities for all staff members.

DSP management should practice positive approaches to staff management designed to increase productivity, minimize turnover, and contribute to a high level of morale.

DSP should use a system for reviewing the job performance of all staff members, including student employees, on a scheduled basis as an integral part of a proactive human resource development process.

DSP should provide special recognition for staff members, including student employees, whose performance is superior as an incentive to all staff members to maximize their potential.

DSP must have a system for administering discipline on an objective and fair basis with a clear focus on human resource development.

DSP must provide procedures for filing, processing,

and hearing employee grievances. All staff members, including students, must be aware of and support the goals, objectives, and philosophy of DSP.

Where collective bargaining agreements exist, DSP management must administer them in good faith and strive to maintain a positive working relationship between management and union staff members.

DSP must comply with applicable laws and regulations and institutional and department policies regarding posting of information for staff members, including students, about their rights and responsibilities.

DSP should have orderly separation procedures that follow institutional policies for processing resignations and involuntary termination of employment.

Part 5. Ethics

Dining Services Programs (DSP) must
- review applicable professional ethical standards and must adopt or develop and implement appropriate statements of ethical practice
- publish and adhere to statements of ethical practice and ensure their periodic review
- orient new personnel to relevant ethical standards and statements of ethical practice and related institutional policies

Statements of ethical standards must
- specify that DSP personnel respect privacy and maintain confidentiality in communications and records as delineated by privacy laws
- specify limits on disclosure of information contained in students' records as well as requirements to disclose to appropriate authorities
- address conflicts of interest, or appearance thereof, by personnel in the performance of their work
- reflect the responsibility of personnel to be fair, objective, and impartial in their interactions with others
- reference management of institutional funds
- reference appropriate behavior regarding research and assessment with human participants, confidentiality of research and assessment data, and students' rights and responsibilities
- include the expectation that personnel confront and hold accountable other personnel who exhibit unethical behavior
- address issues surrounding scholarly integrity

DSP personnel must
- employ ethical decision making in the performance of their duties
- inform users of programs and services of ethical obligations and limitations emanating from codes and laws or from licensure requirements
- recognize and avoid conflicts of interest that could adversely influence their judgment or objectivity and, when unavoidable, recuse themselves from the situation

- perform their duties within the scope of their position, training, expertise, and competence
- make referrals when issues presented exceed the scope of the position

Part 6. Law, Policy, and Governance

Dining Services Programs (DSP) must be in compliance with laws, regulations, and policies that relate to their respective responsibilities and that pose legal obligations, limitations, risks, and liabilities for the institution as a whole. Examples include constitutional, statutory, regulatory, and case law; relevant law and orders emanating from codes and laws; and the institution's policies.

DSP must have access to legal advice needed for personnel to carry out their assigned responsibilities.

DSP must inform personnel, appropriate officials, and users of programs and services about existing and changing legal obligations, risks and liabilities, and limitations.

DSP must inform personnel about professional liability insurance options and refer them to external sources if the institution does not provide coverage.

DSP must have written policies and procedures on operations, transactions, or tasks that have legal implications.

DSP must regularly review policies. The revision and creation of policies must be informed by best practices, available evidence, and policy issues in higher education.

DSP must have procedures and guidelines consistent with institutional policy for responding to threats, emergencies, and crisis situations. Systems and procedures must be in place to disseminate timely and accurate information to students, other members of the institutional community, and appropriate external organizations during emergency situations.

Personnel must neither participate in nor condone any form of harassment or activity that demeans persons or creates an intimidating, hostile, or offensive environment.

DSP must purchase or obtain permission to use copyrighted materials and instruments. References to copyrighted materials and instruments must include appropriate citations.

DSP must inform personnel about internal and external governance organizations that affect programs and services.

Part 7. Diversity, Equity, and Access

Within the context of each institution's mission and in accordance with institutional policies and applicable codes and laws, Dining Services Programs (DSP) must create and maintain educational and work environments that are welcoming, accessible, inclusive, equitable, and free from harassment.

DSP must not discriminate on the basis of disability; age; race; cultural identity; ethnicity; nationality; family educational history (e.g., first generation to attend college); political affiliation; religious affiliation; sex; sexual orientation; gender identity and expression; marital, social, economic, or veteran status; or any other basis included in institutional policies and codes and laws.

DSP structure should reflect an unbiased commitment to diversity and maximize the potential of all staff members, including students.

DSP must

- advocate for sensitivity to multicultural and social justice concerns by the institution and its personnel
- ensure physical, program, and resource access for all constituents
- modify or remove policies, practices, systems, technologies, facilities, and structures that create barriers or produce inequities
- ensure that when facilities and structures cannot be modified, they do not impede access to programs, services, and resources
- establish goals for diversity, equity, and access
- foster communication and practices that enhance understanding of identity, culture, self-expression, and heritage
- promote respect for commonalities and differences among people within their historical and cultural contexts
- address the characteristics and needs of diverse constituents when establishing and implementing culturally relevant and inclusive programs, services, policies, procedures, and practices
- provide personnel with diversity, equity, and access training and hold personnel accountable for applying the training to their work
- respond to the needs of all constituents served when establishing hours of operation and developing methods of delivering programs, services, and resources
- recognize the needs of distance and online learning students by directly providing or assisting them to gain access to comparable services and resources

DSP should acknowledge that it serves a multicultural community and provide products and services that recognize this ethnic and cultural diversity.

DSP should plan promotions that recognize religious or ethnic events, considering student body diversity, institutional support, and community diversity.

Part 8. Internal and External Relations

Dining Services Programs (DSP) must reach out to individuals, groups, communities, and organizations internal and external to the institution to

- establish, maintain, and promote understanding

and effective relations with those that have a significant interest in or potential effect on the students or other constituents served by the programs and services

- garner support and resources for programs and services as defined by the mission
- collaborate in offering or improving programs and services to meet the needs of students and other constituents and to achieve program and student outcomes
- engage diverse individuals, groups, communities, and organizations to enrich the educational environment and experiences of students and other constituents
- disseminate information about the programs and services

Promotional and descriptive information must be accurate and free of deception and misrepresentation.

DSP must have procedures and guidelines consistent with institutional policy for

- communicating with the media
- distributing information through print, broadcast, and online sources
- contracting with external organizations for delivery of programs and services
- cultivating, soliciting, and managing gifts
- applying to and managing funds from grants

DSP must comply with these standards even when contracted for or outsourced by the institution.

DSP should make a positive contribution to the educational, social, and economic development of the campus and local community.

The success of DSP is dependent on the maintenance of good relationships with students, faculty, administrators, alumni, the community at large, contractors, and support agencies. Staff members should encourage participation in campus programs by relevant groups.

When appropriate within the policies and procedures of the institution and department, DSP should sponsor campus and community nonprofit activities to promote goodwill and enhance the nonprofit mission of the community organization.

DSP departmental managers should encourage staff members, including students, to volunteer for community nonprofit and campus causes and activities in the name of the department to promote the community image of the department and enhance the quality of life of the volunteers.

Part 9. Financial Resources

Dining Services Programs (DSP) must have funding to accomplish the mission and goals.

In establishing and prioritizing funding resources, DSP must conduct comprehensive analyses to determine

- unmet needs of the unit

- relevant expenditures
- external and internal resources
- impact on students and the institution

DSP must use the budget as a planning tool to reflect commitment to the mission and goals of the programs and services and of the institution.

DSP must administer funds in accordance with established institutional accounting procedures.

DSP must demonstrate efficient and effective use and responsible stewardship of fiscal resources consistent with institutional protocols.

Financial reports must provide an accurate financial overview of the organization and provide clear, understandable, and timely data upon which personnel can plan and make informed decisions.

Procurement procedures must

- be consistent with institutional policies
- ensure that purchases comply with laws and codes for usability and access
- ensure that the institution receives value for the funds spent
- consider information available for comparing the ethical and environmental impact of products and services purchased

DSP must have in place an effective system of financial accountability controls to ensure responsible fiscal management.

The institution should recognize that when outsourced, the food service provider has a reasonable expectation of making profit.

DSP should prepare annual operating budgets to project income and expenses for the year for each component of the operation and break down the budget to accurately forecast financial performance by accounting periods. DSP should strive to balance revenue and institutional expectations to provide necessary and desirable services.

DSP must use an accounting system that accurately accounts for all income and expenses, as approved by the institution, the department's controller, and auditors, as applicable.

Part 10. Technology

Dining Services Programs (DSP) must have technology to support the achievement of their mission and goals. The technology and its use must comply with institutional policies and procedures and with relevant codes and laws.

DSP must use technologies to

- provide updated information regarding mission, location, staffing, programs, services, and official contacts to students and other constituents in accessible formats
- provide an avenue for students and other

constituents to communicate sensitive information in a secure format
- enhance the delivery of programs and services for all students

DSP must
- back up data on a regular basis
- adhere to institutional policies regarding ethical and legal use of technology
- articulate policies and procedures for protecting the confidentiality and security of information
- implement a replacement plan and cycle for all technology with attention to sustainability
- incorporate accessibility features into technology-based programs and services

When providing student access to technology, DSP must
- have policies on the use of technology that are clear, easy to understand, and available to all students
- provide information or referral to support services for those needing assistance in accessing or using technology
- provide instruction or training on how to use the technology
- inform students of implications of misuse of technologies

DSP should use an objective process for evaluating technology needs and staying current with appropriate new information technologies. Areas for consideration include menu and inventory management, nutritional analysis, catering, event management, point-of-sale systems, concessions management, accounting systems, email, office production systems and services, and other specialty software such as that used for time and attendance.

DSP should make appropriate selections of technology systems, including hardware and software, to meet clearly-defined needs within budgetary limitations.

DSP should use a system for maintaining electronic and other computerized equipment and software.

Part 11. Facilities and Equipment

Dining Services Programs' (DSP) facilities must be intentionally designed and located in suitable, accessible, and safe spaces that demonstrate universal design and support the program's mission and goals.

Facilities must be designed to engage various constituents and promote learning.

Personnel must have workspaces that are suitably located and accessible, well equipped, adequate in size, and designed to support their work and responsibilities.

The design of the facilities must guarantee the security and privacy of records and ensure the confidentiality of sensitive information and conversations. Personnel must be able to secure their work.

DSP must incorporate sustainable practices in use of facilities and purchase of equipment. Facilities and equipment must be evaluated on an established cycle and be in compliance with codes, laws, and accepted practices for access, health, safety, and security.

When acquiring capital equipment, DSP must take into account expenses related to regular maintenance and life cycle costs.

The facilities managed by DSP must be in full compliance with applicable federal, state/provincial, and local building codes, as well as institutional policies.

DSP should share dining facility spaces for campus programs and events, such as study halls and social events.

DSP should take extra precautions to provide a secure environment for customers and staff members.

DSP should have a capital improvement budget that supports the long-term strategic plan.

DSP must comply with all applicable federal, state/provincial, and local statutes, regulations, and codes when undertaking capital improvements, including new construction, renovations, and equipment installation.

DSP should use current sources of information in planning for capital equipment purchases, installation, and implementation to support the mission of the department within applicable federal, state/provincial, and local codes and regulations.

DSP facilities must be accessible, clean, attractive, properly designed, well-maintained, comfortable, conducive to a positive dining experience, and must have appropriate safety and security features.

DSP must maintain a high level of facilities sanitation through effective housekeeping.

DSP should have ongoing programs of planned and preventive maintenance to extend the life of facilities and equipment, ensure optimum working condition, and enhance safety and appearance.

Spaces must include adequate areas for seating as well as for service, preparation, storage, and receiving of food, and for disposal of waste.

DSP should design its facilities to support the mission of the department with optimum efficiency, while enhancing customer and staff satisfaction.

DSP must have a program for managing solid and liquid waste that complies with federal, state/provincial, and local regulations and coordinates the program with other solid and liquid waste efforts of the institution or community.

The focus of all capital improvement projects should be on designing for the future, based on the best available information and projections concerning future enrollment, shifts in student housing patterns, changes in the diversity of the student body, trends in college and university dining services, and market research of the off-campus dining service trends in the surrounding community.

Part 12. Assessment

Dining Services Programs (DSP) must develop assessment plans and processes.

Assessment plans must articulate an ongoing cycle of assessment activities.

DSP must
- **specify programmatic goals and intended outcomes**
- **identify student learning and development outcomes**
- **employ multiple measures and methods**
- **develop manageable processes for gathering, interpreting, and evaluating data**
- **document progress toward achievement of goals and outcomes**
- **interpret and use assessment results to demonstrate accountability**
- **report aggregated results to respondent groups and stakeholders**
- **use assessment results to inform planning and decision-making**
- **assess effectiveness of implemented changes**
- **provide evidence of improvement of programs and services**

DSP should conduct market research such as comparing prices, offerings, menu, hours, and service levels.

DSP should promote a positive relationship with all internal and external customers, especially students, and openly solicit comments from all customers about how to improve the dining services program.

DSP must also evaluate customer satisfaction.

DSP must employ ethical practices in the assessment process.

DSP must have access to adequate fiscal, human, professional development, and technological resources to develop and implement assessment plans.

General Standards revised in 2014;
DSP content developed in 2006

Disability Resources and Services
CAS Contextual Statement

Professionals who serve disabled students have had pivotal roles in expanding access to college and university campus environments by encouraging colleagues and administration to adopt the pedagogical principles and practices of Universal Design (UD), Universal Design for Instruction (UDI), and in playing key roles in transforming sociopolitical consciousness of disability (Vance, Lipsitz, & Parks, 2014). In the 21st century, disability is now viewed as a form of diversity and a part of the range of natural expression of difference in the human condition rather than a deficiency by definition.

The language of disability has also undergone changes over time in response to ever-emerging scholarship from the field of disability studies as well as from the perspectives of social justice and disability advocacy. Further influences on the language of disability flow from concepts of universal design, which emphasize universal access through intentional design and barrier removal, thus moving toward equality of experience for all individuals and removing distinctions and stigmas of disability.

Person-first language has been used extensively since the second half of the 20th century and is typically seen in the phrases "persons with disabilities" or "students with disabilities." More recently, disability rights advocates and disability studies scholars have endorsed use of disability-first language when referring to a group of persons who have disabling impairments, using the term "disabled persons" with pride and ownership, recognizing that disability is a social construct. In the 2013 revision of the CAS Disability Resources and Services (DRS) standards and guidelines, person-first terminology is used when referencing individuals, and disability-first terminology is used when referencing groups. It is important that DRS professionals and institutional administrators be alert to the evolving language of disability and its implications for and impacts on the design and delivery of resources and services.

Prior to the mid-20th century in the United States, disabled college students were supported primarily by *rehabilitation* services. In the rehabilitation model college personnel and family members primarily assisted students by attempting to reduce barriers in postsecondary educational environments. However, buildings were not physically accessible, texts in accessible formats such as braille were limited, and most aspects of campus life remained inaccessible to disabled students.

Many U.S. veterans returning from World War II who were recently injured (wounded warriors) sought college educations and began a process of opening doors that coincided with the Disability Rights Movement (Church, 2009). Other voices for change included disability and independent living advocates like Ed Roberts, Judy Heumann, and Justin Dart, who knew that colleges needed to make their campuses and programs more accessible by removing, not merely reducing barriers, if disabled individuals were to have true equal opportunities for education.

The Rehabilitation Act of 1973, which included Section 504 subpart E, stipulated that recipients of federal funds could not deny access or admission based solely on disability and must provide auxiliary aids and services to accommodate for a person's disability. The Americans with Disabilities Act (ADA) of 1990, amended in 2008, expanded and further clarified the rights of persons with disabilities to equal access and accommodation in public and private spheres (ADA, 2008). Disability rights and inclusive education are also international human rights issues as seen in the 2008 United Nations Convention on the Rights of People with Disabilities (United Nations, 2008). Some countries have nationwide laws such as the Americans with Disabilities Act; others, like Canada, have enacted disability laws in their provinces or regions.

In the 1970s and 1980s, U.S. postsecondary institutions began to establish offices and departments to address the access needs of disabled students (Linton, 1998). These offices, aligned with student affairs or academic affairs, facilitated academic adjustments and modifications for disabled students. Services included administering tests when extra time or other accommodations were needed, arranging for sign language interpreters, securing accessible instructional materials, and coordinating room assignments in residence halls. The medical, or individual rehabilitation, model of disability was the framework for much of this early disability services work on campuses. As a result of these early initiatives, work of the disability services professional is now linked with all sectors of the campus community in a collaborative network that includes study abroad, residence life, food service, security, administration, financial aid, diversity, career services, library services, academic advising, and other campus services.

The Association of Handicapped Student Service Personnel in Postsecondary Education (AHSSPPE) was established in 1977 as a professional association for individuals working in disability resource and service offices around the U.S. In 1992 AHSSPPE became the Association on Higher Education And Disability (AHEAD, www.ahead.org), reflecting progress both in nomenclature and breadth of mission. With over 2,800 U.S. and international members, AHEAD is the principal professional resource for disability professionals in higher education. Driven by its vision, "education and societal environments that value disability and embody equality of opportunity," AHEAD provides professional development, professional engagement and networking, information, and technical assistance; has 38 state and multi-state affiliate groups around the U.S. in addition to an international affiliate program; and is active with allied international organizations sharing common missions. AHEAD produces a refereed publication, the *Journal on Postsecondary Education and Disability*.

Disability services professionals serving in colleges and universities have varied educational and career backgrounds, including counseling, social work, education, psychology, rehabilitation, and disability studies. The majority of directors and coordinators of disability resource and service departments have master's degrees, and many have doctorates across these academic disciplines (Kasnitz, 2011).

In the 21st century, colleges and universities are being challenged to provide inclusive education to an expanding population of disabled students (U.S. Department of Education, 2008). The number of disabled students attending colleges and universities continues to grow (U.S. Government Accountability Office, 2009). Special education under the Individuals with Disabilities Education Act (IDEA) has resulted in higher enrollment of disabled students at postsecondary institutions than a couple of decades ago (Wagner, Newman, Cameto, Garza, & Levine, 2005). Learning disability is the most prevalent type of disability, both in the PK-12 system and at the postsecondary level (Kasnitz, 2011).

In postsecondary settings, in order to qualify for accommodations, students must self-identify as having a disability, and they must do so through disability resources and services or other designated office. Some students who experience disability could benefit from accommodations but for various reasons do not self-identify. Students who are wounded warriors or from other countries are examples of those who may not request disability accommodations. The use of UDI as a pedagogical practice benefits all students, especially those who choose not to disclose disability.

Postsecondary disability services professionals are transitioning from a perspective of strict compliance to a resource-oriented model. This transition is in compliance with ADA regulations, as amended in 2008, and in alignment with emerging models of student development theory and disability philosophy. However, they continue to be aware that other campus departments and staff must provide equal access for disabled students (Colker & Grossman, 2014). Disability resources and services offices vary in size. AHEAD's guideline is that each campus must have appropriate levels of full-time professional staff in these roles; rarely can this be accomplished by just one person.

Challenges for institutions of higher education and disability services professionals and departments are numerous. They include retrofitting and adapting poorly designed services, programs, and offerings where accessibility by all students was not a consideration at inception; adapting to a new and emerging population of disabled students with, such as wounded warriors who do not self-identify as disabled; adapting to the rapidly evolving world of technology, in particular to technology designed for access by persons with disabilities; securing or facilitating use of accessible instructional materials; facilitating equal access in online course management systems; and educating campus personnel regarding the shared institutional responsibilities of creating just, equitable, and usable environments through the elimination of barriers in any and all areas of the academic experience.

References, Readings, and Resources

American Council on Education (ACE). (2011). *Accommodating student veterans with traumatic brain injury and post-traumatic stress disorder: Tips for campus faculty and staff*. Retrieved from http://www.acenet.edu/news-room/Documents/Accommodating-Student-Veterans-with-Traumatic-Brain-Injury-and-Post-Traumatic-Stress-Disorder.pdf

Americans With Disabilities Act of 1990, as Amended, 42 U.S.C. 12101 *et seq.* (2008). Retrieved from http://access-board.gov/about/laws/ADA.htm

Colker, R. & Grossman, P.D. (2014). The Law of Disability Discrimination for Higher Education Professionals. San Francisco, CA: LexisNexis.

Church, T. E. (2009). *Veterans with disabilities: Promoting success in higher education*. Available at http://www.ahead.org/publications#bo16

Kasnitz, D. (2011). *The 2010 biennial AHEAD survey of disability services and resource professionals in higher education*. Retrieved from http://www.ahead.org/uploads/membersarea/Final%20AHEAD%202010%20Biennial%20Initial%20Report.docx

Linton, S. (1998). *Claiming disability: Knowledge and identity*. New York, NY: New York University Press.

Madaus, J., Miller, W., & Vance, M. L. (2009). Veterans with disabilities in postsecondary education. *Journal of Postsecondary Education and Disability, 22*(1), 10-17.

Rehabilitation Act of 1973, Section 504 as amended, 29 U.S.C 794 *et seq.* (1973). Subpart E retrieved from http://ed.gov/policy/rights/reg/ocr/edlite-34cfr104.html#E

United Nations. (2008). *Convention on the rights of persons with disabilities*. Retrieved from http://www.un.org/disabilities/convention/conventionfull.shtml

United States Department of Education. (2008). *The Higher Education Opportunity Act (Public Law 110-315)*. Retrieved from www.pacer.org/tatra/TheHigherEducationOpportunityAct.doc

United States Government Accountability Office. (2009, October). *Higher education and disability: Education needs a coordinated approach to improve its assistance to schools in supporting students*. Washington, DC: Author. Retrieved from http://www.gao.gov/new.items/d1033.pdf

Vance, M. L., Lipsitz, N. & Parks, K (2014). *Beyond the Americans with Disabilities Act: Inclusive policy and practice for higher education*. Washington, DC: National Association of Student Personnel Administrators.

Vance, M. L., & Miller, W. (2009). Serving wounded warriors: Current practices in postsecondary education. *Journal of Postsecondary Education and Disability, 22*(1), 18-35.

Vance, M. L., Miller, W. K., & Grossman, P. D. (2010, Fall). What you need to know about 21st-century college military veterans. *Leadership Exchange*. NASPA - Student Affairs Administrators in Higher Education. Retrieved from http://www.naspa.org/kc/dckc/A_Veteran_Friendly_Campus.pdf

Contextual Statement Contributors
Current Edition:
Jean Ashmore, Rice University, AHEAD
Bea Awoniyi, Santa Fe College, AHEAD
Mary Lee Vance, University of California Berkeley, AHEAD

Previous Editions:
Beth Hunsinger, Community College of Baltimore Maryland, AHEAD
Bill Scales, University of Maryland, College Park, AHEAD
Jean Ashmore, Rice University, AHEAD
Jim Kessler, University of North Carolina at Chapel Hill
Kate Broderick, Old Dominion University, assisted by David J. Thomas, AHEAD
Peggy Hayeslip, Johns Hopkins University
Sam Goodin, University of Michigan

Disability Resources and Services
CAS Standards and Guidelines

The primary mission of Disability Resources and Services (DRS) is to provide leadership and facilitate equal access to all institutional opportunities for disabled students.

To accomplish its mission, DRS must perform three duties:
- provide institution-wide advisement, consultation, and training on disability-related topics, including legal and regulatory compliance, universal design, and disability scholarship
- collaborate with partners to identify and remove barriers to foster an all-inclusive campus
- provide individual services and facilitate accommodations to students with disabilities

Because disability touches all aspects of higher education, DRS should be at the forefront as institutional policies are developed and implemented and as systems evolve. Through collaboration with institutional allies, networks, and community partners, DRS leadership contributes to the development of equitable higher education experiences for all disabled students.

DRS must develop, disseminate, implement, and regularly review their missions, which must be consistent with the mission of the institution and with applicable professional standards. The mission must be appropriate for the institution's students and other constituents. Mission statements must reference student learning and development.

To achieve their mission, Disability Resources and Services (DRS) must contribute to
- students' formal education, which includes both the curriculum and the co-curriculum
- student progression and timely completion of educational goals
- preparation of students for their careers, citizenship, and lives
- student learning and development

To contribute to student learning and development, DRS must
- identify relevant and desirable student learning and development outcomes
- articulate how the student learning and development outcomes align with the six CAS student learning and development domains and related dimensions
- assess relevant and desirable student learning and development
- provide evidence of impact on outcomes
- articulate contributions to or support of student learning and development in the domains not

- specifically assessed
- use evidence gathered to create strategies for improvement of programs and services

STUDENT LEARNING AND DEVELOPMENT DOMAINS AND DIMENSIONS

Domain: knowledge acquisition, integration, construction, and application
- Dimensions: understanding knowledge from a range of disciplines; connecting knowledge to other knowledge, ideas, and experiences; constructing knowledge; and relating knowledge to daily life

Domain: cognitive complexity
- Dimensions: critical thinking, reflective thinking, effective reasoning, and creativity

Domain: intrapersonal development
- Dimensions: realistic self-appraisal, self-understanding, and self-respect; identity development; commitment to ethics and integrity; and spiritual awareness

Domain: interpersonal competence
- Dimensions: meaningful relationships, interdependence, collaboration, and effective leadership

Domain: humanitarianism and civic engagement
- Dimensions: understanding and appreciation of cultural and human differences, social responsibility, global perspective, and sense of civic responsibility

Domain: practical competence
- Dimensions: pursuing goals, communicating effectively, technical competence, managing personal affairs, managing career development, demonstrating professionalism, maintaining health and wellness, and living a purposeful and satisfying life

[LD Outcomes: See *The Council for the Advancement of Standards Learning and Development Outcomes* statement for examples of outcomes related to these domains and dimensions.]

DRS must be
- intentionally designed
- guided by theories and knowledge of learning and development
- integrated into the life of the institution
- reflective of developmental and demographic profiles of the student population
- responsive to needs of individuals, populations with distinct needs, and relevant constituencies
- delivered using multiple formats, strategies, and

contexts
- designed to provide universal access

DRS must collaborate with colleagues and departments across the institution to promote student learning and development, persistence, and success.

The scope of DRS must include the following five program components:
- appropriate and relevant office policies, procedures, and practices
- individual consultation, accommodation, and service
- proactive dissemination of information
- institution-wide education, consultation, and advocacy
- guidance and technical assistance to the institution on disability-related laws and regulations

DRS may be assigned responsibilities for performing these five program components for faculty, staff, or visitors.

Through appropriate and relevant office policies, procedures, and practices DRS must
- clearly articulate both the rights and responsibilities of the institution for providing accommodations, aids, or services and the rights and responsibilities of individuals identifying as disabled and seeking accommodation
- establish and promulgate processes for disabled students to self-identify, to seek and obtain specific accommodations, aids, and services, and to grieve accommodation decisions
- establish methods for informing faculty members and other identified institutional personnel of students' rights to specific DRS-identified accommodation(s), when requested by students
- establish a process for involving faculty members and identified institutional personnel in determining the reasonableness of identified accommodations
  DRS should support students in learning how to advocate for themselves and discuss who needs to know their DRS-recognized accommodations.
- develop relevant office policies, procedures, and processes that minimize extra burdens for disabled students

Through individual consultation, accommodation, and service DRS must
- engage in an interactive process with each student to understand how his or her disability intersects with the institutional environment and how accommodation(s) would reduce barriers
  DRS may request access to information about the student's disability from external sources, such as health care providers or psychoeducational evaluators and focus those requests on a need to understand the disability in the higher-education context.
- ensure that accommodations do not

fundamentally alter essential components of the course, program, activity, or experience
- monitor the utilization and effectiveness of individual accommodations
- be available to consult with students, faculty, and staff as needed

Through proactive dissemination of information DRS must
- inform the institutional community of the location of disability services
- inform the institutional community of key individuals to contact to request accommodations
- inform the institutional community of the processes to follow in seeking accommodations
- inform the institutional community of the availability and location of equipment and technology useful to students with disabilities
- ensure that the community is provided with accessible wayfinding information
- promote inclusion of information about DRS resources and services in institutional publications, including but not limited to recruitment materials, student and faculty handbooks, brochures, departmental websites, and catalogs

Through institution-wide education, consultation, and advocacy DRS must
- promote and support equitable and inclusive campus environments
  This includes active involvement with campus leaders responsible for curricular, co-curricular, technological, physical, and policy environments. DRS should collaborate with faculty members and faculty developers to support inclusive pedagogy. DRS should collaborate with faculty to infuse disability content into the curriculum, such as literary works by disabled authors, linguistic development of braille or ASL, accessibility in architecture, disability in film, and the disability experience in social sciences.
- provide guidance to faculty members in providing reasonable and effective accommodations
- participate with academic decision-makers to ensure that policies do not have the effect of discriminating against students with disabilities
- provide consultation and training on disability-related topics across the institution
  Relevant entities may include admissions and registration, housing and residential life programs, career services, leadership programming, communications, risk management, facilities and renovation, purchasing, website design and management, parking and transportation, human resources, and distance education and study abroad experiences.
- advocate for disabled students to have access to the same level of service from campus offices as is available to non-disabled students and to receive from DRS only those services not provided

elsewhere by the institution

To reduce the need for individual accommodations, DRS staff members should consult and collaborate with faculty and other institutional personnel to explore design solutions for disability-related barriers to minimize differential treatment of students with disabilities.

- **actively foster the development of a campus culture that values the diversity of disability and that values disability as a core component of diversity**
- **proactively encourage the design of campus environments that welcome disabled students**
- **advocate for inclusion of a commitment across institutional departments**

Through guidance and technical assistance to the institution on disability-related laws and regulations, DRS must

- **provide guidance, advice, and technical assistance that informs and enables the institution to meet all applicable laws and regulations**
- **apprise key administrators of emerging issues relative to disability and access that may impact the institution**
- **ensure that students with disabilities receive reasonable and appropriate accommodations, aids, and services to have equal access to all institutional programs, services, and activities**

  In providing institutional guidance and technical assistance for fulfilling legal and regulatory commitments, DRS should convey that regulations reflect minimum standards, which are not always adequate to achieve full access.
- **foster academic experiences that are as similar as possible to the experiences of non-disabled students**

Part 3. Organization and Leadership

To achieve program and student learning and development outcomes, Disability Resources and Services (DRS) must be purposefully structured for effectiveness. DRS must have clearly stated and current

- goals and outcomes
- policies and procedures
- responsibilities and performance expectations for personnel
- organizational charts demonstrating clear channels of authority

DRS must be situated within the institutional structure so that it has organizational leadership with authority to advise the institution effectively on its obligations.

DRS should involve advisory bodies that include students, faculty, and staff members with disabilities.

Leaders must model ethical behavior and institutional citizenship.

Leaders with organizational authority for DRS must provide strategic planning, management and supervision, and program advancement.

Strategic Planning
- **articulate a vision and mission that drive short- and long-term planning**
- **set goals and objectives based on the needs of the populations served, intended student learning and development outcomes, and program outcomes**
- **facilitate continuous development, implementation, and assessment of program effectiveness and goal attainment congruent with institutional mission and strategic plans**
- **promote environments that provide opportunities for student learning, development, and engagement**
- **develop, adapt, and improve programs and services in response to the changing needs of populations served and evolving institutional priorities**
- **include diverse perspectives to inform decision making**

Management and Supervision
- **plan, allocate, and monitor the use of fiscal, physical, human, intellectual, and technological resources**
- **manage human resource processes including recruitment, selection, professional development, supervision, performance planning, succession planning, evaluation, recognition, and reward**
- **influence others to contribute to the effectiveness and success of the unit**
- **empower professional, support, and student personnel to become effective leaders**
- **encourage and support collaboration with colleagues and departments across the institution**
- **encourage and support scholarly contributions to the profession**
- **identify and address individual, organizational, and environmental conditions that foster or inhibit mission achievement**
- **use current and valid evidence to inform decisions**
- **incorporate sustainability practices in the management and design of programs, services, and facilities**
- **understand appropriate technologies and integrate them into programs and services**
- **be knowledgeable about codes and laws relevant to programs and services and ensure that programs and services meet those requirements**
- **assess and take action to mitigate potential risks**

Program Advancement
- **advocate for and actively promote the mission and goals of the programs and services**
- **inform stakeholders about issues affecting practice**
- **facilitate processes to reach consensus where wide support is needed**
- **advocate for representation in strategic planning initiatives at divisional and institutional levels**

Leaders of DRS must keep abreast of best practices within

the field of disability resources and services, changes in the understandings of disability, and changes in laws and regulations that pertain to disability in higher education.

DRS must monitor emerging disability subpopulations and analyze shifts in utilization of disability services.

DRS leaders must use information on best practices and current research to advise their institution and community on means to achieve inclusive education through universal design, removal of barriers, accessible technology, and instructional practices that can minimize the need for individual accommodation.

Part 4. Human Resources

Disability Resources and Services (DRS) must be staffed adequately by individuals qualified to accomplish mission and goals.

DRS must have access to technical and support personnel adequate to accomplish their mission.

Within institutional guidelines, DRS must
- establish procedures for personnel recruitment and selection, training, performance planning, and evaluation
- set expectations for supervision and performance
- provide personnel access to continuing and advanced education and appropriate professional development opportunities to improve their competence, skills, and leadership capacity
- consider work/life options available to personnel (e.g., compressed work schedules, flextime, job sharing, remote work, or telework) to promote recruitment and retention of personnel

Administrators of DRS must
- ensure that all personnel have updated position descriptions
- implement recruitment and selection/hiring strategies that produce a workforce inclusive of under-represented populations
- develop promotion practices that are fair, inclusive, proactive, and non-discriminatory

Specialized DRS personnel, whether contract or staff, must have appropriate qualifications and applicable certifications.

Specialized DRS personnel may include sign language interpreters, real-time translators, braille transcribers, adaptive technology experts, and those who prepare alternative instructional materials for the institution.

DRS should actively seek to hire individuals with disabilities.

Personnel responsible for delivery of DRS must have written performance goals, objectives, and outcomes for each year's performance cycle to be used to plan, review, and evaluate work and performance. The performance plan must be updated regularly to reflect changes during the performance cycle.

Results of individual personnel evaluations must be used to recognize personnel performance, address performance issues, implement individual and/or collective personnel development and training programs, and inform the assessment of programs and services.

DRS personnel, when hired and throughout their employment, must receive appropriate and thorough training.

DRS support staff must be given training on the DRS mission to remove barriers within the institution through consultation, collaboration, and accommodation as well as on models of disability and concepts of universal design.

All DRS staff members should receive training in basic access technologies and accessible content-creation techniques.

DRS personnel, including student employees and volunteers, must have access to resources or receive specific training on
- institutional policies pertaining to functions or activities they support
- privacy and confidentiality policies
- laws regarding access to student records
- policies and procedures for dealing with sensitive institutional information
- policies and procedures related to technology used to store or access student records and institutional data
- how and when to refer those in need of additional assistance to qualified personnel and have access to a supervisor for assistance in making these judgments
- systems and technologies necessary to perform their assigned responsibilities
- ethical and legal uses of technology

DRS personnel must engage in continuing professional development activities to keep abreast of the research, theories, legislation, policies, and developments that affect their programs and services.

Administrators of DRS must ensure that personnel are knowledgeable about and trained in safety, emergency procedures, and crisis prevention and response. Risk management efforts must address identification of threatening conduct or behavior and must incorporate a system for responding to and reporting such behaviors.

DRS personnel must be knowledgeable of and trained in safety and emergency procedures for securing and vacating facilities.

PROFESSIONAL PERSONNEL

DRS professional personnel either must hold an earned graduate or professional degree in a field relevant to their position or must possess an appropriate combination of educational credentials and related work experience.

Designated staff members may serve as practicum instructors or intern supervisors.

INTERNS OR GRADUATE ASSISTANTS

Degree- or credential-seeking interns or graduate assistants must be qualified by enrollment in an appropriate field of study and relevant experience. These students must be trained and supervised by professional personnel who possess applicable educational credentials and work experience and have supervisory experience. Supervisors must be cognizant of the dual roles interns and graduate assistants have as both student and employee.

Supervisors must
- adhere to parameters of students' job descriptions
- articulate intended learning outcomes in student job descriptions
- adhere to agreed-upon work hours and schedules
- offer flexible scheduling when circumstances necessitate

Supervisors and students must both agree to suitable compensation if circumstances necessitate additional hours.

STUDENT EMPLOYEES AND VOLUNTEERS

Student employees and volunteers must be carefully selected, trained, supervised, and evaluated. Students must have access to a supervisor. Student employees and volunteers must be provided clear job descriptions, pre-service training based on assessed needs, and continuing development.

Part 5. Ethics

Disability Resources and Services (DRS) must
- review applicable professional ethical standards and must adopt or develop and implement appropriate statements of ethical practice
- publish and adhere to statements of ethical practice and ensure their periodic review
- orient new personnel to relevant ethical standards and statements of ethical practice and related institutional policies

DRS staff members who are licensed or certified in other professions must recognize and apply the professional ethical standards appropriate to their role and function at the institution.

All DRS staff members must respect the private nature of personal disability information in all elements of work and in relations with all institutional personnel.

To maintain ethical standards within their work, DRS staff members must
- have a current understanding of disability as put forth by disability studies scholarship and the disability community and continually explore these conceptual frameworks
- have an appreciation of disability as a valued aspect of diversity and as an integral part of the institution and postsecondary educational experience
- include disabled students in creating equitable

and inclusive environments for the institution, including policy, procedure, and program development

Statements of ethical standards must
- specify that DRS personnel respect privacy and maintain confidentiality in communications and records as delineated by privacy laws
- specify limits on disclosure of information contained in students' records as well as requirements to disclose to appropriate authorities
- address conflicts of interest, or appearance thereof, by personnel in the performance of their work
- reflect the responsibility of personnel to be fair, objective, and impartial in their interactions with others
- reference management of institutional funds
- reference appropriate behavior regarding research and assessment with human participants, confidentiality of research and assessment data, and students' rights and responsibilities
- include the expectation that personnel confront and hold accountable other personnel who exhibit unethical behavior
- address issues surrounding scholarly integrity

DRS personnel must
- employ ethical decision making in the performance of their duties
- inform users of programs and services of ethical obligations and limitations emanating from codes and laws or from licensure requirements
- recognize and avoid conflicts of interest that could adversely influence their judgment or objectivity and, when unavoidable, recuse themselves from the situation
- perform their duties within the scope of their position, training, expertise, and competence
- make referrals when issues presented exceed the scope of the position

Part 6. Law, Policy, and Governance

Disability Resources and Services (DRS) must be in compliance with laws, regulations, and policies that relate to their respective responsibilities and that pose legal obligations, limitations, risks, and liabilities for the institution as a whole. Examples include constitutional, statutory, regulatory, and case law; relevant law and orders emanating from codes and laws; and the institution's policies.

DRS must have access to legal advice needed for personnel to carry out their assigned responsibilities.

DRS must inform personnel, appropriate officials, and users of programs and services about existing and changing legal obligations, risks and liabilities, and limitations.

DRS must inform personnel about professional liability insurance options and refer them to external sources if the institution does not provide coverage.

DRS must have written policies and procedures on operations, transactions, or tasks that have legal implications.

DRS must regularly review policies. The revision and creation of policies must be informed by best practices, available evidence, and policy issues in higher education.

DSR must have procedures and guidelines consistent with institutional policy for responding to threats, emergencies, and crisis situations. Systems and procedures must be in place to disseminate timely and accurate information to students, other members of the institutional community, and appropriate external organizations during emergency situations.

Personnel must neither participate in nor condone any form of harassment or activity that demeans persons or creates an intimidating, hostile, or offensive environment.

DRS must purchase or obtain permission to use copyrighted materials and instruments. References to copyrighted materials and instruments must include appropriate citations.

DRS must inform personnel about internal and external governance organizations that affect programs and services.

DRS staff members must take advantage of professional development and continuing education opportunities to stay informed of changes in laws and regulations as well as best professional practices that pertain to the DRS function in higher education.

DRS must, in consultation and collaboration with legal counsel where appropriate, develop policies and procedures that reflect best professional practices and guidance from applicable higher education disability laws and regulations.

Higher education institutions must adhere to appropriate laws and regulations in appointing a designated disability compliance officer for the entire institution.

The function of disability compliance officer is not necessarily assigned to DRS. If the director of DRS functions as compliance official for the institution, another campus administrator should be designated to handle grievances directed at DRS.

DRS must collaborate with the designated institutional disability compliance official to promote and support non-discriminatory practices, equal opportunities, and reasonable accommodations for those who utilize the institution's programs or services.

Part 7. Diversity, Equity, and Access

Within the context of each institution's mission and in accordance with institutional policies and applicable codes and laws, Disability Resources and Services (DRS) must create and maintain educational and work environments that are welcoming, accessible, inclusive, equitable, and free from harassment.

DRS must not discriminate on the basis of disability; age; race; cultural identity; ethnicity; nationality; family educational history (e.g., first generation to attend college); political affiliation; religious affiliation; sex; sexual orientation; gender identity and expression; marital, social, economic, or veteran status; or any other basis included in institutional policies and codes and laws.

DRS must
- advocate for sensitivity to multicultural and social justice concerns by the institution and its personnel
- ensure physical, program, and resource access for all constituents
- modify or remove policies, practices, systems, technologies, facilities, and structures that create barriers or produce inequities
- ensure that when facilities and structures cannot be modified, they do not impede access to programs, services, and resources
- establish goals for diversity, equity, and access
- foster communication and practices that enhance understanding of identity, culture, self-expression, and heritage
- promote respect for commonalities and differences among people within their historical and cultural contexts
- address the characteristics and needs of diverse constituents when establishing and implementing culturally relevant and inclusive programs, services, policies, procedures, and practices
- provide personnel with diversity, equity, and access training and hold personnel accountable for applying the training to their work
- respond to the needs of all constituents served when establishing hours of operation and developing methods of delivering programs, services, and resources
- recognize the needs of distance and online learning students by directly providing or assisting them to gain access to comparable services and resources

DRS staff members must actively foster disability as a positive and integral part of the institution's diversity.

The values and practices of DRS should advance the philosophy that human variation is natural and vital in the development of dynamic communities; inclusion and equal participation are matters of social justice; accessible and usable design is a shared responsibility essential for equity and full participation; and disability is a sociopolitical construct that includes people with a variety of conditions who share common experiences.

Part 8. Internal and External Relations

Disability Resources and Services (DRS) must reach out to individuals, groups, communities, and organizations internal and external to the institution to

- establish, maintain, and promote understanding and effective relations with those that have a significant interest in or potential effect on the students or other constituents served by the programs and services
- garner support and resources for programs and services as defined by the mission
- collaborate in offering or improving programs and services to meet the needs of students and other constituents and to achieve program and student outcomes
- engage diverse individuals, groups, communities, and organizations to enrich the educational environment and experiences of students and other constituents
- disseminate information about the programs and services

DRS must maintain a high degree of visibility within the institution.

DRS must serve as liaison to institutional units on disability-related matters to foster the design of accessible experiences and consult on reasonable and effective accommodations.

DRS must work collaboratively with all institutional units that may provide direct services to disabled students, such as testing centers, dedicated programs, and grant programs.

DRS should partner with these offices to promote inclusive education initiatives.

DRS must maintain information about community resources that serve the disability community and make appropriate referrals.

Community resources include offices of vocational rehabilitation, veterans' centers, school districts, and transition specialists, diagnosticians, and others.

DRS must ensure that access is considered in institutional policy decisions either by participating on campus-wide committees or by ensuring that a disability perspective is represented.

In its role as institutional leader on disability-related matters, DRS must promote non-cumbersome, interactive processes for students to identify as disabled and request accommodations whether directly through DRS or to other institutional offices.

DRS must identify institutional policies, practices, technologies, and environments that negatively impact disabled persons and propose strategies for removing the resulting barriers to access.

Proactive DRS consultation with institution-wide units on development of inclusive, non-discriminatory policies, practices, and language may positively affect people who do not self-disclose disability, thereby creating a welcoming culture of inclusion.

In working with institutional partners, DRS must engage in an ongoing practice of identifying barriers in the curricular, co-curricular, physical, information, technology, and policy environments and work collaboratively to ensure equal access.

Promotional and descriptive information must be accurate and free of deception and misrepresentation.

DRS must have procedures and guidelines consistent with institutional policy for
- communicating with the media
- distributing information through print, broadcast, and online sources
- contracting with external organizations for delivery of programs and services
- cultivating, soliciting, and managing gifts
- applying to and managing funds from grants

Part 9. Financial Resources

Disability Resources and Services (DRS) must have funding to accomplish the mission and goals.

In establishing and prioritizing funding resources, DRS must conduct comprehensive analyses to determine
- unmet needs of the unit
- relevant expenditures
- external and internal resources
- impact on students and the institution

The allocation of DRS financial resources must be adequate to support the infrastructure of service delivery, ensure that accommodations determined to be reasonable are fully funded, and meet the obligations of the institution under relevant laws and regulations.

Although funding models may vary, institutions must not deny the provision of auxiliary aids and services based on funding, unless the aids and services constitute an undue financial burden.

In considering undue financial burden, an institution should look at its overall budget and not the DRS budget alone.

Funding for accommodations should come from a centralized institutional source and be administered by DRS.

DRS budget expenses must include recognition of accommodation expenses that vary with enrollment.

Administrators should recognize that accommodation costs can increase quickly and significantly and that providing accommodations is an institution-wide obligation.

DRS must regularly estimate variable accommodation expenses based on the institution's population of disabled students and advise administration of these estimates to ensure provision of accommodation to fulfill institutional obligations.

Disability Resources and Services (DRS) must use the budget as a planning tool to reflect commitment to the mission and goals of the programs and services and of the institution.

DRS must administer funds in accordance with established institutional accounting procedures.

DRS must demonstrate efficient and effective use and responsible stewardship of fiscal resources consistent with institutional protocols.

Financial reports must provide an accurate financial overview of the organization and provide clear, understandable, and timely data upon which personnel can plan and make informed decisions.

Procurement procedures must
- be consistent with institutional policies
- ensure that purchases comply with laws and codes for usability and access
- ensure that the institution receives value for the funds spent
- consider information available for comparing the ethical and environmental impact of products and services purchased

Part 10. Technology

Disability Resources and Services (DRS) must have technology to support the achievement of their mission and goals. The technology and its use must comply with institutional policies and procedures and with relevant codes and laws.

DRS must advocate for assistive and adaptive technology that ensures access.

DRS must use technologies to
- provide updated information regarding mission, location, staffing, programs, services, and official contacts to students and other constituents in accessible formats
- provide an avenue for students and other constituents to communicate sensitive information in a secure format
- enhance the delivery of programs and services for all students

DRS should be consulted to ensure that selected student learning technology will work effectively for those who utilize assistive technology.

DRS must
- back up data on a regular basis
- adhere to institutional policies regarding ethical and legal use of technology
- articulate policies and procedures for protecting the confidentiality and security of information
- implement a replacement plan and cycle for all technology with attention to sustainability
- incorporate accessibility features into technology-based programs and services

DRS must have access to personnel knowledgeable in the use and support of current and appropriate assistive technology.

DRS should secure and maintain assistive technology

resources suitable to the academic environment. Examples of assistive technology include assistive listening devices, note-taking devices, e-text readers, speech-to-text software, text-to-speech software, and screen readers.

DRS must be timely in securing or arranging for assistive technology necessary for a student's access to curricular materials.

DRS must collaborate with decision-makers to ensure that technology is accessible, usable, and compatible with assistive technologies and that institutional technology procurement practices factor in accessibility, usability, and compatibility with assistive technologies.

DRS must promote systematic review and evaluation of institutional websites, course management systems, electronic course materials, adopted software, and hardware for accessibility.

DRS must apprise institutional leadership of emerging issues and guidance from governmental agencies related to the use and adoption of technology to ensure accessibility of campus instructional and infrastructure platforms, programs, and hardware.

When providing student access to technology, DRS must
- have policies on the use of technology that are clear, easy to understand, and available to all students
- provide information or referral to support services for those needing assistance in accessing or using technology
- provide instruction or training on how to use the technology
- inform students of implications of misuse of technologies

Part 11. Facilities and Equipment

Disability Resources and Services' (DRS) facilities must be intentionally designed and located in suitable, accessible, and safe spaces that demonstrate universal design and support the program's mission and goals.

Facilities must be designed to engage various constituents and promote learning.

Personnel must have workspaces that are suitably located and accessible, well equipped, adequate in size, and designed to support their work and responsibilities.

The design of the facilities must guarantee the security and privacy of records and ensure the confidentiality of sensitive information and conversations. Personnel must be able to secure their work.

DRS must incorporate sustainable practices in use of facilities and purchase of equipment. Facilities and equipment must be evaluated on an established cycle and be in compliance with codes, laws, and accepted practices for access, health, safety, and security.

When acquiring capital equipment, DRS must take into

account expenses related to regular maintenance and life cycle costs.

DRS must include these features:
- accessible offices and program spaces
- appropriate space for alternative media production
- adequate and appropriate spaces when administering accommodated exams
- conference room and training space adequate to accommodate persons who use wheelchairs and scooters
- nearby availability of accessible rest rooms, water fountains, elevators or ramps, and corridors
- adequate accessible parking convenient to the facility
- multisensory emergency warning devices.
- access to institutional student database
- database resources for DRS record keeping and report generation

Part 12. Assessment

Disability Resources and Services (DRS) must develop assessment plans and processes.

Assessment plans must articulate an ongoing cycle of assessment activities.

DRS must
- specify programmatic goals and intended outcomes
- identify student learning and development outcomes
- employ multiple measures and methods
- develop manageable processes for gathering, interpreting, and evaluating data
- document progress toward achievement of goals and outcomes
- interpret and use assessment results to demonstrate accountability
- report aggregated results to respondent groups and stakeholders
- use assessment results to inform planning and decision-making
- assess effectiveness of implemented changes
- provide evidence of improvement of programs and services

DRS must employ ethical practices in the assessment process.

DRS must have access to adequate fiscal, human, professional development, and technological resources to develop and implement assessment plans.

A student data collection system must be used to document and analyze utilization of DRS services.

DRS data systems may be developed or purchased.

Data collected should reflect the number and demographics of students who use the office, their identified disabilities, accommodations used and requested, and other pertinent data to reflect the work of DRS. Data should be collected and reported annually with comparative analysis to earlier years' data. Retention, attrition, and graduation data of students using DRS services should be compiled and compared with institutional averages. DRS assessments should measure student satisfaction with DRS services, student perceptions of the institutional climate relative to disability, and student learning outcomes specific to DRS.

DRS should consider assessing the institutional disability climate, including data from faculty, administrators, and students with and without disabilities.

DRS should collect data on the effectiveness of its resources and services from students and institutional colleagues. Suggestions for improvement and feedback on the effectiveness of collaborations, trainings, and consultation should be collected and analyzed to support program development.

All DRS assessment findings should be used to inform resource allocations for future development.

DRS should collaborate with other departments on campus, such as institutional research, in developing evaluation reports.

General Standards revised in 2014;
DRS content developed/revised in 1986, 1997, 2003, & 2013

Education Abroad Programs and Services

CAS Contextual Statement

Students in the United States have been traveling abroad for higher education for centuries, but study abroad as we know it today officially began in the 1920's with Junior Year Abroad programs (Hoffa, 2007). More recently, there has been a sharp upward trend in U.S. students studying abroad. According to the Institute of International Education's 2013 *Open Doors* publication, during the 2011-2012 academic year a record 283,332 students from colleges and universities in the United States participated in an education abroad program for academic credit. This represents a 3.4 percent increase over the previous year; U.S. study abroad has grown 76 percent over the past ten years.

In addition to the increase in participation, there have been other recent trends. Students have been choosing destinations outside of Western Europe more frequently than before for their study abroad experiences, and they have been choosing short-term (one semester or shorter) study abroad programs much more frequently than yearlong programs. Besides the student numbers listed in *Open Doors*, U.S. students participated in experiential, volunteer, service-learning, and internship programs abroad. The visible trend toward greater interest and participation in education abroad among college students, both in the U.S. and in other countries, has been concurrent with the proliferation of education abroad opportunities. Education abroad participants may now choose from a variety of programs that differ according to program location, type, duration, academic focus, method of instruction, and coordinating entity. Given the array of programs and the increasing interest in global education among students, their parents, educational institutions, as well as in governments in countries throughout the world, the need for Education Abroad Programs and Services (EAPS) to have and meet standards cannot be overstated.

For more than 40 years, guidelines and standards for providing EAPS have been developed by various groups, such as NAFSA: Association of International Educators, the Council on International Educational Exchange, the Institute for International Education, the Institute for the International Education of Students, The Forum on Education Abroad, and accreditation bodies such as the Middle States Association. The Forum is registered as the Standards Development Organization for education abroad with the U.S. Department of Justice and Federal Trade Commission. CAS drew heavily on the publications of these groups in developing the CAS standards for EAPS. See the Resources section below for access to these organizations and some of their standards materials. They provide essential perspectives to any standards assessment of an education abroad office or organization. On college and university campuses, EAPS responsibilities may be centralized in one office or dispersed among multiple schools and departments across the institution. Education abroad directors and advisers must be familiar with a broad spectrum of campus services, processes, and systems, including but not limited to academic advising services, financial aid, registration, residence life, health services, counseling services, off-campus regulations and guidelines, disability services, risk management, legal affairs and export control, judicial affairs, career services, alumni services, and development.

In times of global and economic uncertainty, education abroad directors and advisers must pay special attention to matters of safety, security, currency and market fluctuations, and access to financial assistance. These matters are of concern to students and their families as well as to those responsible for program development and management.

Assessment is a critical aspect of ensuring the integrity of EAPS. Among other areas, EAPS should systematically assess student learning and development outcomes. Research and practice in assessment and evaluation in study abroad programs have grown considerably, and there are many resources available to EAPS providers.

Some education abroad opportunities are administered by the student's home campus, some by other institutions, and some by international educator organizations. Whenever the programs are not administered by the home campus, the EAPS is responsible for investigating and approving the programs before allowing students to participate in and receive credit through them. The following standards and guidelines are aimed at home-country campus-based offices, although non-campus based EAPS organizations and overseas institutions will find many of the sections helpful. The provision of Education Abroad Programs and Services has become a global enterprise.

References, Readings, and Resources

Alliance for International Educational and Cultural Exchange: http://www.alliance-exchange.org/

American Council on Education. (n.d.). *Assessing international learning.* http://www.acenet.edu/news-room/Pages/ACEFIPSE-Project-on-Assessing-International-Learning.aspx

Association for Studies in International Education: http://www.asie.org/index.htm

Bolen, M., Ed. (2007) *A guide to outcomes assessment in study abroad.* Carlisle, PA: Forum on Education Abroad.

Brockington, J. L., Hoffa W. W., and Martin, P.C. (2005). *NAFSA's guide to education abroad for advisers and administrators (3rd ed.). Washington, DC: NAFSA.*

Center for Global Education: http://globaled.us/index.asp

Forum on Education Abroad: http://www.forumea.org/

Forum on Education Abroad: *Standards of good practice for education abroad,* 4th edition, 2011. Available at http://www.forumea.org/resources/standards-of-good-practice

Frontiers, The Interdisciplinary Journal of Study Abroad: http://www.frontiersjournal.com/

Hoffa, W. W. (2007). A history of U.S. study abroad: Beginnings to 1965. A Special Publication of *Frontiers: The Interdisciplinary Journal of Study Abroad* and *The Forum on Education Abroad.* Lancaster, PA.

IES Abroad Model Assessment Program (MAP): http://www.
  iesabroad.org/study-abroad/advisors-faculty/ies-abroad-map/
  map-for-study-abroad

Institute of International Education, http://www.iienetwork.org/

Institute of International Education. *Open Doors (published annually)*
  available at http://www.iie.org/Research-and-Publications/
  Open-Doors

NAFSA: Association of International Educators: http://www.nafsa.
  org/

NAFSA's Statement of Ethical Principles: http://www.nafsa.org/
  Learn_About_NAFSA/Governance_Documents/Ethics_And_
  Principles/Statement_Of_Ethics/NAFSA_s_Statement_of_
  Ethical_Principles/

NAFSA's Curriculum integration of education abroad
  (2012). http://www.nafsa.org/interactive/core/orders/product.
  aspx?catid=2&prodid=403

Spencer, S. E., & Tuma, K. (Eds.). (2007). *The guide to successful
  short-term programs abroad (2ⁿᵈ ed.).* Washington, DC: NAFSA:
  Association of International Educators.

*Strengthening study abroad: Recommendations for effective
  institutional management.* (2008). Washington, DC: NAFSA:
  Association of International Educators. Available at http://www.
  nafsa.org/imsa

Contextual Statement Contributors

Current Edition:
Lorie Johns Páulez, Georgia Institute of Technology
Adriane van Gils-Pierce, Clark University

Previous Editions:
Emily Gorlewski, Western Illinois University
Susan Komives, University of Maryland, ACPA
Sandy Tennies, NAFSA
Zaneeta Daver, University of Maryland, ACPA

Education Abroad Programs and Services
CAS Standards and Guidelines

Part 1. Mission

Education Abroad Programs and Services (EAPS) facilitate and oversee student participation in educational experiences that occur in countries outside the institution's home country.

EAPS must develop, disseminate, implement, and regularly review their missions, which must be consistent with the mission of the institution and with applicable professional standards. The mission must be appropriate for the institution's students and other constituents. Mission statements must reference student learning and development.

The EAPS overall mission and goals should address the following components:
- program constituents
- program values
- desired learning outcomes
- support for students prior to, during, and after their education abroad experiences
- collaboration with internal and external stakeholders
- support for the institution's mission and strategic plan

Part 2. Program

To achieve their mission, Education Abroad Programs and Services (EAPS) must contribute to
- students' formal education, which includes both the curriculum and the co-curriculum
- student progression and timely completion of educational goals
- preparation of students for their careers, citizenship, and lives
- student learning and development

To contribute to student learning and development, EAPS must
- identify relevant and desirable student learning and development outcomes
- articulate how the student learning and development outcomes align with the six CAS student learning and development domains and related dimensions
- assess relevant and desirable student learning and development
- provide evidence of impact on outcomes
- articulate contributions to or support of student learning and development in the domains not specifically assessed
- use evidence gathered to create strategies for improvement of programs and services

STUDENT LEARNING AND DEVELOPMENT
DOMAINS AND DIMENSIONS

Domain: knowledge acquisition, integration, construction, and application
- Dimensions: understanding knowledge from a range of disciplines; connecting knowledge to other knowledge, ideas, and experiences; constructing knowledge; and relating knowledge to daily life

Domain: cognitive complexity
- Dimensions: critical thinking, reflective thinking, effective reasoning, and creativity

Domain: intrapersonal development
- Dimensions: realistic self-appraisal, self-understanding, and self-respect; identity development; commitment to ethics and integrity; and spiritual awareness

Domain: interpersonal competence
- Dimensions: meaningful relationships, interdependence, collaboration, and effective leadership

Domain: humanitarianism and civic engagement
- Dimensions: understanding and appreciation of cultural and human differences, social responsibility, global perspective, and sense of civic responsibility

Domain: practical competence
- Dimensions: pursuing goals, communicating effectively, technical competence, managing personal affairs, managing career development, demonstrating professionalism, maintaining health and wellness, and living a purposeful and satisfying life

[LD Outcomes: See *The Council for the Advancement of Standards Learning and Development Outcomes* statement for examples of outcomes related to these domains and dimensions.]

EAPS must be
- intentionally designed
- guided by theories and knowledge of learning and development
- integrated into the life of the institution
- reflective of developmental and demographic profiles of the student population
- responsive to needs of individuals, populations with distinct needs, and relevant constituencies
- delivered using multiple formats, strategies, and contexts
- designed to provide universal access

EAPS must collaborate with colleagues and departments across the institution to promote student learning and development, persistence, and success.

The EAPS should facilitate student participation in a variety of types of education abroad programs such as

- programs where the student mobility is from the home institution (the school at which the student is seeking the degree) to a host institution (the school outside the institution's home country at which the student receives instruction and services while abroad)
- reciprocal institutional exchanges where students from the home institution trade places with students from the host institution
- faculty-led study abroad programs
- research abroad programs for credit
- international service learning programs for credit
- opportunities to participate in work, internship or volunteer experiences abroad
- short-term, semester-long, and academic-year-long programs
- consortia programs that involve two or more institutions
- programs administered outside the institution by international education organizations

To fulfill its mission and goals effectively, EAPS must include the following elements:

- **Clear and consistent academic policies and guidelines for home and host institutions**

  Admissions policies and procedures should be clearly articulated to students. Academic policies and procedures for awarding credit and understanding course grade equivalencies should also be clearly articulated to students before they depart for an education abroad program. Guidance with course selection should be offered regarding course transferability and equivalency. Coursework should be appropriately challenging; course requirements and methods of evaluating performance should be clearly stated; feedback should be provided to students periodically, in keeping with host country norms. Opportunities should be provided that allow the learning that occurs as a result of the EAPS experience to be integrated into subsequent educational experiences.

- **Curricular and co-curricular opportunities that are related to the mission and purpose of the specific education abroad program**

  The curricular and co-curricular components of each education abroad opportunity should make effective use of the location and resources of the host country; students should be encouraged to engage with the host culture and to reflect on the differences and similarities between the intellectual, political, cultural, spiritual, and social institutions of the home and host countries. Students' curricular and co-curricular experiences should contribute to their appreciation and respect for cultural differences in general. Students should be encouraged to immerse themselves in the host culture, interact with host nationals, practice and improve their language and intercultural communication abilities, and reflect on their value systems in the context of living in another culture.

  EAPS should provide opportunities for internships, service-learning, and other field study experiences that are related to the mission and purpose of the specific education abroad program. EAPS should incorporate opportunities to synthesize the learning that occurs as a result of these out-of-classroom experiences into future educational and life experiences.

  Where field opportunities exist, they must be appropriately supervised and evaluated and must relate to the mission of the EAPS and institution. Awarding of credit for internships or field studies must be consistent with the policies of the home institution.

- **Pre-departure advising and orientation programs**

  Pre-departure advising and orientation sessions must inform students about program requirements, academic credit and transfer policies, visa and passport requirements, and housing and travel arrangements, as well as financial, health, liability, insurance, safety, and security information. International students at the home institution must be advised to determine their re-entry status. Students must be asked directly and encouraged strongly to share information about any on-going health concerns before departing for their program locations. Home and host institution codes of conduct that apply to students while abroad must be clearly articulated; consequences of not following these codes of conduct must be clearly defined and communicated. Students must be provided with an introduction to intercultural communication and preparation for the cultural transition, including resources on culture shock and cultural adjustment. Orientation programs must identify resources for students so that they may educate themselves about the culture, customs, and laws of the host countries. EAPS must provide students with the contact the information of their home country's embassy or consulate at their host site.

  Students should be advised to utilize the appropriate campus or community resources (e.g., travel medicine, financial aid, immigration status) before departure.

- Information about student financial assistance

- On-going advising and support services for students while they are abroad

  On-going advising and support services throughout

the duration of the education abroad program should be provided either through the home or host institution.

- Re-entry support and orientation programs for returning students

  Upon return, re-entry programs and services must support re-acculturation to the home country, relationships, and the institution.

- Returning students should be encouraged to integrate their experience abroad into their continued learning, including sharing their stories and experiences with other students, faculty members, and staff members.

- Returning students should be offered re-entry programming including academic and emotional support, debriefs, and opportunities to stay connected with the international community on campus.

- Returning students should be offered workshops or other forms of assistance in capturing their education abroad experiences on their resumes and in articulating transferable skills during interviews with potential employers.

- Returning students should be offered opportunities to remain involved with the Education Abroad office by volunteering to assist new students going abroad, assisting with Education Abroad fairs, and with pre-departure orientations.

- Where possible, participation in work study or internship opportunities should be made available in the Education Abroad office to returning students.

Part 3. Organization and Leadership

To achieve program and student learning and development outcomes, Education Abroad Programs and Services (EAPS) must be purposefully structured for effectiveness. EAPS must have clearly stated and current

- goals and outcomes
- policies and procedures
- responsibilities and performance expectations for personnel
- organizational charts demonstrating clear channels of authority

Leaders must model ethical behavior and institutional citizenship.

Leaders with organizational authority for EAPS must provide strategic planning, management and supervision, and program advancement.

Strategic Planning
- articulate a vision and mission that drive short- and long-term planning
- set goals and objectives based on the needs of the populations served, intended student learning and

development outcomes, and program outcomes
- facilitate continuous development, implementation, and assessment of program effectiveness and goal attainment congruent with institutional mission and strategic plans
- promote environments that provide opportunities for student learning, development, and engagement
- develop, adapt, and improve programs and services in response to the changing needs of populations served and evolving institutional priorities
- include diverse perspectives to inform decision making

Management and Supervision
- plan, allocate, and monitor the use of fiscal, physical, human, intellectual, and technological resources
- manage human resource processes including recruitment, selection, professional development, supervision, performance planning, succession planning, evaluation, recognition, and reward
- influence others to contribute to the effectiveness and success of the unit
- empower professional, support, and student personnel to become effective leaders
- encourage and support collaboration with colleagues and departments across the institution
- encourage and support scholarly contributions to the profession
- identify and address individual, organizational, and environmental conditions that foster or inhibit mission achievement
- use current and valid evidence to inform decisions
- incorporate sustainability practices in the management and design of programs, services, and facilities
- understand appropriate technologies and integrate them into programs and services
- be knowledgeable about codes and laws relevant to programs and services and ensure that programs and services meet those requirements
- assess and take action to mitigate potential risks

Program Advancement
- advocate for and actively promote the mission and goals of the programs and services
- inform stakeholders about issues affecting practice
- facilitate processes to reach consensus where wide support is needed
- advocate for representation in strategic planning initiatives at divisional and institutional levels

EAPS leaders should establish working relationships with institutional agents, such as provosts, academic deans, department chairs, risk managers, academic advisors, scholarship/fellowship advisors, financial aid officers, registrar, offices that work with underrepresented populations, career services, and student affairs professionals on the home campus to promote programs and engender support.

To fulfill its mission and goals effectively, EAPS must
- provide leadership for integrating education abroad into the wider administrative and academic structure of the institution
- efficiently and effectively administer the programs they coordinate
- advise students appropriately, based on their interests, needs, financial ability, language proficiency, and academic background, as they choose an education abroad program

EAPS should be coordinated across the institution, with common guidelines for policies and procedures

EAPS should be supported philosophically and financially by institutional leadership.

EAPS should ensure that their work is in direct support of the institution's mission and strategic plan.

Information about education abroad opportunities and related institutional policies must be easily available.

Part 4. Human Resources

Education Abroad Programs and Services (EAPS) must be staffed adequately by individuals qualified to accomplish mission and goals.

EAPS must have access to technical and support personnel adequate to accomplish their mission.

Within institutional guidelines, EAPS must
- establish procedures for personnel recruitment and selection, training, performance planning, and evaluation
- set expectations for supervision and performance
- provide personnel access to continuing and advanced education and appropriate professional development opportunities to improve their competence, skills, and leadership capacity
- consider work/life options available to personnel (e.g., compressed work schedules, flextime, job sharing, remote work, or telework) to promote recruitment and retention of personnel

Administrators of EAPS must
- ensure that all personnel have updated position descriptions
- implement recruitment and selection/hiring strategies that produce a workforce inclusive of under-represented populations
- develop promotion practices that are fair, inclusive, proactive, and non-discriminatory

Personnel responsible for delivery of programs and services must have written performance goals, objectives, and outcomes for each year's performance cycle to be used to plan, review, and evaluate work and performance. The performance plan must be updated regularly to reflect changes during the performance cycle.

Results of individual personnel evaluations must be used to recognize personnel performance, address performance issues, implement individual and/or collective personnel development and training programs, and inform the assessment of programs and services.

EAPS personnel, when hired and throughout their employment, must receive appropriate and thorough training.

EAPS personnel, including student employees and volunteers, must have access to resources or receive specific training on
- institutional policies pertaining to functions or activities they support
- privacy and confidentiality policies
- laws regarding access to student records
- policies and procedures for dealing with sensitive institutional information
- policies and procedures related to technology used to store or access student records and institutional data
- how and when to refer those in need of additional assistance to qualified personnel and have access to a supervisor for assistance in making these judgments
- systems and technologies necessary to perform their assigned responsibilities
- ethical and legal uses of technology

EAPS personnel must engage in continuing professional development activities to keep abreast of the research, theories, legislation, policies, and developments that affect their programs and services.

Administrators of EAPS must ensure that personnel are knowledgeable about and trained in safety, emergency procedures, and crisis prevention and response. Risk management efforts must address identification of threatening conduct or behavior and must incorporate a system for responding to and reporting such behaviors.

EAPS personnel must be knowledgeable of and trained in safety and emergency procedures for securing and vacating facilities.

PROFESSIONAL PERSONNEL

Professional personnel either must hold an earned graduate or professional degree in a field relevant to their position or must possess an appropriate combination of educational credentials and related work experience.

EAPS staff should have experience living or studying abroad. Entry into the profession by educators from a variety of academic backgrounds is encouraged.

EAPS professional staff members must be knowledgeable and competent in the following areas:
- cultural competence
- experiential education
- legal affairs and risk management
- intercultural communication
- culture shock, reverse culture shock, and cultural

adjustment
- student advising and counseling
- emergency and crisis management
- budgetary and financial management
- collaboration with academic stakeholders at home and at host institutions
- organizational policies (e.g., admissions, credit transfer, financial aid, travel regulations, immigration policies, insurance)
- pre-departure and re-entry issues
- travel and living abroad
- higher education administration
- technology (e.g., application and data management systems, virtual communication)
- country specific health, safety, and security concerns

EAPS professional staff members should be knowledgeable and competent in such areas as
- foreign language(s)
- countries, cultures, and regions where their students most frequently study (e.g. culture, customs, language, art, geography, political system, economic system, history, traditions, values, laws)
- other countries' educational systems
- human development
- marketing and promoting education abroad programs
- Unites States export control, or equivalent
- program development
- academic advising

INTERNS OR GRADUATE ASSISTANTS

Degree- or credential-seeking interns or graduate assistants must be qualified by enrollment in an appropriate field of study and relevant experience. These students must be trained and supervised by professional personnel who possess applicable educational credentials and work experience and have supervisory experience. Supervisors must be cognizant of the dual roles interns and graduate assistants have as both student and employee.

Supervisors must
- adhere to parameters of students' job descriptions
- articulate intended learning outcomes in student job descriptions
- adhere to agreed-upon work hours and schedules
- offer flexible scheduling when circumstances necessitate

Supervisors and students must both agree to suitable compensation if circumstances necessitate additional hours.

STUDENT EMPLOYEES AND VOLUNTEERS

Student employees and volunteers must be carefully selected, trained, supervised, and evaluated. Students must have access to a supervisor. Student employees and volunteers must be provided clear job descriptions, pre-service training based on assessed needs, and continuing development.

Part 5. Ethics

Education Abroad Programs and Services (EAPS) must
- review applicable professional ethical standards and must adopt or develop and implement appropriate statements of ethical practice
- publish and adhere to statements of ethical practice and ensure their periodic review
- orient new personnel to relevant ethical standards and statements of ethical practice and related institutional policies

Statements of ethical standards must
- specify that EAPS personnel respect privacy and maintain confidentiality in communications and records as delineated by privacy laws
- specify limits on disclosure of information contained in students' records as well as requirements to disclose to appropriate authorities
- address conflicts of interest, or appearance thereof, by personnel in the performance of their work
- reflect the responsibility of personnel to be fair, objective, and impartial in their interactions with others
- reference management of institutional funds
- reference appropriate behavior regarding research and assessment with human participants, confidentiality of research and assessment data, and students' rights and responsibilities
- include the expectation that personnel confront and hold accountable other personnel who exhibit unethical behavior
- address issues surrounding scholarly integrity

EAPS home and host staff members must have ethical guidelines in place for advising and interacting with students and their families.

EAPS personnel must
- employ ethical decision making in the performance of their duties
- inform users of programs and services of ethical obligations and limitations emanating from codes and laws or from licensure requirements
- recognize and avoid conflicts of interest that could adversely influence their judgment or objectivity and, when unavoidable, recuse themselves from the situation
- perform their duties within the scope of their position, training, expertise, and competence
- make referrals when issues presented exceed the scope of the position

EAPS home and host staff members must have ethical and unbiased procedures in place for terminating an individual's participation.

Termination procedures should be made public and provided to participants prior to their participation in an education abroad program. Termination procedures should include refund and cancellation policies and procedures.

Part 6. Law, Policy, and Governance

Education Abroad Programs and Services (EAPS) must be in compliance with laws, regulations, and policies that relate to their respective responsibilities and that pose legal obligations, limitations, risks, and liabilities for the institution as a whole. Examples include constitutional, statutory, regulatory, and case law; relevant law and orders emanating from codes and laws; and the institution's policies.

EAPS staff members must know where to refer program participants for information on host country laws and host institution policies and procedures.

EAPS staff members must make participants aware of home institution consequences of breaking these laws, policies, and procedures.

EAPS must have access to legal advice needed for personnel to carry out their assigned responsibilities.

EAPS must inform personnel, appropriate officials, and users of programs and services about existing and changing legal obligations, risks and liabilities, and limitations.

EAPS must inform personnel about professional liability insurance options and refer them to external sources if the institution does not provide coverage.

EAPS must have written policies and procedures on operations, transactions, or tasks that have legal implications.

EAPS must regularly review policies. The revision and creation of policies must be informed by best practices, available evidence, and policy issues in higher education.

EAPS must have procedures and guidelines consistent with institutional policy for responding to threats, emergencies, and crisis situations. Systems and procedures must be in place to disseminate timely and accurate information to students, other members of the institutional community, and appropriate external organizations during emergency situations.

EAPS staff members must develop collaborative relationships with relevant home and host institutional departments (e.g., general counsel, student conduct programs) in order to assess and minimize risk and develop appropriate resources for students.

EAPS must work with risk management personnel to ensure that proper insurance coverage is secured by all program participants, faculty, and staff.

Faculty, staff and students must attend orientations/trainings before departure for an overseas program sponsored by the [SB3] institution

The home institution should obtain the host institution's crisis management plan.

Insurance should include emergency medical, medical evacuation, repatriation of remains, and security evacuation coverage.

Personnel must neither participate in nor condone any form of harassment or activity that demeans persons or creates an intimidating, hostile, or offensive environment.

EAPS must purchase or obtain permission to use copyrighted materials and instruments. References to copyrighted materials and instruments must include appropriate citations.

EAPS must inform personnel about internal and external governance organizations that affect programs and services.

EAPS staff members must ensure that expectations for participant conduct—including but not limited to drug and alcohol abuse, sexual assault and harassment, academic integrity, and social conduct—are clearly articulated in program materials and in pre-departure and on-site orientations.

Part 7. Diversity, Equity, and Access

Within the context of each institution's mission and in accordance with institutional policies and applicable codes and laws, Education Abroad Programs and Services (EAPS) must create and maintain educational and work environments that are welcoming, accessible, inclusive, equitable, and free from harassment.

EAPS must not discriminate on the basis of disability; age; race; cultural identity; ethnicity; nationality; family educational history (e.g., first generation to attend college); political affiliation; religious affiliation; sex; sexual orientation; gender identity and expression; marital, social, economic, or veteran status; or any other basis included in institutional policies and codes and laws.

EAPS must
- advocate for sensitivity to multicultural and social justice concerns by the institution and its personnel
- ensure physical, program, and resource access for all constituents
- modify or remove policies, practices, systems, technologies, facilities, and structures that create barriers or produce inequities
- ensure that when facilities and structures cannot be modified, they do not impede access to programs, services and resources
- establish goals for diversity, equity, and access
- foster communication and practices that enhance understanding of identity, culture, self-expression, and heritage
- promote respect for commonalities and differences among people within their historical and cultural contexts
- address the characteristics and needs of diverse constituents when establishing and implementing culturally relevant and inclusive programs,

- services, policies, procedures, and practices
- provide personnel with diversity, equity, and access training and hold personnel accountable for applying the training to their work
- respond to the needs of all constituents served when establishing hours of operation and developing methods of delivering programs, services, and resources
- recognize the needs of distance and online learning students by directly providing or assisting them to gain access to comparable services and resources

EAPS should encourage underrepresented students (e.g., gender, ethnicity, age, disability, marital status, socioeconomic status, academic major, religious affiliation, sexual orientation) to apply and participate in education abroad programs.

EAPS should collaborate with appropriate offices to attract and serve underrepresented students on education abroad programs.

EAPS must intentionally foster students' understanding of cross-cultural differences and encourage participants to reflect on these differences at home, in the host country and abroad.

EAPS staff members must actively work with all interested participants to select an education abroad program suitable to their needs, skills, and eligibility.

Part 8. Internal and External Relations

Education Abroad Programs and Services (EAPS) must reach out to individuals, groups, communities, and organizations internal and external to the institution to

- establish, maintain, and promote understanding and effective relations with those that have a significant interest in or potential effect on the students or other constituents served by the programs and services
- garner support and resources for programs and services as defined by the mission
- collaborate in offering or improving programs and services to meet the needs of students and other constituents and to achieve program and student outcomes
- engage diverse individuals, groups, communities, and organizations to enrich the educational environment and experiences of students and other constituents
- disseminate information about the programs and services

Promotional and descriptive information must be accurate and free of deception and misrepresentation.

EAPS must have procedures and guidelines consistent with institutional policy for

- communicating with the media
- distributing information through print, broadcast, and online sources
- contracting with external organizations for

delivery of programs and services
- cultivating, soliciting, and managing gifts
- applying to and managing funds from grants

EAPS staff members should collaborate with

- departments on the home campus (i.e., academic departments and programs, registrar, academic affairs, financial aid, financial services, student affairs, international student and scholar services, admissions, career advising, clinical health services, counseling services, institutional advancement, disability services, multicultural centers, residential life)
- consulates of host countries
- home country embassies and consulates abroad
- faculty members at home and abroad who teach or do research in fields related to home institution education abroad opportunities
- administrative staff at the host institution responsible for students from abroad
- external program providers

EAPS staff members should collaborate with third-party program providers as appropriate to sustain existing programs and establish new opportunities to increase the diversity of options for students.

EAPS should encourage interested individuals (faculty members or other campus personnel) to become involved in education abroad by suggesting possible opportunities, proposing specific programs, or presenting and encouraging discussions about education abroad.

Agreements between EAPS and other institutions to promote education abroad, whether exchange agreements or co-sponsorship of programs, should be supportive of the institution's overall mission and collaborative with regard to academic objectives and standards.

EAPS should ensure that faculty members, administrators, staff members, and students are aware of education abroad opportunities.

EAPS should work to ensure that programs are accurately described in advisory and promotional materials and that their purposes, financial implications, and educational objectives are clearly stated.

Part 9. Financial Resources

Education Abroad Programs and Services (EAPS) must have funding to accomplish the mission and goals.

In establishing and prioritizing funding resources, EAPS must conduct comprehensive analyses to determine

- unmet needs of the unit
- relevant expenditures
- external and internal resources
- impact on students and the institution

EAPS must use the budget as a planning tool to reflect

commitment to the mission and goals of the programs and services and of the institution.

EAPS must administer funds in accordance with established institutional accounting procedures.

EAPS must demonstrate efficient and effective use and responsible stewardship of fiscal resources consistent with institutional protocols.

Financial reports must provide an accurate financial overview of the organization and provide clear, understandable, and timely data upon which personnel can plan and make informed decisions.

Procurement procedures must
- be consistent with institutional policies
- ensure that purchases comply with laws and codes for usability and access
- ensure that the institution receives value for the funds spent
- consider information available for comparing the ethical and environmental impact of products and services purchased

EAPS should offer education abroad programs to students at affordable costs.

EAPS should consider grant writing and fundraising efforts to increase their financial resources, including funding for need-based student scholarships.

EAPS should encourage their institution to create institutional education abroad scholarships and grants, both need and merit-based.

EAPS should work directly with development officers and alumni affairs to target alumni groups, class reunion committees and other groups as appropriate to secure additional funding.

Part 10. Technology

Education Abroad Programs and Services (EAPS) must have technology to support the achievement of their mission and goals. The technology and its use must comply with institutional policies and procedures and with relevant codes and laws.

EAPS must use technologies to
- provide updated information regarding mission, location, staffing, programs, services, and official contacts to students and other constituents in accessible formats
- provide an avenue for students and other constituents to communicate sensitive information in a secure format
- enhance the delivery of programs and services for all students

EAPS must
- back up data on a regular basis
- adhere to institutional policies regarding ethical and legal use of technology

- articulate policies and procedures for protecting the confidentiality and security of information
- implement a replacement plan and cycle for all technology with attention to sustainability
- incorporate accessibility features into technology-based programs and services

When providing student access to technology, EAPS must
- have policies on the use of technology that are clear, easy to understand, and available to all students
- provide information or referral to support services for those needing assistance in accessing or using technology
- provide instruction or training on how to use the technology
- inform students of implications of misuse of technologies

EAPS should prepare students for differences in standards of technology and set expectations for available resources before departure.

EAPS should inform students, faculty, and staff of export control regulations and of research security procedures while abroad.

Part 11. Facilities and Equipment

Education Abroad Programs and Services' (EAPS) facilities must be intentionally designed and located in suitable, accessible, and safe spaces that demonstrate universal design and support the program's mission and goals.

Facilities must be designed to engage various constituents and promote learning.

Personnel must have workspaces that are suitably located and accessible, well equipped, adequate in size, and designed to support their work and responsibilities.

The design of the facilities must guarantee the security and privacy of records and ensure the confidentiality of sensitive information and conversations. Personnel must be able to secure their work.

EAPS must incorporate sustainable practices in use of facilities and purchase of equipment. Facilities and equipment must be evaluated on an established cycle and be in compliance with codes, laws, and accepted practices for access, health, safety and security.

When acquiring capital equipment, EAPS must take into account expenses related to regular maintenance and life cycle costs.

Home and host institutions must provide office facilities to accommodate EAPS goals. Home and host campus facilities must allow for privacy during student advising.

Host institutions must provide student facilities that are safe and secure, and meet student needs.

Residential and non-residential student facilities should be located conveniently at host institutions.

Host institutions should provide equivalent services at similar costs for visiting education abroad students.

Part 12. Assessment

Education Abroad Programs and Services (EAPS) must develop assessment plans and processes.

Assessment plans must articulate an ongoing cycle of assessment activities.

EAPS must
- **specify programmatic goals and intended outcomes**
- **identify student learning and development outcomes**
- **employ multiple measures and methods**
- **develop manageable processes for gathering, interpreting, and evaluating data**
- **document progress toward achievement of goals and outcomes**
- **interpret and use assessment results to demonstrate accountability**
- **report aggregated results to respondent groups and stakeholders**
- **use assessment results to inform planning and decision-making**
- **assess effectiveness of implemented changes**
- **provide evidence of improvement of programs and services**

EAPS must employ ethical practices in the assessment process.

EAPS must have access to adequate fiscal, human, professional development, and technological resources to develop and implement assessment plans.

General Standards revised in 2014;
EAPS content developed/revised in 2005 and 2014

Financial Aid Programs
CAS Contextual Statement

According to National Association of Student Financial Aid Administrator's (NASFAA) *2014 National Student Aid Profile: Overview of 2014 Federal Programs*, more and more Americans have relied on federal student financial assistance programs to assist with college costs. The number of students applying for federal financial assistance rose from 19.4 million in 2007-08 to nearly 31.4 million in 2011-12, a 62 percent increase over five years. Among the multitude of student financial aid sources, the U.S. Federal government provided the majority of student aid, 71 percent (or $238.5 billion dollars), in 2012-13. The Pell Grant program, which provides grants to low-income undergraduates with the greatest demonstrated financial need, provided approximately $35 billion to approximately 9.4 million undergraduate students in 2011-12. *Trends in Student Aid 2014*, from The College Board, also indicated in 2013-14, 58 percent of U.S. federal education loans accounted for all federal student aid and 43 percent of aid from all sources— $62,925 million. Along with federal student aid, other sources of aid were state governments; college and universities; private scholarships and employer programs; and other nonfederal agencies, such as state- or institution-sponsored and private-education loans. The mission of the financial aid office focuses on service to students and stewardship of funds. Practically speaking, the financial aid office assumes primary responsibility on behalf of the institution for compliance with government requirements for financial aid distribution.

An effective and comprehensive aid program must be supported by leaders at the institution who understand the increasing administrative and operational responsibilities, obligations, and the potential liabilities that accompany participation in federal aid programs. It also requires that leaders be aware of the challenges and conflicts imposed on the administration of aid and the delivery of quality services to their students. Leaders can take several steps to ensure that the financial aid program advances the goals of the institution without compromising service quality or program integrity. The consistency between institutional goals and those of the aid program can be evaluated by examining the level of commitment of internal resources, the composition of aid packages, the levels of unmet need, and the extent of commitment to need-based aid.

The establishment and support of goals and measures that ensure high-quality financial aid operations should be a high priority for all institutions. Of equal importance is the institution's responsibility for educating the community about its goals and mission and the role of financial aid in defining and meeting them. Communicating the importance of financial aid to both internal and external constituencies is critical. Presidents, trustees, and others must understand and support the policies of their financial aid programs and serve as effective advocates at the institutional and governmental levels. These advocacy efforts should

- provide opportunities for representatives from all academic and administrative areas of the institution to discuss and help formulate institutional goals;
- coordinate with the financial aid office to develop mission statements and strategic goals that consider its relationship with other offices;
- present the philosophy, purpose, goals and strategies, and the principle governing financial aid awards and disseminate these statements to demonstrate the leadership's support of them and their complementary relationship to broader objectives of the institution;
- provide forums to make known the impact of pending federal and state developments on the institution and the financial aid office; and
- communicate widely the criteria by which financial aid policies are defined and evaluated and create opportunities to highlight program successes and the positive impact they have on students and the broader community.

Institutions committed to these strategies draw upon tools provided by the government, the National Association of Student Financial Aid Administrators (NASFAA), and other non-governmental entities. When institutions encounter conflicting information between the CAS Financial Aid Programs Standards and Guidelines and NASFAA Statement of Ethical Principles, they should defer to the NASFAA Statement of Ethical Principles and Code of Conduct for guidance.

References, Readings, and Resources

Bosshardt, D. I., Lichtenstein, L., Palumbo, G., & Zaporowski, M. P. (2010). Optimization techniques for college financial aid managers. *Journal of Student Financial Aid*, 40(3). Available at: http://publications.nasfaa.org/jsfa/vol40/iss3/3

Conard, L., Holman, S. B., Levy, D., Satterfield, B., & Turner, L. (Eds.) (2012). *You're the director: A guide to leadership in student financial aid.* Washington, DC: National Association of Student Financial Aid.

Davidson, J. C. (2013). Increasing FAFSA completion rates: Research, policies and practices. *Journal of Student Financial Aid*, 43(1). Available at: http://publications.nasfaa.org/jsfa/vol43/iss1/4

MacCallum, M. (2008). Effect of financial aid processing policies on student enrollment, retention and success. *Journal of Student Financial Aid*, 37(2). Available at: http://publications.nasfaa.org/jsfa/vol37/iss2/2

National Association of Student Financial Aid Administrators (NASFAA). (2014). *Statement of ethical principles and code of conduct for financial aid professionals.* Retrieved from: http://www.nasfaa.org/mkt/about/Statement_of_Ethical_Principles.aspx

National Association of Student Financial Aid Administrators (NASFAA). (2014). *National student aid profile: Overview of 2014 federal programs.* Retrieved from: http://www.nasfaa.org/national-profile/

National Association of Student Financial Aid Administrators (NASFAA). (2013). *Preliminary report of the NASFAA reauthorization task force to the membership.* Retrieved from: http://www.nasfaa.org/reauth/

National Association of Student Financial Aid Administrators (NASFAA). (2013). *Reimagining financial aid to improve student access and outcomes.* Retrieved from: http://www.nasfaa.org/radd/

Perna, L. W. (2005). A gap in the literature: The influence of the design, operations, and marketing of student aid programs on college-going plans and behaviors. *Journal of Student Financial Aid 35*(1). Available at: http://publications.nasfaa.org/jsfa/vol35/iss1/1

Spaulding, R. & Olswang, S. (2005) "Maximizing Enrollment Yield through Financial Aid Packaging Policies," *Journal of Student Financial Aid, 35*(1). Available at: http://publications.nasfaa.org/jsfa/vol35/iss1/3

Wolanin, T. R. (2005). Students with disabilities: Financial aid policy issues. *Journal of Student Financial Aid, 35*(1). Available at: http://publications.nasfaa.org/jsfa/vol35/iss1/2

Woolf, N. & Martinez, M. (2013). A financial aid competency model for professional development. *Journal of Student Financial Aid, 43*(2). Available at: http://publications.nasfaa.org/jsfa/vol43/iss2/3

Contextual Statement Contributors:

Current Edition:
Lisa Blazer, University of Texas at San Antonio
Megan McClean, formerly with NASFAA
Charlotte Etier, NASFAA

Previous Editions:
Jan Arminio, Shippensburg University, NACA
Joan H. Crissman, NASFAA
A. Dallas Martin, Jr., NASFAA

Financial Aid Programs
CAS Standards and Guidelines

Part 1. Mission

The mission of Financial Aid Programs (FAP) is to develop, review, and disseminate financial resources and information to students to assist them in achieving their educational goals from pre-enrollment through graduation.

FAP must develop, disseminate, implement, and regularly review their missions, which must be consistent with the mission of the institution and with applicable professional standards. The mission must be appropriate for the institution's students and other constituents. Mission statements must reference student learning and development.

FAP goals must be consistent with the mission, goals, policies, procedures, and characteristics of the institution and compatible with the ability of the institution to provide adequate resources to meet the needs and educational goals of students.

Institutional goals for financial aid must be developed and reviewed regularly. Goals must comply with laws, regulations, policies, and other providers of funding.

Such goals must be consistent with statements of good practices articulated by relevant and appropriate professional associations such as the National Association of Student Financial Aid Administrators and the Canadian Association of Student Financial Aid Administrators.

Part 2. Program

To achieve their mission, Financial Aid Programs (FAP) must contribute to
- students' formal education, which includes both the curriculum and the co-curriculum
- student progression and timely completion of educational goals
- preparation of students for their careers, citizenship, and lives
- student learning and development

To contribute to student learning and development, FAP must
- identify relevant and desirable student learning and development outcomes
- articulate how the student learning and development outcomes align with the six CAS student learning and development domains and related dimensions
- assess relevant and desirable student learning and development
- provide evidence of impact on outcomes
- articulate contributions to or support of student learning and development in the domains not specifically assessed

- use evidence gathered to create strategies for improvement of programs and services

STUDENT LEARNING AND DEVELOPMENT DOMAINS AND DIMENSIONS

Domain: knowledge acquisition, integration, construction, and application
- Dimensions: understanding knowledge from a range of disciplines; connecting knowledge to other knowledge, ideas, and experiences; constructing knowledge; and relating knowledge to daily life

Domain: cognitive complexity
- Dimensions: critical thinking, reflective thinking, effective reasoning, and creativity

Domain: intrapersonal development
- Dimensions: realistic self-appraisal, self-understanding, and self-respect; identity development; commitment to ethics and integrity; and spiritual awareness

Domain: interpersonal competence
- Dimensions: meaningful relationships, interdependence, collaboration, and effective leadership

Domain: humanitarianism and civic engagement
- Dimensions: understanding and appreciation of cultural and human differences, social responsibility, global perspective, and sense of civic responsibility

Domain: practical competence
- Dimensions: pursuing goals, communicating effectively, technical competence, managing personal affairs, managing career development, demonstrating professionalism, maintaining health and wellness, and living a purposeful and satisfying life

[LD Outcomes: See *The Council for the Advancement of Standards Learning and Development Outcomes* statement for examples of outcomes related to these domains and dimensions.]

FAP must be
- intentionally designed
- guided by theories and knowledge of learning and development
- integrated into the life of the institution
- reflective of developmental and demographic profiles of the student population
- responsive to needs of individuals, populations with distinct needs, and relevant constituencies
- delivered using multiple formats, strategies, and contexts
- designed to provide universal access

FAP must collaborate with colleagues and departments across the institution to promote student learning and development, persistence, and success.

FAP must assist students by addressing financial issues that may serve as barriers to enrollment and the achievement of educational goals. Issues include

- Students in Transition

  Financial aid administrators must track student financial aid histories and the impact of past aid on receiving aid in the future.

  FAP personnel should consider that students move from secondary to postsecondary education, from one postsecondary institution to another, from undergraduate to graduate school, as well as return from a period of non-enrollment to formal learning or re-enrollment in the institution.

- Financial Aid Practices

  Practices must establish, promulgate, and implement financial aid criteria that accurately represent the financial needs of the applicant pool, set priorities within the applicant group, and respond with funding to the extent possible.

- Financial Counseling

  Financial counseling must provide services to students for (a) the purpose of providing better understanding of financial aid, (b) financial guidance, (c) individual review of situations that may require special consideration, (d) guidance in academic and financial matters especially as they relate to satisfactory academic progress, and (e) guidance on default management, budgeting, and loan repayment.

FAP leaders should provide information for students, parents/guardians, and families to conduct a cost/benefit analysis of college enrollment.

FAP must
- promote and maintain integrity, accuracy, and timeliness in the delivery of financial aid
- provide comprehensive information and clear policies and procedures for students and their parents/guardians and families to make informed decisions regarding the financing of their education
- clarify the types of financial assistance to the student

Print and online communication must include financial aid deadlines and information on opportunities for financial aid.

Part 3. Organization and Leadership

To achieve program and student learning and development outcomes, Financial Aid Programs (FAP) must be

purposefully structured for effectiveness. FAP must have clearly stated and current
- goals and outcomes
- policies and procedures
- responsibilities and performance expectations for personnel
- organizational charts demonstrating clear channels of authority

Leaders must model ethical behavior and institutional citizenship.

Leaders with organizational authority for FAP must provide strategic planning, management and supervision, and program advancement.

Strategic Planning
- articulate a vision and mission that drive short- and long-term planning
- set goals and objectives based on the needs of the populations served, intended student learning and development outcomes, and program outcomes
- facilitate continuous development, implementation, and assessment of program effectiveness and goal attainment congruent with institutional mission and strategic plans
- promote environments that provide opportunities for student learning, development, and engagement
- develop, adapt, and improve programs and services in response to the changing needs of populations served and evolving institutional priorities
- include diverse perspectives to inform decision making

Management and Supervision
- plan, allocate, and monitor the use of fiscal, physical, human, intellectual, and technological resources
- manage human resource processes including recruitment, selection, professional development, supervision, performance planning, succession planning, evaluation, recognition, and reward
- influence others to contribute to the effectiveness and success of the unit
- empower professional, support, and student personnel to become effective leaders
- encourage and support collaboration with colleagues and departments across the institution
- encourage and support scholarly contributions to the profession
- identify and address individual, organizational, and environmental conditions that foster or inhibit mission achievement
- use current and valid evidence to inform decisions
- incorporate sustainability practices in the management and design of programs, services, and facilities
- understand appropriate technologies and integrate them into programs and services

- be knowledgeable about codes and laws relevant to programs and services and ensure that programs and services meet those requirements
- assess and take action to mitigate potential risks

Program Advancement
- advocate for and actively promote the mission and goals of the programs and services
- inform stakeholders about issues affecting practice
- facilitate processes to reach consensus where wide support is needed
- advocate for representation in strategic planning initiatives at divisional and institutional levels

FAP leaders must advocate for and represent the financial needs of students, the operation and staffing of the financial aid program, and the institution.

FAP leaders should advocate for financial aid programs at the governmental and policy levels and inform lawmakers on financial aid programs and their benefits.

FAP leaders must ensure timely and fair administration of policies regarding financial aid decisions, proper notification, and appeal processes.

A FAP leader with appropriate financial aid experience and training should be designated to lead the FAP staff.

FAP leaders must ensure the development of
- policies and procedures that provide clear descriptions of the administrative processes
- clearly stated criteria used in the decision-making process for awarding financial aid and the source of authority for the criteria employed
- steps for appealing, evaluating, or revising policies and procedures
- an effective system to manage the programs, services, and personnel of the FAP

Part 4. Human Resources

Financial Aid Programs (FAP) must be staffed adequately by individuals qualified to accomplish mission and goals. FAP must have access to technical and support personnel adequate to accomplish their mission.

Within institutional guidelines, FAP must
- establish procedures for personnel recruitment and selection, training, performance planning, and evaluation
- set expectations for supervision and performance
- provide personnel access to continuing and advanced education and appropriate professional development opportunities to improve their competence, skills, and leadership capacity
- consider work/life options available to personnel (e.g., compressed work schedules, flextime, job sharing, remote work, or telework) to promote recruitment and retention of personnel

Administrators of FAP must
- ensure that all personnel have updated position descriptions
- implement recruitment and selection/hiring strategies that produce a workforce inclusive of under-represented populations
- develop promotion practices that are fair, inclusive, proactive, and non-discriminatory

Personnel responsible for delivery of FAP must have written performance goals, objectives, and outcomes for each year's performance cycle to be used to plan, review, and evaluate work and performance. The performance plan must be updated regularly to reflect changes during the performance cycle.

Results of individual personnel evaluations must be used to recognize personnel performance, address performance issues, implement individual and/or collective personnel development and training programs, and inform the assessment of programs and services.

FAP personnel, when hired and throughout their employment, must receive appropriate and thorough training.

Suggested formal training in preparation for professional financial aid employment includes fields such as business administration, computer sciences, information systems, college student affairs, higher education administration, counseling, and other human behavior disciplines; course work may include computer literacy, research and statistical methods, counseling, legal issues of higher education, leadership and management, or any related degree program or certification.

Additional training may include conferences, webinars, workshops, and other specialized training in financial aid, enrollment management, customer/student service, advising, or other higher education fields.

Institutional training for all FAP personnel should include familiarization with campus facilities, publications, academic programs, admission policies, institutional financial aid policies and procedures, and services of the institution.

FAP personnel, including student employees and volunteers, must have access to resources or receive specific training on
- institutional policies pertaining to functions or activities they support
- privacy and confidentiality policies
- laws regarding access to student records
- policies and procedures for dealing with sensitive institutional information
- policies and procedures related to technology used to store or access student records and institutional data
- how and when to refer those in need of additional assistance to qualified personnel and have access to a supervisor for assistance in making these judgments
- systems and technologies necessary to perform their assigned responsibilities

- ethical and legal uses of technology

FAP must ensure that personnel are knowledgeable of and trained on the rights and responsibilities as an employee of the institution.

FAP personnel must engage in continuing professional development activities to keep abreast of the research, theories, legislation, policies, and developments that affect their programs and services.

Administrators of FAP must ensure that personnel are knowledgeable about and trained in safety, emergency procedures, and crisis prevention and response. Risk management efforts must address identification of threatening conduct or behavior and must incorporate a system for responding to and reporting such behaviors.

FAP personnel must be knowledgeable of and trained in safety and emergency procedures for securing and vacating facilities.

PROFESSIONAL PERSONNEL

FAP professional personnel either must hold an earned graduate or professional degree in a field relevant to their position or must possess an appropriate combination of educational credentials and related work experience.

Professional association staffing models may be utilized by FAP leadership to determine appropriate staffing levels.

Professional association publications may be utilized by FAP leadership to determine appropriate compensation for personnel.

Support personnel should be skilled in interpersonal communications, public relations, referral techniques, and dissemination of information. Support personnel with higher technical responsibilities should possess the academic background and experience for effective performance.

INTERNS OR GRADUATE ASSISTANTS

Degree- or credential-seeking interns or graduate assistants must be qualified by enrollment in an appropriate field of study and relevant experience. These students must be trained and supervised by professional personnel who possess applicable educational credentials and work experience and have supervisory experience. Supervisors must be cognizant of the dual roles interns and graduate assistants have as both student and employee.

Supervisors must
- adhere to parameters of students' job descriptions
- articulate intended learning outcomes in student job descriptions
- adhere to agreed-upon work hours and schedules
- offer flexible scheduling when circumstances necessitate

Supervisors and students must both agree to suitable compensation if circumstances necessitate additional hours.

STUDENT EMPLOYEES AND VOLUNTEERS

Student employees and volunteers must be carefully selected, trained, supervised, and evaluated. Students must have access to a supervisor. Student employees and volunteers must be provided clear job descriptions, pre-service training based on assessed needs, and continuing development.

If student employees and volunteers will be assisting students, parents/guardians, and families, they should be trained in public relations, referral techniques, peer counseling, and dissemination of information.

FAP personnel must protect the privacy of students and ensure the confidentiality of personal circumstances.

All FAP personnel should be
- willing to seek out and implement new ideas
- able to translate new ideas into practical methods for improving the overall operation of the financial aid program
- willing to seek out and use new conceptual frameworks, equipment, and technology that bring information to students more clearly and effectively
- aware of relevant developments in higher education and be able to incorporate these developments

Part 5. Ethics

Financial Aid Programs (FAP) must
- review applicable professional ethical standards and must adopt or develop and implement appropriate statements of ethical practice
- publish and adhere to statements of ethical practice and ensure their periodic review
- orient new personnel to relevant ethical standards and statements of ethical practice and related institutional policies

Statements of ethical standards must
- specify that FAP personnel respect privacy and maintain confidentiality in communications and records as delineated by privacy laws
- specify limits on disclosure of information contained in students' records as well as requirements to disclose to appropriate authorities
- address conflicts of interest, or appearance thereof, by personnel in the performance of their work
- reflect the responsibility of personnel to be fair, objective, and impartial in their interactions with others
- reference management of institutional funds
- reference appropriate behavior regarding research and assessment with human participants, confidentiality of research and assessment data, and students' rights and responsibilities
- include the expectation that personnel confront and hold accountable other personnel who exhibit unethical behavior
- address issues surrounding scholarly integrity

When conflict exists between the mission and goals of the institution and the educational goals of the student, students must be given relevant information for decision making.

FAP personnel must

- employ ethical decision making in the performance of their duties
- inform users of programs and services of ethical obligations and limitations emanating from codes and laws or from licensure requirements
- recognize and avoid conflicts of interest that could adversely influence their judgment or objectivity and, when unavoidable, recuse themselves from the situation
- perform their duties within the scope of their position, training, expertise, and competence
- make referrals when issues presented exceed the scope of the position

FAP must avoid misrepresentation as defined by applicable laws, regulations, and policies.

Part 6. Law, Policy, and Governance

Financial Aid Programs (FAP) must be in compliance with laws, regulations, and policies that relate to their respective responsibilities and that pose legal obligations, limitations, risks, and liabilities for the institution as a whole. Examples include constitutional, statutory, regulatory, and case law; relevant law and orders emanating from codes and laws; and the institution's policies.

Financial aid must be awarded in compliance with applicable rules and regulations governing financial aid.

FAP must have access to legal advice needed for personnel to carry out their assigned responsibilities.

FAP must inform personnel, appropriate officials, and users of programs and services about existing and changing legal obligations, risks and liabilities, and limitations.

FAP must inform personnel about professional liability insurance options and refer them to external sources if the institution does not provide coverage.

FAP must have written policies and procedures on operations, transactions, or tasks that have legal implications.

When appropriate, FAP leaders and personnel may need to exercise professional judgment in making exceptions to established financial aid policies. These decisions should be made in a fair and objective manner with supporting documentation that meets the criteria for evidence-based decisions.

FAP must regularly review policies. The revision and creation of policies must be informed by best practices, available evidence, and policy issues in higher education.

FAP must have procedures and guidelines consistent with institutional policy for responding to threats, emergencies, and crisis situations. Systems and procedures must be in place to disseminate timely and accurate information to students, other members of the institutional community, and appropriate external organizations during emergency situations.

Personnel must neither participate in nor condone any form of harassment or activity that demeans persons or creates an intimidating, hostile, or offensive environment.

FAP must purchase or obtain permission to use copyrighted materials and instruments. References to copyrighted materials and instruments must include appropriate citations.

FAP must inform personnel about internal and external governance organizations that affect programs and services.

Part 7. Diversity, Equity, and Access

Within the context of each institution's mission and in accordance with institutional policies and applicable codes and laws, Financial Aid Programs (FAP) must create and maintain educational and work environments that are welcoming, accessible, inclusive, equitable, and free from harassment.

FAP must not discriminate on the basis of disability; age; race; cultural identity; ethnicity; nationality; family educational history (e.g., first generation to attend college); political affiliation; religious affiliation; sex; sexual orientation; gender identity and expression; marital, social, economic, or veteran status; or any other basis included in institutional policies and codes and laws.

FAP must

- advocate for sensitivity to multicultural and social justice concerns by the institution and its personnel
- ensure physical, program, and resource access for all constituents
- modify or remove policies, practices, systems, technologies, facilities, and structures that create barriers or produce inequities
- ensure that when facilities and structures cannot be modified, they do not impede access to programs, services and resources
- establish goals for diversity, equity, and access
- foster communication and practices that enhance understanding of identity, culture, self-expression, and heritage
- promote respect for commonalities and differences among people within their historical and cultural contexts
- address the characteristics and needs of diverse constituents when establishing and implementing culturally relevant and inclusive programs, services, policies, procedures, and practices
- provide personnel with diversity, equity, and access training and hold personnel accountable for applying the training to their work
- respond to the needs of all constituents served when establishing hours of operation and

developing methods of delivering programs, services, and resources

- recognize the needs of distance and online learning students by directly providing or assisting them to gain access to comparable services and resources

FAP staff members should be sensitive to the needs of first generation, nontraditional, under-represented students, and students with special needs.

Part 8. Internal and External Relations

Financial Aid Programs (FAP) must reach out to individuals, groups, communities, and organizations internal and external to the institution to

- establish, maintain, and promote understanding and effective relations with those that have a significant interest in or potential effect on the students or other constituents served by the programs and services
- garner support and resources for programs and services as defined by the mission
- collaborate in offering or improving programs and services to meet the needs of students and other constituents and to achieve program and student outcomes
- engage diverse individuals, groups, communities, and organizations to enrich the educational environment and experiences of students and other constituents
- disseminate information about the programs and services

FAP should maintain relationships with interested groups within the community regarding general and institutional financial aid practices. The community may include grant and scholarship agencies, high schools, and other community outreach programs.

Promotional and descriptive information must be accurate and free of deception and misrepresentation.

FAP must have procedures and guidelines consistent with institutional policy for

- communicating with the media
- distributing information through print, broadcast, and online sources
- contracting with external organizations for delivery of programs and services
- cultivating, soliciting, and managing gifts
- applying to and managing funds from grants

Financial aid and admission decisions must be made independently.

FAP must have access to appropriate information in the student's admission file to assure compliance with applicable rules and regulations and to assist in awarding scholarships.

Part 9. Financial Resources

Financial Aid Programs (FAP) must have funding to accomplish the mission and goals.

In establishing and prioritizing funding resources, FAP must conduct comprehensive analyses to determine

- unmet needs of the unit
- relevant expenditures
- external and internal resources
- impact on students and the institution

FAP must use the budget as a planning tool to reflect commitment to the mission and goals of the programs and services and of the institution.

FAP must administer funds in accordance with established institutional accounting procedures.

FAP must demonstrate efficient and effective use and responsible stewardship of fiscal resources consistent with institutional protocols.

Financial reports must provide an accurate financial overview of the organization and provide clear, understandable, and timely data upon which personnel can plan and make informed decisions.

Procurement procedures must

- be consistent with institutional policies
- ensure that purchases comply with laws and codes for usability and access
- ensure that the institution receives value for the funds spent
- consider information available for comparing the ethical and environmental impact of products and services purchased

Part 10. Technology

Financial Aid Programs (FAP) must have technology to support the achievement of their mission and goals. The technology and its use must comply with institutional policies and procedures and with relevant codes and laws.

FAP must use technologies to

- provide updated information regarding mission, location, staffing, programs, services, and official contacts to students and other constituents in accessible formats
- provide an avenue for students and other constituents to communicate sensitive information in a secure format
- enhance the delivery of programs and services for all students

FAP must

- back up data on a regular basis
- adhere to institutional policies regarding ethical and legal use of technology
- articulate policies and procedures for protecting the confidentiality and security of information
- implement a replacement plan and cycle for all

- technology with attention to sustainability
- incorporate accessibility features into technology-based programs and services

When providing student access to technology, FAP must
- have policies on the use of technology that are clear, easy to understand, and available to all students
- provide information or referral to support services for those needing assistance in accessing or using technology
- provide instruction or training on how to use the technology
- inform students of implications of misuse of technologies

Part 11. Facilities and Equipment

Financial Aid Programs' (FAP) facilities must be intentionally designed and located in suitable, accessible, and safe spaces that demonstrate universal design and support the program's mission and goals.

Facilities must be designed to engage various constituents and promote learning.

Personnel must have workspaces that are suitably located and accessible, well equipped, adequate in size, and designed to support their work and responsibilities.

The design of the facilities must guarantee the security and privacy of records and ensure the confidentiality of sensitive information and conversations. Personnel must be able to secure their work.

FAP must incorporate sustainable practices in use of facilities and purchase of equipment. Facilities and equipment must be evaluated on an established cycle and be in compliance with codes, laws, and accepted practices for access, health, safety and security.

When acquiring capital equipment, FAP must take into account expenses related to regular maintenance and life cycle costs.

Part 12. Assessment

Financial Aid Programs (FAP) must develop assessment plans and processes.

Assessment plans must articulate an ongoing cycle of assessment activities.

FAP must
- specify programmatic goals and intended outcomes
- identify student learning and development outcomes
- employ multiple measures and methods
- develop manageable processes for gathering, interpreting, and evaluating data
- document progress toward achievement of goals and outcomes
- interpret and use assessment results to demonstrate accountability
- report aggregated results to respondent groups and stakeholders
- use assessment results to inform planning and decision-making
- assess effectiveness of implemented changes
- provide evidence of improvement of programs and services

Assessment resources from governmental agencies and professional associations may be used to evaluate financial aid programs and services.

FAP must employ ethical practices in the assessment process.

FAP must have access to adequate fiscal, human, professional development, and technological resources to develop and implement assessment plans.

General Standards revised in 2014;
FAP content developed/revised in 1986, 1997, 2005, and 2014

Fraternity and Sorority Advising Programs
CAS Contextual Statement

Advising undergraduate fraternity and sorority organizations is a multifaceted function within student affairs. Professionals support individual student development and advance organizational and community goals that hopefully align with the educational mission of host institutions. Professionals who advise these organizations must have an understanding of the history and organizational norms of the fraternities and sororities on their campus. Additionally, as the types of fraternities and sororities on a campus often include cultural, professional, and social as well as sometimes academic, service, and identity based (i.e. sexual orientation), it is vital for those who work with these organizations to have a grasp of the role that each chapter can play within a diverse fraternity/sorority community (Barber, Espino, & Bureau, 2015; Johnson, Bradley, Bryant, Morton, & Sawyer, 2008; Kimbrough, 2002; 2003).

Fraternities and sororities are distinctive in their historical and modern day function within higher education. They have been a part of the fabric of student life on some campuses for more than two centuries, but the nature of this relationship is debated (Brown, Parks, & Phillips, 2005; Gregory, 2003; Kimbrough, 2003; Rudolph, 1990; Whipple & Sullivan, 1998). A question to be answered by fraternity/sorority professionals is to what extent these organizations augment the institution's educational mission (Hevel & Bureau, 2015; Barber et al., 2015). Effective Fraternity and Sorority Advising Programs (FSAP), as explained in the CAS Standards, keep this question in the forefront of their mind as they enact programs and deliver resources and services for the fraternity and sorority community on their campus.

Individuals working with Fraternity and Sorority Advising Programs (FSAP) work with a range of stakeholders within and outside of the institution (Association of Fraternity/Sorority Advisors, 2015). Stakeholders include students, alumni, national and international fraternity/sorority staff, volunteer governing bodies of these organizations (e.g., the National Pan-Hellenic Council), parents, police and fire officials, and community members, among others (Mamarchev, Sina, & Heida, 2003). Recent edits to the CAS FSAP Standards reflect the evolving nature of the role of a fraternity/sorority life campus professional (FSL) and have aimed to capture the way in which the position has evolved since the very early days of the functional area: it is no longer acceptable to simply work with chapter leaders. To be successful, a FSAP must engage many in the shared pursuit of aligning the espoused purpose of these organizations to the actions of members.

With this charge in mind, we present the context of supporting fraternity and sorority advising programs using the following model: identify the issues, generate ideas, and act with intention. While simplistic, this model can provide a basis for enacting the CAS Standards for FSAP as professionals support the holistic development of students and promulgate the positive and enduring principles of fraternities and sororities in higher education.

Issues

Postsecondary organizational culture is certainly complex (Kuh & Whitt, 1988). Any collection of organized individuals can provide challenges for student affairs professionals; however, some argue the long-standing traditions in fraternities and sororities can make this culture particularly difficult to manage (Jelke & Kuh, 2003; Kimbrough, 2003; Whipple & Sullivan, 1998). Culture is shaped in part by students but is also molded by stakeholders' influence. Therefore, multiple agents influence issues and opportunities within a fraternity and sorority community. A simple way to look at the issues would be to examine them as internal and external to the fraternity and sorority community.

Internal issues are those that immediate stakeholders must address to support student needs, organizational functions, and community-wide advancement. These include the challenges associated with alcohol misuse and abuse, hazing, recruitment and intake activities, and membership education practices. These issues can be made more complex when there is a lack of collaboration amongst diverse fraternal organizations in the enactment of community policies and procedures.

There are also issues within the international fraternity/sorority system that impact fraternities and sororities on campuses: the management role of umbrella groups, ensuring that professionals have the skills necessary to support fraternities and sororities (such as those outlined in the CAS Standards for Fraternity and Sorority Advising Programs and the AFA Core Competencies for Excellence in the Profession) and a sometimes politically charged and potentially disjointed effort to assess the quality of the undergraduate experience.

There are also opportunities to take an ordinary college experience and transform it into a powerful learning experience. Students learn through involvement in civic engagement, community service, philanthropic activities, leadership development, academic support, and friendships built upon common values. Additionally, some organizations contribute to an individual's personal identity development (Guardia & Evans, 2008). Ultimately these experiences offer students a unique challenge of managing individual and organizational expectations.

External issues are those that influence fraternities and sororities and the FSAP in the larger scope of student affairs, higher education, and society. Challenges include institutional funding and staffing of student affairs functions, accountability and assessment in higher education, assessment of student learning outcomes, and the role of student affairs in supporting the mission of higher education (Sandeen & Barr, 2006). Student Affairs must align its activities with the goal of student learning, development and overall success (Schuh &

Upcraft, 2001); therefore, as a part of a larger student affairs division, FSAP must demonstrate the degree to which this important task is accomplished.

Within society, the perceptions of fraternities/sororities vary. Ardent supporters value the role these organizations can play in the development of students. Critics question how fraternity and sorority life adds value to the student experience (Hevel & Bureau, 2014; Kimbrough, 2003; Parks, 2008). Ultimately, fraternities and sororities influence and are influenced by discourse on all of these issues. Efforts to solve the problems and accentuate the contributions of FSL require new and innovative ideas.

Ideas

If the consistently problematic issues could be easily solved, then the ills of fraternities and sororities would have been cured years ago. There are certainly individuals committed to improving these organizations and aligning them with the mission of higher education. However, students bring with them a world of ideas and expectations about fraternities and sororities. These perceptions and expectations will be difficult to alter. A list of action steps is beyond the scope of this contextual statement; however, the accomplishment of any new idea must involve collaboration, embrace the never-ending process of change, and apply creativity and innovation.

As professionals support the advancement of their respective fraternity and sorority community, some comfort may be found in the idea that many are invested in the future of fraternities and sororities. Partnerships with fellow staff, faculty, alumni volunteers, national/international/fraternity/sorority professionals and volunteers, parents, and local service agencies and businesses can be forged to support the development of the students and the organizations. The FSAP standards certainly can be a launching point for such collaborations.

Applying new ideas can be tricky. However, innovation is required to make change stick in the interfraternal community (Koepsell, 2008). Tactics such as grounding policy discussions in a values-perspective, implementing activities that let students and stakeholders imagine reinventing the fraternity and sorority community, and transforming educational efforts to move from a *symptom approach* (for example, alcohol misuse and abuse) to a broader *disease approach* (people drink too much because they have low self-esteem) could be viewed as innovative. Even small tactics of innovation can make a difference in how fraternities and sororities contribute to the campus environment (Barber, Espino, & Bureau, 2015).

Intentionality

With these issues and ideas in mind, we must be purposeful in our support of the positive development of students in fraternities and sororities. Student development theory is widely applied in student affairs to aid in the explanation of how students function (Hamrick, Evans, & Schuh, 2002; Johnson et al., 2008). Additionally, organizational theory can guide practice in FSAP (Jelke & Kuh, 2003). When practitioners intentionally apply the theoretical foundations

of student affairs, they can be most focused on providing opportunities for student learning and development in the context of the fraternity and sorority community.

In addition to theories, FSAP professionals can be effective in their roles if they understand the models and frameworks that guide good practice. There are many to consider (Barber, Espino, & Bureau, 2015; Gregory, 2003; Marmarchev, Sina, & Heida, 2003). One effective framework is that of assessment. Assessment is one way to be most intentional in how student affairs professionals conduct their work (Sandeen & Barr, 2006). Schuh and Upcraft (2001) provide guidance on how to support assessment in fraternity and sorority communities. If Fraternity and Sorority Advising Program (FSAP) leaders aspire to be more aligned with higher education priorities, it is particularly vital to place the extent to which student learning occurs in fraternities and sororities as a top priority in a FSAP assessment agenda (Bureau, 2011).

Conclusion

Fraternities and sororities can be powerful forums for learning and development. It is the responsibility of those who work with these organizations to apply practices that enable success at both the student and organizational level. The *CAS Standards for Fraternity and Sorority Advising* Programs can be a framework for good practice and an assessment tool to determine the extent to which FSAP meet the needs of the students and other stakeholders with whom they work.

References, Readings, and Resources

Association of Fraternity/Sorority Advisors (AFA, 2015). http://afa1976.org/

Barber, J.P., Espino, M.M., & Bureau, D.A. (2015). Fraternities and sororities: Developing a compelling case for relevance in higher education. In P. Sasso and J. DeVitis (Eds.), *Today's college student.* New York, NY: Peter Lang Press.

Brown, T. L., Parks, G. S., & Phillips, C. M. (2005). *African American fraternities and sororities: The legacy and the vision.* Lexington, KY: The University Press of Kentucky.

Bureau, D. (2011, Summer). Why reinvent the wheel? Using the CAS learning domains and dimensions as a framework for fraternity and sorority advising program learning outcomes. *Perspectives*, 24-26.

Gregory, D. E. (2003). The dilemma facing fraternal organizations at the Millennium. In D. E. Gregory & Associates, *The administration of fraternal organizations on North American campuses,* 1-21. Asheville, NC: College Administration Publications.

Guardia, J.R., & Evans, N.J. (2008). The factors influencing the ethnic identity development of Latino fraternity members at a Hispanic Serving Institution. *Journal of College Student Development, 49,* 163-181.

Hamrick, F. A., Evans, N. J., & Schuh, J. H. (2002). *Foundations of student affairs practice.* San Francisco, CA: John Wiley & Sons.

Hevel, M.S., & Bureau, D.A. (2014). Research driven practice in fraternity and sorority life. *New Directions for Student Services 2014(147),* 23-236.

Jelke, T., & Kuh, G. (2003). High performing fraternities and sororities. In D. E. Gregory & Associates, *The administration of fraternal organizations on North American campuses,* 1-21. Asheville, NC: College Administration Publications.

Johnson, R., Bradley, D., Bryant, L., Morton, D., & Sawyer, D.

(2008). Advising black Greek-letter organizations: A student development approach. In G.S. Parks (Ed.), *Black Greek-letter organizations in the 21st century: The fight has just begun*, pp. 437-458. Lexington, KY: The University Press of Kentucky.

Kimbrough, W. M. (2002, January 22). *Guess who's coming to campus: The growth of Black, Latin and Asian fraternal organizations.* Retrieved from www.naspa.org/constituent-groups/kcs/asian-pacific-isalnders/resources

Kimbrough, W. M. (2003). *Black Greek 101: The culture, customs, and challenges of Black fraternities and sororities.* Madison, NJ: Fairleigh Dickinson University Press.

Koepsell, M. (2008, May). Utilizing community standards to align accountability, assessment and performance. *Essentials*. Retrieved from http://www.fraternityadvisors.org/Essentials/200805_Community_Standards.aspx

Kuh, G. D., & Whitt, E. J. (1988). The invisible tapestry: Culture in American colleges and universities. *ASHE-ERIC Higher Education Report Series*, No. 1. Washington, DC: Association for the Study of Higher Education.

Mamarchev, H. L., Sina, J. A., & Heida, D. E. (2003). Creating and managing a campus oversight plan: Do they work? What are the alternatives? In D. E. Gregory & Associates, *The administration of fraternal organizations on North American campuses*, 1-21. Asheville, NC: College Administration Publications.

Parks, G. S. (2008). *Black Greek-letter organizations in the 21st century: The fight has just begun.* Lexington, KY: The University Press of Kentucky.

Rudolph, F. (1990). *The American college and university* (2nd ed.). Athens, GA: The University of Georgia Press.

Sandeen, A., & Barr, M. J. (2006). *Critical issues for student affairs: Challenges and opportunities.* San Francisco, CA: Jossey-Bass.

Schuh, J. H., & Upcraft, M. L. (2001). *Assessment practice in student affairs: An applications manual.* San Francisco, CA: Jossey-Bass.

Whipple, E. G., & Sullivan, E. G. (1998). Greek-letter organizations: A community of learners? In E. G. Whipple (Ed.), *New challenges for Greek-letter organizations: Transforming fraternities and sororities into learning communities.* San Francisco, CA: Jossey-Bass.

Contextual Statement Contributors
Current Edition:
Jason Bergeron, AFA
Dan Bureau, AFA
Gentry McCreary, AFA
Veronica Moore, AFA

Previous Editions:
Dan Bureau, Indiana University, AFA
Tanner Marcantel, Vanderbilt University
Monica Miranda Smalls, University of Rochester
Emily Perlow, Worcester Polytechnic Institute
Jeremiah Shinn, Indiana University
AFA Executive Board and Staff

Fraternity and Sorority Advising Programs
CAS Standards and Guidelines

Part 1. Mission

The mission of the Fraternity and Sorority Advising Programs (FSAP) is to promote the learning and development of students who affiliate with fraternities and sororities. FSAP must support the fraternity and sorority community in efforts to be a relevant and contributing part of the institution.

To accomplish its mission, FSAP must
- promote the intellectual, physical, emotional, social, spiritual, ethical, civic, and career development of members
- provide education and experience in interpersonal relationships, leadership, group dynamics, and organization development
- promote member involvement in co-curricular activities
- promote sponsorship of and participation in community service, service-learning, and philanthropic projects
- promote an appreciation for differences and development of cross-cultural competencies
- recognize and encourage learning experiences that occur as a result of a diverse fraternity and sorority community
- advocate academic success of all members and for opportunities through which students can integrate in-class and out-of-class learning
- support members› efforts to align actions with espoused organizational mission and values
- collaborate with stakeholders who support the mission, including undergraduate and graduate/alumni members, faculty and other advisors, and organizational staff and/or volunteers,

FSAP must develop, disseminate, implement, and regularly review their missions, which must be consistent with the mission of the institution and with applicable professional standards. The mission must be appropriate for the institution's students and other constituents. Mission statements must reference student learning and development.

Part 2. Program

To achieve their mission, Fraternity and Sorority Advising Programs (FSAP) must contribute to
- students' formal education, which includes both the curriculum and the co-curriculum
- student progression and timely completion of educational goals
- preparation of students for their careers, citizenship, and lives
- student learning and development

To contribute to student learning and development, FSAP must
- identify relevant and desirable student learning and development outcomes
- articulate how the student learning and development outcomes align with the six CAS student learning and development domains and related dimensions
- assess relevant and desirable student learning and development
- provide evidence of impact on outcomes
- articulate contributions to or support of student learning and development in the domains not specifically assessed
- use evidence gathered to create strategies for improvement of programs and services

STUDENT LEARNING AND DEVELOPMENT
DOMAINS AND DIMENSIONS

Domain: knowledge acquisition, integration, construction, and application
- Dimensions: understanding knowledge from a range of disciplines; connecting knowledge to other knowledge, ideas, and experiences; constructing knowledge; and relating knowledge to daily life

Domain: cognitive complexity
- Dimensions: critical thinking, reflective thinking, effective reasoning, and creativity

Domain: intrapersonal development
- Dimensions: realistic self-appraisal, self-understanding, and self-respect; identity development; commitment to ethics and integrity; and spiritual awareness

Domain: interpersonal competence
- Dimensions: meaningful relationships, interdependence, collaboration, and effective leadership

Domain: humanitarianism and civic engagement
- Dimensions: understanding and appreciation of cultural and human differences, social responsibility, global perspective, and sense of civic responsibility

Domain: practical competence
- Dimensions: pursuing goals, communicating effectively, technical competence, managing personal affairs, managing career development, demonstrating professionalism, maintaining health and wellness, and living a purposeful and satisfying life

[LD Outcomes: See *The Council for the Advancement of Standards*

Learning and Development Outcomes statement for examples of outcomes related to these domains and dimensions.]

FSAP must be
- intentionally designed
- guided by theories and knowledge of learning and development
- integrated into the life of the institution
- reflective of developmental and demographic profiles of the student population
- responsive to needs of individuals, populations with distinct needs, and relevant constituencies
- delivered using multiple formats, strategies, and contexts
- designed to provide universal access

FSAP must collaborate with colleagues and departments across the institution to promote student learning and development, persistence, and success.

To support a positive experience that emphasizes the learning and development of members, the FSAP must include educational programming, advising services, and social and recreational programming.

FSAP focus on education must
- enhance new-member and member knowledge, understanding, and competencies essential for academic success, personal and moral development, organizational development, and the practice of leadership
- complement the academic mission of the institution
- complement the efforts of educational programs implemented by international, national, and/or regional organizations when applicable
- address aspects of the fraternity and sorority community that are currently or historically problematic, including applicable laws and institutional policies, housing safety, hazing, alcohol and other drug abuse, sexual harassment, sexual assault, racism, intolerance based on religion or sexual orientation, and other practices and attitudes that diminish human dignity or physical and social security

FSAP should support the development of academic skills and the creation of environments that encourage academic success. FSAP should facilitate the application of knowledge and skills through experiential opportunities provided by the member's chapter and the overall fraternity and sorority community.

Leadership experiences should prepare members to effectively understand and support group processes, particularly the relevant aspects of self-governance, change management, problem solving, dynamics of power and influence, responsibility, accountability, and integrity. Leadership experiences also should enable members to gain knowledge about assessing leadership and management skills.

In their focus on individual chapters, FSAP must

- monitor academic performance of chapter members individually and collectively and recommending programs for scholastic improvement
- meet with chapter leaders to aid in the development of member and chapter goals
- assist members to understand their responsibilities to the group and to the overall community, including emphasis on demonstrating espoused organizational values
- attend new member and chapter meetings as appropriate
- evaluate chapter development and recommend programs for improvement
- provide assistance and advice in planning chapter programs (e.g., new member education, intake activities)
- encourage chapter members' attendance at their organization's leadership conferences and conventions
- support the development of standards and expectations for members
- complement efforts of educational programs offered by international, national, and/or regional organizations when applicable
- attend to the specific needs of chapters without international, national, or regional affiliation, oversight, and support

FSAP focus on the fraternity and sorority community and its immediate stakeholders (e.g., chapter advisors, house corporation members, chapter presidents, institutional administrators, faculty advisors) must include
- advising governing councils and organizations
- advising financial processes
- coordinating life safety, facility management, and risk management programs in conjunction with local agencies
- facilitating or providing resources, including potential presenters of campus or national renown to conduct workshops, programs, retreats, and seminars on relevant topics (e.g., multicultural competence, leadership development, recruitment and intake, risk management)
- monitoring of membership statistics and academic retention by chapter and community (fraternity/sorority and non-fraternity/sorority) for purposes of improving academic support and recommending intervention strategies
- gathering and disseminating information via meetings, websites, newsletters, social media venues, and/or information bulletins to the various entities involved in fraternity and sorority life (e.g., campus involvement and service opportunities)
- providing assistance and advice in planning and assessing fraternity and sorority community programs (e.g., recruitment activities, stepshows, philanthropies, and alumni events)

- organizing and facilitating leadership programs/retreats/workshops
- connecting members to leadership opportunities across campus, in the local community, and within their national or international organizations
- publishing or sharing documents that focus on current events, leadership opportunities, trends, and other information regarding fraternity and sorority life
- providing for recording and archiving information about the fraternity and sorority community and encouraging chapter leaders to do the same for their organizations

FSAP focus on other stakeholders must include
- collaborating with national or international organizations when applicable and appropriate
- connecting faculty, staff, and administrators to fraternity and sorority members
- establishing and coordinating communication with local alumni volunteers
- providing resources for parents/guardians of members
- helping alumni and national and international volunteers support members' meeting of standards
- being available as an information resource for members, alumni, faculty, and administrators

In their focus on social and recreational programming, FSAP must enhance the members' knowledge, understanding, and skills necessary to promote social responsibility and develop a safe and healthy social culture within the fraternity and sorority community.

FSAP must develop appropriate processes for recognition of organizational status or registration by the institution.

Campus chapters should participate in the same student organization registration and recognition process as other campus student groups.

Because fraternities and sororities often have unique relationships with their institutions and operate under dual-authority structures, institutions may assign responsibility for fraternities and sororities to specific offices, departments, or personnel. In such cases, it may be important to articulate how fraternities and sororities are to contribute to the institution and vice versa. This may require a documented relationship statement. When applicable, the relationship statement should be formalized, signed, and disseminated.

The relationship between the institution and its chapters should be defined based upon the unique circumstances for the campus. Areas for consideration may include
- a description of each chapter's responsibility to recognize the shared expectations of and contributions to a productive fraternity/sorority community
- historical relationships
- educational role of fraternities and sororities
- conditions, privileges, and responsibilities of

affiliation
- housing and other facilities
- support and program orientation
- governance and authority (e.g., national and international organization affiliation and expansion, self-governance)
- reference to comprehensive policy documents
- expectations of the institution and the fraternity and sorority community
- accountability to other student governing bodies
- support for organization growth

FSAP expectations of fraternities/sororities should not infringe upon the legal rights of student organizations.

FSAP at campuses where chapters exist without institutional recognition should mitigate any negative influence of these chapters on the campus community and inform stakeholders about the institution's position on these groups.

Part 3. Organization and Leadership

To achieve program and student learning and development outcomes, Fraternity and Sorority Advising Programs (FSAP) must be purposefully structured for effectiveness. FSAP must have clearly stated and current
- goals and outcomes
- policies and procedures
- responsibilities and performance expectations for personnel
- organizational charts demonstrating clear channels of authority

Leaders must model ethical behavior and institutional citizenship.

Leaders with organizational authority for FSAP must provide strategic planning, management and supervision, and program advancement.

Strategic Planning
- articulate a vision and mission that drive short- and long-term planning
- set goals and objectives based on the needs of the populations served, intended student learning and development outcomes, and program outcomes
- facilitate continuous development, implementation, and assessment of program effectiveness and goal attainment congruent with institutional mission and strategic plans
- promote environments that provide opportunities for student learning, development, and engagement
- develop, adapt, and improve programs and services in response to the changing needs of populations served and evolving institutional priorities
- include diverse perspectives to inform decision making

Management and Supervision
- plan, allocate, and monitor the use of fiscal, physical, human, intellectual, and technological

resources

- manage human resource processes including recruitment, selection, professional development, supervision, performance planning, succession planning, evaluation, recognition, and reward
- influence others to contribute to the effectiveness and success of the unit
- empower professional, support, and student personnel to become effective leaders
- encourage and support collaboration with colleagues and departments across the institution
- encourage and support scholarly contributions to the profession
- identify and address individual, organizational, and environmental conditions that foster or inhibit mission achievement
- use current and valid evidence to inform decisions
- incorporate sustainability practices in the management and design of programs, services, and facilities
- understand appropriate technologies and integrate them into programs and services
- be knowledgeable about codes and laws relevant to programs and services and ensure that programs and services meet those requirements
- assess and take action to mitigate potential risks

Program Advancement

- advocate for and actively promote the mission and goals of the programs and services
- inform stakeholders about issues affecting practice
- facilitate processes to reach consensus where wide support is needed
- advocate for representation in strategic planning initiatives at divisional and institutional levels

FSAP must assist members and chapters in understanding their rights and responsibilities as part of the institution.

This may include interpreting institutional policies, administering a conduct system that addresses inappropriate behavior in a manner that safeguards procedural fairness and is consistent with institutional conduct policies, and providing outreach programming to familiarize other departments and community agencies with fraternity and sorority life.

Staff members must avoid situations or actions that may pose conflicts of interest or create the appearance of preferential treatment.

Part 4. Human Resources

Fraternity and Sorority Advising Programs (FSAP) must be staffed adequately by individuals qualified to accomplish mission and goals.

FSAP must have access to technical and support personnel adequate to accomplish their mission.

Within institutional guidelines, FSAP must

- establish procedures for personnel recruitment and selection, training, performance planning,

and evaluation

- set expectations for supervision and performance
- provide personnel access to continuing and advanced education and appropriate professional development opportunities to improve their competence, skills, and leadership capacity
- consider work/life options available to personnel (e.g., compressed work schedules, flextime, job sharing, remote work, or telework) to promote recruitment and retention of personnel

Administrators of FSAP must

- ensure that all personnel have updated position descriptions
- implement recruitment and selection/hiring strategies that produce a workforce inclusive of under-represented populations
- develop promotion practices that are fair, inclusive, proactive, and non-discriminatory

Personnel responsible for delivery of FSAP must have written performance goals, objectives, and outcomes for each year's performance cycle to be used to plan, review, and evaluate work and performance. The performance plan must be updated regularly to reflect changes during the performance cycle.

Results of individual personnel evaluations must be used to recognize personnel performance, address performance issues, implement individual and/or collective personnel development and training programs, and inform the assessment of programs and services.

FSAP personnel, when hired and throughout their employment, must receive appropriate and thorough training.

FSAP personnel, including student employees and volunteers, must have access to resources or receive specific training on

- institutional policies pertaining to functions or activities they support
- privacy and confidentiality policies
- laws regarding access to student records
- policies and procedures for dealing with sensitive institutional information
- policies and procedures related to technology used to store or access student records and institutional data
- how and when to refer those in need of additional assistance to qualified personnel and have access to a supervisor for assistance in making these judgments
- systems and technologies necessary to perform their assigned responsibilities
- ethical and legal uses of technology

FSAP personnel must engage in continuing professional development activities to keep abreast of the research, theories, legislation, policies, and developments that affect their programs and services.

Administrators of FSAP must ensure that personnel are knowledgeable about and trained in safety, emergency procedures, and crisis prevention and response. Risk management efforts must address identification of threatening conduct or behavior and must incorporate a system for responding to and reporting such behaviors.

FSAP personnel must be knowledgeable of and trained in safety and emergency procedures for securing and vacating facilities.

PROFESSIONAL PERSONNEL

FSAP professional personnel either must hold an earned graduate or professional degree in a field relevant to their position or must possess an appropriate combination of educational credentials and related work experience.

Appropriate preparatory graduate level coursework may include organizational behavior and development, oral and written communication, research and evaluation, ethics, appraisal of educational practices, group dynamics, budgeting, counseling techniques, leadership development, learning and human development theories, higher education administration, performance appraisal and supervision, application of information technology, legal issues in higher education, and student affairs.

Effective supervision is critical to the success of the program, with knowledge often required in the areas of housing, dining, accounting, safety and risk management, student conduct, alumni relations, and programming. In addition, professional staff members should have experience in the development and implementation of educational programs for members. FSAP staff should be qualified to work with various internal and external agencies in formulating goals and directions for the chapters and community that are consistent with institutional policies.

INTERNS OR GRADUATE ASSISTANTS

Degree- or credential-seeking interns or graduate assistants must be qualified by enrollment in an appropriate field of study and relevant experience. These students must be trained and supervised by professional personnel who possess applicable educational credentials and work experience and have supervisory experience. Supervisors must be cognizant of the dual roles interns and graduate assistants have as both student and employee.

Supervisors must
- adhere to parameters of students' job descriptions
- articulate intended learning outcomes in student job descriptions
- adhere to agreed-upon work hours and schedules
- offer flexible scheduling when circumstances necessitate

Supervisors and students must both agree to suitable compensation if circumstances necessitate additional hours.

FSAP should utilize paraprofessionals such as graduate assistants and graduate student interns to expand staff

capabilities and provide valuable experience for individuals who have an interest in the field of fraternity and sorority advising.

STUDENT EMPLOYEES AND VOLUNTEERS

Student employees and volunteers must be carefully selected, trained, supervised, and evaluated. Students must have access to a supervisor. Student employees and volunteers must be provided clear job descriptions, pre-service training based on assessed needs, and continuing development.

The level of FSAP staffing services must be established and reviewed regularly with regard to demands, enrollment, diversity of services offered, institutional resources, and other services available on the campus and in the local community.

Part 5. Ethics

Fraternity and Sorority Advising Programs (FSAP) must
- review applicable professional ethical standards and must adopt or develop and implement appropriate statements of ethical practice
- publish and adhere to statements of ethical practice and ensure their periodic review
- orient new personnel to relevant ethical standards and statements of ethical practice and related institutional policies

FSAP must adopt a statement of ethics intended to
- treat fairly prospective students who wish to affiliate with a fraternity/sorority
- eliminate illegal discrimination associated with the selection of members
- uphold applicable standards of conduct expressed by the institution and by the respective national or international organization

Statements of ethical standards must
- specify that FSAP personnel respect privacy and maintain confidentiality in communications and records as delineated by privacy laws
- specify limits on disclosure of information contained in students' records as well as requirements to disclose to appropriate authorities
- address conflicts of interest, or appearance thereof, by personnel in the performance of their work
- reflect the responsibility of personnel to be fair, objective, and impartial in their interactions with others
- reference management of institutional funds
- reference appropriate behavior regarding research and assessment with human participants, confidentiality of research and assessment data, and students' rights and responsibilities
- include the expectation that personnel confront and hold accountable other personnel who exhibit unethical behavior
- address issues surrounding scholarly integrity

FSAP personnel must
- employ ethical decision making in the performance

of their duties

- inform users of programs and services of ethical obligations and limitations emanating from codes and laws or from licensure requirements
- recognize and avoid conflicts of interest that could adversely influence their judgment or objectivity and, when unavoidable, recuse themselves from the situation
- perform their duties within the scope of their position, training, expertise, and competence
- make referrals when issues presented exceed the scope of the position

FSAP staff members should examine the distinct ethical challenges that come with serving the fraternity and sorority community, determine and implement appropriate approaches for addressing such challenges, and model relevant ethical standards in their everyday practice.

Part 6. Law, Policy, and Governance

Fraternity and Sorority Advising Programs (FSAP) must be in compliance with laws, regulations, and policies that relate to their respective responsibilities and that pose legal obligations, limitations, risks, and liabilities for the institution as a whole. Examples include constitutional, statutory, regulatory, and case law; relevant law and orders emanating from codes and laws; and the institution's policies.

FSAP must have access to legal advice needed for personnel to carry out their assigned responsibilities.

FSAP must inform personnel, appropriate officials, and users of programs and services about existing and changing legal obligations, risks and liabilities, and limitations.

FSAP must inform personnel about professional liability insurance options and refer them to external sources if the institution does not provide coverage.

FSAP must have written policies and procedures on operations, transactions, or tasks that have legal implications.

FSAP should involve stakeholders in the administration of policies specific to the fraternity and sorority community.

FSAP may assist chapters and house corporations to identify appropriate levels of insurance.

Contracts with outside vendors must include adherence to ethical standards and institutional policies.

FSAP must regularly review policies. The revision and creation of policies must be informed by best practices, available evidence, and policy issues in higher education.

FSAP must have procedures and guidelines consistent with institutional policy for responding to threats, emergencies, and crisis situations. Systems and procedures must be in place to disseminate timely and accurate information to students, other members of the institutional community, and appropriate external organizations during emergency

situations.

Personnel must neither participate in nor condone any form of harassment or activity that demeans persons or creates an intimidating, hostile, or offensive environment.

FSAP must purchase or obtain permission to use copyrighted materials and instruments. References to copyrighted materials and instruments must include appropriate citations.

FSAP must inform personnel about internal and external governance organizations that affect programs and services.

FSAP must provide information on laws pertinent to the operation of chapters to fraternity and sorority community stakeholders.

FSAP must ensure chapters without international, national, or regional affiliation understand applicable laws and policies.

FSAP must attend to the specific legal and policy issues of chapters without international, national, or regional affiliation, oversight, and support.

FSAP at campuses where chapters exist without institutional recognition should mitigate any negative influence of these chapters on the campus community and inform stakeholders about the institution's position on these groups.

Houses or common rooms that are owned, rented, or otherwise assigned to fraternities and sororities for their use must be managed in accordance with all applicable regulatory and statutory requirements of the host institution, international/national organization, and governmental authorities.

FSAP should establish a process for monitoring public discussions and informal communications, including social media and mobile networks.

Issues such as fire safety, noise control, parking, trash removal, security, facility and property maintenance, and life safety and health code compliance are of particular importance and should be monitored regularly.

FSAP staff members may be the principal representative of the administration to the fraternity and sorority community as well as the principal advocate for the fraternity and sorority community within the administration.

Processes used by the FSAP must emphasize positive working relationships with members and stakeholders.

These relationships may be fostered through the advising and administrative processes used by the FSAP.

The administrative organization of FSAP should reflect the mission and size of the institution. FSAP should be a fully integrated institutional component and organized, resourced, and administered in a manner that permits its stated mission to be fulfilled. The administrative leader of the program should be responsible to the senior student affairs officer or designee.

Part 7. Diversity, Equity, and Access

Within the context of each institution's mission and in accordance with institutional policies and applicable codes and laws, Fraternity and Sorority Advising Programs (FSAP) must create and maintain educational and work environments that are welcoming, accessible, inclusive, equitable, and free from harassment.

FSAP must not discriminate on the basis of disability; age; race; cultural identity; ethnicity; nationality; family educational history (e.g., first generation to attend college); political affiliation; religious affiliation; sex; sexual orientation; gender identity and expression; marital, social, economic, or veteran status; or any other basis included in institutional policies and codes and laws.

FSAP must
- advocate for sensitivity to multicultural and social justice concerns by the institution and its personnel
- ensure physical, program, and resource access for all constituents
- modify or remove policies, practices, systems, technologies, facilities, and structures that create barriers or produce inequities
- ensure that when facilities and structures cannot be modified, they do not impede access to programs, services, and resources
- establish goals for diversity, equity, and access
- foster communication and practices that enhance understanding of identity, culture, self-expression, and heritage
- promote respect for commonalities and differences among people within their historical and cultural contexts
- address the characteristics and needs of diverse constituents when establishing and implementing culturally relevant and inclusive programs, services, policies, procedures, and practices
- provide personnel with diversity, equity, and access training and hold personnel accountable for applying the training to their work
- respond to the needs of all constituents served when establishing hours of operation and developing methods of delivering programs, services, and resources
- recognize the needs of distance and online learning students by directly providing or assisting them to gain access to comparable services and resources

FSAP should cultivate a range of opportunities for students to gain membership into fraternities and sororities that have diverse purposes, including those that are cultural, social, and professional in nature.

FSAP must address the characteristics and needs of a diverse campus population when establishing and implementing policies and procedures.

FSAP must enhance members' knowledge, understanding, skills, and responsibilities associated with being a member of a pluralistic and global society. The program must provide educational efforts that develop appreciation of differences and cross-cultural competencies.

The FSAP should work with members to ensure recruitment and intake processes are accessible to all who choose to take part.

FSAP staff should maintain current knowledge of student demographics and characteristics on their campus and higher education in general.

FSAP should work with members to promote fraternity and sorority membership as a viable involvement option for all student populations. The FSAP should not interfere with the fraternity/sorority's right to select membership based on Title IX criteria and its status as a private organization.

Part 8. Internal and External Relations

Fraternity and Sorority Advising Programs (FSAP) must reach out to individuals, groups, communities, and organizations internal and external to the institution to
- establish, maintain, and promote understanding and effective relations with those that have a significant interest in or potential effect on the students or other constituents served by the programs and services
- garner support and resources for programs and services as defined by the mission
- collaborate in offering or improving programs and services to meet the needs of students and other constituents and to achieve program and student outcomes
- engage diverse individuals, groups, communities, and organizations to enrich the educational environment and experiences of students and other constituents
- disseminate information about the programs and services

Promotional and descriptive information must be accurate and free of deception and misrepresentation.

FSAP must have procedures and guidelines consistent with institutional policy for
- communicating with the media
- distributing information through print, broadcast, and online sources
- contracting with external organizations for delivery of programs and services
- cultivating, soliciting, and managing gifts
- applying to and managing funds from grants

A team approach in working with members in the local chapters should be a common goal of the FSAP when it collaborates with advisors, alumni, house corporations, national or international representatives, and other community stakeholders.

Because alumni can serve as valuable resources, program staff members should encourage and enlist a productive level of alumni involvement and assist with information exchange and collaborative programming efforts.

FSAP should engage faculty and staff members to serve as chapter advisors and serve on committees that focus on institutional issues and policies affecting the fraternity and sorority community.

The FSAP should establish relationships with local nonprofit organizations that provide opportunities for service and philanthropic pursuits and involvement. Programs focused on philanthropic activities and community service/volunteer involvement, that have been traditional components of fraternity and sorority programs, should be developed, maintained, and encouraged. The FSAP should connect fraternity and sorority chapters to opportunities to serve their community.

Part 9. Financial Resources

Fraternity and Sorority Advising Programs (FSAP) must have funding to accomplish the mission and goals.

In establishing and prioritizing funding resources, FSAP must conduct comprehensive analyses to determine
- unmet needs of the unit
- relevant expenditures
- external and internal resources
- impact on students and the institution

FSAP must use the budget as a planning tool to reflect commitment to the mission and goals of the programs and services and of the institution.

FSAP must administer funds in accordance with established institutional accounting procedures.

FSAP must demonstrate efficient and effective use and responsible stewardship of fiscal resources consistent with institutional protocols.

Financial reports must provide an accurate financial overview of the organization and provide clear, understandable, and timely data upon which personnel can plan and make informed decisions.

Procurement procedures must
- be consistent with institutional policies
- ensure that purchases comply with laws and codes for usability and access
- ensure that the institution receives value for the funds spent
- consider information available for comparing the ethical and environmental impact of products and services purchased

In some cases, FSAP may supplement institutional funding from sources such as development, fundraising, grants, and fees for services.

Part 10. Technology

Fraternity and Sorority Advising Programs (FSAP)

must have technology to support the achievement of their mission and goals. The technology and its use must comply with institutional policies and procedures and with relevant codes and laws.

FSAP must use technologies to
- provide updated information regarding mission, location, staffing, programs, services, and official contacts to students and other constituents in accessible formats
- provide an avenue for students and other constituents to communicate sensitive information in a secure format
- enhance the delivery of programs and services for all students

FSAP must
- back up data on a regular basis
- adhere to institutional policies regarding ethical and legal use of technology
- articulate policies and procedures for protecting the confidentiality and security of information
- implement a replacement plan and cycle for all technology with attention to sustainability
- incorporate accessibility features into technology-based programs and services

When providing student access to technology, FSAP must
- have policies on the use of technology that are clear, easy to understand, and available to all students
- provide information or referral to support services for those needing assistance in accessing or using technology
- provide instruction or training on how to use the technology
- inform students of implications of misuse of technologies

FSAP should centralize fraternity and sorority community resources with one website providing links to the websites of each recognized chapter and council along with other relevant sites.

FSAP should provide access to policies, procedures, standards, and relevant fraternity and sorority community documents. These documents provide insight into the operations and performance of the community and should be accessible to stakeholders.

Part 11. Facilities and Equipment

Fraternity and Sorority Advising Programs' (FSAP) facilities must be intentionally designed and located in suitable, accessible, and safe spaces that demonstrate universal design and support the program's mission and goals.

Chapters that maintain facilities should have those living units assessed annually including life safety, sanitation, and quality of life inspections of all housing facilities, kitchens, building electrical systems, heating systems, and fire safety equipment.

Facilities must be designed to engage various constituents and promote learning.

Personnel must have workspaces that are suitably located and accessible, well equipped, adequate in size, and designed to support their work and responsibilities.

FSAP space should be integrated with other institutional student services.

The design of the facilities must guarantee the security and privacy of records and ensure the confidentiality of sensitive information and conversations. Personnel must be able to secure their work.

FSAP must incorporate sustainable practices in use of facilities and purchase of equipment. Facilities and equipment must be evaluated on an established cycle and be in compliance with codes, laws, and accepted practices for access, health, safety, and security.

When acquiring capital equipment, FSAP must take into account expenses related to regular maintenance and life cycle costs.

Part 12. Assessment

Fraternity and Sorority Advising Programs (FSAP) must develop assessment plans and processes.

Assessment plans must articulate an ongoing cycle of assessment activities.

Plans should complement assessment efforts initiated by organizations including the Association of Fraternity/Sorority Advisors (AFA) and umbrella groups.

FSAP must
- **specify programmatic goals and intended outcomes**
- **identify student learning and development outcomes**
- **employ multiple measures and methods**
- **develop manageable processes for gathering, interpreting, and evaluating data**
- **document progress toward achievement of goals and outcomes**
- **interpret and use assessment results to demonstrate accountability**
- **report aggregated results to respondent groups and stakeholders**
- **use assessment results to inform planning and decision-making**
- **assess effectiveness of implemented changes**
- **provide evidence of improvement of programs and services**

Assessment should be conducted to determine the strength of leadership, the fulfillment of the community's purposes and priorities, academic performance (including chapter performance and contributions to retention), the effectiveness of self-governance procedures, individual chapter congruence with institutional and system purposes, the effectiveness of programs, and the availability and stability of resources.

Periodic assessment and evaluation of chapter and governing council needs, goals, and objectives should include chapter vitality and evaluation of each chapter's leadership, self-sufficiency, accountability to purpose, and productive activities.

An institutionally developed annual awards, recognition, or local accreditation program should be used to gauge chapter progress toward community goals.

When research is conducted, topics could include
- how student development is influenced by fraternity or sorority membership
- influence of participation on members' values, ethics, and actions
- skill development among members at various stages of membership
- the effect of participation in fraternities and sororities on members' matriculation, retention, and academic performance and progression
- involvement and influence of alumni advisors
- organizational and community development over time

Results of research and assessment initiatives should be shared with constituents and stakeholders (e.g., students, advisors, alumni, parents, national and international organizations, faculty, staff, and administrators).

FSAP must employ ethical practices in the assessment process.

FSAP must have access to adequate fiscal, human, professional development, and technological resources to develop and implement assessment plans.

General Standards revised in 2014;
FSAP content developed/revised in 1986, 1996, & 2012

Graduate and Professional Student Programs and Services

CAS Contexual Statement

In 2010, the Council of Graduate Schools (CGS) and the Educational Testing Service (ETS) issued *The Path Forward: The Future of Graduate Education in the United States*, a report that asserted that the need for graduate education, and the highly-skilled workforce it produces, is vital to our economic success and competitiveness as a nation and as a global leader (CGS & ETS, 2010). Further, studies have shown that those with graduate degrees earn higher salaries on average as well as face lower levels of unemployment, making this issue also one of individual prosperity (CGS & ETS, 2012). The 2010 document called attention to major problems confronting graduate education, such as the rate of attrition, time to degree, and the challenge of identifying career paths to, during, and after graduate school, especially for minorities and women.

Since the mid-1990s the higher education community has recognized the unique needs, challenges, and experiences of graduate and professional students – a growing and often underserved population. However, efforts to address those needs are complicated by the distinct types of degrees (master's, doctoral, professional, and more recently, the professional science masters); institutional reporting structure (centralized graduate office within a school or college or a campus-wide graduate school); collaborations with other institutional units such as International Student Life, Residence Life, and Career Services; backgrounds of professional administrators; and differences in the student populations served. These factors present unique challenges in the development of standards and guidelines for graduate and professional student programs and services and underscore the need for these standards.

In the last several decades, several notable initiatives occurred to address the challenges of graduate and professional students (Brandes, 2007). They include publications such as *Reshaping the Education of Scientists and Engineers* (Committee on Science, Engineering, and Public Policy, 1995), a report that recommended a more student-centered model of education with attention to diversity and student professional development, and also the first major monograph to address services for graduate and professional students, *Student Services for the Changing Graduate Student Population* (Logan & Isaac, 1995). In 2006, a second monograph, *Supporting Graduate and Professional Students: The Role of Student Affairs* (Guentzel & Elkins Nesheim) was published. Universities such as Harvard, Cornell, and Yale took the lead in the latter half of the 1990s by establishing graduate student centers and appointing student affairs professionals (Brandes, 2007). These new professionals in graduate student affairs provided the vision and impetus for the formation in 1999 of a knowledge

community within NASPA (Student Affairs Administrators in Higher Education) that continues today as the Administrators in Graduate and Professional Student Services (AGAPSS). Following NASPA's lead, ACPA (College Student Educators International) established its Commission for Graduate and Professional School Educators (Brandes, 2007), continuing today as the Commission for Graduate and Professional Student Affairs. In 2008, the National Resource Center for the First-Year Experience and Students in Transition published a monograph, *Graduate Students in Transition: Assisting Students through the First Year*.

The growing awareness of the unique needs of graduate and professional students led the authors of ACPA's and NASPA's seminal publication, *Learning Reconsidered: A Campus-Wide Focus on the Student Experience* (2004) to recommend that "Faculty members, student affairs professionals, academic administrators, and representative graduate students should work together to define strategies and resources that will support the comprehensive, holistic learning of graduate students" (p. 29). Other studies and findings, most notably Elkins Nesheim et al. (2007), also suggest that programs for graduate students are often most successful when delivered through partnerships between student affairs and academic affairs professionals.

Much like the important work Student Affairs practitioners do to create a supportive environment for students on the undergraduate level, similar efforts are needed on the graduate level, with the main differences being an emphasis on career focus and discipline-specific socialization. As noted above, the most crucial areas that the 2010 report addressed were identifying pathways into graduate education and, once enrolled, the issues of attrition and time to degree that are crippling the potential success of countless graduate students.

Emerging topics in graduate and professional student programs and services include:

- recruitment of an increasingly more diverse, multicultural, nontraditional, commuting, part-time and full-time employed graduate and professional student population, including subpopulations such as international students and veterans;
- retention issues including attrition, time to degree, and lack of funding; offering support services to specific populations such as underrepresented, first-generation, and non-traditional students whose career goals are often influenced by family, community, and cultural identity in addition to input from faculty and peers;
- understanding of the variation in types of degrees including master's, doctoral, professional, interdisciplinary, online, and certificate programs;

- academic structural issues such as how to best deliver programs and services (e.g., orientation) while providing experiences that involve and engage students and lead to their professional development; the differences and variety of organizational and reporting structures, services offered, and locations of offices responsible for the provision of services to graduate students; availability of campus student organizations that focus on this population and the opportunity for graduate students to serve the campus community;
- counteracting attitudes that institutions only need to attend to the basic academic experience of graduate and professional students; beliefs that graduate students do not require the student services provided to undergraduates or places and opportunities for community building, involvement, and social integration; the focus of many divisions of student affairs on the undergraduate experience, resulting in lack of resources to address needs of graduate students;
- lack of research on the developmental needs of graduate students and application of developmental theories and recommended practices to this population;
- failure to address mental health, emotional, or stress-related problems including feelings of isolation and the impostor phenomenon that are common among graduate and professional students; groups of students feeling marginalized, e.g., underrepresented, international, nontraditional, and part-time students;
- issues of socialization to the profession including advisor-advisee relationship, departmental issues, peer relationships, and mentorships;
- lack of transparent career pathways including academic job shortages and decline in students pursuing academic careers; the teaching of soft skills such as written and oral communication, cultural and international competencies, and teambuilding; the creation of connections with alumni for professional development;
- lack of funding and financial literacy on the part of students who must navigate complex systems to seek and obtain funding for advanced study;
- the varied knowledge, backgrounds, and experiences of professionals responsible for providing services and support to graduate and professional students; how to build the professional communities such as NASPA's AGAPSS and ACPA's Commission; standards of practice for individuals with primary responsibility for student support services for graduate and professional students.

Members of NASPA's AGAPSS and ACPA's Commission for Graduate and Professional Student Affairs actively participated in the development of these standards and guidelines.

References, Readings, and Resources

ACPA - College Student Educators International, Commission for Graduate and Professional Student Affairs: www.myacpa.org/commgpsa

Association for Graduate Enrollment Management (NAGAP): www.nagap.org

Brandes, L. C. O. (2007). Recent graduate and professional education issues: A timeline. Prepared for NASPA AGAPSS Preconference workshop at Harvard University, March 2007.

Cain, D. L., Marrara, C., Pitre, P. E., & Armour, S. (2003). Support services that matter: An exploration of the experiences and needs of graduate students in a distance learning environment. *Journal of Distance Education, 18*(1), 42-56.

Committee on Science, Engineering and Public Policy. (1995). *Reshaping the education of scientists and engineers.* Washington, DC: National Academy of Sciences.

Council of Graduate Schools and Educational Testing Service. (2010). *The path forward: The future of graduate education in the United States. Report from the Commission on the Future of Graduate Education in the United States.* Princeton, NJ: Educational Testing Service.

Council of Graduate Schools and Educational Testing Service. (2012). *Pathways through graduate school and into careers. Report from the Commission on Pathways Through Graduate School and Into Careers.* Princeton, NJ: Educational Testing Service.

Council of Graduate Schools. (2011). *Findings from the 2011 CGS international graduate admissions survey.* Retrieved from http://www.cgsnet.org/ckfinder/userfiles/files/R_IntlAdm11_II.pdf

Craddock, S., Birnbaum, M., Rodriguez, K., Cobb, C., & Zeeh, S. (2011). Doctoral students and the impostor phenomenon: Am I smart enough to be here? *Journal of Student Affairs Research and Practice, 48*(4), 429-442.

Elkins Nesheim, B., Guentzel, M. J., Kellogg, A. H., McDonald, W. M., Wells, C. A., & Whitt, E. J. (2007). Outcomes for student affairs-academic affairs partnership programs. *Journal of College Student Development, 48*(4), 435-454.

Gardner, S. K., & Barnes, B. J. (2007). Graduate student involvement: Socialization for the professional role. *Journal of College Student Development, 48*(4), 369-387.

Guentzel, M. J., & Elkins Nesheim, B. (2006). *Supporting graduate and professional students: The role of student affairs.* New Directions in Student Services (No.115). San Francisco, CA: Jossey Bass.

Haley, K. J., Jaeger, A. J., & Levin, J. S. (2014). The influence of cultural social identity on graduate student career choice. *Journal of College Student Development, 55*(2), 101-119.

Hesli, V. L., Fink, E. C., & Duffy, D. M. (2003). The role of faculty in creating a positive graduate experience: Survey results from the Midwest region, part II. *Political Science and Politics, 36*(4), 801-804.

Hyun, J. K., Quinn, B. C., Madon, T., & Lustig, S. (2006). Graduate student mental health: Needs assessment and utilization of counseling services. *Journal of College Student Development, 47*(3), 247-266.

Kruger, K. (2005). *Technology in student affairs: Supporting student learning and services.* New Directions in Student Services (No.112). San Francisco, CA: Jossey Bass.

Le, T., & Gardner, S. K. (2010). Understanding the doctoral experience of Asian international students in the science, technology, engineering, and mathematics (STEM) fields: An exploration of one institutional context. *Journal of College Student Development, 51*(3), 252-264.

Logan, A. P., & Isaac, P. D. (1995). *Student services for the changing graduate student population.* New Directions in Student Services (No.42). San Francisco, CA: Jossey Bass.

NASPA - Student Affairs Administrators in Higher Education, Knowledge Community- Administrators in Graduate and Professional Student Services (AGAPSS): www.naspa.org/constituent-groups/kcs/administrators-in-graduate-and-professional-student-services

National Association of Student Personnel Administrators (NASPA) & American College Personnel Association (ACPA). (2004). *Learning reconsidered: A campus-wide focus on the student experience.* Washington, DC: Authors.

Polson, C. J. (2003). Adult graduate students challenge institutions to change. *New Directions for Student Services, 102,* 59-68.

Poock, M. C. (2004). Graduate student orientation practices: Results from a national survey. *NASPA Journal 41*(3), 470-486.

Portnoi, L. M., & Kwong, T. M. (2011). Enhancing the academic experiences of first-generation master's students. *Journal of Student Affairs Research and Practice, 48*(4), 411-427.

Roberts, D. L. (2012). International graduate student mobility in the US: What more can we be doing. *Journal of College & Character, 13,* 1-7.

Tokuno, K. A. (Ed.). *Graduate students in transition: Assisting students through the first year* (Monograph No. 50). Columbia, SC: University of South Carolina, National Resources Center for The First-Year Experience and Students in Transition.

Contextual Statement Contributors

Current Edition:
Lisa Sperling, University of Georgia, NAGAP

Previous Editions:
Lisa Brandes, Yale University, NASPA-AGAPSS
Pat Carretta, George Mason University, NACE
Lori Cohen, George Mason University
Eva DeCourcey, George Mason University
Janice Sutera Wolfe, George Mason University

Graduate and Professional Student Programs and Services

CAS Standards and Guidelines

Part 1. Mission

The mission of Graduate and Professional Student Programs and Services (GPSPS) is to promote academic, personal, and professional growth and development of students enrolled in graduate and professional schools. In support of successful degree completion and achievement of other academic goals, GPSPS must ensure student access to programs and services that address students' needs, provide opportunities for involvement and engagement with students, staff, and faculty members, and facilitate community building and social integration across disciplines. Central to this mission is the necessity to connect students with appropriate resources through collaboration with campus partners and experts when services are not centrally provided by a GPSPS office.

GPSPS must develop, disseminate, implement, and regularly review their missions, which must be consistent with the mission of the institution and with applicable professional standards. The mission must be appropriate for the institution's students and other constituents. Mission statements must reference student learning and development.

Part 2. Program

Graduate and Professional Student Programs and Services (GPSPS) must provide programs and services to meet the academic, personal, and professional needs and interests of graduate and professional students, whether organized as a central office; located within an academic department, school, or college; or offered in collaboration with other student and academic affairs offices. GPSPS must use data about their graduate and professional students and their experiences to tailor programs and services for those students.

GPSPS should offer programs that reflect the diversity of their students. Demographics to consider include heterogeneity of students who are seeking degrees, disciplines studied, and the different types of institutions they have previously attended.

To achieve their mission, GPSPS must contribute to
- students' formal education, which includes both the curriculum and the co-curriculum
- student progression and timely completion of educational goals
- preparation of students for their careers, citizenship, and lives
- student learning and development

To contribute to student learning and development, GPSPS must
- identify relevant and desirable student learning and development outcomes

- articulate how the student learning and development outcomes align with the six CAS student learning and development domains and related dimensions
- assess relevant and desirable student learning and development
- provide evidence of impact on outcomes
- articulate contributions to or support of student learning and development in the domains not specifically assessed
- use evidence gathered to create strategies for improvement of programs and services

STUDENT LEARNING AND DEVELOPMENT DOMAINS AND DIMENSIONS

Domain: knowledge acquisition, integration, construction, and application
- Dimensions: understanding knowledge from a range of disciplines; connecting knowledge to other knowledge, ideas, and experiences; constructing knowledge; and relating knowledge to daily life

Domain: cognitive complexity
- Dimensions: critical thinking, reflective thinking, effective reasoning, and creativity

Domain: intrapersonal development
- Dimensions: realistic self-appraisal, self-understanding, and self-respect; identity development; commitment to ethics and integrity; and spiritual awareness

Domain: interpersonal competence
- Dimensions: meaningful relationships, interdependence, collaboration, and effective leadership

Domain: humanitarianism and civic engagement
- Dimensions: understanding and appreciation of cultural and human differences, social responsibility, global perspective, and sense of civic responsibility

Domain: practical competence
- Dimensions: pursuing goals, communicating effectively, technical competence, managing personal affairs, managing career development, demonstrating professionalism, maintaining health and wellness, and living a purposeful and satisfying life

[LD Outcomes: See *The Council for the Advancement of Standards Learning and Development Outcomes* statement for examples of outcomes related to these domains and dimensions.]

GPSPS must be
- intentionally designed
- guided by theories and knowledge of learning and development
- integrated into the life of the institution
- reflective of developmental and demographic profiles of the student population
- responsive to needs of individuals, populations with distinct needs, and relevant constituencies
- delivered using multiple formats, strategies, and contexts
- designed to provide universal access

GPSPS must collaborate with colleagues and departments across the institution to promote student learning and development, persistence, and success.

Because of the potential impact on graduate student success, GPSPS must offer programs and services that promote students' continued cognitive, emotional, ethical, and social development.

GPSPS must provide opportunities for students to develop knowledge, skills, professional ethics, and values necessary for entry into and progress through the profession or career for which the graduate or professional degree programs offer preparation.

GPSPS must ensure that students have access to programs and services to assist in navigating the issues and coping with stress often associated with the transition into and progress through graduate or professional education. GPSPS must develop support systems for fostering retention and persistence.

Programs should address changes in lifestyle, relationships, work, and finances, as well as isolation and lack of support networks.

GPSPS should provide resources, services, and support to students who are or who become parents during their graduate program and should ensure that policies do not place an unfair burden on students who are parents.

GPSPS must offer programs and services that promote individual and community responsibility, academic integrity, and ethical practices.

GPSPS must advocate that students involved in research, teaching, or clinical work receive supervision and information, guidelines, and training on appropriate practices and policies.

GPSPS should be especially responsive to the needs of international, multicultural, women, and LGBT students and students with disabilities.

GPSPS must include an admissions function or work closely with admissions staff to
- ensure timely dissemination of information and materials
- provide equal access for all prospective students interested in and capable of pursuing graduate or

professional education at the institution
- work with stakeholders to develop enrollment goals, related strategies, and resources that are needed to reach those goals
- coordinate programs for prospective students that present the realities of graduate education and promote deliberate educational planning

GPSPS must orient students to the academic unit, school/college, institution, and community or work closely with appropriate staff and resources to offer information in formats compatible with multiple constituencies, including residential, commuter, and distance learning students.

GPSPS should coordinate a series of orientation activities and transition services for new students that address the realities, norms, and expectations of graduate education; policies and regulations; resources within the academic department or school/college; and other campus and community resources beyond the department or school/college that offer programs and services essential or of interest to their students. GPSPS should provide information about student organizations and other formal or informal support groups and opportunities for involvement for all graduate students and especially for underrepresented students. GPSPS should employ the assistance of advanced graduate and professional students in planning and implementing the orientation program.

GPSPS must offer financial aid services or provide access to appropriate staff and resources to
- provide comprehensive and accurate information for students to make informed decisions on financing their education, managing loans and debt, research and training grants, and other financial matters while in graduate or professional school
- ensure clear and transparent procedures and policies for awarding financial aid
- ensure timeliness of delivery of financial aid offered by the academic department, school/college, or institution

GPSPS must assist students in adjusting to the academic demands of graduate or professional education or provide access to appropriate staff and resources.

GPSPS may
- provide information about grading and other policies; academic writing and citation style; the pace for learning; and other realities about academic demands and performance in their program of study
- provide professional development programs, resources, or referral to services on studying, test-taking, intellectual property, research methodologies, and research protocol
- arrange or facilitate study or tutor groups
- refer students with disabilities to staff or others who can conduct assessments and arrange accommodations
- discuss and clarify educational, career, and life goals and advise on the selection of appropriate courses

and other educational experiences

- provide opportunities to assess appropriateness of academic program choice
- evaluate and monitor student academic progress and the impact on achievement of goals and degree completion
- support or refer students with supervisory, assistantship, or advising issues
- direct students with personal concerns to resources and programs on the campus or in the community
- provide information and referral to programs to improve oral communication and conversation skills
- encourage departments and students to develop strong mentorship programs

GPSPS must offer or provide access to resources that enhance the career and professional development of its students. Program components must be designed for and be reflective of the needs and interests of students.

GPSPS program components should include

- career counseling or coaching
- information and resources on careers, specializations within fields and professions, further education and training opportunities, and fellowships
- opportunities to explore career options available to those with graduate or professional degrees
- opportunities to gain experience related to the field or profession through internships, practicums, summer or part-time jobs, job shadowing, or volunteer work
- job search services
- access to advice and guidance from faculty, peer mentors, alumni, and other professionals
- information and support for travel grants and professional presentations

GPSPS may also encompass

- academic advising
- academic integrity and student conduct
- counseling and psychological services
- assistance with housing on and off campus
- disability services
- professional development programs in teaching, presentation of research, academic and research integrity, thesis and dissertation preparation, grant writing, ethical conduct, preparing future faculty, diversity training, and related topics
- information and advice on applying for scholarships and fellowships
- disciplinary or interdisciplinary scholarly events
- student organizations, governance support, and leadership development
- social and networking activities and programs
- international student programs and services
- multicultural activities and events
- access to sports events, recreation, and fitness and wellness activities
- community service opportunities
- services and accommodations for students with

families including children
- graduation activities
- graduate alumni activities
- post-doctoral training and support services

GPSPS must disseminate relevant information about campus services, programs, and current events in a variety of media and formats.

Access to GPSPS services should be available via the Internet and telephone as well as through other channels of communication appropriate to the institution and community.

GPSPS must facilitate opportunities for community building and multicultural interaction within and across academic units.

GPSPS should offer students opportunities for interaction with faculty and staff members and peers within and outside their fields of study. GPSPS should encourage and support formation of student organizations and activities, multicultural communities, special-interest student organizations, honoraries, mentoring, and leadership programs.

Graduate and professional students should have adequate study, meeting, and lounge spaces that serve as gathering and community building spaces for students from different departments and academic programs. These spaces should encourage and support informal meetings, study groups, quiet study space, student organization activities, and co-curricular programs.

GPSPS should partner with graduate faculty members to offer discipline specific co-curricular programs or collaborate with other departments, faculty members, and staff from related disciplines to offer such programs to a larger population of graduate students.

GPSPS must promote representation of graduate and professional students on all appropriate levels of campus planning, policy-making, budgeting, program delivery, and governance.

GPSPS must advocate for students and empower students to advocate for themselves.

Graduate and professional student advocacy should focus on

- access to comprehensive academic and student support services and information
- recognition of diverse subgroups within the graduate student population
- availability and equitable distribution of funds in support of student organizations, governance, conference travel, and research
- institutional research and assessment that enhance understanding of the demographic characteristics and special needs of graduate and professional students
- provision of on-campus housing designed for graduate and professional students, including housing for married students, students with domestic partners, older single students, and students with

children
- assistance in locating accessible, affordable, and safe off-campus housing
- provision of child care services
- expanded access to libraries, laboratories, and studios as needed days, nights, and weekends throughout the year
- coordination of campus and community transit, parking, and security to access classes, libraries, laboratories, and studios

Part 3. Organization and Leadership

To achieve program and student learning and development outcomes, Graduate and Professional Student Programs and Services (GPSPS) must be purposefully structured for effectiveness. Programs and services must have clearly stated and current
- goals and outcomes
- policies and procedures
- responsibilities and performance expectations for personnel
- organizational charts demonstrating clear channels of authority

Leaders must model ethical behavior and institutional citizenship.

Leaders with organizational authority for the GPSPS must provide strategic planning, management and supervision, and program advancement.

Strategic Planning
- articulate a vision and mission that drive short- and long-term planning
- set goals and objectives based on the needs of the populations served, intended student learning and development outcomes, and program outcomes
- facilitate continuous development, implementation, and assessment of program effectiveness and goal attainment congruent with institutional mission and strategic plans
- promote environments that provide opportunities for student learning, development, and engagement
- develop, adapt, and improve programs and services in response to the changing needs of populations served and evolving institutional priorities
- include diverse perspectives to inform decision making

Management and Supervision
- plan, allocate, and monitor the use of fiscal, physical, human, intellectual, and technological resources
- manage human resource processes including recruitment, selection, professional development, supervision, performance planning, succession planning, evaluation, recognition, and reward
- influence others to contribute to the effectiveness

and success of the unit
- empower professional, support, and student personnel to become effective leaders
- encourage and support collaboration with colleagues and departments across the institution
- encourage and support scholarly contributions to the profession
- identify and address individual, organizational, and environmental conditions that foster or inhibit mission achievement
- use current and valid evidence to inform decisions
- incorporate sustainability practices in the management and design of programs, services, and facilities
- understand appropriate technologies and integrate them into programs and services
- be knowledgeable about codes and laws relevant to programs and services and ensure that programs and services meet those requirements
- assess and take action to mitigate potential risks

Program Advancement
- advocate for and actively promote the mission and goals of the programs and services
- inform stakeholders about issues affecting practice
- facilitate processes to reach consensus where wide support is needed
- advocate for representation in strategic planning initiatives at divisional and institutional levels

GPSPS leaders must collaborate with institutional leaders; academic departments within their college, school, or division; colleagues in other graduate programs at their institution; and with graduate offices, enrollment services, student affairs, academic support services, and alumni affairs for the purpose of developing strategies for connecting students to the larger community and positively affecting graduate student learning and development in and outside the classroom.

Staffing and reporting structures of GPSPS may vary. Whatever the structure, GPSPS should develop collaborative mechanisms, working groups, or relationships to coordinate their work to benefit all graduate and professional students.

Part 4. Human Resources

Graduate and Professional Student Programs and Services (GPSPS) must be staffed adequately by individuals qualified to accomplish mission and goals.

GPSPS must have access to technical and support personnel adequate to accomplish their mission.

Within institutional guidelines, GPSPS must
- establish procedures for personnel recruitment and selection, training, performance planning, and evaluation
- set expectations for supervision and performance
- provide personnel access to continuing and advanced education and appropriate professional development opportunities to improve their

- competence, skills, and leadership capacity
- consider work/life options available to personnel (e.g., compressed work schedules, flextime, job sharing, remote work, or telework) to promote recruitment and retention of personnel

Administrators of GPSPS must
- ensure that all personnel have updated position descriptions
- implement recruitment and selection/hiring strategies that produce a workforce inclusive of under-represented populations
- develop promotion practices that are fair, inclusive, proactive, and non-discriminatory

Personnel responsible for delivery of GPSPS must have written performance goals, objectives, and outcomes for each year's performance cycle to be used to plan, review, and evaluate work and performance. The performance plan must be updated regularly to reflect changes during the performance cycle.

Results of individual personnel evaluations must be used to recognize personnel performance, address performance issues, implement individual and/or collective personnel development and training programs, and inform the assessment of programs and services.

GPSPS personnel, when hired and throughout their employment, must receive appropriate and thorough training.

GPSPS personnel, including student employees and volunteers, must have access to resources or receive specific training on
- institutional policies pertaining to functions or activities they support
- privacy and confidentiality policies
- laws regarding access to student records
- policies and procedures for dealing with sensitive institutional information
- policies and procedures related to technology used to store or access student records and institutional data
- how and when to refer those in need of additional assistance to qualified personnel and have access to a supervisor for assistance in making these judgments
- systems and technologies necessary to perform their assigned responsibilities
- ethical and legal uses of technology

GPSPS personnel must engage in continuing professional development activities to keep abreast of the research, theories, legislation, policies, and developments that affect their programs and services.

Administrators of GPSPS must ensure that personnel are knowledgeable about and trained in safety, emergency procedures, and crisis prevention and response. Risk management efforts must address identification of threatening conduct or behavior and must incorporate a system for responding to and reporting such behaviors.

GPSPS personnel must be knowledgeable of and trained in safety and emergency procedures for securing and vacating facilities.

PROFESSIONAL PERSONNEL

GPSPS professional personnel either must hold an earned graduate or professional degree in a field relevant to their position or must possess an appropriate combination of educational credentials and related work experience.

GPSPS professional staff should be educated in student/academic services in order to design and implement intentional support and services for graduate and professional students.

INTERNS OR GRADUATE ASSISTANTS

Degree- or credential-seeking interns or graduate assistants must be qualified by enrollment in an appropriate field of study and relevant experience. These students must be trained and supervised by professional personnel who possess applicable educational credentials and work experience and have supervisory experience. Supervisors must be cognizant of the dual roles interns and graduate assistants have as both student and employee.

Supervisors must
- adhere to parameters of students' job descriptions
- articulate intended learning outcomes in student job descriptions
- adhere to agreed-upon work hours and schedules
- offer flexible scheduling when circumstances necessitate

Supervisors and students must both agree to suitable compensation if circumstances necessitate additional hours.

STUDENT EMPLOYEES AND VOLUNTEERS

Student employees and volunteers must be carefully selected, trained, supervised, and evaluated. Students must have access to a supervisor. Student employees and volunteers must be provided clear job descriptions, pre-service training based on assessed needs, and continuing development.

Part 5. Ethics

Graduate and Professional Student Programs and Services (GPSPS) must
- review applicable professional ethical standards and must adopt or develop and implement appropriate statements of ethical practice
- publish and adhere to statements of ethical practice and ensure their periodic review
- orient new personnel to relevant ethical standards and statements of ethical practice and related institutional policies

Statements of ethical standards must
- specify that GPSPS personnel respect privacy and

maintain confidentiality in communications and records as delineated by privacy laws

- specify limits on disclosure of information contained in students' records as well as requirements to disclose to appropriate authorities
- address conflicts of interest, or appearance thereof, by personnel in the performance of their work
- reflect the responsibility of personnel to be fair, objective, and impartial in their interactions with others
- reference management of institutional funds
- reference appropriate behavior regarding research and assessment with human participants, confidentiality of research and assessment data, and students' rights and responsibilities
- include the expectation that personnel confront and hold accountable other personnel who exhibit unethical behavior
- address issues surrounding scholarly integrity

GPSPS personnel must

- employ ethical decision making in the performance of their duties
- inform users of programs and services of ethical obligations and limitations emanating from codes and laws or from licensure requirements
- recognize and avoid conflicts of interest that could adversely influence their judgment or objectivity and, when unavoidable, recuse themselves from the situation
- perform their duties within the scope of their position, training, expertise, and competence
- make referrals when issues presented exceed the scope of the position

Part 6. Law, Policy, and Governance

Graduate and Professional Student Programs and Services (GPSPS) must be in compliance with laws, regulations, and policies that relate to their respective responsibilities and that pose legal obligations, limitations, risks, and liabilities for the institution as a whole. Examples include constitutional, statutory, regulatory, and case law; relevant law and orders emanating from codes and laws; and the institution's policies.

GPSPS must have access to legal advice needed for personnel to carry out their assigned responsibilities.

GPSPS must inform personnel, appropriate officials, and users of programs and services about existing and changing legal obligations, risks and liabilities, and limitations.

GPSPS must inform personnel about professional liability insurance options and refer them to external sources if the institution does not provide coverage.

GPSPS must have written policies and procedures on operations, transactions, or tasks that have legal implications.

GPSPS must regularly review policies. The revision and creation of policies must be informed by best practices, available evidence, and policy issues in higher education.

GPSPS must have procedures and guidelines consistent with institutional policy for responding to threats, emergencies, and crisis situations. Systems and procedures must be in place to disseminate timely and accurate information to students, other members of the institutional community, and appropriate external organizations during emergency situations.

Personnel must neither participate in nor condone any form of harassment or activity that demeans persons or creates an intimidating, hostile, or offensive environment.

GPSPS must purchase or obtain permission to use copyrighted materials and instruments. References to copyrighted materials and instruments must include appropriate citations.

GPSPS must inform personnel about internal and external governance organizations that affect programs and services.

Part 7. Diversity, Equity, and Access

Within the context of each institution's mission and in accordance with institutional policies and applicable codes and laws, Graduate and Professional Student Programs and Services (GPSPS) must create and maintain educational and work environments that are welcoming, accessible, inclusive, equitable, and free from harassment.

GPSPS must not discriminate on the basis of disability; age; race; cultural identity; ethnicity; nationality; family educational history (e.g., first generation to attend college); political affiliation; religious affiliation; sex; sexual orientation; gender identity and expression; marital, social, economic, or veteran status; or any other basis included in institutional policies and codes and laws.

GPSPS must

- advocate for sensitivity to multicultural and social justice concerns by the institution and its personnel
- ensure physical, program, and resource access for all constituents
- modify or remove policies, practices, systems, technologies, facilities, and structures that create barriers or produce inequities
- ensure that when facilities and structures cannot be modified, they do not impede access to programs, services, and resources
- establish goals for diversity, equity, and access
- foster communication and practices that enhance understanding of identity, culture, self-expression, and heritage
- promote respect for commonalities and differences among people within their historical and cultural contexts
- address the characteristics and needs of diverse

constituents when establishing and implementing culturally relevant and inclusive programs, services, policies, procedures, and practices

- provide personnel with diversity, equity, and access training and hold personnel accountable for applying the training to their work
- respond to the needs of all constituents served when establishing hours of operation and developing methods of delivering programs, services, and resources
- recognize the needs of distance and online learning students by directly providing or assisting them to gain access to comparable services and resources

Part 8. Internal and External Relations

Graduate and Professional Student Programs and Services (GPSPS) must reach out to individuals, groups, communities, and organizations internal and external to the institution to

- establish, maintain, and promote understanding and effective relations with those that have a significant interest in or potential effect on the students or other constituents served by the programs and services
- garner support and resources for programs and services as defined by the mission
- collaborate in offering or improving programs and services to meet the needs of students and other constituents and to achieve program and student outcomes
- engage diverse individuals, groups, communities, and organizations to enrich the educational environment and experiences of students and other constituents
- disseminate information about the programs and services

The staff of GPSPS must work collaboratively with colleagues in other graduate programs at their institution and with departments including but not limited to graduate offices, enrollment services, international student services, student affairs, academic support services, research and grants offices, development, and alumni affairs.

Promotional and descriptive information must be accurate and free of deception and misrepresentation.

GPSPS must have procedures and guidelines consistent with institutional policy for

- communicating with the media
- distributing information through print, broadcast, and online sources
- contracting with external organizations for delivery of programs and services
- cultivating, soliciting, and managing gifts
- applying to and managing funds from grants

Part 9. Financial Resources

Graduate and Professional Student Programs and Services

(GPSPS) must have funding to accomplish the mission and goals.

In establishing and prioritizing funding resources, GPSPS must conduct comprehensive analyses to determine

- unmet needs of the unit
- relevant expenditures
- external and internal resources
- impact on students and the institution

GPSPS must use the budget as a planning tool to reflect commitment to the mission and goals of the programs and services and of the institution.

GPSPS must administer funds in accordance with established institutional accounting procedures.

GPSPS must demonstrate efficient and effective use and responsible stewardship of fiscal resources consistent with institutional protocols.

Financial reports must provide an accurate financial overview of the organization and provide clear, understandable, and timely data upon which personnel can plan and make informed decisions.

Procurement procedures must

- be consistent with institutional policies
- ensure that purchases comply with laws and codes for usability and access
- ensure that the institution receives value for the funds spent
- consider information available for comparing the ethical and environmental impact of products and services purchased

Part 10. Technology

Graduate and Professional Student Programs and Services (GPSPS) must have technology to support the achievement of their mission and goals. The technology and its use must comply with institutional policies and procedures and with relevant codes and laws.

GPSPS must use technologies to

- provide updated information regarding mission, location, staffing, programs, services, and official contacts to students and other constituents in accessible formats
- provide an avenue for students and other constituents to communicate sensitive information in a secure format
- enhance the delivery of programs and services for all students

GPSPS must

- back up data on a regular basis
- adhere to institutional policies regarding ethical and legal use of technology
- articulate policies and procedures for protecting the confidentiality and security of information
- implement a replacement plan and cycle for all technology with attention to sustainability

- incorporate accessibility features into technology-based programs and services

When providing student access to technology, GPSPS must
- have policies on the use of technology that are clear, easy to understand, and available to all students
- provide information or referral to support services for those needing assistance in accessing or using technology
- provide instruction or training on how to use the technology
- inform students of implications of misuse of technologies

Part 11. Facilities and Equipment

Graduate and Professional Student Programs and Services' (GPSPS) facilities must be intentionally designed and located in suitable, accessible, and safe spaces that demonstrate universal design and support the program's mission and goals.

Facilities must be designed to engage various constituents and promote learning.

Personnel must have workspaces that are suitably located and accessible, well equipped, adequate in size, and designed to support their work and responsibilities.

The design of the facilities must guarantee the security and privacy of records and ensure the confidentiality of sensitive information and conversations. Personnel must be able to secure their work.

GPSPS should advocate for adequate office and work space for research and teaching assistants located where meaningful interactions with students, faculty members, and staff members may take place.

GPSPS should ensure that graduate and professional students have adequate spaces for study groups; for socializing and networking with peers, faculty and staff members; and for holding co-curricular programs and events. These spaces should be for the specific use by graduate and professional students.

GPSPS should provide space for graduate student organizations and governance councils.

GPSPS must incorporate sustainable practices in use of facilities and purchase of equipment. Facilities and equipment must be evaluated on an established cycle and be in compliance with codes, laws, and accepted practices for access, health, safety, and security.

When acquiring capital equipment, GPSPS must take into account expenses related to regular maintenance and life cycle costs.

Part 12. Assessment

Graduate and Professional Student Programs and Services (GPSPS) must develop assessment plans and processes.

These should include assessment of
- demographics and characteristics of the students
- student needs, experiences, and learning outcomes
- overall use of and satisfaction with programs and services
- attrition and persistence rates, such as time to degree completion and reasons for leaving prior to completion
- post-graduation career plans and outcomes
- adherence to national standards
- certification and licensing examination passing rates
- overall satisfaction with services and environment

Assessment plans must articulate an ongoing cycle of assessment activities.

GPSPS must
- specify programmatic goals and intended outcomes
- identify student learning and development outcomes
- employ multiple measures and methods
- develop manageable processes for gathering, interpreting, and evaluating data
- document progress toward achievement of goals and outcomes
- interpret and use assessment results to demonstrate accountability
- report aggregated results to respondent groups and stakeholders
- use assessment results to inform planning and decision-making
- assess effectiveness of implemented changes
- provide evidence of improvement of programs and services

GPSPS must employ ethical practices in the assessment process.

GPSPS must have access to adequate fiscal, human, professional development, and technological resources to develop and implement assessment plans.

General Standards revised in 2014;
GPSPS content developed in 2008

Health Promotion Services
CAS Contextual Statement

Many institutions use Health Promotion Services (HPS) to enhance the learning experience of students and the quality of the academic environment. Institutions also use a comprehensive employee wellness program as the foundation for establishing an environment that values health and wellness as a resource for productivity, learning, and everyday life. Colleges and universities engage students, faculty, and staff in developing personal skills, establishing strong communities, and building environments where well-being advances the capacity to learn, work, and contribute. Many variables (physical facilities, campus master plans, policies, traditions, enrollment demographics, the geography of the surrounding communities, and the employees as faculty or staff) contribute to the environment of an institution of higher education and are essential to using health promotion to bring about health and wellness on a college campus. For context several definitions are needed to understand how health, wellness, health promotion and prevention are interrelated.

The most commonly quoted definition of health was formalized in 1948 by the World Health Organization (WHO); "**Health** is a complete state of physical, mental and social well-being, and not merely the absence of disease or infirmity."

Wellness is defined in the United States, by the President's Council on Physical Fitness and Sports as:

> **Wellness** is not the same as physical fitness. Wellness is what you are- not what you do. Wellness is not a form of alternative medicine. Wellness is a multidimensional state of being describing the existence of positive health in an individual as exemplified by quality of life and sense of well-being. Wellness, clearly understood, can be a useful term for health promotion professionals and for the general public. (Corbin & Pangrazi, 2001)

Health and wellness may be synonymous terms for a state of being and may shift from moment to moment regardless of professional disease or condition diagnosis. Wellness usually has a more detailed list of descriptors for "well-being," often detailing six or more areas (physical, emotional, social, intellectual, spiritual, and occupational) rather than the three areas found in the WHO definition of health (physical, mental, social). Useful definitions of related terms can be found in the WHO "Health Promotion Glossary, New Terms" (Smith, Tang, & Nutbeam, 2006).

Achieving, maintaining, or enhancing a state of health and wellness is guided by a variety of multifaceted processes. One of these processes is health promotion as defined in 1986 by the World Health Organization (WHO) "Ottawa Charter for Health Promotion" as:

> **Health promotion** is the process of enabling people to increase control over, and to improve, their health. To reach a state of complete physical, mental and social well-being, an individual or group must be able to identify and to realize aspirations, to satisfy needs,

and to change or cope with the environment. Health is, therefore, seen as a resource for everyday life, not the objective of living. Health is a positive concept emphasizing social and personal resources, as well as physical capacities. Therefore, health promotion is not just the responsibility of the health sector, but goes beyond healthy life-styles to well-being. (p. 2)

On any given campus, HPS have four essential goals: (a) the realization of the fullest potential of an individual physically, psychologically, socially, spiritually, and economically; (b) the fulfillment of an individual's role expectations in the family, community, place of worship, workplace, and other settings; (c) the achievement of more desirable outcomes for a group or population; and (d) the support and creation of environments that are enhancing of well-being for whole populations regardless of individual variables. These four key points are part of a positive concept emphasizing social and personal resources as well as the capacities of individuals, groups, populations, and environments.

Prevention and wellness enhancement ground the integration of these four essential goals and lead the process that is state-of-the-art HPS. Health promotion is a process that can enhance wellness, reduce risk and prevent negative outcomes. While wellness enhancements build resilience and capacity, **prevention** deters the development of health problems before they occur and therefore reduces risk factors and enhances protective factors. Using the Institute of Medicine Model, there are three subsets of prevention: universal, selective, and indicated.

- Universal prevention is wellness enhancing or risk reducing for broad populations without consideration of individual differences in risk.
- Selective prevention targets sub-populations of individuals identified on the basis of their membership in a group that has elevated risk.
- Indicated prevention is for individuals who are members of a group that exhibit high-risk behaviors (Springer & Phillips, 2006).

In recent history, health is determined objectively by infection, injury, illness or deficiency, while wellness is about subjective capacities and realization of wholeness for individual, community, and environments (Awofeso, 2008). These **Health Promotion Actions** listed in the Ottawa Charter for Health Promotion, provide actions for the process to achieve health and wellness:
- build healthy public policy
- create supportive environments
- strengthen community actions
- develop personal skills
- re-orient healthcare services (i.e., "beyond its responsibility for providing clinical and curative services towards prevention of illness and promotion of health")

All of these actions are essential. Unfortunately, too often the focus of HPS efforts is limited to only developing personal skills and even then only focused on involving some form of communication designed to improve health knowledge; health education that is focused only at the "remembering" level of Bloom's *Taxonomy of Educational Objectives* is never evaluated for actual skill development. Limited resources go to ineffectively informing individuals rather than developing personal skills or any of the other five Health Promotion Actions. The Socio-ecological Model emphasizes the necessity for action at the contextual levels surrounding the individual. In fact, environmental management using policy and the built environment can reduce risk and enhance health without requiring each individual to develop a skill. Each of the five Health Promotion Actions are reinforced with the Socio-ecological Prevention Planning Model (McLeroy, 1988) in that they set individual-level skills and risk factors within complex layers of environment that can add population-level protection and enhancement.

This is important to articulate these definitions in mission and purpose statements, strategic plans, physical location, and resource allocations. It will also be important to describe the health promotion discipline to campus colleagues and to support campus-wide initiatives. Before the development of health promotion in the 1980s when health education was the focus, many professionals were relegated to executing awareness activities, giving presentations, distributing kitschy promotional items, and creating bulletin boards, brochures, and other non-evidence-based activities. Individual education is ineffective in a non-supportive environment. Today, mature health promotion services have much more to offer the campus, placing a great emphasis on gathering population-level surveillance data, universal prevention leadership; theory-based and evidence-informed practice to create the environments in which wellness helps learning happen.

State-of-the-art health promotion not only provides services that develop personal skills but also those that support built environments, enforces public policy, and empowers communities. The most effective work is in universal prevention at the population-level rather than waiting to identify at-risk behavior and then "fixing" one individual at a time. For HPS to engage in the actions listed--personal skills, built environments, policy, and community support—it requires moving beyond the healthcare sector to coalition building, networking, leadership, policy change, and community organizing.

References, Readings, and Resources

Allen, N., Fabiano, P., Hong, L., Kennedy, S., Kenzig, M., Kodama, C., Swinford, P. L., & Zimmer, C. (2007). Introduction to the American College Health Association's "Standards of practice for health promotion in higher education." *Journal of American College Health, 55*(6), 374-379.

American College Health Association [ACHA]. (2014). *Guidelines for hiring health promotion professionals in higher education.* Baltimore, MD. http://www.acha.org/Publications/docs/Hiring_Health_Promotion_Professionals_in_Higher_Ed_May2014.pdf

American College Health Association [ACHA]. (2012). *Standards of practice for health promotion professionals in higher education.*

Baltimore, MD. http://www.acha.org/Publications/docs/Standards_of_Practice_for_Health_Promotion_in_Higher_Education_May2012.pdf

American College Health Association [ACHA]: www.acha.org

Awofeso, N., (2008). *Redefining Health.* Bulletin of the World Health Organization. Retrieved from http://www.who.int/bulletin/bulletin_board/83/ustun11051/en/#

Bloom, B. S., Engelhart, M. D., Furst, E. J., Hill, W. H., & Krathwohl, D. R. (1956). *Taxonomy of educational objectives: The classification of educational goals; Handbook I: Cognitive Domain.* New York, NY: David McKay Co. Inc.

Centers for Disease Control and Prevention. (2007). The social-ecological model: a framework for prevention. Retrieved from http://www.cdc.gov/ncipc/dvp/social-ecological-model_dvp.htm

Gordon, R. S. (1983). An operational classification of disease prevention. *Public Health Reports, 98*(2), 107- 109.

Gullotta, T. P., & Bloom, M. (eds.). (2003). *The encyclopedia of primary prevention and health promotion.* New York, NY: Kluwer/Plenum.

Haddon, W. (1980). Advances in the epidemiology of injures as a basis for public policy. *Public Health Reports, 95*(5), 411-421.

McLeroy, K., Bibeau, D., Steckler, A., & Glanz, K. (1988). An ecological perspective on health promotion programs. *Health Education & Behavior, 15*(4), 351-377.

Miller, J. W. (2005). Wellness: The History and Development. *Spektrum Freizeit, 2005/1*, 84-102.

National Association of Student Personnel Administrators – NASPA. (2010). Leadership for a healthy campus: An ecological approach for student success. Retrieved from http://www.naspa.org/membership/mem/pubs/ebooks/HealthyCampus.pdf

National Wellness Institute, http://www.nationalwellness.org/?page=Six_Dimensions

Nutbeam, D. (1998). Health promotion glossary. *Health Promotion International, 13*(4), 349-364.

O'Donnell, M. P. (1989). Definition of health promotion: Part III: Expanding the definition. *American Journal of Health Promotion, 3*(3), 5.

O'Donnell, M. P. (2011). Editor's notes: Reflections on the 25th anniversary of publishing the American Journal of Health Promotion: People, scientific progress, and missteps. *American Journal of Health Promotion, 25*(4), iv-xi.

Smith, B. J., Tang, K. C., & Nutbeam, D. (2006). WHO health promotion glossary: New terms. *Health Promotion International, 21*(4), 340-345.

Springer, J. F., & Phillips, J. (2006). The IOM Model: A tool for prevention planning and implementation. Prevention Tactics 8:13. Sacramento, CA: Department of Alcohol and Drug Programs. Retrieved from http://casdfsc.org/docs/resources/SDFSC_IOM_Policy.pdf

Swinford, P. (2002). Advancing the health of students: A rationale for college health programs, *Journal of American College Health, 50*(6), 309-312.

Swinford, P., Baral Abrams, G. (2011, May 31). *Benchmark results: Infrastructure and scope of practice for health promotion in higher education.* Annual Meeting. Powerpoint presentation at the Annual Meeting of the American College Health Association, Chicago, IL Retrieved from http://www.acha.org/AnnualMeeting/webhandouts_2012/TH4-320_Swinford_P.pdf

US Department of Health and Human Services –DHHS (2008). *Executive summary - phase I report: recommendations for the framework and format of healthy people 2020.* Retrieved from http://www.healthypeople.gov/hp2020/advisory/PhaseI/summary.htm#_Toc211942897

World Health Organization. (1998). *Health promotion glossary.*

Retrieved from http://www.who.int/hpr/NPH/docs/hp_
glossary_en.pdf

World Health Organization. (1986). *The Ottawa charter for health
promotion.* (pp. 2). Retrieved from http://www.who.int/
healthpromotion/conferences/previous/ottawa/en/index1.html

World Health Organization. (1948). *Preamble to the Constitution of
the World Health Organization as adopted by the International
Health Conference,* New York, 19-22 June 1946, and entered into
force on 7 April 1948

Zimmer, C. G., Hill, M. H., & Sonnad, S. R. (2003). A scope-of-
practice survey leading to the development of standards of
practice for health promotion in higher education. *Journal of
American College Health, 51*(6), 247-54.

Zimmer, C. G. (2002). Health promotion in higher education. In
S Turner & J. Hurley (Eds.), *The history and practice of college
health.* Lexington, KY: The University Press of Kentucky, 311-
327.

<u>**Contextual Statement Contributors**</u>
Current Edition:
Patricia Fabiano, Western Washington University
Susan Kennedy, Pennsylvania State University
Nancy Allen, Michigan State University
Daisye Orr, Washington State Public Health Department
Paula Swinford, University of Southern California, ACHA
Dixie Bennett, Loyola University Chicago, NIRSA
Cathy Kodoma, University of California at Berkeley
Luoluo Hong, Arizona State University
Gina Baral Abrams, Princeton University
Stacy Andes, Villanova University, ACHA

Previous Editions:
Patricia Fabiano, Western Washington University
Susan Kennedy, Pennsylvania State University
Nancy Allen, Michigan State University
Daisye Orr, Washington State Public Health Department
Paula Swinford, University of Southern California
Dixie Bennett, Loyola University Chicago, NIRSA
Cathy Kodoma, University of California at Berkeley
Luoluo Hong, Arizona State University
Gina Baral Abrams, Princeton University
Stacy Andes, Villanova University, ACHA

Health Promotion Services
CAS Standards and Guidelines

Part 1. Mission

The mission and scope of practice of health promotion, sometimes referred to as wellness, must be reflective of the following fundamental assumptions about the role of health in higher education:

- there is a reciprocal relationship between learning and health, as well as a direct connection between the academic mission of higher education and the well-being of students
- in the broadest sense, health encompasses the capacity of individuals and communities to reach their potential
- health transcends individual factors and includes cultural, institutional, socioeconomic, and political influences
- health is not solely a biomedical quality measured through clinical indicators
- health and social justice are inextricably connected
- both individual and environmental approaches to health are critical

Health Promotion Services (HPS) must develop, disseminate, implement, and regularly review their missions, which must be consistent with the mission of the institution and with applicable professional standards. The mission must be appropriate for the institution's students and other constituents. Mission statements must reference student learning and development.

Part 2. Program

To achieve their mission, Health Promotion Services (HPS) must contribute to

- students' formal education, which includes both the curriculum and the co-curriculum
- student progression and timely completion of educational goals
- preparation of students for their careers, citizenship, and lives
- student learning and development

To contribute to student learning and development, HPS must

- identify relevant and desirable student learning and development outcomes
- articulate how the student learning and development outcomes align with the six CAS student learning and development domains and related dimensions
- assess relevant and desirable student learning

and development
- provide evidence of impact on outcomes
- articulate contributions to or support of student learning and development in the domains not specifically assessed
- use evidence gathered to create strategies for improvement of programs and services

STUDENT LEARNING AND DEVELOPMENT DOMAINS AND DIMENSIONS

Domain: knowledge acquisition, integration, construction, and application

- Dimensions: understanding knowledge from a range of disciplines; connecting knowledge to other knowledge, ideas, and experiences; constructing knowledge; and relating knowledge to daily life

Domain: cognitive complexity

- Dimensions: critical thinking, reflective thinking, effective reasoning, and creativity

Domain: intrapersonal development

- Dimensions: realistic self-appraisal, self-understanding, and self-respect; identity development; commitment to ethics and integrity; and spiritual awareness

Domain: interpersonal competence

- Dimensions: meaningful relationships, interdependence, collaboration, and effective leadership

Domain: humanitarianism and civic engagement

- Dimensions: understanding and appreciation of cultural and human differences, social responsibility, global perspective, and sense of civic responsibility

Domain: practical competence

- Dimensions: pursuing goals, communicating effectively, technical competence, managing personal affairs, managing career development, demonstrating professionalism, maintaining health and wellness, and living a purposeful and satisfying life

[LD Outcomes: See *The Council for the Advancement of Standards Learning and Development Outcomes* statement for examples of outcomes related to these domains and dimensions.]

HPS must be

- intentionally designed
- guided by theories and knowledge of learning and development
- integrated into the life of the institution

- reflective of developmental and demographic profiles of the student population
- responsive to needs of individuals, populations with distinct needs, and relevant constituencies
- delivered using multiple formats, strategies, and contexts
- designed to provide universal access

HPS must collaborate with colleagues and departments across the institution to promote student learning and development, persistence, and success.

HPS must advance the health of students and contribute to the creation of an institutional and community climate of health and social justice.

HPS must review health promotion research and theories from interdisciplinary sources as a guide for the development of initiatives.

HPS must articulate the theoretical frameworks used in setting priorities and decision-making to the campus community.

HPS must apply professionally recognized constructs, tested theories, and evidence based strategies to the development of initiatives designed to improve the health of individuals and the campus environment.

HPS must involve students, faculty members, staff members, and community constituents to advance the health of students and to create campus and community environments that support students' health.

HPS professionals should strive to reduce risk, incidence, and severity for individual mental and physical distress, illness and injury; enhance health as a strategy to support student learning; and advocate for safety, social justice, economic opportunity, and human dignity.

HPS must acknowledge that health and social justice are inextricably connected.

HPS professionals should strive to identify and address the complex social, cultural, economic, and political factors that may contribute to or compromise the health of individuals or communities; advocate for inclusive and equal access to resources and services; and eliminate health disparities and increase the quality and years of healthy life for all.

HPS must include both individual and environmental prevention strategies.

HPS professionals should strive to reduce the risk of individual illness and injury, as well as build individual capacity and address larger institutional issues, priority health issues, community factors, and public policies that affect the health of students.

HPS professionals must advance the connection between the academic mission of higher education and the well-being of students.

HPS professionals should support the academic mission of student learning by assisting students in leading healthier lives and engaging individuals who will become political, social, and economic decision makers, thereby advancing the collective health of the community.

Part 3. Organization and Leadership

To achieve program and student learning and development outcomes, Health Promotion Services (HPS) must be purposefully structured for effectiveness. HPS must have clearly stated and current

- goals and outcomes
- policies and procedures
- responsibilities and performance expectations for personnel
- organizational charts demonstrating clear channels of authority

Leaders must model ethical behavior and institutional citizenship.

Leaders with organizational authority for HPS must provide strategic planning, management and supervision, and program advancement.

Strategic Planning
- articulate a vision and mission that drive short- and long-term planning
- set goals and objectives based on the needs of the populations served, intended student learning and development outcomes, and program outcomes
- facilitate continuous development, implementation, and assessment of program effectiveness and goal attainment congruent with institutional mission and strategic plans
- promote environments that provide opportunities for student learning, development, and engagement
- develop, adapt, and improve programs and services in response to the changing needs of populations served and evolving institutional priorities
- include diverse perspectives to inform decision making

Management and Supervision
- plan, allocate, and monitor the use of fiscal, physical, human, intellectual, and technological resources
- manage human resource processes including recruitment, selection, professional development, supervision, performance planning, succession planning, evaluation, recognition, and reward

- influence others to contribute to the effectiveness and success of the unit
- empower professional, support, and student personnel to become effective leaders
- encourage and support collaboration with colleagues and departments across the institution
- encourage and support scholarly contributions to the profession
- identify and address individual, organizational, and environmental conditions that foster or inhibit mission achievement
- use current and valid evidence to inform decisions
- incorporate sustainability practices in the management and design of programs, services, and facilities
- understand appropriate technologies and integrate them into programs and services
- be knowledgeable about codes and laws relevant to programs and services and ensure that programs and services meet those requirements
- assess and take action to mitigate potential risks

Program Advancement
- advocate for and actively promote the mission and goals of the programs and services
- inform stakeholders about issues affecting practice
- facilitate processes to reach consensus where wide support is needed
- advocate for representation in strategic planning initiatives at divisional and institutional levels

Leaders of HPS must also
- develop health-related programs and policies that support student learning
- gather relevant data and review current literature
- develop strategic, operational, and resource utilization plans and policies

Leaders of HPS should advocate for campus-wide understanding of the connections between learning, culture, identity, social justice, and health.

Leaders of HPS should support others in strengthening their health promotion skills.

The HPS director must be placed within the institution's organizational structures so as to be able to promote cooperative interaction with appropriate campus and community entities and to develop the support of high-level administrators for the creation of safe and healthy campus environments. The placement of HPS within the organizational structure must clearly articulate the value of enhancing well-being and health promotion as essential to the overall mission of an institution.

HPS organizational placement should facilitate significant interaction with unit heads in academic and student affairs.

HPS must be located in an organizational structure to best provide for effective programs and services to achieve its mission.

HPS must play a principal role in creating and implementing institutional policies and programs in response to assessed student needs and capabilities.

HPS should function independent of clinical health services to ensure adequate attention is paid to prevention.

Part 4. Human Resources

Health Promotion Services (HPS) must be staffed adequately by individuals qualified to accomplish mission and goals.

HPS must have access to technical and support personnel adequate to accomplish their mission.

Within institutional guidelines, HPS must
- establish procedures for personnel recruitment and selection, training, performance planning, and evaluation
- set expectations for supervision and performance
- provide personnel access to continuing and advanced education and appropriate professional development opportunities to improve their competence, skills, and leadership capacity
- consider work/life options available to personnel (e.g., compressed work schedules, flextime, job sharing, remote work, or telework) to promote recruitment and retention of personnel

Administrators of HPS must
- ensure that all personnel have updated position descriptions
- implement recruitment and selection/hiring strategies that produce a workforce inclusive of under-represented populations
- develop promotion practices that are fair, inclusive, proactive, and non-discriminatory

HPS staffing requirements must be established and reviewed regularly with regard to size of campus, institutional resources, student needs, and interdisciplinary health promotion collaborations on campus.

Personnel responsible for delivery of HPS must have written performance goals, objectives, and outcomes for each year's performance cycle to be used to plan, review, and evaluate work and performance. The performance plan must be updated regularly to reflect changes during the performance cycle.

Results of individual personnel evaluations must be used to recognize personnel performance, address performance issues, implement individual and/ or collective personnel development and training programs, and inform the assessment of programs and services.

HPS personnel, when hired and throughout their employment, must receive appropriate and thorough training.

HPS personnel, including student employees and volunteers, must have access to resources or receive specific training on

- institutional policies pertaining to functions or activities they support
- privacy and confidentiality policies
- laws regarding access to student records
- policies and procedures for dealing with sensitive institutional information
- policies and procedures related to technology used to store or access student records and institutional data
- how and when to refer those in need of additional assistance to qualified personnel and have access to a supervisor for assistance in making these judgments
- systems and technologies necessary to perform their assigned responsibilities
- ethical and legal uses of technology

HPS personnel must engage in continuing professional development activities to keep abreast of the research, theories, legislation, policies, and developments that affect their programs and services.

HPS staff members must participate in training sessions and professional development that address gender, sexual orientation, racial, cultural, religious and/or spiritual, and ethnic sensitivity.

HPS should provide personnel with convenient access to on-line and other reference services that include materials pertinent to the operational, administrative, institutional, and research services offered by the institution.

Specific aspects of professional development should include theories of health promotion, student learning, and student development; assessment and evaluation; service delivery; coalition building; collaboration; and business and financial management.

Administrators of HPS must ensure that personnel are knowledgeable about and trained in safety, emergency procedures, and crisis prevention and response. Risk management efforts must address identification of threatening conduct or behavior and must incorporate a system for responding to and reporting such behaviors.

HPS personnel must be knowledgeable of and trained in safety and emergency procedures for securing and vacating facilities.

PROFESSIONAL PERSONNEL

HPS professional personnel either must hold an earned graduate or professional degree in a field relevant to their position or must possess an appropriate combination of educational credentials and related work experience.

HPS should encourage professional staff members to participate in regular self-reflection, assessment, and professional development planning to improve health promotion practice.

Professional staff members should have appropriate professional preparation and competencies in both theory and evidence-based practice for promoting health, advancing student learning, and contributing to student development.

The director of HPS should have an advanced degree in health education, public health, higher education administration, or other related discipline from an accredited institution.

The preferred qualification for HPS staff members should be an advanced degree from an accredited institution in a relevant discipline such as health education, public health, higher education administration, counseling, or community development with experience in higher education.

INTERNS OR GRADUATE ASSISTANTS

Degree- or credential-seeking interns or graduate assistants must be qualified by enrollment in an appropriate field of study and relevant experience. These students must be trained and supervised by professional personnel who possess applicable educational credentials and work experience and have supervisory experience. Supervisors must be cognizant of the dual roles interns and graduate assistants have as both student and employee.

Supervisors must

- adhere to parameters of students' job descriptions
- articulate intended learning outcomes in student job descriptions
- adhere to agreed-upon work hours and schedules
- offer flexible scheduling when circumstances necessitate

Supervisors and students must both agree to suitable compensation if circumstances necessitate additional hours.

STUDENT EMPLOYEES AND VOLUNTEERS

Student employees and volunteers must be carefully

selected, trained, supervised, and evaluated. Students must have access to a supervisor. Student employees and volunteers must be provided clear job descriptions, pre-service training based on assessed needs, and continuing development.

HPS staff members should be encouraged to demonstrate their commitment to these issues that affect individuals, the campus, and the community by participating in relevant events.

HPS staff members must demonstrate trustworthiness when dealing with sensitive information and a strict regard for confidentiality.

HPS should maintain and financially support an in-service and staff development program, and budgetary support should be available to provide for in-service and professional development activities.

Part 5. Ethics

Health Promotion Services (HPS) must
- review applicable professional ethical standards and must adopt or develop and implement appropriate statements of ethical practice
- publish and adhere to statements of ethical practice and ensure their periodic review
- orient new personnel to relevant ethical standards and statements of ethical practice and related institutional policies

Statements of ethical standards must
- specify that HPS personnel respect privacy and maintain confidentiality in communications and records as delineated by privacy laws
- specify limits on disclosure of information contained in students' records as well as requirements to disclose to appropriate authorities
- address conflicts of interest, or appearance thereof, by personnel in the performance of their work
- reflect the responsibility of personnel to be fair, objective, and impartial in their interactions with others
- reference management of institutional funds
- reference appropriate behavior regarding research and assessment with human participants, confidentiality of research and assessment data, and students' rights and responsibilities
- include the expectation that personnel confront and hold accountable other personnel who exhibit unethical behavior
- address issues surrounding scholarly integrity

HPS personnel must
- employ ethical decision making in the performance of their duties
- inform users of programs and services of ethical obligations and limitations emanating from codes and laws or from licensure requirements
- recognize and avoid conflicts of interest that could adversely influence their judgment or objectivity and, when unavoidable, recuse themselves from the situation
- perform their duties within the scope of their position, training, expertise, and competence
- make referrals when issues presented exceed the scope of the position

Part 6. Law, Policy, and Governance

Health Promotion Services (HPS) must be in compliance with laws, regulations, and policies that relate to their respective responsibilities and that pose legal obligations, limitations, risks, and liabilities for the institution as a whole. Examples include constitutional, statutory, regulatory, and case law; relevant law and orders emanating from codes and laws; and the institution's policies.

HPS must have access to legal advice needed for personnel to carry out their assigned responsibilities.

HPS must inform personnel, appropriate officials, and users of programs and services about existing and changing legal obligations, risks and liabilities, and limitations.

HPS must inform personnel about professional liability insurance options and refer them to external sources if the institution does not provide coverage.

HPS must have written policies and procedures on operations, transactions, or tasks that have legal implications.

HPS must regularly review policies. The revision and creation of policies must be informed by best practices, available evidence, and policy issues in higher education.

HPS must have procedures and guidelines consistent with institutional policy for responding to threats, emergencies, and crisis situations. Systems and procedures must be in place to disseminate timely and accurate information to students, other members of the institutional community, and appropriate external organizations during emergency situations.

Personnel must neither participate in nor condone any form of harassment or activity that demeans persons or creates an intimidating, hostile, or offensive environment.

HPS must purchase or obtain permission to use copyrighted materials and instruments. References to copyrighted materials and instruments must include appropriate citations.

HPS must inform personnel about internal and external governance organizations that affect programs and services.

Part 7. Diversity, Equity, and Access

Within the context of each institution's mission and in accordance with institutional policies and applicable codes and laws, Health Promotion Services (HPS) must create and maintain educational and work environments that are welcoming, accessible, inclusive, equitable, and free from harassment.

HPS must not discriminate on the basis of disability; age; race; cultural identity; ethnicity; nationality; family educational history (e.g., first generation to attend college); political affiliation; religious affiliation; sex; sexual orientation; gender identity and expression; marital, social, economic, or veteran status; or any other basis included in institutional policies and codes and laws.

HPS must

- advocate for sensitivity to multicultural and social justice concerns by the institution and its personnel
- ensure physical, program, and resource access for all constituents
- modify or remove policies, practices, systems, technologies, facilities, and structures that create barriers or produce inequities
- ensure that when facilities and structures cannot be modified, they do not impede access to programs, services, and resources
- establish goals for diversity, equity, and access
- foster communication and practices that enhance understanding of identity, culture, self-expression, and heritage
- promote respect for commonalities and differences among people within their historical and cultural contexts
- address the characteristics and needs of diverse constituents when establishing and implementing culturally relevant and inclusive programs, services, policies, procedures, and practices
- provide personnel with diversity, equity, and access training and hold personnel accountable for applying the training to their work
- respond to the needs of all constituents served when establishing hours of operation and developing methods of delivering programs, services, and resources
- recognize the needs of distance and online learning students by directly providing or assisting them to gain access to comparable

services and resources

HPS should identify any social, cultural, political, and economic disparities that influence the health of students so that any disparities may be adequately addressed to improve equity and access to health-related services.

HPS staff members must demonstrate cultural competency and inclusiveness in advancing the health of individuals and communities.

HPS should design health promotion initiatives that reflect the social, cultural, and economic diversity of students.

HPS should create health promotion mission statements, program policies, staff member recruitment and retention practices, and professional development goals that reflect the social, cultural, and economic diversity of the campus.

HPS should provide leadership for campus-wide understanding of the connection between culture, identity, social justice, and health status.

Part 8. Internal and External Relations

Health Promotion Services (HPS) must reach out to individuals, groups, communities, and organizations internal and external to the institution to

- establish, maintain, and promote understanding and effective relations with those that have a significant interest in or potential effect on the students or other constituents served by the programs and services
- garner support and resources for programs and services as defined by the mission
- collaborate in offering or improving programs and services to meet the needs of students and other constituents and to achieve program and student outcomes
- engage diverse individuals, groups, communities, and organizations to enrich the educational environment and experiences of students and other constituents
- disseminate information about the programs and services

Sustaining partnerships should

- advocate for a shared vision that health promotion is the responsibility of all campus and community members
- develop and participate in campus and community partnerships that advance health promotion initiatives
- use campus and community resources to maximize the effectiveness of health promotion initiatives
- advocate for campus, local, state/provincial, national, and international policies that address campus and community health issues

- institutionalize health promotion initiatives through inclusion in campus strategic planning and resource allocation processes

Promotional and descriptive information must be accurate and free of deception and misrepresentation.

Health Promotion Services (HPS) must have procedures and guidelines consistent with institutional policy for
- **communicating with the media**
- **distributing information through print, broadcast, and online sources**
- **contracting with external organizations for delivery of programs and services**
- **cultivating, soliciting, and managing gifts**
- **applying to and managing funds from grants**

To ensure success, HPS must maintain productive relations with students, faculty members, staff members, alumni, the community at large, contractors, and support agencies.

HPS staff members should participate actively with their institutions in designing policies and practices and developing further resources and services that have direct effects on the health of the campus population.

HPS should work closely with the senior administrators to ensure the meeting of institutional goals and objectives.

HPS should establish relationships with a wide range of constituencies, such as student affairs professionals, faculty members, and student groups, to promote collaboration and serve as a resource.

HPS should foster relationships with academic units and campus professionals in residence halls, recreational facilities, student activities, and athletics, where appropriate.

HPS should foster reciprocal relationships with clinical health services and counseling services to refer students for medical concerns and to serve as colleagues and consultants.

Part 9. Financial Resources

Health Promotion Services (HPS) must have funding to accomplish the mission and goals.

In establishing and prioritizing funding resources, HPS must conduct comprehensive analyses to determine
- **unmet needs of the unit**
- **relevant expenditures**
- **external and internal resources**
- **impact on students and the institution**

HPS must use the budget as a planning tool to reflect commitment to the mission and goals of the programs and services and of the institution.

HPS must administer funds in accordance with

established institutional accounting procedures.

Funding for HPS should be provided and sustained by the institution's budget or through a designated health fee applied to all enrolled students.

HPS must demonstrate efficient and effective use and responsible stewardship of fiscal resources consistent with institutional protocols.

Financial reports must provide an accurate financial overview of the organization and provide clear, understandable, and timely data upon which personnel can plan and make informed decisions.

Procurement procedures must
- **be consistent with institutional policies**
- **ensure that purchases comply with laws and codes for usability and access**
- **ensure that the institution receives value for the funds spent**
- **consider information available for comparing the ethical and environmental impact of products and services purchased**

Part 10. Technology

Health Promotion Services (HPS) must have technology to support the achievement of their mission and goals. The technology and its use must comply with institutional policies and procedures and with relevant codes and laws.

HPS must use technologies to
- **provide updated information regarding mission, location, staffing, programs, services, and official contacts to students and other constituents in accessible formats**
- **provide an avenue for students and other constituents to communicate sensitive information in a secure format**
- **enhance the delivery of programs and services for all students**

HPS must
- **back up data on a regular basis**
- **adhere to institutional policies regarding ethical and legal use of technology**
- **articulate policies and procedures for protecting the confidentiality and security of information**
- **implement a replacement plan and cycle for all technology with attention to sustainability**
- **incorporate accessibility features into technology-based programs and services**

When providing student access to technology, HPS must
- **have policies on the use of technology that are clear, easy to understand, and available to all students**
- **provide information or referral to support**

services for those needing assistance in accessing or using technology
- provide instruction or training on how to use the technology
- inform students of implications of misuse of technologies

Part 11. Facilities and Equipment

Health Promotion Services' (HPS) facilities must be intentionally designed and located in suitable, accessible, and safe spaces that demonstrate universal design and support the program's mission and goals.

Facilities must be designed to engage various constituents and promote learning.

Personnel must have workspaces that are suitably located and accessible, well equipped, adequate in size, and designed to support their work and responsibilities.

The design of the facilities must guarantee the security and privacy of records and ensure the confidentiality of sensitive information and conversations. Personnel must be able to secure their work.

HPS must incorporate sustainable practices in use of facilities and purchase of equipment. Facilities and equipment must be evaluated on an established cycle and be in compliance with codes, laws, and accepted practices for access, health, safety, and security.

To promote holistic health, the facilities of HPS should include
- a safe, functional, effective, and conveniently located positive environment for students, faculty and staff members, and community partners
- office space that is functionally autonomous rather than housed as a component of other units on campus
- office space that is physically separate from clinical health services
- quality space to ensure maximum effectiveness in providing health promotion resources for the campus community
- adequate meeting space for training student volunteers and supporting their work
- adequate physical facilities, equipment, and technology to monitor and report population health status data

When acquiring capital equipment, HPS must take into account expenses related to regular maintenance and life cycle costs.

Part 12. Assessment

Health Promotion Services (HPS) must develop assessment plans and processes.

Assessment plans must articulate an ongoing cycle of assessment activities.

HPS must
- specify programmatic goals and intended outcomes
- identify student learning and development outcomes
- employ multiple measures and methods
- develop manageable processes for gathering, interpreting, and evaluating data
- document progress toward achievement of goals and outcomes
- interpret and use assessment results to demonstrate accountability
- report aggregated results to respondent groups and stakeholders
- use assessment results to inform planning and decision-making
- assess effectiveness of implemented changes
- provide evidence of improvement of programs and services

Assessment and evaluation should include
- data gathered from published research on international, national, state/provincial, local, and campus health priorities
- population-based assessment of health status, needs, and assets of students
- environmental assessment of campus-community health needs and resources
- measurable goals and objectives for health promotion initiatives

HPS should report evaluation data and research results to students, faculty members, staff members, and the campus community.

HPS must employ ethical practices in the assessment process.

HPS must have access to adequate fiscal, human, professional development, and technological resources to develop and implement assessment plans.

General Standards revised in 2014;
HPS content developed/revised in 2006

Housing and Residential Life Programs
CAS Contextual Statement

Although American institutions of higher learning have provided student housing in one form or another since the first colleges were founded (Frederiksen, 1993), the professionalization of those employed in housing was greatly enhanced when the Association of College and University Housing Officers-International (ACUHO-I) held its first annual conference in 1949. This meeting marked a significant step forward in the development of college and university student housing programs as a profession.

Until the middle of the last century, college and university "dormitories" were administered by "housemothers," often under the supervision of deans of men or women. These staff members assumed parental responsibility (in loco parentis) for the students housed in the residence halls. During the 1960s, dramatic changes in laws and education produced changes in the operation of residence halls. Housemothers were replaced by full-time staff with professional training in counseling and administration. These student affairs professionals focused on using the residence hall environment as a tool to complement formal classroom education. Since the 1960s, student housing has become increasingly more specialized and complex. The influence of the residential experience on the lives of students has been widely researched over the years.

> Group living influences maturation by exposing students to a variety of experiences and community-building activities. What distinguishes group living in a campus residence from most other forms of housing is the involvement of both professional and paraprofessional staff members in providing intentional, as opposed to random, educational experiences for students. Students living in residence halls participate in more extracurricular, social, and cultural events; are more likely to graduate; and exhibit greater positive gains in psychosocial development, intellectual orientation, and self-concept than students living at home or commuting. In addition, they demonstrate significantly greater increases in aesthetic, cultural, and intellectual values; social and political liberalism; and secularism. (Schroeder & Mable, 1993)

More recently, the quality of residence halls has been acknowledged as not only essential to the quality of campus life but as an increasingly important factor in attracting students to a given institution. There has been a renaissance in college and university housing with many campuses significantly renovating halls and constructing new facilities to respond to today's students and to better meet expectations. One challenge for housing professionals has indeed been the increasing demand for amenities in residence halls, which is often necessary to not only respond to the needs of today's students but to remain competitive with housing in the local market or with other institutions that are considered peers for enrollment management purposes. Some of the more obvious amenity enhancements include air conditioning, wireless connectivity, and conversion of traditional double loaded corridor rooms to suite style or single room accommodations, including bathrooms.

Another facility enhancement that cannot be overlooked is additions to the safety features provided in housing and residence life programs. In addition to electronic card access found on exterior doors, more programs are adding this feature to the individual room doors to eliminate the need for keys and to facilitate a very timely response, minimizing any threat to building security. Throughout these facility enhancements, housing professionals are continually faced with balancing students' desire for convenience with the university's needs related to security and public safety. Many colleges and universities have added video surveillance capability to exterior doors, stairwells, elevator lobbies, halls, high tech learning facilities, or specialized classrooms while being sensitive to privacy issues on individual floors and rooms. Housing and Residence Life professionals are often members of the campus emergency management and/or threat-assessment teams and play a key role in emergency planning and response.

One of the most impactful concepts in higher education today is that of learning communities; many universities have developed living-learning communities (LLCs) within residential communities as a means to be more intentional about student learning. LLCs provide valuable opportunities to integrate the more formal academic and student life experience, provide increased interaction between students and faculty, and provide critical avenues to enhance campus community building activities and traditions. Living-learning communities can be developed around themes, majors, or concepts. In addition to providing a seamless learning experience and increased student engagement, LLCs are seen as critical to increasing retention, especially from the first to the second year.

College and university student housing operations employ staff members with wide varieties of skills and functions. Areas administered by institutional housing and residence life programs include such functions as

- Apartment, graduate, and family housing
- Fraternities and sororities
- Student conduct and/or contract violations
- Housing for students with disabilities and other special needs
- Conference and guest housing
- Residence Education, including academic initiatives, LLCs, programming, and diversity education
- Facilities management (custodial and maintenance) and capital projects
- Financial planning and administration (assignments, contracting, billing, collections)
- Dining services (including catering and retail venues)

- Administration of in-hall information technology capabilities, media, and facilities (cable TV, various software systems, network and wireless access, computer learning centers, and classrooms)
- Off-campus housing services
- Research and assessment
- Safety and security measures (fire safety, electronic access systems, video surveillance, hall security)
- Identification and "one card" programs

Assessment efforts, particularly incorporating assessment of services, programs, staffing, and student learning, can provide valuable information to housing administrators as they shape their housing and residential life programs. Administrators can work to develop clear student learning outcomes and design assessment to analyze these outcomes. Assessment lenses (e.g., interviews, focus groups, surveys, tracking) can help administrators document student learning and make efforts to improve the residential experience. Association of College and University Housing Officers–International (ACUHO-I), Educational Benchmarking Inc., the National Survey of Student Engagement (NSSE), and National Study of Living-Learning Programs (NSLLP) are examples of national surveys that are often administered to collect assessment data.

Many institutional student-housing operations are self-supported auxiliaries that do not receive financial support from the institution or other public sources; in effect, student housing in that context is an education "business." Privatization of residence halls/collegiate housing is part of the landscape of 21st century housing on college campuses. Some schools have opted to privatize aspects of their residence halls (development, construction, and management), utilizing housing management companies to address residence hall capacity shortages, aging facilities, a desire to house more students on campus, and changing student expectations (Fickes, 2007). Regardless of the status of the operation, planning is usually initiated institution-wide due to the wide scope and function of student housing. Likewise, although housing encompasses many functions, most administrations agree that students are best served when all housing and residential life functions fall under the responsibility of a single administrator, usually the director of housing and/or residential life. When public-private partnerships are undertaken, and "privatized" housing developments have a formal relationship with the college or university and are located on campus, it is expected that these entities follow the same CAS Standards as the institution's program. As higher education prepares students with the knowledge and skills required for the challenges of the 21st century and as learning becomes more a lifetime responsibility, residence halls will continue to be a critical component of the undergraduate experience. The standards and guidelines that follow provide guidance to those who work in this field and accountability to the public they serve.

References, Readings, and Resources

American Association of Higher Education, American College Personnel Association, National Association of Student Personnel Administrators. (1998). *Powerful partnerships: A shared responsibility for learning.* Washington, DC: Authors.

American College Personnel Association. Commission on Housing and Residence Life: http://www.acpa.nche.edu/comms/comm03/index.html

National Association of Student Personnel Administrators (NASPA) & American College Personnel Association (ACPA) (2004). *Learning reconsidered: A campus-wide focus on the student experience.* Washington DC: Authors.

Association of College and University Housing Officers-International (ACUHO-I). (1999). *Educational programming and student learning in college and university residence halls.* Columbus, OH: Author.

Association of College and University Housing Officers-International (ACUHO-I). (1992). *Ethical principles and standards for college and university housing professionals.* Columbus, OH: Author.

Association of College and University Housing Officers - International. (2008b). *Recruitment and retention of entry-level staff in housing and residence life*: A report on activities supported by the ACUHO-I commissioned research program. Columbus, OH: Author.

Blimling, G. S. (1993). New challenges and goals for residential life programs. In R. B. Winston, Jr., S. Anchors, & Associates (Eds.), *Student housing and residential life* (pp. 1-20). San Francisco, CA: Jossey-Bass.

Blimling, G. (1998). *The resident assistant: Applications and strategies for working with college students in residence halls* (5th ed.). Dubuque, IA: Kendall/Hunt.

Dunkel, N. W., & Schreiber, P. J. (1992). Competency development of housing professionals. *Journal of College and University Student Housing, 22*(2), 19-23.

Fickes, M. (2007, November 15). Privatized housing moves on-campus. *College Planning & Management.* ww.peterli.com/archive/cpm/122.shtm.

Frederiksen, C. F. (1993). A brief history of collegiate housing. In R. B. Winston, Jr., & S. Anchors (Eds.), *Student housing and residential life: A handbook for student affairs professionals committed to student development goals* (pp. 167-183). San Francisco, CA: Jossey-Bass.

Keeling, R. P. (Ed.) (2006). *Learning reconsidered 2: Implementing a campus-wide focus on the student experience.* Washington, DC: American College Personnel Association, Association of College and University Housing Officers-International, Association of College Unions-International, National Academic Advising Association, National Association for Campus Activities, National Association of Student Personnel Administrators, National Intramural-Recreational Sports Association.

Kuh, G. D., Sheed, J. D., Whitt, E. J., & Associates. (1991). *Involving colleges: Successful approaches to fostering student learning and development outside the classroom.* San Francisco, CA: Jossey-Bass.

Laufgraben, J. L., Shipiro, N. S., & Associates. (2004). *Sustaining and improving learning communities.* San Francisco, CA: Jossey-Bass.

National Leadership Council for Liberal Education and America's Promise. (2007). *College learning for the new global century.* Washington, DC: Author.

Schroeder, C. C., Mable, P., & Associates. (1993). *Realizing the educational potential of residence halls.* San Francisco, CA: Jossey-Bass.

Schuh, J. (Ed.) (1999*). Educational programming and student learning in college and university residence halls.* Columbus, OH: Association of College and University Housing Officers-International.

The Journal of College and University Student Housing. Published by the Association of College and University Housing

Officers-International (ACUHO-I), 941 Chatham Lane, Suite 318 Columbus, OH 43221-2416 Phone: 614.292.0099 Fax: 614.292.3205

Winston, R. B., Jr., Anchors, S., & Associates. (1993). *Student housing and residential life: A handbook for student affairs professionals committed to student development goals*. San Francisco, CA: Jossey-Bass.

Contextual Statement Contributors

Current Edition:
Carole Henry, Old Dominion University, ACUHO-I
Deb Boykin, The College of William and Mary, ACUHO-I

Previous Editions:
Mike Eyster, University of Oregon

Housing and Residential Life Programs
CAS Standards and Guidelines

Part 1. Mission

The mission of Housing and Residential Life Programs (HRLP) is to provide for a living environment that promotes learning and development in the broadest sense and an emphasis on supporting the academic mission of the institution.

The mission of HRLP must address
- reasonably priced living facilities that are clean, attractive, well-maintained, comfortable, sustainable, and which include contemporary safety features
- programs, services, and experiences occurring in living facilities

Programs that include food services should refer to the CAS Standards and Guidelines for Dining Services. Campuses that utilize residence halls for conferences and other events should refer to the CAS Standards and Guidelines for Conference and Event Programs.

HRLP standards must apply to residence halls, apartment communities, and other facilities that are managed or owned by private operators whenever there is a formal relationship with the institution.

Any off-campus housing services should include referrals to available off-campus housing listings and information about leases, landlord/tenant law, local ordinances, local crime statistics, community resources, and other related information.

HRLP must develop, disseminate, implement, and regularly review their missions, which must be consistent with the mission of the institution and with applicable professional standards. The mission must be appropriate for the institution's students and other constituents. Mission statements must reference student learning and development.

Part 2. Program

To achieve their mission, Housing and Residential Life Programs (HRLP) must contribute to
- students' formal education, which includes both the curriculum and the co-curriculum
- student progression and timely completion of educational goals
- preparation of students for their careers, citizenship, and lives
- student learning and development

To contribute to student learning and development, HRLP must
- identify relevant and desirable student learning and development outcomes

- articulate how the student learning and development outcomes align with the six CAS student learning and development domains and related dimensions
- assess relevant and desirable student learning and development
- provide evidence of impact on outcomes
- articulate contributions to or support of student learning and development in the domains not specifically assessed
- use evidence gathered to create strategies for improvement of programs and services

STUDENT LEARNING AND DEVELOPMENT
DOMAINS AND DIMENSIONS

Domain: **knowledge acquisition, integration, construction, and application**
- Dimensions: **understanding knowledge from a range of disciplines; connecting knowledge to other knowledge, ideas, and experiences; constructing knowledge; and relating knowledge to daily life**

Domain: **cognitive complexity**
- Dimensions: **critical thinking, reflective thinking, effective reasoning, and creativity**

Domain: **intrapersonal development**
- Dimensions: **realistic self-appraisal, self-understanding, and self-respect; identity development; commitment to ethics and integrity; and spiritual awareness**

Domain: **interpersonal competence**
- Dimensions: **meaningful relationships, interdependence, collaboration, and effective leadership**

Domain: **humanitarianism and civic engagement**
- Dimensions: **understanding and appreciation of cultural and human differences, social responsibility, global perspective, and sense of civic responsibility**

Domain: **practical competence**
- Dimensions: **pursuing goals, communicating effectively, technical competence, managing personal affairs, managing career development, demonstrating professionalism, maintaining health and wellness, and living a purposeful and satisfying life**

[LD Outcomes: See *The Council for the Advancement of Standards Learning and Development Outcomes* statement for examples of outcomes related to these domains and dimensions.]

HRLP must be

- intentionally designed
- guided by theories and knowledge of learning and development
- integrated into the life of the institution
- reflective of developmental and demographic profiles of the student population
- responsive to needs of individuals, populations with distinct needs, and relevant constituencies
- delivered using multiple formats, strategies, and contexts
- designed to provide universal access

HRLP must collaborate with colleagues and departments across the institution to promote student learning and development, persistence, and success.

To fulfill its mission, HRLP should provide an environment that supports high academic standards of residents, pursuit of higher GPAs, retention, and persistence toward graduation. Integral to this effort are partnerships with units and offices in the institution such as those that focus on the first-year experience and year-two programs. Initiatives may include establishment of first-year interest groups, early alert intervention programs, and living-learning communities; education of staff members and students about available campus academic resources; informal study groups and tutoring; and other academic initiatives to support student success.

HRLP must provide students with access to opportunities, experiences, and services that facilitate
- seamless learning environments
- development of a sense of identity through educational opportunities
- independence and self-sufficiency through activities and educational opportunities
- development of mature styles of relating to others and living cooperatively with others
- appreciation of cultural differences, perspectives, lifestyles, spirituality, and other forms of diversity
- opportunities for analyzing, forming, and confirming values
- personal growth, reflection, and development
- development of balanced lifestyles embracing wellness
- respect for self, others, and property
- appreciation of new ideas
- development of a sense of justice and fairness
- leadership development, problem-solving, and decision-making
- interaction between students, faculty, and staff
- formation of study groups
- access to academic resources through technology
- acquisition and use of knowledge, skills, and values
- educational and career choices
- learning life skills, e.g., health, personal finance, and time management

HRLP must offer purposeful programs, which may include living-learning communities, designed to integrate curricular and co-curricular experiences that complement and extend classroom learning.

Educational and community development programming, advising and counseling, and administrative activities of the HRLP staff will vary according to assessed student needs, institutional priorities, and the competencies of the staff members.

In education and community development programs, staff members must
- introduce and orient residents to community expectations, facilities, services, emergency protocols, and staff members
- document institutional and residential living policies, procedures, and expectations including the potential consequences for violation
- involve students in programming, policy development, and self-governance
- provide educational programs that focus on awareness of cultural differences, social justice, and self-assessment of possible bias
- offer social, recreational, educational, cultural, spiritual, and community service programs
- promote and provide education about the effects and risks of drug and alcohol use, and other high risk behaviors
- encourage residents to exercise responsibility for their community through confrontation of inappropriate or disruptive behavior
- encourage residents to participate in mediating conflict within the community
- encourage residents to learn about their rights as students, tenants, residents, and consumers
- promote appropriate student use of technological resources

Successful education and community development programs should promote the following outcomes for student participants:
- greater knowledge and skills related to career opportunities
- increased knowledge about institutional resources
- greater commitment to civic engagement
- improved academic performance and higher academic achievement
- stronger collaborative problem-solving skills
- improved demonstration of critical thinking skills
- increased student satisfaction

One approach to promoting education and community development in residence halls is through living-learning communities (LLCs). LLCs are defined as: "programs in which undergraduate students live together in a discrete portion of a residence hall (or the entire hall) and participate in academic and/or extracurricular programming designed especially for them" (National Study of Living-Learning Programs, 2007, p. I-2). LLCs should create more integrated experiences for first-year students by connecting faculty, students, disciplines, and co-curricular experiences.

Living-learning communities can be developed around themes, majors, or concepts. LLCs can be broadly defined academic interest areas (e.g., health professions, foreign languages, or education); based upon a specific major or majors (e.g., engineering or journalism); targeted to specific groups of students (e.g., students in Honors programs, transfer students, first-year students, students in sophomore success programs); or LLCs can be linked with co-curricular interest (e.g., civic engagement or sustainability). Some LLCs offer Freshmen Interest Groups (FIGs) and freshmen seminars.

To facilitate success in the development, design, and administration of LLCs, HRLP should
- ensure that resources are in place before an LLC program is implemented
- explore models of LLCs that support student needs, goals, and fit with the institution's culture
- share responsibility and accountability among various LLC partners by defining roles and duties
- engage in collaborative partnership with academic and student affairs staff to advance LLC development
- facilitate regular communication among academic faculty and staff members, HRLP staff, and other LLC partners (e.g., create an LLC advisory council which includes stakeholders who directly influence the success of the program)
- provide adequate staffing structures for the overall coordination and administration of the program
- ensure appropriate and sustained resources to provide for faculty participation, professional development, stipends, assessment, and technical support
- market programs to various target audiences such as students, parents, faculty, and administrators
- develop mentor programs and use peer advisors for advising, leading study groups, assisting with teaching seminars, or providing programs
- incorporate a strong assessment program, which may include evaluation of learning outcomes, GPAs, retention rates, satisfaction data, co-curricular engagement, student conduct comparisons, and other measures of academic success

To achieve important learning outcomes for students, HRLP staff members should employ the following practices within LLCs:
- identify learning outcomes with strong academic focuses
- incorporate credit-bearing courses, taught specifically for LLC participants, into the LLC curriculum
- create opportunities for students to engage with peers, staff members, and faculty members around academic, vocational, social, and cultural topics germane to the LLC's topic
- incorporate academically oriented co-curricular activities into the LLC, including internships, service-learning experiences, and research opportunities
- provide assistance to faculty members teaching within LLCs to help them maximize the residential environment, which may be unfamiliar to them

- provide dedicated LLC study spaces and/or resource rooms within the residence hall

Successful LLCs should report the following outcomes for student participants, as compared to traditional residence hall students:
- smoother transition to college, both academically and socially
- stronger sense of belonging, including feeling that the institution is less overwhelming
- increased first-to-second year retention
- increased persistence toward graduation
- higher levels of academic self-confidence
- greater integration of students' academic and non-academic lives
- increased participation and engagement in academic and co-curricular programs
- increased involvement in volunteer opportunities and/or enrollment in service-learning courses
- greater likelihood of serving as a mentor for other students
- more frequent integration and application of knowledge from different sources across contexts (e.g., other courses or personal experiences)

Successful LLCs should report the following outcomes regarding faculty and staff participants:
- increased involvement of faculty in the co-curriculum
- greater collaboration among faculty and staff members
- enhanced knowledge about students and their development by faculty members
- increased and enhanced opportunities for faculty rewards and recognition

In advising, counseling, and crisis intervention, HRLP staff members must
- **provide individual advising or counseling support within the scope of their training and expertise and make appropriate referrals to student support services**
- **foster relationships with students that demonstrate genuine interest in students' educational and personal development**

In administrative activities, HRLP staff members must
- **provide policies and procedures to support special populations**
- **encourage residents to participate in evaluating the HRLP**
- **provide information on safety, security, and emergency procedures**
- **create and maintain an environment and atmosphere conducive to educational pursuits**
- **provide emergency response and crisis intervention management in coordination with relevant campus and community resources**
- **ensure that the safety and security of the residents and their property are taken into consideration as policies are developed**

- assess needs of the housing population annually, specifically addressing the needs for special interest programming and for upgrading or modifying facilities

Part 3. Organization and Leadership

To achieve program and student learning and development outcomes, Housing and Residential Life Programs (HRLP) must be purposefully structured for effectiveness. HRLP must have clearly stated and current

- goals and outcomes
- policies and procedures
- responsibilities and performance expectations for personnel
- organizational charts demonstrating clear channels of authority

Leaders must model ethical behavior and institutional citizenship.

Leaders with organizational authority for HRLP must provide strategic planning, management and supervision, and program advancement.

Strategic Planning

- articulate a vision and mission that drive short- and long-term planning
- set goals and objectives based on the needs of the populations served, intended student learning and development outcomes, and program outcomes
- facilitate continuous development, implementation, and assessment of program effectiveness and goal attainment congruent with institutional mission and strategic plans
- promote environments that provide opportunities for student learning, development, and engagement
- develop, adapt, and improve programs and services in response to the changing needs of populations served and evolving institutional priorities
- include diverse perspectives to inform decision making

Management and Supervision

- plan, allocate, and monitor the use of fiscal, physical, human, intellectual, and technological resources
- manage human resource processes including recruitment, selection, professional development, supervision, performance planning, succession planning, evaluation, recognition, and reward
- influence others to contribute to the effectiveness and success of the unit
- empower professional, support, and student personnel to become effective leaders
- encourage and support collaboration with colleagues and departments across the institution
- encourage and support scholarly contributions to the profession

- identify and address individual, organizational, and environmental conditions that foster or inhibit mission achievement
- use current and valid evidence to inform decisions
- incorporate sustainability practices in the management and design of programs, services, and facilities
- understand appropriate technologies and integrate them into programs and services
- be knowledgeable about codes and laws relevant to programs and services and ensure that programs and services meet those requirements
- assess and take action to mitigate potential risks

Program Advancement

- advocate for and actively promote the mission and goals of the programs and services
- inform stakeholders about issues affecting practice
- facilitate processes to reach consensus where wide support is needed
- advocate for representation in strategic planning initiatives at divisional and institutional levels

HRLP must work with institutional leadership to establish and maintain productive working relationships when the management of the HRLP is divided among different agencies within the institution.

A unified organizational structure, including all housing and residential life functions, should be used so as to effectively deliver the services to users and to avoid multiple hierarchical lines of communication and authority.

HRLP must maintain well-structured management functions, including planning, human resources, property management, procurement, contract administration, financial control, and information systems.

Evaluation of the organization must be based upon progress toward the achievement of short-range and long-range organizational goals. Planning must be adequate to project and accommodate both immediate and future needs.

Part 4. Human Resources

Housing and Residential Life Programs (HRLP) must be staffed adequately by individuals qualified to accomplish mission and goals.

HRLP must have access to technical and support personnel adequate to accomplish their mission.

Within institutional guidelines, HRLP must

- establish procedures for personnel recruitment and selection, training, performance planning, and evaluation
- set expectations for supervision and performance
- provide personnel access to continuing and advanced education and appropriate professional development opportunities to improve their competence, skills, and leadership capacity

- consider work/life options available to personnel (e.g., compressed work schedules, flextime, job sharing, remote work, or telework) to promote recruitment and retention of personnel

Administrators of HRLP must

- ensure that all personnel have updated position descriptions
- implement recruitment and selection/hiring strategies that produce a workforce inclusive of under-represented populations
- develop promotion practices that are fair, inclusive, proactive, and non-discriminatory

Personnel responsible for delivery of HRLP must have written performance goals, objectives, and outcomes for each year's performance cycle to be used to plan, review, and evaluate work and performance. The performance plan must be updated regularly to reflect changes during the performance cycle.

Results of individual personnel evaluations must be used to recognize personnel performance, address performance issues, implement individual and/or collective personnel development and training programs, and inform the assessment of programs and services.

HRLP personnel, when hired and throughout their employment, must receive appropriate and thorough training.

HRLP personnel, including student employees and volunteers, must have access to resources or receive specific training on

- institutional policies pertaining to functions or activities they support
- privacy and confidentiality policies
- laws regarding access to student records
- policies and procedures for dealing with sensitive institutional information
- policies and procedures related to technology used to store or access student records and institutional data
- how and when to refer those in need of additional assistance to qualified personnel and have access to a supervisor for assistance in making these judgments
- systems and technologies necessary to perform their assigned responsibilities
- ethical and legal uses of technology

HRLP personnel must engage in continuing professional development activities to keep abreast of the research, theories, legislation, policies, and developments that affect their programs and services.

Administrators of HRLP must ensure that personnel are knowledgeable about and trained in safety, emergency procedures, and crisis prevention and response. Risk management efforts must address identification of threatening conduct or behavior and must incorporate a system for responding to and reporting such behaviors.

HRLP personnel must be knowledgeable of and trained in safety and emergency procedures for securing and vacating facilities.

PROFESSIONAL PERSONNEL

HRLP professional personnel either must hold an earned graduate or professional degree in a field relevant to their position or must possess an appropriate combination of educational credentials and related work experience.

Individual residence halls and apartment communities should be supervised by professional staff members who have earned a master's degree from accredited institutions in a field of study such as college student affairs, college counseling, or higher education administration.

Desirable characteristics for professional, pre-professional, and paraprofessional staff members include demonstrated skills of leadership and communication, maturity, a well-developed sense of responsibility, sensitivity to individual differences, a positive self-concept, an understanding of how to promote student learning and academic success, and an obvious interest and enthusiasm for working with students.

INTERNS OR GRADUATE ASSISTANTS

Degree- or credential-seeking interns or graduate assistants must be qualified by enrollment in an appropriate field of study and relevant experience. These students must be trained and supervised by professional personnel who possess applicable educational credentials and work experience and have supervisory experience. Supervisors must be cognizant of the dual roles interns and graduate assistants have as both student and employee.

Supervisors must

- adhere to parameters of students' job descriptions
- articulate intended learning outcomes in student job descriptions
- adhere to agreed-upon work hours and schedules
- offer flexible scheduling when circumstances necessitate

Supervisors and students must both agree to suitable compensation if circumstances necessitate additional hours.

STUDENT EMPLOYEES AND VOLUNTEERS

Student employees and volunteers must be carefully selected, trained, supervised, and evaluated. Students must have access to a supervisor. Student employees and volunteers must be provided clear job descriptions, pre-service training based on assessed needs, and continuing development.

HRLP professional staff members must train resident/community assistants and other paraprofessionals to contribute to the accomplishment of the following functions: (a) community development (b) educational programming, (c) administration, (d) group and activity advising, (e) leadership development, (f) student conduct, (g) role modeling, (h) individual assistance and referral,

(i) providing information, (j) crisis intervention, and (k) facilities management.

HRLP staff members must have a working knowledge of all relevant policies and procedures, the rationale for policies and procedures, and the relationship of policies and procedures to the HRLP's mission statement, goals, and objectives.

HRLP position descriptions must include adequate time for planning as well as for program implementation.

HRLP must routinely evaluate conditions of employment for all HRLP staff (e.g., length of contracts, job expectations).

HRLP staff members should have a personal development plan that reflects and supports the goals and objectives of the organization and areas for professional improvement.

HRLP staff members must be knowledgeable about and remain current with respect to the obligations and limitations placed upon the institution by law and institutional policies.

HRLP must ensure that comprehensive planning documents and protocols exist and that annual training occurs for staff members and students for all crisis-related residential circumstances (e.g., individual psychological incidents, fire and evacuation, environmental disasters, medical emergencies, etc.).

A well-developed Business Recovery/Continuity Plan must exist, and HRLP must fully participate in campus crisis management and evaluation.

HRLP staff members must receive adequate training to make appropriate and timely referrals regarding any escalating behavior problems.

Part 5. Ethics

Housing and Residential Life Programs (HRLP) must
- review applicable professional ethical standards and must adopt or develop and implement appropriate statements of ethical practice
- publish and adhere to statements of ethical practice and ensure their periodic review
- orient new personnel to relevant ethical standards and statements of ethical practice and related institutional policies

Statements of ethical standards must
- specify that HRLP personnel respect privacy and maintain confidentiality in communications and records as delineated by privacy laws
- specify limits on disclosure of information contained in students' records as well as requirements to disclose to appropriate authorities
- address conflicts of interest, or appearance thereof, by personnel in the performance of their work
- reflect the responsibility of personnel to be fair,

objective, and impartial in their interactions with others
- reference management of institutional funds
- reference appropriate behavior regarding research and assessment with human participants, confidentiality of research and assessment data, and students' rights and responsibilities
- include the expectation that personnel confront and hold accountable other personnel who exhibit unethical behavior
- address issues surrounding scholarly integrity

HRLP personnel must
- employ ethical decision making in the performance of their duties
- inform users of programs and services of ethical obligations and limitations emanating from codes and laws or from licensure requirements
- recognize and avoid conflicts of interest that could adversely influence their judgment or objectivity and, when unavoidable, recuse themselves from the situation
- perform their duties within the scope of their position, training, expertise, and competence
- make referrals when issues presented exceed the scope of the position

HRLP staff members should remain abreast of ethical codes and practices through involvement in professional associations or other equally effective means.

Part 6. Law, Policy, and Governance

Housing and Residential Life Programs (HRLP) must be in compliance with laws, regulations, and policies that relate to their respective responsibilities and that pose legal obligations, limitations, risks, and liabilities for the institution as a whole. Examples include constitutional, statutory, regulatory, and case law; relevant law and orders emanating from codes and laws; and the institution's policies.

HRLP must have access to legal advice needed for personnel to carry out their assigned responsibilities.

HRLP must inform personnel, appropriate officials, and users of programs and services about existing and changing legal obligations, risks and liabilities, and limitations.

HRLP must inform personnel about professional liability insurance options and refer them to external sources if the institution does not provide coverage.

HRLP must have written policies and procedures on operations, transactions, or tasks that have legal implications.

HRLP must regularly review policies. The revision and creation of policies must be informed by best practices, available evidence, and policy issues in higher education.

HRLP must have procedures and guidelines consistent with institutional policy for responding to threats, emergencies, and crisis situations. Systems and procedures must be in place to disseminate timely and accurate information to students, other members of the institutional community, and appropriate external organizations during emergency situations.

Personnel must neither participate in nor condone any form of harassment or activity that demeans persons or creates an intimidating, hostile, or offensive environment.

HRLP must purchase or obtain permission to use copyrighted materials and instruments. References to copyrighted materials and instruments must include appropriate citations.

HRLP must inform personnel about internal and external governance organizations that affect programs and services.

HRLP must provide a clear and complete written agreement between the resident and the institution that conveys mutual commitments and responsibilities. The agreement must include contract eligibility and duration; room assignments and changes; rates and payment policies; dining options; procedures for canceling, subleasing, or being released from the housing and/or dining agreement; room entry and inspection procedures; and pertinent rules and regulations.

Part 7. Diversity, Equity, and Access

Within the context of each institution's mission and in accordance with institutional policies and applicable codes and laws, Housing and Residential Life Programs (HRLP) must create and maintain educational and work environments that are welcoming, accessible, inclusive, equitable, and free from harassment.

HRLP must not discriminate on the basis of disability; age; race; cultural identity; ethnicity; nationality; family educational history (e.g., first generation to attend college); political affiliation; religious affiliation; sex; sexual orientation; gender identity and expression; marital, social, economic, or veteran status; or any other basis included in institutional policies and codes and laws.

HRLP must
- advocate for sensitivity to multicultural and social justice concerns by the institution and its personnel
- ensure physical, program, and resource access for all constituents
- modify or remove policies, practices, systems, technologies, facilities, and structures that create barriers or produce inequities
- ensure that when facilities and structures cannot be modified, they do not impede access to programs, services, and resources
- establish goals for diversity, equity, and access
- foster communication and practices that enhance understanding of identity, culture, self-expression, and heritage
- promote respect for commonalities and differences

among people within their historical and cultural contexts
- address the characteristics and needs of diverse constituents when establishing and implementing culturally relevant and inclusive programs, services, policies, procedures, and practices
- provide personnel with diversity, equity, and access training and hold personnel accountable for applying the training to their work
- respond to the needs of all constituents served when establishing hours of operation and developing methods of delivering programs, services, and resources
- recognize the needs of distance and online learning students by directly providing or assisting them to gain access to comparable services and resources

Part 8. Internal and External Relations

Housing and Residential Life Programs (HRLP) must reach out to individuals, groups, communities, and organizations internal and external to the institution to
- establish, maintain, and promote understanding and effective relations with those that have a significant interest in or potential effect on the students or other constituents served by the programs and services
- garner support and resources for programs and services as defined by the mission
- collaborate in offering or improving programs and services to meet the needs of students and other constituents and to achieve program and student outcomes
- engage diverse individuals, groups, communities, and organizations to enrich the educational environment and experiences of students and other constituents
- disseminate information about the programs and services

Promotional and descriptive information must be accurate and free of deception and misrepresentation.

HRLP must have procedures and guidelines consistent with institutional policy for
- communicating with the media
- distributing information through print, broadcast, and online sources
- contracting with external organizations for delivery of programs and services
- cultivating, soliciting, and managing gifts
- applying to and managing funds from grants

HRLP must advocate for membership on critical committees, especially those related to crisis response, threat assessment, emergency operations, and business continuity.

HRLP should develop close cooperation with campus and off-campus agencies responsible for university communications, legal counsel, environmental health, emergency management, student conduct, counseling services, academic units, learning assistance, disability services, student health services, student activities, public safety, academic advising, admissions, campus mail, physical plant services, institutional budgeting and planning, computer services, vendors and suppliers of products used in residence and dining halls, and privatized housing operators.

HRLP should establish relationships with a wide range of student groups (e.g., Residence Hall Association, campus student government, LGBT groups, fraternities and sororities, and student organizations which may align with any living-learning communities) to gain input and serve as a resource.

HRLP staff members should be aware of the political implications of housing as a critical institutional asset, its opportunity to contribute to academic programs and the delivery of services, and its effect on attracting and retaining students.

HRLP staff members must develop and maintain staff relationships in a climate of mutual respect, support, trust, and interdependence in recognizing the strengths and limitations of each colleague.

Part 9. Financial Resources

Housing and Residential Life Programs (HRLP) must have funding to accomplish the mission and goals.

In establishing and prioritizing funding resources, HRLP must conduct comprehensive analyses to determine
- **unmet needs of the unit**
- **relevant expenditures**
- **external and internal resources**
- **impact on students and the institution**

HRLP must use the budget as a planning tool to reflect commitment to the mission and goals of the programs and services and of the institution.

HRLP must administer funds in accordance with established institutional accounting procedures.

HRLP must demonstrate efficient and effective use and responsible stewardship of fiscal resources consistent with institutional protocols.

Financial reports must provide an accurate financial overview of the organization and provide clear, understandable, and timely data upon which personnel can plan and make informed decisions.

Procurement procedures must
- **be consistent with institutional policies**
- **ensure that purchases comply with laws and codes for usability and access**
- **ensure that the institution receives value for the funds spent**
- **consider information available for comparing the ethical and environmental impact of products and services purchased**

Procedures should be present to ensure reconciliation

between goods paid for and goods ordered and received.

A portion of fees collected must be dedicated to the immediate support and long-term improvement of housing and residential life programs and facilities. Funding must be available for the continuous upkeep of facilities, equipment and furnishings, on-going repairs, educational programming, and services to residents. Reserves must be available for major maintenance and renovation of housing facilities, replacement of equipment, and other capital improvements.

Student governance units (e.g., hall or campus-wide residential councils) should have access to accounting offices and services to effectively carry out their functions. Dues collected from students for programs and services should be managed within the institution.

Representatives of residence hall and apartment housing communities should be given opportunity to comment on proposed rate increases and the operating budget. Rate increases should be announced well in advance of implementation.

Information regarding the use of HRLP funds should be available to the campus community.

When HRLP is an auxiliary enterprise, additional funds beyond reasonable institutional service charges should not occur without consultation with HRLP senior leadership.

Part 10. Technology

Housing and Residential Life Programs (HRLP) must have technology to support the achievement of their mission and goals. The technology and its use must comply with institutional policies and procedures and with relevant codes and laws.

HRLP must use technologies to
- **provide updated information regarding mission, location, staffing, programs, services, and official contacts to students and other constituents in accessible formats**
- **provide an avenue for students and other constituents to communicate sensitive information in a secure format**
- **enhance the delivery of programs and services for all students**

HRLP must
- **back up data on a regular basis**
- **adhere to institutional policies regarding ethical and legal use of technology**
- **articulate policies and procedures for protecting the confidentiality and security of information**
- **implement a replacement plan and cycle for all technology with attention to sustainability**
- **incorporate accessibility features into technology-based programs and services**

When providing student access to technology, HRLP must
- **have policies on the use of technology that are**

- clear, easy to understand, and available to all students
- provide information or referral to support services for those needing assistance in accessing or using technology
- provide instruction or training on how to use the technology
- inform students of implications of misuse of technologies

Technology systems should be used to create and sustain cost reduction and efficiency improvement measures. HRLP should consider the use of electronic security systems including access control, video surveillance, and intercommunication systems as part of a unified integrated security management system. HRLP should provide a formal written policy to regulate the use of and provide guidelines for video surveillance cameras and systems for residential facilities and consider the use, retention, and dissemination of surveillance records along with student privacy issues.

HRLP must make appropriate use of social networking and other web-based communication programs and techniques.

Part 11. Facilities and Equipment

Housing and Residential Life Programs' (HRLP) facilities must be intentionally designed and located in suitable, accessible, and safe spaces that demonstrate universal design and support the program's mission and goals.

Facilities must be designed to engage various constituents and promote learning.

Personnel must have workspaces that are suitably located and accessible, well equipped, adequate in size, and designed to support their work and responsibilities.

The design of the facilities must guarantee the security and privacy of records and ensure the confidentiality of sensitive information and conversations. Personnel must be able to secure their work.

HRLP must incorporate sustainable practices in use of facilities and purchase of equipment. Facilities and equipment must be evaluated on an established cycle and be in compliance with codes, laws, and accepted practices for access, health, safety, and security.

When acquiring capital equipment, HRLP must take into account expenses related to regular maintenance and life cycle costs.

The location and layout of the facilities must be sensitive to the needs of transgender persons.

The HRLP must ensure that the physical environment is attractive, conducive to academic success and other learning outcomes, functional, in compliance with codes, and equipped adequately with safety features. Individual rooms and apartments must be furnished and equipped to accommodate the designated number of occupants.

Adequate space must be provided for student study, community development, and group meetings. Public, common, study, recreational areas, fitness rooms, and computer labs when provided must be adequately furnished and maintained to accommodate the number of users.

Residential facilities should include private offices for counseling, advising, interviewing, or other meetings of a confidential nature as well as office, reception, and storage space sufficient to accommodate assigned staff, supplies, equipment, library resources, conference rooms, classrooms, and meeting spaces.

Custodial services programs must be required to provide a clean and orderly environment in all housing facilities and to minimize the introduction of hazardous or toxic materials into the residential environment. All community bathrooms, as well as public areas, must be cleaned and sanitized at least daily on weekdays.

A weekend custodial services program should be in place.

Sufficient space for custodial equipment and storage must be available in close proximity to the assigned custodial area.

Pest management practices must be implemented in all housing and food service areas.

Maintenance and renovation programs must be implemented in all housing operations and include four major areas: (a) a preventive maintenance program designed to realize or exceed the projected life expectancy of the equipment and facilities, (b) a program designed to repair or upgrade equipment, facilities, and building systems as they become inoperable or obsolete, (c) a renovation program that modifies physical facilities and building systems to make them more sustainable, flexible, accessible, effective, attractive, efficient, and safe, and (d) a program designed to provide emergency response 24 hours a day.

Periodic inspections and audits must be made to (a) ensure compliance with fire and safety codes; (b) identify and address potential safety and security hazards (e.g., fire extinguishers charged, sprinkler systems and exit doors working properly, automatic door closers, lighting outside buildings, potential hazards identified and corrected, etc.) and (c) adhere to campus efforts to improve energy efficiency. Data from inspections must be used for repair and replacement schedules.

A system of access control must be in place to provide for frequent monitoring of all associated hardware and identifying potential security hazards related to key/card inventory by stringently controlling the use of master keys/access cards.

Systematically planned equipment replacement programs must exist for furnishings, mechanical, and electrical systems; maintenance equipment; carpeting and other flooring; window coverings; and dining equipment where applicable.

Painting must be conducted on the basis of current need and a preplanned cyclical schedule.

Waste disposal, recycling, and handling and storage of chemicals and hazardous materials must be in compliance with laws and regulations for health, safety, and environmental protection requirements. HRLP staff members must identify work-place hazards and strive to minimize the risk to employees through education, training, and provision of personal protective equipment.

Grounds, including streets, walks, recreational areas, and parking lots, must be attractively maintained, with attention given to safety features.

Principles of sustainability should be incorporated into the operation and renovation of existing facilities and construction of new facilities. These principles should include but are not limited to a strong energy conservation program, an organized recycling program, choices of furnishings and floor coverings, as well as advancement of the principles of a carbon-neutral environment.

Student housing construction project planning must be responsive to the current and future needs of residents. HRLP staff members must be involved in the design and development of new housing construction.

Students should be consulted on the design and development of new housing construction, renovations, and capital improvements.

A master plan for maintaining and renovating all facilities must exist and include timelines for addressing specific needs.

Laundry facilities must be provided within or in close proximity to living areas, be well-maintained, and reasonably priced.

Suggestions from residents must be regularly and consistently sought and considered regarding physical plant improvements and renovations to college/university housing and dining facilities.

A systematic evaluation of student satisfaction of residential facilities must be in place.

An up-to-date inventory of housing property and furnishings must be maintained.

Physical plant renovations must be scheduled to minimize disruption to residents and diners. During the academic and summer terms adequate communication regarding closings should be coordinated and provided to users.

Acceptable accommodations and amenities must be provided for professional live-in staff members with appropriate consideration for the following needs: adequate living space for the staff member and any family, furnishings and equipment, telecommunications package, appropriate access, and parking.

Part 12. Assessment

Housing and Residential Life Programs (HRLP) must develop assessment plans and processes.

Assessment plans must articulate an ongoing cycle of assessment activities.

HRLP should regularly assess its programs and services.

HRLP must
- specify programmatic goals and intended outcomes
- identify student learning and development outcomes
- employ multiple measures and methods
- develop manageable processes for gathering, interpreting, and evaluating data
- document progress toward achievement of goals and outcomes
- interpret and use assessment results to demonstrate accountability
- report aggregated results to respondent groups and stakeholders
- use assessment results to inform planning and decision-making
- assess effectiveness of implemented changes
- provide evidence of improvement of programs and services

Qualitative methods may include questionnaires and focus groups. Quantitative measures may include data on housing capacity, occupancy, and retention; student conduct; damages; facility assessments; demographics; programming; and analysis of student GPAs (academic class, sex, building type, LLCs, etc.). Data should be used to develop projections related to new construction, renovation of existing facilities, new initiatives, and room rates.

At least once annually residents must be invited to anonymously evaluate the performance of their Resident Assistants and other student staff members who serve in their residences.

HRLP must employ ethical practices in the assessment process.

HRLP must have access to adequate fiscal, human, professional development, and technological resources to develop and implement assessment plans.

General Standards revised in 2014
HRLP content developed/revised in 1986, 1992, 1997, 2004, & 2013

International Student Programs and Services
CAS Contexual Statement

In 2013-2014, the number of international students at colleges and universities in the United States increased to 866,502, an eight percent increase over the previous year (IIE, 2014). International students studying in the United States pursue undergraduate and graduate degrees as well as English-language training; they are drawn to this country because of the high quality programs and the wide range of academic options offered. International students bring with them rich experiences and unique cross-cultural perspectives that help to internationalize the campus and give American students, faculty, staff and the local community first-hand opportunities to learn about the world. International students face unique challenges as they attempt to adjust to a different campus life and culture, master written and spoken languages, comply with immigration regulations, meet the requirements of their academic programs, and prepare to begin their careers., often while balancing the complexities of managing family or extended family concerns occurring thousands of miles away.

The International Student Programs and Services (ISPS) functions and roles on campuses vary greatly. Some ISPS offices may serve only a handful of students, while others serve thousands as well as the academic departments that enroll and depend on these students. Some offices only serve international students; other offices serve international students, visiting scholars, and US students studying abroad. As more institutions open campuses in other countries, ISPS may be responsible for helping prepare institutional officials from both countries for the cross-cultural, procedural, and governmental issues that could arise. International student and scholar advising is a robust profession with a specialized body of knowledge and any number of necessary key skill sets, including those listed below.

It is important for international student and scholar advisers to be current on immigration regulations and policies. International Student Programs and Services (ISPS) are charged with record keeping and reporting that is required for an institution to remain in compliance with immigration regulations. Advisers need to effectively communicate these regulations to students, scholars, and key campus community members; establish and maintain working relationships with individuals on and off-campus to address and advocate for students' and scholars' needs; be competent in crisis intervention in case of illness or serious legal, financial, or personal problems; have strong cross-cultural competencies to allow them to interact effectively with students and scholars from diverse cultures; understand how to develop effective and creative social and cultural programming; and prioritize and manage time and resources.

Advisers frequently serve as the liaison between international students and scholars and all those with whom these students and scholars come into contact, including faculty members, students, and staff; local citizens; officials of host country and foreign government agencies; and the student's sponsor or family at home to represent the students' best interests and advise them accordingly. Advisers should be knowledgeable and articulate about host country culture and how it differs from the cultures of other countries and should understand the social and psychological processes of cross-cultural adjustment. They should be familiar with the educational systems and political, economic, historical, and social issues and trends framing the contexts of the countries from which their students come. Considering the various cultural norms that advisers navigate with their students and the community members of the host campus, advisors should have access to ongoing training to develop cross-cultural competencies.

As more campuses continue to emphasize internationalization efforts, International Student Programs and Services (ISPS) should be prepared to step forward and initiate partnerships that will advance these goals. Collaboration with education abroad, admissions, international studies and international education, and student affairs organizations will sustain these efforts. Although this statement and the accompanying standards and guidelines are mostly focused on international students studying in the U.S., many of the challenges and other aspects described may also apply to any students who are studying outside their home country.

References, Readings, and Resources

Albrecht, T. (Ed.). (2015). *Crisis management in a cross-cultural setting: International student and scholar services.* Washington, DC: NAFSA.

Althen, G. (Ed.). (1994). *Learning across cultures.* Washington, DC: NAFSA.

Assaf, M., & Gentile, L. (Eds.). (2014). *Basic F-1 procedures for beginners.* Washington, DC: NAFSA.

Bennett, M. (Ed.). (2013). *Basic concepts of intercultural communication: Paradigms, principles and practices.* (2nd ed.). Washington, DC: NAFSA.

Choudaha, R., & Schulmann, P. (2014). *Bridging the gap: Recruitment and retention to improve international student experiences.* Washington, DC: NAFSA.

Czarnawska, I. (2001). *The Aliens: Being a Foreign Student* [video]. Boston, MA: Intercultural Press.
    - In this film, six international students are interviewed about their experiences coming to the United States and attending a U.S. American college.

Feagles, S. (Ed.) (1999). (CD). *A guide to educational systems around the world.* Washington, DC: NAFSA.

Gooding, M., & Wood, M. (Eds.). (2006). *Finding your way:*

navigational tools for international student and scholar advisers. Washington, DC: NAFSA.

Hastings, C.E. (2012). *Collaborative partnerships: sponsored student programs.* Washington, DC: NAFSA.

Institute of International Education (IIE) (2014). *Open Doors Report on International Educational Exchange.* New York, NY: Author.

Institute of International Education: http://www.iie.org

Intercultural Press: http://www.interculturalpress.com

Lanier, A., & Davis, J. (2005). *Living in the U.S.A.* (6th ed.). Yarmouth, ME: Intercultural Press.

NAFSA: Association of International Educators: http://www.nafsa.org

NAFSA Resource Page for ISPS:

http://www.nafsa.org/Find_Resources/Supporting_International_ Students_And_Scholars/International_Students_and_Scholars/

Network NAFSA's community platform for International Student and Scholar Services: http://network.nafsa.org/home

NAFSA Adviser's Manual On-line: http://www.nafsa.org/am

NAFSA's Statement of Ethical Principles:

http://www.nafsa.org/Learn_About_NAFSA/Governance_ Documents/Ethics_And_Principles/Statement_Of_Ethics/ NAFSA_s_Statement_of_Ethical_Principles/

U. S. Citizenship and Immigration Services: http://www.uscis.gov

O'Connell, B. (Ed.). (1994). *Foreign student education at two-year colleges.* Washington, DC: NAFSA.

Ogami, N. (1986). *Cold water* [video]. Yarmouth, ME: Intercultural Press.
- This movie is about cross-cultural adaptation and culture shock and includes a comprehensive instructional guide. Twelve Boston University international students (plus one U.S. American student and three cross-cultural specialists) are interviewed about the experience of living and studying in a new culture.

Open Doors Report (Published annually by the Institute of International Education): http://www.iie.org/research-and-publications/open-doors/data

Ritchie, M. (2013). *Advising international students with disabilities.* Washington, DC: NAFSA.

Storti, C. (1998). *Figuring foreigners out: A practical guide.* Yarmouth, ME: Intercultural Press.

Wolfe. J. (2014). *Improving international student experiences.* Washington, DC: NAFSA.

U.S. Immigration and Customs Enforcement: http://www.ice.gov

U.S. Department of Homeland Security: http://www.dhs.gov

U.S. Department of State: http://travel.state.gov

Contextual Statement Contributors

Current Edition:

Erin Hillis, Rhodes College

Mihaela Metianu, Florida Atlantic University

Joann Ng Hartmann, NAFSA: Association of International Educators

Ali Soltanshahi, Iowa State University

Previous Editions:

Louis Gecenok, San Jose State University

Monica Sharp, University of Oklahoma

International Student Programs and Services
CAS Standards and Guidelines

Part 1. Mission

The mission of International Student Programs and Services (ISPS) is to provide support and assistance necessary for international students to achieve their educational goals and to ensure institutional compliance with governmental immigration regulations. The ISPS must provide the documents for students to enter the country and maintain their legal status.

ISPS must develop, disseminate, implement, and regularly review their missions, which must be consistent with the mission of the institution and with applicable professional standards. The mission must be appropriate for the institution's students and other constituents. Mission statements must reference student learning and development.

Part 2. Program

To achieve their mission, International Student Programs and Services (ISPS) must contribute to
- students' formal education, which includes both the curriculum and the co-curriculum
- student progression and timely completion of educational goals
- preparation of students for their careers, citizenship, and lives
- student learning and development

To contribute to student learning and development, ISPS must
- identify relevant and desirable student learning and development outcomes
- articulate how the student learning and development outcomes align with the six CAS student learning and development domains and related dimensions
- assess relevant and desirable student learning and development
- provide evidence of impact on outcomes
- articulate contributions to or support of student learning and development in the domains not specifically assessed
- use evidence gathered to create strategies for improvement of programs and services

STUDENT LEARNING AND DEVELOPMENT DOMAINS AND DIMENSIONS

Domain: knowledge acquisition, integration, construction, and application
- **Dimensions: understanding knowledge from a range of disciplines; connecting knowledge to other knowledge, ideas, and experiences; constructing knowledge; and relating knowledge to daily life**

Domain: cognitive complexity
- **Dimensions: critical thinking, reflective thinking, effective reasoning, and creativity**

Domain: intrapersonal development
- **Dimensions: realistic self-appraisal, self-understanding, and self-respect; identity development; commitment to ethics and integrity; and spiritual awareness**

Domain: interpersonal competence
- **Dimensions: meaningful relationships, interdependence, collaboration, and effective leadership**

Domain: humanitarianism and civic engagement
- **Dimensions: understanding and appreciation of cultural and human differences, social responsibility, global perspective, and sense of civic responsibility**

Domain: practical competence
- **Dimensions: pursuing goals, communicating effectively, technical competence, managing personal affairs, managing career development, demonstrating professionalism, maintaining health and wellness, and living a purposeful and satisfying life**

[LD Outcomes: See *The Council for the Advancement of Standards Learning and Development Outcomes* statement for examples of outcomes related to these domains and dimensions.]

ISPS must be
- **intentionally designed**
- **guided by theories and knowledge of learning and development**
- **integrated into the life of the institution**
- **reflective of developmental and demographic profiles of the student population**
- **responsive to needs of individuals, populations with distinct needs, and relevant constituencies**
- **delivered using multiple formats, strategies, and contexts**
- **designed to provide universal access**

ISPS must collaborate with colleagues and departments across the institution to promote student learning and development, persistence, and success.

ISPS should provide the campus and larger community with multiple and varied opportunities for discussion to maximize learning, to minimize cultural conflict, or to deal with conflict.

ISPS must

- assess the needs of the international student population and set priorities among those needs
- offer or provide access to professional services for students in the areas of immigration and other government regulations, financial matters, employment, obtaining health care insurance, navigating the health care system, host-country language needs, and personal and cultural concerns
- assure institutional compliance with government regulations and procedures, including record-keeping and reporting responsibilities
- interpret immigration policies to the campus and local communities
- develop and offer educational programs to the campus community to enhance positive interaction between domestic and international students, to develop sensitivity regarding cultural differences and international student needs, and to assist in the understanding of adjustment to a host country's educational system and culture
- orient international students to the expectations, policies, and culture of the institution and to the educational system and culture of the host country
- facilitate the enrollment and retention of international students
- prepare students for re-entry and cultural re-adjustment related to the students' return home
- provide appropriate referrals for students whose individual needs may be in conflict with the home culture
- provide appropriate and timely referral services to other relevant agencies
- determine the educational goals; developmental levels; and social, emotional, and cultural needs of individual international students and specific populations
- collaborate effectively with other services areas, student organizations, and academic departments to meet international students' needs
- facilitate international students' participation in campus life
- advocate to all areas of the institution for the needs of international students
- facilitate sensitivity within the institution and the community at large to the cultural needs of international students

Part 3. Organization and Leadership

To achieve program and student learning and development outcomes, International Student Programs and Services (ISPS) must be purposefully structured for effectiveness. ISPS must have clearly stated and current

- goals and outcomes
- policies and procedures
- responsibilities and performance expectations for personnel

- organizational charts demonstrating clear channels of authority

Leaders must model ethical behavior and institutional citizenship.

Leaders with organizational authority for ISPS must provide strategic planning, management and supervision, and program advancement.

Strategic Planning

- articulate a vision and mission that drive short- and long-term planning
- set goals and objectives based on the needs of the populations served, intended student learning and development outcomes, and program outcomes
- facilitate continuous development, implementation, and assessment of program effectiveness and goal attainment congruent with institutional mission and strategic plans
- promote environments that provide opportunities for student learning, development, and engagement
- develop, adapt, and improve programs and services in response to the changing needs of populations served and evolving institutional priorities
- include diverse perspectives to inform decision making

Management and Supervision

- plan, allocate, and monitor the use of fiscal, physical, human, intellectual, and technological resources
- manage human resource processes including recruitment, selection, professional development, supervision, performance planning, succession planning, evaluation, recognition, and reward
- influence others to contribute to the effectiveness and success of the unit
- empower professional, support, and student personnel to become effective leaders
- encourage and support collaboration with colleagues and departments across the institution
- encourage and support scholarly contributions to the profession
- identify and address individual, organizational, and environmental conditions that foster or inhibit mission achievement
- use current and valid evidence to inform decisions
- incorporate sustainability practices in the management and design of programs, services, and facilities
- understand appropriate technologies and integrate them into programs and services
- be knowledgeable about codes and laws relevant to programs and services and ensure that programs and services meet those requirements
- assess and take action to mitigate potential risks

Program Advancement

- advocate for and actively promote the mission and

goals of the programs and services

- inform stakeholders about issues affecting practice
- facilitate processes to reach consensus where wide support is needed
- advocate for representation in strategic planning initiatives at divisional and institutional levels

Institutional compliance issues must be considered in creating and maintaining effective office organization structure and management.

The institution should be aware of and ready to respond to government requirements for enrolling international students. For instance, the institution may be required to designate specific employees who will ensure institutional compliance with government immigration regulations.

Part 4. Human Resources

International Student Programs and Services (ISPS) must be staffed adequately by individuals qualified to accomplish mission and goals.

ISPS must have access to technical and support personnel adequate to accomplish their mission.

Within institutional guidelines, ISPS must

- establish procedures for personnel recruitment and selection, training, performance planning, and evaluation
- set expectations for supervision and performance
- provide personnel access to continuing and advanced education and appropriate professional development opportunities to improve their competence, skills, and leadership capacity
- consider work/life options available to personnel (e.g., compressed work schedules, flextime, job sharing, remote work, or telework) to promote recruitment and retention of personnel

Administrators of ISPS must

- ensure that all personnel have updated position descriptions
- implement recruitment and selection/hiring strategies that produce a workforce inclusive of under-represented populations
- develop promotion practices that are fair, inclusive, proactive, and non-discriminatory

Personnel responsible for delivery of ISPS must have written performance goals, objectives, and outcomes for each year's performance cycle to be used to plan, review, and evaluate work and performance. The performance plan must be updated regularly to reflect changes during the performance cycle.

Results of individual personnel evaluations must be used to recognize personnel performance, address performance issues, implement individual and/or collective personnel development and training programs, and inform the assessment of programs and services.

ISPS personnel, when hired and throughout their employment, must receive appropriate and thorough training.

ISPS personnel, including student employees and volunteers, must have access to resources or receive specific training on

- institutional policies pertaining to functions or activities they support
- privacy and confidentiality policies
- laws regarding access to student records
- policies and procedures for dealing with sensitive institutional information
- policies and procedures related to technology used to store or access student records and institutional data
- how and when to refer those in need of additional assistance to qualified personnel and have access to a supervisor for assistance in making these judgments
- systems and technologies necessary to perform their assigned responsibilities
- ethical and legal uses of technology

ISPS personnel must engage in continuing professional development activities to keep abreast of the research, theories, legislation, policies, and developments that affect their programs and services.

Administrators of ISPS must ensure that personnel are knowledgeable about and trained in safety, emergency procedures, and crisis prevention and response. Risk management efforts must address identification of threatening conduct or behavior and must incorporate a system for responding to and reporting such behaviors.

ISPS personnel must be knowledgeable of and trained in safety and emergency procedures for securing and vacating facilities.

ISPS professional staff members must be knowledgeable about research and practice in areas related to international student programs and services and stay abreast of developments in policies, laws, and regulations affecting international students.

ISPS professional staff members must have an understanding of and demonstrate appreciation for various cultures served in the student population.

ISPS professional staff members must possess the required interpersonal skills and be competent in the areas of effective communication, group facilitation, leadership training and development, and crisis intervention.

ISPS professional staff members should be familiar with multicultural theory, organizational development, counseling theory and practice, group dynamics, leadership development, human development, and research and evaluation. ISPS professional staff members should have proficiency in a second language and extended travel and/or living experiences abroad.

PROFESSIONAL PERSONNEL

ISPS professional personnel either must hold an earned

graduate or professional degree in a field relevant to their position or must possess an appropriate combination of educational credentials and related work experience.

INTERNS OR GRADUATE ASSISTANTS

Degree- or credential-seeking interns or graduate assistants must be qualified by enrollment in an appropriate field of study and relevant experience. These students must be trained and supervised by professional personnel who possess applicable educational credentials and work experience and have supervisory experience. Supervisors must be cognizant of the dual roles interns and graduate assistants have as both student and employee.

Supervisors must
- adhere to parameters of students' job descriptions
- articulate intended learning outcomes in student job descriptions
- adhere to agreed-upon work hours and schedules
- offer flexible scheduling when circumstances necessitate

Supervisors and students must both agree to suitable compensation if circumstances necessitate additional hours.

ISPS should hire graduate assistants and interns with an interest in international student programs and services. These individuals expand staff abilities, provide peer role models, and gain valuable pre-professional experience. Particular attention should be given to preparing assistants and interns to be sensitive to cultural differences and the special needs of international students.

STUDENT EMPLOYEES AND VOLUNTEERS

Student employees and volunteers must be carefully selected, trained, supervised, and evaluated. Students must have access to a supervisor. Student employees and volunteers must be provided clear job descriptions, pre-service training based on assessed needs, and continuing development.

Part 5. Ethics

International Student Programs and Services (ISPS) must
- review applicable professional ethical standards and must adopt or develop and implement appropriate statements of ethical practice
- publish and adhere to statements of ethical practice and ensure their periodic review
- orient new personnel to relevant ethical standards and statements of ethical practice and related institutional policies

ISPS must also make exceptions to privacy and confidentiality of information contained in students' education records when mandated by governmental regulations and legislation.

In the United States, this includes the U.S. Department of Homeland Security or the U.S. Department of State.

Statements of ethical standards must

- specify that ISPS personnel respect privacy and maintain confidentiality in communications and records as delineated by privacy laws
- specify limits on disclosure of information contained in students' records as well as requirements to disclose to appropriate authorities
- address conflicts of interest, or appearance thereof, by personnel in the performance of their work
- reflect the responsibility of personnel to be fair, objective, and impartial in their interactions with others
- reference management of institutional funds
- reference appropriate behavior regarding research and assessment with human participants, confidentiality of research and assessment data, and students' rights and responsibilities
- include the expectation that personnel confront and hold accountable other personnel who exhibit unethical behavior
- address issues surrounding scholarly integrity

ISPS personnel must
- employ ethical decision making in the performance of their duties
- inform users of programs and services of ethical obligations and limitations emanating from codes and laws or from licensure requirements
- recognize and avoid conflicts of interest that could adversely influence their judgment or objectivity and, when unavoidable, recuse themselves from the situation
- perform their duties within the scope of their position, training, expertise, and competence
- make referrals when issues presented exceed the scope of the position

Part 6. Law, Policy, and Governance

International Student Programs and Services (ISPS) must be in compliance with laws, regulations, and policies that relate to their respective responsibilities and that pose legal obligations, limitations, risks, and liabilities for the institution as a whole. Examples include constitutional, statutory, regulatory, and case law; relevant law and orders emanating from codes and laws; and the institution's policies.

ISPS staff must be well versed in and remain current on immigration laws and regulations that impact students. ISPS staff must understand and be able to communicate short-term issues related to and long-term impacts of immigration tracking systems, such as SEVIS, the Student and Exchange Visitor Information System.

ISPS staff must also be familiar with constitutional issues of due process, with rights and responsibilities afforded international students, and with privacy laws, and staff must be able to communicate such to students.

ISPS must have access to legal advice needed for personnel to carry out their assigned responsibilities.

Staff members should establish and maintain positive working relationships with the institution's legal counsel.

ISPS must inform personnel, appropriate officials, and users of programs and services about existing and changing legal obligations, risks and liabilities, and limitations.

ISPS must inform personnel about professional liability insurance options and refer them to external sources if the institution does not provide coverage.

ISPS must have written policies and procedures on operations, transactions, or tasks that have legal implications.

ISPS must regularly review policies. The revision and creation of policies must be informed by best practices, available evidence, and policy issues in higher education.

ISPS must have procedures and guidelines consistent with institutional policy for responding to threats, emergencies, and crisis situations. Systems and procedures must be in place to disseminate timely and accurate information to students, other members of the institutional community, and appropriate external organizations during emergency situations.

Personnel must neither participate in nor condone any form of harassment or activity that demeans persons or creates an intimidating, hostile, or offensive environment.

ISPS must purchase or obtain permission to use copyrighted materials and instruments. References to copyrighted materials and instruments must include appropriate citations.

ISPS must inform personnel about internal and external governance organizations that affect programs and services.

Part 7. Diversity, Equity, and Access

Within the context of each institution's mission and in accordance with institutional policies and applicable codes and laws, International Student Programs and Services (ISPS) must create and maintain educational and work environments that are welcoming, accessible, inclusive, equitable, and free from harassment.

ISPS must not discriminate on the basis of disability; age; race; cultural identity; ethnicity; nationality; family educational history (e.g., first generation to attend college); political affiliation; religious affiliation; sex; sexual orientation; gender identity and expression; marital, social, economic, or veteran status; or any other basis included in institutional policies and codes and laws.

ISPS must
- advocate for sensitivity to multicultural and social justice concerns by the institution and its personnel
- ensure physical, program, and resource access for all constituents
- modify or remove policies, practices, systems, technologies, facilities, and structures that create barriers or produce inequities

- ensure that when facilities and structures cannot be modified, they do not impede access to programs, services, and resources
- establish goals for diversity, equity, and access
- foster communication and practices that enhance understanding of identity, culture, self-expression, and heritage
- promote respect for commonalities and differences among people within their historical and cultural contexts
- address the characteristics and needs of diverse constituents when establishing and implementing culturally relevant and inclusive programs, services, policies, procedures, and practices
- provide personnel with diversity, equity, and access training and hold personnel accountable for applying the training to their work
- respond to the needs of all constituents served when establishing hours of operation and developing methods of delivering programs, services, and resources
- recognize the needs of distance and online learning students by directly providing or assisting them to gain access to comparable services and resources

ISPS must orient international students to the culture of the host country and promote and deepen international students' understanding of cross-cultural differences while building cross-cultural competencies.

ISPS should encourage coordinated efforts to promote multicultural sensitivity and the elimination of prejudicial behaviors in all functional areas.

Considering the long-term wellbeing of both individual international students and the institution's international educational exchange programs, ISPS staff members must anticipate and balance the wants, needs, and requirements of students with institutional policies, laws, and sponsors.

ISPS staff members should develop procedures to respond to anticipated conflicts between the needs of individual international students and institutional policies, governmental laws and regulations, or sponsor policies.

ISPS staff members should develop systems to address unanticipated conflicts between the needs of individual international students and institutional policies, governmental laws and regulations, or sponsor policies.

ISPS staff members must demonstrate a high degree of cross-cultural competency and sensitivity, while treating differences between value systems and cultures non-judgmentally and avoiding use of pejorative stereotypical statements.

Part 8. Internal and External Relations

International Student Programs and Services (ISPS) must reach out to individuals, groups, communities, and organizations internal and external to the institution to
- establish, maintain, and promote understanding and effective relations with those that have a

significant interest in or potential effect on the students or other constituents served by the programs and services

- garner support and resources for programs and services as defined by the mission
- collaborate in offering or improving programs and services to meet the needs of students and other constituents and to achieve program and student outcomes
- engage diverse individuals, groups, communities, and organizations to enrich the educational environment and experiences of students and other constituents
- disseminate information about the programs and services

Promotional and descriptive information must be accurate and free of deception and misrepresentation.

ISPS must have procedures and guidelines consistent with institutional policy for

- communicating with the media
- distributing information through print, broadcast, and online sources
- contracting with external organizations for delivery of programs and services
- cultivating, soliciting, and managing gifts
- applying to and managing funds from grants

ISPS professional staff must be aware of and respond to changes in government activity affecting international students.

ISPS professional staff members should establish and maintain a positive working relationship with the institutional government liaison. Staff members should participate in advocacy as appropriate and necessary.

Part 9. Financial Resources

International Student Programs and Services (ISPS) must have funding to accomplish the mission and goals. In establishing and prioritizing funding resources, ISPS must conduct comprehensive analyses to determine

- unmet needs of the unit
- relevant expenditures
- external and internal resources
- impact on students and the institution

ISPS must use the budget as a planning tool to reflect commitment to the mission and goals of the programs and services and of the institution.

ISPS must administer funds in accordance with established institutional accounting procedures.

ISPS must demonstrate efficient and effective use and responsible stewardship of fiscal resources consistent with institutional protocols.

Financial reports must provide an accurate financial overview of the organization and provide clear, understandable, and timely data upon which personnel can plan and make informed decisions.

Procurement procedures must

- be consistent with institutional policies
- ensure that purchases comply with laws and codes for usability and access
- ensure that the institution receives value for the funds spent
- consider information available for comparing the ethical and environmental impact of products and services purchased

When considering a special student fee as a means of supporting international student programs and services, ISPS should carefully review the related ethical issues of such a fee and bring them to the attention of appropriate institutional leaders.

Part 10. Technology

International Student Programs and Services (ISPS) must have technology to support the achievement of their mission and goals. The technology and its use must comply with institutional policies and procedures and with relevant codes and laws.

ISPS must use technologies to

- provide updated information regarding mission, location, staffing, programs, services, and official contacts to students and other constituents in accessible formats
- provide an avenue for students and other constituents to communicate sensitive information in a secure format
- enhance the delivery of programs and services for all students

ISPS must

- back up data on a regular basis
- adhere to institutional policies regarding ethical and legal use of technology
- articulate policies and procedures for protecting the confidentiality and security of information
- implement a replacement plan and cycle for all technology with attention to sustainability
- incorporate accessibility features into technology-based programs and services

When providing student access to technology, ISPS must

- have policies on the use of technology that are clear, easy to understand, and available to all students
- provide information or referral to support services for those needing assistance in accessing or using technology
- provide instruction or training on how to use the technology
- inform students of implications of misuse of technologies

Part 11. Facilities and Equipment

International Student Programs and Services' (ISPS) facilities must be intentionally designed and located in suitable, accessible, and safe spaces that demonstrate universal design and support the program's mission and goals.

Facilities must be designed to engage various constituents and promote learning.

Personnel must have workspaces that are suitably located and accessible, well equipped, adequate in size, and designed to support their work and responsibilities.

The design of the facilities must guarantee the security and privacy of records and ensure the confidentiality of sensitive information and conversations. Personnel must be able to secure their work.

ISPS must incorporate sustainable practices in use of facilities and purchase of equipment. Facilities and equipment must be evaluated on an established cycle and be in compliance with codes, laws, and accepted practices for access, health, safety, and security.

When acquiring capital equipment, ISPS must take into account expenses related to regular maintenance and life cycle costs.

Part 12. Assessment

International Student Programs and Services (ISPS) must develop assessment plans and processes.

Assessment plans must articulate an ongoing cycle of assessment activities.

ISPS must
- specify programmatic goals and intended outcomes
- identify student learning and development outcomes
- employ multiple measures and methods
- develop manageable processes for gathering, interpreting, and evaluating data
- document progress toward achievement of goals and outcomes
- interpret and use assessment results to demonstrate accountability
- report aggregated results to respondent groups and stakeholders
- use assessment results to inform planning and decision-making
- assess effectiveness of implemented changes
- provide evidence of improvement of programs and services

ISPS must employ ethical practices in the assessment process.

ISPS must have access to adequate fiscal, human, professional development, and technological resources to develop and implement assessment plans.

General Standards revised in 2014;
ISPS content developed/revised in 1996 & 2008

Internship Programs
CAS Contextual Statement

In the 1960s, with its social upheaval, a movement gained considerable momentum to make the college curriculum more relevant and to apply the knowledge of theoretical disciplines to address societal problems. As higher education institutions revamped their curricula, they began to recognize that supervised learning experiences, defined as internships, outside the classroom were relevant to the educational process and to student development. Thoughtful structuring and assessment of outcomes took on new meaning with the prospect of these learning experiences also being available for academic credit.

The National Society for Experiential Education (NSEE), the primary professional association focused on internships and other forms of experiential student learning, was established in 1978 with the merging of the Society for Field Experience and National Center for Public Service Internship Programs. Among others, experiential education organizations include the Cooperative Education and Internship Association, the Association for Experiential Education, NAFSA: Association of International Educators, the National Association of Colleges and Employers, and Campus Compact.

Although professionalism in experiential education has developed significantly in the past decade, the establishment of the CAS Internship Programs standards is of compelling importance to the field. They define an internship within the context of an academic institution of higher education. They emphasize that within both academic and co-curricular areas careful thought, planning, administration, implementation, and feedback are important to the entire learning process and that intentionality of purpose and sufficient resources to achieve those goals need to be available to accomplish the established outcomes of the learning experience.

Increasingly, discipline-based academic associations have developed best practices for internships within their fields. NSEE has a series of training modules, the Experiential Education Academy, to guide academics and others designing internships and which awards a certificate of recognition. A goal of internship-focused organizations has been to advance the practice and to advocate for the inclusion of experiential and related forms of active or engaged learning, within and outside the classroom or campus setting, and to establish appropriate principles, standards and ethics to guide the work.

As a result of the efforts of these organizations, reinforced by demands of students and parents for a more applied curriculum, internships have become an integral part of a college education at both two and four year institutions. In part what identifies a quality internship, as it does other experiential "high impact practices" (AAC&U), is the degree of faculty or professional staff direction and support of the process and the expectation for student self-study that together enable the intern to "learn by doing" and to reflect upon that "doing" to achieve specific learning outcomes (Kuh, 2008).

What distinguishes an intern from a volunteer is the intentional learning shaped by experiential pedagogy (Sweitzer & King, 2014). Assessment feedback for student learning and the clarification of the relationship of an internship experience to its specific learning outcomes are essential. Additionally, the development of this experiential learning environment provided by the internship is the responsibility of the student, the student's academic program, the institution, and the internship site partner (Inkster & Ross, 1995; 1998). Each shares in the responsibility to ensure that the experience addresses intentional and collaboratively framed learning outcomes that are sufficiently rigorous to warrant academic credit or to ensure personal developmental outcomes (Hesser, 2014).

The type of internship experience sanctioned by an institution may vary. Some emphasize a form of cooperative education in which compensation for professional work is a high expectation and where credit for the experience is not necessarily expected. Some may involve a heavily supervised semester or summer-long experience which may or may not award academic credit. Others may utilize a form of externship, which is similar to short-term, field-based learning with minimal or limited interaction with an organization. Regardless of the structure and as a result of the application of CAS standards to include liability concerns and the application of CAS standards, an increasing number of institutions are now taking a more active role in evaluating placements and in incorporating their institutional expectations into the internship process.

It should be noted that the U.S. Department of Labor's Wage and Hours Divisions' interpretation of the Federal Fair Labor Standards Act has addressed the legal expectations of internships and internship programs; this attention has generated significant conversation about the responsibilities and ethics of program offerings. The Department has stated that if an employment relationship is deemed to exist, the intern must be paid at least the required minimum wage and any appropriate overtime compensation. With regard to the issue of paid versus unpaid interns, recent court decisions seem to have broadened the protection of companies using unpaid interns when internships are designed chiefly for educational purposes and the majority of the benefit derived from the experience is to the intern (Glatt v. Fox Searchlight Pictures Inc., 2015; Wang v. Hearst Corp, 2015).

Legal cases are clarifying national and regional expectations of acceptable practice in internship programs. Educational institutions using CAS and other standards of good practice are helping address these complex matters by educating staff members, students, and internship sites regarding pedagogy, expectations, and the law. Internship program directors should consult with institutional officials on legal and business matters as part of their application of the CAS Standards to their programs.

Setting standards for internship programs establishes benchmarks for administrators, faculty, and staff members that identify a quality internship and an effective learning experience. Within this framework, it is also important to address the similarities and differences of an academic internship within academic affairs and a co-curricular internship supported by a student affairs division. The CAS Internship Program standards take into account the importance of establishing standards within each of these areas to meet student development, academic, career, and personal goals. Additionally, these standards assume there is sufficient communication between the two areas to ensure that appropriate expertise is utilized across divisions and throughout the campus.

Of considerable significance is the intent of CAS to support the concept that the Internship Programs standards apply to all internship offerings regardless of their placement within academic, student services, or individualized settings within or external to the institution. It should be noted that many colleges and universities are establishing coordinating committees to ensure viability of learning outcomes and to address issues of risk management in their IP offerings. As they consider internships a "high impact" component of students' curricula, the need to adequately train professional staff and faculty as they guide students' experiential education is an essential institutional duty for knowledgeable and professional delivery of programmatic services.

To minimize the risk associated with off-campus internships, there is a trend for institutions to select third-party organizations with personnel who are expert in these programmatic areas to place and to supervise students. Appropriate evaluation of the performance of these organizations, moreover, must be an integral part of the internship process and incorporate relevant CAS criteria to assure adherence to institutional and best practice internship program expectations.

Another new development in the field has been the creation of virtual internships, during which students engage in communication, special projects, and other activities while not located at the primary internship site. Still in its infancy, this type of internship gives greater flexibility to the student who cannot afford to live in another city or to take time away from employment or from one's campus. As the convenience of such arrangements becomes more attractive, institutions will have to learn to adapt their evaluation of such arrangements and to consider the impact of these offerings on their ability to supervise, support, and assess the intended learning (Wortham, 2014). Additionally, as this form of internship begins to overlap into the field of distance learning there may be complex issues with federal and state authorization of these programs which may be quite impactful for higher education. The current revision of the CAS standards provides guidance for these new challenges.

Internships and other forms of experiential education have become fully accepted as part of the college experience. Many new faculty members are former interns who understand the value of an internship and understand appropriate methods of measuring student performance. More off-campus agencies and site partners understand the law and the necessity to provide substantive work and responsibilities to the student intern. More financial assistance is available either through the institution or the placement site to help cover students' costs. Technology is providing career centers, internship offices, or off-campus programs with the ability to more efficiently and effectively evaluate additional placement opportunities and to match student interest and internship requirements with appropriate placements. Additionally, the implementation of online portfolio systems allows more involvement by students in their development and in assessment of their learning when all participants in the internship experience collaborate.

All the developments seen in the evolution of experiential learning, reinforced by the application of uniform standards available through CAS and use of rigorous experiential pedagogy, will provide internship programs the ability to offer comprehensive learning experiences grounded within the application of effective experiential education methods.

The reader is encouraged to recognize that the CAS Internship Programs standards compliment and support other CAS standards. Among others, the CAS standards for Career Services, Academic Advising Programs, Civic Engagement and Service-Learning Programs, and Education Abroad Programs include components supportive of comprehensive internship offerings in higher education.

References, Readings, and Resources

American Association of Colleges and Universities: https://www. aacu.org

Association for Experiential Education: http://www.aee.org

Campus Compact: http://www.compact.org

Chickering, A. W. (1977). Experience and learning: An introduction to experiential learning. Rochelle, NY: Change Magazine Press.

Cooperative Education and Internship Association, http://www. ceiainc.org.

Glatt v. Fox Searchlight Pictures, Inc., No. 13-4478-cv (2d Cir. July 2, 2015).

Hesser, G. (2014). *Strengthening experiential education: A New Era.* Mount Royal, NJ: National Society for Experiential Education.

Inkster, R. P., & Ross, R. G. (1998). *The internship as partnership: A handbook for businesses, nonprofits, and government agencies.* Raleigh, NC: National Society for Experiential Education.

Inkster, R. P., & Ross, R. G. (1995). *The internship as partnership: A handbook for campus based coordinators and advisors.* Raleigh, NC: National Society for Experiential Education.

Kendall, J. C., Duley, J. S., Little, T. C., Permaul, J. S., & Rubin, S. (1986). *Strengthening experiential education within your institution.* Raleigh, NC: National Society for Internships and Experiential Education.

Kiser, P. M. (2000). *Getting the most out of your internship: Learning from experience.* Belmont, CA: Wadsworth/Thomson Learning.

Kolb, D. A. (1984). *Experiential learning: Experience as the source of learning and development.* Upper Saddle River, NJ: Prentice-Hall.

Kuh, G. D. (2008) *High-Impact educational practices: What they are, who has access to them, and why they matter.* Washington, DC: American Association of Colleges and Universities.

NAFSA: Association of International Educators: http://www.nafsa. org

National Association of Colleges and Employers: https://www.naceweb.org

National Council for State Authorization Reciprocity Agreements: http://www.nc-sara.org

National Society for Experiential Education, http://www.nsee.org__

Stanton, T., & Ali, K. (1994). *The experienced hand: A student manual for making the most of an internship*. (2nd ed.). New York, NY: Carroll Press.

Sweitzer, H. F., & King, Mary A. (2014). *The successful internship: Transformation and empowerment in experiential learning*. (4th ed.). Boston, MA: Cengage Learning.

U.S. Department of Labor, Wage and Hour Division, Fact Sheet #71, April 2010. Retrieved from http://www.dol.gov/whd/regs/compliance/whdfs71.htm

United States International Council on Disabilities (USICD). (2015, May*). Engaging Interns with Disabilities at International Organizations*. Washington, DC: Author. Retrieved from http://67.199.83.28/doc/Engaging%20Interns%20with%20Disabilities%20at%20International%20Organizations%20%28Beta%29%20May%202015.pdf

Wang v. Hearst Corp., No 13-4480-cv (2d Cir. July 2, 2015).

Wortham, J. (2013, January 30). "Virtually There: Working Remotely." *The New York Times*. Retrieved from http://www.nytimes.com/2013/02/03/education/edlife/virtual-internships.html

Contextual Statement Contributors

Current Edition:
Eugene J. Alpert, The Washington Center for Internships and Academic Seminars, NSEE
James Walters, The Walters Group, NSEE

Previous Editions:
Eugene J. Alpert, The Washington Center for Internships and Academic Seminars, NSEE

Internship Programs
CAS Standards and Guidelines

Part 1. Mission

The primary mission of Internship Programs (IP) is to engage students in planned, educationally-related work and learning experiences that integrate knowledge and theory with practical application and skill development in a professional setting.

IP must develop, disseminate, implement, and regularly review their missions, which must be consistent with the mission of the institution and with applicable professional standards. The mission must be appropriate for the institution's students and other constituents. Mission statements must reference student learning and development.

Part 2. Program

To achieve their mission, Internship Programs (IP) must contribute to

- students' formal education, which includes both the curriculum and the co-curriculum
- student progression and timely completion of educational goals
- preparation of students for their careers, citizenship, and lives
- student learning and development

To contribute to student learning and development, IP must

- identify relevant and desirable student learning and development outcomes
- articulate how the student learning and development outcomes align with the six CAS student learning and development domains and related dimensions
- assess relevant and desirable student learning and development
- provide evidence of impact on outcomes
- articulate contributions to or support of student learning and development in the domains not specifically assessed
- use evidence gathered to create strategies for improvement of programs and services

STUDENT LEARNING AND DEVELOPMENT DOMAINS AND DIMENSIONS

Domain: knowledge acquisition, integration, construction, and application

- Dimensions: understanding knowledge from a range of disciplines; connecting knowledge to other knowledge, ideas, and experiences; constructing knowledge; and relating knowledge to daily life

Domain: cognitive complexity

- Dimensions: critical thinking, reflective thinking, effective reasoning, and creativity

Domain: intrapersonal development

- Dimensions: realistic self-appraisal, self-understanding, and self-respect; identity development; commitment to ethics and integrity; and spiritual awareness

Domain: interpersonal competence

- Dimensions: meaningful relationships, interdependence, collaboration, and effective leadership

Domain: humanitarianism and civic engagement

- Dimensions: understanding and appreciation of cultural and human differences, social responsibility, global perspective, and sense of civic responsibility

Domain: practical competence

- Dimensions: pursuing goals, communicating effectively, technical competence, managing personal affairs, managing career development, demonstrating professionalism, maintaining health and wellness, and living a purposeful and satisfying life

[LD Outcomes: See *The Council for the Advancement of Standards Learning and Development Outcomes* statement for examples of outcomes related to these domains and dimensions.]

IP must be

- intentionally designed
- guided by theories and knowledge of learning and development
- integrated into the life of the institution
- reflective of developmental and demographic profiles of the student population
- responsive to needs of individuals, populations with distinct needs, and relevant constituencies
- delivered using multiple formats, strategies, and contexts
- designed to provide universal access

IP must collaborate with colleagues and departments across the institution to promote student learning and development, persistence, and success.

Learning goals of IP must

- be clear about the educational purpose and expected student learning outcomes of the internship experience
- encourage the learner to test assumptions and hypotheses about the outcomes of decisions and actions taken, then weigh the outcomes against past learning and future implications
- develop and document intentional goals and objectives for the internship experience and

measure learning outcomes against these goals and objectives

- maintain intellectual rigor in the field experience

IP must

- ensure that the participants enter the experience with sufficient foundation to support a successful experience
- engage students in appropriate and relevant internships that facilitate practical application of theory and knowledge
- provide the learner, the facilitator, and any organizational partners with important background information about each other and about the context and environment in which the experience will operate
- articulate the relationship of the internship experience to the expected learning outcomes
- determine criteria for internship sites and train appropriate internship personnel to ensure productive and appropriate learning opportunities for students
- ensure that all parties engaged in the experience are included in the recognition of progress and accomplishment

When course credit is offered for an internship, the credit must primarily be for learning, not just for the practical work completed at the internship. Whether the internship is for credit or not, the focus must be on learning and educational objectives, not just on hours accrued at the site.

IP must offer a wide range of internship experiences appropriate for students at various developmental levels, abilities, and with various life circumstances.

Examples may include older students, commuter students, parents, part-time students, fully employed students, and students with disabilities.

IP must initiate collaborative relations among faculty and staff members within the institution for the design and implementation of internship experiences. They must also develop partnerships with external organizations to meet student learning and development outcomes and the organizations' needs.

Whether integrated into a course, completed as an independent study, or designed for co-curricular learning or personal development, internships should encourage practical application of knowledge and theory, development of skills and interests, and exploration of career options in a professional setting. Internships may be for pay or non-pay, for credit or non-credit, and for a variety of lengths or terms. IP experiences could include the following:

Discipline-specific course-based internships: These can be designed to achieve a variety of student learning outcomes relevant to the course and discipline within which the internship is based, including introducing students to career opportunities as a critical aspect of their college education and their chosen field of study, enabling students to learn what types of work within their chosen field of study best

suit their interests, and helping students to understand the different career opportunities available to them both inside and outside their curriculum. These experiences should be part of the academic curriculum for credit.

Student-initiated internships: These internships can be designed to enable students to explore internship opportunities within or outside their course of study and their discipline, to apply knowledge learned in their academic program to practice in different situations and venues, and to gain exposure to a broader array of internship experiences than a course- or discipline-based internship might allow. These experiences, if approved in advance, should be considered for academic credit. These experiences could also add to co-curricular learning and personal development.

Short-term internships: These internship programs offer students the opportunity to explore career opportunities through internships without the long-term commitment required by a quarter-term program, academic semester, or year. Typically these occur during week-long breaks or during the short sessions between fall and spring semesters and summer (i.e., January or May term). These experiences can be integrated into the academic curriculum or serve as a co-curricular experience, for credit or not-for-credit, in the student's discipline, or in a broader learning context.

Paid internships: Whether integrated into a course, completed as independent-study, or planned during the summer or semester breaks, these internships are designed to provide students with exposure to career opportunities within a paid employment environment. Structured within a real-world context, students are encouraged to apply theory and knowledge in the career setting while receiving financial compensation for their work and time.

Internship experiences must be described in a syllabus or plan.

The internship course syllabus or plan for academic or co-curricular experiences should describe

- purpose of the internship
- desired learning and development outcomes of the internship for all participants
- assignments that link the internship to academic, career, or personal goals
- opportunities to reflect on one's personal reactions to internship experiences
- logistics (e.g., time required, transportation, materials required, access to services and resources, credit/non-credit, paid/unpaid, financial costs, and benefits)
- roles and responsibilities of students and site personnel
- risk management procedures
- supervision and accommodation requirements by institution personnel and internship site
- evaluation of the internship experience and assessment of the extent to which desired outcomes were achieved
- course requirements (if for credit), including criteria for grading

Part 3. Organization and Leadership

To achieve program and student learning and development outcomes, Internship Programs (IP) must be purposefully structured for effectiveness. IP must have clearly stated and current
- goals and outcomes
- policies and procedures
- responsibilities and performance expectations for personnel
- organizational charts demonstrating clear channels of authority

Leaders must model ethical behavior and institutional citizenship.

Leaders with organizational authority for IP must provide strategic planning, management and supervision, and program advancement.

Strategic Planning
- articulate a vision and mission that drive short- and long-term planning
- set goals and objectives based on the needs of the populations served, intended student learning and development outcomes, and program outcomes
- facilitate continuous development, implementation, and assessment of program effectiveness and goal attainment congruent with institutional mission and strategic plans
- promote environments that provide opportunities for student learning, development, and engagement
- develop, adapt, and improve programs and services in response to the changing needs of populations served and evolving institutional priorities
- include diverse perspectives to inform decision making

Management and Supervision
- plan, allocate, and monitor the use of fiscal, physical, human, intellectual, and technological resources
- manage human resource processes including recruitment, selection, professional development, supervision, performance planning, succession planning, evaluation, recognition, and reward
- influence others to contribute to the effectiveness and success of the unit
- empower professional, support, and student personnel to become effective leaders
- encourage and support collaboration with colleagues and departments across the institution
- encourage and support scholarly contributions to the profession
- identify and address individual, organizational, and environmental conditions that foster or inhibit mission achievement
- use current and valid evidence to inform decisions
- incorporate sustainability practices in the management and design of programs, services, and facilities
- understand appropriate technologies and integrate them into programs and services
- be knowledgeable about codes and laws relevant to programs and services and ensure that programs and services meet those requirements
- assess and take action to mitigate potential risks

Program Advancement
- advocate for and actively promote the mission and goals of the programs and services
- inform stakeholders about issues affecting practice
- facilitate processes to reach consensus where wide support is needed
- advocate for representation in strategic planning initiatives at divisional and institutional levels

Part 4. Human Resources

Internship Programs (IP) must be staffed adequately by individuals qualified to accomplish mission and goals.

IP must have access to technical and support personnel adequate to accomplish their mission.

Within institutional guidelines, IP must
- establish procedures for personnel recruitment and selection, training, performance planning, and evaluation
- set expectations for supervision and performance
- provide personnel access to continuing and advanced education and appropriate professional development opportunities to improve their competence, skills, and leadership capacity
- consider work/life options available to personnel (e.g., compressed work schedules, flextime, job sharing, remote work, or telework) to promote recruitment and retention of personnel

Administrators of IP must
- ensure that all personnel have updated position descriptions
- implement recruitment and selection/hiring strategies that produce a workforce inclusive of under-represented populations
- develop promotion practices that are fair, inclusive, proactive, and non-discriminatory

Personnel responsible for delivery of IP must have written performance goals, objectives, and outcomes for each year's performance cycle to be used to plan, review, and evaluate work and performance. The performance plan must be updated regularly to reflect changes during the performance cycle.

Results of individual personnel evaluations must be used to recognize personnel performance, address performance issues, implement individual and/or collective personnel development and training programs, and inform the assessment of programs and services.

IP personnel, when hired and throughout their employment, must receive appropriate and thorough training.

IP personnel, including student employees and volunteers, must have access to resources or receive specific training on

- **institutional policies pertaining to functions or activities they support**
- **privacy and confidentiality policies**
- **laws regarding access to student records**
- **policies and procedures for dealing with sensitive institutional information**
- **policies and procedures related to technology used to store or access student records and institutional data**
- **how and when to refer those in need of additional assistance to qualified personnel and have access to a supervisor for assistance in making these judgments**
- **systems and technologies necessary to perform their assigned responsibilities**
- **ethical and legal uses of technology**

IP personnel must engage in continuing professional development activities to keep abreast of the research, theories, legislation, policies, and developments that affect their programs and services.

Administrators of IP must ensure that personnel are knowledgeable about and trained in safety, emergency procedures, and crisis prevention and response. Risk management efforts must address identification of threatening conduct or behavior and must incorporate a system for responding to and reporting such behaviors.

IP personnel must be knowledgeable of and trained in safety and emergency procedures for securing and vacating facilities.

PROFESSIONAL PERSONNEL

IP professional personnel either must hold an earned graduate or professional degree in a field relevant to their position or must possess an appropriate combination of educational credentials and related work experience.

To facilitate the process of identifying internship sites, professional development of staff and faculty members engaged in IP should include enhancing their ability to

- identify the compatibility between site needs and student interests
- build relationship with business, organizations, institutions, and other career and professional settings
- establish and maintain collaborative relationships with academic and other units on campus
- understand career and workforce trends

To ensure goal achievement of the IP experience, the professional development of staff and faculty members engaged in IP should include

A. Development of assessment skills:
- access previous evaluations of internship sites and make appropriate recommendations as to the learning value of the internship

- develop, implement, and evaluate internship and learning goals
- ensure the time commitment for the internship is appropriate
- ensure that the time spent at internships produces an appropriate balance between the objectives of the site and the learning objectives of the student
- match the unique needs of students and internship sites

B. Proper communication with students:
- prepare, mentor, and monitor students to fulfill internship requirements according to legal and risk management policies
- clarify the responsibilities of students, the institution, and internship sites

C. Enhancement of student learning:
- engage students in internship experiences to enhance student learning and exposure to career opportunities
- use active learning strategies that are effective in achieving identified learning outcomes
- engage students in structured opportunities for self-reflection and reflection on the internship experience
- sustain genuine and active commitment of students, the institution, and internship sites
- educate, train, and support students to apply learning from internship experiences to future endeavors

D. Management skills:
- foster participation by and with diverse populations
- develop fiscal and other resources for program support

INTERNS OR GRADUATE ASSISTANTS

Degree- or credential-seeking interns or graduate assistants must be qualified by enrollment in an appropriate field of study and relevant experience. These students must be trained and supervised by professional personnel who possess applicable educational credentials and work experience and have supervisory experience. Supervisors must be cognizant of the dual roles interns and graduate assistants have as both student and employee.

Supervisors must
- **adhere to parameters of students' job descriptions**
- **articulate intended learning outcomes in student job descriptions**
- **adhere to agreed-upon work hours and schedules**
- **offer flexible scheduling when circumstances necessitate**

Supervisors and students must both agree to suitable compensation if circumstances necessitate additional hours.

STUDENT EMPLOYEES AND VOLUNTEERS

Student employees and volunteers must be carefully selected, trained, supervised, and evaluated. Students must have access to a supervisor. Student employees and

volunteers must be provided clear job descriptions, pre-service training based on assessed needs, and continuing development.

Part 5. Ethics

Internship Programs (IP) must

- review applicable professional ethical standards and must adopt or develop and implement appropriate statements of ethical practice
- publish and adhere to statements of ethical practice and ensure their periodic review
- orient new personnel to relevant ethical standards and statements of ethical practice and related institutional policies

Statements of ethical standards must

- specify that IP personnel respect privacy and maintain confidentiality in communications and records as delineated by privacy laws
- specify limits on disclosure of information contained in students' records as well as requirements to disclose to appropriate authorities
- address conflicts of interest, or appearance thereof, by personnel in the performance of their work
- reflect the responsibility of personnel to be fair, objective, and impartial in their interactions with others
- reference management of institutional funds
- reference appropriate behavior regarding research and assessment with human participants, confidentiality of research and assessment data, and students' rights and responsibilities
- include the expectation that personnel confront and hold accountable other personnel who exhibit unethical behavior
- address issues surrounding scholarly integrity

IP personnel must

- employ ethical decision making in the performance of their duties
- inform users of programs and services of ethical obligations and limitations emanating from codes and laws or from licensure requirements
- recognize and avoid conflicts of interest that could adversely influence their judgment or objectivity and, when unavoidable, recuse themselves from the situation
- perform their duties within the scope of their position, training, expertise, and competence
- make referrals when issues presented exceed the scope of the position

All IP faculty and staff members responsible for supervising internship activities must monitor student performance and alter placements as needed.

Part 6. Law, Policy, and Governance

Internship Programs (IP) must be in compliance with laws, regulations, and policies that relate to their respective responsibilities and that pose legal obligations, limitations, risks, and liabilities for the institution as a whole. Examples include constitutional, statutory, regulatory, and case law; relevant law and orders emanating from codes and laws; and the institution's policies.

IP must have access to legal advice needed for personnel to carry out their assigned responsibilities.

IP must inform personnel, appropriate officials, and users of programs and services about existing and changing legal obligations, risks and liabilities, and limitations.

IP staff and faculty members and internship site personnel engaged in internships must be knowledgeable about and responsive to laws and regulations that relate to their respective responsibilities.

IP must inform personnel about professional liability insurance options and refer them to external sources if the institution does not provide coverage.

IP must have written policies and procedures on operations, transactions, or tasks that have legal implications.

IP must regularly review policies. The revision and creation of policies must be informed by best practices, available evidence, and policy issues in higher education.

IP must have procedures and guidelines consistent with institutional policy for responding to threats, emergencies, and crisis situations. Systems and procedures must be in place to disseminate timely and accurate information to students, other members of the institutional community, and appropriate external organizations during emergency situations.

IP staff members must establish, review, and disseminate company safety and emergency procedures and policies for the work site and accompanying residential facility.

Personnel must neither participate in nor condone any form of harassment or activity that demeans persons or creates an intimidating, hostile, or offensive environment.

IP must purchase or obtain permission to use copyrighted materials and instruments. References to copyrighted materials and instruments must include appropriate citations.

IP must inform personnel about internal and external governance organizations that affect programs and services.

Part 7. Diversity, Equity, and Access

Within the context of each institution's mission and in accordance with institutional policies and applicable codes and laws, Internship Programs (IP) must create and maintain educational and work environments that are welcoming, accessible, inclusive, equitable, and free from harassment.

IP must not discriminate on the basis of disability; age; race; cultural identity; ethnicity; nationality; family educational history (e.g., first generation to attend college); political affiliation; religious affiliation; sex; sexual orientation; gender identity and expression; marital, social, economic, or veteran status; or any other basis included in institutional policies and codes and laws.

IP must
- advocate for sensitivity to multicultural and social justice concerns by the institution and its personnel
- ensure physical, program, and resource access for all constituents
- modify or remove policies, practices, systems, technologies, facilities, and structures that create barriers or produce inequities
- ensure that when facilities and structures cannot be modified, they do not impede access to programs, services, and resources
- establish goals for diversity, equity, and access
- foster communication and practices that enhance understanding of identity, culture, self-expression, and heritage
- promote respect for commonalities and differences among people within their historical and cultural contexts
- address the characteristics and needs of diverse constituents when establishing and implementing culturally relevant and inclusive programs, services, policies, procedures, and practices
- provide personnel with diversity, equity, and access training and hold personnel accountable for applying the training to their work
- respond to the needs of all constituents served when establishing hours of operation and developing methods of delivering programs, services, and resources
- recognize the needs of distance and online learning students by directly providing or assisting them to gain access to comparable services and resources

IP staff members must select sites that adhere to this nondiscrimination standard.

Part 8. Internal and External Relations

Internship Programs (IP) must reach out to individuals, groups, communities, and organizations internal and external to the institution to
- establish, maintain, and promote understanding and effective relations with those that have a significant interest in or potential effect on the students or other constituents served by the programs and services
- garner support and resources for programs and services as defined by the mission
- collaborate in offering or improving programs and services to meet the needs of students and other constituents and to achieve program and student outcomes
- engage diverse individuals, groups, communities, and organizations to enrich the educational environment and experiences of students and other constituents

- disseminate information about the programs and services

These agencies include government, private business, and nonprofit organizations at the local, national, or international level.

If there is more than one campus unit that facilitates internship experiences, those offices should share information and collaborate as appropriate.

IP should develop productive working relationships with a wide range of campus agencies.

Promotional and descriptive information must be accurate and free of deception and misrepresentation.

IP must have procedures and guidelines consistent with institutional policy for
- communicating with the media
- distributing information through print, broadcast, and online sources
- contracting with external organizations for delivery of programs and services
- cultivating, soliciting, and managing gifts
- applying to and managing funds from grants

IP must be concerned about issues of risk management and consult with appropriate campus offices and officials to insure proper procedures.

IP flourishes best when the institution as a whole is engaged as part of its surrounding community. IP should advocate for the institution to share its resources with its community and to develop a wide range of mutually beneficial campus-community partnerships. The "community" may include individuals and organizations beyond the immediate physical location of the campus and include state/provincial, national, and international relationships.

Part 9. Financial Resources

Internship Programs (IP) must have funding to accomplish the mission and goals.
In establishing and prioritizing funding resources, IP must conduct comprehensive analyses to determine
- unmet needs of the unit
- relevant expenditures
- external and internal resources
- impact on students and the institution

IP must use the budget as a planning tool to reflect commitment to the mission and goals of the programs and services and of the institution.

IP must administer funds in accordance with established institutional accounting procedures.

IP must demonstrate efficient and effective use and responsible stewardship of fiscal resources consistent with institutional protocols.

Financial reports must provide an accurate financial overview of the organization and provide clear, understandable, and timely data upon which personnel can plan and make informed decisions.

Procurement procedures must
- be consistent with institutional policies
- ensure that purchases comply with laws and codes for usability and access
- ensure that the institution receives value for the funds spent
- consider information available for comparing the ethical and environmental impact of products and services purchased

Part 10. Technology

Internship Programs (IP) must have technology to support the achievement of their mission and goals. The technology and its use must comply with institutional policies and procedures and with relevant codes and laws.

IP must use technologies to
- provide updated information regarding mission, location, staffing, programs, services, and official contacts to students and other constituents in accessible formats
- provide an avenue for students and other constituents to communicate sensitive information in a secure format
- enhance the delivery of programs and services for all students

IP must
- back up data on a regular basis
- adhere to institutional policies regarding ethical and legal use of technology
- articulate policies and procedures for protecting the confidentiality and security of information
- implement a replacement plan and cycle for all technology with attention to sustainability
- incorporate accessibility features into technology-based programs and services

When providing student access to technology, IP must
- have policies on the use of technology that are clear, easy to understand, and available to all students
- provide information or referral to support services for those needing assistance in accessing or using technology
- provide instruction or training on how to use the technology
- inform students of implications of misuse of technologies

Part 11. Facilities and Equipment

Internship Programs' (IP) facilities must be intentionally designed and located in suitable, accessible, and safe spaces that demonstrate universal design and support the program's mission and goals.

Facilities must be designed to engage various constituents and promote learning.

Personnel must have workspaces that are suitably located and accessible, well equipped, adequate in size, and designed to support their work and responsibilities.

The design of the facilities must guarantee the security and privacy of records and ensure the confidentiality of sensitive information and conversations. Personnel must be able to secure their work.

IP must incorporate sustainable practices in use of facilities and purchase of equipment. Facilities and equipment must be evaluated on an established cycle and be in compliance with codes, laws, and accepted practices for access, health, safety, and security.

When acquiring capital equipment, IP must take into account expenses related to regular maintenance and life cycle costs.

Part 12. Assessment

Internship Programs (IP) must develop assessment plans and processes.

Assessment plans must articulate an ongoing cycle of assessment activities.

IP must
- specify programmatic goals and intended outcomes
- identify student learning and development outcomes
- employ multiple measures and methods
- develop manageable processes for gathering, interpreting, and evaluating data
- document progress toward achievement of goals and outcomes
- interpret and use assessment results to demonstrate accountability
- report aggregated results to respondent groups and stakeholders
- use assessment results to inform planning and decision-making
- assess effectiveness of implemented changes
- provide evidence of improvement of programs and services

IP must employ ethical practices in the assessment process.

IP must have access to adequate fiscal, human, professional development, and technological resources to develop and implement assessment plans.

IP must regularly evaluate, assess, and respond appropriately regarding the extent to which internship sites add to student learning.

General Standards revised in 2014;
IP standards developed in 2006

Learning Assistance Programs
CAS Contextual Statement

Formal and informal learning assistance has been essential to student success and retention since the opening of the first U.S. colleges (Arendale, 2010; Maxwell, 1997). The reading clinics, intensive writing, and study methods laboratories of the 1930s and 1940s and self-help programs, learning modules, and programmed instruction of the 1950s and 1960s formed part of the historical foundation for learning assistance programs (Arendale, 2004, 2010; Carino, 1995; Enright, 1975; Lissner, 1990; Sullivan, 1980). In the U.S., more holistic learning assistance grew out of demographic shifts in student populations in the 1970s, spearheaded in colleges and universities on the West Coast (Christ, 1980; Walker, 1980) and in the Midwest, coupled with a growing national sense of college as a necessary part of a complete education.

This open-university revolution, which broadened admissions to students who had not traditionally sought or been admitted to academically-oriented postsecondary institutions, meant that learning assistance centers expanded their missions to keep the open door to college from becoming a revolving door. The growth of academic success programs across the U.S. and Canada into and through the 1980s was consistent with traditional American ideals of democratic education and equal opportunity. With the passage of the Americans with Disabilities Act in 1990, the last decade of the 20th century saw comprehensive academic support become a standard part of the postsecondary landscape. In the early 21st century, learning assistance has continued to evolve, as the 2008 ADAAA (ADA Amendments Act), rapid demographic shifts, global recruitment of students, and developments in cognitive science have resulted in new and unique challenges in designing appropriate postsecondary learning environments. Learning assistance programs address mismatches between these (and all) students and faculty assumptions, expectations, and practices in order to align learning and instruction and thereby enhance students' academic engagement.

Contemporary learning assistance programs (LAPs) facilitate student learning, development, and academic success (Ryan & Glenn, 2004; Stone & Jacobs, 2008) by assisting students in developing appropriate strategies and behaviors to increase learning efficiency (Dansereau, 1985). Through a combination of student support programs, tutoring, and developmental courses in reading, writing, mathematics, and study strategies, students' particular academic needs can be addressed (Armstrong, Stahl, & Boylan, 2014; Flippo & Caverly, 2009; Hodges, Simpson, & Stahl, 2009). Participation in learning assistance programs and services can also improve student retention (Beal, 1980; Ryan & Glenn, 2004) and academic engagement, providing the kinds of rewarding interactions that foster student intellectual and social growth (Tinto, 1987, 2004). The LAP may serve all students at the institution or targeted populations from first-year through graduate and professional students, as well as faculty, staff, administrators, and students in the community (Kerstiens, 1995). The general trend has been to serve students in a wider variety of settings. LAPs uniquely complement classroom and online instruction by encouraging communities of learning on campus, making learning accessible to students, and helping students make the most of their intellectual opportunities.

Learning assistance programs usually provide individualized instruction (tutoring, mentoring, academic coaching, and counseling; Truschel & Reedy, 2009) that accommodate students' learning preferences, learning goals, and current development. Learning centers may also provide Supplemental Instruction (SI), Structured Learning Assistance (SLA), Peer Led Team Learning (PLTL), and a variety of other programs and services that help students master content and learn how to learn. Sometimes the LAP provides or partners with credit and non-credit courses, including developmental education, tutor and mentor training courses or workshops, first-year seminars, linked courses, and learning strategies instruction. LAPs support students in bridge programs and learning communities; in emporium, companion, co-requisite, and workshop environments; and in accelerated and just-in-time support situations. These programs are intentionally diverse because they are designed and implemented to be consistent with institutional missions as well as educational best practices. Ideally, the LAP operates "at the crossroads of academic affairs, student affairs, and enrollment management" (Arendale, 2010, p. 3).

High-quality learning assistance programs are characterized by a focus on processes and strategies of learning, intellectual development, and effective assessment of academic performance. These programs respect students' cultures while acquainting them with the conventions, discourses, and expectations of higher education. LAPs also engage faculty, staff, students, and administrators in broader conversations about academic success. To augment professional expertise, LAP professionals often train student and paraprofessional staff to provide services (e.g., peer tutoring and mentoring, study groups, SI, SLA, PLTL); the learning and development of student staff, as well as of student clients, thus become important parts of the mission.

Learning assistance programs have increasingly embraced the need for summative and formative assessment of effectiveness, ranging from the measurement of individual student outcomes to pioneering research in teaching and learning (Norton & Agee, 2014). Programs and learning assistance professionals also enjoy growing partnerships with other institutional departments and external organizations who promote data-informed decision-making processes coupled with research in teaching and learning.

CAS Standards provided the impetus for certification and professional development programs in learning assistance. In 1989, the College Reading and Learning Association (CRLA) initiated International Tutor Training Program Certification to ensure minimum standards for tutor training. Nine years later CRLA developed International Mentor Training Program Certification. The *CRLA Handbook for Training Peer Tutors and Mentors* (Agee & Hodges, 2012) provides examples of best practices that meet certification standards. The National Association for Developmental Education (NADE) developed the *NADE Self-Evaluation Guides* (Clark-Thayer, 1995; Clark-Thayer & Putnam Cole, 2009), which provide for a self-study process relevant for developmental coursework programs, tutoring services programs, course-based learning assistance programs, and teaching and learning processes. Firmly grounded in the self-study process from the *Guides,* NADE certification requires programs to incorporate rigorous data analyses in their decision-making processes. All three certification programs as well as programs certifying tutors and tutor trainers (ATP, 2015) and learning center leadership (NCLCA, 2015) are endorsed by the Council of Learning Assistance and Developmental Education Associations (CLADEA), through which six organizations continue to examine and approve certifications in the field.

References, Readings, and Resources

Agee, K., & Hodges, R. (Eds.). (2012). *Handbook for training peer tutors and mentors.* Mason, OH: Cengage Learning.

Arendale, D. R. (2004). Mainstreamed academic assistance and enrichment for all students: The historical origins of learning assistance centers. *Research for Educational Reform, 9*(4), 3-20.

Arendale, D. R. (2010). *Access at the crossroads: Learning assistance in higher education.* ASHE Higher Education Report, *35*(6). San Francisco, CA: Jossey-Bass.

Armstrong, S. L., Stahl, N. A., & Boylan, H. R. (2014). *Teaching developmental reading: Historical, theoretical, and practical readings* (2nd ed.). Boston, MA: Bedford/St. Martin's.

Association for the Tutoring Profession: www.myatp.org, *Synergy*

Association for the Tutoring Profession (ATP). (2015). *ATP certification levels and requirements.* Retrieved from http://www.myatp.org/certification/

Association of Colleges for Tutoring and Learning Assistance, www.actla.info

Beal, P. E. (1980). Learning centers and retention. In O. T. Lenning & D. L. Wayman (Eds.), *New roles for learning assistance* (pp. 59-73). San Francisco, CA: Jossey-Bass.

Carino, P. (1995). Early writing centers: Toward a history. *The Writing Center Journal, 15*(2), 103-115.

Christ, F. L. (1980). Learning assistance at a state university: A cybernetic model. In K. V. Lauridsen (Ed.), *New directions for college learning assistance: Examining the scope of learning centers* (pp. 45-56). San Francisco, CA: Jossey-Bass.

Christ, F., Sheets, R., & Smith, K. (Eds.). (2000). *Starting a learning assistance center: Conversations with CRLA members who have been there and done that.* Clearwater, FL: H&H.

Clark-Thayer, S. (1995). *The NADE self-evaluation guides: Models for assessing learning assistance/developmental education programs.* Clearwater, FL: H&H.

Clark-Thayer, S., & Putnam Cole, L. (Ed.). (2009). *NADE self-evaluation guides: Best practice in academic support programs* (2nd ed.). Clearwater, FL: H&H.

College Reading and Learning Association, www.crla.net, *Journal of College Reading and Learning*

Council of Learning Assistance and Developmental Education Associations, www.cladea.net

Dansereau, D. F. (1985). Learning strategy research. In J. W. Segal, S. F. Chipman, & R. Glaser (Eds.), *Thinking and learning skills: Relating learning to basic research* (pp. 209-240). Hillsdale, NJ: Erlbaum.

Enright, G. (1975). College learning skills: Frontierland origins of the learning assistance center. In R. Sugimoto (Ed.), *College learning skills today and tomorrowland: Proceedings of the Eighth Annual Conference of the Western College Reading Association* (pp. 81-92).

ETL Project, Enhancing Teaching-Learning Environments in Undergraduate Courses, www.etl.tla.ed.ac.uk/project.html

Flippo, R. F., & Caverly, D. C. (Eds.). (2009). *Handbook of college reading and study strategy research* (2nd ed.). New York, NY: Routledge.

Hodges, R., Simpson, M. L., & Stahl, N. A. (2012). *Teaching strategies in developmental education: Readings on theory, research, and best practice.* Boston, MA: Bedford/St. Martin's.

Journal of Academic Language and Learning: journal.aall.org.au/

Journal of Learning Development in Higher Education: www.aldinhe.ac.uk/ojs/index.php?journal=jldhe

Journal of Adolescent and Adult Literacy: www.reading.org/general/Publications/Journals/jaal.aspx

Learning Specialists Association of Canada: www.learningspecialists.ca/

Kerstiens, G. (1995). A taxonomy of learning support services. In S. Mioduski & G. Enright (Eds.), *Proceedings of the 15th and 16th Annual Institutes for Learning Assistance Professionals* (pp. 48-51).

Lissner, L. S. (1990). The learning center from 1829 to the year 2000 and beyond. In R. M. Hashway (Ed.), *Handbook of Developmental Education* (pp. 128-154). New York, NY: Praeger.

LRNASST listserv archives, www.lists.ufl.edu/archives/lrnasst-l.html

LSCHE, Learning Support Centers in Higher Education web portal, www.lsche.net

Maxwell, M., Ed. (1994). *From access to success: A book of readings on college developmental education and learning assistance programs.* Clearwater, FL: H&H.

Maxwell, M. (1997). *Improving student learning skills: A new edition.* Clearwater, FL: H&H.

National Association for Developmental Education, www.nade.net, *NADE Digest* and *NADE Monograph Series*

National Center for Developmental Education, Appalachian State University, www.ncde.appstate.edu, *Journal of Developmental Education* and *Research in Developmental Education*

National College Learning Center Association, www.nclca.org, *The Learning Assistance Review*

National College Learning Center Association (NCLCA). (2015). *Learning center leadership certification.* Retrieved from http://nclca.org/certification.htm

Norton, J., & Agee, K. S. (2014). *Assessment of learning assistance programs: Supporting professionals in the field.* Retrieved from http://www.crla.net/index.php/publications/crla-white-papers

Oxford Learning Institute, Oxford University, http://www.learning.ox.ac.uk/

Ryan, M. P., & Glenn, P. A. (2004). What do first-year students need most: Learning strategies instruction or academic socialization? *Journal of College Reading & Learning, 34*(2), 4-28.

Stone, M. E., & Jacobs, G. (Eds.). (2008). *Supplemental Instruction: Improving first-year student success in high-risk courses* (Monograph No. 7, 3rd ed.). Columbia, SC: University of South Carolina, National Resource Center for The First-Year Experience and Students in Transition.

Sullivan, L. L. (1980). Growth and influence in the learning center movement. In K. V. Lauridsen (Ed.), *Examining the scope of learning centers* (pp. 1-8). San Francisco, CA: Jossey-Bass.

Tinto, V. (1987). *Leaving college: Rethinking the causes and cures of student attrition.* Chicago, IL: University of Chicago Press.

Tinto, V. (2004). *Student retention and graduation: Facing the truth, living with the consequences.* Retrieved from http://www.pellinstitute.org/downloads/publications-Student_Retention_and_Graduation_July_2004.pdf

Trammell, J. (2005). Learning about the learning center: Program evaluation for learning assistance programs. *The Learning Assistance Review, 10*(2), 31-40.

Truschel, J., & Reedy, D. L. (2009). National survey—What is a learning center in the 21st century? *The Learning Assistance Review, 14*(1), 9-22.

Walker, C. (1980). The learning assistance center in a selective institution. In K. V. Lauridsen (Ed.), *New directions for college learning assistance: Examining the scope of learning centers* (pp. 57-68). San Francisco, CA: Jossey-Bass.

Contextual Statement Contributors

Current Edition:

Karen S. Agee, University of Northern Iowa

Patricia Mulcahy-Ernt, University of Bridgeport

Jane Neuburger, Syracuse University

Jan Norton, University of Iowa

Karen Patty-Graham, Southern Illinois University Edwardsville

Melissa Thomas, College of Charleston

Linda Thompson, Harding University

John K. Trammell, Randolph-Macon College

Dominic Voge, Princeton University

Learning Assistance Programs
CAS Standards and Guidelines

The primary mission of Learning Assistance Programs (LAP) must be to provide students with resources and opportunities to improve their ability to learn and to achieve academic success.

LAP must develop, disseminate, implement, and regularly review their missions, which must be consistent with the mission of the institution and with applicable professional standards. The mission must be appropriate for the institution's students and other constituents. Mission statements must reference student learning and development.

LAP must collaborate with faculty members, staff, and administrators in addressing the learning needs, academic performance, and retention of students.

Models of LAP vary, but must have the following goals:
- ensure that students are the central focus of the program
- assist students in achieving their personal potential for learning
- introduce students to the academic expectations of the institution, the faculty members, and the culture of higher education
- help students develop positive attitudes toward learning and confidence in their ability to learn
- foster students' personal responsibility and accountability for their own learning
- provide a variety of instructional approaches appropriate to the skill levels and learning styles of students
- assist students in applying newly learned skills and strategies to their academic work
- support the academic standards and requirements of the institution

Models of LAP should also share the following common goals:
- provide instruction and services that address the cognitive, affective, and sociocultural dimensions of learning
- provide to faculty members, staff, and administrators, both services and resources that enhance and support student learning, instruction, and professional development

To achieve their mission, Learning Assistance Programs (LAP) must contribute to
- students' formal education, which includes both the curriculum and the co-curriculum
- student progression and timely completion of educational goals
- preparation of students for their careers, citizenship, and lives
- student learning and development

To contribute to student learning and development, LAP must
- identify relevant and desirable student learning and development outcomes
- articulate how the student learning and development outcomes align with the six CAS student learning and development domains and related dimensions
- assess relevant and desirable student learning and development
- provide evidence of impact on outcomes
- articulate contributions to or support of student learning and development in the domains not specifically assessed
- use evidence gathered to create strategies for improvement of programs and services

STUDENT LEARNING AND DEVELOPMENT DOMAINS AND DIMENSIONS

Domain: knowledge acquisition, integration, construction, and application
- Dimensions: understanding knowledge from a range of disciplines; connecting knowledge to other knowledge, ideas, and experiences; constructing knowledge; and relating knowledge to daily life

Domain: cognitive complexity
- Dimensions: critical thinking, reflective thinking, effective reasoning, and creativity

Domain: intrapersonal development
- Dimensions: realistic self-appraisal, self-understanding, and self-respect; identity development; commitment to ethics and integrity; and spiritual awareness

Domain: interpersonal competence
- Dimensions: meaningful relationships, interdependence, collaboration, and effective leadership

Domain: humanitarianism and civic engagement
- Dimensions: understanding and appreciation of cultural and human differences, social responsibility, global perspective, and sense of civic responsibility

Domain: practical competence
- Dimensions: pursuing goals, communicating effectively, technical competence, managing personal affairs, managing career development, demonstrating professionalism, maintaining health and wellness, and living a purposeful and

satisfying life

[LD Outcomes: See *The Council for the Advancement of Standards Learning and Development Outcomes* statement for examples of outcomes related to these domains and dimensions.]

LAP must be
- **intentionally designed**
- **guided by theories and knowledge of learning and development**
- **integrated into the life of the institution**
- **reflective of developmental and demographic profiles of the student population**
- **responsive to needs of individuals, populations with distinct needs, and relevant constituencies**
- **delivered using multiple formats, strategies, and contexts**
- **designed to provide universal access**

LAP must collaborate with colleagues and departments across the institution to promote student learning and development, persistence, and success.

The scope of programs and services must be determined by the needs of the student populations whom LAP are charged to serve.

LAP should serve all students at the institution. Individual LAP may serve specific populations such as culturally and ethnically diverse students, international and English-as-a-second-language students, student athletes, returning students, students with disabilities, and those provisionally admitted or on academic probation.

LAP should provide instruction and services for the development of reading, mathematics and quantitative reasoning, writing, critical thinking, problem-solving, technological literacy, scientific literacy, and learning strategies. Other programs may include subject-matter tutoring, course-based instructional programs such as Supplemental Instruction, time management programs, college success courses, first-year student seminars, and preparation for graduate and professional school admissions tests and for professional certification requirements.

In recognition of the fact that all students do not learn in the same manner, modes of delivering learning assistance programs should be diverse, including individual and group instruction and/or tutoring, cooperative learning, peer assisted learning, and accelerated learning. A variety of instructional media such as print, electronic, and skills laboratories should be incorporated. Instruction and programs may be delivered traditionally or via technology, either on or off site.

Formal and informal screening or diagnostic procedures must be conducted to identify the knowledge, skills, and motivation that students need to develop to achieve the level of proficiency prescribed or required by the institution, program, or instructor.

Assessment results must be shared with the student to formulate recommendations and a plan of instruction.

LAP should provide systematic feedback to students concerning their progress in reaching cognitive and affective goals; teach methods of self-regulation; and give students practice in applying and transferring skills and strategies learned through the LAP.

LAP professional staff must have access to institutional databases with student information relevant to its work.

LAP must promote, either directly or by referral, the cognitive and affective skills that influence learning, such as stress management, test anxiety reduction, assertiveness, time management, concentration, and motivation.

LAP must refer students to appropriate campus and community resources for assistance with personal problems, learning disabilities, financial difficulties, and other areas of need that may be outside the purview or beyond the expertise of the learning assistance program.

LAP must promote an understanding among campus community members of the learning needs of the student population.

Actions to promote this understanding may include
- establishing advisory boards consisting of members from key segments of the campus community
- holding periodic informational meetings and consulting with staff, faculty members, and administrators
- participating in staff and faculty development and inservice programs on curriculum and instructional approaches that address the development of learning skills, attitudes and behaviors, and the assessment of student learning outcomes
- encouraging the use of learning assistance program resources, materials, instruction, and services as integral or supplemental classroom activities
- conducting inclass workshops that demonstrate the application of learning strategies to course content
- disseminating information that describes programs and services, hours of operation, and procedures for registering or scheduling appointments
- training and supervising paraprofessionals and pre-professionals to work in such capacities as tutors, peer mentors, and other group leaders, such as Supplemental Instruction (SI) leaders
- providing jobs, practicums, courses, internships, mentoring, and assistantships for students interested in learning assistance and related careers
- collaborating with other community groups and educational institutions to provide college preparation assistance

Part 3. Organization and Leadership

To achieve program and student learning and development outcomes, Learning Assistance Programs (LAP) must be purposefully structured for effectiveness. LAP must have clearly stated and current
- **goals and outcomes**
- **policies and procedures**

- responsibilities and performance expectations for personnel
- organizational charts demonstrating clear channels of authority

Leaders must model ethical behavior and institutional citizenship.

Leaders with organizational authority for LAP must provide strategic planning, management and supervision, and program advancement.

Strategic Planning
- articulate a vision and mission that drive short- and long-term planning
- set goals and objectives based on the needs of the populations served, intended student learning and development outcomes, and program outcomes
- facilitate continuous development, implementation, and assessment of program effectiveness and goal attainment congruent with institutional mission and strategic plans
- promote environments that provide opportunities for student learning, development, and engagement
- develop, adapt, and improve programs and services in response to the changing needs of populations served and evolving institutional priorities
- include diverse perspectives to inform decision making

Management and Supervision
- plan, allocate, and monitor the use of fiscal, physical, human, intellectual, and technological resources
- manage human resource processes including recruitment, selection, professional development, supervision, performance planning, succession planning, evaluation, recognition, and reward
- influence others to contribute to the effectiveness and success of the unit
- empower professional, support, and student personnel to become effective leaders
- encourage and support collaboration with colleagues and departments across the institution
- encourage and support scholarly contributions to the profession
- identify and address individual, organizational, and environmental conditions that foster or inhibit mission achievement
- use current and valid evidence to inform decisions
- incorporate sustainability practices in the management and design of programs, services, and facilities
- understand appropriate technologies and integrate them into programs and services
- be knowledgeable about codes and laws relevant to programs and services and ensure that programs and services meet those requirements
- assess and take action to mitigate potential risks

Program Advancement
- advocate for and actively promote the mission and goals of the programs and services
- inform stakeholders about issues affecting practice
- facilitate processes to reach consensus where wide support is needed
- advocate for representation in strategic planning initiatives at divisional and institutional levels

LAP leaders must be knowledgeable about issues, trends, theories, research, and methodologies related to student learning and retention.

LAP leaders should
- participate in institutional planning, policy, procedural, and fiscal decisions that affect learning assistance for students
- seek opportunities for additional funding, resources, and facilities, as needed
- represent the learning assistance program on institutional committees
- collaborate with leaders of academic departments and support services in addressing the learning needs and retention of students
- be involved in research, publication, presentations, consultation, and activities of professional organizations
- communicate with professional colleagues in the learning assistance field and related professions
- promote and advertise their programs and services

The mission and goals of LAP, the needs and demographics of their clients, and their institutional role should determine where the unit is located in the organizational structure of the institution. Learning assistance programs are frequently organized as units in the academic affairs or the student affairs division.

Regardless of where LAP is positioned within the organization structure, it must communicate and collaborate with a network of key units across the institution to ensure coordination of related functions, programs, services, policies, and procedures, and to expedite student referrals.

LAP should have a broadly constituted advisory board to share information and make suggestions to strengthen the program.

LAP must provide written goals, objectives, and anticipated outcomes for each program and service.

Written procedures should exist for collecting, processing, and reporting student assessment and program data.

LAP must hold regularly scheduled meetings to share information; coordinate the planning, scheduling, and delivery of programs and services; identify and discuss potential and actual problems and concerns; and collaborate on making decisions and solving problems.

Part 4. Human Resources

Learning Assistance Programs (LAP) must be staffed

adequately by individuals qualified to accomplish mission and goals.

LAP must have access to technical and support personnel adequate to accomplish their mission.

Within institutional guidelines, LAP must
- establish procedures for personnel recruitment and selection, training, performance planning, and evaluation
- set expectations for supervision and performance
- provide personnel access to continuing and advanced education and appropriate professional development opportunities to improve their competence, skills, and leadership capacity
- consider work/life options available to personnel (e.g., compressed work schedules, flextime, job sharing, remote work, or telework) to promote recruitment and retention of personnel

Staff and faculty who hold a joint appointment with LAP must be committed to the mission, philosophy, goals, and priorities of the program and must possess the necessary expertise for assigned responsibilities.

Administrators of LAP must
- ensure that all personnel have updated position descriptions
- implement recruitment and selection/hiring strategies that produce a workforce inclusive of under-represented populations
- develop promotion practices that are fair, inclusive, proactive, and non-discriminatory

Personnel responsible for delivery of LAP must have written performance goals, objectives, and outcomes for each year's performance cycle to be used to plan, review, and evaluate work and performance. The performance plan must be updated regularly to reflect changes during the performance cycle.

Results of individual personnel evaluations must be used to recognize personnel performance, address performance issues, implement individual and/or collective personnel development and training programs, and inform the assessment of programs and services.

LAP personnel, when hired and throughout their employment, must receive appropriate and thorough training.

LAP personnel, including student employees and volunteers, must have access to resources or receive specific training on
- institutional policies pertaining to functions or activities they support
- privacy and confidentiality policies
- laws regarding access to student records
- policies and procedures for dealing with sensitive institutional information
- policies and procedures related to technology used to store or access student records and institutional data
- how and when to refer those in need of additional assistance to qualified personnel and have access to a supervisor for assistance in making these judgments
- systems and technologies necessary to perform their assigned responsibilities
- ethical and legal uses of technology

Administrative and technical staff should be knowledgeable about changes in programs, services, policies, and procedures in order to expedite smooth and efficient assistance to students. Appropriate staff development opportunities should be available.

LAP personnel must engage in continuing professional development activities to keep abreast of the research, theories, legislation, policies, and developments that affect their programs and services.

Administrators of LAP must ensure that personnel are knowledgeable about and trained in safety, emergency procedures, and crisis prevention and response. Risk management efforts must address identification of threatening conduct or behavior and must incorporate a system for responding to and reporting such behaviors. LAP personnel must be knowledgeable of and trained in safety and emergency procedures for securing and vacating facilities.

LAP professionals must be knowledgeable of the policies and procedures to be followed for internships and practicums as required by students' academic departments.

PROFESSIONAL PERSONNEL

LAP professional personnel either must hold an earned graduate or professional degree in a field relevant to their position or must possess an appropriate combination of educational credentials and related work experience.

Relevant disciplines include English, reading, mathematics, student affairs professional preparation, student development, higher education, counseling, psychology, or education.

LAP professionals should be competent and experienced in
- the content areas in which they teach, conduct labs, or provide assistance
- learning theory, instruction and assessment, and the theory and professional standards of practice for their areas of specialization and responsibility
- understanding the unique characteristics and needs of the populations they assist and teach
- demonstrating the ability to adjust pedagogical approaches according to the learning needs and styles of their students, the nature of the learning task, and the content of academic disciplines across the curriculum
- working with college students with different learning styles and abilities, including those with disabilities
- writing and communicating at a professional level
- working in culturally and academically diverse environments
- consulting, collaborating, and negotiating with staff,

faculty members, and administrators of academic and student affairs units
- designing, implementing, and utilizing instructional strategies, materials, and technologies
- training, supervising, and mentoring paraprofessionals and pre-professionals
- identifying and establishing lines of communication for student referral to other institutional and student support units

INTERNS OR GRADUATE ASSISTANTS

Degree- or credential-seeking interns or graduate assistants must be qualified by enrollment in an appropriate field of study and relevant experience. These students must be trained and supervised by professional personnel who possess applicable educational credentials and work experience and have supervisory experience. Supervisors must be cognizant of the dual roles interns and graduate assistants have as both student and employee.

Supervisors must
- adhere to parameters of students' job descriptions
- articulate intended learning outcomes in student job descriptions
- adhere to agreed-upon work hours and schedules
- offer flexible scheduling when circumstances necessitate

Supervisors and students must both agree to suitable compensation if circumstances necessitate additional hours.

STUDENT EMPLOYEES AND VOLUNTEERS

Student employees and volunteers must be carefully selected, trained, supervised, and evaluated. Students must have access to a supervisor. Student employees and volunteers must be provided clear job descriptions, pre-service training based on assessed needs, and continuing development.

Roles and responsibilities of LAP and those of the academic department should be clearly defined.

Faculty members assigned to LAP must be informed about the implications for tenure and promotion.

Part 5. Ethics

Learning Assistance Programs (LAP) must
- review applicable professional ethical standards and must adopt or develop and implement appropriate statements of ethical practice
- publish and adhere to statements of ethical practice and ensure their periodic review
- orient new personnel to relevant ethical standards and statements of ethical practice and related institutional policies

Specific attention must be given to properly orienting and advising student staff about matters of confidentiality. Clear statements must be distributed and reviewed with student staff regarding what information is not appropriate for them to access or communicate.

Statements of ethical standards must
- specify that LAP personnel respect privacy and maintain confidentiality in communications and records as delineated by privacy laws
- specify limits on disclosure of information contained in students' records as well as requirements to disclose to appropriate authorities
- address conflicts of interest, or appearance thereof, by personnel in the performance of their work
- reflect the responsibility of personnel to be fair, objective, and impartial in their interactions with others
- reference management of institutional funds
- reference appropriate behavior regarding research and assessment with human participants, confidentiality of research and assessment data, and students' rights and responsibilities
- include the expectation that personnel confront and hold accountable other personnel who exhibit unethical behavior
- address issues surrounding scholarly integrity

LAP personnel must
- employ ethical decision making in the performance of their duties
- inform users of programs and services of ethical obligations and limitations emanating from codes and laws or from licensure requirements
- recognize and avoid conflicts of interest that could adversely influence their judgment or objectivity and, when unavoidable, recuse themselves from the situation
- perform their duties within the scope of their position, training, expertise, and competence
- make referrals when issues presented exceed the scope of the position

Because LAP staff work with students' academic coursework, they must be knowledgeable of policies related to academic integrity, plagiarism, student code of conduct, students' rights and responsibilities and other similar policies. All staff members must be cognizant of the implications of these policies.

Statements or claims made about outcomes that can be achieved from participating in learning assistance programs and services must be truthful and realistic.

LAP funds acquired through grants and other noninstitutional resources must be managed according to the regulations and guidelines of the funding source and the institution.

Part 6. Law, Policy, and Governance

Learning Assistance Programs (LAP) must be in compliance with laws, regulations, and policies that relate to their respective responsibilities and that pose legal obligations, limitations, risks, and liabilities for the institution as a whole. Examples include constitutional, statutory, regulatory, and case law; relevant law and orders emanating from codes and laws; and the institution's policies.

LAP must have access to legal advice needed for personnel to carry out their assigned responsibilities.

LAP must inform personnel, appropriate officials, and users of programs and services about existing and changing legal obligations, risks and liabilities, and limitations.

LAP must inform personnel about professional liability insurance options and refer them to external sources if the institution does not provide coverage.

LAP must have written policies and procedures on operations, transactions, or tasks that have legal implications.

LAP must regularly review policies. The revision and creation of policies must be informed by best practices, available evidence, and policy issues in higher education.

LAP must have procedures and guidelines consistent with institutional policy for responding to threats, emergencies, and crisis situations. Systems and procedures must be in place to disseminate timely and accurate information to students, other members of the institutional community, and appropriate external organizations during emergency situations.

Personnel must neither participate in nor condone any form of harassment or activity that demeans persons or creates an intimidating, hostile, or offensive environment.

LAP must purchase or obtain permission to use copyrighted materials and instruments. References to copyrighted materials and instruments must include appropriate citations.

LAP must inform personnel about internal and external governance organizations that affect programs and services.

Staff development programs should be available to educate LAP staff of changing legal obligations.

Part 7. Diversity, Equity, and Access

Within the context of each institution's mission and in accordance with institutional policies and applicable codes and laws, Learning Assistance Programs (LAP) must create and maintain educational and work environments that are welcoming, accessible, inclusive, equitable, and free from harassment.

LAP must not discriminate on the basis of disability; age; race; cultural identity; ethnicity; nationality; family educational history (e.g., first generation to attend college); political affiliation; religious affiliation; sex; sexual orientation; gender identity and expression; marital, social, economic, or veteran status; or any other basis included in institutional policies and codes and laws.

LAP must

- advocate for sensitivity to multicultural and social justice concerns by the institution and its personnel

- ensure physical, program, and resource access for all constituents
- modify or remove policies, practices, systems, technologies, facilities, and structures that create barriers or produce inequities
- ensure that when facilities and structures cannot be modified, they do not impede access to programs, services, and resources
- establish goals for diversity, equity, and access
- foster communication and practices that enhance understanding of identity, culture, self-expression, and heritage
- promote respect for commonalities and differences among people within their historical and cultural contexts
- address the characteristics and needs of diverse constituents when establishing and implementing culturally relevant and inclusive programs, services, policies, procedures, and practices
- provide personnel with diversity, equity, and access training and hold personnel accountable for applying the training to their work
- respond to the needs of all constituents served when establishing hours of operation and developing methods of delivering programs, services, and resources
- recognize the needs of distance and online learning students by directly providing or assisting them to gain access to comparable services and resources

The program should facilitate student adjustment to the academic culture of the institution by orienting students to the practices, resources, responsibilities, and behaviors that contribute to academic success.

The instructional content, materials, and activities of learning assistance programs should provide opportunities to increase awareness and appreciation of the individual and cultural differences of students, staff, and faculty members.

Part 8. Internal and External Relations

Learning Assistance Programs (LAP) must reach out to individuals, groups, communities, and organizations internal and external to the institution to

- establish, maintain, and promote understanding and effective relations with those that have a significant interest in or potential effect on the students or other constituents served by the programs and services
- garner support and resources for programs and services as defined by the mission
- collaborate in offering or improving programs and services to meet the needs of students and other constituents and to achieve program and student outcomes
- engage diverse individuals, groups, communities, and organizations to enrich the educational environment and experiences of students and other constituents

- disseminate information about the programs and services

Promotional and descriptive information must be accurate and free of deception and misrepresentation.

LAP must have procedures and guidelines consistent with institutional policy for
- communicating with the media
- distributing information through print, broadcast, and online sources
- contracting with external organizations for delivery of programs and services
- cultivating, soliciting, and managing gifts
- applying to and managing funds from grants

LAP should
- be integrated into the academic program of the institution
- establish communication with academic units and student services
- collaborate with appropriate academic departments and faculty members when providing course-based learning assistance
- encourage the exchange of ideas, knowledge, and expertise
- provide mutual consultation, as needed, on student cases
- expedite student referrals to and from the LAP
- collaborate on programs and services that efficiently and effectively address student needs
- have representation on institutional committees relevant to the mission and goals of the program such as committees on retention, orientation, basic skills, learning communities, first-year student seminars, probation review (e.g., academic, financial aid), academic standards and requirements, curriculum design, assessment and placement, and professional development
- solicit and use trained volunteers from the local community to contribute their skills and talents to the services of the learning assistance program, consistent with the LAP mission and goals and the institution's risk management policies
- provide training and consultation to communitybased organizations, e.g., literacy associations, corporate training, and school-to-college transitions, initiatives, and programs

Part 9. Financial Resources

Learning Assistance Programs (LAP) must have funding to accomplish the mission and goals.

In establishing and prioritizing funding resources, LAP must conduct comprehensive analyses to determine
- **unmet needs of the unit**
- **relevant expenditures**
- **external and internal resources**
- **impact on students and the institution**

Adequate funds should be provided for the following

budget categories: staff and student salaries, general office functions, student assessment and instructional activities, data management and program evaluation processes, staff training and professional development activities, instructional materials and media, and instructional and office technology.

LAP must use the budget as a planning tool to reflect commitment to the mission and goals of the programs and services and of the institution.

LAP must administer funds in accordance with established institutional accounting procedures.

LAP must demonstrate efficient and effective use and responsible stewardship of fiscal resources consistent with institutional protocols.

A financial analysis of costs and available resources must be completed before implementing new programs or changing existing ones. This analysis must include an assessment of the impact on students served prior to making significant changes.

Opportunities for additional funding should be pursued; however, these sources should not be expected to supplant institutional funding.

Financial reports must provide an accurate financial overview of the organization and provide clear, understandable, and timely data upon which personnel can plan and make informed decisions.

Procurement procedures must
- **be consistent with institutional policies**
- **ensure that purchases comply with laws and codes for usability and access**
- **ensure that the institution receives value for the funds spent**
- **consider information available for comparing the ethical and environmental impact of products and services purchased**

Part 10. Technology

Learning Assistance Programs (LAP) must have technology to support the achievement of their mission and goals. The technology and its use must comply with institutional policies and procedures and with relevant codes and laws.

LAP must use technologies to
- **provide updated information regarding mission, location, staffing, programs, services, and official contacts to students and other constituents in accessible formats**
- **provide an avenue for students and other constituents to communicate sensitive information in a secure format**
- **enhance the delivery of programs and services for all students**

Electronic systems for scheduling and record keeping must be secure.

Such systems should be integrated with institutional systems.

LAP must

- back up data on a regular basis
- adhere to institutional policies regarding ethical and legal use of technology
- articulate policies and procedures for protecting the confidentiality and security of information
- implement a replacement plan and cycle for all technology with attention to sustainability
- incorporate accessibility features into technology-based programs and services

When providing student access to technology, LAP must

- have policies on the use of technology that are clear, easy to understand, and available to all students
- provide information or referral to support services for those needing assistance in accessing or using technology
- provide instruction or training on how to use the technology
- inform students of implications of misuse of technologies

Part 11. Facilities and Equipment

Learning Assistance Programs' (LAP) facilities must be intentionally designed and located in suitable, accessible, and safe spaces that demonstrate universal design and support the program's mission and goals.

Facilities must be designed to engage various constituents and promote learning.

Personnel must have workspaces that are suitably located and accessible, well equipped, adequate in size, and designed to support their work and responsibilities.

Facilities and equipment should support the instructional, service, and office functions of the learning assistance program. Facilities should include flexible space to accommodate different delivery modes and student needs. Consideration should be given to universal instructional design in creating classrooms, labs, resource rooms, media and computer centers, and group and onetoone tutorial space to support instruction. Adequate space should be provided for quiet areas to support testing and other activities that require concentration.

There must be adequate and secure storage for equipment, supplies, instructional and testing materials, and confidential records.

Environmental conditions such as appropriate acoustics, lighting, ventilation, heating, and air-conditioning should enhance the teaching/learning process.

The design of the facilities must guarantee the security and privacy of records and ensure the confidentiality of sensitive information and conversations. Personnel must be able to secure their work.

LAP must incorporate sustainable practices in use of facilities and purchase of equipment. Facilities and equipment must be evaluated on an established cycle and

be in compliance with codes, laws, and accepted practices for access, health, safety, and security.

When acquiring capital equipment, LAP must take into account expenses related to regular maintenance and life cycle costs.

Part 12. Assessment

Learning Assistance Programs (LAP) must develop assessment plans and processes.

Assessment plans must articulate an ongoing cycle of assessment activities.

LAP must

- specify programmatic goals and intended outcomes
- identify student learning and development outcomes
- employ multiple measures and methods
- develop manageable processes for gathering, interpreting, and evaluating data
- document progress toward achievement of goals and outcomes
- interpret and use assessment results to demonstrate accountability
- report aggregated results to respondent groups and stakeholders
- use assessment results to inform planning and decision-making
- assess effectiveness of implemented changes
- provide evidence of improvement of programs and services

Qualitative methods may include standard evaluation forms, questionnaires, interviews, focus groups, observations, or case studies, with input solicited from faculty members, staff, and students.

Quantitative measurements range from data on an individual student's performance to data on campus retention rates and success for various cohorts. Quantitative methods may include followup studies on students' grades in targeted courses, gain scores, grade point averages, graduation, reenrollment, and retention figures. Program effectiveness may also be measured by comparing data of learning assistance program participants and nonparticipants. Quantitative program measures may include data on the size of the user population, numbers utilizing particular services and number of contact hours, sources of student referrals to the program, or numbers of students who may be on a waiting list or who have requested services not provided by the learning assistance program. Quantitative data should be collected within specific time periods as well as longitudinally to reveal trends.

LAP should have the ability to collect and analyze data through its own resources as well as through access to appropriate data generated by the institution.

Periodic evaluations of LAP or services may be performed by on-campus experts and outside consultants. Evaluations should be disseminated to appropriate administrators and constituencies.

LAP should conduct periodic selfassessments, utilizing selfstudy processes endorsed by professional organizations. The assessments should examine the quality of services provided as well as the potential impact on student learning over time. Additionally, learning outcomes associated with LAP instructional courses should reflect what students learn or do better as a result of being exposed to course materials and instructional strategies.

Various means of individual assessment should be conducted for the purpose of identifying the learning needs of the students and guiding them to appropriate programs and services. Assessment results should be communicated to students confidentially, honestly, and sensitively. Students should be advised and directed to appropriate, alternative educational opportunities when there is reasonable cause to believe that students may not be able to meet requirements for academic success.

LAP should periodically review and revise its goals and services based on evaluation outcomes and based on changes in institutional goals, priorities, and plans. Data that reveal trends or changes in student demographics, characteristics, needs, and outcomes should be utilized for learning assistance program short and longterm planning.

LAP must employ ethical practices in the assessment process.

LAP must have access to adequate fiscal, human, professional development, and technological resources to develop and implement assessment plans.

General Standards revised in 2014;
LAP content developed/revised in 1986, 1996, & 2007

Lesbian, Gay, Bisexual, and Transgender Programs and Services

CAS Contexual Statement

In referencing lesbian, gay, bisexual, and transgender people, the acronym *LGBT* has become standard on most campuses. It should be understood, however, to be broadly inclusive of many related identities with nomenclature going far beyond these four terms. These may include people who identify as queer, questioning, intersex, pansexual, fluid, asexual, genderqueer, agender, gender nonconforming men who have sex with men (MSM), and women who have sex with women (WSW). It also includes people who identify with terms rooted primarily in communities of color, such as same gender loving (SGL) in African American communities, *khush* in South Asian populations, and *two spirit* among American Indian peoples. Gender identity, gender expression, and sexual orientation are the main identities being addressed by these terms.

From the late 1960s when the first Student Homophile Association formed at Columbia University, LGBT students made themselves visible on college campuses in ever increasing numbers. Positive institutional responses have usually begun with adding sexual orientation to non-discrimination policies and, typically much later, gender identity and gender expression. Over time, institutions have added services and programs that address the specific needs of LGBT students.

Dedicated resources delivered through a unit created specifically for that purpose began in 1971 when the University of Michigan created a Human Sexuality Office with a one-room office, two quarter-time positions, and a small budget (Burris, n.d.). Growth in the number of campuses with such units was slow initially and accelerated exponentially in the late 1990s and early years of the twenty-first century. Higher education professionals began to organize to provide support and information, share common practices, and otherwise develop this specialty first within existing professional organizations such as the Standing Committee for Lesbian, Gay, Bisexual, and Transgender Awareness within ACPA and the Gay, Lesbian, Bisexual, and Transgender Knowledge Community within NASPA. The professional organization that has best met the needs of these educators—the Consortium of Higher Education LGBT Resource Professionals (lgbtcampus.org)—was officially founded in 1997 within the context of an advocacy organization known as the National LGBTQ Task Force. An advocacy element continues to be part of the work of these professionals, and the Consortium continues to be the most vital organization supporting them.

Services and programs addressing the specific needs of LGBT students may be delivered by a LGBT Resource Center through a unit with a broader mission such as a Multicultural Center, a Gender and Sexuality Center, or other organizational structures. Regardless of how the needs of LGBT students are addressed, two basic principles are observed: (a) all units must be responsible for meeting the needs of LGBT students within their functional areas and (b) some identifiable unit must be responsible for addressing the needs of LGBT students globally, including those needs that require a specific, articulated mission to address their unique needs. Also, regardless of organizational structure (LGBT Resource Center, Multicultural Center), these standards and guidelines apply.

Successful LGBT programs target individual students while creating and maintaining a healthy LGBT campus community. Such programs also have a responsibility to serve the entire campus community, including staff, faculty, alumni, and parents. Depending on location, these programs may also serve the broader off-campus community.

Although recruitment and retention of students are central issues, it is difficult to produce statistical data similar to those that are used in developing and assessing programs for recruitment and retention of other populations. Unlike questions about race and sex, questions about gender identity, gender expression, and sexual orientation are not routinely asked. Best practices for collecting these data have begun to emerge for sexual orientation, although many different approaches exist for gender identity and gender expression (SMART, 2009). Now that there is developing a degree of consensus regarding how to gather these data, it remains to be seen if higher education will find appropriate means for routinely collecting the data.

In the absence of institution-specific data, we must rely on individual studies generally produced by researchers who examine these issues nationally within the United States. For example, the ongoing collection of data about LGBT students in K-12 environments show continuing problems of hostile school climate, absenteeism, lowered educational aspirations and academic achievement, and poorer psychological well-being (Kosciw, Greytak, Diaz, & Bartkiewicz, 2010). The existing data indicate these problems continue and are compounded after LGBT students step onto college campuses (Rankin, Weber, Blumenfeld, & Frazer, 2010). In particular, LGBT students report significantly higher rates of harassment and discrimination than their non-LGBT peers. This is especially true for students with multiple minority identities including LGBT students of color, LGBT international students, and LGBT first generation students. These data demonstrate that LGBT students are among the most likely to experience conduct that interferes with their ability to live and learn on campus.

None of the data regarding harassment, discrimination, and hostile climate for LGBT college students comes as a surprise to the professionals working in this area. It is from the collective wisdom of these professionals that CAS standards emerge.

References, Readings, and Resources

Burris, N. (n.d.). *History of the Spectrum Center.* Retrieved from
http://spectrumcenter.umich.edu/about/history

Kosciw, J., Greytak, E., Diaz, E., & Bartkiewicz, M. (2010). *The 2009
national school climate survey.* New York, NY: Gay, Lesbian and
Straight Education Network.

Rankin, S., Weber, G., Blumenfeld, W., & Frazer, S. (2010). *2010
state of higher education for lesbian, gay, bisexual & transgender
people.* Charlotte, NC: Campus Pride.

Sexual Minority Assessment Research Team (SMART). (2009). *Best
practices for asking questions about sexual orientation on surveys.*
Los Angeles, CA: The Williams Institute.

Contextual Statement Contributor

Current Edition:
Luke Jensen, University of Maryland, College Park

Previous Edition:
Ronni Sanlo, LGBT, University of California at Los Angeles

Lesbian, Gay, Bisexual, Transgender Programs and Services
CAS Standards and Guidelines

Part 1. Mission

The mission of the Lesbian, Gay, Bisexual, Transgender Programs and Services (LGBT Programs and Services) must be to
- promote academic and personal growth of all LGBT and questioning students
- build and maintain campus LGBT communities
- advance access and equity in higher education
- establish and maintain coalitions with other campus constituencies and allies to create a more socially just institution and community
- offer programs to educate the campus about sexual orientation and gender identity and expression

Programming should address how sexual orientation and gender identity and expression differ in concept while remaining intertwined in daily life.

The term *LGBT* includes a broad spectrum of identities in addition to the four terms comprising the acronym.

LGBT Programs and Services must develop, disseminate, implement, and regularly review their missions, which must be consistent with the mission of the institution and with applicable professional standards. The mission must be appropriate for the institution's students and other constituents. Mission statements must reference student learning and development.

The mission of LGBT Programs and Services and the goals of its initiatives must be based on assessment of the needs of and campus climate for LGBT students. LGBT Programs and Services must select priorities among those needs and respond accordingly.

LGBT Programs and Services must not be the only institutional unit meeting the needs of LGBT students.

All institutional units should share responsibility for identifying and meeting the needs of LGBT students and eliminating prejudicial behaviors.

Part 2. Program

To achieve their mission, Lesbian, Gay, Bisexual, Transgender Programs and Services (LGBT Programs and Services) must contribute to
- students' formal education, which includes both the curriculum and the co-curriculum
- student progression and timely completion of educational goals
- preparation of students for their careers, citizenship, and lives
- student learning and development

To contribute to student learning and development, LGBT Programs and Services must
- identify relevant and desirable student learning and development outcomes
- articulate how the student learning and development outcomes align with the six CAS student learning and development domains and related dimensions
- assess relevant and desirable student learning and development
- provide evidence of impact on outcomes
- articulate contributions to or support of student learning and development in the domains not specifically assessed
- use evidence gathered to create strategies for improvement of programs and services

STUDENT LEARNING AND DEVELOPMENT
DOMAINS AND DIMENSIONS

Domain: knowledge acquisition, integration, construction, and application
- Dimensions: understanding knowledge from a range of disciplines; connecting knowledge to other knowledge, ideas, and experiences; constructing knowledge; and relating knowledge to daily life

Domain: cognitive complexity
- Dimensions: critical thinking, reflective thinking, effective reasoning, and creativity

Domain: intrapersonal development
- Dimensions: realistic self-appraisal, self-understanding, and self-respect; identity development; commitment to ethics and integrity; and spiritual awareness

Domain: interpersonal competence
- Dimensions: meaningful relationships, interdependence, collaboration, and effective leadership

Domain: humanitarianism and civic engagement
- Dimensions: understanding and appreciation of cultural and human differences, social responsibility, global perspective, and sense of civic responsibility

Domain: practical competence
- Dimensions: pursuing goals, communicating effectively, technical competence, managing personal affairs, managing career development, demonstrating professionalism, maintaining health and wellness, and living a purposeful and satisfying life

[LD Outcomes: See *The Council for the Advancement of Standards Learning and Development Outcomes* statement for examples of outcomes related to these domains and dimensions.]

LGBT Programs and Services must be

- intentionally designed
- guided by theories and knowledge of learning and development
- integrated into the life of the institution
- reflective of developmental and demographic profiles of the student population
- responsive to needs of individuals, populations with distinct needs, and relevant constituencies
- delivered using multiple formats, strategies, and contexts
- designed to provide universal access

LGBT Programs and Services must collaborate with colleagues and departments across the institution to promote student learning and development, persistence, and success.

LGBT Programs and Services must promote student learning and development outcomes of particular concern to LGBT students:

- realistic self-appraisal, self-understanding, and self-respect
- identity development
- effective leadership

LGBT Programs and Services must promote and advocate for services addressing the unique needs of LGBT students that are generally offered by other functional areas:

- individual and group psychological counseling
  - coming-out support with particular attention to multiple identities, especially race, ethnicity, disability, religion, family-of-origin issues, and to internalized homophobia and biphobia
  - support for individuals facing difficulties regarding gender identity and expression and for those experiencing internalized transphobia
  - services for victims, survivors, and perpetrators of homophobia, biphobia, and transphobia
  - services to address family issues
  - services to address dating issues for those who date only people of the same sex, who may date individuals of either sex, and who are transgender or may date someone who is transgender
  - services to address domestic and relationship violence
  - services to address body image concerns
  - support for LGBT victims of hate crimes
  - support for the education and recovery of perpetrators of hate crimes
  - support for understanding racial, ethnic, national, cultural, and religious issues and differences

- health services
  - health forms with inclusive language
  - LGBT health issues brochures
  - safer sex information for LGBT people
  - safer sex supplies
  - HIV/STD testing services with intake and follow-up protocols appropriate for LGBT people
  - sex-specific services for those whose sex and gender may not align (e.g., pap smears for female-bodied individuals who identify as male)
  - access to or referral for hormone therapy
  - inclusion of transgender specific health care coverage by any insurance offered by the institution

- career services
  - job search preparation
  - information on LGBT-friendly employers
  - employer mentoring programs for LGBT students
  - information on LGBT issues in the workplace, including coming out and transitioning on the job

- academic advising, including support of students' educational choices

- public safety
  - training for police officers and other public safety officials to respond appropriately when an LGBT person is involved in any incident
  - avoidance of re-victimization of LGBT students who have experienced bias
  - management of incidents related to bias against LGBT individuals

- admissions and registration, including maintenance of records and documentation that facilitates a change in name and sex and supports individuals who are in the process of transitioning with the use of a preferred name

- housing and residential life
  - housing assignments that respect students' gender when it conflicts with their legal sex
  - the availability of married student housing options for same sex couples

- library services, including library and research guides for students interested in LGBT issues, especially when they cross traditional lines of academic disciplines

- facilities, including restroom and locker room policies and facilities that accommodate and support individuals who are transitioning or whose appearance may not fit a traditional male/female division

- recreational sports and intercollegiate athletics,

including intramural, club, and varsity sports and other recreational opportunities that include and support individuals who do not fit into traditional sex segregated categories

- student life, activities, and organizations
  - o access to opportunities for membership in student activities, including fraternities and sororities
  - o supportive culture for LGBT students
  - o support for LGBT students engaged in these activities

LGBT Programs and Services must promote resources that may not be the logical responsibility of other functional areas:

- identification of and networking with role models and mentors
- identification of courses with LGBT specific content especially at institutions with no LGBT studies or similar programs
- support of LGBT students in achieving academic success
- identification of supports for families of LGBT students
- identification of appropriate religious and faith communities
- support of international LGBT students
- identification of global LGBT laws and practices that may affect students studying abroad

LGBT Programs and Services must promote issues regarding the overall climate and general support for LGBT students on the campus as a whole:

- advocacy for the creation and maintenance of a campus climate that is free from harassment and violence
- training for students, staff, and faculty members in providing a supportive environment
- training and support for allies
- identification of environmental conditions that negatively influence student welfare and advocacy for their solutions
- creation within the institution of policies and procedures that promote and maintain a hospitable climate

Additionally, LGBT Programs and Services must work to assure equitable access to and involvement in all educational programs.

Particular attention should be given to financial aid, athletic scholarships, fraternity and sorority life, employment opportunities, and campus engagement and co-curricular activities on campus.

LGBT Programs and Services must promote learning opportunities for LGBT students and for all students on issues regarding sexual orientation and gender identity and expression.

LGBT Programs and Services must include examination

of the intersection of sexual orientation, gender identity, and gender expression with race, class, gender, disability, ethnicity, religion, and age.

LGBT Programs and Services must promote the knowledge base of all students on issues regarding sexual orientation and gender identity and expression.

LGBT Programs and Services must assist other functional areas to meet the needs of LGBT students, because all institutional units share responsibility for meeting the needs of LGBT students.

LGBT Programs and Services must support campus efforts to eliminate prejudicial behavior based on sexual orientation and/or gender identity and expression.

LGBT Programs and Services should work closely with campus compliance officers or other campus officials charged with enforcing nondiscrimination policies and charged with promoting broad diversity efforts.

LGBT Programs and Services must educate the campus community when decisions or policies may affect LGBT students; publicize services, events, and issues of concern to LGBT students; and sponsor events that meet educational, personal, physical, and safety needs of LGBT students and their allies.

LGBT Programs and Services should take the following actions:

- encourage awareness of off campus networks and other support systems for LGBT students, including affiliation with local, state or provincial, regional, and national organizations
- increase campus awareness of the complex identity issues inherent in the lives of LGBT students
- publicize and celebrate the accomplishments of LGBT students, faculty, staff, and alumni
- represent LGBT concerns and issues on campus-wide committees
- promote scholarship, research, and assessment on LGBT issues
- encourage campus-wide inclusion of LGBT students and avoidance of negative stereotyping in campus media.

LGBT Programs and Services must address the needs of all LGBT students inclusive of their race, class, socio-economic status, gender, disability, ethnicity, religion, age, and degree or enrollment status. In addition, LGBT Programs and Services must plan for and recognize the diversity among the LGBT student population.

LGBT Programs and Services should partner with other institutional efforts to recognize and celebrate other areas of diversity such as race, ethnicity, gender, and disability.

LGBT Programs and Services must advocate for the human rights of LGBT persons to promote a more socially just institution and community.

LGBT Programs and Services should work with campus

administration in outreach to local, state/provincial, and federal or national leaders to effect positive change for LGBT people in education, employment, and other issues with a direct relevance for campus life.

Part 3. Organization and Leadership

To achieve program and student learning and development outcomes, Lesbian, Gay, Bisexual, Transgender Programs and Services (LGBT Programs and Services) must be purposefully structured for effectiveness. LGBT Programs and Services must have clearly stated and current
- goals and outcomes
- policies and procedures
- responsibilities and performance expectations for personnel
- organizational charts demonstrating clear channels of authority

Leaders must model ethical behavior and institutional citizenship.

Leaders with organizational authority for LGBT Programs and Services must provide strategic planning, management and supervision, and program advancement.

Strategic Planning
- articulate a vision and mission that drive short- and long-term planning
- set goals and objectives based on the needs of the populations served, intended student learning and development outcomes, and program outcomes
- facilitate continuous development, implementation, and assessment of program effectiveness and goal attainment congruent with institutional mission and strategic plans
- promote environments that provide opportunities for student learning, development, and engagement
- develop, adapt, and improve programs and services in response to the changing needs of populations served and evolving institutional priorities
- include diverse perspectives to inform decision making

Management and Supervision
- plan, allocate, and monitor the use of fiscal, physical, human, intellectual, and technological resources
- manage human resource processes including recruitment, selection, professional development, supervision, performance planning, succession planning, evaluation, recognition, and reward
- influence others to contribute to the effectiveness and success of the unit
- empower professional, support, and student personnel to become effective leaders
- encourage and support collaboration with colleagues and departments across the institution
- encourage and support scholarly contributions to the profession
- identify and address individual, organizational, and environmental conditions that foster or inhibit mission achievement
- use current and valid evidence to inform decisions
- incorporate sustainability practices in the management and design of programs, services, and facilities
- understand appropriate technologies and integrate them into programs and services
- be knowledgeable about codes and laws relevant to programs and services and ensure that programs and services meet those requirements
- assess and take action to mitigate potential risks

Program Advancement
- advocate for and actively promote the mission and goals of the programs and services
- inform stakeholders about issues affecting practice
- facilitate processes to reach consensus where wide support is needed
- advocate for representation in strategic planning initiatives at divisional and institutional levels

Program leaders must possess the academic preparation, experience, abilities, professional interests, competencies essential for the efficient operation of the office as charged, as well as the ability to identify additional areas of concern about LGBT students.

LGBT Programs and Services leaders should have coursework in organizational development, counseling, group dynamics, leadership development, student and human development, LGBT studies, multicultural education, women's studies, higher education, and research and assessment.

LGBT Programs and Services leaders should
- participate in institutional planning, policy, procedural, and fiscal decisions that affect LGBT students
- seek opportunities for additional funding, resources, and facilities, as needed
- represent the interests of LGBT students on relevant institutional committees
- collaborate with leaders of academic departments and support services in addressing the learning needs and retention of students
- be involved in research, publication, presentations, consultation, and activities of professional organizations
- interact with professional colleagues from LGBT Programs and Services units at other institutions
- participate with relevant LGBT community organizations
- promote and advertise their programs and services

Whether as a separate unit or as part of a unit with a broader scope, LGBT Programs and Services must be structured to promote academic and personal growth of LGBT students.

LGBT Programs and Services must play a major role in implementing institutional programs developed in response to the assessed needs of LGBT students.

Access to the policymakers of the institution should be readily available.

LGBT Programs and Services must be afforded the opportunity to organize in a manner that is efficient and best promotes equity concerns.

Emphasis should be placed on achieving an organization in which services are not limited to a specific group of LGBT students (e.g., solely undergraduate students) but inclusive of many groups that make up a campus community (e.g., undergraduate, graduate, and prospective students, alumni, faculty, staff, and families).

Regardless of where LGBT Programs and Services are positioned within the organizational structure, they must be empowered to work with all functional areas of the institution to meet the needs of LGBT students and eliminate prejudicial behaviors. All institutional units share responsibility for meeting the needs of LGBT students in their area of service.

Part 4. Human Resources

Lesbian, Gay, Bisexual, Transgender Programs and Services (LGBT Programs and Services) must be staffed adequately by individuals qualified to accomplish mission and goals.

LGBT Programs and Services must have access to technical and support personnel adequate to accomplish their mission.

Within institutional guidelines, LGBT Programs and Services must

- establish procedures for personnel recruitment and selection, training, performance planning, and evaluation
- set expectations for supervision and performance
- provide personnel access to continuing and advanced education and appropriate professional development opportunities to improve their competence, skills, and leadership capacity
- consider work/life options available to personnel (e.g., compressed work schedules, flextime, job sharing, remote work, or telework) to promote recruitment and retention of personnel

Where LGBT Programs and Services is part of a unit with a broader scope, such as a multicultural center or college union, it must be adequately staffed to promote academic and personal growth of LGBT students.

Staff members should have adequate time for student advising, reporting and updating institutional information, contact with faculty members and staff, staff meetings, training, supervision, personal and professional development, and consultation with other experts. Similarly, teaching, administration, research, and other responsibilities should be identified as relevant staff functions.

Administrators of LGBT Programs and Services must

- ensure that all personnel have updated position descriptions
- implement recruitment and selection/hiring strategies that produce a workforce inclusive of under-represented populations
- develop promotion practices that are fair, inclusive, proactive, and non-discriminatory

Personnel responsible for delivery of LGBT Programs and Services must have written performance goals, objectives, and outcomes for each year's performance cycle to be used to plan, review, and evaluate work and performance. The performance plan must be updated regularly to reflect changes during the performance cycle.

Results of individual personnel evaluations must be used to recognize personnel performance, address performance issues, implement individual and/or collective personnel development and training programs, and inform the assessment of programs and services.

LGBT Programs and Services personnel, when hired and throughout their employment, must receive appropriate and thorough training.

LGBT Programs and Services personnel, including student employees and volunteers, must have access to resources or receive specific training on

- institutional policies pertaining to functions or activities they support
- privacy and confidentiality policies
- laws regarding access to student records
- policies and procedures for dealing with sensitive institutional information
- policies and procedures related to technology used to store or access student records and institutional data
- how and when to refer those in need of additional assistance to qualified personnel and have access to a supervisor for assistance in making these judgments
- systems and technologies necessary to perform their assigned responsibilities
- ethical and legal uses of technology

LGBT Programs and Services personnel must engage in continuing professional development activities to keep abreast of the research, theories, legislation, policies, and developments that affect their programs and services.

LGBT Programs and Services must provide opportunities for professional development including but not limited to additional credit courses, seminars, and access to current research.

Additionally, staff members should participate in appropriate professional organizations and should have the budgetary support to do so. Staff members should be encouraged to participate in community activities related to the student population being served.

Administrators of LGBT Programs and Services must ensure that personnel are knowledgeable about and trained in safety, emergency procedures, and crisis prevention and response. Risk management efforts must address identification of threatening conduct or behavior and must incorporate a system for responding to and reporting such behaviors.

LGBT Programs and Services personnel must be knowledgeable of and trained in safety and emergency procedures for securing and vacating facilities.

PROFESSIONAL PERSONNEL

LGBT Programs and Services professional personnel either must hold an earned graduate or professional degree in a field relevant to their position or must possess an appropriate combination of educational credentials and related work experience.

Program staff members should have a combination of graduate course work, formal training (including LGBT issues), and supervising experience.

INTERNS OR GRADUATE ASSISTANTS

Degree- or credential-seeking interns or graduate assistants must be qualified by enrollment in an appropriate field of study and relevant experience. These students must be trained and supervised by professional personnel who possess applicable educational credentials and work experience and have supervisory experience. Supervisors must be cognizant of the dual roles interns and graduate assistants have as both student and employee.

Supervisors must
- adhere to parameters of students' job descriptions
- articulate intended learning outcomes in student job descriptions
- adhere to agreed-upon work hours and schedules
- offer flexible scheduling when circumstances necessitate

Supervisors and students must both agree to suitable compensation if circumstances necessitate additional hours.

STUDENT EMPLOYEES AND VOLUNTEERS

Student employees and volunteers must be carefully selected, trained, supervised, and evaluated. Students must have access to a supervisor. Student employees and volunteers must be provided clear job descriptions, pre-service training based on assessed needs, and continuing development.

Support staff should have a thorough knowledge of the institution and be able to perform office and administrative functions, including receiving visitors and identifying issues. Special emphasis should be placed on development of skills in the areas of public relations, information delivery, identification problems, and referral protocols.

All LGBT Programs and Services staff members must be responsive to and knowledgeable about LGBT issues with special attention to rapidly changing trends in working with transgender individuals and to the intersection of sexual orientation and gender identity and expression with other elements of identity.

LGBT Programs and Services staff members must ensure that the privacy of students' sexual orientation and gender identity and expression are protected.

The staffing, level, and diversity of services must be established and reviewed regularly with regard to service demands, enrollment, user surveys, institutional resources and climate, and other student services available on the campus and in the local community.

LGBT Programs and Services staff must be open to and interested in working with LGBT students.

Part 5. Ethics

Lesbian, Gay, Bisexual, Transgender Programs and Services (LGBT Programs and Services) must
- review applicable professional ethical standards and must adopt or develop and implement appropriate statements of ethical practice
- publish and adhere to statements of ethical practice and ensure their periodic review
- orient new personnel to relevant ethical standards and statements of ethical practice and related institutional policies

Statements of ethical standards must
- specify that LGBT Programs and Services personnel respect privacy and maintain confidentiality in communications and records as delineated by privacy laws
- specify limits on disclosure of information contained in students' records as well as requirements to disclose to appropriate authorities
- address conflicts of interest, or appearance thereof, by personnel in the performance of their work
- reflect the responsibility of personnel to be fair, objective, and impartial in their interactions with others
- reference management of institutional funds
- reference appropriate behavior regarding research and assessment with human participants, confidentiality of research and assessment data, and students' rights and responsibilities
- include the expectation that personnel confront and hold accountable other personnel who exhibit unethical behavior
- address issues surrounding scholarly integrity

LGBT Programs and Services personnel must
- employ ethical decision making in the performance of their duties
- inform users of programs and services of ethical obligations and limitations emanating from codes and laws or from licensure requirements

- recognize and avoid conflicts of interest that could adversely influence their judgment or objectivity and, when unavoidable, recuse themselves from the situation
- perform their duties within the scope of their position, training, expertise, and competence
- make referrals when issues presented exceed the scope of the position

LGBT Programs and Services staff members must ensure that the privacy of individuals' sexual orientation and gender identity and expression is protected.

Information should be released only at the written request of a student who has full knowledge of the nature of the information that is being released and of the parties to whom it is being released. Instances of limited confidentiality should be clearly articulated. The decision to release information without consent should occur only after careful consideration and under the conditions described above.

Part 6. Law, Policy, and Governance

Lesbian, Gay, Bisexual, Transgender Programs and Services (LGBT Programs and Services) must be in compliance with laws, regulations, and policies that relate to their respective responsibilities and that pose legal obligations, limitations, risks, and liabilities for the institution as a whole. Examples include constitutional, statutory, regulatory, and case law; relevant law and orders emanating from codes and laws; and the institution's policies.

LGBT Programs and Services **must** have access to legal advice needed for personnel to carry out their assigned responsibilities.

LGBT Programs and Services **must** inform personnel, appropriate officials, and users of programs and services about existing and changing legal obligations, risks and liabilities, and limitations.

LGBT Programs and Services must inform personnel about professional liability insurance options and refer them to external sources if the institution does not provide coverage.

LGBT Programs and Services must have written policies and procedures on operations, transactions, or tasks that have legal implications.

LGBT Programs and Services must regularly review policies. The revision and creation of policies must be informed by best practices, available evidence, and policy issues in higher education.

LGBT Programs and Services must have procedures and guidelines consistent with institutional policy for responding to threats, emergencies, and crisis situations. Systems and procedures must be in place to disseminate timely and accurate information to students, other members of the institutional community, and appropriate external organizations during emergency situations.

Personnel must neither participate in nor condone any form of harassment or activity that demeans persons or creates an intimidating, hostile, or offensive environment.

LGBT Programs and Services must purchase or obtain permission to use copyrighted materials and instruments. References to copyrighted materials and instruments must include appropriate citations.

LGBT Programs and Services must inform personnel about internal and external governance organizations that affect programs and services.

Resources should be available to educate LGBT Programs and Services staff on changing legal obligations.

Part 7. Diversity, Equity, and Access

Within the context of each institution's mission and in accordance with institutional policies and applicable codes and laws Lesbian, Gay, Bisexual, Transgender Programs and Services (LGBT Programs and Services) must create and maintain educational and work environments that are welcoming, accessible, inclusive, equitable, and free from harassment.

LGBT Programs and Services must not discriminate on the basis of disability; age; race; cultural identity; ethnicity; nationality; family educational history (e.g., first generation to attend college); political affiliation; religious affiliation; sex; sexual orientation; gender identity and expression; marital, social, economic, or veteran status; or any other basis included in institutional policies and codes and laws.

LGBT Programs and Services must
- advocate for sensitivity to multicultural and social justice concerns by the institution and its personnel
- ensure physical, program, and resource access for all constituents
- modify or remove policies, practices, systems, technologies, facilities, and structures that create barriers or produce inequities
- ensure that when facilities and structures cannot be modified, they do not impede access to programs, services, and resources
- establish goals for diversity, equity, and access
- foster communication and practices that enhance understanding of identity, culture, self-expression, and heritage
- promote respect for commonalities and differences among people within their historical and cultural contexts
- address the characteristics and needs of diverse constituents when establishing and implementing culturally relevant and inclusive programs, services, policies, procedures, and practices
- provide personnel with diversity, equity, and access training and hold personnel accountable for applying the training to their work
- respond to the needs of all constituents served when establishing hours of operation and

developing methods of delivering programs, services, and resources

- recognize the needs of distance and online learning students by directly providing or assisting them to gain access to comparable services and resources

LGBT Programs and Services staff should display a statement of commitment or non-discrimination within physical office space as well as in LGBT Programs and Services electronic and print communications.

Part 8. Internal and External Relations

Lesbian, Gay, Bisexual, Transgender Programs and Services (LGBT Programs and Services) must reach out to individuals, groups, communities, and organizations internal and external to the institution to

- establish, maintain, and promote understanding and effective relations with those that have a significant interest in or potential effect on the students or other constituents served by the programs and services
- garner support and resources for programs and services as defined by the mission
- collaborate in offering or improving programs and services to meet the needs of students and other constituents and to achieve program and student outcomes
- engage diverse individuals, groups, communities, and organizations to enrich the educational environment and experiences of students and other constituents
- disseminate information about the programs and services

LGBT Programs and Services should pay particular attention to relationships with alumni, the community at large, contractors, vendors, and support agencies.

LGBT Programs and Services must collaborate with campus referral agencies for LGBT students, staff, faculty, and administration (e.g., multicultural, student affairs, visitor services, women's centers, special academic support units, campus security, health centers, counseling centers, religious programs, and career services).

LGBT Programs and Services must establish relationships with a wide range of student groups (e.g., LGBT student association, student government association, fraternities and sororities, and athletics) to promote visibility and to serve as a resource to the entire campus community.

LGBT Programs and Services must foster relationships with academic units (especially in LGBT studies, ethnic studies, women's studies, higher education, counseling and human services, and student affairs) and with campus professionals (e.g., student activities, athletics, commuter affairs, and residential life).

LGBT Programs and Services staff should be actively involved in appropriate campus networks to effectively participate in

the establishment of institution-wide policies and practices and to collaborate with other staff and faculty to provide services.

LGBT Programs and Services must have adequate access to institutional legal counsel and legal staff of relevant professional organizations.

Where adequate LGBT resources are not available on campus, LGBT Programs and Services must establish and maintain close working relationships with off-campus community LGBT agencies that provide such services as counseling, community involvement, and health care.

An advisory board made up of students, faculty, staff, alumni, and community members may be established to advise, support, and guide the LGBT Programs and Services.

Promotional and descriptive information must be accurate and free of deception and misrepresentation.

LGBT Programs and Services must have procedures and guidelines consistent with institutional policy for

- communicating with the media
- distributing information through print, broadcast, and online sources
- contracting with external organizations for delivery of programs and services
- cultivating, soliciting, and managing gifts
- applying to and managing funds from grants

Part 9. Financial Resources

Lesbian, Gay, Bisexual, Transgender Programs and Services (LGBT Programs and Services) must have funding to accomplish the mission and goals.

In establishing and prioritizing funding resources, LGBT Programs and Services must conduct comprehensive analyses to determine

- unmet needs of the unit
- relevant expenditures
- external and internal resources
- impact on students and the institution

Funding for LGBT Programs and Services must be equitable in relationship to other comparable Programs and Services.

LGBT Programs and Services must use the budget as a planning tool to reflect commitment to the mission and goals of the programs and services and of the institution.

LGBT Programs and Services must administer funds in accordance with established institutional accounting procedures.

LGBT Programs and Services must demonstrate efficient and effective use and responsible stewardship of fiscal resources consistent with institutional protocols.

Financial reports must provide an accurate financial overview of the organization and provide clear, understandable, and timely data upon which personnel can plan and make informed decisions.

Procurement procedures must
- be consistent with institutional policies
- ensure that purchases comply with laws and codes for usability and access
- ensure that the institution receives value for the funds spent
- consider information available for comparing the ethical and environmental impact of products and services purchased

Funding for LGBT Programs and Services may come from a variety of sources, including grant money, student government funds or fees, foundation donations, alumni development initiatives, and government contracts; however non-institutional funding should not be expected to supplant institutional funding.

Part 10. Technology

Lesbian Gay, Bisexual, Transgender Programs and Services (LGBT Programs and Services) must have technology to support the achievement of their mission and goals. The technology and its use must comply with institutional policies and procedures and with relevant codes and laws.

LGBT Programs and Services must use technologies to
- provide updated information regarding mission, location, staffing, programs, services, and official contacts to students and other constituents in accessible formats
- provide an avenue for students and other constituents to communicate sensitive information in a secure format
- enhance the delivery of programs and services for all students

LGBT Programs and Services must
- back up data on a regular basis
- adhere to institutional policies regarding ethical and legal use of technology
- articulate policies and procedures for protecting the confidentiality and security of information
- implement a replacement plan and cycle for all technology with attention to sustainability
- incorporate accessibility features into technology-based programs and services

When providing student access to technology, LGBT Programs and Services must
- have policies on the use of technology that are clear, easy to understand, and available to all students
- provide information or referral to support services for those needing assistance in accessing or using technology
- provide instruction or training on how to use the technology
- inform students of implications of misuse of technologies

Information about LGBT programs, services, and resources must be available in electronic formats.

LGBT Programs and Services should also provide multiple contact points using instant messaging services and social networking sites to provide access to potential visitors who prefer to be anonymous when seeking information, services, guidance, and advice.

Part 11. Facilities and Equipment

Lesbian, Gay, Bisexual, Transgender Programs and Services' (LGBT Programs and Services) facilities must be intentionally designed and located in suitable, accessible, and safe spaces that demonstrate universal design and support the program's mission and goals.

Facilities must be designed to engage various constituents and promote learning.

Personnel must have workspaces that are suitably located and accessible, well equipped, adequate in size, and designed to support their work and responsibilities.

The design of the facilities must guarantee the security and privacy of records and ensure the confidentiality of sensitive information and conversations. Personnel must be able to secure their work.

LGBT Programs and Services must incorporate sustainable practices in use of facilities and purchase of equipment. Facilities and equipment must be evaluated on an established cycle and be in compliance with codes, laws, and accepted practices for access, health, safety, and security.

LGBT Programs and Services should maintain a physical and social environment that facilitates appropriate attention to safety factors. In addition, private, individual, and group meeting space should be provided.

LGBT Programs and Services should have access to resources for research, including access to private computer space.

When acquiring capital equipment, LGBT Programs and Services must take into account expenses related to regular maintenance and life cycle costs.

Part 12. Assessment

Lesbian, Gay, Bisexual, Transgender Programs and Services (LGBT Programs and Services) must develop assessment plans and processes.

Assessment plans must articulate an ongoing cycle of assessment activities.

LGBT Programs and Services must
- specify programmatic goals and intended outcomes
- identify student learning and development outcomes
- employ multiple measures and methods
- develop manageable processes for gathering, interpreting, and evaluating data

- document progress toward achievement of goals and outcomes
- interpret and use assessment results to demonstrate accountability
- report aggregated results to respondent groups and stakeholders
- use assessment results to inform planning and decision-making
- assess effectiveness of implemented changes
- provide evidence of improvement of programs and services

Both internal and external on-going evaluations are encouraged as part of a thoughtful plan of continuous evaluation of the LGBT Programs and Services mission and goals. Periodic reports, statistically valid research, outside reviews, and studies exploring student needs and opinions should be utilized.

LGBT Programs and Services must employ ethical practices in the assessment process.

LGBT Programs and Services must have access to adequate fiscal, human, professional development, and technological resources to develop and implement assessment plans.

General Standards revised in 2014;
LGBT Programs and Services content developed/revised in 2000 &
2010

Master's Level Student Affairs Professional Preparation Programs

CAS Contexual Statement

Master's-level professional preparation programs provide individuals entering the field of student affairs the requisite knowledge, perspectives, and skills to serve students and foster their learning and development. Aside from acquiring skills and knowledge, students that complete a master's program in student affairs are socialized into the field. They learn about the culture of the profession and the values that guide it. These preparation programs may have different foci, including administration, counseling, or student development; all, however, should prepare students to work in a wide variety of functional areas within higher education. Although this diversity of preparation programs is valuable to the field, a set of shared standards is essential to serve as a foundation for all programs. The primary value of the CAS student affairs professional preparation standard is to assist in ensuring that an academic program is offering what the profession, through representative consensus, has deemed necessary to graduate prepared student affairs and student services professionals.

Standards for the professional education of student affairs practitioners have largely been established during the past five decades. In 1964 the Council of Student Personnel Associations in Higher Education (COSPA) drafted *A Proposal for Professional Preparation in College Student Personnel Work*, which subsequently evolved into *Guidelines for Graduate Programs in the Preparation of Student Personnel Workers in Higher Education*, dated March 5, 1967. The change in title from "proposal for" in the 1964 version to "guidelines for" in the fourth revision exemplifies the movement from a rather tentative statement of what professional preparation should entail to one asserting specific guidelines that should be followed in graduate education programs. A final statement, popularly recognized as the COSPA Report, was actually published some time after the dissolution of the Council (1975).

During this period, others concerned with the graduate education of counselors and other helping professionals established counselor education standards and explored the possibilities for accrediting graduate academic programs. A moving force in this effort was the Association of Counselor Educators and Supervisors (ACES), a division of the American Personnel and Guidance Association (APGA), now called the American Counseling Association (ACA). In 1978, ACES published a set of professional standards to accredit counseling and personnel services education programs. APGA recognized ACES as its official counselor education accrediting body and moved to establish an inter-association committee to guide counselor education program accreditation activity and the review and revision of the ACES/APGA preparation standards. In response to

this initiative, the American College Personnel Association (ACPA) established an *ad hoc* Preparation Standards Drafting Committee to create a set of standards designed to focus on the special concerns of student affairs graduate education. At its March 1979 meetings, the ACPA Executive Council adopted the Committee's statement entitled "Standards for the Preparation of Counselors and College Student Affairs Specialists at the Master's Degree Level."

ACPA then initiated a two-pronged effort in the area of professional standards. One was a collaborative effort with the National Association of Student Personnel Administrators (NASPA) to establish a profession-wide program of standards creation, and the other was a concerted effort to work under the then-APGA organizational umbrella to establish an agency for the accreditation of counseling and student affairs preparation programs. The former initiative resulted in the creation of the Council for the Advancement of Standards in Higher Education (CAS) and the latter in the establishment of the Council for the Accreditation of Counseling and Other Related Educational Programs (CACREP), an academic program-accrediting agency. Both the CAS and CACREP professional preparation standards reflected the influence of the ACPA standards for student affairs preparation.

The foregoing process was a prelude to the *CAS Masters-Level Student Affairs Professional Preparation Program Standards and Guidelines*, which follow. A major value of graduate standards is that they provide criteria by which an academic program of professional preparation can judge its educational efforts. Whether used for accreditation or program development and improvement purposes, standards provide faculty, staff, administrators, and students alike a tool to measure a program's characteristics against a set of well-conceived criteria designed to ensure educational quality.

The CAS standards for student affairs graduate programs were revised in 2012 and offer standards and guidelines based on profession-wide inter-association collaboration. Topics addressed in the standards include the program's mission; recruitment and admission policies and procedures; curriculum policies; pedagogy; the curriculum; equity and access; academic and student support; professional ethics and legal responsibilities; and program evaluation. The standards recognize that each program must also be responsive to the host department and institution. The standards support the need for life-long learning and professional development for all professionals. The ACPA and NASPA document of *Professional Competency Areas for Student Affairs* (2011) is a useful guide for professional preparation and professional development.

Curriculum standards are organized around Foundation Studies, Professional Studies, and Supervised Practice. Foundation Studies pertains to the historical and philosophical foundations of higher education and student affairs. This includes historical documents of the profession such as *Learning Reconsidered I and II (2004, 2006), Student Personnel Point of View* (ACE, 1937), *Return to the Academy* (Brown, 1972), the *Student Learning Imperative* (ACPA, 1996), *Principles of Good Practice* (Blimling & Whitt, 1999), *Powerful Partnerships* (Joint Task Force, 1998), and *Reasonable Expectations* (Kuh et al, 1994) among others. Professional Studies pertains to student development theory, student characteristics, the effects of college on students, individual and group interventions, the organization and administration of student affairs, and assessment, evaluation, and research. Supervised Practice includes practica, internships, and externships under professionally supervised work conditions.

There are a number of emerging trends influencing today's professional preparation programs. Students entering these programs are more diverse than they have been in the past. More adult students have entered preparation programs as advanced degrees become more important for promotion and advancement. Changes in higher education, such as the increased emphasis on accountability, including assessment of graduate learning outcomes, are influencing curriculum. The changing demographics of college students have required expanded discussion in areas such as student learning and development theory, program development, and cultural competency. Graduates of professional preparation programs need to be ready to document the impact of programs and services they provide. The tools of the profession are changing; technology from hardware to software to social media is having a significant impact on how we connect with students and do our work. Finally, there is an emerging discussion of professionalism in the field, including consideration of the ACPA/NASPA Professional Competencies. Standards for preparation programs provide anchors guiding students with a strong foundation while adapting to emerging issues affecting the field.

Two groups that exist to support and promote the preparation of professionals are the Commission for Professional Preparation of ACPA and NASPA's Faculty Fellows. The Association for the Study of Higher Education (ASHE) has a commission on graduate preparation that has drafted standards for the study of higher education as a discipline. Through the use of the CAS Professional Preparation standards, programs can ensure that what the field has deemed appropriate education will produce succession student affairs and services professionals.

References, Readings, and Resources

ACPA: College Student Educators International. Commission for Professional Preparation: http://www.myacpa.org/comm/profprep/

ACPA/NASPA (2011). *Professional competency areas for student affairs*. Washington, DC: Author. http://www2.myacpa.org/img/Professional_Competencies.pdf

American College Personnel Association (1996). The student learning imperative: Implications for student affairs. *Journal of College Student Development, 37,* 118-122.

American College Personnel Association (ACPA) (March/April 1996). Special issue: The student learning imperative. *Journal of College Student Development, 37*(2), 118-122.

Association of Counselor Educators and Supervisors (ACES). (1978). *Standards for the preparation of counselors and other personnel services specialists at the master's degree level*. Washington, DC: Author.

Blimling, G. S. & Whitt, E. J. (1999). *Good practice in student affairs*. San Francisco, CA: Jossey-Bass.

Brown, R. D. (1972). Student development in tomorrow's higher education - A return to the academy. *Student Personnel Series, 16.* Washington, DC: American College Personnel Association.

Bryant, W. A., Winston, R. B. Jr., & Miller, T. K. (Eds.) (1991). Using professional standards in student affairs, No. 53. *New Directions for Student Affairs.* San Francisco, CA: Jossey-Bass.

Cooper, D. L., Saunders, S. A., Winston, R. B., Jr., Hirt, J. B., Creamer, D. G., Janosik, S, M. (2002). *Learning through supervised practice in student affairs.* New York, NY: Taylor Francis.

Council of Student Personnel Associations (COSPA). (1964). *A proposal for professional preparation in college student personnel work*. Unpublished manuscript, Indianapolis: Author.

Council of Student Personnel Associations (COSPA). (March, 1967). *Guidelines for graduate programs in the preparation of student personnel workers in higher education*. Unpublished manuscript, Washington, DC: Author.

Council of Student Personnel Associations (COSPA). (1975). Student development services in post-secondary education. *Journal of College Student Personnel, 16,* 524-528.

Evans, N., & Phelps Tobin, C. (1996). *State of the art of preparation and practice in student affairs: Another look.* Lanham, MD: University Press of America.

Joint Task Force of Student Learning. (1998). *Powerful partnerships: A shared responsibility for learning.* Washington, DC: American Association for Higher Education.

Kuh, G. D. (1994). *Reasonable expectations: Renewing the educational compact between institutions and students.* Washington, DC: National Association of Student Personnel Administrators.

Magolda, P & Carnaghi, J. (Eds.). (2004). *Job one: Experiences of new professionals in student affairs.* New York, NY: University Press of America.

National Association of Student Personnel Administrators (NASPA). (1987). *A perspective on student affairs: A statement issued on the 50th anniversary of the student personnel point of view.* Washington, DC: Author.

National Student Affairs Archives, Bowling Green State University, http://www.bgsu.edu/colleges/library/cac/bib/page39347.html

Schuh, J., Jones, S. R., & Harper, S. (Eds.) (2010). *Student services: A handbook for the profession* (5th ed). San Francisco, CA: Jossey-Bass.

Stringer, J. & McClelland, G. (Eds.) (2009). *The handbook of student affairs administration (3rd ed.)*. San Francisco, CA: Jossey-Bass.

Whitt, E. J., Carnaghi, J. E., Matkin, J., Scalese-Love, P., & Nestor, D. (1990). Believing is seeing: Alternative perspectives on a statement of professional philosophy for student affairs. *NASPA Journal, 27*, 178-184.

Winston, R. B. Jr., Creamer, D. G., Miller, T. K., & Associates (2001). *The professional student affairs administrator: Educator, leader, and manager*. Philadelphia, PA: Taylor and Francis.

Contextual Statement Contributors

Current Edition:

Gavin Henning, New England College, ACPA

Previous Editions:

Gavin Henning, New England College, ACPA

Susan R. Komives, University of Maryland, ACPA

Jan Arminio, Shippensburg University, NACA

Master's Level Student Affairs Professional Preparation Programs

CAS Standards and Guidelines

Part 1. Mission and Objectives

The mission of professional preparation programs must be to prepare persons through graduate education for professional positions in student affairs practice in higher education. Each program mission must be consistent with the mission of the institution offering the program.

Program missions should reflect particular emphases, such as administration, counseling, student learning and development, student cultures, social justice, or other appropriate emphases as long as the standards herein are met.

The program's mission may include inservice education, professional development, research, and consultation for student affairs professional staff members working at the institution.

Each professional preparation program must publish a clear statement of mission, objectives, and desired outcomes prepared by the program faculty in consultation with collaborating student affairs professionals and relevant advisory committees. The statement must be readily available to current and prospective students and to appropriate faculty and staff members and agencies. It must support accurate assessment of student learning and program effectiveness. The statement must be reviewed periodically.

This review may be conducted with the assistance of stakeholders, including current students and faculty, graduates of the program, student affairs professionals, and personnel in cooperating entities such as practicum or internship sites, affiliated academic departments, other institutions, or employers.

The program faculty should consider recommendations of governing bodies and professional groups concerned with student affairs when developing, revising, and publishing the program's mission and objectives. The mission and objectives should reflect consideration of the current issues and needs of society, higher education, and student populations served. Personnel in cooperating agencies and faculty members with primary assignments in other disciplines should be aware of and should be encouraged to work toward the achievement of the program's mission and stated objectives.

The mission and objectives should specify both mandatory and elective areas of study. The mission and objectives may address socialization into the field as well as recruitment, selection, retention, employment recommendations, curriculum, instructional methods assessment, research activities, administrative policies, and governance.

Part 2. Recruitment and Admission

Accurate descriptions of the graduate program, including the qualifications of its faculty and records of students' persistence, degree completion, and subsequent study and employment, must be made readily available for review by both current and prospective students.

Students selected for admission to the program must meet the institution's criteria for admission to graduate study. Program faculty members must make admission decisions using written criteria that are disseminated to all faculty members and to prospective students.

Students admitted to the program should demonstrate academic capability interpersonal skills, demonstrated interest in the program, commitment to pursuing a career in student affairs, the potential to serve a wide range of students of varying developmental levels and backgrounds, and the capacity to be open to self-assessment and growth. Criteria known to predict success in the program should be used in selection of candidates. Students from diverse backgrounds should be encouraged to apply.

Admission goals and practices must reflect the need to achieve a diverse group of program students with recruitment of underrepresented student applicants where deemed appropriate by the program.

Admissions materials must be clear about criteria for particular student status, such as full-time students, currently employed students, or students seeking distance learning opportunities, and the manner in which such preferences may affect admissions decisions.

Design of admissions materials, from informational brochures to Internet resources and forms, must ensure they are useable by persons utilizing varied access means and tools.

Universal design concepts should be incorporated to develop admissions materials that pertain to, appeal to, and are useable by all prospective applicants.

Faculty members in institutions that are signatories to the Council for Graduate School's *Resolution Regarding Graduate Scholars, Fellows, Trainees and Assistants* must comply with the April 15th acceptance deadline for graduate student admission decisions, including graduate student employment or fellowship offers made by the graduate program.

Faculty members should encourage those offering employment to graduate students to abide by the acceptance deadline.

Faculty members at non-signatory institutions should also comply with the Council for Graduate School policy.

Part 3. Curriculum Policies

The preparation program must specify its curriculum and graduation requirements in writing and distribute them to prospective students. The program must conform to institutional policy and must be fully approved by the institution's administrative unit responsible for graduate programs. The institution must employ faculty members with credentials that reflect professional knowledge, ability, and skill to teach, advise, produce scholarship, and supervise students.

Any revisions to the publicized program of studies must be published and distributed to students in a timely fashion. Course syllabi must be available that reflect purposes, teaching/learning methods, and outcome objectives.

All prerequisite studies and experiences should be identified clearly in course descriptions and syllabi.

To accomplish the goals of the curriculum as outlined later in this document, a program must include an equivalent total of 40-48 semester credit hours or two years of full-time academic study.

Programs should provide opportunities for part-time study.

Appropriate consideration and provisions for curriculum adjustments should be made for students with extensive student affairs experience.

Distance learning opportunities may be used in the program.

Distance learning, including distance degree programs, must comply with all standards herein.

Successful completion of the program must be based on achievement of clearly articulated learning goals and outcomes.

Programs must demonstrate that the full curriculum, as outlined in Part 5 of these standards and guidelines, is covered and that graduates have mastered relevant competencies.

There must be a sequence of basic to advanced studies. Any required associated learning experiences must be included in the required program of studies.

Associated learning experiences may include comprehensive examinations, portfolios, service-learning, internship/practicum, and research requirements.

Opportunity for students to develop understandings and skills beyond minimum program requirements must be provided through elective course options, supervised individual study, and/or enrichment opportunities.

Programs should encourage students to take advantage of special enrichment opportunities and education that encourages learning beyond the formal curriculum, e.g., experiences in student affairs organizations, professional associations and conferences, and outreach projects.

An essential feature of the preparation program must be to foster an appreciation of intellectual inquiry in faculty members and students, as evidenced by active involvement in producing and using research, evaluation, and assessment information in student affairs.

Research, program evaluation, and assessment findings should be used frequently in instructional and supervised practical experience offerings. The study of methods of inquiry should be provided in context of elected program emphasis, such as administration, counseling, student learning and development, student cultures, or other program options.

Part 4. Pedagogy

Each program and all faculty members must indicate their pedagogical philosophy and strategies in the appropriate program media. Faculty members must accommodate multiple student learning styles.

Teaching approaches must be employed that lead to the accomplishment of course objectives, achievement of student learning outcomes, and evaluation by academic peers for the purpose of program improvement.

Pedagogy should employ principles of universal design for learning principles to meet the educational needs of all students and minimize the need for individual accommodations.

Teaching approaches include active collaboration, service-learning, problem-based learning, community-based learning, experiential learning, and constructivist learning. Faculty members should use multiple teaching strategies.

Part 5. The Curriculum

All programs of study must include (a) foundational studies, (b) professional studies, and (c) supervised practice. Demonstration of necessary knowledge and skill in each area is required of all program graduates.

Programs should use capstone experiences as a culminating activity.

Foundational studies must include the study of the historical and philosophical foundations of higher education and student affairs.

Professional studies must include (a) student learning and development theories, (b) student characteristics and the effects of college on students, (c) individual and group strategies, (d) organization and administration of student affairs, and (e) assessment, evaluation, and research.

Supervised practice must include practicums and/or internships consisting of supervised work involving at least two distinct experiences.

The curriculum described above represents areas of study and should not be interpreted as specific course titles. The precise nature of courses should be determined by a variety of factors, including institutional mission, policies and practices, faculty judgment, current issues, and student needs. It is important that appropriate courses be available within the institution or from another institution, but it is not necessary that all be provided directly within the department or college in which the program is located administratively. Although all areas of study must be incorporated into the academic program, the precise nature of study may vary by institution, program emphasis, and student preference. The requirements for demonstration of competence and minimum knowledge in each area should be established by the faculty and regularly reviewed to assure that students are learning the essentials that underlie successful student affairs practice. A formal comprehensive examination or other culminating assessment project designed to provide students the opportunity to exhibit their knowledge and competence toward the end of their programs of study is encouraged.

Programs of study may be designed to emphasize one or more distinctive perspectives on student affairs such as educational program design, implementation, and evaluation; individual and group counseling and advising; student learning and human development; and/or administration of student affairs in higher education. Such program designs should include the most essential forms of knowledge and groupings of skills and competencies needed by practicing professionals and should be fashioned consistent with basic curriculum requirements. The wide range of expertise and interest of program faculty members and other involved and qualified contributors to curriculum content should be taken into account when designing distinctive perspectives in programs of study.

Each program must specify the structure of its degree options including which courses are considered core, thematic, required, and elective.

A "core" course is one that is principal to the student affairs preparation program. Theme courses are those that center on a common content area (such as introduction to student development theory, the application of student development theory, and using student development theory for environmental assessment).

Programs may structure their curriculum according to their distinctive perspectives and the nature of their students to ensure adequacy of knowledge in foundation, professional, and supervised experience studies.

Adoption and selection of instructional materials must give consideration to accessibility features to ensure they are useable by all students.

Part 5a: Foundational Studies

This component of the curriculum must include study in the historical, philosophical, ethical, cultural, and research foundations of higher education that informs student affairs practice.

Graduates must be able to reference historical and current

documents that state the philosophical foundations of the profession and to communicate the relevance of these documents to current student affairs practice.

Graduates must also be able to articulate the values of the profession that are stipulated or implied in these documents and indicate how these values guide practice.

These values should include educating the whole student, treating each student as a unique individual, offering seamless learning opportunities, and ensuring the basic rights of all students.

This standard encompasses studies in other disciplines that inform student affairs practice, such as cultural contexts of higher education; governance, public policy, and finance of higher education; the impact of environments on behavior, especially learning; history of higher education for majority, minority and disabled students, and international education and global understanding, including the implications of internationalization. Studies in this area should emphasize the diverse character of higher education environments including minority-serving institutions. The foundational studies curriculum component should be designed to enhance students' understanding of higher education systems and exhibit how student affairs programs are infused into the larger educational picture.

Graduates must be knowledgeable about and be able to apply a code of ethics or ethical principles sanctioned by a recognized professional organization that provides ethical guidance for their work.

Part 5b: Professional Studies

This component of the curriculum must include studies of basic knowledge for practice and all programs must encompass at least five related areas of study including (a) student learning and development theories; (b) student characteristics and effects of college on students; (c) individual and group strategies; (d) organization and administration of student affairs; and (e) assessment, evaluation, and research.

Other areas of study, especially when used as enrichment or cognate experiences, are encouraged. Studies in disciplines such as sociology, psychology, political science, public administration, disability studies, and ethnic studies, for example, may be helpful to students depending upon the particular program emphasis.

Communication skills and use of technology as a learning tool must be emphasized in all the professional studies areas listed above.

Subpart 5b.1: Student Learning and Development Theory

This component of the curriculum must include studies of student development theories and research relevant to student learning and personal development. There must be extensive examination of theoretical perspectives that describe students' growth in the areas of intellectual, moral, ego, psychosocial, career, and spiritual development; racial,

cultural, ethnic, gender, abilities, socioeconomic status, and sexual identity; the intersection of multiple identities; and learning styles throughout the late adolescent and adult lifespan. Study of collegiate environments and how person-environment interactions affect student learning and development must also be required.

Graduates must be able to demonstrate the ability to use and critique appropriate theory to understand, support, and advocate for student learning and development by assessing needs and creating opportunities for learning and development.

This component should include studies of and research about human development from late adolescence through the adult life span and models and processes for translating theory and research into practice. Studies should stress differential strengths and applications of student development theories relative to student age, gender, ethnicity, race, culture, sexual identity and expression, abilities, spirituality, national origin, socioeconomic status, and resident/commuter status. Studies should also include specialized theories of learning and development particular to certain populations or groups.

Subpart 5b.2: Student Characteristics and Effects of College on Students

This component of the curriculum must include studies of student characteristics, how such attributes influence student educational and developmental needs, and effects of the college experience and institutional characteristics on student learning and development.

Graduates must be able to demonstrate knowledge of how student learning and learning opportunities are influenced by student characteristics and by collegiate environments so that graduates can design and evaluate learning experiences for students.

This area should include studies of the following: effects of college on students, campus climate, satisfaction with the college experience, student involvement in college, student culture, campus environment, and factors that correlate with student persistence and attrition. This curriculum component should include, but is not limited to, student characteristics such as age, gender, ethnicity, race, religion, sexual identity and expressions, academic ability and preparation, learning styles, socioeconomic status, national origin, immigrant status, abilities, developmental status, cultural background and orientation, transfer status, and family situation. Also included should be the study of specific student populations such as residential, commuter, distance learner; part-time and full-time; transfer; first generation; student-athlete; fraternity/sorority member; adult learner; active duty military and veteran; and international.

Subpart 5b.3: Individual and Group Strategies

This component of the curriculum must include studies, techniques, and methods of advising and helping skills as well as assessing, designing, implementing, and evaluating developmentally appropriate strategies with individuals

and organizations.

Graduates must be able to demonstrate knowledge and skills necessary to design and evaluate effective educational interventions for individuals and groups. Graduates must be able to identify and appropriately refer persons who need additional resources.

This curriculum component should include opportunities for study, skill building, and strategies for the implementation of advising, counseling, disciplining, instructing, mediating, arbitrating, and facilitating to assist individuals and groups. The program of study should include substantial instruction in counseling skills, helping skills, and group dynamics. Students should be exposed to a variety of theoretical perspectives, provided opportunities to practice individual and group interventions, and receive extensive supervision and feedback. Intervention skills are complex and require periods of time to practice under supervised conditions.

Programs of study should include instruction in individual and group techniques and practices for addressing personal crises as well as problem solving, self-assessment, and growth needs. Further, studies should include problem analyses, intervention design, and subsequent evaluation. Studies should emphasize theory plus individual and group strategies that are appropriate for and applicable to diverse populations.

Subpart 5b.4: Organization and Administration of Student Affairs

This component of the curriculum must include studies of organizational, management, and leadership theory and practice; student affairs functions, organizational models, and partnerships; legal issues in higher education; human and organizational resources; and professional issues, ethics, and standards of practice in the context of diverse institutional types.

Graduates must be able to identify and apply leadership, organizational, and management practices that assist institutions in accomplishing their missions.

This curriculum component should include opportunities for the study of student affairs programs and services including but not limited to those for which CAS has developed standards and guidelines. Studies of organizational culture; collaboration and partnerships; budgeting, finance, and resource management; planning; technology as applied to organizations; and the selection, supervision, development, and evaluation of staff should be included as well.

Subpart 5b.5: Assessment, Evaluation, and Research

This component of the curriculum must include the study of assessment, evaluation, and research that centers on evidence-based practice to further accountability and continuous improvement. Studies must include assessment planning and design, outcome development, both qualitative and quantitative research methodologies, measurement of learning processes and outcomes, assessment of environments and organizations,

measurement of program and environment effectiveness, effective reporting, and critiques of published studies.

Graduates must be able to critique a study or evaluation and be able to design, conduct, and report on a sound research study, assessment study, or program evaluation, all grounded in the appropriate literature. Graduates must be able to use assessment results to inform and improve professional practice and student learning.

Graduates must be aware of research ethics and legal implications of research, including the necessity of adhering to a human subjects review.

This curriculum component should include studies of the design of student learning and developmental outcomes, assessment of student needs and developmental attributes, satisfaction studies, the assessment of educational environments that influence student learning, the assessment of resource effectiveness, and the assessment of student outcomes of the educational experience particular to student affairs work. This curriculum component also should include studies of program evaluation models and processes suitable for use in evaluating the impact of a wide range of programs and services. Students should be introduced to methodologies and techniques of quantitative and qualitative research, plus the philosophical foundations, assumptions, methodologies, and criteria of worthiness of both. Students should understand their roles, responsibilities, and personal perspectives as researchers. Students should be familiar with prominent research in student affairs that has greatly influenced the profession.

Part 5c: Supervised Practice

A minimum of 300 hours of supervised practice, consisting of at least two distinct experiences, must be required. Students must gain exposure to both the breadth and depth of student affairs work. Students must gain experience in developmental work with individual students and groups of students in program planning, implementation, or evaluation; staff training, advising, or supervision; and administration functions or processes.

Supervision must be provided onsite by competent professionals, who are approved by, and working in cooperation with qualified program faculty members. Onsite supervisors must provide direct regular supervision and evaluation of students' experiences and comply with all ethical principles and standards of the ACPA - College Student Educators International, NASPA – Student Affairs Administrators in Higher Education, and other recognized professional associations.

Qualified student affairs professionals possessing appropriate student affairs education and experience should be invited to sponsor and supervise students for practicum, internship, and assistantship experiences. Typical qualifications include at least a master's degree in student affairs or a related area of professional study, and a minimum of one year of successful full-time post-master's professional experience and experience at that institution.

Site supervisors must be approved in advance by program faculty. Program faculty must offer clear expectations of learning goals and supervision practices to site supervisors. Site supervisors must involve students in developing reasonable, attainable, and measureable learning outcomes from their practical experiences.

Supervised practice includes practicums and internships consisting of supervised work completed for academic credit in student programs and services in higher education including higher education organizations. The exposure of students to diverse settings and work with diverse clientele or populations should be encouraged.

Because individual supervision of students in practicums and internships is laborious for faculty with this instructional responsibility, supervision must be limited to a small group of students per faculty member to enable close regular supervision. Students must be supervised closely by faculty individually, in groups, or both.

When determining practicum and internship course loads, faculty members who provide direct practicum or internship supervision during any academic term should receive instructional credit for the equivalent of one academic course for each small group. Likewise, students enrolled in such internships should receive academic credit.

A graduate assistantship in programs and services in higher education, which provides both substantive experience and professional supervision, may be used in lieu of a practicum or internship. To ensure effectiveness, faculty members responsible for assuring quality learning outcomes should work closely with graduate assistantship supervisors in students' assignment and evaluation processes. Appropriate consideration and provisions should be made for students with extensive experience in student affairs.

Preparation of students for practicums and internships is required. Practicums and internship experiences must be reserved for students who have successfully completed a sequence of courses pertaining to basic foundational knowledge of professional practice. Before participating in practicums and internships, students must demonstrate basic knowledge and skills in interpersonal communication, consultation, and referral skills. Students must comply with all ethical principles and standards of appropriate professional associations.

Preparation of students for supervised practice may be accomplished through special pre-practicum seminars, laboratory experiences, and faculty tutorials as well as coursework.

Disability accommodations needed during supervised practice should be approached collaboratively between the student and his or her graduate practicum advisor, including site personnel if necessary.

Graduates must develop and maintain personal plans for professional development and habits that support life-long learning.

Student membership in professional associations should be expected. Attendance at professional conferences, meetings, or other professional development opportunities should also be encouraged and supported.

Since the allocation of students in supervised practice experiences represents distribution of institutional resources and by their nature can be political, care should be given to ensure a fair and equitable allocation. The selection and assignment process should ensure that student educational needs are met and that sponsoring programs and supervisors are equally respected so that promised commitments are honored throughout the supervised practice.

Part 6. Equity and Access

A graduate program must adhere to the spirit and intent of equal opportunity in all activities. The program must foster an inclusive community in which diversity is viewed as an ethical responsibility. The program must implement practices of universal design in its services, programs, and facilities. Programs that indicate in their admissions materials convenience and encouragement for distance learners or working students must provide services, classes, and resources that respond to the needs of evening, part-time, distance, and commuter students.

Programs and services must not discriminate on the basis of disability; age; race; cultural identity; ethnicity; nationality; family educational history (e.g., first generation to attend college); political affiliation; religious affiliation; sex; sexual orientation; gender identity and expression; marital, social, economic, or veteran status; or any other basis included in institutional policies and codes and laws.

Graduate programs must be provided on a fair, equitable, and non-discriminatory basis in accordance with institutional policies and with all applicable statutes and regulations.

Graduate programs must maintain an educational and work environment free from discrimination in accordance with law and institutional policy.

Graduate programs must modify or remove policies, practices, facilities, structures, systems, and technologies that create barriers access, discriminate, or produce inequities.

Programs and services must recognize the needs of distance learning students by providing appropriate and accessible services and resources or by assisting students to gain access to other appropriate services and resources in students' geographic regions.

Consistent with the mission and goals, programs must take action to remedy situations in which student enrollment and staffing are not representative of diversity.

The program should recognize the important educational opportunities that diversity among its students and faculty brings to student affairs preparation. Therefore, programs

should encourage the recognition of and adherence to the diversity of all who are allied with the educational program.

Part 7. Academic and Student Support

Institutions must provide sufficient faculty and staff members, resource materials, advising, career services, student financial support, facilities, technology, and funding resources for the program.

Outcome indicators should be developed, such as student and faculty retention, student-faculty ratio, and availability of assistantships to determine that the program has adequate resources.

Part 7a: Faculty and Staff Members

The institution must provide adequate faculty and support staff members for the various aspects of the student affairs graduate program.

The institution must provide an academic program coordinator who is qualified by preparation and experience to manage the program.

The program coordinator or administrative director should have responsibility for managing the program's day to day operations, convening the program faculty as required, developing curriculum, and generally administering the preparation program within the context of the academic unit to which it is assigned. This individual should be the person responsible for guiding faculty teaching assignments, establishing and maintaining connections with student affairs staff members who serve as practicum/internship site supervisors or in adjunct teaching roles, guiding general program activities, and representing the program to internal and external constituencies.

Faculty assignments must demonstrate a commitment to the preparation of student affairs professionals. Sufficient full-time core faculty members must be devoted to teaching and administering the program to produce not only employable students but also students capable of designing, creating, and implementing learning opportunities.

At least one faculty member must be designated full-time to the program. Faculty must be adequate for the student enrollment and nature of the program requirements.

Faculty members should be available according to a reasonable faculty-student ratio that permits quality teaching, advising, supervision, research, and professional service. A core faculty member is one who identifies principally with the preparation program. Primary teaching responsibility in the program is recognized when core faculty member's instructional responsibilities are dedicated half-time or greater to teaching the program's curriculum. Devoted full-time to the program is defined as a faculty member whose institutional responsibilities are fully dedicated to the program. Teaching loads should be established on the basis of institutional policy and faculty assignments for service, research, and supervision. A system within the program and the institution should exist for involving professional practitioners who are qualified to assist with program responsibilities such as teaching and advising. Collaboration between full-time faculty members and student affairs practitioners is recommended for the instruction, advisement, and practicum and internship supervision of students in the preparation program. Student affairs practitioners should be consulted in the design, implementation, and evaluation of the preparation program, particularly regarding practicum and internship requirements.

Faculty members must be skilled as teachers and knowledgeable about student affairs in general, plus current theory, research, and practice in areas appropriate to their teaching or supervision assignments.

Faculty members must also have current knowledge and skills appropriate for designing, conducting, and evaluating learning experiences using multiple pedagogies.

Faculty members must specify how and when they are available to students in the program.

Faculty members must act in accordance with ethical principles and standards of good practice disseminated by recognized professional organizations.

The institution must provide opportunity and resources for the continuing professional development of program faculty members. To ensure that faculty members can devote adequate time to professional duties, the academic program must have sufficient clerical and technical support staff.

Technical support must be of sufficient quality and quantity to meet the technical needs of the program. Equipment sufficient for electronic communications and Internet use is essential.

Technical support should include regular training in software upgrades and new hardware developments, hardware and software repairs, virus protection, access to the Internet, online journals, courseware, presentation software, accessible teaching and learning software/hardware, e-text access and library resource access.

Classroom facilities should have the capacity to offer classes using electronic technologies.

Adjunct and part-time faculty must be qualified and adequately trained to serve as teachers, advisors, and internship supervisors.

Adjuncts and part-time faculty should be informed about institutional policies and procedures, provided access to program resources and faculty, and given feedback about their performance.

Faculty, staff, and affiliated faculty should be familiar with their institution's emergency management, threat assessment, and classroom safety policies and procedures.

Part 7b: Resource Materials

Adequate resource materials must be provided to support
the curriculum.

Resources may include career information; standardized tests and technical manuals; and materials for simulations, structured group experiences, human relations training, and data-based interventions for human and organization development. In addition, resources may include instruments and assessment tools that measure development, and leadership from various theoretical points of view and materials that facilitate leadership, organizational design, management style, intercultural sensitivity, conflict management, and time management development. Resources should include software that allows for the analysis of qualitative and quantitative data.

Adequate library resources must be provided for the program including current and historical books, periodicals, online journals, search mechanisms, and other media for the teaching and research aspects of the program. Library resources must be accessible to all students and must be selected carefully, reviewed, and updated periodically by the program faculty.

The library resources should be available days, evenings, and weekends and should include adequate interlibrary loan services, Education Resources Information Center (ERIC), and similar data sources, computerized search capabilities, and photocopy services. The most recent version of the *CAS Professional Standards for Higher Education* should be in the library collection.

Research support must be adequate for both program faculty and students.

Computing services, data collection and storage services, research design consultation services, and adequate equipment for transcription should be available in support of research activities of both students and faculty members. The program should provide students with individualized research project development, implementation, and training on the use of equipment and resources.

Part 7c: Advising

Faculty members must provide high quality academic and professional advising.

Academic advising must be viewed as a continuous process of clarification and evaluation.

Academic advising should include, but is not limited to, development of suitable educational plans; selection of appropriate courses and other educational experiences; clarification of professional and career goals; knowledge of and interpretation of institutional and program policies, procedures, and requirements; knowledge of course contents, sequences, and support resources; evaluation of student progress; referrals to and use of institutional and community support services; support for and evaluation of scholarly endeavors including research and assessment; and knowledge and interpretation of professional ethics and standards.

Advisors should

- be able to engage in research advising using both qualitative and quantitative methodologies when directing student research such as a thesis;
- be readily available to students and should possess abilities to facilitate a student's career exploration, self-assessment, decision-making, and responsible behavior in interactions with others;
- be able to guide the student's self-assessment utilizing the CAS Characteristics for Individual Excellence and other statements of professional competencies established in the field of student affairs; and
- be able to the use the interpretation of the scores of assessment tools used in the advising process.

The number of faculty advisees should be monitored and adjusted as necessary to ensure that faculty can give adequate attention to all advisees.

Part 7d: Career Services

The institution must provide career assistance, either by institutional career services or by the program faculty.

Students should be assisted in clarifying objectives and establishing goals; exploring the full range of career possibilities; disclosing disability and requesting workplace accommodations; preparing for the job search including presenting oneself effectively as a candidate for employment; and making the transition from graduate student to professional practitioner. Faculty members should collaborate with campus career service providers to develop an active program of assistance, including acquiring job listings; the preparation of credentials such as recommending applications, correspondence, and résumés; development of employment interview skills; identification of appropriate job search networks including professional associations; selection of suitable positions; and communication of ethical obligations of those involved in the employment process. Ideally, these services should be available to graduates throughout their professional careers.

Part 7e: Student Financial Support

Students must be informed about the availability of graduate assistantships, fellowships, work-study, research funding, travel support, and other financial aid opportunities.

Graduate assistantships should be made available to students to provide both financial assistance and opportunities for supervised work experience. Travel support should be made available for students to engage in professional development activities.

Part 7f: Facilities and Funding Resources

The institution must provide facilities accessible to all students and a budget that ensures continuous operation of all aspects of the program.

A program office should be located in reasonable proximity to faculty offices, classrooms, and laboratory facilities. Adequate and appropriate space, equipment, and supplies should be provided for faculty members, staff members, and graduate assistants. There should be facilities for advising, counseling, and student development activities that are private, adequate in size, and properly equipped. Special facilities and equipment may include audio and video recording devices, one-way observation rooms, small group rooms, and computer labs. Adequate classroom, seminar, and laboratory facilities to meet program needs also should be available. Adequate office and technical equipment should be provided including access to email and other relevant technological resources. For online learning, resources and tools should be available to fulfill the responsibilities described above.

Part 8. Professional Ethics and Legal Responsibilities

Faculty members must comply with institutional policies and ethical principles and standards of ACPA – College Student Educators International, NASPA – Student Affairs Administrators in Higher Education, American Association of University Professors, and the CAS Statement of Shared Ethical Principles. Faculty members must demonstrate the highest standards of ethical behavior and academic integrity in all forms of advising, teaching, research, publication, and professional service and must instruct students in ethical practice and in the principles and standards of conduct of the profession.

Ethical expectations of graduate students must be disseminated in writing on a regular basis to all students.

Ethical principles and standards of all relevant professional organizations should be consulted and used as appropriate. An ethical climate should prevail throughout the preparation program wherein faculty members model appropriate ethical behavior at all times for students to experience, observe, and emulate. Faculty members should present various theoretical positions and encourage students to make comparisons and to develop personally meaningful theoretical positions. Faculty members are expected to ensure that educational experiences focusing on self-understanding and personal growth are voluntary or, if such experiences are program requirements, that reasonable effort is made to inform prospective students of them prior to admission to the program. Students should be held accountable for appropriate ethical behavior at all times with special attention paid to the ethics components of the various CAS functional area standards when students participate in related practicum and internship assignments.

Faculty members must strive to ensure the fair and impartial treatment of students and others.

Faculty members must maintain ethical relationships with students exemplifying respect and the ideals of pedagogy.

Faculty members must not teach, supervise, or advise any student with whom they have an intimate relationship. When a student enters an academic program having a

pre-existing intimate relationship with a faculty member, both must notify a third party, such as a department chair, to monitor the pedagogical relationship and assign appropriate teaching, supervisory, and advising responsibilities.

Graduate program faculty members must evaluate annually all students' progress and suitability for entry into the student affairs profession. Evaluation of students' ethical behaviors must be included. Faculty members must keep students informed about their progress toward successful program completion.

Through continual evaluation and appraisal of students, faculty members are expected to be aware of ethically problematic student behaviors, inadequate academic progress, and other behaviors or characteristics that may make a student unsuitable for the profession. Appropriate responses leading to remediation of the behaviors related to students' academic progress or professional suitability should be identified, monitored, evaluated, and shared with individual students as needed. Faculty members are expected, in cases of significant problematic behaviors, to communicate to the student the problems identified and the remediation required to avoid being terminated from the preparation program. After appropriate remediation has been proposed and evaluated, students who continue to be evaluated as being evaluated as poorly suited for the profession, making poor academic progress, or having demonstrated ethically problematic behaviors should be dismissed from the preparation program following appropriate due process procedures of the institution.

If termination is enforced, faculty members must explain to the student the grounds for the decision.

Faculty members must ensure that privacy is maintained of all communication and records considered to be educational records unless written permission is given by the student or when the disclosure is allowable under the law and institutional policy.

Faculty members must respond to requests by students for recommendations for employment or further study. When endorsement cannot be provided for a particular position, the student must be informed of the reason for non-endorsement.

Faculty members should base endorsements on knowledge of the student's academic performance, competencies, skills, and personal characteristics.

Each candidate should be informed of procedures for endorsement, certification, registry, and licensure, if applicable.

Faculty members must inform all students of the institutional and program policies regarding graduate student liability.

Program policy should be established to ensure that all students are periodically informed of their liabilities and options for protection. Programs may wish to establish

policies requiring students to hold membership in particular professional associations and to purchase liability insurance prior to entering into practicums or internships.

Part 9. Program Evaluation

Planned procedures for continuing evaluation of the program must be established and implemented, and the evaluation information must be used for appropriate program enhancements.

Criteria for program evaluation should include knowledge and competencies learned by students, employment rates of graduates, professional contributions to the field made by graduates, and quality of faculty teaching, advising, and research. The process for program evaluation should be transparent and shared with stakeholders. Evaluation of program effectiveness should reflect evidence obtained from current and former students; course evaluations; supervisors from institutions and agencies employing graduates of the program; and personnel in accrediting agencies during formal reviews.

Review of policies and procedures relating to recruitment, selection, retention, and career services should be included in program evaluations. The timing and regularity of evaluations should be determined in accordance with institutional policy or program needs. Generally, the length of time between comprehensive program evaluations by the program faculty should not exceed five years.

Results of assessments and evaluations must be used to identify needs and interests in revising and improving the program; recognizing faculty, staff, and student performance; maximizing resource efficiency and effectiveness; improving student achievement of learning and development outcomes; and improving student persistence and success.

Preparation Program content developed/revised in 1979, 1986, 1997, 2002, and 2012

Multicultural Student Programs and Services
CAS Contexual Statement

The evolution of Multicultural Student Programs and Services in American higher education must be examined within the historical influence of segregation (Kupo, 2011). "Systems of power, privilege, and oppression have created a need for multicultural student services on college campuses as a remedy for communities that have historically been barred from receiving formal primary, secondary, and higher education" (Kupo, 2011, p. 14). The powerful effects of racism, segregation, and discrimination in U.S. education are apparent in disparities in enrollment, retention, and graduation rates of historically marginalized groups (Bonilla-Silva, 2009). Additionally, the remnants of exclusionary practices continue to impact institutional climates for racial/ethnic diversity on campuses (Valencia, Garcia, Flores, & Juarez, 2004). Historical events have not only shaped institutional structures, they have also shaped attitudes in a way that impacts both the access and experience of underrepresented students in higher education.

Each racial/ethnic identity has unique cultural histories within the context of American higher education. "The intersections of shared histories of oppression must be acknowledged at the outset of a conversation about the development of services meant to redress that oppressive history" (Kupo, 2011, p. 25). For American Indian students, forced assimilation through boarding schools requiring the abandonment of all cultural identity is part of that history. For other students of color, wholesale exclusion was the law of the land. Minoritized students have gained access to predominantly White institutions (PWI) primarily by way of coercive legal mandate. *Tape v. Hurley* (1885), *Mendez v. Westminster School District of Orange County* (1946), and the groundbreaking *Brown v. Board of Education of Topeka* (1954) reveal the fervor and fortitude demonstrated by countless scholars, attorneys, activists, and every-day families to force open to doors of the ivory tower to all. Longstanding legacies of exclusion shaped institutional climates, practices, traditions, and policies in ways that made colleges and universities hostile environments for those who did not identify as White, Christian, economically privileged men (Kupo, 2011).

Multicultural Student Programs and Services (MSPS) were born of cultural centers emerging during the Black student movement of the late 1960s and early 1970s in which students held institutions accountable, demanding that their experiences be reflected and supported in the cultural, academic, and social aspects of the university milieu (Patton, 2010). The work of MSPS started from Black cultural centers and evolved to include other racial/ethnic populations with a mission "rooted in bringing voice, support, and celebration to college students, particularly those from racially underrepresented populations" (Patton, 2010, p. xiv). In this way, MSPS units sprang forth to support institutions ill prepared and/or resistant to serving expanded student populations. MSPS were initially created to respond to the

needs of these new students and to support their existence within a structure that was not built with them in mind. On many campuses, the very presence of a designated MSPS is the result of hard-won advocacy by students, faculty, and staff often many years in the making. It is important for practitioners doing this work to know and understand the specific institutional history of the campus of which the MSPS is a part. Whether celebrated or taboo, these narratives are often a critical determinant of the unique structure and purpose of the MSPS. Each university story is different and so too is the MSPS. The resulting work represents and reflects the exponential complexity of institutional history, regional differences, organizational structure, and institution type. With this degree of variability, MSPS should use the standards that follow as guided by their unique setting and institutional needs. These standards will focus on general programs and services for historically marginalized and oppressed students. For standards related to programs and services for other historically marginalized students see the CAS Standards for Lesbian, Gay, Bisexual, and Transgender Programs; Women's and Gender Programs; and Disability Resources and Services.

In the contemporary collegiate setting, MSPS offer proactive programming and services that seek to create welcoming environments marked by inclusive excellence where all students can thrive. This may include, but is not limited to, supporting cultural or identity based student organizations; providing diversity, inclusion, and social justice education for the campus community; advocating for the needs of multicultural students; supporting historically marginalized students in amplifying their voice and developing agency; honoring, celebrating, and validating the experiences and cultures of multicultural students in the larger campus environment; seeking to remove barriers that negatively impact the academic success, retention, graduation rates, and engagement of students of color; recruiting underrepresented students; engagement with and service to the local community; creating a safe community of care for underrepresented students; and connecting students to campus/community resources and support services including tutoring, personal counseling, financial aid counseling, career development, and others. MSPS balance the need for honoring target-only space and creating the conditions that allow students to feel a sense of belonging and acceptance within the larger campus environment as well. Both dimensions are dually important and necessary to student racial/ethnic identity development.

MSPS play a critical role in campus diversity, inclusion, and social justice efforts, but cannot be effective without the active engagement, financial investment, and partnership of the full campus community including all levels of administration, faculty, and staff. Some MSPS organize services to address specific racial identities, while others seek to serve all under-represented and oppressed students collectively. Some have autonomous facilities and budgets that include programming, advising, and community space, whereas others are located under the auspices of other campus entities such as the campus union or housing and residence life.   Due to the often disconnected nature of institutional organizational structures that force students to parse their identities, MSPS should partner often with offices and centers that serve the needs of women, students who identity as LGBTQIA, international students, first-generation students, and other marginalized social identities. An intersectional approach that makes it possible for students to acknowledge the unique and dynamic interplay between all of their social identities is essential. Strong MSPS are essential to the holistic engagement of students and thus, institutional recruitment, retention, and graduation rates. One way in which colleges and universities demonstrate their commitment to diversity, inclusion, and social justice is through the level of support they provide to the MSPS.

MSPS are as necessary today as they were when they were originally established. MSPS practitioners are valuable and important members of the higher educational enterprise exhibiting the necessary cultural competency vital to their work and a host of skills, abilities, and competencies rendering them effective educators, advocates, fundraisers, event planners, advisors, counselors, activists, and fiscal stewards with and on behalf of students. Critical race theorists assert that racism is inherent in society and intricately woven into the fabric of American culture (Delgado, 2000). Higher education is not immune. MSPS support students and endeavor to move their institutions forward to new levels of inclusive excellence. Patton (2010) summarized,

> Although some progress has been made, literature over the past few decades has consistently confirmed that students of color face discrimination and feelings of isolation within predominantly White collegiate spaces, whether the classroom, the residence hall, or the student union. Their daily interactions with peers, faculty, and administrators in these diverse settings are often clear reminders that as students of color, their experiences, culture, and mere presence are often dismissed, unacknowledged, or treated as invisible. (p. xvii)

Often described as homes away from home, MSPS were and continue to be safe havens. They contribute to developing and sustaining campus environments that welcome all students. In so doing, MSPS provide support and guidance to multicultural students in a way that makes it possible for them to pursue their educational goals, make meaning of their experiences, develop agency, and thrive on campus, as members of the local community, and as empowered people of color in the world.

References, Readings, and Resources

Adams, M., Bell, L. A., & Griffin, P. (Eds.). (2007). *Teaching for diversity and social justice* (2nd ed.). New York, NY: Routledge.
Association for Black Culture Centers (Includes African American, Latino, Native American, & Asian American Centers). http://

www.abcc.net/
Bonilla-Silva, E. (2009). *Racism without racists: Colorblind racism and the persistence of racial inequality in the United States* (3rd ed.). Lanham, MD: Rowman & Littlefield.
Brown v. Board of Education of Topeka, 347 U.S. 483 (1954).
Delgado, R. (2000). *Critical race theory: The cutting edge.* Philadelphia, PA: Temple University Press.
Hord, F. E. (2005). *Black culture centers: Politics of survival and identity.* Chicago, IL: Third World Press.
Jones, S. R. & Abes, E. S. (2013). *Identity development of college students: Advancing frameworks for multiple dimensions of identity.* San Fransisco, CA: Jossey-Bass.
Kupo, V. L. (2011). Remembering our past to shape our future. In D. L. Stewart (Ed.), *Multicultural student services on campus: Building bridges, re-visioning community.* (pp. 13-28). Sterling, VA: Stylus Publishing.
Mendez v. Westminster School District of Orange County, 64 F. Supp. 544 Decision (1946).
The National Conference on Race & Ethnicity in American Higher Education: https://www.ncore.ou.edu/
Patton, L. D. (2010). A call to action: Historical and contemporary reflections on the relevance of campus culture centers in higher education. In. L. D. Patton (Ed.), *Culture centers in higher education: Perspectives on identity, theory, and practice.* (pp. xiii-xvii). Sterling, VA: Stylus Publishing.
Patton, L. D. (Ed.). (2010). *Culture centers in higher education: Perspectives on identity, theory, and practice.* Sterling, VA: Stylus Publishing.
Tape v. Hurley, 66 Cal. 473 (Supreme Court of California, 1885).
Valencia, R. A., Garcia, S. R., Flores, H., & Juarez, J. R., Jr. (2004). *Mexican American and the law.* Tucson, AZ: The University of Arizona Press.
Wijeysinghe, C. L., & Jackson, III, B. W. (2012). *New perspectives on racial identity development: Integrating emerging frameworks* (2nd ed.). New York, NY: New York University Press.

Contextual Statement Contributors
Current Edition:
Zoe M. Johnson, The University of Georgia

Previous Editions:
Andrea Reeve, COE, University of Wyoming
Christopher Davis, COE
Jan Arminio, Shippensburg University

Multicultural Student Programs and Services
CAS Standards and Guidelines

Part 1. Mission

Multicultural Student Programs and Services (MSPS) must promote academic and personal growth of traditionally underserved students, work with the entire campus to create an institutional and community climate of justice, promote access and equity in higher education, and offer programs that educate the campus about diversity.

MSPS must develop, disseminate, implement, and regularly review their missions, which must be consistent with the mission of the institution and with applicable professional standards. The mission must be appropriate for the institution's students and other constituents. Mission statements must reference student learning and development.

MSPS must assist the institution in developing shared goals and creating a sense of common community that serves all its constituents fairly and equitably and is marked by
- access to academic, social, cultural, recreational, and other groups and activities
- opportunities for intentional interaction and engagement
- integration

MSPS must encourage the institution to hold units responsible for meeting the needs of traditionally underserved students in their area of responsibility; this includes under-represented or oppressed students, such as students of color; lesbian, gay, bisexual and transgender students; and students with disabilities.

Institutions may have more than one MSPS organization. Each of these MSPS organizations' missions may address the needs of a particular student group or groups. These missions should be complementary. If only one MSPS organization exists, the mission should address the needs of students of the many cultural and oppressed groups.

In addition, MSPS should encourage all units to include explicitly in their mission serving a wide range of underserved students fairly and equitably.

Part 2. Program

To achieve their mission, Multicultural Student Programs and Services (MSPS) must contribute to
- students' formal education, which includes both the curriculum and the co-curriculum
- student progression and timely completion of educational goals
- preparation of students for their careers, citizenship, and lives
- student learning and development

To contribute to student learning and development, MSPS must

- identify relevant and desirable student learning and development outcomes
- articulate how the student learning and development outcomes align with the six CAS student learning and development domains and related dimensions
- assess relevant and desirable student learning and development
- provide evidence of impact on outcomes
- articulate contributions to or support of student learning and development in the domains not specifically assessed
- use evidence gathered to create strategies for improvement of programs and services

STUDENT LEARNING AND DEVELOPMENT DOMAINS AND DIMENSIONS

Domain: knowledge acquisition, integration, construction, and application
- Dimensions: understanding knowledge from a range of disciplines; connecting knowledge to other knowledge, ideas, and experiences; constructing knowledge; and relating knowledge to daily life

Domain: cognitive complexity
- Dimensions: critical thinking, reflective thinking, effective reasoning, and creativity

Domain: intrapersonal development
- Dimensions: realistic self-appraisal, self-understanding, and self-respect; identity development; commitment to ethics and integrity; and spiritual awareness

Domain: interpersonal competence
- Dimensions: meaningful relationships, interdependence, collaboration, and effective leadership

Domain: humanitarianism and civic engagement
- Dimensions: understanding and appreciation of cultural and human differences, social responsibility, global perspective, and sense of civic responsibility

Domain: practical competence
- Dimensions: pursuing goals, communicating effectively, technical competence, managing personal affairs, managing career development, demonstrating professionalism, maintaining health and wellness, and living a purposeful and satisfying life

[LD Outcomes: See *The Council for the Advancement of Standards Learning and Development Outcomes* statement for examples of outcomes related to these domains and dimensions.]

MSPS must be
- intentionally designed
- guided by theories and knowledge of learning and development
- integrated into the life of the institution
- reflective of developmental and demographic profiles of the student population
- responsive to needs of individuals, populations with distinct needs, and relevant constituencies
- delivered using multiple formats, strategies, and contexts
- designed to provide universal access

MSPS must collaborate with colleagues and departments across the institution to promote student learning and development, persistence, and success.

MSPS must be based on models, approaches, or theories that address students across developmental levels.

MSPS must provide educational programs and services for all students that focus on awareness of cultural differences, cultural commonalties, privilege, and identity; self-assessment of cultural awareness and possible prejudices; and changing prejudicial, oppressive, and stereotypical attitudes or behavior.

MSPS may support other institutional functional areas such as recruitment, career services, academic advising, counseling, health services, and alumni relations.

MSPS must promote academic success of students by
- offering distinctive programs that introduce students to a community network and teach students how to negotiate processes within the institution (e. g., registration, academic advising, financial aid, housing, campus employment)
- assisting them to determine and assess their educational goals and academic skills
- providing support services that assist in achieving educational goals and attaining or refining academic skills
- informing students of educational opportunities, such as internships, special scholarship opportunities, study abroad programs, research, seminars, and conferences
- promoting intellectual, career, social, ethical, and social justice development
- networking with staff and faculty members
- connecting them to campus networks and groups and organizations.

MSPS should act as a liaison for referrals and interventions with staff and faculty members and administrators on behalf of students when appropriate.

MSPS must promote personal growth of students by
- enhancing students' understanding of their own culture, heritage, and identities
- enhancing students' understanding of cultures, heritages, and identities other than their own
- providing opportunities for students to establish

satisfying interpersonal relationships
- providing opportunities for interactions, exchange of ideas, and reflection

MSPS must work to create an engaging climate for students by advocating for and encouraging students to take advantage of the following opportunities:
- campus and community service including leadership opportunities
- practice in leadership including training, education, and development
- access to appropriate mentors and role models
- shared inter- and intra-social experiences

MSPS must work to create a just campus climate by
- challenging tacit and overt prejudices or discrimination against students
- coordinating efforts to promote multicultural sensitivity and the elimination of prejudicial behaviors
- facilitating desired changes with the cooperation of other campus entities
- identifying and addressing impediments to the growth and development of full participation of students

If institutional practices or policies have prejudicial effects, staff members must bring these facts to the attention of the proper authorities in the institution and work to change them.

MSPS must offer to the campus community programs that increase multicultural awareness, knowledge, and skills by
- promoting and enhancing the understanding of a variety of cultures and historical experiences
- promoting and enhancing the understanding of privilege, power, and prejudicial and stereotypical assumptions
- promoting and enhancing identity development
- teaching skills on how to combat racism, homophobia, sexism, and other forms of discrimination
- complementing the academic curricula

MSPS must serve as a resource for multicultural training, education, and development.

Educational programs may be provided in collaboration with efforts by academic and student affairs units and other program support services. Staff members in MSPS should coordinate their efforts with academic and student affairs units and other support services. Various dimensions of students' cultures, such as history, philosophy, worldview, literature, and various forms of communication and artistic expression, should be explored. Human relations programs should be designed to assist faculty members, staff members, and students in developing more tolerance, understanding, and ability to relate to others around issues of privilege; age; color; creed; cultural heritage; disability; ethnicity; gender identity; nationality; political affiliation; religious affiliation;

sex; sexual orientation; or social, economic, marital, or veteran status.

Activities that attempt to promote students' development should be based upon assessments and should reflect unique dimensions of the multicultural student experience.

MSPS must assist students across the range of their experiences at the institution.

These areas may include
- monitoring scholastic progress of groups and individual students and recommending strategies for improvement
- providing workshops, programs, retreats, and seminars on relevant topics and encouraging attendance at activities and services sponsored by other campus offices
- encouraging student attendance at conferences, meetings, and programs
- advising student organizations that advance the equality and interests of specific groups (e. g., Black/African American students, Asian/Pacific Islander students, Latino/a students, Native students, LGBT students, and allies), editorial staffs of multicultural publications, fraternal groups, pre-professional clubs, and program councils
- providing assistance and advice in planning multicultural student celebrations (e.g., Black/African American History Month, Kwanzaa, Stonewall Anniversary, Day of Silence, Take Back the Night, Transgender Day of Remembrance)
- assisting multicultural student groups or individuals in identifying and gaining access, where appropriate, to institutional services such as printing, bulk mailing, and computer services
- providing a directory of multicultural faculty and staff members
- providing a directory of faculty and staff members who have agreed to provide mentoring and assistance
- publishing a newsletter, website, or other means of focusing on current events, leadership opportunities, and other relevant information

Part 3. Organization and Leadership

To achieve program and student learning and development outcomes, Multicultural Student Programs and Services (MSPS) must be purposefully structured for effectiveness. MSPS must have clearly stated and current
- **goals and outcomes**
- **policies and procedures**
- **responsibilities and performance expectations for personnel**
- **organizational charts demonstrating clear channels of authority**

Leaders must model ethical behavior and institutional citizenship.

Leaders with organizational authority for MSPS

must provide strategic planning, management and supervision, and program advancement.

Strategic Planning
- **articulate a vision and mission that drive short- and long-term planning**
- **set goals and objectives based on the needs of the populations served, intended student learning and development outcomes, and program outcomes**
- **facilitate continuous development, implementation, and assessment of program effectiveness and goal attainment congruent with institutional mission and strategic plans**
- **promote environments that provide opportunities for student learning, development, and engagement**
- **develop, adapt, and improve programs and services in response to the changing needs of populations served and evolving institutional priorities**
- **include diverse perspectives to inform decision making**

Management and Supervision
- **plan, allocate, and monitor the use of fiscal, physical, human, intellectual, and technological resources**
- **manage human resource processes including recruitment, selection, professional development, supervision, performance planning, succession planning, evaluation, recognition, and reward**
- **influence others to contribute to the effectiveness and success of the unit**
- **empower professional, support, and student personnel to become effective leaders**
- **encourage and support collaboration with colleagues and departments across the institution**
- **encourage and support scholarly contributions to the profession**
- **identify and address individual, organizational, and environmental conditions that foster or inhibit mission achievement**
- **use current and valid evidence to inform decisions**
- **incorporate sustainability practices in the management and design of programs, services, and facilities**
- **understand appropriate technologies and integrate them into programs and services**
- **be knowledgeable about codes and laws relevant to programs and services and ensure that programs and services meet those requirements**
- **assess and take action to mitigate potential risks**

Program Advancement
- **advocate for and actively promote the mission and goals of the programs and services**
- **inform stakeholders about issues affecting practice**
- **facilitate processes to reach consensus where wide support is needed**
- **advocate for representation in strategic planning initiatives at divisional and institutional levels**

MSPS leaders must base their work on models and approaches that are theory-based and data driven.

MSPS must be located in an organizational structure that can best provide for effective programs and services for achievement of its mission.

Wherever located MSPS should collaborate and form close alliances with student affairs.

In response to assessed student needs, MSPS must play a principal role in creating and implementing institutional policies and programs.

Part 4. Human Resources

Multicultural Student Programs and Services (MSPS) must be staffed adequately by individuals qualified to accomplish mission and goals.

MSPS must have access to technical and support personnel adequate to accomplish their mission.
Within institutional guidelines, MSPS must
- establish procedures for personnel recruitment and selection, training, performance planning, and evaluation
- set expectations for supervision and performance
- provide personnel access to continuing and advanced education and appropriate professional development opportunities to improve their competence, skills, and leadership capacity
- consider work/life options available to personnel (e.g., compressed work schedules, flextime, job sharing, remote work, or telework) to promote recruitment and retention of personnel

Administrators of MSPS must
- ensure that all personnel have updated position descriptions
- implement recruitment and selection/hiring strategies that produce a workforce inclusive of under-represented populations
- develop promotion practices that are fair, inclusive, proactive, and non-discriminatory

Personnel responsible for delivery of MSPS must have written performance goals, objectives, and outcomes for each year's performance cycle to be used to plan, review, and evaluate work and performance. The performance plan must be updated regularly to reflect changes during the performance cycle.

Results of individual personnel evaluations must be used to recognize personnel performance, address performance issues, implement individual and/or collective personnel development and training programs, and inform the assessment of programs and services.

MSPS personnel, when hired and throughout their employment, must receive appropriate and thorough training.

MSPS personnel, including student employees and volunteers, must have access to resources or receive specific training on
- institutional policies pertaining to functions or activities they support
- privacy and confidentiality policies
- laws regarding access to student records
- policies and procedures for dealing with sensitive institutional information
- policies and procedures related to technology used to store or access student records and institutional data
- how and when to refer those in need of additional assistance to qualified personnel and have access to a supervisor for assistance in making these judgments
- systems and technologies necessary to perform their assigned responsibilities
- ethical and legal uses of technology

MSPS personnel must engage in continuing professional development activities to keep abreast of the research, theories, legislation, policies, and developments that affect their programs and services.

Administrators of MSPS must ensure that personnel are knowledgeable about and trained in safety, emergency procedures, and crisis prevention and response. Risk management efforts must address identification of threatening conduct or behavior and must incorporate a system for responding to and reporting such behaviors.

MSPS personnel must be knowledgeable of and trained in safety and emergency procedures for securing and vacating facilities.

PROFESSIONAL PERSONNEL

MSPS professional personnel either must hold an earned graduate or professional degree in a field relevant to their position or must possess an appropriate combination of educational credentials and related work experience.

MSPS professional staff members must possess the requisite multicultural knowledge, awareness, and skills.

MSPS professional staff should possess the awareness that cultural differences are valuable.

MSPS professional staff should value the significance of their own cultural heritage and understand that of different cultures. They should have insight into the interpersonal process of how one's own behavior impacts others. They should be aware of when change is necessary for the realization of a positive and just campus.

MSPS professional staff must have knowledge about identity development and the intersections of various aspects of diversity (i.e., race and class, race and gender, race and sexual orientation) on identity development and the acculturation process.

MSPS professional staff must know how various groups experience the campus and what institutional and societal barriers limit their access and their success.

MSPS professional staff must know how culture affects verbal and non-verbal communication. Professional staff must be knowledgeable about research and practice in areas appropriate to their programming with students.

MSPS professional staff must be skilled in identifying cultural issues and assessing their impact.

MSPS professional staff must be able to develop empathetic and trusting relationships with students.

MSPS professional staff must recognize individual, cultural, and universal similarities.

MSPS professional staff must be able to make culturally appropriate interventions to seek to optimize learning experiences for students.

MSPS professional staff must demonstrate respect for cultural values.

The professional staff of MSPS should reflect the various student cultures involved in MSPS.

In addition to professional staff being knowledgeable in their areas of responsibility, they should be knowledgeable about career planning and development, health promotion, group facilitation, leadership training and development, workshop design, social-interpersonal development, individual and group counseling, and campus resources.

MSPS professional staff should complete specific coursework in organizational development, counseling theory and practice, identity development theory, group dynamics, leadership development, human development, and research and assessment.

MSPS professional staff must have a personal commitment to justice and social change.

INTERNS OR GRADUATE ASSISTANTS

Degree- or credential-seeking interns or graduate assistants must be qualified by enrollment in an appropriate field of study and relevant experience. These students must be trained and supervised by professional personnel who possess applicable educational credentials and work experience and have supervisory experience. Supervisors must be cognizant of the dual roles interns and graduate assistants have as both student and employee.

Supervisors must
- adhere to parameters of students' job descriptions
- articulate intended learning outcomes in student job descriptions
- adhere to agreed-upon work hours and schedules
- offer flexible scheduling when circumstances necessitate

Supervisors and students must both agree to suitable compensation if circumstances necessitate additional hours.

The use of graduate assistants and interns should be

encouraged to expand staff abilities, provide peer role models, and give valuable pre-professional experience. Particular attention should be given to preparing all pre-professional assistants to be especially sensitive to cultural differences of focus populations.

STUDENT EMPLOYEES AND VOLUNTEERS

Student employees and volunteers must be carefully selected, trained, supervised, and evaluated. Students must have access to a supervisor. Student employees and volunteers must be provided clear job descriptions, pre-service training based on assessed needs, and continuing development.

Student employees and volunteers from multicultural groups should be utilized.

Student employees must be assigned responsibilities that are within their scope of competence.

Training and activities for student employees could include retreats, leadership classes, and workshops.

Part 5. Ethics

Multicultural Student Programs and Services (MSPS) must
- review applicable professional ethical standards and must adopt or develop and implement appropriate statements of ethical practice
- publish and adhere to statements of ethical practice and ensure their periodic review
- orient new personnel to relevant ethical standards and statements of ethical practice and related institutional policies

Statements of ethical standards must
- specify that MSPS personnel respect privacy and maintain confidentiality in communications and records as delineated by privacy laws
- specify limits on disclosure of information contained in students' records as well as requirements to disclose to appropriate authorities
- address conflicts of interest, or appearance thereof, by personnel in the performance of their work
- reflect the responsibility of personnel to be fair, objective, and impartial in their interactions with others
- reference management of institutional funds
- reference appropriate behavior regarding research and assessment with human participants, confidentiality of research and assessment data, and students' rights and responsibilities
- include the expectation that personnel confront and hold accountable other personnel who exhibit unethical behavior
- address issues surrounding scholarly integrity

MSPS personnel must
- employ ethical decision making in the performance of their duties
- inform users of programs and services of ethical

obligations and limitations emanating from codes and laws or from licensure requirements

- recognize and avoid conflicts of interest that could adversely influence their judgment or objectivity and, when unavoidable, recuse themselves from the situation
- perform their duties within the scope of their position, training, expertise, and competence
- make referrals when issues presented exceed the scope of the position

Part 6. Law, Policy, and Governance

Multicultural Student Programs and Services (MSPS) must be in compliance with laws, regulations, and policies that relate to their respective responsibilities and that pose legal obligations, limitations, risks, and liabilities for the institution as a whole. Examples include constitutional, statutory, regulatory, and case law; relevant law and orders emanating from codes and laws; and the institution's policies.

MSPS must have access to legal advice needed for personnel to carry out their assigned responsibilities.

MSPS must inform personnel, appropriate officials, and users of programs and services about existing and changing legal obligations, risks and liabilities, and limitations.

MSPS must inform personnel about professional liability insurance options and refer them to external sources if the institution does not provide coverage.

MSPS must have written policies and procedures on operations, transactions, or tasks that have legal implications.

MSPS must regularly review policies. The revision and creation of policies must be informed by best practices, available evidence, and policy issues in higher education.

MSPS must have procedures and guidelines consistent with institutional policy for responding to threats, emergencies, and crisis situations. Systems and procedures must be in place to disseminate timely and accurate information to students, other members of the institutional community, and appropriate external organizations during emergency situations.

Personnel must neither participate in nor condone any form of harassment or activity that demeans persons or creates an intimidating, hostile, or offensive environment.

MSPS must purchase or obtain permission to use copyrighted materials and instruments. References to copyrighted materials and instruments must include appropriate citations.

MSPS must inform personnel about internal and external governance organizations that affect programs and services.

Part 7. Diversity, Equity, and Access

Within the context of each institution's mission and in accordance with institutional policies and applicable codes and laws, Multicultural Student Programs and Services (MSPS) must create and maintain educational and work environments that are welcoming, accessible, inclusive, equitable, and free from harassment.

MSPS must not discriminate on the basis of disability; age; race; cultural identity; ethnicity; nationality; family educational history (e.g., first generation to attend college); political affiliation; religious affiliation; sex; sexual orientation; gender identity and expression; marital, social, economic, or veteran status; or any other basis included in institutional policies and codes and laws.

MSPS must

- advocate for sensitivity to multicultural and social justice concerns by the institution and its personnel
- ensure physical, program, and resource access for all constituents
- modify or remove policies, practices, systems, technologies, facilities, and structures that create barriers or produce inequities
- ensure that when facilities and structures cannot be modified, they do not impede access to programs, services, and resources
- establish goals for diversity, equity, and access
- foster communication and practices that enhance understanding of identity, culture, self-expression, and heritage
- promote respect for commonalities and differences among people within their historical and cultural contexts
- address the characteristics and needs of diverse constituents when establishing and implementing culturally relevant and inclusive programs, services, policies, procedures, and practices
- provide personnel with diversity, equity, and access training and hold personnel accountable for applying the training to their work
- respond to the needs of all constituents served when establishing hours of operation and developing methods of delivering programs, services, and resources
- recognize the needs of distance and online learning students by directly providing or assisting them to gain access to comparable services and resources

Part 8. Internal and External Relations

Multicultural Student Programs and Services (MSPS) must reach out to individuals, groups, communities, and organizations internal and external to the institution to

- establish, maintain, and promote understanding and effective relations with those that have a significant interest in or potential effect on the

students or other constituents served by the programs and services
- garner support and resources for programs and services as defined by the mission
- collaborate in offering or improving programs and services to meet the needs of students and other constituents and to achieve program and student outcomes
- engage diverse individuals, groups, communities, and organizations to enrich the educational environment and experiences of students and other constituents
- disseminate information about the programs and services

MSPS professional staff members must coordinate, or where appropriate, collaborate with staff and faculty members and other staff in providing services and programs to meet the needs of multicultural students.

MSPS must identify and address retention issues of underserved populations and advocate for the creation of welcoming surrounding community.

This could include MSPS involvement in community collaborations and coalitions that confront racism, sexism, and homophobia. Community services necessities should be available for all students.

Promotional and descriptive information must be accurate and free of deception and misrepresentation.

MSPS must have procedures and guidelines consistent with institutional policy for
- communicating with the media
- distributing information through print, broadcast, and online sources
- contracting with external organizations for delivery of programs and services
- cultivating, soliciting, and managing gifts
- applying to and managing funds from grants

Part 9. Financial Relations

Multicultural Student Programs and Services (MSPS) must have funding to accomplish the mission and goals.

In establishing and prioritizing funding resources, MSPS must conduct comprehensive analyses to determine
- unmet needs of the unit
- relevant expenditures
- external and internal resources
- impact on students and the institution

MSPS must use the budget as a planning tool to reflect commitment to the mission and goals of the programs and services and of the institution.

MSPS must administer funds in accordance with established institutional accounting procedures.

MSPS must demonstrate efficient and effective use and responsible stewardship of fiscal resources consistent with

institutional protocols.

Financial reports must provide an accurate financial overview of the organization and provide clear, understandable, and timely data upon which personnel can plan and make informed decisions.

Procurement procedures must
- be consistent with institutional policies
- ensure that purchases comply with laws and codes for usability and access
- ensure that the institution receives value for the funds spent
- consider information available for comparing the ethical and environmental impact of products and services purchased

As programs grow and student diversity increases, institutions should increase financial support.

Part 10. Technology

Multicultural Student Programs and Services (MSPS) must have technology to support the achievement of their mission and goals. The technology and its use must comply with institutional policies and procedures and with relevant codes and laws.

MSPS must use technologies to
- provide updated information regarding mission, location, staffing, programs, services, and official contacts to students and other constituents in accessible formats
- provide an avenue for students and other constituents to communicate sensitive information in a secure format
- enhance the delivery of programs and services for all students

MSPS must
- back up data on a regular basis
- adhere to institutional policies regarding ethical and legal use of technology
- articulate policies and procedures for protecting the confidentiality and security of information
- implement a replacement plan and cycle for all technology with attention to sustainability
- incorporate accessibility features into technology-based programs and services

When providing student access to technology, MSPS must
- have policies on the use of technology that are clear, easy to understand, and available to all students
- provide information or referral to support services for those needing assistance in accessing or using technology
- provide instruction or training on how to use the technology
- inform students of implications of misuse of technologies

Part 11. Facilities and Equipment

Multicultural Student Programs and Services' (MSPS) facilities must be intentionally designed and located in suitable, accessible, and safe spaces that demonstrate universal design and support the program's mission and goals.

Facilities must be designed to engage various constituents and promote learning.

Wherever it is located, MSPS should provide a safe haven for students. In addition, MSPS should provide a place for all students to learn to become more multi-culturally competent.

Personnel must have workspaces that are suitably located and accessible, well equipped, adequate in size, and designed to support their work and responsibilities.

Adequate space should be provided for a resource library, private individual consultations, group workshops, and work areas for support staff. Many of the activities offered by MSPS require the same level of privacy as individual and group counseling.

The design of the facilities must guarantee the security and privacy of records and ensure the confidentiality of sensitive information and conversations. Personnel must be able to secure their work.

MSPS must incorporate sustainable practices in use of facilities and purchase of equipment. Facilities and equipment must be evaluated on an established cycle and be in compliance with codes, laws, and accepted practices for access, health, safety, and security.

When acquiring capital equipment, MSPS must take into account expenses related to regular maintenance and life cycle costs.

Part 12. Assessment

Multicultural Student Programs and Services (MSPS) must develop assessment plans and processes.

Assessment plans must articulate an ongoing cycle of assessment activities.

General evaluation of the multicultural student programs and services must be conducted on a regularly scheduled basis. MSPS must solicit evaluative data from current multicultural students.

MSPS must
- specify programmatic goals and intended outcomes
- identify student learning and development outcomes
- employ multiple measures and methods
- develop manageable processes for gathering, interpreting, and evaluating data
- document progress toward achievement of goals and outcomes
- interpret and use assessment results to

demonstrate accountability
- report aggregated results to respondent groups and stakeholders
- use assessment results to inform planning and decision-making
- assess effectiveness of implemented changes
- provide evidence of improvement of programs and services

Assessments may involve many methods. Survey instruments, interviews, behavioral observations, or some combination of these methods may be appropriate in a given institution.

MSPS should solicit evaluative and developmental data from alumni.

Assessments must be conducted in a manner to assure an effective response.

MSPS should consult with the population to be assessed on the nature of the assessment.

MSPS should assess the degree of congruence between students' educational goals and offerings of the institution and communicate the results of the assessment to appropriate decision makers.

MSPS must employ ethical practices in the assessment process.

MSPS must have access to adequate fiscal, human, professional development, and technological resources to develop and implement assessment plans.

General Standards revised in 2014;
MSPS (formerly Minority Student Programs) content developed/ revised in 1986, 1997, & 2006

Orientation Programs
CAS Contextual Statement

To understand current trends in orientation programs, it is helpful to view today's practice within an historical context. The history of orientation programs in the United States is virtually as old as the history of the country's colleges and universities. In the 1640s at Harvard, dons and tutors were expected to "counsel and befriend the young lads" in order to support them in their transition to college (Morrison, 1936). More formal orientation programming can be traced to both Harvard and Boston College in 1888 (Butts, 1971; Drake, 1966). Harvard is credited with creating a system by which current students supported new students in their transition to college (Upcraft, Gardner, & Associates, 1989), a model that persists today. Later in the 19th century, Harvard institutionalized faculty-student contact by assigning faculty members educational and administrative responsibilities outside the classroom.

Today's orientation programs have responded to changing demographics by modifying institutional agendas. Programs have evolved from simply providing students with individualized faculty attention to focusing on important issues and responding to the needs of an increasingly diverse student and family population. Many programs rely extensively on highly trained and motivated peer groups (orientation leaders) in the achievement of the orientation mission. Today there exists a professional organization called the Association for Orientation, Transition and Retention in Higher Education (NODA). Founded in 1976 and a founding member of CAS in 1977, NODA provides education, leadership, and professional development in the field of student orientation, transition, and retention.

Today, most orientation programs provide a clear and cogent introduction to the intellectual, cultural, and social facets of the institution. Orientation is viewed as an important tool for student recruitment, acculturation, and retention (Jacobs, 2003). Most institutions include academic advising and registration for classes in their orientation programs as an impetus for active participation. Many institutions are implementing continuing orientation programs via a first-year experience program and/or course (Perigo & Upcraft, 1989). Because of social and demographic changes and to address the needs of students, colleges and universities are taking steps to encourage student and parent/guardian and family attendance by expanding orientation programs beyond the singular academic perspective to address many issues of wider interest and concern related to matriculation, student support services, and campus life. A growing trend has been the high level of attendance at orientation programs by parents/guardians and families who often are very involved in the transition process (Merriman, 2007). To better address these needs, many institutions deliver parent/guardian and family orientation programs as a complement to student programs.

One of the most important changes seen over the past several decades is that orientation is now viewed as a comprehensive process rather than as a singular program. Examples include programs lasting from one day to a week in length, welcome weeks, and other activities that engage students in a variety of ways to introduce them to the expectations, culture, and traditions of the institution. Increasingly colleges and universities are developing more expansive and extended orientation programs that begin with post-acceptance communication and continue throughout the first year. These programs address the diverse transitional needs of students and their families.

What trends will guide future approaches to orientation programs? It is certain that acculturation and retention will continue to be a major focus in the development of orientation programs. Orientation professionals will need to evaluate ways to deliver orientation content as new technologies emerge that change how, when, and where students learn. Funding for orientation programs will continue to be a matter of concern. Demographic changes in institutions of higher education and society at large will require new institutional and programmatic responses. Likewise, attempts to foster environments responsive to the individual needs of students and families will have a significant effect on orientation programming. Increasingly, students are non-traditional, older, working, married, part-time, and living away from campus. Maintaining current orientation and transitional programs by simply reacting to change does little to address the interests of all constituents. For example, as on-line education grows, institutions must envision new types of orientation programs to help students succeed in a technology-based, asynchronous learning environment that requires new ways of communicating with classmates and instructors. New and creative programs and methodologies must be assessed if the personal and educational needs of new students and their families are to be met.

Research, assessment, and evaluation are vital to effective orientation programs and must include evidence of program impact both immediate and longitudinal on the achievement of student learning and developmental outcomes. The CAS Orientation Programs Standards and Guidelines that follow have utility for national and international institutions and provide criteria by which to evaluate the quality, effectiveness, and appropriateness of orientation programs.

References, Readings, and Resources

Butts, T. H. (1971). *Personnel service review: New practices in student orientation.* Retrieved from ERIC database. (ED057416)

Drake, R. W. (1966). *Review of the literature for freshmen orientation practices in the United States.* Fort Collins, CO: Colorado State University. Retrieved from ERIC database. (ED030920).

Jacobs, B. (2003). New student orientation in the twenty-first century. In G. Kramer & Associates (Eds.), *Student academic services,* 127-146, San Francisco, CA: Jossey-Bass.

Merriman, L. (2007). Managing parents 101: Minimizing interference and maximizing good will. *Leadership Exchange, 5* (1), 14–19.

Harlow, H. F. (1983). Fundamentals for preparing psychology journal articles. *Journal of Comparative and Physiological Psychology, 55,* 893-896.

Hatch, C. & Skipper, T. (2004). *Empowering parents of first-year college students: A guide for success.* National Resource Center for First Year Experience and Student in Transition. Columbia, SC: University of South Carolina.

Perigo, D., & Upcraft, M. (1989). Orientation programs. In M. L. Upcraft, J. N. Gardner, & Associates (Eds.), *The freshman year experience,* 82-94, San Francisco, CA: Jossey-Bass.

Upcraft, M. L., Gardner, J. N., & Associates. (1989). *The freshman year experience.* San Francisco, CA: Jossey-Bass.

Designing successful transitions: A guide for orienting students to college (3rd ed.). Columbia, SC: University of South Carolina.

NODA - Association for Orientation, Transition and Retention in Higher Education: www.nodaweb.org

NODA - Association for Orientation, Transition and Retention in Higher Education Directors Data Bank. Retrieved from www.nodaweb.org/?page=Databank

NODA - Association for Orientation, Transition and Retention in Higher Education: *The Orientation Review.* Retrieved from www.nodaweb.org

NODA - Association for Orientation, Transition and Retention in Higher Education: *Orientation Planning Manual.* Minneapolis: University of Minnesota.

Contextual Statement Contributors

Current Edition
Deb Boykin, William & Mary, ACUHO-I
Ann Hower, University of Michigan, NODA
Deanie Kepler, Southern Methodist University, AHEPPP
Janet Marling, National Association for the Study of Transfer Students, ASTS
Jeffrey Pittman, Regent University, NACAS
Jim Walters, Montgomery College - Takoma Park/Silver Spring, NSEE

Previous Editions:
Ann Hower, University of Michigan, NODA
Gerry Strumpf, University of Maryland, College Park, NODA
Chris Boyer, NODA
Ralph Busby, Stephen F. Austiin State University, NODA

Orientation Programs
CAS Standards and Guidelines

Part 1. Mission

Orientation Programs (OP) must facilitate the transition of new students into the institution; prepare students for the institution's educational opportunities and student responsibilities; and initiate the integration of new students into the intellectual, cultural, and social facets of the institution. Central to the mission of OP is the inclusion of parents/guardians and families in support of the new student. OP must also contribute to institutional enrollment management, including retention.

OP must develop, disseminate, implement, and regularly review their missions, which must be consistent with the mission of the institution and with applicable professional standards. The mission must be appropriate for the institution's students and other constituents. Mission statements must reference student learning and development.

Part 2. Program

To achieve their mission, Orientation Programs (OP) must contribute to

- students' formal education, which includes both the curriculum and the co-curriculum
- student progression and timely completion of educational goals
- preparation of students for their careers, citizenship, and lives
- student learning and development

To contribute to student learning and development, OP must

- identify relevant and desirable student learning and development outcomes
- articulate how the student learning and development outcomes align with the six CAS student learning and development domains and related dimensions
- assess relevant and desirable student learning and development
- provide evidence of impact on outcomes
- articulate contributions to or support of student learning and development in the domains not specifically assessed
- use evidence gathered to create strategies for improvement of programs and services

STUDENT LEARNING AND DEVELOPMENT DOMAINS AND DIMENSIONS

Domain: knowledge acquisition, integration, construction, and application

- Dimensions: understanding knowledge from a range of disciplines; connecting knowledge to other knowledge, ideas, and experiences; constructing knowledge; and relating knowledge to daily life

Domain: cognitive complexity

- Dimensions: critical thinking, reflective thinking, effective reasoning, and creativity

Domain: intrapersonal development

- Dimensions: realistic self-appraisal, self-understanding, and self-respect; identity development; commitment to ethics and integrity; and spiritual awareness

Domain: interpersonal competence

- Dimensions: meaningful relationships, interdependence, collaboration, and effective leadership

Domain: humanitarianism and civic engagement

- Dimensions: understanding and appreciation of cultural and human differences, social responsibility, global perspective, and sense of civic responsibility

Domain: practical competence

- Dimensions: pursuing goals, communicating effectively, technical competence, managing personal affairs, managing career development, demonstrating professionalism, maintaining health and wellness, and living a purposeful and satisfying life

[LD Outcomes: See *The Council for the Advancement of Standards Learning and Development Outcomes* statement for examples of outcomes related to these domains and dimensions.]

OP must be

- intentionally designed
- guided by theories and knowledge of learning and development
- integrated into the life of the institution
- reflective of developmental and demographic profiles of the student population
- responsive to needs of individuals, populations with distinct needs, and relevant constituencies
- delivered using multiple formats, strategies, and contexts
- designed to provide universal access

OP must collaborate with colleagues and departments across the institution to promote student learning and development, persistence, and success.

OP must aid students and their parents/guardians and families in understanding the nature and purpose of higher education, the mission of the institution, and their membership in the community. OP must articulate the institution's expectations of students and provide information that clearly identifies relevant administrative policies, procedures, and programs to enable students to make well-reasoned and well-informed choices.

Such expectations may include scholarship, integrity, conduct, financial obligations, and the ethical use of technology.

OP should design and facilitate opportunities for new students to discuss their expectations and perceptions of the institution and to clarify their personal and educational goals.

OP must inform students about the institution's history, traditions, and culture to facilitate affinity and integration.

OP must provide new students, as well as their parents/guardians and families, with information about laws and policies regarding educational records and other protected information.

OP should emphasize the independence of students in accomplishing their goals while acknowledging their interdependence with their peers and families.

OP must use qualified faculty members, staff, or peer advisors to explain class scheduling, registration processes, and campus life.

OP should assist students in the selection of appropriate courses and course levels, making use of relevant placement examinations, entrance examinations, and academic records.

OP must inform new students, as well as their parents/guardians and families, about the availability of institutional services and programs. Information about personal health, disability resources, safety, and security must also be included.

OP must design and facilitate intentional opportunities for new students to interact with fellow new students as well as continuing students, faculty, and staff members.

OP must provide information about the physical layout of the campus, including the location and purposes of campus facilities, support services, co-curricular venues, and administrative offices. For students enrolling in online programs, OP must provide information about how to access virtual support services and administrative offices.

OP must provide information about technology resources used to conduct institutional business and scholarly work including information about student information systems, library resources, electronic databases, email, and online course software.

Information about how to manage responsible and ethical use of institutional technology resources should also be presented.

OP must introduce students to the learning and development opportunities that will occur throughout

the collegiate experience.

OP should continue as a process to address transitional events, issues, and needs. The orientation process should include pre-enrollment, entry, and post-matriculation services and programs.

Components of OP may include welcome programs, credit and non-credit courses, seminars, adventure programs, service-learning experiences, summer or common reading programs, living-learning communities, interest groups, web-based educational opportunities, comprehensive mailings, electronic communications, and campus visitations and may be administered through multiple institutional offices.

OP must address the characteristics and needs of diverse student populations when establishing programs, services, procedures, and practices.

OP should take into account needs of international students as well as students enrolled in online programs when designing and delivering programs.

First-year, transfer, and entering graduate students, as well as their parents/guardians and families, should be served as distinct populations.

OP should collaborate with offices that coordinate supplemental orientation programs.

Part 3. Organization and Leadership

To achieve program and student learning and development outcomes, Orientation Programs (OP) must be purposefully structured for effectiveness. OP must have clearly stated and current
- **goals and outcomes**
- **policies and procedures**
- **responsibilities and performance expectations for personnel**
- **organizational charts demonstrating clear channels of authority**

Leaders must model ethical behavior and institutional citizenship.

Leaders with organizational authority for OP must provide strategic planning, management and supervision, and program advancement.

Strategic Planning
- articulate a vision and mission that drive short- and long-term planning
- set goals and objectives based on the needs of the populations served, intended student learning and development outcomes, and program outcomes
- facilitate continuous development, implementation, and assessment of program effectiveness and goal attainment congruent with institutional mission and strategic plans
- promote environments that provide opportunities

for student learning, development, and engagement

- develop, adapt, and improve programs and services in response to the changing needs of populations served and evolving institutional priorities
- include diverse perspectives to inform decision making

Management and Supervision

- plan, allocate, and monitor the use of fiscal, physical, human, intellectual, and technological resources
- manage human resource processes including recruitment, selection, professional development, supervision, performance planning, succession planning, evaluation, recognition, and reward
- influence others to contribute to the effectiveness and success of the unit
- empower professional, support, and student personnel to become effective leaders
- encourage and support collaboration with colleagues and departments across the institution
- encourage and support scholarly contributions to the profession
- identify and address individual, organizational, and environmental conditions that foster or inhibit mission achievement
- use current and valid evidence to inform decisions
- incorporate sustainability practices in the management and design of programs, services, and facilities
- understand appropriate technologies and integrate them into programs and services
- be knowledgeable about codes and laws relevant to programs and services and ensure that programs and services meet those requirements
- assess and take action to mitigate potential risks

Program Advancement

- advocate for and actively promote the mission and goals of the programs and services
- inform stakeholders about issues affecting practice
- facilitate processes to reach consensus where wide support is needed
- advocate for representation in strategic planning initiatives at divisional and institutional levels

Coordination of OP must occur even though a number of offices may be involved in the delivery of structured activities.

All institutional offices involved in program delivery should be involved in the review of administrative policies and procedures as related to their roles within the orientation program.

The size, nature, and complexity of the institution should guide the administrative scope and structure of OP.

Part 4. Human Resources

Orientation Programs (OP) must be staffed adequately by individuals qualified to accomplish mission and goals.

OP must have access to technical and support personnel adequate to accomplish their mission.

Within institutional guidelines, OP must

- establish procedures for personnel recruitment and selection, training, performance planning, and evaluation
- set expectations for supervision and performance
- provide personnel access to continuing and advanced education and appropriate professional development opportunities to improve their competence, skills, and leadership capacity
- consider work/life options available to personnel (e.g., compressed work schedules, flextime, job sharing, remote work, or telework) to promote recruitment and retention of personnel

Faculty member involvement in the development and delivery of OP is crucial to its success. Faculty members should be included as part of the overall planning and, where possible, staffing.

Administrators of OP must

- ensure that all personnel have updated position descriptions
- implement recruitment and selection/hiring strategies that produce a workforce inclusive of under-represented populations
- develop promotion practices that are fair, inclusive, proactive, and non-discriminatory

Personnel responsible for delivery of OP must have written performance goals, objectives, and outcomes for each year's performance cycle to be used to plan, review, and evaluate work and performance. The performance plan must be updated regularly to reflect changes during the performance cycle.

Results of individual personnel evaluations must be used to recognize personnel performance, address performance issues, implement individual and/or collective personnel development and training programs, and inform the assessment of programs and services.

OP personnel, when hired and throughout their employment, must receive appropriate and thorough training.

OP personnel, including student employees and volunteers, must have access to resources or receive specific training on

- institutional policies pertaining to functions or activities they support
- privacy and confidentiality policies
- laws regarding access to student records
- policies and procedures for dealing with sensitive

institutional information

- policies and procedures related to technology used to store or access student records and institutional data
- how and when to refer those in need of additional assistance to qualified personnel and have access to a supervisor for assistance in making these judgments
- systems and technologies necessary to perform their assigned responsibilities
- ethical and legal uses of technology

OP personnel must engage in continuing professional development activities to keep abreast of the research, theories, legislation, policies, and developments that affect their programs and services.

Administrators of OP must ensure that personnel are knowledgeable about and trained in safety, emergency procedures, and crisis prevention and response. Risk management efforts must address identification of threatening conduct or behavior and must incorporate a system for responding to and reporting such behaviors.

OP personnel must be knowledgeable of and trained in safety and emergency procedures for securing and vacating facilities.

PROFESSIONAL PERSONNEL

OP professional personnel either must hold an earned graduate or professional degree in a field relevant to their position or must possess an appropriate combination of educational credentials and related work experience.

INTERNS OR GRADUATE ASSISTANTS

Degree- or credential-seeking interns or graduate assistants must be qualified by enrollment in an appropriate field of study and relevant experience. These students must be trained and supervised by professional personnel who possess applicable educational credentials and work experience and have supervisory experience. Supervisors must be cognizant of the dual roles interns and graduate assistants have as both student and employee.

Supervisors must
- adhere to parameters of students' job descriptions
- articulate intended learning outcomes in student job descriptions
- adhere to agreed-upon work hours and schedules
- offer flexible scheduling when circumstances necessitate

Supervisors and students must both agree to suitable compensation if circumstances necessitate additional hours.

STUDENT EMPLOYEES AND VOLUNTEERS

Student employees and volunteers must be carefully selected, trained, supervised, and evaluated. Students must have access to a supervisor. Student employees and volunteers must be provided clear job descriptions, preservice training based on assessed needs, and continuing development.

Student staff must be informed as to the limits of their authority, the expectation for appropriate role modeling, and their potential influence on new students.

Part 5. Ethics

Orientation Programs (OP) must
- review applicable professional ethical standards and must adopt or develop and implement appropriate statements of ethical practice
- publish and adhere to statements of ethical practice and ensure their periodic review
- orient new personnel to relevant ethical standards and statements of ethical practice and related institutional policies

Statements of ethical standards must
- specify that OP personnel respect privacy and maintain confidentiality in communications and records as delineated by privacy laws
- specify limits on disclosure of information contained in students' records as well as requirements to disclose to appropriate authorities
- address conflicts of interest, or appearance thereof, by personnel in the performance of their work
- reflect the responsibility of personnel to be fair, objective, and impartial in their interactions with others
- reference management of institutional funds
- reference appropriate behavior regarding research and assessment with human participants, confidentiality of research and assessment data, and students' rights and responsibilities
- include the expectation that personnel confront and hold accountable other personnel who exhibit unethical behavior
- address issues surrounding scholarly integrity

OP personnel must
- employ ethical decision making in the performance of their duties
- inform users of programs and services of ethical obligations and limitations emanating from codes and laws or from licensure requirements
- recognize and avoid conflicts of interest that could adversely influence their judgment or objectivity and, when unavoidable, recuse themselves from the situation
- perform their duties within the scope of their position, training, expertise, and competence
- make referrals when issues presented exceed the scope of the position

Part 6. Law, Policy, and Governance

Orientation Programs (OP) must be in compliance with laws, regulations, and policies that relate to their respective responsibilities and that pose legal obligations, limitations, risks, and liabilities for the institution as a whole. Examples include constitutional, statutory, regulatory, and case law; relevant law and orders emanating from codes and laws; and the institution's policies.

OP must have access to legal advice needed for personnel to carry out their assigned responsibilities.

OP must inform personnel, appropriate officials, and users of programs and services about existing and changing legal obligations, risks and liabilities, and limitations.

OP must inform personnel about professional liability insurance options and refer them to external sources if the institution does not provide coverage.

OP must have written policies and procedures on operations, transactions, or tasks that have legal implications.

OP must regularly review policies. The revision and creation of policies must be informed by best practices, available evidence, and policy issues in higher education.

OP must have procedures and guidelines consistent with institutional policy for responding to threats, emergencies, and crisis situations. Systems and procedures must be in place to disseminate timely and accurate information to students, other members of the institutional community, and appropriate external organizations during emergency situations.

Personnel must neither participate in nor condone any form of harassment or activity that demeans persons or creates an intimidating, hostile, or offensive environment.

OP must purchase or obtain permission to use copyrighted materials and instruments. References to copyrighted materials and instruments must include appropriate citations.

OP must inform personnel about internal and external governance organizations that affect programs and services.

Part 7. Diversity, Equity, and Access

Within the context of each institution's mission and in accordance with institutional policies and applicable codes and laws, Orientation Programs (OP) must create and maintain educational and work environments that are welcoming, accessible, inclusive, equitable, and free from harassment.

OP must not discriminate on the basis of disability; age; race; cultural identity; ethnicity; nationality; family educational history (e.g., first generation to attend college);

political affiliation; religious affiliation; sex; sexual orientation; gender identity and expression; marital, social, economic, or veteran status; or any other basis included in institutional policies and codes and laws.

OP must

- advocate for sensitivity to multicultural and social justice concerns by the institution and its personnel
- ensure physical, program, and resource access for all constituents
- modify or remove policies, practices, systems, technologies, facilities, and structures that create barriers or produce inequities
- ensure that when facilities and structures cannot be modified, they do not impede access to programs, services, and resources
- establish goals for diversity, equity, and access
- foster communication and practices that enhance understanding of identity, culture, self-expression, and heritage
- promote respect for commonalities and differences among people within their historical and cultural contexts
- address the characteristics and needs of diverse constituents when establishing and implementing culturally relevant and inclusive programs, services, policies, procedures, and practices
- provide personnel with diversity, equity, and access training and hold personnel accountable for applying the training to their work
- respond to the needs of all constituents served when establishing hours of operation and developing methods of delivering programs, services, and resources
- recognize the needs of distance and online learning students by directly providing or assisting them to gain access to comparable services and resources

Part 8. Internal and External Relations

Orientation Programs (OP) must reach out to individuals, groups, communities, and organizations internal and external to the institution to

- establish, maintain, and promote understanding and effective relations with those that have a significant interest in or potential effect on the students or other constituents served by the programs and services
- garner support and resources for programs and services as defined by the mission
- collaborate in offering or improving programs and services to meet the needs of students and other constituents and to achieve program and student outcomes
- engage diverse individuals, groups, communities, and organizations to enrich the educational environment and experiences of students and other

- constituents
- disseminate information about the programs and services

Orientation should be an institution-wide process of planning and implementation that systematically involves student affairs, academic affairs, and other administrative units, such as parent and family programs, public safety, physical plant, athletics, college bookstore, and the business office.

Promotional and descriptive information must be accurate and free of deception and misrepresentation.
Orientation Programs (OP) must have procedures and guidelines consistent with institutional policy for
- communicating with the media
- distributing information through print, broadcast, and online sources
- contracting with external organizations for delivery of programs and services
- cultivating, soliciting, and managing gifts
- applying to and managing funds from grants

Part 9. Financial Resources

Orientation Programs (OP) must have funding to accomplish the mission and goals.

In establishing and prioritizing funding resources, OP must conduct comprehensive analyses to determine
- unmet needs of the unit
- relevant expenditures
- external and internal resources
- impact on students and the institution

OP must use the budget as a planning tool to reflect commitment to the mission and goals of the programs and services and of the institution.

OP must administer funds in accordance with established institutional accounting procedures.

OP must demonstrate efficient and effective use and responsible stewardship of fiscal resources consistent with institutional protocols.

Financial reports must provide an accurate financial overview of the organization and provide clear, understandable, and timely data upon which personnel can plan and make informed decisions.

Procurement procedures must
- be consistent with institutional policies
- ensure that purchases comply with laws and codes for usability and access
- ensure that the institution receives value for the funds spent
- consider information available for comparing the ethical and environmental impact of products and services purchased

OP should be funded through institutional resources. In addition to institutional funding, other sources may be considered, including state appropriations, student fees, user fees, donations, contributions, concession and store sales, rentals, and dues.

When overnight programs require students and their parents/guardians and families to stay on campus, room and board costs may be recovered directly from participants.

Resources, such as grants, loans, or fee waivers should be available to those students and their families who are unable to afford the cost associated with orientation.

Part 10. Technology

Orientation Programs (OP) must have technology to support the achievement of their mission and goals. The technology and its use must comply with institutional policies and procedures and with relevant codes and laws.

OP must use technologies to
- provide updated information regarding mission, location, staffing, programs, services, and official contacts to students and other constituents in accessible formats
- provide an avenue for students and other constituents to communicate sensitive information in a secure format
- enhance the delivery of programs and services for all students

OP must
- back up data on a regular basis
- adhere to institutional policies regarding ethical and legal use of technology
- articulate policies and procedures for protecting the confidentiality and security of information
- implement a replacement plan and cycle for all technology with attention to sustainability
- incorporate accessibility features into technology-based programs and services

When providing student access to technology, OP must
- have policies on the use of technology that are clear, easy to understand, and available to all students
- provide information or referral to support services for those needing assistance in accessing or using technology
- provide instruction or training on how to use the technology
- inform students of implications of misuse of technologies

Part 11. Facilities and Equipment

Orientation Programs' (OP) facilities must be intentionally designed and located in suitable, accessible, and safe spaces that demonstrate universal design and support the program's mission and goals.

Facilities must be designed to engage various constituents and promote learning.

Personnel must have workspaces that are suitably located and accessible, well equipped, adequate in size, and designed to support their work and responsibilities.

The design of the facilities must guarantee the security and privacy of records and ensure the confidentiality of sensitive information and conversations. Personnel must be able to secure their work.

OP must incorporate sustainable practices in use of facilities and purchase of equipment. Facilities and equipment must be evaluated on an established cycle and be in compliance with codes, laws, and accepted practices for access, health, safety, and security.

When acquiring capital equipment, OP must take into account expenses related to regular maintenance and life cycle costs.

Cooperation from the campus community is necessary to provide appropriate facilities to implement orientation programs.

Whenever possible, a single accessible location to house personnel and provide adequate workspace should be conveniently located and suitable for its high level of interaction with the public.

Institutions should give OP priority in scheduling or reserving campus facilities for formal orientation programming.

Part 12. Assessment

Orientation Programs (OP) must develop assessment plans and processes.

Assessment plans must articulate an ongoing cycle of assessment activities.

OP must
- specify programmatic goals and intended outcomes
- identify student learning and development outcomes
- employ multiple measures and methods
- develop manageable processes for gathering, interpreting, and evaluating data
- document progress toward achievement of goals and outcomes
- interpret and use assessment results to demonstrate accountability
- report aggregated results to respondent groups and stakeholders
- use assessment results to inform planning and decision-making
- assess effectiveness of implemented changes
- provide evidence of improvement of programs and services

A representative cross-section of appropriate people from the campus community should be involved in reviews of orientation programs.

OP must employ ethical practices in the assessment process.

OP must have access to adequate fiscal, human, professional development, and technological resources to develop and implement assessment plans.

General Standards revised in 2014;
OP content developed/revised in 1986, 1996, 2005, & 2013

Parent and Family Programs
CAS Contextual Statement

Parent involvement at the college level is not a new concept. Parents and families of college students have been involved in campus life since the first child set off to engage in higher learning. How the parental and family involvement manifested itself within the life of the institution has changed throughout the history of higher education. Beginning with the basic tenet of *in loco parentis*, as expressed through the faculty as monitors of student behavior, to the uprising of student rights as expressed in the Family Education Rights and Privacy Act (FERPA) of the 1970s, to a campus environment of *in consortio cum parentibus* (Henning 2007), parents and families have made their influence known with faculty, staff, and administrators on campuses across the nation.

As early as 1920, Mothers' Clubs and Dads' Clubs were active at such universities as Texas A & M, Southern Methodist University, and Stanford University. These early organizations, which sought to bring the stability and security of the family home to the campus, became the foundations of and models for the parent and family organizations active today on these and many other American campuses. As they evolved, these early groups began to incorporate fundraising for campus improvements and scholarships into their clubs' agendas. The Stanford Mothers' Club, after two years of taking convalescing students into their own homes, decided to provide and fund a Men's and a Women's Rest Home that, after 35 years, became part of the permanent Stanford Student Health facilities. This is an example of how parents and family members working with faculty, staff, and administrators established an understanding of the mutual roles necessary to serve students well. Examples such as this have led to the development of today's Parent and Family Programs offices.

Research overwhelmingly demonstrates that parent involvement in children's learning is positively related to achievement. Further, the research shows that the more intensively parents are involved in their children's learning, the greater the achievement effects. At the elementary school level, "family involvement is linked broadly with school achievement across different socioeconomic and ethnic groups" (Harvard Family Research Project, Winter 2006-2007, p. 3).

Students' perceptions of their parents' values about achievement are strongly related to motivation and competence (Harvard Family Research Project, Spring 2007). Family involvement during adolescence is a predictor of such positive outcomes as school success and positive social and emotional outcomes.

Adolescents with supportive parents have higher grade point averages, and they exhibit higher rates of self-reliance, identity formation, school performance, and positive career-planning aspirations, They are more likely to discuss information with their parents that will keep them out of trouble, and they have higher rates of college enrollment (Harvard Family Research Project, Spring 2007).

During the college years, family support continues to be critical. Traditional student development theories support separation from the family for the purpose of individuation and developing as an independent adult. In contrast, other theories suggest that family involvement continues to have a positive effect during the college years, even supporting the goals of individuation. Attachment theory, for example, suggests that for students leaving home, having parents as a secure base may actually support rather than threaten the development of competence and autonomy (Kenny & Donaldson, 1992).

Research proves that parent/family involvement is an important resource that improves a student's productivity (Astone, Nathanson, Schoen, & Kim, 1999; Bourdieu & Passeron, 1977; Coleman, 1988; Lareau, 2001; Lin, 2001; Perna & Titus, 2005). Students bring a bank of social capital to their college experience that is earned through their involvement with family, school and community friends, and high school teachers. Some of the positive influences of this social capital include engagement with students' schools and communities, supportive families, and greater trust in the institution (Goddard, 2003). Successful college admittance at selective institutions rarely occurs without a structural network that includes a high level of commitment and involvement from a student's parents and family (Perna & Titus, 2005). Therefore, creating an environment for overall student success should include a mutually beneficial and appropriate parent and family program. The Parent Program Director at one of the country's largest public institutions says, "When we treat parents as valued partners and give them information about student development, they can be our best allies in student success, retention, and graduation" (Savage, 2007, personal communication).

Parents and families of undergraduate students are important stakeholders in institutions of higher education. Most importantly, evidence demonstrates that students benefit from the involvement of their parents in their education more now than ever before (National Survey of Student Engagement, Annual Report 2007). Additionally, parents have a significant emotional and financial investment in their student's success. Finally, parents discuss the effectiveness and quality of the institution in their communities with friends, prospective students, donors, voters, and taxpayers. When an institution commits to involving parents in appropriate and effective ways, it produces an outcome of parental support for student success and a group of life-long advocates eager to promote and support its vision and mission.

The mission of Parent and Family Programs should be the success and development of the college undergraduate student through education, communication, and the collaboration of the wisdom of parents and families with the expertise and wisdom of the university and its resources. The CAS standards and guidelines that follow provide a basis for institutional self-assessment and program development.

References, Readings, and Resources

Astone, N. A. , Nathanson, C. A., Schoen, R., & Kim, Y. J. (1999). Family demography, social theory, and investment in social capital. *Population and Development, 25*, 1–31.

Bourdieu, P., & Passeron, J. (1977). *Reproduction in education, society and culture.* (Nice, R., Trans.). Beverly Hills, CA: Sage.

Coleman, J. S. (1988). Social capital in the creation of human capital. *The American Journal of Sociology, 94*, S95-120.

Goddard, R. D. (2003). Relational networks, social trust, and norms: A social capital perspective on students' chances of academic success. *Educational Evaluation and Policy Analysis, 25*(1), 59–74.

Harvard Family Research Project, Winter 2006-2007. *Family involvement in elementary school children's education.* No. 2 in a series. Retrieved from http://www.hfrp.org/publications-resources/publications-series/family-involvement-makes-a-difference/family-involvement-in-elementary-school-children-s-education

Harvard Family Research Project, Spring 2007. *Family Involvement in middle and high school students' education.* No. 3 in a series. Retrieved from http://www.hfrp.org/publications-resources/publications-series/family-involvement-makes-a-difference/family-involvement-in-middle-and-high-school-students-education

Henning, G. (2007). Is in corsortio cum parentibus the new in loco parentis? *NASPA Journal, 44*(3), 538–560.

Horvat, E. M. & Lareau, A. (1999). Moments of social inclusion and exclusion: Race, class, and cultural capital in family-school relationships. *Sociology of Education, 72*, 37–53.

Kenny, M. and Donaldson, G.A. (1992). The relationship of parental attachment and psychological separation to the adjustment of first-year college women. *Journal of College Student Development, 33*(5), 431-438.

Lareau, A. (2001). Linking Bourdieu's concept of capital to the broader field: The case of family-school relationships. In B. J. Biddle (Ed.), *Social Class, Poverty, and Education: Policy and Practice* (pp. 77-100). New York: Routledge Falmer.

Lin, N. (2001). Building a network theory of social capital. In N. Lin, K. Cook, & R. S. Burt, (Eds.), *Social capital: Theory and research* (pp. 3–30). New York, NY: Aldine de Gruyter.

National Survey of Student Engagement Annual Report. (2007). Retrieved from http://nsse.iub.edu/NSSE_2007_Annual_Report/docs/withhold/NSSE_2007_Annual_Report.pdf

Perna, L. W., & Titus, M. A. (2005). The relationship between parental involvement as social capital and college enrollment: An examination of racial and ethnic group differences. *Journal of Higher Education, 76*(5), 485–518.

Contextual Statement Contributors

Current Edition:
Marjorie Savage, University of Minnesota
Kristine E. Stewart, Miami University

Previous Editions:
Marjorie Savage, University of Minnesota
Kristine E. Stewart, Miami University

Parent and Family Programs
CAS Standards and Guidelines

Part 1. Mission

The mission of Parent and Family Programs (PFP) is to build collaboration between parents and families and the institution for the common goals of student learning, development, and success.

PFP must develop, disseminate, implement, and regularly review their missions, which must be consistent with the mission of the institution and with applicable professional standards. The mission must be appropriate for the institution's students and other constituents. Mission statements must reference student learning and development.

Inherent in the mission statement should be a vision for students and their families to develop lifelong affinity for the institution and its initiatives.

Part 2. Program

To achieve their mission, Parent and Family Programs (PFP) must contribute to
- students' formal education, which includes both the curriculum and the co-curriculum
- student progression and timely completion of educational goals
- preparation of students for their careers, citizenship, and lives
- student learning and development

To contribute to student learning and development, PFP must
- identify relevant and desirable student learning and development outcomes
- articulate how the student learning and development outcomes align with the six CAS student learning and development domains and related dimensions
- assess relevant and desirable student learning and development
- provide evidence of impact on outcomes
- articulate contributions to or support of student learning and development in the domains not specifically assessed
- use evidence gathered to create strategies for improvement of programs and services

STUDENT LEARNING AND DEVELOPMENT DOMAINS AND DIMENSIONS

Domain: knowledge acquisition, integration, construction, and application
- Dimensions: understanding knowledge from a range of disciplines; connecting knowledge to other knowledge, ideas, and experiences; constructing knowledge; and relating knowledge to daily life

Domain: cognitive complexity
- Dimensions: critical thinking, reflective thinking, effective reasoning, and creativity

Domain: intrapersonal development
- Dimensions: realistic self-appraisal, self-understanding, and self-respect; identity development; commitment to ethics and integrity; and spiritual awareness

Domain: interpersonal competence
- Dimensions: meaningful relationships, interdependence, collaboration, and effective leadership

Domain: humanitarianism and civic engagement
- Dimensions: understanding and appreciation of cultural and human differences, social responsibility, global perspective, and sense of civic responsibility

Domain: practical competence
- Dimensions: pursuing goals, communicating effectively, technical competence, managing personal affairs, managing career development, demonstrating professionalism, maintaining health and wellness, and living a purposeful and satisfying life

[LD Outcomes: See *The Council for the Advancement of Standards Learning and Development Outcomes* statement for examples of outcomes related to these domains and dimensions.]

PFP must be
- intentionally designed
- guided by theories and knowledge of learning and development
- integrated into the life of the institution
- reflective of developmental and demographic profiles of the student population
- responsive to needs of individuals, populations with distinct needs, and relevant constituencies
- delivered using multiple formats, strategies, and contexts
- designed to provide universal access

PFP must collaborate with colleagues and departments across the institution to promote student learning and development, persistence, and success.

PFP must help families maintain a connection to the institution.

PFP should provide programming and services in person and online, information about issues related to student learning and development, and opportunities to interact with other families and students.

Programming and services may include parent and family orientation programs, parent and family weekends, move-in and send-off events, educational workshops and seminars, newsletters, and fundraising. Other programs should be specifically reflective of the institutional history, traditions, and culture.

PFP must

- distribute information on a timely basis to take advantage of the impact of naturally occurring developmental stages experienced by students and families
- encourage parents and families to work with their student so that the student will learn to access institutional resources independently
- assist parents and families to investigate and navigate institutional resources, services, and programs
- collaborate with essential campus partners
- consider diverse perspectives in developing parent and family programs
- provide information for faculty members and staff to help them interact effectively with parents and families and understand their expectations
- advocate for the appropriate distribution of emergency information to parents and families in accordance with institutional policy

Programming should address topics such as

- educational planning (academic advising, selection of major)
- standards of academic progress and other academic policies
- career planning
- student budgeting and money management
- educational costs, financial aid, and financial planning
- health and wellness
- resources to support students with disabilities
- resources through visitor services
- institutional support services (study skills, tutoring, and other learning assistance programs)
- diversity, multicultural, and international programs and services
- membership in a diverse community and interactions across differences
- involvement in co-curricular activities
- campus safety
- global citizenship
- on-campus, off-campus, commuter, or distance learner student issues
- information related to the transition to college and the potential change in family dynamics
- organization and roles of the institution's administration
- realistic parent and family expectations of their student
- appropriate levels of involvement with their student and the institution
- campus policies on rights and responsibilities, conduct, and access to educational records

Part 3. Organization and Leadership

To achieve program and student learning and development outcomes, Parent and Family Programs (PFP) must be purposefully structured for effectiveness. PFP must have clearly stated and current

- goals and outcomes
- policies and procedures
- responsibilities and performance expectations for personnel
- organizational charts demonstrating clear channels of authority

Leaders must model ethical behavior and institutional citizenship.

Leaders with organizational authority for PFP must provide strategic planning, management and supervision, and program advancement.

Strategic Planning

- articulate a vision and mission that drive short- and long-term planning
- set goals and objectives based on the needs of the populations served, intended student learning and development outcomes, and program outcomes
- facilitate continuous development, implementation, and assessment of program effectiveness and goal attainment congruent with institutional mission and strategic plans
- promote environments that provide opportunities for student learning, development, and engagement
- develop, adapt, and improve programs and services in response to the changing needs of populations served and evolving institutional priorities
- include diverse perspectives to inform decision making

Management and Supervision

- plan, allocate, and monitor the use of fiscal, physical, human, intellectual, and technological resources
- manage human resource processes including recruitment, selection, professional development, supervision, performance planning, succession planning, evaluation, recognition, and reward
- influence others to contribute to the effectiveness and success of the unit
- empower professional, support, and student personnel to become effective leaders
- encourage and support collaboration with colleagues and departments across the institution
- encourage and support scholarly contributions to the profession
- identify and address individual, organizational, and environmental conditions that foster or inhibit mission achievement
- use current and valid evidence to inform decisions
- incorporate sustainability practices in the

management and design of programs, services, and facilities

- understand appropriate technologies and integrate them into programs and services
- be knowledgeable about codes and laws relevant to programs and services and ensure that programs and services meet those requirements
- assess and take action to mitigate potential risks

Program Advancement

- advocate for and actively promote the mission and goals of the programs and services
- inform stakeholders about issues affecting practice
- facilitate processes to reach consensus where wide support is needed
- advocate for representation in strategic planning initiatives at divisional and institutional levels

PFP should maintain a website that can be accessed from the institution's home page to address the information needs of parents and families.

PFP must be located in an organizational structure that can best provide for effective programs and services for achievement of its mission.

Such locations may include student affairs, enrollment management, or advancement.

Part 4. Human Resources

Parent and Family Programs (PFP) must be staffed adequately by individuals qualified to accomplish mission and goals.

PFP staff should include full-time professionals.

PFP must have access to technical and support personnel adequate to accomplish their mission.

Within institutional guidelines, PFP must

- establish procedures for personnel recruitment and selection, training, performance planning, and evaluation
- set expectations for supervision and performance
- provide personnel access to continuing and advanced education and appropriate professional development opportunities to improve their competence, skills, and leadership capacity
- consider work/life options available to personnel (e.g., compressed work schedules, flextime, job sharing, remote work, or telework) to promote recruitment and retention of personnel

Administrators of PFP must

- ensure that all personnel have updated position descriptions
- implement recruitment and selection/hiring strategies that produce a workforce inclusive of under-represented populations
- develop promotion practices that are fair, inclusive, proactive, and non-discriminatory

Personnel responsible for delivery of PFP must have written performance goals, objectives, and outcomes for each year's performance cycle to be used to plan, review, and evaluate work and performance. The performance plan must be updated regularly to reflect changes during the performance cycle.

Results of individual personnel evaluations must be used to recognize personnel performance, address performance issues, implement individual and/or collective personnel development and training programs, and inform the assessment of programs and services.

PFP personnel, when hired and throughout their employment, must receive appropriate and thorough training.

PFP personnel, including student employees and volunteers, must have access to resources or receive specific training on

- institutional policies pertaining to functions or activities they support
- privacy and confidentiality policies
- laws regarding access to student records
- policies and procedures for dealing with sensitive institutional information
- policies and procedures related to technology used to store or access student records and institutional data
- how and when to refer those in need of additional assistance to qualified personnel and have access to a supervisor for assistance in making these judgments
- systems and technologies necessary to perform their assigned responsibilities
- ethical and legal uses of technology

PFP should have sufficient and specifically trained staff to support technology including the maintenance of program websites, social networks, communication systems, and developing emerging technology.

PFP must also receive specific training on the Health Insurance Portability & Accountability Act (HIPAA) if appropriate for institutional policies.

PFP personnel must engage in continuing professional development activities to keep abreast of the research, theories, legislation, policies, and developments that affect their programs and services.

PFP staff should pursue opportunities for support, professional development, and networking.

Administrators of PFP must ensure that personnel are knowledgeable about and trained in safety, emergency procedures, and crisis prevention and response. Risk management efforts must address identification of threatening conduct or behavior and must incorporate a system for responding to and reporting such behaviors.

PFP personnel must be knowledgeable of and trained in safety and emergency procedures for securing and vacating

facilities.

PROFESSIONAL PERSONNEL

PFP professional personnel either must hold an earned graduate or professional degree in a field relevant to their position or must possess an appropriate combination of educational credentials and related work experience.

INTERNS OR GRADUATE ASSISTANTS

Degree- or credential-seeking interns or graduate assistants must be qualified by enrollment in an appropriate field of study and relevant experience. These students must be trained and supervised by professional personnel who possess applicable educational credentials and work experience and have supervisory experience. Supervisors must be cognizant of the dual roles interns and graduate assistants have as both student and employee.

Supervisors must
- adhere to parameters of students' job descriptions
- articulate intended learning outcomes in student job descriptions
- adhere to agreed-upon work hours and schedules
- offer flexible scheduling when circumstances necessitate

Supervisors and students must both agree to suitable compensation if circumstances necessitate additional hours.

STUDENT EMPLOYEES AND VOLUNTEERS

Student employees and volunteers must be carefully selected, trained, supervised, and evaluated. Students must have access to a supervisor. Student employees and volunteers must be provided clear job descriptions, pre-service training based on assessed needs, and continuing development.

Part 5. Ethics

Parent and Family Programs (PFP) must
- review applicable professional ethical standards and must adopt or develop and implement appropriate statements of ethical practice
- publish and adhere to statements of ethical practice and ensure their periodic review
- orient new personnel to relevant ethical standards and statements of ethical practice and related institutional policies

Statements of ethical standards must
- specify that PFP personnel respect privacy and maintain confidentiality in communications and records as delineated by privacy laws
- specify limits on disclosure of information contained in students' records as well as requirements to disclose to appropriate authorities
- address conflicts of interest, or appearance thereof, by personnel in the performance of their work

- reflect the responsibility of personnel to be fair, objective, and impartial in their interactions with others
- reference management of institutional funds
- reference appropriate behavior regarding research and assessment with human participants, confidentiality of research and assessment data, and students' rights and responsibilities
- include the expectation that personnel confront and hold accountable other personnel who exhibit unethical behavior
- address issues surrounding scholarly integrity

PFP personnel must
- employ ethical decision making in the performance of their duties
- inform users of programs and services of ethical obligations and limitations emanating from codes and laws or from licensure requirements
- recognize and avoid conflicts of interest that could adversely influence their judgment or objectivity and, when unavoidable, recuse themselves from the situation
- perform their duties within the scope of their position, training, expertise, and competence
- make referrals when issues presented exceed the scope of the position

Part 6. Law, Policy, and Governance

Parent and Family Programs (PFP) must be in compliance with laws, regulations, and policies that relate to their respective responsibilities and that pose legal obligations, limitations, risks, and liabilities for the institution as a whole. Examples include constitutional, statutory, regulatory, and case law; relevant law and orders emanating from codes and laws; and the institution's policies.

PFP must have access to legal advice needed for personnel to carry out their assigned responsibilities.

PFP must inform personnel, appropriate officials, and users of programs and services about existing and changing legal obligations, risks and liabilities, and limitations.

PFP that use volunteers must provide appropriate training and support to ensure that guidelines and legal standards are followed.

PFP must inform personnel about professional liability insurance options and refer them to external sources if the institution does not provide coverage.

PFP must have written policies and procedures on operations, transactions, or tasks that have legal implications.

PFP must regularly review policies. The revision and creation of policies must be informed by best practices, available evidence, and policy issues in higher education.

PFP must have procedures and guidelines consistent with institutional policy for responding to threats, emergencies, and crisis situations. Systems and procedures must be in place to disseminate timely and accurate information to students, other members of the institutional community, and appropriate external organizations during emergency situations.

Personnel must neither participate in nor condone any form of harassment or activity that demeans persons or creates an intimidating, hostile, or offensive environment.

PFP must purchase or obtain permission to use copyrighted materials and instruments. References to copyrighted materials and instruments must include appropriate citations.

PFP must inform personnel about internal and external governance organizations that affect programs and services.

Part 7. Diversity, Equity, and Access

Within the context of each institution's mission and in accordance with institutional policies and applicable codes and laws, Parent and Family Programs (PFP) must create and maintain educational and work environments that are welcoming, accessible, inclusive, equitable, and free from harassment.

PFP must not discriminate on the basis of disability; age; race; cultural identity; ethnicity; nationality; family educational history (e.g., first generation to attend college); political affiliation; religious affiliation; sex; sexual orientation; gender identity and expression; marital, social, economic, or veteran status; or any other basis included in institutional policies and codes and laws.

PFP must
- advocate for sensitivity to multicultural and social justice concerns by the institution and its personnel
- ensure physical, program, and resource access for all constituents
- modify or remove policies, practices, systems, technologies, facilities, and structures that create barriers or produce inequities
- ensure that when facilities and structures cannot be modified, they do not impede access to programs, services, and resources
- establish goals for diversity, equity, and access
- foster communication and practices that enhance understanding of identity, culture, self-expression, and heritage
- promote respect for commonalities and differences among people within their historical and cultural contexts
- address the characteristics and needs of diverse constituents when establishing and implementing culturally relevant and inclusive programs, services, policies, procedures, and practices
- provide personnel with diversity, equity, and access training and hold personnel accountable for applying the training to their work
- respond to the needs of all constituents served

when establishing hours of operation and developing methods of delivering programs, services, and resources
- recognize the needs of distance and online learning students by directly providing or assisting them to gain access to comparable services and resources

PFP should include statements related to disability and equal opportunity laws in all print and electronic materials in accordance with institutional policy.

PFP should respect the diversity of the families of students, acknowledging the many different cultures and backgrounds represented by the families, including non-traditional family structures such as single parent households and foster families.

PFP should educate parents and families in general about all aspects of diversity in the college community and within society and be prepared to identify resources for support both on campus and locally as needed.

PFP staff must be knowledgeable of current trends and changing demographics of their institution as well as how they relate at the national level.

PFP should include programming for the unique family needs of student populations such as commuter, transfer, foster, homeless, international, LGBT, and first generation students.

PFP should provide access to the institution's policies and procedures and resources in multiple language formats including printed forms for families who do not have technology.

Part 8. Internal and External Relations

Parent and Family Programs (PFP) must reach out to individuals, groups, communities, and organizations internal and external to the institution to
- establish, maintain, and promote understanding and effective relations with those that have a significant interest in or potential effect on the students or other constituents served by the programs and services
- garner support and resources for programs and services as defined by the mission
- collaborate in offering or improving programs and services to meet the needs of students and other constituents and to achieve program and student outcomes
- engage diverse individuals, groups, communities, and organizations to enrich the educational environment and experiences of students and other constituents
- disseminate information about the programs and services

PFP should create a role for parents and family members within the institution through a parent/families organization, association, or club. Such a group should develop family affinity for the institution, offer referral to programs and services, and provide opportunities for parents and families to have input on institutional matters affecting their students. A staff member of the institution should be charged with supporting and advising such an organization.

PFP should inform family members about issues that impact the health, well-being, and success of students through a variety of delivery methods communication methods, including newsletters, e-newsletters, websites, social networking, and educational programming. This material should display appropriate institutional branding.

PFP should provide a parents and family resource guide or handbook to address student-life topics of priority to the institution (e.g., drug and alcohol abuse, service-learning and study abroad opportunities, research opportunities, financial literacy, health and wellness), resources and benefits available to parents and families, institutional policies and procedures, the academic calendar, and support services for students and their families.

Promotional and descriptive information must be accurate and free of deception and misrepresentation.

PFP must have procedures and guidelines consistent with institutional policy for
- **communicating with the media**
- **distributing information through print, broadcast, and online sources**
- **contracting with external organizations for delivery of programs and services**
- **cultivating, soliciting, and managing gifts**
- **applying to and managing funds from grants**

PFP should be represented on the institutional crisis response team. PFP should advocate for appropriate information to be sent to parents in the event of an emergency or campus crisis in accordance with institutional procedures.

Part 9. Financial Resources

Parent and Family Programs (PFP) must have funding to accomplish the mission and goals.

In establishing and prioritizing funding resources, PFP must conduct comprehensive analyses to determine
- **unmet needs of the unit**
- **relevant expenditures**
- **external and internal resources**
- **impact on students and the institution**

PFP may supplement institutional funding by developing revenue from sources such as fundraising, grants, and fees for services provided.

PFP must use the budget as a planning tool to reflect commitment to the mission and goals of the programs and services and of the institution.

PFP must administer funds in accordance with established institutional accounting procedures.

PFP must demonstrate efficient and effective use and responsible stewardship of fiscal resources consistent with institutional protocols.

Financial reports must provide an accurate financial overview of the organization and provide clear, understandable, and timely data upon which personnel can plan and make informed decisions.

Procurement procedures must
- **be consistent with institutional policies**
- **ensure that purchases comply with laws and codes for usability and access**
- **ensure that the institution receives value for the funds spent**
- **consider information available for comparing the ethical and environmental impact of products and services purchased**

Part 10. Technology

Parent and Family Programs (PFP) must have technology to support the achievement of their mission and goals. The technology and its use must comply with institutional policies and procedures and with relevant codes and laws.

PFP must use technologies to
- **provide updated information regarding mission, location, staffing, programs, services, and official contacts to students and other constituents in accessible formats**
- **provide an avenue for students and other constituents to communicate sensitive information in a secure format**
- **enhance the delivery of programs and services for all students**

PFP must
- **back up data on a regular basis**
- **adhere to institutional policies regarding ethical and legal use of technology**
- **articulate policies and procedures for protecting the confidentiality and security of information**
- **implement a replacement plan and cycle for all technology with attention to sustainability**
- **incorporate accessibility features into technology-based programs and services**

When providing student access to technology, PFP must
- **have policies on the use of technology that are clear, easy to understand, and available to all students**
- **provide information or referral to support services for those needing assistance in accessing or using technology**
- **provide instruction or training on how to use the technology**
- **inform students of implications of misuse of technologies**

Part 11. Facilities and Equipment

Parent and Family Programs' (PFP) facilities must be intentionally designed and located in suitable, accessible, and safe spaces that demonstrate universal design and support the program's mission and goals.

Facilities must be designed to engage various constituents and promote learning.

Personnel must have workspaces that are suitably located and accessible, well equipped, adequate in size, and designed to support their work and responsibilities.

The design of the facilities must guarantee the security and privacy of records and ensure the confidentiality of sensitive information and conversations. Personnel must be able to secure their work.

PFP must incorporate sustainable practices in use of facilities and purchase of equipment. Facilities and equipment must be evaluated on an established cycle and be in compliance with codes, laws, and accepted practices for access, health, safety, and security.

When acquiring capital equipment, PFP must take into account expenses related to regular maintenance and life cycle costs.

Part 12. Assessment

Parent and Family Programs (PFP) must develop assessment plans and processes.

Assessment plans must articulate an ongoing cycle of assessment activities.

PFP must
- specify programmatic goals and intended outcomes
- identify student learning and development outcomes
- employ multiple measures and methods
- develop manageable processes for gathering, interpreting, and evaluating data
- document progress toward achievement of goals and outcomes
- interpret and use assessment results to demonstrate accountability
- report aggregated results to respondent groups and stakeholders
- use assessment results to inform planning and decision-making
- assess effectiveness of implemented changes
- provide evidence of improvement of programs and services

PFP should employ multiple methods to evaluate and assess the program's effectiveness in meeting the needs of families.

PFP must employ ethical practices in the assessment process.

PFP must have access to adequate fiscal, human, professional development, and technological resources to develop and implement assessment plans.

General Standards revised in 2014;
PFP content developed/revised in 2010

Recreational Sports Programs
CAS Contextual Statement

The concept and practice of providing activities to enhance student growth during college is grounded in various student developmental theories and postulates. Among the most noted are theories related to identity development (Chickering, 1969; Marcia, 1966); cognitive process (Perry, 1968), moral development (Kohlberg & Hersh, 1977; Gilligan, 1982); spirituality and authenticity (Chickering, Dalton, & Stamm, 2006); interpersonal and intrapersonal changes (Knefelkamp, Widick, & Parker, 1978); and gender identity (McCewan, 1996). Student services practice also focuses on involvement and engagement in on and off-campus curricular and co-curricular activities as a method to enhance student retention and success (Astin, 1984; Pascarella & Terrenzini, 2005; Tinto, 1994). *Learning Reconsidered* provided and galvanized the recent focus on student service based learning by defining learning as "a comprehensive, holistic, transformative activity that integrates academic learning and student development, processes that have often been considered separate and even independent of each other" (NASPA & ACPA, 2004, p. 2). The context in which development, engagement, and learning occurs on a college campus is important and ranges from the curricular offerings connected with academic units to those associated with co-curricular units provided by a myriad of student services, including recreational sports.

Student involvement in sports activities has been part of the college experience since the earliest days of the colonial colleges. Organized by students, sports activities were considered a diversion from the rigors of academic life and limited to competitive activities between classmates within the institution. More formalized "intramurals," a term derived from the Latin words *intra*, meaning within, and *muralis*, meaning walls, began in U.S. colleges and universities during the 19th century and were, for the first part of that century, almost exclusively the only form of structured competition for students (Mueller, 1971). By the century's mid-point interest in competitive sport intensified and intercollegiate athletics was born, overshadowing intramural contests as the primary sport engagement focus on campus.

A resurgence of the intramural movement occurred in the late 19th and early 20th centuries and was formalized by the construction of the first dedicated intramural facilities in 1913, and the employment of professional staff members focused on providing increasingly popular sport related programs. The formation of a national professional organization for intramural sports directors first occurred in 1950 when the National Intramural Association (NIA) was formed (NIRSA, 2006; Clark, 1978).

Over-time, intramural programs diversified to broader recreational pursuits and participation increased. The rise in popularity of aerobic exercise and a societal push toward greater gender equity, including implementation of Title IX of the Education Amendments of 1972, produced an influx of women into competitive athletics resulting in even higher levels of interest and participation for varied recreational pursuits. The NIA changed its name in 1975 to the National Intramural and Recreational Sports Association (NIRSA) to reflect the "sport-for-all" mindset held by the organization's membership. Separate standards and guidelines for specializations are governed by professional organizations associated with the specific functional area and/or published by NIRSA. As programs continued to grow and gain both student and institutional support, additional multi-faceted facilities were built, many exclusively, for recreational sports activities. By the late 1980s, the field of recreational sports witnessed a period of rapid growth in programs and the advent of new and better campus facilities for physical activities.

The beginning of the 21st Century found even greater expansion of collegiate recreational sports opportunities and facilities, reaching an estimated combined enrollment of 7.1 million students, with an estimated 5.3 million students considered heavy or regular users of established programs and facilities (NIRSA, 2005). New construction and refurbishing of existing facilities continues unabated and has helped to provide needed services to students to enhance their growth and maturation, particularly in the areas of health, fitness, and wellness. NIRSA reported that, between 2005–2010, at least $3.17 billion will be spent in new construction and renovations for indoor campus recreational sports facilities at 333 NIRSA member institutions at an average cost of $14.2 million. Total student enrollment for the reporting colleges and universities is 3.8 million (NIRSA, 2005).

During this period of tremendous growth, recreational sports programs experienced changed perceptions about institutional roles and standards of practice. Recreational sports programs are placed under the administrative auspices of a division of student affairs at 72 percent of NIRSA member institutions (Franklin, 2007), though some programs are found within a variety of other administrative structures including intercollegiate athletic departments, academic programs, and business units. NIRSA suggests that, while organizational designs vary among institutions, the full realization of recreational sports contributions to any campus depends upon institutional commitment to that endeavor.

NIRSA (2004) found that, at schools with established campus recreational sports departments, 75 percent of students participated in recreational sports programs and that participation in these programs was a key determinant of college satisfaction, success, recruitment, and retention. Student participation also encouraged the development of critical thinking skills and the creation of problem-solving strategies, honed decision-making skills, enhanced creativity, and promoted the synthesis and integration of information into all aspects of their lives. In this way, students both perform more effectively in an academic environment and flourish throughout all phases of the collegiate experience.

Research also found that recreational sports programs contributed to the development of a student's positive self-image, awareness of strengths, increased tolerance and self-control, stronger social interaction skills, and maturity. These programs have been endorsed by institutions for their value in helping students maintain good physical and mental health by providing a respite from rigorous academic work and in teaching recreational skills with a carryover for leisure time exercise throughout life.

Viewed as an essential component of higher education, the field of recreational sports has grown into a dynamic organized profession contributing to the educational process through the enhancement of students' physical, mental, social, and emotional development. Recreational sports practitioners provide quality co-curricular opportunities to enhance the overall growth and development of students by remaining grounded to a commitment to student development and learning; a set of ethical codes and standards; and continuous professional improvement.

References, Readings, and Resources

Astin, A. W. (1984). Student involvement: A developmental theory for higher education. *Journal of College Student Personnel, 25,* 297-308.

Chickering, A. W. (1969). Education and identity. San Francisco, CA: Jossey-Bass.

Chickering, A. W., Dalton, J. C., & Stamm, L. (2006). *Encouraging authenticity and spirituality in higher education.* San Francisco, CA: Jossey-Bass.

Clarke, J. S. (1978). *Challenge and change: A history of the development of the National Intramural and Recreational Sports Association* 1950-1976. West Point, NY: Leisure Press.

Franklin, D. S. (2007). Student development and learning in campus recreation: Assessing recreational sports directors' awareness, perceived importance, application of and satisfaction with CAS standards. (Doctoral dissertation). Retrieved from ProQuest Digital Dissertations database. (Publication No. AAT 3269236).

Gilligan, C. (1982). *In a different voice: Psychological theory and women's development.* Cambridge, MA: Harvard University Press.

Hossler, D., Bean, J. P., & Associates. (1990). *The strategic management of college enrollments.* San Francisco, CA: Jossey-Bass.

Keeling, R. P. (Ed.) (2006). *Learning reconsidered 2: Implementing a campus-wide focus on the student experience.* Washington, DC: American College Personnel Association, Association of College and University Housing Officers-International, Association of College Unions-International, National Academic Advising Association, National Association for Campus Activities, National Association of Student Personnel Administrators, National Intramural-Recreational Sports Association.

Knefelkamp, L. L., Widick, C., & Parker, C. A. (1978). Applying new developmental findings. *New Directions for Student Services, 4,* 69-78. San Francisco, CA: Jossey-Bass.

Kohlberg, L., & Hersh, R. H. (1977). Moral development: A review of the theory. *Theory into Practice. 16,* 53-59

Marcia, J. E. (1966). Development and validation of ego-identity status. *Journal of Personality and Social Psychology, 3,* 551-558.

Mueller, P. (1971). *Intramurals: Programming and administration* (4th ed.). New York, NY: Ronald Press Co.

Mull, R. F., Bayless, K. G., & Ross, C. M. (1987). *Recreational sports programming.* North Palm Beach, FL: The Athletic Institute.

National Association of Student Personnel Administrators (NASPA) & American College Personnel Association (ACPA). (2004). *Learning reconsidered: A campus-wide focus on the student experience.* Washington, DC: Authors.

National Center for Education Statistics. (October, 2003). *College/University Enrollment as Found in Projections of Education Statistics to 2013.* Washington, DC: Author.

National Intramural Recreational Sports Association, (NIRSA) website: www.nirsa.org.

National Intramural-Recreational Sports Association. (1996). *General and specialty standards for collegiate recreational sports.* Champaign, IL: Human Kinetics.

National Intramural-Recreational Sports Association. (2004). *The value of recreational sports in higher education – Impact on student enrollment, success, and buying power.* Champaign, IL: Human Kinetics.

National Intramural-Recreational Sports Association. (2005). *Collegiate recreational sports facility construction report.* Champaign, IL: Human Kinetics.

Pascarella, E. T., & Terrenzini, P. T. (2005). *How college affects students: A third decade of research.* San Francisco, CA: Jossey-Bass.

Perry, W. G. (1968). *Forms of intellectual and ethical development in the college years: A scheme.* New York, NY: Holt, Rinehart & Winston.

Tinto, V. (1994). *Leaving college: Rethinking the causes and cures of student attrition* (2nd ed.). Chicago, IL: University of Chicago Press.

Contextual Statement Contributors
Current Edition:
Doug Franklin, Ohio University

Previous Editions:
Dixie Bennett, Loyola University Chicago

Recreational Sports Programs
CAS Standards and Guidelines

The mission of Recreational Sports Programs (RSP) must be to enhance the mind, body, and spirit of students and other eligible individuals by providing programs, services, and facilities that are responsive to the physical, social, recreational, and lifelong educational needs of the campus community as they relate to health, fitness, and learning.

To accomplish this mission, RSP should
- provide programs and services for participants that are conducive to the development of holistic health, particularly fitness and wellness
- provide comprehensive programs and services in a variety of program formats that reflect and promote the diversity of participant interests, needs, and ability levels
- provide participation, employment, and leadership opportunities designed to enhance learning, growth, and development
- provide participation, employment, and leadership opportunities designed to increase interaction and understanding among individuals from various backgrounds
- contribute to the public relations efforts of the institution, including the recruitment and retention of students, faculty members, and staff members
- facilitate service-learning opportunities for students
- work in collaboration with academic units to facilitate professional preparation opportunities for students
- provide programs, facilities, and equipment that are delivered in a safe, healthy, clean, accessible, and enjoyable environment
- ensure the effective administration, operation, and stewardship of all aspects of the RSP, working in collaboration with other services, programs, campus affiliates (e.g., faculty, staff, alumni, guests, families, general public), and academic units where appropriate

RSP must develop, disseminate, implement, and regularly review their missions, which must be consistent with the mission of the institution and with applicable professional standards. The mission must be appropriate for the institution's students and other constituents. Mission statements must reference student learning and development.

To achieve their mission, Recreational Sports Programs

(RSP) must contribute to
- students' formal education, which includes both the curriculum and the co-curriculum
- student progression and timely completion of educational goals
- preparation of students for their careers, citizenship, and lives
- student learning and development

To contribute to student learning and development, RSP must
- identify relevant and desirable student learning and development outcomes
- articulate how the student learning and development outcomes align with the six CAS student learning and development domains and related dimensions
- assess relevant and desirable student learning and development
- provide evidence of impact on outcomes
- articulate contributions to or support of student learning and development in the domains not specifically assessed
- use evidence gathered to create strategies for improvement of programs and services

STUDENT LEARNING AND DEVELOPMENT DOMAINS AND DIMENSIONS

Domain: knowledge acquisition, integration, construction, and application
- Dimensions: understanding knowledge from a range of disciplines; connecting knowledge to other knowledge, ideas, and experiences; constructing knowledge; and relating knowledge to daily life

Domain: cognitive complexity
- Dimensions: critical thinking, reflective thinking, effective reasoning, and creativity

Domain: intrapersonal development
- Dimensions: realistic self-appraisal, self-understanding, and self-respect; identity development; commitment to ethics and integrity; and spiritual awareness

Domain: interpersonal competence
- Dimensions: meaningful relationships, interdependence, collaboration, and effective leadership

Domain: humanitarianism and civic engagement
- Dimensions: understanding and appreciation of cultural and human differences, social responsibility, global perspective, and sense of civic

responsibility

Domain: practical competence

- **Dimensions: pursuing goals, communicating effectively, technical competence, managing personal affairs, managing career development, demonstrating professionalism, maintaining health and wellness, and living a purposeful and satisfying life**

[LD Outcomes: See *The Council for the Advancement of Standards Learning and Development Outcomes* statement for examples of outcomes related to these domains and dimensions.]

RSP must be

- **intentionally designed**
- **guided by theories and knowledge of learning and development**
- **integrated into the life of the institution**
- **reflective of developmental and demographic profiles of the student population**
- **responsive to needs of individuals, populations with distinct needs, and relevant constituencies**
- **delivered using multiple formats, strategies, and contexts**
- **designed to provide universal access**

RSP must collaborate with colleagues and departments across the institution to promote student learning and development, persistence, and success.

RSP must reflect the needs and interests of students and other eligible users.

Valid indicators include needs assessment surveys, research findings, and documented best practices.

RSP, in collaboration with other campus units and community providers when appropriate, should design programs and services through participation, employment, volunteerism, and leadership opportunities to encourage, enhance, and highlight the value of learning outcomes.

RSP should utilize various program delivery formats including

- informal - to provide for self-directed, individualized approach to participation. Specific times and facility locations should be reserved to provide a variety of self-directed individual or small group participation opportunities.
- intramural - to provide structured contests, challenges, meets, tournaments, and leagues for participants within the institution
- club - to provide opportunities for individuals to organize around a common interest. Opportunities should be available to students for a variety of interests within or beyond the institution.
- instructional - to provide individualized or group learning opportunities, knowledge, and skills through activity sessions, lessons, clinics, workshops,

and various media

- extramural - to provide structured tournaments, contests, and meets between campus participants and other institutions

In addition to these program formats, the RSP may utilize specialized designations to describe programs or service delivery, including aquatics, fitness, wellness, outdoor, special events, special populations, and facilities.

Program planning and implementation process must be inclusive and include

- **equitable participation for men and women, with opportunities to participate at various levels of ability and disability**
- **interpretation of institutional policies and procedures**
- **a variety of opportunities that reflect and address cultural diversity**
- **participant involvement in shaping program content and procedures**
- **co-recreational activity with opportunities to participate at various levels of ability and disability**

Program operational planning and implementation process must include

- **participant safety through the use of rules, regulations, and facilities management**
- **effective risk management policies, procedures, and practices**
- **supervision of recreational sports activities and facilities**
- **facility coordination and scheduling**
- **consultation with groups and organizations for sport and fitness programming**
- **training of office and field staff**
- **conflict resolution management protocols**
- **procedures for the inventory, maintenance, and use and security of equipment**
- **recognition for participants, employees, and volunteers**
- **publicity, promotion, and media relations**
- **volunteerism in service delivery and leadership**
- **customer service practices**
- **promotion of socially responsible behaviors**

Part 3. Organization and Leadership

To achieve program and student learning and development outcomes, Recreational Sports Programs (RSP) must be purposefully structured for effectiveness. RSP must have clearly stated and current

- **goals and outcomes**
- **policies and procedures**
- **responsibilities and performance expectations for personnel**
- **organizational charts demonstrating clear channels of authority**

Leaders must model ethical behavior and institutional citizenship.

Leaders with organizational authority for RSP must provide strategic planning, management and supervision, and program advancement.

Strategic Planning

- articulate a vision and mission that drive short- and long-term planning
- set goals and objectives based on the needs of the populations served, intended student learning and development outcomes, and program outcomes
- facilitate continuous development, implementation, and assessment of program effectiveness and goal attainment congruent with institutional mission and strategic plans
- promote environments that provide opportunities for student learning, development, and engagement
- develop, adapt, and improve programs and services in response to the changing needs of populations served and evolving institutional priorities
- include diverse perspectives to inform decision making

Management and Supervision

- plan, allocate, and monitor the use of fiscal, physical, human, intellectual, and technological resources
- manage human resource processes including recruitment, selection, professional development, supervision, performance planning, succession planning, evaluation, recognition, and reward
- influence others to contribute to the effectiveness and success of the unit
- empower professional, support, and student personnel to become effective leaders
- encourage and support collaboration with colleagues and departments across the institution
- encourage and support scholarly contributions to the profession
- identify and address individual, organizational, and environmental conditions that foster or inhibit mission achievement
- use current and valid evidence to inform decisions
- incorporate sustainability practices in the management and design of programs, services, and facilities
- understand appropriate technologies and integrate them into programs and services
- be knowledgeable about codes and laws relevant to programs and services and ensure that programs and services meet those requirements
- assess and take action to mitigate potential risks

Program Advancement

- advocate for and actively promote the mission and goals of the programs and services
- inform stakeholders about issues affecting practice
- facilitate processes to reach consensus where wide support is needed
- advocate for representation in strategic planning initiatives at divisional and institutional levels

RSP leaders also must

- empower student staff and participants to build their own leadership skills
- value diversity through effective recruitment and retention of professional and student staff
- identify organization values and innovative opportunities
- establish risk management, technology, and marketing plans
- establish strategic, operational, and resource utilization plans
- manage facility resources
- advocate for financial and physical resources

RSP leaders must educate other institutional leaders about the significant differences in mission among intercollegiate athletics, physical education and recreation academic units, and the recreational sports programs.

Leaders should establish effective working relationships throughout their institution, with special emphasis on those units that impact, affect, or support the mission of the RSP. Leaders should actively seek opportunities for collaboration that may result in partnerships that benefit the institution as well as the RSP.

Members of the campus community should be involved in the selection, design, governance, and administration of programs and facilities. Students and other eligible users may be involved through participant, employee, and living unit committees, councils, and boards.

The organizational placement of recreational sports within the institution should ensure the accomplishment of the program's mission.

To fulfill its mission and goals effectively, RSP must maintain well-structured management functions, including planning, personnel, property and risk management, emergency response, purchasing, contract administration, marketing, financial control, and information systems.

A short and long range planning document that specifies goals, objectives, student learning outcomes, strategies, and timelines should be developed to provide direction for the program. This plan should be reviewed annually.

Purchasing and property management procedures should be designed to ensure value for money spent, security for equipment and supplies, and maintenance of property inventories.

Other areas for consideration in determining structure and

management of the RSP should include
- size, nature, and mission of the institution
- scope of recreational sports programs
- philosophy and method of service delivery
- financial resources
- availability and characteristics of facilities

Part 4. Human Resources

Recreational Sports Programs (RSP) must be staffed adequately by individuals qualified to accomplish mission and goals.

RSP must have access to technical and support personnel adequate to accomplish their mission.

Within institutional guidelines, RSP must
- establish procedures for personnel recruitment and selection, training, performance planning, and evaluation
- set expectations for supervision and performance
- provide personnel access to continuing and advanced education and appropriate professional development opportunities to improve their competence, skills, and leadership capacity
- consider work/life options available to personnel (e.g., compressed work schedules, flextime, job sharing, remote work, or telework) to promote recruitment and retention of personnel

Administrators of RSP must
- ensure that all personnel have updated position descriptions
- implement recruitment and selection/hiring strategies that produce a workforce inclusive of under-represented populations
- develop promotion practices that are fair, inclusive, proactive, and non-discriminatory

Personnel responsible for delivery of RSP must have written performance goals, objectives, and outcomes for each year's performance cycle to be used to plan, review, and evaluate work and performance. The performance plan must be updated regularly to reflect changes during the performance cycle.

Results of individual personnel evaluations must be used to recognize personnel performance, address performance issues, implement individual and/or collective personnel development and training programs, and inform the assessment of programs and services.

RSP personnel, when hired and throughout their employment, must receive appropriate and thorough training.

RSP personnel, including student employees and volunteers, must have access to resources or receive specific training on
- institutional policies pertaining to functions or activities they support
- privacy and confidentiality policies
- laws regarding access to student records
- policies and procedures for dealing with sensitive institutional information
- policies and procedures related to technology used to store or access student records and institutional data
- how and when to refer those in need of additional assistance to qualified personnel and have access to a supervisor for assistance in making these judgments
- systems and technologies necessary to perform their assigned responsibilities
- ethical and legal uses of technology

Technical and support staff includes those positions with an expertise in such areas as customer service, facility/equipment maintenance and operations, marketing, information technology, fundraising, research, and business services.

RSP personnel must engage in continuing professional development activities to keep abreast of the research, theories, legislation, policies, and developments that affect their programs and services.

Administrators of RSP must ensure that personnel are knowledgeable about and trained in safety, emergency procedures, and crisis prevention and response. Risk management efforts must address identification of threatening conduct or behavior and must incorporate a system for responding to and reporting such behaviors.

RSP personnel must be knowledgeable of and trained in safety and emergency procedures for securing and vacating facilities.

PROFESSIONAL PERSONNEL

RSP professional personnel either must hold an earned graduate or professional degree in a field relevant to their position or must possess an appropriate combination of educational credentials and related work experience.

INTERNS OR GRADUATE ASSISTANTS

Degree- or credential-seeking interns or graduate assistants must be qualified by enrollment in an appropriate field of study and relevant experience. These students must be trained and supervised by professional personnel who possess applicable educational credentials and work experience and have supervisory experience. Supervisors must be cognizant of the dual roles interns and graduate assistants have as both student and employee.

Supervisors must
- adhere to parameters of students' job descriptions
- articulate intended learning outcomes in student job descriptions
- adhere to agreed-upon work hours and schedules

- offer flexible scheduling when circumstances necessitate

Supervisors and students must both agree to suitable compensation if circumstances necessitate additional hours.

RSP should provide graduate assistant and/or internship opportunities to enhance professional preparation experiences. Desirable characteristics of interns and graduate assistants should include: knowledge of the principles and philosophy of recreational sports, demonstrated skills on leadership and communication, a well-developed sense of responsibility, sensitivity to individual differences, academic success, enthusiasm for working with students, and an understanding of current issues facing students.

STUDENT EMPLOYEES AND VOLUNTEERS

Student employees and volunteers must be carefully selected, trained, supervised, and evaluated. Students must have access to a supervisor. Student employees and volunteers must be provided clear job descriptions, pre-service training based on assessed needs, and continuing development.

RSP should develop mechanisms designed to recognize employees and volunteers. These efforts should recognize contributions, improvements, and involvement.

Part 5. Ethics

Recreational Sports Programs (RSP) must
- review applicable professional ethical standards and must adopt or develop and implement appropriate statements of ethical practice
- publish and adhere to statements of ethical practice and ensure their periodic review
- orient new personnel to relevant ethical standards and statements of ethical practice and related institutional policies.

Statements of ethical standards must
- specify that RSP personnel respect privacy and maintain confidentiality in communications and records as delineated by privacy laws
- specify limits on disclosure of information contained in students' records as well as requirements to disclose to appropriate authorities
- address conflicts of interest, or appearance thereof, by personnel in the performance of their work
- reflect the responsibility of personnel to be fair, objective, and impartial in their interactions with others
- reference management of institutional funds
- reference appropriate behavior regarding research and assessment with human participants, confidentiality of research and assessment data, and students' rights and responsibilities
- include the expectation that personnel confront and hold accountable other personnel who exhibit

unethical behavior.
- address issues surrounding scholarly integrity

Ethical standard statements utilized by relevant professional associations should be reviewed in the formulation of RSP ethical standards.

RSP personnel must
- **employ ethical decision making in the performance of their duties**
- **inform users of programs and services of ethical obligations and limitations emanating from codes and laws or from licensure requirements**
- **recognize and avoid conflicts of interest that could adversely influence their judgment or objectivity and, when unavoidable, recuse themselves from the situation**
- **perform their duties within the scope of their position, training, expertise, and competence**
- **make referrals when issues presented exceed the scope of the position**

Part 6. Law, Policy, and Governance

Recreational Sports Programs (RSP) must be in compliance with laws, regulations, and policies that relate to their respective responsibilities and that pose legal obligations, limitations, risks, and liabilities for the institution as a whole. Examples include constitutional, statutory, regulatory, and case law; relevant law and orders emanating from codes and laws; and the institution's policies.

To address and minimize the risks inherent in RSP, a comprehensive risk management plan must be implemented.

Development and implementation of a risk management plan should include: identification of appropriate certifications, training and development of personnel, development and implementation of emergency action and critical incident plans, accident care and documentation, participant waivers and consents, participant conduct policies, and the inspection, supervision, and care of facilities and equipment.

RSP must have access to legal advice needed for personnel to carry out their assigned responsibilities.

Recreational sports professionals should understand legal responsibilities related to individual rights and liability including but not limited to due process, employment procedures, equal opportunity, civil rights and liberties, and liability of wrongful or negligent acts.

RSP should conduct a periodic audit of its policies and practices with university counsel and risk management officials.

RSP must inform personnel, appropriate officials, and users of programs and services about existing and changing legal obligations, risks and liabilities, and limitations.

RSP must inform personnel about professional liability insurance options and refer them to external sources if the institution does not provide coverage.

RSP must have written policies and procedures on operations, transactions, or tasks that have legal implications.

RSP must regularly review policies. The revision and creation of policies must be informed by best practices, available evidence, and policy issues in higher education.

RSP must have procedures and guidelines consistent with institutional policy for responding to threats, emergencies, and crisis situations. Systems and procedures must be in place to disseminate timely and accurate information to students, other members of the institutional community, and appropriate external organizations during emergency situations.

Personnel must neither participate in nor condone any form of harassment or activity that demeans persons or creates an intimidating, hostile, or offensive environment.

RSP must purchase or obtain permission to use copyrighted materials and instruments. References to copyrighted materials and instruments must include appropriate citations.

RSP must inform personnel about internal and external governance organizations that affect programs and services.

Part 7. Diversity, Equity, and Access

Within the context of each institution's mission and in accordance with institutional policies and applicable codes and laws, Recreational Sports Programs (RSP) must create and maintain educational and work environments that are welcoming, accessible, inclusive, equitable, and free from harassment.

RSP must not discriminate on the basis of disability; age; race; cultural identity; ethnicity; nationality; family educational history (e.g., first generation to attend college); political affiliation; religious affiliation; sex; sexual orientation; gender identity and expression; marital, social, economic, or veteran status; or any other basis included in institutional policies and codes and laws.

RSP must
- advocate for sensitivity to multicultural and social justice concerns by the institution and its personnel
- ensure physical, program, and resource access for all constituents
- modify or remove policies, practices, systems, technologies, facilities, and structures that create barriers or produce inequities
- ensure that when facilities and structures cannot be modified, they do not impede access to programs, services, and resources
- establish goals for diversity, equity, and access
- foster communication and practices that enhance understanding of identity, culture, self-expression, and heritage
- promote respect for commonalities and differences among people within their historical and cultural contexts
- address the characteristics and needs of diverse constituents when establishing and implementing culturally relevant and inclusive programs, services, policies, procedures, and practices
- provide personnel with diversity, equity, and access training and hold personnel accountable for applying the training to their work
- respond to the needs of all constituents served when establishing hours of operation and developing methods of delivering programs, services, and resources
- recognize the needs of distance and online learning students by directly providing or assisting them to gain access to comparable services and resources

RSP must adhere to applicable government standards and legal directives regarding access.

RSP must define the eligible user population, with consideration given to such groups as undergraduate and graduate students, faculty members, staff, retirees, alumni, and the general public.

RSP should
- consider the impact of fees and charges on access to programs and services
- participate in establishing institutional facility scheduling policies to support and encourage appropriate and equitable utilization of resources

In support of diversity, RSP must
- publish, post, and circulate a statement to articulate a commitment to diversity in programs, services, and staffing
- recruit, hire, and seek to retain a diverse professional and student staff
- include diversity education for its employees and volunteers
- reach out to diverse and under-represented populations through such means as surveys, assessments, focus groups, and campus organizations to identify needs and interests used in program design and delivery and in student employment practices

Part 8. Internal and External Relations

Recreational Sports Programs (RSP) must reach out to individuals, groups, communities, and organizations internal and external to the institution to

- establish, maintain, and promote understanding and effective relations with those that have a significant interest in or potential effect on the students or other constituents served by the programs and services
- garner support and resources for programs and services as defined by the mission
- collaborate in offering or improving programs and services to meet the needs of students and other constituents and to achieve program and student outcomes
- engage diverse individuals, groups, communities, and organizations to enrich the educational environment and experiences of students and other constituents
- disseminate information about the programs and services

Promotional and descriptive information must be accurate and free of deception and misrepresentation.

RSP must have procedures and guidelines consistent with institutional policy for
- communicating with the media
- distributing information through print, broadcast, and online sources
- contracting with external organizations for delivery of programs and services
- cultivating, soliciting, and managing gifts
- applying to and managing funds from grants

RSP should establish advisory councils to facilitate communication and collaboration with other campus and community units to improve programs and services. Representatives should be solicited from a variety of units and should represent diverse users. This may include representatives from student organizations, student union, clinical health services, health promotion services, counseling services, campus information visitor services, career services, student government, faculty and staff governance councils, conference services, residence halls/apartments, cultural centers, fraternity and sorority affairs, academics, campus police/public safety, athletics, alumni affairs, financial affairs, and physical plant. Community organizations may include hospitals and recreation and fitness centers.

Part 9. Financial Resources

Recreational Sports Programs (RSP) must have funding to accomplish the mission and goals.

In establishing and prioritizing funding resources, RSP must conduct comprehensive analyses to determine
- unmet needs of the unit
- relevant expenditures
- external and internal resources
- impact on students and the institution

RSP must use the budget as a planning tool to reflect

commitment to the mission and goals of the programs and services and of the institution.

RSP must administer funds in accordance with established institutional accounting procedures.

RSP must demonstrate efficient and effective use and responsible stewardship of fiscal resources consistent with institutional protocols.

Financial reports must provide an accurate financial overview of the organization and provide clear, understandable, and timely data upon which personnel can plan and make informed decisions.

Procurement procedures must
- be consistent with institutional policies
- ensure that purchases comply with laws and codes for usability and access
- ensure that the institution receives value for the funds spent
- consider information available for comparing the ethical and environmental impact of products and services purchased

Institutional funds for RSP should be allocated to ensure long-term viability. Sources of income may include governmental appropriations, student fees (e.g., general, recreational, or health), user fees, donations, contributions, sponsorships, fines, entry fees, rentals, grants, contracts, dues, concessions, and retail sales.

If student funds from any source are dedicated to RSP, those funds should be designated for programs and services that directly benefit students, and the students should retain first priority for the use of facilities, programs, equipment, and services.

The budget process must include consideration of all expenses that are incurred in order to produce a quality RSP.

Expenses include but are not limited to programs and operations, human resource processes and labor costs, support area expenses (e.g., technology, facility support, member services, marketing, research and development), equipment replacement, capital improvement, administrative cost recovery, and reserve account allocations.

Expenditures should be based upon departmental and institutional goals and protocols, periodic needs assessments, and cost/benefit analysis.

All members of RSP staff should be accountable for financial and other resources.

Part 10. Technology

Recreational Sports Programs (RSP) must have technology to support the achievement of their mission and goals. The technology and its use must comply with institutional

policies and procedures and with relevant codes and laws.

RSP must use technologies to
- provide updated information regarding mission, location, staffing, programs, services, and official contacts to students and other constituents in accessible formats
- provide an avenue for students and other constituents to communicate sensitive information in a secure format
- enhance the delivery of programs and services for all students

RSP must
- back up data on a regular basis
- adhere to institutional policies regarding ethical and legal use of technology
- articulate policies and procedures for protecting the confidentiality and security of information
- implement a replacement plan and cycle for all technology with attention to sustainability
- incorporate accessibility features into technology-based programs and services

When providing student access to technology, RSP must
- have policies on the use of technology that are clear, easy to understand, and available to all students
- provide information or referral to support services for those needing assistance in accessing or using technology
- provide instruction or training on how to use the technology
- inform students of implications of misuse of technologies

Part 11. Facilities and Equipment

Recreational Sports Programs' (RSP) facilities must be intentionally designed and located in suitable, accessible, and safe spaces that demonstrate universal design and support the program's mission and goals.

Facilities must be designed to engage various constituents and promote learning.

Personnel must have workspaces that are suitably located and accessible, well equipped, adequate in size, and designed to support their work and responsibilities.

The design of the facilities must guarantee the security and privacy of records and ensure the confidentiality of sensitive information and conversations. Personnel must be able to secure their work.

RSP must incorporate sustainable practices in use of facilities and purchase of equipment. Facilities and equipment must be evaluated on an established cycle and be in compliance with codes, laws, and accepted practices for access, health, safety, and security.

When acquiring capital equipment, RSP must take into account expenses related to regular maintenance and life cycle costs.

The institution must provide adequate indoor and outdoor facilities with a documented facility usage schedule that includes prioritized blocks of time for RSP to accommodate the needs and interests of the campus community. The use of the facilities must be coordinated to provide efficient and effective utilization.

The schedule should be disseminated to all user groups and reviewed periodically.

Institutions should use available research and assessment data when assessing facility needs. Consideration should be given to sustainability and to a balance of facilities that support the program delivery formats of RSP. Examples of such facilities include swimming pools, strength and cardiovascular training facilities, multi-purpose activity spaces, multi-use fields, nature trails, group exercise and dance rooms, challenge adventure facilities, martial arts mat/studio rooms, personal training rooms, mind-body studios, health and wellness labs, skateboard and rollerblade venues, and racquet sport courts. Facilities should provide activity areas that are diverse as well as flexible and spaces for such support activities as offices, member services, repair rooms, locker/shower rooms, and storage.

Social space should be provided for users to encourage socialization and an inclusive environment. Examples of such facilities include lounges, lobbies, or food service areas.

Renovation, design, and development of facilities must adhere to applicable laws.

RSP may also refer to separate standards and guidelines for specializations governed by professional organizations for the use of facilities.

Technology resources including software and hardware as well as resources for training should be available to support RSP.

RSP must provide equipment adequate to meet the needs of participants.

Institutions should use available research and other assessment data when assessing technology and equipment needs.

RSP must require personal protective equipment and safety devices as appropriate.

Processes must be established for determining needs, inspecting, cleaning, maintaining, repairing, and replacing equipment.

RSP must establish appropriate policies and procedures for responding to emergency situations, especially where RSP facilities, personnel, and resources could assist the institution.

Part 12. Assessment

Recreational Sports Programs (RSP) must develop assessment plans and processes.

Assessment plans must articulate an ongoing cycle of assessment activities.

RSP must

- specify programmatic goals and intended outcomes
- identify student learning and development outcomes
- employ multiple measures and methods
- develop manageable processes for gathering, interpreting, and evaluating data
- document progress toward achievement of goals and outcomes
- interpret and use assessment results to demonstrate accountability
- report aggregated results to respondent groups and stakeholders
- use assessment results to inform planning and decision-making
- assess effectiveness of implemented changes
- provide evidence of improvement of programs and services

Evaluation procedures should yield evidence relative to student/staff recruitment and retention, the achievement of program goals, scope of program offerings, responsiveness to expressed interests, program attendance and effectiveness, participant satisfaction, cost effectiveness, quality of facilities, equipment use and maintenance, staff performance, recruitment and retention, and data as a result of benchmarking against other programs.

Data sources should include student and other eligible users and nonusers. Data should include program evaluations and internal or external assessments and should be maintained in the office of the RSP administrator. They should be accessible to planners of subsequent programs.

RSP should pursue best practices and meaningful research to review and improve programs and services.

RSP must employ ethical practices in the assessment process.

RSP must have access to adequate fiscal, human, professional development, and technological resources to develop and implement assessment plans.

General Standards revised in 2014;
RSP content developed/revised in 1986, 1996, & 2007

Registrar Programs and Services
CAS Contextual Statement

Registrars, at least in function, were the first administrative positions created after institutional presidents. The position dates back to the end of the 12th century in Europe, and the title "registrar" first appeared at Oxford University in 1446.

Registrars were the original, all-purpose campus administrators. The role initially developed from the faculty, with a primary function of being an administrative officer supporting the academic functions of the institution. Multiple functions, including admitting students, collecting tuition, keeping records of faculty meetings, and maintaining student records, were included in the job responsibilities. The registrar has always been somewhat of a generalist—and still is today, even if the role is not quite as diverse as it was a few hundred years ago.

Organizationally, the Registrar's Office is most often found in either Academic Affairs or Student Affairs. Because the position evolved out of the faculty, it was and still is integrated with academic issues. There has been an ebb and flow of the Registrar's Office between Academic Affairs and Student Affairs, depending upon where other academic support services, such as financial aid and admission, have been located.

The Office of the Registrar supports the academic mission of institutions through providing services (either in person or virtually) such as course set up and subsequent registration opportunity, classroom assignment, establishment and enforcement of educational policy, academic record creation and maintenance, institutional compliance with state and federal regulations, records privacy education and regulation, grade processing, transfer credit evaluation, transcripts and certification of enrollment, degree progress monitoring, data management and reporting (i.e., graduation rates, degree progress data, course demand, predictive analytics), degree clearance and diploma preparation, and graduation ceremonies. The exact set of responsibilities within the Office of the Registrar varies widely by institutional type, size, and reporting structure.

Registrars across the United States face a broad array of challenges, including the continued importance of advancing institutional diversity and accommodating the needs of students whose diverse identities and backgrounds entail historical barriers to educational opportunities. As pressure to expand access to higher education leads to federal initiatives such as the expansion of community college access, registrars will have to respond to the increase in demands for services and support. Furthermore, the competing agendas of state and federal governments have led to increasing uncertainty vis-à-vis the regulations and mandates to which registrars must adhere.

One current challenge for registrars lies in the treatment of undocumented immigrants' applications; regulations vary from state to state, as does the impact on access to higher education for students of color. While registrars do not set policy or lobby state legislatures, they are responsible for maintaining applicants and students' records and may provide support for applicants who are unfamiliar with their own rights and responsibilities under the law. Registrars serving undocumented students are challenged to inform themselves about the specific needs and experiences of undocumented students, ensure their staff are culturally competent to understand the needs of this population, and keep informed of changes in state and federal regulations governing the treatment of undocumented applicants and matriculated students (uLEAD, 2015). Under the Obama Administration, the Deferred Action for Childhood Arrivals policy (DACA) is an example of the challenge of the interaction and enforcement of state and federal laws (USCIS, 2014). Whereas the federal government pursued a more inclusive treatment of DACA students, state governors and legislatures reacted by reaffirming existing policies that contrasted with the federal order (Aguilar, 2012; Schwartz, 2012). In these examples, and others related to issues like name change policies for transgender students, the role of the registrar can be crucial in the relationship of students to the institution.

As a service provider, registrars' offices face the trends and challenges that all of higher education is currently experiencing. Quickly evolving technologies require the office to be mindful of new and improved ways of doing business; however, being nimble is a challenge because competing campus projects continually stretch information technology resources. Technology is not a panacea, and as budgets shrink, technology can only replace a portion of the functions that people used to perform. State and federal calls for accountability and outcomes-based assessment land squarely in registrars' offices as these offices have significant responsibility for reporting relevant information. Students increasingly demand integrated services, so the office must work closely with areas that it may not have in the past. Beyond the integration of services, registrars are challenged to support online and distance learning, while navigating the rise-and-fall of technology fads like MOOCs (Jordan, 2014) and the technological innovations they spur (Siemens, 2012).

Pressure to address the cost-effectiveness of higher education has led to more than just the MOOC model. Hope (2015) identified emerging "competency-based" programs that are designed to increase student learning while simultaneously reducing cost. Competency-based models leverage technology to support a model of education that prioritizes students' demonstration of mastery of the content over credit hours earned or time spent in instruction (Competency Based Education Network, 2015; U.S. Department of Education, 2015). Registrars will be faced with determining how to accommodate such programs, as well as addressing the potential challenges posed by them. The registrar's office has typically been associated only with transcripts and related record-keeping, but the function of the registrar today is more integral to the institution; the standards that follow reflect this broad, important role.

References, Readings, and Resources

Aguilar, J. (2012, August 20). Perry: "Deferred Action" doesn't change state policies. *Texas Tribune*, Retrieved from http://www.texastribune.org/2012/08/20/perrydeferred-action-does-not-change-state-policie/.

American Association of Registrars and Admissions Officers (AACRAO): www.aacrao.org\

Competency Based Education Network (2015). *Competency-based education*. Retrieved from http://www.cbenetwork.org/competency-based-education/.

Fisher v. University of Texas at Austin, 570 U.S. (2013).

Hope, J. (2015). Be ready for the challenges of competency-based programs. *The Successful Registrar, 15*, 5-8.

Jordan, K. (2014). Initial trends in enrolment and completion of Massive Open Online Courses. *The International Review of Research in Open and Distance Learning, 15*(1), 133-159.

Kaplin, W. E., & Lee, B. A. (2006). *The law of higher education* (4th ed., Vol. 1-2). San Francisco, CA: Jossey-Bass.

Lauren, B. (2006). *The registrar's guide: Evolving best practices in records and registration*. Washington, DC: American Association of Collegiate Registrars and Admissions Officers.

Pace, H. L. (2011). The evolving office of the registrar. *College and University, 86*(3), 3-7.

Rooker, L. (Ed.), Falkner, T. M., Hicks, D. J., Myers, B. A, & Shirley, S. *2010 FERPA Guide*, American Association of Collegiate Registrars and Admissions Officers.

Schwartz, D. (2012, August 15). Jan Brewer signs executive order denying state benefits to children of undocumented immigrants. *Huffington Post*. Retrieved from http://www.huffingtonpost.com/2012/08/15/jan-brewer-executive-order_n_1785482.html.

Siemens, G. (2012). MOOCs are really a platform. Elearnspace blog. http://www.elearnspace.org/blog/2012/07/25/moocs-are-really-a-platform/

uLEAD – National Forum on Higher Education for the Public Good. (2015). *Resources.* Retrieved from http://uleadnet.org/content/overview

U.S. Citizenship & Immigration Services (USCIS). (2014). *Deferred Action for Childhood Arrivals Process - Frequently Asked Questions.* Retrieved from http://www.uscis.gov/humanitarian/consideration-deferred-action-childhood-arrivals-process/frequently-asked-questions#what%20is%20DACA.

U.S. Department of Education. (2015). *Competency-based learning or personalized learning*. Retrieved from http://www.ed.gov/oii-news/competency-based-learning-or-personalized-learning.

Contextual Statement Contributors
Current Edition
Andrew M. Wells, University of Georgia

Previous Editions:
Tina Falkner, University of Minnesota
Brad Myers, The Ohio State University

Registrar Programs and Services
CAS Standards and Guidelines

Part 1. Mission

The mission of Registrar Programs and Services (RPS) is to maintain stewardship and integrity of student academic records and manage student and institutional academic policies. Therefore, RPS must
- maintain student academic records in perpetuity
- collaborate with complementary services regarding enrollment management functions
- coordinate academic calendars and academic registration
- support academic advising activities
- interpret, implement, and ensure compliance with policies and procedures related to academic record-keeping
- provide accurate individual and aggregate data to internal and external constituencies

Such constituencies needing data may include but are not limited to offices of institutional research, assessment, or enrollment management; faculty members and administrators; accreditation or certification agencies; athletic associations with whom the institution holds membership; entities providing services for veterans or students with special needs; and provincial/state/federal government agencies, such as Homeland Security in the US.

RPS must develop, disseminate, implement, and regularly review their missions, which must be consistent with the mission of the institution and with applicable professional standards. The mission must be appropriate for the institution's students and other constituents. Mission statements must reference student learning and development.

Part 2. Program

To achieve their mission, Registrar Programs and Services (RPS) must contribute to
- students' formal education, which includes both the curriculum and the co-curriculum
- student progression and timely completion of educational goals
- preparation of students for their careers, citizenship, and lives
- student learning and development

To contribute to student learning and development, RPS must
- identify relevant and desirable student learning and development outcomes
- articulate how the student learning and development outcomes align with the six CAS student learning and development domains and related dimensions
- assess relevant and desirable student learning and

development
- provide evidence of impact on outcomes
- articulate contributions to or support of student learning and development in the domains not specifically assessed
- use evidence gathered to create strategies for improvement of programs and services

STUDENT LEARNING AND DEVELOPMENT
DOMAINS AND DIMENSIONS

Domain: knowledge acquisition, integration, construction, and application
- Dimensions: understanding knowledge from a range of disciplines; connecting knowledge to other knowledge, ideas, and experiences; constructing knowledge; and relating knowledge to daily life

Domain: cognitive complexity
- Dimensions: critical thinking, reflective thinking, effective reasoning, and creativity

Domain: intrapersonal development
- Dimensions: realistic self-appraisal, self-understanding, and self-respect; identity development; commitment to ethics and integrity; and spiritual awareness

Domain: interpersonal competence
- Dimensions: meaningful relationships, interdependence, collaboration, and effective leadership

Domain: humanitarianism and civic engagement
- Dimensions: understanding and appreciation of cultural and human differences, social responsibility, global perspective, and sense of civic responsibility

Domain: practical competence
- Dimensions: pursuing goals, communicating effectively, technical competence, managing personal affairs, managing career development, demonstrating professionalism, maintaining health and wellness, and living a purposeful and satisfying life

[LD Outcomes: See *The Council for the Advancement of Standards Learning and Development Outcomes* statement for examples of outcomes related to these domains and dimensions.]

RPS must be
- intentionally designed
- guided by theories and knowledge of learning and development
- integrated into the life of the institution
- reflective of developmental and demographic

profiles of the student population
- responsive to needs of individuals, populations with distinct needs, and relevant constituencies
- delivered using multiple formats, strategies, and contexts
- designed to provide universal access

RPS must collaborate with colleagues and departments across the institution to promote student learning and development, persistence, and success.

RPS must
- treat students courteously with respect for them as individuals
- ensure that relevant policies and procedures, including record changes, are communicated effectively to students, faculty members, and other affected constituents
- provide accurate information to all constituents
- provide timely service to all constituents
- ensure the accuracy and reliability of the data collected and distributed
- provide for the maintenance, upkeep, security, integrity, and proper dissemination of academic information
- develop and implement effective and secure processes for exchange of transcripts between institutions
- provide leadership on the implementation of cooperative academic programs, articulation agreements, and other programs involving academic credit
- ensures that cooperative agreements articulate the responsibility for student support and services and the appropriate student conduct policies
- develop a workable disaster recovery plan that will allow RPS to function in the event of catastrophic circumstances
- educate the institutional community with regard to the security and release of student data

In support of the overall mission of the institution, and when responsibility is assigned, RPS must
- provide leadership for developing and maintaining the student record data base and archival files
- provide campus leadership for the application of information technology to academic processes, records, and information
- ensure that the security and confidentiality of student record data are maintained throughout the institution
- contribute to the enrollment management efforts of the institution
- provide a registration process for enrolling students in classes each term, which may include the calculation of tuition and fees
- verify student academic eligibility for graduation, honors, academic probation, or dismissal
- coordinate course schedules to provide information on courses and sections being offered

in any given term with their day, time, location, and delivery formats
- coordinate the scheduling of appropriate space and resources for classes, including non-classroom-based courses
- manage the transfer of matriculating student records from admissions to RPS
- document approved transfer credit
- verify records for graduation for the preparation and distribution of diplomas
- provide information about courses, programs, policies, and procedures for the development of institutional publications, websites, and other educational materials
- provide information on academic regulations, policies, and procedures including appeals processes
- certify student enrollment status (e.g., veterans services, rehabilitation services, student loans, insurance, athletic eligibility, residency status)
- provide reports as required (e.g., class rosters, grade rosters, grade reports, transcripts, committee needs)
- provide appropriate institutional access to academic records and information
- prepare statistical reports (as needed for institutional research, enrollment management, assessment, and other purposes, e.g., enrollment projections, retention, attrition, and graduation rates)

If responsibility for other student records, policies, procedures, or regulations is assigned to the RPS, those matters should be handled in accordance with the standards above.

RPS may also be responsible for the academic calendar, coordinate the arrangements for commencement, and provide administrative support to the faculty governance bodies.

RPS should develop appropriate policies and procedures for allowing students to be referenced by a preferred name.

Part 3. Organization and Leadership

To achieve program and student learning and development outcomes, Registrar Programs and Services (RPS) must be purposefully structured for effectiveness. RPS must have clearly stated and current
- goals and outcomes
- policies and procedures
- responsibilities and performance expectations for personnel
- organizational charts demonstrating clear channels of authority

Leaders must model ethical behavior and institutional citizenship.

Leaders with organizational authority for RPS must provide strategic planning, management and supervision, and program advancement.

Strategic Planning
- articulate a vision and mission that drive short- and long-term planning
- set goals and objectives based on the needs of the populations served, intended student learning and development outcomes, and program outcomes
- facilitate continuous development, implementation, and assessment of program effectiveness and goal attainment congruent with institutional mission and strategic plans
- promote environments that provide opportunities for student learning, development, and engagement
- develop, adapt, and improve programs and services in response to the changing needs of populations served and evolving institutional priorities
- include diverse perspectives to inform decision making

Management and Supervision
- plan, allocate, and monitor the use of fiscal, physical, human, intellectual, and technological resources
- manage human resource processes including recruitment, selection, professional development, supervision, performance planning, succession planning, evaluation, recognition, and reward
- influence others to contribute to the effectiveness and success of the unit
- empower professional, support, and student personnel to become effective leaders
- encourage and support collaboration with colleagues and departments across the institution
- encourage and support scholarly contributions to the profession
- identify and address individual, organizational, and environmental conditions that foster or inhibit mission achievement
- use current and valid evidence to inform decisions
- incorporate sustainability practices in the management and design of programs, services, and facilities
- understand appropriate technologies and integrate them into programs and services
- be knowledgeable about codes and laws relevant to programs and services and ensure that programs and services meet those requirements
- assess and take action to mitigate potential risks

Program Advancement
- advocate for and actively promote the mission and goals of the programs and services
- inform stakeholders about issues affecting practice
- facilitate processes to reach consensus where wide support is needed
- advocate for representation in strategic planning initiatives at divisional and institutional levels

RPS leaders must
- ensure that newly adopted technologies meet

standards of data integrity and accuracy
- be sensitive to the special needs of students such as part-time students, non-traditional students, students with disabilities, LGBT students, students of various ethnic and cultural groups, distance learners, students studying off campus, international students, and students who restrict information access under privacy laws
- be sensitive to the special needs of faculty members including those teaching abroad and those using distance learning or other alternative delivery systems

RPS leaders should have
- the skill to motivate and inspire staff members to develop a team atmosphere
- fiscal management skills
- the ability to identify and apply relevant information technology
- strong communication, customer relationship, and service management skills

RPS leaders should
- maintain awareness of changing technology and how it applies to RPS; communicate changes to others and educate them about rationale for adopting technologies
- assess decision-making and problem-solving models and select those most appropriate to the institutional milieu
- incorporate student input in decision-making, as appropriate
- serve as a catalyst in institution-wide partnerships due to the broad scope of RPS responsibilities
- demonstrate a philosophy of service to students and the institution
- maintain awareness of the changing ways people identify and how they name their identities to include references to race, ethnicity, gender identity, and sexual orientation
- provide leadership in institutional compliance with federal, state/provincial, and local regulations

RPS must identify and be responsive to external constraints and requirements that impact unit operation (e.g., implications of local, state/provincial, and federal regulations, governing body policies, union agreements, accreditation, professional associations, athletic conference requirements).

RPS should
- develop an organizational chart that identifies cooperative interrelationships with other institutional units and those outside the institution (e.g., institutions with cooperative programs or agreements, study abroad partnerships)
- coordinate programs and services with other institutional personnel, offices, functions, and activities
- collaborate with other enrollment management offices

- establish clear and concise criteria for decision-making and define primary responsibility when more than one unit is involved

Part 4. Human Resources

Registrar Programs and Services (RPS) must be staffed adequately by individuals qualified to accomplish mission and goals.

RPS must have access to technical and support personnel adequate to accomplish their mission.

Within institutional guidelines, RPS must
- establish procedures for personnel recruitment and selection, training, performance planning, and evaluation
- set expectations for supervision and performance
- provide personnel access to continuing and advanced education and appropriate professional development opportunities to improve their competence, skills, and leadership capacity
- consider work/life options available to personnel (e.g., compressed work schedules, flextime, job sharing, remote work, or telework) to promote recruitment and retention of personnel

Administrators of RPS must
- ensure that all personnel have updated position descriptions
- implement recruitment and selection/hiring strategies that produce a workforce inclusive of under-represented populations
- develop promotion practices that are fair, inclusive, proactive, and non-discriminatory

Personnel responsible for delivery of RPS must have written performance goals, objectives, and outcomes for each year's performance cycle to be used to plan, review, and evaluate work and performance. The performance plan must be updated regularly to reflect changes during the performance cycle.

Results of individual personnel evaluations must be used to recognize personnel performance, address performance issues, implement individual and/or collective personnel development and training programs, and inform the assessment of programs and services.

RPS personnel, when hired and throughout their employment, must receive appropriate and thorough training.

RPS personnel, including student employees and volunteers, must have access to resources or receive specific training on
- institutional policies pertaining to functions or activities they support
- privacy and confidentiality policies
- laws regarding access to student records
- policies and procedures for dealing with sensitive institutional information
- policies and procedures related to technology used to store or access student records and institutional data
- how and when to refer those in need of additional assistance to qualified personnel and have access to a supervisor for assistance in making these judgments
- systems and technologies necessary to perform their assigned responsibilities
- ethical and legal uses of technology

On-going training and staff development should be designed to enhance and broaden understanding of roles and responsibilities within the office and the institution. The support staff should be skilled in interpersonal communications, public relations, knowledge of campus resources, dissemination of information, and the handling of complex and detailed activities. Development for the support staff should include adequate initial training to be able to represent the institution in their office function in a competent, professional, and educational manner.

RPS personnel must engage in continuing professional development activities to keep abreast of the research, theories, legislation, policies, and developments that affect their programs and services.

Administrators of RPS must ensure that personnel are knowledgeable about and trained in safety, emergency procedures, and crisis prevention and response. Risk management efforts must address identification of threatening conduct or behavior and must incorporate a system for responding to and reporting such behaviors.

RPS personnel must be knowledgeable of and trained in safety and emergency procedures for securing and vacating facilities.

PROFESSIONAL PERSONNEL

RPS professional personnel either must hold an earned graduate or professional degree in a field relevant to their position or must possess an appropriate combination of educational credentials and related work experience.

INTERNS OR GRADUATE ASSISTANTS

Degree- or credential-seeking interns or graduate assistants must be qualified by enrollment in an appropriate field of study and relevant experience. These students must be trained and supervised by professional personnel who possess applicable educational credentials and work experience and have supervisory experience. Supervisors must be cognizant of the dual roles interns and graduate assistants have as both student and employee.

Supervisors must
- adhere to parameters of students' job descriptions
- articulate intended learning outcomes in student job descriptions
- adhere to agreed-upon work hours and schedules
- offer flexible scheduling when circumstances necessitate

Supervisors and students must both agree to suitable compensation if circumstances necessitate additional hours.

STUDENT EMPLOYEES AND VOLUNTEERS

Student employees and volunteers must be carefully selected, trained, supervised, and evaluated. Students must have access to a supervisor. Student employees and volunteers must be provided clear job descriptions, pre-service training based on assessed needs, and continuing development.

Specific titles and reporting structures will vary based on institutional mission, goals, and objectives. RPS should report to a senior officer in academic affairs, student affairs, or enrollment management.

Part 5. Ethics

Registrar Programs and Services (RPS) must
- review applicable professional ethical standards and must adopt or develop and implement appropriate statements of ethical practice
- publish and adhere to statements of ethical practice and ensure their periodic review
- orient new personnel to relevant ethical standards and statements of ethical practice and related institutional policies

RPS offices must develop appropriate protocols regarding such disclosure of information and must ensure that all staff members, including students, are trained to understand and follow department policies.

Basic principles of privacy and confidentiality must govern both electronic and paper communications and records. RPS must ensure that the institution has a written policy and published statement regarding confidentiality of records and procedures for access, release, and challenge of educational records, and that the means for enforcement are clearly delineated.

Statements of ethical standards must
- specify that RPS personnel respect privacy and maintain confidentiality in communications and records as delineated by privacy laws
- specify limits on disclosure of information contained in students' records as well as requirements to disclose to appropriate authorities
- address conflicts of interest, or appearance thereof, by personnel in the performance of their work
- reflect the responsibility of personnel to be fair, objective, and impartial in their interactions with others
- reference management of institutional funds
- reference appropriate behavior regarding research and assessment with human participants, confidentiality of research and assessment data, and students' rights and responsibilities
- include the expectation that personnel confront and hold accountable other personnel who exhibit unethical behavior

- address issues surrounding scholarly integrity

RPS personnel must
- employ ethical decision making in the performance of their duties
- inform users of programs and services of ethical obligations and limitations emanating from codes and laws or from licensure requirements
- recognize and avoid conflicts of interest that could adversely influence their judgment or objectivity and, when unavoidable, recuse themselves from the situation
- perform their duties within the scope of their position, training, expertise, and competence
- make referrals when issues presented exceed the scope of the position

Part 6. Law, Policy, and Governance

Registrar Programs and Services (RPS) must be in compliance with laws, regulations, and policies that relate to their respective responsibilities and that pose legal obligations, limitations, risks, and liabilities for the institution as a whole. Examples include constitutional, statutory, regulatory, and case law; relevant law and orders emanating from codes and laws; and the institution's policies.

RPS must have access to legal advice needed for personnel to carry out their assigned responsibilities.

RPS must inform personnel, appropriate officials, and users of programs and services about existing and changing legal obligations, risks and liabilities, and limitations.

RPS must inform personnel about professional liability insurance options and refer them to external sources if the institution does not provide coverage.

RPS must have written policies and procedures on operations, transactions, or tasks that have legal implications.

RPS must regularly review policies. The revision and creation of policies must be informed by best practices, available evidence, and policy issues in higher education.

RPS must have procedures and guidelines consistent with institutional policy for responding to threats, emergencies, and crisis situations. Systems and procedures must be in place to disseminate timely and accurate information to students, other members of the institutional community, and appropriate external organizations during emergency situations.

Personnel must neither participate in nor condone any form of harassment or activity that demeans persons or creates an intimidating, hostile, or offensive environment.

RPS must purchase or obtain permission to use copyrighted materials and instruments. References to copyrighted materials and instruments must include appropriate citations.

RPS must inform personnel about internal and external governance organizations that affect programs and services.

RPS must provide leadership in the development of institutional policies related to educational information and appropriate legal issues, especially privacy laws. RPS must ensure that the institution has written policies on all RPS transactions that may have legal implications.

Relevant areas include privacy laws (e.g., Family Educational Rights and Privacy Act (FERPA) in the USA); affirmative action policies; certification of academic transcript information; academic and disciplinary sanctions and dismissals; parental access to records; refund policies; fraudulent records; name changes; gender transitioning; record-keeping practices; facility scheduling policies; access to student information systems; residency status determination; student enrollment status; policies on applicant and student criminal or judicial history; requests for information from government or law enforcement agencies (e.g., in the USA, those related to Homeland Security or the Solomon Amendment); security procedures; social security number usage; court orders; and subpoenas. RPS leaders should meet with the institution's legal counsel regularly to review all relevant documents for clarity and to determine that current regulations are being followed.

RPS must have procedures to keep staff members informed of all requirements related to the maintenance of academic records. RPS must ensure that procedures and forms used to implement regulations must be developed and regularly reviewed to assure fulfillment of institutional requirements.

RPS staff should meet with the institution's legal counsel periodically to review all relevant documents for clarity and to determine that current regulations are being followed. Some of the relevant areas that should be reviewed include affirmative action policies; certification of academic transcript information; academic and disciplinary sanctions and dismissals; parental access to records; privacy laws; refund policies; fraudulent records; name changes; gender transitioning; record-keeping practices; facility scheduling policies; access to student information systems; residency status determination; student enrollment status; policies on applicant and student criminal or judicial history; requests for information from government or law enforcement agencies (e.g., those related to Homeland Security or the Solomon Amendment in the USA); security procedures; social security number usage; court orders; and subpoenas.

Part 7. Diversity, Equity, and Access

Within the context of each institution's mission and in accordance with institutional policies and applicable codes and laws, Registrar Programs and Services (RPS) must create and maintain educational and work environments that are welcoming, accessible, inclusive, equitable, and free from harassment.

RPS must not discriminate on the basis of disability;

age; race; cultural identity; ethnicity; nationality; family educational history (e.g., first generation to attend college); political affiliation; religious affiliation; sex; sexual orientation; gender identity and expression; marital, social, economic, or veteran status; or any other basis included in institutional policies and codes and laws.

RPS must

- advocate for sensitivity to multicultural and social justice concerns by the institution and its personnel
- ensure physical, program, and resource access for all constituents
- modify or remove policies, practices, systems, technologies, facilities, and structures that create barriers or produce inequities
- ensure that when facilities and structures cannot be modified, they do not impede access to programs, services, and resources
- establish goals for diversity, equity, and access
- foster communication and practices that enhance understanding of identity, culture, self-expression, and heritage
- promote respect for commonalities and differences among people within their historical and cultural contexts
- address the characteristics and needs of diverse constituents when establishing and implementing culturally relevant and inclusive programs, services, policies, procedures, and practices
- provide personnel with diversity, equity, and access training and hold personnel accountable for applying the training to their work
- respond to the needs of all constituents served when establishing hours of operation and developing methods of delivering programs, services, and resources
- recognize the needs of distance and online learning students by directly providing or assisting them to gain access to comparable services and resources

Part 8. Internal and External Relations

Registrar Programs and Services (RPS) must reach out to individuals, groups, communities, and organizations internal and external to the institution to

- establish, maintain, and promote understanding and effective relations with those that have a significant interest in or potential effect on the students or other constituents served by the programs and services
- garner support and resources for programs and services as defined by the mission
- collaborate in offering or improving programs and services to meet the needs of students and other constituents and to achieve program and student outcomes
- engage diverse individuals, groups, communities, and organizations to enrich the educational

environment and experiences of students and other constituents
- disseminate information about the programs and services

Relevant constituencies include administrators, faculty members, students, alumni, and the public, as well as other institutions with which there are articulation agreements, cooperative programs, or transfer of students.

Promotional and descriptive information must be accurate and free of deception and misrepresentation.

RPS must have procedures and guidelines consistent with institutional policy for
- communicating with the media
- distributing information through print, broadcast, and online sources
- contracting with external organizations for delivery of programs and services
- cultivating, soliciting, and managing gifts
- applying to and managing funds from grants

RPS must provide leadership to the institution to set standards regarding interpretation of policy and appropriate dissemination of information.

Part 9. Financial Resources

Registrar Programs and Services (RPS) must have funding to accomplish the mission and goals.

In establishing and prioritizing funding resources, RPS must conduct comprehensive analyses to determine
- unmet needs of the unit
- relevant expenditures
- external and internal resources
- impact on students and the institution

RPS must use the budget as a planning tool to reflect commitment to the mission and goals of the programs and services and of the institution.

RPS must administer funds in accordance with established institutional accounting procedures.

RPS must demonstrate efficient and effective use and responsible stewardship of fiscal resources consistent with institutional protocols.

Financial reports must provide an accurate financial overview of the organization and provide clear, understandable, and timely data upon which personnel can plan and make informed decisions.

Procurement procedures must
- be consistent with institutional policies
- ensure that purchases comply with laws and codes for usability and access
- ensure that the institution receives value for the funds spent
- consider information available for comparing the ethical and environmental impact of products and services purchased

RPS leaders must comply with the institution's financial policies that could affect the budget, with required accounting reports that track expenditures, and with policies governing unused funds.

Expenses specific to RPS responsibilities may include purchase and maintenance of customized software systems, adequate security of electronic and hard-copy data, and appropriate back-up systems for all data.

Part 10. Technology

Registrar Programs and Services (RPS) must have technology to support the achievement of their mission and goals. The technology and its use must comply with institutional policies and procedures and with relevant codes and laws.

RPS must use technologies to
- provide updated information regarding mission, location, staffing, programs, services, and official contacts to students and other constituents in accessible formats
- provide an avenue for students and other constituents to communicate sensitive information in a secure format
- enhance the delivery of programs and services for all students

RPS must
- back up data on a regular basis
- adhere to institutional policies regarding ethical and legal use of technology
- articulate policies and procedures for protecting the confidentiality and security of information
- implement a replacement plan and cycle for all technology with attention to sustainability
- incorporate accessibility features into technology-based programs and services

When providing student access to technology, RPS must
- have policies on the use of technology that are clear, easy to understand, and available to all students
- provide information or referral to support services for those needing assistance in accessing or using technology
- provide instruction or training on how to use the technology
- inform students of implications of misuse of technologies

Backup copies of important documentation such as transcripts, the student data base, and the processes for accessing the back-ups must be stored off site in the event of a natural disaster or damage to the records.

RPS should provide to other offices and departments appropriate access to store or retrieve data on students they serve.

Part 11. Facilities and Equipment

Programs and services' facilities must be intentionally designed and located in suitable, accessible, and safe spaces that demonstrate universal design and support the program's mission and goals.

Facilities must be designed to engage various constituents and promote learning.

When RPS is responsible for determining facilities usage outside the immediate office, policies and procedures must be developed and disseminated with respect to the assignment of such space.

Personnel must have workspaces that are suitably located and accessible, well equipped, adequate in size, and designed to support their work and responsibilities.

The design of the facilities must guarantee the security and privacy of records and ensure the confidentiality of sensitive information and conversations. Personnel must be able to secure their work.

RPS must incorporate sustainable practices in use of facilities and purchase of equipment. Facilities and equipment must be evaluated on an established cycle and be in compliance with codes, laws, and accepted practices for access, health, safety, and security.

When acquiring capital equipment, RPS must take into account expenses related to regular maintenance and life cycle costs.

Part 12. Assessment

Registrar Programs and Services (RPS) must develop assessment plans and processes.

Assessment plans must articulate an ongoing cycle of assessment activities.

RPS must
- specify programmatic goals and intended outcomes
- identify student learning and development outcomes
- employ multiple measures and methods
- develop manageable processes for gathering, interpreting, and evaluating data
- document progress toward achievement of goals and outcomes
- interpret and use assessment results to demonstrate accountability
- report aggregated results to respondent groups and stakeholders
- use assessment results to inform planning and decision-making
- assess effectiveness of implemented changes
- provide evidence of improvement of programs and services

Student input should be incorporated into program improvement and policy development.

RPS must employ ethical practices in the assessment process.

RPS must have access to adequate fiscal, human, professional development, and technological resources to develop and implement assessment plans.

General Standards revised in 2014;
RPS content developed/revised in 1995 & 2008

Sexual Violence-Related Programs and Services
CAS Contexual Statement

Introduction

Sexual Violence-Related Programs and Services operate under the assumption that (a) all students deserve to learn in an environment free from violence and (b) students cannot learn if they do not feel safe. College campuses are generally statistically safer than the communities in which they are located, yet sexual violence is a particular risk for the 18-24 age group (especially college women) in both the United States and Canada (DeKeseredy & Kelly, 1993; Fisher, Cullen & Turner, 2000; Krebs, Lindquist, Warner, Fisher, & Martin, 2014). Research continues to demonstrate a steady trend of college-aged individuals in the United States who have experienced sexual violence (Black et al., 2011; Centers for Disease Control and Prevention [CDC], 2012). Clearly there is a need for colleges and universities to have established Sexual Violence-Related Programs and Services, policies and protocols in order to respond to incidents of sexual violence but also to prevent and reduce the risk of its occurrence.

In the context of these standards, CAS is using the term *sexual violence* to include the following: physical sexual acts perpetrated against a person's will or where a person is incapable of giving consent (e.g., due to the person's age or use of alcohol or other drugs, or because a disability prevents the person from having the capacity to legally consent). This includes rape, sexual assault, sexual battery, sexual abuse, and sexual coercion, and may also include incidents of sexual harassment, stalking, domestic, dating and intimate partner violence during which any of these occur but are not, in and of themselves, necessarily sexual violence. Sexual violence can be committed by institutional employees, other students, or third parties. All such acts are prohibited by federal law including Title IX, criminal law, and institutional policies, as well as by the laws in virtually all U.S. states.

In the context of these standards, CAS uses the term *survivor* to describe a person who has lived through one or more experience of sexual violence.

In the context of these standards, CAS uses the term *complainant* to describe a person who formally reports to institutional authorities that they have been the target of sexual violence; and uses the term *respondent* to describe a person who has been accused of but not yet found responsible for sexual violence.

Historical Context

Historians of sexual violence activism in the United States suggest that the call to action on college and university campuses stems from a much longer history of the rape crisis movement in the United States in the post-Civil War era (Greensite, 2009). The movement to address sexual violence on college campuses was largely in response to an increase in the number of survivors willing to report incidents on campus, not necessarily to police or senior administrators, but to student affairs professionals and academic advisors. Sexual Violence-Related Programs and Services, begun

on some college campuses in the early 1970s, were frequently associated with health care, health promotion/education or women's advocacy centers. Mostly run by forward thinking staff in these areas, along with student volunteers, those staffing these programs developed their early expertise from students' own experiences and the experiences of their friends. In those early days, the research literature to guide sexual violence response practices was scarce; it was not until Burgess and Holmstrom (1974) coined the term *rape trauma syndrome* that advocates and counselors had a meaningful theoretical framework to understand the experiences of sexual violence survivors.

At the time, campus advocates partnered with community rape crisis centers to provide needed support services and education. Those at the forefront of the movement lobbied for the first campus-based rape crisis center at the University of Maryland in 1972, a women's studies program and rape crisis center at the University of Pennsylvania in 1973, and campus-wide prevention programs for the University of California system in 1976 (Heldman & Brown, 2014).

The 1980s brought increasing attention to the issue of campus sexual violence. Receiving media attention for the first time in 1985, *Ms.* Magazine published "Date Rape: A Campus Epidemic" which featured the groundbreaking research of Dr. Mary Koss. This three-year study of more than 7,000 students at 35 schools would challenge the misconception that rape was an act perpetrated by strangers, that the vast majority of sexual assaults were being committed by someone known to the survivors. Then, in the spring of 1987, the Santa Monica Rape Treatment Center experienced a sudden increase in the number of survivors seeking support for sexual assaults occurring on college campuses. This surge in survivors seeking support resulted in a report entitled "Sexual Assault on Campus: What Colleges Can Do" (Adams & Abarbanel, 1988) intended to assist colleges and universities in establishing effective prevention, education and assistance programs for survivors of sexual violence. As the 1980s would come to a close, Robin Warshaw published *I Never Called It Rape* (1988), a book of personal accounts from survivors around the country that confirmed Koss's research (Heldman & Brown, 2014).

By the mid-1990s many campuses began to address dating and domestic violence. Even at that time however, many institutions refrained from providing assistance or programs on domestic and dating violence because of the common misperception that this type of violence only happened in heterosexual marital relationships and not in the dating or casual context that better characterized the experiences of the general undergraduate population (Bogal-Allbritten & Allbritten, 1991). Since that time, society has developed a more complex understanding of violence in relationships with the term *intimate partner violence* (CDC, 2011) used to reference any acts of physical, psychological, emotional or economic harm, or threats of harm against a current or former partner with or without sexual intimacy between those involved, including harm against individuals in same-sex relationships.

In recent decades, misperceptions about *who* commits acts of sexual violence and in *what context* they occur still persist that promulgate stranger rape as the common scenario on campus and in the broader community (McMahon, 2011; Lisak & Miller, 2002). However, most acts of campus sexual violence are committed by individuals who are known to the survivor rather than by a stranger. Additionally, research continues to establish that the "undetected rapist" – the male who commits repeated acts of sexual violence which often go unreported - is likely responsible for the majority of campus sexual violence (Lisak & Miller, 2002; Abbey & McAuslan, 2004).

Legislation

Federal legislation, regulations and sub-regulatory guidance have influenced Sexual Violence Programs around the United States and in Canada over recent decades. The following bulleted list provides a snapshot of the various acts, guidance and other materials that have impacted the evolving climate around sexual violence on U.S. campuses:

- **1972**: Congress passed into law *Title IX of the Education Amendments of 1972* (Title IX) which prohibits discrimination on the basis of sex for federally funded education programs and activities.
- **1990**: The *Jeanne Clery Disclosure of Campus Security Policy and Campus Crime Statistics Act* (also known as the Campus Security Act or the Clery Act), was signed into law. It required institutions of higher education to annually report certain incidents of crime to the DOE.
- **1992**: The Clery Act was amended in 1992 to include the *Campus Sexual Assault Victim's Bill of Rights* that requires all colleges and universities receiving federal funding to promulgate sexual assault policies that provide victims with a set of basic rights, such as access to counseling and other services. The amendments also mandated that colleges and universities develop and offer programs specifically aimed at preventing sexual assault.
- **1994**: Congress passed the *Violence Against Women Act* (VAWA), and federal funds were made available five years later through campus grants to prevent violence against women.
- **1997**: OCR produced the "Sexual Harassment Guidance: Harassment of Students by School Employees, Other Students or Third Parties" which was grounded in the legal authority that sexual harassment of students can be a form of sex discrimination covered by Title IX.
- **2001**: OCR produced the "Revised Sexual Harassment Guidance: Harassment of Students by School Employees, Other Students or Third Parties" which served as an update to the 1997 document to reflect subsequent Supreme Court cases relating to sexual harassment in schools. In all other

regards, the document remained the same, in that it reinforces that schools should recognize and respond effectively to the sexual harassment of students as a condition of receiving federal financial assistance.

- **2010**: The Center for Public Integrity published a report entitled "Sexual Assault on Campus: A Frustrating Search for Justice." The report was the culmination of a two-year study examining how institutions of higher education handled cases of sexual assault through the surveying of 152 campus crisis clinics and services, interviews with 50 former and current college student survivors, data analysis of 10 years' worth of Title IX complaints and Clery violations filed through the DOE.
- **2011**: OCR produced a "Dear Colleague Letter" which offered sub-regulatory guidance that the requirements of Title IX pertaining to sexual harassment are also applicable to sexual violence. The letter went on to discuss Title IX requirements as they relate to student-on-student sexual harassment, including sexual violence, and explained institutional responsibility to take immediate and effective steps to stop sexual violence and to take proactive efforts to prevent it from happening again.
- **2013**: Congress passed the *Violence Against Women Reauthorization Act* (VAWA) which contains language from the drafted Campus SaVE Act in section 304. This legislation introduced new federal requirements for colleges and universities and resulted in a number of amendments to the Clery Act. At the same time, President Obama created a task force on campus sexual assault; Congress introduced laws which would require institutions to increase their vigilance of and services to campuses; and state leaders in Virginia and elsewhere across the country focused more resources to combat this threat.
- **2014**: OCR published a frequently asked questions document which clarified their 2011 "Dear Colleague Letter;" VAWA, in which section 304 contains campus provisions, went into effect on October 1, 2014. In the Spring of this year the Office of the President released its White House "Not Alone" Web site (www.notalone.gov) aimed at supporting survivors of sexual violence on campus which contains additional non-binding guidance and support including a policy checklist, Title IX Coordinator job description, interim and support measures for survivors, and definitions of prohibited conduct to help institutions achieve success in addressing the complex issues surrounding sexual violence on campus. In the Fall the White House Task Force announced a companion public service campaign "It's On Us" (itsonus.org) largely aimed at engaging college men, intended to change campus culture and encourage individuals to prevent sexual violence before it happens.
- **2015**: By the summer of 2015, the amendments to the Clery Act, as outlined in section 304 of

VAWA, went into effect and required colleges and universities to do the following: maintain statistics regarding the number of incidents of dating violence, domestic violence, sexual assault, and stalking; disclose "unfounded" crime reports in campus annual security reports; revise the definition of rape according to the Federal Bureau of Investigation (FBI) definition; revise the categories of bias for the purposes of Clery reporting to include gender identity and to separate ethnicity and national origin; describe ongoing prevention and awareness programs and their evaluation as well as those targeting incoming students and new employees; describe each type of disciplinary proceeding, including all steps (e.g., how to file a complaint), timelines and decision-making processes; list all possible sanctions for a finding of responsibility; outline all protective and interim measures available following a report; and provide a prompt, fair, and equitable process for both the complainant(s) and respondent(s).

Canadian Context. Prior to 1983, Canadian law and legal processes significantly impacted someone's decision to report sexual violence and to pursue legal action. The following bulleted list provides a snapshot of the various changes that have impacted the evolving climate around sexual violence on Canadian campuses:

- Until 1983, crimes of sexual assault were gender-specific; there were separate offenses for indecent assault of a male and female, as defined in the *Criminal Code.*
- In 1983 and again in 1992, the *Criminal Code* was amended to eradicate myths and stereotypes inherent in the legal process.
- The current *Criminal Code* does not distinguish between rape and sexual assault. The passage of Bill C-127 introduced a three-tier definition of sexual assault characterized by the degree of seriousness (defined by level of physical violence associated with the crime).
- In March 2015, the Ontario government released its action plan related to sexual violence and the Council of Ontario Universities (COU) released its framework for sexual violence policies and protocols.

Sexual violence is commonly believed to be the most underreported form of violence. The U.S. Department of Justice found that fewer than 5% of female college students who are sexually assaulted report the matter to school authorities or law enforcement (Karjane, Fisher, & Cullen, 2005). Research demonstrates a variety of factors that contribute to low levels of reporting. The college campus is often characterized by high levels of victimization and a pervasive cultural acceptance of rape myths which create an environment where survivors often feel disempowered and alienated, particularly in the wake of sexual violence (ACHA, 2006). Therefore, it is particularly important that campuses are transparent about identifying and training mandatory reporters and the availability of confidential campus and community-based options. Additionally, institution-wide

policies, including specific written protocols for offices and departments across campus can be an effective approach to enhancing transparency and consistency as necessary for full campus community engagement. Such intentionally designed policies serve as a statement of an institution's commitment to preventing and responding to acts of sexual violence.

While federal legislation in both the U.S. and Canada has dedicated much of its guidance to creating a climate supportive of reporting sexual violence, it also encourages campuses to employ conduct processes that ensure all parties involved in reports of sexual violence on campus are treated in an integrated and consistent manner, are treated with dignity and respect, and that prompt responsive action is taken to stop, prevent recurrence, and address the effects of sexual violence. This need for fair, prompt and equitable processes is further highlighted by a growing number of students who have filed complaints and/or sued their respective institutions for what they have deemed to be biased and ineffective campus conduct processes. Balancing the rights and responsibilities of the complainant(s), respondent(s), and the institution is challenging for campuses, particularly with regard to protecting confidentiality while also maintaining campus safety.

As a result of increased federal attention to sexual violence on college campuses in the U.S. and Canada, more and more institutions are creating new positions (e.g., Title IX Coordinator), new offices (e.g., Violence Prevention and Response), and/or programs (e.g., employee training) dedicated to the issue. Recent legislation has heightened campus attention to compliance; the CAS Sexual Violence-Related Programs and Services Standards seek to challenge institutions to approach the issue of sexual violence from a broader perspective through sustainable, community-wide, evidence-informed strategies that draws upon the rich history of those working to prevent and address sexual violence for many decades. Sexual Violence-Related Programs and Services also challenge colleges and universities to move beyond strategies that reduce the risk for victimization to a broader approach to ending sexual violence.

Prevention. All levels of prevention are necessary to stop the occurrence of sexual violence. The goal of prevention is to change the social climate so that sexual violence is not tolerated and root causes for its occurrence are eliminated. Comprehensive prevention consists of well-timed and well-executed strategies that incorporate sociopolitical analysis of the anti-rape movement, a multidimensional systematic approach to increasing awareness, and promoting healthy behaviors central to public health and safety. Prevention strategies include assessment of campus climate (including normative attitudes, perceptions and behaviors related to sexual violence); application of the current research to provide evidence-informed approaches; training students, staff and faculty to intervene appropriately and effectively; community organizing around gender equality issues; policy creation and revision to reflect gender equity; and norms clarification that support healthy, consensual relationships.

Reducing risk of victimization. Strategies for reducing the risk of victimization are the most common form of sexual violence education on campuses (O'Donohue, Yeater, & Fanetti, 2003), yet they also may inadvertently promote deeply engrained victim-blaming attitudes and perceptions. These strategies have a philosophic and programmatic focus on decreasing incidents of sexual violence through activities that focus on steps a person can take to protect themselves, what friends can do to help reduce the risk of sexual violence among their peers, and bystander intervention strategies which try to change attitudes and beliefs about sexual violence and increase the likelihood that someone will intervene in the future. It is important that these strategies are informed by the best available evaluation and evidence to minimize the risk for victim-blaming.

Reducing risk for perpetration. Strategies for reducing the risk for perpetration are also critical in preventing sexual violence. Studies have demonstrated that at least 10% of male college students have perpetrated sexual violence in the preceding year (Abbey & McAuslan, 2004; Thompson, Koss, Kingree, Goree, & Rice, 2011; White & Smith, 2004). Risk factors for perpetration, such as attitudes toward gender roles and sexual activity, peer influences and norms related to sexual activity, acceptance of rape myths and rape-supportive beliefs, and high-risk alcohol use (Harrell et al, 2009), contribute to a greater likelihood of male perpetration. Identifying and targeting these factors and particular high-risk male populations may further reduce risk for perpetration, both at the institutional level and at earlier stages of adolescent development (Kingree & Thompson, 2014; Carr & VanDeusen, 2004; Abbey & McAuslan, 2004).

Alcohol and sexual violence. The majority of sexual assaults on campus involve alcohol (Krebs et al., 2007). The *Campus Sexual Assault Study* (Krebs et al., 2007) indicates that frequency of high-risk drinking (4 or more drinks in one sitting) is positively correlated with experiences of incapacitated sexual assault since entering college. Therefore, it is critical that efforts to address high-risk alcohol use incorporate implications for sexual violence prevention for reducing the risk of both victimization and perpetration and to ensure that policies (e.g., amnesty policies), protocols (e.g., campus safety official response systems), and procedures (e.g., conduct review boards) are informed by the relationship between alcohol and sexual violence. Regardless of the circumstances, high-risk alcohol use is not an excuse for sexual violence. Concerns also exist regarding the use of other drugs to facilitate incapacitation and sexual violence.

Summary

Although Sexual Violence-Related Programs and Services provide expertise on campus sexual violence, this work cannot be successfully undertaken without the active support and participation at all levels of the institution. Coordinated prevention and response should include campus and community-based services and resources, and should engage students, staff, faculty and administrators.

Notes

[1] CAS does not espouse specific legal and student conduct language and encourages campuses to consult state, provincial and federal law and institutional policies for clear definition of terms.

References, Readings and Resources

Abbey, A. & McAuslan, P. (2004). A longitudinal examination of male college students' perpetration of sexual assault. *Journal of Consulting and Clinical Psychology*, 72, 747-756.

Adams, A. & Abarbanel, G. (1988). *Sexual assault on campus: What colleges can do.* Santat Monica, CA: Rape Treatment Center Santa Monica.

American College Health Association. American College Health Association-National College Health Assessment: http://www.acha-ncha.org

American College Health Association. (2011, December). *Position statement on preventing sexual violence on college campuses.* Retrieved from http://www.acha.org/Publications/docs/ACHA_Statement_Preventing_Sexual_Violence_Dec2011.pdf

Black, M. C., Basile, K. C., Breiding, M. J., Smith, S. G., Walters, M. L., Merrick, M. T., Chen, J., & Stevens, M. R. (2011). The national relationship and sexual violence survey (NISVS): 2010 summary report. Atlanta, GA: National Center for Injury Prevention and Control, Centers for Disease Control and Prevention.

Bogal-Allbritten, R. & Allbritten, W. (1991). Courtship violence on campus: A nationwide survey of student affairs professionals. *NASPA Journal of Student Affairs Practice and Research*, 28, 312-318.

Burgess, A. W. & Holmstrom, L. L. (1974). Rape trauma syndrome. *The American Journal of Psychiatry, 131*(9), 981-986.

Carr, J., & VanDeusen, K.M. (2004). Risk factors for male sexual aggression on college campuses. *Journal of Family Violence, 19,* 279-289.

Centers for Disease Control and Prevention. National Intimate Partner and Sexual Violence Survey. http://www.cdc.gov/violenceprevention/nisvs/summary_reports.html

Centers for Disease Control and Prevention. (2009). *Understanding intimate partner violence: Fact Sheet.* Retrieved from http://www.cdc.gov/ViolencePrevention/sexualviolence/defintion.html

Center for Public Integrity. (2010). *Sexual assault on campus: A frustrating search for justice.* Retrieved from http://cloudfront-files-1.publicintegrity.org/documents/pdfs/Sexual%20Assault%20on%20Campus.pdf

DeKeseredy, W. & Kelly, K. (1993). The incidence and prevalence of women abuse in Canadian university and college dating relationships. *Canadian Journal of Sociology*, 18, 137-159.

Fisher, B., Cullen, F., Turner, M. (2000). *The sexual victimization of college women.* U.S. Department of Justice, Office of Justice Programs, National Institute of Justice. Retrieved from http://www.ncjrs.gov/pdffiles1/nij/182369.pdf.

Harrell, M.C., Castaneda, L.W., Adelson, M., Gaillot, S., Lynch, C., & Pomeroy, A. (2009). *A compendium of sexual assault research.* National Defense Research Institute. Retrieved from http://www.rand.org/content/dam/rand/pubs/technical_reports/2009/RAND_TR617.pdf

Heldman, C. & Brown, B. (2014). *Campus rape: A brief history of sexual violence activism in the U.S.* Washington, D.C.: Ed Act Now Rally.

Karjane, H., Fisher, B. & Cullen, F. (2005). *Sexual assault on campus: What colleges and universities are doing about it.* National Institute of Justice. Retrieved from http://www.ncjrs.gov/pdffiles1/nij/205521.pdf

Kingree, J.B., & Thompson, M. (2014). A comparison of risk factors for alcohol-involved and alcohol-uninvolved sexual aggression perpetration. *Journal of Interpersonal Violence.* Advance online publication. doi:10.1177/086260514540806

Koss, M. (1985). *Date Rape: A Campus Epidemic.*

Krebs, C., Lindquist, C., Warner, T., Fisher, B., Martin, S. (2007). *The campus sexual assault (CSA) study.* Retrieved from www.ncjrs. gov/pdffiles1/nij/grants/221153.pdf

Lisak, D. & Miller, P.M. (2002). Repeat rape and multiple offending among undetected rapists. *Violence and Victims, 17,* 73-84.

Mahoney, P. & Williams, L.M. (1998). "Sexual assault in marriage: Prevalence, correlates, and treatment of wife rape," in eds. J.J. Jasinski and L.M. Williams, *Partner Violence: A Comprehensive Review of 20 Years of Research,* Thousand Oaks, CA: Sage, 113-162.

McMahon, S. (2011). *Changing perceptions of sexual violence over time.* Applied Research Paper, National Online Resource Center on Violence Against Women. Retrieved from http://www.vawnet.org/Assoc_Files_VAWnet/AR_ChangingPerceptions.pdf

METRAC. (2014). *Sexual assault policies on campus: A discussion paper.* Retrieved from http://www.metrac.org/wp-content/uploads/2014/11/final.formatted.campus.discussion.paper_.26sept14.pdf

National Center on Safe Supportive Learning Environments. U.S. Department of Education. http://safesupportivelearning.ed.gov/

O'Donohue, W., Yeater, E. A., & Fanetti, M. (2003). Rape prevention with college males: The role of rape myth acceptance, victim empathy and outcome expectancies. *Journal of Interpersonal Violence, 18,* 513-531.

Office of the President. (2014). *Checklist for campus sexual misconduct policies.* Retrieved from https://www.notalone.gov/assets/checklist-for-campus-sexual-misconduct-policies.pdf

Office of the President. (2014). *Sample language and definitions of prohibited conduct for a school's sexual misconduct policy.* Retrieved from https://www.notalone.gov/assets/definitions-of-prohibited-conduct.pdf

Office of the President. (2014). *Sample language for interim and supportive measures to protect students following an allegation of sexual misconduct.* Retrieved from https://www.notalone.gov/assets/interim-and-supportive-measures.pdf

Office of the President. (2014). *Sample language for title IX coordinator's role in sexual misconduct policy.* Retrieved from https://www.notalone.gov/assets/role-of-title-ix-coordinator.pdf

Office for Civil Rights. U.S. Department of Education. (1997). *Sexual harassment guidance: Harassment of students by school employees, other students and third parties.* Retrieved from http://www2.ed.gov/about/offices/list/ocr/docs/sexhar01.html

Office for Civil Rights. U.S. Department of Education. (2001). *Revised sexual harassment guidance: Harassment of students by school employees, other students and third parties.* Retrieved from http://www2.ed.gov/about/offices/list/ocr/docs/shguide.html

Office for Civil Rights. U.S. Department of Education. (2011). *Dear colleague letter.* Retrieved from http://www2.ed.gov/print/about/offices/list/ocr/letters/colleague201104.html

Ontario Women's Directorate. (January 2013). *Developing a response to sexual violence: A resource guide for Ontario's colleges and universities.* Ontario, Canada. Full text available at http://www.women.gov.on.ca/owd/docs/campus_guide.pdf

Sinozich, S. & Langton, L. (2014). *Rape and sexual assault victimization among college-age females, 1995-2013.* U.S. Department of Justice, Office of Justice Programs, The Bureau of Justice Statistcs. Full text available at http://www.bjs.gov/content/pub/pdf/rsavcaf9513.pdf

Thompson, M., Koss, M., Kingree, J., Goree, J., & Rice, J. (2011). A prospective meditational model of sexual aggression among college men. *Journal of Interpersonal Violence, 26,* 2716-2734.

Warshaw, R. (1988). *I never called it rape.* New York, NY: Harper & Row Publishers.

White, J. & Smith, P. (2004). Sexual assault perpetration and re- perpetration: From adolescence to young adulthood. *Criminal Justice and Behavior, 31,* 182-202.

Contextual Statement Contributors
Current Edition:
Stacy Andes, Villanova University, ACHA
Sara Bendoraitis, American University, Consortium
S. Daniel Carter, VTV Family Outreach Foundation
Jill Dunlap, University of California - Santa Barbara
Doug Franklin, Private Consultant, NIRSA
Dennis Gregory, Old Dominion University, SACSA
Deanie Kepler, Southern Methodist University, AHEPPP
Alison Kiss, Clery Center for Security on Campus
Ruth Anne Koenick, Rutgers University - New Brunswick
Regina Lawson, Wake Forest University, IACLEA
Melissa Mahan, Texas A&M - San Antonio, NCCP
Mollie M. Monahan-Kreishman, Independent Consultant Addressing Sexual Violence in Higher Education
Marcelle Mullings, York University
Mary-Jeanne Raleigh, University of North Carolina at Greensboro, ACCA
Dana Scaduto, Dickinson College
Cathy Seasholes, University of Wisconsin - Milwaukee, NWSA
Michael Webster, McDaniel College

Previous Editions:
Holly Ennis, Rutgers University
Sara Bendoraitis, American University, Consortium
Ruth Anne Koenick, Rutgers University
Rebecca Morrow, Idaho State University, NWSA
Sandra Ortman-Tomlin, Gateway Community and Technical College
Mary-Jeanne Raleigh, St. Mary's College of Maryland, ACCA
William Smedick, Johns Hopkins University, NACA

Sexual Violence-Related Programs and Services
CAS Standards and Guidelines

The mission of Sexual Violence-Related Programs and Services (SV-RPS) is to end sexual violence on campus and to engage the campus community in creating a safe, supportive, and responsive environment for all members affected when sexual violence occurs.

SV-RPS must provide, directly or through collaboration, a range of crisis intervention, advocacy, education, training, and prevention programs and services that meet the needs of the institutions and individuals they serve including survivors, complainants, respondents, and all members of the campus community

SV-RPS must develop, disseminate, implement, and regularly review their missions, which must be consistent with the mission of the institution and with applicable professional standards. The mission must be appropriate for the institution's students and other constituents. Mission statements must reference student learning and development.

To accomplish this mission SV-RPS must
- address the needs and experiences of individuals across all social and personal identities
- employ supportive and survivor-centered care that avoids victim-blaming attitudes, practices, and beliefs
- provide information and resources to survivors about the broad range of options available to them, including but not limited to, pursuing action in the criminal justice system; pursuing action through the code of conduct; obtaining emergency and follow-up health care; accessing counseling services; and receiving advocacy assistance with living, work, and academic concerns
- provide and/or facilitate access to the range of available services as a way of supporting the choices made by the survivor regardless of whether the survivor chooses to seek disciplinary and/or legal action
- provide services to respondents to assure compliance with laws regarding equal treatment of both the complainant and respondent
- educate the institutional community on issues of sexual violence and current campus climate

Institutions should examine the primary purpose of SV-RPS programs and develop the appropriate approach that reflects their institutional needs while assuring compliance with laws, regulations, policies, procedures and guidelines, and a commitment to creating a campus free of sexual violence.

To achieve their mission, Sexual Violence-Related Programs and Services (SV-RPS) must contribute to
- students' formal education, which includes both the curriculum and the co-curriculum
- student progression and timely completion of educational goals
- preparation of students for their careers, citizenship, and lives
- student learning and development

To contribute to student learning and development, SV-RPS must
- identify relevant and desirable student learning and development outcomes
- articulate how the student learning and development outcomes align with the six CAS student learning and development domains and related dimensions
- assess relevant and desirable student learning and development
- provide evidence of impact on outcomes
- articulate contributions to or support of student learning and development in the domains not specifically assessed
- use evidence gathered to create strategies for improvement of programs and services

STUDENT LEARNING AND DEVELOPMENT DOMAINS AND DIMENSIONS

Domain: knowledge acquisition, integration, construction, and application
- Dimensions: understanding knowledge from a range of disciplines; connecting knowledge to other knowledge, ideas, and experiences; constructing knowledge; and relating knowledge to daily life

Domain: cognitive complexity
- Dimensions: critical thinking, reflective thinking, effective reasoning, and creativity

Domain: intrapersonal development
- Dimensions: realistic self-appraisal, self-understanding, and self-respect; identity development; commitment to ethics and integrity; and spiritual awareness

Domain: interpersonal competence
- Dimensions: meaningful relationships, interdependence, collaboration, and effective leadership

Domain: humanitarianism and civic engagement
- Dimensions: understanding and appreciation of cultural and human differences, social responsibility, global perspective, and sense of civic responsibility

Domain: practical competence

- **Dimensions: pursuing goals, communicating effectively, technical competence, managing personal affairs, managing career development, demonstrating professionalism, maintaining health and wellness, and living a purposeful and satisfying life**

[LD Outcomes: See *The Council for the Advancement of Standards Learning and Development Outcomes* statement for examples of outcomes related to these domains and dimensions.]

SV-RPS must be

- **intentionally designed**
- **guided by theories and knowledge of learning and development**
- **integrated into the life of the institution**
- **reflective of developmental and demographic profiles of the student population**
- **responsive to needs of individuals, populations with distinct needs, and relevant constituencies**
- **delivered using multiple formats, strategies, and contexts**
- **designed to provide universal access**

SV-RPS must collaborate with colleagues and departments across the institution to promote student learning and development, persistence, and success.

In collaboration with faculty, staff, and students, SV-RPS must

- **implement policies regarding sexual violence that serve as a statement of the institution's commitment to preventing and responding to acts of sexual violence**
- **monitor the use and enforcement of these policies**
- **obtain institutional support for SV-RPS during the creation and enforcement of these policies**

Policies should define sexual assault, dating violence, domestic violence, intimate partner violence, sexual harassment and stalking. Policies should contain rules and regulations for faculty, staff and student members' conduct, as well as all possible sanctions for unacceptable behavior, the rights and responsibilities of complainant(s) and respondent(s), and procedures for responding to reports of sexual violence.

Policies must be widely communicated in a variety of methods to staff members, faculty members, and students.

SV-RPS must provide direct training, in-service programs, and updates about changes to policy and law on a regular basis.

SV-RPS must determine protocols for response and support.

Protocols should be created so that response to a report of sexual violence is organized, seamless, and survivor-centered. Protocols should ensure that complainants and respondents get timely, respectful treatment in a supportive manner.

These protocols may also be included in the aforementioned policies and should be distributed to all involved in responding to reports of sexual violence. Protocols should comply with all laws and regulations. Protocols, like policies, should be widely publicized to all faculty, staff and students at the institution. These protocols should address

- training requirements for all faculty and staff, especially those in key student contact areas and campus law enforcement and security personnel
- use and role of advocates when sexual violence is suspected or known to have occurred
- mandated reporting and who mandated reporters are for purposes of Clery Act compliance, Title IX compliance, and/or other governmental mandates
- who, how and when different individuals and offices should be notified of a report of sexual violence, including information sharing with outside entities (e.g., media, parents and relatives, campus community)
- providing services to students who do not wish to report the crime to law enforcement or campus authorities
- procedures for reporting to institutional and law enforcement authorities based on legal requirements, including avenues for confidential as well as anonymous reporting
- procedures for investigating reports of sexual violence
- the role of campus law enforcement and security personnel and procedures to be followed when investigations involve local law enforcement or prosecutors office
- who keeps records, what information should and should not be documented, and who has access to these records
- development of a coordinated communication plan amongst all individuals, institutional entities and community services involved in responding to a report of sexual violence
- development of communication plans between the institution and complainant(s) and the institution and respondent(s)
- procedures for special populations such as students who are minors and international students
- availability of medical and mental health services
- procedures for collecting forensic and medical evidence
- availability of legal support for both the complainant and respondent
- the role of external organizations such as local shelters or services, if any
- housing policies for on-campus students who need to be relocated
- institutional withdrawal policies to allow flexibility for meeting survivor needs
- student conduct procedures for those found responsible for acts of violence, including how a report will be investigated
- statement regarding the fact that both complainant and respondent will be treated equally and fairly

- procedures for the implementation of sanctions and consequences for respondents found responsible for violations of institutional policy around sexual violence
- a comprehensive list of all possible sanctions for students found responsible for perpetrating sexual violence

Appropriate institutional authorities should be involved in the enforcement of such policies in an effort to ensure that all departments involved in response are aware of their role and follow the protocols.

Services must be provided without concern for whether a person seeks legal or student conduct intervention.

People respond to trauma differently and it is imperative that SV-RPS provide services that address the diverse responses that survivors, complainants and respondents experience.

SV-RPS must
- **promise confidentiality only if it can be guaranteed**
- **inform all individuals of their rights, including complainants and respondents, and ensure that they have all the information needed to make informed decisions about what is right for them**
- **provide access to emergency support at all times, even during non-business hours**
- **provide referrals to counseling and other key services to survivors, complainants and respondents**
- **offer services to all students**

Research indicates that prevention efforts are the most effective approach for institutions to eliminate sexual violence on their campuses. Prevention efforts should be multifaceted and include diverse approaches to issues and learning styles.

Programs to prevent perpetration and victimization should be designed to improve knowledge and attitudes that correspond to the origins of sexual violence (such as adherence to societal norms supportive of sexual violence, attitudes toward gender roles and sexual activity, acceptance of rape myths and rape-supportive beliefs), build skills for respectful interactions, and empower participants to become agents of change. Sexual violence prevention should address attitudes about sexual violence, the impact of gender roles, healthy relationships, consent, conflict resolution, respect for personal boundaries, and skill building for these topics.

These programs should address (a) the issue of sexual violence against the individual, the relationship, the community, and societal values and (b) the root cause of sexual violence by challenging attitudes and behaviors that support a culture of violence. One common aspect of prevention programs is an effort to engage men on campus to promote a healthy concept of masculinity as well as to develop allies that stand up against sexual violence.

Training must cover policies and protocols as well as information about the nature of these crimes, legal responsibilities of individuals and groups, and other important elements of prevention.

Comprehensive training on issues related to sexual violence, including but not limited to sexual assault, dating violence, domestic violence, intimate partner violence, stalking, and sexual harassment must be available to all members of the campus community with special attention to the training needs of staff in roles most likely to interact with survivors, complainants and respondents.

Part 3. Organization and Leadership

To achieve program and student learning and development outcomes, Sexual Violence-Related Programs and Services (SV-RPS) must be purposefully structured for effectiveness. SV-RPS must have clearly stated and current
- **goals and outcomes**
- **policies and procedures**
- **responsibilities and performance expectations for personnel**
- **organizational charts demonstrating clear channels of authority**

Leaders must model ethical behavior and institutional citizenship.

Leaders with organizational authority for SV-RPS must provide strategic planning, management and supervision, and program advancement.

Strategic Planning
- articulate a vision and mission that drive short- and long-term planning
- set goals and objectives based on the needs of the populations served, intended student learning and development outcomes, and program outcomes
- facilitate continuous development, implementation, and assessment of program effectiveness and goal attainment congruent with institutional mission and strategic plans
- promote environments that provide opportunities for student learning, development, and engagement
- develop, adapt, and improve programs and services in response to the changing needs of populations served and evolving institutional priorities
- include diverse perspectives to inform decision making

Management and Supervision
- plan, allocate, and monitor the use of fiscal, physical, human, intellectual, and technological resources
- manage human resource processes including recruitment, selection, professional development, supervision, performance planning, succession planning, evaluation, recognition, and reward
- influence others to contribute to the effectiveness and success of the unit
- empower professional, support, and student personnel to become effective leaders
- encourage and support collaboration with colleagues and departments across the institution
- encourage and support scholarly contributions to

the profession

- identify and address individual, organizational, and environmental conditions that foster or inhibit mission achievement
- use current and valid evidence to inform decisions
- incorporate sustainability practices in the management and design of programs, services, and facilities
- understand appropriate technologies and integrate them into programs and services
- be knowledgeable about codes and laws relevant to programs and services and ensure that programs and services meet those requirements
- assess and take action to mitigate potential risks

Program Advancement

- advocate for and actively promote the mission and goals of the programs and services
- inform stakeholders about issues affecting practice
- facilitate processes to reach consensus where wide support is needed
- advocate for representation in strategic planning initiatives at divisional and institutional levels

SV-RPS leaders must

- promote cooperation from other units in providing services for complainants and respondents (e.g., law enforcement and counseling services)
- work with other departments to send a message that sexual violence of any kind is not acceptable
- model a fair and balanced approach when responding to incidents of sexual violence
- encourage campus administration to be a critical voice concerning sexual violence, and to advocate for fair and balanced policies and processes for complainant(s) and respondent(s)

Part 4. Human Resources

Sexual Violence-Related Programs and Services (SV-RPS) must be staffed adequately by individuals qualified to accomplish mission and goals.

SV-RPS must have access to technical and support personnel adequate to accomplish their mission.

Within institutional guidelines, SV-RPS must

- establish procedures for personnel recruitment and selection, training, performance planning, and evaluation
- set expectations for supervision and performance
- provide personnel access to continuing and advanced education and appropriate professional development opportunities to improve their competence, skills, and leadership capacity
- consider work/life options available to personnel (e.g., compressed work schedules, flextime, job sharing, remote work, or telework) to promote recruitment and retention of personnel

Administrators of SV-RPS must

- ensure that all personnel have updated position descriptions
- implement recruitment and selection/hiring strategies that produce a workforce inclusive of under-represented populations
- develop promotion practices that are fair, inclusive, proactive, and non-discriminatory

Personnel responsible for delivery of SV-RPS must have written performance goals, objectives, and outcomes for each year's performance cycle to be used to plan, review, and evaluate work and performance. The performance plan must be updated regularly to reflect changes during the performance cycle.

Results of individual personnel evaluations must be used to recognize personnel performance, address performance issues, implement individual and/or collective personnel development and training programs, and inform the assessment of programs and services.

SV-RPS personnel, when hired and throughout their employment, must receive appropriate and thorough training.

SV-RPS personnel, including student employees and volunteers, must have access to resources or receive specific training on

- institutional policies pertaining to functions or activities they support
- privacy and confidentiality policies
- laws regarding access to student records
- policies and procedures for dealing with sensitive institutional information
- policies and procedures related to technology used to store or access student records and institutional data
- how and when to refer those in need of additional assistance to qualified personnel and have access to a supervisor for assistance in making these judgments
- systems and technologies necessary to perform their assigned responsibilities
- ethical and legal uses of technology

SV-RPS personnel must engage in continuing professional development activities to keep abreast of the research, theories, legislation, policies, and developments that affect their programs and services.

Administrators of SV-RPS must ensure that personnel are knowledgeable about and trained in safety, emergency procedures, and crisis prevention and response. Risk management efforts must address identification of threatening conduct or behavior and must incorporate a system for responding to and reporting such behaviors.

SV-RPS personnel must be knowledgeable of and trained in safety and emergency procedures for securing and vacating facilities.

PROFESSIONAL PERSONNEL

SV-RPS professional personnel either must hold an earned

graduate or professional degree in a field relevant to their position or must possess an appropriate combination of educational credentials and related work experience.

INTERNS OR GRADUATE ASSISTANTS

Degree- or credential-seeking interns or graduate assistants must be qualified by enrollment in an appropriate field of study and relevant experience. These students must be trained and supervised by professional personnel who possess applicable educational credentials and work experience and have supervisory experience. Supervisors must be cognizant of the dual roles interns and graduate assistants have as both student and employee.

Supervisors must
- adhere to parameters of students' job descriptions
- articulate intended learning outcomes in student job descriptions
- adhere to agreed-upon work hours and schedules
- offer flexible scheduling when circumstances necessitate

Supervisors and students must both agree to suitable compensation if circumstances necessitate additional hours.

STUDENT EMPLOYEES AND VOLUNTEERS

Student employees and volunteers must be carefully selected, trained, supervised, and evaluated. Students must have access to a supervisor. Student employees and volunteers must be provided clear job descriptions, pre-service training based on assessed needs, and continuing development.

Employees and volunteers should have sensitivity for survivors, complainants and respondents, regardless of their identities, and for their privacy; inform all parties of the limits to their confidentiality; and provide them with information regarding confidential support services.

Licensed professional counselors and pastoral counselors are exempt reporters and therefore have statutory and ethical responsibilities regarding non-disclosure of sexual violence in the performance of their job-related duties. Training must be available for persons who fall into categories where confidentiality is expected or required by state or provincial law. Additionally, training must be available for faculty, staff and students regarding mandatory reporting requirements and what is considered a confidential role.

Part 5. Ethics

Sexual Violence-Related Programs and Services (SV-RPS) must
- review applicable professional ethical standards and must adopt or develop and implement appropriate statements of ethical practice
- publish and adhere to statements of ethical practice and ensure their periodic review
- orient new personnel to relevant ethical standards and statements of ethical practice and related institutional policies

Statements of ethical standards must
- specify that SV-RPS personnel respect privacy and maintain confidentiality in communications and records as delineated by privacy laws
- specify limits on disclosure of information contained in students' records as well as requirements to disclose to appropriate authorities
- address conflicts of interest, or appearance thereof, by personnel in the performance of their work
- reflect the responsibility of personnel to be fair, objective, and impartial in their interactions with others
- reference management of institutional funds
- reference appropriate behavior regarding research and assessment with human participants, confidentiality of research and assessment data, and students' rights and responsibilities
- include the expectation that personnel confront and hold accountable other personnel who exhibit unethical behavior
- address issues surrounding scholarly integrity

SV-RPS personnel must
- employ ethical decision making in the performance of their duties
- inform users of programs and services of ethical obligations and limitations emanating from codes and laws or from licensure requirements
- recognize and avoid conflicts of interest that could adversely influence their judgment or objectivity and, when unavoidable, recuse themselves from the situation
- perform their duties within the scope of their position, training, expertise, and competence
- make referrals when issues presented exceed the scope of the position

Part 6. Law, Policy, and Governance

Sexual Violence-Related Programs and Services (SV-RPS) must be in compliance with laws, regulations, and policies that relate to their respective responsibilities and that pose legal obligations, limitations, risks, and liabilities for the institution as a whole. Examples include constitutional, statutory, regulatory, and case law; relevant law and orders emanating from codes and laws; and the institution's policies.

SV-RPS must have access to legal advice needed for personnel to carry out their assigned responsibilities.

SV-RPS must inform personnel, appropriate officials, and users of programs and services about existing and changing legal obligations, risks and liabilities, and limitations.

SV-RPS must inform personnel about professional liability insurance options and refer them to external sources if the institution does not provide coverage.

SV-RPS must have written policies and procedures on operations, transactions, or tasks that have legal implications.

SV-RPS must regularly review policies. The revision and creation of policies must be informed by best practices, available evidence, and policy issues in higher education.

SV-RPS must have procedures and guidelines consistent with institutional policy for responding to threats, emergencies, and crisis situations. Systems and procedures must be in place to disseminate timely and accurate information to students, other members of the institutional community, and appropriate external organizations during emergency situations.

SV-RPS must determine policies for disclosure of incidents to family members and other individuals in accordance with relevant laws and practices.

Personnel must neither participate in nor condone any form of harassment or activity that demeans persons or creates an intimidating, hostile, or offensive environment.

SV-RPS must purchase or obtain permission to use copyrighted materials and instruments. References to copyrighted materials and instruments must include appropriate citations.

SV-RPS must inform personnel about internal and external governance organizations that affect programs and services.

SV-RPS staff must be knowledgeable about changes in relevant laws and practices.

In the U.S., these include, but are not limited to, Family Educational Rights and Privacy Act (FERPA), the Jeanne Clery Disclosure of Campus Security Policy and Campus Crime Statistics Act (Campus Security Act) and newly revised regulations (2014), Title IX of the Education Amendments of 1972 (Title IX) plus sub-regulatory guidance issues in 2011 and 2014, the Violence Against Women Act (VAWA) Reauthorization and, specifically, Section 304 which deals with campus sexual assault and related issues and has amended the Clery Act, the U.S. Department of Education Office for Civil Rights, and The Department of Justice Office of Violence Against Women, as well as existing and forthcoming material from the White House.

Part 7. Diversity, Equity, and Access

Within the context of each institution's mission and in accordance with institutional policies and applicable codes and laws, Sexual Violence-Related Programs and Services (SV-RPS) must create and maintain educational and work environments that are welcoming, accessible, inclusive, equitable, and free from harassment.

SV-RPS must not discriminate on the basis of disability; age; race; cultural identity; ethnicity; nationality; family educational history (e.g., first generation to attend college); political affiliation; religious affiliation; sex; sexual orientation; gender identity and expression; marital, social, economic, or veteran status; or any other basis included in institutional policies and codes and laws.

SV-RPS must

- advocate for sensitivity to multicultural and social justice concerns by the institution and its personnel
- ensure physical, program, and resource access for all constituents
- modify or remove policies, practices, systems, technologies, facilities, and structures that create barriers or produce inequities
- ensure that when facilities and structures cannot be modified, they do not impede access to programs, services, and resources
- establish goals for diversity, equity, and access
- foster communication and practices that enhance understanding of identity, culture, self-expression, and heritage
- promote respect for commonalities and differences among people within their historical and cultural contexts
- address the characteristics and needs of diverse constituents when establishing and implementing culturally relevant and inclusive programs, services, policies, procedures, and practices
- provide personnel with diversity, equity, and access training and hold personnel accountable for applying the training to their work
- respond to the needs of all constituents served when establishing hours of operation and developing methods of delivering programs, services, and resources
- recognize the needs of distance and online learning students by directly providing or assisting them to gain access to comparable services and resources

SV-RPS must provide services to individuals of all identities and address culturally-specific needs.

SV-RPS should educate the campus community about myths and stereotypes associated with sexual violence.

Part 8. Internal and External Relations

Sexual Violence-Related Programs and Services (SV-RPS) must reach out to individuals, groups, communities, and organizations internal and external to the institution to

- establish, maintain, and promote understanding and effective relations with those that have a significant interest in or potential effect on the students or other constituents served by the programs and services
- garner support and resources for programs and services as defined by the mission
- collaborate in offering or improving programs and services to meet the needs of students and other constituents and to achieve program and student outcomes
- engage diverse individuals, groups, communities, and organizations to enrich the educational environment and experiences of students and other constituents
- disseminate information about the programs and

services

Promotional and descriptive information must be accurate and free of deception and misrepresentation.

SV-RPS must have procedures and guidelines consistent with institutional policy for
- communicating with the media
- distributing information through print, broadcast, and online sources
- contracting with external organizations for delivery of programs and services
- cultivating, soliciting, and managing gifts
- applying to and managing funds from grants

SV-RPS must build and maintain strong, mutually beneficial working relationships with administrative, co-curricular, and academic departments across the institution as well as with community organizations to create a campus environment intolerant of sexual violence, especially as directed towards marginalized individuals and groups, and to strengthen the campus's comprehensive response to sexual violence.

SV-RPS must collaborate with on- and off-campus partners to create institutional policies, procedures, and programs to work toward the elimination of sexual violence on campus and the provision of effective sexual violence-related support services.

SV-RPS should provide technical assistance and capacity building to departments across the institution in order to facilitate the institutionalization of policies, structures and practices in those departments, reflecting their commitment to a sexual violence-free campus.

Part 9. Financial Resources

Sexual Violence-Related Programs and Services (SV-RPS) must have funding to accomplish the mission and goals.

Permanent institutional funding should be allocated for the continuing operation and staffing of SV-RPS.

In establishing and prioritizing funding resources, SV-RPS must conduct comprehensive analyses to determine
- unmet needs of the unit
- relevant expenditures
- external and internal resources
- impact on students and the institution

SV-RPS must use the budget as a planning tool to reflect commitment to the mission and goals of the programs and services and of the institution.

SV-RPS must administer funds in accordance with established institutional accounting procedures.

SV-RPS must demonstrate efficient and effective use and responsible stewardship of fiscal resources consistent with institutional protocols.

Financial reports must provide an accurate financial overview of the organization and provide clear, understandable, and timely data upon which personnel can

plan and make informed decisions.

Procurement procedures must
- be consistent with institutional policies
- ensure that purchases comply with laws and codes for usability and access
- ensure that the institution receives value for the funds spent
- consider information available for comparing the ethical and environmental impact of products and services purchased

Part 10. Technology

Sexual Violence-Related Programs and Services (SV-RPS) must have technology to support the achievement of their mission and goals. The technology and its use must comply with institutional policies and procedures and with relevant codes and laws.

SV-RPS must use technologies to
- provide updated information regarding mission, location, staffing, programs, services, and official contacts to students and other constituents in accessible formats
- provide an avenue for students and other constituents to communicate sensitive information in a secure format
- enhance the delivery of programs and services for all students

SV-RPS must
- back up data on a regular basis
- adhere to institutional policies regarding ethical and legal use of technology
- articulate policies and procedures for protecting the confidentiality and security of information
- implement a replacement plan and cycle for all technology with attention to sustainability
- incorporate accessibility features into technology-based programs and services

When providing student access to technology, SV-RPS must
- have policies on the use of technology that are clear, easy to understand, and available to all students
- provide information or referral to support services for those needing assistance in accessing or using technology
- provide instruction or training on how to use the technology
- inform students of implications of misuse of technologies

SV-RPS should be aware of methods in which technology can be used by individuals to perpetrate acts of sexual aggression, gain access to and/or control over potential targets for sexual violence. Examples include unwanted communication via e-mails, text messages, and chat requests; tracking individuals via global positioning systems (GPS); covertly installing spyware on a person's computer; unauthorized posting of pictures; and information or messages in Internet chat rooms or on websites, including social networking sites.

Because issues of power and control are inherent in sexual violence, individuals often keep close watch on the actions and movements of others and may do so through such means as monitoring of email accounts and online use, including tracking the history of websites visited. SV-RPS should undertake efforts to maintain the privacy of those who access the program's website. Instructions on how to erase one's Internet history and cookies should be provided to all who visit the SV-RPS website, making less likely someone's ability to discern the sites someone visited. If possible, the website should include a quick escape button in the event that someone should walk in on another person while they are accessing the website. Websites should state the limits of confidentiality.

SV-RPS staff members should take into account the ability to maintain confidentiality and safety when using technology. Additionally, the use of social media and networks as well as other communication methods such as text messaging, and blogging should be conducted with privacy in mind.

SV-RPS should pursue technology applications that increase their ability to provide services to survivors.

Part 11. Facilities and Equipment

Sexual Violence-Related Programs and Services' (SV-RPS) facilities must be intentionally designed and located in suitable, accessible, and safe spaces that demonstrate universal design and support the program's mission and goals.

Facilities must be designed to engage various constituents and promote learning.

Personnel must have workspaces that are suitably located and accessible, well equipped, adequate in size, and designed to support their work and responsibilities.

The design of the facilities must guarantee the security and privacy of records and ensure the confidentiality of sensitive information and conversations. Personnel must be able to secure their work.

SV-RPS must incorporate sustainable practices in use of facilities and purchase of equipment. Facilities and equipment must be evaluated on an established cycle and be in compliance with codes, laws, and accepted practices for access, health, safety, and security.

When acquiring capital equipment, SV-RPS must take into account expenses related to regular maintenance and life cycle costs.

SV-RPS must create and maintain an environment that assures confidentiality, privacy, and trust.

SV-RPS should have a location and layout that minimizes unintended interaction between complainants and respondents and which offers adequate privacy to protect their identities.

Facilities should be equipped to provide spaces for counseling and other confidential conversations, which might include soundproofing or other efforts to protect confidentiality. A reception area with a private waiting room should also be available if counseling or other private meetings are held regularly.

SV-RPS should have training facilities with proper technology and space for student groups such as peer educators to meet and conduct business. -

Part 12. Assessment

Sexual Violence-Related Programs and Services (SV-RPS) must develop assessment plans and processes.

Assessment plans must articulate an ongoing cycle of assessment activities.

SV-RPS must

- specify programmatic goals and intended outcomes
- identify student learning and development outcomes
- employ multiple measures and methods
- develop manageable processes for gathering, interpreting, and evaluating data
- document progress toward achievement of goals and outcomes
- interpret and use assessment results to demonstrate accountability
- report aggregated results to stakeholders
- use assessment results to inform planning and decision-making
- assess effectiveness of implemented changes
- provide evidence of improvement of programs and services

SV-RPS should collaborate with other departments to assess relevant campus climate **concerns** related to sexual violence issues.

SV-RPS must employ ethical practices in the assessment process.

SV-RPS must have access to adequate fiscal, human, professional development, and technological resources to develop and implement assessment plans.

General Standards revised in 2014;
SV-RPS content (formerly Sexual Assault and Relationship Violence Prevention Programs) developed/revised in 2012 and 2015

Student Conduct Programs
CAS Contextual Statement

Colleges' and universities' need to correct and discipline student behavior "is as old as higher education itself, dating back to the nascent University of Paris almost 800 years ago" (Dannells, 1988, p. 127). Student conduct has also been one of the most persistent, controversial, and contested areas in all of higher education (Dannells, 1997; Waryold & Lancaster, 2013).

The history and evolution of student discipline in American higher education, in many respects, mirrors the development of American colleges and universities (Smith, 1994). When America's first colleges were founded, there were no borders between an institution's charge to develop students' intellects and to supervise their moral and ethical growth (Rudolph, 1962/1990). Over the last century, the diminishing role of faculty in student life, the growth of the student affairs field, and the increasing scope of legal directives have transformed the ways institutions address and manage student misconduct on campus (Dannells, 1997; Waryold & Lancaster, 2013).

The origins of the student personnel movement in the late 1800s and early 1900s grew directly out of institutional needs to address student incivility as well as a renewed focus on holistic education (American Council on Education, 1937; Waryold & Lancaster, 2013). Court decisions like *Dixon v. Alabama State Board of Education* (1961), legislative enactments like the Family Educational Rights & Privacy Act (FERPA), and the numerous judicial decisions and government directives that followed have necessitated that all institutions, public and private, must utilize conduct policies practices that are substantively clear, procedurally sound, and fundamentally fair. While students at public institutions are afforded these protections through the Constitution's due process clause, private institutions are not required to abide by Constitutional mandates; even so, almost all private institutions have adopted similar protections to ensure their procedures are fair and to avoid treating students in an unlawful, arbitrary and capricious manner during the adjudication process (Lake, 2013; Smith, 2011; Waryold & Lancaster, 2013). As a result, institutions have increasingly relied on specialists to manage campus disciplinary processes.

Student conduct specialists began organizing and professionalizing their area in the early 1970s. The ACPA Commission for Student Conduct and Legal Issues began in 1973 and remains active today (ACPA, 2014). In 1987, the Association of Student Conduct Administration (ASCA, then called the Association of Student Judicial Affairs) was founded and now sponsors an annual conference (with over 1,000 attendees), holds annual week-long training institutes for conduct professionals of all levels, and has promulgated ethical principles and professional standards to guide the profession (ASCA, 1993; Waryold & Lancaster, 2013). ASCA became a member institution of CAS in 1990.

Today, student conduct programs on college campuses must balance three complex, interconnected goals, as reflected in the Preamble to the ASCA Constitution and Bylaws (ASCA, 1988/2012). Student conduct programs should be:
- Community-focused,
- Learning-centered, and
- Procedurally sound.

Although balancing these goals can be difficult and challenging, they can and must be integrated into student conduct practice (Gehring, 2001; Pavela & Pavela, 2012).

Community-focused. Student conduct programs must reflect the unique needs, characteristics, and values of their individual institutions and campus communities (King, 2009). As such, they must set forth clear standards for their particular community and also ensure protection for *all* students within that community. As Bennett, Gregory, Loschiavo, and Waller (2014) advised, "students who may have been harmed, students who are accused of causing harm, and the rest of the student body" must all be "treated with care, concern, honor, and dignity" (p. 1). Conduct programs must also recognize that campus culture and environmental factors influence students' attitudes and behavior -- both positively and negatively (Harper, Harris, & Mmeje, 2005; McCabe, Treviño, & Butterfield, 2001; Waryold & Lancaster, 2013). Finally, conduct officials are increasingly being asked to utilize their expertise to help their campus communities manage students who may pose threats to themselves or others through threat assessment and behavioral intervention teams (Dunkle, Silverstein, & Warner, 2008).

Learning-centered. Student conduct programs must also uphold the primacy of the educational mission of colleges and universities by ensuring that student learning and development are central (but not necessary the only) goals of the disciplinary process (Baldizian, 1998; Bennett et al., 2014; Dannells, 1997). Student conduct programs should, whenever feasible, seek to prioritize educational processes and outcomes for students while also ensuring the safety and integrity of the learning environment for all students. Despite these goals, research has shown that many students going through conduct processes learn little from their experience (Howell, 2005). The imperative, therefore, is to identify and utilize conduct practices and interventions that have a demonstrable effect on students' knowledge, values, and behavior.

Procedurally sound. Student conduct programs must ensure that their policies and practices are procedurally sound. Although institutions must comply with legal and judicial authority (including procedural and substantive due process, legislative mandates, and regulatory directives), student conduct processes also have a moral and ethical duty to ensure their processes are inclusive, socially just, and multipartial (Holmes, Edwards, & DeBowes, 2009; Lopez-Phillips & Trageser, 2008). Student conduct programs should consider adopting a range of practices and resolution options that may be more socially just and learning-focused, including those incorporating dialogue, mediation, and restorative justice principles (Schrage & Thompson, 2009). Recent research demonstrates that sound conduct procedures (i.e., those that are perceived as fair and those utilizing restorative justice practices) produce more positive learning outcomes for students going through them (Karp & Sacks, 2014; King, 2012).

In pursuing these goals, student conduct programs must also navigate various external influences. Student disciplinary systems on college and university campuses have increasingly come under the scrutiny of campus stakeholders, government agencies, advocacy groups, and the press (Bartholet et al., 2014; Binkley, Wagner, Riepenhoff, & Gregory, 2014; Gehring, 1998; U.S. Department of Education, 2011, 2014). High profile instances of college misconduct and violence (including deadly episodes of hazing and alcohol abuse, criminal charges against student-athletes, and national focus of the prevalence of campus sexual assault) have highlighted the importance of student conduct within the institutional setting.

Student conduct practitioners in today's environment must be knowledgeable about a number of federal mandates that have a direct impact on their work within an institution. Federal laws such as FERPA, the Drug Free Schools and Communities Act, the Jeanne Clery Disclosure of Campus Security and Campus Crime Statistics Act (originally known as the Student Right-to-Know Act and Campus Security Act of 1990), the Campus Sexual Violence Elimination Act of 2013, and recent amendments to the Violence Against Women Act (VAWA) all contain provisions specifically targeting conduct policies and practices. Directives regarding sexual misconduct and Title IX from the Department of Education's Office for Civil Rights (2011, 2014), as well as the White House Task Force to Protect Students from Sexual Assault (2014), demonstrate that governmental scrutiny of campus safety is a current reality – one that does not appear to be diminishing in the future.

In addition to external influence at the governmental level, advocacy groups are also working to shape the status of modern student conduct administration. For example, compare the aspirations of two separate special interest groups that are especially critical of modern student conduct practice: The Clery Center for Security on Campus (formerly, Security on Campus) and the Foundation for Individual Rights in Education (FIRE). While the Clery Center has sought to strengthen and enhance student conduct regulations and other campus safety protocols, FIRE believes that current conduct practices are too abusive and accuse institutions of trampling the Constitutional rights of students -- particularly those accused of infractions (Clery Center, 2012; FIRE, 2013).

Additional external factors impacting student conduct practice include state and national pressure on higher education institutions to demonstrate their effectiveness (Banta & Palomba, 2015) and increasing levels of parental involvement (Cullaty, 2011; de Carvalho, 2014). Current student conduct practitioners must also stay aware of trends within the profession, including the principles underlying threat assessment, behavioral intervention, restorative justice,

and motivational interviewing.

Ultimately, these CAS Standards are presented to help student conduct programs achieve their primary goals while navigating external responsibilities. Through the use of the learning domains and dimensions, higher education professionals can ensure learning occurs while students participate in conduct processes. These Standards provide a framework for the development of well-functioning and exceptional conduct programs. Finally, the Standards give conduct professionals a roadmap for fulfilling their ethical and professional obligations as well as identifying competencies and skills needed to successfully implement their programs.

References, Readings, and Resources

ACPA - College Student Educators International. (2014). *Commission for Student Conduct and Legal Issues history.* Retrieved from http://www.acpa.nche.edu/commission-student-conduct-and-legal-issues-history

American Council on Education (1937). *The student personnel point of view: A report of a conference on the philosophy and development of student personnel work in colleges and universities.* Washington, DC: Author. Retrieved from http://www2.bgsu.edu/sahp/pages/1937STUDENTPERSONNELnew.pdf

Association for Student Conduct Administration. (1993). *Ethical principles and standards of conduct.* College Station, TX: Author. Retrieved from http://theasca.membershipsoftware.org/files/Governing%20Documents/Ethical%20Principles%20and%20Standards%20of%20Conduct.pdf

Association for Student Conduct Administration. (2012). *Bylaws.* College Station, TX: Author. Available from http://www.theasca.org/documents (Originally adopted 1988)

Baldizan, E. M. (1998). Development, due process, and reduction: Student conduct in the 1990s. In D. L. Cooper & J. M. Lancaster (Eds.), *Beyond law and policy: Reaffirming the role of student affairs* (New Directions for Student Services, no. 82; pp. 29-37). San Francisco: Jossey-Bass. doi: 10.1002/ss.8203

Banta, T. W., & Palomba, C. A. (2015). *Assessment essentials: Planning, implementing, and improving assessment in higher education.* San Francisco, CA: Jossey-Bass.

Bartholet, E., Brewer, S., Clark, R., Dershowitz, A., Desan, C., Donahue, C., ... Wilkins, D. (2014, Oct. 15). Rethink Harvard's sexual harassment policy [Open letter]. *Boston Globe.* Retrieved from http://www.bostonglobe.com/opinion/2014/10/14/rethink-harvard-sexual-harassment-policy/HFDDiZN7nU2UwuUuWMnqbM/story.html

Bennett, L., Gregory, D. M., Loschiavo, C., & Waller, J. (2014). *Student conduct administration & Title IX: Gold standard practices for resolution of allegations of sexual misconduct on college campuses* [White paper]. College Station, TX: Association for Student Conduct Administration. Retrieved from http://www.theasca.org/Files/Publications/ASCA%202014%20Gold%20Standard%20Report.pdf

Binkley, C., Wagner, M., Riepenhoff, J. & Gregory, S. (2014, Nov. 23). College disciplinary boards impose slight penalties for serious crimes. *The Columbus Dispatch.* Retrieved from http://www.dispatch.com/content/stories/local/2014/11/23/campus-injustice.html

Clery Center for Security on Campus. (2012). *Our mission.* Retrieved from http://clerycenter.org/our-mission

Cullaty, B. (2011). The role of parental involvement in the autonomy development of tradition-age college students. *Journal of College*

Student Development, 52(4), 425-439. doi:10.1353/csd.2011.0048

Dannells, M. (1988). Discipline. In A. L. Rentz & G. L. Saddlemire (Eds.), *Student affairs function in higher education* (pp. 127-154). Springfield, IL: Charles C. Thomas.

Dannells, M. (1997). *From discipline to development: Rethinking student conduct in higher education* (ASHE-ERIC Higher Education Report, Vol. 25, No. 2). Washington, DC: George Washington University Graduation School of Education and Human Development.

de Carvalho, M. E. P. (2014). *Rethinking family-school relations: A critique of parental involvement in schooling.* New York, NY: Psychology Press.

Dixon v. Alabama State Board of Education, 294 F.2d 150 (5th Cir.), *cert. denied,* 368 U.S. 930 (1961).

Dunkle, J. H., Silverstein, S. B., Warner, S. L. (2008). Managing violent and other troubling students: The role of threat assessment teams on campus. *Journal of College and University Law, 34*, 585-635. Retrieved from http://heinonline.org/HOL/LandingPage?handle=hein.journals/jcolunly34&div=25&id=&page=

Foundation for Individual Rights in Education. (2013). *Mission.* Retrieved from http://www.thefire.org/about-us/mission/

Gehring, D. D. (1998). The frog in the pot: External influence on higher education. In D. L. Cooper & J. M. Lancaster (Eds.), *Beyond law and policy: Reaffirming the role of student affairs* (New Directions for Student Services, No. 82; pp. 3-14). San Francisco, CA: Jossey-Bass. doi:10.1002/ss.8201

Gehring, D. D. (2001). The objectives of student conduct and the process that's due: Are they compatible? *NASPA Journal, 38*(4), 466-481. doi:10.2202/1949-6605.1155

Harper, S. R., Harris, F., III, & Mmeje, K. (2005). A theoretical model to explain the overrepresentation of college men among campus judicial offenders: Implications for campus administrators. *NASPA Journal, 42*(4), 565-588. doi:10.2202/1949-6605.1541

Holmes, R. C. Edwards, K., & DeBowes, M. M. (2009). Why objectivity is not enough: The critical role of social justice in campus conduct and conflict work. In J. M. Schrage & N G. Giacomini (Eds.), *Reframing campus conflict: Student conduct practice through a social justice lens* (pp. 50-64). Sterling, VA: Stylus.

Howell, M. T. (2005). Students' perceived learning and anticipated future behaviors as a result of participation in the student judicial process. *Journal of College Student Development, 46*, 374-392. doi:10.1353/csd.2005.0035

Karp, D. R. & Sacks, C. (2014). Student conduct, restorative justice, and student development: Findings from the STARR project: A student accountability and restorative research project. *Contemporary Justice Review, 17*(2), 154-172. doi:0282580.2014.915140

King, R. H. (2012). Student conduct administration: How students perceive the educational value and procedural fairness of their disciplinary experiences. *Journal of College Student Development, 53*, 563-580. doi:10.1353/csd.2012.0058

King, T. L. (2009). Endorsement. In J. M. Schrage & N. G. Giacomini (Eds.), *Reframing campus conflict: Student conduct practice through a social justice lens* (pp. xiii-xiv). Sterling, VA: Stylus.

Lake, P. F. (2013). *The rights and responsibilities of the modern university: The rise of the facilitator university* (2nd ed.). Durham, NC: Carolina Academic Press.

Lopez-Phillips, M. & Trageser, S. P. (2008). Development and diversity: A social justice model. In J. M. Lancaster & D. M. Waryold (Eds.), *Student conduct practice: The complete guide for student affairs professionals* (pp. 119-134). Sterling, VA: Stylus.

McCabe, D. L., Treviño, L. K., & Butterfield, K. D. (2001). Cheating in academic institutions: A decade of research. *Ethics & Behavior, 11*(3), 219-232. doi:10.1207/S15327019EB1103_2

Pavela, G. & Pavela, G. (2012). The ethical and educational imperative of due process. *Journal of College and University Law, 38*, 567-627. Retrieved from http://heinonline.org/HOL/Page?handle=hein.journals/jcolunly38&div=22&g_sent=1&collection=journals

Rudolph, F. (1990). *The American college and university: A history.* Athens, GA: University of Georgia Press. (Original work published in 1962)

Schrage, J. M. & Thompson, M. C. (2009). Providing a spectrum of resolution options. In J. M. Schrage & N G. Giacomini (Eds.), *Reframing campus conflict: Student conduct practice through a social justice lens* (pp. 65-84). Sterling, VA: Stylus.

Smith, D. B. (1994). Student discipline in American colleges and universities: A historical overview. *Educational Horizons, 72*(2), 78-85.

Smith, P. (2011). Due process, fundamental fairness, and judicial deference: The illusory difference between state and private educational institution disciplinary legal requirements. *University of New Hampshire Law Review, 9*, 443-468. Retrieved from http://law.unh.edu/assets/images/uploads/publications/unh-law-review-vol-09-no3-smith.pdf

U.S. Department of Education, Office for Civil Rights. (2011, Apr. 4). *Dear colleague letter: Sexual violence.* Washington, DC: Author. Retrieved from http://www2.ed.gov/about/offices/list/ocr/letters/colleague-201104.html

U.S. Department of Education, Office for Civil Rights. (2014, Apr. 29). *Questions and answers on Title IX and sexual violence.* Washington, DC: Author. Retrieved from http://www2.ed.gov/about/offices/list/ocr/docs/qa-201404-title-ix.pdf

Waryold, D. M., & Lancaster, J. M. (Eds.) (2013). *The state of student conduct: Current forces and future challenges: Revisited.* College Station, TX: Association for Student Conduct Administration.

White House Task Force to Protect Students from Sexual Assault. (2014). *Not alone: The first report of the White House Task Force to Protect Students from Sexual Assault.* Washington, DC: The White House. Retrieved from http://www.whitehouse.gov/sites/default/files/docs/report_0.pdf

Contextual Statement Contributors

Current Edition:

Marc H. Shook, LaGrange College, ASCA

Jim Neumeister, Loyola University Chicago, ASCA

Previous Editions:

John Wesley Lowery, Indiana University of Pennsylvania, ASCA

John Zacker, University of Maryland, ASCA

Marc H. Shook, LaGrange College, ASCA

Student Conduct Programs
CAS Standards and Guidelines

Part 1. Mission

Student Conduct Programs (SCP) promote community standards, safety, and student learning through educational outreach and processes that aid in the resolution of violations of institutional policies, rules, or regulations. SCP's policies, practices, and systems must be: (a) community-focused, (b) learning centered, and (c) procedurally sound.

The standards set forth below are intended to cover individual and organizational disciplinary systems/procedures as well as the resolution of academic and non-academic instances of misconduct.

SCP must develop, disseminate, implement, and regularly review their missions, which must be consistent with the mission of the institution and with applicable professional standards. The mission must be appropriate for the institution's students and other constituents. Mission statements must reference student learning and development.

The goals of SCP must address the institution's need to
- develop, disseminate, interpret, and enforce institutional policies and procedures regarding student as well as group/organizational behavioral expectations
- protect the rights of students who have been victims of misconduct as well as those accused of misconduct
- ensure that all students, faculty, staff, or community members involved in the administration of the student conduct program are sufficiently prepared and trained
- respond to student behavioral concerns in an unbiased, fair, and reasonable manner
- facilitate the process of individuals and organizations taking responsibility for their assigned roles in the conduct system
- provide learning experiences for students whose conduct may not be consistent with institutional expectations as well as for those students who participate in the operations of the student conduct system
- initiate and encourage outreach activities that serve to educate the community about the student conduct program and individual responsibilities within the program
- balance the needs and interests of individuals with the needs and interests of the institution, the community, and others who may have an interest in the matter or outcome

Part 2. Program

To achieve their mission, Student Conduct Programs (SCP) must contribute to
- students' formal education, which includes both the curriculum and the co-curriculum
- student progression and timely completion of educational goals
- preparation of students for their careers, citizenship, and lives
- student learning and development

To contribute to student learning and development, SCP must
- identify relevant and desirable student learning and development outcomes
- articulate how the student learning and development outcomes align with the six CAS student learning and development domains and related dimensions
- assess relevant and desirable student learning and development
- provide evidence of impact on outcomes
- articulate contributions to or support of student learning and development in the domains not specifically assessed
- use evidence gathered to create strategies for improvement of programs and services

STUDENT LEARNING AND DEVELOPMENT DOMAINS AND DIMENSIONS

Domain: knowledge acquisition, integration, construction, and application
- Dimensions: understanding knowledge from a range of disciplines; connecting knowledge to other knowledge, ideas, and experiences; constructing knowledge; and relating knowledge to daily life

Domain: cognitive complexity
- Dimensions: critical thinking, reflective thinking, effective reasoning, and creativity

Domain: intrapersonal development
- Dimensions: realistic self-appraisal, self-understanding, and self-respect; identity development; commitment to ethics and integrity; and spiritual awareness

Domain: interpersonal competence
- Dimensions: meaningful relationships, interdependence, collaboration, and effective leadership

Domain: humanitarianism and civic engagement

- Dimensions: understanding and appreciation of cultural and human differences, social responsibility, global perspective, and sense of civic responsibility

Domain: practical competence

- Dimensions: pursuing goals, communicating effectively, technical competence, managing personal affairs, managing career development, demonstrating professionalism, maintaining health and wellness, and living a purposeful and satisfying life

[LD Outcomes: See *The Council for the Advancement of Standards Learning and Development Outcomes* statement for examples of outcomes related to these domains and dimensions.]

SCP must be

- **intentionally designed**
- **guided by theories and knowledge of learning and development**
- **integrated into the life of the institution**
- **reflective of developmental and demographic profiles of the student population**
- **responsive to needs of individuals, populations with distinct needs, and relevant constituencies**
- **delivered using multiple formats, strategies, and contexts**
- **designed to provide universal access**

SCP must collaborate with colleagues and departments across the institution to promote student learning and development, persistence, and success.

SCP must establish, manage, promote, and regularly review policies and practices that govern the student conduct program. Such policies and practices must be provided in accessible formats and made available in both printed and web-based forums.

All processes, procedures, and practices governed by this statement must be fair, equitable, and procedurally sound, and must be administered in compliance with appropriate institutional, regulatory, and legal standards. Likewise, policies and practices must be reviewed on an annual basis to determine if recent law or policy changes necessitate any update or revision to the statement.

Procedures and processes provide for substantive and procedural due process at public institutions of higher education and fundamental fairness at private institutions.

A single institution may have multiple statements and procedures based on the overall structure of the student conduct system. Multiple statements should exist if different offices, departments, or programs take individual responsibility for varying components of the overall program, such as academic versus non-academic misconduct or individual versus organizational misconduct.

Statements of processes, procedures, and practices must

include

- a clear statement of the institution's behavioral expectations and standards for students
- the identity of each office, department, or program that has responsibility for addressing student misconduct, specifically including alleged instances of academic and non-academic misconduct
- a description of the authority, philosophy, scope, and core components of the student conduct program
- the manner in which an SCP addresses and resolves incidents of student misconduct
- whether acts of sexual violence, relationship violence, and stalking are covered under the general resolution processes or in a separate institutional policy.
- procedures for the review and resolution of allegations of student misconduct, including identifying multiple pathways or alternative resolution processes that may be used or requested by the student
- a clear description of possible sanctions that may be imposed
- appeal procedures (if provided)
- procedures for interim, summary, or emergency actions
- policies governing the maintenance, confidentiality, and disclosure of records pertaining to alleged instances of student misconduct
- the evidentiary standard that will be used in the resolution of the matter should be preponderance of evidence
- if there are separate or distinct resolution processes then those must be made available to all students

Examples of distinct processes within a campus community include: acts of individual misconduct, group/organizational misconduct, academic misconduct, non-academic misconduct, and misconduct occurring on-campus, in campus residence halls, or off/away from campus.

Government regulations dictate that the preponderance of evidence standard must be used to determine the resolution of acts of sexual violence, relationship violence and stalking.

This statement should include:

- the scope of authority for each office, department, or program involved in the administration of the student conduct program, including which policies and regulations are enforced by each
- the scope of authority of each office, department, or program to address misconduct in the context of where the misconduct occurs or outside of times when a student is actively enrolled and/or present

at the institution, including education study abroad, internships, exchange programs, during times classes are not in session, or during a period that student is not actively enrolled

- a clear description of the relationship between each student conduct program and law enforcement agencies (both on- and off-campus), including guidelines as to when SCPs will contact law enforcement authorities
- information regarding the impact, if any, decisions by external bodies (such as a criminal court) may influence the outcome of a student conduct program decision
- any role faculty, staff, and students may play in the adjudication of disciplinary infractions
- the role that restorative justice will play in the resolution (if any)
- the rights of the students to have assistance in navigating the student conduct process both before, during, and after the allegation of misconduct is made as well as a statement on the role that advisors or legal counsel may play in the process
- how the SCP will go about maintaining and destroying documents and records pertaining to an allegation of misconduct

All statements of SCP policies and practices must be disseminated to and be easily accessed by all members of the institutional community.

Dissemination methods should include electronic media, institutional catalog, student handbook, admission/ registration materials, orientation programming, and first-year experience courses. Methods should be accessible to all students.

Governmental and state regulations (in the U.S.) may dictate that the institution also train the institutional community on some aspects of the statement, such as reporting instances of sexual harassment or sexual violence.

The outcomes and/or sanctions imposed as a result of institutional action must be educational and developmental and not solely punitive, appropriately and equitably assigned, address the overall safety needs of those involved in the process as well as the general campus community, and attend to any impacts and harms of the behavior on the community or others.

SCP must provide on-going case management, including the enforcement of outcomes and sanctions, assessing the developmental processes that have been affected, and ensuring that students are directed to appropriate services for support and assistance.

Use of Adjudication/Appeals Boards

Although under no legal or regulatory requirement to do so, a number of institutions use adjudication/appeal boards (also often known as hearing boards or panels) to resolve allegations of student misconduct. These panels, typically consisting of students, faculty, and staff can provide educational and developmental benefits for both the accused student and the individuals serving on the board/panel.

Roles and functions of adjudication/appeal boards may include

- reviewing referrals and concerns
- interpreting misconduct allegations and identifying if any specific policies, rules, or regulations were likely violated
- conducting preliminary meetings and gathering information pertinent to a formal allegation of misconduct
- advising students and other interested parties on their rights and responsibilities
- engaging in substantive discussions with students about relevant ethical issues
- scheduling, coordinating, and conducting resolution proceedings
- reviewing decisions and outcomes
- maintaining accurate written records of the entire proceeding
- referring information to other offices, parties, or student conduct authorities when applicable
- following up on sanctions to ensure that they have been implemented
- following up with students and other interested parties to ensure awareness of available support services
- establishing and implementing a procedure for maintenance and disclosure of conduct-related records
- assessing student conduct procedures, policies, and outcomes
- participating on governance-related committees associated with student conduct, except when a conflict of interest will result
- conducting education and outreach efforts of the SCP

When using an adjudication/appeal board, initial and in-service training of all members must be provided. This training must include all institutional officials or agents who serve on the adjudication/appeal board and individuals who serve in other positions related to the operation of the SCP.

In order for adjudication/appeal boards to fulfill their roles and functions, initial training should include

- an overview of all conduct policies and procedures
- an explanation of the operation of the conduct processes at all levels including their scope of authority
- an overview of the institution's philosophy on student conduct and the adjudication/appeal board's role in the process
- roles and functions of all student conduct authorities/

bodies and their members
- review of individual and institutional rights and responsibilities, including institutional and legal requirements
- information on weighing of evidence, appropriate questioning, determining credibility and standard of proof as required topics
- an explanation of outcomes and sanctions
- an explanation of pertinent ethics, including confidentiality of student conduct records and addressing bias as well as conflict of interest in the student conduct process
- a description of available personal counseling programs and referral sources
- an outline of conditions that may involve interactions with external enforcement officials, attorneys, witnesses, parents or family members, and the media
- an overview of development and interpersonal issues likely to arise among college students

Based on the particular scope of the adjudication/appeal board, some specialized training may be required or needed to assist the board fulfill their obligations on campus; topics could include sexual violence, alcohol/drug issues, and hazing.

In-service training should include participation in relevant and on-going workshops, seminars, and conferences. A library containing current resources about the student conduct program should be made available.

Part 3. Organization and Leadership

To achieve program and student learning and development outcomes, Student Conduct Programs (SCP) must be purposefully structured for effectiveness. SCP must have clearly stated and current
- goals and outcomes
- policies and procedures
- responsibilities and performance expectations for personnel
- organizational charts demonstrating clear channels of authority

Leaders must model ethical behavior and institutional citizenship.

Leaders with organizational authority for the SCP must provide strategic planning, management and supervision, and program advancement.

Strategic Planning
- articulate a vision and mission that drive short- and long-term planning
- set goals and objectives based on the needs of the populations served, intended student learning and development outcomes, and program outcomes
- facilitate continuous development,

implementation, and assessment of program effectiveness and goal attainment congruent with institutional mission and strategic plans
- promote environments that provide opportunities for student learning, development, and engagement
- develop, adapt, and improve programs and services in response to the changing needs of populations served and evolving institutional priorities
- include diverse perspectives to inform decision making

Management and Supervision
- plan, allocate, and monitor the use of fiscal, physical, human, intellectual, and technological resources
- manage human resource processes including recruitment, selection, professional development, supervision, performance planning, succession planning, evaluation, recognition, and reward
- influence others to contribute to the effectiveness and success of the unit
- empower professional, support, and student personnel to become effective leaders
- encourage and support collaboration with colleagues and departments across the institution
- encourage and support scholarly contributions to the profession
- identify and address individual, organizational, and environmental conditions that foster or inhibit mission achievement
- use current and valid evidence to inform decisions
- incorporate sustainability practices in the management and design of programs, services, and facilities
- understand appropriate technologies and integrate them into programs and services
- be knowledgeable about codes and laws relevant to programs and services and ensure that programs and services meet those requirements
- assess and take action to mitigate potential risks

Program Advancement
- advocate for and actively promote the mission and goals of the programs and services
- inform stakeholders about issues affecting practice
- facilitate processes to reach consensus where wide support is needed
- advocate for representation in strategic planning initiatives at divisional and institutional levels

Part 4. Human Resources

Student Conduct Programs (SCP) must be staffed adequately by individuals qualified to accomplish mission and goals.

Staffing models may be influenced by Governmental mandates.

SCP must have access to technical and support personnel adequate to accomplish their mission.

Within institutional guidelines, SCP must
- establish procedures for personnel recruitment and selection, training, performance planning, and evaluation
- set expectations for supervision and performance
- provide personnel access to continuing and advanced education and appropriate professional development opportunities to improve their competence, skills, and leadership capacity
- consider work/life options available to personnel (e.g., compressed work schedules, flextime, job sharing, remote work, or telework) to promote recruitment and retention of personnel

Administrators of SCP must
- ensure that all personnel have updated position descriptions
- implement recruitment and selection/hiring strategies that produce a workforce inclusive of under-represented populations
- develop promotion practices that are fair, inclusive, proactive, and non-discriminatory

Personnel responsible for delivery of SCP must have written performance goals, objectives, and outcomes for each year's performance cycle to be used to plan, review, and evaluate work and performance. The performance plan must be updated regularly to reflect changes during the performance cycle.

Results of individual personnel evaluations must be used to recognize personnel performance, address performance issues, implement individual and/or collective personnel development and training programs, and inform the assessment of programs and services.

SCP personnel, when hired and throughout their employment, must receive appropriate and thorough training.

SCP personnel, including student employees and volunteers, must have access to resources or receive specific training on
- institutional policies pertaining to functions or activities they support
- privacy and confidentiality policies
- laws regarding access to student records
- policies and procedures for dealing with sensitive institutional information
- policies and procedures related to technology used to store or access student records and institutional data
- how and when to refer those in need of additional

assistance to qualified personnel and have access to a supervisor for assistance in making these judgments
- systems and technologies necessary to perform their assigned responsibilities
- ethical and legal uses of technology

SCP personnel must engage in continuing professional development activities to keep abreast of the research, theories, legislation, policies, and developments that affect their programs and services.

Administrators of SCP must ensure that personnel are knowledgeable about and trained in safety, emergency procedures, and crisis prevention and response. Risk management efforts must address identification of threatening conduct or behavior and must incorporate a system for responding to and reporting such behaviors.

SCP personnel must be knowledgeable of and trained in safety and emergency procedures for securing and vacating facilities.

PROFESSIONAL PERSONNEL

SCP professional personnel either must hold an earned graduate or professional degree in a field relevant to their position or must possess an appropriate combination of educational credentials and related work experience.

A qualified member of the institution must be designated as the person responsible for student conduct programs.

Multiple people may be responsible at an institution that uses different offices for the resolution of individual versus group misconduct or academic versus non-academic misconduct.

The designee and any other professional staff member in the student conduct programs should, at a minimum, possess the following
- specialized training in student learning and development; this training could be achieved through a formal academic program or through professional development activities once in the field
- a clear understanding of the institutional and legal/ regulatory requirements governing the student conduct process
- knowledge sufficient to confer with students, community members, and other parties involved in student conduct proceedings, including attorneys, as well as other aspects of the student conduct program
- an interest in and commitment to the welfare and development of students as well as the greater community
- demonstrated skills in working with decision-making processes, conflict management, motivational interviewing, as well as alternative dispute resolution practices
- the ability to communicate and interact with others regardless of disability; age; race; cultural

identity; ethnicity; nationality; family educational history (e.g., first generation to attend college); political affiliation; religious affiliation; sex; sexual orientation; gender identity and expression; marital, social, economic, or veteran status
- understanding of the requirements relative to privacy/confidentiality and security of student conduct records
- the ability to create an atmosphere where students and other interested or involved parties feel free to ask questions and obtain assistance
- awareness of trends in facilitating best practices in conduct such as behavioral intervention, restorative justice, and motivational interviewing

INTERNS OR GRADUATE ASSISTANTS

Degree- or credential-seeking interns or graduate assistants must be qualified by enrollment in an appropriate field of study and relevant experience. These students must be trained and supervised by professional personnel who possess applicable educational credentials and work experience and have supervisory experience. Supervisors must be cognizant of the dual roles interns and graduate assistants have as both student and employee.

Supervisors must
- adhere to parameters of students' job descriptions
- articulate intended learning outcomes in student job descriptions
- adhere to agreed-upon work hours and schedules
- offer flexible scheduling when circumstances necessitate

Supervisors and students must both agree to suitable compensation if circumstances necessitate additional hours.

STUDENT EMPLOYEES AND VOLUNTEERS

Student employees and volunteers must be carefully selected, trained, supervised, and evaluated. Students must have access to a supervisor. Student employees and volunteers must be provided clear job descriptions, pre-service training based on assessed needs, and continuing development.

Student members of peer review and adjudication boards should be representative of the institution's student body as a whole, reflecting the diversity of the community.

Undergraduate students who participate on peer review boards or who assist the SCP may be awarded academic credit based on approval from the institution and appropriate supervision from a trained member of the professional staff. Clear objectives and assignments should be created to ensure that a student's grade for this participation is in no way influenced by decision-making on a particular student conduct matter.

Part 5. Ethics

Student Conduct Programs (SCP) must
- review applicable professional ethical standards and must adopt or develop and implement appropriate statements of ethical practice
- publish and adhere to statements of ethical practice and ensure their periodic review
- orient new personnel to relevant ethical standards and statements of ethical practice and related institutional policies

Statements of ethical standards must
- specify that SCP personnel respect privacy and maintain confidentiality in communications and records as delineated by privacy laws
- specify limits on disclosure of information contained in students' records as well as requirements to disclose to appropriate authorities
- address conflicts of interest, or appearance thereof, by personnel in the performance of their work
- reflect the responsibility of personnel to be fair, objective, and impartial in their interactions with others
- reference management of institutional funds
- reference appropriate behavior regarding research and assessment with human participants, confidentiality of research and assessment data, and students' rights and responsibilities
- include the expectation that personnel confront and hold accountable other personnel who exhibit unethical behavior
- address issues surrounding scholarly integrity

SCP personnel must
- employ ethical decision making in the performance of their duties
- inform users of programs and services of ethical obligations and limitations emanating from codes and laws or from licensure requirements
- recognize and avoid conflicts of interest that could adversely influence their judgment or objectivity and, when unavoidable, recuse themselves from the situation
- perform their duties within the scope of their position, training, expertise, and competence
- make referrals when issues presented exceed the scope of the position

Part 6. Law, Policy, and Governance

Student Conduct Programs (SCP) must be in compliance with laws, regulations, and policies that relate to their respective responsibilities and that pose legal obligations, limitations, risks, and liabilities for the institution as a whole. Examples include constitutional, statutory, regulatory, and case law; relevant law and orders emanating from codes and laws; and the institution's policies.

SCP must have access to legal advice needed for personnel to carry out their assigned responsibilities.

SCP must inform personnel, appropriate officials, and users of programs and services about existing and changing legal obligations, risks and liabilities, and limitations.

SCP must inform personnel about professional liability insurance options and refer them to external sources if the institution does not provide coverage.

SCP must have written policies and procedures on operations, transactions, or tasks that have legal implications.

SCP must regularly review policies. The revision and creation of policies must be informed by best practices, available evidence, and policy issues in higher education.

Institutions should review annually the rules and policies pertaining to student conduct; a crucial aspect of this review is determining of new governmental or state regulations (in the U.S.) have occurred since the last review that would dictate a change in current rules or policies.

SCP must have procedures and guidelines consistent with institutional policy for responding to threats, emergencies, and crisis situations. Systems and procedures must be in place to disseminate timely and accurate information to students, other members of the institutional community, and appropriate external organizations during emergency situations.

Personnel must neither participate in nor condone any form of harassment or activity that demeans persons or creates an intimidating, hostile, or offensive environment.

SCP must purchase or obtain permission to use copyrighted materials and instruments. References to copyrighted materials and instruments must include appropriate citations.

SCP must inform personnel about internal and external governance organizations that affect programs and services.

SCP staff should remain informed and provide training on all governmental mandates impacting the practice of student conduct.

In the U.S., these include, but are not limited to, Family Educational Rights and Privacy Act (FERPA), the Jeanne Clery Disclosure of Campus Security Policy and Campus Crime Statistics Act (Campus Security Act) and newly revised regulations (2014), Title IX of the Education Amendments of 1972 (Title IX) plus sub-regulatory guidance issues in 2011 and 2014, the Violence Against Women Act (VAWA) Reauthorization and, specifically, Section 304 which deals with campus sexual assault and related issues and has amended the Clery Act, the U.S. Department of Education Office for Civil Rights, and The Department of Justice Office of Violence Against Women.

SCP staff in the United States should remain informed and provide training on all state mandates impacting the practice of student conduct. Examples of state laws include those specific to firearms and drug possession.

Part 7. Diversity, Equity, and Access

Within the context of each institution's mission and in accordance with institutional policies and applicable codes and laws, Student Conduct Programs (SCP) must create and maintain educational and work environments that are welcoming, accessible, inclusive, equitable, and free from harassment.

SCP must not discriminate on the basis of disability; age; race; cultural identity; ethnicity; nationality; family educational history (e.g., first generation to attend college); political affiliation; religious affiliation; sex; sexual orientation; gender identity and expression; marital, social, economic, or veteran status; or any other basis included in institutional policies and codes and laws.

SCP must

- advocate for sensitivity to multicultural and social justice concerns by the institution and its personnel
- ensure physical, program, and resource access for all constituents
- modify or remove policies, practices, systems, technologies, facilities, and structures that create barriers or produce inequities
- ensure that when facilities and structures cannot be modified, they do not impede access to programs, services, and resources
- establish goals for diversity, equity, and access
- foster communication and practices that enhance understanding of identity, culture, self-expression, and heritage
- promote respect for commonalities and differences among people within their historical and cultural contexts
- address the characteristics and needs of diverse constituents when establishing and implementing culturally relevant and inclusive programs, services, policies, procedures, and practices
- provide personnel with diversity, equity, and access training and hold personnel accountable for applying the training to their work
- respond to the needs of all constituents served when establishing hours of operation and developing methods of delivering programs, services, and resources
- recognize the needs of distance and online learning students by directly providing or assisting them to gain access to comparable services and resources

Part 8. Internal and External Relations

Student Conduct Programs (SCP) must reach out to individuals, groups, communities, and organizations internal and external to the institution to

- establish, maintain, and promote understanding and effective relations with those that have a significant interest in or potential effect on the students or other constituents served by the programs and services
- garner support and resources for programs and services as defined by the mission
- collaborate in offering or improving programs and services to meet the needs of students and other constituents and to achieve program and student outcomes
- engage diverse individuals, groups, communities, and organizations to enrich the educational environment and experiences of students and other constituents
- disseminate information about the programs and services

Promotional and descriptive information must be accurate and free of deception and misrepresentation.
SCP must have procedures and guidelines consistent with institutional policy for

- communicating with the media
- distributing information through print, broadcast, and online sources
- contracting with external organizations for delivery of programs and services
- cultivating, soliciting, and managing gifts
- applying to and managing funds from grants

Representatives of the student conduct system should meet regularly with pertinent constituencies (e.g., student government, student development offices, staff, faculty members, academic administrators, Title IX coordinator(s), public safety, legal counsel, local police, district attorneys, service providers, Multicultural Student Programs, Women and Gender Programs, LGBT centers) to exchange information concerning their respective operations and to identify ways to work together to prevent behavior problems as well as correct existing ones. Such collaborative effort might include educational programs.

Part 9. Financial Resources

Student Conduct Programs (SCP) must have funding to accomplish the mission and goals.

In establishing and prioritizing funding resources, SCP must conduct comprehensive analyses to determine

- unmet needs of the unit
- relevant expenditures
- external and internal resources
- impact on students and the institution

SCP must use the budget as a planning tool to reflect commitment to the mission and goals of the programs and services and of the institution.

SCP must administer funds in accordance with established institutional accounting procedures.

SCP must demonstrate efficient and effective use and responsible stewardship of fiscal resources consistent with institutional protocols.

Financial reports must provide an accurate financial overview of the organization and provide clear, understandable, and timely data upon which personnel can plan and make informed decisions.
Procurement procedures must

- be consistent with institutional policies
- ensure that purchases comply with laws and codes for usability and access
- ensure that the institution receives value for the funds spent
- consider information available for comparing the ethical and environmental impact of products and services purchased

Part 10. Technology

Student Conduct Programs (SCP) must have technology to support the achievement of their mission and goals. The technology and its use must comply with institutional policies and procedures and with relevant codes and laws.

SCP must use technologies to

- provide updated information regarding mission, location, staffing, programs, services, and official contacts to students and other constituents in accessible formats
- provide an avenue for students and other constituents to communicate sensitive information in a secure format
- enhance the delivery of programs and services for all students

SCP must

- back up data on a regular basis
- adhere to institutional policies regarding ethical and legal use of technology
- articulate policies and procedures for protecting the confidentiality and security of information
- implement a replacement plan and cycle for all technology with attention to sustainability
- incorporate accessibility features into technology-based programs and services

When providing student access to technology, SCP must

- have policies on the use of technology that are clear, easy to understand, and available to all students
- provide information or referral to support services for those needing assistance in accessing or using

technology
- provide instruction or training on how to use the technology
- inform students of implications of misuse of technologies

Part 11. Facilities and Equipment

Student Conduct Programs' (SCP) facilities must be intentionally designed and located in suitable, accessible, and safe spaces that demonstrate universal design and support the program's mission and goals.

Facilities must be designed to engage various constituents and promote learning.

Personnel must have workspaces that are suitably located and accessible, well equipped, adequate in size, and designed to support their work and responsibilities.

The design of the facilities must guarantee the security and privacy of records and ensure the confidentiality of sensitive information and conversations. Personnel must be able to secure their work.

SCP must incorporate sustainable practices in use of facilities and purchase of equipment. Facilities and equipment must be evaluated on an established cycle and be in compliance with codes, laws, and accepted practices for access, health, safety, and security.

When acquiring capital equipment, SCP must take into account expenses related to regular maintenance and life cycle costs.

SCP must have access to facilities of sufficient size and arrangement to ensure privacy of records, meetings, and interviews.

The facilities should include a private office where individual consultations and conferences with those involved in conduct actions may be held, a meeting room for small groups, a library or resource area, and a secure location for student conduct records. The facilities should also be designated to promote the personal safety of the individuals involved in the SCP (e.g., multiple methods of egress, panic buttons).

Part 12. Assessment

Student Conduct Programs (SCP) must develop assessment plans and processes.

Assessment plans must articulate an ongoing cycle of assessment activities.

SCP must
- specify programmatic goals and intended outcomes
- identify student learning and development outcomes
- employ multiple measures and methods

- develop manageable processes for gathering, interpreting, and evaluating data
- document progress toward achievement of goals and outcomes
- interpret and use assessment results to demonstrate accountability
- report aggregated results to respondent groups and stakeholders
- use assessment results to inform planning and decision-making
- assess effectiveness of implemented changes
- provide evidence of improvement of programs and services

SCP must employ ethical practices in the assessment process.

SCP must have access to adequate fiscal, human, professional development, and technological resources to develop and implement assessment plans.

Evaluation of SCP should include
- periodic performance evaluations of peer review boards in use
- on-going assessment and evaluation of training programs and publications
- periodic review of applicable state and governmental regulations and laws to ensure compliance

Assessment and evaluation activities should include
- review of student conduct authorities' adherence to the institution's guidelines
- general impressions of the student conduct system according to students, faculty members, staff members, and the general community
- developmental and learning outcomes for students and members of peer review boards (if any are in existence at the institution)
- annual trends in staff caseload, rates of recidivism, types of offenses, and efficacy of sanctions
- effects of programming designed to prevent behavioral problems
- effectiveness of special population peer review boards (e.g., sexual violence, student organization, residence hall boards)

General Standards revised in 2014;
SCP content (formerly Judicial Programs and Services) developed/
revised in 1986, 1996, 2005, and 2015.

Student Leadership Programs
CAS Contextual Statement

Many college mission statements contain commitments to develop citizen leaders or prepare students for professional and community responsibilities in a global context. Throughout the history of higher education, however, leadership development has been targeted primarily toward students holding leadership positions, such as student government officials, officers in fraternities and sororities, and resident assistants. Consequently, only a handful of students had a genuine opportunity for focused experience in leadership development.

During the 1970s, many colleges refocused efforts on leadership development when events such as the Watergate scandal caused institutions to ponder how they taught ethics, leadership, and social responsibility. Subsequent initiatives such as the women's and African-American civil rights movements and adult reentry programs increased access to college. New forms of campus shared governance, coupled with a focus on intentional student development, led to new forms of leadership development through programs such as assertiveness training, emerging leaders' retreats, and leadership targeted toward specific populations.

By the 1970s, professional associations were becoming increasingly interested in broad-based leadership efforts. Several associations, including the American College Personnel Association (ACPA), National Association of Student Personnel Administrators (NASPA), National Association for Campus Activities (NACA), and National Association for Women in Education (NAWE), expanded projects and initiatives with a leadership focus. Burns' seminal book, *Leadership* (1978), brought new energy with its discussion of transformational leadership grounded in values and moral purpose. Thinking about leadership expanded in the 1980s and 1990s to include such perspectives as cultural influences, service learning, social change, and spirituality. Leadership educators focused on developing leadership models with applicability to the college context. Two such models, the Social Change Model of Leadership (SCM) (HERI, 1996) and the Relational Leadership Model (Komives, Lucas, & McMahon, 1996), have been widely adopted.

This shift to colleges developing not just better, but more leaders, has resulted in leadership education efforts directed toward the entire student body. Because students experience leadership in many different settings—in and out of the classroom, on and off campus, through social media, virtually every student engages in some type of activity that involves the practice of leadership. Regardless of differences in academic discipline, organizational affiliation, cultural background, or geographical location, students must be better prepared to serve as citizen-leaders in a global community. The role of student affairs professionals in this arena is to help students understand their experiences and to facilitate their learning so that they become effective contributors to their communities. Comprehensive leadership programs should be based on an active learning pedagogy where learning is situated in students' experiences, where students are validated as knowers, and where there is mutually constructed meaning (Baxter Magolda, 1999).

The Inter-Association Leadership Project brought student affairs leadership educators together in the mid-1980s to create and sustain a leadership agenda. By the end of the decade, higher education's commitment to leadership was clear—with over 600 campuses teaching leadership courses. Special leadership centers were created, such as the Jepson School of Leadership Studies at the University of Richmond and the McDonough Leadership Center at Marietta College, as well as special programs, including the National LeaderShape Institute. In 1992 the National Clearinghouse for Leadership Programs (NCLP) was established at the University of Maryland, and a co-sponsored series of symposia encouraged leadership educators to identify a leadership agenda for the new millennium. Projects funded by the Kellogg, Pew, and Lilly Foundations; FIPSE; and the federal Eisenhower Leadership grant program have also focused broad-based attention on leadership development. By late 1990s, there were over 800 college leadership programs.

The International Leadership Association (ILA) was established in 1999 to bring a global lens to leadership education; ILA developed a set of guiding questions to inform curricular leadership development. The Association of Leadership Educators, largely agricultural and community-based leadership faculty, has a focus on college students. Other leadership institutes serve the leadership educator professional; for example, NCLP and the NACA host the annual summer leadership educators' symposium, and NCLP in partnership with NASPA and ACPA now hosts the Leadership Educators Institute, a bi-annual program for entry and mid-level leadership educators. NCLP and the Association of College Unions International (ACUI) had a webinar series, and NACA developed a set of student leadership competencies. A detailed history of the evolution of leadership education can be found in the *Handbook for Student Leadership Development* (Komives, 2010).

The *CAS Student Leadership Program Standards and Guidelines* can be used to help professionals provide comprehensive leadership programs and enhance students' learning opportunities. Leadership for positional leaders will still occur within specific functional areas such as student activities and residence life; campuses that seek to develop a comprehensive leadership program will recognize the need to make intentional leadership development opportunities available to all students through coordinated campus-wide efforts. Research contains developmental models (e.g., Leadership Identity Development model; Komives, Owen, Longerbeam, Mainella, & Osteen, 2005) that can guide intentional practice. Further, an international Multi-Institutional Study of Leadership has established normative data using the SCM (see www.nclp.umd.edu).

Leadership is an inherently relational process of working with others to accomplish a goal or to promote change. Most leadership programs seek to empower students to enhance their self-efficacy as leaders and understand how they can make a difference, whether as positional leaders or active participants in a group or community process. Leadership development involves self-awareness and understanding of others, values and diverse perspectives, organizations, and change. Leadership also requires competence in establishing purpose, working collaboratively, and managing conflict. Institutions can initiate opportunities to study leadership and to experience a range of leadership-related activities designed to intentionally promote desired outcomes of student leadership learning.

References, Readings, and Resources

Astin, H., & Astin, A. (Eds.). (2000). *Leadership reconsidered: Engaging higher education in social change.* Battle Creek, MI: W.K. Kellogg Foundation.

Baxter Magolda, M. B. (1999). *Creating contexts for learning and self-authorship: Constructive-developmental pedagogy.* Nashville, TN: Vanderbilt University Press.

Boatman, S. (1987). *Student leadership development: Approaches, methods, and models.* Columbia, SC: National Association for Campus Activities.

Boatman, S. (1992). *Supporting student leadership: Selections from the student development series.* Columbia, SC: National Association for Campus Activities.

Brungardt, C. (1996). The making of leaders: A review of the research in leadership development and education. *Journal of Leadership Studies, 3*(3), 81-95.

Center for Creative Leadership, www.ccl.org. Publisher of periodic sourcebooks.

Concepts & connections: A newsletter for leadership educators. The National Clearinghouse for Leadership Programs, www.nclp.umd.edu.

Guthrie, K. & Osteen, L. (Eds). (2012). *Developing student leadership capacity.* New Directions for Student Services. San Francisco, CA: Jossey-Bass.

HERI (1996). *A social change model of leadership development: Guidebook version III.* Los Angeles: University of California Los Angeles Higher Education Research Institute.

Journal of Leadership Education, Association for Leadership Education, http://www.leadershipeducators.org/

Komives, S. R., Lucas, N., & McMahon, T. (1998). *Exploring leadership.* San Francisco: Jossey-Bass.

Komives, S. R., Owen, J. E., Longerbeam, S., Mainella, F. C., & Osteen, L. (2005). Developing a leadership identity: A grounded theory. *Journal of College Student Development, 46,* 593-611.

Komives, S. R., Dugan, J., Owen, J. E., Slack, C., & Wagner, W. (Eds). (2011). *Handbook for student leadership development (2nd ed.).* A publication of the National Clearinghouse for Leadership Programs. San Francisco, CA: Jossey-Bass.

Leadership Quarterly. JAI Press. http://www.journals.elsevier.com/the-leadership-quarterly/

Murray, J. I. (1994). *Training for student leaders.* Dubuque, IA: Kendall/Hunt.

Roberts, D. C. (1981). *Student leadership programs in higher education.* Carbondale, IL: American College Personnel Association.

Zimmerman-Oster, K., & Burkhardt, J. C. (1999). *Leadership in the making: Impact and insights from leadership development programs in U. S. colleges and universities.* Battle Creek, MI: W. K. Kellogg Foundation.

Contextual Statement Contributors
Current Edition:
Susan Komives, University of Maryland, ACPA

Previous Editions:
Jan Arminio, Shippensburg University, NACA
Susan Komives, University of Maryland, ACPA
Julie Owen, George Mason University, NCLP
Craig Slack, University of Maryland, NCLP

Student Leadership Programs
CAS Standards and Guidelines

Part 1. Mission

The mission of Student Leadership Programs (SLP) must be to prepare students to engage in the process of leadership. To accomplish this mission, the program must

- be grounded in the belief that leadership can be learned
- be based upon clearly stated principles, values, and assumptions
- use multiple leadership theories, models, and approaches
- provide students with opportunities to develop and enhance a personal philosophy of leadership that includes understanding of self, others, and community, and acceptance of responsibilities inherent in community membership
- promote intentional student involvement and learning in varied leadership experiences
- acknowledge effective leadership behaviors and processes
- be inclusive and accessible, by encouraging and seeking out underrepresented populations

SLP must develop, disseminate, implement, and regularly review their missions, which must be consistent with the mission of the institution and with applicable professional standards. The mission must be appropriate for the institution's students and other constituents. Mission statements must reference student learning and development.

Student leadership development must be an integral part of the institution's educational mission.

The SLP mission should be developed in collaboration with appropriate and multiple constituents interested in leadership development.

SLP should seek an institution-wide commitment that transcends the boundaries of the units specifically charged with program delivery.

Part 2. Program

To achieve their mission, Student Leadership Programs (SLP) must contribute to

- students' formal education, which includes both the curriculum and the co-curriculum
- student progression and timely completion of educational goals
- preparation of students for their careers, citizenship, and lives
- student learning and development

To contribute to student learning and development, SLP must

- identify relevant and desirable student learning and development outcomes
- articulate how the student learning and development outcomes align with the six CAS student learning and development domains and related dimensions
- assess relevant and desirable student learning and development
- provide evidence of impact on outcomes
- articulate contributions to or support of student learning and development in the domains not specifically assessed
- use evidence gathered to create strategies for improvement of programs and services

STUDENT LEARNING AND DEVELOPMENT DOMAINS AND DIMENSIONS

Domain: knowledge acquisition, integration, construction, and application

- Dimensions: understanding knowledge from a range of disciplines; connecting knowledge to other knowledge, ideas, and experiences; constructing knowledge; and relating knowledge to daily life

Domain: cognitive complexity

- Dimensions: critical thinking, reflective thinking, effective reasoning, and creativity

Domain: intrapersonal development

- Dimensions: realistic self-appraisal, self-understanding, and self-respect; identity development; commitment to ethics and integrity; and spiritual awareness

Domain: interpersonal competence

- Dimensions: meaningful relationships, interdependence, collaboration, and effective leadership

Domain: humanitarianism and civic engagement

- Dimensions: understanding and appreciation of cultural and human differences, social responsibility, global perspective, and sense of civic responsibility

Domain: practical competence

- Dimensions: pursuing goals, communicating effectively, technical competence, managing personal affairs, managing career development, demonstrating professionalism, maintaining health and wellness, and living a purposeful and satisfying life

[LD Outcomes: See *The Council for the Advancement of Standards Learning and Development Outcomes* statement for examples of outcomes related to these domains and dimensions.]

SLP must be

- **intentionally designed**
- **guided by theories and knowledge of learning and development**
- **integrated into the life of the institution**
- **reflective of developmental and demographic profiles of the student population**
- **responsive to needs of individuals, populations with distinct needs, and relevant constituencies**
- **delivered using multiple formats, strategies, and contexts**
- **designed to provide universal access**

SLP must collaborate with colleagues and departments across the institution to promote student learning and development, persistence, and success.

SLP must be comprehensive in nature and provide opportunities for students to develop leadership knowledge and skills. SLP staff must design learning environments reflective of the institutional mission, organizational context, learning goals, and intended audience. Programs must have clear theoretical foundations and be based upon well-defined principles, values, and assumptions. Programs must facilitate students' self-awareness, their capacity for collaboration, and their ability to engage within multiple contexts while understanding diverse perspectives.

Key components of SLP must include the following: opportunities for students to develop the competencies required for effective leadership; multiple delivery formats, strategies, and contexts; and collaboration with campus and community partners. These components are described in more detail below.

A. **SLP must provide opportunities for students to develop the competencies required for effective leadership.**

   SLP must advance student competencies in the categories of foundations of leadership; personal development; interpersonal development; and the development of groups, organizations, and systems. Suggested content for each of these categories follows.

   Foundations of leadership should include
   - historical perspectives on leaders, leadership, and leadership development
   - established and evolving theoretical, conceptual, and philosophical frameworks of leadership
   - the distinction between management and leadership
   - diverse approaches to leadership including positional (leadership-follower dynamics) and non-positional (collaborative-process models)
   - theories and strategies of change
   - the integrative and interdisciplinary nature of leadership
   - cross-cultural and global approaches to leadership

   Personal development should include

   - an awareness and understanding of various leadership styles and approaches
   - exploration of a personal leadership philosophy, including personal values exploration, leadership identity development, and reflective practice
   - connection of leadership to social identities and other dimensions of human development, such as psychosocial, cognitive, moral, and spiritual development
   - leadership skill development, including accessing and critiquing sources of information, ethical reasoning and decision making, oral and written communication skills, critical thinking and problem-solving, cultural competence, goal setting and visioning, motivation, creativity, and risk-taking

   Interpersonal development should include
   - movement from dependent or independent to interdependent relationships
   - development of self-efficacy for leadership
   - recognition of the influences on leadership of multiple aspects of identity, such as race, gender identity and expression, sexual orientation, class, disability, nationality, religion, and ethnicity

   Development of groups, organizations, and systems should include
   Group competencies:
   - team building
   - developing trust
   - group roles, group dynamics, and group development
   - group problem-solving, conflict management, and decision-making
   - shared leadership and collaboration
   Organizational competencies:
   - organizational planning, communication, and development
   - organizational culture, values, and principles
   - organizational politics and political systems
   - organizational lifecycles, sustainability, and stewardship
   - methods of assessing and evaluating organizational effectiveness
   Systems competencies:
   - understanding and critiquing of systems and human behavior within systems including functional and dysfunctional practices
   - coalition-building and other methods of systemic change
   - civic and community engagement
   - leadership across diverse organizations, environments, and contexts

B. **SLP must provide multiple delivery formats, strategies, and contexts. SLP must be intentionally designed to meet the developmental needs of participants across** diverse contexts. SLP programs must be based on principles of active learning.

Examples of delivery formats include retreats, conferences, credit-bearing courses, workshops, internships, panel discussions, case studies, films, lectures, simulations, mentor programs, adventure training, assessment tools, portfolios, and participation in local, regional, and national associations. Consideration should be given to on-line delivery methods.

SLP should provide strategies that may include training, education, and development. SLP *training* refers to activities designed to improve individual performance within specific roles; *education* consists of activities designed to provide improve the overall leadership knowledge of an individual; and *development* involves activities and environments that encourage growth and increasing complexity.

SLP should provide strategies that involve programs and services that are *open* to all students, *targeted* to a specific group of students, and aimed at students with *positional* leadership roles.

SLP should include multiple *contexts* for leadership development, such as diverse academic and career fields, campus organizations and committees, employment and internship settings, community involvement and service-learning, family, international settings, and social and religious organizations.

C. **SLP must collaborate with campus and community partners**

SLP must involve a diverse range of partners in the planning, delivery, and assessment of programs and services.

This group may include faculty members, students, staff members, group advisors, community members, and on- and off-campus organizations.

SLP should consider collaborating with a broad range of campus departments, community groups, schools, and businesses to increase awareness of leadership programs, fiscal and human resources, and access to additional sources of leadership expertise.

Part 3. Organization and Leadership

To achieve program and student learning and development outcomes, Student Leadership Programs (SLP) must be purposefully structured for effectiveness. SLP must have clearly stated and current
- goals and outcomes
- policies and procedures
- responsibilities and performance expectations for personnel
- organizational charts demonstrating clear channels of authority

Leaders must model ethical behavior and institutional citizenship.

Leaders with organizational authority for SLP must provide strategic planning, management and supervision, and program advancement.

Strategic Planning
- articulate a vision and mission that drive short- and long-term planning
- set goals and objectives based on the needs of the populations served, intended student learning and development outcomes, and program outcomes
- facilitate continuous development, implementation, and assessment of program effectiveness and goal attainment congruent with institutional mission and strategic plans
- promote environments that provide opportunities for student learning, development, and engagement
- develop, adapt, and improve programs and services in response to the changing needs of populations served and evolving institutional priorities
- include diverse perspectives to inform decision making

Management and Supervision
- plan, allocate, and monitor the use of fiscal, physical, human, intellectual, and technological resources
- manage human resource processes including recruitment, selection, professional development, supervision, performance planning, succession planning, evaluation, recognition, and reward
- influence others to contribute to the effectiveness and success of the unit
- empower professional, support, and student personnel to become effective leaders
- encourage and support collaboration with colleagues and departments across the institution
- encourage and support scholarly contributions to the profession
- identify and address individual, organizational, and environmental conditions that foster or inhibit mission achievement
- use current and valid evidence to inform decisions
- incorporate sustainability practices in the management and design of programs, services, and facilities
- understand appropriate technologies and integrate them into programs and services
- be knowledgeable about codes and laws relevant to programs and services and ensure that programs and services meet those requirements
- assess and take action to mitigate potential risks

Program Advancement
- advocate for and actively promote the mission and goals of the programs and services
- inform stakeholders about issues affecting practice
- facilitate processes to reach consensus where wide support is needed
- advocate for representation in strategic planning

initiatives at divisional and institutional levels

An individual or team should be designated with responsibility for the coordination of the leadership program, including allocation and maintenance of resources and creating leadership opportunities.

SLP are organized in a variety of offices and departments in student and academic affairs, and in other administrative areas. An advisory group with representatives from the involved areas and other relevant campus and community partners should be established for the purpose of communication and consultation.

Part 4. Human Resources

Student Leadership Programs (SLP) must be staffed adequately by individuals qualified to accomplish mission and goals.

SLP must have access to technical and support personnel adequate to accomplish their mission.

Within institutional guidelines, SLP must
- establish procedures for personnel recruitment and selection, training, performance planning, and evaluation
- set expectations for supervision and performance
- provide personnel access to continuing and advanced education and appropriate professional development opportunities to improve their competence, skills, and leadership capacity
- consider work/life options available to personnel (e.g., compressed work schedules, flextime, job sharing, remote work, or telework) to promote recruitment and retention of personnel

Administrators of SLP must
- ensure that all personnel have updated position descriptions
- implement recruitment and selection/hiring strategies that produce a workforce inclusive of under-represented populations
- develop promotion practices that are fair, inclusive, proactive, and non-discriminatory

Personnel responsible for delivery of SLP must have written performance goals, objectives, and outcomes for each year's performance cycle to be used to plan, review, and evaluate work and performance. The performance plan must be updated regularly to reflect changes during the performance cycle.

Results of individual personnel evaluations must be used to recognize personnel performance, address performance issues, implement individual and/or collective personnel development and training programs, and inform the assessment of programs and services.

SLP personnel, when hired and throughout their employment, must receive appropriate and thorough training.

SLP personnel, including student employees and volunteers, must have access to resources or receive specific training on
- institutional policies pertaining to functions or activities they support
- privacy and confidentiality policies
- laws regarding access to student records
- policies and procedures for dealing with sensitive institutional information
- policies and procedures related to technology used to store or access student records and institutional data
- how and when to refer those in need of additional assistance to qualified personnel and have access to a supervisor for assistance in making these judgments
- systems and technologies necessary to perform their assigned responsibilities
- ethical and legal uses of technology

SLP personnel must engage in continuing professional development activities to keep abreast of the research, theories, legislation, policies, and developments that affect their programs and services.

SLP staff serving as leadership educators must be knowledgeable about learning theories and their implications for student development, program design, and assessment.

Program staff should engage in continuous discovery and understanding of student leadership models, research, theories, and definitions through on-going study and professional development activities.

Administrators of SLP must ensure that personnel are knowledgeable about and trained in safety, emergency procedures, and crisis prevention and response. Risk management efforts must address identification of threatening conduct or behavior and must incorporate a system for responding to and reporting such behaviors.

SLP personnel must be knowledgeable of and trained in safety and emergency procedures for securing and vacating facilities.

PROFESSIONAL PERSONNEL

SLP professional personnel either must hold an earned graduate or professional degree in a field relevant to their position or must possess an appropriate combination of educational credentials and related work experience.

Professional staff or faculty involved in leadership programs should possess
- knowledge of the history of and current trends in leadership theories, models, and philosophies
- an understanding of the contextual nature of leadership
- knowledge of organizational development, group dynamics, strategies for change, and principles of community

- knowledge of how social identities and dimensions of diversity influence leadership
- experience in leadership development
- the ability to work with diverse range of students
- the ability to create, implement and evaluate student learning as a result of leadership programs
- the ability to effectively organize learning opportunities that are consistent with students' stages of development
- the ability to use reflection in helping students understand leadership concepts
- the ability to develop and assess student learning outcomes

INTERNS OR GRADUATE ASSISTANTS

Degree- or credential-seeking interns or graduate assistants must be qualified by enrollment in an appropriate field of study and relevant experience. These students must be trained and supervised by professional personnel who possess applicable educational credentials and work experience and have supervisory experience. Supervisors must be cognizant of the dual roles interns and graduate assistants have as both student and employee.

Supervisors must
- adhere to parameters of students' job descriptions
- articulate intended learning outcomes in student job descriptions
- adhere to agreed-upon work hours and schedules
- offer flexible scheduling when circumstances necessitate

Supervisors and students must both agree to suitable compensation if circumstances necessitate additional hours.

STUDENT EMPLOYEES AND VOLUNTEERS

Student employees and volunteers must be carefully selected, trained, supervised, and evaluated. Students must have access to a supervisor. Student employees and volunteers must be provided clear job descriptions, pre-service training based on assessed needs, and continuing development.

Part 5. Ethics

Student Leadership Programs (SLP) must
- review applicable professional ethical standards and must adopt or develop and implement appropriate statements of ethical practice
- publish and adhere to statements of ethical practice and ensure their periodic review
- orient new personnel to relevant ethical standards and statements of ethical practice and related institutional policies

Statements of ethical standards must
- specify that SLP personnel respect privacy and maintain confidentiality in communications and records as delineated by privacy laws
- specify limits on disclosure of information

contained in students' records as well as requirements to disclose to appropriate authorities
- address conflicts of interest, or appearance thereof, by personnel in the performance of their work
- reflect the responsibility of personnel to be fair, objective, and impartial in their interactions with others
- reference management of institutional funds
- reference appropriate behavior regarding research and assessment with human participants, confidentiality of research and assessment data, and students' rights and responsibilities
- include the expectation that personnel confront and hold accountable other personnel who exhibit unethical behavior
- address issues surrounding scholarly integrity

SLP personnel must
- employ ethical decision making in the performance of their duties
- inform users of programs and services of ethical obligations and limitations emanating from codes and laws or from licensure requirements
- recognize and avoid conflicts of interest that could adversely influence their judgment or objectivity and, when unavoidable, recuse themselves from the situation
- perform their duties within the scope of their position, training, expertise, and competence
- make referrals when issues presented exceed the scope of the position

SLP staff members must ensure that facilitators have appropriate training, experience, and credentials. Expertise and certification, where appropriate, are essential in the administration and interpretation of personality, developmental, and leadership assessment instruments.

Part 6. Law, Policy, and Governance

Student Leadership Programs (SLP) must be in compliance with laws, regulations, and policies that relate to their respective responsibilities and that pose legal obligations, limitations, risks, and liabilities for the institution as a whole. Examples include constitutional, statutory, regulatory, and case law; relevant law and orders emanating from codes and laws; and the institution's policies.

SLP must have access to legal advice needed for personnel to carry out their assigned responsibilities.

SLP must inform personnel, appropriate officials, and users of programs and services about existing and changing legal obligations, risks and liabilities, and limitations.

SLP must inform personnel about professional liability insurance options and refer them to external sources if the institution does not provide coverage.

SLP must have written policies and procedures on operations, transactions, or tasks that have legal implications.

SLP must regularly review policies. The revision and creation of policies must be informed by best practices, available evidence, and policy issues in higher education.

SLP must have procedures and guidelines consistent with institutional policy for responding to threats, emergencies, and crisis situations. Systems and procedures must be in place to disseminate timely and accurate information to students, other members of the institutional community, and appropriate external organizations during emergency situations.

Personnel must neither participate in nor condone any form of harassment or activity that demeans persons or creates an intimidating, hostile, or offensive environment.

SLP must purchase or obtain permission to use copyrighted materials and instruments. References to copyrighted materials and instruments must include appropriate citations.

SLP must inform personnel about internal and external governance organizations that affect programs and services.

SLP must advocate for student involvement in institutional governance.

Part 7. Diversity, Equity, and Access

Within the context of each institution's mission and in accordance with institutional policies and applicable codes and laws, Student Leadership Programs (SLP) must create and maintain educational and work environments that are welcoming, accessible, inclusive, equitable, and free from harassment.

SLP must not discriminate on the basis of disability; age; race; cultural identity; ethnicity; nationality; family educational history (e.g., first generation to attend college); political affiliation; religious affiliation; sex; sexual orientation; gender identity and expression; marital, social, economic, or veteran status; or any other basis included in institutional policies and codes and laws.

SLP must

- advocate for sensitivity to multicultural and social justice concerns by the institution and its personnel
- ensure physical, program, and resource access for all constituents
- modify or remove policies, practices, systems, technologies, facilities, and structures that create barriers or produce inequities
- ensure that when facilities and structures cannot be modified, they do not impede access to programs, services, and resources
- establish goals for diversity, equity, and access
- foster communication and practices that enhance understanding of identity, culture, self-expression, and heritage
- promote respect for commonalities and differences among people within their historical and cultural contexts

- address the characteristics and needs of diverse constituents when establishing and implementing culturally relevant and inclusive programs, services, policies, procedures, and practices
- provide personnel with diversity, equity, and access training and hold personnel accountable for applying the training to their work
- respond to the needs of all constituents served when establishing hours of operation and developing methods of delivering programs, services, and resources
- recognize the needs of distance and online learning students by directly providing or assisting them to gain access to comparable services and resources

SLP must provide students with the opportunity to
- recognize the influences of aspects of social identity on personal and organizational leadership
- examine social identities, multiple identities, and other aspects of development and how they influence experiences in different contexts
- develop multicultural awareness, knowledge, and skills

Part 8. Internal and External Relations

Student Leadership Programs (SLP) must reach out to individuals, groups, communities, and organizations internal and external to the institution to
- establish, maintain, and promote understanding and effective relations with those that have a significant interest in or potential effect on the students or other constituents served by the programs and services
- garner support and resources for programs and services as defined by the mission
- collaborate in offering or improving programs and services to meet the needs of students and other constituents and to achieve program and student outcomes
- engage diverse individuals, groups, communities, and organizations to enrich the educational environment and experiences of students and other constituents
- disseminate information about the programs and services

Promotional and descriptive information must be accurate and free of deception and misrepresentation.

SLP must have procedures and guidelines consistent with institutional policy for
- communicating with the media
- distributing information through print, broadcast, and online sources
- contracting with external organizations for delivery of programs and services
- cultivating, soliciting, and managing gifts
- applying to and managing funds from grants

Part 9. Financial Resources

Student Leadership Programs (SLP) must have funding to accomplish the mission and goals.

In establishing and prioritizing funding resources, SLP must conduct comprehensive analyses to determine
- unmet needs of the unit
- relevant expenditures
- external and internal resources
- impact on students and the institution

SLP must use the budget as a planning tool to reflect commitment to the mission and goals of the programs and services and of the institution.

SLP must administer funds in accordance with established institutional accounting procedures.

SLP must demonstrate efficient and effective use and responsible stewardship of fiscal resources consistent with institutional protocols.

Financial reports must provide an accurate financial overview of the organization and provide clear, understandable, and timely data upon which personnel can plan and make informed decisions.

Procurement procedures must
- be consistent with institutional policies
- ensure that purchases comply with laws and codes for usability and access
- ensure that the institution receives value for the funds spent
- consider information available for comparing the ethical and environmental impact of products and services purchased

Funding for SLP may come from a variety of sources, including institutional funds, grants, student fees, fees for services, individual donors, academic departments, course fees, and government contracts. Where possible, institutional funding should be allocated regularly and consistently for the operation of leadership programs.

Part 10. Technology

Student Leadership Programs (SLP) must have technology to support the achievement of their mission and goals. The technology and its use must comply with institutional policies and procedures and with relevant codes and laws.

SLP must use technologies to
- provide updated information regarding mission, location, staffing, programs, services, and official contacts to students and other constituents in accessible formats
- provide an avenue for students and other constituents to communicate sensitive information in a secure format
- enhance the delivery of programs and services for all students

SLP must
- back up data on a regular basis
- adhere to institutional policies regarding ethical and legal use of technology
- articulate policies and procedures for protecting the confidentiality and security of information
- implement a replacement plan and cycle for all technology with attention to sustainability
- incorporate accessibility features into technology-based programs and services

When providing student access to technology, SLP must
- have policies on the use of technology that are clear, easy to understand, and available to all students
- provide information or referral to support services for those needing assistance in accessing or using technology
- provide instruction or training on how to use the technology
- inform students of implications of misuse of technologies

Part 11. Facilities and Equipment

Student Leadership Programs' (SLP) facilities must be intentionally designed and located in suitable, accessible, and safe spaces that demonstrate universal design and support the program's mission and goals.

Facilities must be designed to engage various constituents and promote learning.

SLP offices and programming space should be conveniently located on campus and designed to facilitate maximum interaction among students, faculty members, and staff.

Personnel must have workspaces that are suitably located and accessible, well equipped, adequate in size, and designed to support their work and responsibilities.

The design of the facilities must guarantee the security and privacy of records and ensure the confidentiality of sensitive information and conversations. Personnel must be able to secure their work.

SLP must incorporate sustainable practices in use of facilities and purchase of equipment. Facilities and equipment must be evaluated on an established cycle and be in compliance with codes, laws, and accepted practices for access, health, safety, and security.

When acquiring capital equipment, SLP must take into account expenses related to regular maintenance and life cycle costs.

Part 12. Assessment

Student Leadership Programs (SLP) must develop assessment plans and processes.

Assessment plans must articulate an ongoing cycle of assessment activities.

SLP must

- specify programmatic goals and intended outcomes
- identify student learning and development outcomes
- employ multiple measures and methods
- develop manageable processes for gathering, interpreting, and evaluating data
- document progress toward achievement of goals and outcomes
- interpret and use assessment results to demonstrate accountability
- report aggregated results to respondent groups and stakeholders
- use assessment results to inform planning and decision-making
- assess effectiveness of implemented changes
- provide evidence of improvement of programs and services

Assessment efforts should include

- student needs
- student satisfaction
- student learning outcomes
- overall program evaluation

Assessment efforts should be linked to strategic planning efforts including the articulation of a clear program mission, vision, and values; theoretical orientation; and short- and long-term goals.

SLP must employ ethical practices in the assessment process.

SLP must have access to adequate fiscal, human, professional development, and technological resources to develop and implement assessment plans.

General Standards revised in 2014;
SLP content developed/revised in 1996 & 2009

Transfer Student Programs and Services
CAS Contextual Statement

The increasing number of students moving between institutions, coupled with national and international attention focused on degree completion, shows the importance of examining higher education programs and services that enhance the success of transfer students. This document establishes guidelines for institutions as they develop and execute policies and procedures related to services for transfer students. Because there is no prototypical transfer student, each institution must determine the approach for providing services that best fits its mission and resources. Therefore, this document is not prescriptive but is intended to define the scope of services needed to create a transfer-friendly culture that meets students' individual goals. The concepts within these standards are applicable for "sending" and "receiving" institutions as well as any transfer scenario.

Transfer includes various pathways, including (a) lateral transfer (transfer to the same type of institution, e.g., 2-year to 2-year, as the one in which a student is currently or previously enrolled); (b) vertical transfer (transferring from a 2-year institution to a four-year institution with the intent of completing a bachelor's degree); or (c) reverse transfer (transfer from a 4-year institution to a 2-year institution) (Poisel & Marling, 2011). It is not uncommon for students to "swirl" between and among institutions taking courses from more than one institution either simultaneously or consecutively as they attempt to achieve their educational goals. The services mentioned within these standards are expected to address all types of transfer students, including those enrolled in online courses.

The numbers of college students in the United States on a transfer track at a community college or as transfer students at a 4-year campus account for one-third of entering students (NACAC, 2010). In California, the number of transfer students moving from 2-year to 4-year institutions is the same as those moving in the reverse direction (Hagedorn, 2010). Nearly 60 percent of college graduates in the U.S. have attended more than one college or university (Adelman, 2009). Although not all of these individuals are considered transfer students, the high percentage underscores the importance of developing sound practices to facilitate transfer student success.

Not only are transfer students a large percentage of the higher education population but postsecondary institutions are also being challenged by legislatures throughout the U.S. and Canada to increase degree completion rates. U.S. President Obama has set a national goal that "America will regain its lost ground and have the highest proportion of students graduating from college in the world by 2020" (http://www.whitehouse.gov/issues/education/). The National Governors Association has urged colleges and universities to produce improved outcome and progress metrics, including the tracking of transfer students (Reyna, 2010). An emphasis on student mobility is not limited to the U.S., as demonstrated by efforts on behalf of the European Action Scheme for the Mobility of University Students (Erasmus), University Mobility in Asia Pacific (UMAP) (Junor & Usher, 2008), the British Columbia Council on Admissions and Transfer (BCCAT), and other provincial associations (Stewart & Martinello, 2012).

Although moving from a 2-year to 4-year institution is the most prevalent transfer pathway (Handel, 2011), it is important to note that the CAS standards and guidelines for transfer student programs and services are intended to apply to the services available to all transfer students, regardless of their institutions of origin, credential acquisition, or educational goals. For example, it is recommended that community colleges and 4-year institutions collaborate to develop a reverse awarding of degrees process by which students earning enough credits for their associate's degree post-transfer are reverse-awarded their associate's degree by their community college. This is just one example of how the provision of services for transfer students is quite complex. These standards aspire to provide for a range of scenarios about the transfer process.

Understandably, there is an underlying focus on degree completion. Increasing the persistence and graduation rates of transfer students is accomplished by effectively preparing students for planned and unplanned transitions between institutions; helping them anticipate areas where change is more likely to occur; and identifying early in the process their personal, academic, financial, and social goals as well as factors that may inhibit or facilitate success. Early intervention is critical to mitigating the negative effects of transfer shock (Thurmond, 2007), a temporary dip in grade point average during the first and sometimes second semester post transfer (Hills, 1965).

Prior to the last decade, there was a dearth of literature about transfer issues; however, a number of studies since that time have produced valuable information about the migration patterns and success rates of transfer students (Jacobs, Cutright, Niebling, Simon, & Marling, 2010). As a result, transfer student issues have secured a firm place on the national higher education agenda (NACAC, 2010).

Most notably, researchers (Handel, 2009, 2011; Handel & Herrera, 2007; Jain, Herrera, Bernal, & Soloranzo, 2001) have brought into focus the need for community colleges to create a transfer-going culture that respects students' academic goals while creating well-articulated and -communicated pathways for pursuing a baccalaureate degree. Similarly, 4-year colleges and universities are encouraged to provide a transfer-receptive culture that respects students' previous experiences and offers services tailored to their unique needs. All institutions are encouraged to set high expectations for transfer student success and degree completion and ensure that policies and practices lead to positive outcomes. The literature on transfer student success provides good examples of such policies and practices.

To better understand how services for transfer students can be infused into institutional culture, Taylor Smith and Miller (2009) explored the characteristics, practices, and policies of community colleges that contribute to success of students prior to and after transferring to a 4-year institution. Studying six community college campuses, they found programs appearing to contribute to higher-than-expected transfer rates had three common characteristics: structured academic pathway, student-centered culture, and culturally sensitive leadership. Taylor Smith and Miller's recommendations for implementing positive practices and strategies include

- collaborative campus programming
- administrative offices as support and service centers
- data-driven decision making
- faculty engagement in the transfer process
- rewards for personnel who value students
- a culture of performance and accountability

Yet, more must be done to support students' transition between institutions and to strengthen the transfer pathway. Handel (2011) offered three strategies for 4-year institutions: (a) create an institution-wide vision that includes transfer students, (b) value transfers in outreach, admission, and academic and student affairs comparably to first-year students, and (c) understand that the needs of transfer students may be different from those of first-year students. The report (Handel, 2011) also addressed initiating or improving transfer at 4-year colleges and universities through the following recommendations:

- provide explicit institutional leadership and commitment to the transfer pathway
- offer ongoing outreach and preparation for staff and students
- implement user-friendly admission and enrollment processes
- educate on financial aid options
- strengthen the connection of student and academic affairs resources, programs, and services

The successful provision of services for transfer students requires intra- and inter-institutional collaboration among multiple stakeholders across functional lines focused on facilitating transfer student success. It is critical to have a unified and widely communicated institutional approach to providing transfer students services that may result in provision of services directly by a designated department (e.g., a transfer center) or as a function of multiple departments. To facilitate seamless transfer, it is also important to consider creating state/provincial approaches to service delivery and policy. To this end, the CAS standards and guidelines are intended to be aspirational, with the understanding that implementation will vary by state/region/province in response to existing policies, practices, and resources.

References, Readings, and Resources

American Association of Community Colleges (AACC). (2011). *Community college fast facts*. Retrieved from http://www.aacc.nche.edu/AboutCC/Documents/FactSheet2011.pdf

Berger, J. B., & Malaney, G. D. (2003). Assessing the transition of transfer students from community colleges to a university. *NASPA Journal, 40*(4), 1-23. Retrieved from http://www.eric.ed.gov/PDFS/ED453489.pdf

Braxton, J. M. (2003). Student success. In S. R. Komives & D. B. Woodard, Jr., & Associates (Eds.), *Student services: A handbook for the profession* (4th ed., pp. 317-338). San Francisco, CA: Jossey-Bass.

Grites, T. J., & Rondeau, S. (2011). Creating effective transfer initiatives. In T. Brown, M. C. King, & P. Stanley (Eds.), *Fulfilling the promise of the community college: Increasing first-year student engagement and success* (Monograph No. 56, pp. 83-97). Columbia, SC: University of South Carolina, National Resource Center for the First-Year Experience and Students in Transition.

Handel, S. J. (2011). *Improving student transfer from community colleges to four-year institutions—The perspective of leaders from baccalaureate granting institutions*. New York, NY: The College Board.

Handel, S. J. (2009). Transfer and the part-time student: The gulf separating community colleges and selective universities. *Change: The Magazine of Higher Learning, 41*(4), 48-53.

Handel, S. J. (2007). Transfer students apply to college, too. How come we don't help them? *Chronicle of Higher Education, 54*(9), B20.

Handel, S. J., & Herrera, A. (2006, June). *Pursuing higher education access and achievement: Case studies in the development of "transfer-going" cultures*. Prepared for the Jack Kent Cooke National Forum, Washington, DC. Retrieved from http://professionals.collegeboard.com/profdownload/pursuing-higher-education_handel-herrera.pdf

Hills, J. (1965, Spring) Transfer shock: The academic performance of the transfer student. *The Journal of Experimental Education, 33*(3). Retrieved from http://www.jstor.org/stable/20156766?seq=1#page_scan_tab_contents

Jacobs, B. C. (2010). Making the case for orientation: A vice president's perspective. In J. Ward (Ed.), *Designing successful transitions: A guide to orienting students to college* (Monograph No. 13, 3rd ed., pp. 29-39). Columbia, SC: University of South Carolina, National Resource Center for the First-Year Experience and Students in Transition.

Jacobs, B. C. (2009). The swirling, whirling world of transfer student orientation. In M. A. Sedotti & M. J. Payne (Eds.), *Orientation planning manual* (pp. 11-16). Minneapolis, MN: National Orientation Directors Association.

Jacobs, B. C., Cutright, M., Niebling, G. F., Simon, J. F., & Marling, J. L. (Eds.) (2010). *Exploring promising practices in transfer student services: A Texas initiative*. Denton, TX: University of North Texas, National Institute for the Study of Transfer Students

Jacobs, B. C., Lauren, B., Miller, M., & Nadler, D. (Eds.) (2004). *The college transfer student in America: The forgotten student*. Washington, DC: American Association of Collegiate Registrars and Admissions Officers (AACRAO).

Jain, D., Herrera, A., Bernal, S., & Solorzano, D. (2011). Critical race theory and the transfer function: Introducing a transfer receptive culture. *Community College Journal of Research and Practice, 35*, 252-266.

Junor, S., & Usher, A. (2008). Student mobility and credit transfer: A national and global survey. Educational Policy Institute, Virginia Beach, VA. Retrieved from http://www.educationalpolicy.org/publications/pubpdf/credit.pdf

Laanan, F. S. (2007). Studying transfer students. Part II: Dimensions of transfer students' adjustment. *Community College Journal of Research and Practice, 31*, 37-59.

Marling, J. L. (Ed.) (2013). Collegiate Transfer: Navigating the New Normal. *New Directions for Higher Education*, Vol. 162. San Francisco, CA: Jossey-Bass

Marling, J., & Jacobs, B. C. (2010). Effective orientation for transfer students. In M. A. Poisel & S. Joseph (Eds.), *Transfer students in higher education: Building a rationale for policies, programs, and services that foster student success* (pp. 71-88). Columbia, SC: University of South Carolina, National Resource Center for the First Year Experience and Students in Transition.

National Association for College Admission Counseling (NACAC). (2010, April). *Special report on the transfer admission process*. Arlington, VA: Author. Retrieved from http://www. nacacnet.org/PublicationsResources/Research/Documents/ TransferFactSheet.pdf

National Institute for the Study of Transfer Students (NISTS). (2011).

Poisel, M. A., & Marling, J. L. (2011, October). *Strategies for transition: Facilitating transfer student success.* Pre-Conference workshop presented at the Students in Transition Conference for the National Resource Center for the First Year Experience and Student in Transition, Saint Louis, MO.

Reyna, R. (2010). *Complete to compete: Common college completion metrics*. Washington, DC: National Governors Association. Retrieved from http://www.nga.org/files/live/sites/NGA/files/ pdf/1007COMMONCOLLEGEMETRICS.PDF

Stewart, J., & Martinello, F. (2012). Are transfer students different? An examination of first year grades and course withdrawals. *Canadian Journal of Higher Education, 42*(1), pp. 25-42.

Taylor Smith, C., & Miller, A. (2009). *Bridging the gaps to success: Promising practices for promoting transfer among low-income and first-generation students*. Washington DC: The Pell Institute for the Study of Opportunity in Higher Education. Retrieved from http://www.pellinstitute.org/downloads/publications-Bridging_ the_Gaps_to_Success_2009.pdf

Thurmond, K. C. (2007). *Transfer shock: Why is a term forty years old still relevant?* Retrieved from NACADA Clearinghouse of Academic Advising Resources Website: http://www.nacada.ksu. edu/Clearinghouse/AdvisingIssues/Transfer-Shock.htm

Townsend, B. K., & Wilson, K. (2006). "A hand hold for a little bit": Factors facilitating the success of community college transfer students to a large research university. *Journal of College Student Development, 47*, 439-456. doi:10.1353/csd.2006.0052

Contextual Statement Contributors

Current Edition:
Janet L. Marling, University of North Texas, NISTS
Jan Hillman, University of North Texas, NISTS
Bonita C. Jacobs, North Georgia College, NISTS
Marsha Miller, Kansas State University

Previous Editions:
Janet L. Marling, University of North Texas, NISTS
Jan Hillman, University of North Texas, NISTS
Bonita C. Jacobs, North Georgia College, NISTS
Marsha Miller, Kansas State University

Transfer Student Programs and Services
CAS Standards and Guidelines

The mission of Transfer Student Programs and Services (TSPS) is to aid in the successful transfer, persistence, and graduation of transfer students. To accomplish the mission, TSPS must facilitate seamless pathways among and within institutions to support transfer students at all stages of their transitions.

Through the provision of TSPS, the institution's culture becomes one that is supportive and inclusive of transfer students.

TSPS must develop, disseminate, implement, and regularly review their missions, which must be consistent with the mission of the institution and with applicable professional standards. The mission must be appropriate for the institution's students and other constituents. Mission statements must reference student learning and development.

To achieve their mission, Transfer Student Programs and Services (TSPS) must contribute to
- students' formal education, which includes both the curriculum and the co-curriculum
- student progression and timely completion of educational goals
- preparation of students for their careers, citizenship, and lives
- student learning and development

To contribute to student learning and development, TSPS must
- identify relevant and desirable student learning and development outcomes
- articulate how the student learning and development outcomes align with the six CAS student learning and development domains and related dimensions
- assess relevant and desirable student learning and development
- provide evidence of impact on outcomes
- articulate contributions to or support of student learning and development in the domains not specifically assessed
- use evidence gathered to create strategies for improvement of programs and services

STUDENT LEARNING AND DEVELOPMENT DOMAINS AND DIMENSIONS

Domain: knowledge acquisition, integration, construction, and application
- Dimensions: understanding knowledge from a range of disciplines; connecting knowledge to other knowledge, ideas, and experiences; constructing knowledge; and relating knowledge to daily life

Domain: cognitive complexity
- Dimensions: critical thinking, reflective thinking, effective reasoning, and creativity

Domain: intrapersonal development
- Dimensions: realistic self-appraisal, self-understanding, and self-respect; identity development; commitment to ethics and integrity; and spiritual awareness

Domain: interpersonal competence
- Dimensions: meaningful relationships, interdependence, collaboration, and effective leadership

Domain: humanitarianism and civic engagement
- Dimensions: understanding and appreciation of cultural and human differences, social responsibility, global perspective, and sense of civic responsibility

Domain: practical competence
- Dimensions: pursuing goals, communicating effectively, technical competence, managing personal affairs, managing career development, demonstrating professionalism, maintaining health and wellness, and living a purposeful and satisfying life

[LD Outcomes: See *The Council for the Advancement of Standards Learning and Development Outcomes* statement for examples of outcomes related to these domains and dimensions.]

TSPS must be
- intentionally designed
- guided by theories and knowledge of learning and development
- integrated into the life of the institution
- reflective of developmental and demographic profiles of the student population
- responsive to needs of individuals, populations with distinct needs, and relevant constituencies
- delivered using multiple formats, strategies, and contexts
- designed to provide universal access

TSPS must collaborate with colleagues and departments across the institution to promote student learning and development, persistence, and success.

TSPS must
- serve as a contact for transfer students throughout the application, acceptance, and transfer processes
- connect students to appropriate institutional academic and behavioral policies and procedures

- facilitate cooperation between institutions to help students align their programs of study to enable a timely and successful transfer
- advocate for improvement of institutional articulation agreements and/or curricular alignment depending on the particular institution's policies
- know how to apply applicable laws, regulations, and policies related to the successful transfer of students
- inform key partners about policies and practices that maximize transfer student success
- provide access to professional advisors, faculty members, counselors, and staff support to help transfer students engage in and develop college and long-term academic, career, and life goals
- advocate for equitable enrollment and flexible class scheduling and delivery methods
- review informational materials for accessible and accurate information about transfer policies, processes, scholarships and affordability, course equivalencies, and programs
- disseminate informational material to transfer students and to institutional personnel supporting transfer students
- participate in recruitment events to communicate with prospective students about transfer and articulation
- collaborate with partners to prioritize programming specific to the needs of transfer students during the first-year and throughout their time at the institution
- collaborate with stakeholders to address transfer student success, retention, and degree completion

TSPS programming should address topics that are pivotal to the successful transfer of students to and from their institution.

Particular attention should be paid to programming specific to the transfer student's first year. Topics could include

- demographics of the institution's transfer students (including first-generation and veteran status)
- institutional academic support services and other learning assistance programs
- eligibility for and promotion of leadership opportunities and awards for students
- student money management, academic resources, financial aid, and scholarships
- living options (both on and off campus), learning communities, and theme halls

TSPS should ensure that the institution provides support for transfer-intending students and current transfers by offering the following opportunities:

- advising regarding the institution's admission process and application for admission
- assistance as needed in orientation and academic advising
- early-alert systems, intrusive advising, academic

support, transfer-year seminars and student success courses, peer mentoring, and other transition services

TSPS should provide informal transcript evaluations so that prospective students can gauge their academic standing before committing to an institution.

TSPS should work with Residence Life/Housing to develop opportunities for new residential transfer students to be paired with or mentored by other transfer students

Part 3. Organization and Leadership

To achieve program and student learning and development outcomes, programs Transfer Student Programs and Services (TSPS) and services must be purposefully structured for effectiveness. Programs and services must have clearly stated and current

- goals and outcomes
- policies and procedures
- responsibilities and performance expectations for personnel
- organizational charts demonstrating clear channels of authority

TSPS cross-functional and divisional reporting lines must be located in the organizational department or division that can best provide effective programming and services for achievement of the mission.

Leaders must model ethical behavior and institutional citizenship.

Leaders with organizational authority for TSPS must provide strategic planning, management and supervision, and program advancement.

Strategic Planning

- articulate a vision and mission that drive short- and long-term planning
- set goals and objectives based on the needs of the populations served, intended student learning and development outcomes, and program outcomes
- facilitate continuous development, implementation, and assessment of program effectiveness and goal attainment congruent with institutional mission and strategic plans
- promote environments that provide opportunities for student learning, development, and engagement
- develop, adapt, and improve programs and services in response to the changing needs of populations served and evolving institutional priorities
- include diverse perspectives to inform decision making

Management and Supervision

- plan, allocate, and monitor the use of fiscal, physical, human, intellectual, and technological resources

- manage human resource processes including recruitment, selection, professional development, supervision, performance planning, succession planning, evaluation, recognition, and reward
- influence others to contribute to the effectiveness and success of the unit
- empower professional, support, and student personnel to become effective leaders
- encourage and support collaboration with colleagues and departments across the institution
- encourage and support scholarly contributions to the profession
- identify and address individual, organizational, and environmental conditions that foster or inhibit mission achievement
- use current and valid evidence to inform decisions
- incorporate sustainability practices in the management and design of programs, services, and facilities
- understand appropriate technologies and integrate them into programs and services
- be knowledgeable about codes and laws relevant to programs and services and ensure that programs and services meet those requirements
- assess and take action to mitigate potential risks

TSPS leaders should

- be involved in research, publication, presentations, consultation, and relevant professional organizations
- communicate with professional colleagues in the transfer student field and related areas

TSPS leaders should provide informational resources that are easily accessed and that address the informational needs of transfer students and their families.

Program Advancement

- advocate for and actively promote the mission and goals of the programs and services
- inform stakeholders about issues affecting practice
- facilitate processes to reach consensus where wide support is needed
- advocate for representation in strategic planning initiatives at divisional and institutional levels

TSPS leaders should

- identify examples of successful transfer students, including those who transferred from a community college, and integrate them as able into the operations of TSPS
- work with institutional leaders to plan courses and course sections to accommodate transfer student degree plans
- collaborate with key partners to influence institutional planning, policy, procedural, and fiscal decisions that affect transfer student articulation
- provide a voice for transfer student concerns on institutional committees

TSPS leaders must serve as role models for transfer student transition to a new institution.

Part 4. Human Resources

Transfer Student Programs and Services (TSPS) must be staffed adequately by individuals qualified to accomplish mission and goals.

TSPS professional staff members must possess the skills and competencies needed to provide assistance to prospective and enrolled transfer students.

TSPS may include, but should not be limited to, the following competencies:

- effective advocacy for prospective and enrolled students
- ethical and objective presentation of the institution's programs and opportunities, including careful and concerned analysis of student goals
- clear understanding of likely student-institution compatibility
- guidance in responsible decision-making in the selection of an institution or degree program
- ability to explain and contextualize relevant academic policies and practices
- ability to articulate relevant cost and financial aid issues, especially since these may differ from policies at the student's current institution
- ability to manage human and fiscal resources, including creative thinking in the augmentation of these resources through strong collaboration skills and fundraising

At least one dedicated institutional employee should be identified as the primary contact and resource for transfer students and their families.

TSPS must have access to technical and support personnel adequate to accomplish their mission.

Within institutional guidelines, TSPS must

- establish procedures for personnel recruitment and selection, training, performance planning, and evaluation
- set expectations for supervision and performance
- provide personnel access to continuing and advanced education and appropriate professional development opportunities to improve their competence, skills, and leadership capacity
- consider work/life options available to personnel (e.g., compressed work schedules, flextime, job sharing, remote work, or telework) to promote recruitment and retention of personnel

Administrators of TSPS must

- ensure that all personnel have updated position descriptions
- implement recruitment and selection/hiring strategies that produce a workforce inclusive of under-represented populations
- develop promotion practices that are fair, inclusive, proactive, and non-discriminatory

Personnel responsible for delivery of TSPS must have

written performance goals, objectives, and outcomes for each year's performance cycle to be used to plan, review, and evaluate work and performance. The performance plan must be updated regularly to reflect changes during the performance cycle.

Results of individual personnel evaluations must be used to recognize personnel performance, address performance issues, implement individual and/or collective personnel development and training programs, and inform the assessment of programs and services.

TSPS personnel, when hired and throughout their employment, must receive appropriate and thorough training.

TSPS personnel, including student employees and volunteers, must have access to resources or receive specific training on

- institutional policies pertaining to functions or activities they support
- privacy and confidentiality policies
- laws regarding access to student records
- policies and procedures for dealing with sensitive institutional information
- policies and procedures related to technology used to store or access student records and institutional data
- how and when to refer those in need of additional assistance to qualified personnel and have access to a supervisor for assistance in making these judgments
- systems and technologies necessary to perform their assigned responsibilities
- ethical and legal uses of technology

TSPS personnel must engage in continuing professional development activities to keep abreast of the research, theories, legislation, policies, and developments that affect their programs and services.

TSPS professional staff should have knowledge of theories of student learning, development, and transition.

Administrators of TSPS must ensure that personnel are knowledgeable about and trained in safety, emergency procedures, and crisis prevention and response. Risk management efforts must address identification of threatening conduct or behavior and must incorporate a system for responding to and reporting such behaviors.

TSPS personnel must be knowledgeable of and trained in safety and emergency procedures for securing and vacating facilities.

PROFESSIONAL PERSONNEL

TSPS professional personnel either must hold an earned graduate or professional degree in a field relevant to their position or must possess an appropriate combination of educational credentials and related work experience.

TSPS professional staff should be knowledgeable in the areas of transition issues, barriers to transfer, financial aid, and testing.

INTERNS OR GRADUATE ASSISTANTS

Degree- or credential-seeking interns or graduate assistants must be qualified by enrollment in an appropriate field of study and relevant experience. These students must be trained and supervised by professional personnel who possess applicable educational credentials and work experience and have supervisory experience. Supervisors must be cognizant of the dual roles interns and graduate assistants have as both student and employee.

Supervisors must
- adhere to parameters of students' job descriptions
- articulate intended learning outcomes in student job descriptions
- adhere to agreed-upon work hours and schedules
- offer flexible scheduling when circumstances necessitate

Supervisors and students must both agree to suitable compensation if circumstances necessitate additional hours.

STUDENT EMPLOYEES AND VOLUNTEERS

Student employees and volunteers must be carefully selected, trained, supervised, and evaluated. Students must have access to a supervisor. Student employees and volunteers must be provided clear job descriptions, pre-service training based on assessed needs, and continuing development.

TSPS staff members should demonstrate knowledge of and sensitivity to the needs of non-traditional students, traditionally under-represented groups, academically underprepared students, international students, and veterans.

Staff members who provide services for transfer students should have working relationships with advisors, faculty, counselors, and staff as they help students think about academic, career, and life goals.

TSPS should include faculty in the development and delivery of programs for transfer students.

Part 5. Ethics

Transfer Student Programs and Services (TSPS) must
- review applicable professional ethical standards and must adopt or develop and implement appropriate statements of ethical practice
- publish and adhere to statements of ethical practice and ensure their periodic review
- orient new personnel to relevant ethical standards and statements of ethical practice and related institutional policies

Statements of ethical standards must
- specify that TSPS personnel respect privacy and maintain confidentiality in communications and records as delineated by privacy laws

- specify limits on disclosure of information contained in students' records as well as requirements to disclose to appropriate authorities
- address conflicts of interest, or appearance thereof, by personnel in the performance of their work
- reflect the responsibility of personnel to be fair, objective, and impartial in their interactions with others
- reference management of institutional funds
- reference appropriate behavior regarding research and assessment with human participants, confidentiality of research and assessment data, and students' rights and responsibilities
- include the expectation that personnel confront and hold accountable other personnel who exhibit unethical behavior
- address issues surrounding scholarly integrity

TSPS personnel must

- employ ethical decision making in the performance of their duties
- inform users of programs and services of ethical obligations and limitations emanating from codes and laws or from licensure requirements
- recognize and avoid conflicts of interest that could adversely influence their judgment or objectivity and, when unavoidable, recuse themselves from the situation
- perform their duties within the scope of their position, training, expertise, and competence
- make referrals when issues presented exceed the scope of the position

TSPS staff members must work to create institutional culture, policies, curriculum, and standards that positively support the success of transfer students

TSPS staff members must

- refrain from challenging another institution's services or information even if those services or information may be different from their own policies or programs
- avoid falsely representing their institution and academic standing for the sole reason of securing the transfer student's admittance

TSPS documents used by admissions, academic advising and counseling, orientation, housing, personal counseling and testing, the registrar, and international student services must be accurate and handled with confidentiality.

Part 6. Law, Policy, and Governance

Transfer Student Programs and Services (TSPS) must be in compliance with laws, regulations, and policies that relate to their respective responsibilities and that pose legal obligations, limitations, risks, and liabilities for the institution as a whole. Examples include constitutional, statutory, regulatory, and case law; relevant law and orders emanating from codes and laws; and the institution's policies.

TSPS staff members must understand and know how to apply appropriate laws, regulations, and policies that are specific to transfer students; including guaranteed admission policies, core curriculum policies, matriculation and articulation agreements, and policies specific to diverse student populations including veterans and first-generation students, and other agreements within and among institutions.

TSPS must have access to legal advice needed for personnel to carry out their assigned responsibilities.

TSPS must inform personnel, appropriate officials, and users of programs and services about existing and changing legal obligations, risks and liabilities, and limitations.

TSPS must inform personnel about professional liability insurance options and refer them to external sources if the institution does not provide coverage.

TSPS must have written policies and procedures on operations, transactions, or tasks that have legal implications.

TSPS must regularly review policies. The revision and creation of policies must be informed by best practices, available evidence, and policy issues in higher education.

TSPS must have procedures and guidelines consistent with institutional policy for responding to threats, emergencies, and crisis situations. Systems and procedures must be in place to disseminate timely and accurate information to students, other members of the institutional community, and appropriate external organizations during emergency situations.

Personnel must neither participate in nor condone any form of harassment or activity that demeans persons or creates an intimidating, hostile, or offensive environment.

TSPS must purchase or obtain permission to use copyrighted materials and instruments. References to copyrighted materials and instruments must include appropriate citations.

TSPS must inform personnel about internal and external governance organizations that affect programs and services.

TSPS staff members must ensure that all transfer policies, including an appeals process, are publicly available for review prior to the student's commitment to transfer.

TSPS should encourage 2-year and 4-year institutions to collaborate in the development of policies and processes to reverse-award associate degrees to students.

Part 7. Diversity, Equity, and Access

Within the context of each institution's mission and in accordance with institutional policies and applicable codes and laws, Transfer Student Programs and Services (TSPS) must create and maintain educational and work environments that are welcoming, accessible, inclusive, equitable, and free from harassment.

TSPS must not discriminate on the basis of disability; age; race; cultural identity; ethnicity; nationality; family educational history (e.g., first generation to attend college); political affiliation; religious affiliation; sex; sexual orientation; gender identity and expression; marital, social, economic, or veteran status; or any other basis included in institutional policies and codes and laws.

TSPS must

- advocate for sensitivity to multicultural and social justice concerns by the institution and its personnel
- ensure physical, program, and resource access for all constituents
- modify or remove policies, practices, systems, technologies, facilities, and structures that create barriers or produce inequities
- ensure that when facilities and structures cannot be modified, they do not impede access to programs, services, and resources
- establish goals for diversity, equity, and access
- foster communication and practices that enhance understanding of identity, culture, self-expression, and heritage
- promote respect for commonalities and differences among people within their historical and cultural contexts
- address the characteristics and needs of diverse constituents when establishing and implementing culturally relevant and inclusive programs, services, policies, procedures, and practices
- provide personnel with diversity, equity, and access training and hold personnel accountable for applying the training to their work
- respond to the needs of all constituents served when establishing hours of operation and developing methods of delivering programs, services, and resources
- recognize the needs of distance and online learning students by directly providing or assisting them to gain access to comparable services and resources

All transfer-related marketing and forms must clearly state student rights and responsibilities in the transfer process. Practices must be congruent with institutional policies on equal opportunity access.

TSPS should respect the diversity of students and their families, acknowledging the many different cultures and backgrounds represented by these individuals, and be prepared to identify resources for support both on campus and locally as needed.

TSPS should provide access to the institution's policies and procedures and resources in multiple language formats, including printed forms for families who do not have informational technology.

Part 8. Internal and External Relations

Transfer Student Programs and Services (TSPS) must reach out to individuals, groups, communities, and organizations internal and external to the institution to

- establish, maintain, and promote understanding and effective relations with those that have a significant interest in or potential effect on the students or other constituents served by the programs and services
- garner support and resources for programs and services as defined by the mission
- collaborate in offering or improving programs and services to meet the needs of students and other constituents and to achieve program and student outcomes
- engage diverse individuals, groups, communities, and organizations to enrich the educational environment and experiences of students and other constituents
- disseminate information about the programs and services

TSPS must develop and maintain collaborative relationships between sending and receiving institutions.

TSPS must develop and maintain a relationship with those responsible for the orientation of new students.

TSPS should collaborate with those in charge of new student orientation programs and courses to meet the specific needs of transfer students.

TSPS must be aware of governmental units responsible for laws, policies, and regulations relevant to transfer matriculation and maintain relationships with them.

TSPS should partner with academic unit leadership to develop course acceptance and course applicability plans by major.

TSPS should partner with the academic and enrollment management functions to ensure timely evaluation and application of earned credits.

TSPS should advise prospective and enrolled transfer students about their responsibilities in achieving their goals.

TSPS should work with parent and family programs to inform family members about issues that impact the health, well-being, and success of students through a variety of communication methods.

TSPS should work with parent and family programs to provide a resource guide or handbook to address student-life topics of priority to the institution (e.g., drug and alcohol use, service-learning and study abroad opportunities, research opportunities, financial literacy, health and wellness), resources and benefits available to parents and families, institutional policies and procedures, the academic calendar, and support services.

Promotional and descriptive information must be accurate

and free of deception and misrepresentation.

TSPS must have procedures and guidelines consistent with institutional policy for
- communicating with the media
- distributing information through print, broadcast, and online sources
- contracting with external organizations for delivery of programs and services
- cultivating, soliciting, and managing gifts
- applying to and managing funds from grants

Part 9. Financial Resources

Transfer Student Programs and Services (TSPS) must have funding to accomplish the mission and goals.

In establishing and prioritizing funding resources, TSPS must conduct comprehensive analyses to determine
- unmet needs of the unit
- relevant expenditures
- external and internal resources
- impact on students and the institution

TSPS must use the budget as a planning tool to reflect commitment to the mission and goals of the programs and services and of the institution.

TSPS must administer funds in accordance with established institutional accounting procedures.

TSPS must demonstrate efficient and effective use and responsible stewardship of fiscal resources consistent with institutional protocols.

Financial reports must provide an accurate financial overview of the organization and provide clear, understandable, and timely data upon which personnel can plan and make informed decisions.

Procurement procedures must
- be consistent with institutional policies
- ensure that purchases comply with laws and codes for usability and access
- ensure that the institution receives value for the funds spent
- consider information available for comparing the ethical and environmental impact of products and services purchased

TSPS should be funded at the same cost/student ratio as services for the institution's first-time, first-year student population.

TSPS may supplement institutional funding through the development of revenue sources such as fundraising, grants, and fees for services provided.

Part 10. Technology

Transfer Student Programs and Services (TSPS) must have technology to support the achievement of their mission and goals. The technology and its use must comply with institutional policies and procedures and with relevant codes and laws.

TSPS staff members should be trained in transfer specific technologies, including but not limited to digital transcript services.

TSPS must use technologies to
- provide updated information regarding mission, location, staffing, programs, services, and official contacts to students and other constituents in accessible formats
- provide an avenue for students and other constituents to communicate sensitive information in a secure format
- enhance the delivery of programs and services for all students

TSPS must
- back up data on a regular basis
- adhere to institutional policies regarding ethical and legal use of technology
- articulate policies and procedures for protecting the confidentiality and security of information
- implement a replacement plan and cycle for all technology with attention to sustainability
- incorporate accessibility features into technology-based programs and services

When providing student access to technology, TSPS must
- have policies on the use of technology that are clear, easy to understand, and available to all students
- provide information or referral to support services for those needing assistance in accessing or using technology
- provide instruction or training on how to use the technology
- inform students of implications of misuse of technologies

If the institution equips first-time first-year students with specific technology, then the institution should provide new transfer students with the same technology.

Part 11. Facilities and Equipment

Transfer Student Programs and Services' (TSPS) facilities must be intentionally designed and located in suitable, accessible, and safe spaces that demonstrate universal design and support the program's mission and goals.

Facilities must be designed to engage various constituents and promote learning.

Personnel must have workspaces that are suitably located and accessible, well equipped, adequate in size, and designed to support their work and responsibilities.

The design of the facilities must guarantee the security and privacy of records and ensure the confidentiality of sensitive information and conversations. Personnel must be able to secure their work.

TSPS must incorporate sustainable practices in use of facilities and purchase of equipment. Facilities and equipment must be evaluated on an established cycle and be in compliance with codes, laws, and accepted practices for access, health, safety, and security.

When acquiring capital equipment, TSPS must take into account expenses related to regular maintenance and life cycle costs.

Part 12. Assessment

Transfer Student Programs and Services (TSPS) must develop assessment plans and processes.

Assessment plans must articulate an ongoing cycle of assessment activities.

TSPS must
- specify programmatic goals and intended outcomes
- identify student learning and development outcomes
- employ multiple measures and methods
- develop manageable processes for gathering, interpreting, and evaluating data
- document progress toward achievement of goals and outcomes
- interpret and use assessment results to demonstrate accountability
- report aggregated results to respondent groups and stakeholders
- use assessment results to inform planning and decision-making
- assess effectiveness of implemented changes
- provide evidence of improvement of programs and services

TSPS must collaborate with appropriate partners to conduct research and collect data regarding transfer students. Results must be shared with students, staff, and faculty at both sending and receiving institutions.

TSPS should work to ensure there are processes to monitor and report annual persistence and graduation rates for all types of transfer students, including community college graduates and non-graduates as well as those who transfer from 4-year institutions.

TSPS should employ multiple methods to assess program effectiveness in meeting the needs of transfer-intending and current transfer students.

TSPS should partner with institutional research/assessment personnel to ensure that assessment efforts are tracked.

TSPS must employ ethical practices in the assessment process.

TSPS must have access to adequate fiscal, human, professional development, and technological resources to develop and implement assessment plans.

General Standards revised in 2014;
TSPS content developed in 2012

TRIO and Other Educational Opportunity Programs
CAS Contextual Statement

Students from low-income and first-generation (neither parent has a baccalaureate degree) backgrounds historically have had limited access to higher education. Realizing that the ideal of American higher education must provide opportunities for all students to attend higher education, federal and state legislation has been enacted to mitigate some of the inequities to access and higher education completion. Fifty years ago, the Higher Education Act of 1965 authorized federal student financial aid. This was the *first time* that Federal scholarship monies would be distributed based on a student's low-income status. Also in the HEA Title IV, the first TRIO program, Talent Search was created to inform students about the new federal financial aid opportunities. In the 1960's, few high school and college personnel had experience working with diverse populations of young adults in higher education. Hence, Section 408 of the Higher Education Act authorized "Contracts to Encourage the Full Utilization of Educational Talent (CEFUET, later called Talent Search)", for marketing and outreach to disseminate information about the availability of federal financial aid and how to apply for it.

Since then, a variety of educational opportunity programs have developed at the state, federal, and community levels to increase student college access; assist with transitioning to higher education; and support college persistence, academic achievement, and success-completion in higher education. These college Access and Success Programs primarily provide support to students from lower income, first-generation, and other student groups underrepresented in higher education. Additionally, schools, colleges, foundations, corporations, and non-profit and other organizations fund scholarship, pre-college preparation and college support-success programs.

The TRIO Programs are the largest of the federally-funded Access and Success Programs designed to motivate and support students from disadvantaged backgrounds to prepare for, enroll, persist, transfer from two to four-schools, and graduate from postsecondary institutions. TRIO includes seven student programs providing academic and other support for students from low-income families and are first-generation. In addition, the TRIO legislation provides for professional development training opportunities specific to staff working in the TRIO functional area. TRIO programs serve students beginning in middle school and provide support through postsecondary education, including preparation for graduate-doctoral studies.

The TRIO programs are authorized under the U. S. Higher Education Act of 1965, Title IV, Part A, Subpart 2. FEDERAL TRIO PROGRAMS, and most recently reauthorized by the Higher Education Opportunity Act in August 2008. The Higher Education Act currently is in the process of another reauthorization beginning in 2015. Eligibility criteria for these programs are primarily based on low income (families at or below 150% of poverty level) and first-generation status. The concept of first-generation was first introduced as a new TRIO

eligibility criteria in the 1980 Higher Education Amendments. TRIO projects are funded through competitive grant applications, in five-year cycles. In 2014-2015 there are 2,787 TRIO projects hosted by 1,000 higher education institutions, schools, and community organizations and agencies. In 2014-15, TRIO programs serve 759,094 pre-college and postsecondary students.

The initial three TRIO programs included Talent Search, created in 1965 as part of the Higher Education Act; Upward Bound, which emerged from the Economic Opportunity Act of 1964 as part of President Johnson's War on Poverty and originally housed in the Office of Economic Opportunity; and Student Support Services, in 1968. The term "TRIO" referred to these three original federal programs. The Higher Education Amendments of 1972 added Educational Opportunity Centers, and the 1986 Amendments authorized the Ronald E. McNair Post-Baccalaureate Achievement Program. Veteran's Upward Bound, created in 1972, addressed educational concerns for the large number of returning Vietnam Veterans with low educational attainment; and the Upward Bound Math-Science Program was created in 1990 to address the STEM achievement gaps for low-income and first-generation students.

The Gaining Early Awareness and Readiness for Undergraduate Programs (Gear Up) were authorized in the Higher Education Amendments of 1998, and although not TRIO programs, also provide precollege preparation for low-income students. TRIO and Gear Up are administered by the U. S. Department of Education, Office of Postsecondary Education, Division of Student Services Higher Education Programs.

TRIO and Gear Up Program Descriptions

- **Educational Opportunity Centers (EOC)** provide counseling and information about college admissions and financial aid to qualified adults, with the goal of increasing the number of adult participants who enroll in or continue a program of post-secondary education. Services include advising; counseling; provision of information about educational opportunities and financial assistance; financial and economic literacy; assistance with completing applications for college admissions; testing and financial aid; coordinating with educational institutions and community partnerships; and provision of referrals, tutoring, and mentoring. EOC projects may be sponsored by higher education institutions or community organizations. In 2014-2015, there are 126 EOC's serving 189,733 students.

- **The Ronald E. McNair Post-baccalaureate Achievement Program (McNair)** prepares eligible undergraduates to enter doctoral studies. The goal of McNair is to increase graduate-doctoral degree attainment by students from low-income, first-generation, and designated underrepresented groups. Services include faculty mentoring, scholarly activities to prepare students for doctoral study, summer research internships, tutoring, counseling, assistance with securing graduate program admission and financial aid, preparation for GRE exams, and other activities that enhance successful entry to and persistence in graduate programs, and doctoral degree attainment. McNair projects are sponsored by higher education institutions. In 2014-15, 151 Mc Nair projects serve 4,293 students.

- **The Student Support Services program (SSS)** provides academic support for low-income, first-generation students, including students with disabilities, to motivate students to complete post-secondary education with the goal of increasing participant college retention and graduation rates and to facilitate two-year college student transition to four-year institutions. Activities include basic skills instruction and tutoring; academic, career and personal counseling; financial literacy information; assistance with graduate school admission; mentoring; special services for students with limited English proficiency or are homeless or aged out of foster care systems; cultural activities; and academic support for students with disabilities. SSS projects are sponsored by higher education institutions and in 2014-2015, 1,027 projects serve 202,492 students.

- **The Talent Search program** identifies, motivates, and assists participants in middle and high school to complete high school and enter and persist in higher education. Talent Search also serves high school dropouts by encouraging them to reenter the educational system. The goal is to increase the number of youth from disadvantaged backgrounds who complete high school and enroll in post-secondary education. Talent Search serves sixth to twelfth grade students with early college planning; academic, financial, career, and personal counseling; tutoring; information about post-secondary education and college visits; completing college admissions and financial aid applications; preparation for college entrance exams; mentoring; and family involvement activities. Talent Search projects are sponsored by higher education institutions, community agencies or organizations and schools. In 2014-15, 450 Talent Search projects serve 310,747 students.

- **Upward Bound (UB)** is comprised of three programs, with intensive college preparatory projects designed to provide high school participants and military veterans with college preparation and skills to complete high school, (or in VUB, preparation for college ready) matriculate to postsecondary, and earn a post-secondary degree. Upward Bound provides academic instruction and enrichment activities throughout the calendar year, including summer academic-year programs at college campuses. Other services include study skills; academic, financial, and personal counseling; tutoring; cultural and social activities; college visits, assistance with college entrance and financial aid applications; and preparation

for college entrance exams. In 2014-15, 814 Classic Upward Bound projects served 61,458 students; 162 UB Math Science projects served 10,034 students; and 49 Veteran's Upward Bound served 6,566 students.

- **The Veterans Upward Bound program (VUB)** serves military veterans who are preparing to enter post-secondary education.

- **The Upward Bound Math/Science Program (UBMS)** encourages students to pursue postsecondary degrees in math and science through intensive math and science curricula and experiences, computer instruction, and research activities. Upward Bound projects are sponsored by institutions of higher education, local education agencies, nonprofit organizations, other organizations and/or agencies, state education agencies.

Gaining Early Awareness and Readiness for Undergraduate Programs (GEAR UP) is a competitive grant program of the U.S. Department of Education that increases the number of low-income students who are prepared to enter and succeed in postsecondary education by providing States and local community-education partnerships six-to-seven year grants to offer support services to high-poverty, middle and high schools. The program serves at least one grade level of students, beginning no later than the 7th grade, following them through high school graduation and their first year in college. GEAR UP provides early college awareness and support activities including tutoring, mentoring, academic preparation, financial education and college scholarships to improve access to higher education for low income, minority and disadvantaged first-generation students and their families. GEAR UP funds are also used to provide college scholarships to low-income students. The program mandates cooperation among K-12 schools, institutions of higher education, local and state education entities, businesses and community-based organizations. The GEAR UP initiative was authorized by Title IV of the 1998 Amendments to the Higher Education Act of 1965 (HEA) and was signed into public law (P.L.105-244) in 1998, and reauthorized through the Higher Education Opportunity Act, 2008.

State Sponsored College Access and Success Programs: Some states support educational opportunity – college access and success programs designed to increase access to higher education for lower income, first-generation, and/or students historically underrepresented in higher education. An example is the "New Jersey Educational Opportunity Fund created by law in 1968 to ensure meaningful access to higher education for those who come from backgrounds of economic and educational disadvantage. The Fund assists low-income New Jersey residents who are capable and motivated but lack adequate preparation for college study." In addition to supplemental financial aid to help cover college costs, the Fund supports a wide array of campus-based outreach and support services at 28 public and 13 independent institutions to facilitate college persistence and completion.

In addition to federal and state access and success programs, numerous foundation, corporate, and non-profit organizations fund scholarship and/or pre-college access and preparation programs. Examples of these include the Lumina Foundation, the I Have a Dream Foundation, Daniels Fund Scholars, Gates Millennium Scholars, National College Access Network programs such as the Ohio College Access Network, Jack Kent Cooke Foundation Scholars. The Denver Scholarship Foundation is an example of a PromiseNet organization—a place-based community program that provides the promise of a scholarship and a network of services to increase college access and success among low-income students and contributes to community economic development by providing access to postsecondary education.

TRIO and College Access and Success Professional Associations:

The Council for Opportunity in Education (COE) is the national *professional association* representing over 6,000+ TRIO, Gear Up and other college access and success program personnel. COE sponsors professional development activities including national conferences, symposia, workshops, publications, grant proposal writing workshops, TRIO training, and TRIO and access-success program research through the Pell Institute for the Study of Opportunity in Higher Education. COE advocates for TRIO programs and students and acts as liaison to the US Department of Education for TRIO programs. Other *professional associations* representing college access and success programs include the National College Access Network (NCAN) and the Educational Opportunity Fund Association of New Jersey. COE provides leadership with CAS in recognizing a need for and developing the first set of TRIO and Other EOP Standards and Guidelines in 1999; revised in 2008, and promotes their use for TRIO and other college access and success programs.

Trends:

Current trends expand federally funded TRIO and Gear Up programs and other educational opportunity programs to include the array of College Access and Success Programs, encouraging collaboration and partnerships amongst the college access and success community. The Council for Opportunity in Education provides funding for state TRIO programs to network and collaborate with other state college access and success programs and state departments of education and higher education to increase the numbers of low-income, first-generation, and other student groups underrepresented in higher education preparing for, enrolling and completing college; and to decrease the educational achievement gaps for these populations.

Another trend is the recognition of a need for, and the development of specialized professional development and higher education graduate level courses and programs specific to professionals working in the college access and success functional area. This increased recognition of the functional professional area also influences TRIO and other Access and Success Program staff to use the CAS TRIO and Other Educational Opportunity Program Standards and Guidelines.

References, Readings, and Resources

Council for Opportunity in Education: www.coenet.us

National College Access Network: http://www.collegeaccess.org/

Pell Institute for the Study of Opportunity in Higher Education: www.pellinstitute.org

U. S. Department of Education Office of Postsecondary Education Gear Up: http://www2.ed.gov/programs/gearup/index.html

U. S. Department of Education Office of Postsecondary Education TRIO Programs: http://www2.ed.gov/about/offices/list/ope/trio/index.html

Groutt, J. (2003). Milestones of TRIO history, Part 1 and Part 2. Reprinted from *Opportunity Outlook: The Journal of the Council for Opportunity in Education.*

Institute for Higher Education Policy Film Series (2013). *Access to attainment, an access agenda for 21st century college students.* Washington, DC.

Pell Institute (2015). *Indicators of higher education equity in the United States: 45 year trend report*, Washington, DC.

Perna, L & Jones, A. P. (2013). *The state of college access and completion: Improving college success for students from underrepresented groups.* Routledge: New York, New York.

Wolanin, T. (April, 1997). The history of TRIO: Three decades of success and counting. *NCEOA Journal*, pp. 2-4.

Contextual Statement Contributors

Current Edition:
Andrea Reeve, Colorado State University, COE

Previous Editions:
Andrea Reeve, Colorado State University, COE

TRIO and Other Educational Opportunity Programs
CAS Standards and Guidelines

The mission of TRIO and Other Educational Opportunity Programs (TOEOP) is to encourage and assist people who are traditionally under-represented in postsecondary education because of income, family educational background, disability, or other relevant federal, state/provincial, or institutional criteria, in the preparation for, entry to, and completion of a postsecondary degree.

To accomplish this mission, TOEOP must
- serve as advocates for access to higher education
- address the developmental needs of the individuals served
- provide services to assist individuals in developing and achieving educational goals
- assist individuals in acquiring the necessary skills, knowledge, and attributes to enter and complete a postsecondary education
- provide an environment that recognizes the diversity of backgrounds and learning styles of the individuals served
- develop collaborative relationships with institutions, organizations, schools, parents and families, and communities to promote an environment conducive to the completion of a postsecondary degree

TOEOP must develop, disseminate, implement, and regularly review their missions, which must be consistent with the mission of the institution and with applicable professional standards. The mission must be appropriate for the institution's students and other constituents. Mission statements must reference student learning and development.

TOEOP mission statements must be consistent with the mission and goals of the relevant governmental or other external grant or funding agency.

To achieve their mission, TRIO and Other Educational Opportunity Programs (TOEOP) must contribute to
- students' formal education, which includes both the curriculum and the co-curriculum
- student progression and timely completion of educational goals
- preparation of students for their careers, citizenship, and lives
- student learning and development

To contribute to student learning and development, TOEOP must
- identify relevant and desirable student learning and development outcomes
- articulate how the student learning and

development outcomes align with the six CAS student learning and development domains and related dimensions
- assess relevant and desirable student learning and development
- provide evidence of impact on outcomes
- articulate contributions to or support of student learning and development in the domains not specifically assessed
- use evidence gathered to create strategies for improvement of programs and services

STUDENT LEARNING AND DEVELOPMENT DOMAINS AND DIMENSIONS

Domain: knowledge acquisition, integration, construction, and application
- Dimensions: understanding knowledge from a range of disciplines; connecting knowledge to other knowledge, ideas, and experiences; constructing knowledge; and relating knowledge to daily life

Domain: cognitive complexity
- Dimensions: critical thinking, reflective thinking, effective reasoning, and creativity

Domain: intrapersonal development
- Dimensions: realistic self-appraisal, self-understanding, and self-respect; identity development; commitment to ethics and integrity; and spiritual awareness

Domain: interpersonal competence
- Dimensions: meaningful relationships, interdependence, collaboration, and effective leadership

Domain: humanitarianism and civic engagement
- Dimensions: understanding and appreciation of cultural and human differences, social responsibility, global perspective, and sense of civic responsibility

Domain: practical competence
- Dimensions: pursuing goals, communicating effectively, technical competence, managing personal affairs, managing career development, demonstrating professionalism, maintaining health and wellness, and living a purposeful and satisfying life

[LD Outcomes: See *The Council for the Advancement of Standards Learning and Development Outcomes* statement for examples of outcomes related to these domains and dimensions.]

TOEOP must be
- intentionally designed

- guided by theories and knowledge of learning and development
- integrated into the life of the institution
- reflective of developmental and demographic profiles of the student population
- responsive to needs of individuals, populations with distinct needs, and relevant constituencies
- delivered using multiple formats, strategies, and contexts
- designed to provide universal access

TOEOP must collaborate with colleagues and departments across the institution to promote student learning and development, persistence, and success.

TOEOP must provide activities that support the matriculation, achievement, persistence, success, and graduation of their students, as relevant to the mission of their specific program.

TOEOP must address their specific learning objectives and the allowable activities of each program.

Programs, services, and activities for students involved in specific TOEOP should be relevant to the demographic profile of individuals served. Programs, services, and activities should provide or ensure access to academic support services such as academic instruction; tutoring; English as a Second Language (ESL) activities; collaborative learning opportunities; Supplemental Instruction; development of oral and written communication skills; assessment of academic needs, skills, and individual plans to provide appropriate interventions; monitoring of academic progress; preparation for proficiency and entrance exams; academic advising; opportunities for national and international study exchange; research internships; and opportunities to present and publish program reports or research.

TOEOP should implement unique programming as well as utilize and coordinate with programming at their institutions, agencies, schools, or communities.

Part 3. Organization and Leadership

To achieve program and student learning and development outcomes, TRIO and Other Educational Opportunity Programs (TOEOP) must be purposefully structured for effectiveness. TOEOP must have clearly stated and current

- goals and outcomes
- policies and procedures
- responsibilities and performance expectations for personnel
- organizational charts demonstrating clear channels of authority

Leaders must model ethical behavior and institutional citizenship.

Leaders with organizational authority for TOEOP must provide strategic planning, management and supervision, and program advancement.

Strategic Planning

- articulate a vision and mission that drive short- and long-term planning
- set goals and objectives based on the needs of the populations served, intended student learning and development outcomes, and program outcomes
- facilitate continuous development, implementation, and assessment of program effectiveness and goal attainment congruent with institutional mission and strategic plans
- promote environments that provide opportunities for student learning, development, and engagement
- develop, adapt, and improve programs and services in response to the changing needs of populations served and evolving institutional priorities
- include diverse perspectives to inform decision making

Management and Supervision

- plan, allocate, and monitor the use of fiscal, physical, human, intellectual, and technological resources
- manage human resource processes including recruitment, selection, professional development, supervision, performance planning, succession planning, evaluation, recognition, and reward
- influence others to contribute to the effectiveness and success of the unit
- empower professional, support, and student personnel to become effective leaders
- encourage and support collaboration with colleagues and departments across the institution
- encourage and support scholarly contributions to the profession
- identify and address individual, organizational, and environmental conditions that foster or inhibit mission achievement
- use current and valid evidence to inform decisions
- incorporate sustainability practices in the management and design of programs, services, and facilities
- understand appropriate technologies and integrate them into programs and services
- be knowledgeable about codes and laws relevant to programs and services and ensure that programs and services meet those requirements
- assess and take action to mitigate potential risks

Program Advancement

- advocate for and actively promote the mission and goals of the programs and services
- inform stakeholders about issues affecting practice
- facilitate processes to reach consensus where wide support is needed
- advocate for representation in strategic planning initiatives at divisional and institutional levels

TOEOP leaders must be knowledgeable about issues, trends, theories, research, and methodologies related to student learning and retention, especially with regard to populations served by their programs.

TOEOP leaders should
- participate in institutional or organizational planning, policy, procedural, and fiscal decisions that affect program and student goal achievement
- seek opportunities for additional funding, resources, and facilities, as needed
- represent the TOEOP on institutional or organizational committees
- promote community environments, where relevant to the program, services, or activities, that result in multiple opportunities for student learning and development
- collaborate with leaders of other programs to address learning needs and persistence of program participants
- educate others within the institution and community about the characteristics, challenges, and persistence of populations served by their programs

TOEOP leaders must collect, understand, and use data to make program decisions as well as to communicate to constituents about the relevance of the program within the context of the institution's or organization's mission, goals, and objectives.

TOEOP leaders should cultivate relationships with colleagues in their own and related professional disciplines. TOEOP leaders should be involved in research, publication, presentations, consultation, and participation in professional development opportunities.

TOEOP must be placed in the institution's organizational structure to ensure visibility, promote cooperative interaction with appropriate campus or community entities, and enlist the support of senior administrators.

Part 4. Human Resources

TRIO and Other Educational Opportunity Programs (TOEOP) must be staffed adequately by individuals qualified to accomplish mission and goals.

TOEOP must have access to technical and support personnel adequate to accomplish their mission.

Within institutional guidelines, TOEOP must
- establish procedures for personnel recruitment and selection, training, performance planning, and evaluation
- set expectations for supervision and performance
- provide personnel access to continuing and advanced education and appropriate professional development opportunities to improve their competence, skills, and leadership capacity
- consider work/life options available to personnel (e.g., compressed work schedules, flextime, job sharing, remote work, or telework) to promote recruitment and retention of personnel

Administrators of TOEOP must
- ensure that all personnel have updated position descriptions
- implement recruitment and selection/hiring strategies that produce a workforce inclusive of under-represented populations
- develop promotion practices that are fair, inclusive, proactive, and non-discriminatory

The size, scope, and role of the program staff depend on the mission of TOEOP and the populations served. Staffing should be based on the needs of the students or participants and the resources available. TOEOP should employ a diverse staff to provide readily identifiable role models for students and to enrich the learning community. When possible, the staff should reflect the characteristics of the population being served.

Personnel responsible for delivery of TOEOP must have written performance goals, objectives, and outcomes for each year's performance cycle to be used to plan, review, and evaluate work and performance. The performance plan must be updated regularly to reflect changes during the performance cycle.

Results of individual personnel evaluations must be used to recognize personnel performance, address performance issues, implement individual and/or collective personnel development and training programs, and inform the assessment of programs and services.

TOEOP personnel, when hired and throughout their employment, must receive appropriate and thorough training.

TOEOP personnel, including student employees and volunteers, must have access to resources or receive specific training on
- institutional policies pertaining to functions or activities they support
- privacy and confidentiality policies
- laws regarding access to student records
- policies and procedures for dealing with sensitive institutional information
- policies and procedures related to technology used to store or access student records and institutional data
- how and when to refer those in need of additional assistance to qualified personnel and have access to a supervisor for assistance in making these judgments
- systems and technologies necessary to perform their assigned responsibilities
- ethical and legal uses of technology

TOEOP personnel must engage in continuing professional development activities to keep abreast of the research, theories, legislation, policies, and developments that affect their programs and services.

TOEOP should provide continuing professional development opportunities for staff such as in-service training programs,

TRIO professional training seminars, participation in professional conferences, workshops, mentoring, job shadowing, or other continuing education activities.

TOEOP staff should contribute to the knowledge and practice of the profession through presentations, research, or publications.

Administrators of TOEOP must ensure that personnel are knowledgeable about and trained in safety, emergency procedures, and crisis prevention and response. Risk management efforts must address identification of threatening conduct or behavior and must incorporate a system for responding to and reporting such behaviors.

TOEOP personnel must be knowledgeable of and trained in safety and emergency procedures for securing and vacating facilities.

PROFESSIONAL PERSONNEL

TOEOP professional personnel either must hold an earned graduate or professional degree in a field relevant to their position or must possess an appropriate combination of educational credentials and related work experience.

TOEOP professionals must possess a combination of knowledge and experience applicable to their work with individuals who are traditionally under-represented in postsecondary education.

TOEOP professional staff members should possess
- effective oral and written communication skills
- an understanding of the culture, heritage, social context (e.g., socioeconomic standing, rural vs. urban) and learning styles of the persons served by the program
- leadership, management, organizational, and human relations skills
- ability to work effectively with individuals of diverse backgrounds and ages
- openness to new ideas coupled with flexibility and willingness to change

INTERNS OR GRADUATE ASSISTANTS

Degree- or credential-seeking interns or graduate assistants must be qualified by enrollment in an appropriate field of study and relevant experience. These students must be trained and supervised by professional personnel who possess applicable educational credentials and work experience and have supervisory experience. Supervisors must be cognizant of the dual roles interns and graduate assistants have as both student and employee.

Supervisors must
- adhere to parameters of students' job descriptions
- articulate intended learning outcomes in student job descriptions
- adhere to agreed-upon work hours and schedules
- offer flexible scheduling when circumstances necessitate

Supervisors and students must both agree to suitable compensation if circumstances necessitate additional hours.

STUDENT EMPLOYEES AND VOLUNTEERS

Student employees and volunteers must be carefully selected, trained, supervised, and evaluated. Students must have access to a supervisor. Student employees and volunteers must be provided clear job descriptions, pre-service training based on assessed needs, and continuing development.

TOEOP should hire student employees and volunteers from groups traditionally under-represented in higher education.

Part 5. Ethics

TRIO and Other Educational Opportunity Programs (TOEOP) must
- review applicable professional ethical standards and must adopt or develop and implement appropriate statements of ethical practice
- publish and adhere to statements of ethical practice and ensure their periodic review
- orient new personnel to relevant ethical standards and statements of ethical practice and related institutional policies

Statements of ethical standards must
- specify that TOEOP personnel respect privacy and maintain confidentiality in communications and records as delineated by privacy laws
- specify limits on disclosure of information contained in students' records as well as requirements to disclose to appropriate authorities
- address conflicts of interest, or appearance thereof, by personnel in the performance of their work
- reflect the responsibility of personnel to be fair, objective, and impartial in their interactions with others
- reference management of institutional funds
- reference appropriate behavior regarding research and assessment with human participants, confidentiality of research and assessment data, and students' rights and responsibilities
- include the expectation that personnel confront and hold accountable other personnel who exhibit unethical behavior
- address issues surrounding scholarly integrity

TOEOP personnel must
- employ ethical decision making in the performance of their duties
- inform users of programs and services of ethical obligations and limitations emanating from codes and laws or from licensure requirements
- recognize and avoid conflicts of interest that could adversely influence their judgment or objectivity and, when unavoidable, recuse themselves from the situation

- perform their duties within the scope of their position, training, expertise, and competence
- make referrals when issues presented exceed the scope of the position

Part 6. Law, Policy, and Governance

TRIO and Other Educational Opportunity Programs (TOEOP) must be in compliance with laws, regulations, and policies that relate to their respective responsibilities and that pose legal obligations, limitations, risks, and liabilities for the institution as a whole. Examples include constitutional, statutory, regulatory, and case law; relevant law and orders emanating from codes and laws; and the institution's policies.

TOEOP sponsored by community-based agencies or organizations must also adhere to their comparable standards.

TOEOP must have access to legal advice needed for personnel to carry out their assigned responsibilities.

TOEOP must inform personnel, appropriate officials, and users of programs and services about existing and changing legal obligations, risks and liabilities, and limitations.

TOEOP must inform personnel about professional liability insurance options and refer them to external sources if the institution does not provide coverage.

TOEOP must have written policies and procedures on operations, transactions, or tasks that have legal implications.

TOEOP must regularly review policies. The revision and creation of policies must be informed by best practices, available evidence, and policy issues in higher education.

TOEOP must have procedures and guidelines consistent with institutional policy for responding to threats, emergencies, and crisis situations. Systems and procedures must be in place to disseminate timely and accurate information to students, other members of the institutional community, and appropriate external organizations during emergency situations.

Personnel must neither participate in nor condone any form of harassment or activity that demeans persons or creates an intimidating, hostile, or offensive environment.

TOEOP must purchase or obtain permission to use copyrighted materials and instruments. References to copyrighted materials and instruments must include appropriate citations.

TOEOP must inform personnel about internal and external governance organizations that affect programs and services.

Part 7. Diversity, Equity, and Access

Within the context of each institution's mission and in accordance with institutional policies and applicable codes and laws, TRIO and Other Educational Opportunity Programs (TOEOP) must create and maintain educational and work environments that are welcoming, accessible, inclusive, equitable, and free from harassment.

TOEOP must not discriminate on the basis of disability; age; race; cultural identity; ethnicity; nationality; family educational history (e.g., first generation to attend college); political affiliation; religious affiliation; sex; sexual orientation; gender identity and expression; marital, social, economic, or veteran status; or any other basis included in institutional policies and codes and laws.

TOEOP must

- advocate for sensitivity to multicultural and social justice concerns by the institution and its personnel
- ensure physical, program, and resource access for all constituents
- modify or remove policies, practices, systems, technologies, facilities, and structures that create barriers or produce inequities
- ensure that when facilities and structures cannot be modified, they do not impede access to programs, services, and resources
- establish goals for diversity, equity, and access
- foster communication and practices that enhance understanding of identity, culture, self-expression, and heritage
- promote respect for commonalities and differences among people within their historical and cultural contexts
- address the characteristics and needs of diverse constituents when establishing and implementing culturally relevant and inclusive programs, services, policies, procedures, and practices
- provide personnel with diversity, equity, and access training and hold personnel accountable for applying the training to their work
- respond to the needs of all constituents served when establishing hours of operation and developing methods of delivering programs, services, and resources
- recognize the needs of distance and online learning students by directly providing or assisting them to gain access to comparable services and resources

TOEOP must adhere to eligibility criteria set by funding sources.

Part 8. Internal and External Relations

TRIO and Other Educational Opportunity Programs (TOEOP) must reach out to individuals, groups, communities, and organizations internal and external to the institution to

- establish, maintain, and promote understanding and effective relations with those that have a significant interest in or potential effect on the students or other constituents served by the programs and services
- garner support and resources for programs and

services as defined by the mission
- collaborate in offering or improving programs and services to meet the needs of students and other constituents and to achieve program and student outcomes
- engage diverse individuals, groups, communities, and organizations to enrich the educational environment and experiences of students and other constituents
- disseminate information about the programs and services

TOEOP must seek collaborative relations with program area schools, community organizations, government agencies, and students' families.

Promotional and descriptive information must be accurate and free of deception and misrepresentation.

TOEOP must have procedures and guidelines consistent with institutional policy for
- communicating with the media
- distributing information through print, broadcast, and online sources
- contracting with external organizations for delivery of programs and services
- cultivating, soliciting, and managing gifts
- applying to and managing funds from grants

TOEOP must include a public relations component to regularly inform the institution, communities, agencies, and schools about their missions, services, and outcomes.

Part 9. Financial Resources

TRIO and Other Educational Opportunity Programs (TOEOP) must have funding to accomplish the mission and goals.

In establishing and prioritizing funding resources, TOEOP must conduct comprehensive analyses to determine
- unmet needs of the unit
- relevant expenditures
- external and internal resources
- impact on students and the institution

TOEOP must use the budget as a planning tool to reflect commitment to the mission and goals of the programs and services and of the institution.

TOEOP must administer funds in accordance with established institutional accounting procedures.

TOEOP must demonstrate efficient and effective use and responsible stewardship of fiscal resources consistent with institutional protocols.

TOEOP must know and adhere to governmental and agency fiscal regulations regarding funding.

Financial reports must provide an accurate financial overview of the organization and provide clear, understandable, and timely data upon which personnel can plan and make informed decisions.

Procurement procedures must
- be consistent with institutional policies
- ensure that purchases comply with laws and codes for usability and access
- ensure that the institution receives value for the funds spent
- consider information available for comparing the ethical and environmental impact of products and services purchased

Opportunities for additional funding should be pursued; however, these sources should not be expected to supplant current funding.

TOEOP should negotiate with their institutions to provide additional funding to support areas underfunded by their grants.

Part 10. Technology

TRIO and Other Educational Opportunity Programs (TOEOP) must have technology to support the achievement of their mission and goals. The technology and its use must comply with institutional policies and procedures and with relevant codes and laws.

TOEOP must use technologies to
- provide updated information regarding mission, location, staffing, programs, services, and official contacts to students and other constituents in accessible formats
- provide an avenue for students and other constituents to communicate sensitive information in a secure format
- enhance the delivery of programs and services for all students

TOEOP must
- back up data on a regular basis
- adhere to institutional policies regarding ethical and legal use of technology
- articulate policies and procedures for protecting the confidentiality and security of information
- implement a replacement plan and cycle for all technology with attention to sustainability
- incorporate accessibility features into technology-based programs and services

When providing student access to technology, TOEOP must
- have policies on the use of technology that are clear, easy to understand, and available to all students
- provide information or referral to support services for those needing assistance in accessing or using technology
- provide instruction or training on how to use the technology
- inform students of implications of misuse of technologies

TOEOP must promote alternate access to information

in formats accessible for participants and their families, especially when technology is not available to them.

TOEOP should advocate for and facilitate access to technology for program participants and their families. Technology should be employed to promote TOEOP, to provide academic and other student services, to assist participants with career exploration and the processes related to postsecondary transitions (e.g., admissions, financial aid, course registration, housing), and to communicate with students including those at outreach locations. Programs should intentionally model for their students the use of technology.

Part 11. Facilities and Equipment

TRIO and Other Educational Opportunity Programs' (TOEOP) facilities must be intentionally designed and located in suitable, accessible, and safe spaces that demonstrate universal design and support the program's mission and goals.

Facilities must be designed to engage various constituents and promote learning.

TOEOP facilities must be physically located to promote visibility of the programs and to ensure coordination with other campus or organizational programs and services.

Personnel must have workspaces that are suitably located and accessible, well equipped, adequate in size, and designed to support their work and responsibilities.

The design of the facilities must guarantee the security and privacy of records and ensure the confidentiality of sensitive information and conversations. Personnel must be able to secure their work.

TOEOP must incorporate sustainable practices in use of facilities and purchase of equipment. Facilities and equipment must be evaluated on an established cycle and be in compliance with codes, laws, and accepted practices for access, health, safety, and security.

When acquiring capital equipment, TOEOP must take into account expenses related to regular maintenance and life cycle costs.

Part 12. Assessment

TRIO and Other Educational Opportunity Programs (TOEOP) must develop assessment plans and processes.

Assessment plans must articulate an ongoing cycle of assessment activities.

TOEOP must
- specify programmatic goals and intended outcomes
- identify student learning and development outcomes
- employ multiple measures and methods
- develop manageable processes for gathering, interpreting, and evaluating data
- document progress toward achievement of goals and outcomes
- interpret and use assessment results to demonstrate accountability
- report aggregated results to respondent groups and stakeholders
- use assessment results to inform planning and decision-making
- assess effectiveness of implemented changes
- provide evidence of improvement of programs and services

Assessments, evaluations, and annual program performance reports must be conducted in accordance with conditions required by applicable sponsoring agreements.

Assessments, evaluations, or annual evaluation reports should be made available, when appropriate, to the program's various stakeholders, such as relevant campus offices, external agencies, area schools, community organizations, and program advisory committees and boards.

TOEOP must employ ethical practices in the assessment process.

TOEOP must have access to adequate fiscal, human, professional development, and technological resources to develop and implement assessment plans.

General Standards revised in 2014;
TOEOP content developed/revised in 1999 & 2008

Undergraduate Admissions Programs and Services
CAS Contexual Statement

Offices of undergraduate admissions play a central role in higher education, and are typically the link between K-12 and postsecondary institutions (Stewart, 1998). Admissions personnel act as ambassadors of an institution and serve as liaisons to students in secondary schools. Indeed, the primary role of undergraduate admissions is to "tell prospective students about the institution and its programs, as well as to recruit, screen, and accept applicants" (Dungy, 2003, p. 343).

Historically, the admissions function grew out of the expansion of higher education in the nineteenth century. Legislation like the Morrill Acts of 1862 and 1890, which designated federal land in each state for the purpose of establishing colleges that specialized in agriculture and mechanical arts, represented a new perspective on educational access and dramatically increased the number and types of higher education institutions (Coomes, 2000; Thelin, 2003). No admissions offices existed in early higher education; faculty members were typically responsible for any decisions regarding admission (Henderson, 1998).

In the late 1800s, institutions began to push for standardized admissions criteria (Henderson, 1998). Selective admissions processes began in the 1920s, as the number of applicants increased (Thelin, 2003) and as institutions outlined criteria for future students. The College Entrance Examination Board created the Scholastic Aptitude Test (SAT), a measure of high school students' preparedness for high school education (Hurtado, 2003). Private institutions began to recruit prospective students, making that process even more selective (Schulz & Lucido, 2011).

In the early part of the twentieth century, an increase in staff dedicated to admissions work necessitated the need for professional identity and organization. The American Association of Collegiate Registrars and Admissions Officers (formerly the American Association of Collegiate Registrars) formed in 1910, "to serve and advance higher education by providing leadership in academic and enrollment services" (AACRAO, 2015, para. 1; see also Dungy, 2003; Schulz & Lucido, 2011). The National Association for College Admissions Counseling (NACAC), formed in 1937, focuses on the role of the students in the admissions process, citing a mission to serve "students as they make choices about pursuing postsecondary education" (NACAC, 2015, para. 1; see also Dungy, 2003; Schulz & Lucido, 2011).

Throughout the early twentieth century, enrollments continued to rise through the Great Depression and post-World War II (Coomes, 2000; Thelin, 2003). To help manage this growth, a new administrative position emerged in higher education: deans of admissions. Deans of admissions were responsible for assessing whether applicants were adequately prepared for admission, and they are credited with the introduction of objective measures to "examine the quality of applicants for admission" (Coomes, 2000, p. 7). In addition,

the push for standardized admissions criteria led to the creation of admissions offices in institutions across higher education, relieving the faculty of the burden of admissions decisions (Henderson, 1998).

College admissions growth continued into the late 1970s, when high school graduation rates declined and college enrollment plateaued (Casteen, 1998). Institutions of higher education now competed for students. The evolution of admissions offices and personnel responsibilities was predicated upon this competition for enrollment. Undergraduate admissions staff employed new skills, such as marketing, in their recruitment strategies (Casteen, 1998; Johnson, 2000).

Today, marketing has become an essential aspect of admissions and enrollment work, which has "drawn admissions officers into institutional activities other than conventional admissions work…[such as] new academic programs, on athletics, on the design and operation of dormitories, on fund-raising, and other matters because these professionals know the prospective student market so well" (Casteen, 1998, p. 8). NACAC and AACRAO also outline specific core values of personnel working in admissions and enrollment services, including professionalism, collaboration, trust, education, integrity, fairness and equity, respect for others, and social responsibility (AACRAO, 2015; NACAC, 2014).

Undergraduate admissions can occupy different places in the organizational structure of an institution; some place admissions within student affairs, while others include it in enrollment management (Dungy, 2003). The enrollment management structure "brings together often disparate functions having to do with recruiting [students], funding, tracking, retaining and replacing students as they move toward, within, and way from the university" (Maguire, 1976, p. 16). In this organizational model, undergraduate admissions offices are often coupled with the university registrar and financial aid. Additionally, reporting structures vary by institution; some admissions offices report to the provost, to a vice president, or directly to the president (Dungy, 2003).

Admissions officers are responsible for the recruitment and selection of applicants. Applications are reviewed and evaluated on a series of predictors: traditional academic predictors (e.g., high school grades, rank, GPA, admissions tests), characteristics and background (e.g., gender; race/ ethnicity; socioeconomic status; alumni ties; high school size, type, and quality; aid application), goals and future plans, supplemental achievement predictors (e.g., honors and achievements), and admissions ratings (e.g., interviews, special talents and attributes) (The College Board, 2002). In general, application decisions are based upon rich and complex processes, and each applicant should be reviewed in the context of their own unique history and characteristics, tied to the mission, vision, and goals of the institution (The College Board, 2002).

Changing trends and student demographics continue to influence admissions practices. NACAC reports that more institutions are using early action or early decision application processes, and that more institutions employ a wait list for applicants (Clinedinst, Hurley, & Hawkins, 2012). New practices have emerged in recent years, as well, including "on the spot" admission and "priority applications" (Clinedinst, Hurley, & Hawkins, 2012). Undergraduate admissions professionals adapt to changing trends in the system and the environment, are experts on students and applicants, and are often the first interaction students have with a university.

The Undergraduate Admissions Programs and Services Standards and Guidelines that follow offer admissions professionals guidance about their role in the institution and help them prepare to respond effectively to the complex demands of their profession.

References, Readings, and Resources

American Association of Collegiate Registrars and Admissions Officers. (2015). *Ethics and practice.* Retrieved from http://www.aacrao.org/home/about/ethics-and-practice

Casteen, J. (1998). Perspectives on admissions. In C. C. Swann & S. E. Henderson (Eds.), *Handbook for the college admissions profession* (pp. 7-10). Westport, CT: Greenwood Press.

Clinedinst, M. E., Hurley, S. F., & Hawkins, D. A. (2012). *State of college admission (2012 report).* Arlington, VA: National Association of College Admissions Counseling.

Coomes, M. D. (2000). The historical roots of enrollment management. In M. Coomes (Ed.), *The role student aid plays in enrollment management.* New Directions for Student Services: No. 89. San Francisco, CA: Jossey-Bass.

Dungy, G. J. (2003). Organization and functions of student affairs. In S. Komvies (Ed.), *Student services: A handbook for the profession* (pp. 339-357). San Francisco, CA: Jossey-Bass.

Henderson, S. E. (1998). A historical view of an admissions dilemma: Seeking quantity or quality in the student body. In C. C. Swann & S. E. Henderson (Eds.), *Handbook for the college admissions profession* (pp. 11-26). Westport, CT: Greenwood Press.

Hurtado, S. (2003). Institutional diversity in American higher education. In S. Komvies (Ed.), *Student services: A handbook for the profession* (pp. 23-44). San Francisco, CA: Jossey-Bass.

Johnson, A. L. (2000). The evolution of strategic enrollment management: A historical perspective. *Journal of College Admission, 166,* 4-11.

Maguire, J. (1976). To the organized go the students. *Bridge Magazine, 39*(1), p. 16-20.

National Association of College Admissions Counselors. (2014). *Statement of principles of good practice.* Retrieved from http://www.nacacnet.org/about/Governance/Policies/Documents/SPGP_10_4_2014_FINAL.pdf

National Association of College Admissions Counselors. (2015). *About NACAC.* Retrieved from http://www.nacacnet.org/about/Pages/default.aspx

Schulz, S. A. & Lucido, J. A. (2011). *Enrollment management, inc.: External influences on our practice.* Los Angeles, CA: USC Center for Enrollment Research, Policy, and Practice. Retrieved from http://files.eric.ed.gov/fulltext/ED537409.pdf

Stewart, D. (1998). Perspectives on educational reform. In C. C. Swann & S. E. Henderson (Eds.), *Handbook for the college admissions profession* (pp. 3-6). Westport, CT: Greenwood Press.

The College Board. (2002). *Best practices in admissions decisions: A report on the third College Board Conference on admissions models.* Retrieved from https://research.collegeboard.org/sites/default/files/publications/2012/7/misc2002-1-best-practices-admissions-decisions.pdf

Thelin, J. R. (2003). Historical overview of American higher education. In S. Komvies (Ed.), *Student services: A handbook for the profession* (pp. 3-22). San Francisco, CA: Jossey-Bass.

Contextual Statement Contributors

Current Edition:
Danielle Vitale, The University of Georgia

Previous Editions:
Eric White, Penn State University
Christine Schneikart-Luebbe, Wichita State University
Kevin Kruger, NASPA
Lori Reesor, University of Kansas
Jan Arminio, NACA, Shippensburg University
Joyce Smith, NACAC

Undergraduate Admissions Programs and Services
CAS Standards and Guidelines

The mission of Undergraduate Admissions Programs and Services (UAPS) is to enroll undergraduate applicants who will, both individually and collectively, benefit from the collegiate learning environment through academic and personal enrichment and development.

UAPS must recruit, admit, and encourage enrollment of applicants whose academic and personal credentials are consistent with the overall priorities and mission of the institution.

This may include applicants who may be underprepared for post-secondary study.

To accomplish this mission UAPS must
- assess and evaluate the abilities, needs, and expectations of prospective students as they move from secondary to postsecondary education, as they move from one postsecondary institution to another, or as they return from a period of non-enrollment
- establish, promulgate, and implement admission criteria that accurately represent the mission, goals, purposes and resources of the institution, and that accommodate the abilities, needs, and interests of potential students
- clearly and accurately present the mission, goals, policies, procedures, facilities, and characteristics of the institution
- develop and regularly review enrollment goals for admission with appropriate individuals within the institution

UAPS must develop, disseminate, implement, and regularly review their missions, which must be consistent with the mission of the institution and with applicable professional standards. The mission must be appropriate for the institution's students and other constituents. Mission statements must reference student learning and development.

To achieve their mission, Undergraduate Admissions Programs and Services (UAPS) must contribute to
- students' formal education, which includes both the curriculum and the co-curriculum
- student progression and timely completion of educational goals
- preparation of students for their careers, citizenship, and lives
- student learning and development

To contribute to student learning and development, UAPS must

- identify relevant and desirable student learning and development outcomes
- articulate how the student learning and development outcomes align with the six CAS student learning and development domains and related dimensions
- assess relevant and desirable student learning and development
- provide evidence of impact on outcomes
- articulate contributions to or support of student learning and development in the domains not specifically assessed
- use evidence gathered to create strategies for improvement of programs and services

STUDENT LEARNING AND DEVELOPMENT DOMAINS AND DIMENSIONS

Domain: knowledge acquisition, integration, construction, and application
- Dimensions: understanding knowledge from a range of disciplines; connecting knowledge to other knowledge, ideas, and experiences; constructing knowledge; and relating knowledge to daily life

Domain: cognitive complexity
- Dimensions: critical thinking, reflective thinking, effective reasoning, and creativity

Domain: intrapersonal development
- Dimensions: realistic self-appraisal, self-understanding, and self-respect; identity development; commitment to ethics and integrity; and spiritual awareness

Domain: interpersonal competence
- Dimensions: meaningful relationships, interdependence, collaboration, and effective leadership

Domain: humanitarianism and civic engagement
- Dimensions: understanding and appreciation of cultural and human differences, social responsibility, global perspective, and sense of civic responsibility

Domain: practical competence
- Dimensions: pursuing goals, communicating effectively, technical competence, managing personal affairs, managing career development, demonstrating professionalism, maintaining health and wellness, and living a purposeful and satisfying life

[LD Outcomes: See *The Council for the Advancement of Standards Learning and Development Outcomes* statement for examples of outcomes related to these domains and dimensions.]

UAPS must be
- **intentionally designed**
- **guided by theories and knowledge of learning and development**
- **integrated into the life of the institution**
- **reflective of developmental and demographic profiles of the student population**
- **responsive to needs of individuals, populations with distinct needs, and relevant constituencies**
- **delivered using multiple formats, strategies, and contexts**
- **designed to provide universal access**

UAPS must collaborate with colleagues and departments across the institution to promote student learning and development, persistence, and success.

UAPS must develop recruitment and admission procedures and strategies designed to establish and meet the institution's enrollment plan and diversity goals.

UAPS should have recruitment plans for targeted groups such as
- first generation
- TRIO-eligible and other underrepresented populations
- veterans
- international

UAPS must accurately represent and promote their institutions by providing current information about academic majors and degree programs. Information must include factual and accurate descriptions of majors, minors, concentrations and/or interdisciplinary offerings, information about bridge programs, dual high school/college enrollment programs, diploma, certificate, and other special admissions programs.

UAPS must clearly articulate the requirements of admission and enrollment processes.

These should include processes for the first-year and transfer students, including secondary school preparation, standardized testing, financial aid, housing, and notification deadlines and refund procedures.

UAPS should establish procedures to review and admit, as appropriate, applicants with criminal and disciplinary records in compliance with local, state/provincial, and federal law.

UAPS must clearly explain the process by which applicants bring credit to the institution including transfer credit or life experience, if applicable at the institution.

UAPS must be responsible for the accurate representation and promotion of the admission calendar, separate admissions to majors, academic offerings, financial aid and cost of attendance, housing application and deposit deadlines, and other related services.

UAPS must offer recruitment opportunities including community venues for potential adult students.

UAPS should utilize currently enrolled students, alumni, staff, and faculty members in the recruitment process. Examples include ambassador programs, tour guides, student panels, faculty interviews, or other opportunities for prospective students and their families to interact with current students and faculty.

UAPS should use a variety of strategies to introduce postsecondary opportunities to students and their families.

UAPS must provide students, families, and secondary schools with comprehensive information about costs of attendance and opportunities for financial aid.

The cost of attendance should include course materials, fees, and other non-tuition related expenses.

UAPS must include a current and accurate admission calendar in publications and websites. If the institution offers special admission options, the publication must define these programs and state deadlines dates, notification dates, required deposits, and refund policies.

Special admission options may include Early Admission, Early Action, Early Decision, wait lists, or Restrictive Early Admission.

UAPS should provide current wait-listed applicants notification outlining the number of students from the previous year offered admission, the number who accepted spaces, the number of offered places on the wait list, as well as the availability of financial aid and housing.

UAPS must have policies and procedures for managing special admissions requests from politically sensitive constituencies, such as legislators, governing board members, donors, and alumni.

UAPS offices must have policies and procedures for managing applications and communicating to students who do not meet traditional admission criteria.

Part 3. Organization and Leadership

To achieve program and student learning and development outcomes, Undergraduate Admissions Programs and Services (UAPS) must be purposefully structured for effectiveness. UAPS must have clearly stated and current
- **goals and outcomes**
- **policies and procedures**
- **responsibilities and performance expectations for personnel**
- **organizational charts demonstrating clear channels of authority**

Leaders must model ethical behavior and institutional citizenship.

Leaders with organizational authority for UAPS must provide strategic planning, management and supervision, and program advancement.

Strategic Planning
- **articulate a vision and mission that drive short- and long-term planning**

- set goals and objectives based on the needs of the populations served, intended student learning and development outcomes, and program outcomes
- facilitate continuous development, implementation, and assessment of program effectiveness and goal attainment congruent with institutional mission and strategic plans
- promote environments that provide opportunities for student learning, development, and engagement
- develop, adapt, and improve programs and services in response to the changing needs of populations served and evolving institutional priorities
- include diverse perspectives to inform decision making

Management and Supervision
- plan, allocate, and monitor the use of fiscal, physical, human, intellectual, and technological resources
- manage human resource processes including recruitment, selection, professional development, supervision, performance planning, succession planning, evaluation, recognition, and reward
- influence others to contribute to the effectiveness and success of the unit
- empower professional, support, and student personnel to become effective leaders
- encourage and support collaboration with colleagues and departments across the institution
- encourage and support scholarly contributions to the profession
- identify and address individual, organizational, and environmental conditions that foster or inhibit mission achievement
- use current and valid evidence to inform decisions
- incorporate sustainability practices in the management and design of programs, services, and facilities
- understand appropriate technologies and integrate them into programs and services
- be knowledgeable about codes and laws relevant to programs and services and ensure that programs and services meet those requirements
- assess and take action to mitigate potential risks

Program Advancement
- advocate for and actively promote the mission and goals of the programs and services
- inform stakeholders about issues affecting practice
- facilitate processes to reach consensus where wide support is needed
- advocate for representation in strategic planning initiatives at divisional and institutional levels

UAPS leaders should provide training, orientation, and consultation assistance to faculty members, administrators, staff, institution officials (e.g., trustees), and high school and transfer counselors to assist them in responding to the enrollment needs of students and their families.

UAPS must function as an independent unit or as part of an overall enrollment management structure.

Part 4. Human Resources

Undergraduate Admissions Programs and Services (UAPS) must be staffed adequately by individuals qualified to accomplish mission and goals.

UAPS must have access to technical and support personnel adequate to accomplish their mission.

Within institutional guidelines, UAPS must
- establish procedures for personnel recruitment and selection, training, performance planning, and evaluation
- set expectations for supervision and performance
- provide personnel access to continuing and advanced education and appropriate professional development opportunities to improve their competence, skills, and leadership capacity
- consider work/life options available to personnel (e.g., compressed work schedules, flextime, job sharing, remote work, or telework) to promote recruitment and retention of personnel

Administrators of UAPS must
- ensure that all personnel have updated position descriptions
- implement recruitment and selection/hiring strategies that produce a workforce inclusive of under-represented populations
- develop promotion practices that are fair, inclusive, proactive, and non-discriminatory

UAPS staff must recognize and appreciate individual differences among students and integrate an understanding of this information into the recruitment relationship.

Examples of these differences may include aptitude, intelligence, age, interests, first generation, socio-economic status, cultures and cultural identities, and achievements.

Personnel responsible for delivery of UAPS must have written performance goals, objectives, and outcomes for each year's performance cycle to be used to plan, review, and evaluate work and performance. The performance plan must be updated regularly to reflect changes during the performance cycle.

Results of individual personnel evaluations must be used to recognize personnel performance, address performance issues, implement individual and/or collective personnel development and training programs, and inform the assessment of programs and services.

UAPS personnel, when hired and throughout their employment, must receive appropriate and thorough training.

UAPS personnel, including student employees and volunteers, must have access to resources or receive specific training on

- institutional policies pertaining to functions or activities they support
- privacy and confidentiality policies
- laws regarding access to student records
- policies and procedures for dealing with sensitive institutional information
- policies and procedures related to technology used to store or access student records and institutional data
- how and when to refer those in need of additional assistance to qualified personnel and have access to a supervisor for assistance in making these judgments
- systems and technologies necessary to perform their assigned responsibilities
- ethical and legal uses of technology

UAPS personnel must engage in continuing professional development activities to keep abreast of the research, theories, legislation, policies, and developments that affect their programs and services.

Administrators of UAPS must ensure that personnel are knowledgeable about and trained in safety, emergency procedures, and crisis prevention and response. Risk management efforts must address identification of threatening conduct or behavior and must incorporate a system for responding to and reporting such behaviors.

UAPS personnel must be knowledgeable of and trained in safety and emergency procedures for securing and vacating facilities.

PROFESSIONAL PERSONNEL

UAPS professional personnel either must hold an earned graduate or professional degree in a field relevant to their position or must possess an appropriate combination of educational credentials and related work experience.

Professional staff in UAPS should have knowledge in the following areas:
- institutional curriculum offerings
- student involvement options
- referrals for appropriate institutional community resources in response to particular needs
- various levels of academic preparation and ability
- life planning
- financial aid opportunities and deadlines
- academic advising and student orientation programs and activities

Professional staff members in UAPS should be competent in providing assistance to prospective students regarding their educational goals, including, but not limited to,
- ethical and objective presentation of the institution's programs and opportunities
- careful and concerned analysis of each student's goals
- responsible decision-making in the selection of an institution
- knowledge of admission issues and concerns

INTERNS OR GRADUATE ASSISTANTS

Degree- or credential-seeking interns or graduate assistants must be qualified by enrollment in an appropriate field of study and relevant experience. These students must be trained and supervised by professional personnel who possess applicable educational credentials and work experience and have supervisory experience. Supervisors must be cognizant of the dual roles interns and graduate assistants have as both student and employee.

Supervisors must
- adhere to parameters of students' job descriptions
- articulate intended learning outcomes in student job descriptions
- adhere to agreed-upon work hours and schedules
- offer flexible scheduling when circumstances necessitate

Supervisors and students must both agree to suitable compensation if circumstances necessitate additional hours.

STUDENT EMPLOYEES AND VOLUNTEERS

Student employees and volunteers must be carefully selected, trained, supervised, and evaluated. Students must have access to a supervisor. Student employees and volunteers must be provided clear job descriptions, pre-service training based on assessed needs, and continuing development.

UAPS staff should possess individual and group communication skills to assist students and their families in the admissions process.

UAPS staff should have an understanding of the psychology of adolescents, young adults, and adult learners, as well as concepts of student development and learning.

UAPS staff must demonstrate an awareness of and sensitivity to the unique social, cultural, and economic circumstances of students including but not limited to age; cultural heritage; disability; ethnicity; gender identity and expression; nationality; political affiliation; race; religious affiliation; sex; sexual orientation; economic, marital, social, or veteran status; and any other bases included in applicable laws.

UAPS staff must have an understanding of the proper administration and uses of standardized tests and be able to interpret test scores and test-related data to students, parents, families, educators, institutions, agencies, and the public.

Examples include, but are not limited to, the following tests: The ACT, ACT PLAN, CLEP, DANTES, GED, Preliminary SAT/National Merit Scholarship Qualifying Test (PSAT/NMSQT), SAT I and SAT II, and Advanced Placement exams.

UAPS staff must be able to interpret transcripts with honors courses, AP or CLEP credits, when evaluating undergraduate applications.

UAPS staff must have an understanding of the needs of students with unique pre-collegiate experiences when evaluating undergraduate applications.

Examples of experiences and characteristics include home schooling, foster youth and homeless, international education, GED graduation, veterans, undocumented, and International Baccalaureate programs.

UAPS must provide appropriate training for staff involved with the processing of admission applications, including data integrity, transcript authentication, file management, customer service, and the use of technology in the admission process.

UAPS staff should remain current in emerging recruitment strategies, including the use of call centers, tele-counseling, on-line and social media, and the use of paid and volunteer staff in the recruitment process.

Part 5. Ethics

Undergraduate Admissions Programs and Services (UAPS) must

- review applicable professional ethical standards and must adopt or develop and implement appropriate statements of ethical practice
- publish and adhere to statements of ethical practice and ensure their periodic review
- orient new personnel to relevant ethical standards and statements of ethical practice and related institutional policies

Statements of ethical standards must

- specify that UAPS personnel respect privacy and maintain confidentiality in communications and records as delineated by privacy laws
- specify limits on disclosure of information contained in students' records as well as requirements to disclose to appropriate authorities
- address conflicts of interest, or appearance thereof, by personnel in the performance of their work
- reflect the responsibility of personnel to be fair, objective, and impartial in their interactions with others
- reference management of institutional funds
- reference appropriate behavior regarding research and assessment with human participants, confidentiality of research and assessment data, and students' rights and responsibilities
- include the expectation that personnel confront and hold accountable other personnel who exhibit unethical behavior
- address issues surrounding scholarly integrity

UAPS personnel must

- employ ethical decision making in the performance of their duties
- inform users of programs and services of ethical obligations and limitations emanating from codes and laws or from licensure requirements
- recognize and avoid conflicts of interest that could adversely influence their judgment or objectivity and, when unavoidable, recuse themselves from the situation
- perform their duties within the scope of their position, training, expertise, and competence
- make referrals when issues presented exceed the scope of the position

UAPS staff and volunteers must not disseminate biased, unflattering, and/or potentially inaccurate information about other secondary or postsecondary institutions, their admission criteria, their curricular offerings, or other related information.

UAPS staff must be compensated in the form of a fixed salary, rather than commissions or bonuses based on the number of students recruited, and must not contract with secondary school personnel for remunerations for referred students.

UAPS staff must not offer or accept any reward or remuneration from a college, university, agency, or organization for placement or recruitment of students.

UAPS must cite the source and year of study when institutional publications and communications reference academic programs, academic rigor or reputations, or athletic rankings.

Except for Early Decision programs, UAPS must not require or ask secondary schools to indicate the order of prospective students' college or university preferences, and must not require or ask candidates to indicate the order of their college or university preferences.

UAPS must not offer exclusive incentives that provide opportunities for students applying or admitted under Early Decision that are not available to students admitted under other admission options.

Examples of incentive programs include special residence halls, honors programs, full need-based financial aid packages, or special scholarships in addition to any other promise of an advantage in the admission process if student(s) convert from Regular Admission to Early Decision.

Categories might include student athletes, underprepared students, veterans, or those with a unique talent.

UAPS must develop and use notification practices that protect the confidentiality of an applicant's admission or denial status. Specific efforts must be made to protect privacy when using web based technologies or group email announcements.

Part 6. Law, Policy, and Governance

Undergraduate Admissions Programs and Services (UAPS) must be in compliance with laws, regulations, and policies that relate to their respective responsibilities and that pose legal obligations, limitations, risks, and liabilities for the institution as a whole. Examples include constitutional, statutory, regulatory, and case law; relevant law and orders emanating from codes and laws; and the institution's policies.

UAPS staff members must establish policies with respect to the release of student names during the admission process. Any policy that authorizes the release of students' names must indicate that the release be made only with the students' permission and be consistent with applicable laws and regulations.

UAPS must abide by regulations in the *Family Educational Rights and Privacy Act* (FERPA), or other applicable privacy laws when developing policies that authorize the release of student names during the admission process.

UAPS must have access to legal advice needed for personnel to carry out their assigned responsibilities.

UAPS must inform personnel, appropriate officials, and users of programs and services about existing and changing legal obligations, risks and liabilities, and limitations.

UAPS must inform personnel about professional liability insurance options and refer them to external sources if the institution does not provide coverage.

UAPS must have written policies and procedures on operations, transactions, or tasks that have legal implications.

UAPS must regularly review policies. The revision and creation of policies must be informed by best practices, available evidence, and policy issues in higher education.

UAPS must have procedures and guidelines consistent with institutional policy for responding to threats, emergencies, and crisis situations. Systems and procedures must be in place to disseminate timely and accurate information to students, other members of the institutional community, and appropriate external organizations during emergency situations.

Personnel must neither participate in nor condone any form of harassment or activity that demeans persons or creates an intimidating, hostile, or offensive environment.

UAPS must purchase or obtain permission to use copyrighted materials and instruments. References to copyrighted materials and instruments must include appropriate citations.

UAPS must inform personnel about internal and external governance organizations that affect programs and services.

Part 7. Diversity, Equity, and Access

Within the context of each institution's mission and in accordance with institutional policies and applicable codes and laws, Undergraduate Admissions Programs and Services (UAPS) must create and maintain educational and work environments that are welcoming, accessible, inclusive, equitable, and free from harassment.

UAPS must not discriminate on the basis of disability; age; race; cultural identity; ethnicity; nationality; family educational history (e.g., first generation to attend college); political affiliation; religious affiliation; sex; sexual orientation; gender identity and expression; marital, social, economic, or veteran status; or any other basis included in institutional policies and codes and laws.

UAPS must
- advocate for sensitivity to multicultural and social justice concerns by the institution and its personnel
- ensure physical, program, and resource access for all constituents
- modify or remove policies, practices, systems, technologies, facilities, and structures that create barriers or produce inequities
- ensure that when facilities and structures cannot be modified, they do not impede access to programs, services, and resources
- establish goals for diversity, equity, and access
- foster communication and practices that enhance understanding of identity, culture, self-expression, and heritage
- promote respect for commonalities and differences among people within their historical and cultural contexts
- address the characteristics and needs of diverse constituents when establishing and implementing culturally relevant and inclusive programs, services, policies, procedures, and practices
- provide personnel with diversity, equity, and access training and hold personnel accountable for applying the training to their work
- respond to the needs of all constituents served when establishing hours of operation and developing methods of delivering programs, services, and resources
- recognize the needs of distance and online learning students by directly providing or assisting them to gain access to comparable services and resources

Students inquiring about disability services accommodations must be referred to the appropriate institution staff and resources.

UAPS must accurately describe and depict images of the diversity of the institution in admission material and media.

Part 8. Internal and External Relations

Undergraduate Admissions Programs and Services (UAPS) must reach out to individuals, groups, communities, and organizations internal and external to the institution to
- establish, maintain, and promote understanding and effective relations with those that have a significant interest in or potential effect on the

students or other constituents served by the programs and services
- garner support and resources for programs and services as defined by the mission
- collaborate in offering or improving programs and services to meet the needs of students and other constituents and to achieve program and student outcomes
- engage diverse individuals, groups, communities, and organizations to enrich the educational environment and experiences of students and other constituents
- disseminate information about the programs and services

Promotional and descriptive information must be accurate and free of deception and misrepresentation.

UAPS must work collaboratively with institutional marketing and communications departments in developing publications, websites, video, and other related media that accurately represent the institution to prospective students and their families.

UAPS must work collaboratively with academic departments throughout the recruitment and enrollment process. UAPS staff must provide appropriate training to faculty and campus administrators about the admissions process and their role in the recruitment process.

UAPS must provide appropriate training to alumni and other volunteers who participate in the recruitment process to delineate their role in representing the institution with prospective students and their families.

UAPS must work collaboratively with the registrar and institutional research staff when analyzing yield and conversion rates and other related data for admitted students.

UAPS should coordinate and provide linkages to other campus units such as housing and residential life, campus and visitor information services, financial aid, orientation, registrar, student activities, athletics, academic advising, campus bookstore, student accounts, academic support, disability services, counseling, and career services.

UAPS should identify students deficient in required academic skills and preparation and refer to the appropriate campus units.

UAPS must have procedures and guidelines consistent with institutional policy for
- communicating with the media
- distributing information through print, broadcast, and online sources
- contracting with external organizations for delivery of programs and services
- cultivating, soliciting, and managing gifts
- applying to and managing funds from grants

Part 11. Facilities and Equipment

Undergraduate Admissions Programs and Services (UAPS) must have funding to accomplish the mission and goals.

In establishing and prioritizing funding resources, UAPS must conduct comprehensive analyses to determine
- unmet needs of the unit
- relevant expenditures
- external and internal resources
- impact on students and the institution

UAPS must use the budget as a planning tool to reflect commitment to the mission and goals of the programs and services and of the institution.

UAPS must administer funds in accordance with established institutional accounting procedures.

UAPS must demonstrate efficient and effective use and responsible stewardship of fiscal resources consistent with institutional protocols.

UAPS should have processes to waive admission application fees for prospective students who meet institutionally defined criteria.

Financial reports must provide an accurate financial overview of the organization and provide clear, understandable, and timely data upon which personnel can plan and make informed decisions.

Procurement procedures must
- be consistent with institutional policies
- ensure that purchases comply with laws and codes for usability and access
- ensure that the institution receives value for the funds spent
- consider information available for comparing the ethical and environmental impact of products and services purchased

Part 10. Technology

Undergraduate Admissions Programs and Services (UAPS) must have technology to support the achievement of their mission and goals. The technology and its use must comply with institutional policies and procedures and with relevant codes and laws.

UAPS must use technologies to
- provide updated information regarding mission, location, staffing, programs, services, and official contacts to students and other constituents in accessible formats
- provide an avenue for students and other constituents to communicate sensitive information in a secure format
- enhance the delivery of programs and services for all students

UAPS staff should have expertise in utilizing appropriate technologies in recruiting students, including, but not limited to, social networking, broadcast text messages, instant messaging, electronic financial aid resources, and student record-keeping.

UAPS must

- back up data on a regular basis
- adhere to institutional policies regarding ethical and legal use of technology
- articulate policies and procedures for protecting the confidentiality and security of information
- implement a replacement plan and cycle for all technology with attention to sustainability
- incorporate accessibility features into technology-based programs and services

When providing student access to technology, UAPS must

- have policies on the use of technology that are clear, easy to understand, and available to all students
- provide information or referral to support services for those needing assistance in accessing or using technology
- provide instruction or training on how to use the technology
- inform students of implications of misuse of technologies

Part 11. Facilities and Equipment

Undergraduate Admissions Programs and Services' (UAPS) facilities must be intentionally designed and located in suitable, accessible, and safe spaces that demonstrate universal design and support the program's mission and goals.

Facilities must be designed to engage various constituents and promote learning.

Personnel must have workspaces that are suitably located and accessible, well equipped, adequate in size, and designed to support their work and responsibilities.

The design of the facilities must guarantee the security and privacy of records and ensure the confidentiality of sensitive information and conversations. Personnel must be able to secure their work.

UAPS must incorporate sustainable practices in use of facilities and purchase of equipment. Facilities and equipment must be evaluated on an established cycle and be in compliance with codes, laws, and accepted practices for access, health, safety, and security.

When acquiring capital equipment, UAPS must take into account expenses related to regular maintenance and life cycle costs.

UAPS should encourage the maintenance of attractive and appealing campus facilities that complement the recruitment and admissions process as well as a welcome facility that provides appropriate first stop information and greeting service to all visitors.

Part 12. Assessment

Undergraduate Admissions Programs and Services (UAPS) must develop assessment plans and processes.

Assessment plans must articulate an ongoing cycle of assessment activities.

UAPS must

- specify programmatic goals and intended outcomes
- identify student learning and development outcomes
- employ multiple measures and methods
- develop manageable processes for gathering, interpreting, and evaluating data
- document progress toward achievement of goals and outcomes
- interpret and use assessment results to demonstrate accountability
- report aggregated results to respondent groups and stakeholders
- use assessment results to inform planning and decision-making
- assess effectiveness of implemented changes
- provide evidence of improvement of programs and services

UAPS must employ ethical practices in the assessment process.

UAPS must have access to adequate fiscal, human, professional development, and technological resources to develop and implement assessment plans.

UAPS must employ data-based strategic enrollment management principles when identifying prospective students.

Predictive modeling should be used to identify prospective students and yield data when evaluating the effectiveness of specific recruitment programs and admissions strategies.

Feedback about admission processes should be sought from relevant participants including prospective students, faculty members, staff, and families.

General Standards revised in 2014;
AP content developed/revised in 1987, 1997, & 2010

Undergraduate Research Programs
CAS Contextual Statement

The history of undergraduate research mirrors the history of higher education itself. Many of the principles found in modern-day undergraduate research echo features of the tutorial model of education: close academic connections between students and faculty, mentorship and apprenticeship, problem solving, and experiential learning (Lucas, 1994). As universities expanded along with access to college, undergraduate research emerged as a way to continue educational practices of the past in a new educational environment with greater size and scale.

The beginnings of undergraduate research programs are not seen in "a" history, but rather in the histories of disciplines, professional organizations, and governmental agencies that recognized the value of including undergraduate students in the research enterprise. The National Science Foundation administered a formal program for undergraduate research from 1958-1981, and since 1986 has offered support via the Research Experiences for Undergraduates (REU) program (National Science Foundation, n.d.). Efforts within disciplines to recognize and promote undergraduate research led to the development of two cross-disciplinary national organizations: the Council on Undergraduate Research (CUR) and the National Conferences on Undergraduate Research (NCUR). CUR was formed in 1978 by a group of chemistry professors and now includes individual and institutional members from more than 900 colleges and universities (CUR, n.d.-b). NCUR began in 1987 as an interdisciplinary conference for undergraduate students from across the United States to present their research and scholarship (CUR, n.d.-c), complementing the introduction of undergraduate poster sessions at professional meetings. The two organizations merged in October 2010 (CUR, n.d.-a) to provide comprehensive resources for faculty and students engaged in undergraduate research.

The history of undergraduate research programs emerging as institutional units is also varied, as there is no singular preferred structure or model. Undergraduate research offices vary in their location within an institution (reporting to a provost, lead research administrator, or dean, among other possibilities), as well as in their own organizational structure (led by a full-time or part-time faculty or professional staff member, often supported by other professional and/or student staff). A volume by Kinkead and Blockus (2012) delineates common elements of undergraduate research offices and provides examples to illustrate variation across institutions. The range of possible models signals the importance of tailoring an undergraduate research program or office to the mission, core values, needs, and resources of the particular institution it serves.

As undergraduate research has evolved as a field, basic tenets have emerged that are shared regardless of academic discipline or institution type. First, research is broadly defined so that it encompasses all types of scholarly and creative activities present at an institution. CUR defines undergraduate research as, "an inquiry or investigation conducted by an undergraduate student that makes an original intellectual or creative contribution to the discipline" (n.d.-b). This underscores the idea that students are contributing meaningful work to a discipline rather than participating in a simulation exercise divorced from "real" research. Undergraduate research is genuine participation in the activity of a discipline. Students learn the processes, habits of mind, and principles of scholarship used by faculty researchers through active participation in original inquiry. The contributions made by undergraduates can be seen in the papers and other works that they publish, the creative work they perform and exhibit, and the presentations they make at regional, national, and international meetings and conferences.

Undergraduate research has also been identified as a high-impact practice for student learning and development, indicating the important role undergraduate research can play in the college experience (Kuh, 2008). Collaborative research with faculty allows for extended interaction, frequent feedback about performance, and opportunities to synthesize and apply learning, all of which support student engagement and, thereby, persistence and retention. Undergraduate researchers develop and/or refine aspirations for graduate education and deepen their understandings of research methods and procedures. Students also report that undergraduate research fosters the development of broadly applicable skills, such as critical thinking, communication, collaboration, and problem solving. See Laursen et al. (2010) for a review of research on student outcomes and a detailed analysis of students' gains from participating in intensive summer research experiences in the sciences.

In 2014, CUR adopted five strategic pillars that serve as benchmarks for undergraduate research programs and signposts for future directions in program development. They will be discussed in turn with regard to current trends and challenges in the field.

1. Integrating and Building Undergraduate Research into Curriculum and Coursework
As colleges and universities strive to involve more students in high-impact educational practices like undergraduate research, they may encounter challenges relating to scale and capacity. Curriculum and coursework represent promising avenues for involving more students in research experiences through such approaches as problem-based learning or extended, collaborative projects within learning community contexts. Refer to Karukstis and Elgren (2007) for a discussion of curricular elements and structures, as well as institutional practices, which contribute to a "research-supportive" curriculum.

2. Assessment of the Impact of Undergraduate Research
The *CAS* Standards and Guidelines for undergraduate research programs include a section on assessment and evaluation

in recognition of the importance of assessing achievement of undergraduate research program goals and intended learning outcomes for students. Assessment will have primary implications in the local context, suggesting ways of improving programs and services, but institutional assessment efforts can benefit from – and, in turn, can inform – developments in the field of undergraduate research. Established instruments, such as the Undergraduate Research Student Self-Assessment (URSSA) (Hunter, Weston, Laursen, & Thiry, 2009), the Survey of Undergraduate Research Experiences (SURE) (Lopatto, 2004), and SUNY-Buffalo State's Longitudinal Student Outcomes Evaluation (Singer & Zimmerman, 2012), provide a mechanism for collecting data across programs and time points which can be usefully combined with other approaches, such as interviews and focus groups. See Laursen (2015) for a review of current assessment studies and suggestions for future directions in program evaluation.

3.   Diversity and Inclusion in Undergraduate Research
Diversity and inclusion, as reflected in the *CAS* standards for diversity, equity, and access, are critical issues in undergraduate research. A growing body of research documents efforts to expand participation among students from underrepresented groups, from different types of institutions, at early stages of their academic careers, and across the full range of academic disciplines (Boyd & Wesemann, 2009). Such initiatives are of critical importance in engaging students of diverse backgrounds in academic inquiry, which can influence the shape and content of that inquiry along with the paths pursued by those students in college and beyond.

4.   Innovation and Collaboration in Undergraduate Research
Collaboration in undergraduate research can take many forms, such as working as part of an interdisciplinary team or contributing to a cross-institutional faculty research collaboration. Institutions are now experimenting with other collaborative models, exploring partnerships with businesses and non-profit organizations to design research projects related to real-world needs. These efforts may be supported by intra-institutional partnerships with service learning, extension services, or other allied units. A related trend is the growing emphasis on entrepreneurship and innovation at universities, as evidenced by the development of makerspaces, business incubators, and entrepreneurship centers. Entrepreneurship experiences share many elements in common with undergraduate research – hands-on work on a project with no predetermined outcome, often in collaboration with team members – and may represent new opportunities for executing or applying research.

5.   Internationalization and Undergraduate Research
International research exchanges and collaborations are concrete illustrations of the global nature of contemporary research. International fieldwork experiences can benefit undergraduate research in a variety of fields, from conservation biology to linguistics, anthropology to civil engineering. Logistical challenges associated with international work may be addressed most effectively through collaboration with other campus offices with expertise in study abroad, travel, and international affairs. The internationalization of undergraduate research bears great potential for enhancing students' global learning, appreciation of diversity, and engagement with the difficult problems and questions that transcend borders.

References, Readings, and Resources

Boyd, M. K., & Wesemann, J. L. (Eds.) (2009). *Broadening participation in undergraduate research: Fostering excellence and enhancing the impact.* Washington, DC: Council on Undergraduate Research.

Council on Undergraduate Research. (n.d.-a). *CUR and NCUR join forces.* Retrieved from http://www.cur.org/about_cur/history/cur_and_ncur/

Council on Undergraduate Research. (n.d.-b). *Fact sheet.* Retrieved from http://www.cur.org/about_cur/fact_sheet/

Council on Undergraduate Research. (n.d.-c). *NCUR: National conferences on undergraduate research.* Retrieved from http://www.cur.org/conferences_and_events/student_events/ncur/

Council on Undergraduate Research. (2014). *CUR strategic pillars.* Retrieved from http://www.cur.org/about_cur/strategicpillars/

Hunter, A.-B., Weston, T. J., Laursen, S. L., & Thiry, H. (2009). URSSA: Evaluating student gains from undergraduate research in science education. *Council on Undergraduate Research Quarterly, 29*(3), 15-19.

Karukstis, K. K., & Elgren, T. E. (2007). *Developing & sustaining a research-supportive curriculum: A compendium of successful practices.* Washington, DC: Council on Undergraduate Research.

Kinkead, J., & Blockus, L. (Eds.). (2012). *Undergraduate research offices & programs: Models & practices.* Washington, DC: Council on Undergraduate Research.

Kuh, G. D. (2008). *High-impact educational practices: What they are, who has access to them, and why they matter.* Washington, DC: Association of American Colleges and Universities.

Laursen, S. L. (2015). Assessing undergraduate research in the sciences: The next generation. *Council on Undergraduate Research Quarterly, 35*(3), 9-14.

Laursen, S., Hunter, A.-B., Seymour, E., Thiry, H., & Melton, G. (2010). *Undergraduate research in the sciences: Engaging students in real science.* San Francisco, CA: Jossey-Bass.

Lopatto, D. (2004). Survey of undergraduate research experiences (SURE): First findings. *Cell Biology Education, 3*(4), 270-277.

Lucas, C. J. (1994). *American higher education: A history.* New York, NY: St. Martin's Griffin.

National Science Foundation. (n.d.). *A timeline of NSF history, 1986 – December 1: Undergraduate research.* Retrieved from http://www.nsf.gov/news/special_reports/history-nsf/1986_undergrads.jsp

Singer, J., & Zimmerman, B. (2012). Evaluating a summer undergraduate research program: Measuring student outcomes and program impact. *Council on Undergraduate Research Quarterly, 32*(3), 40-47.

Contextual Statement Contributors

Current Edition:
Caroline E. McGuire, University of Connecticut
Jennifer Lease Butts, University of Connecticut

Previous Editions:
Dorothy Mitstifer, ACHS

Undergraduate Research Programs
CAS Standards and Guidelines

Part 1. Mission

The primary mission of Undergraduate Research Programs (URP) is to engage students in investigative and creative activity to experience firsthand the processes of scholarly exploration and discovery. Undergraduate research is an inquiry or investigation conducted by an undergraduate student to examine, create, and share new knowledge in the context of disciplinary and interdisciplinary traditions.

URP must develop, disseminate, implement, and regularly review their missions, which must be consistent with the mission of the institution and with applicable professional standards. The mission must be appropriate for the institution's students and other constituents. Mission statements must reference student learning and development.

Part 2. Program

To achieve their mission, Undergraduate Research Programs (URP) must contribute to

- students' formal education, which includes both the curriculum and the co-curriculum
- student progression and timely completion of educational goals
- preparation of students for their careers, citizenship, and lives
- student learning and development

To contribute to student learning and development, URP must

- identify relevant and desirable student learning and development outcomes
- articulate how the student learning and development outcomes align with the six CAS student learning and development domains and related dimensions
- assess relevant and desirable student learning and development
- provide evidence of impact on outcomes
- articulate contributions to or support of student learning and development in the domains not specifically assessed
- use evidence gathered to create strategies for improvement of programs and services

STUDENT LEARNING AND DEVELOPMENT DOMAINS AND DIMENSIONS

Domain: knowledge acquisition, integration, construction, and application

- Dimensions: understanding knowledge from a range of disciplines; connecting knowledge to other knowledge, ideas, and experiences; constructing knowledge; and relating knowledge to daily life

Domain: cognitive complexity

- Dimensions: critical thinking, reflective thinking, effective reasoning, and creativity

Domain: intrapersonal development

- Dimensions: realistic self-appraisal, self-understanding, and self-respect; identity development; commitment to ethics and integrity; and spiritual awareness

Domain: interpersonal competence

- Dimensions: meaningful relationships, interdependence, collaboration, and effective leadership

Domain: humanitarianism and civic engagement

- Dimensions: understanding and appreciation of cultural and human differences, social responsibility, global perspective, and sense of civic responsibility

Domain: practical competence

- Dimensions: pursuing goals, communicating effectively, technical competence, managing personal affairs, managing career development, demonstrating professionalism, maintaining health and wellness, and living a purposeful and satisfying life

[LD Outcomes: See *The Council for the Advancement of Standards Learning and Development Outcomes* statement for examples of outcomes related to these domains and dimensions.]

URP must be

- intentionally designed
- guided by theories and knowledge of learning and development
- integrated into the life of the institution
- reflective of developmental and demographic profiles of the student population
- responsive to needs of individuals, populations with distinct needs, and relevant constituencies
- delivered using multiple formats, strategies, and contexts
- designed to provide universal access

URP must collaborate with colleagues and departments across the institution to promote student learning and development, persistence, and success.

URP must

- create an active learning environment supportive of scholarship and research
- integrate research activities with professional and liberal education
- create an infrastructure to recognize and reward research excellence and successful completion of

research
- create a collegial climate in which to conduct research
- allow students to define their interests within the context of the research activity
- promote intellectual rigor and student intellectual growth and development
- require an appropriate report of the student's completed work
- provide opportunities for research dissemination

URP must encourage research that is commensurate with practice in the disciplines and enables students to recognize work that is original, current, and significant.

URP must establish mechanisms for individual or small-group mentoring on a regular basis that is based on the intellectual readiness of students. Mentoring must address research design; appropriate forms of data collection, verification, and analysis; information retrieval; oversight of research on human subjects; and appropriate forms of written and oral scholarly communication.

URP must ensure that students are made aware that disciplines and publications have specific authorship policies and ethical standards and are provided resources to identify those relevant to their research.

URP should provide opportunities for undergraduate students to present their research to peers, faculty members, professionals, and appropriate others and to participate in undergraduate and disciplinary research conferences. These may include institutional, local, regional, national, and international meetings.

URP should offer opportunities for academic credit for research activity where applicable.

URP should offer a range of research experiences appropriate for students at various developmental levels, abilities, and with various life circumstances.

Because a particular research activity may not be appropriate for every student, a range of options should be provided so that all students may find appropriate opportunities. Examples of such opportunities may include first-year experiences, living-learning programs, honors programs, graduation requirements, general education courses, major requirements, capstone courses, and community-based research. These illustrative examples are not mutually exclusive. An undergraduate research activity may involve two or more of these. Activities may be initiated by students, faculty members, programs, or institutions.

Part 3. Organization and Leadership

To achieve program and student learning and development outcomes, Undergraduate Research Programs (URP) must be purposefully structured for effectiveness. URP must have clearly stated and current
- goals and outcomes
- policies and procedures

- responsibilities and performance expectations for personnel
- organizational charts demonstrating clear channels of authority

Leaders must model ethical behavior and institutional citizenship.

Leaders with organizational authority for URP must provide strategic planning, management and supervision, and program advancement.

Strategic Planning
- articulate a vision and mission that drive short- and long-term planning
- set goals and objectives based on the needs of the populations served, intended student learning and development outcomes, and program outcomes
- facilitate continuous development, implementation, and assessment of program effectiveness and goal attainment congruent with institutional mission and strategic plans
- promote environments that provide opportunities for student learning, development, and engagement
- develop, adapt, and improve programs and services in response to the changing needs of populations served and evolving institutional priorities
- include diverse perspectives to inform decision making

Management and Supervision
- plan, allocate, and monitor the use of fiscal, physical, human, intellectual, and technological resources
- manage human resource processes including recruitment, selection, professional development, supervision, performance planning, succession planning, evaluation, recognition, and reward
- influence others to contribute to the effectiveness and success of the unit
- empower professional, support, and student personnel to become effective leaders
- encourage and support collaboration with colleagues and departments across the institution
- encourage and support scholarly contributions to the profession
- identify and address individual, organizational, and environmental conditions that foster or inhibit mission achievement
- use current and valid evidence to inform decisions
- incorporate sustainability practices in the management and design of programs, services, and facilities
- understand appropriate technologies and integrate them into programs and services
- be knowledgeable about codes and laws relevant to programs and services and ensure that programs and services meet those requirements
- assess and take action to mitigate potential risks

Program Advancement
- advocate for and actively promote the mission and goals of the programs and services
- inform stakeholders about issues affecting practice
- facilitate processes to reach consensus where wide support is needed
- advocate for representation in strategic planning initiatives at divisional and institutional levels

URP leaders must promote a research environment that recognizes and respects all aspects of diversity. This includes research topics and the recruitment, access, and full participation of diverse students in research activity.

Part 4. Human Resources

Undergraduate Research Programs (URP) must be staffed adequately by individuals qualified to accomplish mission and goals.

URP must have access to technical and support personnel adequate to accomplish their mission.

Within institutional guidelines, URP must
- establish procedures for personnel recruitment and selection, training, performance planning, and evaluation
- set expectations for supervision and performance
- provide personnel access to continuing and advanced education and appropriate professional development opportunities to improve their competence, skills, and leadership capacity
- consider work/life options available to personnel (e.g., compressed work schedules, flextime, job sharing, remote work, or telework) to promote recruitment and retention of personnel

URP should offer training for individuals who mentor undergraduate researchers about research policies and procedures, URP goals and opportunities, and the diversity of student learning styles.

Administrators of URP must
- ensure that all personnel have updated position descriptions
- implement recruitment and selection/hiring strategies that produce a workforce inclusive of under-represented populations
- develop promotion practices that are fair, inclusive, proactive, and non-discriminatory

URP personnel responsible for delivery of programs and services must have written performance goals, objectives, and outcomes for each year's performance cycle to be used to plan, review, and evaluate work and performance. The performance plan must be updated regularly to reflect changes during the performance cycle.

Results of individual personnel evaluations must be used to recognize personnel performance, address performance issues, implement individual and/or collective personnel development and training programs, and inform the assessment of programs and services.

URP personnel, when hired and throughout their employment, must receive appropriate and thorough training.

URP personnel, including student employees and volunteers, must have access to resources or receive specific training on
- institutional policies pertaining to functions or activities they support
- privacy and confidentiality policies
- laws regarding access to student records
- policies and procedures for dealing with sensitive institutional information
- policies and procedures related to technology used to store or access student records and institutional data
- how and when to refer those in need of additional assistance to qualified personnel and have access to a supervisor for assistance in making these judgments
- systems and technologies necessary to perform their assigned responsibilities
- ethical and legal uses of technology

URP personnel must engage in continuing professional development activities to keep abreast of the research, theories, legislation, policies, and developments that affect their programs and services.

The professional development of staff and faculty members engaged in URP should address
- identification of the compatibility between research activities and student interests
- establishment and maintenance of relationships with academic and other units on campus
- development, implementation, and assessment of learning goals
- preparation, mentoring, and monitoring of students involved in research experiences
- use of active learning strategies
- education and support of students to apply learning from research experiences to future endeavors

Administrators of URP must ensure that personnel are knowledgeable about and trained in safety, emergency procedures, and crisis prevention and response. Risk management efforts must address identification of threatening conduct or behavior and must incorporate a system for responding to and reporting such behaviors.

URP personnel must be knowledgeable of and trained in safety and emergency procedures for securing and vacating facilities.

PROFESSIONAL PERSONNEL

URP professional personnel either must hold an earned graduate or professional degree in a field relevant to their position or must possess an appropriate combination of educational credentials and related work experience.

INTERNS OR GRADUATE ASSISTANTS

Degree- or credential-seeking interns or graduate assistants must be qualified by enrollment in an appropriate field of study and relevant experience. These students must be trained and supervised by professional personnel who possess applicable educational credentials and work experience and have supervisory experience. Supervisors must be cognizant of the dual roles interns and graduate assistants have as both student and employee.

Supervisors must
- adhere to parameters of students' job descriptions
- articulate intended learning outcomes in student job descriptions
- adhere to agreed-upon work hours and schedules
- offer flexible scheduling when circumstances necessitate

Supervisors and students must both agree to suitable compensation if circumstances necessitate additional hours.

STUDENT EMPLOYEES AND VOLUNTEERS

Student employees and volunteers must be carefully selected, trained, supervised, and evaluated. Students must have access to a supervisor. Student employees and volunteers must be provided clear job descriptions, pre-service training based on assessed needs, and continuing development.

Part 5. Ethics

Undergraduate Research Programs (URP) must
- review applicable professional ethical standards and must adopt or develop and implement appropriate statements of ethical practice
- publish and adhere to statements of ethical practice and ensure their periodic review
- orient new personnel to relevant ethical standards and statements of ethical practice and related institutional policies

Statements of ethical standards must
- specify that URP personnel respect privacy and maintain confidentiality in communications and records as delineated by privacy laws
- specify limits on disclosure of information contained in students' records as well as requirements to disclose to appropriate authorities
- address conflicts of interest, or appearance thereof, by personnel in the performance of their work
- reflect the responsibility of personnel to be fair, objective, and impartial in their interactions with others
- reference management of institutional funds
- reference appropriate behavior regarding research and assessment with human participants, confidentiality of research and assessment data, and students' rights and responsibilities

- include the expectation that personnel confront and hold accountable other personnel who exhibit unethical behavior
- address issues surrounding scholarly integrity

Policies and procedures must guard against potential physical and psychological harm to human subjects of research.

URP personnel must
- employ ethical decision making in the performance of their duties
- inform users of programs and services of ethical obligations and limitations emanating from codes and laws or from licensure requirements
- recognize and avoid conflicts of interest that could adversely influence their judgment or objectivity and, when unavoidable, recuse themselves from the situation
- perform their duties within the scope of their position, training, expertise, and competence
- make referrals when issues presented exceed the scope of the position

URP staff members must acknowledge authorship based on disciplinary guidelines and practices.

Part 6. Law, Policy, and Governance

Undergraduate Research Programs (URP) must be in compliance with laws, regulations, and policies that relate to their respective responsibilities and that pose legal obligations, limitations, risks, and liabilities for the institution as a whole. Examples include constitutional, statutory, regulatory, and case law; relevant law and orders emanating from codes and laws; and the institution's policies.

URP must have access to legal advice needed for personnel to carry out their assigned responsibilities.

URP must inform personnel, appropriate officials, and users of programs and services about existing and changing legal obligations, risks and liabilities, and limitations.

URP must inform personnel about professional liability insurance options and refer them to external sources if the institution does not provide coverage.

URP must have written policies and procedures on operations, transactions, or tasks that have legal implications.

URP must regularly review policies. The revision and creation of policies must be informed by best practices, available evidence, and policy issues in higher education.

URP must have procedures and guidelines consistent with institutional policy for responding to threats, emergencies, and crisis situations. Systems and procedures must be in place to disseminate timely and accurate information to students, other members of the institutional community, and appropriate external organizations during emergency situations.

Personnel must neither participate in nor condone any form of harassment or activity that demeans persons or creates an intimidating, hostile, or offensive environment.

URP must purchase or obtain permission to use copyrighted materials and instruments. References to copyrighted materials and instruments must include appropriate citations.

URP must inform personnel about internal and external governance organizations that affect programs and services.

Part 7. Diversity, Equity, and Access

Within the context of each institution's mission and in accordance with institutional policies and applicable codes and laws, Undergraduate Research Programs (URP) must create and maintain educational and work environments that are welcoming, accessible, inclusive, equitable, and free from harassment.

URP must not discriminate on the basis of disability; age; race; cultural identity; ethnicity; nationality; family educational history (e.g., first generation to attend college); political affiliation; religious affiliation; sex; sexual orientation; gender identity and expression; marital, social, economic, or veteran status; or any other basis included in institutional policies and codes and laws.

URP must

- advocate for sensitivity to multicultural and social justice concerns by the institution and its personnel
- ensure physical, program, and resource access for all constituents
- modify or remove policies, practices, systems, technologies, facilities, and structures that create barriers or produce inequities
- ensure that when facilities and structures cannot be modified, they do not impede access to programs, services, and resources
- establish goals for diversity, equity, and access
- foster communication and practices that enhance understanding of identity, culture, self-expression, and heritage
- promote respect for commonalities and differences among people within their historical and cultural contexts
- address the characteristics and needs of diverse constituents when establishing and implementing culturally relevant and inclusive programs, services, policies, procedures, and practices
- provide personnel with diversity, equity, and access training and hold personnel accountable for applying the training to their work
- respond to the needs of all constituents served when establishing hours of operation and developing methods of delivering programs, services, and resources
- recognize the needs of distance and online learning

students by directly providing or assisting them to gain access to comparable services and resources

Part 8. Internal and External Relations

Undergraduate Research Programs (URP) must reach out to individuals, groups, communities, and organizations internal and external to the institution to

- establish, maintain, and promote understanding and effective relations with those that have a significant interest in or potential effect on the students or other constituents served by the programs and services
- garner support and resources for programs and services as defined by the mission
- collaborate in offering or improving programs and services to meet the needs of students and other constituents and to achieve program and student outcomes
- engage diverse individuals, groups, communities, and organizations to enrich the educational environment and experiences of students and other constituents
- disseminate information about the programs and services

Promotional and descriptive information must be accurate and free of deception and misrepresentation.

URP must have procedures and guidelines consistent with institutional policy for

- communicating with the media
- distributing information through print, broadcast, and online sources
- contracting with external organizations for delivery of programs and services
- cultivating, soliciting, and managing gifts
- applying to and managing funds from grants

Part 9. Financial Resources

Undergraduate Research Programs (URP) must have funding to accomplish the mission and goals.

In establishing and prioritizing funding resources, URP must conduct comprehensive analyses to determine

- unmet needs of the unit
- relevant expenditures
- external and internal resources
- impact on students and the institution

URP should seek funding to increase undergraduate research activities that involve a wide range of students and disciplines.

URP must use the budget as a planning tool to reflect commitment to the mission and goals of the programs and services and of the institution.

URP must administer funds in accordance with established institutional accounting procedures.

URP must demonstrate efficient and effective use and responsible stewardship of fiscal resources consistent with institutional protocols.

Financial reports must provide an accurate financial overview of the organization and provide clear, understandable, and timely data upon which personnel can plan and make informed decisions.

Procurement procedures must
- be consistent with institutional policies
- ensure that purchases comply with laws and codes for usability and access
- ensure that the institution receives value for the funds spent
- consider information available for comparing the ethical and environmental impact of products and services purchased

Part 10. Technology

Undergraduate Research Programs (URP) must have technology to support the achievement of their mission and goals. The technology and its use must comply with institutional policies and procedures and with relevant codes and laws.

URP must use technologies to
- provide updated information regarding mission, location, staffing, programs, services, and official contacts to students and other constituents in accessible formats
- provide an avenue for students and other constituents to communicate sensitive information in a secure format
- enhance the delivery of programs and services for all students

URP must
- back up data on a regular basis
- adhere to institutional policies regarding ethical and legal use of technology
- articulate policies and procedures for protecting the confidentiality and security of information
- implement a replacement plan and cycle for all technology with attention to sustainability
- incorporate accessibility features into technology-based programs and services

When providing student access to technology, URP must
- have policies on the use of technology that are clear, easy to understand, and available to all students
- provide information or referral to support services for those needing assistance in accessing or using technology
- provide instruction or training on how to use the technology
- inform students of implications of misuse of technologies

Part 11. Facilities and Equipment

Undergraduate Research Programs' (URP) facilities must be intentionally designed and located in suitable, accessible, and safe spaces that demonstrate universal design and support the program's mission and goals.

Facilities must be designed to engage various constituents and promote learning.

Personnel must have workspaces that are suitably located and accessible, well equipped, adequate in size, and designed to support their work and responsibilities.

The design of the facilities must guarantee the security and privacy of records and ensure the confidentiality of sensitive information and conversations. Personnel must be able to secure their work.

URP must incorporate sustainable practices in use of facilities and purchase of equipment. Facilities and equipment must be evaluated on an established cycle and be in compliance with codes, laws, and accepted practices for access, health, safety, and security.

When acquiring capital equipment, URP must take into account expenses related to regular maintenance and life cycle costs.

Part 12. Assessment

Undergraduate Research Programs (URP) must develop assessment plans and processes.

Assessment plans must articulate an ongoing cycle of assessment activities.

URP must
- specify programmatic goals and intended outcomes
- identify student learning and development outcomes
- employ multiple measures and methods
- develop manageable processes for gathering, interpreting, and evaluating data
- document progress toward achievement of goals and outcomes
- interpret and use assessment results to demonstrate accountability
- report aggregated results to respondent groups and stakeholders
- use assessment results to inform planning and decision-making
- assess effectiveness of implemented changes
- provide evidence of improvement of programs and services

URP must employ ethical practices in the assessment process.

URP must have access to adequate fiscal, human, professional development, and technological resources to develop and implement assessment plans.

General Standards revised in 2014;
URP content developed in 2007

Veterans and Military Programs and Services
CAS Contextual Statement

The purpose of Veterans and Military Programs and Services (VMPS) is to provide support for student veterans, military personnel, military family members, and family members receiving veterans' benefits through the GI Bill (and similar programs in Canada) that are affiliated with an institution of higher education. The need for such support is evidenced by the experiences of personnel impacted by their involvement in the Global War on Terrorism (GWOT), Operation Enduring Freedom (OEF), Operation Iraqi Freedom (OIF), and other service-related actions, who have been subject to sudden mobilization and demobilization. The VMPS standards and guidelines were developed to be as inclusive as possible without being prescriptive and are designed to provide the greatest latitude for VMPS providers to serve clientele.

Although VMPS is relatively new to higher education, colleges have had a relationship with military service since the founding of the United States. Thomas Jefferson indicated, "[we] must train and classify the whole of our male citizens, and make military instruction a regular part of collegiate education. We can never be safe till this is done" (University of Virginia, 2010). Jefferson believed education and military service to be key elements of a democratic society and signed legislation establishing the United States Military Academy in 1802. In the Rockfish Gap Report, Jefferson outlined plans for the University of Virginia and identified the need for military training in geometry and architecture (1818). In 1824, the Board of Visitors authorized the institution's faculty to hire a military instructor to drill and train the students (Bruce, 1917, p. 117). Other state-based colleges with military training programs included Virginia Military Institute (1839) and The Citadel in South Carolina (1842). Formalizing military training on college campuses was established with the Morrill Act of 1862, which brought about the development of the land-grant university systems and with it the placement of military training programs, the precursor to the modern Reserve Officer Training Programs or ROTC.

After World War I, Canada created the Department of Soldiers' Civil Re-establishment and provided subsistence allowances and educational grants (Mosch, 1975), and the United States provided educational benefits for disabled veterans as part of the Rehabilitation law of 1919 (Olson, 1974). Several states, including Arkansas, California, Colorado, Illinois, Minnesota, New York, North Dakota, Oregon, and Wisconsin offered free or reduced tuition and other education benefits to World War I veterans (Mosch, 1975).

In 1944 US President Franklin D. Roosevelt signed into law the Servicemen's Readjustment Act (1944). This legislation, known as the GI Bill, provided tuition assistance and subsistence to support educational pursuits for returning WWII veterans. Considered a grand experiment in education (Olson, 1973), the GI Bill is one of the most influential acts to impact education and society (Wolfe, 2001) and served as the catalyst for mass education in the United States. In 1946, James Bryant Conant, Harvard President, stated the GI Bill was "a heartening sign that the democratic process of social mobility is energetically at work, piercing the class barriers that, even in America, have tended to keep a college education the prerogative of the few" (Altschuler & Blumin, 2009, p. 95). The Veteran's Rehabilitation Act (VRA) or Canadian GI Bill was administered unevenly by provinces but had similar effects for Canadian veterans (Lemieux & Card, 1998). A key outcome of the GI Bill was the development of student advisement centers to support veterans (Altschuler & Blumin, 2009). GI bills have followed each conflict since World War II, including specific bills for the Korean and Vietnam Wars, and are now staples to military service.

In 1973 the US Army adopted the Total Force Concept (TFC), increasing the reliance on reserve components for both combat and combat support and making reservists and guardsmen more susceptible to recall. Also in 1973 the draft ended for US males and an all-volunteer military was established. The volunteer military created an increased focus on recruitment incentives such as Voluntary Education Programs (VEP), which offer tuition assistance, counseling, classroom facilities, and other systems to support voluntary education; the Student Loan Repayment (SLR), which offers loan repayment for service to both active and reserve military service personnel; and the Simultaneous Membership Program (SMP), which allows guard and reserve enlisted personnel to join college and university Reserve Officer Training Corps (ROTC) programs.

Colleges and universities, eager to demonstrate their accessibility to military personnel and their families, sought alignment with Servicemembers Opportunity Colleges (SOC). SOC is affiliated with the American Association of State Colleges and Universities (AASCU) in partnership with the Department of Defense (DOD) and active and reserve components of the military services to increase and enhance postsecondary education opportunities for military service members. To be SOC eligible an institution must develop a system for reasonable transfer of credit, reduce academic residency requirements, provide credit for military training and experience, and give credit for nationally-recognized testing programs.

Recent wars in Iraq and Afghanistan have raised the visibility of veterans, military personnel, and their families on college campuses. The numbers of veterans from these conflicts (now the third longest in US history), the educational benefits of the Montgomery and Post 9-11 GI bills, and the use of VEP and SLR as recruitment incentives will continue to have major impacts on higher education.

Professional associations have been established to assist in the professional development of administrators providing services to veterans, military service members, and their families matriculating through higher education:

- The National Association of Veteran Program Administrators (NAVPA) serves individuals working in the growing field of veterans' educational support and has been instrumental in the development of the CAS Standards and Guidelines for Veterans and Military Programs and Services. NAVPA members are service providers and VCOs on US campuses seeking to promote professional competency and efficiency in veterans educational programs.
- The National Association of Veterans Upward Bound Project Personnel (NAVUBPP) is the professional association for personnel associated with these programs. Veterans Upward Bound projects are funded by the US Department of Education and serve eligible veterans across the nation.
- Founded in 2008, the Student Veterans Association (SVA) works to develop new student groups, coordinate between existing student groups, and advocate on behalf of student veterans at the local, state, and national levels. SVA consists of an executive staff and campus-based student veterans groups that coordinate programs, enhance networking, and assist in the transition to higher education. The SVA published a *Veterans Center Handbook*, available from the association's website, which identifies concerns, provides resources, and outlines steps for developing a center.
- The NASPA Veterans Knowledge Community identifies and advances best practices for veterans' programs.

References, Readings, and Resources

Ackerman, R.T. & DiRamio, D. (Eds.). (2009). *Creating a veteran-friendly campus: Strategies for transition and success. New Directions for Student Services, No. 126.* San Francisco, CA: Jossey-Bass.

Altschuler, G. C., & Blumin, S. M. (2009). *The GI Bill: A new deal for veterans.* Oxford, UK: Oxford University Press.

Bruce, P. A. (1920) *History of the University of Virginia: The lengthened shadow of one man. Vol. II.* New York, NY: The MacMillan Company.

Cook, B. J., & Kim, Y. (2009). *From soldier to student: Easing the transition of service members on campus.* Washington, DC: ACE, SOC, AASCU, NASPA, NAVPA.

Lemieux, T., & Card, D. (1998). *Working paper: Education, earnings, and the Canadian GI Bill.* Cambridge, MA: National Bureau of Economic Research.

McMurray, A. J. (2007). College students, the GI Bill, and the proliferation of online learning: A history of learning and contemporary challenges. *The Internet and Higher Education, 10,* pp. 143-150.

Mosch, T. R. (1975). *The GI Bill: A breakthrough in educational and social policy in the United States.* Hicksville, NY: Exposition Press.

National Association of Student Personnel Administrators, Veterans Knowledge Community: http://www.naspa.org/kc/veterans/

National Association of Veterans Personnel Administrators, http://www.navpa.org/index.htm

Olson, K. W. (1974). The GI Bill, the veterans, and the colleges. Lexington, KY: University Press of Kentucky.

Olson, K. W. (1973). The GI Bill and higher education: Success and surprise. *American Quarterly, 25,* pp. 596-610.

Servicemembers Opportunity Colleges: http://www.soc.aascu.org/

Student Veterans Association: http://www.studentveterans.org/about/

United States Military Academy: http://www.usma.edu/history.asp

University of Virginia. (2010). *Thomas Jefferson on politics and government: 47. The military and the militia.* Retrieved from http://etext.virginia.edu/jefferson/quotations/jeff1480.htm

Veterans Upward Bound: http://navub.org/article/index.php?article_id=8&mainmenu_id=7_

Wolfe, M. P. (2001). Reflections on the most important educational developments of the 20th century: Kappa Delta Pi laureates. *Educational Forum, 65,* 146-163.

Contextual Statement Contributors
Current Edition:
Douglas Franklin, Ohio University, NIRSA

Previous Editions:
Douglas Franklin, Ohio University, NIRSA

Veterans and Military Programs and Services

CAS Standards and Guidelines

Part 1. Mission

The primary mission of Veterans and Military Programs and Services (VMPS) must be to provide, facilitate, or coordinate programs and services for student veterans, military service members, and their family members. VMPS must identify student veterans and military service members and establish a community that connects and supports this population.

Family members include veterans' and service members' spouses/partners and children as well as survivors of veterans.

VMPS must develop, disseminate, implement, and regularly review their missions, which must be consistent with the mission of the institution and with applicable professional standards. The mission must be appropriate for the institution's students and other constituents. Mission statements must reference student learning and development.

Part 2. Program

Veterans and Military Programs (VMPS) must assist student veterans, military service members, and their family members with

- transitions from military service to higher education
- issues related to deployment of active duty students or call up for students affiliated with National Guard and Reserve Units
- integration into institutions and campus life
- reintegration following activation
- establishment of procedures to facilitate progress toward educational goals

VMPS should include admissions support, orientation, financial aid, housing and logistics, advising and mentoring, and learning communities.

VMPS should develop systems to establish and maintain communications between the institution and deployed students.

VMPS must collaborate with key departments to streamline campus administrative procedures for student veterans and military service members, particularly those preparing for or returning from deployments.

VMPS must provide support and advisement for student veteran organizations and veteran advisory groups on campus.

The VMPS should establish an advisory group to assist in developing a campus responsiveness plan for returning veterans and their family members. Membership of veteran advisory groups may include representatives from the offices of admissions, financial aid, registrar, counseling services, disability services, and health services.

VMPS should facilitate the development of a campus-wide community of student veterans, military service members, and their family members to provide opportunities to connect with their peers.

VMPS must provide, directly or in collaboration with other institutional units, education and training for faculty and staff on issues relevant to student veterans, military service members, and their family members.

VMPS should facilitate workshops and seminars for the campus community regarding the needs and issues facing student veterans, military service members, and their family members.

VMPS must obtain, distribute, and provide referrals to current information on educational benefits for veterans.

VMPS must work with the veteran certifying official and make available certifying paperwork for student veterans, military service members, and their family members for all applicable educational benefits.

To achieve their mission, VMPS must contribute to
- students' formal education, which includes both the curriculum and the co-curriculum
- student progression and timely completion of educational goals
- preparation of students for their careers, citizenship, and lives
- student learning and development

To contribute to student learning and development, VMPS must
- identify relevant and desirable student learning and development outcomes
- articulate how the student learning and development outcomes align with the six CAS student learning and development domains and related dimensions
- assess relevant and desirable student learning and development
- provide evidence of impact on outcomes
- articulate contributions to or support of student learning and development in the domains not specifically assessed
- use evidence gathered to create strategies for improvement of programs and services

STUDENT LEARNING AND DEVELOPMENT DOMAINS AND DIMENSIONS

Domain: knowledge acquisition, integration, construction, and application
- Dimensions: understanding knowledge from a range of disciplines; connecting knowledge

to other knowledge, ideas, and experiences; constructing knowledge; and relating knowledge to daily life

Domain: cognitive complexity
- Dimensions: critical thinking, reflective thinking, effective reasoning, and creativity

Domain: intrapersonal development
- Dimensions: realistic self-appraisal, self-understanding, and self-respect; identity development; commitment to ethics and integrity; and spiritual awareness

Domain: interpersonal competence
- Dimensions: meaningful relationships, interdependence, collaboration, and effective leadership

Domain: humanitarianism and civic engagement
- Dimensions: understanding and appreciation of cultural and human differences, social responsibility, global perspective, and sense of civic responsibility

Domain: practical competence
- Dimensions: pursuing goals, communicating effectively, technical competence, managing personal affairs, managing career development, demonstrating professionalism, maintaining health and wellness, and living a purposeful and satisfying life

[LD Outcomes: See *The Council for the Advancement of Standards Learning and Development Outcomes* statement for examples of outcomes related to these domains and dimensions.]

VMPS must be
- intentionally designed
- guided by theories and knowledge of learning and development
- integrated into the life of the institution
- reflective of developmental and demographic profiles of the student population
- responsive to needs of individuals, populations with distinct needs, and relevant constituencies
- delivered using multiple formats, strategies, and contexts
- designed to provide universal access

VMPS must collaborate with colleagues and departments across the institution to promote student learning and development, persistence, and success.

Part 3. Organization and Leadership

Veterans and Military Programs and Services (VMPS) leaders must be knowledgeable about and responsive to the needs and experiences of student veterans, military service members, and their family members. VMPS must advise decision-makers and advocate for institutional policies and procedures that address these issues.

VMPS leaders should have a working knowledge of relevant governmental organizational structures and processes to advocate for student veterans, military service members, and their families.

To achieve program and student learning and development outcomes, VMPS must be purposefully structured for effectiveness. VMPS must have clearly stated and current
- goals and outcomes
- policies and procedures
- responsibilities and performance expectations for personnel
- organizational charts demonstrating clear channels of authority

Leaders must model ethical behavior and institutional citizenship.

Leaders with organizational authority for VMPS must provide strategic planning, management and supervision, and program advancement.

Strategic Planning
- articulate a vision and mission that drive short- and long-term planning
- set goals and objectives based on the needs of the populations served, intended student learning and development outcomes, and program outcomes
- facilitate continuous development, implementation, and assessment of program effectiveness and goal attainment congruent with institutional mission and strategic plans
- promote environments that provide opportunities for student learning, development, and engagement
- develop, adapt, and improve programs and services in response to the changing needs of populations served and evolving institutional priorities
- include diverse perspectives to inform decision making

Management and Supervision
- plan, allocate, and monitor the use of fiscal, physical, human, intellectual, and technological resources
- manage human resource processes including recruitment, selection, professional development, supervision, performance planning, succession planning, evaluation, recognition, and reward
- influence others to contribute to the effectiveness and success of the unit
- empower professional, support, and student personnel to become effective leaders
- encourage and support collaboration with colleagues and departments across the institution
- encourage and support scholarly contributions to the profession
- identify and address individual, organizational, and environmental conditions that foster or inhibit mission achievement
- use current and valid evidence to inform decisions

- incorporate sustainability practices in the management and design of programs, services, and facilities
- understand appropriate technologies and integrate them into programs and services
- be knowledgeable about codes and laws relevant to programs and services and ensure that programs and services meet those requirements
- assess and take action to mitigate potential risks

Program Advancement
- advocate for and actively promote the mission and goals of the programs and services
- inform stakeholders about issues affecting practice
- facilitate processes to reach consensus where wide support is needed
- advocate for representation in strategic planning initiatives at divisional and institutional levels

VMPS must serve as a primary point of contact to serve student veterans, military service members, and their family members. In institutions with multiple service providers, the VMPS must collaborate to ensure resources and support.

Institutions with small numbers of military members and veterans should maximize services by collaborating with other post-secondary institutions and community agencies.

Part 4. Human Resources

Veterans and Military Programs and Services (VMPS) must be highly visible to student veterans, military service members, and their family members with at least one staff member to serve as an institutional single point of contact to coordinate services, provide advice, and advocate for students with issues related to their military experiences and student status.

VMPS must be staffed adequately by individuals qualified to accomplish mission and goals.

VMPS staff must possess the knowledge and skills to assist student veterans, military service members, and their family members with transition and orientation to campus and to address the needs of veterans with disabilities.

VMPS staff should have experience with issues related to student veterans, military service members, and their family members.

VMPS should identify and promote student employment opportunities and career transition opportunities to support student veterans, military service members, and their family members. When possible, VMPS should identify and hire students eligible for work-study programs for veterans.

VMPS must have access to technical and support personnel adequate to accomplish their mission.

Within institutional guidelines, VMPS must
- establish procedures for personnel recruitment and selection, training, performance planning, and evaluation
- set expectations for supervision and performance
- provide personnel access to continuing and advanced education and appropriate professional development opportunities to improve their competence, skills, and leadership capacity
- consider work/life options available to personnel (e.g., compressed work schedules, flextime, job sharing, remote work, or telework) to promote recruitment and retention of personnel

Administrators of VMPS must
- ensure that all personnel have updated position descriptions
- implement recruitment and selection/hiring strategies that produce a workforce inclusive of under-represented populations
- develop promotion practices that are fair, inclusive, proactive, and non-discriminatory

Personnel responsible for delivery of VMPS must have written performance goals, objectives, and outcomes for each year's performance cycle to be used to plan, review, and evaluate work and performance. The performance plan must be updated regularly to reflect changes during the performance cycle.

Results of individual personnel evaluations must be used to recognize personnel performance, address performance issues, implement individual and/or collective personnel development and training programs, and inform the assessment of programs and services.

VMPS personnel, when hired and throughout their employment, must receive appropriate and thorough training.

VMPS personnel, including student employees and volunteers, must have access to resources or receive specific training on
- institutional policies pertaining to functions or activities they support
- privacy and confidentiality policies
- laws regarding access to student records
- policies and procedures for dealing with sensitive institutional information
- policies and procedures related to technology used to store or access student records and institutional data
- how and when to refer those in need of additional assistance to qualified personnel and have access to a supervisor for assistance in making these judgments
- systems and technologies necessary to perform their assigned responsibilities
- ethical and legal uses of technology

VMPS personnel must engage in continuing professional development activities to keep abreast of the research, theories, legislation, policies, and developments that affect their programs and services.

Administrators of VMPS must ensure that personnel are knowledgeable about and trained in safety, emergency procedures, and crisis prevention and response. Risk management efforts must address identification of threatening conduct or behavior and must incorporate a system for responding to and reporting such behaviors.

VMPS personnel must be knowledgeable of and trained in safety and emergency procedures for securing and vacating facilities.

PROFESSIONAL PERSONNEL

VMPS professional personnel either must hold an earned graduate or professional degree in a field relevant to their position or must possess an appropriate combination of educational credentials and related work experience.

INTERNS OR GRADUATE ASSISTANTS

Degree- or credential-seeking interns or graduate assistants must be qualified by enrollment in an appropriate field of study and relevant experience. These students must be trained and supervised by professional personnel who possess applicable educational credentials and work experience and have supervisory experience. Supervisors must be cognizant of the dual roles interns and graduate assistants have as both student and employee.

Supervisors must
- adhere to parameters of students' job descriptions
- articulate intended learning outcomes in student job descriptions
- adhere to agreed-upon work hours and schedules
- offer flexible scheduling when circumstances necessitate

Supervisors and students must both agree to suitable compensation if circumstances necessitate additional hours.

STUDENT EMPLOYEES AND VOLUNTEERS

Student employees and volunteers must be carefully selected, trained, supervised, and evaluated. Students must have access to a supervisor. Student employees and volunteers must be provided clear job descriptions, pre-service training based on assessed needs, and continuing development.

Part 5. Ethics

Veterans and Military Programs and Services (VMPS) must
- review applicable professional ethical standards and must adopt or develop and implement appropriate statements of ethical practice
- publish and adhere to statements of ethical practice and ensure their periodic review
- orient new personnel to relevant ethical standards and statements of ethical practice and related institutional policies

Statements of ethical standards must
- specify that VMPS personnel respect privacy and

maintain confidentiality in communications and records as delineated by privacy laws
- specify limits on disclosure of information contained in students' records as well as requirements to disclose to appropriate authorities
- address conflicts of interest, or appearance thereof, by personnel in the performance of their work
- reflect the responsibility of personnel to be fair, objective, and impartial in their interactions with others
- reference management of institutional funds
- reference appropriate behavior regarding research and assessment with human participants, confidentiality of research and assessment data, and students' rights and responsibilities
- include the expectation that personnel confront and hold accountable other personnel who exhibit unethical behavior
- address issues surrounding scholarly integrity

VMPS personnel must
- employ ethical decision making in the performance of their duties
- inform users of programs and services of ethical obligations and limitations emanating from codes and laws or from licensure requirements
- recognize and avoid conflicts of interest that could adversely influence their judgment or objectivity and, when unavoidable, recuse themselves from the situation
- perform their duties within the scope of their position, training, expertise, and competence
- make referrals when issues presented exceed the scope of the position

Part 6. Law, Policy, and Governance

Veterans and Military Programs and Services (VMPS) must be aware of applicable laws affecting student veterans, military service members, and their family members, including educational benefits. VMPS must refer student veterans to the institution's veterans benefits certifying official for application and certification of benefits.

VMPS should maintain awareness of changes to entitlement programs and statute-based tuition discounting such as tuition benefits and communicate these to student veterans, military service members, and their family members.

VMPS must be in compliance with laws, regulations, and policies that relate to their respective responsibilities and that pose legal obligations, limitations, risks, and liabilities for the institution as a whole. Examples include constitutional, statutory, regulatory, and case law; relevant law and orders emanating from codes and laws; and the institution's policies.

VMPS must have access to legal advice needed for personnel to carry out their assigned responsibilities.

VMPS must inform personnel, appropriate officials, and

users of programs and services about existing and changing legal obligations, risks and liabilities, and limitations.

VMPS must inform personnel about professional liability insurance options and refer them to external sources if the institution does not provide coverage.

VMPS must have written policies and procedures on operations, transactions, or tasks that have legal implications.

VMPS must regularly review policies. The revision and creation of policies must be informed by best practices, available evidence, and policy issues in higher education.

VMPS must have procedures and guidelines consistent with institutional policy for responding to threats, emergencies, and crisis situations. Systems and procedures must be in place to disseminate timely and accurate information to students, other members of the institutional community, and appropriate external organizations during emergency situations.

Personnel must neither participate in nor condone any form of harassment or activity that demeans persons or creates an intimidating, hostile, or offensive environment.

VMPS must purchase or obtain permission to use copyrighted materials and instruments. References to copyrighted materials and instruments must include appropriate citations.

VMPS must inform personnel about internal and external governance organizations that affect programs and services.

Part 7. Diversity, Equity, and Access

Veterans and Military Programs and Services (VMPS) must coordinate with units providing disability related services to ensure access to relevant programs and services for veterans with disabilities.

VMPS should coordinate with units providing disability related services about the use of services by veterans and military service members assumed to have a disability but lacking documentation.

VMPS should work with students to obtain required disability documentation in accordance with the institution's documentation guidelines for students with disabilities.

Within the context of each institution's mission and in accordance with institutional policies and applicable codes and laws, VMPS must create and maintain educational and work environments that are welcoming, accessible, inclusive, equitable, and free from harassment.

VMPS must not discriminate on the basis of disability; age; race; cultural identity; ethnicity; nationality; family educational history (e.g., first generation to attend college); political affiliation; religious affiliation; sex; sexual orientation; gender identity and expression; marital, social, economic, or veteran status; or any other basis included in institutional policies and codes and laws.

VMPS must

- advocate for sensitivity to multicultural and social justice concerns by the institution and its personnel
- ensure physical, program, and resource access for all constituents
- modify or remove policies, practices, systems, technologies, facilities, and structures that create barriers or produce inequities
- ensure that when facilities and structures cannot be modified, they do not impede access to programs, services, and resources
- establish goals for diversity, equity, and access
- foster communication and practices that enhance understanding of identity, culture, self-expression, and heritage
- promote respect for commonalities and differences among people within their historical and cultural contexts
- address the characteristics and needs of diverse constituents when establishing and implementing culturally relevant and inclusive programs, services, policies, procedures, and practices
- provide personnel with diversity, equity, and access training and hold personnel accountable for applying the training to their work
- respond to the needs of all constituents served when establishing hours of operation and developing methods of delivering programs, services, and resources
- recognize the needs of distance and online learning students by directly providing or assisting them to gain access to comparable services and resources

In this context, diverse groups include partners of disabled and deceased service members and single parents. VMPS should coordinate provision of services to diverse military service members with various organizations, centers, and other appropriate venues on campus that serve those populations.

Part 8. Internal and External Relations

Veterans and Military Programs and Services (VMPS) must reach out to individuals, groups, communities, and organizations internal and external to the institution to

- establish, maintain, and promote understanding and effective relations with those that have a significant interest in or potential effect on the students or other constituents served by the programs and services
- garner support and resources for programs and services as defined by the mission
- collaborate in offering or improving programs and services to meet the needs of students and other constituents and to achieve program and student outcomes
- engage diverse individuals, groups, communities, and organizations to enrich the educational environment and experiences of students and other

constituents
- disseminate information about the programs and services

Promotional and descriptive information must be accurate and free of deception and misrepresentation.

VMPS must have procedures and guidelines consistent with institutional policy for
- communicating with the media
- distributing information through print, broadcast, and online sources
- contracting with external organizations for delivery of programs and services
- cultivating, soliciting, and managing gifts
- applying to and managing funds from grants

VMPS must work with the office of admissions to coordinate and address the needs and issues of student veterans, military members, and their matriculated family members.

VMPS should advocate for the inclusion of questions on the admission application regarding anticipated status at the time of enrollment – active duty, veteran, member of the Guard or reserve, or military dependent.

VMPS should advocate for consideration of military experience and training in admissions decisions.

VMPS must advocate for flexible policies to deal with the deployment of military service members and work with the institutional registrar to ensure the effectiveness of withdrawal and course-completion procedures, including withdrawals, incomplete grades, and awarding of partial credit.

VMPS must work with academic services to facilitate advising, tutoring assistance, and supplemental instruction for student veterans, military service members, and their matriculated family members.

VMPS must advocate for awarding credit for previous military training and experience.

Articulation agreements should use documents similar to the American Council of Education Guide to the Evaluation of Educational Experiences in the Armed Services.

VMPS should be aware of national testing programs such as College Level Examination Program (CLEP), DANTES Subject Standardized Tests (DSST), and Excelsior College Examinations (ECE).

VMPS must advocate for clear and facilitative articulation agreements between home institutions and colleges and universities providing education to military members serving on active duty.

Articulation agreements should avoid both excessive loss of previously earned credit and duplication of coursework.

VMPS should advocate for policies that consider and recognize civilian courses taken and formal training obtained while in the military.

VMPS should coordinate with various institutional departments to facilitate the resolution of grades from students' final semesters and the potential posthumous awarding of degrees for students who die while in military service.

VMPS must work with the campus career services and other units to identify or develop specific programs and opportunities that support career planning and employment.

VMPS must work with campus units to encourage student veterans, military service members, and their family members in campus-wide social and cultural events, academic programs, orientation programs, and other activities designed to ease the transition to campus life.

VMPS should work with student affairs and other co-curricular units to tailor some programs to meet the specific needs of student veterans, military service members, and their family members.

VMPS must assist student veterans, military service members, and their family members to find appropriate on- and off-campus psychological counseling and mental health care service providers and advocate for specialized training for campus providers dealing with mental health issues affecting this population.

VMPS should advocate for institutional counseling resources to be knowledgeable of veterans' issues, e.g., Post-Traumatic Stress Disorder (PTSD), Combat Stress Reaction (CSR), and Traumatic Brain Injury (TBI), and post deployment transition challenges.

VMPS must advocate for and work with the bursar to ensure deferment of tuition and fees for students when education benefits are delayed beyond normal payment due dates or for military withdrawals due to activation.

VMPS may advocate for tuition discounting for student veterans, military service, members, and their matriculated family members.

VMPS should assist in addressing the financial aid needs and issues of student veterans, military service members, and their family matriculated members.

VMPS should collaborate with the institution's foundation and development offices to identify or establish scholarships for veterans and other financial support pools and establish procedures for their disbursement to qualified students.

When an institution has determined that it can provide the necessary services, VMPS must participate in institutional recruitment efforts, including establishment of marketing and outreach strategies to enroll student veterans, military service members, and their family members.

VMPS should work with institutional outreach services such as lifelong learning and distance education units to bring academic programs to mobilized and deployed military service members.

VMPS may advocate for reducing academic residency requirements by eliminating on-campus degree requirements, supporting 100 percent on-line degrees and eliminating final-year or semester-in-residence requirements for student veterans, military service members, and matriculated family members.

VMPS staff must establish a working relationship with the institutional veterans benefits certifying official, if this position is separate from VMPS.

VMPS must work with the Veterans Affairs offices and serve as liaisons between the campus and the Veterans Affairs education office in providing services for student veterans.

VMPS should coordinate opportunities for recruitment, academic advising, and admissions counseling with military bases and National Guard units in the area.

VMPS should communicate with programs and services at peer institutions to develop and implement additional best practices to serve veterans, military service members, and their families.

Part 9. Financial Resources

Veterans and Military Programs and Services (VMPS) must have funding to accomplish the mission and goals.

In establishing and prioritizing funding resources, VMPS must conduct comprehensive analyses to determine
- **unmet needs of the unit**
- **relevant expenditures**
- **external and internal resources**
- **impact on students and the institution**

VMPS must use the budget as a planning tool to reflect commitment to the mission and goals of the programs and services and of the institution.

VMPS must administer funds in accordance with established institutional accounting procedures.

VMPS must demonstrate efficient and effective use and responsible stewardship of fiscal resources consistent with institutional protocols.

Financial reports must provide an accurate financial overview of the organization and provide clear, understandable, and timely data upon which personnel can plan and make informed decisions.

Procurement procedures must
- **be consistent with institutional policies**
- **ensure that purchases comply with laws and codes for usability and access**
- **ensure that the institution receives value for the funds spent**
- **consider information available for comparing the ethical and environmental impact of products and services purchased**

Adequate funds should be provided for the following budget categories: staff and student salaries, general office functions, student assessment activities, data management and program evaluation processes, staff training and professional development activities, instructional materials and media, information technology, and office technology.

VMPS should explore state/provincial or federal funding sources or write grant proposals to support the service. In the event the VMPS receives a start-up grant, a financial plan should be developed to sustain the operation after the term of the grant.

External funding sources should not be expected to supplant institutional funding.

Part 10. Technology

Veterans and Military Programs and Services (VMPS) must have technology to support the achievement of their mission and goals. The technology and its use must comply with institutional policies and procedures and with relevant codes and laws.

VMPS must use technologies to
- **provide updated information regarding mission, location, staffing, programs, services, and official contacts to students and other constituents in accessible formats**
- **provide an avenue for students and other constituents to communicate sensitive information in a secure format**
- **enhance the delivery of programs and services for all students**

VMPS must
- **back up data on a regular basis**
- **adhere to institutional policies regarding ethical and legal use of technology**
- **articulate policies and procedures for protecting the confidentiality and security of information**
- **implement a replacement plan and cycle for all technology with attention to sustainability**
- **incorporate accessibility features into technology-based programs and services**

When providing student access to technology, VMPS must
- **have policies on the use of technology that are clear, easy to understand, and available to all students**
- **provide information or referral to support services for those needing assistance in accessing or using technology**
- **provide instruction or training on how to use the technology**
- **inform students of implications of misuse of technologies**

VMPS must maintain an Internet presence with information to ease the transition of student veterans, military service members, and their families into higher education. VMPS web pages must provide timely and

accurate information regarding programs and services offered by the institution and must connect the student to external resources for veterans.

Communication must be accurate in describing program requirements and pre-requisites, costs, payment and refund policies, partnerships with military or government agencies, and occupational opportunities for program graduates.

VMPS web information should include links to governmental veterans administration agencies and institutional web links with services for student veterans, military service members, and their families.

VMPS should advocate for technology that supports distance learning for mobilized or deployed students.

Part 11. Facilities and Equipment

Veterans and Military Programs and Services' (VMPS) facilities must be intentionally designed and located in suitable, accessible, and safe spaces that demonstrate universal design and support the program's mission and goals.

The VMPS center should be centrally located and in proximity to institutional student support services.

VMPS should establish a dedicated physical space where student veterans military service members and their family members can congregate, seek academic support services, and complete assigned coursework. The space should be safe, with easily identifiable and accessible exits, and located near the VMPS center and other student organization offices.

Facilities must be designed to engage various constituents and promote learning.

Personnel must have workspaces that are suitably located and accessible, well equipped, adequate in size, and designed to support their work and responsibilities.

The design of the facilities must guarantee the security and privacy of records and ensure the confidentiality of sensitive information and conversations. Personnel must be able to secure their work.

VMPS must incorporate sustainable practices in use of facilities and purchase of equipment. Facilities and equipment must be evaluated on an established cycle and be in compliance with codes, laws, and accepted practices for access, health, safety, and security.

When acquiring capital equipment, VMPS must take into account expenses related to regular maintenance and life cycle costs.

Part 12. Assessment

Veterans and Military Programs and Services (VMPS) must develop assessment plans and processes.

Assessment plans must articulate an ongoing cycle of assessment activities.

VMPS must

- specify programmatic goals and intended outcomes
- identify student learning and development outcomes
- employ multiple measures and methods
- develop manageable processes for gathering, interpreting, and evaluating data
- document progress toward achievement of goals and outcomes
- interpret and use assessment results to demonstrate accountability
- report aggregated results to respondent groups and stakeholders
- use assessment results to inform planning and decision-making
- assess effectiveness of implemented changes
- provide evidence of improvement of programs and services

VMPS must employ ethical practices in the assessment process.

VMPS must have access to adequate fiscal, human, professional development, and technological resources to develop and implement assessment plans.

General Standards revised in 2014;
VMPS content developed/approved in 2010

Women's and Gender Programs and Services
CAS Contextual Statement

Sexism persists in North American colleges and universities, revealing itself in institutional structures, policies, and practices, as well as campus cultures that privilege some and disadvantage others. For many generations, North American colleges and universities were open only to a discrete subset of men. This legacy of gender inequity continues to shape the college experience, despite women students now being the numerical majority on most campuses (Allen, Dean, & Bracken, 2008); as Vlasnik points out, "the *quantity* of women in higher education is a different discussion than the *quality* of their experience" (2011, p. 24). Women and men experience college differently (Sax, 2008), and traditional gender socialization narrows access and opportunities on campuses in ways that reinforce stereotypes and disproportionately limit women and other campus constituents facing gender-based oppression. The term *women* is inclusive of all individuals who identify as women and the term *men* is inclusive of all individuals who identify as men, regardless of their biological sex or sex assigned at birth. The intersection of sexism with other forms of systematic oppression further impacts the collegiate experience for all. Addressing these and related issues by supporting women and individuals of all gender identities, educating the campus community about women's and gender issues, and advocating for gender equity at the institutional level are just some of the unique roles that Women's and Gender Programs and Services (WGPS) play in the academy.

Women's and Gender Programs and Services refer to campus offices that advance gender equity and support women and other campus constituents facing gender-based oppression. These offices include women's centers, centers for gender, offices for women, and other units in higher education settings that address gender-related issues and concerns. Such programs are housed within colleges and universities across the U.S., including public and private institutions, two-year and four-year schools, historically black colleges and universities, tribal institutions, Hispanic-serving institutions, Asian American- and Pacific Islander-serving institutions, institutions serving deaf and hard of hearing students, and those serving blind and visually impaired students. Approximately 500 such programs exist in U.S. higher education (National Women's Studies Association, n.d., in Vlasnik, 2010); similar organizations also exist in higher education in other countries. The first women's center in the U.S. was established in 1960 at the University of Minnesota (Bonebright, Cottledge, & Lonnquist, 2012) at the cusp of an era of tremendous change in higher education. WGPS serve as catalysts and leaders of positive institutional change; women's centers, one form of WGPS, have been named the "very heart of feminist engagement with the academy" (Marine, 2011, p. 16).

Women's and Gender Programs and Services are established on campuses as a result of concerns about gender equity raised by students, administrators, faculty, staff, alumnae/alumni, and community members. Informed by women's, African American, LGBT+ (lesbian, gay, bisexual, transgender, and sexual and gender minorities), and other civil rights movements, WGPS are developed to respond to individual and institutional needs to support women and other campus constituents facing gender-based oppression in achieving their educational goals, encouraging engaging in broader fields of study and promoting into leadership positions, and advancing issues of gender equity in higher education. In addition, WGPS have initiated important conversations about masculinities, men's roles as allies, and the specific needs of transgender women, transgender men, and other individuals facing gender-based oppression. Reporting lines for Women's and Gender Programs and Services differ among institutions, with some embedded in the missions and services of divisions of student affairs and others with reporting lines reflecting other institutional organizational structures such as academic affairs or diversity/multicultural affairs (see Goettsch, Linden, Vanzant, & Waugh, 2012, for discussion of structures and name changes).

In recent decades, scholars and practitioners have debated the use of the term *women* both in the field of women's and gender studies as well as in naming campus centers, offices, and programs that address gender issues. Some prioritize the importance of directly naming the primary target of sexism and gender discrimination by using the term *women* (as in women's center). Others assert that use of the term *women* reproduces an essentialist framework that privileges a monolithic category of women while the term *gender* (as in gender studies and gender equity center) is more inclusive of all individuals and their diverse experiences of gender, and of gender-based inequity and discrimination. For some, the term *gender* in program names also more explicitly draws attention to masculinities and services for men and gender diverse individuals, which women's centers have provided to varying degrees. Others have observed that replacing the term *women* with *gender* could erase the history of the struggle to put women's lives and experiences at the center of attention, opening the door to co-opting the goals of that movement and shifting resources, energy, and attention away from addressing the status of women (Berger & Radeloff, 2011). There is a similarly complex dialogue regarding the naming, configuration, and delivery of programs and services at the intersection of gender and sexuality.

In 2015, CAS chose to change the name of the functional area from "Women Student Programs and Services" to "Women's and Gender Programs and Services." The addition of *gender* to the name acknowledges the above debate regarding the use of the terms *women* and *gender* in program names. The elimination of *student* acknowledges the broader focus of some programs to include faculty, staff, alumnae/alumni, and/or community members in their missions. The name change for this functional area does not compel campus-based programs or units to alter their names; institutions should name WGPS units to reflect the unique mission, needs, history, and culture of their institution.

Women's and Gender Programs and Services have varied missions that express the unique cultures and goals of the institutions within which they reside. Most of them include in their mission the need to address equity, including institutional change; education, including equal access, affordability, recruitment, retention, and professional development; support and advocacy; personal safety; and the development of community (Kunkel, 1994, 2002). There is no single form for WGPS, yet there are many shared commitments, tenets, goals, and practices. In 2010, Ohio women's centers created and published a shared philosophy statement that for the first time brought diverse centers and programs together to self-define their collective work. It reads in full:

> Women's centers reflect the unique needs of their institutions and communities, yet share a commitment to historically underserved individuals and groups. Additionally, women's centers play a leadership role in understanding the changing workplace and preparing members of the university community to engage successfully with an increasingly complex world. Women's centers are integral to transforming institutions into inclusive environments; through community-building, advocacy, education, support, and research, they encourage the full participation and success of women. (Vlasnik, 2010, p. 5)

The statement points to the ongoing importance and impact of WGPS on their institutions and on individuals of all gender identities.

Supporting the success of women students and other campus constituents facing gender-based oppression involves working with individuals of all gender identities to raise awareness about and contribute to cultural change related to gender issues more broadly, and addressing concerns that affect all members of a campus community and beyond, including alumnae/alumni, community organizations and the public at large. Additionally, the unique experiences of women and other constituents facing gender-based oppression require that WGPS—regardless of their reporting structures—engage with every element of campus life, including collaborating with academic, administrative, student affairs, and other co-curricular units, as well as student-based organizations. Women's and Gender Programs and Services are informed by a broad range of academic disciplines and professions. It is important to note that WGPS draw on information from scholars and practitioners whose work is often interdisciplinary in nature, foregrounds an analysis of power and privilege, and recognizes the impact of intersectionality on research, teaching, and activism. In addition, WGPS serve as locations for exploring the connection between theory and practice. This exploration is also predicated on their connections to a wide range of activist movements. Ultimately, WGPS are dedicated to advancing knowledge of how historical and current imbalances of power among genders impact equity issues, both on campus and in society, with the goal of helping all people to reach their full potential.

When Women's and Gender Programs and Services were first founded, they tended to focus on access (i.e., assisting women in gaining entrance into academic institutions both as students and personnel), equity, and the tenets outlined by Kunkel (1994, 2002). Addressing barriers to access and equity remain central to the missions of WGPS. However, because the manifestations of these issues on contemporary campuses have changed, WGPS have responded to address the following current issues and concerns:

- Supporting access for and the success of specific groups of women who remain underrepresented in higher education (e.g., Buford, 1988; Chuang, 2010; Keller & Rogers, 1983);
- Fostering the full integration of women and other constituents facing gender-based oppression once they are on campus;
- Advocating for equity and critiquing and challenging social constructions of gender
- Exploring and deepening their relationships with academic programs, particularly women's and gender studies (e.g., Cook, 1998; Green, 2002; Parker & Freedman, 1999; Zaytoun Byrne, 2000);
- Educating about and exploring the fluidity and diversity of gender identities and expressions;
- Challenging the explicit and implicit biases and stereotypes that continue to hinder women's academic and career progress in higher education leadership and male-dominated fields such as science, technology, engineering and math (Hill, Corbett, & St. Rose, 2010);
- Responding to the expanding participation in the discourse around masculinities, and cultivating partnerships in which men self-define and act as allies for gender equity and social justice;
- Exploring leadership, internationalization, and technology in their programs and services (Davie, 2002; see Bonebright et al., 2012);
- Building the field of WGPS work by focusing on the professional development, preparation, and experiences of WGPS staff (e.g., Marine, 2011; Vlasnik & DeButz, 2013); and
- Continuing to identify and explore emerging issues and concerns related to women, gender, and gender equity on college and university campuses.

While Women's and Gender Programs and Services work to address the above issues, WGPS do so in their historical context and roots in social justice, community activism, and social change efforts, as well as in student development theory and administrative leadership practice.

Acknowledging the immense potential of higher education to improve the lives of people of all gender identities and gender expressions, WGPS translate the richness of feminist and womanist community organization- and movement-based work to college and university settings, demonstrating the relevance of women and their many contributions to all aspects of higher education. Through support, advocacy, and education, WGPS address sexual assault and other forms of power-based personal violence, sexual harassment, gender discrimination, sexism, cisgenderism, and other barriers to student academic achievement that disproportionately impact the success of women and other students facing gender-based oppression. With a commitment to the continuous examination of power, privilege, interlocking oppressions, and the intersection of gender with other identities, WGPS seek to support and advocate for the positive educational experiences of all members of college and university communities while simultaneously maintaining a specific focus on gender and women. As a result of this intersectional framework, traditionally under-served, underrepresented, and marginalized populations across gender identities engage in and benefit from WGPS. Individuals whose salient identity may not be gender often gravitate towards the educational and activist activities and/or seek support and advocacy provided by WGPS in order to succeed on campus.

Obtaining and sustaining funding and resources sufficient to fully actualize the missions of Women's and Gender Programs and Services remains one of the most significant challenges facing these programs. This is a particular concern in light of women comprising the majority of students enrolled in colleges and universities in the U.S. but the minority of faculty in the senior ranks and individuals in academic and administrative leadership positions. Coalition work, which is both integral to WGPS and a method for addressing limited resources, strategically engages partners in WGPS work to dismantle intersecting oppression, deepen the quality and impact of their work, and advance shared priorities and projects that serve their constituents and institutions. WGPS assume leadership roles in advocating for campus climate assessments and policy change at the institutional level and in forming collaborations to accelerate institutional changes so that campuses are inclusive of all their members.

References, Readings, and Resources

Allen, J. K., Dean, D. R., & Bracken, S. J. (2008). *Most college students are women: Implications for teaching, learning, and policy*. Sterling, VA: Stylus.

American Association of University Women, http://www.aauw.org

Berger, M. T., & Radeloff, C. (2011). *Transforming scholarship: Why women's and gender studies students are changing themselves and the world*. New York, NY: Routledge.

Bonebright, D. A., Cottledge, A. D., & Lonnquist, P. (2012). Developing women leaders on campus: A Human Resources-Women's Center partnership at the University of Minnesota. *Advances in Developing Human Resources, 14*(1), 79-95. doi: 10.1177/1523422311429733

Buford, C. (1988, Summer). Multicultural programming in a university women's center. *Initiatives, 51*(2/3), 31-35.

Campus Women Lead, http://www.aacu.org/campuswomenlead

Chuang, I. (2010, July). Asian women students' group: Success through mutual support. *Women in Higher Education, 19*(7), 19.

College and University Professional Association for Human Resources (CUPA-HR): http://www.cupahr.org/surveys

College Student Educators International (ACPA) Standing Committee for Women: http://www.myacpa.org/scw

Cook, S. (1998, April). Women's center partners with academics for reality. *Women in Higher Education, 7*(4), 20.

Davie, S. L. (2002). Drawing new maps. In S. L. Davie (Ed.), *University and college women's centers: A journey toward equity* (pp. 447-458). Westport, CT: Greenwood Press.

Goettsch, J., Linden, A., Vanzant, C., & Waugh, P. (2012, June). *Campus women's centers for the twenty-first century: Structural issues and trends* (Issue Brief No. 03). Cincinnati, OH: Greater Cincinnati Consortium of Colleges and Universities and Southwestern Ohio Council for Higher Education. Retrieved from http://www.gcccu.org/committees/womens-studies.cfm and https://soche.org/members/councils-and-committees/womens-centers-committee

Green, D. (2002, November). Experiential learning connects women's studies to centers. *Women in Higher Education, 11*(11), 27.

Hill, C., Corbett, C., & St. Rose, A. (2010). *Why so few? Women in science, technology, engineering and math*. Washington, D.C.: American Association of University Women.

Keller, M. J., & Rogers, J. L. (1983, November). The awareness, impressions, and use of a campus women's center by traditional and nontraditional women students. *Journal of College Student Personnel, 24*(6), 550-556.

Kunkel, C. A. (1994). Women's needs on campus: How universities meet them. *Initiatives, 56*(2), 15-28.

Kunkel, C. A. (2002). Starting a women's center: Key issues. In S. L. Davie (Ed.), *University and college women's centers: A journey toward equity* (pp. 65-78). Westport, CT: Greenwood Press.

Marine, S. (2011). Reflections from "professional feminists" in higher education: Women's and gender centers at the start of the twenty-first century. In P. A. Pasque & S. Errington Nicholson (Eds.), *Empowering women in higher education and student affairs: Theory, research, narratives, and practice from feminist perspectives* (pp. 15-31). Sterling, VA: Stylus Publishing.

National Council for Research on Women (NCRW): www.ncrw.org

National Women's Studies Association (NWSA): www.nwsa.org

NWSA Women's Centers Committee Blog: nwsawcc.wordpress.com/

Parker, J., & Freedman, J. (1999). Women's centers/women's studies programs: Collaborating for feminist activism. *Women's Studies Quarterly, 27*(3/4), 114-121.

Sax, L. J. (2008). *The gender gap in college: Maximizing the developmental potential of men and women*. San Francisco, CA: Jossey-Bass.

Student Affairs Administrators in Higher Education (NASPA) Center for Women: http://www.naspa.org/constituent-groups/groups/center-for-women

Student Affairs Administrators in Higher Education (NASPA) Women in Student Affairs (WISA) Knowledge Community: http://www.naspa.org/constituent-groups/kcs/women-in-student-affairs

Vlasnik, A. L. (2010, May). *Ohio women's centers: Statement of philosophy* (Issue Brief No. 01). Cincinnati, OH: Greater Cincinnati Consortium of Colleges and Universities and Southwestern Ohio Council for Higher Education. Retrieved from http://www.gcccu.org/committees/womens-studies.cfm and https://soche.org/members/councils-and-committees/womens-centers-committee

Vlasnik, A. L. (2011). Historical constructs of gender and work: Informing access and equity in U.S. higher education. In J. L. Martin (Ed.), *Women as leaders in education: Succeeding despite inequity, discrimination, and other challenges: Vol. 1. Women's leadership in higher education* (pp. 23-44). Santa Barbara, CA: Praeger.

Vlasnik, A. L., & DeButz, M. D. (2013, December). *Professional competencies of women's center staff* (Issue Brief No. 04). Cincinnati, OH: Greater Cincinnati Consortium of Colleges and Universities and Southwestern Ohio Council for Higher Education. Retrieved from http://www.gcccu.org/committees/womens-studies.cfm and https://soche.org/members/councils-

and-committees/womens-centers-committee

Women's Centers in U.S. Higher Education Bibliography: http://www.nwsa.org/research

WRAC-L: The Women's Resource and Action Centers Group: http://nwsawcc.wordpress.com/wrac-l/

Zaytoun Byrne, K. (2000). The roles of campus-based women's centers. *Feminist Teacher, 13*(1), 48-60.

Contextual Statement Contributors

Current Edition:

Jane Goettsch, Miami University

Kathleen Holgerson, University of Connecticut

Rebecca Morrow, West Virginia School of Osteopathic Medicine, NWSA

Kathy Rose-Mockry, University of Kansas

Cathy Seasholes, University of Wisconsin - Milwaukee, NWSA

Amber L. Vlasnik, Wright State University

Previous Editions:

Brenda Bethman, Texas A&M University

Chimi Boyd, North Carolina Central University

Janine Cavicchia, Western Illinois University

Peg Lonnquist, University of Minnesota

Corrie Martin, University of the Pacific

Rebecca Morrow, Idaho State University

Ellen Plummer, Virginia Tech University

Beth Rietveld, Oregon State University

Claire K. Robbins, University of Maryland

Cathy Seasholes, University of Wisconsin – Milwaukee

Nora Spencer, Vanderbilt University

Amber L. Vlasnik, Wright State University

Jennifer Wies, Xavier University

Women's and Gender Programs and Services
CAS Standards and Guidelines

The purpose of Women's and Gender Programs and Services (WGPS) is to advance gender equity, educate the campus community about women's and gender issues, and promote a supportive and safe environment for women and all campus constituents facing gender-based oppression.

The term women is inclusive of all individuals who identify as women and the term men is inclusive of all individuals who identify as men, regardless of their biological sex or sex assigned at birth. College and university campuses have youth visitors/participants and some WGPS work directly with youth so in these Standards the term women is also inclusive of girls, when relevant.

Education, advocacy and support should serve as the guiding framework for WGPS service delivery, partnerships and priorities.

WPGS must develop, disseminate, implement, and regularly review their missions, which must be consistent with the mission of the institution and with applicable professional standards. The mission must be appropriate for the institution's students and other constituents. Mission statements must reference student learning and development.

To achieve their mission, Women's and Gender Programs and Services (WGPS) must contribute to
- students' formal education, which includes both the curriculum and the co-curriculum
- student progression and timely completion of educational goals
- preparation of students for their careers, citizenship, and lives
- student learning and development

To contribute to student learning and development, WGPS must
- identify relevant and desirable student learning and development outcomes
- articulate how the student learning and development outcomes align with the six CAS student learning and development domains and related dimensions
- assess relevant and desirable student learning and development
- provide evidence of impact on outcomes
- articulate contributions to or support of student learning and development in the domains not specifically assessed
- use evidence gathered to create strategies for improvement of programs and services

STUDENT LEARNING AND DEVELOPMENT DOMAINS AND DIMENSIONS

Domain: knowledge acquisition, integration, construction, and application
- Dimensions: understanding knowledge from a range of disciplines; connecting knowledge to other knowledge, ideas, and experiences; constructing knowledge; and relating knowledge to daily life

Domain: cognitive complexity
- Dimensions: critical thinking, reflective thinking, effective reasoning, and creativity

Domain: intrapersonal development
- Dimensions: realistic self-appraisal, self-understanding, and self-respect; identity development; commitment to ethics and integrity; and spiritual awareness

Domain: interpersonal competence
- Dimensions: meaningful relationships, interdependence, collaboration, and effective leadership

Domain: humanitarianism and civic engagement
- Dimensions: understanding and appreciation of cultural and human differences, social responsibility, global perspective, and sense of civic responsibility

Domain: practical competence
- Dimensions: pursuing goals, communicating effectively, technical competence, managing personal affairs, managing career development, demonstrating professionalism, maintaining health and wellness, and living a purposeful and satisfying life

[LD Outcomes: See *The Council for the Advancement of Standards Learning and Development Outcomes* statement for examples of outcomes related to these domains and dimensions.]

WGPS must be
- intentionally designed
- guided by theories and knowledge of learning and development
- integrated into the life of the institution
- reflective of developmental and demographic profiles of the student population
- responsive to needs of individuals, populations with distinct needs, and relevant constituencies
- delivered using multiple formats, strategies, and contexts
- designed to provide universal access

WGPS must emphasize the needs of women and all

constituents facing gender-based oppression including transgender women, transgender men, and gender diverse individuals.

WGPS must collaborate with colleagues and departments across the institution to promote student learning and development, persistence, and success.

WGPS must collaborate with colleagues and departments across the institution to promote an inclusive campus climate free of discrimination, harassment, and other barriers to success.

WGPS must incorporate dimensions of identity beyond gender identity and expression, such as race; ethnicity; nationality; religious affiliation; sexual orientation; disability; age; and relationship, social, economic, or veteran status into programs and services.

WGPS must actively work to eliminate problems of power and privilege within WGPS work.

WGPS must promote unrestricted access for full involvement of women and all constituents facing gender-based oppression.

WGPS must provide programs and services that actualize the core tenets of the WGPS mission to address gender equity through education, advocacy, and support.

Education
WGPS must provide educational programs, offer experiential opportunities, and engage in informal education that

- promote awareness of the ways gender is culturally constructed and how this shapes society and the individual experience
- increase understanding of systems of social privilege and oppression and the interrelationship between sexism and the systems of power and privilege associated with other marginalized social identities and experiences
- empower participants to create strategies for success within existing social structures
- elevate participants' capacity to confront and transform individual and institutionalized inequality and discrimination
- help campus constituencies identify and create equitable practices
- empower students and other constituents served by the WGPS mission to engage in gender-related activist causes
- facilitate attitudinal and behavioral change

WGPS should support scholarship and research on women and gender including individual projects and work pursued in collaboration with relevant academic departments and other entities.

WGPS should collaborate on the provision of service learning and internship opportunities aligned with the mission to promote gender equity.

Advocacy
WGPS must provide opportunities for individuals within the institution to collectively transform institutional culture related to improving the lives of women and all people facing gender-based oppression.

To address the institutional environment, WGPS must

- advocate for a campus culture that eliminates barriers, prejudice, and bigotry, and creates a hospitable climate for women and all constituents facing gender-based oppression
- advocate for institutional accountability for assessing and monitoring campus climate in areas of gender bias and discrimination
- collaborate with on- and off-campus partners to create institutional policies, procedures, and programs to work toward the elimination of gender bias and discrimination
- advocate for the elimination of institutional policies and practices that result in an inequitable impact on students or employees based on their gender identity and/or gender expression
- advocate for curricular change to consistently and comprehensively include the concerns and contributions to society of women and all people facing gender-based oppression

WGPS should provide gender-related expertise, critique, and perspective on legal issues, institutional policy, and applicable laws related to women and gender, such as those associated with gender discrimination including sexual assault and other forms of sexual violence, intimate partner violence, stalking, sexual harassment, pregnancy, and work life accommodations. In addition, WGPS should serve as an institutional resource on how laws and policies may have a disparate impact based on gender.

WGPS should advance gender justice through opportunities for involvement in local, regional, national, and global action initiatives related to improving the lives of women and all people facing gender-based oppression.

Support
WGPS must provide advocacy ~~to~~ for/with individuals as a form of direct support.

WGPS must provide opportunities that create support systems and communication networks for women and all constituents facing gender-based oppression.

WGPS must provide culturally appropriate and relevant information, resources, and referrals for promoting the success, health and holistic well-being of all constituents served by the WGPS mission including those from under-represented or under-served communities.

WGPS must address the provision of culturally appropriate and relevant support services including crisis intervention, counseling, advocacy, resources, accommodation, referrals and information about related institutional practices and policies to individuals who experience gender equity, bias, discrimination or hostile climate concerns in institutional learning, working and living environments, and to constituents who experience sexual assault and other forms of sexual violence, intimate partner violence, stalking, sexual harassment, and pregnancy discrimination.

WGPS must provide information about the availability of adequate, accessible, affordable, and flexible child and family care.

Part 3. Organization and Leadership

To achieve program and student learning and development outcomes, Women's and Gender Programs and Services (WGPS) must be purposefully structured for effectiveness. WGPS must have clearly stated and current
- goals and outcomes
- policies and procedures
- responsibilities and performance expectations for personnel
- organizational charts demonstrating clear channels of authority

Leaders must model ethical behavior and institutional citizenship.

Leaders with organizational authority for WGPS must provide strategic planning, management and supervision, and program advancement.

Strategic Planning
- articulate a vision and mission that drive short- and long-term planning
- set goals and objectives based on the needs of the populations served, intended student learning and development outcomes, and program outcomes
- facilitate continuous development, implementation, and assessment of program effectiveness and goal attainment congruent with institutional mission and strategic plans
- promote environments that provide opportunities for student learning, development, and engagement
- develop, adapt, and improve programs and services in response to the changing needs of populations served and evolving institutional priorities
- include diverse perspectives to inform decision making

Management and Supervision
- plan, allocate, and monitor the use of fiscal, physical, human, intellectual, and technological resources
- manage human resource processes including recruitment, selection, professional development, supervision, performance planning, succession planning, evaluation, recognition, and reward
- influence others to contribute to the effectiveness and success of the unit
- empower professional, support, and student personnel to become effective leaders
- encourage and support collaboration with colleagues and departments across the institution
- encourage and support scholarly contributions to the profession
- identify and address individual, organizational, and environmental conditions that foster or inhibit mission achievement
- use current and valid evidence to inform decisions
- incorporate sustainability practices in the management and design of programs, services, and facilities
- understand appropriate technologies and integrate them into programs and services
- be knowledgeable about codes and laws relevant to programs and services and ensure that programs and services meet those requirements
- assess and take action to mitigate potential risks

Program Advancement
- advocate for and actively promote the mission and goals of the programs and services
- inform stakeholders about issues affecting practice
- facilitate processes to reach consensus where wide support is needed
- advocate for representation in strategic planning initiatives at divisional and institutional levels

WGPS must be organized and integrated within the institution in order to serve multiple constituencies effectively and in ways that demonstrate an institutional commitment to promoting gender equity and women's success.

WGPS should play a principal role in creating and implementing gender-related institutional policies and structures.

WGPS should undertake periodic reviews of gender-related campus needs in order to determine the needs of key constituencies across the organization and beyond, for example, students, faculty and staff, alumnae/i, community, and others. Such reviews will help WGPS adjust their missions, priorities, and activities.

WGPS must advocate for opportunities and advancement within the institution for their mission-defined constituents and integrate an understanding of power and privilege as influences on these constituents' access to advancement.

In the case of student-run WGPS, student leaders should have access to policy and decision makers of the institution.

Recognizing that WGPS operate within institutional

hierarchies, WGPS must incorporate feminist (e.g., non-hierarchical and collaborative) approaches to leadership and organizational structures, the value of consensus building, and the importance of multiple and diverse voices in decision making into their operations.

WGPS should function as discrete operational units with their own identities.

Part 4. Human Resources

Women's and Gender Programs and Services (WGPS) must be staffed adequately by individuals qualified to accomplish mission and goals.

WGPS personnel must demonstrate a commitment to the equity and inclusion practices upon which WGPS work is modeled.

WGPS personnel must engage with the larger WGPS community in order to support each other, promote best practices, build the WGPS field, and maintain an awareness of current issues and concerns facing WGPS.

WGPS personnel must have the experience, skills, knowledge base and understanding of the philosophy and needs inherent in WGPS work to support and advance the work of the unit.

In the selection and training of personnel, special emphasis should be placed on skills and competencies in the areas of diversity, customer service, creating a welcoming and inclusive environment, confidentiality, problem identification, crisis response and management, public relations, information dissemination, problem identification, and referral. A thorough knowledge of the institution, its various offices, and relevant community resources is important.

All WGPS personnel, as vital members of the team, should be encouraged to share their viewpoints, contribute to planning, and fulfill their duties in a way that acknowledges their agency, regardless of their status and position.

WGPS staff positions must be classified and compensated adequately and on a level commensurate with equivalent positions in other units.

WGPS must have access to technical and support personnel adequate to accomplish their mission.

Within institutional guidelines, WGPS must
- establish procedures for personnel recruitment and selection, training, performance planning, and evaluation
- set expectations for supervision and performance
- provide personnel access to continuing and advanced education and appropriate professional development opportunities to improve their competence, skills, and leadership capacity
- consider work/life options available to personnel (e.g., compressed work schedules, flextime, job sharing, remote work, or telework) to promote recruitment and retention of personnel

Administrators of WGPS must
- ensure that all personnel have updated position descriptions
- implement recruitment and selection/hiring strategies that produce a workforce inclusive of under-represented populations
- develop promotion practices that are fair, inclusive, proactive, and non-discriminatory

Personnel responsible for delivery of WGPS must have written performance goals, objectives, and outcomes for each year's performance cycle to be used to plan, review, and evaluate work and performance. The performance plan must be updated regularly to reflect changes during the performance cycle.

Results of individual personnel evaluations must be used to recognize personnel performance, address performance issues, implement individual and/or collective personnel development and training programs, and inform the assessment of programs and services.

WGPS personnel, when hired and throughout their employment, must receive appropriate and thorough training.

WGPS personnel, including student employees and volunteers, must have access to resources or receive specific training on
- institutional policies pertaining to functions or activities they support
- privacy and confidentiality policies
- laws regarding access to student records
- policies and procedures for dealing with sensitive institutional information
- policies and procedures related to technology used to store or access student records and institutional data
- how and when to refer those in need of additional assistance to qualified personnel and have access to a supervisor for assistance in making these judgments
- systems and technologies necessary to perform their assigned responsibilities
- ethical and legal uses of technology

WGPS personnel must engage in continuing professional development activities to keep abreast of the research, theories, legislation, policies, and developments that affect their programs and services.

Administrators of WGPS must ensure that personnel are knowledgeable about and trained in safety, emergency procedures, and crisis prevention and response. Risk management efforts must address identification of threatening conduct or behavior and must incorporate a system for responding to and reporting such behaviors.

WGPS personnel must be knowledgeable of and trained in safety and emergency procedures for securing and vacating facilities.

PROFESSIONAL PERSONNEL

WGPS professional personnel either must hold an earned graduate or professional degree in a field relevant to their position or must possess an appropriate combination of educational credentials and related work experience.

WGPS professional personnel must have demonstrated commitment to advocacy on gender equity issues.

WGPS professional personnel should be knowledgeable about the field's historical context and roots in social justice, community activism, and social change efforts.

INTERNS OR GRADUATE ASSISTANTS

Degree- or credential-seeking interns or graduate assistants must be qualified by enrollment in an appropriate field of study and relevant experience. These students must be trained and supervised by professional personnel who possess applicable educational credentials and work experience and have supervisory experience. Supervisors must be cognizant of the dual roles interns and graduate assistants have as both student and employee.

Supervisors must
- adhere to parameters of students' job descriptions
- articulate intended learning outcomes in student job descriptions
- adhere to agreed-upon work hours and schedules
- offer flexible scheduling when circumstances necessitate

Supervisors and students must both agree to suitable compensation if circumstances necessitate additional hours.

STUDENT EMPLOYEES AND VOLUNTEERS

Student employees and volunteers must be carefully selected, trained, supervised, and evaluated. Students must have access to a supervisor. Student employees and volunteers must be provided clear job descriptions, pre-service training based on assessed needs, and continuing development.

Part 5. Ethics

Women's and Gender Programs and Services (WGPS) must
- review applicable professional ethical standards and must adopt or develop and implement appropriate statements of ethical practice
- publish and adhere to statements of ethical practice and ensure their periodic review
- orient new personnel to relevant ethical standards and statements of ethical practice and related institutional policies

Statements of ethical standards must
- specify that WGPS personnel respect privacy and maintain confidentiality in communications and records as delineated by privacy laws
- specify limits on disclosure of information contained in students' records as well as requirements to disclose to appropriate authorities

- address conflicts of interest, or appearance thereof, by personnel in the performance of their work
- reflect the responsibility of personnel to be fair, objective, and impartial in their interactions with others
- reference management of institutional funds
- reference appropriate behavior regarding research and assessment with human participants, confidentiality of research and assessment data, and students' rights and responsibilities
- include the expectation that personnel confront and hold accountable other personnel who exhibit unethical behavior
- address issues surrounding scholarly integrity

WGPS should be a confidential reporting option as relates to gender-based discrimination, harassment, and violence.

WGPS personnel must
- employ ethical decision making in the performance of their duties
- inform users of programs and services of ethical obligations and limitations emanating from codes and laws or from licensure requirements
- recognize and avoid conflicts of interest that could adversely influence their judgment or objectivity and, when unavoidable, recuse themselves from the situation
- perform their duties within the scope of their position, training, expertise, and competence
- make referrals when issues presented exceed the scope of the position

When engaging in advocacy work, WGPS personnel must empower individuals and support them in making their own decisions.

WGPS personnel should clearly articulate within the institution the expectations of the advocacy framework under which they and their units operate. The advocacy framework includes the potential that a constituent's choices may result in outcomes that meet the constituent's needs but which may be antithetical to the expectations of other individuals or the institutional structure.

WGPS should help constituents to understand the complexities of higher education institutions, including any limitations on the activist activities of WGPS personnel, while still empowering constituents to critically develop, implement and evaluate their own activist agendas.

Part 6. Law, Policy, and Governance

Women's and Gender Programs and Services (WGPS) must be in compliance with laws, regulations, and policies that relate to their respective responsibilities and that pose legal obligations, limitations, risks, and liabilities for the institution as a whole. Examples include constitutional, statutory, regulatory, and case law; relevant law and orders emanating from codes and laws; and the institution's policies.

WGPS must have access to legal advice needed for personnel to carry out their assigned responsibilities.

WGPS must inform personnel, appropriate officials, and users of programs and services about existing and changing legal obligations, risks and liabilities, and limitations.

WGPS should provide gender-related expertise, critique, and perspective on legal issues, institutional policy and applicable laws related to women and gender, such as those associated with gender discrimination including sexual assault and other forms of sexual violence, intimate partner violence, stalking, sexual harassment, pregnancy and work life accommodations, including but not exclusive to, in the US, Title IX, Title VII, FMLA, and the Clery Act (the Campus Security Act), as well as serve as an institutional resource on how other laws and policies may have a disparate impact based on gender.

WGPS must inform personnel about professional liability insurance options and refer them to external sources if the institution does not provide coverage.

WGPS must have written policies and procedures on operations, transactions, or tasks that have legal implications.

WGPS must regularly review policies. The revision and creation of policies must be informed by best practices, available evidence, and policy issues in higher education.

WGPS must have procedures and guidelines consistent with institutional policy for responding to threats, emergencies, and crisis situations. Systems and procedures must be in place to disseminate timely and accurate information to students, other members of the institutional community, and appropriate external organizations during emergency situations.

Personnel must neither participate in nor condone any form of harassment or activity that demeans persons or creates an intimidating, hostile, or offensive environment.

WGPS must purchase or obtain permission to use copyrighted materials and instruments. References to copyrighted materials and instruments must include appropriate citations.

WGPS must inform personnel about internal and external governance organizations that affect programs and services.

Part 7. Diversity, Equity, and Access

Within the context of each institution's mission and in accordance with institutional policies and applicable codes and laws, Women's and Gender Programs and Services (WGPS) must create and maintain educational and work environments that are welcoming, accessible, inclusive, equitable, and free from harassment.

WGPS must not discriminate on the basis of disability; age; race; cultural identity; ethnicity; nationality; family educational history (e.g., first generation to attend college); political affiliation; religious affiliation; sex; sexual orientation; gender identity and expression; marital, social, economic, or veteran status; or any other basis included in institutional policies and codes and laws.

WGPS must

- advocate for sensitivity to multicultural and social justice concerns by the institution and its personnel
- ensure physical, program, and resource access for all constituents
- modify or remove policies, practices, systems, technologies, facilities, and structures that create barriers or produce inequities
- ensure that when facilities and structures cannot be modified, they do not impede access to programs, services, and resources
- establish goals for diversity, equity, and access
- foster communication and practices that enhance understanding of identity, culture, self-expression, and heritage
- promote respect for commonalities and differences among people within their historical and cultural contexts
- address the characteristics and needs of diverse constituents when establishing and implementing culturally relevant and inclusive programs, services, policies, procedures, and practices
- provide personnel with diversity, equity, and access training and hold personnel accountable for applying the training to their work
- respond to the needs of all constituents served when establishing hours of operation and developing methods of delivering programs, services, and resources
- recognize the needs of distance and online learning students by directly providing or assisting them to gain access to comparable services and resources

WGPS must be intentional about addressing intersecting identities in WGPS educational programs and services as well as in institutional policies and practices.

WGPS must provide gender-related expertise, critique, and perspective on issues of diversity, equity, and access and how these issues are addressed in institutional policies and practices.

WGPS should provide expert assistance with the implementation and development of systems of accountability of the diversity, equity, and access standard across all functional areas.

Part 8. Internal and External Relations

Women's and Gender Programs and Services (WGPS) must reach out to individuals, groups, communities, and organizations internal and external to the institution to

- establish, maintain, and promote understanding and effective relations with those that have a significant interest in or potential effect on the

students or other constituents served by the programs and services

- garner support and resources for programs and services as defined by the mission
- collaborate in offering or improving programs and services to meet the needs of students and other constituents and to achieve program and student outcomes
- engage diverse individuals, groups, communities, and organizations to enrich the educational environment and experiences of students and other constituents
- disseminate information about the programs and services

In keeping with their mission, priorities and available resources, WGPS should address concerns that affect members of the community beyond the institution, including alumnae/ alumni, community organizations and the public at large.

WGPS must build and maintain strong, mutually beneficial working relationships with co-curricular and academic departments across the institution as well as with community organizations.

WGPS's campus and community collaborative relationships should be ongoing, allowing strategic engagement to develop productive dialog, express common concerns and shared goals, and generate collective action. These relationships should be non-hierarchical, value differing perspectives, involve consensus-building, and facilitate increased visibility of the gender-related needs of WGPS constituents.

WGPS must be open to receiving feedback to ensure the mutuality of relationships with other entities.

In line with its advocacy framework, when making referrals, WGPS should actively facilitate successful connections, engagement and outcomes for the person referred.

WGPS should provide expert assistance and capacity building to departments across the institution as well as community organizations in order to facilitate the integration of gender equity into their policies, structures and practices with the goal of further reinforcing the institutionalization of gender equity.

Promotional and descriptive information must be accurate and free of deception and misrepresentation.

WGPS must have procedures and guidelines consistent with institutional policy for

- **communicating with the media**
- **distributing information through print, broadcast, and online sources**
- **contracting with external organizations for delivery of programs and services**
- **cultivating, soliciting, and managing gifts**
- **applying to and managing funds from grants**

Part 9. Financial Resources

Women's and Gender Programs and Services (WGPS) must

have funding to accomplish the mission and goals.

Permanent institutional funding should be allocated for the continuing operation and staffing of WGPS.

Permanent institutional funding must be commensurate with other units/departments that have similar scope.

WGPS should leverage institutional resources, including federally and other sponsored programs' personnel, to create and execute diversified funding plans that utilize internal and external funding sources to result in financial stability for WGPS.

In establishing and prioritizing funding resources, WGPS must conduct comprehensive analyses to determine

- **unmet needs of the unit**
- **relevant expenditures**
- **external and internal resources**
- **impact on students and the institution**

As human resources are the primary vehicle to accomplishing goals, WGPS should prioritize the maintenance of human resources, including student workers.

WGPS must use the budget as a planning tool to reflect commitment to the mission and goals of the programs and services and of the institution.

WGPS must administer funds in accordance with established institutional accounting procedures.

WGPS must demonstrate efficient and effective use and responsible stewardship of fiscal resources consistent with institutional protocols.

Financial reports must provide an accurate financial overview of the organization and provide clear, understandable, and timely data upon which personnel can plan and make informed decisions.

Procurement procedures must

- **be consistent with institutional policies**
- **ensure that purchases comply with laws and codes for usability and access**
- **ensure that the institution receives value for the funds spent**
- **consider information available for comparing the ethical and environmental impact of products and services purchased**

WGPS personnel should be an integral part of appropriate campus networks to participate effectively in the determination of institutional financial priorities and the allocation of funding resources.

WGPS should provide gender-related expertise, critique, and perspective on financial policies and practices and the distribution of financial resources related to women and gender, including pay equity.

Part 10. Technology

Women's and Gender Programs and Services (WGPS) must have technology to support the achievement of

their mission and goals. The technology and its use must comply with institutional policies and procedures and with relevant codes and laws.

WGPS must use technologies to
- provide updated information regarding mission, location, staffing, programs, services, and official contacts to students and other constituents in accessible formats
- provide an avenue for students and other constituents to communicate sensitive information in a secure format
- enhance the delivery of programs and services for all students

WGPS must
- back up data on a regular basis
- adhere to institutional policies regarding ethical and legal use of technology
- articulate policies and procedures for protecting the confidentiality and security of information
- implement a replacement plan and cycle for all technology with attention to sustainability
- incorporate accessibility features into technology-based programs and services

When providing student access to technology, WGPS must
- have policies on the use of technology that are clear, easy to understand, and available to all students
- provide information or referral to support services for those needing assistance in accessing or using technology
- provide instruction or training on how to use the technology
- inform students of implications of misuse of technologies

Technological resources must be allocated for the continuing operation of WGPS commensurate with other units/departments that have similar scope.

WGPS should provide expert consultation on the development and implementation of institutional policies and procedures that focus on responding to the negative effects of technology that may result in a disproportionately harmful impact for some users based on their actual or perceived gender identity and/or expression (e.g., electronic stalking, cyberbullying). WGPS should elevate institutional awareness about these policies and procedures.

WGPS should advocate for policies and procedures that monitor institutional technological spaces in order to identify in a timely way potentially harmful technological issues, including hostile environments.

WGPS should proactively engage with institutional technology authorities to ensure that there are resources available to respond quickly and effectively to any negative effects of technology.

WGPS should proactively engage with institutional

technology authorities to review emerging technologies for their potential opportunities and risks in order to promote positive usage.

Part 11. Facilities and Equipment

Women's and Gender Programs and Services' (WGPS) facilities must be intentionally designed and located in suitable, accessible, and safe spaces that demonstrate universal design and support the program's mission and goals.

Facilities must be designed to engage various constituents and promote learning.

WGPS should provide gender-related expertise, critique, and perspective on the location and design of facilities to ensure safe, inclusive, and welcoming environments such as appropriately equipped lactation spaces, gender inclusive restrooms and other gender-specific and family-friendly facilities.

Personnel must have workspaces that are suitably located and accessible, well equipped, adequate in size, and designed to support their work and responsibilities.

WGPS facilities must also include private meeting areas and a welcoming communal space.

The design of the facilities must guarantee the security and privacy of records and ensure the confidentiality of sensitive information and conversations. Personnel must be able to secure their work.

WGPS must incorporate sustainable practices in use of facilities and purchase of equipment. Facilities and equipment must be evaluated on an established cycle and be in compliance with codes, laws, and accepted practices for access, health, safety, and security.

When acquiring capital equipment, programs and services must take into account expenses related to regular maintenance and life cycle costs.

Part 12. Assessment

Women's and Gender Programs and Services (WGPS) must develop assessment plans and processes.

Assessment plans must articulate an ongoing cycle of assessment activities.

WGPS must
- specify programmatic goals and intended outcomes
- identify student learning and development outcomes
- employ multiple measures and methods
- develop manageable processes for gathering, interpreting, and evaluating data
- document progress toward achievement of goals and outcomes
- interpret and use assessment results to demonstrate accountability

- report aggregated results to respondent groups and stakeholders
- use assessment results to inform planning and decision-making
- assess effectiveness of implemented changes
- provide evidence of improvement of programs and services

WGPS must employ ethical practices in the assessment process.

WGPS must have access to adequate fiscal, human, professional development, and technological resources to develop and implement assessment plans.

WGPS should analyze institutional data to identify gender-related disparities and issues and use this data to inform decision-making about WGPS priorities.

WGPS should engage in campus climate assessment initiatives, independently or collaboratively, with particular attention to eliciting information about gender-related disparities and concerns.

General Standards revised in 2014;
WGPS content (formerly Women Student Programs and Services)
developed/revised in 1992, 1997, 2005, and 2015

Appendix A
CAS Member Associations - July 2015

Association	Member Since
ACPA: College Student Educators International (ACPA)	1979
American College Counseling Association (ACCA)	1993
American College Health Association (ACHA)	1995
Association for Student Conduct Administration (ASCA, formerly ASJA)	1990
Association of College and University Housing Officers-International (ACUHO-I)	1979
Association of College Honor Societies (ACHS)	2004
Association of College Unions International (ACUI)	1979
Association of Collegiate Conference and Events Directors-International (ACCED-I)	1999
Association of Fraternity/Sorority Advisors (AFA)	1981
Association of Higher Education Parent/Family Program Professionals (AHEPPP)	2010
Association on Higher Education and Disability (AHEAD)	1981
Canadian Association of College and University Student Services (CACUSS)	1994
College Media Association (CMA)	2011
College Reading and Learning Association (CRLA)	1993
Collegiate Information and Visitor Services Association (CiVSA)	1998
Consortium of Higher Education LGBT Resource Professionals (Consortium)	1999
Cooperative Education and Internship Association (CEIA)	2009
Council for Opportunity in Education (COE)	1994
International Association of Campus Law Enforcement Administrators (IACLEA)	2009
NACADA: National Academic Advising Association (NACADA)	1981
NAFSA: Association of International Educators (NAFSA)	1989
NASPA: Student Affairs Administrators in Higher Education (NASPA)	1979
National Association for Campus Activities (NACA)	1979
National Association for Developmental Educators (NADE)	1992
National Association of College and University Food Services (NACUFS)	2004
National Association of College Auxiliary Services (NACAS)	1998
National Association of Colleges and Employers (NACE)	1979
National Association of College Stores (NACS)	2005
National Association of Student Affairs Professionals (NASAP)	2004
National Association of Student Financial Aid Administrators (NASFAA)	1991
National Clearinghouse for Commuter Programs (NCCP)	1980
National Clearinghouse for Leadership Programs (NCLP)	2004
National College Learning Center Association (NCLCA)	2015
National College Testing Association (NCTA)	2015
National Council on Student Development (NCSD)	1979
National Institute for the Transfer Students (NISTS)	2010
NIRSA: Leaders in Collegiate Recreation (NIRSA)	1981
NODA: Association for Orientation, Transition, and Retention in Higher Education (NODA)	1979
National Society for Experiential Education (NSEE)	2004
National Women's Studies Association (NWSA)	2006
Southern Association for College Student Affairs (SACSA)	1982

Appendix B
CAS Preamble
Approved by the CAS Board of Directors
November 18, 1994
Washington, DC

"Let us raise a standard to which the wise and honest can repair."
- George Washington, 1787

The CAS Purpose

The Council for the Advancement of Standards in Higher Education (CAS) develops and promulgates standards that enhance the quality of a student's total learning experience in higher education. CAS is a consortium of associations in higher education whose representatives achieve consensus on the nature and application of standards that guide the work of practitioners. CAS derives its authority from the prestige and traditional influence of its member associations and from the consensus of those members in establishing requirements for high-quality practice.

The CAS philosophy is grounded in beliefs about excellence in higher education, collaboration between teacher and learner, ethics in educational practice, student development as a major goal of higher education, and student responsibility for learning. Taken together, these beliefs about practice shape the vision for all CAS endeavors.

- The beliefs about excellence require that all programs and services in institutions of higher education function at optimum level.
- The beliefs about collaboration require that learning be accomplished in concert by students and educators.
- The beliefs about ethics require that all programs and services be carried out in an environment of integrity and high ideals.
- The beliefs about student development require that the student be considered as a whole person in the context of a diverse population and a diversity of institutions, that outcomes of education be comprehensive, and that the total environment be structured to create opportunities for student involvement and learning.
- The beliefs about responsibility require that the institution recognize the rights and responsibilities of students as its citizens and that it provide an array of resources and learning opportunities that enable students to exercise their responsibility to take full advantage of them.

CAS collectively develops, examines, and endorses standards and guidelines for program and service areas in higher education. The CAS approach to ensuring quality educational experiences is anchored in the assumption that its standards and guidelines can be used in a variety of ways to enhance institutional quality. They can, for example, be used for design of programs and services, for determination of the efficacy of programs, for staff development designed to enhance the skills of those providing professional services, for programmatic self-assessment to assure institutional effectiveness, and for self-regulation purposes.

Background

The Council for the Advancement of Standards in Higher Education was established in 1979 as the Council for the Advancement of Standards for Student Services/Development Programs, a consortium of professional associations representing student affairs practitioners committed to assuring quality programs and services for students. Members of 32 established professional associations directed their interests, talents, and resources to develop and promulgate professional standards and guidelines based on state-of-the-art thinking about educational programs and services. From the beginning, CAS employed an open process of consensus-building among the representatives of member associations as the primary tool for producing its standards and guidelines.

The Council published the original set of 16 functional area standards and the academic preparation standards in 1986, with a grant from American College Testing (ACT). In 1988, CAS developed a Self-Assessment Guide (SAG) for each set of functional area standards to facilitate program assessment and evaluation. Each SAG is an operational version of a functional area standard designed to provide practitioners with a detailed instrument for self-assessment.

The Council's current name and expanded mission were adopted in 1992, to be inclusive of all programs for students in higher education, including those serving undergraduate, graduate, traditional, and nontraditional students. CAS now oversees the development of standards for new service areas and the systematic review and periodic revision of existing standards and guidelines.

The CAS Approach to Self-Regulation and Self-Assessment

Self-regulation is an internally motivated and directed institutional process devoted to the creation, maintenance, and enhancement of high-quality programs and services. CAS believes this approach is preferable to externally motivated regulation, because those within an institution generally have the clearest perceptions of its mission, goals, resources, and capabilities. The

essential elements of self-regulation include
- institutional culture that values involvement of all its members in decision making
- quality indicators that are determined by the institution
- standards and guidelines in quality assurance
- collection and analysis of data on institutional performance
- commitment to continuing improvement that presupposes freedom to explore and develop alternative directions for the future

The success of self-regulation depends on mutual respect between an institution and its members. Within the self-regulated institution, individual accomplishments are valued, goals are based on shared vision, systems are open and interactive, processes are carried out in a climate of mutual trust and caring, conflicts are mediated in the best interests of the entire community, and achievements are recognized and rewarded. Such an environment stimulates individual and group initiatives and fosters self-determination of goals. In a self-regulating environment, members identify quality indicators in consultation with a variety of internal and external constituencies and stakeholders, including professional associations.

These indicators may include professionally derived standards, such as those of CAS, which comprise the views of many professional practitioners and professional associations. Self-regulation relies on the willingness and capacity of the organization to examine itself meticulously, faithfully, and reliably, and then to assemble the pertinent results of that examination into coherent reports that constituents can comprehend and use. Such reports are essential for recording the evidence assembled in self-study, for displaying synthesis and analysis of information, for fostering the broad participation of members in the self-regulation process, and for registering benchmark results and conclusions for future reference.

Finally, the self-regulation process relies on the institution's capacity to modify its own practices as needed. A culture that supports self-regulation must operate in a climate that permits members to make independent choices among reasonable alternatives. These choices constitute a commitment to constant improvement of educational practices and of the health of the organization.

References

American College Personnel Association (ACPA). (March/April 1996). Special issue: The student learning imperative. *Journal of College Student Development, 37*(2).

Council for the Advancement of Standards (CAS). (1986). *CAS standards and guidelines for student service/development programs.* Iowa City, IA: American College Testing Program.

Eaton, J. S. (March/April 2001). Regional accreditation reform: Who is served? *Change Magazine,* 39-45.

Miller, T. K., & Prince, J. S. (1976). *The future of student affairs: A guide to student development for tomorrow's higher education.* San Francisco, CA: Jossey-Bass.

Appendix C
Protocol for Developing New CAS Standards and Guidelines

The protocol for developing new standards has been devised to be a broad-based and inclusive process. It encompasses an internal-external-internal drafting procedure that is outlined below.

Identify the Functional Area. The CAS Executive Committee with the approval of the CAS Board of Directors identifies and defines the functional area for which a CAS standard is to be written. Individuals, professional entities, or a group of concerned professional practitioners can propose new standards by considering and providing responses to the following list of CAS Evaluation Questions for Selecting New Standards:

1. Is there a trend toward a distinct functional area?
2. Is there consistency in practice across multiple institutions?
3. Is there a clear need for these standards within higher education?
4. Would creating these standards match the CAS mission and purpose to enhance student learning?
5. Are there policies, practices, and structures that are increasingly unique?
6. Is there a body of literature?
7. Would new standards be different enough from existing standards?
8. Would an expansion of existing standards address this need?
9. Are additions to the general standards more appropriate as an approach to address this need?
10. Are there professionals interested in supporting the development of the standards?
11. Is there a group of professionals working to support the functional area?
12. Is there a professional association related to the proposed standard?

CAS should identify standards created by one or more organizations outside of CAS and seek involvement and cooperation in developing new CAS standards and guidelines for that functional area. If such organizations decide not to join the development process, CAS will move forward. The CAS Board of Directors must agree by majority vote to sponsor development of a new professional standard.

Charge a Development Committee for New Standards Creation. Once the CAS Board of Directors approves the development of a new CAS functional area standard, a Development Committee of three to five CAS directors (or alternate directors) is appointed and charged by the CAS president to guide the development process. If further help is needed, committee members with functional area expertise from outside of CAS can be added. The chair cannot be a representative of a professional association that has significant interest in the new standard. However, at least one person on the committee must be connected with the functional area to serve as an expert and play a significant role in ensuring that the standards demonstrate contemporary quality practices. Development Committee appointments are made after the spring CAS Board of Directors meeting and followed by a New Committee Chair Training Program. The Development Committee members work with the CAS Executive Committee's Member-at-Large for Standards Development to establish an Internet-based space for document storage, references related to the functional area, and committee collaboration. The Development Committee may request copies of existing CAS standards with similarities to the new functional area be placed online along with a copy of the current CAS General Standards.

Develop Initial Draft. Usually, the chair and area expert craft the initial draft with feedback and suggestions from Development Committee members. If a professional association connected with the functional area has already written a standard, it is used in the creation of the first draft. The CAS General Standards are used as the foundation for newly developed functional area standards.

Solicit Internal Review and Comment. The CAS Development Committee identifies all CAS member associations with a significant interest in the new functional area standard. The first draft of the standards is sent to CAS directors of identified organizations with a request that they provide timely and substantive recommendations and feedback. The Development Committee then creates a second draft based on feedback from these CAS directors. A minimum of two months should be allowed for the writing of the second draft.

Solicit External Expert Review and Comment. The CAS Development Committee must identify expert functional area professionals for their review of the second draft of the new standards. To achieve diversification, the committee should consider institution size, location, and type (e.g., 4-year/2-year, public/private, historically underrepresented, etc.). In addition, the Development Committee solicits feedback from practitioners through online professional lists, organizational web pages, and the database of users collected from purchasers of CAS materials. CAS directors are consulted for names of professionals/colleagues who are currently filling related positions or with connections and interest in the new standards under development. The goal is to receive feedback from at least five experts within two months.

Incorporate comments into a third draft document. The Development Committee evaluates all substantive feedback and recommendations from experts (compiled electronically) and provides its own well-considered ideas for the development of the third draft of the functional area standards and guidelines. This draft should be prepared within one year after the beginning of the development process.

Executive Committee Review and Approve. The CAS Development Committee submits a final standards draft along with an updated version of the contextual statement to the CAS Editor approximately six weeks prior to the next scheduled CAS Executive Committee meeting. The proposed new standards and contextual statement are reviewed by the CAS Editor for accuracy and completeness and then forwarded to the CAS Executive Committee for review at least two weeks before the meeting. The Development Committee chair and/or area expert presents the draft to the Executive Committee in person or by electronic conference. The CAS Executive Committee reviews the draft and can either return it for further work by the Development Committee or formulate a penultimate draft to be sent to the CAS Board of Directors for final review and approval. This penultimate draft should be sent to the CAS directors no later than 45 days before the board meeting.

Full CAS Board of Directors Review, Consider, and Approve. The CAS Board of Directors reviews the penultimate draft of the new standards and contextual statement and provides substantive feedback and suggestions to the Development Committee at least two weeks prior to the CAS Board of Directors meeting. The Development Committee reviews and discusses this feedback and prepares alternate language and/or feedback and answers to questions prior to the board meeting. The chair of the Development Committee submits all materials, including a summary of any areas of substantive feedback, to the Executive Committee for review prior to presentation of the new standards and contextual statement to the CAS Board of Directors. The chair of the Development Committee, along with the functional area expert, formally presents the new standards to the CAS directors following a training program that clarifies the process and specific roles at the meeting. Following final review and discussion, the CAS Board of Directors votes to adopt the new standards and guidelines. This process should be completed within eighteen months after beginning the development process.

Publish. The new Standards and Guidelines, upon adoption by the Board of Directors and final review by the Development Committee chair, are submitted to the Editor to format the CAS Self-Assessment Guide for distribution to the profession at large. Upon completion, the Standards and Guidelines and contextual statement will be published in the next *CAS Professional Standards for Higher Education* book along with the appropriate contextual statement. The standards will be made available as a separate publication on the CAS website and linked to appropriate CAS member associations' websites. The completion of the new Standards and Guidelines from the beginning of the process through publication should take no longer than two years. The committee chair also is asked to provide guidance for marketing, including identifying interested professional association information and providing quotes for press releases. If during final editing and review there are any substantial changes, this document will be returned to the Board of Directors for approval. The CAS secretary maintains the official version of the final approved standards and guidelines.

Development Process Timeline

Event Chronology	Time Allotted	Total Time
Evaluate potential new function area standard	3 months	3 months
Development Committee chair and committee members identified and trained	2 months	5 months
Initial draft created	3 months	8 months
Solicit internal CAS review and comment	2 months	10 months
Create a second draft	2 months	12 months
Solicit external expert review and comment	2 months	14 months
Create a third draft	2 months	16 months
Draft is submitted for review to the Executive Committee	1 month	17 months
Executive Committee approved draft is distributed to Directors for review. Initial feedback from directors received by Development Committee and Executive Committee	1 months	18 months
Substantial items reviewed by Development Committee and reported to the Executive Committee and prepared for discussion at Board Meeting	0.5 month	19 months

Appendix C
Protocol for Revising Existing CAS Standards and Guidelines

The CAS Board of Directors systematically initiates a review of approximately five CAS Functional Area Standards and Guidelines per year within a projected 11-year planning cycle. The standards revision protocol was developed to be a broad-based and inclusive process. It encompasses the internal-external-internal drafting procedure outlined below. Member associations with interest in the functional area(s) under review are called upon to provide functional area expert committee members and reviewers.

Initial Review: When standards are scheduled for revision, the CAS president appoints and charges a Revision Committee. The revision process includes the following components and actions:

1. The committee consists of a chair to guide the revision process and at least two other CAS directors or alternates.
2. The chair cannot be a representative of a professional association with a significant interest in the standard.
3. At least one person connected with the functional area serves on the committee as an area expert and plays a considerable role in ensuring that the revised standards demonstrate contemporary language and quality practices.
4. Revision Committee appointments are made after the spring CAS Board of Directors meeting and followed by training for new committee chairs.
5. The Revision Committee works with the CAS Executive Committee's Member-at-Large for Standards Development to establish an Internet-based space for document storage, references related to the functional area, and committee collaboration.
6. The Revision Committee receives a copy of the existing standards, updated to reflect the current CAS General Standards.
7. The chair works with the functional area expert to identify an initial list of experts in the field for a high level review of the existing standards.
8. The Revision Committee circulates the existing standards with general standards updates to its members and identified experts to determine if a substantial revision is necessary or whether an editorial revision will be adequate.

Editorial Standards Revision: An editorial revision of existing standards includes

1. basic word, punctuation, and grammatical corrections
2. alteration of phrases for purposes of improved clarity
3. modification required by changes in general standards
4. presentation/format changes
5. non-substantive word changes

After determining an editorial revision is most appropriate, the Revision Committee begins work on creating a first draft to be distributed to the identified functional area experts for review. The use of other experts in the field usually is not necessary for an editorial revision.

1. After receiving expert feedback and integrating final updates from committee members, a revised set of standards and updated contextual statement is submitted to the CAS Executive Committee.
2. The Revision Committee chair and/or functional area expert presents the draft to the Executive Committee in person or by an electronic conference, as needed.
3. The CAS Executive Committee reviews the revised draft, formulates a penultimate draft, and either returns the standards and contextual statement to the Revision Committee for further work (including undertaking a substantial standards revision) or forwards it to the full CAS Board of Directors for review and possible approval at a regular meeting.
4. The penultimate draft, clearly identifying changes from the original version of the standards and contextual statement, is sent to the Board of Directors no later than 45 days before a board meeting.
5. The directors return substantive feedback or suggestions at least two weeks before the Board of Director's meeting so the Revision Committee has time to consider and prepare responses or alternate suggestions.
6. The chair of the Revision Committee submits all materials, including a summary of any areas of substantive feedback, to the Executive Committee for review prior to presentation of the revised standards to the CAS Board of Directors.
7. The chair of the Revision Committee, along with the functional area expert, formally presents the revised standards to the CAS Board of Directors.
8. A short training program prior to the meeting explains and clarifies the facilitation process.
9. An editorial revision should take approximately six months to complete from the beginning of the review process.

Substantial Standards Revision: After deciding that a substantial revision is required, the Revision Committee begins work on creating an initial draft. The revision process includes the following actions:

1. Usually the creation of the initial draft is lead by the chair and functional area expert with feedback and suggestions from other committee members.
2. The Revision Committee polls CAS member associations to determine those that have a significant interest in the

standard under revision and contact those CAS directors for review and feedback of the initial draft.

3. The chair and functional area expert also take the lead in identifying an expanded and diverse list of experts who can be asked to review and provide feedback about the initial draft. To achieve diversification, they should consider institutional size, location, and type (e.g., 4-year/2-year, public/private, historically underrepresented, etc.).

4. The chair of the Revision Committee contacts non-member professional associations, who have a significant interest in the standards under revision, to seek their involvement and review of the revised standards. It is also recommended that the committee gather feedback from practitioners through online professional lists, organizational web pages, and the database of users collected from purchasers of CAS materials.

5. Once a list of experts and interested parties is completed, the Chair requests that those individuals review the initial draft of the revised standard and give feedback and suggestions.

6. Committees are encouraged to include 10 external or internal experts in the review and comment process. An intern or graduate student may assist in compiling this material into a useful format for the committee.

7. The Revision Committee uses collected feedback and suggestions to prepare a second draft of the revised standards.

8. Once the committee is comfortable with the second draft, the revised standards and updated/revised contextual statement is submitted to the Editor to forward to the CAS Executive Committee.

9. The Revision Committee chair and/or functional area expert presents the draft to the Executive Committee in person or by electronic conference.

10. The CAS Executive Committee reviews the draft and formulates a penultimate draft to either return to the Revision Committee for further work or send to the full board for review and possible approval at a regular meeting.

11. The penultimate draft, clearly identifying all substantive changes from the original version of the standards, is sent to the Board of Directors no later than 45 days before a board meeting. The directors must return any substantive feedback or suggestions to the Revision Committee Chair and CAS Executive Committee at least two weeks before the Board of Directors meeting so that the Revision Committee has time to consider and prepare responses or alternate suggestions.

12. The chair of the Revision Committee submits all materials, including a summary of any areas of substantive feedback, to the Executive Committee for review prior to presentation of the revised standards to the CAS Board of Directors.

13. A short training program prior to the meeting explains and clarifies the facilitation process.

14. The chair of the Revision Committee along with the functional area expert presents the revised standards to the CAS Board of Directors.

15. This revision process should be completed within one year.

Publication: The newly revised standards and contextual statement, upon adoption by the CAS Board of Directors, is sent by the CAS secretary to the Editor for final editing and formatting the *CAS Self Assessment Guide*. Upon completion, the revised standards will be published in the next *CAS Professional Standards for Higher Education* book along with the appropriate contextual statement. In addition, it will be made available as a separate publication on the CAS website and linked to appropriate CAS member association websites. If during final editing and review there are any substantial proposed changes, this document will be returned to the Board of Directors for approval. A substantial standards revision should take approximately 12 months. The CAS secretary maintains the official version of the final approved standards and guidelines.

Revision Process Timeline – Editorial Review

Event Chronology	Time Allotted	Total Time
Revision Committee chair and committee members identified and trained	2 months	2 months
Decision made as to whether the Revision Committee will complete an editorial or substantial review	1 month	3 months
First draft completed by Revision Committee	2 months	5 months
Experts identified and first draft distributed for feedback	1 month	6 months
Draft is submitted for review to the Executive Committee	1 month	7 months
Executive Committee approved draft is distributed to Directors for review. Initial feedback from directors received by Development Committee and Executive Committee	1 month	8 months
Substantial items reviewed by Development Committee and reported to the Executive Committee and prepared for discussion at Board Meeting	0.5 month	8.5 months

Revision Process Timeline – Substantial Review

Event Chronology	Time Allotted	Total Time
Revision Committee chair and committee members identified and trained	2 months	2 months
Decision made as to whether the Revision Committee will complete an editorial or substantial review	1 month	3 months
First draft completed by Revision Committee	2 months	5 months
Experts identified and first draft distributed for feedback	1 month	6 months
Experts return feedback and second draft is written by Revision Committee	3 months	9 months
Draft is submitted for review to the Executive Committee	1 month	10 months
Executive Committee approved draft is distributed to Directors for review. Initial feedback from directors received by Development Committee and Executive Committee	1 months	11 months
Substantial items reviewed by Development Committee and reported to the Executive Committee and prepared for discussion at Board Meeting	0.5 months	11.5 months

Appendix D
Glossary of Terms

accreditation. A "process of external quality review created and used by higher education to scrutinize colleges, universities and programs for quality improvement" (Eaton, 2011, p. 3). Accreditation is divided into two types - institutional and specialized. Although both are designed to assure fundamental levels of quality, the former focuses on the institution as a whole while the latter focuses on academic pre-professional or specialty professional programs such as law, business, psychology, and education, or services such as counseling centers within the institution. Campus communities typically use a self-assessment process to prepare for accreditation team visits. Although the CAS standards can provide a foundation for accreditation self-study, CAS is not an accrediting body.

administrators of programs and services. Individuals with oversight or responsibility for implementing functional area programs and services.

assessment. "Actions taken to gather, analyze, and interpret information and evidence to support the effectiveness of institutions, departments, divisions, or agencies" (Timm, Barham, McKinney, & Knerr, 2013, p. 86) and to use data gathered through the process to improve overall quality, practice, and decision-making.

assessment plan. An "intentionally developed sequence of activities that ensures coherence from program planning through implementation and assessment of outcomes" (Barham & Dean, 2013, p. 7).

benchmark. A criterion used for comparison to measure and evaluate a program or service; a reference point.

best practice. A phrase used to refer to a method, approach, or program that is thought to represent an aspirational level of achievement; in informal usage, the determination often has no assessment or vetting associated with it. CAS standards are not intended to represent best practices except in the sense that they are identified through a widely-informed development and consensus process; they instead represent a threshold of good practice that is meant to be essential and achievable across settings.

Blue Book. The informal name for the printed publication entitled *CAS Professional Standards for Higher Education* that presents the CAS General Standards and standards and guidelines for functional areas and preparation programs. The first iteration of the CAS Blue Book was published in 1986; in recent years a new edition has been published every three years.

boilerplate. Informal term used by CAS referring to the General Standards when they appear within individual functional area standards.

CAS. The Council for the Advancement of Standards in Higher Education (CAS) is a consortium of over 40 higher education professional associations representing over 100,000 professionals, many with international constituencies. CAS promotes the use of its professional standards for the development, assessment, and improvement of quality student learning, programs, and services. CAS was established in 1979 with the purpose of helping to foster and enhance student learning, development, and achievement at institutions of higher education through the development and promulgation of professional standards of practice. Prior to 1992, the consortium's name was the Council for the Advancement of Standards for Student Services/Development Programs.

CAS Board of Directors. The body of representatives from professional higher education associations in the U.S. and Canada that have joined the CAS consortium, pay annual dues, and keep their memberships informed about CAS standards and related initiatives. Although each member association may designate two official representatives (Director and Alternate) to act on its behalf at CAS Board meetings, each association has only one vote during Board meetings. All new or revised standards must have the approval of the full Board, generally by consensus.

CAS Executive Committee. The body of CAS officers, including president, past-president, president-elect, secretary, treasurer, and members at large elected by the CAS Board of Directors. The Executive Director and Editor serve ex-officio. This body is responsible for specific leadership and business operations of CAS, including managing finances and keeping records of all meetings. The CAS Executive Committee meets periodically to address CAS governance issues, consider standards drafts prior to Board review, and manage the business of the Council between Board meetings.

CAS member association. One of the higher education professional associations that has joined CAS and contributes to the work of the Board through its representatives.‑

CAS Public Director. An individual elected by the CAS Board of Directors to represent the public at large. CAS by-laws call for the appointment of public directors who do not represent a specific functional area or professional association but rather view higher education from a broader perspective.

CAS standards and guidelines. Published criteria and related statements and information designed to provide personnel within college and university programs and services with established practices against which to benchmark, build, evaluate, and self-assess programs and services within a specific unit. The CAS standards and guidelines are made up of all functional area standards, the Masters-Level Student Affairs Professional Preparation Program Standards, and the General Standards.

certification. Official recognition by a governmental or professional body attesting that an individual practitioner demonstrates knowledge and can apply learned skills to meet established standards or criteria. Criteria most often include formal academic preparation in prescribed content areas and a period of supervised practice with successful completion of a standardized test of the practitioner's knowledge. CAS does not offer individual credentials of any kind.

compliance. Adherence to a standard of practice or preparation. Compliance with the CAS standards implies that an institution or program meets or exceeds the fundamental essential criteria established for a functional area program, service, or masters-level professional preparation program.

constituents. Those who benefit from or are affected by programs and services. Constituents may include prospective and current students, parents, alumni, faculty, other institution personnel, visitors to the institution, members of the community, employers, and government officials.

criterion categories. Functional area standards are divided into twelve criterion categories (i.e., parts) that help focus assessment efforts. The twelve criterion categories include: mission; program; organization and leadership; human resources; ethics; law, policy, and governance; diversity, equity, and access; internal and external relations; financial resources; technology; facilities and equipment; and assessment.

dimensions. See **student learning and development domains and dimensions**.

domains. See **student learning and development domains and dimensions**.

evaluation. A process that "applies judgment to data that are gathered and interpreted through assessment" (Palomba & Banta, 1999, p. 4). The terms assessment and evaluation are often used in tandem to represent the process of collecting, analyzing, and interpreting data that is then used to judge the outcome of a process or achievement of a goal.

functional area. A distinct grouping of activities, programs, and services within higher education that can be differentiated from other groups (e.g., departments) by its purpose, mission, focus, policies, practices, staff, budget, and the professional interests and backgrounds of its practitioners. In many cases, functional areas are what are often referred to as offices or departments, but CAS uses the term functional area to indicate a program or service that may not have the separate organizational structure typically associated with a department. Examples of functional areas include academic advising, housing and residential life, leadership, and internships. Typically, one or more professional associations represent a functional area on the CAS Board.

functional area standards and guidelines. The set of specific standards and guidelines, with the embedded general standards, that apply to one functional area program or service. Often referred to as the CAS Standards for (insert functional area name). In 2015 there are 43 sets of CAS functional area Standards.

General Standards. The essential level of practice agreed on by the profession at large, as represented by CAS, which applies to all functional area programs and services. The General Standards are a core, global set of standards that articulate common expectations (e.g., expectations that are relevant across all higher education institutions and their programs and services regardless of their specialties). The General Standards espouse student learning and development as fundamental to mission and program. Each general standard is embedded in every set of functional area standards. These boilerplate criteria are presented in bold type and use the auxiliary verb "must," as do all CAS standards. Note: General Standards are capitalized when referring to the document that lists all general standard statements. The term general standards is not capitalized when referring to a specific general standard statement embedded within functional area standards.

guideline. A statement used to clarify or amplify professional standards. Although not essential for acceptable practice, a guideline provides institutions with a description of enhanced practice that can assist in establishing, assessing, and improving programs and services. Guidelines help programs and services move beyond the essential standards to more fully address the needs of students or the institution. CAS guidelines use the auxiliary verbs "should" and "may" and appear in regular (i.e., not bold) typeface.

institutional programs and services. Refers to the higher education functional areas and the professional preparation programs that CAS supports with standards and guidelines. These institutional programs and services may reside in student affairs, academic affairs, academic units, auxiliary services, enrollment services, and other higher education operational units. A key component of their mission is the provision of programs and services to students in support of learning and development.

learning and development outcomes. Statements that describe significant and measurable change occurring in students as a direct result of their interaction with an educational institution and its programs and services. Learning and development outcomes identify what the learners will know, appreciate, and/or be able to do as a result of engaging with the program or service (UCONN, para. 10). The CAS standards identify six broad student learning and development *domains*, as well as related *dimensions*, or elements of the domains, that students should accomplish as a result of their higher education experiences. Institutional programs and services must assess achievement of learning and development outcomes.

outcomes, student learning. See **learning and development outcomes**.

outcomes, program/programmatic. See **program outcomes**.

personnel. Refers to all individuals who are involved in the functional area, inclusive of employees across structures of pay (i.e., salaried, stipend, hourly staff); unpaid academic and non-academic interns and volunteers; part-time and full-time; permanent and limited term. Replaces the term *faculty and staff* which appeared in earlier editions of the standards.

Professional Preparation Program Standards. A set of standards developed and promulgated for purposes of providing master's level student affairs administration programs with criteria to guide the professional education and preparation of entry-level practitioners in student affairs.

program. Refers to either: (a) organizational, a departmental level administrative unit or sub-unit (e.g., the orientation program); or (b) activity, such as an invited lecture, a workshop, a social event, or a series of organized presentations over time (e.g., a "lunch and learn" program).

program outcome. A measure of the results of a program or service-level goal (e.g., increased satisfaction); often used to include operational outcomes, which represent elements of the program's functioning (e.g., cost per student).

quality assurance. Activities, processes, and initiatives that are intended to ensure that those accessing available programs and services will benefit from them and achieve intended outcomes. The CAS self-assessment approach is a form of quality assurance.

Self-Assessment Guide (SAG). An operational version of the CAS standards and guidelines designed to provide users with an assessment tool that can be used for self-study or self-assessment purposes. A SAG is available for each functional area for which a CAS standard exists.

self-study. An internal process by which institutions and programs evaluate their quality and effectiveness in reference to established criteria such as the CAS standards and guidelines. This process, often used to prepare for institutional and specialty accreditation, results in a formal report presenting the findings of the internal evaluation implemented by institutional employees. For accreditation purposes, this report is then validated by an external committee of peers from comparable institutions or programs.

self-regulation. The recommended process by which the CAS standards and guidelines can best be used to assess and evaluate institutional programs and services. This approach calls for institutions and programs to establish, maintain, and enhance the quality of their offerings and environments by using the standards to evaluate themselves. CAS believes that each institution and its programs can and should seek to assess, evaluate, and identify ways to improve its own practices rather than relying on external agencies to do so.

standard. A statement framed within the context of a functional area or professional preparation program designed to provide practitioners with criteria against which to judge the quality of the programs and services offered. Each individual criterion statement, or standard, reflects an essential level of practice that, when met, represents quality practice and performance that any college or university could reasonably achieve. Each CAS standard statement (e.g., **Programs and services must develop, disseminate, implement, and regularly review their missions**) uses an auxiliary verb (i.e., "must"), is presented in bold print, and is agreed upon by the CAS Board of Directors, representing higher education at large.

standards. The generic term used for a set of CAS standards and guidelines designed for a functional area or professional preparation program (e.g., Career Services Standards). The term *standards* is also applied to the compilation of all sets of functional area and professional preparation program standards and guidelines that are published as *CAS Professional Standards for Higher Education* (i.e., the Blue Book).

student learning and development. Individual growth that is an intended outcome of engaging with functional area programs and services. Student learning and development refers to the changes that result when students are exposed to new experiences, concepts, information, and ideas; the knowledge, understanding, and personal growth are generated, in this context, from interactions with higher education learning environments.

student learning and development domains and dimensions. Known as "CAS domains," they represent six broad categories of student learning and development outcomes: knowledge acquisition, construction, integration, and application; cognitive complexity; intrapersonal development; interpersonal competence; humanitarianism and civic engagement; and practical competence. To comply with CAS standards, institutional programs and services must identify relevant and desirable outcomes from these domains, assess their achievement, and articulate how the programs or services contribute to each of the domains. Each domain includes a number of more specific outcome dimensions, and CAS also provides examples of outcome statements.

universal access/design. Application of principles, theories, research, and practices intended to make products, communications, facilities, campus grounds, environments, learning (in and out of the classroom), programs, and services accessible and usable by people of all ages and abilities.

References

Davis Barham, J, & Dean, L. A. (2013). Introduction: The foundation. In D. Timm, J. Davis Barham, K. McKinney, & A. R. Knerr (Eds.), *Assessment in practice: A companion guide to the ASK standards* (pp. 3-8). Washington, DC: ACPA-College Student Educators International. Available from http://www.myacpa.org/commae

Eaton, J. S. (2011, August). *An overview of U.S. accreditation.* Council for Higher Education Accreditation. Retrieved from http://chea.org/pdf/Overview%20of%20US%20Accreditation%2003.2011.pdf

Palomba, C. A., & Banta, T. W. (1999). *Assessment essentials: Planning, implementing, and improving assessment in higher education.* San Francisco: Jossey-Bass.

Timm, D. M., Davis Barham. J., McKinney, K., & Knerr, A. R. (2013). *Assessment in practice: A companion guide to the ASK standards.* Washington, DC: ACPA-College Student Educators International. Available from http://www.myacpa.org/commae

UCONN. (2014). Assessment primer: Goals, objectives and outcomes. Retrieved from http://assessment.uconn.edu/primer/goals1.html

Appendix E
FAQ: Frequently Asked Questions about CAS and Its Initiatives

1. **Why does CAS write standards?**
    One criterion for being a profession is the existence of a set of professional standards to guide and judge practice. Without standards there would be few if any criteria established that institutions and their programs and services could use to judge their quality. CAS was established to develop and promulgate the standards necessary to achieve educational excellence.

2. **What utility do the CAS Standards and Guidelines have for practitioners?**
    The CAS standards are multi-purpose in nature. They can be used to study and evaluate institutional divisions of student affairs and the various student program and service areas common across institutions. Likewise, they can be used for professional development purposes to ensure that staff members comprehend their roles and functions and develop the level of knowledge and skill essential for good practice. Also, the CAS standards can be used to guide the development of new or enhanced functional areas designed to provide students with additional learning and development opportunities.

3. **Can I use the CAS standards for regional or other accreditation purposes?**
    Institutions undergoing accreditation self-studies will find the CAS standards most useful. Because CAS functional area standards are invariably more comprehensive than regional accreditation criteria, a self-study using the CAS standards will provide ample documentation that can be used as evidence of compliance with accreditation criteria.

4. **How are CAS projects funded?**
    CAS dues for member organizations have been maintained at a low annual fee since the Council's inception in 1979. Consequently, CAS has come to rely upon sale of professional publications as its primary source of funding. As a non-profit organization, CAS can accept tax-exempt contributions from individuals as well as grants from philanthropic foundations.

5. **How can I obtain the CAS publications and what are their costs?**
    All available CAS publications, along with current costs and payment options, are listed on the CAS web site, www.cas.edu. Current publications include the *CAS Professional Standards for Higher Education* and the Self Assessment Guides (SAGs), and bundled sets are available. The SAGs are available only as an electronic download. Questions can be addressed to the CAS Executive Director at executive_director@cas.edu or (202) 862-1400.

Nuts and Bolts

6. **Why does CAS call them "functional areas" instead of using a more common term?**
    The areas for which CAS publishes standards represent functions on campuses; in some cases, these are commonly organized in departments or offices (e.g., housing and residential life, counseling), but in other cases, the function may be distributed across multiple offices or only one part of a department's total scope (e.g., assessment services, internships). The term "functional area" is used as an inclusive term to encompass the wide range of functions on campus.

7. **What are the General Standards? How are they different than the standards for my functional area?**
    A number of expectations for practice are common to all functional areas, and these commonalities demand inclusion in all CAS standards. The General Standards form the core of each set of functional area standards; they are embedded verbatim in each set. The functional area standards also include *specialty standards*, which address criteria unique to that function. The CAS General Standards are reviewed and revised prior to the publication of each new edition of the *CAS Professional Standards for Higher Education*, so that all standards are routinely updated

8. **Why is there both bold and regular print in the standards for my area?**
    A CAS standard, which is printed in bold-faced type, is considered to be essential to successful professional practice and uses the auxiliary verb "must." Compliance with the CAS standards indicates that a program meets essential criteria as described in each standard statement and that there is tangible evidence available to support that fact. The regular print is used for the guidelines (see 9. below).

9. **What are guidelines? How are they different from Standards?**
    A CAS guideline, printed in light-face type, is a statement that clarifies or amplifies a CAS standard. Although not required for achieving compliance, CAS guidelines are designed to offer suggestions and illustrations that can assist programs and services to more fully address the learning and development needs of students. CAS guidelines use the auxiliary verbs "should" and "may."

10. **What is the appropriate citation format for referencing the CAS Professional Standards in Higher Education?**
    APA format citation (subsections should follow the citation format for chapters in a book):
    Council for the Advancement of Standards in Higher Education. (2015). *CAS professional standards for higher education* (9th ed.). Washington, DC: Author.

11. **Where will I find the CAS standards and guidelines?**
CAS publishes two versions of its standards, one in text format and another in workbook format designed for use in self-studies. *CAS Professional Standards for Higher Education* (2015, sometimes known as the "CAS Blue Book") provides an introduction to CAS, its mission, initiatives, and the principles upon which it was founded, as well as guidance in using the standards. Individual functional area standards accompanied by introductory contextual statements are included, along with the General Standards, *CAS Learning and Development Outcomes*, the *CAS Characteristics of Individual Excellence*, and the *CAS Statement of Shared Ethical Principles*. In addition, for use in programmatic self-studies, there is a CAS Self-Assessment Guide (SAG) for each set of standards. These assessment workbooks include the standards along with a series of "criterion measure" statements used to judge the level of program compliance with the standard. The CAS SAGs are available electronically via the CAS Online Store in a download format and through a partnership with Campus Labs (www.campuslabs.com).

12. **Where will I find information about using the CAS standards and guidelines?**
An outline of how to put the CAS standards to work is included in Chapter 2 of the *CAS Professional Standards for Higher Education* (2015), and each functional area SAG has an introductory section that describes how to apply the SAG for self-study purposes. The SAG download also contains a PowerPoint presentation and additional resources to help train users. PowerPoint presentations are also available on the CAS website.

13. **How many CAS standards and guidelines are currently in place? Where can I find the list?**
As of August 2015, CAS had developed 43 sets of functional area standards and guidelines and one set of student affairs master's level preparation program standards. They are listed in the Table of Contents of *CAS Professional Standards for Higher Education* and in the Standards section on the CAS website at www.cas.edu.

14. **How do I find standards for an area not listed in the CAS materials? How does CAS suggest we assess those areas?**
Although the CAS General Standards were not designed to stand alone, they illustrate commonalities that exist among the many student-focused programs and services throughout higher education. If you are seeking a starting point for assessing programs and services for which CAS standards are not available, you might use the General Standards as a template.

15. **I downloaded CAS standards for one functional area from a member association's website. Where can I get a copy of a set of standards for a different functional area?**
CAS provides each of its member associations with the opportunity to link to two sets of CAS functional standards on its website. Associations determine where to place these links at their own discretion; some are available only for members of those associations. You may purchase the most recent *CAS Professional Standards for Higher Education* book to obtain the standards. In addition, standards revised since the publication of the last book can be purchased individually through the CAS Online Store.

Conducting Program Reviews

16. **Why use CAS standards to evaluate my program rather than using another approach (e.g., benchmarks)?**
The CAS standards were developed and adopted by knowledgeable representatives from a wide range of higher education organizations. They represent a profession-wide perspective about what constitutes good practice. Additionally, if multiple areas at an institution all use the CAS standards, the General Standards will offer consistency and a common language across different programs and services.

17. **What are the advantages of self-assessment? What is the CAS perspective on self-assessment as opposed to external review?**
Self-assessment (or program review) offers a meaningful opportunity for practitioners to be reflective. The results of self-studies can be organized into reports that divisions and institutions can use to enhance the student experience and guide continuous improvement and strategic planning, as well as to support accreditation efforts. The CAS founders believed that, given good tools, campus professionals are in the best position to evaluate their programs and services, in light of the local context.

18. **Can I make photocopies of the materials for all the members of the review team(s)?**
At this time, you are able to purchase downloadable files of CAS Self-Assessment Guides to share on a secure connection for your institutional colleagues. There is no additional license.

CAS materials are copyrighted, and the copyright permits use by the division or office that purchases them. They may not be posted on a publicly-searchable website. The materials represent CAS intellectual property, and sales comprise the majority of our revenue. As a non-profit entity, this allows us to support the continued work of the organization. Users are expected to abide by legal and ethical guidelines for fair and appropriate use.

19. **How long does a typical division or individual program self-study take to complete?**
The time required to complete the self-study process varies greatly with size and complexity of institutions and programs.

In most instances, it will take from 6 to 9 months to complete a comprehensive division or campus-wide self-study, while a single administrative unit functional area program self-study may well be completed in approximately 3 to 6 months. One of the major time-consuming factors of any self-study is the data collection process in which documentary evidence is obtained and organized into a usable format. More time will be required if the documentary evidence has not already been collected.

20. **Can a partial program self-study using less than a full functional area standard be implemented?**
Each CAS standard is organized into 12 parts. These individual program components can be used on stand-alone bases for targeted program self-studies or for program development purposes. That is, a partial self-study using selected components may be desirable for some programs to consider. It should be understood, however, that a full program assessment cannot be accomplished using less than the complete functional area standard, and a functional area cannot be considered to be in compliance with CAS standards if all the component parts are not evaluated.

21. **Does CAS offer certification or accreditation?**
CAS does not function as a certification or accreditation agency. Rather, CAS encourages institutions and their functional area programs to follow a self-regulation" approach wherein program evaluation self-studies are implemented for internal assessment purposes.

22. **Are institutions in jeopardy if they fail to meet the CAS standards and guidelines?**
CAS standards are provided for institutions to use within the context of a self-regulation process. Although compliance with the standards evidences "good practice" that is recognized profession-wide, there are no external sanctions for non-compliance. However, institutions that do not meet the CAS standards will likely discover that their programs and services fail to function effectively or to meet the needs of their students.

23. **Does CAS provide institutional staff training programs and workshops?**
The CAS national office can provide information about CAS officers and board members who are well qualified to provide staff development training workshops and programs for institutions, or to consult about use of the CAS materials. Training materials for local use are also provided on the CAS website.

CAS Process and Operations

24. **How does one become a member of CAS?**
Because CAS is a consortium of professional organizations, there are no individual memberships currently available. The CAS Board of Directors is composed of representatives from member organizations, and each member association has one vote on CAS business. Organizational membership information is available from the CAS national office.

25. **How often are CAS functional area standards and guidelines revised?**
CAS policy calls for every functional area standard to be reviewed periodically on a 10-year basis for purposes of determining whether a revision is needed. Individuals or organizations who believe a given standard is in need of revision are invited to contact CAS to make such recommendations. Additionally, the General Standards are generally revised every three years, and that revision is then embedded in all of the functional area standards.

26. **Does CAS have a presence at national association meetings?**
Because CAS is a consortium of professional associations, each member association is responsible for providing its membership with information about the availability and use of CAS standards. Most member associations include CAS-related presentations at their conventions. Several CAS officers and directors are available upon request to provide CAS workshops or programs sponsored by professional organizations. CAS-oriented programs have been offered at numerous national and international conferences in recent years.

27. **My association has already established professional standards. What can CAS provide that we don't already have?**
Many professional associations have established standards for their constituent members, some of which are quite comparable to CAS standards. In general, CAS standards are designed to be used in every type and size of higher educational institution and were created for this broad user base. A primary benefit of the CAS standards is the fact that CAS represents a profession-wide effort to develop, promulgate, and encourage use of its professional standards. Consequently, the professional credibility of the CAS standards and guidelines tends to exceed those proffered by a single organization. If an institution or division uses the CAS standards to study more than one functional area, use of CAS ensures that the areas to be examined and the criteria will be consistent across areas.

28. **I think CAS needs to develop standards for a new functional area. How can I learn if CAS is working on my area of interest or make a recommendation?**
CAS maintains a growing list of functional areas that have been recommended for developing new standards. Individuals or CAS Directors can make suggestions for new standards directly to the CAS President. These suggestions will be considered by the Executive Committee and evaluated using a series of questions to assess whether practice in the area has developed to a point where it is consistent enough to be codified in standards.

Appendix F
CAS Accolades and Additional Resources

"CAS has represented the most comprehensive standards for functional areas in higher education for the past 30 years. Research has shown that, throughout that period of time, the standards promulgated by CAS have had an overall positive impact on student services by promoting program self-assessment, advancing program improvement, and providing guidance for the creation of environments where student development can flourish. Yet, CAS has not rested on its laurels and continues to innovate. In this latest edition of the standards, student learning is placed at the forefront, reminding all higher education professionals that the highest standard of quality requires attention beyond compliance, efficiency, and the bottom line."

- Dallin George Young is Assistant Director for Research, Grants, and Assessment at the National Resource Center for The First-Year Experience and Students in Transition at the University of South Carolina

"We use the CAS standards to help in the essential process of reflection upon our practices in a myriad of areas within student affairs, allowing us to use a common set of standards from which our very unique story can resonate and emerge. Using the standards is an excellent beginning point of a shared understanding of what we do – and the process by which we utilize the standards, in program review, for example, gives us a coherent way to understand how we can best move forward intentionally."

– Daniel W. Newhart is Director of Student Affairs Research, Evaluation, and Planning at Oregon State University

"All departments in our division of student affairs conduct program reviews every five years. CAS provides us the resources to conduct the reviews for a wide variety of functional areas, and I know that I can count on the standards to be the current and best practices for us to evaluate our programs and services. Completing program reviews with the CAS standards is comprehensive and invaluable in helping us evaluate where we are and where we need to be and helps departments in strategic planning. The standards also are a great resources for developing new programs to best meet the needs of our students."

- Martha Glass is Director of Assessment and Professional Development at Virginia Tech

Related CAS Materials Available
at http://www.cas.edu

CAS Professional Standards for Higher Education (9th ed.) e-book
The ninth edition of *CAS Professional Standards for Higher Education* is now also available as an e-book. Information about purchasing the appropriate format for your needs can be found at http://www.cas.edu/store_home.asp.

Complete Set of Self-Assessment Guides (SAGs)
The downloadable electronic package contains all 44 functional area SAGs and contextual statements, a PowerPoint for presentations, and resources on conducting self-assessment.*

CAS-Campus Labs Program Review
As part of a relationship with Campus Labs, CAS self-assessment guides are available through the Campus Labs program review platform. The CAS-Campus Labs module contains all 44 functional area SAGs and contextual statements. Campus Labs members also gain access to a PowerPoint for presentations and resources on conducting self-assessment. Contact Campus Labs (www.campuslabs.org) for information, pricing details, or a demonstration.*

Individual Self-Assessment Guides (SAGs)
For use in program reviews, CAS Self-Assessment Guide (SAG) can be individually purchased for individual functional areas. These downloadable assessment workbooks include the standards and guidelines along with a series of criterion statements used to judge the level of program compliance with the standard.*

> *Each electronic SAG file includes a contextual statement; instructions for conducting self-assessment using the SAG; and self-assessment instrument comprised of criterion statements, rating scales, and evaluation forms for compiling assessment and planning improvements.